PRAISE FOR

General Lee's Army

"Joseph T. Glatthaar brings a fresh and revealing perspective to the much-studied history of Robert E. Lee and the Army of Northern Virginia. Prodigious research, a meticulous use of statistical information, and analytical acuity mark this book, which abounds with surprising information about the makeup of the army, its casualties, and the quality of its leadership. This is now the indispensable first place to go for anyone interested in Lee, his army, and their storied campaigns."

—Gary W. Gallagher, author of *The Confederate War*

"This is a splendid piece of work, buttressed by wondrously thorough research in a vast array of primary material, and destined to be a great classic."

—Robert K. Krick, author of *Stonewall Jackson at Cedar Mountain*

"A unique, often controversial description of Lee's soldiers, their background, and the conditions under which they fought."

—*Kirkus Reviews*

"This well-written work provides much food for thought for all Civil War buffs."

—*Publishers Weekly*

"[Glatthaar] punctures a few necessary holes in the Lee myth."

—*Des Moines Register*

"Glatthaar's conclusions challenge the notion that the war in the South was a rich man's war and a poor man's fight with support for slavery concentrated among the Southern upper class."

—*News & Record* (Greensboro, NC)

"Perceptive and fascinating history. . . . The strength of *General Lee's Army* lies in Glatthaar's exploration of the personal experiences of individual soldiers . . . he carefully tracks the soldiers' transformation from greenhorns to suffering masses . . . a fine blend of scholarly research and you-are-there history. Glatthaar brings new life to the drive of the Dixie soldiers, while never neglecting their bonds to the sins of the South."

—*The Christian Science Monitor*

General Lee's Army

———◆———

From Victory to Collapse

JOSEPH T. GLATTHAAR

FREE PRESS

New York London Toronto Sydney

FREE PRESS
A Division of Simon & Schuster, Inc.
1230 Avenue of the Americas
New York, NY 10020

First Free Press trade paperback edition March 2009

FREE PRESS and colophon are trademarks of Simon & Schuster, Inc.

For information about special discounts for bulk purchases,
please contact Simon & Schuster Special Sales at
1-800-456-6798 or business@simonandschuster.com

The Simon & Schuster Speakers Bureau can bring authors to your live event.
For more information or to book an event contact the Simon & Schuster Speakers Bureau at 866-248-3049 or visit our website at www.simonspeakers.com

Book design by Ellen R. Sasahara

Manufactured in the United States of America

1   3   5   7   9   10   8   6   4   2

The Library of Congress has catalogued the hardcover edition as follows:

Glatthaar, Joseph T.
General Lee's army: from victory to collapse / Joseph T. Glatthaar.
p. cm.
1. Confederate States of America. Army of Northern Virginia.   2. United
States—History—Civil War, 1861–1865—Campaigns.   3. Virginia—
History—Civil War, 1861–1865—Campaigns.   4. Lee, Robert E. (Robert
Edward), 1807–1870—Military leadership.   5. United States—History—
Civil War, 1861–1865—Regimental histories.   6. Soldiers—Confederate
States of America—Attitudes.   7. Soldiers—Confederate States of America—
Psychology.   8. Soldiers—Confederate States of America—Social conditions.
I. Title.
E470.2.G58   2008
973.7'42—dc22   2007023724

ISBN-13:   978-0-684-82787-2
ISBN-10:   0-684-82787-5
ISBN-13:   978-1-4165-9697-4 (pbk)
ISBN-10:   1-4165-9697-6 (pbk)

For Jackie, Who Deserves It

CONTENTS

———◦◦———

LIST OF MAPS

PROLOGUE

I N MID-MAY 1864, Theodore Lyman, a Union officer on Maj. Gen. George G. Meade's staff, attempted to dispel the rumors that Robert E. Lee and his Army of Northern Virginia were beaten. Lee "is a brave and skilful soldier and he will fight while he has a division or a day's rations left." Of the soldiers in the Army of Northern Virginia, Lyman wrote admiringly, "These Rebels are not half-starved and ready to give up—a more sinewy, tawny, formidable-looking set of men could not be. In education they are certainly inferior to our native-born people; but they are usually very quick-witted within their own sphere of comprehension; and they know enough to handle weapons with terrible effect. Their great characteristic is their stoical manliness; they never beg, or whimper, or complain; but look you straight in the face, with as little animosity as if they never heard a gun." After three years of hard war against vastly superior Union strength and resources, the Army of Northern Virginia was still a deadly combat force. Not surprisingly to Lyman, it would take eleven more months of brutal fighting to subdue Lee's army.[1]

This is a study of that "sinewy, tawny, formidable-looking set of men," as well as their "brave and skilful" commander, Lee. The saga of Lee's army especially tells the broader story of the entire Civil War, because if you understand why his men fought, what hardships they endured, how they managed so much success against the vastly superior enemy, how they came close to winning, and why they lost, you understand fundamentally the war itself.

In order to see such a wide angle, this book reaches back more than a year before Lee assumed command of those troops, when they soldiered under Joseph E. Johnston in the Shenandoah Valley, Pierre Gustave Toutant Beauregard in Northern Virginia, or John Bankhead Magruder along the peninsula between the York and James rivers. Half of all the soldiers who ever served in the Army of Northern Virginia left home to don the Confederate uniform in 1861, and nearly three of every four enlisted before Lee assumed command. What made this army so special, however, was the combination of its soldiers and its new commander, Lee, in June 1862. Over the next few months, as Lee and his army drove the Union forces away from the gates of Richmond and reclaimed nearly all of Virginia for the Confederacy, he won the hearts of the soldiers and the Confederate people. The Army of Northern Virginia became Lee's army, and the soldiers took great pride in being part of it.

General Lee's Army is based on contemporary evidence, specifically official documents and manuscripts and published letters and diaries of some 4,000 soldiers, tapping memoirs sparingly and only when the contemporary record supports those assertions. When I began this project in 1989, I concluded that postwar memoirs usually reflected more about the times in which their authors had written them than the war itself. In an attempt to settle various scholarly disputes and to guard against cherry-picking my evidence, I developed a statistically representative sample of Lee's men, from compiled service records, census records, state tax records, family histories, obituaries, pension files, and other sources. This information has enabled me to address some of the most important questions, many of them answered unsatisfactorily by previous scholars, about who these soldiers and their families were and what their wartime experiences were like, including background, slave ownership, occupation, wealth, family, desertion, conscription, illnesses, casualties, and many more. To the extent that statistics are cited in the narrative, unless otherwise noted, they came from this sample.

This book is not an examination of the army from the top down, with an occasional colorful anecdote to uplift the narrative, nor is it exclusively a study from the bottom up, a depiction solely of life from the perspective of the common soldier. I have sought to blend those two approaches in order to develop important issues that influenced the motivations, attitudes, feelings, and conduct of officers and enlisted men throughout the course of the war. The book also highlights the interactions between soldiers and loved ones at home. To study the army in isolation from the home front, especially in a war to repel invaders, would be to ignore one of the most powerful influences on soldiers. Men entered the army in large part to defend their "civil rights" and protect loved ones and their homes from Union invasion. What occurred in the army influenced lives on the home front, and what took place on the home front affected soldiers in the field. As Lee explained to Jefferson Davis in early 1864 about the two fronts, "They are one in reality & all for the Country."[2]

Many believed that the Confederacy never really stood a chance against the Union's overwhelming numbers of men and industrial strength. Yet that belief ignores the different aims of the two sides. For the Union to win, it had to invade and subjugate the Rebels. For the Confederates to win independence, they merely had to convince the Union to stop trying to conquer them.

Confederate president Jefferson Davis formulated a strategy for independence that called on the Confederacy's armies to punish enemy forces as they invaded Rebel territory, in hopes that severe losses would convince the Federals that the price in lives and treasure for restoring the Union was too severe. No Confederate army fulfilled that strategy as well as the Army of Northern Virginia. For four years, it held the larger Union Army of the Potomac at bay, and on several occasions it took the war into Yankeedom. General Lee's army came far closer to winning the war than any other Confederate field command. Among soldiers and civilians, it became the embodiment of the Rebel cause. When Ellen Renshaw House, a fervent Confederate amid a hotbed of pro-Union sentiment in East Tennessee, learned the Army of Northern Virginia had surrendered at Appomattox Court House, she reconciled herself to the news by recording, "we have depended too much on Gen Lee[,] too little on God, & I believe God has suffered his surrender to show us he can use other means than Gen Lee to affect his ends." Lee's unparalleled success amid Confederate disasters in other theaters elevated his men to symbols of the independent Confederacy and, indeed, came close to convincing the Union to give up the fight. In the late stages of the war, as disaster upon disaster befell the Confederate people, many still clung to hope that Lee and his army might somehow stave off the horrible defeat that finally became inevitable. As long as Lee and his army survived, the Confederate States of America lived. When the Union crushed the Army of Northern Virginia, the rebellion was over.[3]

Lee and the Army of Northern Virginia were the greatest nationalizing institution in the Confederacy. Their experiences reflected the strengths and weaknesses of the Confederacy. Soldiers brought cultural notions and values from home that shaped the way they felt and performed their duties as soldiers. The internal and external problems that ultimately caused the Confederacy to collapse were reflected within that army. In short, Lee's army explains both why the Confederacy almost won, and why it lost.[4]

In 1944, Douglas Southall Freeman completed his two-decade-long investigation of the Army of Northern Virginia. After a four-volume biography of its principal commander, Robert E. Lee, and three more tomes on Lee's senior officers entitled *Lee's Lieutenants*, Freeman provided a brilliant and seemingly exhaustive treatment of the uppermost echelons of the Confederacy's premier army. Yet a most enthusiastic critic noticed that there was still room for work on the Army of Northern Virginia. The reviewer for the *New York Times* wrote that there was one more fruitful avenue of investigation, from the ground level. "Future historians," he admonished, "will be well advised to turn to 'men and morale' as the one rewarding field of study remaining to that army—rather than attempting further studies of strategy and tactics."[5]

Since then, scholars and enthusiasts have written thousands of books on various aspects of Lee and the Army of Northern Virginia, but no one has embarked upon a major investigation of the army throughout the entire war. That is the intention of this book.[6]

In all cases, I have kept the quotations and spellings the same, although I have capitalized the first letter for each new sentence to avoid unnecessary distraction to the reader.

GENERAL LEE'S ARMY

Chapter 1

———◦⊂◦⊃◦———

COMEDY OF ERRORS,
TRAGEDY OF TRIUMPH

E VEN THOUGH James Thomas Petty had resided in Washington, D.C., for years, he always identified himself as a Virginian. When it came time to choose sides in the sectional crisis, Thomas, as his friends called him, had no difficulty. He left the Union for the Confederate States of America just as Virginia did.

Born in 1836 in Falmouth, Virginia, Thomas lived there and in Front Royal, Virginia, in the shadow of the Blue Ridge Mountains during his youth. His father, James S. Petty, was a tailor by trade, and not a notably successful one at that. In 1860, at age fifty-three, James Petty owned no land and held personal property worth a meager $150.00. Although he never made much money, James and his wife, Margaret, emphasized schooling for their children. At fourteen, Thomas could have helped to ease the financial woes of the family by seeking employment. Instead, his family scrimped while Thomas secured a superior education, which reaped dividends for the rest of his life.[1]

Avoiding his father's craft and, for that matter, other forms of manual labor, young Thomas gravitated toward the nation's capital in the early 1850s in search of employment. With support from his father's family, he found employment as a clerk, earning decent wages with the promise of economic mobility and financial security. A bright and pleasant lad, about medium height with hazel eyes and dark hair, Thomas carved out a strong network of friends and connections in and around Washington. He socialized broadly, forging relationships with other aspiring young men from modest backgrounds, and with quite a number of single young women.[2]

On January 1, 1861, Petty called on President James Buchanan to offer him a happy New Year. "Poor Old Buck!" he jotted in his diary. "He looks careworn, and the effects of 'Secession' are visible in his countenance." Barely a week earlier, South Carolina had voted to withdraw from the Union, and rumblings from other slave states suggested that more would follow.[3]

Along with other Washingtonians, Petty rejoiced when rumors circulated that Senator John Crittenden's committee had eked out a compromise. It would have overseen the adoption of perpetually binding constitutional amendments that would secure slavery forever and guarantee slavery in territories south of the Missouri Compromise line, 36°, 30'. "A mountain seemd removed from every heart," he exulted. But that, too, quickly unraveled.[4]

Soon, the electricity of the times seized him, as it did hundreds of thousands of others. The thrill of momentous events, the culmination of decades of struggle over the legality and geography of slavery, was so exciting that it clouded his mind to solutions and consequences. "The South," he proclaimed joyously, "is in a blaze." On behalf of the Commonwealth of Virginia, he argued with friends so vociferously that he had to avoid political discussions to preserve his bond with them. When Fort Sumter in Charleston harbor fell to Rebel gunners in mid-April, he erupted with joy. Soon thereafter, when Virginia seceded, he announced his decision: "All my friends nearly condemn me but believing I'm right I still cry hurrah for Old Virginia! Whither she goes I'll follow."[5]

Although neither Petty nor his parents had slaves, many people he knew from days as a youth and an adult did—his uncle in Front Royal owned a dozen. Slaveholding was a Southern right, and Petty detested "Black Republicans" for their goals of stripping Southerners of their civil liberties as the Constitutional Convention of 1787 had reaffirmed. He took great pride in his standing as *"Virginian & a Southerner."*[6]

By mid-April, Petty had written his parents to inform them where he stood on the national crisis. A week later, he arrived in Front Royal, determined to enlist in the army. Two of his cousins had already left for Harpers Ferry to serve in the Warren Rifles, and he decided to join them. Before the month was out, Thomas Petty drilled on the green in front of Christ Episcopal Church in Alexandria, where George Washington and Robert E. Lee had worshiped.

It did not take long before Petty's officers discovered the value of his clerking talents. After a stint as recorder for a court-martial, duty that earned him the praise of the judge advocate, his captain asked him to prepare the company rolls. Soon, the brigade commissary sought his labor, and a struggle for Petty's services ensued that went all the way to the brigade commander, Brig. Gen. James Longstreet. Longstreet directed that Petty should remain with his regiment.[7]

In mid-July, a Union army of 32,000 under Brig. Gen. Irvin McDowell marched southward toward the main Confederate body that guarded Manassas Junction, where the Manassas Gap Railroad from Front Royal intersected the Orange & Alexandria Railroad. Advanced Rebel units fell back in the face of the large Union column, joining forces with other elements of Brig. Gen. P. G. T. Beauregard's command behind a sluggish, fairly shallow stream with steep banks called Bull Run, about one and a half miles from Manassas Junction.

Petty's regiment, the 17th Virginia Infantry, had only pulled its component companies together in late June. Along with the rest of Longstreet's Brigade, it guarded Blackburn's Ford across Bull Run, on the right of Beauregard's line.

About noon on July 18, the lead column of the Union command approached, placing the entire regiment under fire for the first time. To open the contest, Union artillery hurled projectiles to the left of the brigade. Soon, the fire drifted on top of the 17th. As the soldiers hugged the ground for protection, Federal infantrymen deployed and delivered volleys at the Rebel line. Some soldiers panicked and began withdrawing to the rear. Suddenly, Longstreet rode among them. A large and powerful man who appeared like a giant on horseback, Longstreet's imperturbability amid enemy gunfire reassured the raw troops and restored order. Others held their ground but nervously fidgeted with their firing hammers, itching for a chance to respond in kind. Once Confederates countered with volleys of their own, many of them regained composure. The mere act of defending themselves, and the physical activity of loading and firing, dissipated skittishness among the inexperienced volunteers.

In haste, soldiers loaded and fired, but not in accordance with the procedures officers had taught the men. Perspiration streamed down on the warm day, combining with gunpowder to form a black batter on their faces. Hands, too, took on a charcoal hue from careless pouring of gunpowder into musket barrels. Most men were soon barely recognizable. Hours passed in what appeared to be only seconds. One soldier recalled little of the fight, except his captain parading behind them directing their fire, and his shooting a Yankee some seventy yards out. For that act of killing, he shed no tears of remorse. "Well, I was fighting, for my house, and he had no business there," he wrote.[8]

Three times the Yankees tried to drive off the Rebel defenders, and three times they fought them back. Finally, Rebel volleys suppressed Federal rifle fire enough to allow three companies from the 17th Virginia to rush across Bull Run. Popping up on the Union flank, they delivered withering blasts that forced the attackers into retreat.

Despite some shaky moments, Longstreet's Brigade, and the 17th Virginia Infantry, acquitted themselves well in their first firefight. All told, Longstreet's command suffered seventy casualties while inflicting eighty-three on the attackers. One member of the 17th was killed, with another eighteen wounded. Petty gazed on the corpse of the only fatality, Tom Sangster, of Alexandria. "A triumphant smile rested like a ray of sunshine upon his marble-like features," he commented. At least some of those casualties, Petty complained, were victims of friendly fire. Frightened men shot first and identified targets later. "Just say boo!" grumbled Petty the day after, "& pop goes a gun at whoever is before them."[9]

Petty himself witnessed no action that day. Off on an errand for his regimental commander, he returned after the fighting was done. Chagrined by his own absence, and perhaps a bit embarrassed, Petty extracted a promise from his colonel two days later that he could return to his company for the remainder of the campaign. Next time, he would not miss the fight.

Yet the next time, the true Battle of First Manassas on July 21, was even more embarrassing for Petty. Deployed as skirmishers in advance of the Rebel

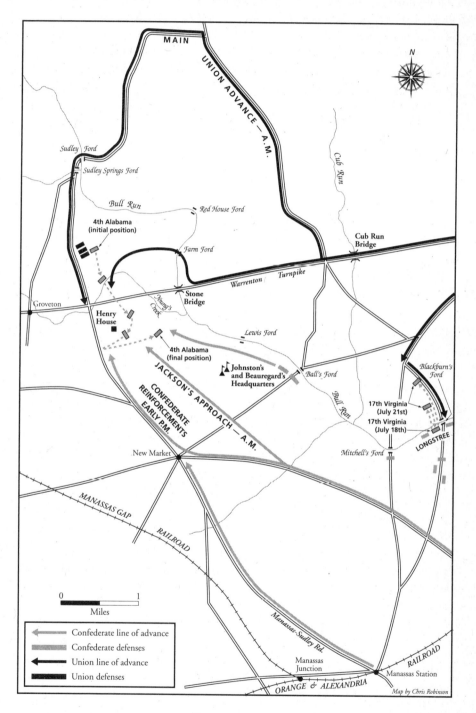

First Manassas

army, Petty and his captain were nearly captured. While running back to Rebel lines, they both stumbled and fell into Bull Run. As Petty plunged into the water, his musket slipped from his grasp. His body crashed into a rock just below the surface, bruising him badly, and as he rolled away, he knocked his captain back under. Completely saturated, the two struggled with each other and the current to stand once more. Hastily, Petty felt around for his weapon, without success. He was suddenly unarmed and in the midst of the largest battle yet fought on the North American continent. Petty limped back to Confederate trenches to secure another rifled musket. By the time he returned to the company, his captain had realized that Petty's bruise was severe enough to prevent him from moving quickly. He ordered the private back to camp. Petty hobbled off to a commanding hill, and from 11:00 A.M. until 5:00 P.M., watched the battle from safety. The simultaneous roar of musketry and artillery from both sides must have stunned the green soldier. One eyewitness described it to his father by writing, "It was one continual thunder upon thunder until the Earth seemed to shake its very foundations." By very late afternoon, eruptions of gunfire slowly dissipated, and as darkness settled on the field, Petty returned to the trenches.[10]

For Thomas Petty and many others, the start of the war was a comedy of errors, more slapstick than drama. His story is a useful reminder that any single narrative of the war, any story of one united army defeating another, obscures as much as it clarifies. War is the sum total of its individual stories, from comedy to romance to drama to tragedy.

The only way to develop the full story of a war is to tell a number of its individual stories, while keeping them in balance. The Confederacy had some Thomas Pettys, but it had many more Jesse Jordans. Jordan and his comrades in the 4th Alabama Infantry experienced the harsh realities of war at First Manassas. A twenty-one-year-old from Huntsville, Alabama, Jordan had grown up in a very wealthy slaveholding family. His father, a planter, held personal property and real estate worth $50,000, a staggering sum in 1860. With all the opportunities that opulence often offers, Jesse received excellent academic preparation, which culminated in the study of law at the University of Virginia. When the secession crisis erupted, he had just hung his shingle in his hometown.[11]

Like many other wealthy individuals, Jesse felt a great sense of obligation, too. Thoughtful and sensitive by nature, he never questioned the moral legitimacy of the "peculiar institution." Jesse had grown up in a slave-owning environment, and his family had prospered in it. The Jordans had enjoyed all the rights and benefits of a free white society in Alabama, and with those privileges came the responsibility to defend it. "My country desires my services & she must have it," he explained to his sister. "I am bound to her by a solemn oath." Duty demanded that he pick up the sword "for the defence of the rights of my injured country."[12]

In the spring of 1861, Jordan enlisted as a private in a company of infantrymen that formed in his native Madison County. Ultimately called Company I,

4th Alabama Infantry, the "North Alabamians" assembled with the other prospective companies from around Alabama in Dalton, Georgia, in early May, where the men swore an oath to serve for a year. After a raucous election for field-grade officers and a rousing send-off by the neighboring Georgians, the men in the 4th Alabama entrained for Lynchburg, Virginia. To ease Private Jordan's military burden, his father sent along a young male family slave, who would act as his body servant, cooking his meals, washing his clothes, and running various errands for him. Three days of travel placed Jordan and his comrades in the Virginia Theater, and by mid-month they joined Brig. Gen. Barnard Bee's brigade of Johnston's army in Harpers Ferry, along the Potomac River.[13]

Nagging Jordan was a premonition that he would never see his family again. "I am going to the tented field," he informed his sister, "going to leave Mother, Father, Sisters & Brothers with the expectation of never returning." The idea of dying did not haunt him. He accepted death as likely, but an unyielding sense of responsibility and honor overrode any uneasiness. Warfare, he noted, was a horrible thing, yet he could not dodge his duty. "What unhappiness to us, & devastation to the human race," he acknowledged. "Husbands obliged to leave their wives, & their dear children[,] Mothers to part with their sons, & sisters with their brothers." Still, he must serve "for the defence of the rights of my injured country; & if ever I forsake her in her hour of need may the God of my fathers forsake me in that Eternal day."[14]

At Harpers Ferry, soldiers drilled in the warm Virginia sun, mastering the basic tactical formations that they must assume on the battlefield. The officers in the 4th Alabama marched and paraded their men anywhere from six to eight hours per day. They honed tactical maneuvers and instilled a sense of unity and élan, but drilling alienated troops from their colonels and major.[15]

Nor were regimental officers the only targets of criticism. When Johnston deemed the occupation of Harpers Ferry too precarious and withdrew his command to the southwest, epithets against him gushed forth from the men in the 4th Alabama. "This thing of *falling back* as General Johnston calls it does not suit the temper of our men and you never heard any one 'cussed' as he was by the whole army when the orders came to retreat to Winchester," a private in Jordan's regiment noted. Several weeks later, as the Federals occupied Martinsburg, Virginia, a chorus of curses spewed forth once more, this time both at the Yankees for declining to give battle and at Johnston for refusing to attack the invaders. Thus, when Johnston removed his command from the area south of Winchester in mid-July, some soldiers interpreted the movement as another retreat, until he circulated an order informing them that they would march to Piedmont and board trains to reinforce Beauregard's columns at Manassas Junction. The men responded to the news with throaty cheers and a new spring in their step. The prospect of battle largely stifled dissent, except from those who feared they would not reach Bull Run in time for the fight.[16]

Serving to the west in the Shenandoah Valley, Jordan's regiment was shuttled by train to reinforce Beauregard's command around Bull Run. By the late morning on July 20, the 4th Alabama had arrived at Manassas Junction, nearly 600 strong. A two-mile march positioned the regiment near Ball's Ford, to the west of the anticipated area of attack. Just how nervous Jordan felt that evening, just how restlessly he slept that night, he never recorded. By early morning, Jordan and his Alabama comrades had awakened and shifted quickly in a northwesterly direction to aid fellow Confederates in blocking the wide Union flank attack. They advanced into a cornfield just beyond Buck Hill. Within minutes, Yankee infantry columns appeared, and the men of the 4th Alabama began exchanging fire. As more and more Federals deployed, the regimental commander pulled his men back to a position behind the hill's crest. Using the terrain as protection, the troops would rise up, deliver a volley, and hug the earth again. For close to ninety minutes, the 4th Alabama held its ground, behaving calmly under heavy fire. The endless hours of drill and discipline reaped dividends. One private in the regiment thought his comrades were "the coolest men I ever saw we were all the time talking of the incidents of the fight even while the men were being wounded on every side." Some laughed at near misses.[17]

At Buck Hill, Jordan suffered a mild gunshot wound to the head. A minie ball creased his scalp and drew blood, but did not damage his skull, and he remained at his post. Under such heavy fire, sustaining only this "small wound," he considered himself very lucky. "God only knows how I escaped being killed," he elaborated to his sister, "for never did hail fall faster around me than did the balls & shells & upon my right, left & before me I could see my poor comrades fall as they were."[18]

With vastly greater numbers, the Federal forces outflanked the Confederate troops there and forced them to retire to a new position, just north of the Warrenton Turnpike. They did not hold this ground for long. Once again, superior Union strength compelled the 4th Alabama to fall back. This time, they mistook attacking Yankees as friends, and allowed them to approach too closely to repulse their advance. "We had been there but a short time," Jordan described, "before we were flanked upon the right & left by an over whelming number of the enemy, supposed to [be] at first our friends." Their escape, he suggested, required divine interposition. "Nothing but Gods providence ever enabled us to escape without the destruction of every mans life."[19]

Across the turnpike the 4th Alabama raced, regrouping with great difficulty east of the famous Henry House. There, General Bee called on them to rally and support Brig. Gen. Thomas Jonathan Jackson's forces. The men moved forward, some 250 strong, but an artillery battery sliced a part of the regiment off from the rest, and in its divided, worn-out state, it could do little more than help fortify the line. Fortunately, the Confederates rushed substantial numbers from the center and right of their line to strengthen the left, and invaluable reinforcements from Johnston's army arrived by train in the nick of time. Building upon Jackson's and Bee's position, they extended beyond the Union flank and launched a devastating counterattack. While these Confederates, flush with the thrill of victory and disordered from their effective assault, attempted to organize a pursuit from the jumbled units, the exhausted Alabamians finally retired.[20]

In its first fight, the 4th Alabama had endured a terrible beating. Forty officers and men were killed, and another 157 suffered wounds. In one company alone, 58 entered the battle, and 33 were killed or wounded. Only 25 emerged unscathed, and "of these nearly every man was either struck by a spent ball [a round that lacked enough force to penetrate the skin] or had holes shot through his hat or clothes," wrote one of its members. Jordan, stunned by the magnitude of the losses and bewildered by his own survival, concluded that "the prayers of my mother & other loved ones at home must have protected me from all harm." Even though the 4th Alabama served throughout the war in what ultimately became the Army of Northern Virginia, the regiment never lost as many men in a single fight as it did that July day. One-third of the regiment were casualties that day. Only at the Battle of the Wilderness, in May 1864, would its percentage of casualties actually exceed that total.

Throughout the war, three of every four Confederates in Lee's army were either killed in action, died of disease, wounded, or captured. Petty would manage to survive the war. In the Seven Days' Campaign of June and July 1862, he was taken prisoner. Yankees shipped him to Fort Columbus in New York and then to Fort Warren in Boston, where locals gawked at him and his comrades. Barely a month after he fell into Union hands, Federals exchanged him for a Yankee prisoner of war. Petty returned to the 17th Virginia in time for the Maryland invasion that fall, and he remained with his regiment, except for an illness, until July 1863. For the next thirteen months, Petty served as a clerk for the brigade commissary. Those skills may have saved his life: They kept him out of the meat grinder known as the Overland Campaign of 1864. With the Confederacy desperate for manpower, Petty returned to the line later that year; during the remaining months of the Petersburg siege, he lived on meager rations, and trench warfare gradually broke him down, yet he completed his wartime service with the 17th, signing a parole at Lynchburg, Virginia, in April 1865.[21]

In contrast, almost 30,000 officers and men were killed in action or mortally wounded, and Jesse Jordan was among them. As he had feared, on June 27, 1862, at Gaines's Mill, Virginia, in the same campaign where Petty was captured, Jordan sustained a mortal wound while assaulting a Federal battery. Comrades bore his body to a nearby church, which the Rebels had converted into a field hospital. He died with his body servant at his side. He was buried in a marked grave, before his mother, Mary, could travel from Huntsville to

Richmond to retrieve her son's body. With the help of the family slave, she disinterred Jesse's remains and placed them in a casket. They escorted the body back to Huntsville, where she held a fitting burial for her son.[22]

Thomas Petty and Jesse Jordan were two of 200,000-odd officers and men who served in Lee's army. These men comprised a substantial part of a great human canvas, on which was painted a tragic and terrible picture called the American Civil War.

Chapter 2

SECESSION AND MOBILIZING
FOR WAR

BOTH THOMAS PETTY and Jesse Jordan entered military service to defend rights that the Constitution bequeathed to them, the very same basis upon which their home states of Virginia and Alabama seceded from the Union: They acted to protect the institution of slavery. The Army of Northern Virginia fought for many reasons, but the events that led to its formation clarified the key factor of the Civil War: It was fought over slavery.

Since the Revolutionary era, and particularly in the four decades before the Civil War, tensions over slavery had heightened. Northerners, who often held the same racial prejudices as Southerners, envisioned no role for slavery in the nation's future; Southern whites could not imagine life without it. As Northerners challenged Southerners on slavery on moral, economic, and social grounds with increasing aggressiveness, Southerners clung to the institution more tenaciously. In time, the dispute ripped apart virtually every major national organization or institution and, ultimately, the United States of America.

By the late 1850s, various disputes had escalated the sectional strains to an almost feverish pitch. Northerners in Congress who cared nothing about slavery joined forces with their Southern colleagues to pass the Kansas-Nebraska Act, which rescinded the decades-old Missouri Compromise. Instead of a division of the Louisiana Purchase into free and slave territories along 36°, 30', a concept called popular sovereignty—the vote of the people who resided there—determined whether these areas north of 36°, 30', would permit slave ownership or not. The backlash among Northern voters drove the last nail into the coffin of a dying Whig Party. In its place rose the Republican Party, dedicated to blocking the extension of slavery and, many Southerners believed, to the abolitionist goal of the eradication of slavery everywhere. In the Kansas Territory, violence erupted between proslavery and antislavery elements, with Northerners and Southerners alike pouring manpower and resources to tilt the scales in their favor. The U.S. Supreme Court entered the battleground on the side of slaveholders when it ruled in *Dred Scott v. Sanford* (1857) that blacks were not citizens and that slaveholders could take their property (slaves) into any territory. The decision rubbed against both the Republican Party plank of free soil and the Democratic Party stance of popular sovereignty. Republicans and many Northern Democrats dismissed the ruling as mere *obiter dicta*, a nonbinding court opinion, which infuriated Southerners all the more.[1]

Southern outrage peaked after a bizarre scheme to destroy the institution of slavery violently. John Brown had earned a reputation as a fanatical abolitionist who took matters into his own hands when he and a small band of followers murdered five proslavery neighbors in Kansas in 1856. In October 1859, Brown appeared at Harpers Ferry, Virginia, at the head of a group of twenty-one to strike a mighty blow for abolitionism. His scheme called for the party to seize the arsenal there and for slaves to rush to his column of loyalists, receive arms, and join his army of liberators. For protection, they would take prominent locals as hostages. Brown and his small band would then march southward, freeing more slaves and placing weapons in their hands, until they had crushed the entire institution of slavery. In truth, Brown may have envisioned the group as martyrs for the cause of freedom. He planned for no contingencies in case things went awry, and took no care to haul or secure provisions. It was almost as if Brown wanted to be captured.[2]

With such incompetent planning, Brown and his comrades botched the effort at Harpers Ferry. Although they did secure the arsenal, they allowed a train to pass, and word about what they had done quickly circulated. Virginia called out its ill-trained militia, and the U.S. government sent Lt. Col. Robert E. Lee with a party of marines to retake the arsenal. Lee and his marines stormed the engine room where Brown and his henchmen had holed up. Two conspirators were killed, and all the rest captured, including a wounded Brown.

Southerners howled over Brown's attempt to launch a massive slave uprising; his trial for murder and inciting insurrection only fueled their fears. Had Brown behaved in an obviously deranged fashion, had he raved in the defendant's chair or mumbled incoherently, he could have been dismissed as a lunatic. But Brown's lucid testimony convinced Southerners that there could be many more fanatics like John Brown up north, just waiting to try some other means of destroying slavery. The *Richmond Enquirer* called the event the beginning of the "irrepressible conflict" that New York senator William Seward had foreseen in 1858. Governor William H. Gist of South Carolina predicted that "Harper's Ferry is the truthful illustration of the first act in the drama to be performed on a Southern theatre."[3]

State governments embraced active steps to strengthen their defensive capabilities. Each state ordered a massive upgrade of its militia system and authorized vast expenditures for home defense. In Virginia, numerous militia companies formed while others resumed recruitment and regular drilling in the aftermath of John Brown's Raid. The governor of Florida, conceding that his state militia had deteriorated to a lowly condition, urged its restoration. "The militia should be thoroughly organized, armed and officered to be able to render efficient service in cases of sudden and pressing emergency," he instructed the state legislature. In Louisiana, the governor recommended a "complete reorganization of the militia," with a program "so clear, stringent and comprehensive that evasion would be impossible." His Alabama counterpart sought similar improvements in his state troops, but his words hinted that he had more in mind than simply suppressing slave revolts. "Seeing the disorganization of our state militia," he explained, "I have encouraged the formation of volunteer companies," which Alabama could employ beyond state borders more easily than militia. And create them they did. As a Virginian boasted, "volunteer companies were forming all over the South."[4]

Southern state governments sought to provide them with the very best arms and equipment, too. No longer relying on individuals to bring their antiquated or impractical firearms from home, states sought standardized, higher-quality weapons. In the winter of 1859–60, the Mississippi legislature investigated the quality of its weapons and determined "The State of Mississippi to be in a very poor condition for the defence of her Constitutional rights, if a contingency should occur." The legislature allocated $150,000 for the purchase of new weapons. The Alabama governor proposed the stockpiling and effective maintenance of an armory. "The recent developments at Harper's Ferry," he explained, "admonish us of the propriety of the State being ready, at all times, to protect the lives and property of her citizens." In response, the legislature set up a joint committee, whose recommendations exceeded the governor's requests. The Militia Committee sought the arming at state expense of the students at Tuskegee Collegiate Institute and the construction of an arsenal, a gunpowder mill, and a munitions factory. For future consideration, the joint committee also suggested the creation of a state military academy. Similarly, the Louisiana legislature authorized the creation of a state arsenal in Alexandria. Virginia promptly held "deliberations for the organization & arming the militia," an official gathering that Lieutenant Colonel Lee agreed to attend, and its militia system expanded rapidly. For added security, the legislature appropriated $320,000 to refurbish the old Virginia Manufactory Armory.[5]

Several states also sought to punish the North. Southern governors began to talk to one another about passing state laws that would levy a tax on Northern manufactured goods in Southern states. As one prominent Virginian explained, "by touching the pocket nerve" they hoped to "constrain the conservative part of the Yankees to keep the rest in order."[6]

John Brown's Raid convinced many Southerners that the Union offered them no real protection and that slaveholding states must to look to one another for security. A joint resolution in Florida called for the legislature to open communications with the Border States and to inform them that the people of Florida viewed them as the "van guard of our Constitutional rights" and pledged support to "stay the tide of aggressions." In an effort to tone down its fury over the raid, the legislature chose this more moderate version over an alternative wording that asserted its attachment to the Union "would be scarcely an atom in the scale against the perpetual maintenance of our system of African slave labor."[7]

Fully a year before secession, the South was preparing for war. Authorities in Alabama cryptically hinted about their intentions, promoting the development of a vastly improved militia, "so that in case of emergency, we might be provided with as many well trained officers and men, as possible, as a nucleus around which to rally." Just weeks after the Harpers Ferry raid, in his opening remarks for a new legislative session, Gov. William McWillie of Mississippi argued that "in view of our Federal relations" the state needed to arm the militia, particularly the new volunteer companies. "The mouth of the cannon and the glitter of steel," McWillie justified, "are arguments of power much stronger than those of the brain." After laying out his program for security in his January 1860 report, Louisiana governor Robert Wickliffe predicted, "If my suggestions are carried out, the State will be upon a war footing, at small expense."[8]

Although various Southerners and state entities had threatened secession over the years, never before had the discussions and assertions taken on such an ominous tone. Long before election day, slave states began to mull over secession. A joint resolution in Louisiana stated baldly that the election of a Republican president in the upcoming 1860 election would signal "the final destruction and overthrow of everything held most sacred and dear in the South." The State of Alabama spoke more bluntly. There, the governor concurred with a Senate proposal to discuss secession if a "Black Republican" were elected president.[9]

Southerners had a lengthy list of grievances against the free states. For several decades, abolitionists had agitated for emancipation, and Northerners had attempted to block the expansion of slavery into the territories. If the South accepted the North's position, it was tantamount to admitting slavery was wrong. The issue, many Southerners believed, was a canard. As the *Report of the Joint Committee of the General Assembly of Virginia on the Harpers Ferry Outrages, 26 January 1860* explained, "The whole argument against the *extension* of slavery is soon, by a very slight deflection, made to bear against the *existence* of slavery, and thus the anti-extension idea is merged in that of abolition." Non-extentionists were abolitionists in disguise.[10]

Southerners also found Personal Liberty Laws particularly odious. The U.S. Constitution authorized Congress to legislate on the return of fugitive slaves. In the Compromise of 1850, Congress had passed a tough new fugitive slave law, which placed the burden on blacks to prove they were free even though they could not testify on their own behalf and offered financial inducements for special commissioners to convict. Northern states responded by passing new Personal Liberty Laws, which undercut the process by providing certain rights for blacks whom Southern whites or their agents had seized as runaway slaves. In some instances, these laws forbade state and local officials from cooperating in the process. Not only did these Personal Liberty Laws effectively neutralize the constitutional rights of Southern slaveholders, but they also made free territories all the more unacceptable. If neighboring territories or states refused to enforce fugitive slave laws, then those areas could become havens for runaways, leading to a breakdown of slavery in areas that buffered free soil.

Worst of all, the Republican Party had become powerful in the North, a region with nearly twice as many people as the slave states. Republicans avowed their goal of restricting slavery's expansion, a euphemism in the minds of Southerners for abolitionism. As the governor of Alabama described, the Republican Party's "leading and publicly arrived project is the destruction of the institution of slavery as it exists in the slaveholding states." The party's agenda also included a series of economic and political planks that would largely benefit growth in the Northern states, such as a protective tariff and a homestead law that would give free land on the frontier to anyone who would settle it. At best these policies were lukewarm toward the vast majority of the South, and in some cases they would injure Southerners by making them pay higher prices for imported goods.[11]

To be sure, Southerners had other grievances against the North. Southern whites viewed their region as rural and dominated by agriculture; the North was more urbanized, more heavily industrialized. Southerners believed the tariff promoted Northern manufacturing at their expense, protecting Northern products and compelling Southerners to buy higher-priced, inferior domestic goods. More generally, while Northerners advocated a stronger central government, the South stood for states' rights.

In fact, these issues were not quite so simple and clear-cut. Even though twenty-two of twenty-five of the largest cities were in the North, two of every three farms were also in Northern states. Some Southern groups, such as sugar growers, relished the tariff, because it protected them from foreign competition. Feared retaliatory tariffs that would hinder the sales of Southern agricultural products overseas never really materialized. And many Northerners, perhaps even a majority, believed in states' rights. Certainly Northerners employed states' rights concepts when it suited them, as with the Personal Liberty Laws. Differences in philosophy represented shades, not clear demarcations.

Still, slavery was the one issue that neither section could skirt. When Lincoln won the presidency without receiving a single Electoral College vote from Southern states, South Carolina passed an ordinance of secession. Within several months, Georgia, Florida, Alabama, Mississippi, Louisiana, and Texas followed suit.

Their official justifications for leaving the Union offer unshakable proof that their principal motive was to protect and preserve slavery. South Carolina justified secession in a twenty-five-hundred-word history of slavery and Northern interference with it. The Georgia Secession Convention offered a similar rationale. "For twenty years past," its representatives noted, "the abolitionists and their allies in the Northern States have been engaged in constant efforts to subvert our institutions and to excite insurrection and servile war among us." To avoid any confusion over its motives, the State of Mississippi bluntly asserted, "Our position is thoroughly identified with the institution of slavery—the greatest material interest of the world." Texas explained that it had joined the Union "as a commonwealth holding, maintaining and protecting the institution known as negro slavery—the servitude of the African to the white race within her limits." Because Northerners threatened that right, Texans voted to separate from the Union.[12]

The South also began to mobilize for war. Most voters and government officials knew that the Union might not let them leave peaceably. Others, like Robert Stafford, a student at Auburn in Alabama, resigned himself to war as a certainty. "War is no trivial affair when you come to sum up the whole," he penned his sister, "but I am ready any time in whatsoever way I can [to] render assistance to our common cause." In anticipation of strife, states called out the militia and began to raise yet more volunteer units. There was no shortage of the willing.[13]

Four years earlier, in anticipation of just such a fight over secession, future division commander Stephen Dodson Ramseur, at the time a West Point cadet, called for the construction of arsenals and armories and the stockpiling of war materiel. At the time, no one heeded his proposal. By 1860, the political and emotional climate had changed. A month before Georgia took its vote—even before South Carolina left the Union—Governor Joseph E. Brown sent an official north to purchase arms, ammunition, and accouterments. Paul J. Semmes, a militia officer and future brigade commander in Lee's army, purchased artillery, pistols, and large quantities of artillery and musket ammunition, including gunpowder. Even as trouble seemed more and more imminent, Northern companies like Du Pont sold gunpowder and musket and cannon ammunition to Semmes. As early as January 1861, months before Virginia seceded, Governor John Letcher had proposed a significant expansion of the militia, above and beyond its enlarged levels. On the local level, county courts allocated money to purchase improved firearms and gunpowder, in case of war. At the University of Virginia, students organized themselves into companies, as they did on college campuses throughout the South. "Our two companies now number about 80 apiece," boasted John Davis at the beginning of March, "& we are getting to be pretty well drilled, as we drill $1\frac{1}{4}$ hours every evening." Mississippians, who had organized volunteer companies at a rate of two per month after John Brown's Raid, suddenly formed seven to eight companies of fifty to sixty men each week in November, December, and early January.[14]

By February 1861, representatives from the original seven seceding states had gathered in Montgomery, Alabama, to form the Confederate States of America. Despite entreaties from those seven, and attempts to justify their participation by calling for solidarity among the slaveholders, the other slave states decided to wait and see how the federal government attempted to resolve the crisis.

In April 1861, after political and military maneuvering on both sides, Confederate batteries hurled artillery projectiles at a partially completed bastion in

South Carolina called Fort Sumter. For twenty-four hours, the garrison withstood the bombardment. Only when it appeared that fires from heated shot endangered the fort's crew did the Union commander raise the white flag of surrender.

Once President Abraham Lincoln learned of the attack on Federal troops, he called out 75,000 militiamen to suppress the rebellion. The announcement convinced Virginia, North Carolina, Tennessee, and Arkansas to pass ordinances of secession, and within weeks their fellow slave states welcomed them into the new Confederacy. Confedcrate president Jefferson Davis could not wait that long. Just days after the Virginia convention voted to secede, a month before voters could ratify that decision, Davis had rushed forward regiments to protect the state, a huge industrial and agricultural gem that bordered the free states. A warrior by training, with extensive experience on the Military Affairs Committees of both U.S. houses of Congress and as secretary of war, Davis knew Virginia and the Richmond area would be an important battleground, and he would commit all the resources he could reasonably muster to protect it. He was already planning to form what would become the Army of Northern Virginia.[15]

Chapter 3

⎯⎯◦◦⎯⎯

THE VOLUNTEERS OF '61

"ALL IS IN EXCITEMENT HEAR—," Jesse Jordan proclaimed from Huntsville, Alabama, "war—war—war is the continued topics of evrydays conversation." In neighboring Georgia, the same fever had seized everyone, so H. W. Barclay recalled: "It seemed to me that the people were crazy and we were wild crazy." Even in Virginia, slow to secede from the Union, passions ran high. "I have heard only one sentiment," wrote a visitor in language reminiscent of Jordan, "& that is war! war! war!" He told his mother back home, "Virginia is all ablaze and Lincoln will never wave the sceptre of despotism over the sons of the old Dominion." On street corners, in shops, over dinner tables, the sectional strife dominated conversations. Prognostications, secondhand news, rumors, and more coursed through discussions, energizing the citizenry as never in their lifetimes. In early 1861, men could not sign up to fight quickly enough, and when all the slots were taken, those turned away were heartbroken. "If you all get into a fight before I get there," teased a jealous friend, "you will get whipped certain & sure."[1]

Armed with passion and little else, the "Boys of '61" enlisted in two great waves. Of the initial volunteers, some had been a part of prewar militia units; others volunteered as their state seceded from the Union. They entered the armed services in that first *rage militaire*, when passions gushed forward and everyone had war on the brain. Only a handful predicted a lengthy struggle in those early days—and those farsighted few who did, like President Davis, could never have convinced a cocksure congress otherwise—and the government established most terms of service for a year, although some military units signed on for the war. The second great rush occurred in the aftermath of the Battle of First Manassas. The euphoria of that first victory stirred hundreds of thousands, and the Confederate Congress tapped into the overflowing spirit and authorized the creation of a new round of volunteer units. This time, Congress acted more circumspectly, extending terms of service to up to thirty-six months in length.[2]

Volunteers came in varying ages, with all sorts of backgrounds. John T. Bivins of Milledgeville, Georgia, was one of the youngest. He slipped off with-

17

out his parents' permission and enlisted at fourteen, an extremely tender age for someone to actually serve in the infantry, and not as a drummer boy. His father pleaded for his son's release, taking his case all the way to Davis. "He belongs to his Country, but *take him at 18* & thereby give me a chance to qualify him by education and maturity to Service his Country well," Will Bivins wrote. Davis saw that the lad was shipped home, but not before he had served more than six months in the Confederate army. On the opposite end of the age scale stood Edmund Ruffin, sexagenarian farmer and Fire-Eater who carried a musket at First Manassas and then realized that he could not cope with the physical demands of military service. The average age for volunteers in 1861 was twenty-five; the median, or middle age, was twenty-four. Only one in every seven enlistees that first year was eighteen or younger, and fewer than a third were twenty-one or younger.[3]

Although the bulk of the enlistees were in their midtwenties or older, almost three of every four were single. As a group, unmarried men had the least responsibility in society, and generally they could detach from work and personal obligations more easily to serve in the army. James D. Gilliam of Amherst County, Virginia, was a twenty-two-year-old laborer living with his mother. One of seven children, he had three adult brothers who were still at home, which enabled him to enlist in the Lynchburg Artillery in April, knowing that his siblings would look after her. Despite his very different background, William Herring had a similar situation. Herring grew up in a large and wealthy slaveholding family with plenty of brothers and sisters to assist their father in managing a twenty-three-slave plantation. Instead, he had opted to farm for a neighbor. When the war broke out, Herring had no real obligations or concerns about family welfare. He was twenty-four, unmarried, and the owner of five slaves, so he joined the 3rd North Carolina Cavalry to defend the institution that generated such a good income for him and his family.[4]

More surprising was that nearly one in every four men who enlisted in 1861 left behind a wife and children, a difficult proposition for the entire family. James W. Dickinson, a mattress maker in Campbell County, Virginia, had a young wife and a three-year-old baby. Fortunately, he also had a sister who lived with them, and she could help ease the burden on his wife. With considerable property at risk, thirty-four-year-old Elbert Leech could not resist the call to arms, and he joined the 26th Alabama Infantry as a captain. Unlike Dickinson, however, Leech left his wife with enormous responsibility. She had to oversee their five children, the farm, and sixteen slaves. Had Leech not possessed enormous confidence in his wife's ability to manage all those affairs, he probably would have hesitated to join the army. Her capability of overseeing the farm paved the way for his military service. John M. Tilley of Crawfordsville, Georgia, had a wife, three young children, and a dozen slaves on a large farm. "I believe that it will be rather to my benefit to be away from home," Tilley commented to his wife in midsummer 1861 after enlisting in the 15th Georgia. "You & Dock will get everything in such good order & the negroes in such good training that I feel I'll have nothing to do when I get home."[5]

Among enlistees of 1861, half the men had no accumulated wealth, according to the 1860 census, yet the average personal wealth was $1,615, a considerable sum at the start of the war. Very wealthy individuals more than compensated for their poorer comrades. But because so many of the soldiers were just starting out in life, their personal wealth did not adequately reflect their background or their access to money and property. Quite a number of soldiers had grown up in comfortable middle- and upper-class households and still resided with their parents or relatives. Others, for employment or to learn a trade, had moved into the homes of wealthy families, where they enjoyed the comforts of an opulent lifestyle despite their status as an employee. More reflective of the average soldier's true financial status was a combination of the wealth of the individual soldier and, if he lived at home, his family. By adding those two categories, the average total estate soared to $6,882, a figure that positioned these men at the edge of the wealthy class. The median combined wealth climbed to $1,365, a figure that placed them comfortably in the middle class. Although twenty-year-old George Webb of Baton Rouge, Louisiana, merely worked as a farm hand for the family and had no wealth of his own, his mother, Amelia, was worth almost $40,000, and the family held title to twenty slaves. Ganam S. Lyons, twenty-six years of age, had only $100 worth of money and property to his name. Still, he farmed alongside his father on Alabama soil worth $800. With his father's additional property valued at $600, the Lyonses lived a middle-class lifestyle.[6]

For those volunteers who still lived at home, if one combines their personal wealth with their family's net worth, the picture appears very different. What emerges from an examination of that combined wealth is a huge range among these men. The ratio of soldiers and their families who had total assets under $300 was about one-third, the same as those who were worth more than $5,000, a truly substantial sum in 1860. One in every five enlistees and their families had accumulated wealth that surpassed $10,000; one in five were worth nothing, too. Rich and poor shouldered arms in equal proportions in 1861, and the middle lot of them were certainly from solid, middle-class backgrounds.[7]

If one includes nonfamily wealth within their households, the figure for the average household rose to a staggering $11,205, while the median wealth increased dramatically to $3,500, or an upper-middle-class lifestyle. At the time of the secession crisis, John T. Kerfoot studied at Columbia College in Washington, D.C. His widowed mother owned one slave and was worth $1,500. Still, she resided in the home of John Smith, who may have been related to her. Smith claimed ownership of fifteen slaves and over $50,000 as his net worth, providing a quality of life that was a far cry from what John and his mother could afford on their total assets.[8]

Even more revealing was their attachment to slavery. Among the enlistees in 1861, slightly more than one in ten owned slaves personally. This compared favorably to the Confederacy as a whole, in which one in every twenty white persons owned slaves. Yet more than one in every four volunteers that first year lived with parents who were slaveholders. Combining those soldiers who owned slaves with those soldiers who lived with slaveholding family members, the proportion rose to 36 percent. That contrasted starkly with the 24.9 percent, or one in every four households, that owned slaves in the South, based on the 1860 census. Thus, volunteers in 1861 were 42 percent more likely to own slaves themselves or to live with family members who owned slaves than the general population.[9]

The attachment to slavery, though, was even more powerful. One in every ten volunteers in 1861 did not own slaves themselves but lived in households headed by nonfamily members who did. This figure, combined with the 36 percent who owned or whose family members owned slaves, indicated that almost one of every two 1861 recruits lived with slaveholders. Nor did the direct exposure stop there. Untold numbers of enlistees rented land from, sold crops to, or worked for slaveholders. In the final tabulation, the vast majority of the volunteers of 1861 had a direct connection to slavery. For slaveholder and nonslaveholder alike, slavery lay at the heart of the Confederate nation. The fact that their paper notes frequently depicted scenes of slaves demonstrated the institution's central role and symbolic value to the Confederacy.[10]

More than half the officers in 1861 owned slaves, and none of them lived with family members who were slaveholders. Their substantial median combined wealth ($5,600) and average combined wealth ($8,979) mirrored that high proportion of slave ownership. By comparison, only one in twelve enlisted men owned slaves, but when those who lived with family slave owners were included, the ratio exceeded one in three. That was 40 percent above the tally for all households in the Old South. With the inclusion of those who resided in nonfamily slaveholding households, the direct exposure to bondage among enlisted personnel was four of every nine. Enlisted men owned less wealth, with combined levels of $1,125 for the median and $7,079 for the average, but those numbers indicated a fairly comfortable standard of living. Proportionately, far more officers were likely to be professionals in civil life, and their age difference, about four years older than enlisted men, reflected their greater accumulated wealth.[11]

The war was a great leveler. Howlit Irvin, a prewar student and the son of the former lieutenant governor of Georgia, owned nothing in 1860, but his father possessed nearly $170,000 in wealth, including an estate with 117 slaves. His father died in an explosion that year, and Howlit and his brother took over the family plantation. At the opposite end of the financial ladder, William R. Phillips, a twenty-seven-year-old laborer from Portsmouth, Virginia, had a wife, a child, and $20 to his name. Both Irvin and Phillips served as privates in artillery batteries in 1861.[12]

Slightly fewer than one in every twenty of these Rebels was foreign-born. With a combined median wealth of $0 and an average combined wealth of

$803, most were poorer than the Southern-born Confederates. The bulk of the foreign-born were men like Patrick Brennan, who had left his native Ireland and gravitated to the urban area of Savannah, where he found employment as an unskilled laborer. Brennan, a twenty-one-year-old, was single and had no accumulated wealth. William Forner, an immigrant from the German state of Baden, found employment as a butcher for Lewis Eichner, a master butcher in Baltimore who had wealth totaling $3,500. The twenty-two-year-old Forner had yet to leave his mark and claimed no appreciable wealth.[13]

Yet some of the immigrants had amassed considerable wealth by 1860. Frank Potts, a lieutenant in the 1st Virginia Infantry, joined the rebellion to "exact respect from our Northern enemy, and recognition from the nations of the earth." A prewar merchant grocer who had accumulated an impressive $8,000 of property including two slaves, Potts had established himself well in Richmond society, taking a Virginian as his bride. Potts's captain, John Dooley, fled Ireland for America after the failed Revolution of 1848. A prewar merchant as well, Dooley estimated his wealth in real estate and personal property at nearly $100,000, with seven slaves.[14]

Frederick Law Olmsted, an unusually perceptive traveler in the prewar South, believed racial animosity bound the poorer immigrants to the slave-holding cause. "No native can exceed, in idolatry to Slavery, the mass of the ignorant foreign-born laborers," Olmsted insisted. "Their hatred of the negro is proportionate to the equality of their intellect and character to his; and their regard for Slavery, to their disinclination to compete with him in a fair field." Harsh racial attitudes and a fear of competition—along with the steady pay for military service that lured many poor folks—could easily explain the consider-able rush to arms by immigrants.[15]

No doubt, the issue of abolitionism played an important role among those without slaves, who would lose their elevated status and be forced to compete with blacks if emancipation occurred. This same consideration would certainly have resonated among foreign-born slaveholders. But quite a number of immigrants had ties to the failed European Revolution of 1848. Either they or their parents had fled their native land in the wake of the revolt for freedom, and it sensitized them to the powers of tyranny in government. Dooley's son, also named John, could not understand how a soldier who had fought in the Revolution of 1848 could fight for the Federals and "consistently turn his back on his principles and for the pitiful hire of a few dollars do all in his power to crush a brave people asserting their right of self government." It boggled his mind that someone who had endured that struggle could now "engage in the cause of tyranny, fighting against honesty, Justice, and right." Although another sol-dier, an English immigrant, was not inspired by the same event, he nonetheless embraced the same stance. After living in the United States for some years, and residing in Mississippi when the war broke out, he joined the Confederate army because of the "inherent love of liberty which animates every English heart." His "manhood" would not permit him to "stand idly by, and gaze upon the despotism which a blind and fanatical majority sought to thrust upon an unoffending and almost helpless minority." Immigrant James Sheeran, a Catholic chaplain for the 14th Louisiana and fervent advocate for the Confederacy, joined the army with an absolutely clear conscience. "Abe Lincoln has perjured himself by violating the Constitution since his introduction into office," the priest insisted, and that was enough grounds to lead him to aid the rebellion.[16]

Having embraced Southern life and Southern people, and having been adopted by them, immigrants felt a powerful attachment to the Confederacy. In February 1861, Bavarian native Philip Kohn wrote his immigrant son Theodore, reminding him that "I got him away from the old world, from the old 'rust' fatherland, so that he has not to serve as a soldier-slave for an unjust cause." Theodore begged to differ. He had lived a few years in South Carolina, and Southern life had imbued him with such deep affection for his adopted homeland that he volunteered in 1861. Louis Leon, a German by birth and a prewar clerk, fought for four years, and when the war ended, he refused to concede anything. The only grudge he bore was the defeat. "I shall now close this diary in sorrow," he wrote defiantly, "but to the last I shall say that, although but a private, I still say our Cause was just, nor do I regret one thing that I have done to cripple the North." While ethnic groups formed their own companies, such as Dooley's Irishmen or the French and Irish in Louisiana regiments that came to Virginia in 1861, many immigrants, like Leon and Kohn, integrated in local units, regardless of ethnic background.[17]

Throughout the entire war, just under 5 percent of all soldiers who served in the Virginia Theater with what ultimately became the Army of Northern Virginia were born in Northern states. In the random sample of 600 men, not one owned slaves, and only one lived with parents who did. They tended to be poorer than many of their comrades, with a combined median wealth of $0 and an average of $2,875, mirroring the paucity of slave ownership. Yet they fought, and in the course of that experience quite a number of them exhibited an unusual degree of loyalty to the Confederacy. Perhaps they lived up to the notion that the most obstinate advocate is often the recent convert. Having resided in the North and the South, it is also possible that they weighed both societies and preferred life in the South. They may also have been unusually sensitive to criticism from family and friends up north. In their letters to loved ones in the North, they defended their decision to side with the Confederacy by criticizing the Union in harsh, almost shrill terms.[18]

Frank Dunbar Ruggles left Massachusetts for New Orleans and worked as a clerk for a master shoemaker, who also hailed from the Old Bay State. Ruggles responded to the call in May 1861 and joined the Washington Artillery, destined for Virginia. Not until the fall of 1862 did he have an opportunity to send a letter legally across lines to his father. A decade ago, he wondered, who would have guessed that any dispute "would cause men to take up arms, Father against Son, & Brother against Brother, thereby forever severing ties not only of friendship but of blood." He thought, "Truly the people of the North are bereft of reason." Ruggles warned his father, "Many doubtless with you are sincere in their belief of the righteousness of their Cause, but with *us* we are a *unit* in the firm conviction that our Cause is a just & holy one & 'Thrice armed is he whose cause is just.'" He concluded his letter with the words, "Trusting and Praying that God may open the eyes of the blind families of the North to a true view of their condition & intentions, that their ears may be opened to the popular Voice of the South which only asks of them the Rights, to be let alone & allowed to depart from a Union which is no longer a Union, in peace."[19]

Native New Yorker Dewees Ogden, who enlisted in the Richmond Howitzers, had moved to Mississippi before the war, but had returned to New York for a visit when Lincoln declared the Southern states in rebellion. He slipped down to Virginia, where he joined a militia cavalry company and then entered Confederate service. His stance alongside his adopted countrymen outraged his family, and the sharp criticism and character assassinations caught his younger sisters in the middle. Evidently, his father even put a price on his son's head. It was the "verdict of the *'whole family'*" that he should suffer severe punishment for his "treason desertion and ingratitude." Ogden did not care what his relatives said about him, "provided they will aim directly at me and not through my little sisters." He chided Northerners, especially his family, for their behavior during the sectional tensions and secession crisis. He felt they had lost all perspective and cast aside all values. "Had I not seen ministers forget their calling and their master in denunciations of what they fancied a prostrate people?" he questioned his uncle. "Had I not seen *gentlemen* forget their training while they stooped to felonies and justified them with a catch word [beauty or booty]? . . . Had I not seen delicate women forget their womanhood while they applauded crimes & atrocities that nature must shudder at? Had I not *known* a father who set a price upon the head of his rebel son?"[20]

When Northern-born Rebel Anderson Merchant wrote a letter to his mother, it had an entirely different tone. Although he refused to yield an inch in support of the Confederacy, Merchant perceived his mother as an emotional caretaker who would empathize with her son's decision. "Do not feel sad my dearest Mother because your son has, and will be fighting on a different side from all his relations," Merchant begged. "Your son Andy feels he is acting right." He urged her to patch his relationship up with his father and a family friend, whom he was "fighting up against." Merchant then appealed to her, "My dearest Mother if you have any influence, endeavor to stop a War which is unnatural and which is the unjust one waged by the North on the South."[21]

Even individuals from Border States like Maryland sometimes found it difficult to join with their fellow Confederates. Union crackdowns on dissent prevented Rebel supporters from organizing openly, and patrols and troops built up in the southern part of the state sometimes made the Potomac River boundary between Maryland and Virginia seem like an ocean. One Marylander tried to slip off to Confederate lines, all the time living in fear of apprehension by Union authorities. The first time he tried to run off, his father caught him at the Washington Depot. Worried that his son would live like "white negroes" in the army, "My father threatened me with personal violence" if he ever tried that again. The wrath of his father did not discourage him, though. At the beginning of August, he and about twenty others took off for Rebeldom. "I was very much scared they would find out my destination and arrest me," he recorded in his diary. They went by boat across the Potomac River, and his friend, Clinton James, was caught. He eluded authorities and made it into Confederate lines, where he joined the 1st Maryland Artillery.[22]

Before Federals had overrun large portions of the Confederacy and cut off soldiers from their families, these Rebel soldiers of Northern birth were among the very few in the army who had no family support structure, and their comrades in arms appreciated that plight. Virginian James Langhorne asked that his mother or sister sew a shirt for "one of my best friends," a "high-toned gentleman and I really love him." The young officer explained that "he is fighting against the State that gave him birth, Father, Mother Bro. & Sister and for what[?] because he thinks our cause is just." His father came down to Harpers Ferry by private conveyance and implored him to resign and come north. His mother pleaded with him to reconsider, too, but she could not persuade him. "He could not give up the loyal principals of his noble heart & made the sacrifice of all family connection." Langhorne requested the shirt as a small token, because "such sacrifices as these ought to be rewarded." After all, "he has not the sweet assurance that we have that we are fighting for 'our own, our native land,' but he is fighting for justice which is inspiration enough for a noble soul like his."[23]

Those adopted Southerners lacked that reciprocal relationship between soldiers and the home front. The men in Rebel gray pledged to protect the folks at home from invaders who sought to disrupt their lives, steal their property, and deprive them of civil liberties. In return, soldiers expected the people back home to provide for the army, to support them physically, spiritually, and emotionally, and to look after their loved ones who must cope without them. But with companies and batteries raised on the local level, these units also generated a powerful communal interest. This military service and the threat of invasion drew the Southern people together as nothing else could. While a majority of the population endorsed secession, many Southerners who initially opposed or hesitated to support it came around to the cause, simply because their children, relatives, and neighbors were suddenly in harm's way. With loved ones at risk, they could not turn their back on Confederate independence or the war. Once those men marched off to the front, private views became secondary to their welfare and success. William Blackford of Virginia retained his staunch Unionist sympathies until his sons and nephews joined the Confederate army. Confronted with a choice, he could not turn his back on his family, Blackford confided in his diary, "So I have a deep personal interest in the strife." Weighing the various concerns, personal opinions seemed inconsequential compared to the lives of people Southerners had known and cared for over the years.[24]

In their towns and communities, people came together to raise and support military units. They adopted unusual names for their military organizations, like the Dismal Swamp Rangers, the Conecuh Guards, the Ft. Browder Roughs, or the Panola Vindicators, to reflect their localities. Over time, those stylish titles would fade, as companies banded into regiments and a letter replaced the old designation, but that local attachment remained inviolate.[25]

Once soldiers assembled, their companies, batteries, or regiments had an opportunity to choose officers. Election day was usually quite an event. Candidates frequently curried favor by plying the men with whiskey, which made for a raucous affair. Companies from various sections of the state colluded to ensure the election of certain individuals. The victors saw this horse trading of commissions as part and parcel of the American political tradition; the losers cried foul. Rarely, though, did the protesters ever get satisfaction. In Jesse Jordan's 4th Alabama, there was so much maneuvering, lobbying, and manipulation that regimental officer selection more closely resembled a political convention than a military organization. In Company A, 18th Virginia, a small group held a caucus and prepared a slate. They nominated one another and won the election by voting as a bloc against the wishes of a tough orderly sergeant who had alienated them.[26]

Resentfulness and sensitivity over the outcome of the election often spilled over into service. Officers and enlisted men stirred the pot of discontent against other officers, as military life did not measure up to expectations and army discipline offended sensitive souls. Protesters circulated petitions for the relief of officers, as the men of the 4th Alabama did with their regimental commander, or they so undercut the authority of an officer that he lost all credibility with his command. Shrewd general officers dismissed the complaints unless soldiers accused the officer of violations of army regulations, just as Johnston had done with the 4th Alabama. In the 15th Virginia Infantry, the regimental commander quashed incipient protests by reminding the soldiers, "the Officers of the Companies have been elected by themselves and if they have failed in their Selection they have nobody to blame but themselves." He then informed them that the issue was now beyond their control. Meetings and letters to remove officers were illegal and soldiers would be punished for it.[27]

In the end, the troops did not choose all that badly. Despite the political maneuvers and occasional improper behavior, companies and regiments usually selected individuals for leadership posts who had prior military experience or training. They chose Mexican War veterans and former students at West Point, Virginia Military Institute, the South Carolina Military Academy (now generally called The Citadel), and other military academies, whenever available, for leadership positions. At least these individuals knew basic tactics and organization. Ultimately, volunteers who had attended any of the various schools contributed mightily to the army's development that first year and throughout the entire war. The 28th North Carolina Infantry elected James H. Lane, a Virginia Military Institute graduate and a professor at the North Carolina Military Institute, as regimental colonel. "Every man, officer and soldier, in the whole camp is anxious for your acceptance," wrote a regimental spokesman. "Most of us are 'Mountain Boys,' and we trust that we do not disgrace the home from which we came." They believed that "all that we need is a 'first rate' colonel to mould us to his own ideas." At the time, Lane was a lieutenant colonel in the 1st North Carolina Infantry, and he had no connection with the 28th. Nonetheless, he accepted the offer and led the 28th North Carolina as its regimental and then its brigade commander.[28]

One Confederate assessed the process of selecting officers shrewdly, stating, "Men are as intelligent in camp as at home, and can vote as intelligently for their officers as they can for members of Congress." Well over 700 former students at Virginia Military Institute served as officers in the war, most of them in the Virginia Theater and nearly all of them elected to office. The North Carolina Military Institute performed a similar function for its state. Early in the war governors from both states called out their cadet corps to act as drillmasters for recruits at the state rendezvous camps in Richmond and Raleigh, and later many of those cadets received commissions as officers in their state units through the election process. Conversely, when soldiers chose unwisely, there was recourse. In mid-June 1861, Lee advised Beauregard to notify the governor whenever he had incompetent officers. Later, army commanders used general courts-martial to weed out poor officers, and eventually Congress authorized the formation of boards to examine and make recommendations on the fitness of officers.[29]

With officers chosen, time at home was short. After a local sendoff consisting of banquets, speeches, hugs, kisses, and emotional farewells, the new regiments and batteries departed for the front. Some of the Virginia units marched to rendezvous points like Harpers Ferry, Manassas Junction, or Richmond. Soldiers from other states or more distant points in Virginia normally traveled by train. The thrill and novelty of a lengthy trip, the huge outpouring of affection and enthusiasm from strangers along the way, the nervous energy and anticipation at the start of a great adventure, and the boisterousness of exclusive male company who were stuck in tight confines made the trip a raucous, sometimes riotous affair.

Those initial units that passed through Unionist country had to keep up their guard at all times. Rumors circulated that Unionists planned to waylay them, and officers directed the men to travel with loaded weapons in readiness for a fight. By contrast, Sam Melton of South Carolina, who served on Milledge L. Bonham's brigade staff, described his trip to Virginia on a troop train in April as an uplifting experience. Women waved handkerchiefs and cried out "God's speed" as they chugged past, and the outpouring of enthusiasm lifted the volunteers to new heights of emotion and enthusiasm. Everyone seemed to be behind them and the cause, and the public reaction, particularly among women, inspired the soldiers. "It is astonishing what effect the waving of a woman's hand kerchief has upon a soldier," he elucidated. "They all cheered it with deafening peals, every time they saw it: and I verily believe a woman with a hand kerchief could send one entire little army to perdition."[30]

At least Melton and his comrades rode the rails in the cool of April. Men in other commands packed into small passenger and box cars in spring and summer heat, at times almost gasping for some fresh air or a comforting breeze. The foul smells from excessive perspiration, tobacco smoke, and burnt timber overpowered all other senses, and the only escape appeared to be the roofs or platform cars. There smoke and cinders played havoc with them, along with nature's elements. When men in the 12th Georgia arrived in Virginia, "with nothing to protect us from the sun, dust and smoke," quipped one of their own, " 'twas hard to tell whether we were from Georgia or Africa." The 48th Georgia had traveled by train from Dalton, Georgia, to Bristol, Tennessee. That rugged country even got the better of their train. On several occasions, the men had to get off the cars and push them upgrade.[31]

Lafayette McLaws, future division commander, entrained in Augusta bound for Virginia on what amounted to the trip through hell. At Branchville, South Carolina, his train took on 116 volunteers from Lowndes County, Georgia, and "from that time, there was an end to all individuality." They surrounded him, "dressed and undressed as suited their humor or degree of heat." Soldiers pulled off their shoes, and as the late June heat increased, "the *feetid* odor was tremendous." He could not understand "the insane idea peculiar to volunteers" that they had to cheer all passersby. At each stop, everyone rushed out to get water, and when the conductor cried, "get aboard," several of these Georgians would call back, "I cant find a board but can get a shingle if you want one!" to which the men roared in hilarity—time after time. The next day, train officials placed the volunteers in the baggage cars, but the day after, the men returned "and the odors and the singing and the patriotic yelling was truly remarkable," commented McLaws. All in all, he assessed them as fine-looking men and reasonably well behaved, largely due to their captain.[32]

The officers of the 14th Louisiana Infantry did not maintain much control over their men. Some troops had smuggled whiskey on board the train and got drunk before they disembarked for the evening at Grand Junction, Tennessee. Although the regimental commander ordered all drinking establishments closed and placed guards outside them, the drunken soldiers slipped through windows and continued their consumption of spirits. When guards tried to stop them, the drunken mob turned hostile and disarmed them. Fortunately, the Confederacy's inability to provide for its men at this stage of the war proved for once to be a boon. Intoxicated and eager for trouble, few of the troublemakers had arms, and none had ammunition. The regimental commander had enough sense to issue ammunition only to the officers.

As the mutineers poured out onto the street, officers fired into the crowd and dropped several men, but rioters chased them into a hotel and then set fire to the building. While officers and reliable troops rushed to the rescue and extinguished the flames, inebriated soldiers stormed the smoldering hotel and ransacked it. The colonel jumped into the fray, discharging his pistol into the crowd to restore order. Two looters were hit, but one sergeant who was attempting to aid the officers fell, too, at the hands of his colonel's misdirected shot. With the aid of fellow officers, the regimental commander eventually drove the drunken plunderers into the street. The struggle continued to rage for about an hour, until the riotous soldiers—too tired from fighting and too drunk to continue their resistance—succumbed to overwhelming force. They had enlisted to fight Yankees; instead, seven lay dead with nineteen more wounded in the melee, all by officers on their own side.[33]

WHEN JAMES LANGHORNE of the 4th Virginia Infantry arrived in Winchester after a train ride with his regiment from Richmond, he admitted to his mother, "Ma I begin to think I am a soldier in earnest." The Confederacy had assembled quite an impressive array of talent in Virginia in 1861. Cadmus Wilcox, a West Pointer and Regular Army officer who had written a prewar book on the impact of rifled weapons on tactics, observed to his sister, "We have the best portion of the old army, I mean not in numbers, but in talent." His only question mark was the effectiveness of "a number of Brigadier generals from civil life who do not know a great deal." On the whole, the officers and enlisted men on the regimental and battery levels were a motivated, spirited lot, but not the traditional sort of mix. "The men in the ranks here are not soldiers such as are seen in ordinary Wars," noted a soldier stationed in Virginia. "You will find a Father and all his sons and sons in law and Grandsons in one company." When Thomas Rowland, a Virginia cavalryman, scanned the regimental rows and tented fields, he observed different faces and backgrounds but the same inspired look. "You would be surprised to see what men we have in the ranks," he informed his mother in May 1861, "cool headed farmers, & men of property & family, men who will give all they have & devote their lives to the cause of their native state." This was not so much an army of the poor with an educated and opulent officer corps. It was instead largely an army of property, primarily soldiers who either owned land or a business themselves or lived in a household where their family did. This was an army that risked everything—families, property, and slaves that had taken them and their ancestors lifetimes to accumulate.[34]

Perhaps President Davis expressed it best when he told a small group that he anticipated a long war, but believed the character of the Confederate soldier would win in the end. "We will do all that can be done by pluck and muscle, endurance, and dogged courage—dash and red-hot patriotism." But as Davis also knew, even highly motivated soldiers had their limits. That level of commitment would wear down over years of suffering and sacrifices. Even red-hot patriotism burned out eventually.[35]

Chapter 4

---◦◦◦---

WHY THEY ENLISTED

O N JULY 25, 1861, four days before the Panola Guards entrained
for Virginia as Company G, Cobb's Legion, the women of Georgia Female College in Macon presented a flag to the men. Before the student
body and sundry townsfolk, Miss Josie V. Thrasher, spokesperson for the students, reminded the soldiers, "The Constitution, which was framed by our
fathers for the peace, happiness, and well being of the whole country, which
recognizes distinctly, and almost in so many words, the right of property in our
servants; and spreads its broad folds equally over South and North; has been
subverted by Republican fanaticism." To these powerful words, Capt. Gazaway
L. B. Knight pledged, "We go to meet the enemy on the borders, and aid in
driving them back. We go to ensure his never setting foot upon our soil, and
to keep afar from those we love the horrors and misseries of war." He accepted
the colors, vowing, "On the field of battle it shall float in the thickest of the
fight" and "it shall never trail dishonored." In the course of defending them,
Knight suffered two wounds and ultimately received a medical discharge from
Confederate service.[1]

Two months earlier, Rev. Dr. Benjamin Moore Palmer had the privilege
of speaking at City Hall in New Orleans, at the departure ceremony for the
Washington Artillery, also bound for Virginia. Palmer thundered: "It is a war of
defence against wicked and cruel aggression; a war of civilization against a ruthless barbarism, which would dishonor the dark ages; a war of religion against
a blind and bloody fanaticism. It is war for your homes and your firesides—for
your wives and your children—for the land which the Lord has given us for a
heritage. It is a war for the maintenance of the broadest principle for which
a free people can contend—for the right of self-government." Some eighty-five years earlier, their ancestors had fought for the same cause. Now, Palmer
insisted, it was their turn.

These speeches—one from an educated young woman, a response from
a volunteer company commander, and a third by a prominent Louisianan—
suggested diverse yet powerful motives for Confederate enlistment. Because
the Confederate states had seceded to protect slavery, Thrasher, among many,

viewed the war as an extension of that effort. Soldiers bore arms to preserve the "peculiar institution." For others, like Captain Knight, the principal mission was to defend hearth and home. Dr. Palmer viewed the concept of self-determination as paramount, although he also emphasized the traditional role of military forces in protecting a nation and its loved ones from invaders. Still, for other men, personal considerations weighed heavily in their determination to volunteer. By swapping civilian garb for Confederate gray, those who struggled financially in peacetime found steady employment. And for some, particularly youthful prospects, the temptations of travel and adventure proved too alluring to resist.[2]

An Irish-born private named William Mooney, the jokester of Company E, 12th Georgia Infantry, played up the stereotype of his feisty ancestry when he quipped to his mates, "A short time ago he bought a negro, he says, to have something to fight for." Underlying Mooney's effort at humor rested a fundamental truth. As Lt. William E. Smith of the 4th Georgia Infantry noted, "Without slavery, there would not have been at the time any reasons for break up [of] the old government, [and] with it, there was an eternal strife[,] dispute and quarrell between the North & South." If the Rebel states seceded to protect slavery, and the Union attempted to prevent secession, then those who owned slaves, or had a direct connection to the institution, certainly had the most at stake in Confederate independence.[3]

In fact, Southerners who resided in slaveholding households turned out in disproportionate numbers to fight in Virginia, comprising four of every nine men. If one includes those who rented land from slaveholders, or whose principal clients were slaveholders and whose livelihood depended on slave labor, the figure soars well above half the soldiers. With so much of their personal wealth and investment at risk, or with their economic well-being in jeopardy, it is no small wonder that these men fought.[4]

Beyond those who lived with, worked with, or derived their principal income from slavery or slaveholders, it was imperative that the remaining population established an attachment to the "peculiar institution." Without full participation and cooperation from the entire community, slavery could not survive. If then were any sign of weakness, if any individual turned a blind eye to runaway slaves or failed to vigilantly enforce local standards for supervision of bondsmen, the institution could begin to crumble. In order to retain the goodwill and cooperation of others in the community, slaveholders assumed certain responsibilities and concerns for their neighbors. One of the ways they could help out family, friends, and neighbors was with their additional labor. Thomas Petty's father, James, did not own slaves, but Uncle John Petty did. Since young Petty's father and uncle lived in the same town, and the families were close, Thomas's father could borrow one of his brother's thirteen slaves any time he needed one. Along similar lines, James B. W. Foster, who joined the 2nd North Carolina Cavalry in 1861, did not own slaves, but all four of the families that lived around him did. If Foster ever fell on hard times physically, or if he undertook a project that required additional labor for a day or two, one of them could lend him a slave. It would be the neighborly thing to do, and it would ensure that Foster continued to look out for slaveholder interests. In other instances, absence of economies of scale made it impractical for small farmers to own a cotton gin or to transport their cash crops to market themselves. Slaveholders filled the void by helping their neighbors. A Southerner need not own slaves personally to benefit from them. Virtually everyone had a kinsman or friend who would lend or hire out bondsmen temporarily.[5]

Most white Southerners hoped to own slaves one day. The addition of a single slave to a household increased productivity and profits dramatically. So lucrative, in fact, was slavery that the price of bondsmen rose 70 percent in the decade before the Civil War. Slave ownership, wealth, social standing, and power melded together in the pre–Civil War South. Because virtually every opulent Southerner owned slaves, the institution rested at the core of financial, social, and political success. For those on the outside looking in, the quickest route to acquiring wealth, climbing the social ladder, and gaining influence in the community was by saving enough money to purchase a slave.[6]

As an added reinforcement, a deep and powerful sense of racial superiority strengthened nonslaveholder commitment and active support for the war. In a speech on the U.S. Senate floor in 1858, James Henry Hammond of South Carolina explained that in all societies "there must be a class to do the menial duties, to perform the drudgeries of life." This group "constitutes the very mudsill of society." In the North, it was the wage slave; in the South, it was the African slave. Either way, the lowly performed essential, basic tasks so that others—in the South, all white people—did not have to tackle demeaning duties. They could enjoy freedom and bask in their elevated status.[7]

In 1860, J. D. B. DeBow, a Southern intellectual and the editor of the influential periodical *DeBow's Review*, insisted that slavery was "an interest of the whole community," not just slaveholders. "*The non-slaveholder of the South preserved the status of the white man, and is not regarded as an inferior or a dependent,*" DeBow argued. They had a full voice in the selection of their political leaders, and through their labor they contributed to the economic well-being of the entire South. Whites who did not own slaves nonetheless upheld the virtues and sustained the superiority of their race. For those reasons, he felt justified in asserting that "the interest of the poorest non-slaveholder among us is to make common cause with, and die in the last trenches in defence of, the slave property of his more favored neighbor."[8]

Both Hammond and DeBow played the race card skillfully. Far too sophisticated for crass racial arguments, they shrewdly packaged their case in terms of social elevation, virtue, and financial well-being. Since the latter half of the seventeenth century, slaveholders had used race as a means of building allegiances with lower-and middle-class whites and preventing the poor from joining forces with blacks against the wealthy. By reminding all whites of the inferiority of African-Americans, slaveholders built strong bridges with non-slaveholding whites.[9]

As SOUTHERN STATES seceded and braced for armed attempts by Northerners to keep them in the Union, rich, middle class, and poor alike prepared to resist. "Virginia is united as one man, in the spirit of lofty defiance; and this includes all classes," pronounced Presbyterian cleric Robert Lewis Dabney, who would serve on Stonewall Jackson's staff. According to a member of the 4th Virginia Cavalry, it was the race card that motivated many less-fortunate soldiers. They believed that Northerners intended to force racial changes on them that were anathema to their fundamental beliefs. "Our poor men of the southern army say it is to free the negro and make the negro equal with the poor man of the southern states and have free mixed schools and a negro can marry a white girl and etc.," he recorded, "and the men are saying they will wade in blood to their chins before such a thing shall happen to our people."[10]

Steeped as they were in the history of their Revolutionary ancestors, Southerners were sensitive to any perceived threat to their rights. When the Union attempted to prevent the Southern states from seceding and forming their own Confederacy, many southerners married the two distinct civil liberties—slave ownership and self-determination—under a solitary banner that they commonly referred to as "their rights." Richard Henry Watkins of the 3rd Virginia Cavalry reminded his wife that he went off to war so that "we may be permitted to have our own form of government and our own social institutions and regulate our own domestic affairs." Along similar lines, Robert Haile of the 55th Virginia Infantry recorded in his diary that he was willing to suffer "any and every hardship, rather than submit to Abolitionists who are invading our soil seeking to destroy that which our fore fathers gained for us 'Liberty.'" Paraphrasing Patrick Henry's immortal words, he proclaimed, "Our battle cry should be liberty or death." Southerners' sense of honor demanded nothing less.[11]

Like the race card, this linking of slaveholding and liberty broadened the base of opposition to abolitionism and the Republican Party. Southerners knew that the Founding Fathers had rebelled from Great Britain and established the federal government for the security of life, liberty, and property. They perceived Lincoln and his Republican cohorts as politicians who were hostile to their enjoyment of those rights. People united to form governments in order to protect civil liberties. Since Southerners could no longer look to the central government for protection, in their eyes it served no purpose. Why should Southerners recognize the power and authority of a government that not only failed to protect people's liberties, but actually sought to strip people of them? A Marylander who ultimately commanded a brigade in Virginia believed that the election of 1860 indicated the Republicans would soon control all three branches of government. Reminiscent of the great Southern politician John

C. Calhoun, he believed that slave states needed "Something that will give security to the minority against the absolute power of the majority for all time, to come for all parties and for all sections." Without that guarantee, every state that "values its rights should secede."[12]

Southern whites frequently reminded themselves and loved ones at home of the worthy nature of their liberties. "Nothing can be too hard, no sacrifice to[o] great, when Liberty is at stake," noted a Georgian in 1861. "It will cost us much suffering," predicted a Virginia cavalryman before First Manassas, "but no people ever preserved their liberties without encountering such trials in their history." Semiliterate Milton Barrett tried to reassure his mother not to worry about his brother and him in the army; rather, be proud that her sons were fighting for the most noble reason, liberty. "If you to[r]ment a tall let hit be be cose you have not twenty engage in the glouris cose," he scribbled in a letter home.[13]

Many also picked up weapons to fulfill a central duty of both the government and the individual, to protect citizens from invaders. Not long before he enlisted in the 2nd Louisiana Infantry, Albert Batchelor, a student at Kentucky Military Institute, discussed this sense of duty with his mother. "I think the time is not far off, before my servises as humble as they are, will be needed in defence of Southern rights, in defence of our firesides and homes," he announced. "Yes 'tis sweet to die for one's country so also is it sweet to die for one's parents brothers and sisters."[14]

The same spirit of public duty operated on a family level. More than merely an act of love, it was a societal expectation that adults protect their families and their homes. For many volunteers, the idea of shielding the home from invaders was a central reason for their willingness to serve. All their hopes, all their dreams, all that they loved and had worked for were tied up in it. Home represented a sanctuary, a place where loved ones were contented, secure, and comfortable. Any threat or unwelcome entry into that household was a violation, a kind of moral outrage. As a Georgian reminded his wife, "our homes our fireside our land and negroes and even the virtue of our fair ones is at stake."[15]

For Virginians, with their native state as the battleground of the war, the distinction between defense of the nation and defense of the family blurred. "I feel that it is for you that I fight," a member of the 53rd Virginia Infantry explained to his wife, "that while I render my country service I am as a shield between my love, my darling & danger." The longer Union troops occupied portions of Virginia, the more outraged and, in some cases, humiliated Virginia soldiers felt. "It makes the blood boil in me when I think of an envading army being allowed to sleep two nights in Va without some attempt to drive them out," a fiery James Langhorne erupted to his father.[16]

Nor did individuals have to fight at their own doorstep to shield loved ones from invaders. They could fulfill those duties to their nation and their families by joining the army and serving elsewhere. An Arkansan justified his military service to his wife when he penned, "I feel that if we fail to resist Lincoln here the war will be transferred to our own doors." A Mississippian serving in Virginia did not enjoy military life, "But as it is, I joyfully embrace it as a means of repelling a dastardly, plundering oppressive and cowardly foe from our homes and borders," he remarked to his mother. "I grasp it as the only means of preserving all that is near and dear to me—home, family, friends and country."[17]

Political divisions, opposition to secession, even any tensions between slaveholders and nonslaveholders seemed inconsequential in the face of a Yankee invasion. Southerners banded with one another, so a North Carolina soldier fumed, "to drive them from the soil polluted by their footsteps." From these newfound bonds of mutual protection, Southerners began to forge a Confederate identity. They started to see themselves not just as citizens of their own states, but also as residents of the Confederate States of America, with a national army to protect them. As an Alabamian commented to his girlfriend in June 1861, just before he shipped off to Virginia and the war front, "when a Southron's home is threatened the spirit of resistance is irrepressable."[18]

Notions of Southern honor linked fundamental motivations of liberty, slaveholding, self-determination, and protection of hearth and home. An idea with strong European roots, honor was a concept that Southern whites adapted to meet the peculiar circumstances of the slaveholding South. Honor was a reflection of how others viewed a person. Individuals whose conduct lived up to society's most elevated values held the greatest honor or reputation; those who did not conduct themselves according to those values were regarded with low esteem and therefore lacked honor. Among the wide array of qualities that determined whether an individual had honor, at the core rested honesty, integrity, courage, and self-respect.[19]

A man of honor came out to perform his duty and remained at his post, in spite of hardships. "Be of good cheer & keep a stout heart, My dearest and best wife," Georgian John M. Tilley wrote to his wife before the Battle of First Manassas. "If I fall or die don't grieve over me as one entirely lost—You will know that you interposed no selfish objections to your husband doing his duty & I would were I a woman vastly prefer to be a true man's widow than some men's wives." Private Jeremiah Tate of the 5th Alabama Infantry vowed to his sister, "it shall never be said that Jery was a coward & wood not fight for his cuntry." As the war dragged on, and hardships compounded, honor sustained them. Many soldiers realized that if they survived the war, they had to live with their wartime behavior. Soldiers had joined companies and batteries with neighbors and friends, and they could not endure the shame of returning to that community, having deserted or shirked their duty. Personal reputation meant more to them than life itself. "I expect to be a man of Honor to our country at the risk of my life," wrote another Georgian in autumn 1863. "I don't want to be a disgrace to myself nor my relations." A Tennessean felt the same way. "I have one glorious consolation," he admitted to his father, "that as long as a yankee can stand the war for my subjugation, I can stand it for my honor and liberty."[20]

Honor reflected more than how others treated an individual. It had a collective component, and Southern whites felt that the North had exhibited little respect for them. Two months before his state seceded, a future Virginia soldier grumbled in revealing language: "The northerners have ignored southern principals and treated them with as much disrespect as it is possible for them to do and [by] their treatment to southern principals they nullify the constitution." James Langhorne of the 4th Virginia attempted to console his mother in advance in case he lost his life in the war. "Rest assured if any thing happens to me you will be immediately informed of it," her teenage son explained, "and if I die in this fight Ma I intend to die *worthy of* the Mother that bore me and of the Father that taught me to be a *free man*, & to have honor." He insisted that this was "a noble & just cause" and "if the north subjugates the South I never want to live to be 21 years old." When he reached legal maturity, "I want to breath[e] the breath of a freeman or not breath[e] at all." The prospect of defeat hung like a pall over the heads of Confederate soldiers. "We would be humbled, down trodden and disgraced people not entitled to the respect of anybody and have no respect for ourselves," a South Carolinian wrote home. "In fact, we would be the most wretched and abject people on the face of the Earth." A conquered people were undeserving of honor.[21]

With all the emphasis on dishonor, Southerners could not help but compare their plight and status with that of their bondsmen. A slave had no rights. He lived a life in which others dictated for him. He had no honor, no integrity, because a man with honor would not tolerate that status for a moment. Anyone without rights, without liberty, was nothing more than a slave to those who denied those rights. When Jefferson Davis challenged the Southern people, "Will you be slaves or will you be independent?" he struck a resonant chord. Acceptance of Federal control was tantamount to "slavery and degradation," a South Carolinian argued. "Better to die freemen," penned a Texan, "than to live slaves." A poem on the masthead of a Virginian's letter to his mother explained the sentiment and its ties to honor well:

> *Far better to perish with honor.*
> *Far better to go to the grave.*
> *And better to die as a freeman,*
> *Than to live as a Northerner's slave.*[22]

Although most of the men who volunteered in 1861 embraced the slaveholding ideology and all its trappings, and although most of them felt keenly the violation of their sense of honor and genuinely believed that Northerners threatened their civil liberties and sought to deny them the right of self-determination, money and adventure may have also influenced some Southerners to enlist. One in every four soldiers and their families had a combined total wealth of $250 or less, and slightly more than three in ten owned total assets of $500 or less. Low-paying, sporadic employment in civil life offered few prospects for many Southerners. Before rampant inflation made paper money practically worthless, payment of eleven dollars per month plus meals and clothing for a private soldier were attractive, especially if he was unwed. Good service in defense of the new country might offer a chance to establish valuable contacts and create postwar opportunities that would have been unavailable otherwise.[23]

For others, military service provided a chance to travel. Many soldiers, especially younger men, perceived the war as the great adventure of their generation. Among the 1861 enlistees, one in twenty was born abroad, and at the time of enlistment only slightly more than one in every six resided in a state different from the one in which they were born. Eighty percent of the men who would ultimately serve in the army in Virginia and who entered the service in 1861 were born and lived in the same state. Many had remained in the same neighborhood, and an area with a radius of twenty miles circumscribed their world. The war offered a chance to escape. Some boarded a train for the first time on the trip to Virginia. Many gazed upon the Appalachian Mountains en route, and verified for themselves the lushness of the Shenandoah Valley. They trod on the same dirt as illustrious Founding Fathers George Washington, Thomas Jefferson, and James Madison. Volunteers toured Richmond, the capital of Virginia. They visited St. John's Church, where another Virginia son, Patrick Henry, proclaimed, "Give me liberty, or give me death."[24]

Most enlistees in 1861 had been mere boys during the United States' last great war, against Mexico. Fathers, uncles, even older brothers who were veterans had regaled them with war tales, and the power of those stories fueled youthful questions about themselves. Combat provided individuals with that rare chance to test their manhood, to measure themselves against their peers. Young men wanted to know how well they would stand up under the tremendous strain of battle. Military experience could instill confidence, foster leadership skills, or shatter them. Despite the risks of physical or emotional damage, despite the chance they could emerge from the war a cripple or with a damaged reputation, they had to know how they would perform.[25]

For those with more maturity, perceptions of manhood stemmed from their sense of honor. They must serve their country, and do so well—behave like a man by performing their duties credibly, courageously, and without complaint—lest others view them as dishonored, as something less than a man. Buttressed by a belief in the nobility of their cause, Southern soldiers, whether older or younger, viewed combat as "the field of honour." A thirty-five-year-old Virginia planter and army private explained to his wife that he wanted to come home to be with her and the children, but only under two conditions: The army had to establish peace with an independent Confederacy, and "I have acted the part of a man, and of a good soldier." When a Texan's sister asked if he fought for pay or accolades, he replied, "I am fighting for patriotism, but if there is any glory connected with it I want to get my share of it."[26]

Among younger volunteers, as their lives shifted from teenage years to adulthood, military service hastened that transformation. James Langhorne confessed to his mother in May 1861 that "with youthful, and boyish feelings at heart I find it a little difficult at times to keep them down." Still, he insisted, "Ma I am truly in the full capasity of a man I am treated as such & consequently expected to act as such." Six weeks later, the man had supplanted the teenager, as Langhorne expressed his eagerness for the fight and an opportunity to demonstrate his newfound manhood. "The chances at stake are '*glory* or the grave' 'victory or death,'" he swaggered to his father, "these are the feelings that animates every heart."[27]

For most young men, anticipating a full adulthood ahead of them, military service provided an initial opportunity to prove themselves. For older men, those who struggled in life, it might be their last chance to turn life around. When thirty-one-year-old Henry Lethcoe enlisted in the 48th Virginia Infantry in June 1861, he reported his occupation as laborer. The previous year, Lethcoe had served an extended tour in jail at Abingdon, Virginia, the hometown of army commander Joseph Johnston. The army may have been his last opportunity to break from his old record. Unfortunately, in Lethcoe's case, past was prologue. He served out his year-long tour and re-enlisted in February 1862. Thirteen months later, Lethcoe found his way back to jail, this time one controlled by the Confederate army. Authorities caught him absent without leave.[28]

VIRTUALLY ALL THOSE who enlisted in 1861, perhaps even Lethcoe himself, believed that they had embarked on a magnificent undertaking. A Confederate soldier called the South "*This New Jerusalem*" and considered the Confederacy "the last hope of free Government." Similarly, a Georgia private thought, "We are living in the midst of the grandest revolution ever known in the annals of the world." He expected the Confederacy to "become a nation among the nations of earth, designed, in the hands of God, to fulfill a glorious destiny." Much as colonists viewed England during the Revolution, a Virginia cavalryman depicted the United States as "the old corrupt and rotten Republic." Volunteers described their service in the noblest of terms, as did Private J. V. Fuller of Mississippi when he wrote his wife, "I feel that I am fighting for your liberty and the liberty and privaliges of my little children." It was a goal, so a Louisiana soldier admitted, for which he would give up his life. "Our cause is a glorious & holy one," he declared, "and I for one am willing that my bones shall bleach the sarced [sacred] soil of Virginia in driving the envading host of tyrants from our soil." The seceding states were bound together, and the public outpouring convinced soldiers that all the people were behind them. "It does really appear to me that every man, woman, child and negro is determined to resist until death," a Georgian penned for a newspaper with considerable hyperbole. More reflective of true support was a Virginian who wrote his brother, "we look upon it as a just caus and we are united man and women all contribute." A flood of young and middle-aged men volunteered, far more than the Confederacy could handle. Those males who remained home could grow food or produce equipment that would aid the soldiers.[29]

Women supported the war effort enthusiastically, applauding those who offered their services and shaping the public will wholly behind the war effort. "If the men were all like the Ladies we would Whip old lincon before Tomorrow night," a Georgian predicted in May 1861. A "Daughter of 'Old Virginia'" informed readers of the *Richmond Enquirer* that although women could not shoulder arms, "We can encourage and we can endure—encourage our soldiers, and endure patiently and cheerfully the privations and hardships that must, without doubt, fall to our lot." Women should ratify soldiers' decision to fight with words and deeds. Not only should they inspire men to serve, the author insisted, but they should provide for the soldier, encourage morality in camp, fill their void at home, and bear hardships without complaint. Everyone must contribute, as Lucy Butler commented in her diary. "Our needles are our weapons," she jotted, "and we have a part to perform as well as the rest."[30]

With this level of unity and zeal, and the meritorious nature of their struggle, Confederates of any religious bent believed that they would march into battle with the ultimate weapon on their side. Although no human could predict God's designs, the idea that God would aid their enemy or even remain neutral seemed absurd. Edmund Kirby Smith, West Point graduate and chief of staff for Johnston, assuaged his mother's uneasiness when he wrote, "We feel our cause is just and Providence in its good time will bring it to a prosperous conclusion." How could a great and almighty God not ensure that they achieved their worthy object? So firmly were they convinced of a divine sanction for slavery, so resolved were they that God would endorse those in a struggle for civil liberty, that for the men of 1861 the war took on elements of a crusade. "You must not dear Martha grieve for me," counseled a North Carolinian, "but remember that the Struggle we are engaged in is a noble and a just one and that God is on our side and if he is for us who can be against us." An all-powerful God on the side of the Confederacy provided both reassurance and confidence. "We believe the God of battles is with us and victory must crown our efforts," a Mississippi soldier comforted his aunt. "There is Something truly Sublime in a Christian warrior fighting in a just cause," noted a North Carolinian. One woman wrote her husband in the army in Virginia that this was a holy cause, and that his sacrifices on behalf of the Confederacy would cleanse him in the eyes of God. She acknowledged that the hardships were difficult for both of them, but "if you only come out of this war purified and an 'Israelite indeed in whom there is no guile' we will all be amply repaid for all our privations and separations."[31]

For those Southerners with limited ties to God and religion, a secular ideal fortified them in the same ways. They believed in liberty and progress as the tide of history. To see the great strides in civil liberties over the last two hundred years, they had only to look at Western history for proof. It seemed absurd that a people who were fighting for their rights and willing to commit themselves wholeheartedly to the goal could lose. "Remember that science and numbers are feeble in opposition to the determined valor of men who are fighting for their homes," a general reminded his men. "They can not conquer men determined to be free and to throw off the yoke of an oppressive despotism," a Virginian asserted. More than just the tide of history, the American political and judicial system imbued Southerners with an implicit faith in justice, a kind of optimism that, ultimately, the correct outcome would result. Southerners carried this notion over to the war. "*We are right!*" pronounced a Mississippian, "and sooner or later *right* must triumph!"[32]

Less than a century earlier, their ancestors had fought and won a war for independence against a nation with vastly superior manpower and resources. Everywhere they turned in Virginia, Confederates observed evidence of those dramatic days that would guide them through the hardships of war. Like the original revolutionaries, they sought independence and preservation of their liberties. George Washington became their model—a citizen who picked up his sword and risked all for freedom. Henry's immortal words fired their hearts. Occasionally, they glimpsed Robert E. Lee, a Confederate general and the son of the Revolutionary War hero "Light Horse" Harry Lee, or John A. Washington, descendant of the first president's brother. The sites and people reminded them of their obligation to preserve that legacy.[33]

Yet the lessons they extracted from the War for Independence also reminded them of their role as torchbearers for freedom. Just as Revolutionary War veterans had fought to secure liberty for their descendants, so they must preserve it for future generations. "Little did they think that within less than a century, after they had achieved for us a glorious independence," mused a Mississippian about the Revolutionary warriors, "their native soil would be invaded by the descendants of those who in the time that 'tried men's souls,' they met with confidence in the council chamber of the nation." Nor could they have imagined that less than eight decades later, "the fields where once they fought together against a common enemy should afterwards be whitened by the tents of the defenders of that liberty for which they toiled and sacrificed their lives." A Georgia soldier thought that the Revolutionary fathers had taught their descendants to assume an obligation for themselves and future generations. They were to resist oppression, to preserve the independence they had earned, and to govern themselves. "If THEY could not endure a tax on tea because it violated a sacred principle," he wondered, "how could WE submit to be governed by those whose steady determination is to sacrifice our happiness, and even our lives, in the abolition of an institution guaranteed to us by the constitution of our fathers?"[34]

This interest in the work of their Revolutionary War ancestors raised a question: Why was the North fighting them? A Virginian recounted a humorous conversation between a soldier in his company and a Union officer.

When the Federal soldier asked what the Rebel fought for, he said, "I fought for Eleven dollars a month, what did you fight for?"

To this the Yankee replied, "Well I fought for a principle."

The Confederate private then responded, "I always thought both sides were right—fighting for what they wanted most, I lacked money and you wanted principle."[35]

Their ancestors had fought a war for self-government. How could Northerners have forgotten that event just a few generations ago? A small group of abolitionists, they understood, fomented war because they would go to any lengths to destroy slavery. John Brown's raid had taught them that. But what about the vast majority of Northerners, who had no ties to abolitionism? Why would they not respect Southern rights to freedom? Southern soldiers could not see how their leaving the Union affected Northerners.

Confederates of 1861 arrived at a simple conclusion. Since Union soldiers had no legitimate cause, they must be Hessians—paid mercenaries, foreigners whom the North induced to serve for money—like the troops from the German states whom the Crown paid to serve in the American Revolution. Perhaps there was a sprinkling of militant abolitionists as officers, but the vast majority of Union soldiers had no motive other than lucre. "The army of the North must all be fanatics or hirelings to undergo the hardships of war with no better cause than they have," a member of the 13th Virginia Infantry recorded in his diary. A Georgia soldier could not wait to fight "the mercenaries of a Despotic tyrant, who has without a cause forced upon him the alternative of resistance or servilism." Troops wrongly referred to the Union command as a "Hessian Army," one "composed for the most part of foreign hirelings." Another soldier compared Federals to waves of barbarous Germanic tribesmen, bent on snuffing out their sophisticated civilization, with no goals other than booty and the enslavement of white Southerners. "Abraham Lincoln Sent Hordes of Goths and Vandals to over run our beloved South," he scribbled in a diary, "to Subjugate us and take freedom and our homes and property from us." Confederates, a private in the 8th Georgia explained to his sister, were fighting for "a pure motive," while Northerners served for pay, because no one could fight to suppress the liberties of another except for pecuniary reward.[36]

In the face of invaders who possessed such spurious motives, volunteers in 1861 could not understand why all Southerners did not come forward to fight. "A southerner is a madman or a coward not to enlist," asserted a Virginian. A cavalryman who struggled with his spelling nonetheless conveyed a potent message to his wife when he wrote, "1 will fite the[m] as long as I have a drop of blod." More skillfully, a Georgian expressed his sentiments to his mother, penning, "I expect to stand my hand in the Cause as long as I can for I am now sold to Jeff Davis and I expect to serve him till he discharges me in honor or till I die." In an effort to bring his unit up to full strength, a soldier reminded an officer, "Life is short at best. The times are pregnant with momentous events. Be an actor in the day of trial." Even as early as mid-1861, soldiers began to draw distinctions between those who served and those who remained at home, and they wanted no rewards or advantages to go to those who refused to fight for hearth, home, and cause. "My dear sisters," a Georgia infantryman admonished, "I as an elder brother want you not to name [for marriage] no young man whoo will not volunter any fight for the writs [rights] of his country, but wait and take one whoo has faught for the liberties and freddom of thier country." With a brother at war, those must have been difficult words to reject.[37]

They would fight until the last shot was fired or until the enemy struck them down. And when they fell, they expected their children to take their place. A Virginia officer instructed his wife to "teach our boys to think of me as a father who willingly risked his life in defence of the great principles of civil liberty when they were assailed by a tyrant, and train them so to love freedom that they may be prepared, whenever the necessity arises, to imitate my example." Along similar lines, a member of South Carolina's Hampton Legion informed his wife that he hoped when "darling Jimmie" grew up he would "take his Father's place in the field and fight until he dies, rather than be a slave. *Yea*, worse than a slave to Yankee Masters." A North Carolina soldier offered advice directly to his son. In a letter to "Captain," his pet name for the boy, he "hoped that no such necessity will arise," but if he fell in battle, "you must follow my footsteps in this respect and shoulder a musket as soon as you are large enough to carry one, and to fight the Yankees to the last." They would carry the torch for this generation, and their sons must be ready to pick it up for the next as the price for freedom.[38]

Chapter 5

---◎---

BECOMING SOLDIERS

A LL DAY LONG, they tossed up breastworks and planted field guns to cover the York River. By mid-May, the weather in Virginia had begun to get warm, and direct sunlight and reflections off the water badly burned their white winter skin. While the farmers, mechanics, and laborers in the group earned calloused hands and relative immunity to aches and pains from manual labor, a number of volunteers were wealthy or students. In their minds, digging ditches was slave work. They would do it because of the crisis, as an act of patriotism, but they did not like the labor and refused to relinquish their God-given right to grumble about demeaning tasks, throbbing backs, and blistered hands. They also labored out of fear. Visions of Federal warships sailing upriver haunted their waking and sleeping hours, and they hoped their efforts would protect them in the upcoming fight.[1]

"We all went to sleep last night expecting nothing else but that some larger war vessel would be upon us before this morning," Virginia artillerist James Williams revealed to his aunt, "and that we would have to run or all be killed." After enduring a long night of fitful sleep, they arose to an intelligence report that warned of an impending attack. A steamer soon approached, but from the opposite direction, with replacement troops and an order for them to return to Richmond. The men were furious. "I was just mad enough to wring old [Governor] Letchers head off," Williams complained. But they obeyed the orders. The men climbed aboard, and the steamer chugged upriver toward the state capital. Before they reached Richmond, however, new orders arrived, directing their command to return to Gloucester Point on the York River. The annoyance of moving back and forth, the evident lack of planning and orderly procedures, and the frustration of nearly losing a chance to confront their detested foe proved too much. "It is enough to provoke any one to death," Williams grumbled, "and our men are almost worn out of all patience."[2]

Williams's experience reflected the frustration and utter chaos in those early months of the war. Troops rushed to the Virginia Theater from across the Confederacy, eager to defend the Old Dominion. Unfortunately, neither Virginia nor the Confederacy was quite ready for the tidal wave of volunteers that swept over them. Lacking satisfactory equipment, Confederate officials had to send troops to the front inadequately armed and accoutered. Field commanders, none of whom had experience leading large bodies of men, struggled to deploy their resources effectively, and they frequently second-guessed their own decisions. As one officer grumbled, his battery, the Richmond Howitzers, was "marched and countermarched like a parcel of 'Wandering Jews' doomed to never rest or stay in one place for a week."[3]

On April 20, 1861, Governor John Letcher offered former U.S. Army colonel Robert E. Lee the position of commander of Virginia Forces, and Lee promptly accepted. When the Confederate government took over the war effort there, the secretary of war confirmed Lee's authority. A highly respected officer with a first-rate mind, Lee brought to the job clear thinking and sound judgment. Forecasting the logical routes of invasion correctly, he built up Confederate forces at the northern end of the Shenandoah Valley around Harpers Ferry and in northern Virginia near a railroad intersection called Manassas Junction. Lee also ensured that authorities located troops and guns along the banks of major riverways to obstruct the advance of any Union forces by water.[4]

While Lee positioned troops in locations where reinforcements could be easily transported, he could not perform mobilization miracles. Transforming a country onto a war footing proved a complicated process, particularly as the revolutionaries were attempting to create a new government and nation simultaneously. Even though states had built up their militias and stockpiled some weapons over the last eighteen months, these were mere baby steps in preparation for large-scale war. The state and national governments needed a huge influx of troops to shield both the northern border and the lengthy coastline of Virginia, and the explosion of enthusiasm for war assured an ample supply of volunteers early in the war. The men were willing, yet the soldiers who arrived in Virginia lacked all sorts of basic equipment. Rather than detain them in Richmond until they had outfitted everyone satisfactorily, authorities rushed them to the front as rapidly as they could or assembled them along the rail lines in places like Lynchburg. They would forward weapons and material as soon as they became available.[5]

Shortly after Virginia seceded, military officials in Richmond had realized that it would take some time to provide troops with all the essentials for military service, and the state urged volunteers to carry these necessities with them. They advised soldiers to bring their own weapons, "one extra pair of good walking shoes, one blanket, and such other light conveniences as they can easily carry themselves on the march." A month later, as troops from other states poured into Virginia, Confederate authorities continued to wrestle with the same problems. "In my opinion, we are in a bad fix," Lee's military secretary informed a friend. "Troops come here daily from the South with no arms and we have none to give them but the old flint lock musket." He considered it the gravest problem confronting the Confederacy: "We want arms, not men."

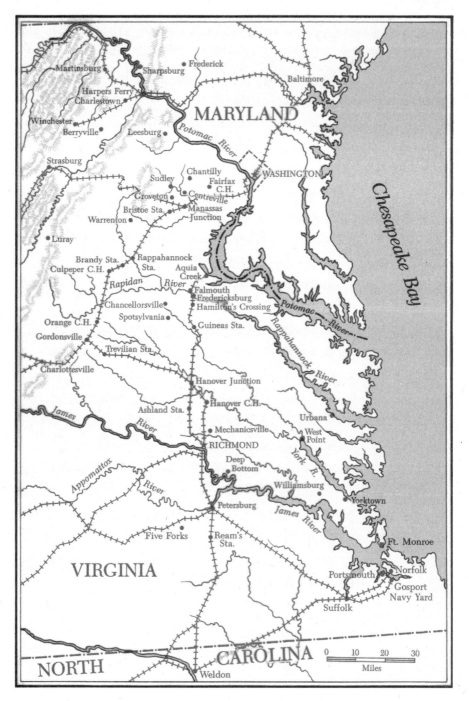

Virginia Theater

As fast as ordnance personnel could work, they converted flintlocks into per-cussion weapons—muskets that used a percussion cap filled with fulminate of mercury to spark the gunpowder and propel the round—but it still took time. Since John Brown's raid, state governments had purchased quality weapons, but governors naturally wanted to keep the best firearms for home defense.[6]

Fortunately, Lee had an efficient officer at his ready disposal. Colonel Thomas J. Jackson, a West Point graduate in 1846, had been quite a hero in the Mexican War. Eventually opting for a teaching job instead of the every-day routine of the Regular Army, Jackson settled in Lexington, Virginia, as an instructor at VMI. Tall, medium build, with steel-blue eyes, Jackson was an awkward fellow made all the more odd by his peculiar practices and intense religious convictions. The owner of six slaves, Jackson ensconced himself in the Lexington community, where people thought very well of him, despite his peculiarities. Students pulled pranks on him and ridiculed him behind his back, largely because of his eccentricities and his dreadful teaching style—his lec-tures consisting of memorizing the textbook and reciting it to the students. But students also knew that "Tom Fool" Jackson was a superb soldier, and when the secession crisis hit, they rallied around him. He led the VMI cadets to Rich-mond, where they began to teach drill to recruits. His presence and efficiency reinforced Lee's high opinion of him, and before April was out, Jackson was bound for Harpers Ferry, to assume command and develop defenses there.[7]

At a time when few others seemed willing to make decisions, Jackson filled the power vacuum. Lee authorized Jackson to call for volunteer companies in the adjacent seven counties and to organize them into regiments, which Jackson did. In accordance with Lee's instructions, Jackson prepared defensive positions to hold the town and began dismantling the machinery at the arsenal and moving it to a more secure location. Since the arsenal manufactured rifled muskets that the Confederate army desperately needed, Jackson continued their production as long as it was safe. To accumulate weapons for the soldiers, Jackson offered locals five dollars for the best weapons, largely rifled muskets pilfered from the arsenal or issued to local militiamen.

Jackson formulated and executed decisions and kept Lee abreast of what he had done. When Jackson exceeded his authority, as he did when he occupied the better defensive terrain on the north side of the Potomac River in early May, in effect invading Maryland, Lee had him withdraw without any sharp rebuke. Lee had placed him in authority, and Jackson would exercise it to the best of his ability. He was exactly what Lee needed.[8]

Jackson's independent command was short-lived. In mid-May, President Davis appointed Joseph E. Johnston as commander of the troops near Harp-ers Ferry. Doubtless the selection pleased Lee, who had known Johnston vir-tually all his life. A decade after the war, Johnston described his relationship with Lee by writing, "we were as intimate as boys & youths ever are; and were closely associated the first ten years of manhood." Johnston's father had served under Lee's father during the Revolutionary War, and the two young men had attended West Point as classmates. Both worked in the Corps of Engineers in the Regular Army and fought bravely in Mexico. Lee exhibited great warmth for Johnston, and he assumed the feelings were mutual.

They were not. While Johnston may have liked Lee, he was jealous of him. Lee's father had been a hero and leader; Johnston's father had been a staff officer. Lee had graduated second in their class; Johnston ranked thirteenth. Johnston bolstered his reputation as a soldier in the Mexican War; Lee emerged as the rising star in the army. The one-sided competition was too much for Johnston. He reveled in Lee's failures—one person described him as "so exuberant he could not hide it"—and it did not take long before Johnston had converted some of his staff into private Lee bashers as well.[9]

Of medium height, with a slight build that belied his physical strength, Johnston's broad forehead, bald head, high cheekbones, and tapered cheeks and jaw gave him a cerebral appearance. Soldiers marveled at his imperial air, that "striking & military appearance." A Georgian thought Johnston looked the part of a general, describing him as a "tolerably large man, well formed & sits his horse like a statue." Johnston's cousin, Thomas Preston, who served on his staff, sized him up well when he wrote his wife, "Genl. Johnston is careful of his men & his reputation, & will risk neither rashly." Johnston once went hunting with Wade Hampton, future Confederate cavalry commander in Lee's army, and another prominent South Carolinian, Hamilton Boykin. Boykin described Johnston as a likeable fellow but a "dead failure" as a hunter. "He was a capital shot," Boykin related, "better than Wade or I," but Johnston was "too fussy, too hard to please, too cautious, too much afraid to miss and risk his fine reputation for a crack shot." While Hampton and Boykin each had a heavy bag full of birds by the end of the day, Johnston never fired. "Either the birds flew too high or too low—the dogs were too far or too near—things never did suit exactly." Johnston waited for "the exactly right time and place" and it "never came."[10]

At Harpers Ferry, Johnston did not like the position and wanted to fall back, but he also did not want to order the retreat himself and suffer a decline in his reputation. Within two days of his arrival, he determined that it was "untenable by us at present against a strong enemy." Two days later, Johnston reiterated, "This place cannot be held against an enemy who would venture to attack it." He wanted the authority to withdraw and merge his command with a larger army. Lee replied that officials in Richmond knew the difficulties, but they still wanted Johnston to hold Harpers Ferry. "Its abandonment," Lee explained, "would be depressing to the cause of the South." The Davis administration preferred that Johnston hold Harpers Ferry as long as possible and fall back only when an attack was imminent. Johnston feared that an evacuation of Harpers Ferry as the enemy approached would besmirch his reputation, and he reminded them that a retreat in the face of a skilled army was a difficult proposition at best.

Johnston, then, could not let the matter drop. He engaged in a tautological debate about his mission and insisted, "Would not the loss of five or six thousand men be more so?" He had fallen victim to the notion that the problem of inexperience that his army suffered could not possibly afflict the enemy army. Ultimately, the adjutant general, Samuel Cooper, directly authorized Johnston to evacuate the area and to destroy the arsenal there when he believed the enemy was turning him. A testy Johnston barked back, "nothing in my correspondence with my military superiors makes me obnoxious to the charge of desiring that the responsibility of my official acts should be borne by any other person than myself." Johnston withdrew from Harpers Ferry on his own orders the day before, but his response was patently dishonest.[11]

Along the more direct avenue of invasion from Washington, D.C., toward Manassas Junction, the commanders better understood the intent of Richmond authorities. Virginia governor Letcher requested Philip St. George Cocke to take charge of the Department of the Potomac with the rank of brigadier general. Cocke had graduated from West Point sixth in the class of 1832. After two years in the artillery service, he resigned his commission to take over his family estates. A fabulously wealthy man, by 1860 Cocke owned property and slaves in Virginia and Mississippi worth nearly $1.6 million. Intelligent, courtly, and high-minded, he devoted much of his time to public service, especially to promoting progressive agricultural practices. When Letcher placed him in charge of all areas bounded by the Potomac River, three days before Lee took over as commander of all Virginia forces, he could not refuse.[12]

Despite the overwhelming responsibilities, Cocke took charge much like Jackson did, but he had even more obstacles in his path. Technically, Jackson's command should have been under Cocke's authority, but because of the distance and necessary haste, and perhaps because of Lee's confidence in Jackson's abilities, Jackson reported directly to Lee. Jackson built and Johnston inherited a force of 8,000 soldiers, of whom 7,300 were "able to go into combat, well armed." Cocke concentrated his efforts on building up and training forces in the central portion of Virginia, along the Alexandria–Manassas Junction axis, directly across from Washington, D.C., where the principal Union army prepared for invasion. Two weeks before Johnston took command, Cocke had only 1,100 infantry, artillery, and cavalry, one quarter of whom had no arms. In early June, with volunteers continuing to build up troop strength, the force consisted of 6,000 effective troops. By then, an estimated 12,000 to 15,000 Federal troops had crossed the Potomac River and occupied Alexandria and the surrounding area.[13]

As soon as Cocke received Letcher's orders to take command along the Potomac, he headed for Alexandria. So hasty was his departure that he still wore his "plantation dress." From the 300 soldiers he found there, Cocke began to build up forces and a defense. He realized that he could never hold Alexandria in the event of a large-scale Union advance, but he believed he could scout, gather information on the enemy, and train his troops. Lee expected Cocke to call out volunteers, organize them into regiments, and set up schools of instruction for the troops. Alexandria was situated on the bulge of the Potomac River, and a pincer movement could easily trap the troops in the town. Instead of calling for a withdrawal, Cocke positioned soldiers well out on the flanks to protect his rear. He communicated with the commander to the southeast to cooperate, and he proposed a course of action similar to one that Lee had already adopted: amass mobile forces at Manassas Junction and Winchester, so that they could reinforce Harpers Ferry or the Alexandria-Manassas area by rail rapidly. If the Union army invaded, Cocke would fall back, all the while harassing the enemy and obstructing his advance. No one could expect him to do more, and it was precisely what Lee wanted.[14]

In the course of all this active service, Cocke suffered two slights at the hands of the state and national governments. Letcher had appointed Cocke a brigadier general, but before the Constitutional Convention adjourned, it passed an ordinance that required its own approval for all generals' ranks, and it placed a limit on the number of general officers. Cocke lost his rank in the shuffle and instead received a colonelcy. Because subordinates had received commissions in the Provisional Army of the Confederacy, they suddenly outranked Cocke, and he lost his assignment as well. Lee apologized and tried to mollify him. "I do not consider that either rank or position are necessary to bestow upon you honor, but believe that you will confer honor on the position." Lee felt sure that Cocke would continue to "advance the cause" and "promote the interests of the service, which you have so much at heart." Fortunately for the Confederacy, Cocke endured the insults and remained with the army. At the Battle of First Manassas, Cocke commanded a brigade skillfully and made several tactical decisions that keyed Rebel success. Snake-bitten once again, however, Cocke saw the credit due him go largely to Beauregard.[15]

Little more than a week after Cocke received his demotion, the Confederate government assigned Brig. Gen. Milledge L. Bonham, a South Carolina politician with Mexican War experience, as commander. The Southern states would have been better off with Cocke. Bonham overstretched his forces, and when the Federals began their touted "Forward to Richmond" campaign with an advance on Manassas Junction in July, he retreated hastily, abandoning baggage and equipment that the Confederacy sorely needed. It would not be the only time that poor planning cost the Rebel army valuable materiel.[16]

Ten days after Bonham's appointment, Davis placed Beauregard in overall authority along the "Alexandria Line." Of medium height, stockily built, with black hair and dark complexion, Beauregard possessed boundless energy and a fancy for elaboration. One soldier applauded his appearance, reporting home, "I have seen prettier men than beauregard in south carolina all tho he is a smart keen looking man." Exceedingly bright, Beauregard graduated second in the West Point class of 1846, before his twentieth birthday. In the Mexican War, he distinguished himself alongside Lee on Maj. Gen. Winfield Scott's staff. In one instance, both he and Lee were nearly killed when a guard on their side fired first and challenged second. His good fortune, however, did not last long. Beauregard sustained two wounds in the fighting there and earned a pair of brevets for heroism. After he returned to the Corps of Engineers, political connections helped him secure the superintendency of West Point in January 1861. In the shortest tenure in that institution's history, Beauregard's appointment was revoked after less than a week for outspoken support for the Confederacy, and within days he resigned from the army. He soon became a household name throughout the South for overseeing the shelling of Fort Sumter.[17]

For the most part, soldiers loved him. There was more than a hint of flamboyance in him—President Davis joked that when they had someone who was "so fine" they did not know what to do with him, they sent the fellow to Beauregard's staff—and that showiness played well with the troops. Too energetic to sit behind a desk all day, Beauregard got out, inspected his command, and ordered improvements in works and training personally. His activity and powers of observation impressed the men. "My gracious what an eye he has," a Virginian remarked. "He looks like he could see through an inch board." Within days, he had troops throwing up trenches around Manassas, but while other commanders had alienated their troops with strenuous manual labor, this effort strengthened their opinion of Beauregard. In those early days, soldiers believed that if Beauregard ordered it, then it was sound military practice. "Every day covinces us more and more that Beauregard is *the General* of the ages," penned a Georgian to his uncle. "We have the most implicit confidence in anything that he does."[18]

Two days after his arrival in the Manassas area, Beauregard sized up his situation for Davis. The current defensive position required more troops than he had. He could prepare a new line, around Bull Run, but to hold that would require 10,000 to 15,000 men, and he only had 6,000 effectives. If the enemy advanced in large force, he would have to retire toward Richmond, "with the intention of arresting him whenever and wherever the opportunity shall present itself." Like Johnston, he assumed the Federal force would have "all the advantages of arms, numbers, and discipline." He had a trump card, however. He commanded a motivated soldiery. "My troops are not only willing, but are anxious, to meet the enemies of our country under all circumstances," he asserted with characteristic bravado.[19]

While Beauregard may have overrated his enemy, he assessed his own troops, and Johnston's, exactly. Both commands suffered from a dearth of equipment. They lacked arms, and many of the weapons that soldiers carried were badly dated. There was also a serious ammunition shortage in those early days, and it worried both Beauregard and Johnston. Many of the officers could not drill the men because they did not know the tactics themselves. Both commands desperately needed competent field officers and staff officers who could handle the paperwork properly, to improve the flow of information and provide Beauregard and Johnston with precise data on army needs. As Johnston's chief of staff, Edmund Kirby Smith, commented, "Words cannot express our deplorable condition here, unprovided, unequiped, unsupplied with ammunition and provisions." He concluded, "The utter confusion and ignorance presiding in the councils of the authorities that were is without parallel."[20]

"Everything is *hurry scurry* here," wrote a lieutenant colonel to his wife. "Galoping riding marching & countermarching all the time night & day." Everyone was trying to do their best, yet very few actually knew what they were doing, or were supposed to be doing. An Alabamian described his first night-time picket duty with his brother, Bolling Hall, and a friend, Jim Oliver. They advanced about one mile from camp and positioned themselves about 150 yards from each other. "We were all new hands at this Kind of duty and of course did not pass the night without some rare scenes," he explained. "I challenged a dog Bolling a rabbit." Oliver "came near shooting a trooper who had the countersign." All three thought the woods were crawling with Yankees. Afterward, Oliver admitted, "every bush he heard crack he tortured into some Yankee cocking his musket to shoot him."[21]

Officers with prior military experience or training had huge advantages over the others. At least they knew drill and had observed how to compel a body of volunteers to learn tactics and behave like soldiers. Many officers, however, knew little more than their soldiers. They had been on familiar terms with their men before the war, and now had to control and discipline them and teach them drill, all the while learning to do it themselves. "Sallie you can scarcely firm an idea, of the difficulties responsibilities and labours of a Captains position in times like these," a Virginia cavalryman described with exasperation. "To keep 60 or 70 raw, undisciplined troops in proper subjection—to instruct them, attend to all their wants—to gratify and deny them—to keep up their spirits—to punish and reward and all the while retain their respect and regard is no easy task I assure you." Officers had to teach respect and discipline and impose some distance between themselves and enlisted men with whom they had been familiar. They also had to remind themselves that these were volunteers who had made great personal sacrifices to serve their country, and that officers must exhibit patience and tolerance for ignorance or mistakes.[22]

They drilled hour after hour, day after day, practicing the tactical maneuvers that they would use in combat so that the motions would become second nature to them. Only then could officers rest assured that amid the chaos of combat, their men could execute tactical movements. "We drill six times a day in the hot sun," a Virginian reported, "and such a black set of fellows you never saw in your life, if I was to come home you would think I was some Cols. waiting boy." His regimental commander, Col. Ambrose Powell Hill, emphasized squad-and company-level drills whenever possible. Once they mastered these small-unit maneuvers, they graduated to battalion and eventually regiment drill. Lieutenant James Langhorne applauded the training regimen. "We drill 5 times a day, and have military carried out to the strict letter of the law," Langhorne informed his mother. "It bothers some of the men very much to come down to such strict discipline but it is just what I like." His 4th Virginian Infantry served in Jackson's Brigade, and on July 16, Langhorne reported that its leader "had his whole brigade drilling at a charge bayonets double quick time for the last week." Five days later, those same men assaulted a Union battery at First Manassas with bayonets and "drove them before us like chaff before the wind," the young lieutenant boasted.[23]

The drill and discipline pulled units together. It hardened them for the battlefield experience and it created an élan within companies, regiments, and even brigades. Soldiers, who already identified with their companies from recruitment on the local level, began to see themselves as a group. One soldier out of line, one man fouling up a drill, and the entire company, regiment, even brigade looked sloppy. For all to achieve, each individual component must succeed, and each person must rely on everyone else to perform effectively.

Meanwhile, the administration continued to funnel more troops, arms, and ammunition to the field commands. They may not have received the kind of quality weapons that their enemy possessed, but most infantrymen carried serviceable muskets, and artillerists manned reasonably good guns. What the cavalry lacked in firearms, it compensated for with high-quality horses. By July 11, Beauregard reported his troop strength at 18,401, with well over 16,000 infantrymen, a force larger than Johnston's Army of the Shenandoah, with more than 12,000 soldiers. They came from as far away as Texas and as near as local volunteers.[24]

Within the brigade and certainly within the larger field commands, soldiers gained exposure to fellow volunteers from other states and regions. In this early part of the war, competition took on a friendly tone. Soldiers did not criticize the differences among them; they appreciated everyone's willingness to serve in Virginia, and the atmosphere was more one of curiosity and amusement than anything else. South Carolina troops told a group of Virginians that "they intend to lead the attack on Washington and only wish us to follow them." When they left for Alexandria, they said their farewells and invited the Virginians to dine on lamb at the Willard Hotel in a few days. The Louisianans caused quite a stir when they brought a young woman with them. According to Thomas Petty, "She had a bowie knife & pistol & wicker covered canteen." The troops from Texas, too, were a big hit. Soldiers marveled at their marksmanship and horseback-riding skills. A South Carolinian also admired their courage. "Those Texans are the most perfect daredevils in the world," he insisted to his wife.[25]

"A soldier's life is much harder than I expected when I left home," confessed a Mississippian, "thought that I knew something about it but found it quite to the contrary." A Virginian agreed with the burdens, but perceived a silver lining in the cloud. "The change from a child of luxury to a soldier where there was no organization was exceedingly severe but the novelty was more agreeable than the hardships were unpleasant," he determined.[26]

ON THE VERGE of the Battle of First Manassas, an Alabamian began to figure out the mysteries of military service. "I am getting along a great deal better than I expected," he noted. "I found this to be the motto for a soldier—'Do your whole duty and nothing but your duty and keep silent.'" After the trials and hardships, they were fast transforming into soldiers. They were becoming an army.[27]

Chapter 6

————◦○◦————

"TO SLAUGHTER ONE ANOTHER
LIKE BRUTES"

\

F ROM THEIR POSITION far to the rear, some Alabama troops could faintly
hear sporadic rifle and cannon fire from the Battle of Big Bethel Church
in June 1861. With each musket or cannon concussion, the men began to curse
"loudly & deeply" in frustration. A member of the regiment recorded, "They
swear the enemy nor any one else *'will ever find us.'*" After enlisting in the army
and traveling all the way to Virginia, the Alabamians expressed fear that they
might miss the biggest event of their lifetime. They had come to prove themselves in battle, both as individuals and as a group, and they desperately sought
an opportunity to do so.[1]

As with the Alabamians, an element of fear drove Lt. Col. Edward T. H.
Warren of Virginia, yet unlike his fellow soldiers from the Deep South, he
derived his motivation from the concept of honor. Perhaps because he was
older, eagerness for combat did not drive him; it was the presence of Union
troops on Virginia soil and their conduct that disturbed and offended him. "I
dont exactly like the idea of standing on the defensive like a whiped cur," Warren revealed to his wife, "while our vile wicked and degraded enemy is marching through our land ruthlessly destroying everything in their way, murdering
our men, insulting our women, Stealing our negroes & every thing else they
can lay their hands on." He then declared, "I feel like striking back often   I
am not only struck but spit on." As they advanced, the Northern army pillaged
and brutalized, and if Southerners did not drive them from their homeland,
they would lose all self-respect. Military mission and personal honor demanded
that a man protect those who were most vulnerable—women, children, and
the elderly—from acts of violence and aggression. To attempt valiantly and to
fail brought no dishonor. But falling back without a fight, as the Army of the
Shenandoah under Johnston did, uncovering Confederate homes and subjecting fellow citizens and their property to brutal enemy violations, begot humiliation.[2]

Still another type of fear stemmed from failure. Officials had stationed Carolinians who composed Bonham's brigade far to the north to defend the area around Fairfax. Once the Union army advanced toward Manassas Junction, the Carolina soldiers received orders to fall back to Bull Run in such haste that they had to destroy or abandon all sorts of equipment. The fault lay more with improper planning at the general's level than anything else, but the men thought they could never live down the stigma of retreat against Yankees. As a South Carolinian explained to his father, the soldiers believed they would be "forever disgraced and all the bright hopes of Laurels which were expected to be won by many a gallent heart on the soil of Virginia were about to be vanished."[3]

Whether they were concerned that they would miss the war, burdened by the shame of not protecting the defenseless, or embarrassed for retreating quickly, none of these Confederates expressed fear of the enemy. Others may have felt insecure about how they would measure up individually in combat, but very few had any doubts about the outcome of the fight. Organizational chaos and substandard arms and equipment meant little to these men. Southern soldiers were convinced of their superiority over the Yankees. Two weeks before the Battle of First Manassas, a Mississippi captain, Charles F. Hamer, boasted, "We can whip 3000 yanks with our company." A private in the company justified the cocky assertion by explaining to his mother, "He knows that the Yazoo boys has got the right kind of sand in their craws." James Langhorne boasted in a similar vein to his mother: "There is not a man in the Southern Army, who does not in his heart believe that he can whip three Yankees, he would consider it beneath his manhood to count upon whipping a less number in any sort of a fight." The Union's attempt to conquer them boggled Langhorne's mind. "How they can ever hope to subdue us is beyond my comprehension." So convinced was he of Southern superiority that he even doubted the entire world could defeat them in ten years.[4]

For Hamer, Langhorne, and many others, the supremacy of the Southern slave society over the Northern free world lay at the root of this belief. Slavery promoted the elevation and evolution of the entire white population. Because it removed them from menial tasks, as Hammond had argued in his "Mudsill" speech, slavery enabled white men to develop superior qualities and enhanced self-confidence and self-respect, all of which, they thought, made them better soldiers. By raising the white population above the pedestrian elements of life, Southern society could concentrate on instilling honor, pride, courage, and individualism in its white males. Moreover, the burden of caring for and overseeing slaves, they believed, fostered leadership and supervision skills that would benefit its husbands and sons in battle.

Southerners also claimed superior breeding. They argued that they descended from Virginia cavaliers who themselves were descended from Normans. Yankee ancestors stemmed from Saxons and after them the Puritans. In fact, few Southerners had cavalier lineage, and intermixture among Normans,

Saxons, and other peoples over dozens of generations had diluted any Norman blood that pulsed through their veins. Nonetheless, they believed it so. No one should have been surprised, they asserted, that their superior breeding and superior culture and upbringing would produce superior soldiers who would overcome Yankee advantages in manpower and material. As the *Charleston Mercury* described the Southern advantages over Yankees and the inevitable Rebel success, "The onset of Southern men, accustomed to the use of weapons, bred in the habit of command and with the sentiment of honor, and fighting under the influence of principle and enthusiasm and vengeance, have proved irresistible."[5]

In an effort to ease his wife's trepidation, South Carolinian Sam Melton proposed the corollary argument: The North's army was incompetent. "The amount of lead shot away in every battle is equal to the weight of every man killed and wounded. It is strange, yet true. And when we know that the Yankees shoot wilder than any other soldier in the world," he proposed further, "we must conclude that the calculation must be made even more liberally." In the minds of Southern whites, the North consisted largely of effete abolitionists and oppressed laborers, predominantly foreigners by birth and therefore inferior stock. Without any vested interest in Northern society, these deluded workers, so Southerners thought, had weak attachments to the Union cause.[6]

The victory at the Battle of First Manassas merely confirmed these sentiments throughout the South. "We have won the greatest victory that has ever been recorded in history," pronounced a euphoric Mississippi soldier who fought that day. An overjoyed Georgia officer, stationed near the Virginia coast, sensed the Confederate triumph reflected divine will. "I believe God is on our side," he justified to his brother. Even a hardened warrior like Robert E. Lee admitted, "I almost wept for joy at the glorious victory achieved by our brave troops on the 21st."[7]

Although the Yankees actually had far fewer troops on the battlefield that day, Southerners convinced themselves that they had whipped a much greater enemy force. Johnston believed the flank attack alone consisted of 35,000 Federals, and Beauregard calculated the entire Union army at 54,140 men. Captain Edward Porter Alexander, one of the savviest officers in the Confederate army, estimated Union strength at 63,000.[8]

Not surprisingly, troops who missed the battle felt slighted, and some were downright bitter. The men in the 9th Georgia Infantry raced from the Shenandoah Valley, and even though the rest of the brigade arrived in time to see some combat, they missed it. "Many were the curses long loud and deep that were given to Gen Johnson by our troops for detaining us from battle," grumbled an embittered soldier. Men in the 13th Virginia jumped off the train and raced to the sound of gunfire. A private reported that "the dust was so thick that we could not see a man five paces immediately in front of us." Choking on dirt and craving water to soothe parched mouths, they eagerly rushed onward nevertheless. Stragglers and wounded called out to them to "pick off the red pants

[11th New York Infantry (Zouaves) and 14th New York Infantry], that they had injured us more than any other part of the enemy." But to their great dismay, they never got the chance. By the time they reached the main battlefield, their comrades had swept the field. The only Yankees in red pants that they met were prisoners of war.[9]

Victorious Rebels lifted their hearts and minds to a kindly God, who had guided their arms to victory. A soldier in Thomas Petty's regiment claimed "a kind Providence has hovered around our little band and protected it from the many dangers which have surrounded us." He concluded by admitting, "Yes, I fully appreciate the kindness of Him who has the power to do all things." Even one of the heroes of the hour, Thomas J. Jackson, who earned his nickname "Stonewall" for his stout defense here, informed his wife, "Yesterday we fought a great battle, & gained a great victory, for which all the glory is due to God alone."[10]

Drained by ten hours of fighting and several days of intermittent sleep, soldiers collapsed from exhaustion that first night. But for days and weeks afterward, troops traded tales around campfires, critiquing performances and awarding honor and blame to various officers and men. In letters home, too, they described their experiences and emotions throughout that bloody day. What emerged from these conversations and missives was recognition that reality shattered preconceived notions of battle, and the aftermath of combat proved far more gruesome than almost any of them could have imagined.[11]

Private J. W. Reid of the 4th South Carolina Infantry described the battle as "heaven and earth coming together." What stuck in Reid's mind most, what he anticipated least, was the incredible and continual roar of combat. He asked his family to "picture to yourself at least one hundred thousand men, all loading and firing as fast as they could." The sound was almost deafening. "The cannons," he elaborated, "although they make a great noise, were nothing more than pop guns compared with the thundering noise of the thousands of muskets."[12]

Fear, a topic they had discussed thoroughly in camps over the weeks and months before battle, had suddenly taken on life. Alabama private Jeremiah Tate had heard rumors of the devastating impact of artillery on the minds of ground troops. After his baptism by fire, Tate dismissed its psychological power, asserting, "I feel as unconsirned as if I was going a sqirl hunting." Like Tate, Capt. Hamilton Couper of the 8th Georgia Infantry defied all the precombat predictions. "All the stuff you hear about the feelings of a man in battle is *bosh*," he asserted. "You are too busy to have much feelings about anything." Thomas Goree from Texas disagreed with his comrades-in-arms. "But to be honest," he confessed to his mother, "I will say that I was pretty badly frightened. And it was time to be when you could constantly see men being killed and wounded in but a few paces of where I was." Another soldier confided that he mouthed all the prayers he could recall, even the ones from childhood, to sustain him through the ordeal.[13]

For all the posturing and braggadocio, no one knew how he or anyone else would measure up in combat until that moment arrived. Later in the war, as hardships compounded and the prolonged stress of battle wore down nearly everyone, soldiers proved more forgiving, especially in cases where men had previously stood steadfast and performed their duty well. In their first fight, however, officers and men took note of those who dodged their responsibilities and hid or broke for the rear. A lieutenant told his father the captain got ill "when we got within a mile of the battle ground" and he had to take command of the company. Lieutenant Colonel Edward Warren reported that two officers in his regiment acted badly and resigned from the army immediately after the battle. No one tried to stop them. A South Carolinian may have expressed it best when he grumbled, "Heart disease is getting very common here—the kind that I call chicken heart disease."[14]

Nor did soldiers have to fight to become unnerved by the battle. When word of the Battle of First Manassas reached the troops of the 4th Battalion Georgia Infantry, destined for the Virginia Theater, "some of our bold men became *weak in the knees* and wanted to sneak back home," a soldier informed his wife. They bombarded the surgeon with claims of sickness, rheumatism, constitutional debility, and "a parcel of falsehoods," anything to get the physicians to declare them unfit for duty.[15]

Over the next four years, this army would fight almost two dozen battles that eclipsed First Manassas in the number of casualties and troops engaged. Yet coming as it did so early in the war, and because they lacked physical, emotional, and psychological preparation, the battle absolutely stunned the participants and those who arrived shortly afterward. As one perceptive soldier commented in disillusionment after scanning the residue of battle, "I came to the conclusion that it was the most foolish thing imaginable for two civilized nations thus to meet and slaughter one another like brutes." The reality of battle shattered their illusions.[16]

Fighting ended late in the afternoon, and before anyone could make much sense from the victory, the sun had set. That night, a bright moon revealed just a part of the devastation, but soon clouds rolled in, and before the shift from night to day, a steady rain began to fall, one that continued all the next day. Throughout the night, Confederate troops could hear the groans and cries for help. By morning, soldiers had their first true glimpse of the disastrous victory. With light, they could affix faces to those gasps, and the dead and dying suddenly became all too human, the scene all too real. "Oh the indescribable horrors of the battle field!" exclaimed a Virginia lieutenant colonel. "Men shot all to pieces & shri[e]king for water & assistance, horses moaning in the agonies of death! Some of the men were awfully mangled." Although the 1,500 Rebel casualties received priority, a number of them remained on the field throughout the night and well into the morning. Some Federal wounded spent days there, not out of vengeance, but simply because the overworked Rebel medical staff could not get around to them.[17]

Within twenty-four hours of the battle, the field transformed from grue-some to ghastly. An Alabama captain who arrived too late for the fight wandered about the terrain in utter shock. "You could see where the battle had been the hottest," he jotted in a diary, "at every half dozen paces the body of a mangled Yankee laying gory and putrifying, and otherwise extremely revolting," most of them shot through the stomach or chest and facedown. "Horses, too, lay in abundance, and the millions of green flys that buzzed and blew over their swollen and putrid bodies render the scenes truly disgusting & sickening." Brazen birds picked away, too, he noted. Soldiers drove them off, but they quickly returned or found another carcass upon which to feast.[18]

Once again, Confederate dead merited priority, and burying Union troops and animals was almost an afterthought. Close to 900 soldiers gave their lives in the battle, along with hundreds of animals. Burial of so many men took time. An Alabama private walked the battlefield five days afterward, counting twenty-eight dead horses near Henry Hill alone. "The dead bodies of our men had been buried or removed from the field," he wrote; "those of the enemy lay where they fell, presenting a horrid and ghastly spectacle, and creating a stench almost intolerable."[19]

A Virginia cavalryman took a wounded prisoner he had captured to a hospital. On his return, "we past dead and wounded men (Yankees) all along the road they were beging for water." The sight so appalled him that he admitted, "I felt very Sorry for them though they were enemies."[20]

One of the soldiers who arrived just after the battle commented in his diary on how hardened he had become since joining the army. "One grows used to looking upon human suffering & misery so that it produces little or no effect upon him. Our noble dead seemed sacred sacrifices on the alter of liberty." Lieutenant Henry Franklin wrote his parents "with bleeding heart" to report and "mourn the loss of several of the Monroe Guards." These were people he had known virtually his entire life, and it crushed him to think of them and the pain this news would cause in their families and community.[21]

A North Carolina infantryman lost a cousin, Paisley White, in the fight. White had been sick, but he refused to drop out of the column, insisting, "I want a pop at the confounded Yankees." White suffered three wounds early in the battle and fell into Federal hands. Some Yankees threatened to execute him, but another talked them out of it. "Let the damned dog die as he is," White recounted. Around 10:00 P.M., Confederates found White and carried him to a hospital, some six miles away. By then, explained White's cousin, "flies had blowed his wounds and filled them with loathsome creatures." He died several days later.[22]

In a war that divided a nation and families, it was inevitable that Confederates sometimes shed tears for Yankee deaths. A Georgian witnessed a Rebel "weeping bitterly and wringing his hands over the stiff and blackened cor[p]se of his brother who fell on the other side." In "a sight that was truly piteous to behold," the Confederate soldier showed them letters his brother had written him, "full of kindness." The Georgian concluded by writing, "This civil war is a terrible thing."[23]

With so many casualties, medical personnel were overwhelmed, and the care that wounded received was scandalous. Dr. Hunter McGuire, Stonewall Jackson's friend and physician, went among the battlefield wounded that first night, ministering to their physical needs as best he could. Most of the injuries were from musket shots, and they fired massive .58 or .69 rounds, which inflicted grisly wounds. Unfortunately, there were too few Dr. McGuires to diagnose and prioritize cases on the field. A dearth of ambulances consigned the wounded to ride in "rough wagons, over rough roads," a chaplain recorded. "Their sufferings can better be imagined, than expressed." A horseman observed similar scenes, writing home, "There was more suffering than I can describe and never want to see again." They converted homes, schools, any kind of structures into hospitals. Overwhelmed by the sheer number of cases, officials shipped wounded by rail to the University of Virginia. Authorities there converted a large commencement hall into a hospital, and filled it.[24]

Rather than leave the wounded exposed to the elements, they took them to any shelter, including barns with livestock. Doctors seldom made the rounds there, but when they did, their skills frequently could not make a difference. A Mississippi soldier suffered a gunshot wound to the head. They carried him to a barn converted into a hospital, and rested him on some hay. According to an eyewitness, for five days "he lay there thousands of maggots in his head, crying continually 'Worse; Worser; worser!' unconscious of everything else."[25]

Angels of mercy, like Jesse Jordan's mother, Mary, came to the rescue. She had traveled from Huntsville, Alabama, to Virginia to care for sick soldiers, as her own mother had done in the Revolutionary War. When she heard that her son had been wounded badly in the fight, she immediately set out for Manassas. Two days later, Mary arrived, inquiring about Jesse. Despite all the sick and injured she had seen, it was the first time since she arrived in Virginia that she gave way to her feelings and sank beneath the weight of sorrow. When she saw that her boy had suffered only a slight wound, Mary was overjoyed. With wounded and sick under her care, Jesse accompanied her on the train to Culpeper. "I never had any idea she could stand & witness the groans of the dying & crying of the wounded but she stands it like a soldier," he boasted. Mary admitted to her son, "It is a wonder she is not gray, for since she left home she never witnessed such a sight in her life."[26]

At least Mary Jordan was in a position to ascertain the truth about her son's injuries quickly. Others had to wait, and at times the news was not so joyous. Private Willie P. Mangum, Jr., from a prominent Southern family, appeared to dodge a critical wound when a Yankee bullet struck a pocket Bible and glanced away from his heart. Several days later, though, he died from the musket shot anyway. Edmund Kirby Smith, who had served as Johnston's chief of staff, commanded a brigade at First Manassas that arrived from the Valley just in time to turn the tide of the battle. As he led several of his regiments to the front, Col. Joseph B. Kershaw rode up to request that he extend the line on the South Carolinians' left. Before Smith could respond, he swooned in his saddle and collapsed off his horse. A Union musket ball had crashed into his shoulder and exited near the spine. Stories circulated widely that Smith had been killed, spawning an emotional nightmare for his mother and his soon-to-be bride. They learned the truth a few days later. Three weeks after the battle, Smith informed his mother that he "read my obituary with but little satisfaction." Evidently, the experience compelled him to re-examine his priorities. In mid-September, Smith was spotted shopping in Richmond for an engagement ring for his girlfriend and the two married soon afterward.[27]

In addition to the hundreds of Federals killed and the 500 left wounded on the battlefield, the Confederates captured 900 Yankees. For the first time since the outbreak of hostilities, Rebel troops had an opportunity to confront Union soldiers personally. Yankees "are such mean, nasty, vulgar looking objects," declared a Georgia infantryman. Another soldier, from Virginia, had read a "specimen of Yankee letters" that circulated among Confederates and spoke with prisoners of war. Not one letter, he argued, "is from an educated person but all low flung and vulgar." Among the prisoners, "but one that I have heard of is a gentleman but all talk as the lowest class." Since the Rebel cause had such overwhelming merits, they could not imagine why Northerners would seek to subjugate them. When they asked Yankees why they fought, the responses, so Southerners deemed, were foolish, and the individuals were either misguided or devoid of morals. Claims such as fighting to preserve the Union made little sense to Rebels if that Union did not protect civil liberties. "They are not only the most deluded people on earth," a Georgian proclaimed after interviewing several wounded Federal soldiers, "but they are the most degraded people under the canopy of Heaven."[28]

The Confederacy seized an enormous number of weapons and equipment that its soldiers badly needed. In the rout, Rebel troops captured twenty-eight artillery pieces, most of them superior to anything they had in their military arsenal, thirty-seven caissons loaded with artillery ammunition, and more than five dozen artillery horses. Littered on the ground among the bodies and along the line of retreat were approximately five thousand rifled muskets, sundry army wagons, and half a million small-arms cartridges, more than replenishing the ammunition they had expended in the battle. As Federals retreated, many in panic, they discarded enormous quantities of impedimenta. A Virginia cavalryman involved in the pursuit assessed the prize to his wife: "For twelve miles the road was literally strewn with every description of Baggage, Wagons, Ambulances, Barrels of Sugar, Crackers, ground coffee &c thousands of Axes, spades shovels picks Arms by the thousands—clothing of every description—cooking utensils—in fact every thing." For the poorly equipped Rebel soldiers, the haul was truly a bonanza. "They were most luxuriously equipped for soldiers," a captain explained to a friend, "& their losses in the above respects are great helps to us."[29]

Confederate soldiers knew they had won a great victory, and the public reaction to the Battle of First Manassas was overwhelming. Thoughtful military minds realized that there would be more battles like this one before the North acknowledged the South's independence. But for the time being, soldiers cherished the idea that they had been a part of a great battle. Civilians at home, hoping to live vicariously through the army and soldiers with whom they were acquainted, also wanted something that would enable them to share the success, some item that would attach them both physically and emotionally to the battlefield.

Soldiers and civilian visitors took to heart the axiom, "to the victor go the spoils." They soon learned that in addition to clothing and shoes, which Rebels could use, Yankees often carried such valuables as watches, rings, and money. By rifling through the pockets of the dead, wounded, and prisoners, individuals could pick up some money and marketable items to supplement their meager pay.[30]

Even more gruesome, soldiers and civilians sought trophies. They began collecting macabre mementos to send home, often at the request of loved ones. A Georgian shipped teeth from the lower jaw of a Yankee to his father; a staff officer offered to send a woman a Yankee scalp. "I send you Some hair off the head of a New York Zouave," a Virginian wrote a woman. "I could have sent a skull just dug up but it was too large." Blacks openly hawked bones of Yankees to Confederates and visitors as keepsakes. A month after the battle, relic seekers had so plundered the field that they had stripped much of the evidence of a great clash of arms. Only skeletons of horses, shattered trees, and scarred houses offered obvious reminders of that horrible day.[31]

For soldiers, this was a way of demonstrating the collective battlefield accomplishments of Confederate forces, almost a means of bragging about their combat prowess. It indicated how effectively they could dehumanize the enemy, and in a warped version of masculinity, it attempted to tell the people at home how hardened they had become. For the recipient, the human keepsake helped them to live vicariously through the soldier. The gruesome article brought the war into their home, enabling them to feel more a part of the great struggle for slavery and independence. As a trophy, the piece of human anatomy represented their hatred and low regard for Northerners.[32]

According to a Georgia private, this desecration of the fallen was a black stain on the record of Confederate forces. "I am sorry to say that I saw Confederate soldiers digging them up[,] taking their skulls and other bones." He personally witnessed some twenty Rebels, including an old friend, unearthing bodies for relics. Another friend told him that he saw a cavalryman who pried apart "the chin of a Yankee and was wearing the lower jaw bone as a spur." He reassured himself that others at home and in the army grounded themselves in moral values. "I know you agree with me that this is a degree of barbarism more worthy of savages in the dark ages than our nation at this enlightened period," he wrote. "I am glad to say such proceedings are discountenanced by a vast majority of us."[33]

All told, the Confederates had performed extremely well at First Manassas. They had superior numbers, but the Federal soldiers carried rifled muskets, which gave them greater accuracy and more than triple the range of the Confederates, who largely employed smooth-bore muskets. From long distances, the Confederates simply had to endure the Union rifle fire, but during the course of the battle, they closed with the enemy and more than neutralized the Union advantage. Nervous soldiers on both sides fired too high, but because the Union weapons were sighted for three hundred yards, the angle of trajectory would naturally have caused the projectile to travel above the heads of close-in targets. Despite a lack of marksmanship training in the army, it was apparent to Johnston and others that their soldiers had fired more accurately than the enemy. "Our men require less instruction in shooting than in any other Military exercise," assessed Johnston after the battle. Although Confederate soldiers had fired too high, Johnston deemed that "the consequence more of excitement than of want of skill." Southern white men learned to shoot well at home, and "It is one of our great advantages over the Northern people," the general informed Davis.[34]

While some officers floundered in their first genuine test, others rose to the occasion and earned newfound or enhanced respect with the men. Those who stood tall on that day forged a powerful bond with their soldiers, and those who performed poorly lost face. When a lieutenant took over for his captain, he "gave satisfaction with the men & officers," and he soon supplanted his superior officer for company command. Wade Hampton, the fabulously wealthy South Carolinian who organized the Hampton Legion, drove his men hard to get to Manassas in time for the battle and then fought valiantly. "I am very glad to feel that I have the confidence of my men," he wrote to a family friend after the battle, "& I know that they will follow me anywhere." Without this initial success, and the self-assurance that the experience instilled in him, Hampton might not have evolved into one of the truly great cavalry commanders in the war.[35]

Most important, Confederates interpreted the victory at First Manassas as a reaffirmation of the supremacy of Confederates over Yankees. A captain in a Virginia regiment believed, "This may be as much owing to the superior class of men in our army as to anything else." While Southern society produced individuals of character who stood firmly in the face of danger, "the material of the Enemies army is of the low grade." Confederates demonstrated that superior character when they launched successful assaults on the Union line. "The Yankees cannot stand a *Charge*," a Louisianan scrawled to a girlfriend.

"They have a Horror of cold steel in any form & at the first charge they *invariably Run*."[36]

Johnston, who had largely commanded Northerners and foreigners in the Regular Army, placed little stock in arguments that elevated one society over the other. Instead, he viewed motivation as the key. He perceived Rebel superiority as "due solely to the spirit with which they fight, a spirit excited by patriotism & consciousness of the magnitude of the stake." At the heart of combat ability, Johnston argued, "is the difference between men fighting for independence—to drive back invasion—& those who will hire for eleven dollars a month." Like most Confederates, Johnston believed that the South fought for their rights—slavery and self-government. Since the North possessed no true cause, everyone who entered its army was a hired hand.[37]

EVEN THOUGH THE Confederates routed the Yankees at First Manassas, the battle exposed some problems that, if they continued to develop, would prove devastating to the Rebel war effort. In the course of the fight, part of the line of the 18th Mississippi Infantry reformed behind the 5th South Carolina Infantry, and when the order to fire came, the men of the 18th "poured in upon me heavy fires of musketry, cutting us up sadly," reported Col. Micah Jenkins. During the heat of battle, soldiers formed lines sloppily and failed to distinguish friend from foe. The diversity of uniforms among Rebels that day added to their woes. Those concerns, however, were classic problems for inexperienced soldiers.[38]

From an organizational standpoint, the Confederate leadership realized that it needed more cavalry to exploit infantry and artillery success. Johnston and Beauregard fought with too few horse soldiers, and when the infantry swept the Yankees from the field, they lacked enough cavalry to pursue effectively. Traditionally, armies had employed cavalry for scouting, raids, and attacks on a retreating foe. Although the advent of rifled weapons reduced the effectiveness of mounted attacks and pursuit, the shattered and panicked Federal soldiers would have been easy pickings for a larger, efficient cavalry command. As Johnston reported to Davis with but slight exaggeration, "An adequate force of cavalry would have made it decisive."[39]

One of the greatest problems that the Confederate commanders experienced was the diminishment of combat power due to shirkers and soldiers who escorted wounded comrades to the rear. As President Davis reached the field, he encouraged dozens if not hundreds of able-bodied men to rally and return to their commands. Lieutenant John Bratton, whose 6th South Carolina Infantry arrived just at the tail end of the rout, discovered in the rear huge numbers of "wounded and the rascally stragglers, who got enough and quit." Left unchecked, the practice could result in disaster, and Johnston and Beauregard determined to halt it. Two weeks after the battle, Beauregard suggested that the surest way to check the practice was to ensure that "a moral stain *must* be attached to all who leave the field of battle without the authority of the officer of a company." He wanted a roll call before units left the battlefield, and "all who are absent *without such authority* or *being wounded*, must be held by their comrades as poltroons & cowards." Later that year, Johnston issued a General Order that prohibited soldiers from escorting wounded comrades to the rear. The severe nature of the penalties for violators demonstrated the seriousness of the problem. "Offenders against this order will be punished with instant death on the spot, and at any hand, for desertion and cowardice."[40]

Many of these difficulties derived from the age-old problem of converting volunteers into soldiers. The bulk of the men had enlisted only three months before, and while most of them exhibited tremendous courage, they were by no means veterans. "It must be confessed too," Johnston confidentially wrote the president, "that the victory disorganized our volunteers as utterly as a defeat would do in an army of regulars." They had fought aggressively, and had carried the day, but Johnston's soldiers had neglected to follow through to its utmost conclusion. "Every body, officers & privates, seemed to think that he had fulfilled all his obligations to country—& that before attending to any further call of duty, it was his privilege to look after his friends, procure trophies, or amuse himself." Not until several days after Davis had returned to Richmond were officials able to reassemble the troops. Johnston and Beauregard had discussed this lack of discipline, and, "This trait in the volunteer character gives us great anxiety," he concluded. "It deprives one of the hope of achieving any thing like the battle of Rivoli," a reference to Napoleon's crushing blow to the Austrians more than six decades earlier.[41]

In analyzing the situation after First Manassas, President Davis explained, "Our difficulty was not to get men, but arms with which to provide them." Victory and control of the battlefield offered the Confederacy an opportunity to supply its armies with the best weapons and equipment that the Union had to offer. Politicians, officers, and men learned that the spoils of battlefield success provided the surest way to meet the needs of the field commands.[42]

Soldiers, too, discovered the lucrative nature of Civil War battlefields. Yankees could provide shoes and coats to protect them from the elements, food to fill their stomachs, superior weapons to fight future battles, and personal plunder such as money and jewelry to supplement private's pay. Unless the Confederate government could find another way to clothe, equip, and pay these soldiers properly, the demand for plunder could significantly detract from the combat effectiveness of the army.

The Battle of First Manassas, fought just three months after Virginia, North Carolina, Tennessee, and Arkansas seceded, had forced Rebel troops into combat long before they were ready. Against a tired and untrained enemy, Confederate soldiers relied on their aggressive spirit, courage, and familiarity with firearms to defeat the Yankees. Although the fight exposed green troops to combat, the victory also gave Rebels a false sense of confidence and an unbalanced perception of military service. Over the succeeding months, they would learn painful lessons about army life. When the novelty of service and the thrill of battle dissipated, they would have to cope with day-to-day living on a tented field, with all its hardships: exposure to weather, drilling in every condition, tedious duties, utter boredom, devastating illnesses, inadequate food and clothing, and unwanted discipline. They would discover that war-making was not only about combat. Its realities extended far beyond the battlefield into camps, factories, fields, and homes, affecting lives, treasures, and dreams across the Confederate States and extracting untold sacrifices from soldiers and civilians alike.

Chapter 7

"A GREAT CANVASS CITY"

"NEARLY *Ten Thousand Soldiers*," marveled a twenty-seven-year-old Alabamian in November 1861. "Oh! I never saw as many human beings in my life nor never expect to see as many again as long as I live (that is in such a small place.)." In his eyes, "it was the most magnificent sight on earth." From atop a nearby hill, a lieutenant scanned the panorama and spotted "no less than sixteen Regiments" in their camps. "Think what a splendid view they present," he wrote to his bride, "how the canvass glistens in the sunlight; and how the white tents far away in the distance, dotting the green plain of pines, seem like great white swans on some far off water."[1]

For all their motivation and prior training, Confederate officers and men who served in Virginia had no inkling of the scale and scope of the Civil War armies, or of the problems they would encounter in building them. None of them had ever served in an army larger than 10,000—the one Winfield Scott led in his advance on Mexico City. By the end of July 1861, the Confederate command at Manassas Junction alone numbered 30,000. The flood of military personnel and civilians taxed the agricultural and production base beyond its capacity, and railroads and roads struggled to deliver the necessary food and supplies to the army. Commanding and controlling these men, especially with the spirit of independence and individuality that they had absorbed from civil life, proved extremely burdensome, and in some cases almost impossible. And the consequences were dire. Misguided notions about war at virtually all levels inflicted painful, sometimes fatal, lessons. Southerners thought life on their farms and in rural areas nurtured good character and soldierly qualities, but they were less ready for many of the hardships and hazards than their urban compatriots.

In organizing an army in northern Virginia, Confederates were actually forming what a Georgian described as "a great canvass city," with all the complexities and troubles of an urban environment. By the summer of 1861, that army around the Centerville-Manassas axis was larger than Richmond in 1860. It would continue to increase in manpower strength until, by the summer of 1862, it was more than twice the size of prewar Richmond.[2]

Confederates had very little experience coping with urban life. Richmond was the twenty-fifth-largest city in the United States in 1860, ranking immediately behind Troy, New York. New Orleans at number 6 and Charleston at 22 were the only other cities in seceding states that outranked Richmond. At the start of the war, barely one of every twenty-five Confederate citizens lived in cities with 10,000 people or more.

Military demands forced soldiers to mass in densely packed areas. Immediately after the Battle of First Manassas, Confederate troops spent considerable time digging fortifications in case the Union attacked again. For days afterward, they remained on the field, living in heavy concentration. Rebel soldiers alone—excluding civilians and slaves—numbered close to 10,000 per square mile. By comparison, 1860 Richmond had a population density of about 6,000 per square mile. A little over a week later, the army dispersed along a fifteen-mile front, which reduced the density to 2,000–3,000 men per square mile, still a heavy concentration. By December, the department had 76,000 officers and men present, with soldiers crammed into a nine-square-mile area around Centerville.[3]

To make matters worse, nonmilitary personnel crowded into the area. Many of the troops brought slaves as servants to care for their personal needs. Visitors flocked to Manassas to meet with loved ones and see for themselves this giant and triumphant army that their fledgling nation had created. Others came to scavenge for mementos. All of them taxed supplies and occupied valuable cargo space on trains and wagons. Even worse, some brought illnesses with them, which spread to the army.

The bivouacs, clumped together so tightly, acted as a biological time bomb. Medical studies have discovered a very high correlation between population density and the rate of illness. With soldiers packed into these camps, both Yankees and Rebels would suffer from a high incidence of sickness.

What made these Rebel camps particularly lethal was that the troops came almost exclusively from rural areas, where they had little exposure to these deadly agents. By the time city dwellers reached adulthood, they had survived bouts with the usual assortment of childhood illnesses such as measles, mumps, and chicken pox, and many of them had endured the likes of typhoid fever and other potentially lethal ailments. All had developed resistance to them. If their ancestors had come from urban areas, they inherited resistance to some illnesses, what medical scholars call seasoning. Most farmers, however, had none of this resistance. In camp, living in tight proximity to thousands of others, and with huge numbers of soldiers drawing from the same water supply, disease spread like wildfire.

CITY RESIDENTS FORMED a relatively small portion of the army in Virginia. A sampling of the troops reveals that most soldiers came from rural areas and had various experiences with disease. One in seventeen soldiers came from communities with more than 10,000 inhabitants before the war. Of those urbanites, almost half were foreigners by birth. Most of them eked out meager livings—as did unwed Barry Lynch, a Louisianan of Irish descent who found employment as a hook and ladder keeper for a New Orleans firefighter company and had no appreciable wealth. Lynch enlisted in the Washington Artillery as a private. By contrast, Georgia-born Addison Tinsely, who was the same age as Lynch and also single, worked as a bookkeeper in a commercial house in Savannah and still lived at home. His father was a bank officer, and Addison's parents had accumulated considerable property and nine slaves. Tinsley served as a private in the 8th Georgia Infantry for the entire war. Perhaps the most unusual was Daniel Girand Wright of Baltimore, who served in various Virginia and Maryland units as an officer and enlisted man. Born in Rio de Janeiro, Brazil, to a prominent American father and a Brazilian mother, Wright studied law before the war and lived at home. His parents maintained no slaves but did employ four Irish and one free black as housekeepers and cooks. Wright managed to survive the war and become a prominent jurist in Baltimore.[4]

George S. High was not so lucky. A Tennessean by birth, the thirty-one-year-old High worked as an overseer on a farm of nineteen slaves near Starkville, Mississippi. He enlisted that May in the 13th Mississippi Infantry and traveled with his comrades to Virginia, where he was stricken with the measles. High tried to fight it, but he succumbed that same year, debilitated by fever and wracking bronchial ailments. He left behind a twenty-five-year-old widow and three small children.[5]

Illness struck down more Rebels than did Yankee bullets in 1861. Shortly after the Battle of First Manassas, a Virginia captain complained, "A sick man with fever is just as much [in] danger of dying as the wounded man if any thing more so." By December 1861, a North Carolinian who had fought in First Manassas spoke from a position of knowledge when he asserted, "It is a fact that the Battlefield is far less to be dreaded than the sickness in Camp."[6]

No one could have anticipated the astounding numbers of sick. In June, a Mississippian complained that his regiment had 350 to 400 ill. In mid-August, the 5th North Carolina reported 800 sick out of a total of 1,100 men. Eight men turned out for dress parade in one company; everyone else was incapacitated by health problems. The 7th Georgia could assemble 300 of the original regiment for dress parade, and of those 300, about 100 were too sick to perform active duty. In October, Brig. Gen. John Magruder implored the mayor of Williamsburg to let him use churches as temporary hospitals for the men in the 13th Alabama. Out of 800 soldiers, only 143 were fit for duty, and he lacked housing to protect them from the elements. "As summer diseases pass away," commented a young North Carolinian, "Winter ones takes its place." In December, the 14th Alabama had 500 sick troops. Nearly all the healthy ones had to devote their day to caring for the ill. That January, out of 700 on the rolls in the 8th Virginia, only 264 could assemble for duty. At one point, army commander Joseph E. Johnston complained to President Davis that of the 45,000 men he had with the army, almost 10,000 were sick, and that did not include 5,000 who were in hospitals away from camp.[7]

Both Johnston and Beauregard alerted Davis that childhood illnesses, especially measles, afflicted their troops in epidemic proportions. With soldiers in close confinement in camp, the malady spread from one contagious soldier to the next, and there seemed no way to check it. Because measles has an incubation period of nine to eleven days, by the time its victims exhibited the telltale symptoms of skin blotches, they had already spread it to others. Nine of every ten persons without immunity who come in close contact with carriers catch the ailment. Those units raised in rural areas, where few had exposure to it, suffered worse. Virtually the entire 11th Alabama Infantry caught it. From Richmond, General Lee warned a physician that outbreaks particularly affected Arkansas and Tennessee soldiers, who had lived in comparative isolation much of their lives. A member of the 7th Tennessee Infantry concurred. "Henry, it is a *fine* thing that we had the measles before we entered the army. I don't know of but one or two that have any health since they have had the measles," he informed his brother. "Nearly all have died after they had the measles." One soldier who survived his bout with measles contracted it just before the Confederates fell back from northern Virginia to Bull Run. "I would give out ever step but I knowed it would not do to stop," he explained to his mother, "for the yankes was comeing on be hind." It was not just the fever that could elevate to 105° but the severe respiratory infection, especially pneumonia and bronchitis, that killed or incapacitated soldiers.[8]

Along with measles, the greatest scourge in the army was typhoid fever. The bacteria that causes typhoid fever spread through feces, which contaminated water and food. Those soldiers who ingested the bacteria suffered fevers ranging from 103° to 104°. Victims sometimes died from these high temperatures, or they contracted pneumonia in their weakened state and died of what surgeons called typhoid pneumonia. Even when soldiers managed to recover from typhoid fever, they often continued to act as carriers and contaminated the water supply with their feces or by failing to wash their hands properly and then tainting foods.

At the time, no one knew what caused typhoid fever. Some Georgia troops concluded that it "was caused by the build up of carbonic acid produced by respiration," so they ventilated their tents. A North Carolina regimental surgeon complained to Lee that half the officers and almost two-thirds of the privates, some 500 men, had fallen victim to illness, especially typhoid fever and typhoid pneumonia. In his desperate struggle to check the affliction, the physician could not determine if it was the result of "vicissitudes of weather, change in climate, exposure, or want of variety of diet." The surgeon admitted he had exhausted his supplies and, by implication, his own resourcefulness. A captain in the 14th Louisiana Infantry took his case directly to his commander in chief. He explained to Davis that after designating his men to minor detail assignments, illness left him with only four healthy soldiers. "The Regimental

Surgeon seems unable to treat the disease successfully," he wrote the president. "The men have become alarmed and very much dispirited. The disease advances steadily on & every man seems doomed to fall before its fatal stroke." The captain called it an epidemic and urged the president to transfer his men farther south.[9]

The least excusable illness in the army was scurvy, because its causes were well known. When an individual did not consume enough vitamin C over a prolonged period, his body could no longer produce collagen. Blood vessels began to deteriorate, teeth loosened and fell out, and soldiers eventually hemorrhaged. Since the late eighteenth century, physicians had known that after five months without "antiscorbutics" in citrus fruits, scurvy would set in. In January 1862, the army medical director notified his superiors, "Already has this disease made its appearance and prompt measures should be taken to arrest its progress." He alerted them "to the urgent necessity of issuing anti-scorbutics to the troops in the field. Unless this be done," he insisted, "scurvy will become quite prevalent in the Army in the course of the next few months."[10]

Although the medical world was on the cusp of major breakthroughs, physicians in the early 1860s cured very few illnesses, and surgical success was marginal at best. In many instances, competent and caring nurses offered the best medical attention, simply by keeping soldiers and hospitals clean and providing good nourishment and comfort for recovery. Unfortunately, there were too few Mary Jordans. Johnston assigned one soldier for every ten patients to act as nurses, but that was not much of a solution. Soldiers could not yet care for themselves, let alone fellow troops. When the department medical director attempted to secure free blacks as nurses, his solution ran at cross purposes with Johnston's policy of reducing logistical burdens by preventing any more blacks from entering the department.[11]

Efforts to remove the sick and place them in hospitals merely shifted the site of agony. It took twenty-four to thirty-six hours to transport sick and injured soldiers by train from Manassas Junction to Charlottesville, where officials had temporarily converted university areas into hospital facilities. Seldom did they receive food or care on the trip, according to a physician. Others traveled to Richmond, a fourteen-hour journey on what one soldier called "filthy cattle cars." It was small wonder that soldiers deserted the hospital trains.[12]

Understaffed, overcrowded, overworked, and overwhelmed, medical staff were blamed for the neglect and suffering. As one soldier noticed, "the army is a poor place for sick and wounded men." John Apperson, a skilled hospital steward, contracted typhoid fever. "I lay from Wednesday until Sunday with little or no attention, food, or medicine," he recorded in his journal. A friend tried to get him a sick furlough and take him away from the army, but the surgeon refused, and he continued to wallow in unattended misery. Finally, on Sunday, his uncle arrived and took him home. Another soldier visited a Staunton, Virginia, hospital, and was outraged. "I never saw such utter neglect to sick men in my life," he vented in a letter to his cousin. "Men rolling about in their dirty clothes not a change of clothes nor any one to bathe their aching bones." A volunteer physician insisted, "The Doctors either do not understand their business or they do not do their duty. The sick in many instances certainly receive very poor attention." He complained about the care of one particular soldier to an officer, and this instigated an official inquiry. After checking into the matter, the investigating officer determined, "this man died more like a hog than a human being."[13]

One group of patients took their case directly to President Davis. "Disease is wasting away the glorious Army of the Potomac,'" they grumbled. "We have lost *10 times* as many men by sickness as by warfare." One-fifth of the army suffered from illness, with "no additional means used to prevent the spread of the fearful pestilence. We humbly protest that three fourths of the surgeons of the army are wholly unfit for their positions." The surgeons, they claimed, were political appointees who did not order or enforce the most elementary steps in sanitation.[14]

In time, soldiers hardened emotionally to the death of comrades from disease, but those initial fatalities affected Confederates badly. "I never regretted the death of a stranger so much in all my life," confessed a Mississippian upon the death of Joe Griffith, one of the most popular men in his unit. Death became so widespread that one soldier predicted, "those Yankees are going to try to whip with *disease* instead of the Powder." The burial dirge became more familiar than "Dixie," as Confederates regularly laid comrades to rest. "Every day or so we hear the Band commence playing a sad burial tune very suddenly," a soldier informed his parents; "we know then that some poor boy's spirit has departed."[15]

The Confederate troops unwittingly created a sanitary nightmare for themselves. The best means of preventing illness was to select healthy campsites and to police camps rigorously, but these practices were neglected.

In the early 1840s, a physician named John H. Griscom embarked on a path-breaking study of sanitary conditions for the laboring class in New York City. Griscom blamed the high rate of disease on poor sanitary and living conditions. It took a few years to convince authorities, but Northern cities began to clean streets, build sewage lines, remove waste, and in general concern themselves with proper sanitation. The same month that the war broke out, a group of Northerners formed the U.S. Sanitary Commission, based on a model in the Crimean War. The Sanitary Commission acted as an advisory and watchdog group to ensure that Union officials preserved the health and welfare of the men.[16]

By contrast, the South lagged far behind. Farms on which most Southerners lived had few serious sanitary problems. To measure up to mid-nineteenth-century standards, they needed to know little more than to not build the

---

*Under Johnston, the army was called the Army of the Potomac, the same name as its Federal opposing army.

outhouse next to the well and to keep the livestock out of the house. Since Joseph Lister did not develop his germ theory and antiseptics until after the war, widely accepted practices demanded little else to maintain a healthy environment.

This lackadaisical attitude spilled over into military service. Severe sanitation problems erupted in the aftermath of the Battle of First Manassas. The Confederates were unprepared to cope with the thousands of killed and wounded soldiers and animals. Human and animal bodies lay on the field decaying for days and days. The smell, recorded a Georgia captain, resembled a "butcher's pen." Millions of flies, thousands of scavenging birds, and untold numbers of vermin overran the area and picked at the remains, spreading all sorts of bacteria and viruses.[17]

Two days after the battle, a Virginian wrote home, "Wee will Hav to burry the Yankeys today to keep them from stinking us to death." After Confederates interred their comrades, they dug graves for Union soldiers, but officers failed to supervise the efforts carefully, and in most instances they simply tossed some shovelfuls of dirt over the bodies. A month later, complained a Mississippian, "the recent rains had washed much of the dirt off, and it was nothing unusual to see hands or feet exposed." The signs of the battle were visible for miles and "The stench was unbearable."[18]

In Bull Run, which most soldiers tapped for their water, dead Yankees and horses rotted, breeding pestilence. Nine days after the battle, a Mississippian and his comrades had to wade across the rivulet. He complained that they "were much annoyed by the bad smell of the water, as we crossed below the battlefield, and the creek was perfectly impregnated with the smell of the bodies of dead men, & horses. As soon as I could," he continued, "I went to a spring branch, and washed off the smell, & put on clean clothes." Interred bodies contaminated the groundwater and the river, tainting the water supply for thousands of Confederates weeks after the battle. A member of Jesse Jordan's 4th Alabama recorded in his journal that his regiment drew all its water from Bull Run, "a muddy, sluggish branch in which, *madam rumor* says, there were lying a number of dead Yanks." After some days, "The stench created by the dead carcasses, both of horses and Yanks, soon became so intolerable, that the Regiment was forced to seek a more congenial clime." Not quite so fortunate, the 7th Louisiana Infantry remained on the battlefield and continued to suffer the consequences. In August alone, two-thirds of the men fell ill, primarily with fevers and diarrhea. They camped along Bull Run, and men complained of unusually severe cramping and diarrhea. Johnston eventually recognized the problem, blaming bad water problems for "a great deal of sickness among our troops," but he maintained regiments near the battlefield nonetheless.[19]

Creeks and streams always run along the lowest piece of ground; soldiers almost always fortified on the high ground. When they dug trenches, soldiers covered the grass and promoted runoff. Without well-located and universally used sinks—holes dug in the ground to serve as toilets for the men—soldiers relieved themselves just outside the defensive position. Rains then washed the waste down into the streams, contaminating the water supply.

Unaccustomed to much discipline and unschooled in field hygiene, troops' proper sanitary practices lapsed as they responded anywhere to nature's call. The surgeon in the 7th Louisiana believed the "decomposition of dead Yankees" intensified the contamination problem, but its principal origin rested with poorly located sinks. "The sinks were too near, and not often covered with dirt," which fouled the air and tainted the water. Medical officers called for the digging and regular use of sinks, but enforcement was lax. Two years later, a soldier complained of the same problem. "On rolling up my bed this morning," he penned home, "I found I had been lying in—I wont say what—something that didn't smell like milk & peaches."[20]

Sloppy sanitary conditions continued to plague the army. The department medical director complained in mid-November that offal from the slaughter pens and camp kitchens was not buried daily and that soldiers did not dig sinks "at such a distance from camp as to prevent the deleterious effects of miasma naturally arising from the deposits." Two months later, the Second Corps medical director grumbled that the troops failed to bury offal and dead horses, and "The use of privates seems to have become a matter of Regimental history, and the claim of commanders to approval for observances of the Regulations in this respect appears to be entirely based upon the past." That month, the First Corps assigned a *"Police Officer"* with a party of men for daily duty to ensure proper practices in camp. Eight days later, however, an inspector uncovered the same unsanitary problems: failing to bury offal, poor location and maintenance of sinks, and interring deceased horses in the vicinity of camp.[21]

The army needed high-ranking officers to elevate camp sanitation to the level of a crusade, yet far too few did so. Rare indeed were officers like Brig. Gen. Jubal Early, who not only provided guidance on how to dig trenches for the disposal of butchers' discards and how to cover them properly each day, but also assigned the officer of the day for each regiment in his brigade the responsibility of inspecting the sites during that tour of duty. Early demanded written reports of all violations. He also directed officers to attend to sinks. If they caught soldiers not using them properly, officers were "to require such persons to remove all offensive matter to the *Sinks* and keep the same in good order."[22]

Despite their days in the countryside, Confederate soldiers had little experience living outdoors. Often they positioned camps in unhealthy locations or among clumps of trees and then proceeded to chop them down for firewood. What they did not realize was that an adult tree drinks up about thirty gallons of water a day. Without the timber for drainage, they converted their camps into mudbaths. "I thought I had some very respectable muddy roads in Alabama," a soldier wrote, "but Virginia mud, is so decidedly muddy, of such unmitigated depth and stickiness as to render comparison impossible." Some complained that it was ankle deep in their tents.[23]

Nor did soldiers demonstrate much interest in caring for themselves in camp. Removed from traditional social controls, soldiers neglected personal cleanliness. Troops seldom bathed and infrequently shaved. One soldier, who refused to trim his facial growth, informed his girlfriend that "one might as well kiss a Scrub Broom or a duster as myself." Dirt and mud—the Virginia form that had no parallel—dusted and caked onto uniforms, yet soldiers continued to wear them, undeterred by the filth. Charles S. Venable, a future staff officer for Robert E. Lee, visited his brother-in-law and described him as "very well and big and fat and greasy and did not seem to want anything in the world but some clean water." A soldier in the 2nd Georgia Infantry depicted himself to his parents as "not quite as dirty as a New Orleans Zouave but I've seen many a cleaner negro." Compared to his peers, however, he glistened. "You ought to see some of the soldiers in this regiment," he exclaimed. "Some of them I dont believe have had on a clean shirt in two months, one of them told me he had'nt washed himself *since he left home* (more than three months ago), he was decidedly one of the 'great unwashed.'" Part of the blame rested with the quartermaster department, which failed to issue soap for two months, but soldiers used it sparingly even when soap was readily available.[24]

When it came to food preparation, nearly all the troops were clueless. At home, cooking had been women's work. Some in camp had the benefit of servants, but those blacks were usually selected on the basis of loyalty and hardiness, rather than culinary expertise. The burden, then, fell largely on the men, and as the volunteers soon learned, burnt fingers were the least of their worries. A Georgia private grumbled of eating biscuits so hard "i could nock a bull down with one." One mess stole what they thought was a container of lard and baked biscuits with it. After they had gobbled down a few each, someone came along and notified them they had pilfered tallow to make candles, not lard. One of the group thought the tallow biscuits were "very good" and proposed that they continue using it, but his mess voted him down. A soldier named Bacon had quite a time baking bread. "The first time I made up dough," he explained to a friend, "I had a mess of it; stuck to my hands and I hardly could get it off. Then I tried to bake it, but I could not get it done; some was burnt up and some was raw." He concluded by remarking, "what a mess I had." Another soldier complained to his aunt, "The only thing that hurts me is the food I have to eat. It keeps my stomach out of order all the time. The bread is burned out side & raw in side, & the meat is so strong & salt[y] that I dont pretend to eat it. The two comprise our bill of fare."[25]

Stringy pork, salt-drenched beef, and flour and occasional coffee without sugar were standard rations. Soldiers attempted to supplement that diet by buying items from hawkers, begging from locals, or stealing. In time, troops picked the area clean, which meant they had to subsist almost exclusively on government-issued food, and with their culinary incompetence, they managed to convert good ingredients into bad food and bad ingredients into even worse fare. As a group of soldiers grumbled to the president, "The horrid mixtures which pass in our army for bread are enough to destroy the health of any army that uses them." The problem became so serious that Johnston and Beauregard blamed the poor cooking for the massive diarrhea outbreaks. Beauregard informed Davis that in his opinion, portable kitchens and cooked food would be more valuable than a regimental surgeon. "Many of the volunteers," he commented with dismay, "cannot even cook a potato." Both generals sought ovens built to furnish soldiers with decent bread a few times per week. Yet in November and again in January 1862, the army medical director complained about the quality of bread baked in camp, arguing that it "is generally of the worst possible description, and most prolific of disease."[26]

With little experience living outdoors, regardless of their backgrounds, most soldiers struggled to perform the most elementary tasks. Such chores as building proper campfires could turn into quite an ordeal. Troops burned themselves by tossing on too many logs, roasting their feet and singeing their hair. In one instance, a huge, roaring fire that the men had built shot embers that landed on the socks of a sleeping soldier. When they burned through the clothing, he leaped up and slapped at them, which only made it worse. "I never saw such jumping as he did in my life, and never laughed so much," a comrade reported. The next morning, the soldier had a huge burn blister on his shin. Even more dangerous was the mistake of some men in the Rockbridge Artillery, who positioned their fire too close to some woods. In the cold January air, they piled on too many logs, and the roaring flames spread to the trees. Frantic troops had to scurry about to remove the animals, guns, ammunition chests, and nearly a ton of gunpowder before the flames consumed them.[27]

Nor were volunteers accustomed to carrying loaded firearms on a regular basis. While most of them had experience with firearms hunting game, and occasionally shooting at targets, they had very little day-to-day experience carrying weapons. All too often careless soldiers left their muskets loaded, with percussion caps on the firing nipple. A slight jarring of the hammer would hurl a projectile through camps, occasionally with fatal consequences. A soldier in the 5th Alabama Infantry was practicing the manual of arms when his musket exploded "& blode alittle boys head off," according to a witness. In the 2nd Virginia, a musket accidentally discharged, the ball passing through the chest of one man and lodging in the abdomen of another. "It is much harder, I think, to die by the hand of friend, than by that of an enemy," a member of the regiment suggested. Others did not bother to remove the powder and ball before cleaning the weapon, or were careless in the loading process. A captain in the 1st Arkansas Infantry accidentally shot himself in the thigh, and he felt humiliated. "If I have been shot by a Yankee I would not have cared a bit, but to shoot myself in gloriously just when my servises were likely to be needed is mortifying in the extreme," he confessed to his wife.[28]

Quite a number of Rebels, regardless of rank, brought pistols with them. Unstable when loaded, these weapons discharged far too frequently in camp, usually maiming or killing the owner, but sometimes taking someone else's life.

Private Gilbert Nicholson in the 4th Alabama was loading his pistol in camp when he accidentally let the hammer slip. The gun fired, and the ball severed the spine of Powhatan Baptist, a popular young soldier who was just lounging on the ground. Before he died, Baptist forgave Nicholson and said that "he knows Gilbert suffers more than he does." The problem with pistols discharging unintentionally became so serious that a Georgia officer wrote an Atlanta newspaper, urging volunteers to leave those weapons at home.[29]

All told, these were harsh and frequently fatal lessons for volunteers. Brigadier General Lafayette McLaws, a hardened soldier who rose to command a division, believed that military life was so alien to their civilian experience that it exacted a temporary change. According to McLaws, "the necessities of a Soldiers life makes him selfish to such a degree that until custom makes him an adept in that way of living he cares for no one but himself, and very often cares nothing for himself." They might look after a friend, McLaws conceded, but otherwise they exhibited surprising insensitivity to the plight of comrades.[30]

Although McLaws may have overstated his argument, particularly about soldiers' concern for their comrades, there was more than a hint of truth in it. The army attempted to strip volunteers of all semblance of individualism and imposed on them a world of regimen, routine, and limitations. Their natural inclination was to respond in selfish ways, until army life became second nature to them. Soldiers also believed that because the military world drew them away from social norms, and called upon them to kill fellow men on behalf of their citizens and country, they could willfully transgress other social constructs. Personal hygiene was the least of it. Personal convenience rose above good judgment. Eventually, soldiers realized that lazy shortcuts for digging and using sinks sometimes generated severe consequences. It took time, but troops came to the realization that a little extra effort in camp saved lives.

Ultimately the men learned to adapt to military ways so thoroughly that civilian life seemed like the aberration. Some soldiers and units resisted more than others. Louisiana troops rioted and committed acts of violence repeatedly, until the army executed several of them for mutiny and murder and placed numerous others under arrest. Texas regiments, composed of rough-and-tumble individualists, required the firm and powerful hand of an imposing officer like John Bell Hood to coerce them into proper conduct. But even with these men, the transformation occurred, and they became excellent soldiers. The key was to instill discipline and forge unit cohesion without squashing all remnants of individualism and self-esteem. Southerners brought with them a cockiness, a confidence in their military abilities, a pride in themselves and their way of life that would sustain them through hardships and combat. To eliminate that would be to strip them of much of their competitiveness.[31]

The volunteers of 1861 learned some lessons the hard way during their initial year of service. By September, men who knew nothing about the culinary arts before the war could boast, perhaps with a slip of the pen, "I have got so that I can bake frustrate [first rate] Soda bread," or could write to a brother,

"I flatter myself that I can cook Beef Stake as good as any woman and I can Bake first rate." Later in the war, a Georgian would admit to his wife, "Many a soldier can now realize the value of woman's work that thought but little or nothing about it before the war commenced."[32]

From these harsh experiences the volunteers of 1861 hardened, so that as the spring of 1862 approached, they had mastered much of the art of soldiering in camp. These vital lessons not only benefited them, but would also aid succeeding waves of recruits. Through firsthand knowledge born largely of trial and error, veterans of 1861 could shield newcomers from some of the harshest elements of army life and impart lessons from personal experience, which would save lives and ease the transition from civilian to soldier.

Chapter 8

———◦◦◦———

KEEPING THE ARMY TOGETHER

O N THE FINAL day of summer in 1861, a fair-haired farmer named Daniel J. Hileman lay in camp, pining for closure to this infernal war. A native son of Rockbridge County and a resident of Stonewall Jackson's hometown of Lexington, the twenty-five-year-old private echoed the sentiments of his more famous townsman. "It will never be ended except by fighting & the sooner we do it the better," he grumbled. "I despise inaction."[1]

Twenty-six year-old bachelor James A. Maddox echoed Hileman's frustration. A prewar overseer on his father's huge farm in western Georgia, Maddox let his impatience get the best of him. "We did not come here to lie in camps, and do nothing," he griped.[2]

If Maddox wished for action, he would see plenty of it. By the war's end, he would bear scars from wounds received in three separate battles. But in 1861 Hileman and Maddox expressed the impatience of thousands of their comrades throughout the summer and fall months. They had come out to protect slavery, their rights as free men, and their loved ones. The sooner they battled it out, the sooner they could return home.

As the year wound to a close, the descending winter chill was symbolic. Amid the boredom and hardships of camp life, many men's burning passion for war and glory flickered out. As the frozen ground began to thaw in 1862, the Confederate government confronted the possibility that its veteran army might very well dissolve.

After First Manassas, both sides built up large armies in the Virginia Theater. What followed was a kind of phony war, with Yankees and Rebels staring at one another and doing nothing. The Union replaced its army commander, Irvin McDowell, with a reputed dynamo, Maj. Gen. George B. McClellan. Unlike McDowell, McClellan did not lose any battles with his army that summer and fall, because he did not venture any. This Yankee inaction played right into the hands of Confederate commander Joseph Johnston, whose personal predilections, military responsibilities, and limited resources dovetailed into a policy of watch and see. Johnston's sole proposal for an offensive, which he, Beauregard, and Maj. Gen. Gustavus W. Smith presented to Davis in the beginning of October, required more weapons and "seasoned" reinforcements than the Confederacy had available.[3]

Confident and aggressive by nature, and buoyant after the victory at First Manassas, Rebel officers and men found stagnation almost too much to endure. Major General Earl Van Dorn, a division commander in Virginia, likened the behavior of Johnston and McClellan to "two old women always quarrelling and daring one another but afraid to 'hitch.'" The same frustration seized future corps commander Ambrose Powell Hill, when he wrote his wife that fall, "We are still lying on our oars, in a perfect state of sluggishness, so far as the cause is concerned." In November, a well-connected South Carolinian, Louis Gourdin Young, unburdened himself to his uncle. "I am getting very, very tired looking at the enemy and doing nothing more," he bristled. Young affixed blame on military and civilian leadership, asserting, "It seems to me that we are as wanting in enterprise as the Yankees."[4]

Days blended into weeks and months. "What would a soldier not do and undergo for a variety or rather a change, from the regular routine attending a regular camp?" pondered a Louisianan who answered himself, "anything and every thing." Drill, guard duty, and cooking composed the daily regimen; variety consisted of digging defensive works or tinkering with existing fortifications. The rest of the time, the army simply waited. It was small wonder that Private Hileman complained, "This eternal routine of drilling a little going on guard occasionally & cooking day after day & week after week just kills me."[5]

On rare occasions, the rhythmic thumping of the long roll shattered the humdrum. For a few fleeting moments, soldiers actually thought the enemy was near, that the great battle for independence was upon them. The entire camp erupted in a swarm of activity, until word spread of false intelligence or they assembled for battle, only to learn that their officers were conducting a test. Like premature cries of wolf, these false alarms became annoying, and in no time, soldiers reacted to the drum roll much as they did to other duties, with no enthusiasm.[6]

But the problem was more than just "this dull, monotinous, lasy camp life," so bemoaned one soldier; exposure to harsh weather compounded their woes. In the summertime, it was not nearly as bad. A pale-skinned soldier could complain that the hot Virginia sun "burnt all the skin off my ears," or Lt. James Langhorne might tan so deeply that he could joke about switching races. "I am as black as it is possible for a white person to get. I think if I get a half shade darker I will be no longer classed among persons of that complexion." During the warm-weather season, heavy rains could saturate soldiers and make the performance of their duties uncomfortable, too. A North Carolina captain observed a sentinel executing his duty amid a torrential shower that fell "with perfect fury on his head." He described the man as "the picture of despair," soaked completely to the skin. The guard looked at the officer and said, "'Who would'nt be a soldier?'"[7]

Yet November to February was something else entirely. Plummeting temperatures, sleet, and snow elevated difficulties and discomfort exponentially. "We are soldiering in reality now," explained a Virginian to his father in mid-November. "It is very severe on us during this cold weather." The standard shelter, Army-issue tents, offered little aid in battling the elements. Mississippian Will Crutcher explained to his wife that in a heavy rain "tents are no more protection than one of your fine cambric pocket hankerchief might be for an Elephant," offering little protection from the harsh aspects of Virginia winters.[8]

Those who suffered most, quite understandably, came from the Deep South, where snowfall and bitter cold were anomalies. In December, Alabamian Bolling Hall went to sleep in a drizzle and woke up several hours later to find that he was now bedded in a stream of runoff three inches deep. Hall, by this time a hardening soldier, simply rolled over and fell back asleep. When he awoke the next morning, rain had changed to sleet and snow, and he noticed a glaze of ice coating tree trunks and branches. Someone walked by and started laughing at him. Hall borrowed a looking glass, and he discovered why. His hair had icicles dangling from it.[9]

As winter descended, virtually everyone knew that McClellan would not advance—especially as the Yankee general had squandered ideal campaigning weather in the fall—except for the individual who counted most, army commander Joe Johnston. Despite pleas from his most trusted subordinates, Johnston hesitated to order the men into winter quarters, wherein many could build shanties with fireplaces some slight distance to the rear for protection from the elements. Although soldiers would have ample time to reoccupy their frontline positions in the event of a Union attack as long as the advanced troops on picket duty did their job, Johnston erred on the side of caution. He looked toward short-term defense, and troops suffered. Some men did not go into winter quarters until late January.[10]

Nor did winter camps signal an end to active campaigning. In northwestern Virginia, Jackson perceived an opportunity to regain the lower or northernmost portion of the Shenandoah Valley and drive occupying Federals back across the Potomac River. The movement required the combination of two Confederate commands and a surprise attack on Federal forces. Unfortunately, January weather refused to cooperate, and sleet, snow, and bitter cold impaired Rebel advances and enabled the Union troops to escape. A Virginia soldier likened the campaign to a bad dream in which "he is straining every nerve & muscle in a desperate struggle, but something ever intervenes to thwart his efforts and paralyze his strength." In this instance, "bad weather or something else over which we have no control always comes and prevents us from achieving any positive good." According to an artillerist, the campaign bordered on a nightmare. It snowed one night, and during the march the sun melted it, but after sunset it turned cold and everything froze hard. The artillery horses slipped and fell often the next day on the sheet of ice. "Going uphill," explained a member of the Rockbridge Artillery, "soldiers had to push & coming down-hill they had to restrain the guns from sliding over the horses."[11]

The harsh elements, endless structure and routine, and separation from loved ones, particularly during the holiday season, weighed heavily on the men. In a huge understatement just before Christmas, Russell Strickland suggested that this "*livlyhood* business, of Soldiering, is not, in every respect as pleasant—& as comfortable—as a man might imagine." The regimentation, the deprivation of their most fundamental rights to control their own lives and to question everything, made soldiers feel more like machines than humans. "We eat when we are told, and we work as we are told, asking no questions," grumbled an Alabamian. "We are machines—" insisted a Georgian, "have no use for THINKING—only ACTING." Theodore Fogle of the 2nd Georgia Infantry hated the way his officers and the army in general treated him. "I don't like the idea of being ordered about like a slave, & being treated as a mere tool or machine," he complained to his sister. "I think I am a reasonable being, but some fools in authority think that a private soldier has no right to think atall."[12]

Like Fogle, other soldiers could not help but compare their plight to the status of slaves. That dichotomy between freedom and slavery, a comparison that weighed heavily on the minds of Southern whites during the secession crisis, never drifted far from soldiers' thoughts. In the army, they were well aware of the irony that, as one Virginian asserted, "I am sure there is no field negro that has not more liberty than we have."[13]

Almost everything about the army sought to strip away any semblance of individuality and rights. It was part of the adaptation and training process. "I have come to the conclusion that a private soldier has no earthly business with an opinion," a Louisiana lieutenant divulged to his mother, "and that an Officer is to have one only to be divulged with great circumspection, and under peculiar circumstances, and to hold it merely *as* an opinion, a myth, a *nothing*." Struggle though they might, ultimately, most troops yielded some freedom, but they did so grudgingly, and they continually battled against army regimentation to regain it.[14]

Many soldiers grew disillusioned with the inconsiderate and at times vulgar behavior of their comrades-in-arms. Since the men in uniform sacrificed on behalf of their nation, they believed that others should contribute to their comfort, and quite a number of troops had no compunction about taking from civilians without permission from owners or without the authorization of their officers. The consequence of this rationalization was wholesale destruction and widespread pilfering of civilian property. In mid-September, a Georgian informed his wife that "everything as far as I have been from Manassas is desolation, fences destroyed, corn fields laid waste, orchards stripped, gardens broken down." He then vowed, "Let me always if I must do it fight for Georgia outside her limits." Seven months later, a Virginian expressed his disgust at the condition of northern Virginia when he wrote his wife, "The stories of out rage, theft & destruction by our men are truly horrible. Women have escaped thus far," he conceded, "but property of every kind is taken without hesitation." Officials issued order after order attempting to check this misconduct, without success. The basic hypocrisy of it all did not elude concerned soldiers. Here they were, serving in the army and fighting in defense of civil liberties, especially threats to property rights, while many of them violated the property rights of fellow citizens with impunity.[15]

Camp life revealed everyone's mettle, and in most instances, the sight was not pretty. "Man's opinion of man is not improved by constant contact in camp life," noted a Virginian. An Alabamian admitted to his sister, "I have learned more of human nature since being in the army, than I ever did before." Unfortunately, he uncovered "a man's true character. Selfishness is the principal characteristic." Another soldier considered his comrades a pack of "theaves an[d] dogs." Of some men in camp, he wrote, "I say men but if I had substuted [sic] dogs it would have suted much better."[16]

Several volunteers concluded that the absence of women prompted the unfortunate behavior. More than simply the moral keepers, women were the civilizing force in Southern society. They prevented males from degenerating into baser beings. Private Daniel Hileman confessed, "I have often heard it said that man when taken away from female society will soon become like a brute, & I am forced by experience to acknowledge it to be true." While reflecting on camp life, Virginia private James S. Newman, a prewar teacher, "was struck by the influence of women upon the opposite sex." Regrettably, he had to admit that without women, "society would be even worse than the camp." Newman believed that, "Were it not for the letters received from them by the soldiers they would become perfect barbarians in six months." He saw clear evidence of their impact in the conduct of soldiers who corresponded with females. Yet as one soldier complained, not all female contact was necessarily conducive to sound moral conduct. Soldiers brought prostitutes, posing as their wives, into camp. His proof rested with men from Richmond and Lynchburg, who recognized the women and knew the ladies' marital status and trade.[17]

As they sat around camp, stewing over all the hardships, frustrations, and annoyances, soldiers soured on the experience of military life and were prompted to discourage others from serving. "I would advise all my friends unless the[y] wish to live like negroes to stay at home," a Mississippian instructed his father. "I know if there is another war this chicken wont be *thar* when they enlist." North Carolinian Willie Williams approved of his brother Baldy coming to his regiment, but not brother John. "Bro J. would not be able to charge bayonets with some of the giant Irishmen in Lincoln's army," he explained. Georgian Eli Landers feared what illnesses would do to his brother and warned him, "Pole, don't you volunteer for God's sake for I know enough about camps to know that your constitution ain't strong enough to stand camp life." Perhaps Alabamian Jeremiah Tate employed the most potent effort at dissuasion. He wrote his mother, "Tell Thompson to stay home & take care of the widows I will kill Yankees enough for me & him both."[18]

Anticipating the breakup of its armies in the spring if troops did not re-enlist, the Confederate government launched a campaign to retain their services. It offered opportunities to reorganize and to elect new officers if soldiers would only re-enlist for two more years or the war's duration. As an added inducement, troops who extended their service would receive a bounty and a furlough, too. The initial response was tepid. Troops were reluctant to commit themselves to a continued life of unknown hardship, high risk, and restrictions on their rights, what one Alabama veteran described as "a leap into the dark." A Georgian expressed no interest in extending his term of service. "I am fighting for independence," he noted sagely, "but have only made a slave of myself in the effort." A lieutenant feared not one hundred men in his regiment would re-enlist. "They assign as a reason that the Government has shown an utter indifference to their comfort health or lives," he wrote the president.[19]

Soldiers resented the fact that they had endured burdens and sacrificed while many others who were fully capable of serving lived in the safety and comfort of their homes. They had done their duty; now, it was time for others to stand in their place. An Alabamian explained to his father, "I don't think it is right for us to reenlist for the war when there are men at home who have done nothing & are more able to be in the army, than we are." He concluded by demanding, "Let them come & try it a while." Resentment had bubbled up to the point that one Virginian insisted, "I would not hesitate a moment to reenlist if I thought my going would not stop some militiaman from coming."[20]

Married soldiers, especially those with children at home, as well as those who shouldered unusual responsibilities for their families, such as an elder son who cared for his widowed mother, hesitated to commit themselves to further service. The previous spring, they had wrestled with conflicting obligations to community, state, nation, and family, and had elected to serve for a year. Once that time expired, they had always assumed, they would return home, while someone else took their place. The idea of extending that term of service seemed both burdensome to their families and unjust to themselves. Private Richard Bryant, a prewar farmer, left a bride and two sons behind when he joined the 18th Virginia Infantry. In January 1862, he told his wife that the consequences worried him, but all the "Volunteers say they are going home when their twelve months expires and the Militia must take their turn."[21]

Confederate soldiers came from a largely patriarchical world, in which the eldest male, usually the father, wielded a disproportionate amount of power over the family. This was particularly true for younger men, but even those in their midtwenties regularly sought the opinion of their fathers in any grave matter. Quite a number of 1861 volunteers preferred to go home and consult their fathers in person. Despite pressure from his messmates to extend his service, twenty-four-year-old S. Bartlett Waring resisted. "I simply told them that

I did not intend to leap before I looked—nor is it my intention to bind or compromise myself in any manner," he explained to sister Cora. Waring planned to return home and discuss everything with his father first before making such an important decision. Eighteen-year-old George Lee Robertson, from a wealthy Texas family, implored his father for consent to let him re-enlist for the war. "How do you think I would feel," he asked, "to see our company start for the wars and me stay here with my hands in my pockets[?]"[22]

To keep the army together in these critical times, just a couple of months away from the spring campaign season, respected officers, including generals, sold the re-enlistment package to soldiers through personal appeals to companies and regiments. Major General John Bankhead Magruder, whose nickname of "Prince John" reflected his penchant for theatrics, exploited his reservoir of talent, exhorting his men, "Your country, invaded by an insolent foe, again demands your help." He reminded them "your homes are violated—your firesides polluted by the presence of a mercenary foe, or silent in their desolation." Their ancestors had borne great burdens in defense of freedom, some of them serving for six or seven years, and they must do the same to preserve their rights. If the men had any doubts, he told them, "let us remember that truth is Eternal, and that God is just. His arm is our trust, and the great Ruler of Nations and of men, will protect the right and crown with victory the noble and the brave." Col. Evander M. Law of the 4th Alabama Infantry delivered a short yet powerful speech to the men, and according to a soldier, "I never saw such a reaction in men in my whole life." In his company alone forty men re-enlisted on the spot, and the entire regiment reacted with equal fervor. Among those who extended was Jesse Jordan.[23]

In time, a sizable proportion of the volunteers of 1861 elected to remain in the service of their own volition. Some retained the same passion that had seized them a year earlier. "I want to see our men rally to the rescue of their country with the Watch word liberty or death," announced a Georgian. "We will die or be freemen." Another soldier, a North Carolinian, felt he had not accomplished what he had intended in his first year of service, and he would need more time in uniform. "I want to kill one yankey before I return."[24]

YET THE CONFEDERATE government could not rely solely on inducements to spur re-enlistment. According to Secretary of War George W. Randolph, the 1861 volunteers had soured on the army, and Union inactivity lulled them into a false sense of security. At the very time that Federal forces were coming together, Rebel commands were dissolving and discipline was breaking down. "The plan of voluntary enlistment having failed to preserve the organization, and to recruit the strength of our armies at a time when the safety of the country required both to be effected," Randolph justified to the president, "a resort to the draft or conscription was the only alternative." In April 1862, the Confederate government passed a law, which Davis endorsed, that directed states to enroll all males between eighteen and thirty-five for conscription, except for those who had legal exemptions. Draftees would serve a term of three years, unless the war ended sooner. All one-year enlistees from 1861 would remain in the service for an additional two years.[25]

The mere consideration of a conscription bill in Congress sparked re-enlistments. The men of 1861 feared that a draft would take them again and require them to serve three more years, so enlistment for two more years seemed "the best of two evils." Others worried that if they went home and risked the draft, invariably, the government would take them, and then they would be compelled to serve in some other unit. It was that fear of serving with strangers, apart from his first-year comrades upon whom he could rely, that drove Spencer Barnes, a prewar miller from North Carolina, to admit to his father, "I hate to be thrown into another company."[26]

More than simply returning to the old unit and serving alongside comrades, quite a few soldiers perceived opportunity in the conscription law. With a draft and unit reconstitution, the door opened for individuals who sought commissions as officers. According to the law, re-enlisted troops could select their own officers, which placed all original commission holders in jeopardy of losing their rank and created fresh possibilities for aspiring officeholders. Lieutenant Colonel Edward T. H. Warren of the 10th Virginia Infantry had been acting regimental commander for an extended period while the colonel recovered from a lengthy illness. Having grown accustomed to the position and responsibility, he worried that the colonel would return and beat him out in the election. His fears proved unfounded, as his troops chose him to be the new colonel. For Pvt. John S. Foster of 2nd Georgia Battalion Infantry, the conscription law offered hope. A pampered twenty-year-old from a well-to-do slaveholding family, he had tired of enlisted service and sought a lieutenancy in his regiment. "If this war lasts I must get a commission," he admitted. "Patriotism may do to talk about but comfort must be had or I cannot live in this country." His comrades elected not to fulfill his aspirations, and he served throughout the war as a private.[27]

Many commission holders feared that the men would cast aside proven officers with their ballots, or that the elections would become simply popularity contests. Wade Hampton, who would rise to command the cavalry in the Army of Northern Virginia, disapproved of the idea of balloting for officers, explaining, "The best officers are sometimes left out because they are strict." A fellow South Carolinian also worried that "a good many of the old officers will be turned out and *worse* ones put in their stead. As a general rule," he continued, "the officers who have discharged their duties properly are not popular with their men and those who have allowed most privileges and have been least efficient, are the men who will be elected."[28]

On days of election, when "a great many men got gloriously *tight*" from whiskey, a tabulation of the ballots resulted in a major overhaul, if not an overthrow, of the command structure in some regiments. In the 7th Georgia Infantry, the men retained or promoted approximately one in every four officers and ousted the rest from the commissioned ranks. In the 2nd Georgia Infantry, the total was closer to half. Complaints, particularly from those who lost out, were rampant. "Some of the companies have elected good men," William Preston Johnston asserted of the 1st Kentucky Infantry, "but most have elected worthless hounds." The 18th North Carolina Infantry replaced twenty-seven of forty officers. According to the new regimental commander, "Many of the officers elect were reported 'incompetent' by a Board of Examination."[29]

Yet the flow of liquor did not damage the judgment of the soldiers as much as critics of the system indicated. One-third of all field-grade officers (colonels, lieutenant colonels, and majors) lost their positions. While some competent colonels and majors failed in re-election, the men retained most of the skilled ones and promoted quality captains to fill vacancies. Many aged or sickly field-grade officers, along with some proven incompetents and shabby leaders, lost their posts in the election shuffle. According to Frank Gaillard of the 2nd South Carolina (Palmetto) Infantry, who rose from lieutenant to major in the election four months later, his company commander was a disaster. "The men are very much dissatisfied with Capt. [William H.] Casson, through duplicity and insincerity and other qualities, equally uncommendable, he has become very unpopular." Casson was subsequently elevated to major by seniority, but when re-election time rolled around, he rightfully lost his position.[30]

On the company level, occasionally a private won a commission as a lieutenant, but soldiers most often elevated a junior lieutenant or a skilled noncommissioned officer to the position of captain or lieutenant. Wiley P. Robertson, a twenty-year-old from a prominent slaveholding family, had served as a corporal in Company A, 13th North Carolina Infantry, until his comrades elected him as the third lieutenant in the reorganization. Young Robertson held the post for only two months; in late June, he was killed in action. Thomas Beall, a slave-owning farmer from Davidson County, North Carolina, was chosen as a third lieutenant when Company I, 14th North Carolina Infantry, was first organized. In the re-organization election, he defeated Jesse Hargrave, the original company commander and an extremely wealthy planter with fifty-four slaves, for the captaincy. In a random sample of seventeen regiments and batteries—approximately one-tenth of all the regiments and batteries in Virginia on April 30, 1862—the men voted out of office just under 23 percent.[31]

Individuals who lost their commissions in the election could stay with the regiment, but very few did. They were given an opportunity to resign from the service, and most took it. As a Virginia officer explained of a lieutenant who failed to win re-election, "it would be very hard for him to Serve as a private in the same company where he had been for 12 months an officer." Another officer, however, believed that those who resigned had "disgraced themselves," particularly the individuals who had pressed their soldiers to re-enlist. "We have too many men who will fight in office but not out of it," he regretted. A number of those officers who lost in re-election went home yet ended up commanding troops in new units, bringing the skills and lessons they had learned earlier in the war to their new position. In the 16th North Carolina, for example, ten of the officers who lost elections ultimately served in other regiments; six from the 21st North Carolina later commanded. Those officers became the building blocks for new regiments. Lieutenant William Madison Keith failed for re-election because he was under arrest for shooting a waiter. He resigned, evidently won his court battle, and later served as a captain in the 64th North Carolina.[32]

A few individuals, such as Captain John C. Gilmer of the 21st North Carolina, stood for and won re-election, but refused the commission. They sought the election victory as vindication for their good service but preferred to serve as enlisted men in the company.[33]

On the whole, the election worked reasonably well. Twelve-month recruits had served long enough to know that they needed individuals with genuine leadership talent as their commissioned officers. Inevitably, persons from prominent families who were instrumental in forming the regiment or battery received the initial support for positions of leadership, but the true test was in the field. Some measured up, while others failed, and the election offered a chance to weed out incompetents. Martinets learned a valuable lesson in dealing with volunteers. They commanded citizen-soldiers, individuals who would perform their duties in this crisis but had no interest in further military service. To treat them brutally, to lord it over them solely because an individual possessed rank, alienated the troops from the army and the revolutionary cause and choked the lifeblood—their spirit and motivation—out of these volunteers.

For all its obvious faults and the turmoil it created, the election system offered opportunities for promising talents to rise in rank and authority. Among those who resigned, the aged and the infirm could no longer serve anyway, and their extended absence from the army placed additional burdens on officers and men. The election process eased them out of the army and enabled the Confederate government to replace them with individuals who were capable of performing the duties properly. In the 42nd Virginia, eleven officers lost their commissions, but of these, six had been sick and absent from the regiment for extended periods. In a more complicated situation, three more had suffered wounds that placed them in the hospital or on furlough for extended lengths of time. In the 42nd Virginia, the most important factor in winning re-election was a continued presence with the men, doing one's duty.[34]

To avoid implementation of that first draft, states rushed to create new military units to reach their manpower quotas. Many of those who failed to win re-election joined these new regiments and batteries as officers, bringing with them knowledge of the army, tactics, and the military system. In the course of that first year of service, they also had learned some difficult lessons, the growing pains of leadership, which they had acquired largely at the expense of their original command. The new units offered a second chance for these officers, overseeing men who carried none of the negative baggage from that first command experience. Not only did the old commands have officers in whom the men had faith, their own choice, but these new units that joined the army in Virginia had experienced officers who could prepare the recruits for the horrors and hardships of the 1862 campaign season.[35]

At a critical time in the war, just before the Yankee spring and summer offensive of 1862, the conscription act held the army together and brought forth large numbers of additional troops to help it. Politicians and citizens croaked over the illegality of the legislation, and many soldiers grumbled that their retention in service beyond twelve months was a severe injustice. Yet the Confederacy could not have survived the 1862 campaigns without the veterans, and it compelled states to produce fresh regiments when their nation needed them.

The conscription act also helped to spread military obligations to a portion of society that might not have donned the Rebel uniform otherwise. For some time, tensions had built up among soldiers over the notion that they were carrying a disproportionate, if not the entire, burden for the rebellion. A Virginia soldier noticed that whenever the troops in his regiment passed civilians of military age, the men began hooting at them. They opened with a barrage of "Melish," a shortened version of the word militia. "With this and other jeering remarks," the soldier noted, "he becomes very much abashed and frequently insulted, but he must curb his anger the best he can for to show it is only adding fuel to the fire." As Congress began debating a draft, another soldier queried his aunt, "What do the Malitia say about going into the war?" He opined, "I think it is time they wer striking for the *green graves* of *their sires*, God and their native land." The conscription act publicized their obligations and would drive them to enlist, or its enforcement would compel them to serve. Either way, able-bodied white males would join the ranks and carry their fair share of military duties and hardships.[36]

Thanks to the conscription act, the volunteers of '61 had many new reinforcements. The Confederate government now had large forces in Virginia, and many veterans who knew the ropes. As one private explained to his mother, attempting to alleviate her concern but reflecting his acceptance of military life, "My Cotrig [cartridge] Box makes a soft pillow, the Mother Earth makes a easy bed, the heavens makes a good shelter, the Lord is a Good Genral." They were ready to fight.[37]

Chapter 9

CLASHES WITHIN THE
HIGH COMMAND

E DMUND KIRBY SMITH's lengthy service experience and extensive contacts made him a shrewd observer of the Confederacy's high command. A West Point graduate and well-regarded Regular Army officer whom Secretary of War Jefferson Davis had designated as a rising star in the 1850s, Smith resigned his commission when his native Florida seceded from the Union. Appointed as Johnston's chief of staff, Smith gained a huge reputation by his timely arrival with reinforcements at First Manassas, where he immediately suffered a severe wound. The *Richmond Dispatch* dubbed Smith "the Blucher in that glorious victory for the South," an allusion to the aid that Prussian field marshal gave to the Duke of Wellington against Napoleon at Waterloo.[1]

Promoted to major general and division commander under Beauregard, Smith recovered enough to return to active duty at the end of October 1861, three months after the fight. Within days he realized that the rapport between the military and political high command had soured. "There is not that cordiality of feelings, that confidence & freedom of intercourse between our Generals in the field, and the President and authorities at Richmond, which should exist in the present critical state of the country," he confided to his new bride. During Smith's absence, Beauregard and Johnston had independently run afoul of President Davis. In each case, problems stemmed largely from personality clashes and different perceptions of the role and duties of generals in the field and the commander in chief.[2]

Both Beauregard and Johnston had emerged from a Regular Army world in which most officers proclaimed political neutrality, yet all of them were part of the political system. While military men in the prewar army sometimes dabbled in politics, and their duties often drew them into it, most officers insisted that they sought to stay clear of it. But officers were inherently political animals. Whether they received their commissions from the president directly out of civilian life or via an appointment to West Point from a local congressman or senator, all of them were beholden to politicians. As they rose in rank, politicians weighed in heavily to secure promotions, choice assignments, or other advantages for their favorite officers. Beauregard and Johnston were no different in exploiting those ties.[3]

During the Civil War, lines between the political and military worlds blurred even more than usual. Politicians and Regular Army officers alike coveted and employed the same types of connections. Politicos perceived military service as an opportunity to win glory and enhance their standing among voters and fellow legislators. Through their extensive contacts with colleagues, quite a number secured commissions at ranks well beyond their levels of military knowledge and experience. They necessarily embraced notions that leadership in the political world differed little from leadership in the army, and that tactics and regulations were learned skills, something they could certainly master. From their perspective, they were just as qualified for general's rank as were captains and majors in the peacetime Regular Army.

On the flip side, career officers sought politicians who would look after them in the halls of government, lobby for their advancement, and promote their welfare and that of their soldiers. These military men selected many of their staff members based on family connections and access to political power. By extending appointments to the sons or nephews of prominent politicians, general officers built ties between their military family at headquarters and some distinguished political families across the Confederacy. Young people almost always leaped at these opportunities for a staff position, which placed them at the heart of military decision-making and provided a freer lifestyle than service at a comparable rank in traditional combat arms. From the vantage point of a general's headquarters, the staffer had access to valuable military information and gossip, which he could convey to the politician within the context of innocuous family letters. For their part, politicians enjoyed the friendship of successful general officers and benefited from the pipeline of fresh information, independent from official versions.

Occasionally, though, politicians themselves sought temporary staff posts with prominent military officers just to be at the center of planning and command decisions during a great battle or campaign. In that way, they could be a part of the war without undertaking extensive training and labor. As the fighting dragged into its second and third years, and as the government systematized and scrutinized staff appointments, the practice of employing politicians as temporary staffers disappeared. But in the early stages of the war, before the War Department strictly enforced its own policies, politicians often served in the Virginia Theater. This practice ultimately caused Beauregard's relationship with Davis to deteriorate.[4]

Shortly after the Battle of First Manassas, Beauregard grew irritated over transportation and provisions for the army. He instructed his chief of commissary, a lieutenant colonel, to complain directly to the Confederate president that supplies were becoming "alarmingly reduced." When that achieved no results, Beauregard decided to circumvent military channels entirely and bring congressional pressure to bear. Grandiose by nature and prone to flamboyant excesses in writing, he dashed off a letter of complaint to two former volunteer aides, William Porcher Miles and James Chesnut, both of whom were serving in the Confederate Congress.

Beauregard knew full well that he had mailed a politically charged missive masquerading as a letter among friends. After grumbling over shortages for his troops, Beauregard claimed that "The want of food and transportation has made us lose all the fruits of our victory. We ought at this moment to be in or about Washington"; instead, the army was "anchored" at Manassas. "From all accounts," he insisted in summary, "Washington could have been taken up to the 24th instant, by twenty thousand men! Only think of the brilliant results we have lost by the two causes referred to!" When Miles read this outrageous pack of exaggerations to Congress, it struck like a bombshell. Beauregard not only indicted the commissary and quartermaster departments for gross incompetence but painted Davis and his administration as inept at best and insensitive to the cause at worst.[5]

Congress immediately passed a resolution by Chesnut seeking an explanation from Davis. In reply, Davis asserted that the Commissary Department's condition was "as good as was reasonable to expect." The movement of troops and munitions had monopolized the railroads in recent days, Davis explained, but he had directed an inquiry to rectify any supply difficulties.[6]

Supplies and transportation were legitimate problems for the army. Yet Beauregard's methods suggested that his motivations extended beyond concern for his veterans. His heavy-handed foray into the traditional political world also stemmed from a sense of his own achievements. He had commanded the batteries at Fort Sumter and had largely overseen the fight at First Manassas. Public adulation for these triumphs poured forth from across the Confederacy, and in his mind, these successes earned him special consideration. The Louisianan thought that the needs and requisitions from his army should have priority over others. When his staff officer sought more supplies, and the Commissary Department failed to meet his needs promptly, Beauregard decided to teach those bureaucrats a lesson.

What Beauregard failed to grasp was the degree of Davis's sensitivity to criticism. As a longtime politician who had experienced successes and failures, Davis possessed an unusually thin skin. When Varina Howell, Davis's future bride, first met him, she noted with some dissatisfaction that he simply assumed that "everybody agrees with him when he expresses an opinion." As she got to know him better, Varina attributed this flaw to the fact that "he was abnormally sensitive to disapprobation." She believed that "Even a child's disapproval discomposed him." Since Davis could not endure criticism, he camouflaged this fear by accepting as fact that everyone agreed with him.[7]

Davis nevertheless responded to Beauregard's veiled criticism with unusual restraint. In a kindly intoned letter, Davis explained that he did not realize how serious the supply problem had become, and that neither he, the quartermaster general, nor the commissary general felt the criticism was just. He reminded Beauregard of the utter chaos in the aftermath of the Rebel victory at First Manassas, which prevented any organized pursuit, and he advised the general that it was unwise to open the way for criticism "after the event." As a means of reassuring Beauregard, the president closed with the words, "With sincere esteem, I am, your friend."[8]

A brief, contrite statement and a vow to work with the president to improve army logistics would have been the appropriate response. Instead, Beauregard dodged responsibility and engaged in sheer sophistry, which only made matters worse. He regretted "exceedingly" that Miles had read the letter to Congress and insisted that it was not his intention to imply that Davis had been remiss in support of the troops. He flattered the president with the assertion, "You have done more than could be expected of you for this army." He even claimed never to have suggested that the army could have pursued the Federals and captured Washington within two days of the fight were it not for inadequate supplies and transportation. Beauregard concluded with a flowery depiction of himself as a genuine citizen-soldier, a Civil War Cincinnatus who fought not for glory, but to protect his homeland.[9]

Beauregard ineptly managed to revive smoldering embers after Davis had tried to extinguish them. He offered a series of disingenuous arguments and denials, foolishly parsed words with a nitpicker like Davis, a man who also happened to be his commander in chief, and then concluded with a trite, melodramatic flourish. Still, in Davis's mind, the regrettable episode did not outweigh Beauregard's contributions to the Rebel cause. He knew just how flamboyant and eccentric the Louisiana general could be, and he was willing to move beyond the annoyance as long as Beauregard learned his lesson. Unfortunately for both men, the general did not.

Ten weeks later, Beauregard landed in a new mess, once again his own creation. When Beauregard prepared his report of the Manassas Campaign, a nine-thousand-word epic, he opened with a discussion of a plan he proposed through a staff officer, Congressman Chesnut, calling for Confederate forces to concentrate and take the offensive against the Federals as they pressed southward from Washington. After attacking the Yankee army, "with the inevitable result, as I submitted, of his complete defeat and the destruction or capture of his army," he then proposed to return to the Shenandoah Valley and rout the Union command that had opposed Johnston's forces. Peeling off reinforcements to help defeat McClellan's columns in western Virginia, the combined Rebel troops would then capture Washington and liberate Maryland. Davis, Lee, and Adjutant General Cooper heard the oral briefing and rejected the scheme.

Beauregard presented the fanciful proposal as eminently achievable. He also impugned Davis as commander in chief by suggesting that the president had turned down what he offered as a viable opportunity to restore oppressed Marylanders to the Confederacy and perhaps win the war in one swoop. To make matters worse, once the battle report of First Manassas arrived in Richmond, bureaucrats at the War Department neglected to forward it to the president, so that Davis only learned of its existence and the inclusion of Beauregard's bizarre scheme when he read a synopsis in the press.[10]

Politicians, newspapermen, and citizens howled; Congress ultimately initiated an investigation by requesting a copy of the full report, to see if the newspaper summaries were accurate. Davis, this time stung sharply by the uproar, immediately marshaled evidence to vindicate his position. Dismayed that the report "seemed to be an attempt to exalt yourself at my expense," the president demanded that Beauregard provide written proof of his proposal. He directed that Lee and Cooper draft their recollections of what had transpired, and he requested that Congressman Chesnut convey his remembrances as well. Chesnut offered the most detailed summary of the meeting, repeating almost verbatim the contents of his written report to Beauregard a day afterward. Davis, Lee, and Cooper recalled the basic elements of the proposal and their sound reasons why they rejected the plan, which Beauregard had predicated on exaggerated Confederate numbers, wishful thinking about Union reactions to the approach of enemy troops, and supposition of a string of crushing Rebel victories.[11]

Beauregard attempted to extricate himself from his newest jam with a letter to a Richmond newspaper, but its obtuseness and transparent melodrama did little to stifle the unrest. He then penned a missive to Davis, assuring him that it was not the general's intention to diminish the president's reputation. Still, he refused to withdraw his assertion that Chesnut had delivered a viable plan, which the president had rejected. Eventually, the War Department sent all the materials to Congress, and when the legislative body agreed to publish the battle report, it compromised and dropped Beauregard's section on the plan and Davis's critical response.[12]

The controversy marked a serious break between Davis and Beauregard. As Chesnut concluded his letter to the president, he urged the commander in chief not to give credence to the "unwise babbling" or malicious attacks against him, but it was not in Davis's constitution to resist the impulse. He could not move beyond Beauregard's intent. "My confidence and friendship for General Beauregard have been unmistakably manifest," he elaborated to Chesnut, "and none can regret more than myself the error he has committed in bringing extraneous matter into his report of a battle, without any perceivable motive for doing so which is consistent with the good opinion I entertained of him." In the president's eyes, he had befriended Beauregard, and the general had stabbed him in the back.[13]

Beauregard had a series of other clashes with Richmond authorities as well. He regularly referred to himself as commander of a corps. When the acting secretary of war, Judah Benjamin, pointed out in early October that there was no congressional authorization for a corps, and that Beauregard was instead second in command of the army, Beauregard took offense and requested reassignment. Before that dust settled, Beauregard tried to create a rocket battery. Once the acting secretary of war learned of this, he wrote Beauregard a firm legal opinion that only Congress had authority to authorize the formation of units. Sensitive of transgressions by one branch into the domain of another, the lawyerly Benjamin ascribed no ill motives to Beauregard's act; he simply assumed that Beauregard had not read the law. Benjamin, a wealthy Louisiana lawyer and planter who had begun to ingratiate himself with Davis as a loyal and indispensable advisor, harbored some mistrust for the judgment of military officers and earned a deserved reputation for unnecessary interference. But in this instance, he merely acted the part of a responsible secretary of war, executing the laws of the land. Yet Beauregard took grave offense at both the content and the legalistic tone of the reply, insisting that he deserved better treatment based on his service to the Confederacy. At this point, Davis intervened.[14]

Davis's soothing letter was dated October 25, five days before the president learned of the report on First Manassas. He tried to calm Beauregard, while endorsing Benjamin's rulings. Once the Manassas conflict erupted, a wise person would have let the squabble with Benjamin drop. Yet on November 5, in the midst of the larger controversy, Beauregard accepted Davis's reassurance that Benjamin bore no ill will but insisted that if Benjamin, his superior in the government, pointed out errors, he must do so "in a proper tone and style." Then, in a back-handed swipe at both Benjamin and Davis, he expressed hope that the administration would not let legalisms, or as the Louisiana general described it, "straight-jackets of the law," get in the way of Beauregard and the army prosecuting the war. This was too much for Davis. In a coolly intoned letter, the president informed Beauregard that he did not feel competent to advise Benjamin in matters of style, but that he and the secretary of war had every obligation to scrutinize the legal aspects of official decisions. "You surely did not intend to inform me that your army and yourself are outside the limits of the law," Davis penned forcefully. "It is my duty to see that the laws are faithfully executed, and I cannot recognize the pretension of any one that their restraint is too narrow for him." When Beauregard disregarded congressional law, the secretary had not just a right but an obligation to "inform you of the error committed."[15]

Beauregard had let his runaway ego impair his judgment, and he had finally run afoul of the president, who had tried to be his earnest friend. By the end of January, well before the campaigns of 1862 heated up, the War Department transferred him out west.[16]

IN JOHNSTON'S CASE, it was not so much his political ineptness that led to difficulties with the president. Although he did commit a major political blunder during his tenure in Virginia—challenging the competence of Acting Secretary of War Benjamin in a conversation with several congressmen at a Richmond dinner party—most of his disastrous forays, such as snuggling up to Davis's archenemies, occurred after he vacated command in the Army of the Potomac. Johnston's troubles with the commander in chief stemmed largely from his own tender ego, his notions of command prerogatives, and his administrative failures, which, when combined with Davis's abruptness and impersonality, caused difficulties between them. Unlike Beauregard, Johnston maintained a working relationship with Davis, but it was marred by either miscommunication or, in numerous instances, a lack of communication, problems that did not exist before the Battle of First Manassas.[17]

The first signs of trouble appeared shortly after the battle at Bull Run, when Johnston expressed his contention that he was the ranking officer in the Confederate army. It began when Lee forwarded an officer for Johnston's staff. Although Lee was trying to be helpful, he should have discussed the individual with Johnston first. Johnston bristled. Not only had Lee interfered with his staff, but Johnston claimed that he outranked Lee. When Davis read Johnston's justification for refusing the officer, the president endorsed the letter with a single word, "Insubordinate." Days later, Johnston challenged another order from Lee. Again, the directives intruded on Johnston's command authority, and because he outranked Lee, "such orders I cannot regard, because they are illegal." Once again, Davis affixed the notation "Insubordinate" to the message.[18]

Since Johnston's days at West Point, where fellow cadets nicknamed him "Colonel" for his officious, domineering, albeit thoroughly competent ways, Johnston had striven to be the best. Everything he undertook, he worked at diligently, until he mastered it. Johnston became a crack shot and an expert swordsman. He studied the military art indefatigably, demonstrating a depth of knowledge by 1860 that surpassed everyone in the Regular Army save Winfield Scott. Under fire, he exhibited courage that was second to none. Because of his extraordinary accomplishments and his willingness to play the role of master, younger officers gravitated toward him magnetically. In assessing his former commander, Edmund Kirby Smith wrote privately, "Johnson's brain soars above all that surrounds it." Edward Porter Alexander, probably the most brilliant and talented young officer in the Confederate army, later described Johnston as "a great soldier." Alexander conjectured that "as long as he lived I never had a warmer or kinder friend than Gen. Johnston, nor he a more affectionate admirer than I." The great Confederate cavalryman, James Ewell Brown Stuart, referred to Johnston as his best friend, and James Longstreet, long after Lee had replaced Johnston as commander in Virginia, yearned for a return to service under him.[19]

Yet this passion to achieve also spilled over into a relentless competition to best his peers, with military rank as the yardstick. Throughout his Regular Army career, Johnston went to extraordinary lengths to receive promotions and brevets (essentially an honorary elevation in rank for outstanding service that brought little increase in responsibility and no additional pay or commission), and on two occasions he clearly fractured the rules to get them. In 1837,

Johnston resigned his commission as an artillery lieutenant because "Many of my juniors by luck got before me on the army list," he complained to a relative. Accepting a job as a civilian engineer for the army, in January 1838 he exhibited wonderful leadership under fire against the Seminoles. When he returned to the Regular Army six months later, the War Department awarded him a brevet for that action, a decision that the adjutant general later ruled was without precedent and without the authority of law. Still, no one took it away from him. In the Mexican War, Johnston fought gallantly with a temporary regiment. As a temporary lieutenant colonel, he received a brevet to colonel, and in his capacity as a Regular Army officer, he received a brevet to major for the same action and another one to lieutenant colonel for later service. Unsatisfied, Johnston demanded that the War Department recognize the brevet colonelcy, in effect, granting him two brevets for the same action. The War Department declined, but Johnston continued to fight it until finally, a new secretary of war, John B. Floyd, who also happened to be related to Johnston through marriage, ruled in his favor. Even his good friend and West Point classmate Lee, who rarely criticized others, admitted to his son that Johnston knew this decision violated the practice of brevets.[20]

In June 1860, President James Buchanan appointed Johnston the quartermaster general of the U.S. Army. The new position held the rank of brigadier general of staff, which meant that if Johnston vacated the assignment, he would revert to his permanent rank of lieutenant colonel of cavalry. Not surprisingly, the clash between Johnston and Lee that generated Davis's comment of "Insubordinate" revolved around that rank. As the highest-grade officer to resign from the U.S. Army and join the Confederate army, Johnston assumed he would continue as the senior officer. He justified this contention by citing a law that preserved the date and commission from the U.S. Army. But the issue was not so simple. Davis, a legalistic stickler, also had to factor in another law eight days earlier, which stated that a commission or brevet in one corps, or branch of service, did not equate to the same rank and standing in another branch of service, and that soldiers must perfom duty at the rank in that branch of service. In essence, the section meant that because Johnston had vacated a staff position for duty with troops in the field, the law required Davis to base his Confederate seniority on his highest rank with troops, which was lieutenant colonel of cavalry. Two other officers, Albert Sidney Johnston and Lee, as colonels in the U.S. Army, had outranked Johnston in the cavalry. Cooper, the adjutant general in the Confederacy, held that post in the U.S. Army before the war and had the earliest date on his colonelcy commission. Because Cooper remained in the same staff position, he retained his seniority. Thus, when the War Department released the order of rank for Generals, Davis and the secretary of war correctly determined it as Cooper, Albert Sidney Johnston, Lee, and Joseph E. Johnston.[21]

Once Johnston caught a whiff that he ranked fourth in the Confederate army, he erupted with a two-thousand-word epistle to Davis, staking his claim to "first general in the Armies of the Southern Confederacy." In painstaking detail, Johnston made his case, concluding that the reduction of his rank "is a blow aimed at me only." He drew his sword for the Confederacy, "not for rank or fame, but to defend the sacred soil," yet he nonetheless complained that Davis's decision "seeks to tarnish my fair fame as a soldier and a man, earned by more than thirty years of laborious and perilous service." Beauregard had received promotion to general for his service at Manassas, Johnston grumbled, but "care seems to be taken to exclude the idea that I had any part in winning our triumph." The order of rank was illegal.[22]

The lecture struck a nerve with Davis. The Confederate president had obeyed the will of Congress precisely. In response, Davis acknowledged receipt of Johnston's letter and registered his opinion that "Its language is, as you say, unusual; its arguments and statements utterly one-sided, and its insinuations as unfounded as they are unbecoming." Unfortunately, Davis's terse response explained nothing, leading Johnston to believe he was correct. And over the years, Davis worsened the problem by putting forth several different rationales for the ranking.[23]

The two men had known each other since West Point days. Davis encouraged a friendly relationship between president and a leading general, assuming that they would collaborate on strategy and operations, and he welcomed Johnston's input on military policies. Early in the war, the president had specifically encouraged Johnston to "write whenever your convenience will permit, and give me fully both information and suggestions." After Johnston's eruption over rank, Davis's warmth evaporated, and his dealings with the general took on a more official tone that did not encourage free and effective exchange. Still, as a president with considerable military expertise, he expected Johnston to keep him informed.

That expectation clashed with Johnston's view of command. Just as South Carolina nullified federal law within its borders, so Johnston felt he could delay indefinitely certain presidential policies that interfered with the execution of his fundamental duties. The general clung tenaciously to what he perceived as his entitlements as a leading general and his prerogatives as an army commander. He suspected excessive interference in directives from Richmond officials, and he became increasingly uncommunicative with his commander in chief. If Davis knew what Johnston was doing, he might intrude, so the best way to have a free hand, Johnston believed, was to keep the president in the dark. Over time, brick by brick, commander in chief and commanding general erected a barrier between them that obscured intentions, impaired collaboration, and fostered confusion.[24]

Davis and Johnston had very different approaches to the war. Above all else, Johnston feared failure caused by his own error. He dreaded the idea of being caught unprepared in the event of a Union advance, and he sought a concentration of forces and a heightened state of readiness at all times to prevent it. "I am an enemy to much distribution of troops," he explained to Stonewall Jackson.

Instead of engaging enemy columns near the border under anything less than ideal circumstances, the Virginia general much preferred to sacrifice real estate and wait until he could fight the Federals on favorable terms. Prudent to the point of excess, Johnston detested policies that granted furloughs and dreaded his troops going into winter quarters because that would impair his ability to fight at any given moment.[25]

His commander in chief, by contrast, advocated a different approach to defense, one based on initiative, and he embraced a military program that weighed long-term factors against immediate readiness. The president hoped to "resist invasion as far as may be practicable, and repel the invaders whenever and however it may be done." Because citizens and soldiers lived along avenues of invasion, Davis believed the Confederacy could not yield territory unless it was absolutely necessary. To Johnston's former chief of staff, the president explained that the revolutionary nature of this war dictated adjustments in traditional military practices. "The general truth that power is increased by the concentration of an army is, under our peculiar circumstances, subject to modification," he advised. "The evacuation of any portion of territory involves not only the loss of supplies, but in every instance has been attended by a greater or less loss of troops, and a general, therefore, has in each case a complete problem to solve." As Federal forces penetrated Rebel territory, they not only deprived the Confederacy of resources in that area, but also promoted desertion among Confederate soldiers who had loved ones there. Thus, Davis believed the Confederacy had to disperse forces to discourage enemy invasion, and when the Federals launched a major advance, Rebel troops would have to employ their interior lines to concentrate for battle.[26]

The single exception to Johnston's reactive approach occurred on October 1, 1861, when the general, prodded by Beauregard and Maj. Gen. Gustavus W. Smith, conferred with Davis about a possible movement into Maryland. If Davis could supplement the Army of the Potomac with an additional 20,000 seasoned troops, plus vast increases in transportation and munitions, they could strike into Maryland, perhaps threatening Washington, D.C. Davis liked the concept but explained that the Confederacy possessed no such manpower, arms, and resources. Instead, he suggested a raid. The generals nixed this plan, fearing the strike force could become trapped north of the Potomac River.[27]

Administratively, too, Johnston clashed with Davis over policies. Part of this problem stemmed from sloppiness or neglect of paperwork, problems that should not have befallen a former quartermaster general like Johnston. Most of the time, though, the conflict stemmed from different perceptions of responsibility. While Davis and his secretary of war expected Johnston to obey their directives promptly, Johnston believed that his prerogatives as army commander granted him more leeway to implement policies and form decisions on his own. In early January 1862, Jackson launched an offensive to drive Federals out of north central and western Virginia. After combining with Brig. Gen. W. W. Loring's forces, he marched circuitously to surprise the enemy near Romney, but foul weather delayed his advance and enabled the Yankees to escape. Jackson ordered the men to settle into winter quarters in the Romney area, and soon the grumbling began. Soldiers petitioned for their removal, and a brigade commander and subordinate officers accused Jackson of wasting manpower through excessive exposure to the elements and risking them as Federals built up a presence in Harpers Ferry. Eventually, congressmen complained to the administration, and the president asked Johnston to "examine for yourself into the true state of the case." When Johnston sent his inspector general in his stead, Benjamin on Davis's advice directed Loring's men to fall back to Winchester. With his authority undercut, Jackson submitted his letter of resignation, but not before pressing charges against Loring for neglect of duty and conduct subversive of good order. Johnston requested that Davis remove the Valley District from his command, because "a collision of authority of the honorable Secretary of War and mine might occur at a critical moment." Ultimately, Jackson was dissuaded from resigning and the War Department dropped the charges against Loring. Davis, however, firmly rebuked Johnston for sending an underling on an assignment that he had specifically directed Johnston to undertake. Benjamin had taken the unusual step of issuing an order directly to a field commander, Davis scolded, because Johnston "had failed more than once" to carry out the secretary's instructions. The Valley District would remain within Johnston's purview.[28]

Even more disconcerting to Davis was Johnston's handling of command restructuring. Generally, as companies formed, they grouped into individual regiments in their home states and then traveled to Virginia. In Richmond, authorities hoped to equip them properly and instill basic military training and then send them off to field commands. Unfortunately, reality clashed with sensible planning, and pressing needs for manpower frequently demanded that officials forward them upon arrival to the front, sometimes without arms. At that point, commanders lumped regiments into brigades and then divisions, with no concern for state or regional interests. Nor did the brigade commander necessarily reflect the predominant attachment of the soldiers in his command.

Davis perceived this system as flawed and believed it violated congressional intent. He had been empowered to create brigades and divisions and appoint general officers with legislative approval. The Confederacy needed to exploit allegiance to locality and state, and whenever possible, regiments from states ought to serve in the same brigade, so that all the units would come from Mississippi, or Louisiana, or Georgia. In Davis's view, this would stimulate much greater popular interest back home, publicize the war and the theater of operations, and encourage enlistment. States would take pride in their own brigades and make every effort to maintain their strength through recruitment. It would also help to solve a delicate problem of military patronage. Davis needed to appoint general officers from each of the Confederate states, to spread the most coveted positions across the nation and reinforce each state's commitment to the war. As vacancies occurred through promotion, resignation, or death, the new commission as brigadier general would most likely go to a qualified regimental commander in the brigade, thereby continuing the practice of having a Mississippian command a brigade of Mississippi regiments. Beauregard understood the merits of Davis's arguments, and shortly after the Battle of Manassas he shuffled his regiments, so that six of his eight brigades consisted of regiments from the same state, and the other two had all but one from the same state.

With an eye toward re-enlistment, Davis spoke personally to Johnston about consolidation during a trip to army headquarters in late September, and he continued to press the matter. Yet Johnston temporized. On two occasions, the president had the adjutant general issue orders that reorganized brigades, but Johnston refused to implement them. Finally, in early December, Davis ordered the consolidation of the Mississippi regiments into brigades and a division "without delay." Johnston promptly protested, insisting that nine regiments in transit at once could jeopardize the army, and that the men were already familiar with their defensive positions and their superior officers. The two men were at loggerheads: Davis would not budge, and Johnston justified his delays "in the exercise of the discretion vested in me." Throughout the winter and into the spring the general stalled, and the matter continued to fester with the president, so that at the height of the spring campaign, Davis was still grumbling about reorganizing the army.[29]

The administration and Johnston also battled over re-enlistments, a dispute that reflected concern for immediate readiness versus long-term troop strength. Before Congress proposed conscription, it had offered liberal inducements, including lengthy furloughs, to retain one-year men. Unfortunately, no one sent Johnston a copy of the new law, and he learned of it only when an officer inquired about it. After reading the document, he immediately fired off a message to Benjamin, questioning the sensibleness of the law awarding furloughs "in such numbers as I deem incompatible with the safety of this command." Benjamin urged Johnston to extend furloughs "to the extreme verge of prudence," to ensure "your having under orders a large force of veteran troops when active operations recommence," reminding the general that the road conditions were so bad that Federals could not possibly advance. Johnston, however, resisted implementation of the policy, once again believing that a liberal furlough program would reduce his military strength and jeopardize his army. Already irritated because he had not received a copy of the General Order that announced the law, Johnston erupted when recruiters arrived in his army camps with offers of furloughs. Having endured a series of intrusions in his domain as army commander from Benjamin, Johnston had had enough, and in early March he took his complaints to the president. Once again, they fell on deaf ears. Annoyed by Johnston's unwillingness to reorganize his command, and frustrated with his failure to handle the Jackson-Loring debacle personally, Davis sided with Benjamin, who he claimed had not signed furloughs for soldiers in Johnston's army for a month. Although the president expressed a "readiness to protect your proper authority," he rebuked Johnston for failing to obey the secretary's orders in "so many instances" which were "in nowise the invasion of your prerogative as a commander in the field."[30]

The strain between the principal field general in the East and the commander in chief stemmed primarily from differing strategic perspectives and divergent ideas about command prerogatives. For Johnston, the idea of a concentration of forces implied a comforting level of preparedness. In camp, maintaining a maximum readiness offered him the same sort of security. Reorganization of brigades by states disrupted the command structure and destroyed familiarity among regiments and brigades, both of which could damage the combat effectiveness of his command and impair security. While a re-enlistment program was essential, liberal use of furloughs reduced manpower strength dramatically and, in his eyes, placed his command at risk. Because he believed in an expansive view of command prerogatives, one that granted him the power to delay or decline to enforce laws and directives that interfered with his task of preserving a maximum level of readiness to repel the invaders, he felt entitled to sidestep orders such as reorganization and furloughs. Benjamin's involvement in the Jackson-Loring dispute cut deeply into Johnston's sense of command prerogatives, but it also impeded his ability to concentrate or direct his forces. Johnston could not be held responsible, he complained to Davis, "while the corresponding control is not in my hands."[31]

Amid these clashes, effective communication between general and commander in chief broke down in late February and early March 1862. Out west, a Union brigadier general named Ulysses S. Grant shattered the Confederate cordon defense by seizing Forts Henry and Donelson and capturing most of Donelson's defenders. Piercing the center, Federal forces suddenly threatened Rebel troops to the east and the west and compelled a massive retreat to the southern border of Tennessee, with the abandonment of Nashville, the state capital. Both Davis and Johnston feared that the Union command in the East, with its superior strength, might deliver a similar blow to Confederate forces in Virginia, perhaps even compelling the evacuation of Richmond.

Just three days after the fall of Fort Donelson, Johnston joined Davis and the cabinet to formulate a plan. Although rail connections serviced the main Confederate line, the Manassas-Centerville axis, the region offered no real defensible terrain, and Johnston feared Federals could outflank the position. He preferred to fall back to the Rappahannock River area, which would provide a much more effective barrier. What concerned Johnston, however, was the slow process of retreat. After Beauregard's accusations about neglect for the army, the Confederate supply system stockpiled gargantuan quantities of food and even erected a huge meat-curing plant ten miles to the rear. The army also possessed too much impedimenta, ranging from soldiers' personal items to excess equipment, and it had some heavy guns that would be nearly impossible to remove. If he possessed an army of laborers, he might be able to pull off the move effectively, but as Johnston grumbled, "our Volunteers would not *work*." Johnston feared that muddy roads and inconsistent railroad performance would delay the retreat and tip Federals, who could then exploit the opportunity while their army retreated. "The difficulties," the general believed, "were almost insurmountable." In his concern for the security of his command, Johnston played down the facts that the Union forces might not be ready to exploit the retreat, and that the same problems the Confederates encountered—muddy roads and overtaxed transportation—would also affect the Yankees at least as much.[32]

In the end, Davis directed Johnston to reconnoiter the country in his rear to create a new line of defense. The army would continue to ship excess food and equipment including the heavy guns rearward. Johnston thought he had authority to retreat; the president, in keeping with his strategy of defense as close to the border as possible, had hopes of reinforcing Johnston's army and keeping it in its present defensive position. Davis meant for the line behind the Rappahannock to serve as a fallback position, a precaution Johnston would use only if necessary.[33]

Yet Johnston began his withdrawal of troops on March 7. Rumors of a retreat began to circulate in Richmond, and a newspaper carried an account on March 11. Not until March 13 did Johnston draft a letter to Davis, informing him officially of the retrograde movement. The entire affair smacked of inadequate planning and management. By Johnston's own admission, he destroyed four days' rations and a "corresponding quantity of grain," which had just arrived. More than half the salt meat at the curing plant—perhaps more than a million pounds—was left behind. According to his chief of commissary, another half million pounds spoiled or were damaged by exposure to the elements—enough to feed Johnston's entire army for three weeks. The commanding general also admitted that "Much more than half the regimental property was left and burned." While he deplored the destruction of personal property, "This army had accumulated a supply of baggage like that of Xerxes' myriads," he elaborated. Even worse, he notified Davis that he would "cross the Rapidan and take such a position as you may think best in connection with those of other troops." He hurried the retreat unnecessarily, abandoned or destroyed huge quantities of food and other materials, and failed to lay out his new line in advance.[34]

A Virginia private described the evacuation of Manassas as "such a day as I never saw before. Boxes were burst upon and the contents scattered over the ground Cakes pies cooked fowls and every thing of the Kind were given to all who would receive." A member of Johnston's staff was stunned by what he witnessed. "The destruction of stores of every kind was terrible. Bacon, flour, salt, lard, saddles, shoes clothing were the principle stores." He then confessed to his wife, "Every one is out-raged by this mismanagement & Genl J is chiefly blamed. I fear he has been careless in this matter, & permitted his subalterns to neglect their duty." In their haste to withdraw, soldiers discarded blankets, pillows, oil-cloth shelters, skillets, ovens, and dishes.[35]

As the army retreated, it uncovered thousands of homes to Union forces.

Rather than suffer at the hands of Yankee invaders, many of the residents abandoned the area, taking with them only the possessions they could carry. "As soon as the army had passed," a Georgia private described, "crowds and throngs of citizens in carts wagons buggies carriages and vehicles of all sorts passed by until it seemed that the whole country must be depopulated." The prewar attorney and slave owner added, "I never saw any thing in the worst times of the Indian war to equal it." The scene generated similar sentiments in one of Johnston's staff officers. "Rarely has any sight made me feel sadder," he wrote to his wife. "I just think of the many happy families driven from their homes of comfort many of elegance, & wandering houseless & in poverty thro' the country. The street has teemed with wagons, filled with the little remnant of furniture that could be snatched from the general wrecks." Seizing upon the chaos, some soldiers and civilians entered abandoned homes, took what they wanted, broke furniture and goods, and then left the remainder for the Yankees. Most, however, simply felt humiliated. Later in the war, they would come to accept advance and retreat as normal components of warfare. But at this stage, soldiers viewed retreat as a failure to fulfill their primary mission, to protect the people and property of Virginia.[36]

When Davis first received Johnston's message, he responded curtly, telling Johnston that he had no idea where he should position his men but it should be as far in advance as possible. Later, he elaborated that he had heard "Alarming reports of great destruction of ammunition, camp equipage, and provisions, indicating a precipitate retreat; but, having heard of no cause for such a sudden movement, I was at a loss to believe it." As for the position, "I had intended that you determine that question," which was why he furnished Johnston with engineers. For all intents, communication between the principal army commander and his commander in chief had broken down. Only the belief they had in the Confederate cause, and their longstanding respect and faith in each other, kept their relationship from breaking down completely.[37]

With spring campaigning about to begin, and his relationship with Johnston deteriorating, Davis needed a trusted advisor to help him plan and oversee military activities and operations throughout the Confederacy. For a month, he had wanted to recall an officer, but enemy threats in his sector prevented a change of command. Finally, he could wait no longer. The president called Robert E. Lee back to Richmond for consultation, and on March 13, Davis appointed him military advisor to the president, charged "with the conduct of military operations in the armies of the Confederacy." Lee could discuss military matters with the president, help formulate policies and plans, and communicate with generals in the field—all areas where the president needed assistance.

The appointment came on the same day that Lincoln gave McClellan approval for a movement by water to Fort Monroe, on the Peninsula between the York and James rivers. Confederate forces in Virginia would soon meet the enemy.[38]

Chapter 10

⸺◦◦⸺

PLAYING TROOPS
LIKE FIREFLIES

"THERE IS NO doubt the enemy are here in force," announced an Alabama colonel to Maj. Gen. John Bankhead Magruder on March 24, "and, though it may not be reasonable that they will tell their designs, yet have not come for nothing." Magruder promptly relayed the news to authorities in Richmond, explaining, "The enemy are in very great force at Fort Monroe, Newport News, and between those places," perhaps more than 35,000. The long-awaited spring offensive of 1862 had begun.[1]

For several months, McClellan had planned to land a large force behind Johnston's Manassas-Centerville line and march inland, preferably at Urbanna, interposing his columns between the Rebel army and Richmond. Johnston, McClellan explained, would have to attack him. But when Johnston's army fell back behind the Rappahannock in early March, he nullified McClellan's scheme. As an alternative, the Union general opted for Fort Monroe, on the peninsula between the York and James rivers. With Federal naval support and supplies hauled by ship, McClellan planned to drive up the Peninsula and seize Richmond, smashing enemy opposition in the process. What Magruder's men had observed was just the first portion of McClellan's massive army.

The completion of the ironclad CSS *Virginia*, formerly the USS *Merrimack*, at Norfolk Navy Yard on the James River temporarily scuttled McClellan's plans. The Confederates had salvaged the partially destroyed Union warship and ingeniously applied four inches of wrought-iron bars to its twenty-two-inch oak timbers. On March 8, on its maiden combat voyage, the *Virginia* sank one Union warship and ran another aground, forcing its surrender. The success of the *Virginia* cheered Southerners and panicked Northerners, especially those along the eastern seaboard. But the next day, the *Virginia* encountered the Union's own version of an ironclad, the USS *Monitor*. In what appeared to onlookers as a battle between a floating barn roof (*Virginia*) and a cheese box on a raft (*Monitor*), the ships slugged it out for several hours, with neither able to inflict significant damage. Their rounds could not penetrate the iron

104

shields, and the greater speed and maneuverability of the *Monitor* negated the superior firepower of the *Virginia*. By the end of the day, the *Monitor* had called off the fight, but the Federals had at least stalemated the *Virginia*. The *Virginia* returned to Norfolk, where it dominated passage up the James River. With control of the rest of the seas restored to the Federals, McClellan could proceed with the movement of his army by water.[2]

As the long line of blue-clad soldiers shuffled off the landing areas at Fort Monroe to join the 14,000-man garrison there, the Confederacy reacted cautiously. Back in December, Johnston had predicted just such a move, and the idea had not caught the Rebel high command by any great surprise. Yet the Rebels did not want to rush troops to the Peninsula, only to find out that the Federals had perpetrated a ruse, and Johnston's withdrawal had opened the door to a Union advance from Washington. The same spring thaw and rainfall that generated mud gumbo in northern and central Virginia would also impede any Yankee movement from Fort Monroe and buy the Rebels some time. Lee called on Johnston to prepare to move between 20,000 and 30,000 men, but simultaneously to hold his present line.[3]

This placed the burden of defense temporarily on the controversial Magruder. One soldier perceived his commander as gentlemanly. "His eye is keen as a hawks," he described to his mother, "—straight nose black hair— thin lips, perfectly straight, and a mustache with each coal-black hair pointing straight from the middle of his upper lip." Graduating from West Point a year behind Lee and Johnston, Magruder had seen extensive combat in the Regular Army, but his reputation as a dandy—he was nicknamed Prince John—may have led others to underestimate his abilities and impeded his advance. He talked incessantly and pronounced his Rs like Ws, making him the butt of jokes. The Confederacy commissioned him a colonel and assigned him to the Peninsula, where he fought well in a firefight at Big Bethel in June 1861, earning promotions to brigadier and then major general. Yet Magruder suffered from the rumor mill. In early January 1862, Daniel Harvey Hill, a cantankerous if talented soldier who fought with him at Bethel, lamented to his wife, "Poor Magruder, I hear he has taken to opium and has destroyed his mind."[4]

In command on the Peninsula since the previous spring, Magruder had been preparing two sets of defensive positions, one behind the Warwick River around Yorktown, and another farther up the Peninsula near Williamsburg. Because he employed his men so regularly in digging fortifications, the troops nicknamed him "King of Spades," a term some soldiers later applied to Lee. Magruder was prepared to block the Union advance and even launch a counterattack, but to do either he would need additional manpower.[5]

Lee hustled 3,600 reinforcements to the Peninsula, but before shifting large numbers of troops, authorities in Richmond attempted to divine the Union's intentions. Meanwhile, Magruder had to fend off ever-increasing numbers of Federals. The assignment required more than simply a "King of Spades"; it also called on Magruder to tap his sense of showmanship, to play the role of "Jack of

Spades." His defenses consisted of a variety of earthworks that stretched from Mulberry Island on the James River northward to Yorktown on the York River. To cover the obvious land approaches, Confederates had erected dams at various locations on the Warwick River to flood the area. One hundred and forty carefully positioned artillery pieces raked fire over land and sea routes. With additional fortifications on the north bank at Gloucester Point, Magruder's men could block advances up the York River. Along the James River, the *Virginia* would prevent any Federal attempt to land forces farther upriver, and Maj. Gen. Benjamin Huger's command at Norfolk would obstruct efforts to march overland and shuttle across the James. All in all, Magruder had established a formidable defense. Still, by his own estimate, he needed another 10,000 troops to defend properly.[6]

As Yankees approached to within eyesight and earshot of the works, Magruder executed a brilliant piece of deception. He had troops marching back and forth along the line, sometimes visible to the enemy, sometimes disappearing and popping up elsewhere, to convince Federals that he had more defenders. A Louisianan claimed that in one twenty-four-hour period, his men traveled from Yorktown to the extreme right flank on the James River six times, to dupe the enemy. Other Yankee observers heard train whistles, cheers, and the report of guns in celebration, as if a trainload of reinforcements had just arrived. As the perceptive diarist Mary Chesnut described, "he played his ten thousand before McClellan like fireflies and utterly deluded him." Whether Magruder intended to do so or not, Confederate prisoners of war buttressed his bluff by escalating the number of defenders fourfold to their captors and suggesting that Johnston was on the way with tens of thousands more. McClellan reacted cautiously and advanced in a conventional siege approach, when Magruder had only 14,000 soldiers in his path.[7]

The Union advance convinced Lee that McClellan intended to use the Peninsula as the principal theater of operations. On March 27, Richmond authorities had requested that Johnston send the 10,000 men that Magruder required. When no significant Federal force pressed down from Washington, Lee concluded that the major campaign had shifted to the Peninsula, and on April 4 he directed Johnston to bring his entire command to the Yorktown area. Eight days later, to ensure full cooperation among the various Confederate commands in the region, Davis placed Johnston in charge.[8]

As Johnston's soldiers passed through the Confederate capital, locals cheered and feted them, a suitable sendoff for the heroes who would save the seat of government. But for many of them, this was the first great march in their military career, from the Rappahannock to the Peninsula. "I have travelled about 150 miles, almost every bit of which was performed on nature's carriage, otherwise most commonly called 'shank's mare,'" grumbled one soldier. Nor did matters improve when they arrived near Yorktown. The Peninsula campaign exposed them to trench warfare, a grind worse than anything they had experienced previously. "Of all the hardships through which we have passed," complained seventeen-year-old Pvt. John Scurry to his sister in mid-May, "the last few weeks' experience has completely thrown former privations 'in the shade.'" The defenses themselves were reasonably strong. As a Virginian crowed, "we can whip ten to one easy if they advance on us." It was exposure to the elements and shortages that took their toll. Rain and cold, calf-deep mud in the trenches, two to three hours of sleep a night, and front-line service with almost no respite enervated the men. Because no one was allowed to build fires for cooking, they subsisted on a daily diet of raw, pickled pork and hard biscuit. Muddy roads so impeded the movement of supplies that on some days troops went hungry. A clearcut mission to save the capital inspired the men and sustained a high morale, but it was demanding duty.[9]

Even before he examined the defenses, Johnston expressed opposition to a campaign around Yorktown. Fearful that a joint Union army-navy operation would bypass his forces and trap them on the Peninsula, Johnston much preferred to fall back behind the Chickahominy River near Richmond and fight for the city there, views he had made clear to the president. In fact, Johnston underestimated the effectiveness of land-based batteries against gunboats, and he overestimated the power of large siege guns against well-fortified positions.[10]

On April 13, Johnston inspected the Yorktown works. All he could find was fault to support his opinion. After examining the line, he complained to Lee that Magruder's young engineers had erected various positions in the wrong locations, which made them susceptible to attack, and Union forces could turn the Rebels out of Gloucester Point or shell them into submission with gunboats and force passage up the York River. The defenses were so weak, Johnston assessed, that "No one but McClellan could have hesitated to attack." He proposed that the Rebels in the Peninsula fall back to the vicinity of Richmond and the president order the concentration of all Confederate troops from Virginia, North Carolina, South Carolina, and Georgia in defense of the capital.[11]

This idea of abandoning the Peninsula without a fight clashed with Davis's own views, and the president decided to hold a meeting to thrash out an operational plan. In attendance were Davis, his secretary of war George Randolph, Lee, Johnston, and several of Johnston's top generals. Johnston presented his case for retreating behind the Chickahominy and drawing on reinforcements from hundreds of miles away to defeat the enemy. His generals endorsed that approach. But Lee and Randolph objected. By stripping defenders as far south as Savannah, the Confederacy would open those major ports to ready conquest, and by retreating from Yorktown, the Confederacy would have to abandon Norfolk with its outstanding navy yard, scuttling the ironclad *Virginia*. Lee also believed that by fighting in such a restrictive area as the Peninsula, the Confederacy could better neutralize overwhelming Union manpower and technological superiority. After some give and take, Davis ordered Johnston to defend along the Yorktown line as long as he could.[12]

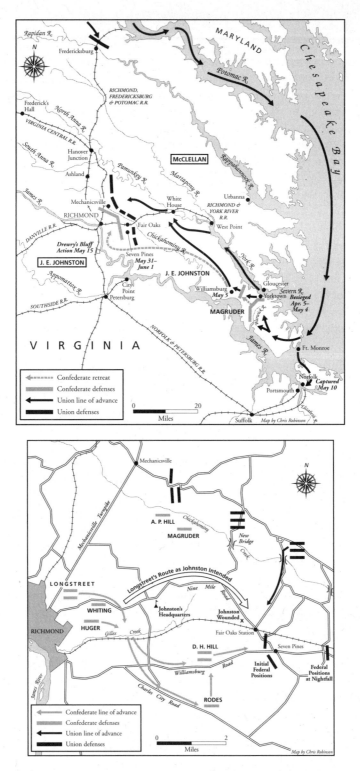

Peninsula to Richmond, including Seven Pines

The decision by the president to side with Lee and Randolph marked a vital moment in Lee's wartime career. Although Davis had never lost faith in Lee's ability or performance, many critics considered him a flop. Various political and military persons, including Johnston and his staff, believed that Lee had temporized excessively and planned poorly in fielding the defense of Virginia early in the war. When Lee finally received a field command in western Virginia in 1861, he did not exert control over political generals, and he formulated an operational concept that was too difficult for inexperienced officers and men to execute. After extensive maneuvering in foul weather and difficult terrain, he retreated without delivering a significant blow. Rumors swirled throughout Richmond that the Virginian lacked the strength of will to command troops effectively. Davis then sent Lee to Georgia and South Carolina to oversee defenses there, in part because the job demanded an expert engineer, but perhaps also to remove Lee from the Richmond cauldron. But as the president's relationship with Johnston slowly deteriorated, Davis realized that he needed Lee's advice more and more, and he brought him back to Richmond in time for the spring campaign season. By now adopting Lee's arguments on the defense on the Peninsula, Davis gave Lee the kind of endorsement he needed to take on a more active role in operations in the Virginia Theater. Barely a week after that meeting in Richmond, Lee intervened with Jackson to plan one of the most extraordinary campaigns of the war.[13]

Since Jackson's unsuccessful effort to strike the enemy in the Romney campaign, and his ensuing squabble with Loring and the acting secretary of war, he had remained on the defensive near Winchester with instructions to protect the Shenandoah Valley. Loring's men loathed him, and brawls broke out regularly between Loring's men and Jackson's troops. Fortunately, the War Department had the foresight to transfer Loring and all of his troops, except the Virginia units. With an easing of tensions, the Stonewall Brigade helped to set the tone for the remaining units in the Valley. Its men adored their former commander, booming out cheers whenever they saw him, and in time their enthusiasm spread to the other brigades.[14]

Early in March, a relative by marriage, Daniel Harvey Hill, accurately described Jackson's situation as "*very, very, very* critical." That month, 35,000 Federals under command of Maj. Gen. Nathaniel P. Banks advanced on Jackson's command at Winchester. With only 4,600 troops, Jackson opted to evacuate the city on March 12. Still, the soldiers under Jackson knew their commander would not suffer the loss lightly. "Old Banks thought to distinguished himself by bagging 'Old Jack,'" a Virginia private with extraordinary prescience explained to his sister the next day, "but he finds an affinity between Gen. Jackson & the Irishman's Flea—'When he goes to put his finger on him he aint thar,' & I'll bet my head 'agin' a rotten rail that if old Banks comes up the Valley very far he will get into a bag himself." Ten days later, the Confederate general launched a surprise strike on Banks's columns at Kernstown, south of Winchester. Rebel cavalry had reported a Union retreat, with a rear guard exposed, and Jackson hoped to crush it. Unfortunately for the Confederates, the intelligence was faulty, and Jackson had attacked a Federal force double his size. Initially, the Rebels drove the bluecoats back, but as the Union columns deployed more effectively, they extended beyond Jackson's flanks. Rather than suffer the capture of his men, the Stonewall Brigade commander, Brig. Gen. Richard B. Garnett, withdrew, ending the fight and earning Jackson's wrath and his own removal.[15]

At Kernstown, Jackson had acted boldly, and based on false information, he struck a much larger force. His command suffered well over 700 casualties, more than a third of them captured. But from this failure emerged some positive signs for the Rebels. Morale among the troops and their faith in Jackson was unshaken. "The Yankees gained the day," a Virginian justified to his mother, "but we are not beaten yet." The fight at Kernstown also focused the attention of Washington officials on the safety of the nation's capital. Rather than the 73,000 defenders that McClellan had claimed, the Yankees actually had under 30,000 for Washington's defense. Unwilling to risk the loss of the city, even if the chances were small, Lincoln responded by freezing large numbers of reinforcements departing for the Peninsula.[16]

This shift alerted Lee to a way of diverting resources from McClellan's command. The Union army on the Peninsula totaled approximately 100,000, with smaller commands in the theater—Maj. Gen. Irvin McDowell advancing on Fredericksburg with 40,000, Brig. Gen. C. C. Augur commanding 5,000 in the Fredericksburg vicinity, Banks in the Valley at 35,000, and Maj. Gen. John C. Frémont west of the Valley in charge of 19,000—providing another 100,000. Against this, Johnston had approximately 50,000 on the Peninsula; in the Shenandoah Valley, some light reinforcements bumped Jackson's tally to 6,000. Between Brandy Station and Gordonsville were 8,500 troops, commanded by a bald-headed, long-nosed, little fellow with two decades of Regular Army service named Richard S. Ewell. Ewell was so stressed over dealing with the eccentric Jackson that he suffered severe headaches and dyspepsia, to the point where he complained to a niece, "As an Irishman would say, 'I'm kilt entirely.'" Brigadier General Edward "Allegheny" Johnson, who according to one of his men "regards a shower of Minnie Balls Just about as little as a mule would a slight hail storm," guarded the Staunton area with 2,800. Finally, the athletic and intelligent Brig. Gen. Charles W. Field led a column of 2,500 men at Fredericksburg. If the Federals could merge several of their commands, they could overwhelm the Confederates with triple the number of troops.[17]

With little hope of the Rebels in Virginia securing more than a modest number of reinforcements, Lee had to figure out a way of combining his forces against isolated Union commands and transforming small battles into major triumphs. Northern public opinion was crucial to the war. If the Federals could be convinced that the price for victory was too high, or that they could not conquer the Confederacy, their war effort would collapse. The Confederacy did not have to crush the Union; it had only to convince the Northern states to stop shooting and allow the Confederacy to remain independent. It was a brilliant strategy because it gave the Confederacy a much greater chance of victory. Lee also knew that Lincoln, a politician with limited military knowledge, believed above all else the Union could least afford to lose Washington to the Confederacy. The North could replace manpower; the fall of Washington, however, would trigger shock waves that could dissolve public support for the entire war effort. Lincoln thus took excessive precautions to defend the city, and Lee intended to exploit them. Jackson would serve as the centerpiece of this operation.[18]

It was the start of one of the most exciting periods of the struggle for the army in Virginia. In a series of blows, they shifted the momentum and started the army on a course toward driving Federal troops from Virginia and perhaps winning the war. Wisely, Lee had no intention of managing Jackson's movements and fights. He had recently told Johnston that as an experienced soldier and the commander on the scene, he must make the decisions, that Lee could only advise him. As a result of Jackson's Mexican War service and his aggressiveness in command at First Manassas, Romney, and Kernstown, he had earned that respect. Lee could lay out the options and offer recommendations, but he refused to micromanage the campaign. Circumstances in the field changed daily, sometimes hourly or minute by minute. A good field commander understood his army and its morale, the capabilities of his subordinate officers, the terrain, the weather, and numerous other factors that influenced planning and execution. Lee, from his perch in Richmond, knew none of this. The individual in charge at the scene, whom the government entrusted with command, occupied the best position to judge. Because Jackson had long exhibited a willingness to make difficult decisions and execute them, Lee had faith in him.[19]

After baiting Jackson with a warning that he must either use Ewell's nearby forces or lose them to someone else, Lee waited a few days and then spelled out his agenda. "I have hoped in the present divided condition of the enemy's forces that a successful blow may be dealt them by a rapid combination of our troops before they can be strengthened themselves either in their position or by re-enforcements." He preferred a thrust against Banks, but a Jackson-Ewell attack on Federals around Warrenton, northwest of Fredericksburg, offered a viable second option. Either plan would relieve the pressure on the defenders near Fredericksburg, which Lee had just bolstered with 8,000 fresh troops in case McDowell advanced from Fredericksburg against Richmond. "The blow, wherever struck, must be successful, be sudden and heavy," Lee coached. "The troops used must be efficient and light," the perfect mission for Jackson's command. Lee then concluded by defining each of their roles in the campaign: "I cannot pretend at this distance to direct operations depending on circumstances unknown to me and requiring the exercise of discretion and judgment as to time and execution, but submit these suggestions for your consideration."[20]

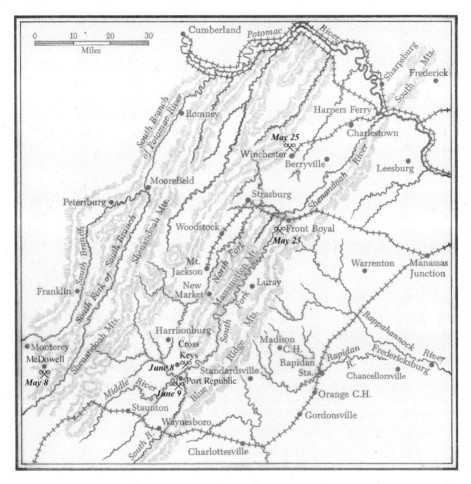

Valley Campaign

As Jackson debated his options with Lee and Ewell, the Federals forced him into action. A Union advance threatened Jackson's supply base, and the eccentric general had to act quickly, with Lee's endorsement. To prevent Banks from pressing southward, Jackson adopted a roundabout route to Staunton, joined forces with "Allegheny" Johnson's small command, and pushed on to the town of McDowell in western Virginia. There, he repulsed a Union assault in a fight that left one Virginian to record secretly, "I pray to God that I never get into another one as hot as that one." Effective pursuit by his exhausted troops along muddy roads proved impossible, but it mattered little. Jackson's men had forced the enemy back to Franklin and essentially out of the theater of war for a month.[21]

After defeating Federal troops at McDowell, Jackson hoped to turn on Banks's command and drive him from the Valley. Lee agreed. Banks appeared weaker than they had assumed, and the combination of Jackson's and Ewell's forces might enable Jackson to clear him from Virginia soil. Two days later, Lee again urged Jackson to strike Banks. A decisive Confederate victory might eliminate the Union threat in the Valley and draw reinforcements from Fredericksburg or McClellan's army near Richmond. "Whatever movement you make against Banks," Lee advised, "do it speedily, and if successful drive him back toward the Potomac, and create the impression, as far as practicable, that you design threatening that line."[22]

Just as Jackson prepared to unite with Ewell and strike after Banks, conflicting orders nearly undid the entire campaign. Technically, Jackson and Ewell were part of Johnston's department, and even though Johnston had taken charge personally on the Peninsula, he still commanded Ewell and Jackson. Lee perceived both a void and an opportunity and filled it, yet Johnston never relinquished command or responsibility. Thus, Jackson and Ewell attempted to please two bosses, whose directives sometimes clashed. Earlier in the campaign, Ewell had privately grumbled about being pulled in several directions at once. Jackson stepped in to take charge of Ewell's men and assumed full responsibility for his actions. This time, Johnston directed Ewell either to attack Union troops heading to Maj. Gen. Irvin McDowell in northern Virginia or to reinforce his army near Richmond. "We want troops here," Johnston stated emphatically. After some discussion about what to do, Jackson telegraphed Lee for guidance. Evidently, Lee ran interference with Johnston, opening the door for Jackson's movement. Once Johnston learned of the full picture, he endorsed Jackson's plan as well.[23]

During the height of the McDowell campaign, Jackson's trademark—lengthy and circuitous marches that would enable him to surprise the enemy—took its toll on his men, eliciting complaints after they had covered 140 miles. Yet a twenty-mile march would become child's play in Jackson's next campaign. With cavalry acting as a screen, Jackson slipped through the gap in Massanutten Mountain undetected, rendezvoused with Ewell's forces, and headed northward. On May 23, his men surprised and crushed a Union detachment at Front Royal. According to one Confederate, he and his comrades struck at 4:00 P.M. and "kept it up as long as we could see to run after the Yankees and fire a gun for the Yankees commenced runing soon after our guns opened fire upon them." In the course of the fight, one of those great anomalies of civil war occurred: the Confederate 1st Maryland Infantry helped to capture nearly the entire Union 1st Maryland Infantry.[24]

Suddenly, Banks and his soldiers around Strasburg discovered Jackson's army a scant dozen miles to his east, when he had assumed his Confederate foe was closing from the south. After some hours of indecision, Banks ordered a retreat to Winchester. The next day, Jackson pursued. With Confederate troops nipping at the Yankees' heels, Banks's troops dumped clothing, equipment, and stores to lighten their load. Only plundering by Rebel cavalry and infantry, causing delays (to Jackson's mortification) saved Banks's army from a horrible thrashing.

All night, with but a brief respite, Jackson drove his army to seize the high ground southwest of Winchester. Jackson was determined to prevent the previous day's breakdown in discipline from happening a second time. At daylight, he deployed for an attack. Confederate forces applied pressure along the line, and a devastating assault by Brig. Gen. Richard Taylor's Louisiana Brigade caved in the Union right flank and ultimately the entire position. Confederates raced through the streets of Winchester, amid "shouts and applause of the ladies," in pursuit of fleeing bluecoats. "To the day of my death I shall never forget the scene that greeted our delighted eyes, created in us the wildest enthusiasm, and nerved us for the fray," an artillerist described to his mother. "On all sides,— from windows, on the side walks, and porches were throngs of the fair young ladies, and hospitable matrons, old men and children hurrahing and shouting for joy; waving handerkerchiefs, bonnets and hats; and some of the fair ones even weeping and laughing by turns, for joy at our arrival, and their being rid of the detested Yankee rule." As Jackson came up the road, men pressed around him and whooped in delight. Jackson, who "seemed much affected," uncovered his head and bowed repeatedly in acknowledgment as he rode past.[25]

Yet again, complete success eluded Jackson. Exhaustion, confusion in triumph, and the unwillingness of Ewell's subordinate to execute a direct order from Jackson permitted Banks to slip away. Still, Jackson captured a fourth of Banks's command, along with assorted supplies and equipment. By midday on May 26, the beleaguered Union army clambered across the Potomac River and gazed back from Maryland on the Rebel columns.

Banks's whipping and chaotic retreat suddenly spurred Lincoln to action. No longer fearful for Washington, the Union president instead perceived an opportunity. Lincoln directed Frémont to march from his camp near Moorefield, Virginia, through a gap in Shenandoah Mountain, across Little North Mountain, and occupy Strasburg. McDowell's Corps east at Fredericksburg, which was destined for McClellan's army, now would converge hastily on Strasburg as well. With a head start on Jackson and a little luck, the two Union commands could seal off the Rebel escape route toward the south. Several days of good marching were all they needed. Yet it was a trap: the plan of Lee and Jackson, to draw resources and manpower away from McClellan, was working.

After his victory at Winchester, Jackson devoted the next two days to a well-deserved rest for his troops and then marched lazily toward Harpers Ferry. By May 28, he had learned of Lincoln's plot to trap his army, but the temptation of threatening a raid into Maryland proved too much. Not until May 30 did Jackson awake to the gravity of his situation. By then, it was almost too late. Employing the Stonewall Brigade as his rear guard, he directed one of the great forced marches of the war. McDowell's Federals, commanded by Brig. Gen. James Shields, had already retaken Front Royal, and Frémont was closing in on Strasburg. This desperate predicament would have discomposed most commanders, but not Jackson. He calmly calculated a solution, one that demanded extraordinary labor from a volunteer army. With cavalry blocking Frémont's troops and an infantry brigade checking Shields's division, the remainder of his army surged through the opening along the pike toward Strasburg. By noon of June 1, the elusive Jackson had slipped through the Yankee president's trap.[26]

Lincoln had summed up the Valley Campaign as "a question of legs," and as usual he was right. Rumors that the Yankees might cut them off and capture them spurred Jackson's troops to march as they had never done before. Despite a double-wide column of wagons eight miles long, loaded with captured goods, and an additional 2,300 Union prisoners, elements of Jackson's army marched over thirty miles in a day.[27]

But the race was not over. Shields's division took the road east of Massanutten Mountain and Frémont pursued along the Valley Turnpike. Yet again, the Federals were no match for Jackson's "foot cavalry." Although heavy rains slowed Jackson's march, they impeded Federal progress even more, and Jackson's horsemen destroyed the spans across the North and South forks of the Shenandoah River.

Neither the harrowing escape nor the rout of Banks's army quelled Jackson's ardor for battle. Most commanders would have retreated to safety, yet Jackson refused to do so. He began to form a plan to deal with the Federals piecemeal—strike one Yankee column and then the other, before they could unite. If he burned the bridge across the South Fork near Conrad's Station, and then occupied the town of Port Republic, he would hold the vital crossroads. By controlling the bridge and the shallows there, Jackson could keep the Union commands apart.[28]

Over two days, Jackson did battle both Union columns. Unfortunately, the Yankees failed to cooperate fully in his scheme, and Jackson narrowly avoided personal capture and nearly had his little army routed. In the end, his forces rocked Frémont and punished Shields, but the battle at Port Republic cost him more than he bargained for—more than 1,100 casualties. Neither side indicated willingness to extend the fight. Jackson's weary men loaded the trophies of battle into wagons and marched off to a gap in the Blue Ridge, euphoric from their exploits, relieved in their escape, and exhausted from their arduous campaign. Yet they were still watchful, as both Federal commands drifted northward, uncovering Confederate territory as they went.[29]

The achievements of Jackson and his followers were nothing short of phenomenal. Over the course of six weeks they had fought five battles and sundry skirmishes against three separate Union commands, in every instance outmarching their opponents. The campaign caused such mayhem for the Northern army that Lincoln personally devised a plan and committed troops to catch Jackson, delaying invaluable reinforcements to McClellan's army.

Amid applause from all quarters, Lee heaped praise on Jackson for his leadership during the campaign. "Your march to Winchester has been of great advantage, and has been conducted with your accustomed skill and boldness," he acclaimed. Three days later, after news of the fights around Port Republic reached Richmond, Lee rejoiced in Jackson's achievements. "Your recent successes have been the cause of the liveliest joy in this army as well as the country," Lee declared. "The admiration excited by your skill and boldness has been constantly mingled with solicitude for your situation."[30]

Equally if not more importantly, Jackson's reputation with his men soared. "This is one of the most brilliant moves of the war," proclaimed a Virginia private after the fall of Winchester, "& old Jack will be a greater man than ever." By the end of the campaign, soldiers rejoiced in their accomplishments and those of their commander. Georgian Ujanirtus Allen predicted they would rest a few days and then they "will be away, away, like a meteor and fall upon the anemy at some exposed position—dealing such a blow as will remind him that the 'Valley fox' Stonewall Jackson is again at his old pranks." Alabamian Barnett Cody informed his sister, "it takes a person with an iron Constitution to stand his marches," but he was convinced, "If all our Generals was like Jackson this war would not last long." Even Jackson's critics confessed satisfaction. "I believe that General Jackson is one of the keenest Generals in the South," penned a North Carolina private to his parents, "and I know that he is the most successful one, but he is terrible hard on his men. He very often marches them day and night, but he always accomplishes his aim." Success made hardship tolerable.[31]

FOR ALL JACKSON's achievements in the Shenandoah Valley, they would have proved meaningless if the Confederacy had lost Richmond. On the Peninsula east of the Confederate capital, Johnston struggled to deal with McClellan's massive command. Just as the Union completed the positioning of its heavy siege guns, Johnston determined to retreat from Yorktown. He wanted to withdraw nearer to Richmond and fortify, while a rear guard under his trusted subordinate Longstreet would cover the retreat. Yet extricating some 55,000 soldiers with artillery and wagons over muddy roads at night, in the face of the enemy, proved exceedingly complicated. Faulty staff work and delays by some division commanders created considerable angst at headquarters. Still, Johnston, overseeing his fourth retreat in a year, executed this evacuation with unusual skill, leaving behind some antiquated artillery guns and little more.[32]

Longstreet maintained a defensive line for the Confederacy along some incomplete works near Williamsburg, with artillery and most of an infantry brigade occupying the central field work called Fort Magruder. But he made what could have been a disastrous error. No one bothered to ask Magruder about the layout of fortifications, and Longstreet, unfamiliar with the defenses, left open a crossing near a dam to the north. On May 5, pursuing Yankee columns and artillery from the southeast hammered Confederates around Fort Magruder; in response, Longstreet tapped the brigades of Cadmus Wilcox, Ambrose Powell Hill, and George Pickett to roll up the enemy flank.

The evening before, Pvt. William R. Smith in the 17th Virginia in Hill's Brigade pondered his fate: "The faces of the men are stern and serious, and anxiety sits brooding on every brow." In his case, "home, parents, friends, and all associations of former days, come sweeping down the paths of memory." Most of all, though, he wondered what would happen to him the next day. Smith and his fellow soldiers entered the fight on the right flank after Wilcox's men stirred up a hornet's nest of bluecoats. Through thickets and woods they drove back the Federals. Rain, smoke, and fog limited visibility to about fifty yards, but they continued to press the Federals with additional support from Pickett's brigade. When ammunition supplies were exhausted, Smith and his comrades rushed across a clearing with fixed bayonets, once more driving back the Yankees from their position, enabling the Confederate men to replenish their ammunition from enemy dead and wounded.[33]

On the northern part of the line, Federal troops pushed across the unguarded dam and threatened the defenders at Fort Magruder. From the west, however, emerged a brigade under a crusty old West Pointer turned lawyer named Jubal Early. A reluctant secessionist, Early fought with all the ferocity and hatred of a recent convert. Around 5:00 P.M., his men rushed forward impetuously to seal off the penetration. Unity broke down amid the dense undergrowth and timber, and when part of the brigade tried to cross an open field, it ran smack into a larger Union force, well positioned and fortified by eight artillery guns. Reinforcements rushed in to extricate their comrades, but they were no match for the Union troops. Two of every three men in the 5th North Carolina Infantry went down in the fight, and barely more than one in five of its officers escaped uninjured. Early himself took a minie ball to the shoulder. Had the Union not bungled its command and control, failing to commit more troops to this front earlier in the afternoon, it could have spelled disaster for Longstreet's Confederates.[34]

For many soldiers, the Battle of Williamsburg eclipsed Manassas in danger and brutality. Captain Henry T. Owen, a company commander in Pickett's Brigade, told his wife that his men fired so fast and furiously that they ran out of cartridges and had to replenish them with dead soldiers' ammunition. "Manassas did not come half up to this and the balls rattled against trees around us like hail upon window panes." Another soldier in the 19th Virginia described how "We killed the Yankees in piles, they were laying sometimes as many as 15 & twenty in a place, and it was almost impossible to walk without treading on them." He believed the Battle of Manassas "was nothing" compared to Williamsburg in casualties over a small area of land. Both sides suffered nearly as many casualties as at First Manassas, with far fewer men who actually fought.[35]

As Confederate troops fell back toward their capital, they passed clusters of forlorn residents abandoned to their enemy. Worse, Rebel cavalry had specific instructions to take or consume all food and material that the Yankee army could use. "Our Cavalry service has got to be *odious*," griped an embarrassed staff officer. "Continually in the rear of the Army, we have to subsist by plundering and stealing, and many a home has been made desolate by the approach of Stuart's Cavalry." While he regretted the plight of these local citizens, there was little he could do. "The standing order is *impress* everything that may fall into Enemy's hands."[36]

Johnston had hoped to call a halt to the retreat around Barhamsville, near the head of the York River, but his evacuation of the Yorktown lines created a ripple effect. Once he withdrew from Yorktown, Norfolk with its prized navy yard became untenable. The South Carolinian Benjamin Huger began taking steps to evacuate men and equipment and to scuttle the CSS *Virginia*. Its commander hoped to bring it nearer to Richmond, but the *Virginia*'s deep draft prevented it from passing over the sand bars. This opened the James River for penetration by the Union navy, and Johnston, fearing that the Federals could land forces under gunboat cover in his rear, now decided to fall back within the confines of the Chickahominy River, a handful of miles east of Richmond.

Although Johnston had picked up reinforcements, he still felt that he lacked the strength to launch a successful attack. Better to wait until McClellan committed a mistake, then seize on the opportunity, he explained. But as McClellan's army approached Richmond, the pressure mounted for Johnston to act. He first proposed an attack on the extreme right Union flank. McClellan had extended his wing to meet McDowell's Corps of 40,000, advancing south from Washington. Reconnaissance the day before by Gustavus Smith indicated that the Union forces had taken a good defensive position. Smith was confident that an attack could carry the line, but it would also be a bloody affair. That evening, cavalryman James Ewell Brown Stuart reported that McDowell had halted his advance and diverted troops to the Shenandoah Valley in response to Jackson's rout of Banks, and Johnston called off the attack. Yet Johnston neglected to notify authorities in Richmond that he had canceled the assault, so the following morning, Davis and Lee had ridden out to check up on the progress of the fight. The president was dismayed to learn the news.

As the campaign extended from April into May, Johnston had become increasingly uncommunicative about his plans with the president or Lee.

Having suffered what he believed to be interference by the president, he was not about to place his army and his reputation in the hands of Davis. As he explained to a friend, Sen. Louis T. Wigfall, some eighteen months later, "I did not consult with the president as commander of the Va army because it seemed to me that to do so would be to transfer my responsibilities to his shoulders. I could not consult him without adopting the course he might advise, so that to ask his advice would have been, in my opinion, to ask him to command for me." Nor could Johnston take Lee into his confidence. Despite many years of friendship, Lee's position was an extension of the president's power as commander in chief, and private solicitations of advice would place Lee in a very awkward position.[37]

After terminating the assault on the Union's northern flank, Johnston returned to a scheme he had contemplated earlier: attacking isolated Union forces. McClellan had positioned three of his corps on the opposite side of the Chickahominy, a small waterway that carved through swampland filled with a tangle of trees and vines, but two corps remained on the Confederate side of the river. One of those corps, commanded by a former West Point instructor and Winfield Scott's military secretary, Brig. Gen. Erasmus Keyes, was well in advance of the other, and particularly vulnerable. Johnston formulated a simple plan to destroy Keyes's command. While a small portion of the army would keep all other Federal troops at bay, Johnston hoped to concentrate twenty-two brigades against six of the Yankees' infantry brigades and some of their artillery batteries.[38]

On the surface, everything seemed to work to the Confederates' advantage. The road network ideally supported the attack. A northern route, Nine Mile Road, crossed the Richmond and York River Railroad at Fair Oaks Station and extended to the right flank of Keyes's position at a crossroads called Seven Pines. The Williamsburg Road led to the center of the Federal line at Seven Pines, where D. H. Hill would oversee the fight. The Charles City Road branched along a dirt road to Seven Pines, enabling Huger's three brigades to roll up the Union left flank. The two divisions of Brig. Gen. Samuel Heintzelman's corps that were on the Richmond side of the Chickahominy could lend support to Keyes, but they were some distance away. Heavy rains that fell the night before offered an additional bonus, swelling the Chickahominy and making it treacherous for Federals to cross.

In theory, it was a simple plan: On May 31, Hill would fix the enemy while the other columns hit both flanks. Yet in execution, everything unraveled. Fear that Hill lacked satisfactory punch prompted Confederates to alter the plan. One of his brigades, commanded by the talented Alabaman Robert Rodes, was blocking along the Charles City Road. Johnston agreed that as Huger advanced, he would relieve Rodes, who would then march his brigade northward, joining on Hill's southernmost flank. This was an unnecessary complication on the morning of a battle; the relief should have taken place the evening before.

Much more serious was a shocking example of administrative incompetence by Johnston. He should have drafted a single order for the battle, which informed all major participants of everyone's mission, routes of attack, and timing. Instead, he issued two vague orders to Huger, neither of which informed the South Carolinian that a battle would take place. Gustavus Smith's stock had plummeted in Johnston's eyes, and although Johnston sent Smith perhaps the best-written instructions of all, they were not very detailed. Johnston's chosen replacement for command of Smith's division, William H. C. Whiting, received identical orders. Whiting's troops would support the attack that Longstreet would lead. D. H. Hill, who would spearhead the attack in the center, at least knew his own mission and took precautions to ensure that officers issued dry ammunition to the men and that everyone wore a strip of white cloth to limit friendly fire amid the woods.[39]

The most egregious failure occurred with Longstreet. The large, unflappable West Point graduate had earned the trust of Johnston as an excellent combat commander. The two conferred extensively and Longstreet was assigned to oversee his, Smith's, and Huger's troops. Yet somehow he, too, emerged from that meeting with a completely convoluted notion of what Johnston intended. Rather than advance directly east along Nine Mile Road and angle down through Fair Oaks Station on the Union right flank, Longstreet led his men on an early-morning march directly south, cutting behind the Confederate line and then swinging over along the Charles City Road, cutting off Huger's men, who started their advance late. Longstreet and Huger proceeded to argue, first over the order of march along the Charles City Road (in this case, possession was nine-tenths of the law, and Longstreet's men were there first), and then over whose commission predated whose, so they could determine who was the ranking officer in that sector. In both cases, Huger yielded temporarily.[40]

Hill, who had expected to lead the attack around 8:00 A.M., was stalled until Rodes's brigade arrived. Rodes, meanwhile, was waiting for Huger to relieve him before moving his command to Hill's flank. When Whiting reported to Johnston that Longstreet's men blocked his intended route, the commanding general assumed it was the tail end of Longstreet's division marching east along Nine Mile Road. He never would have imagined that Longstreet had directed his division to march south for the Rebel right flank. Johnston finally sent an aide on Nine Mile Road to find Longstreet. The officer rode so far in search of Confederate troops that he traveled straight into Yankee lines and was captured.

Hill, meanwhile, could not endure the delay any longer. Never a patient man, Hill paced and fumed. After extensive confusion and miscommunication, he directed Rodes to bring his brigade, but he would not even wait for its arrival. About 1:00 P.M., five hours later than Johnston had intended, the Confederate attack began in the center, with no troops along either flank. Fighting aggressively, assailing the enemy amid mounting losses, the attackers routed the Yankees from their advanced line and pushed on to the second one. To the south, Longstreet completely mismanaged the attack, finally getting Huger in position to fight but with instructions to await further orders. None came. In desperation, Hill cobbled together his own flank attack, spearheaded by a skillful, self-promoting South Carolinian named Micah Jenkins. Jenkins swung around the Union right and crashed through several weak positions, ultimately gaining control of the Williamsburg Road by nightfall. With Rodes's men pressing from the west, Union resistance around Seven Pines buckled and then collapsed. It took a titanic effort on the part of Yankee officers to halt the flight and reform the line, a mile and a half east of Seven Pines.[41]

Back at headquarters, Johnston knew nothing and heard nothing. Late that morning, Lee, who could not stand the idea of sitting at a desk in Richmond while a major battle might be taking place several miles away, rode out to investigate. The day before, he had offered his services through a staff officer to Johnston, to act in any capacity the general saw fit, but Johnston demurred. Around 3:00 P.M., Lee thought he heard musketry fire. His West Point classmate and friend listened and insisted it was simply some sporadic artillery rounds.

Not until 4:00 P.M. did Johnston learn of the fight. An aide had arrived from Longstreet's headquarters to inform him that the attack had driven the Federal line back a couple of miles, but they sure could use some support from the northern flank. Johnston rushed out of headquarters to oversee Whiting's advance along Nine Mile Road personally, hoping the late flank attack would be the *coup de grace*. What Johnston did not know was that Union reinforcements had finally crossed the Chickahominy floodwaters on a rickety span called Grapevine Bridge, and Whiting's men ran smack into them. Try as they might, his men could not dislodge the Federals. Around 6:00 P.M., Johnston called off the attacks and directed his men to sleep on their arms.[42]

From his advanced position with Whiting's command, Johnston observed the fight with shot and shells falling all around him. Unflinching under fire, he had frequently generated admiration from eyewitnesses for his calm demeanor in battle. On this day, however, after Johnston teased a staff officer for trying to dodge enemy fire, a musket ball zipped through the air and crashed into his shoulder. Moments later, a shell exploded in front of his horse. Shell shards penetrated his chest and thigh, and the concussion toppled Johnston from his mount.[43]

As they bore Johnston to the rear, Jefferson Davis and Robert E. Lee rode up. The president had come from Richmond to see the battle for himself and had reached Johnston's headquarters just as the general had rushed off to supervise Whiting's command. The two had not spoken. Davis and Lee spotted the stretcher bearers carrying the wounded commander from the field. When Davis approached, Johnston opened his eyes, smiled, and offered his hand to the president. He told Davis he did not know how badly he was injured, but he feared a spinal injury. "The poor fellow bore his suffering most heroically," Davis informed his wife. In time, Johnston would recover, but he would never serve in the Virginia Theater again.[44]

Command devolved on Gustavus Smith, a man with a tremendous reputation for intellect and judgment. Sixth in his West Point Class of 1842, the Kentuckian Smith served as an engineer and had two tours as an instructor at West Point, where his wife, an acclaimed beauty, captivated class after class of cadets. Johnston described Smith as "a man of high ability, fit to command in chief," and when he thought Davis had transferred Smith out west, he squawked mightily. Smith's staff believed he "is easily the *chief*, the highest, most towering military genius of the South." When the war broke out, he was street commissioner in New York City. A bout with paralysis forced him south for treatment. The Federal government misconstrued his intentions and deemed him an enemy, so Smith offered his services to the Confederacy.

While Smith brought great talent into the Confederate army, he suffered two drawbacks: He had never commanded troops in battle at any level, and under great stress, he lapsed into physical paralysis.[45]

Smith deemed the attack on Seven Pines a failure and wanted to fall back to the defenses of Richmond. Lee urged him to continue the fight. Only ten of twenty-two brigades had seen action, yet the Rebel forces, almost exclusively Hill's men, had driven the enemy back two and a half miles. With the momentum they had created, the fresh troops available, and the high water in the Chickahominy, Lee thought it was an opportunity worth pursuing. Smith, who by now was increasingly feeling the ill effects of stress, so much that by June 2 he would suffer paralysis in his arm, tried to renew the offensive on June 1, but the problem of miscommunication in high command that had plagued Johnston the day before afflicted him. Once again, Hill attacked on a limited scale, no one supported him, and the Federals checked his advance.[46]

In two days of fighting, the Confederacy had racked up over 6,000 casualties, including the army's commander, with little to show for it. They had inflicted some 5,000 casualties on the enemy, and had driven them back a couple of miles, but McClellan's army still loomed as a threat to Richmond, and the Confederates had to fall back to their old position. The thousands of quality rifled muskets and ten cannons that Confederate troops seized did little to ease the pain of their losses.

AFTER JOHNSTON'S WOUNDING, Davis and Lee met with Smith to plan for the next day. Davis probably suspected that Smith was not the right person for the job of army commander, and the meeting confirmed it. As the two men—commander in chief and de facto general-in-chief—rode slowly in the darkness, Davis turned and informed Lee that he intended to assign him as the next commander. It was now Lee's army.[47]

Chapter 11

LEE IN COMMAND

JOHNSTON'S SERIOUS WOUND "rendered it necessary in the opinion of the Pres: that I should take his place," Lee informed his daughter-in-law Charlotte on June 2. "I wish his mantle had fallen on an abler man, or that I was able to drive our enemies back to their homes." Although Lee wrote his son's wife with the obligatory modesty, he was not alone in doubting his ability to accomplish the task of driving the Federal army away from the gates of Richmond.[1]

Lee came from the Old Army, where he had built a reputation as a golden boy. Few men of his age could compete with his pedigree. The son of Revolutionary War hero "Light Horse" Harry Lee, he was descended from one of the most powerful families of Virginia. Although his family fell on hard times when his father's career and wealth degenerated, young Robert made a name for himself at West Point, graduating second in the class of 1829. He entered the Corps of Engineers, as befitted a cadet of his rank and intellectual ability, where he continued to impress those around him. He also took time to marry a Custis, which linked him through marriage to George Washington. In the Mexican War, Lee proved time and again that he was a man of great courage and sound judgment, emerging from the war with the best reputation of all the junior officers in the Regular Army. With commanding general Winfield Scott as his mentor, Lee enjoyed choice assignments and, by mid-nineteenth-century army standards, rapid promotion for a field officer. Appointed superintendent of West Point, he vacated his position before his term of service officially ended to take over as lieutenant colonel of the newly created 2nd U.S. Cavalry, which Secretary of War Jefferson Davis stocked with choice officers. At the time, Edmund Kirby Smith, who also earned a promotion to join the same regiment, called Lee "the most accomplished officer and gentleman in the army." By early 1861, Lee had received promotion to colonel and regimental commander. Not long before, he had led the party that crushed John Brown's Raid on Harpers Ferry. In the midst of the secession crisis, Scott offered Lee command of the principal field army, which he declined in order to join with his native Virginia.[2]

The Prussian military officer and observer Justus Scheibert noted of Lee, "he made the impression not of a soldier, but of a man of affairs." Endowed with a brilliant mind, Lee was devoted to education and intellectual growth. He knew both French and Latin, and he read extensively, particularly military history. Lee had also mastered the social banter of the parlor and was comfortable in any setting.[3]

By the time of the Civil War, volunteers anticipated that Lee would be the mastermind of the Confederate victory. D. H. Hill informed his wife in June 1861, "Genl Lee came down here yesterday. The enthusiasm of our men over him was very amusing. They made all sorts of noises to express their delight and cut up very much like a parcel of school-boys." A Virginia cavalryman called Lee "my beau ideal of a military chief" despite "the sternest expression of countenance I ever saw." Two months later, a Tennessean described a visit by Lee to his command. "He is a fine looking, old fellow weighs about 160 lbs Heavy set full breasted Keen Dark Grey Eye Heavy *Mustache*." Lee, he concluded, "has a commanding military bearing." In time, Lee's hair would gray, and he would grow his trademark "whiskers as white as cotton," as a South Carolinian described them.[4]

Yet within certain circles, an undercurrent of doubt flowed about Lee. By May 1861, after observing Lee for six years, Edmund Kirby Smith had come to the conclusion that he lacked the ability for large-scale command, describing his selection to head Virginia forces as "unfortunate." Smith, like numerous others, was put off by Lee's slowness to come to a decision. Sam Melton, who served on Brig. Gen. Milledge L. Bonham's staff and had a very favorable impression of the Virginia general, informed his wife in May 1861 that Lee "is a splendid officer; slow—too slow, but thoroughly accomplished." In a letter that has become almost famous for its misreading of the man, South Carolina governor Francis W. Pickens announced to Bonham just before First Manassas, "The truth is Lee is not with us at heart, or he is a common man, with good looks, and too cautious for practical Revolution." Even Lee's trusted staff member Walter H. Taylor admitted later in the war to his future bride that Lee's slowness to arrive at a decision frustrated him. "He is too undecided," Taylor grumbled, "takes too long to firm his conclusions." What these supporters and early critics missed, however, was the distinction between caution and thoroughness. Lee liked to gather all the information before deciding on a course of action. While he could and did make snap judgments, he knew that instant decisions were more likely to be wrong decisions.[5]

Lee's greatest strength as a military commander stemmed from his vision and his mastery of the operational art of war—the ability to use military forces in campaigns or major operations to achieve strategic goals in a theater of war. Over the course of three and a half decades of military service, from active duty in Mexico and the Confederacy, readings on the Napoleonic Wars, and mature reflection, Lee had sharpened his skills as a campaign planner. He could see how each command related to another, and how he could employ them in combination to achieve success. Lee also had an uncanny talent for anticipating movements of the enemy. As a trained engineer and student of war for many years, Lee understood the possibilities that confronted his opponents. By perceiving those options and studying their decisions, he gained insight into the minds of enemy leaders. He analyzed how they reacted to particular circumstances and used that information to predict how they would respond to specific situations that he created.[6]

Army command was both a learned science and an art that few can master. In the prewar army, Lee had never led more than a regiment, and it would take time to make the leap to army command. Like other soldiers in the war, he would have to learn on the job, and those harsh lessons usually cost lives and sometimes territory. As Lee quickly discovered, the Rebel public and its soldiery had extremely high expectations and were not very forgiving of failure.

In Lee's first major field-command assignment, he had to coordinate three separate columns in the rugged terrain of western Virginia. Two of these commanders were prominent politicians with limited military experience—Henry A. Wise and John B. Floyd. The other was Brig. Gen. William W. Loring, a veteran of the Mexican War who had lost an arm there. He had a good reputation as a soldier, but at least one individual challenged his character when he confronted Loring with improper behavior with Mexican boys. Lee formed a complicated plan, far too difficult for Loring and the politicos to execute, particularly in the mountainous country under poor weather conditions. With his command mired in mud, Lee could not deliver a powerful blow, and eventually his men retreated. Though the Confederates had shielded the Virginia and Tennessee Railroad, the campaign was otherwise a bust.[7]

Fueled by excessively optimistic tales in the newspapers as the campaign was unfolding, soldiers and civilians alike reacted as if Lee had committed some monstrous and irreversible blunder. The press and public howled over Lee's incompetence. Edward A. Pollard, a Richmond newspaperman and a sharp critic of the Davis administration, wrote, "The most remarkable circumstance of this campaign was, that it was conducted by a general who had never fought a battle, who had a pious horror of guerrillas, and whose extreme tenderness of blood induced him to depend exclusively upon the resources of strategy, to essay the achievement of victories without the cost of life." A student at West Point when Lee was superintendent, Ben Allston reported to his father that people called Lee a dirt dauber, a small insect that leaves a soiled trail in its wake. "Slow he unquestionably is, and he has disappointed a host of friends," Allston asserted, "but still he is there in command & must be upheld, until we find one who we are sure will do better than he has done." Alexander C. Haskell, a family friend of the Lees, described to his mother satirical sketches he had seen of Lee, "with a double barrel spy glass in one hand, and a spade in the other reconnoitering the position of the enemy." The caption read, "to retreat a little & throw up fortifications, the instant he set eyes upon them." Haskell believed, "This is unjust to a fine officer, but it does somewhat exhibit his very cautious policy." Evidence indicates that some officers drew up a petition to have him removed, probably around this time, but Lee's friends "made it disappear without his enemies knowing it," Gen. Braxton Bragg mentioned to Beauregard's brother.[8]

Lee responded privately to his critics with a twinge of sarcasm. "I am sorry, as you say, that the movements of our armies cannot keep pace with the expectations of the editors of the papers," he commented to his wife. Those vicious attacks unquestionably damaged Lee's reputation to the point that Davis decided to send Lee away from Richmond. The defense of Charleston and South Carolina, Georgia, and Florida was unquestionably an important mission, and the job did require engineering skills, but there were more essential duties for one of five full generals in the Confederacy. To save Lee's reputation, however, he had to leave Richmond and let the frenzy die out.[9]

Lee succeeded in his new assignment. Drawing on his engineering, organizational, and leadership talents, Lee erected an impressive network of defenses. He convinced Confederate soldiers that tossing up dirt in the right locations could save lives, cities, and property. Constantly inspecting the works, Lee earned the admiration of his soldiers and local civilians for his attention to detail and his awareness of their labors. When Davis recalled him to Richmond for consultation and then placed him in charge of "military operations in the armies of the Confederacy," a soldier in the 14th South Carolina, defending his native state, confessed to his wife, "I am very sorry for it, for I had more confidence in him than in all other Generals together." The *Charleston Mercury*, a venomous antiadministration paper if ever there was one, applauded Lee's elevation. "The people are far more cheerful, in consequence of the fine weather, and the fact that Lee is to be made Commanding General, and to organize victory for us." It then suggested that had Lee been in place months ago, the Confederacy would never have lost Forts Henry and Donelson in Tennessee. Six days later, the *Mercury* reiterated that optimism: "Under Lee's prudent management we expect that our affairs will soon begin to look brighter."[10]

Yet memories in Virginia were long, and noncombat achievements in South Carolina and Georgia altered few opinions. "The appointment of Genl Lee as chief military advisor of the Presdt. looks like a fatal mistake," Thomas Preston of Johnston's staff commented. He thought Lee's "traits of mind" would prove more problematic than they were the previous year. "May God in mercy protect us." Catherine Edmondston, a North Carolinian and unusually perceptive diarist, held nothing but contempt for Lee. "He is too timid, believes too much in masterly inactivity, finds 'his strength' too much in 'sitting still,'" she recorded. Even Lee's counterpart on the Union side, McClellan, rejoiced when he thought that Lee, in his new position, would replace Johnston as field commander. "I prefer Lee to Johnston—" he elaborated to Lincoln, "the former is *too* cautious & weak under grave responsibility—personally brave & energetic to a fault, he yet is wanting in moral firmness when pressed by heavy responsibility & is likely to be timid & irresolute in action."[11]

On June 1, Davis relieved Lee "temporarily" from his duties as military advisor and directed him to take command of the Confederate forces in eastern Virginia and North Carolina. Lee's initial mission was obvious: He had to drive the Union forces away from the Confederate capital. Of all the Rebel cities, Richmond was the one the fledgling nation could least afford to lose. As the nation's capital, it had come to symbolize the independent Confederacy, and even if every high-ranking official escaped capture, its fall would spell disaster for Rebel morale. Recent Federal successes had generated a momentum, and the loss of Richmond would be a terrible blow from which the Confederacy could never recover. The city was also a major industrial and transportation hub. Richmond facilities manufactured more than half of all the ammunition in the Confederacy. Tredegar Iron Works produced cannons and rails in numbers greater than anywhere else. Four major railroads flowed into the city, and dozens of small machine shops and workplaces for skilled labor contributed to the war effort. With the fall of Richmond, Rebel forces would have to fall back to southwest Virginia and abandon most of the state, uncovering huge areas of agriculture, livestock, and citizens to Union control.[12]

Immediately, Lee began placing his stamp on the army. As Davis's chief military advisor, he understood the military needs and mobilization capacity of the entire Confederacy, certainly better than Johnston or any other army commander. Lee also knew how and to what degree Southerners could contribute to the nation's defense. His assignment had been to oversee the entire war effort, a job that had given him rare insights into Union production and manpower capabilities. Thus, he realized that his command would have to alter its practices if it were to withstand the overwhelming resources of the Federals.

From his days as head of Virginia forces, his visits to the front, and his service in South Carolina, Lee had developed a feel for the men under his command. He understood what motivated his troops because he shared a commitment to the same cause. Despite four years at West Point and almost thirty in federal service, for Lee the United States was an important but not a principal attachment. Over the four years preceding secession, Lee spent approximately two years in his home at Arlington. There, he rebuilt ties to his family and his native state. By 1861, he viewed himself as a Lee, a Virginian, and a Southerner. All were part of the same identity. He absorbed the same Southern values that were ingrained in his soldiers. Like most Southern whites, Lee endorsed the institution of slavery, and as a slave owner he enjoyed its benefits during his time in Virginia.

As Davis's military advisor, he had adopted a nationalist perspective. Immediately after the fall of Forts Henry and Donelson, Lee complained of Southern complacency and explained his sense of the commitment the Confederate government must secure from its population. "The victories of the enemy increase & Consequently the necessity of increased energy & activity on our part," he penned. "Our men do not seem to realize this, & the same supineness & Carelessness of their duties Continue. If it will have the effect of arousing them &

imparting an earnestness & boldness to their work, it will be beneficial to us. If not we shall be overun [sic] for a time, & must make up our minds to great suffering." He concluded with the powerful words, "All must be sacrificed to the country."[13]

Lee also understood the great value that culture placed on honor and courage. Society demanded that their males act aggressively in war, in defense of homes, rights, and honor. Lee knew that he and his subordinate officers could exploit that aggressiveness and spirit of commitment to offset Union superiority in manpower and equipment. Yet Lee also realized that certain vital wartime duties did not come readily to Southerners. Southern culture encouraged qualities such as individualism and discouraged discipline and subordination, all of which would impair the creation of an effective fighting force. He and his fellow commanders would have to compel them to act as a team and to function in a subordinate and disciplined environment. To win independence, Confederate soldiers must exhibit a level of discipline and sacrifice that few had known in peacetime.

Lee's first act included the establishment of a new name for his forces. Johnston had called the primary field command in Virginia the Army of the Potomac, the same as its Federal counterpart. In October 1861, Davis consolidated three entities—the Potomac District headed by Beauregard, the Aquia District under Maj. Gen. Theophilus Holmes, and the Valley District under Jackson—into the new Department of Northern Virginia, with Johnston as its commander. While Davis and others occasionally referred to it as the Army of Northern Virginia, the name never stuck. In Lee's first announcement as the new commander, in Special Orders, No. 22, on June 1, he informed the troops that he was certain "every man has resolved to maintain the ancient fame of the Army of Northern Virginia and the reputation of its general," Joseph E. Johnston. In time, the Army of Northern Virginia became synonymous with its new commander.[14]

Within days of taking over, Lee took steps to improve the health, comfort, and well-being of his troops. He routinized the distribution of provisions and required division commanders to scrutinize the work of subordinates. Johnston's staff was not particularly adept at administration, and its neglect of procedure and paperwork filtered downward, resulting in sloppiness, occasional neglect, and a squandering of precious resources. Rations arrived so infrequently that men in the Orange Battery resorted to trapping rats, soaking them in clear water overnight, and frying them for breakfast the next day. Lee worked to ensure that no soldiers wanted for food and basic supplies and that the army cut down on waste. He complained to the quartermaster general that "This army has with it in the field little or no protection from weather." What the men needed were small fly tents to shelter them and reduce sickness from exposure, and he proposed that cutting the larger tents "would answer the purpose." He also circulated directives to all officers to pay attention to the "health and comfort of the men under command, and spare unnecessary exposure and fatigue."

Certainly soldiers must perform their duties, but what he sought was the elimination of unnecessary labors that might impair the health of the men, so that everyone would be ready for battle. Lee even authorized whiskey rations, at the discretion of division commanders, "when deemed essential to the health of the men, from inclemency of the weather or exposure in the swamps." These steps would improve the quality of life for soldiers, boost morale, and elevate soldiers' confidence of officers who must lead them into battle.[15]

Lee also called on officers and men to be vigilant in their efforts to conserve valuable materiel. He knew the productive capability of the Confederacy and the difficulty of procuring replacement items. Four days into the job, he warned officers that they must reduce the amount of supplies lost. "The increasing difficulty in replacing them," he directed, "makes greater watchfulness and care necessary in their preservation." One week later, he rebuked his command for squandering specific resources. The quartermaster had issued plenty of tents during the past year, many of which soldiers had destroyed or discarded carelessly. "The means of supply are becoming more limited while the demand continues great," he warned.[16]

When fundamental items like barrels started to run short, Lee ordered his troops to recycle them, rather than allocate valuable manpower to chopping trees, planing lumber, and building new barrels. Even more critical was wasted ammunition, a great Confederate concern throughout the war. Soldiers carried packages of cartridges in their pockets and unintentionally damaged them. Only when entering combat, Lee advised, should soldiers carry ammunition in their pockets. He ordered ordnance sergeants to collect and send to Richmond damaged cartridges and to inspect troops to guarantee compliance.[17]

Damage and destruction of public property was another problem. On his daily rides, Lee explained, he "has observed with concern in passing through Camps, too much disregard to the proper preservation of public property." He was "firmly convinced that our success is mainly dependent upon the economical and proper appropriation of public property at all times." If the Confederates were going to win this war, they needed to husband precious resources. They had very little margin for error, compared to their Northern enemy.[18]

Lee also focused on intelligence. He instructed subordinate officers to accumulate information on the Federals and their positions. Confederates scoured Northern newspapers for plans and units, so they could estimate Federal strength accurately. Conversely, Lee did not hesitate to request that the Confederate secretary of war see to it that newspapers kept certain movements out of print.[19]

Lee's predecessor, Johnston, had taken no steps to prepare detailed maps of the Virginia Theater. As soon as Lee took the reins, it began to happen. Chief Engineer Walter H. Stevens installed Albert H. Campbell as head of the Commission of Engineers and Draughtsmen, with the duty of preparing maps that showed "the R.Rds. [railroads] Stage Farm Rds, Water Courses, Woods, Clearings, farm houses, Ponds, Marshes, & Commanding Elevations." It would take time to complete maps with this level of detail, and none would affect the outcome of the battle for Richmond, but detailed maps would provide invaluable information for future operations.[20]

As Lee began to formulate plans, he sent cavalry commander James Ewell Brown Stuart on a reconnaissance around the Union left flank, to determine its vulnerability. In flamboyant style, Jeb Stuart, as the public came to know him, and his horse soldiers rode completely around McClellan's line, destroying supplies, seizing prisoners, causing mayhem, and gathering priceless information. The movement electrified Southerners. "Gen. J.E.B. Stuart just returned from the most daring & brilliant achievement of the war," pronounced a major. "The moral effect of this act," an artillerist explained to his wife, "must act finely on our forces and must tend to intimidate their men." Then, mixing his nicknames, he unwittingly forecast Lee's plan when he wrote, "I suppose they think 'Stonehouse Jackson' must have come down from the mountains."[21]

Lee adopted an aggressive approach to check efforts on the part of Federals to strengthen their lines. As a trained engineer, he knew that it would be almost impossible for the Federals to haul huge guns over the soft, muddy earth along the Peninsula and the Chickahominy. They would have to ship them to the front by the York River Railroad. Lee sought the construction of a huge, iron-plated, mounted gun, similar to something the navy might employ, to shell the railroad. Until the gun arrived, the army commander directed his sharpshooters and artillerists to pester the enemy as much as possible, as "enemy work parties must be arrested."[22]

While his men hampered Union progress on their works, Lee decided he must employ his other troops in building and improving their own works. Yet by doing so, he challenged a naive cultural perspective on warfare. "Our people are opposed to work," the general wrote Davis. "Our troops, officers, Community & press, All ridicule & resist it." It was the very means by which McClellan was closing in on Richmond. "Why should we leave to him the whole advantage of laborers," he wondered. "Combined with valor fortitude & boldness, of which we have no fair proportion, it should lead us to Success." After describing how the Romans combined fortifications and fighting so skillfully, he concluded, "There is nothing so military as labour, & nothing so important to our army as to Save the lives of its soldiers." Three days into his command, he ordered each division to assign 300 men to work under the supervision of engineer officers to dig earthworks, make sharpened, crossed logs called abatis, and build other obstructions and fortifications. Soldiers resented the labor, but Lee did not care. In addition to the work details, he required division commanders to see to it that officers and men "strengthen their positions in the most perfect manner with redoubts, barricades, abatis, rifle pits, &c., so that everyone had a hand in the manual labor." By mid-June, an officer jotted in his diary, "the whole front is one rifle pit, & many little redoubts." The trenches had a banquette or ledge about two to three feet off the bottom, so that soldiers could walk freely and then step up to shoot at the Yankees. To the rear, Lee saw to it that the secretary of war impressed one in every four slaves from five counties to the west to build more works in safer locations near Richmond.[23]

When Lee assumed command of the army, he believed the battle for Richmond was a only few weeks or a month away. He had to bolster his ranks to offset the numerical advantage of McClellan's army. The general requested that the secretary of war restore soldiers on temporary duty with medical and quartermaster departments and reduce cavalry details. Nor would he allow partisan organizations—semiauthorized cavalry units that functioned as guerrillas—to draw troops from his regiments. With Lee's encouragement, his chief of artillery, an Episcopal clergyman and West Point graduate, William N. Pendleton, culled the unattached artillery around Richmond, with a view to transferring extra guns and personnel to field batteries. As troop strength increased, Lee demanded manpower reports on the tenth, twentieth, and last day of every month.[24]

Richmond teemed with soldiers who were absent from their units, and the number of stragglers had reached epidemic proportions. According to D. H. Hill, "There are hundreds and thousands of skulkers, who are dodging off home or lying a round the brothels[,] gambling saloons & drinking houses of Richmond." Lee directed Stuart to send a company of horsemen each day to scour the capital in search of absent troops, and to coordinate with the provost marshal there. On one raid, the cavalry netted large numbers of soldiers who were attending the theater. "I am glad they were caught in no worse place than the Theatre," wrote the theatrical Magruder. "Men who in times like these can have a stomach for amusement must necessarily make good fighters." Yet much to Hill's chagrin, authorities failed to halt the flow, and troops continued to sneak out of camp and into Richmond for theater and other, less culturally elevating activities.[25]

In the Battle of Seven Pines, an ugly problem again resurfaced: Soldiers left combat for ammunition, plundering, or fear, and thus reduced the critical number of men who fired their weapons. A day after the fight, Brig. Gen. William H. C. Whiting tried to bring pressure to bear from within the division to check the practice. "In some instances the skulking has been shameful & the Brig. Genl. Comdg. [Commanding] hopes that those brave men who stood the fire & more than that patiently endured the great privations of the past three days, will assist him, in bringing these laggards if not to a sense of duty, to a sense of shame," he urged. Likewise, Longstreet rebuked his men for plundering in the middle of the battle. "It is a source of deep regret however that gallant soldiers after thus taking the entire position of the enemy should have endangered our captured stronghold by so far forgetting themselves as to desert their ranks for plunder," he fumed. The following day, he announced that no officer below the rank of brigadier general could send a man from the battlefield. Lee then reinforced these steps. To check the flagrant straggling and plundering, and to keep troops with their commands, Lee charged each regimental commander with creating a provost guard, consisting of a lieutenant, a noncommissioned officer, and ten privates. He also directed that "No Officer is authorized to withdraw his command from its position in line of battle to procure ammunition," a problem that appeared all too frequently at Seven Pines. Division commanders were to enforce this and to see that ammunition was brought forward to the troops.[26]

Lee even tackled Davis's pet project, the reorganization of brigades by states. Johnston had stalled throughout the winter months, and now Lee would have to implement the changes himself. Personally, Lee wrote the president, "I fear the result." Nor did he think it would best serve the cause. He would prefer to command a brigade with regiments from different states. "I think it could be better controulled, more emulation would be excited & there would be less combination against authority." He realized that officers "looking to political preferment would prefer it, & it may be more agreeable to the men. The latter consideration," he elaborated, "has much weight with me." In the end, though, because the commander in chief wanted it, and because it "may be in conformity to the spirit of the land," he would "attempt what can be done." With existing brigades, "It must necessarily be slow & will require much time," especially since they stood with their backs to Richmond. "All new brigades I will endeavour so to arrange." Lee then issued a circular, alerting the army to the law and calling on division commanders to let him know if it "can be made prospectively and progressively, but without embarrassment to the operations of the army."[27]

All the while, Lee kept Davis informed of what he was doing and what he planned to do. The day after Davis placed Lee in command officially, he had asked the general, "please keep me advised as frequently as your engagements will permit of what is passing before and around you." Lee needed no prodding. Having spent months at Davis's side, he knew the president wanted to be kept informed. Lee's attention to important detail comforted Davis, who wrote to his wife, "Lee is working systematically[,] co-operating cordially and the army is said to feel the beneficial effect of it."[28]

Others were not so optimistic. Since February, the Confederacy had suffered setback after setback and soldiers and civilians affixed blame to general officers. After the command fiasco at Seven Pines, William Preston Johnston, the president's aide and the son of Gen. Albert Sidney Johnston, grumbled to his wife, "The trouble is we have *no Generals.*" With Lee now in command of the army, his spirits were buoyed a bit. Young Johnston believed Lee possessed patience, administrative ability, absolute integrity, and an unshakeable commitment to the Confederacy. His disadvantage was that he neither knew the officers so well, nor did they know him. No ringing endorsement, young Johnston concluded, "I hope more from him, than I did from [Joseph E.] Johnston." After conferring with Lee on June 1, Pendleton, the chief of artillery, revealed his pleasure with the new army commander. "I liked very much his tone & bearing in the conference I had with him the evening before last," Pendleton penned his wife two days later. "His head seems clear & his heart strong." Lee had two great problems, the clergyman turned general explained to his wife: He must shield Richmond and then whip McClellan and the Yankees. Unfortunately, protection of Richmond imposed considerable restrictions on Lee's options for defeating the Federals. "Few men have ever borne a greater weight than that which now rests upon his shoulders," he conveyed solemnly. Others expressed lingering doubts about Lee as a field commander. A knowledgeable staff officer jotted in his diary, "One week since real fighting ceased & Genl Lee took command—not so sanguine of our defeating McClellan as when he first came up." The following week, an acerbic D. H. Hill offered the same old refrain. "Genl Lee is so slow and cautious," he complained to his wife.[29]

The flurry of reforms and duties impressed few other people in or out of the army. This was certainly an army that wanted Lee to succeed, and desperately needed him to succeed, but its officers and men had serious doubts about him. After a long and difficult winter, with a retreat from northern Virginia to Yorktown and now to the gates of Richmond and only one major attack, a more subdued mood had descended on the troops. Few even mentioned Lee's appointment in letters and diaries. They grumbled over the manual labor, affixing Magruder's old nickname "King of Spades" on Lee, but otherwise revealed shockingly little about him, his appointment, and changes in the army. Rare was the soldier like Pvt. Samuel Oakey, a twenty-two-year-old prewar blacksmith from Virginia, who, after three weeks under his new commander, was convinced this one was better. "General Lee is more vigilant than Johnson was," he alerted his cousin. "Lee wont give up an inch of ground to the Enemy without contesting it."[30]

Soldiers fixated on the trenches as a sign that Lee would only engage the enemy on the defensive. Still embracing a naive sense of honor and combat, the notion of fighting behind fortifications did not sit well with them. "The very idear of two large armys only separated by a small stream to be entrenching themselves is out of the question," jotted Capt. Robert G. Haile of the 55th Virginia Infantry. "I go in for their meeting each other in open ground and fight it out and be done with it."[31]

Civilians seemed even less impressed with Lee and his approach to warfare. Catherine Edmondston, from a North Carolina slaveholding family, offered no kind words for Lee. "I do not much like him, he 'falls back' too much," she commented. After listing his failures in western Virginia and South Carolina, Edmondston jabbed at him, "His nick name last summer was '*old-stick-in-the-mud.*' There is mud enough now in and about our lines, but pray God he may not fulfill the whole of his name." Mary Chesnut, the well-connected South Carolina diarist, recorded, "Lee is King of Spades. They are all once more digging for dear life." She believed the Confederacy's only hope was Stonewall Jackson's conjuring up some of his martial magic. Like so many Southerners, she thought fighting behind earthworks and frequent retreats cut the heart out of the soldiers. "Our chiefs contrive to dampen and destroy the enthusiasm of all who go near them. So much entrenching and falling back destroys the morale of any army," she pinpointed. "This everlasting retreating, it kills the hearts of the men."[32]

The press, which had bashed Lee after the western Virginia campaign, continued to rail about him. John Moncure Daniel, editor of the *Richmond Examiner*, drew upon his poison pen to express his dismay at the way Lee handled the crisis. "As for this city," he spat sarcastic venom, "if its fate depends on a game in which '*spades are trumps*,' played by two eminent hands of the old army, each knowing every thing that the other knows, there is no doubt but that the Confederate Government will, sooner or later, be spaded out of Richmond." Even the editors of the *Richmond Enquirer*, a wartime rag that seldom criticized the government, believed the "instincts and genius of the Southern troops" were "peculiarly suited to attack." So virulent were the sentiments, and so obstinate were those claims, that Davis feared the worst. "Politicians, Newspapers, and uneducated officers have created such a prejudice in our army against labor that it will be difficult until taught by sad experience."[33]

Lee had a clear course of action in mind. What neither civilians nor soldiers knew was that Lee had done so much preparation with the intention of assuming the offensive. He oversaw the provisioning and improved the comfort of troops, so that they would enter the campaign well rested. He husbanded resources for the fight, and gathered intelligence to plan his attack. By harassing the enemy, he attempted to keep their works from being completed, and he drew together the maximum number of men for the fight. He dug fortifications not so much to counter McClellan's advance as to free large numbers of soldiers for an attack, while a small portion of the army held Yankees at bay. Lee meant to fight.

Chapter 12

THE BATTLE FOR RICHMOND: THE SEVEN DAYS' CAMPAIGN

A FTER A LENGTHY trip from the Georgia coast, Brig. Gen. Alexander R. Lawton and his Georgian regiments had barely arrived at the Shenandoah Valley when Jackson ordered an about-face, and away they marched. On foot and by train they traveled to a destination that even Lawton did not know until they arrived.

Personally, Lawton much preferred the march to the rails. Huge wagon trains clogging the roads for miles around gave him his first taste of being part of a "'grand army.'" Lawton thrilled at the sight of masses of soldiers and enormous lines of animals and conveyances stretched out for miles and miles, creeping up the hillsides and snaking their way to the valley floors.

Lawton graduated thirteenth in his West Point class in 1839, but he resigned the next year for a career in law and politics. By 1860, he had achieved unusual financial success, with eight slaves and almost $65,000 worth of property. Like so many West Point graduates, though, Lawton never truly got the army out of his blood, and he took command of the 1st Georgia and seized Fort Pulaski for his home state before it had even seceded.

Jackson's senior by five years, Lawton had never met the man until June 1862. Although they rode together on the rail cars, Stonewall seldom spoke and conveyed no military information to Lawton, leaving the Georgian to muse that "He is very silent & mysterious." A week after joining Jackson's command, Lawton explained to his wife, "My impressions of him do not differ from what I expected—great energy & will, without much system." He believed Jackson was personally "capable of any amounts of endurance," yet, Lawton complained, "he is rather indifferent to the comfort of his troops, & they are broken down very fast," a problem that would haunt him in the coming week. Had Jackson not expressed sensitivity to the cheers of women as they passed, Lawton might have considered him less than fully human.[1]

Both men were on a great mission, one Lee had designed shortly after taking over as army commander. "Should there be nothing requiring your attention in the valley, so as to prevent your leaving it for a few days," Lee tempted Jackson on June 6, "and you can make arrangements to deceive the enemy and impress him with the idea of your presence, please let me know, that you may unite at the decisive moment with the army near Richmond." Several days later, Lee elaborated. He would send Jackson reinforcements, of which Lawton's Brigade was a part, and he wanted Jackson to move quickly through Ashland and sweep down behind McClellan's right flank, while Lee's army attacked in the front. Lee felt confident the blow would compel McClellan to abandon his strong works and retreat. When Jeb Stuart returned from his sweep around McClellan's army and reported the Union right flank to be vulnerable, Lee locked into the scheme. It was a brilliant and simple concept, but one fraught with difficulty to execute because of the timing and the need to preserve the element of surprise.[2]

On June 23, around noon, Jackson strode into Mary Dabbs's house on Nine Mile Road outside Richmond. Lee pumped his hand, and minutes later, Longstreet, A. P. Hill, and Jackson's brother-in-law D. H. Hill joined them. Lee had called them together because they were the team that would execute a massive turning movement. After some conversation, everyone agreed on the timetable. Stuart's cavalry would shield Jackson's flank as he penetrated McClellan's rear. Once A. P. Hill heard gunfire, signaling Jackson's arrival in the enemy rear, he would attack the well-fortified Yankees at Mechanicsville. Pressure from behind should unloosen the Federal position. As the attacks peeled back Union defenders, Lee hoped to strike them during their withdrawal with Longstreet's men. D. H. Hill would support his brother-in-law in the movement. Fearful of a letup, Lee instructed everyone to press on toward Cold Harbor, where they would sever McClellan's supply line. The meeting adjourned around sunset. Jackson, having ridden fifty-two miles in the last fourteen hours, arose, mounted his horse, and galloped off into the darkness.[3]

The next day, Lee issued a General Order that carefully laid out the missions of each commander, with timetables. Lee wanted no such confusion as Johnston had suffered at Seven Pines. The entire enterprise was fraught with risk. Lee planned to hurl almost 60,000 men against and behind the Union right flank, while holding three-fourths of McClellan's army at bay with a third of his army, using the trenches to augment their strength. Lee gambled that the "Little Napoleon," as Northerners nicknamed McClellan, would fall back, rather than attack, but if he did go forward, the commands of Magruder and Huger, supported by some troops from Theophilus Holmes, would have to hold out until the others inflicted so much damage that the Federals would have to retreat.[4]

When the morning of June 26 arrived, the aggressive A. P. Hill heard nothing from Jackson. Hours passed, and still no word or sound. By midafternoon, neither Hill nor Lee could wait much longer. The army was vulnerable now that the great bulk of its troops were positioned to the north. Finally, around 3:00 P.M., Hill crossed the Chickahominy and struck the Federals in a frontal attack. At least it would distract the Yankees, and surely Jackson would support him soon. For several hours, Rebel troops hammered away at well-positioned Union soldiers. The Federals occupied the high ground beyond Beaver Dam Creek, behind earthworks and supported by artillery. The Rebels could barely make a dent. Mercifully, darkness called a halt to the attacks.[5]

The key element in the plan, Jackson's attack on the flank and rear, had fallen way behind schedule. The extremely long march, along muddy roads and hauling too much weight, from cooler temperatures of the Great Valley and into the hot, humid, rolling hills of the piedmont, proved too much. Jackson's soldiers simply could not keep pace with their general's expectations. That same huge column of men and wagons that convinced Lawton he was part of something monumental also indicated that the head and the tail had stretched too far apart, forcing the front to delay while the rear closed the gap.

Lawton was also wrong about Jackson. There were limits to his endurance, and Jackson had exceeded them. Riding to Lee's headquarters and back to the army, attending to so much detail, and sleeping little, Jackson's judgment had become impaired. His extraordinary strength of character, with the power to will his army into spectacular marches, was too weak to extract superhuman effort now from his footsore and weary soldiers.

Yet all was not disaster for Lee and his plan; it was just a little behind schedule. By nightfall, Jackson had finally positioned himself on the Yankee flank. Although the Union detected his presence, the execution of a withdrawal took so long that the Confederates captured numerous prisoners the next morning. As the Federals pulled back from the high ground near Beaver Dam Creek, Rebel troops poured across the Chickahominy with room to deploy and pursue.

Once again, the Union forces secured a position on high ground behind a waterway, this time Boatswain's Swamp, and they strengthened it with rifle pits and cut trees. For the second day in a row, Jackson's command was tardy, this time reaching the battlefield in the late afternoon. Meanwhile, Rebel comrades from A. P. Hill's and Longstreet's commands struck time after time, but could not push the Yankees from their strong works. Finally, near sunset, with Confederates pressing all along the line, men from the Texas Brigade roared through Boatswain's Swamp and clambered up the steep slope to crack the Union line. At the opposite end, Jackson's men also broke through, and the Yankee line collapsed. In the Battle of Gaines's Mill, Lee's army won a clear victory. Still, it paid a heavy price. Some 9,000 Confederates were among the casualties, while inflicting 6,000 losses on the outnumbered Yankees.

As the Federals rolled back from their positions along the Chickahominy, fresh troops took up a blocking position at Savage's Station and to the west, near the old Seven Pines battlefield. McClellan hoped they could hold long enough for him to remove supplies from the base near the York River railhead and get them, along with some battered Federal soldiers, across White Oak Swamp. Lee, sensing an opportunity to deal a huge blow, tried to sandwich the

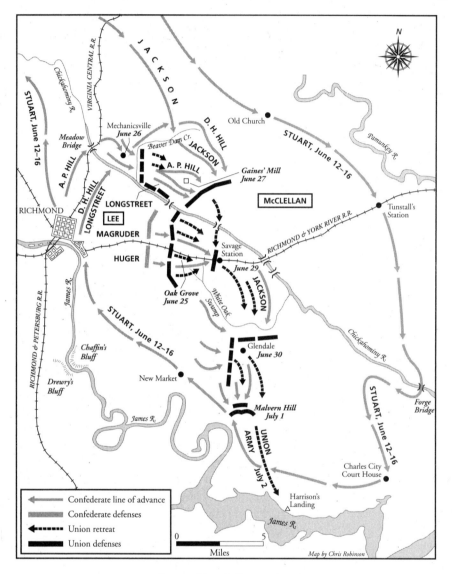

Seven Days' Campaign

Federal defenders between Magruder's columns, already south of the Chickahominy, and Jackson's troops, which would have to rebuild bridges over the Chickahominy to move south toward White Oak Swamp. Huger would have to advance toward the crossroad to Glendale, and Longstreet and A. P. Hill would have to rush west toward the James River and then back to the southeast below Huger to deliver a crunching blow on Glendale.

Although Lee had high hopes for the attack, timing and coordination were so complicated that even a veteran army would have struggled to execute it effectively, and neither his staff nor his key subordinates rose to the challenge. Conflicting orders and vague information detained Jackson to protect the bridge crossings, and Magruder, without Jackson's support, advanced timorously and committed only a portion of his troops to battle. The fight itself was vicious, with Georgians and Mississippians inflicting over 200 casualties in twenty minutes, but the results proved inconclusive.[6]

The next day, June 30, Lee's army again failed to coordinate effectively. Neither Huger nor Jackson exhibited much initiative—Huger acted hesitantly while Jackson may have been too exhausted to formulate command decisions—which pushed the burden onto Longstreet's and A. P. Hill's soldiers. They advanced along the Long Bridge Road toward Glendale, where they encountered stiff resistance. The battle seesawed as Confederates assaulted and seized portions of the Union line, only to lose them to a counterattack. At times, fighting degenerated to hand-to-hand. As nightfall descended, the Rebels seized a critical battery and held it, compelling the bluecoats to withdraw. In the Battle of Frayser's Farm, as Confederates called it, the two sides racked up 6,400 casualties combined.

Time after time, Lee had attempted to crush a portion of the Union army, and in each instance the Federals had managed to escape. The next morning, the Confederates discovered Union forces occupying a beautiful, wheat-covered slope called Malvern Hill. Lee knew that as the Federals retreated closer and closer to the James River, Federal gunboats would augment Union firepower considerably, making it nearly impossible to defeat them. This would be his last opportunity to deliver a powerful blow. For the defense, the Federals had occupied an outstanding position, with steep declines on three sides, and for the first time the entire army, with artillery and siege guns, had consolidated.

Lee intended to create artillery crossfire to silence enemy batteries and soften the position, and then have infantry assault up the slope. Once again, his command could not concentrate at the right time and in the right place. Artillery stretched far to the rear and never reached position in sufficient numbers to silence anything. Those batteries that did open fire suffered horribly from overwhelming Union firepower. Nonetheless, Magruder ordered Lewis Armistead, a Regular Army officer from North Carolina, to lead his brigade forward, followed by others, and begin a series of piecemeal assaults. Some intrepid souls actually stormed to the crest in the face of overwhelming fire;

most were mowed down along the slope or fell to the ground, unwilling to advance farther, and made their way back when they thought it was safe. Mercifully, the attack started late in the day and darkness brought it to a halt. With over 5,600 Confederate casualties strewn across the field, the cantankerous D. H. Hill did not miss the mark by much when he exclaimed twenty-five years later, "It was not war—it was murder."[7]

The next day, Union forces evacuated Malvern Hill, falling back to a position on the James River, with protection from their gunboats and ready access to supplies. Lee personally examined the new position and determined that an attack would prove too costly. After seven days of fighting, Rebel soldiers were exhausted, especially Jackson's command. Lee posted a cavalry force to monitor Federal behavior and withdrew his weary men closer to Richmond, where resupply and reorganization would become easier.[8]

At the time, both sides perceived this as series of independent fights, and they referred to it as the Seven Days' Battles or the Seven Days' Campaign. Future generations, however, would view it more precisely as one large battle, taking place over the course of seven days with fighting at various locations. In the course of that struggle, Lee's army had driven the Federals, who could literally scan the landscape westward and observe church spires in Richmond, away from the Confederate capital to a sanctuary on the James River some twenty miles away. The victory had shattered the Union skein of victories stretching back to the invasion of coastal islands in North Carolina and including the fall of New Orleans, Nashville, and Forts Henry and Donelson, Shiloh, and the evacuation of the Peninsula. The Battle of Seven Days was the most cataclysmic of the war to date, with 13,000 more losses than the bloody Battle of Shiloh. Union and Confederate armies combined to inflict more than 36,000 casualties on each other, approximately the same number of people who resided in Richmond in 1860.

Neither First Manassas, nor Williamsburg, nor even Seven Pines prepared the combatants for what they witnessed in this struggle. The scale and scope of the fighting, and the sheer brutality of it, crushed all sorts of myths they had conjured about themselves. The Battle of Seven Days jolted virtually everyone who participated in it. While many soldiers fought effectively, some individuals and entire commands broke down.

Never before had so many of these Rebels witnessed the utter calamity of the battlefield. Even those who had fought before were overwhelmed. "We used to think that the battle of Manassas was a great affair," scribbled prewar clerk Pvt. Charles Kerrison home, "but it was mere child's play compared with those in which we have been lately engaged." His regiment, the 2nd South Carolina Rifles, had been in the thick of the fights at Gaines's Mill and Frayser's Farm, and lost 149 men. Other regiments had lost as many soldiers at First Manassas or Seven Pines. What distinguished the Seven Days' Battle was the widespread devastation in human lives and private property. Twenty-five-year-old prewar mechanic Pvt. Jasper A. Gillespie in the 45th Georgia wrote to his wife, "I have heard talk of war & read of war but never could realize its horrors until I experienced it. I have been in 4 fights in one week & marched all the time, have seen thousands of dead men & horses, and even the Woods cut to peaces by the heavy Artilery." Another soldier, a Virginian, testified to his sister that he witnessed a solid cannonball bore directly through the center of a tree at least two feet thick and still have enough power to sever a man's head. In the wake of this level of violence and destruction, Gillespie believed only divine interposition had saved him. "I feel more humble & thank ful to Almighty God than ever before, thus far he has let better men fall & spared me, which Only God could do, as the amount of Lead and Iron that rained about me it seamed meracilous [miraculous] that I was saved."[9]

Prewar farmer and slaveholder Lt. Col. Robert H. Gray of the 22nd North Carolina instructed his father, "A man who has not been in a battle can have no idea of it; in fact a picture of a terrible thunderstorm looks & is about as much like the reality as a description of a battle is like the real affair." Not only had it shattered their prewar and prebattle images of the grandeur of combat, it exploded personal myths about the individual and warfare. One soldier offered a litany of his personal peacetime disasters—he had fallen out of a runaway streetcar, had a stampede of mules run over him, nearly drowned, and had his father take him behind the house for a cowhide whipping—and wrote that nothing unnerved him like this battle. It was his first experience under fire, and he confessed to becoming "wobbly." Private Christopher P. Poppenheim of Hampton's Infantry Legion felt an "indescribiable" combination of "extreame excitement and an indiferance to death" before the fighting. Once he began shooting his rifled musket, he became cooler and calmer by focusing on his duty. "I am then preparred to die at any minute, and expect every ball that I hear coming to be for me, and am astonished when it passes that it did not hit me." At least these projectiles traveled so fast that he could not see them. "I have often heard and seen a shell coming," Poppenheim attested, "and thought that I was up the *spout* and was very glad when it passed very near and did not hit me."[10]

To the shock of many soldiers, who assumed that Southerners possessed an inherent martial instinct, quite a number lacked Poppenheim's calm. The steely determination expressed in many letters vanished at the critical moment. They "wobbled" and then fled from the scene or dodged battle with or without some excuse. Soldiers wandered off from their command, or slipped behind and never made it to the front lines. Others escorted a wounded comrade rearward at the first opportunity in order to leave the battlefield and still justify their conduct in honorable terms. Large portions or entire regiments broke and ran, or fell back and refused to re-enter the fight. Those who remained behind and performed their duty were embarrassed over the shirking, skulking, and downright cowardly behavior. Colonel Alfred H. Colquitt of Georgia, owner of 176 slaves before the war and commander of a brigade in the battle, complained to a friend, "you would be surprised to know how many skulked behind and returned to camp under pretense of sickness." His brigade engaged heavily at Gaines's Mill, and by the time they entered the fight at Malvern Hill, "I witnessed acts of cowardice that is disgraceful to Southern character." He insisted, "If the enemy had known what an unaccountable panic would seize on our men as they came under fire, they would have cut us up, but they were just as bad off." Stunned by the widespread misconduct and dismayed by a society that could produce so many scamps, Colquitt admitted, "I was discouraged and demoralized." He concluded, "This is the secret history of the fight which you will not see published."[11]

For many regiments, this was their first battle, and it showed. In early June, Wylie Scott of the 57th Virginia expressed doubts over the ability of his comrades to execute in combat. "Our Regiment is not composed of the best material by any means," he explained, "and I think the first battle we get into none will be left to report how many are missing for we are running stock." The officers, he complained, knew little of their duties and "stand low in the estimation of the men." When they finally did see some action, at Malvern Hill, "our Brigade run like the dickence long before we got to the enemy," he described, "a perfect pell mell." Guns and hats "were strewn in our stampede in all directions."[12]

In fact, Scott's regiment and brigade actually did suffer heavy losses before and during their stampede rearward, and they were not the only commands that fell apart. During a precursor to the Seven Days' Battle, a sharp struggle for some woods around King's School House or Oak Grove on June 25, Lt. Col. Samuel Walkup of the 48th North Carolina Infantry had a terrible time trying to control his men. As with Scott's command, this was their initial exposure to combat. Approaching the picket line, their brigade commander ordered them to lie down and wait. Stress mounted. "Some of our Regt. suddenly took sick and fell back to the rear." Finally, the remainder stood up and pressed on toward some woods. Enemy fire grew heavy, and several key members of the 48th went down. Again, soldiers hugged the ground, drawing heavy fire, unable to return it without excessive exposure. Under pressure, Walkup's command dissolved. He realized that of the 450 he had taken into the fight, only a few dozen remained. Some dodged to the rear and collected behind a woodpile; others fled toward a house, defended by artillery. Unable to hold the position with so few men, Walkup fell back toward the stacks of firewood, where he tried to reorganize his command and lead it back into the fight. At that time, Brig. Gen. Robert Ransom rode up and scolded him with the question, " 'Col. Walkup, what does this all mean?' " Walkup explained he was trying to rally the men, but they were not budging. Ransom then pulled a pistol and stormed behind the woodpile, threatening to shoot anyone who refused to reform. Unfortunately, the target for his accusation of cowardice was a wounded major.

Walkup twice ordered the color bearer to come out so that the troops would rally around him, and both times he dodged the duty. After some squabbling, an officer volunteered to take the flag, and with Ransom alongside, Walkup and some 100 men re-entered the fight. Bolstered by reinforcements from

The Valley Pike was a major thoroughfare that Jackson and later Lee exploited. The road was macadamized, with small stones covering it. Macadamized roads eased wagon movements all year round but took a horrible toll on bare feet and shoes. *National Archives*

Confederate winter quarters at Manassas in 1862. Soldiers became adept at erecting structures from logs, planed wood, and other materials to keep themselves warm during the cold weather, when campaigning became very difficult. *Library of Congress*

This is an 1862 sketch by A. C. Redwood, perhaps the best Confederate sketch artist during the war, of an artillerist in Virginia leaning on his piece. His nice new uniform would soon become threadbare, and replacement garments seldom matched. Like so many of his comrades, he may have gone barefoot for a time. *Author's collection*

This sketch depicts Confederate soldiers crossing the Potomac River during the raid into Maryland in 1862. Soldiers removed their shoes, rolled up their pants, and waded across the river. *Battles and Leaders of the Civil War, vol. 2, p. 621*

The Richmond Arsenal produced the bulk of the ordnance for the Army of Northern Virginia. The photograph depicts the arsenal shortly after the explosion and fire that killed forty-three female employees and injured another twenty-five. The arsenal shut down temporarily, forcing Lee to replenish his supply with artillery ammunition from South Carolina. Shells from South Carolina played a significant role in the outcome of the Battle of Gettysburg. *Library of Congress*

The Confederate prison called Castle Thunder in Richmond was a converted warehouse. "You her [hear] a heap of talk a bowt that place a being such a bad place," one soldier explained to his wife. "I had as soon bee in thar as any other place in Richmon." Imprisonment there may have saved his life. It kept him out of the Gettysburg campaign. *Library of Congress*

A slave family fleeing with Pope's army as it retreated northward. The advance of the Union army offered slaves a chance to escape to freedom. *Library of Congress*

Confederate entrenchments along the Orange Plank Road in the Battle of the Wilderness in May 1864. The photograph gives a good sense of the denseness of the trees and tangled brush. *Library of Congress*

Confederate works around Petersburg. Logs and earth offered protection from enemy fire. Summer heat turned the dirt floors into a choking dust. During rainy periods, mud, pools of water, and even ice formed, making soldiers, particularly barefoot men, extremely uncomfortable. *Library of Congress*

As this sketch demonstrates, Confederate soldiers regularly plundered dead and wounded Yankees for clothing, equipment, food, and valuables. Some even robbed from their own dead and wounded. *Pictorial War Record: Battles of the Late Civil War*

This sketch depicts the formidable works at Hatcher's Run during the Petersburg Campaign. Soldiers on both sides became very good at erecting strong works with earth and timber. *Harper's Pictorial History of the Civil War*

These Confederate works around Petersburg provide a glimpse of the conditions in which Lee's soldiers lived from summer 1864 until early April 1865. Gabions—sticks woven together into huge baskets that were filled with earth—served as walls for bombproofs. *Library of Congress*

A dead Confederate soldier, probably a North Carolinian in Ewell's Corps, had fought from behind breastworks in action near Spotsylvania on May 19, 1864. *Library of Congress*

This Confederate soldier, probably a North Carolinian in Ewell's Corps, was killed in action near Spotsylvania on May 19, 1864. *Library of Congress*

These Confederate soldiers, probably North Carolinians in Ewell's Corps, were killed in fighting near Spotsylvania on May 19, 1864. Federal soldiers in the background lined them up for burial. Note the variation and quality of their clothing, compared with that of the Union troops. *Library of Congress*

This chilling photograph depicts a barefoot Confederate soldier, perhaps as young as fourteen, who was killed outside a bombproof in the trenches of Fort Mahone southeast of Petersburg on April 2, 1865. *Library of Congress*

other regiments, they drove back the Federals and cleared the woods. The regiment suffered 105 casualties. In his after-action report, Ransom praised the unit, reminding his superiors that it had organized just two months earlier and claiming, "I am happy to have witnessed its courage." Walkup, in his diary, had very different words for them.[13]

In the case of the 48th North Carolina, as time would prove, it did not possess an unusual number of shirkers and cowards. Walkup's regiment suffered problems with the way the men were introduced into battle and the critical casualties it took. Had the generals brought them up from the rear and thrown them into the fight immediately, the men might have held fast. Instead, they lay down in the rear of the picket lines and watched as stretcher bearers and fellow soldiers carried dead and wounded men through the line. That anguish, combined with the usual fears about entering battle for the first time, unnerved large numbers of troops. When key officers went down with wounds, or were killed outright, soldiers lost the critical, stabilizing force in their companies. Lacking faith in their officers' successors, the men refused to return to combat, despite pleas and threats. Scattered across the battlefield were similar breakdowns of cohesion and command authority.

In a short time, memory transformed failure into achievement and camouflaged misdeed with heroism. As D. R. E. Winn, a wealthy prewar physician and officer in the 4th Georgia Infantry, commented wryly, "Scores of incidents of the battle will never cease to be fabricated while men's brains can conjure up a chimera." With frequent retelling, soldiers absorbed and incorporated one another's stories into their own. "Loud and constant are the tales told of incidents that were and things that never were," Winn elaborated, "by men who saw & men who didn't see, by men whom others saw in the battle and men whom nobody saw in the battle but many saw miles away." The cataclysmic nature of the fight and the passion of the human mind to build acceptance and to gain vindication combined to form a new, inclusive reality.[14]

Yet there was no hiding the destruction of Seven Days'. Huge patches of timber had been mowed down to man-sized heights. Weapons were left scattered over the ground, with Confederate troops swapping their old muskets for superior Yankee firearms. Federal troops piled up knapsacks for body cover. In their haste to abandon the field, the Yankees left their personal possessions behind. "The men pilage them unmercifully," a Virginian alerted his mother, "and what they do not want they throw away." As Rebel attackers overran Union encampments, troops ransacked them, too. "In many instances fire had been applied to tents & property," commented a South Carolinian, "but very often hundreds of quarters were left just as they had been used—half-written letters lying upon desks unclosed and inky pens dashed down in flight."[15]

Bodies, both human and animal, littered the field. Once Rebel troops cleared an area of enemy troops, ambulance after ambulance hauled the wounded to hospitals. "Now came the busiest time of the surgeons," recorded physician James R. Boulware of South Carolina. In no time, he had a two-acre lot filled with casualties. Because the Confederates ultimately gained possession of the entire battlefield in Seven Days', thousands of Union wounded fell into their hands. "The dead and wounded of the yankies lay unburied and uncared for for three or four days," Pvt. Charles Kerrison alerted his sister, "our men and surgeons having enough to do to attend to our own."[16]

The nature of much of the fighting during the Seven Days' was close range, leaving bodies of Union and Confederates interspersed on the ground. In the heat of late June Virginia, flesh rapidly decomposed, overpowering the senses. Two days after Malvern Hill, a Rebel soldier reported that Yankee dead lay all over a ten-mile area. Rebels had not gotten around to burying the Yankees yet, "and the field smells so bad that I don't know how we will live if we stay here long." Several days later, Georgia captain William Plane informed his wife, "The air is putrid with decaying bodies of men & horses." Ten days after the fighting had ceased, a North Carolina soldier marching from the front toward Richmond insisted the rancid scent had not abated. "It was almost enough to take ones breath (the awful smell)," he told a girlfriend.[17]

The entire scene—the sights, the sounds, the smells, the destruction, and the killing and maiming of thousands of soldiers and animals—beggared description. Nothing in American history had approached the human disaster of the Seven Days', and the magnitude of the cataclysm stunned even the most dedicated soldiers. Wade Hampton, a superb cavalry commander, admitted to a family friend, "The sight of that fearful 'battle week' were enough to quell the passions of the angriest heart." After scanning a field of decaying men and horses, Plane erupted, "My God, My God, what a scourge is war."[18]

Although they continued to believe in the Rebel cause, many no longer found glory in combat. "I have bin in one battle and that satisfied me with war," Pvt. Haban R. Foster confided to his siblings, "and I would beg to be excused next time for I tell you there is no fun in standing and letting an enemy shoot at you with there cannons and shot and shell flying as thick as hail and the grape and canister flying between the shot and shells." Cavalry private Noble J. Brooks was detached on picket duty when the battle began, and in his search to link up with his comrades, he witnessed "heart rending sights": wounded hobbling off the battlefield, soldiers burned from powder explosions, and destruction all around him. "I tell you of a truth," he wrote to his mother, "a battle field is awful." To see "angry warriors rushing upon each other, yelling like so many hell hounds from the infernal regions, with glittering steel and brazen guns, eager for each other's destruction and when you see hundreds of bombs bursting and men falling, horses running away, killing themselves and riders—cannon firing—clouds of smoke and dust rising—cannon balls tearing up the earth and cutting down timber—ambulances and men running hither and thither getting the wounded away, many wounded getting themselves and other wounded away, as bloody as butchered hogs," and all this chaos compounded by the "cracking of thousands of musketry" the "roar-roar" of cannon fire, and the feeling of earth trembling under foot, shattered his faith in humanity. After helping a wounded man to the hospital, he heard a woman cry in anguish over her loss. Suddenly, it dawned on him, "if all the women North and South would come upon the hills and valleys around Richmond and could see at once the many slain of their Fathers, husbands, sons, brothers, and lovers, that their weeping and wailing would be such that it would wring tears from angelic eyes, and that there would be a ten fold greater clamor for peace among them than there ever was for war." Women, he believed, deserved considerable blame for this disaster. "Men love to fight too well to ever need the example and persuasion of women to excite them to war."[19]

Some slacking aside, the Rebel army on the whole fought with a desperate bravery, to the point of foolhardiness. Time after time, they stormed enemy works, armed with muskets and an old fox-hunting cry ultimately called the Rebel Yell, for "encouraging each other and confusing and terrorizing the enemy." Repelled again and again, the Confederates constantly regrouped and renewed their assaults, racking up massive casualties. In the 1st South Carolina Rifles, twenty men left their sickbeds to join comrades in the fight at Gaines's Mill. Against artillery and infantry, they charged with fixed bayonets, fought hand-to-hand. Without support, they were compelled to withdraw. Of the original 515 men in that attack, only 149 returned unscathed. Other regiments suffered almost as much. The 4th Texas Infantry had 253 losses at Gaines's Mill; the 44th Georgia had 335 men killed or wounded at Mechanicsville; at Gaines's Mill and Glendale, the 14th Alabama endured 335 casualties, the 19th Mississippi just ten fewer; in three fights, losses in the 20th North Carolina totaled 380, including 93 killed. "The enemy is giving way everywhere and our boys don't stop for breastworks nor embankments," crowed Virginian Henry Owen to his wife on the second-to-last day of the battle. "The yankee prisoners say our men fight like devils and nothing can stand before such men."[20]

On numerous occasions, extraordinary efforts on the regimental and, occasionally, brigade level bailed out tactical incompetence among senior field commanders. Brigadier and major generals ordered frontal assaults against fortified Yankee positions, hurling men into battle without a clear understanding of what they were up against, and failing to coordinate with adjacent units. Almost no one was innocent. So clouded was Jackson's mind in his exhaustion that nearly twenty months later, an engineer on his staff had to explain the Battle of Gaines's Mill to him. "He says that he never before had a clear idea of that fight," Capt. James Keith Boswell recorded. With Jackson unable to turn the Yankees in a timely fashion, others struck enemy forces in more fortified positions, with Confederate infantry paying an exorbitant price. Only Rebel élan and dash enabled them to carry the day.[21]

Effective communication had broken down in the army under Johnston; Lee failed to restore it. In his first major battle, Lee attempted to direct too many commands, and he could never position them at the right place and the right time. Jackson, Longstreet, D. H. Hill, A. P. Hill, Magruder, Huger, Holmes, McLaws, and Stuart all received orders directly from Lee. This forced

Lee to delve into too many details, to dip into levels of control that an army commander should rarely, if ever, venture. Although he had formulated a wonderful concept, Lee could not stay on top of all nine commanders, and execution stalled.[22]

A lack of effective combat support and staff work worsened the problems for Lee and the army. Even though Virginians composed a substantial portion of the army, and many of them came from the area just east of Richmond, commanders inexcusably suffered from poor guides and inaccurate maps. Lee's staff officers failed to take charge and at times issued confusing orders. With a rapidly advancing front, supply trains could not keep up with their units, and men had to live off anything they could take from the Federals. When soldiers had to plunder Yankee camps for food, it diminished combat strength and impaired effective pursuit. Those not fortunate enough to have access to enemy knapsacks went hungry. On other occasions, ordnance wagons got lost from their artillery batteries or failed to keep up, and when Confederate attacks needed fire support, they received little. Even when they were fully supported, Federal artillery outgunned them. The organization of Confederate artillery, attaching a battery to each brigade and holding a few batteries in reserve, diluted their firepower against massed Yankee artillery. Despite terrain that frequently did not suit the use of artillery, Federals employed it skillfully, while Confederates did not. As Lee's chief of artillery Brig. Gen. William N. Pendleton pithily assessed, "too little was thrown into action at once; too much was left in the rear unused."[23]

Lee himself was dissatisfied with the battle. His troops performed admirably, but he could not manage to deliver a powerful blow to his injured, retreating adversary. To his wife, he admitted, "Our success has not been as great or complete as I could have desired, but God knows what is best for us." In his report after the campaign, Lee stated matters more candidly: "Under ordinary circumstances the Federal Army should have been destroyed." While he did not blame anyone outright, the tone of his campaign correspondence indicated dissatisfaction with the level of aggressiveness of Magruder, Holmes, and Huger. Lee understood that in order to compensate for superior enemy numbers and equipment, his army must maintain the initiative—it must dictate to the best of its ability how, where, and when it fought. He could excuse excessive aggressiveness; he could not excuse timidity.[24]

The campaign taught Lee many lessons about personnel and organization, which he would attempt to correct or improve in the coming weeks. Before the battle began, Confederate authorities had designated Magruder for another assignment. Lee let him go—to the west—as well as Holmes and Huger, who headed south. He may not have engineered their departure, but he did not lift a finger to stop it. Within six weeks, Lee tacitly established two wings in the army, commanded by Jackson and Longstreet, elevating their responsibilities and easing his own burden, allowing him to concentrate on larger concerns. To address the imbalance in artillery effectiveness, Pendleton took charge. He embarked on a plan to reorganize that branch, a project he would complete in early October.[25]

Even though Lee expressed frustration with the outcome of the campaign and dissatisfaction with his own performance, the army had achieved its fundamental goal. As he concluded in his report, "The siege of Richmond was raised, and the object of a campaign, which had been prosecuted after months of preparation at an enormous expenditure of men and money, completely frustrated." The Rebels seized 51 artillery pieces, 31,000 small arms—equal or superior to anything the Confederates carried into battle—10,000 sets of accouterments, and 6,000 knapsacks. Nearly all of those items were usable, and the army badly needed the small arms, especially the rifled muskets.[26]

As the Confederate army pounded away at Federal forces, Lee's reputation rose quickly in the eyes of his soldiers. Occasionally, they caught a glimpse of him, but mostly they only observed his handiwork. Union troops cobbled together defensive positions, and Rebels drove them out; each abandoned Yankee position removed them farther and farther from Richmond. Despite the heavy losses, the sight of bluecoats falling back exhilarated the troops. A man in the 10th Virginia, approaching the scene of fighting at Gaines's Mill, boasted to a cousin, "I never will forget the noble appearance of Lee as he rode by our regiment." At that moment, men from Hood's Texas Brigade had just launched an assault on the Union works. Lee stopped and listened awhile. Then, according to the eyewitness, "his face brightened up as he said, 'we are chasing them now' and on we pitched with redoubled effort." The succeeding day, rock-solid commander and tough critic Maj. Gen. Lafayette McLaws informed his wife, "General Lee is rapidly regaining, if he has not already regained entirely, the confidence of the army and the people as a skillful and even dashing officer." McLaws placed matters in succinct terms when he explained, "The criterion in military matters is success, and up to this hour the combinations of General Lee have been of the most marked, decided, and successful." He then closed with a bit of enthusiastic insight: "You cannot imagine how gratifying is the feeling to Soldiers to know that their Chief is Competent to all positions."[27]

After the battle, once soldiers had a chance to explore the field and examine carefully what the army had achieved, they sang Lee's praises to loved ones at home. "It was consummate generalship that drove McClellan from his fortifications," insisted a Virginian to his wife. Troops affixed no blame for the heavy Rebel losses on the army commander. "General Lee has certainly won his laurels," a Texan wrote. "The plan of the campaign was certainly well conceived, and it was not Genl. Lee's fault that it was not well executed." After the campaign closed, a North Carolina officer described Lee to his father as a "large, stout man, somewhat inclined to corpulency," who "rides from one point to another as quietly as a farmer would ride over his farm." With evident pride, the officer concluded, "He has the reputation of being the best strategist in America."[28]

Because of the public's fixation on Jackson, most civilians assumed that the hero of the Valley Campaign had once again saved Richmond, particularly because he spearheaded the flank attack. A cute joke circulated, asking why McClellan had failed to take Richmond: " 'Because there is a *Stonewall* to climb A *Longstreet* that never turns, two *Hills* to pass and an impassable *Branch* to wade.' " Other versions included a *Pickett* to pass and rough *Rhoades* (Rodes) to travel over. Nowhere could they work *Lee* into that tale.[29]

A major reason civilians failed to credit Lee with success was that newspapers doled out praise to the general stingily. The schizophrenic *Charleston Mercury*, which lost no opportunity to slam President Davis and everyone linked to him, argued that "McCLELLAN has been out-generaled" on July 1 yet one week later bashed Lee for his "blundering manner" of pursuit and insisted that he lacked "practical generalship." Other, less one-sided newspapers emphasized the defeat of McClellan and his grand army rather than the triumph of Lee and his army. When they did focus on Confederates, newspapers described the movements of Jackson, Longstreet, A. P. Hill, Magruder, Huger, and others, ignoring Lee. On June 28, the *Augusta Daily Constitutionalist* reported Jackson in command. In other papers, stories so rarely mentioned Lee that someone could read wartime columns daily and not know he commanded the army. Around the Confederacy, most newspapers drew their stories initially from the Richmond papers, fixating on Jackson and other subordinate commanders.[30]

The first notice of Lee's role in the battle came in a letter to the editor of the *Richmond Enquirer* from someone who was most likely an officer. The individual complained that there was "in certain quarters a disposition to ignore the fact that we owe, in an eminent degree, our recent great victory to General Lee, and to ascribe to others the praise justly due to his admirable and successful strategy." Prompted by this suggestion, the editors of the *Enquirer* finally admitted, "The result of the conflict thus far is a splendid tribute to the capacity of our Commanding General Robert E. Lee." They concluded, "The facts when analysed, as we hope soon to be better able to do, will display a combination of strategy, prudence, vigor, and sagacity in planning the attack, that have rarely been equalled in the history of military operations." Other papers were slow to respond. As late as July 10 and 11, in a two-part series under the title, "The Masterly Strategy and Generalship of Commanders of the Confederate Army," the *Atlanta Southern Confederacy* referred to Lee only once and awarded Johnston equal credit and billing for the success of the Richmond campaign.[31]

Eventually, however, Lee emerged as the hero of the hour. He had taken command at a critical moment, instilled a fresh focus and a new efficiency in his troops, and then whipped the touted Yankee army, driving it twenty miles to the rear and saving the nation's capital. Slow to admit their snub, newspapers eventually came around to praise Lee. On July 14, the editor of the *Richmond Whig* asserted that many civilians had skillfully manipulated the story of Confederate successes and failures, boosting the standing of their favorites and denigrating the reputations of others. Lee was a particular target. "Disparagement, sarcasm and ridicule have made him the mark of many a flying arrow," the paper explained. "Now comes his reward." Lee took the helm with Yankees at the gates of Richmond, and he quietly formed his plan of action and stuck with it, despite doubts and criticism. "He has amazed and confounded his detractors by the brilliancy of his genius, the fertility of his resources, his energy and daring. He has established his reputation forever, and has entitled himself to the lasting gratitude of his country." Lee, who had "met injustice without a murmur, now seems to almost hide from praise."[32]

The image of McClellan's massive army cowering under the protection of Yankee gunboats elicited delight across the Confederacy and restored order to the Southern universe, which had anticipated such great achievements from its soldiers, only to suffer a steady string of setbacks at the hands of the Yankees. A siege would surely have resulted in the fall of Richmond. Without the Confederate industrial hub and the nation's capital, secessionists could not have prosecuted the war for very long. In just thirty days, Lee had completely altered the fortunes of the Confederacy. In the *Atlanta Southern Confederacy*, Corporal James Adair of the 8th Georgia explained to his newspaper audience, "At many times we were in the midst of showers of shot and shell, from which escape seemed impossible. I tried to put my trust in God and Gen. Lee. The former had the power to protect us from the shafts of death hurled at us by the enemy, while the latter led us through Yankee camps, driving back, capturing thousands of Yankees and their 'baggage.' "[33]

From his position outside Richmond, Pvt. Charles Friend admitted that this was the first time since the evacuation of Yorktown that he felt optimistic of Confederate independence. "I do hope that as we have so uncoiled the twists of the great Anaconda," Friend played off the derisive name for Union strategy, "God will vouchsafe us an escape from his embrace and also grant that we may so make them feel the ills of War, that they will most cheerfully consent to our governing ourselves by such laws as we the governed may deem most conducive to our happiness and prosperity." With Richmond safe and Lee at the helm, soldiers in the Army of Northern Virginia looked toward an offensive that took the fight to Yankee territory. That, they believed, would bring the war to a close. At the time, Davis and Lee were plotting just such a campaign.[34]

Chapter 13

———◦●◦———

TAKING WAR TO THE ENEMY

Back in May 1861, seventeen-year-old Private James Williams had expressed dismay over the loss of an opportunity to fight the Yankees in defense of his native state. Fourteen months of time and a lifetime of experience later, he had witnessed enough bloodshed and destruction to demand that the Confederacy exact revenge by going on the offensive. "I take it for granted, and I do hope too, that the policy of our generals now, will be to carry the war to the enemy's country," he wrote to his aunt several days after the close of the Seven Days' Battle. "I want to see Washington, Philadelphia and New York surrender to Confederate authorities and those vile fanatics that inhabit the northern states made to *feel* what war is." The surest way to Confederate independence and peace, Williams believed, was for the Northern public to feel the hard hand of war. "They will never *realize* what war is, until it is carried into their own country and the *people* made to suffer *directly* from the ravages of a hostile army."[1]

This element of hatred, and the passion for revenge that it engendered, spread among nearly all Confederates, regardless of rank. Before the war, many had held Northerners in disdain, and some even despised them. But war enriched their venom and universalized it. In late January 1861, Thomas J. Jackson, professor at Virginia Military Institute, explained to his nephew that if the North "should endeavor to subjugate us, and thus excite our slaves to servile insurrection in which our families will be murdered without quarter or mercy, it becomes us to wage such a war as will bring hostilities to a speedy close," including the practice of showing no quarter—taking no prisoners. Still, Jackson doubted there would be war, and he was not even sure Virginia would have to leave the Union. A year of fighting, however, had darkened Jackson's sentiments dramatically. In early 1862, he endorsed a suggestion to strike at Philadelphia. Several weeks later, Jackson anticipated "war in earnest" in the upcoming spring campaign and believed the Confederacy should "make short work of it." At times, his hatred for Yankees bubbled to the surface. On one occasion, when Ewell complained to him that hogs were rooting around and even eating the Yankee bodies lying just beyond Confederate lines, Jackson injected a macabre quip: "I knew a hog was not particular about what it ate but I gave them credit for having better taste than to eat a Yankee." He once confessed that "the only objection he had to Genl Lee was that he did not hate Yankees enough." Lee, however, bore his own animus toward the Yankees. In mid-1863, when Federals sought permission to disinter dead Federal troops and bring their bodies home, Lee authorized the removal, commenting to his chief surgeon that he " 'did not want a single Yankee on our soil *dead* or *alive.*' "[2]

Other Rebels thirsted for vengeance. "May God avenge us our infernal enemies—and if I ever forgive them it is more than I Expect," a soldier confessed in his diary. He knew that religion taught him to pardon his enemies, but he simply could not do it. "How can one forgive such enemies as we are contending against?" he pondered. "Despoiling us of our property, driving us from our homes & friends and slaying our best citizens on the field are hard crimes to forgive—At any rate," he continued, "let me have a chance to retaliate & then I can forgive with a better grace." Porter Alexander, a West Point graduate in 1857 and an ascending star in the Confederate army, told several officers, " 'It is my greatest comfort to know that I have killed some of them with my own hands, I have shot them with muskets and artillery and have seen them fall and afterwards went there and found them dead.' " He concluded by asserting, " 'if they should kill me today and I had but time for one thought before I died it would be that my account with them was more than even.' "[3]

The loss of Rebel soldiers from combat or disease fueled the intensity. As Georgia private Benjamin Prescott seethed in a letter to his sister over the death of brother Homer, "while my grief was great, like you, my scorn and hatred of the hell hounds, who uselessly wage this bloody and unnatural war, was intensified, like the gathering of wrath against the day of wrath." They had simply sought their right to peaceful independence, the same as their Revolutionary ancestors, and they perceived this invasion as illegitimate and the wartime fatalities as wholly unnecessary.[4]

But this bitterness toward Yankees, this passion to take the war to the enemy, emanated from more than simply the heavy loss of life. While Southerners grieved over deceased or maimed loved ones, most had fortified themselves in anticipation that some would die in the war. The soldiers often counseled folks at home to prepare for such an eventuality. "If it should be his will that I fall in this terrible struggle," instructed Virginia sergeant Thomas Green Penn, "you must my dear ma give me up willingly, and consider me a sacrifice offered up for our dear cause, and consider that it is but the fate of many sons equally as dear to their mothers as yours."[5]

What sparked their fury was failure to accomplish their goal. Confederates had enlisted to secure independence and slavery and to protect loved ones and property, yet Union forces had threatened each of those things. Even though the Army of Northern Virginia had beaten McClellan and his army back from the gates of Richmond, the Union troops had approached to within eyesight of the Rebel capital. Yankees had marched and fought their way through much of Virginia and they still controlled substantial portions of the state. Southern whites could proclaim the existence of a new nation, draft a constitution, and even hold elections, but as long as Union soldiers occupied portions of the Confederacy, they had not achieved true independence, nor had they shielded loved ones from the enemy.

Worse, the institution of slavery had suffered a serious blow in the war, as several hundred slaves per day on average reached sanctuary and freedom behind Federal lines. Early in the war, Union generals and then Congress authorized the seizure of slaves who worked on Confederate military projects, declaring them contraband of war. As these bondsmen arrived at Union lines with families in tow, many Federal officers refused to send their wives and children back into slavery.[6]

Whenever Federal armies penetrated into Confederate states, slaves flocked to them for freedom. While McClellan's army crept up the Peninsula, dozens of slaves from two plantations owned by Edmund Ruffin, the Fire-Eater and oldest Rebel private, deserted the fields for freedom night after night, to the complete mystification of their owner. "Why this property & Malbourne should be especially losers of slaves, cannot be understood," he jotted in dismay, "for nowhere were they better cared for, or better managed & treated, according to their condition of slavery." Each Union military advance uncovered farms, plantations, and towns, and as Rebel authorities fell back, locals lost their ability to keep slaves at home. "They are running away every night & when I go to bed, I expect to find some of ours gone," Virginian Benjamin Fleet recorded in his journal during the campaign. "*Dreadful*, DREADFUL times," he complained forlornly. Another Virginian from Hanover County protested that when Johnston withdrew from the Manassas-Centerville line, he uncovered their homes. Slaves rode off in buggies and carriages, and "We could do nothing but look on and see our property skedaddle." He then concluded with the potent words, "Men went to bed rich and got up poor."[7]

This slow breakdown of their coveted institution aroused Southerners' greatest fear: a loss of control that could lead to servile insurrection. Since the early days of African enslavement in the mainland colonies, Southerners had been wary of slave revolts. John Brown's raid on Harpers Ferry in 1859 brought a heightened awareness and sensitivity to uprisings, and the war elevated the issue from a concern to a real possibility. During late summer 1861, Union Maj. Gen. John C. Frémont declared all slaves of pro-Confederates in Missouri free. Lincoln ultimately overturned the order, but Frémont's action sparked a debate over the merits of emancipation. In fall 1861, several Northern newspapers endorsed arming slaves, and rumors circulated that Lincoln's secretary of war, Simon Cameron, supported the idea. Southerners were incensed. "The hellish atrocity of these wretches exceeds all belief," D. H. Hill vented. "The whole world will be astonished at their baseness." Brigadier General Cadmus Wilcox, a West Point graduate and a leading expert on the rifled musket, insisted Cameron and others "are for raising a servile war if they can. Should they do that," he justified, "we should in no battle Show them any quarter."

Before the opening of the Seven Days' Battle, Longstreet sought to inspire his men for combat through the use of racial fear. He reminded them that Frémont, the Republican presidential candidate in 1856, had declared slaves in Missouri free, and he directly linked emancipation to a slave rebellion. "Already has the hatred of one of their great leaders attempted to make the negro your equal by declaring his freedom," Longstreet pronounced. "They care not for the blood of babes nor carnage of innocent women which servile insurrection thus stirred up may bring upon their heads." By midsummer, the Union army had brought its first blacks officially into military service, confirming Longstreet's deep fears.[8]

Lee's army volunteered to defend loved ones and their property from invaders. Once again, they had not failed completely, but they also had not succeeded. In some areas, Union forces had penetrated a hundred miles into Virginia, exposing thousands of families, their homes, and their personal property to the wrath of Federal soldiers. Rather than confront Union soldiers, citizens had fled, leaving their abandoned property as an inviting target for Federal mayhem. Brigadier General Alexander Lawton informed his wife, "My heart is touched daily at the sad condition of Virginia. The homes that are deserted & families wandering about appeal to us to fight the battle of Virginia." Yankees ransacked homes, shattered china, trashed libraries, broke furniture, confiscated livestock, trampled crops, torched barns, and dismantled fences. Anything they could not or would not take they destroyed or damaged. According to one Rebel soldier who witnessed Union handiwork, "a party of malicious monkeys let loose in the house could not have procured a more ridiculous scene of confusion." Even in churches they drew caricatures of Davis and other Confederate leaders on the walls, accompanied by such threatening words as " 'Death to all traitors thus saith the Lord.' "[9]

These actions did more than simply convince Confederate soldiers how oppressive Yankee rule would be; the destruction and pillaging infuriated them. "If there is one degree of *hell* hotter than an other I think it will be retained for the Vandles who invade our homes, rob & distroy our property," a company-grade officer predicted to his wife. "Our men seem to be desperate on the subject and will fight bravely every opertunity that is offered." The plundering cut to the very core of their sense of masculinity. At the heart of Southern perceptions of manhood, even more central than notions of honor, rested the idea of protecting one's family and property—hearth and home. In nineteenth-century Southern parlance, a man without honor was dishonorable; a man who refused to protect his family and his home was no man at all. When Yankee armies invaded Virginia, and families had to abandon their homes or remained behind to confront Federals alone, Rebels had failed in their fundamental duty, both as soldiers and as men, especially if they made no effort to resist the Union onslaught. Confederate troops were desperate to retaliate because they had endured the humiliation of losing territory and exposing their own people to enemy invaders, thereby suffering two huge blows to their sense of masculinity.[10]

Confederates could not continue to stand on the defensive, await massive Federal advances, and then cobble together forces to repulse them. Each Union invasion uncovered more valuable Confederate terrain, exposing citizens and their property to humiliation and devastation. The Yankees had become too good at soldiering, with too many resources behind them, for Rebels to allow them to seize the initiative. Until the triumph in the Valley and around Richmond, Federals had won a string of victories that had shattered Southern complacency and, in some cases, had shaken Southern confidence. Notions that each Confederate soldier measured better than three or six or even ten Yankees proved absurd. "We have been boasting, and underrating our enemy, who is far superior to us in both force and every appliance of war," a Virginia regimental commander had commented back in February. As Federals advanced near Richmond, any thoughtful soldier in Lee's army knew he was in for a difficult struggle. "I think the fighting is now fully inaugurated and a succession of severe battles may be looked for," predicted Alabama private Otis Smith on the eve of Seven Pines, "and desperate fighting it will be too for however much it has been the fashion to depreciate Northern courage, we have found and shall still find them 'foemen' not unworthy of our steel." In order to win, Smith argued, "We have got to fight and to fight desperately."[11]

Even with the victory at Seven Days', Confederates had to acknowledge Union battlefield performance. By doing so, they elevated their own achievement, but these claims also reflected a new reality: Yankees made pretty good adversaries. "We have had to fight genuine yankies this time and also any quantity of foreigners," announced a South Carolina private to his sister. "The idea that they will not fight is exploded, and it puts our men to their best to whip them." Although many newspapers and some soldiers oversold the extent of the triumph in Seven Days', D. H. Hill's assessment very much reflected Lee's. "He is very far from being as much frightened and demoralized as represented," Hill noted. "The enemy has managed his retreat well & has fought with more desperation on the retreat than he did in his breastworks." A soldier in the Jeff Davis Legion explained to his father, "They are hard to conquer and will not give up yet." If the Confederacy yielded the initiative, overwhelming Federal resources would take their toll and eventually shift the balance to the armies of Lincoln.[12]

OVER THE COURSE of those fifteen months of war, sentiments on the collective nature of Yankee soldiers had blossomed into full-blown race hatred. Southerners perceived Yankees as a distinct set of beings, wholly different in behavior and motivation from themselves. "I don't see why it should be called a *civil* war," wondered a Louisianan. "We are not fighting our own people—but a race which is & has always been antagonistic in every particular to us—of a different country & of different pursuits." Division commander Lafayette McLaws instructed his men about the enemy, "He speaks and acts always for some tangible, interested, selfish motive." William Pegram, the Confederacy's heralded artillerist, referred to the enemy as "this ungodly, fanatical, depraved Yankee race." In the eyes of Southern troops, the Northern population comprised two types: self-centered, money-grubbing, principleless Yankees whose sole concern was to oppress Southerners for their own pathetic motives and the immigrants—worthless, filthy, stupid foreigners whom the Yankees had duped into fighting this war. Private Stephens Smith of the Hampton Legion stooped to give water to a wounded Yankee during Seven Days'. He asked the man what he was fighting for. In broken English, the Federal soldier replied, " 'I fight for the glorious Union and for the Flag which you have insult.' " Smith described him as a "poor ignorant devil" and claimed, "I do not suppose he had been a month in America yet he lay dying on the battle field a victim to the teachings of Lincoln & Seward dependent for his burial to the humanity of those he had come to slay."[13]

In Confederate phraseology, these Yankees were invaders, vandals, mercenaries, hirelings, or Hessians. They had trampled Southern rights, invaded their homeland, wrecked their property, and worst of all, they had done it for the basest motive of all—money. The idea that Federal soldiers could possibly have legitimate motives for fighting to keep the Confederacy in the Union was absurd. Only pecuniary rewards could induce anyone to take up arms against a free people seeking merely to exercise their legitimate rights, hence the label mercenaries, hirelings, and Hessians. They were detestable beings, and Southern soldiers hoped to exact a measure of revenge for their despicable behavior.

A YEAR EARLIER, Secretary of War Leroy Pope Walker had proposed a campaign that would plant the Confederate flag atop the Capitol Building in Washington and perhaps Faneuil Hall in Boston, a suggestion that sparked a firestorm of controversy, North and South. Newspaper editors cried for the Confederate seizure of Washington and the deliverance of Maryland into the Confederacy, yet they did not endorse the capture of Boston or even the invasion of free states. Davis, no idealist, prepared for war yet expressed hope for a peaceful separation and insisted that "all we ask is to be let alone." By the time Seven Days' concluded, sentiments in the Confederacy had shifted dramatically. On July 5, Davis issued a congratulatory order to the "Army of Eastern Virginia," applauding its soldiers for their valiant service and defining for them "your one great objective being to drive the invader from your soil and carry your standards beyond the outer boundaries of the Confederacy, wring from an unscrupulous foe the recognition of your birthright, community independence." Southern newspaper after Southern newspaper applauded and joined Davis's call for an advance into the North. The same day Davis issued his order, the *Richmond Dispatch* ran an editorial arguing, "At the earliest moment the enemy should be made to feel some of the horrors of invasive warfare." The *Mobile Advertiser* urged the Confederate government to invade the North to promote the peace party there. The *Augusta Daily Constitutionalist* blended retribution with sound policy. Its editors thought, "If an invading column can be spared now from Virginia to march across the Potomac and carry the war into the enemy's country, policy and a justifiable spirit of vengeance alike call for an onward movement across the Potomac."[14]

Soldiers in the Army of Northern Virginia, too, were in overwhelming accord. They had personally witnessed the destructive capabilities of Union troops, had looked into the teary eyes of refugees flocking to safety, and had observed the flight of slaves to Yankee sanctuary. A skillful and effective movement north of Maryland would drive the enemy from Confederate soil, salve their injured sense of masculine pride, enable them to reciprocate against the Northern population for the violations their own people had endured, and sour Northern public opinion for the war. An officer in the 57th Virginia wrote in June that he did not think the Confederacy could win the conflict unless its soldiers took the fight into the Northern states. "With an army in Maryland, & from thence marching into Pennsylvania, we will bring the war home to them & teach them the true meaning of the term 'Civil War,' in all its most hideous forms," he commented. "This & nothing else will bring them to their senses." Before the advance across the Potomac River, a Mississippi private predicted that based on the way Confederate troops behaved toward their own citizens, "our people will treat the Northerners most savagely." An Alabamian believed a move into Maryland and Pennsylvania would "bring the war to a close sooner than anything," because "they will then feel the horrors of the war & will be glad to have it ended." All three men had arrived at the opinion that the Confederacy must fight a defensive war by aggressive means.[15]

In fact, Davis had contemplated a movement northward for some time. During the first days of Lee's tenure as army commander, shortly after Jackson routed Banks and occupied the northern portion of the Shenandoah Valley, Jackson had called for reinforcements to launch a raid into Maryland and perhaps Pennsylvania, with the objective of siphoning manpower and resources away from McClellan. Lee and Davis had considered the proposal, and Lee had even directed some troops to bolster Jackson's command in anticipation of a strike across the Potomac River, but the scheme collapsed when Jackson had to fall back as Federals from the east and west converged on his supply line. At the conclusion of Seven Days', when an old friend proposed a campaign into Maryland and perhaps beyond to ease pressure on Richmond and Virginia, Davis endorsed the idea. "Indeed, such has been my purpose for many months," the president wrote, "and I have silently borne criticism on the supposition that I was opposed to offensive war, because to correct the error, would have required disclosure of facts which the public interest demanded should not be revealed." Although they had taken steps to bolster the ranks, they lacked the manpower strength to "ensure the plan's success." Davis assured his friend that "The General [Lee] is fully alive to the advantage of the present opportunity and will I am sure cordially sustain and boldly execute my wishes to the fullest extent of his power."[16]

Lee shared the sentiments of Davis and his soldiers that it was necessary to assume the offensive and take the war into the North, but first he had to deal with two enemy forces. Along the James River, McClellan's army hunkered down under cover of his gunboats. To the north, Lincoln had consolidated the various forces under a single commander, Maj. Gen. John Pope. Pope made pompous promises to impose harsher conditions on civilians in the occupied Confederacy, eliciting hostility from many sources, including Lee, who referred to him as "a miscreant." It was unclear whether the Federals intended to strike out for Richmond again on two fronts or to consolidate both forces into a single thrust on the Rebel capital from the north. One thing was certain in the mind of Lee and his men: The Union army would attempt to seize Richmond again. As a North Carolina private quipped in late July, "they say they will have Richmond or hell is their home and I fere hell will be their home be fore they ever get it." He concluded with the flourish, "god grant them a better place for it will be bad for them to miss richmond & get hell both."[17]

Not long after the end of Seven Days' Battle, Lee took steps to prepare the army for further combat. Unsure whether his people had truly whipped McClellan's army, or whether the Yankees had decided to regroup, reinforce the command, and then attempt another campaign against Richmond, Lee had to prepare for either eventuality. In the aftermath of the fight at Malvern Hill, the Confederate forces were in such a state of chaos that ranking officers believed further operations were impossible. Thousands of Confederates lay strewn across the slope, many in need of burial, with others crying out for medical attention; thousands more straggled away from their commands, either lost, in search of loved ones, or hunting plunder. It would take days for Lee and his subordinate officers to restore order. They buried the dead, cared for the wounded, rested, and refitted, and, perhaps most important, gathered up thousands of stragglers and returned them to their commands. To protect his existing troop strength, Lee canceled all furloughs and sought reinforcements to offset the heavy battlefield losses. The bulk of his army fell back to the vicinity of Richmond, a more central location and better defensive position where authorities could supply his army's needs more readily. Lee also took time to reorganize some brigades by state, in accordance with Davis's longstanding wishes.[18]

With Magruder, Huger, and Holmes gone, Lee decided to restructure his army for the upcoming campaign. Confederate law still did not allow for corps commands, so Lee designated two individuals, Longstreet and Jackson, as wing commanders. Apparently, Longstreet's failure at Seven Pines never came to Lee's attention, and he had handled a large command better than anyone else during Seven Days'. Jackson stumbled repeatedly throughout the campaign to protect Richmond, but his extraordinary service in the Valley, where he had directed an independent command skillfully, earned him the other wing.

For division commanders, Lee tapped individuals who had already served in that capacity and had graduated from West Point. Richard H. Anderson, a West Point graduate who filled in ably as head of the division when Longstreet supervised a battlefield as ranking officer, assumed permanent command with Longstreet's elevation. He joined David R. Jones, who had commanded a brigade at First Manassas and a division along the Peninsula, the redoubtable Lafayette McLaws, and crusty yet skilled D. H. Hill as division commanders under Longstreet. Among Jackson's division commanders was Charles S. Winder, an accomplished Marylander who had led the Stonewall Brigade and succeeded to Jackson's old command during the Seven Days'. Richard S. Ewell, the eccentric former Regular who fought at First Manassas and served Jackson well in the Valley, continued in command of his division.

The newcomer to Jackson's senior leadership was A. P. Hill. After Seven Days', a newspaper article trumpeted the achievements of Hill's division, and by doing so it demeaned the efforts of all other troops. Longstreet drafted some corrections, which he submitted to a different Richmond newspaper under the name of his assistant adjutant general, Moxley Sorrel. Several days later, Sorrel relayed an order to Hill, which the division commander childishly refused to accept or implement because it came from Sorrel. Longstreet then intervened and ordered Hill to obey, and when he refused, Longstreet sent an officer to arrest Hill. Meanwhile, Hill requested that Lee remove him from Longstreet's command, to which Longstreet consented. Lee defused the trouble by shifting Hill's division to Jackson's command.[19]

Lee also consolidated cavalry into a division. Stuart was the obvious choice for cavalry commander and received promotion to major general. Brigade commands went to the wealthy and well-connected South Carolinian Wade Hampton, who had also proven to be an excellent combat leader, and Fitz Lee, Lee's nephew.

As the army sought to recover and reorganize, Federal activity compelled Lee to react. Pope advanced southward from the Washington area to threaten one of Lee's critical supply lines. If Federals seized Gordonsville, they would sever the Virginia Central Railroad, which carried essential foodstuffs from the Shenandoah Valley to Richmond, and the Orange & Alexandria Railroad, which ran northeast toward Washington, D.C. On July 13, Lee ordered Jackson to take two divisions and some cavalry and march northward. His mission was to protect the railroad and to threaten to attack any Union thrust from Fredericksburg on Richmond. Within a week of Jackson's arrival at Gordonsville, Lee had concluded, "Pope is too strong to be allowed to remain so near our communications. He ought to be suppressed if possible." With A. P. Hill's Division and a Louisiana brigade as reinforcements, Lee again instructed Jackson, "I want Pope to be suppressed." In response to problems that had surfaced earlier, Lee counseled Jackson to devote personal attention to the well-being of the troops, consult the division commanders, and keep them informed of his plans. Once Jackson crushed Pope, the commanding general directed him to be prepared to return to Richmond, in the event McClellan advanced.[20]

Several times, Jackson attempted to deliver a blow against Pope but could not position his forces properly. Finally, on August 9, Jackson struck a portion of the Federal command at Cedar Mountain. In a nasty fight, the initial Confederate attack stalled and the initiative shifted to the Federals. The timely arrival of Rebel reinforcements enabled Jackson's combined force to sweep the field. Based on the intensity of fighting over several hours, a veteran thought "it was as great a battle as that of Manassas." One Virginia company entered the battle with thirty-nine men. Seventeen were killed, fifteen more were wounded, and only seven walked away uninjured. Once again, the Yankees had fought well, even hand-to-hand, but "all this was met by our Virginia lads with an ardor and coolness that they could not stand, and therefore retired leaving the field and woods strewed with their killed & wounded." Jackson lost over 1,400 men in the fight, but his army inflicted more than 2,400 casualties on the Yankees.[21]

Within days of Jackson's victory, Lee detected a shift of troops from the James River back north. He reacted boldly. The Lincoln government had abandoned the eastern approach and had elected to unite Pope's forces with McClellan's for a southward advance on Richmond. Lee viewed this as a golden opportunity. If he could combine the bulk of his army stationed around Richmond with Jackson's command, then move quickly while many of McClellan's men were in transit, the Confederates would outnumber Pope and perhaps "suppress" him, as Lee desired. By mid-August, Lee had sent Longstreet's columns to Gordonsville and personally followed shortly after. A plan to trap Pope with his back to the Rappahannock River backfired when Lee's nephew, Fitzhugh Lee, who had no idea of the critical nature of his assignment, dillydallied to gather forage, failed to strike Federal troops swiftly, and neglected to destroy the bridge over the river. Pope fell back across the river. Other attempts to turn Pope's eastern and western flanks went awry, too, due to high water and prompt Union responses.

Once Stuart's horsemen seized some of Pope's correspondence, which provided Lee with Pope's strength and Union intentions, Lee adopted an even bolder course of action. Jackson finally crossed the river and swung on a wide arc through a gap in the Bull Run Mountains, around Pope's army and into the Federal rear. In less than forty-eight hours, Jackson's columns marched more than fifty miles, brushed aside a small Union command at Bristoe Station with the aid of Stuart's cavalry, destroyed the bridge there, and seized Manassas Junction seven miles to the north, with bountiful supplies and Pope's headquarters train.[22]

Lee had divided his forces and sent Jackson's command into Pope's rear, placing it in a precarious position. Union reinforcements from the James River were accumulating in the Washington vicinity. A bold Yankee advance from north and south could trap and crush the isolated Confederates. Jackson

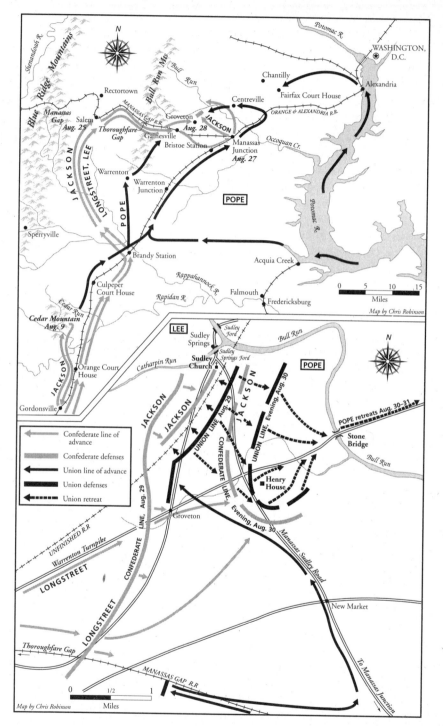

Second Manassas

selected an excellent defensive position, on some high ground shielded by heavy woods and guarded by a railroad cut. Reinforcements could take the same route as Jackson and join him readily, and in the event of a rapid Union concentration against him, his troops could fall back along a road through another gap in the Bull Run Mountains. Nonetheless, Jackson could not hold out for very long, and it was imperative that Longstreet's command unite with him. On the afternoon of August 26, Longstreet's men crossed the Rappahannock and traveled an impressive fourteen miles, but the next day they slowed, covering only six. On the morning of August 28, Longstreet began his advance without much urgency. Lee accompanied Longstreet and made no effort to spur him onward. After outflanking some resistance, Longstreet passed through the mountain gap, so that he could join with Jackson early the next day.

Jackson and his command, meanwhile, had to fend for themselves. On the afternoon of August 28, Jackson left his strong defensive position to attack some unsuspecting troops passing before him. As one of his enlisted men had prophetically advised his father, " 'Old Jack' can't stay within 5 miles of the Yankees without fighting." In no time, an entire Federal division confronted his forces, and in a vicious fight that lasted well into darkness, portions of the two sides hammered each other on open ground. Virtually devoid of any tactics, soldiers stood completely exposed, loading, firing, and absorbing musketry and artillery rounds. One regiment, the 26th Georgia Infantry, lost 72 percent of its men in the nasty slugfest. All told, nearly 2,500 men sustained wounds or were killed before the Federals finally withdrew.[23]

Jackson's attack at Brawner Farm (also called Groveton) convinced Pope that he must concentrate his command and eliminate the pesky Jackson before reinforcements arrived from Longstreet. Early on the following morning, Federals slammed into Jackson's command, and they continued to hammer away all day long. With stout resistance and a skillful deployment of his reserves, Jackson's men fought off enemy attackers, sometimes desperately. Longstreet reached a position west of the battlefield at about 9:00 A.M. and, as his troops arrived, he deployed them for combat. According to Longstreet, "My command was ready to receive any attack after 11 o'clock A.M. and *we all were particularly anxious to bring on the battle after* 12 M.; General Lee more so than the rest." The problem, Longstreet convinced Lee, was two large Union forces, which could bring their arms to bear on his flank if he should attack. All day long his command waited, looking for a chance to enter the fray. Finally, a shift of Union troops away from that left flank enabled Longstreet to launch an evening reconnaissance in force, with a division fortified by two brigades. Despite the darkness, John Bell Hood's command slammed into some Union troops and knocked them pell-mell off the high ground, about a mile south of Jackson's men. Hood had secured some valuable terrain from which to assault the following day.[24]

The next morning opened much like the previous day. Pope hurled column after column at Jackson's troops to pry them loose from their strong position.

According to a North Carolinian, "We slaughtered them like hogs[.] I never saw the like of dead men in all my life." Twice, Federals seized parts of the line. Rebel counterattacks drove the enemy back. When soldiers exhausted their ammunition supply, they resorted to hurling rocks at the Yankees, but they refused to cede that precious ground. The Rebel position had become increasingly desperate.[25]

To aid Jackson, Longstreet increased Col. Stephen Dill Lee's artillery to eighteen guns. From some high ground ideally situated to the south and west of Jackson's line, Lee's gunners pounded Yankee troops as they launched their attacks on the right portion of Jackson's line. Accurate cannon fire mowed down many who tried to cross the artillery front; those fortunate enough to make it across the open ground soon realized they were trapped. Jackson's command confronted them, and Lee's artillery fire prevented anyone from retreating across that treacherous landscape. Twice, Federals organized reserves to bolster the attack against Jackson, and twice the heavy fire of Lee's artillerists halted them from advancing.[26]

Just as Union momentum began to wane, Longstreet seized the moment to unleash his own attack. Wave after wave of screaming Rebel soldiers roared down on the enemy. The Yankees resisted bravely. As one South Carolinian in the charge reported, "The shower of balls, shells, grape, canister & c, as we advanced upon the Yankees at the double quick was perfectly furious, and it seems almost a miracle that any of our Regt escaped." On and on they rushed, shattering the Union ranks. Some men in his regiment captured a Union battery and turned the guns on the retreating foe. "We fought as grandly as any troops in the world," crowed the triumphant South Carolinian.[27]

Longstreet's attack had indeed routed the enemy. Unlike the first battle at Manassas, this time the Federals retained some order, and Pope cobbled together a strong defense near Henry House. Rebel troops continued to pound away, but just when a successful flank attack jeopardized the entire Yankee position, the Confederate advance lost its momentum. The onset of darkness, some confusion in the mind of division commander Maj. Gen. Richard H. Anderson over Longstreet's intention, and a failure to recognize the critical nature of the Union forces combined to convince Anderson not to press the enemy too strongly. Even as Jackson's ragged columns tried their best to squeeze from the north, Pope extricated the remainder of his command.

That night, Lee telegraphed Davis that the army that day had achieved a "SIGNAL VICTORY," but he knew that, again, he had failed to win decisively. Once more, he called on Jackson to undertake a circuitous march to trap Pope's command. Yet Jackson's men could deliver no more. After marching some fifty miles in two days, they had fought the enemy for three consecutive days more, suffering heavy losses. Bone weary and emotionally drained, Jackson's men gutted out a ten-mile march. The next afternoon, at Chantilly, they ran into a reinforced Union corps, and after a nasty little scrape amid heavy rains and lightning, the Confederates called off the pursuit.[28]

"None of the Richmond Battles was half so severe as this one," reported a Georgian to his sister. In victory, Lee's army had suffered some 9,000 losses, most of them on the field around Manassas. So many officers had fallen that a number of regiments marched away from the battlefield five days later under the command of captains. Well over 10,000 Federals were killed or wounded, and another 5,000 were taken as prisoners. "Surely," pined a Georgian, "this field has drunk sufficiently of human blood."[29]

Although the combined losses at Seven Days' were greater, they were not nearly as concentrated as at Second Manassas. Over several square miles of battlefield, nearly 3,000 were dead and perhaps 10,000 or more lay wounded. "I have walk over more ded yankes than ever want to doo agin," confessed a Florida private. Unlike Seven Days', the Manassas battlefield was far removed from Richmond, and the Confederates lacked the trained personnel and the facilities to care for so many fallen soldiers. According to one witness in the Jeff Davis Legion, it took two hundred ambulances five days to remove the wounded Yankees alone. For days, victims "lay among the festering and decaying mass of dead and dying uncared for." Those who could do so crawled under trees for shade and to waterholes for refreshment. His command arrived three days after the battle, and "As we neared the scene of conflict the stench from the already putrifying bodies of men and horses became disagreeable in the extreme."[30]

On September 4, as the Rebel army marched away from the Manassas battlefield, another Virginia private, this one an infantryman, expressed mixed sentiments over leaving behind unburied Yankee dead. "It is bad that the dead Yankees could not be buried as I don't like to see any human being lay on top of the earth and rot, but it is a fit emblem for the invader of our soil for his bones to bleach in the soil he invades, especially of a people that wish to be let along [alone] and settle down to their own peaceful pursuits."[31]

OVER THE COURSE of three months, Lee's army had not only driven a larger and better-equipped Union force away from the gates of Richmond, it had also routed a second army and cleared nearly all of Virginia of Federal presence. The Union retained possession only of pockets of Virginia territory. The Confederate retreats, the hardships, the failures East and West all seemed faint memories, as confidence in Lee and in the soldiers themselves soared. "Our advance to this place (near Bull Run)," staff officer Walter Taylor penned immediately after the battle, "was one of the boldest moves of our so called 'timid' General." North Carolina brigade commander Dorsey Pender, a West Point graduate and former Regular Army officer, evaluated Lee's performance even higher. "Gen. Lee has shown great Generalship and the greatest boldness," he trumpeted to his wife. "There never was such a campaign, not even by Napoleon." A Georgian concurred: "Gen. Lee stands now above all generals in modern history." He announced, "Our men will follow him to the end."[32]

With Union forces reeling from two powerful defeats, Lee finally elected to fulfill Davis's wishes and push northward into Maryland and, he hoped, beyond. Wartime devastation had so debilitated northern Virginia that Lee could not maintain his army there for long. Across the Potomac River he anticipated an abundance of grain fields and livestock to feed his troops and animals. Each day of support that his army drew from Marylanders and Pennsylvanians meant the Confederacy saved that much for itself. Amid those lush farms, Lee believed, his army could feed itself lavishly, while at the same time easing the burden on Southern farmers. By taking the fight across the Potomac, he would draw enemy soldiers from Confederate soil and enable Virginia farmers to harvest their own crops in peace and security. Perhaps he could sustain his forces there far enough into the fall that the Union would not be able to mount another offensive until the spring.[33]

Lee perceived other benefits as well. Freedom for his army to roam across Northern states, with Yankees powerless to check them, could damage the Lincoln administration in the upcoming congressional election. Perhaps the Rebels could even convince the North that the price for reunion was too high.

Lee also perceived a movement into Maryland as a means of broadening the Confederacy's support and bolstering his army. Losses in the two huge fights that summer had depleted his ranks, while the Union had increased its troop strength through recent recruitment efforts. Lee and others hoped to lure thousands of Marylanders, coerced into remaining in the Union, to Confederate banners to offset those wartime casualties. By drawing Union forces out of Virginia, too, Lee opened areas in Virginia once again to recruitment and conscription for his army.[34]

No doubt, his army was ill-supplied for a raid northward. Soldiers lacked proper clothing and shoes, and his army suffered from a shortage of wagons and animals. But Lee, a keen student of military history, fully grasped the psychological element to warfare. Not only had Lee seized the initiative, but the Army of Northern Virginia had also built a momentum. In the eyes of his men, and to an extent in the hearts of Yankee troops, a feeling of success for the Confederacy blossomed—an attitude of Rebel invincibility under Lee's leadership. Now was the time for a bold advance.[35]

Rebel soldiers overwhelmingly rejoiced at the prospect. The mere thought that they had completely reversed fortunes in the East, that they were devouring food and treading on the soil of Yankeedom, intoxicated them. Soldiers stripped off their pants, drawers, shoes, and stockings, holding them aloft with their weapons and ammunition, and plunged into the waist-deep Potomac. An officer thought his men resembled cranes, as they slowly, blindly picked their way across the rocky ford, searching with their feet for some smooth-edged rock on which to step. As they emerged on Maryland soil, "such a yell was never heard," so claimed a Georgia private. Bands struck up "Maryland, My Maryland," to the cheers of soldiers. An officer dipped his pencil into the river, sprinkled some water on his stationery, and then jotted the words, "'God bless the Potomac.'" Baltimorean Osmun Latrobe, one of Longstreet's staff officers, bent down and gulped a big drink to revive his taste for Maryland.[36]

Although everyone speculated, most soldiers had no clue where Lee intended to take them. Some thought Baltimore, others Philadelphia; most believed they would at least cross into Pennsylvania. "I do not understand the programme determined upon by Gen. Lee, but guess we will first clear Maryland of our hated tyrants, and then 'carry the war into Africa,'" a Georgian wrote with revealing phraseology. "The Yankees should be made to taste some of the 'bitter sweets' of their cherished scheme of hostile invasion." In truth, the specifics were no matter for the men; they trusted Lee. As a Rebel soldier explained to his sister, "We all have such confidence in the ability of our General, the valor of our men and the justness of our cause as it makes very little to us which way we go, so we can do our duty to our country."[37]

Elizabeth Phoebe Key Howard, a fifty-eight-year-old Baltimore resident who had five sons in the Confederate army, enjoyed a reunion of sorts. With her husband, a former judge and police commissioner, away, she could not resist the allure of seeing her sons, gone some sixteen months. She and daughter Alice climbed aboard a small carriage and set out for Frederick, fifty miles away. They arrived at the home of a family friend, only to learn that two sons had just left. The provost marshal sent word to them, which they never received, but a family friend, Col. Bradley Johnson, ordered them to report to their mother forthwith. The following morning they showed up, one a major and the other a surgeon. "I have *seen* our boys!" she exclaimed joyously to her husband. They looked good and felt good, described by her as "brown as two buns," although Edward, the surgeon, had exhausted himself caring for wounded at Second Manassas. "I felt as if I was in a dream," she reported. "To tell you what a world of happiness I have enjoyed in the last two or three days would be impossible," she gushed. "We clung to each other" all day long. She missed the three others, but she received detailed reports that all were well.

The next day the army marched off, and she stood alongside her sons, observing the troops and meeting officers and friends. It took four to five hours for Jackson's old division alone to pass. "The Confederate army was a sight that almost overcame me," she admitted. She had seen plenty of Federal troops before, and these men were completely different. "Dirty, (I must say it) bronzed by exposure—marked by hardship & suffering—badly clad from want—yet with a look of firm patient and cheerful endurance and unflinching courage and determination." They were different from any people she had ever seen. "I caught myself wondering what race of men they were." To her mind, "They looked to me not made of flesh and blood but stone and iron." Men "dressed in any thing they can get, except Yankee uniforms," with many of the officers, even generals, attired no better than the men. Dirt and dust coated everyone's clothing and carefully disguised rank. It was one of the great days of her life.[38]

Yet not everyone was as thrilled as Elizabeth Howard to see Confederate troops marching through Maryland. Rather than the anticipated hero's welcome, they received a chilly reception in western Maryland. "You could see disappointment written on the face of every man," an officer informed his mother. Many people boarded themselves inside their homes. Some shopkeepers sold items to soldiers and accepted Confederate money, fearful of upsetting the invading troops. "Others would not take it," one staff officer noted, "but no one was constrained." Women brazenly displayed their support for the Union, to the dismay of soldiers. One woman floated the Stars and Stripes for all Rebels to see. A Texas soldier walked up to her and said, " 'You can wave that air thing but thar aint a man in this town can do it but that I can whip.' " Upon his return to Virginia, a Mississippi private admitted that he and his comrades were terribly disappointed at the public's lack of support. "The country looked as one might imagine Paradise did, after the expulsion," he asserted. "All nature looked verdant & delightful, but no one of the human family was to be seen to enjoy it." A South Carolina officer concluded, "One thing is very sure: the soldier sings 'Maryland, My Maryland' with far less zest than heretofore."[39]

From the fight around Manassas, Pope's forces had fallen back to the Washington defenses, where they consolidated with the remainder of the Army of the Potomac. With Pope's reputation for leadership in tatters, Lincoln turned to McClellan to restore order and instill a fighting spirit once again.

In Virginia, other than the defenses around Washington, Yankees clung only to their garrisons at Martinsburg and Harpers Ferry. Rather than leave them in his rear and perhaps obstruct the Confederate escape route, Lee elected to detach portions of his army to gobble them up. Before Confederate troops arrived, the Yankees at Martinsburg evacuated stores and troops to Harpers Ferry. Lee ordered three columns—Jackson, McLaws, and a division under Brig. Gen. John G. Walker—to converge on the area, seize the high ground overlooking the garrison, and coerce its capitulation. Longstreet's columns and D. H. Hill's division would proceed northward toward Boonsboro, Maryland, with Stuart's cavalry shielding them.

On paper, the plan seemed sensible enough. The capture of Harpers Ferry and its garrison would yield large numbers of prisoners and huge amounts of ordnance that his army badly needed, and it would also clear out almost all remaining Union pockets of resistance on Virginia soil. By dividing an army into so many components with a large enemy presence nearby, a commander usually incurred excessive risks, but in this case Lee believed it would take weeks for the Federals to restore order after the rout at Second Manassas, and he would need to disperse his forces anyway to feed them properly from the countryside.[40]

Lee, for all his deep thought and careful consideration, failed to anticipate several factors that ultimately would undermine his plan. The Confederate army had always suffered from straggling; during the raid into Maryland, however, it reached epidemic proportions. "One great embarrassment," Lee grumbled to Davis, "is the reduction of our ranks from straggling," a crisis that the general blamed on regimental officers. "Our ranks are very much diminished—

I fear from a third to one-half of the original numbers." An officer in the 1st South Carolina Infantry concurred. "If the straggling in our army could only be stopped, it would be worth more than a great victory." Less than a week after the campaign ended, Brig. Gen. Cadmus Wilcox, a thoughtful soldier acting as division head, reported 5,000 soldiers present in a command of over 19,000—almost three soldiers gone for each one who was there.[41]

While the vast majority of troops who wandered away from the army did so to dodge danger and duty, head home, or seek fun and food, many had legitimate reasons for remaining behind. Before crossing into Maryland, Lee left about 900 barefoot soldiers in Winchester. During the campaign, he acquired 4,000–5,000 pairs of shoes for his men in Maryland; still, thousands lacked them. According to one Georgian, "Many of our men did not cross the river for want of shoes, while others preferred to bruise their bare feet on the stony turnpikes of Maryland," which he described as "graded almost like a railroad, thoroughly imbedded with pounded stones." Officers and men who had only recently lost their shoes on the march from Richmond accumulated blisters on the tops and bottoms of their feet—those on the bottom from the rough terrain until their feet calloused, and severe burns and blisters on the top from the sun or the rubbing of tattered shoes.[42]

Although some soldiers skulked in protest over an invasion of Northern states, the great majority of the reliable soldiers rejoiced at the prospect of taking revenge on the Union for its treatment of their beloved South. As a Louisianan expressed, "I suppose our next step, now that we have got the enemy clear out of Virginia, will be an advance on that nice State of Pensylvania and give the barbarous Dutchmen of hers a taste of the horrors they have inflicted upon the citizens of the Valley." While some soldiers certainly had qualms about invading the North in a war for Southern independence, it did not trigger a mass exodus from the army. Moral concerns over invasion proved to be more an after-the-fact justification than a cause for being absent without leave.[43]

Lee assumed that his army would tap the fertile farms of central and western Maryland for livestock and grain, yet once in Maryland, his soldiers discovered few cattle, hogs, or poultry for consumption, forcing the men to live on grain. Virtually none of the farmers had harvested their wheat, and "there is reluctance on the part of millers and others to commit themselves in our favor," Lee complained to Davis. While they did find fifteen hundred barrels of flour in Frederick, that would not last the army for long, and a dearth of wagons and animals prevented him from hauling all of it.[44]

Amid vast cornfields, troops collected ripe corn, but they failed to cook it properly, ate it raw, or consumed spoiled corn, which caused cramps and diarrhea. Campaigning on warm, late summer days, enervation from diarrhea and dehydration took their toll. According to Porter Alexander, a diet of corn and apples "weakened the men, caused sickness & had much to do with the straggling." Many others kept up with the army, but they suffered distress as well. George Templeton Strong, a prominent Northerner who traveled out to

Maryland to assist in caring for wounded soldiers after the campaign, confirmed Alexander's depiction of a debilitated army. "We traced the position in which a rebel brigade had stood and bivouacked in line of battle for a half miles by the thickly strewn belt of green corns husks and cobs, and also *sic venia loquendi*, by a ribbon of dysenteric stools just behind," Strong recorded in his diary.[45]

With his soldiers weakened by sickness and his ranks diminished by a third to a half through straggling, the fate of Lee's raid was almost certain. A discovery on September 13 made matters worse. A Union soldier, poking around a Rebel campsite near Frederick, discovered a paper wrapped around three cigars. As he unraveled the paper, he immediately realized he held a copy of Lee's marching orders. Because D. H. Hill functioned as a semi-independent force, both Jackson and Lee's adjutant Robert H. Chilton had prepared copies of Special Orders, No. 191, dated September 9. Hill had his copy from Jackson, but apparently a staff officer wrapped the duplicate around the cigars, and it fell out of his pocket. Within several hours, the document had reached McClellan's headquarters, where a staff officer verified the order as authentic. Emboldened by the knowledge that Lee had divided his command, McClellan conceived a scheme to isolate and crush Lee's army piecemeal. While Jackson laid siege to Harpers Ferry, Union forces suddenly appeared in strength to brush back Stuart's horsemen and to challenge Hill's troops for control of Turner's Gap at South Mountain. Lee promptly warned McLaws, whose men held the high ground on the north bank of the Potomac River at Harpers Ferry, to beware of a possible Federal advance on his flank, and he dispatched Longstreet to assist Hill. Yet by the time Longstreet's command came to Hill's aid, it was too late. The combative Hill had resisted stoutly, but overwhelming Union superiority had enabled the Yankees to extend beyond both Rebel flanks. Six miles to the south, at Crampton's Gap in South Mountain, Rebel infantry and cavalry could not prevent Union troops from prying their way through the passage. By the night of September 14, Yankees stood only eight miles from Harpers Ferry. In just thirty-six hours, the tide had turned.[46]

Lee elected to fall back to Sharpsburg and recross the Potomac at Shepherdstown. McLaws could unite with him at Sharpsburg, and Jackson would cover the ford at Shepherdstown. From Sharpsburg, some fourteen miles away from Harpers Ferry, Lee could also buy Jackson time by threatening the flank of any Union relief expedition. Jackson did not need much. Securing high ground around Harpers Ferry, Rebel gunners opened on September 15 with a bombardment at dawn. Within a couple of hours, the Union garrison of 11,000 surrendered, along with 73 artillery guns, 13,000 small arms, extensive military stores, and 2,000 blacks, a haul comparable to that at the Confederate surrender at Fort Donelson seven months earlier. Fully cognizant of Lee's situation, Jackson directed A. P. Hill's command to oversee the surrender and remove the captured property, while he led the remainder of his forces on a march all night to Sharpsburg.[47]

Despite the straggling, the illness, and the exhaustion from tough marches,

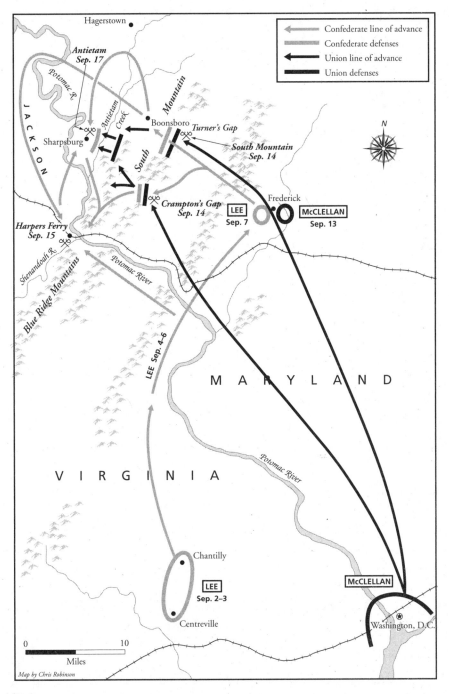

Hagerstown

Antietam
Sep. 17

Potomac R.

J A C K S O N

Sharpsburg

Antietam Creek

Mountain

Boonsboro

Turner's Gap

South Mountain
Sep. 14

South

Harpers Ferry
Sep. 15

Shenandoah R.

Blue Ridge Mountains

Potomac River

Crampton's Gap
Sep. 14

LEE
Sep. 7

Frederick

McCLELLAN
Sep. 13

LEE Sep. 4–6

M A R Y L A N D

V I R G I N I A

Potomac River

Chantilly

LEE
Sep. 2–3

Centreville

McCLELLAN

Washington, D.C.

N

Confederate line of advance
Confederate defenses
Union line of advance
Union defenses

0   10
Miles

Map by Chris Robinson

Raid into Maryland

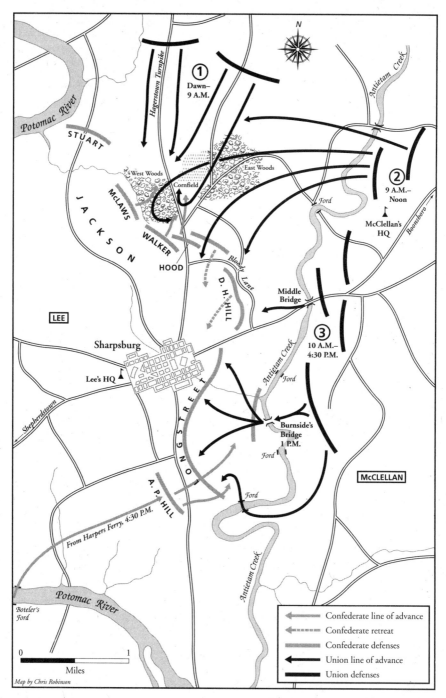

N

Potomac River

Hagerstown Turnpike

STUART

① Dawn–9 A.M.

West Woods

Cornfield

East Woods

J A C K S O N

McLAWS

WALKER

HOOD

Bloody Lane

D. H. HILL

Antietam Creek

Ford

② 9 A.M.–Noon

McClellan's HQ

Boonsboro

Middle Bridge

③ 10 A.M.–4:30 P.M.

LEE

Sharpsburg

Lee's HQ

Antietam Creek

Ford

L O N G S T R E E T

Shepherdstown

Burnside's Bridge 1 P.M.

Ford

McCLELLAN

A. P. HILL

From Harpers Ferry, 4:30 P.M.

Ford

Potomac River

Boteler's Ford

Antietam Creek

0   Miles   1

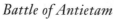

Map by Chris Robinson

Confederate line of advance
Confederate retreat
Confederate defenses
Union line of advance
Union defenses

Battle of Antietam

Lee began to see opportunity instead of misfortune. Word of Jackson's victory invigorated Lee and his army, restoring a sense of Confederate momentum. After receiving the news, one of Longstreet's staff officers pronounced the men "in grand humor for fight." The terrain around Sharpsburg, moreover, strengthened Lee's hope. As Lee's foot-weary troops arrived at the hamlet over the next two days, the commanding general parceled them out among some very strong defensive positions. If he could induce the Federals to attack him, he could keep his own losses down and perhaps inflict a bloody repulse. With Federals reeling from a bitter defeat, he might then have a chance to swing north to Hagerstown and resume the raid. Lee simply did not want to give up on the chance to strike into Pennsylvania and influence the upcoming elections.[48]

In the late afternoon of September 16, some men in Hood's division on the Confederate left exchanged fire with Yankees. The real fight, the bloodiest day in the Civil War, erupted early the following morning and lasted throughout the day in a battle called Sharpsburg by the Confederates and Antietam by the Federals. Assault after assault crashed into various Rebel positions, pressuring Lee's army into critical moments on several occasions. Fortunately, the attacks lacked coordination, and Lee was able to shift troops from one portion of the line to another to stanch the penetration or launch vicious yet costly counterattacks to regain vital ground and avoid disaster. Almost at the closing hour, the Union secured a critical position on the Rebel right and prepared to deliver a crushing blow. A. P. Hill and his men, having covered seventeen miles in seven hours, raced from the rear to snuff out the final Yankee effort.[49]

"The musketry became incessand, and rolled out in tremendous volleys, the artillery thundered, shells exploding men yelling and hurrahing," described a Texas private. Amid this torrent of lead, "Many a poor fellow closed his eyes for the last time with the Setting Sun," wrote a Virginia officer. In twenty minutes, the 30th Virginia Infantry suffered 161 men killed and wounded in the cornfield on the Confederate left. So heavy were the casualties that sister regiments in the brigade refused to advance. The 2nd Georgia Infantry, part of Robert Toombs's brigade that blocked the Union crossing of a bridge over Antietam Creek much of the day, entered the fight with 93 men and exited with only 13 uninjured. "So many of the men were shot down," a Georgian informed his parents, "that the officers filled their places & loaded & fired their guns." Three companies in the 14th North Carolina had no officers standing. The 47th Alabama entered the fight 115 strong and at the end of the day tallied 17 men under the command of a sergeant. The 6th Louisiana Infantry awoke that morning with a dozen officers; by sunset, 5 were dead and all of the others wounded. In total, some 13,000 Confederate soldiers were casualties, including 3 division commanders and almost half the brigade and regimental commanders. It could have been worse. As Jackson instructed McLaws where to deploy his men, a shell landed at their feet, wounding a courier but failing to explode. Had it done so, both Jackson and McLaws would surely have perished.[50]

Although the Union possessed a manpower superiority of two to one, the Confederates' great disadvantage lay in artillery. "Sharpsburg was artillery hell," assessed Colonel Stephen D. Lee. Along similar lines, a South Carolina officer jotted his opinion of the day in his diary: "I pronounce this battle to have been the most terrible in artillery than any one of the preceding fights. I never was so tired of shelling in my life before." He then concluded, "*I hate cannons*." A South Carolinian in McLaws's Division thought the Confederate infantry bested the Yankees, but "Our difficulty (where I was) was in withstanding their terrible artillery." He believed, "Our artillery seemed uncommonly inefficient that day," although he admitted, "they excel us in artillery." The South Carolinian was partially right. Artillerists fought valiantly that day against a Union army with superior weapons. Nearly half of all artillery guns functioned only at short range, and one in every four was a six-pounder, a light piece that did not stand up well on the battlefield, compared to the three-inch rifled gun or the twelve-pounder Napoleon smoothbore. By the end of the day, Lee "urgently" requested long-range guns with "abundant" ammunition, to help offset Union superiority.[51]

Strangely enough, the critical tactical decision concerned artillery, and a cavalryman made it—Jeb Stuart. Since the advance from Richmond, Stuart had tasted both triumphs and embarrassments. In mid-August, a Union raid nearly captured him. He made a hasty escape, leaving behind personal gear. For days afterward, troops chided him with cries, "*where's your hat*" as he rode past. Later in the campaign, he seized Pope's headquarters wagons, along with personal possessions, and had Pope's uniform hung in a shop window in Richmond. At Antietam, Stuart was the only general officer to recognize the key piece of terrain, Nicodemus Heights. The day before the battle, Stuart devoted his time to posting field guns. Three batteries under Maj. John Pelham planted on the hill, supported by some infantrymen, anchored Lee's left. From Nicodemus Heights they poured fire into the flank of attackers, disrupting their columns and easing the pressure on Jackson's beleaguered infantrymen. Ultimately, the artillerists had to withdraw from the heights, but they may have saved Lee's army.[52]

By the end of that terrible day at Antietam, Lee had stabilized his lines, having pulled his left well back. During the night, both sides sent parties to collect their dead and wounded. The next morning, Lee and his army braced for an enemy attack—but it would never come. That night, the army recrossed the Potomac under a light fog and a drizzling rain, which softened the ground and muffled the sounds of wagons and artillery pulled over the roads. Private William L. Claybrooks, wounded at Antietam, marched 130 miles back to Virginia without any attention from a physician. He tied a handkerchief around his wound and walked rearward. "Half the time [I] could not get water to Bathe it with," he complained. At least he could walk. Thousands never left the battlefield, and the Confederates had to haul thousands of others away from it.[53]

Reactions by the soldiers to the Maryland Campaign were mixed. A Virginia officer exclaimed, "our troops so far from being demoralized have acquired new confidence in their commanders." Walter Taylor of Lee's staff believed "the fight of the 17th has taught us the value of our men, who can even when weary with constant marching & fighting & when on short rations, contend with and resist three times their own number." Some kept up their confidence in Lee, but thought he had made a big mistake by fighting at Antietam. Porter Alexander believed that with the vast numerical superiority of the Union forces, the best Lee could have hoped to achieve was a draw. Back on Virginia soil, a forlorn private announced to his aunt, "I do'nt believe that fighting will ever bring peace no way. I never have been so tired of war as I have since I got back." One thing was certain: Soldiers lost all sympathy for Maryland. When a band commenced playing "Maryland, My Maryland," groans and hisses drowned out the tune and compelled the musicians to stop.[54]

Lee had let his combativeness get the best of him. His desire to take his army into Maryland and Pennsylvania and keep them there well into the fall, to draw supplies and influence the upcoming elections, and his confidence in the army's ability to fight outnumbered and defeat the enemy overruled more practical considerations. In two major campaigns, the Army of Northern Virginia had fought and beaten an enemy when the advantages lay with their foe; Lee no doubt viewed Antietam no differently. The fall of Harpers Ferry and the capture of 11,000 prisoners, plus ordnance and supplies, reinforced Lee's faith in the army and its dominance over the Union. Unless his army had routed the Federals and suffered comparatively light losses, though, Lee probably could not have sustained the raid anyway. Unfortunately, the Confederate army could not replace many of the losses.[55]

Yet Lee fought the kind of campaign for which the Confederacy, both soldiers and civilians, had clamored. As one astute soldier noted, "The people have called for an active campaign and Gen. Lee has certainly given it to us."[56]

Chapter 14

——— ◦○◦ ———

A FAILURE OF DISCIPLINE

Private James H. Hoyt stood astonished and disgusted. A thirty-two-year-old painter from Mobile, he had rallied around the flag days after the firing on Fort Sumter by joining the 3rd Alabama Infantry Regiment in 1861. It was the first Alabama regiment to serve in Virginia, and the 3rd had distinguished itself at Seven Pines and Malvern Hill, among its numerous battles. But in Hoyt's eyes, its men were not distinguishing themselves at the moment.

On the battlefield of Fredericksburg in December 1862, he gazed upon hundreds of lifeless, naked Yankee bodies. Rebel troops had swooped down after the fighting and stripped them of everything, emptying their pockets, swiping their shoes, confiscating their pants, shirts, and coats, and removing everything of any possible value. Nearby, six of his comrades hovered over a dying Yankee, waiting for him to expire before they plundered him as well. "I felt ashamed of being a southerner from the way our men acted in sight of the Yankee line," he confessed.[1]

Major General Ambrose P. Burnside, who replaced the temporizing McClellan as commander of the Union Army of the Potomac, had devised a clever stratagem to feint toward Gordonsville and slip eastward and across the Rappahannock River at Fredericksburg. The plan worked—Burnside maneuvered his forces and beat Lee to the river—but pontoon bridging failed to arrive on time, enabling Longstreet and then Jackson to shift their commands into position around the town. Rather than call off the scheme, Burnside elected to bull his way over the river and through Lee's army, a fateful mistake. Under heavy Rebel fire, Yankees bridged crossings and stormed strong Confederate defensive positions. On the Rebel left, Longstreet occupied high ground and fortified his line. The Union attack there was a slaughter. In order to protect themselves, Yankees took extreme measures. "They had actually dragged their dead in a line," a Rebel artillerist described, "piled them up like logs, dug a trench behind & thrown the dirt upon them, & thus made a *fortification* out of *their own dead*." On the left, Jackson took advantage of the natural terrain yet neglected to augment its defenses. His men repulsed the Union assault along most of the line, but in a swampy area, where his defenses were thin,

Union troops penetrated. Reserves rushed forward, and after a vicious fight, they sealed the breach. For two days, opposing sides stared at each other, with wounded and killed crowding no-man's-land. Finally, amid a blustery nighttime rainstorm, Burnside withdrew his forces across the Rappahannock. Confederate losses tallied more than 5,000; Union casualties surpassed 12,600, many of them abandoned on the field. A Virginian informed his father, "one might have walked a ¼ of a mile stepping from dead Ye.[Yankee] to dead Ye. without once touching the ground."[2]

The Civil War was now a heavyweight slugfest. Neither side had momentum and the losses were horrible. There was no room for civility. After the Federals withdrew, Confederate soldiers descended like locusts to pick clean what the Yankees left behind. "As the boys say," crowed a Mississippi private, "Burnside is old Lee's *Quarter Master*." A North Carolina officer commented that "our men went to work robbing the dead without ceremony," while a member of Early's staff explained to his grandmother, "They were stripped to the skin by our Soldiers who have long since lost all delicacy on the subject." A Confederate artillerist penciled in his diary, "All the Yank dead had been stripped of every rag of their clothing and looked like hogs that had been cleaned." In some instances, Confederates dug up buried Yankee dead to get their clothes. Scavengers sought garments, Yankee money, watches, and jewelry. A disgusted Virginian alerted his wife, "A Mississippian cut a dead Yankees finger to get his ring." Nor were these plunderers simply enlisted personnel. A Georgian, thoroughly annoyed by the whole scene, cast scorn on those with commissions as well: "Officers, Cols. Majors, etc, forgot their positions and quarrelled about the distribution of the booty."[3]

This conduct after the Battle of Fredericksburg represented neither unusual behavior nor the limits of Confederate misdeeds. Soldiers had grown accustomed to taking for themselves, to providing for their needs when the government failed to do so. After observing the army take from the enemy for martial purposes, many saw nothing wrong with stripping the dead of anything remotely useful, rifling through the pockets of wounded for valuables, or compelling prisoners of war to "trade" their clothing and equipment for Rebel versions. It had become part of their culture. The problem was that these practices represented a severe breakdown in discipline, which would come back to haunt Confederate troops, especially in a war with such a very narrow margin for error.[4]

Civil War army culture did not flow primarily from top to bottom. Because the high command neglected to establish and enforce an effective military culture, a vacuum formed, and the troops themselves forged one that drew heavily from the civilian world. Military regulations circumscribed their day-to-day existence more rigidly than in civil life, but they could not snuff out vestiges of Southern society.[5]

Most officers came from Southern communities and commanded neighbors, friends, and family. They reflected the values of that society, and most of them had to learn soldiering right alongside their men. Troops elected officers largely from among their own; the officers may have been wealthier and owned slaves more frequently than the majority of enlisted men, but there were plenty of enlisted men who came from rich families. When reorganization and re-election time approached, some strong disciplinarians lost their commissions, but most failed in balloting because they were not around or neglected to attend to the needs of the men.[6]

At the core, virtually all these citizen-soldiers shared the same fundamental beliefs in the rightness of secession and slavery. From society, they inherited Southern honor, an overarching concept that embraced powerful perceptions of manhood, integrity, independence, valor, kinship, and esteem, and among the elite both luxury and generosity. In times of war, a wholehearted allegiance to the spirit of honor would serve its soldiers well. But Southern society also promoted certain qualities that did not benefit the Confederate nation in a war against the better-resourced Union. A lack of discipline and, particularly among the well-to-do, a spirit of profligacy and self-indulgence were acceptable modes of conduct before the war. Closely related to one another, these three behaviors elevated the individual over the group and tolerated conduct in uniform that was not conducive to effective military service. More than simply a spirit of individualism, which the army could harness and convert to military purposes, these qualities diminished the usefulness of the soldier. In the prewar South, an individual who squandered money recklessly was not necessarily scorned. In some circles, he earned praise by distinguishing himself from his penurious, materialistic Northern countrymen. Southerners, particularly males, aspired to fulfill their every impulse and desire, and society tolerated and often encouraged indulgence. Attention to administrative detail and other mundane matters was beneath many of them. Undisciplined conduct, an open expression of passion, or a ready resort to violence were not necessarily considered unbecoming in the prewar South. After all, to adhere to a code of discipline meant that others imposed their will on an individual. Such dominance of the individual smacked of slavery, and Southern whites were extremely sensitive to it. Even in the realm of laws and codes of moral conduct, Southern males abided by them voluntarily, not out of compunction. If society compelled them to obey, then it dominated the individual and deprived him of his manhood, and no self-respecting white Southerner could endure that.[7]

These attitudes and behaviors translated into sloppy, wasteful, and destructive practices that impaired the Confederacy's ability to wage war. Fighting against a better-resourced power, the Rebels had very little room for error. Lee understood this, and during his first month as commander he attempted to break the army of its wasteful and undisciplined ways. Yet for all Lee's efforts, he was merely jousting with windmills. He had inherited an army that had squandered precious equipment and resources and had failed to instill discipline in its soldiery to the point where it had become part of its culture. Long before Lee assumed the reins as army commander, officers under Beauregard and Johnston had set the example by their lack of uniform discipline. Soldiers escaped punishment for the destruction of property and equipment. Officers tolerated or punished mildly other inappropriate behavior short of violence. Three times, soldiers had witnessed the massive destruction of equipment and supplies by order of the commanding general, Joseph E. Johnston. They had seen their comrades wander away from camp and battlefields, plunder in a "promiscuous scramble," and suffer limited repercussions.[8]

Even worse, soldiers pillaged the very people they had volunteered to defend. In a war to protect private property, they stole from civilians. "Our soldiers are committing many shameful outrages which are a disgrace to the country & some ought to, & I hope will be, shot, as examples," Porter Alexander vented to his wife. "The Yankees could be no worse than many of them are." Back in May, a soldier thought both the inefficient commissary department and the unrelenting hardships were "fast demoralizing our men." Other than the personal danger and the loss of slaves that residents faced when Yankees approached, he saw no difference in the way the enemy and the Rebels treated the locals. "The country passed over by our own army is totally destroyed & the most wanton damage frequently committed by our own men," he reported, "farms completely turned out on the commons, stock *killed* by our half famished soldiers—crops trampled down & destroyed & famine for the next year staring the poor farmer in the face." He then predicted, "there certainly must be great suffering in many parts of Virginia during the next twelve months." Brigadier General Alexander Lawton, whose brigade arrived in time for Seven Days' and then continued its service with Lee's army, could not believe what he saw. "Dearest, tell our friends in Georgia they aught to thank God that they are so far removed from the seat of war," he informed her. "We really know nothing there of its devastating effects." In Lawton's opinion, "Our own army is as destructive as the enemy's, & nearly one half the State is a desert."[9]

Long before Lee assumed command, soldiers had embraced the practice of taking what they wanted and acting for their own convenience, with little regard for long-term consequences. In September 1861, as a soldier near Fairfax Court House described to his uncle, "marching through this country we can see fields of corn greatly damaged by soldiers, which would have afforded much grain." By January 1862, conditions around Centerville, the principal line of defense, had declined to the point where it would have been extremely difficult for civilian families to survive. "If you could get a glimpse of this section of the country just now it would call impressively to mind the devastation and waste of war," a staff officer wrote his father. "Fields lay barren Comm ons without fences, or cultivation; farm houses are dismantled of all their ornaments, and comforts, and on ever side is seen wreck and destruction." Wilderness had begun to reclaim the fields, and wild birds and animals had returned in plentiful supply to feed on the vegetation and wildlife. On the march, a company officer compared the troops to "an army worm leaving nothing at all standing." Soldiers "ran through gardens on the road devouring every particle of vegetables," and "wherever a cow or hog were found it was shot down & soon dispatched."[10]

Under Lee, the same type of conduct took place. Just as they had done at First Manassas, Seven Pines, and elsewhere, Rebel troops carried Yankee positions and then abandoned the fight in search of plunder. At Seven Days', thousands broke ranks to seek Yankee booty. At Cedar Mountain, Jackson's men preyed on wounded, "emptying their pockets and stealing their clothes," complained a Louisiana chaplain in disgust. They left some of them "lying naked in the dust." After Second Manassas, soldiers reaped the bounty from thousands of fallen Yankees. Only at Antietam, where they had to evacuate the field, did Confederates leave the fallen undisturbed.[11]

Of course, Rebel troops considered prisoners of war as fair game. Union soldiers carried currency that had far greater purchasing power than C.S.A. money. Confederate soldiers regularly relieved them of that burden. As the war went on and Confederate paper money exponentially deteriorated in value, this became an important means of improving their quality of life. The Federal government also issued superior equipment to its men, and Confederates liked to "trade" for it. "I swaped canteens with a prisoner," a Georgia lieutenant alerted his wife. "Their things are of much better quality than ours and our soldiers are quite eager to get them. The truth is all of them have them." Later in the war, as the Confederate transportation system strained to provide for the men, this source became even more important. From top to bottom, one Rebel soldier depended on the largess of the Federal government. After obtaining a black felt hat that he was "indebted to a Yankee officer for," he boasted, "Thanks to Yank I captured the other day, I have a very good pair of blue pantaloons. The poor rascal begged very hard for his pants, but as mine were in a very dilapidated condition I considered it my duty to trade with him." His boots, which he "captured last July," were now wearing badly, and he was on the lookout for a new pair.[12]

Nor did Rebel plunderers stop at Yankees. A South Carolina officer protested the behavior of some troops, which had suddenly turned against their own comrades. "I am sorry to say that many of our dead were robbed by our soldiers or stragglers during the night," he wrote home. "This is sad, but in such an immense army as we have, there are bad characters along." What he did not realize was that the term "bad characters" encompassed a sizable proportion of the army. During the Seven Days', Pvt. Henri Mugler examined a dead Mississippi soldier with a beautifully scripted letter from a female lying alongside his body. "His pockets had been turned inside out by the Battle Field 'Vultures' who are found in all armies," he complained. "It is a common thing the morning after a battle to find the pockets of the killed turned inside out." When friends found the body of James Hardeman Stuart, a cousin of Jeb Stuart who was serving with the Texas Brigade, soldiers had stripped him of his shirt and drawers.[13]

Toward civilians, Lee's soldiers behaved equally badly, if not worse. "Our men are sometimes as bad as the enemy.—Pulling down and burning fences, pulling down corn and destroying fruit and fruit trees," a private commented in his diary. Having endured hardships and sacrifices on scant rations and with minimal clothing, soldiers began to resent those at home who bore a light burden. Why should not the people at home share, especially when a soldier wanted? A private in an artillery battery believed the soldiers in his brigade "are noted for their plundering and robbery." Coming to terms with the conduct of the army, a Georgia sergeant explained to his sweetheart, "Soldiers will steal or press, as they term it, and there is no use to deny it." By enlisting in the army, soldiers justified, they had brokered a deal with the Confederate people. They had promised to incur risks to defend the Confederacy, and in return, those people had agreed to feed, clothe, equip, and pay them. When the government could not provide for their basic needs, soldiers took it from the people.[14]

Yet their behavior extended beyond necessities. An infantry colonel from Virginia received a letter from his wife, who described how some Confederate cavalry broke into their home, rummaged around, and took what they wanted. When he received the letter, he was "as mad as forty furies." The intruders "are nothing but a set of low bred thieving scoundrels & not fit to be a soldier of the Confederacy," he blasted. After the march into Maryland, Brig. Gen. Dorsey Pender was disgusted with his men. "My dear such a filthy unprincipled set of villains I have never seen," he vented to his wife. "They have lost all honor or decency, all sense of right or respect for property. I have had to strike many with my saber." Rather than act as a shield from destruction, they had become the destroyer.[15]

Ultimately, this level of destructiveness damaged the Rebel cause hugely. Union and Confederate armies proved so damaging that most farmers decided it was no longer worth it to cultivate their fields, only to see armies trample them or pick everything clean. By late September 1862, a Georgian pronounced the portions of the Shenandoah Valley that he traveled as "ruined" and "a perfect desert." In late winter, 1862–63, a Virginia cavalryman stationed in the Valley wondered what would prompt a farmer to devote money and labor to the production of a crop, only to have soldiers take it or government officials confiscate it for a very low price. Three days later, he complained that supplies were short and "no army of any size can long hold this Valley over which 6 armies have gone, unless such protection of the farmers can be given as will Encourage production of breadstuffs this spring." By July 1863, a Florida private in northern Virginia noticed "nearly all the farms are deserted and the country a perfect waste." A Virginia soldier declared Culpeper County "a barren waste— plantation after plantation lay as bare of cultivation as a wilderness," with only a few scattered corn patches dotting the landscape. Near Orange Court House, a Virginia chaplain reported, "The farmers find it impossible to cultivate, with our army trampling over their fields & fences, in every direction, not to speak of the possibility of the Yankees coming in upon them."[16]

"Nothing will disorganize an army more or ruin it more completely than pillage," insisted Napoleon Bonaparte. Plundering on the battlefield and in the countryside, failing to husband valuable materiel, neglecting duties, irresponsible officers, and wandering away in search of spoils or to avoid combat were all symptoms of a severe lack of discipline. In September, Brig. Gen. Cadmus M. Wilcox announced, "we have no discipline in our army, it is but little better than an armed mob," insisting "where our army marches & camps desolation follows." D. H. Hill concurred. "The straggler is generally a thief and always a coward, lost to all sense of shame; he can only be kept in ranks by a strict and sanguinary discipline." At the Battle of Antietam, "More than half of my Brigade went off that day," Dorsey Pender admitted to his wife.[17]

Nor were these solely enlisted men who abandoned their commands and their duties. When Southern honor clashed with instincts of self-preservation, the conflict left casualties in its wake, regardless of rank. Pender complained that in one regiment, six of the ten officers skulked at Antietam. A South Carolina captain enlightened his spouse when he wrote, "You need not think *all* that come out here are entitled to their country's praise, and you would be astonished to know how many officers are dodging behind some various pretexts. I know of a great many," he concluded, "who have not been in any of the battles and will not be in any unless they are driven in." One Mississippian even accused a brigadier general of cowardice at Antietam, hiding behind a stone barn a half mile in the rear and issuing orders that were inappropriate.[18]

Lee fully recognized the scope of the problem. In a revealing letter to the president just days after entering Maryland, he admitted that the army suffered from a severe discipline problem that stemmed from a combination of the way the Confederacy organized units, its premature introduction into combat without adequate training and regimentation, and a series of harsh conditions, hard marches, and frequent campaigns and battles. He believed "the material of which it is composed is the best in the world," and "nothing can surpass the gallantry and intelligence of the main body, but there are individuals who, from their backwardness in duty, tardiness of movement, and neglect of orders, do it no credit." Lee deemed straggling "One of the greatest evils." Some of those who fell out of the march did so from poor health; others "do not wish to be with their regiments, nor to share in their hardships and glories. They are cowards of the army, desert their comrades in times of danger, and fill the houses of the charitable and hospitable on the march." As a solution, Lee proposed military commissions, like those Winfield Scott had run in Mexico, which required fewer officers than a general court-martial and could mete out punishment swiftly and firmly. He also sought effective inspectors general with staff to ensure the timely execution of orders.[19]

By the end of the campaign into Maryland, Lee realized that the discipline problem was extremely serious. A few brigades on line at Antietam constituted barely more than a full-strength company—100 men. Soldiers simply melted into the countryside, wreaking havoc on citizens, performing acts that "are disgraceful to the army and injurious to the cause," Lee asserted. Within ten days after the Battle of Antietam, one cavalry brigade commander, stationed in Winchester and fanning his horsemen throughout the neighboring communities, had picked up and returned to the army between 5,000 and 6,000 stragglers. According to the officer, to avoid the campaign into Maryland some men had thrown away their shoes in order to remain with the barefoot camp in Winchester. The scale of the problem was much larger than Lee had anticipated. "It is impossible as the army is now organized to prevent these acts by orders," he conceded to the president.[20]

Lee and subordinate commanders had taken steps to check misconduct, but they had never developed a thorough plan and enforced it rigorously. After Seven Days', an artillery officer warned his men about the "spirit of depredation" that Lee had personally witnessed. A month later, in an effort to halt straggling on the march and in battle, Lee detailed two men per company to carry wounded to the rear and a subcommand consisting of one officer, two noncommissioned officers, ten privates, and a medical officer to march behind each division and deal with stragglers. These forces proved not nearly strong enough, nor were his efforts to halt straggling all-encompassing. Subordinates such as Brig. Gen. Samuel Garland tried to remind the troops as they advanced northward in Virginia that the same principles of conduct in peacetime applied in wartime. "The standard of good morals had not been altered by our absence from Home, and our present occupation," he counseled them. "To take any article that does not belong to us, without permission or knowledge of the owner, is dishonest and is disgraceful now as much as ever." Likewise, Longstreet issued a circular order as his wing entered Maryland, warning his men against molesting citizens or disturbing their property. He then took steps to prevent these acts, but clearly they were insufficient.[21]

Less than a week after Antietam, Lee informed Longstreet and Jackson that they must alter army culture. He urged them to "infuse a different spirit among our officers, and to inspire them in making every necessary effort to bring about a better state of discipline." They must "impress men and officers with the importance of a change necessary to the preservation of this army and its successful accomplishment of its mission, as its better discipline, greater mobility, and higher inspirations must counterbalance the many advantages over us, both in numbers and material, which the enemy possess." To crack down on straggling or wandering off from camp, he ordered roll calls at reveille, with each soldier appearing with weapons. Officers were to hold weekly inspections, and to pay careful attention to the condition and maintenance of the arms. He shifted the burden of preventing stragglers from the division level down to the brigade. On the march, each brigade would have a guard to "drive up all stragglers, irrespective of commands, and all leaving the ranks." Lee directed regimental commanders to pass up and down the lines periodically on the march, verifying that soldiers remained in their ranks and officers attended to their duties. Once they camped for the evening, the brigade guard assumed responsibility for protecting nearby homes and private property. To eliminate the motivation for soldiers wandering from camp in search of food and clothing, Lee cracked down on sloppy record-keeping within the commands and demanded greater efficiency from the quartermaster and commissary departments. Soldiers who received proper issues of clothing and food, Lee surmised, were less likely to forage on their own. Finally, Lee set up corps provost guards, to whom officers would turn over all stragglers, skulkers, and depredators. He intended to hold ranking officers responsible, directing that they arrest neglectful subordinates or suffer the same consequences themselves.[22]

In order to alter army culture, Lee also had to reconfigure his high command and place responsible, attentive, and skillful officers in place. Congress finally authorized the creation of corps, and Lee proposed his two wing commanders, Longstreet and Jackson, to lead them. Lee merely recommended Longstreet without justification, which indicated that Davis concurred with the choice. In Jackson's case, however, Lee had to sell him to the president. Evidently, Davis had lost faith in Jackson during his Romney campaign and the squabbles that ensued during the winter of 1861–62. While he won kudos for his work in the Valley, his reputation suffered during the Seven Days' Campaign and Cedar Mountain. Perhaps not to the same degree, Lee had his own concerns about Jackson. From his advice when he sent Jackson north from Richmond after Seven Days', Lee hinted at Jackson's shortfalls. He wanted Jackson to care for his men more effectively, communicate better with key subordinates, and whenever possible, turn the enemy's flanks. To Davis on October 2, Lee justified his choice by stating, "My opinion of the merits of Genl. Jackson has been greatly enhanced during this expedition. He is true, honest, and brave, has a single eye to the good of the service, and spares no exertion to accomplish his object."[23]

Much more serious was the turnover at division and brigade levels, positions that Lee deemed critical to effective operation of the army. Over the three months from the opening salvos at Seven Days' to the first shot at Antietam, only 30 percent of division commanders still commanded divisions in Lee's army, and almost four of every ten among brigade commanders had changed. A system of promotion by seniority, not merit, determined who filled these vacancies, depriving Lee of the best talent at critical positions. Efforts to change the process largely failed, but Lee did have an opportunity to elevate selected individuals to brigade and division command with rank, most of whom Congress confirmed.[24]

For a while, high-ranking officers attempted to enforce discipline, with the commanding general leading the way. In early December, Lee ordered Longstreet to assess officers for property damage against citizens for dismantling fences and using them as firewood. "I regard them not only as in the highest degree discreditable, but very injurious to our cause," Lee elaborated. "When we consider the scarcity of labor, and the impossibility of replacing the fencing so as to enable the people to raise enough for their support, the extent of the injury that will result from such actions as this becomes apparent." A new brigade commander, Alfred Iverson, reacted to depredations by instituting a system of roll calls, and anyone absent without authorization would suffer a bucking, a punishment in which officials tied a soldier up in a very uncomfortable position and left him that way for a few hours. Longstreet called on brigade commanders to instruct their men to act with caution while camping. Soldiers had carelessly started too many fires that destroyed woods and fields, to the detriment of the army and the local citizens. As far away as Richmond, authorities picked up stragglers and loafers and, according to a private, were "plasing them in the calaboose un til they can send them to there Regments."[25]

Davis, who well understood the nature and severity of the difficulty, concurred with Lee's approach and took steps to secure the proper changes. In mid-September, he called on Congress to create the military commissions that would allow each field army to handle matters that the articles of war did not cover, mainly trespassing and destroying civilian property. Congress promptly passed a law and Davis signed it October 9. The previous day, Davis had asked Congress to support a system enabling the War Department to bypass seniority and elevate more competent junior officers to brigade and division command. Instead, Congress passed a law on October 13 that allowed a department commander to create a board to pass on the competency of an officer, and when the board determined the officer was unfit for the position, the department commander could suspend him. The next officer by seniority would take the job. The problems of this law, though, were manifest. An officer might serve perfectly well as regimental or brigade commander but would not necessarily execute his duties effectively at a higher level. After suffering the humiliation of being found incompetent at a new rank, the officer could not revert to his old position. The army then lost the services of a perfectly competent officer who was unsuited for higher rank. Nor did the congressional system secure the best-qualified officer for the position, unless he happened to be the next senior person.[26]

Lee first tested the new commanders and disciplinary system in the Fredericksburg Campaign, and it proved a poor start. The army was in the midst of a campaign, and it needed captured weapons, wagons, and equipment to offset the Confederacy's weakness in manufacturing. Including its haul of 9,091 muskets at Fredericksburg, the Rebel army in Virginia had picked up more than 100,000 small arms and 174 artillery pieces of various sizes on battlefields. One soldier testified that fully one-third of all army wagons had "U.S." on them, even the vehicle that carried Lee into Maryland after his horse threw him and he broke both wrists. For weeks, the same soldier and his comrades had eaten hard tack from crates stamped "Cincinnati." The Army of Northern Virginia relied on holding the battlefield to secure the spoils of war.[27]

Its soldiers were no different. In September, an artillery captain called his comrades a "set of ragamiffins" and predicted, "If we don't gain a victory soon or capture Harper's Ferry, so as to get possession of Yankee spoils, our whole army will be naked & barefooted." By mid-November, as early signs of winter appeared, soldiers itched for a fight. "The rebels have all taken up an idea that the Yankee army has just been furnished with new Overcoats & Blankets for the winter," Pvt. James P. Williams explained to his aunt, "& they want to get a few of them before cold weather sets in." About the same time, a Louisianan told his brother not to send warm clothes. If he could not make out with his current issue, "I will supply myself with Yankee clothes the next fight I get into." After every battle they had access to Union knapsacks and all they contained. "Heretofore I would never wear Yankee clothes but as 'necessity is the mother of invention' I will have to pick up the next Yankee knapsack I come across," he wrote. After the Battle of Fredericksburg, a Virginia private explained why the Yankees were naked: "our men stripped the dead bodies to get clothes to Keep them warm." While many, perhaps most, soldiers sought to plunder for personal wealth, they also took from the Yankees out of necessity, because the Confederacy failed to provide for them. "As laurels alone don't keep folks warm in winter," an officer justified spoils to his sister, "the blankets are congenial company with them."[28]

The war, too, had altered the morality of soldiers. If necessity demanded that they strip the dead of weapons, shoes, coats, and blankets for survival, then should they leave the money, watch, and rings? Once they crossed that line, individual soldiers could rationalize all sorts of behavior. Lee had declared September 3 a day of fasting. "As someone had stolen my rations," commented a Georgia private, "I had no difficulty in observing it." A Virginia officer had $1,000 stolen from him one night. "The money was on my person and slipped from me whilst I was asleep at night," he wrote his mother. Certainly every army composed of 70,000 or more soldiers would have its criminal element, but the strains and circumstances of war eroded moral boundaries and broke down self-discipline.[29]

Nor did it help instill effective discipline when officers themselves transgressed the bounds of good judgment. After launching into a tirade over how his soldiers were expert plunderers, Dorsey Pender confessed to his wife, "The officers are nearly as bad as the men." A company commander in the 18th Virginia, and a good officer, thought it was improper for officers to plunder, but he saw nothing wrong with enlisted men doing it. "I rather think an officer is out of place strolling across a battle field in search of plunder and I would rather pay for what I get—" he wrote his wife, "but it is different with the privates and they should be allowed to have all they can carry." Even the stern disciplinarian Stonewall Jackson suffered a lapse of judgment that promoted undisciplined behavior when he captured Pope's supply base at Manassas Junction. Instead of giving his commissary control and having it dole out portions to each soldier, he allowed the men to plunder the train cars loaded with food and other items. Early arrivals gorged themselves, while those who came up late because of other duties got nothing. The unintended lesson was that when it came to plundering, you must get there first to receive your share.[30]

Against vastly superior Union numbers and equipment, Lee realized that the

Confederacy must alter the culture of its army. Only a disciplined, mobile, and inspired Confederate army could counterbalance Federal numbers and equipment. Yet what he found were countervailing forces that resisted change. The resilience of the bottom-up, citizen-soldier culture, the haphazard approach to administration and attention to detail by some of Lee's new appointees, and wartime conditions impaired the effectiveness of the top-down approach. If Lee were to force a change, he needed the entire officer corps as his allies, a difficult proposition at best.[31]

Chapter 15

LEE'S OFFICER CORPS AND ARMY CULTURE

I F LEE HOPED to alter the culture within the army, he needed to enlist the support and vigilance of regimental and company-grade officers. Brigade, division, and corps commanders were too far removed from the soldiers to impose a genuine transformation throughout the army. Company and regimental officers lived within these smaller units, had extensive, everyday contact with the men, and supervised their conduct more intimately than did general officers. Only with their full cooperation could Lee accomplish this reformation.

Yet less than a week after the Battle of Antietam, Lee complained to the secretary of war, "There is great dereliction of duty among the regimental and company officers, particularly the latter, and unless something is done the army will melt away." Nine days later, while seeking solutions to the decline in manpower strength, Lee argued to the president that officers needed to care more for their men, citing numerous areas of neglect and inefficiency. If officers attended to their men better, their physical condition would be stronger, and fewer soldiers would straggle because of physical ailments during the campaigns. "Until the regimental officers can be made to appreciate the necessity of taking care of their men, keeping them under control, attending to their wants and comforts, and enforcing cleanliness, &c., I fear the sanitary condition of the army will not improve," Lee asserted. "It is the want of this attention and provision for comfort that causes our men to break down under hardship."[1]

Since early in the war, the quality of officers had greatly concerned Lee. To Governor John Letcher of Virginia, in September 1861, Lee attempted to convey the vital importance of securing high-caliber individuals as officers for the army. "It is cruelty to the men as well as injury to the country to commit them to incompetent officers," he wrote. Lee had no doubt that Southern society would produce excellent combat soldiers, but unlike so many volunteers, the veteran commander understood that fighting was just one part of soldiering. Lee knew that Southern society did not produce disciplined men who would take orders well. Nor did he expect most Southern men to possess the kinds of leadership skills, judgment, and attention to detail necessary to make good officers. Graduates from West Point, Virginia Military Institute, and The Citadel could provide many quality officers, particularly at the upper levels of command. Lee's great concern was with regiment- and company-grade officers, most of whom would have to come from civil life. The Confederacy had to choose these carefully.[2]

In December 1861, Lee expressed his opinion on the selection of officers to the former governor of South Carolina. "The best troops are ineffectual without good officers," Lee asserted. "Our volunteers, more than any others, require officers whom they can respect and trust." He added, "It would be safe to trust men of the intelligence and character of our volunteers to elect their officers, could they at the time of election realize their dependent condition in the day of battle." Yet this they could not do, and he had witnessed soldiers in the moment of danger repudiate officers of their own choosing and seek others to lead them into battle. "Is it right, then for a State to throw upon its citizens a responsibility which they do not feel and cannot exercise properly?" Instead, he preferred governors, with the advice of legislatures, to appoint field officers for state troops, and the president and Congress to handle those obligations for Confederate commands. The choice only of company-grade officers, Lee implied, would be the domain of the soldiers themselves.[3]

The original laws for the selection of officers rested with individual states, nearly all of which called for some form of election. And Congress was loath to wade into the debate to trim soldiers' rights. As one soldier shrewdly articulated, "Men are as intelligent in camps as at home, and can vote as intelligently for their officers as they can for members of Congress," a notion not lost on politicians. President Davis recognized both the political nature of army building and the inability of anyone to devise a foolproof system. "In the election and appointment of officers for the Provisional Army," he admitted in August 1862, "it was to be anticipated that mistakes would be made and incompetent officers of all grades introduced into the service." Still, Davis confessed, "In the absence of experience, and with no reliable guide for selection, executive appointments as well as elections have been sometimes unfortunate." Soldiers simply had to rely on their best judgment.[4]

But if the Confederacy had to depend on any flawed system, it must also have means of removing incompetent or derelict officers. Early in the war, Lee advised Beauregard to notify the governor whenever he had incompetent officers. Leaving it to politicians, however, was no solution. Superior officers could levy court-martial charges for violations of army regulations, but that did not solve the problem of officers who simply lacked the ability to execute the duties of the commission effectively. For instances of sheer incompetence, the government established examination boards in the conscription law of April 1862. Technically, all officers were supposed to undergo an examination within one year of their promotion, but in a Confederacy that was hard-pressed for manpower in the field, it could not allocate the personnel for boards. In practice, superior officers would press charges of incompetence and an examination board would assess the officer for ability and character.

Congress also employed seniority to check election errors. After the reorganization of 1862, when vacancies occurred, the regiment or battery promoted by seniority and elected only new second lieutenants. Although Lee felt the seniority system restricted his options and imposed incompetent or inferior officers on the troops, under the circumstances it was probably the best alternative. Another option was battlefield recommendations for promotion, but officers seldom nominated enlisted men, and they could only serve in their current company. And as the Confederacy learned very quickly, battlefield prowess by no means encompassed all the essential qualities for effective officership.[5]

Lee's problem was that these officers played a role in creating the very culture that he sought to eradicate. They came from the same community and reflected the same values as their men. In the course of their service they endured the hardships and frustrations of their troops and were more likely to empathize with or tolerate the behavior of their men. Once the war ended, they would return home with their soldiers and work alongside them every day for the rest of their lives. Without powerful incentives, they were not likely to challenge their soldiers, as long as the men fought well.

Throughout the entire war, those who received commissions, through either election or appointment, came largely from wealthy backgrounds, especially compared to the enlisted population. According to a sample, the median wealth of officers was almost triple that of enlisted men, $3,305 compared to $1,125. Half of all officers either owned slaves or lived with immediate family members who owned slaves, and almost two of every three resided in households with slaves. Among those officers elected in 1861, there was a four-year age difference between them and enlisted men. As the war dragged on, that gap closed significantly as the army tapped younger veterans to fill vacancies, so that for the entire war, the difference on average was less than two years. About half of all officers derived their living primarily from the soil—very similar to the figure for enlisted men—but officers were almost two and half times more likely to hold professional jobs than their soldiers. Slightly older and richer, officers were more typically married.[6]

Although there were genuine differences in background between officers and enlisted men, the gaps between them were not all that dramatic. For the entire war, one in every three enlisted men or their families with whom they resided owned slaves, and almost four of every nine lived in households with slaves. Approximately one in every five officers, or their families if they lived with them, possessed less than $800 worth of property. By comparison, five of every nine enlisted men had more than $800 worth of property. Certainly some of those officers may have received good educations and had come from wealthy families. They were just starting out on their own and had not accrued much wealth at that point in their careers. But wartime opportunities were available for soldiers of talent, regardless of family background. Once soldiers had been in combat and endured the hardships of the march and camp life, the ability to lead effectively, rather than personal popularity or family status, emerged as the benchmark for selection as a commissioned officer in elections.[7]

Initially, soldiers reacted strongly to those who attempted to impose a firm dose of discipline on them. A Mississippian resented his strict company commander, complaining in June 1861, "he watches us as if we were negroes instead of Gentlemen." Barely a month later, another Mississippi private confronted his company commander. "He is insulting and overbearing to those who allow it," the soldier reported home. "I had occasion to inform him that I would not submit to any insults or insinuations, and knowing that I was right he quietly stopped." The private insisted that he had obeyed and would continue to obey orders and perform his duty, "But he is required to treat me as a gentleman and he shall." In those early days, both officers and enlisted men struggled to establish boundaries while attempting to master their military duties, and the learning process was sometimes painful.[8]

As soldiers learned their jobs and experienced battle, the kind of nitpicking discipline that may have been necessary early in the war seemed completely out of place. Those who had fought and bled for their country deserved better. By 1863, after the Gettysburg Campaign, while the army rested and refitted in camp, the troops in the 6th South Carolina regularly went over to witness the daily punishment of men in the neighboring 5th South Carolina. The colonel, Asbury Coward, "has some one punished nearly every evening for very trifling offenses," according to an enlisted man. He believed the colonel was "devoid of *humane* feelings." Each night, he had men parading back and forth in front of his headquarters with logs across their shoulders "for mere nothings." The previous evening, a soldier walked in front of the entire regiment with a sign on his back that read, "'a spectator.'" Humiliating or harsh punishments had no place in an army that had fought the momentous campaigns of 1862 and 1863, the writer believed. "Col. Coward is very unpopular with his reg't and I think he should be so until he learns how to treat men right," he concluded.[9]

In most cases, soldiers tolerated bad judgment or poor leadership among officers, unless it became severe. Men in the Jeff Davis Legion called their major, William M. Stone, "'A. No. 1'" to each other and to his face. Stone never knew the joke: "'A' standing for *Ass*." In the case of the 4th Texas Infantry, the governor appointed as a field officer a favorite who knew nothing about military service. Officers and men made him feel extremely uncomfortable and blitzed politicians with requests to have him removed. Just over two months later, the major was killed in action at Gaines's Mill.[10]

Soldiers always had ways to make life more difficult for officers who behaved badly. When a young dandy walked by in all his military finery, a soldier taunted, loud enough for all to hear, "'Great God Almighty! Just look at the brass that feller has got on his coat.'" Private Cornelius McLaurin informed his sister how "We have a good deal of fun some times making these big Officers mark time." One night during a rainstorm, his adjutant forgot the password, and he held him up a half hour, just to annoy the swelled-headed officer. Another recourse was the pen. Soldiers wrote letters home, describing how officers misbehaved or lost proper perspective, and community sentiment pressured them to reform.[11]

When problems became severe, and complaints fell on deaf ears, soldiers tried to handle things themselves. A Louisianan grumbled of an officer who exacted more than simply discipline that "tyranny, cruelty, and wanton maliscussness [maliciousness]" were integral components of his leadership. Evidently, "the threats that were going round reached his ears" because he resigned. In the 9th Virginia, the soldiers served under Maj. Mark B. Hardin, a transfer from the 33rd Virginia Infantry and a VMI graduate, whom one private called "a tyrannical little puppy." Fortunately for Hardin, he lost out in the re-election. "Had we gotten into an engagement with him he would have been riddled with bullets and not yankee ones either," the Virginian informed his parents. A captain in the 8th Florida abandoned his post at Second Manassas, and a general court-martial dismissed him from the service for cowardice. His mother then wrote Jefferson Davis, offering extenuating circumstances. "In raising his Company of this County he had to act very rigidly which caused a great deal of dissatisfaction among his men and several have said they would Kill him if they ever got him in Battle," she claimed.[12]

Favoritism on the part of officers chafed morale. A newly elected colonel rewarded his old company by issuing long muskets and assigning them to duty as sharpshooters and mounted infantry, to the dismay of other companies. "He is playing out in this Regiment fast," one soldier grumbled. Officers occasionally elevated friends improperly, infuriating both displaced officers, whose honor was at stake, and their men, because the decision in some way ignored due process. In a case that reached President Davis, Maj. John Mullins of the 19th Mississippi arbitrarily altered seniority among captains and then had one arrested for refusing duty at a lower rank. An officer disputed an effort by Brig. Gen. James Lane to promote someone over him while he was absent from the regiment. He went to division headquarters, and the staff there suggested he file a written protest. When Lane read the document, "it completely unstrung his nerves" and he began to tremble in rage. "He was the maddest man, I think, I ever saw. But let him broil," the officer detailed to his wife. He was in the right, and his honor would not allow him to back down.[13]

Perhaps even worse were cases of nepotism. From a prisoner of war camp, a soldier protested that the lieutenant colonel, the adjutant, the sergeant major, and the sergeant of ambulances in the 21st Mississippi were brothers. "I think the *policy* of making a family affair, of regimental easy places, is decidedly wrong, and much to be condemned." That kind of policy, he continued, "is well calculated to engender complaining, and discontent among the men, and should therefore be avoided." In the case of eighteen-year-old James R.

Hagood, when he received a promotion from captain to colonel, some soldiers grumbled, because his brother was a general. According to one soldier, "Some of my company went to school with him & speak rather disparagingly of the Col.'s talents." Even worse, he then took command of the brigade as the only colonel present.[14]

Having come from civilian pursuits and entering a war for the defense of their rights, Rebel troops were particularly sensitive to anything that smacked of inferiority or second-class status. Most of them grasped the concept of rank and would obey reasonable orders. Indeed, based on the mixed quality and judgment of officers, enlisted men at times exhibited a surprising degree of tolerance and patience. But nothing sent soldiers more quickly across the line into rebellion or obstruction than flagrant double standards. A private in a North Carolina regiment explained to his father how the men in the company fumed over two of the officers who ordered early morning roll calls and punished soldiers for oversleeping, yet they themselves slept through them. Another private, an eighteen-year-old from a slaveholding family, grumbled over five roll calls a day, "but if our High Officers had it to do there wouldn't be quite as much unnecessary duty for the Private to perform." He then concluded with the assessment, "I tell you men in this war (in *low rank*) as a general thing are imposed on, treated like negroes, only not as good."[15]

Officers raised the ire of enlisted men when they exploited their rank and power for personal benefit. It infuriated soldiers when officers received furloughs in disproportionate numbers compared to privates, or when officers' wives could visit camp and the spouses of enlisted men could not or would not afford the expense. The only way a soldier could see his wife and children was to receive a furlough or to go absent without leave, an offense that could lead to execution by firing squad. "The government ought to bring the privates wives here free of cost," one soldier suggested, but of course that never happened. Complaints ultimately reached Lee's ears, and he mentioned the problem to his nephew, cavalry officer Brig. Gen. Fitz Lee.[16]

Those with the rank of field officer and higher usually had tents to protect them from the elements while they did necessary paperwork, which also did not sit well with junior officers and enlisted men who slept without shelter in cold or rainy weather. General officers and their staffs frequently slept in private homes while their troops spent nights in the open air or under fly tents. Lee was so sensitive to this kind of preferential treatment that he often slept on his rickety field cot in a tent, regardless of weather, much to the chagrin of his staff.[17]

Nor did the discrepancy in the quality of food ingratiate high-ranking officers with their enlisted personnel. In camp or on the march, generals in particular could purchase or receive cooked meals from civilians much more readily than enlisted men or, for that matter, junior officers. One soldier grumbled about his diet of fat meat and hard bread, insisting, "this diate did not always Suit a weak stomache. many a time hav I walked by the Genls. Head Quats. &

see his Servants (Negroes) feasting off fried eggs & ham & beef warm bread & Hot coffee & sugar." Another enlisted man thought it was unfair that Jackson and his staff breakfasted at a private home on buckwheat cakes and sausage while his troops were turned away. Even the ladies exhibited much greater interest in rank, according to an enlisted man. "The girls are like the paper sails they look at the mens coat collars to see who has got the most stars and stripes and the one that got the most he the man for them," he mentioned. He did not blame them, however, because "I think a good deal of them myself and they have a right to do the same."[18]

Especially galling to the soldiers were attempts by officers to impose their choices for promotion on the men. After all, soldiers had selected the existing officers, who should have had faith in the enlisted men's ability to choose their superiors. By attempting to influence, undercut, or preclude their decisions, officers suggested a loss of faith in their men. When an officer tried to promote over the wishes of the men in his regiment, a Texan explained to his sister, "a privet has to put up with what a offser say to him but I think that we will nock the apointmant in the had [head]." In a North Carolina company, the captain selected his cousin, a soldier in another regiment, to serve as orderly sergeant, sending waves of dissatisfaction throughout the enlisted ranks. "We look upon this of the 'Capt[ain]' as most publically declaring that there is no one in our company worthy of the place;" a soldier protested, "or otherwise as most plainly manifesting his (the Capt's) great unfitness in principle and disposition for the responsible office which we conferred upon him."[19]

Soldiers were very sensitive to officers at all levels who fought too aggressively, who ran up casualty lists because it made them appear as more desperate fighters. At higher levels, they often attacked with excessive boldness, pressed fights when prudence dictated a halt, and suffered much greater losses than circumstances warranted. An officer complained of his controversial brigade commander, Brig. Gen. Roger A. Pryor, writing, "He hoped by displaying the largest number of killed and wounded in his Brigade to obtain promotion." The officer believed Pryor had "succeeded" in doing that by exposing his men unnecessarily, getting his regiments confused on the battlefield, and running up a huge tally of killed and wounded. Brigadier General Micah Jenkins, a capable officer and one of Longstreet's favorites, fought audaciously and earned the praise of numerous high-ranking officers, but all at the expense of his troops. One of his soldiers said that Jenkins "would walk forty miles on the skulls of his men to be made Major General."[20]

In small commands, the problem was not so much fighting too aggressively. Seldom did small units have a chance to hold ground or attack when all units around them withdrew. To enhance perceptions of their prowess, officers adopted a system of internal body counts to elevate their total losses. They tabulated every scratch and cut as a casualty to make it appear that they fought desperately. "The number of wounded is swelled I think too much," admitted an artillerist, "from the fact that officers like to make the number of wounded in their company as large as possible, and so report those very slightly wounded." Officers included on the wounded list soldiers who sustained "scratches from pebbles and stones knocked by cannon balls." Evidently, Lee believed this had evolved into a serious problem, making conscientious and competent officers look like butchers and providing misleading information to army headquarters and to the public. In mid-May 1863, he established an official policy for defining wounded in action as only those whose battlefield injury made them "unfit for duty."[21]

Despite the Southern culture of manhood and valor, when issues of honor clashed with instincts of survival, officers did not always conduct themselves honorably. Once an officer had exhibited cowardice, he lost all credibility with his men. Colonel Samuel Henry of the 9th Alabama, a regiment fraught with indiscipline, had charges of cowardice levied against him. A court found him guilty of neglect of duty for "crouching behind logs while his Regiment was engaged in battle and neglecting to exercise the proper control over his command, leaving the officers and men in doubt as to what to do." He then ordered the regiment to retire "when the retreat was uncalled for." In another case, rather than face a court-martial for cowardice, a lieutenant in the Holcombe Legion offered his resignation, stating, "I do not feel competent to discharge the duties of an officer." He left the battlefield in search of water for the men and never returned. Later, he claimed that a piece of shell had struck him, but there was no evidence of the injury.[22]

Other forms of misbehavior caused officers to lose face with the men as well. Colonel V. D. Groner of the 61st Virginia exploded at a musician on Christmas Day unnecessarily, calling him a "d——d half fucked son of a bitch." Groner was exonerated by a general court-martial and ended the war with his regiment. Lieutenant William B. Jones of the 4th North Carolina had not only dodged service with the regiment since Second Manassas but also managed to contract a case of syphilis while he was away.[23]

The honor code often heightened disagreements into troubling, sometimes violent, confrontations. Brigadier General John Magruder got into a squabble with a Virginia captain who had failed to execute a direct order and then tried to resign after the general confronted him. When Magruder refused to accept the resignation because they were on the verge of a fight, the captain insisted he had "inherent rights" that Magruder had violated and he would permit no man to talk to him that way. The captain then stormed off and failed to report to his company, although he evidently was at the scene of the battle at Bethel. In an argument between two officers, a captain in the 3rd Louisiana Infantry Battalion struck a lieutenant and earned himself a court-martial. Much more serious, Maj. John J. Seibels of the 6th Alabama and the regimental surgeon got into a heated argument, which prompted Seibels to punch the surgeon several times. The two men determined to engage in a duel. The infantry officer misfired, while the healer's shot struck Seibels in the left breast, glancing off the bone and passing out his side. It was one of several duels among officers in the army, as some Southerners elevated honor to such a status that they lost sight of their declared enemy, the Yankees.[24]

Without doubt, alcohol abuse emerged as one of the greatest problems among the officer corps. "Constantly exposed to danger and disease," a Virginian wrote home, "the men and (I blush to say it) very many of the officers give way to excess and dissipation, drinking and gambling are carried on to a dreadful extent in the army." In his opinion, "The temptation is great and many, very many are the victims. Would to Heaven I could think it is confined to inferior officers and men but alas! Such I fear is not the case." When the 3rd Alabama advanced in an attack against some Federal troops, only to have the operation canceled, Lieut. Harvey E. Jones went on a bender. In his court-martial for drunkenness and conduct prejudicial to good order, Jones offered as his defense the question whether the news that they would no longer attack "may not have unnerved him." The court exhibited little sympathy for his nerves; it found him guilty and cashiered him. After an absence of several months, Lt. Col. Francis P. Anderson of the 59th Virginia returned to camp "beastly intoxicated" and told the guard, "'boys you can all go and get drunk while in Richmond and whore it as much as you please.'" He then invited the troops to "burn the ranch," or headquarters, and was seen visiting a house of ill repute in Richmond known as Ann Sherman's. Soldiers in a Virginia regiment had grown so accustomed to their lieutenant colonel's drunkenness that one of them commented one day in his diary, "he didn't get drunk, for a wonder."[25]

Greater problems among the officers stemmed not from serious character flaws but rather from bad judgment and poor leadership skills. They entered military service with warped perceptions of officership. All they had to do, so they believed, was follow a simple formula for success: act courageously, with manhood and dignity, and men would follow them. Leadership and fighting were instinctual. Simply study the tactics manual, drill the soldiers, and they would succeed in combat. Yet they lacked executive ability and attention to detail—two qualities that prewar Southern society did not promote.[26]

Civil War armies devoted scant attention to improving and developing leadership skills. Officers mastered basic tactics manuals and followed army regulations, but those volumes failed to guide them through the myriad difficulties of command in the lethal environments of camp and campaign. Social standing and occupation in the civilian world, even political experience, did not necessarily translate into army leadership. Under the stress of military service, some individuals buckled, while others discovered their strength of character. Those who emerged as fine leaders did so more because they possessed the right temperament, energy, values, insights, and sound judgment than because they had genuine experience. In some cases, they honed those traits in civil life in their occupation and social position, but in other instances, these traits were fundamental qualities nurtured in their family with no outlet for expression or effective use in the civilian world. The war offered those individuals an opportunity to showcase leadership talent.[27]

From early in the war, Brig. Gen. D. H. Hill launched a campaign to thwart the misperceptions of officers' duties. While enlisted men dug trenches and erected fortifications around Yorktown, "some officers seem to think that they have nothing to do but stroll & sit about leaving all manual & military duty to be performed by the soldiers." It galled Hill that officers cared only for their "personal comfort" and did not attend to their men. He directed regimental and detachment commanders to "arrest all individuals with commissions who are seeking their ease when soldiers are on duty." Nearly two years later, a private rejoiced to his mother over his new commander. "We are now under Col [R. Snowden] Andrews, who is a strict disciplinarian & makes *Officers* as well as men do their duty."[28]

Returning to his brigade after recovering from his second wound, Brig. Gen. Robert Rodes determined he would institute changes, and in his mind the problem rested with the officers. Rodes called together officers and noncommissioned officers and announced some changes "in a manner quite original, and as forcibly & impressive as original," a private reported. He intended to make his brigade "a model of military discipline with a view to the redemption of the Confederate army from the lethargy of inactivity and carelessness of duty into which it had fallen." Rodes grumbled that some officers were "as incompetent to the proper discharge of their duties as would a 'Miss in her teens.'" No longer would he accept resignations from officers and allow them to leave the service. He would see to it that anyone who offered his sword would return to the ranks and tote a musket. If necessary, Rodes vowed to go through every man in the brigade until he had installed quality officers. He divided each company into six squads, with a noncommissioned officer responsible for ensuring that men washed their hands, faces, and feet at daybreak. Rodes charged company commanders with "'murdering one-third of the men lost in this campaign, by not properly providing them with comfortable clothing, and other necessities to a vigorous campaign.'" They were to report every Sunday morning to him on the condition and needs of their company. He also insisted that officers drill replacements twice per day to get them up to tactical proficiency. There would be inspection every Sunday morning, and the officers would read the Articles of War to the men every Sunday evening. "The new rules have had great effect already," the private asserted, "in making the men more comfortable, & giving the brigade the regularity & precision of old soldiers in the performance of their duty, & even in their private actions."[29]

That sort of willingness to share the burdens paid huge dividends with the men. In order to do his duty fully, to ensure that his soldiers had food and supplies, a Texan explained that he had to labor tirelessly: "a Capt[ain] has to work like a Trojan to accomplish any thing with the various departments (Quartermaster & Commissary)." When the men in an artillery battery had gone thirty-six hours without rations, the officers shared their provisions. "Lieut James Ellett stood over the fire and helped us to cook them, and saw that every man was satisfied," recorded a private in his diary. "Indeed, his kindness will never be forgotten by the men." Other officers walked so that sick men could ride on the march. Although enlisted men usually hurled wisecracks at the soldier, such as "'get down and carry your horse,'" everyone took note of the officer's gesture. In an unusual step on behalf of the men, a Virginia officer instructed his wife to assist the families of any of our men by doling out flour and feed to them. An officer in the 13th Alabama attempted to balance the soldiers' desire to secure battlefield plunder with their duty to fight as a coherent and full-strength unit. At Seven Pines, he kept his command together and prevented plundering and straggling while the battle was on. At nightfall, he let them slip out to the overrun Federal camps and take what they wanted. Soldiers returned with food, clothing, gold, silver, stationery, ink, and all sorts of other items. It was not an ideal military resolution, nor one that Lee would have endorsed, but it worked.[30]

By building rapport through attentiveness and concern for the well-being of the command, these officers established a powerful bond with their soldiers. As one semiliterate private, who described his officers as "cind [kind]," wrote his parents, "our officers is sutch men as wee would stand By and fite for to the last."[31]

Yet officers also had to impose discipline and exert authority. After serving more than a year, a South Carolina officer shrewdly noted, "An officer as a general rule, who does his duty is apt to make some enemies." Few men wanted the burdens of leadership, merely the glory of it. Yet as the South Carolina officer recognized, the two were inseparable. When an individual sought a commission as major, Brig. Gen. Cadmus Wilcox refused to endorse the promotion. "'We want men who are commanding, who will execute the laws, and exercise discipline'—'Men,' said he, 'who are not afraid of loosing popularity.'"[32]

Early in the war, a private in the 2nd Georgia expressed empathy for his regimental commander, even though he declared Col. Paul Semmes "extremely strict" and "disposed to exceed his authority." Semmes had "a rough set of men to manage," a regiment "composed of the roughest sort of material" and "even their officers have to be taught everything." He had hopes that once Semmes straightened out the regiment, he would be able to ease up a bit.[33]

Colonel Dorsey Pender, a West Point graduate in 1846, earned the everlasting respect and admiration of the 6th North Carolina for his firm hand as its leader. "Had he not come to us when he did," a private penned a friend, "our regiment long since would have been disorganized." The soldier admitted "he is very rigid in discipline" but he took great pride in knowing "our regiment is the best drilled in this portion of the Army." Pender established discipline while infusing the regiment with pride. The former Regular Army officer understood that they were volunteer soldiers, brimming with enthusiasm that would wane as days and weeks turned to months and years. He had a small window of opportunity to instill discipline and at the same time make these volunteers feel like soldiers, and through tireless efforts, he accomplished this.[34]

But Pender also had several advantages over most officers. He already knew how to drill and train troops, he possessed well-honed military leadership skills, he had served in combat, and he had come from the Regular Army, not the civilian world. Because the Confederacy raised its military units on the local level, familiarity added to the difficulties of command. As a Georgian complained to his wife when half the regiment reported sick before the Battle of Seven Pines, "our officers have not the nerve to force men to arms, even at this time when the liberties of our country are imperilled." He then concluded that as a general rule, "the officers are totally unfit to command."[35]

Good officers knew that they must establish a boundary line between themselves and the soldiers they commanded. Two months into his brigade command, Brig. Gen. Alfred Iverson attempted to address the chief cause for a lack of discipline, "familiarity and companionship of officers with Soldiers." In an order read to the entire brigade, Iverson attempted to explain to citizen-soldiers why they needed to stamp out the level of familiarity within the brigade. "In military life it does not enter into the question of whether the Private was or was not the equal of the Officer at home," Iverson instructed. In the military world, he was subordinate. "He is not degraded by submitting to the line of demarcation that must, in order to preserve discipline and secure consistence, be drawn between all alike."[36]

More than simply establishing boundaries between the commissioned officers and enlisted men, officers had to know their craft to command effectively. After the initial flurry of activity to learn drill, however, many officers eased up on their studies. Lapses in procedures and policies trickled down to their men, who observed their officers' sloppy approach to military duties and adopted similar behavior. More dutiful officers complained to subordinates that problems existed and called for reform, but nothing changed. It fell to general officers and regimental commanders to make training a top priority. Jackson, for example, demanded that his officers not only master their own responsibilities, but also acquaint themselves with the position above them, in the event they must take over that position during a campaign. The commander of the 23rd North Carolina ordered schools for officers that taught tactics and army regulations five hours per day. Six weeks later, he would hold examinations, and those who failed would go before a Board of Examination on the charge of incompetency. Perhaps the most resourceful effort at improving the troops came from the imaginative mind of Col. Carnot Posey, the acting commander of a Mississippi brigade. Posey ordered his men to fight several sham battles with artillery, to teach his soldiers how to maneuver more effectively with a battery of guns.[37]

In the end, of course, the true test for officers was on the battlefield. Confederate officers felt strong social pressure to lead by example, from the front. In critical moments, when their advance faltered or men began to retreat, many incurred great personal risks. During Seven Days', as his troops began to waver, Brig. Gen. Charles W. Field had his horse shot from under him. Fields picked himself up, drew his sword, and rushed to the front, ordering a charge. His bold action renewed the spirit of his faltering men, who then stormed the Yankee breastworks with a yell and carried them. At Antietam, when the 35th North Carolina attack stalled and the men became confused, Col. Matthew Ransom seized the colors and led the advance. In the face of a massive bombardment, Confederate artillerists Maj. John Pelham and Capts. William Pegram and David McIntosh sustained heavy losses yet held their positions and helped check Union attacks on the Confederate right. Also among the lengthy ranks of officer heroes was Capt. R. R. S. Lawrence of the 44th North Carolina. Despite having a sick furlough in his pocket, he entered a battle with a sergeant nearby to keep him on horseback. He led his men in an attack, reformed them after an ordered retreat, and "called upon his Company not to desert him, as he would Stand by them as long as he was able to Keep his feet." Night fell before they could launch another attack. At the time, Lawrence awaited charges of conduct unbecoming an officer before a general court-martial. The regimental officers submitted a petition on his behalf, arguing that "few officers either with or without a sick leave of absence approved and in his possession would of acted as nobly as he did on this occasion," and requested that the charges be dismissed and the petition of Lawrence's outstanding leadership be read aloud to the entire regiment.[38]

Unfortunately for the Confederacy, officers paid a heavy price for such bold leadership. Almost a quarter of all officers were killed in action, and four of every five officers were either killed or wounded at least once. Officers were more than twice as likely to be killed in battle as were enlisted men, and more than one and a half times more likely to receive a wound. Although army commanders compiled casualty statistics inconsistently, the fights in the spring and summer indicate staggering losses among the officer corps. At Seven Pines, Longstreet's command alone had 61 officers killed, 3 of whom were regimental commanders, and 209 wounded. In Seven Days', slightly incomplete figures suggest that 175 officers were killed, 14 of whom were colonels, and 675 were wounded. Lee's army suffered 133 officers killed at Second Manassas, with an additional 604 officers wounded. Eleven regimental commanders were killed in action there. Antietam was also a huge bloodletting for officers. Some 140 were killed or mortally wounded, 13 of them regimental commanders, and another 649 were wounded. Forty-eight more officers were missing in action, most of them presumably dead. With Jackson's Valley campaign, Cedar Mountain, and South Mountain included, some 600 Confederate officers were killed during those months, with over 2,000 wounded. In those same battles, 20 percent fewer Union officers were killed and 10 percent fewer were wounded, despite far more Yankee officers. The attrition rate for officers in the Army of Northern Virginia was simply disastrous.[39]

By the summer of 1864, the officer corps would suffer close to 1,000 more officers killed since Antietam and another 4,000 wounded. With a finite number of good leaders and capable administrators, the army began to tap lesser men to fill these positions. Many were excellent combat soldiers, but they lacked the kind of judgment and administrative skills that were essential for effective leadership. Few had mastered army regulations, and their knowledge of tactics did not always measure up to the wishes of superior officers. Having served extensively as enlisted men, their degree of familiarity and their unwillingness to guide with a firm hand, especially in a continual combat environment, prevented the army from sustaining, let alone improving, its degree of discipline. As one inspector explained to Confederate headquarters, the extensive fighting stripped away "the best and most efficient men in each command, and in too many companies there is not material left, out of which to make Co. [Company] commanders." Yet there was little the Confederacy could do. At least they were, as Maj. Gen. George Pickett suspected, "gallant and meritorious in action," and soldiers trusted them to lead in battle.[40]

Only in late February 1865 would Congress abolish the election of officers, opening the door for promotion on merit at the second lieutenancy level. By that point, the decision mattered little. Lee's army simply ran out of officers, as the meat-grinder war wound on.[41]

"What our officers most lack is the pains & labour of inculcating discipline," Lee complained to Davis in mid-August 1864. "It is a painful and tedious process, & is not apt to win popular favour. Many officers have too many selfish views to promote to induce them to undertake the task of instructing & disciplining their Commands. To succeed it is necessary to set the example, & this necessarily confines them to their duties, their camp & mess, which is disagreeable & deprives them of pleasant visits, dinners & c." Lee believed his enlisted men lacked discipline, and the officers could not instill it in them because they lacked discipline themselves. It was central to their military culture.[42]

Chapter 16

THE SOLDIERS OF '62

JAMES CAMPBELL HAD itched for a chance to fight the Yankees. A twenty-four-year-old stock raiser, Campbell had migrated to Texas from Ireland in the late 1850s. He settled in Seguin, in a house next to his relative, John Campbell, a wealthy stock raiser and minor slaveholder. James had missed the first calling for volunteers in April 1861, when locals raised a company that authorities designated Company D, 4th Texas. Nothing would keep him from enlisting in 1862. That spring, he joined Company D, stationed in Virginia.[1]

In just a few short years, this immigrant from Ireland had acquired a deep hatred for the Yankees. "I wish that all of tham was in one pile and I had a barl of powder under them and match to sat fiar to," he vented to a family friend. "I would do it quick I think." With a youthful cockiness, Campbell predicted, "I will slaee [slay] Some of tham any how if I got to See tham."[2]

His trip to Virginia was quite an ordeal, but not difficult enough to dampen his spirits. At one point, he had to hike fifty miles from the Mississippi River to the railroad, "but I can walk it to gat to Kill some of linken nits." A series of trains brought him to Richmond just in time for the battles to save the capital. At Gaines's Mill, Campbell's 4th Texas roared down a ravine, swept across a stream and various obstacles, and helped shatter the Union works. In the course of this heroic feat, the regiment lost 250 men, including both its colonels. According to official records, Campbell suffered a slight gunshot wound. Throughout the campaign, Lee's army hammered back the Yankee forces. Campbell claimed the battle would have lasted longer "but the anmy got to the gunbuts in the James river and partacted under the fier of the gun bots and they would not come out from unde tham and the[y] will not comout and fight like white man and when you find tham out and atact tham the will run to the gun botes in dubile quick time and every man for him Salf and the divel for all."[3]

Campbell continued to serve with his regiment, fighting at Second Manassas, South Mountain, Antietam, and Fredericksburg, emerging unscathed. He had great hopes that "I will gat home by christmess and spand aweek in plasher with you and my friends in that country" as the army marched northward from

Richmond. As an 1862 volunteer in an 1861 regiment, however, he had a long wait for a furlough.

When Lincoln replaced McClellan with Burnside, Campbell considered it fortunate for the Rebels. In his opinion, McClellan "is hade and sholders over any ginnarl that the[y] have and the[y] ere shiften about So much that it is imposable for than to [be] siccasful in thair atamps." In May 1863, Campbell demonstrated a keen sense of his rights as a free man when he squawked over an attempt by officers to appoint a new officer without the consent of the men. Four months later, his luck finally ran out. He was killed in action at Chickamauga.[4]

Like Campbell, Marion "Hill" Fitzpatrick was of Irish descent, but his family arrived a century earlier. His father, who died a dozen years before the war, had accumulated considerable wealth and proceeded to lose much of it. Still, the Fitzpatricks were hardly in need, owning four slaves and wealth totaling almost $6,500. Early in 1860, the twenty-five-year-old Fitzpatrick married a sixteen-year-old neighbor named Amanda White. Her pregnancy with their first child prevented him from enlisting in the initial wave of the war. A devoted husband and Southerner, however, he decided he had to serve. "I want this war to end and to be at home as bad as anybody can but I do not believe I could enjoy myself at home such times as these if I was able to do duty," he explained to Amanda on the second anniversary of his military service. "Others would be fighting for their Country and my Country and home while I would be skulking my duty, and it would render me miserable." In May 1862, Fitzpatrick left behind his young wife and toddling son to volunteer as a private in the 45th Georgia Infantry.[5]

Fitzpatrick proved to be an excellent soldier. A cheery attitude and good habits impressed his comrades in camp, and on campaign, he exhibited character and toughness. During the march north to Second Manassas and into Maryland, Fitzpatrick's shoes gave out. Huge blisters and cuts developed on his feet. Despite the pain and bleeding, Fitzpatrick kept up with his command. Twice over the course of the fighting he sustained combat injuries. A partially spent ball bruised him badly in Seven Days', and at Fredericksburg, a ball passed through his haversack and penetrated his skin, probably breaking a rib. He was valiant in combat, and his officers chose him to receive a badge for courage after the Battle of Chancellorsville. Over time he rose from private to sergeant major in his regiment. He also survived bouts with several serious illnesses, including high fever and dysentery. When no other noncommissioned officer volunteered, he stepped forward to take charge of the regimental sharpshooters. He worked them rigorously, improved their marksmanship, and oversaw them in action.[6]

Fitzpatrick's letters home offered touching concern for his wife and child, advising her during hog-killing time, "You must be the man and the woman both now you know." He wrote longingly for his son, whom he barely knew, and wished he could hear his gibberish as the boy struggled to form words. Fitzpatrick also praised the toughness of women like Amanda, who bore sacrifices, fed their family and the soldiers, and kept life as they knew it together. "If it were not for the patriotism and industry of the women the Southern Confederacy would soon come to nothing," he averred to Amanda. "Many a soldier can now realize the value of women's work that thought but little or nothing about it before the war commenced."[7]

Throughout the war, Fitzpatrick preserved a positive outlook. In the face of disaster, he merely strengthened his resolve. After the retreat from Pennsylvania in 1863, when the people at home grew despondent, he asserted, "It just fires me up to fight the harder." Even late in the war, he reminded Amanda just how bad Yankee rule would be. "Pen cannot describe nor tongue tell the degradation and suffering of our people if we ever submit," he insisted. On April 2, 1865, just a week before the end of hostilities, Fitzpatrick suffered a mortal wound. He lasted only four days.[8]

The overwhelming preponderance of 1862 soldiers shared this level of commitment to the Confederate cause. Personal matters usually prevented or discouraged them from joining the army that first year. Prospective soldiers had family or business obligations, or they assumed the war would not last long, and believed that their principal duty rested with their families. By early 1862, however, it had become evident the war would last some time and that the Confederacy needed many more men in uniform. That winter and spring, while the government debated ways of strengthening its armed forces and ultimately embraced a policy of conscription, communities publicized efforts to fill up the old regiments or form new units on the local level, offering fresh opportunities for recruits.

Nearly half of all the soldiers who ultimately served in the Army of Northern Virginia enlisted in 1861, and another third joined in 1862. The soldiers of 1862 entered military service with just as strong a belief in the justness of the Confederate cause, and just as much confidence in victory as their veteran comrades. "It would seem to me impossible, utterly impossible to restore the Union even if the Yankees should succeed in completely overrunning every southern state," a twenty-seven-year-old prewar attorney wrote home. "They could only hold us in subjection by keeping a large standing army in each state which would cost more than holding the country would be to them."[9]

The regional breakdown among the soldiers of 1862 remained almost constant, with roughly two of every five coming from the Lower South and three of five residing in the Upper South. The big shift was the increase in the number of soldiers from Georgia and North Carolina and the decline from the more western states, which now fed their volunteers into the armies closer to home.[10]

Those destined for Virginia understood full well that it would be a principal battleground. After asking his wife to "pray for me that I may return home from the forin land," Floridian Thomas Clark urged her "don't be uneasy a bout me." He admitted, "I don't know whether I shal ever see you a gin in this world if I don't I hop we will meet in the better world to com." Clark succumbed to wounds sustained to the chest and leg at Antietam, leaving a wife and a one-year-old daughter.[11]

The initial rush of 1861 attracted many younger, single men. With fewer critical familial responsibilities, weaker business commitments, and perhaps an enhanced spirit of adventure, they were the Confederacy's "minute men." By 1862, recruitment cut much deeper into traditional elements of Southern white society and lured into uniform persons who generally bore a greater sense of responsibility in their family and community. Married with a child, twenty-six-year-old farmer Hill Fitzpatrick was a fairly typical recruit in 1862. Three of every five soldiers who entered military ranks that year were farmers, while only four in nine of those who had enlisted the previous year derived their living directly from the soil. Fewer of the men of 1862 were professional, skilled, or unskilled workers. More than twice as many were married, and more than twice as many had children. This status as husbands and parents reflected a more subtle shift in age. Even though the majority of men were born after 1835, the percentage of those born before 1836 increased by 27 percent over the previous year. The percentage of foreign-born men, such as James Campbell, declined from almost 5 percent of the 1861 volunteers to barely more than 1 percent.[12]

Slightly older, more rooted in the community, married and often with children, and more frequently farmers by trade, the men of 1862 entered military service having accumulated more wealth and owning more slaves, although the differences were not that pronounced. The median personal and family wealth of 1862 soldiers rose to $1,312, from an 1861 figure of $1,180, both respectable levels. Arthur Wachob, a thirty-year-old farmer from Vernon, Florida, represented the changing demographics rather well. Along with two of his brothers, he enlisted in the 8th Florida Infantry. Wachob left behind a twenty-three-year-old wife to tend to their farm and property valued at around $1,100.

Within the same recruiting year, a wide variation existed among the soldiers, as it had in 1861. Thomas Roderick Dew enlisted in the 47th Virginia Infantry. His comrades elected him corporal. The twenty-five-year-old Dew had a wife and two children. He personally owned an estate worth $54,800, including twenty-two slaves, and his in-laws who lived with them had an additional $70,000 of wealth and forty more slaves. At the other end of the financial scale, Cicero Farrar of Campbelltown, Mississippi, joined the 42nd Mississippi Infantry. Three years older than Dew, Farrar left behind a wife and three children on his small farm worth $272. Those who enlisted in 1862 tended to have a greater concentration of extremes—very wealthy and very poor—whereas the men of 1861 exhibited higher percentages among the middle ranges, from the poor through the well-to-do.[13]

Because more soldiers were married and independent householders, personal slave ownership increased significantly. Eli Mayfield was one of these. A thirty-seven-year-old farmer with a slave, Mayfield joined the 11th Georgia Infantry in April 1862, entrusting the farm to his wife, Amanda. Some 18.2

percent—nearly one in every five—owned at least one slave. Almost four of every nine either owned slaves or resided with their family, which owned slaves. All told, the number of soldiers of 1862 who lived in slaveholding households increased marginally from 45 percent to 48 percent. Thus, ties to slavery and wealth were a bit stronger, but they mirrored the shift in age and life cycle.[14]

Those who entered the army in 1862 with commissions as officers tended to reflect the wealthy, slaveholding interests more than did their own enlisted men. Virtually all of the 1862 officers lived in households with slavery, and three of every four either owned slaves or were part of a family that owned slaves. These figures significantly exceeded those for their enlisted men: Almost two of every five enlisted men or their families owned slaves, and four in nine lived in slaveholding households. Officers of 1862 also had a median wealth that was nearly three times as large as that of their enlisted men.

Compared to officers of 1861, those who joined the service in 1862 had more ties to slavery but less total wealth. Half the officers in 1861 personally owned slaves, but none of them in the sample lived with their families who owned slaves. While the volunteers of 1861 lacked the wealth of those who joined in 1862, the officers of 1861 possessed 60 percent more wealth than their counterparts who entered the following year.[15]

Nonetheless, officers' backgrounds and wealth varied considerably. Dr. Hunter H. Holmes, a married physician who became the assistant surgeon in the 1st North Carolina Cavalry, had $21,000 of property, including sixteen slaves. Twenty-two-year-old lieutenant and later captain Otis Mills of the 56th North Carolina owned nothing, but his father had a large farm with nine slaves. Born in 1840, Thomas J. Corbin had worked in a factory before the war and, according to the 1860 census, had accumulated no wealth. Evidently, the men in the Pittsylvania Artillery saw something in him; they elected him second lieutenant.[16]

Precisely what impact the Conscription Act had on military service in 1862 is difficult to gauge. Approximately half of all soldiers who entered military service in 1862 did so before passage of the Conscription Act, and well over three of every four had taken the oath before its enforcement. Neither Campbell nor Fitzpatrick, for example, expressed any fear over the stigma of conscription. Both men believed deeply in the Confederate cause and joined willingly. Still, the draft undoubtedly coerced others to enlist. In the winter of 1862, the Confederate government established a goal of 6 percent of the total white population in uniform for the duration of the war. Governor Joseph Brown of Georgia called for all militia to assemble on March 4, 1862, and for the state to take volunteers, with a fifty-dollar bounty as an inducement. If Georgia did not secure its lot, he would resort to a draft. Brown's directives generated a rush to enlist in the months from March through May in Georgia, and individuals in other states may have felt a comparable pressure.[17]

Among those who entered the service in the final five months of the year, when communities began to feel conscription's pinch, almost half were twenty-one years old or younger, and many of them were just coming of age. Typical was Seaborn Swann of Athens, Georgia. The son of a farmer who owned two slaves, Seaborn enlisted in the Troup Artillery in November 1862, shortly after celebrating his eighteenth birthday.[18]

Conscription contributed at least one in every thirty soldiers in 1862 and probably more. The majority were small farmers, farmhands, or skilled workers who had not accumulated much in the way of wealth. John P. Givens, a twenty-seven-year-old farmhand and father of two, could boast very little money or property when the draft called him into service with the 48th North Carolina. By contrast, local officials pressed into the army William J. Hope, a well-to-do Virginia farmer and slave renter. Hope, still single at twenty-eight, owned over $2,500 worth of property and lived with his mother, two siblings, and a rich woman who leased her slave as Hope's field hand.[19]

After seven months of service, a South Carolina officer proffered some advice. "George will never regret enlisting as a private but once, and that will be continuously and forever." Military service was nothing but glittering misery. Yet his claim against the cavalry service was a rare grumble. "And of all the branches of service, the most trying, tiresome, wearying, and unreasonably exacting—indeed, degrading, is the Cavalry service," the South Carolinian argued. "I would rather be a low-bred, mangy, cur dog than a trooper." Overall, the second year of the war witnessed a significant increase in volunteers for cavalry. The inability to pursue the routed enemy effectively after First Manassas had demonstrated to military and governmental leadership the need for more horsemen. The cavalry, moreover, had gained in popularity. Most infantry and artillery considered it the easiest branch of the service. Even though cavalrymen had to provide their own horses, they did not have to walk or carry equipment very often, and a horse gave them the means to get out of camp regularly and an opportunity to rustle up some adventure. Most males owned at least one horse, so finances rarely prevented an individual at that stage of the war from joining a cavalry regiment. Stuart's raids generated publicity that fueled interest in the "chivalry," as critics called it. And in the end, cavalrymen did not sustain the same sorts of losses in combat as infantrymen or artillerists. After a cavalry battle with significant casualties, a surprised infantryman explained to his wife, "Cavalry you know, somewhat like the Chinese, not infrequently fight for honor and make a great deal of noise without anybody being hurt, but this battle seems to have been an exception."[20]

On the whole, the men of 1862 had a much more difficult transition to military life. Although they had read stories and letters about the war and had talked to veterans at some length, recruits and draftees had little time to train. Volunteers in 1861 had a lengthy acclimation period into army life, with limited combat exposure, other than First Manassas and a few lesser fights. During what seemed to them like a never-ending hiatus, they trained, drilled in tactics, endured hardships, learned survival techniques in camp life, bonded with comrades, and prepared themselves psychologically for the demands and brutality of active campaigning. The soldiers of 1862 who formed new regiments and batteries, by contrast, traveled to rendezvous camps in their home state in order to organize quickly and receive some basic instruction in tactics. From there, they marched or rode trains to Richmond, where authorities thrust them right into the cauldron of battle. Men who joined or were assigned to old regiments had even less training. Not until the end of October 1862 would Confederate authorities open Camp Lee as a Camp of Instruction. The "green" troops of 1862 benefited from working alongside much more experienced soldiers, but they had a long learning curve and little time.

In June 1862, barely more than a week before the opening salvos of Seven Days', Longstreet reminded his troops of the justness of their cause and then counseled his "fresh and inexperienced troops" on the horrors of battle and how to overcome them. He explained that "though the fiery noise of battle is indeed most terrifying, and seems to threaten universal ruin, it is not so destructive as it seems, and few soldiers after all are slain." He instructed, "Let officers and men, even under the most formidable fire, preserve a quiet demeanor and self-possessed temper." Longstreet admonished his troops, especially the new soldiers, "Keep cool, obey orders, and aim low." Finally, in a shrewd effort to instill confidence and build a sense of cohesion among the newcomers, he urged them, "Remember while you are doing this, and driving the enemy before you, your comrades may be relied on to support you on either side, and are in turn relying upon you."[21]

Despite Longstreet's counsel, no words could prepare the men of 1862 for the disasters they would endure. It was combat on a scale unprecedented in American history. Thrown into the war with little preparation, the losses in the class of 1862 were astounding. Three of every four soldiers were killed, wounded, taken prisoner, or died of disease. James Septimus Ackis, an eighteen-year-old native of Charleston, served in the Brooks Artillery. He suffered wounds at Gettysburg and Spotsylvania and spent two stints as a Yankee prisoner. Conscript John Givens, a resident of Vessel's Ford, North Carolina, was wounded and captured at Antietam. He survived Yankee imprisonment and was exchanged, only to die of diarrhea at Gordonsville in April 1864.[22]

The volunteers of 1861 fared better. Despite the trauma of adjustment to military service, volunteers of 1861 melded into army life at a less frenetic pace than those who entered in 1862. They acquired knowledge of how to care for themselves in camp and in combat more gradually and were better prepared for the massive bloodletting of 1862. Not surprisingly, among the men of 1861 and 1862, the infantry suffered the most. Over the course of the war, nearly three of every four infantrymen—officers and enlisted men—from 1861 were either killed, wounded, prisoners, or died of disease. Among those assigned to infantry regiments in 1862, four of every five suffered the same fate. In both classes, casualties among cavalry were slightly below those of artillery, and lagged far behind infantry.[23]

Not long after he entered military service, Pvt. C. A. Hege sought a way out of the army. "I want you to try to hire a substitute for me if you possibly can," he requested of his father. "I would rather be at home and work like a negro than to be here in camp." Three months later, Hege had begun to make the adjustment to military service. "I like the army life a great deal better than I did when I first came out," he admitted, "but I can tell you it is a hard life any way that you take it." Hege and his comrades stepped almost directly from the civilian world into some of the hottest fighting and longest, most difficult marches in the entire war. As one South Carolina veteran remarked of his regiment's new troops, "They look as if they were at a loss to know what to do." While the veterans put many of the newcomers through a mild hazing process or wondered to each other in utter dismay what this war had come to, there were powerful incentives to assimilate the new soldiers into the regiment or battery. Raw recruits sought to be part of the veteran organization, one that would teach and look after them during campaigns and in camp. Veterans, too, had a powerful motivation to train and integrate these green troops. The more thoroughly they instructed and incorporated them into the command, the more effective the organization would become. Just as Longstreet had advised, recruits had to learn, and veterans needed to absorb them into a coherent unit.[24]

Fully one-third of all soldiers who ever served in the Army of Northern Virginia or its predecessors joined the service in 1862. Like their predecessors, the men of 1862 resisted discipline; it was their nature to do so. More than simply warm bodies and cannon fodder, though, this huge influx of troops acted as a nexus between home and military service. As the men of 1862 entered military service, they helped to replenish those cultural attitudes and practices from home. Qualities and ideals such as honor, integrity, manhood, individuality, profligacy, self-indulgence, and a lack of discipline gained renewed strength among officers and men through exposure to those same characteristics in the recruits.

By the close of the year, the hardships, suffering, and combat accelerated the process of bonding between the men of 1861 and those of 1862. They fought in the most horrific battles the continent had ever seen, marched great distances in the heat of summer and the cold of winter, and endured enormous sacrifices on behalf of the Confederacy. Shared experiences built faith and trust, even among prewar strangers. " 'The barefoot boys' have done some terrible fighting," a Georgian informed his parents. "We are a dirty, ragged set mother, but courage & heroism find many a true disciple among us." He concluded accurately that "our Revolutionary forefathers never suffered nor fought as the 'Rebels' of '61 & '62 have fought & suffered."[25]

Chapter 17

———◦———

SUPPLYING THE ARMY

C APTAIN CHARLES M. Blackford marveled at the commitment and toughness of his comrades-in-arms. A native of Lynchburg, Virginia, Blackford grew up in a wealthy household where his mother opposed slavery and his father opposed secession. His father, a small slaveholder, ultimately came around to the cause out of love for his children and relatives who volunteered; his mother never changed her opinion on slavery, but she failed to persuade Charles. A prosperous lawyer and father of two, he owned nine slaves. Like his siblings, Blackford rushed to defend the Rebel cause, and he rose to become captain of the 2nd Virginia Cavalry. Ultimately, Longstreet tapped his legal talents by appointing him judge for the First Corps courts-martial. As his regiment came off the field, it ran into Jackson's troops marching past. Blackford noticed a mountain of a man with bare feet. He dropped out of the column and approached the fellow, asking where his shoes were and offering to buy him a pair. The soldier "positively declined saying, 'We've whipped those rascals now, I fought them barefooted, and I can fight them barefooted again and whip them too,' and off he marched." The date was December 16, 1862; it was after the Battle of Fredericksburg.[1]

Private James T. Thompson of the 11th Georgia Infantry felt the same. The eldest child in a household of twelve, Thompson gave up farming to enlist in 1861. The Confederacy failed to provide for him and his comrades, but that did not dissuade him from the cause, at least not in March 1862. "The Great Washington went hungry and raged [ragged], lay on the coald, frozen ground without blankets," justified the Georgian, "then why not mee be lik Washington."[2]

The soldiers in the Army of Northern Virginia exhibited extraordinary resilience in the face of wartime adversity. Not only did they fight tremendous battles and march great distances, they did so eating scanty rations, wearing poor clothes and shoes and sometimes none at all, and facing supply problems that taxed the most masterful logisticians.

Before secession, the Southern states had developed a transportation network that serviced distant markets predominantly with nonperishable goods, such as cotton, tobacco, and sugar. More perishable items like fruits, milk, meat, and grain usually came from local markets. Railroads were not built for speed; connecting lines often had different gauges, so that locomotives and cars could not transfer from one track to the other. The road system offered few macadamized and planked turnpikes in a region that experienced substantial precipitation. Dirt thoroughfares became quagmires after rainfall, making travel in the winter and spring particularly burdensome.

Nor was slow movement of goods the only supply problem that confronted Lee's army. Despite Herculean efforts, Southern manufacturing could not provide for all the needs of a large-scale war. The Confederacy would have to rely on importation of selected materials to fulfill its needs beyond what its own people could produce, but as the war went on into a second and third year, the Union blockade began choking off the supply.

In agriculture and other industries, the manpower drain was severe. Although soldiers served a vital function for society, they burdened the economy. As civilians, they produced; as soldiers, they consumed large quantities of food and other products, but made nothing tangible. The war, moreover, opened the door for the flight or confiscation of slaves, a portion of the labor force that the Confederacy could not afford to lose. To sustain its armies in the field, the Confederacy was forced to draw upon a diminishing number of farmers and other workers.

With a narrow margin of error, Confederate soldiers and civilians had to skimp or go without during the long war. Many in Lee's army bore shortages in good spirits, but long-term sacrifices and hardships grated on the soldiers, taxing their patience, discipline, and endurance. Supply had already influenced Lee to strike into Maryland to feed his soldiers and animals and gather other materiel necessary to sustain an army, and as the war extended into its second and third years, logistics would sometimes dictate military decision-making at all levels.

Early in the war, for the most part, active men thought of soldiering as a lazy life, in which they received regular if suspect rations and performed occasional duty. "We are all as fat as hogs and as lazy as adog," commented a Georgia private in 1861, "when the sun shines hot the gress [grease] biles out my socks." McLaws informed his bride that his brother "Hugh is So fat that he has had to cut open his pants for five or six inches in the back." The army had generated such intense public interest that in addition to government-issued rations, soldiers supplemented their diet through packages from home and the purchase or gift of food items from locals.[3]

Clothing tended to be a more troublesome concern that first year of war. After four months of service, shoes and boots began to wear, and initial replacements arrived slowly. A colonel complained through official channels that some seventy men in the 2nd Virginia Cavalry were barefoot. Virginia Lt. Col. E. T. H. Warren noted four days later, "The truth is ¼ of our men are bear footed half of them cannot hide their nakedness but are raged [ragged] as they can be." Fortunately, these were the dog days of summer, when soldiers fighting on the defensive required only modest clothing and could function satisfactorily without shoes. A South Carolinian who fought at First Manassas joked with a friend that he needed new pants, "for I have patched these Old ones until they are more holy than righteous." Strenuous efforts on the part of government officials and loved ones at home provided clothing for the winter months. By the spring, fresh needs arose, and the army had to scramble once again.[4]

Animals and their feed proved by far the greatest supply problem for the army during the first year of war. Even though Southerners owned huge numbers of horses and mules, and cavalrymen brought beautiful horses into service from home, many citizens sold inferior animals to the government. Magruder, with his flair for the dramatic, complained that the artillery horses he received "are almost without *exception* worthless" and "nothing but the *vilest refuse* has been sent here." The army's greater problem was feeding them properly. In those chaotic first months of war, quartermasters bought up hay and forage and shipped it from location to location, so that when a military command arrived in any given area, it could not always procure feed locally. As winter mud delayed wagons hauling feed, animals starved. Harsh cold weather took its toll on the horses and mules, so much so that Beauregard ordered shelters constructed to house them. By spring, the number of animals had depleted so dramatically that Brig. Gen. William N. Pendleton asserted that the artillery alone needed 1,200 more horses, of which the government had provided only a small portion.[5]

As the spring campaigns of 1862 opened, military officials redoubled their efforts to supply the army. High-ranking officers pressured their superiors and government officials for proper provisions, and whenever shoes or clothing became available, lower-ranking officers acted aggressively to secure them. An officer in Trimble's Brigade discovered a stockpile of shoes in a warehouse, and the brigade quartermaster directed his subordinate to seize at least five hundred pairs. "Many of the men of the Regiments of this Brigade are absolutely barefooted, & should it be necessary you will make the strongest representation to the Quartermaster having them in charge," he directed. "The shoes *must be had*."[6]

Still, most soldiers retained an upbeat attitude in the face of adversity. As they prepared for battle—many of them for the very first time—clothing meant comparatively little. Food, muskets, and ammunition assumed top priority. In the works around Richmond, a private described rations that Lee could have employed as a weapon against the Yankees. "The government furnishes us with nothing but a little flour and a little meat that is so very strong that it will Knock a man down as far as fifty yards if he does not hold to a post like grim death to a dead negro." After Antietam, when the army settled down a bit, men resumed their jocular complaining. To prove a point, one soldier applied a hammer to his hardtack, claiming "it is hard bread to have to take a hammer to brake it."[7]

As the brisk fall weather transformed into the bitter cold of winter, soldiers shifted their concern to clothing. The Maryland Campaign merely showcased the problem of inadequate footwear and clothing; it did not solve it. The hardship affected everyone, regardless of background or wealth. As Pvt. James Thompson of the 11th Georgia, himself from a well-to-do family, commented to his parents and siblings, "Thir is pleanty of lawyers and Doctors hear barefooted and nearly necked that used to ware broad cloth and wouldent hardly speek to a common man." Civilian eyewitnesses testified to soldiers' complaints. A woman saw Richard Anderson's division march toward Hanover Junction, and "some of the poor fellows were barefooted." Four days later, another woman commented on the condition of Ewell's Division. "A great many of the men are barefooted; it is cold too; yet as ill-fed & ill-clad as they are, they bear all for Liberty." Brigadier General Cadmus Wilcox wrote his brother in Congress that 5,000 men wanted shoes. When Lee's wife sent a note and a batch of socks she had knitted, Lee admitted, "I shall have no difficulty disposing of the latter & will try & find a man with shoes to put over them." Soldiers from Virginia benefited from ready access to home and could secure critical garments. Those from more distant states seldom had the luxury of overcoats or blankets, let alone shirts, pants, and shoes, shipped from home. Even tents, which could have alleviated some of the hardship at nighttime, were in dreadfully short supply. Fortunately, soldiers could build small but often cozy shanties as winter quarters to protect themselves in the worst months of cold.[8]

Food, too, was at a premium that winter and well into the spring of 1863. Troops had to survive exclusively on rations. No longer could they supplement their diet from local purchases, because those few civilians who remained had nothing to offer. On Christmas Day, 1862, a Virginian informed his parents that for a good mackerel, "I think I'd risk letting a whole company have one fire at me from one hundred yards off." Men lived on half rations or less; coffee was a luxury. After receiving even less food for a couple of weeks, the commissary issued half rations to a Virginia regiment. A soldier, referred to as "'the great Army Demoralizer'" for his constant complaining, debated how to consume this bountiful repast. Finally, he decided to consume a bit then and keep the remainder for the next morning. He was so hungry that all night long the soldier dreamed of army rations. When he awoke the next morning, he discovered that someone had stolen his haversack, and no one had enough to share with him. Nor were rations good quality. Private Louis Leon jotted in his diary one February day, "got one day's rations, hard enough to fell a bull."[9]

There were no easy solutions to the food problem. War had so disrupted wheat production in Virginia that farmers harvested only a quarter of what they did in peacetime. Manpower shortages, campaign disruptions, and wartime refugees limited the number of acres under cultivation, and a part of the crop that farmers did harvest was grown in areas that were cut off from Confederate authorities. In an average year, 800,000 to 1 million bushels of wheat were shipped to Richmond. In 1862, even though the city's population doubled and it became the central conduit for supply to the army, only 250,000 to

300,000 bushels arrived. One full-grown cow provided enough meat to issue a full ration to two hundred soldiers. Securing enough cattle and feeding them properly caused the army endless difficulties, especially in the winter months. By mid-January 1863, the army supply of cattle had dwindled down to enough to last through the end of the month only, and those had become very thin due to insufficient grazing.[10]

The army also suffered from a shortage of animals and wagons. In the Union, a command like the Army of the Potomac had one wagon for every forty men and one horse or mule—many of those for cavalry—for every two to three men. The entire command had 2,500 wagons and 35,000 horses or mules, and those animals consumed approximately 600 tons of hay and fodder per day. Lee's army paled in comparison. One field officer complained that his brigade had only thirty-seven wagons, six of which were worn out. He needed six foraging wagons but had only one, and his brigade also was short at least eight mules or horses. Colquitt's brigade had two-mule teams instead of four mules, except for those that had none at all. Similar hardships afflicted the cavalry. The Hampton Legion, for example, had 200 dismounted men.[11]

Hauling large quantities of food, fodder, and other supplies over the railroad may have offered a viable solution, but by the winter of 1862–63, the Confederacy had so overused its rail system in Virginia that it was becoming increasingly unreliable. Lee's army settled into camp that winter in the Rappahannock River area, and the Richmond, Fredericksburg & Potomac Railroad ran directly there. Unfortunately, the railroad builders did not design it to carry much freight, and the tracks could not sustain the necessary workload. The Virginia Central Railroad, probably the most important railroad in the state and a viable alternative, intersected with the Richmond, Fredericksburg & Potomac at Hanover Junction. From there, it ran to Charlottesville and through the Shenandoah Valley, the richest region for food production in the state. Workers could unload supplies at Hanover Junction and place them on wagons, which would then have to haul them the remaining thirty-five miles, a difficult and demanding proposition in bad weather. Even worse, the condition of the Virginia Central's tracks had declined significantly in just two years of war. Due to overuse and a lack of repair, its "efficiency is *most seriously impaired*," so the railroad president informed Jefferson Davis. In mid-March 1863, the line suffered four derailments in a five-day span, with each incident resulting in the destruction of freight cars and delayed operations. According to the railroad president, a severe shortage of workers exacerbated the overuse problem. The railroad employed only about half the number of laborers that it had before the war. Black railroad workers had run off to the Federals, as had local slaves. Without sufficient workers, the railroad could not cut down enough trees and make ties to secure the rails in position and prevent derailments. To slow the rate of these costly derailments, officials had to reduce the weight in each car by 25 percent and slow the speed.[12]

Into the spring, tight supplies translated into meager rations for the sol-

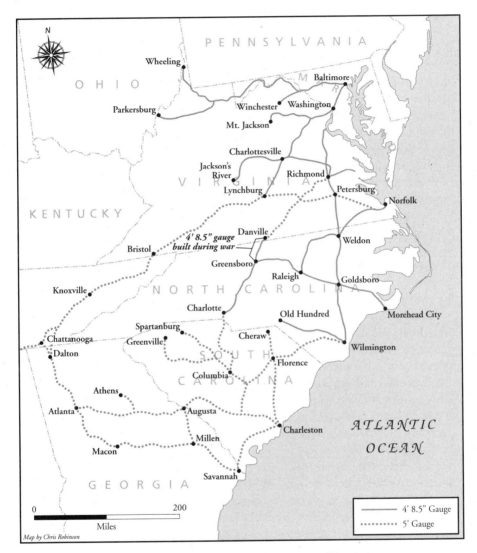

Railroads from Northern Georgia to Virginia,
with different gauges

diers. It took three trains of ten cars or two trains of fifteen cars to carry one million rations, enough for Lee's army for two weeks. The animals for Jackson's Corps alone required four cars of forage per day. With all the demands for the Richmond area and the difficulty of procuring and loading that quantity on a regular basis, Lee's army seldom received enough to meet its basic needs. Soldiers and animals regularly lived on reduced rations. An artilleryman grumbled to his father, "We are pretty bad off now in the eating line we get old rusty bacon & musty flour & not half enough." Joining the chorus was a Virginian, who announced to his wife that they received ¼ lb. of bacon, some bread, and a little rice and molasses per day, which he deemed "not, however, anything like enough." A North Carolinian alerted his father, "I should like to come home to get something to eat for I am starved most to death." Union intelligence learned of the shortages through interrogations of deserters. On the eve of the spring campaign in 1863, Yankee soldiers taunted their Confederate enemies, claiming the Rebels "have a new Gen[eral] in command of our army & say his name is *General Starvation*."[13]

Lee grasped the critical nature of the problem and devoted enormous energy and time to the supply of his army. To his son Custis in early January 1863, Lee intimated that he might have to withdraw from the Rappahannock line. "I am doubtful whether I shall be able to retain my position & may be at last obliged to yield to a greater force than that under Command of Genl. Hooker." By retreating, Lee knew he would give up everything they had gained on the battlefield from August through December, and he feared the ripple effect on morale. In mid-October 1862, Lee had directed commissary and quartermaster officers that if locals refused to sell supplies at the prices established by the government, they should take what was necessary, always leaving enough for family needs, and provide them with certificates stating how much they took and that the individual had refused to sell it to the army. The new procedure did not obtain enough food for man or beast. In December, he warned the secretary of war that the railroads required more energetic management. In response to the problems along the Virginia Central, the army commander requested the secretary of war divert one hundred slaves who worked on fortifications to shift over to the rail line "to prevent it from failing us when we shall most need it." Officers received a directive to reduce transportation "to the lowest limit." He also explained to the quartermaster general in anticipation of the spring campaign, "unless our horses can be brought into good condition disaster must ensue." Lee sent the cavalry to Page County, as it had not sustained the army before, and "the consumption of forage there does not affect the supply for the main army."

Lee informed Jackson and Anderson that the army had no long forage available and instructed them to feed their animals on twigs and bark from poplars, maples, and sweet gums and, rather than tying up horses, let them graze along river and creek bottoms. Most important, Lee detached two divisions and sent them to southeastern Virginia under Longstreet to block a Federal buildup there from advancing on Petersburg and Richmond and severing the vital railroad between Petersburg and Weldon. There, Longstreet's columns could feed themselves, gather critical supplies for the army, and reduce the burden along the Rappahannock by 20 percent.[14]

To provide shoes for the men, Lee took several steps. In November 1862, he withdrew all shoemakers from the ranks—271 of them—and placed them at work making shoes. Officers also encouraged men to convert rawhides from butchered cattle into usable foot coverings. D. H. Hill pushed the alternative so strongly that his men referred to him as "Rawhide Hill."[15]

Over the next year, shoe shortages periodically plagued the army. Soldiers continued to produce their own, or their officers contracted for the men. For some reason, the government kept purchasing shoes, either made at home or abroad, that were too small for the men. Had the shoes been too large, at least soldiers could have wrapped their feet and still used them. In one batch, Lee's army received 10,000 pairs, of which it sent back 3,024 as unfit. They were poorly made, too small, or too low. If footwear did not extend above the ankle, mud sucked them off their feet.[16]

As long as Lee's army remained in Virginia during the 1863 campaign season, it suffered shortages that varied from serious to critical. "Grumbling fills in the courses," admitted a twenty-four-year-old captain, "and laughing at misfortune and tough beef & biscuit, generally makes up the dessert." The standard joke in the army was that the bacon "outranks Gen. Lee." Frustration over food bubbled up in the aftermath of the huge battle along the Rappahannock in late April and early May. A South Carolinian described how the army issued rations for a single day and soldiers had to stretch them out over three. Most men ate their rations over two days and had nothing to eat on the third. "We generally have fast day twice a week," he stated. Some soldiers entered the fight literally with no food in their haversacks. If they overran Yankees, they could eat; otherwise, they went hungry. "It is a cursed shame that after men have done their duty as well as we did marched as hard & fought as hard & drove the Enemy back out of danger that we must suffer for food," erupted a Georgia private. "If this is the stile that the confederacy is going on the war will soon break[,] indeed it is played out." Another soldier grumbled that he had cold bread for dinner, nothing for supper, crackers and water for breakfast, and crackers and wild onions for dinner. "I can eat a day's rations at one meal," he insisted. A North Carolina private doubted the war would last much longer unless the government provided more food, reporting to his brother that "some say that the[y] wood runaway that I thought never would runaway." He admitted, "we can't stand everything & not get half enuf to eat & the[y] wont pay us but if the[y] wood the[re] hant nothing that we can by nowher about here."[17]

By midsummer 1863, clothing shortages once again reached epidemic proportions. "I am getting nearly naked," a soldier revealed to his folks at home. Another, the son of a Confederate senator, described himself to his sister, bottom to top: "My boots were utterly worn out; my pantaloons were all one big hole as the Irishman would say; my coat was like a beggar's and my hat was actually falling to pieces." One regimental commander thought the army needed 30,000 pairs of shoes and estimated half his men were barefoot or almost so. By the late fall, troops still had no tents, no overcoats, and no blankets. With evident admiration for the toughness of his comrades, Sgt. Hill Fitzpatrick stated, "They build a fire and lie down on the ground before it and sleep when it is cold enough to freeze a man well wrapped up." The Confederacy employed 3,000 women to manufacture clothing; it was not nearly enough. Soldiers wore out shoes and garments quicker than the laborers could produce them.[18]

Animals fared even worse. In early August, Lee complained to the secretary of war that the army was receiving only 1,000 bushels of grain per day, nowhere near enough for his artillery and cavalry horses, let alone the wagon train animals. Several weeks later, Lee explained the critical supply situation to the commander-in-chief. "Some days we get a pound of corn per horse, and some days none, some time our limit is 5 lbs. per day per horse." He then closed with the potent words, "You can judge our prospects." Likewise, artillery horses received three to four pounds of corn per day, far too little to sustain them in a condition fit for service. The war had taken such a toll on Virginia agriculture that the Confederacy hauled the corn from Georgia and South Carolina for Lee's army. Ultimately, Lee's army began trading artillery horses with more stationary postings like Petersburg, to secure healthier animals in the event of an active campaign.[19]

Soldiers took matters into their own hands. Early on, they had plundered on the battlefield for money and valuables, weapons, and mementos. By late 1862, they had no choice but to plunder for food and clothing. As cold weather approached once again, soldiers hoped for a battle so that they could clothe themselves properly that winter. "In fact the majority of the troops are Eager for a fight," one staff officer wrote to his father. "The battlefield is the greatest store house of winter equipments & pocket money, and our boys have a 'penchant' for both." A Virginia private and prewar carpenter concurred. "I have Rather bin in hopes if tha ware going to Fight attall that it wood come off for I want Some overcoats and Blankets if our men Whip them I wood Stand a good chance to get Some," he explained to his wife.[20]

Unless they were on the march, soldiers seldom had the chance to swipe food from locals, because there was little left to take by late 1863. Instead, troops turned to their own government to pilfer food. As an Alabama private asserted, "hunger will drive a man to any thing you may Depend." The Confederate government admitted that in 1863 alone, 617,000 pounds of bacon alone were stolen. According to the assistant commissary of subsistence in January 1864, "every shipment of meat is robbed of from 8 to 15 hundred pounds." While civilians certainly took their share, soldiers were also responsible. It was not difficult to board trains, as they moved between eight and ten miles per hour. Soldiers also began placing obstructions on the tracks near Culpepper. Since manpower shortages discouraged the Confederacy from placing guards on the trains, armed soldiers had easy pickings on a halted train. To combat the practice, the Confederacy had to place guards with orders to shoot saboteurs on the spot. The hunger problem became so serious that rumors reached Lee's headquarters of a secret society among men in the army planning to break into the commissary storehouse at Orange Court House.[21]

Soldiers attempted to offset the supply failures by more legitimate means as well. Officers established fishing details, and groups of soldiers, unable to fire their weapons, encircled animals such as rabbits and partridges in order to capture them for meals. Sergeant Hill Fitzpatrick became a fairly expert sewer who repaired his overcoat when it caught fire while he was sleeping. South Carolinian Edwin Kerrison made a hat from a pair of Yankee britches. It "is very dirty & greasy" but serviceable.[22]

As winter descended in late 1863, Pendleton, Lee's chief of artillery, worried. "There seems much suffering in store for us," he predicted to his wife. "The difficulty of feeding our animals where we have to meet the enemy is almost insuperable, and with that difficulty others increase, as feeding our men, whose food horses must draw, and using our cannon which must by horses be moved from place to place." Several months earlier, Lee had to reduce the number of guns in his artillery, because he could not feed the animals. In November, the commanding general complained to Davis, "No Corn was recd here on the 21st & 23rd on the 22d and 24th about five pounds per horse." Two and a half pounds per day was about one-tenth of what the Union was then feeding its horses. In the course of forty days without any campaigning, a cavalry brigade increased the number of its dismounted men from 292 to 681 due to forage shortfalls.[23]

Food for humans, too, was at a premium that winter. The problems were that the government paid half of what farmers could receive on the open market, or less. A member of the Confederate House of Representatives reported that in mid-December 1863, Lee's army had only ten days of meat rations stockpiled, and "Every pound has been sent up." In early January 1864, Davis admitted that the army issued one-quarter of a pound of meat per man per day, and Lee only had one more day's issue on hand. The commissary general urged Lee to impress foodstuffs from locals. Lee rejected the idea of his army seizing food. After fighting hard for several years to earn the confidence and trust of the people, he could not stand to alienate the citizens. As a solution, Lee suggested an alteration of priorities and civilian consumption habits. Soldiers in the field should become the nation's top priority. "If it requires all the meat in the country to support the army," Lee argued, "it should be had, and I believe this could be accomplished by not only showing its necessity, but that all equally contributed, and that it was faithfully applied." If the government could convince the public to consume foodstuffs that "cannot be so well used by the troops in the field," it would save other eatables for his men. But if Lee could not change the practices of his own troops, the chances of adjusting the eating habits of Confederate civilians were nil.[24]

Yet acquiring the food for soldiers was not the sole problem; the government had to transport it along overused and sometimes badly managed rail lines, and then over dirt roads that became almost impassable during wintertime, unless the ground froze solid. Early in December, as the crisis materialized, the government ordered urgent shipments of corn from South Carolina, Georgia, and Alabama to Richmond. By mid-December, large amounts of corn had accumulated in Augusta, Georgia. The first two carloads, however, did not reach Richmond until January 9, 1864. Trains had to travel some five hundred miles, with sundry companies owning parts of the route. Railroads had great difficulty collecting rolling stock and moving those cars over worn rail lines, often at speeds of eight miles per hour, and sometimes shifting to track with different track gauges. The farther Lee had to reach to draw his supplies, the more he taxed the railroad system, and the more wear and tear he caused to the tracks, engines, and cars.[25]

Three weeks before the opening of the spring campaign of 1864, Lee proposed a dramatic policy change to the secretary of war, one that would require a massive intervention into Confederate life. The Confederacy needed to maximize space on trains for supplies to the armies. "The railroads should be at once devoted exclusively to this purpose, even should it be found necessary to suspend all private travel for business or pleasure upon them for the present." The campaign would target Richmond, and Lee suggested that "all the population whose presence would impede or endanger our efforts should be removed, especially that part of it which increases the consumption of public stores, without aiding or strengthening the army." He wanted prisoners, parolees, Federal deserters, and unemployed persons removed from the city, and "every encouragement given to the rest of the non-combatant population to retire, except those whose services may be useful or who will not increase the scarcity of supplies." If the individual did not contribute directly to the war effort through military or government service, production, direct labor, or transportation, the government needed to urge them to leave the Richmond area to conserve supplies for the troops.[26]

The grind of prolonged, attrition warfare against overwhelming Union manpower and economic superiority forced Lee and the Confederacy to consider revolutionary policies. Fortunately, 1864 was a presidential election year in the Union. If they could punish the Federal forces that spring and summer, perhaps they could influence the outcome of the election and secure victory for the peace elements in the North. In order to do that, however, they would have to devise means, such as those proposed by Lee, of maximizing resources and enhancing combat strength.

Soldiers, meanwhile, would have to continue to bear the brunt of shortages. Lee could only blanket them in words of encouragement, assuring them that he spared nothing to provide for their needs. He reminded them that their Revolutionary fathers had born the same suffering in their quest for independence. "Continue to emulate in the future, as you have in the past, their valor in arms, their patient endurance of hardships, their high resolve to be free, which no trial could shake, no bribe seduce, no danger appal[l], and be assured that the just God who crowned their efforts with success, will in his own good time, send down his blessings upon you," he exhorted them. Good words, they were a poor substitute for food or clothing that winter.[27]

Chapter 18

―•○•―

CAMP AND RECREATION

D RUMMERS POUNDED OUT the long roll. Soldiers, hearts thumping, raced to assemble for battle. Mounted field officers positioned themselves in the front. With the enemy two miles off, they planned to lead the advance until their forces neared, at which point they would assume proper combat positions. The brass band struck up a martial tune; its mere sound injected their bloodstreams with bursts of adrenaline and sent tingles down their spines. Despite a long and hard fight the previous day, an impending encounter banished any lingering fatigue among the soldiers in Cadmus Wilcox's Alabama Brigade. By the afternoon, exhaustion would catch up with them. Until then, they would struggle hard and risk all for victory.

About a mile off, they could see the enemy, fully aware of their approach, forming in line of battle to repulse their attack. The Alabamians deployed with skirmishers to the front. Flags fluttered in the wintry breeze. The flagbearers would guide the command, indicating advance, retreat, and rallying positions, a particularly useful device when battlefield sounds drowned out the voices of officers and clouds of smoke obscured sight of men on the ground. The Alabamians, however, entered the fray without the help of artillery. The engagement the day before had battered Cutts's Battery, and they could muster none of its men for duty.

Soon, projectiles hurled through the air, crashing within the ranks. "The fight was desperate," claimed one participant. "Charge after charge was made by both sides," and the air filled with the sounds of "yells, particular to rebels alone." For a while, the enemy held its ground stubbornly, resisting the Alabama onslaught, "but finally we routed them, & drove them from the field," capturing large numbers of prisoners. With colors "triumphantly floating in the breeze & our band playing 'Dixie,'" Wilcox's victorious troops marched back to camp, "all covered with not Glory, but snow."

This was just one of many great snowball fights in the Army of Northern Virginia. The day before, Wilcox's men had fought one another, until at a council of war they agreed to unite against Brig. Gen. Edward Perry's Floridians. The Alabamians attacked that day with the band playing "Come out of the Wilderness." They bombarded the Florida troops, took prisoners, and even offered oaths of allegiance. According to a Florida soldier, the Alabamians supported by Cutts's Battery "presented quite a formidable line of battle." After driving the Floridians from their camp and seizing many prisoners, the victors marched off to the tune of "Bonnie Blue Flag." The next day they fought a rematch.[1]

Massive snowball fights—a regular occurrence in the army when snow fell—offered a wonderful opportunity for men to revert to boys, to take their minds off the hardships of war and to have some good fun together. Since that very first winter, troops in Lee's army had engaged in massive snowball fights. In January 1862, Brig. Gen. Joseph B. Kershaw's South Carolinians joined forces with the Texas Brigade against two brigades of Georgians. All told, some 8,000 men hurled snowballs at one another, until the Texans launched an assault that roared through the defenders' position. Everyone from private to colonel participated.[2]

The Texans were particularly aggressive. According to a Prussian military observer, whenever snow had fallen, anyone who passed near the Texas camp was pelted by a barrage of snowballs. No one was immune, even general officers.[3]

As a snowball warrior reported to his wife in late March 1864 after a battle between Brig. Gen. John R. Cooke's and Brig. Gen. William W. Kirkland's North Carolinians, "there was more laughing and hollowing then I ever herd at one time." In fact, much of camp life was a rollercoaster of emotions and a creative war against boredom.[4]

The tedium of everyday camp life bored soldiers to frustration. "This is a dull stupid life," a major grumbled in 1862, "all day long we are cooped up with nothing to do and every thing to make life disagreeable." Almost two years later, an aggrieved Mississippian vented in his diary, "Still we drag out our weary existence without any prospect of immediate variety." Two months later, the same soldier complained, "Another day is gone & on its face is stamped the same repulsive monotony as the day before." Yet in late August 1861, a soldier in a Virginia regiment explained to his sister, "you all believe that a soldier becomes very sad and gloomy by leaving home but you all are altogether mistaken for we are the liveliest set of men you ever saw together without they had Liquor to drink." Men talked and laughed, others played music and danced, and still more soldiers engaged in all sorts of games. Thirty-two months later, a different Virginian observed similar activities around camp, "some playing the fiddle, some picking the banjo, others beating bones, every fellow doing something and saying something to raise the spirits and drown the sorrow of the weary soldiers." He then explained to a girlfriend, "Yet it all goes in a lifetime, just anything to make the soldier forget his hardships and relieve his troubled mind."[5]

To entertain themselves, soldiers resorted to games from their youth. "Wouldn't you think it funny," an officer queried his younger brother, "to see grown up men playing Roly Poly, & cat and Slingarm and Prisoners Base, and Bullpen, and Pitching horse Shoes all day long[?]" One soldier commented that marbles had become the passion of the 17th Virginia, with officers and enlisted men joining in the contests. Baseball proved quite popular as well. Two Alabama companies squared off for a football game in the snow. Soon the balance of the regiment arrived and broke up the contest by pelting the players with snowballs, starting a melee that lasted for about two hours. Among cavalrymen, horse racing proved very popular. It served as recreation, helped men blow off some competitive steam, and enabled riders to improve their horsemanship skills until severely limited food for the animals made racing unwise. Those who preferred more sedate entertainment took up fishing when the weather suited them.[6]

Reading offered a wonderful solitary outlet for some. More than nineteen of every twenty soldiers in Lee's army were literate to some basic degree. Newspapers, magazines, and books passed through camp, from one set of eyes to the next. A college-educated Mississippian enjoyed "trashy novels," but his favorite in camp was William Shakespeare. Victor Hugo's *Les Misérables* was popular in the army. Troops called it " 'Lee's miserable soldiers.' " A Virginian not only accumulated a small collection of books and magazines, he also made a chess set.[7]

Talented and creative, soldiers developed their own theaters and concerts. The more sophisticated prepared programs, and the performances were so good that they attracted generals and their wives when they were in camp. Minstrel shows were popular forms of entertainment, as were burlesques. One actually included the disrobing of a soldier who played the role of a woman. Those who had the luxury of a duty station near a city, especially early in the war, slipped out of camp to attend cultural events. An Alabamian snuck out on several nights to view amateur minstrels and a concert. Officers caught him and sent him to the guardhouse for twenty-four hours for his absence without leave, but he did not care. He even had a date. "All I can say is that for the same amount of pleasure I will willingly undergo the same penalty any time," he wrote in his diary. As soon as he got out of the guardhouse, he ran the lines again but failed to rendezvous with the woman.[8]

One soldier described his comrades-in-arms to a friend by writing, "common soldiers by name, however, are often times very uncommon soldiers—like common sense." Spirited, fun-loving Southerners amused one another with a wide assortment of pranks and practical jokes. "Our life now is very monotonous," a soldier wrote home, "the boys resort to various expedients to wear away time, the chief one of which I believe is teasing each other." The enlisted men in Crenshaw's battery, evidently with the cooperation of the officers, played a joke on W. G. Walker by holding a fake election for a lieutenancy and selecting him for the post. For several days, everyone kept the joke from him. "He even went so far as to have bars put on his collar and put on airs generally," recorded one of its artillerists. "He was the greatest fool I ever saw."[9]

Around the campfire, soldiers always had to keep up their guard. A little slip and they were apt to become the butt of taunts and laughter. When lovesick Grey Haden of the 4th Alabama asked his buddy earnestly, "Turner did you ever say to your sweet heart—I'd rather die with you than live without?" the others in the group "laughed so hard at Grey that they put him to shame." A group of soldiers in the 5th Virginia decided to spoof their division commander, Maj. Gen. Edward "Allegheny" Johnson. "The whole affair was farcical & amusing in the extreme," recorded an eyewitness. The soldiers who played Johnson and his staff "were resplendently attired in gorgeous uniforms trimmed with red flannell & with immense paper plumes." The general had three stars made from gingerbread on his collar, and his field officers donned spurs "& were dressed like Harlequins." Virtually the entire brigade turned out for the phony review and everyone laughed uproariously. The soldier insisted, "it exemplifies the spirit of the men—buoyant in the extreme."[10]

Except for the first year of the war, camp life during warm weather seldom grew tiresome. The army either prepared for battle or recuperated briefly from recent fights, and troops welcomed relief from the hardships and duress of an active campaign. When heat, rain, and an occasional storm were the worst with which troops in camp had to cope, they were relatively pleased. As the weather began to turn cold, conditions toughened. Soldiers had to sleep in the open air or under modest tents, while rains, snow, and the cycle of freeze and thaw converted dirt roads into impassable mud puddles. In November 1862, Longstreet, vigilant in his care for the men, directed subordinate commanders to "take every method of protecting and guarding their men from the weather in their present exposed position." He ordered officers to keep campfires burning all day long, so that troops not on duty, especially those lacking suitable winter clothing, could warm themselves. At night, he wanted new campfires started close by, "so that the men can make their bivouacs on the earth thus warmed during the day."[11]

When the campaign season ended, army commanders permitted their men to go into winter quarters. Troops erected small cabins from logs, sometimes housing as few as three or four soldiers, other times as many as ten men. The number of trees soldiers cut was staggering. One brigade used 1,800 cords of wood over an eighty-day period. The year before, a different brigade chopped down fifty acres' worth of timber. Each year, the army cleared and burned over 1,000 acres of forest just in the winter months.[12]

In many instances, the finishing touches were quite impressive. Between the logs, soldiers dabbed mud to keep the cold and wind from entering. Initially, inexperienced soldiers relied on dirt floors, which turned to mud quickly. In time, they learned to place hay or planking on the ground and built elevated beds to keep the dampness of the soil from chilling them. For wood and roofing, soldiers often took liberties with nearby structures. Eventually, Lee cracked down on the destruction of private property and actually had inspectors examine nearby areas and assess officers for unnecessary damage to private property.

When one battery dismantled a church to improve their winter quarters, taking pews, planks, doors, and windows, their commander found himself facing a general court-martial. All of the shanties had chimneys to keep warm and cook food. One mess shrewdly employed a railroad handcar to haul stone for a fireplace. Others used bricks from "abandoned" homes or dried mud. All in all, they were not quite home, but they were nonetheless fairly cozy.[13]

Through it all, soldiers endured the hardships of camp and winter with reasonably good spirits. Exchanging tales of battle provided a means of therapy. On a cold and snowy day, a company commander observed some of his men crowded around a campfire. They warmed themselves while discussing "the war, weather, wine and women." There was an unmistakable level of comfort among them. "Upon the whole," the captain assessed, "the soldier is a 'devil may care' jovial kind of fellow and takes things as they come."[14]

Most men, whether married or single, had never lived apart from wives or parents for such a lengthy period. Many had just adopted careers or had recently been married and were loath to leave their world at home; others had not chosen a permanent path and sought adventure, but the hardships of prolonged service made them long for home. Robert H. Jones, who commanded the 22nd Georgia, had not even left the state, yet he still harked back to the time he parted from his wife and children. "O! The pain and anguish of that night," he wrote her, concluding with the words, "If my dying hour had been upon me it seems I could not have felt more sad." After just two months away from his new bride, Pvt. Tazwell Graham, a carpenter from Floyd County, Virginia, pined, "it seems as though it has bee[n] a year since I left home."[15]

As more time passed, family and home took on new meanings. In the minds of soldiers, home represented love, stability, continuity, happiness, peace, and the future, a stark contrast to their current lives of devastation and destruction. "One never knows what home is until they have been away some time, and stands a good chance never to get back again," explained a soldier to his wife. An Arkansan comforted himself by thinking of exactly how everything looked at home, from his wife and children to the slaves and yard. "Every and all things that connects my mind with the endearments of home rush across my thoughts and for the moment I can close my eyes and almost feel your warm breath on my cheek. The touch of your hand in mine and hear the music of your voice." A North Carolina private wanted to turn back the clocks to re-establish life on its old terms. "I hope we may be Spared to reach home again Some time," he wrote his wife, "So we can enjoy our Selfs as we used to & I hope the time is not so far distant when we can meet in peace." They never got the chance. Barely six weeks later, he was killed in action.[16]

Faced with a massive and brutal war, the soldiers used visions of home and loved ones for escapism. "Life in the Army is terribly monotonous and did I not have you to think of, would be unbearable," a fifty-four-year-old Alabama lieutenant who had been born in Kenya wrote his wife. "As you say we can think of each other, and the War cannot deprive us of that." During late March 1863,

Col. Alfred M. Scales received a touching letter from his wife that shattered his emotional resolve. "I was completely unmanned for the moment & tear drops trickled down my cheeks," he confessed to her. A Georgian admitted to his wife, "I frequently withdraw into solitude and enjoy myself in meditation, in thinking of my absent Wife and children and tears course down my cheeks to think that the troubled condition of my native south should demand so cruel a sacrifice of natural feeling." He then concluded with the confession, "On my couch when deep sleep has fallen on others I often shed tears at the cruel separation that divides me from my loved ones."[17]

Thoughts and dreams broke up the lonesomeness of soldier life. "Oh my dear if I could only see you & be with you this morning," a soldier wrote longingly, "I know I would hug & kiss you allmost to death." When Sgt. William G. Parker, a forty-four-year-old father of five and a slaveholder, received a touching letter from his wife, he informed her, "I know of nothing that I can enjoy on earth to equal it." Over and over, he read her letter, until he had practically memorized it, each time poring over the words and reminding himself of the love they conveyed. "I know some call it weakness but I think that is all that is worth calling manly," he expressed to her, "pure affection will move the world in arms."[18]

Unfortunately, both Johnston and then Lee awarded furloughs stingily. Two per one hundred men or two per company was standard practice. By mid-January 1864, when it became clear the Yankees could not advance, Lee finally opened it up to twelve per company. Even then, the rate was slow, and quite a few soldiers went a few years without making it home. At one point, Sgt. John W. Watson of the 47th Virginia could wait no more. He was stationed at Bunker Hill, Virginia, and his wife and children lived only eighty miles away. He could not stop thinking of them and could endure separation no longer. "I will runaway and come home soon as I can get a good chance," he notified his wife. "I hate mity bad to runaway but I want to see you all so bad that I think I shall try that trick if I cant hear from you soon."[19]

The war took such a terrible toll on soldiers in Lee's army that doubts about the future were not pessimistic; they were realistic. North Carolina Pvt. Colier Hamilton jotted a verse to his sister:

> With flaming love I thus reply
> I hope weil meat before I dye.

WITH DIFFICULTY EXPRESSING himself clearly, eighteen-year-old Pvt. James C. Fisher informed his "dear Cossen" that "I would like to sea you all once more before wee die which I hope wee will and if Wee never oh I hope wee will all meat in heaven wher thir is no more War and parting." The hardship of separation convinced many that if they survived they would never leave their families again. "O you don't know how I long to git home to stay with you all the time," a North Carolinian penned his wife. "I do believe we would be two of the happiest people almost in the world for I would never go away and leave you any more." A captain announced that one thing was "certain, and that is a young man answering my description will *tie him self* to the apron string of the prettiest woman in Mississippi—in the person of his wife—and *never never! go away any more.*"[20]

Absence from home was particularly burdensome for soldiers with children. Some fathers never had a chance to know their children. The children were too young to remember their father, and it was heartbreaking for soldiers to know that they could not be part of their own children's lives and upbringing. When Hill Fitzpatrick learned that his little son would go to the door and call out for his father as loud as he could, "I could not help crying like a child," he admitted to his wife. A fellow Georgian felt awful when he learned his child was very ill. His wife sent a lock of the boy's hair to his father. "When i saw my pore little boys hair," wrote the private, "i prest it to my lips an teers floed so forsly [forcefully] that I cold [could] not read for sum time." Several months later, the child died.[21]

Single soldiers, too, longed for those they had left behind. Sweet-talking Pvt. John A. Everett asked his mother to tell all the unattached women in Haynesville, Georgia, "I love them as hard as amule can Buck down hill." An officer in the 58th Virginia longed for Sundays back home, when he went to church "more for the purpose of seeing the girls than for hearing the sermon." He recalled how "during the sermon we cast our eyes wistfully over to the ladies side and went home without knowing the text." Private Robert Stafford could not wait to get home on furlough in two and a half months to feast on home cooking. He instructed his sister, "You must have a plenty of chickens & fruit for me when I get home, for I'm chicken thirsty."[22]

Home consumed much of their thoughts not only during the day; at night, when they dozed off to sleep, they dreamed of home, family, and friends. Social decorum discouraged soldiers from reporting anything erotic. Most merely mentioned having visions of them and their families together, often extremely happy, only to awaken and find themselves alone. "I dream about you and the Children often," a Virginian informed his wife, "and that I am at home But when I wake up find my Self a long ways from there." A lieutenant recorded a dream that his wife and children visited him while the enemy began to attack. He was in the process of bidding them farewell and ushering them to the rear when he awoke, "feeling as miserable as any poor mortal ever did."[23]

Some soldiers reported fearful dreams and wondered if they were premonitions of impending bad events. One soldier dreamed he and his wife were riding horses when they ran into a woman in deep mourning. "I am Fearful it is a bad omen," he suggested. The soldier died of pneumonia several months later. Deep concerns played out in their dreams. An Alabamian on New Year's Day in 1865 described a dream in which he strolled along the banks of a river, when suddenly the water rose so rapidly that he had to run to keep from drowning.[24]

A young, single man had what he recorded as "a very romantic dream." He wandered about through rough, mountainous terrain in search of a peculiar flower of which he had no knowledge. "Singular it was that I should be searching for such a rare object in a rough mountain but there is peculiarity in dreams that events the most improbably always occur," he analyzed.[25]

At night, many dreamed of loved ones and the harshness of separation. Colonel Alfred Scales informed his wife of a dream in which they lay together with her head on his chest when some vile fiend forcibly separated them. Scales rose to brigade command and was wounded twice, survived the war, and was reunited with his wife. After having been away from his wife, Eugenia, for six months, Virginian Richard Bryant dreamed that he and two others were running down some stairs at Monticello when he fell and crashed into a woman's boudoir. "I was in the presence of the prettiest woman you ever saw" and while stammering out an apology he heard some grumbling noises. The woman said it was her father, who had locked her away, and he had to hide or her father would kill him. Just when her father burst into the room, he awoke. "The woman looked like you seven years ago." Bryant perished the following year.[26]

Facing homesickness at camp and death in battle, Lee's army struggled to maintain morale. As Brig. Gen. Dodson Ramseur, himself a newlywed, revealed to his wife, "I sometimes feel like it would not take much persuasion to make me *desert*! How I sympathise with some of my poor fellows who have not seen their Wives & children for two years!" Yet the war still had much to throw at them. Confederate spirits would be sorely tested in 1863 and 1864.[27]

Chapter 19

RELIGION AND MORALITY

S EVERAL WEEKS AFTER the Battle of Antietam, Virginian artillerist John W. Green wrote, "I consider the waste of property the loss of life &c as but little in weight to the *demoralization* that a war causes among a people." In his opinion, the collapse of decency was "the most deplorable consequence of it all. It seems to bury most of the good nature started us with and to give a full play to all the evil that the Father of mischief ever gave us." Colonel John Q. A. Nadenbousch, a wealthy miller and slaveholder, used similar terms to make the same argument. "When I think of the demoralizing effect this war will & is having on our community in corrupting and destroying all society it makes me shudder," he complained to his wife. "It seems as is Satan himself turned loose in the land." Military life is a breeding ground for male vice, and Lee's army was no exception.[1]

Gambling and crass language were rife. When troops had money, such as early in their service and after infrequent paydays, "Immense gambling is going on all over camp," according to a surgeon. During periods of impoverishment, which became all the more frequent as the war extended into its third and fourth years, men played the same card or dice games without cash. By contrast, crude language and bawdy tales required only a mouth. As Capt. William R. Barksdale, a prewar lawyer serving in the 11th Mississippi Infantry, reported to his mother, "I had no idea of the filth and vulgarity of men in camp until I tried this little experiment."[2]

North Carolinian Joseph M. Weller observed that "Drunkenness and profanity are the two evils indulged mostly by Soldiers." Cursing may have been offensive to the ears, but it hurt no one. Alcohol frequently lay at the root of trouble. Writing in March 1862, Private Weller declared, "Whiskey has begun to be the ruination of our army." Large groups of men, many of them young and all of them beyond the control or influence of their parents or wives, seized every opportunity to get roaring drunk. Early in the war, a Virginian noted that "Our boys when kept from whiskey are the very best soldiers, but when it is about they too soon degenerate into a mob." A Mississippi sergeant grumbled that soldiers secured alcohol from the country people "& the officers don't seem to make any efforts to prevent it some rather seem to encourage it by using it themselves." Even as late as October 31, 1864, the army's chief of artillery, William N. Pendleton, an ordained Episcopal minister, wrote the mayor and city council of Petersburg at Lee's request to secure their help in "sepressing the great evil of intemperance, prevailing among a class of our Soldiers in consequence of the facility with which quantities of spirit are obtained & dispensed in your city."[3]

Alcohol frequently led to greater trouble. An Arkansan claimed that some Irishmen in his company secured access to whiskey and in their drunken stupor they threw away their muskets, a matter that became a grave concern as they approached the Manassas battlefield. On a march to the Shenandoah Valley, some wagon drivers got inebriated and mired their teams in deep mud. In another episode, drunken cavalrymen raided a sutler's shop and swiped twelve boxes of tobacco. Frequently, drunkenness resulted in fights and other acts of violence. In early 1864, some troops waiting for a train in Richmond got very drunk on " 'fighting whiskey.' " According to a soldier, "I never saw more fights in the same length of time, in my life."[4]

As the war went on, stealing, too, increased steadily. Not only did soldiers plunder from prisoners and the dead, but with severe shortages, it was almost inevitable that some soldiers would steal basic items from one another. Many men had already crossed the ethical Rubicon, and to take from their own was no giant leap in immorality, especially if they wanted essentials. In January 1862, Jackson's staff officer Sandie Pendleton, the son of Lee's artillery chief, took his boots off at bedtime, only to awake in the morning to find someone had absconded with them. A private in the 16th Georgia had washed his two shirts, and someone stole one of them while they were drying. During the course of the war, Asst. Surg. William H. Taylor had several different horses taken, most likely by cavalrymen whose own horses had been killed. While a Virginia private's messmates went to church, he stayed behind to guard their possessions. "I should like to have gone too," he commented to his mother, "but it is necessary that some one of the mess should stay to watch the thieves, for in these degenerated times, there are a good many of that class of person."[5]

As with most armies throughout history, as soon as troops left their local communities, considerable numbers of men engaged in sexual acts with prostitutes. The 10th Alabama, which authorities stationed in Richmond temporarily, suffered sixty-two new cases of gonorrhea and six of syphilis in July 1861. According to one soldier, whose account was corroborated by others, the Louisiana Tigers brought women in uniform to Virginia with them. Someone told him that the women were the wives of officers, but he did not believe it. Once the army moved away from the cities and into camps, there were camp followers. According to a writer for the *Richmond Enquirer*, a captain turned over to authorities two women in uniform who had accompanied the army for some time. When apprehended, the women argued that they were merely serving their country, and "if all the women of the Confederacy were as patriotick as they the country would have been free long ago." The captain asserted to the journalist that the women were "common camp followers, and that they have been the means of demoralizing several hundred men in his command." They had taken on the disguise as soldiers "to follow the army and hide their iniquity." When a Virginian's wife wanted to visit, he urged her not to come. "I am fearful this country is filled with Prostitutes who pass as soldiers wives" and he did not want her mistaken for one.[6]

Less than two weeks after the Battle of Fredericksburg, Pvt. Tillman F. Beggarly complained to his wife that some of his comrades "git drunk an run after negroes and mien white women but I can till you with a clare conscience I tak[e] no part with them nor I never enten too." His wife, Margaret, replied that she was glad he did not partake in "wicked ways." She then wrote, "I do beg of you for my sake and for your own little children not to join them resist the devil and he will flee you." Sixteen months later, Beggarly again alerted her, "my Dier some of the Boys is doing mity Bad thar is some meen women neer her[e]." Once more, he insisted that he had done nothing, "I gib you my word." One of Pvt. J. C. Penn's friends from home "was walking with a negro girl about the encampment in the presents of the whole Regament." Later, Penn spoke to his friend Sam about it and informed his mother, "if I had my way with him I would have whipped him well."[7]

Yet as a lieutenant colonel grieved, it was more than simply soldiers hiring women for sexual favors. "I was in hope that the demoralization which always follows a war would be confined to the male population, that the inate purity of our girls would at least protect them from all horrors, but it seems not," Edward Warren wrote to his wife. In his hometown of Harrisonburg, Virginia, he learned, four young, single women ranging in ages from fourteen to nineteen were pregnant. Three of the four young ladies came from comfortable or wealthy families. "Of one I expected it & am not at all surprised, but of the others I cant think without a shudder," he admitted. "The grossest licentiousness is every where exhibiting itself." What dismayed Warren most was the way young women cast aside their traditional values in wartime. "We who have been so proud of the virgin inocense & purity of the sex, of their chaste and elegant manners not only in gentlemens society but with each other are suddenly reduced to utter humiliations by seeing the young ladies throwing aside all of their modesty[,] all their chasteness and making vulgar advances to the vagabond soldiery of the South."[8]

Wartime disrupted traditional family and community controls. With a father in the army and mothers managing the entire household and farm or shop, adult supervision often disappeared. In most communities, locals traditionally banded together to enforce codes of conduct, but with so many adults either in military service or filling the void left by others, adult scrutiny was lax.

This decline of familial and social controls caught adolescents and adults unprepared. Tens of thousands of young men poured into Virginia to fight in a war that created tens of thousands of refugees. Virginia households welcomed soldiers, travelers, and loved ones of the sick and wounded, especially early in the war. The introduction of strangers or even family friends into households meant unusual access and interactions. Privacy decreased, creating situations, according to Warren, "where it is impossible for girls not to be occasionally exposed in undress" or for men to pass through the rooms of women.

Even more problematical were hospitals. Community after community clamored to establish a military hospital. Young ladies volunteered for them in large numbers. While ministering to the sick and injured, these young women witnessed soldiers in various situations and unusual conditions. "Some not much over fifteen summers" had to remove men's clothing to bathe or dress their wounds. Later, as the men recovered, the nurses would visit with them regularly—a grateful soldier with the woman who had taken a personal and sympathetic interest in his recovery. As the soldiers improved their health, "moonlight walks occur—crazy ideas of romantic adventure with a soldier boy—then gentle whisperings of pretended love—then a gentle yielding to a gross familiarity which is bad enough—but who can be surprised if worse comes," Warren wrote.[9]

As Warren recognized, "all this promiscuous mingling together of the sexes, of good and bad occurs under a very highly excited state of public mind." Love and hate, passion and listlessness, thrill and boredom, fear and composure, energy and exhaustion swirled. Soldier and civilian could offer one another some comfort from the emotional strain of war, and they could ease the physical discomfort as well.[10]

For all his insights, Warren never quite grasped the importance of the separation of the sexes during wartime. As a regimental commander, he certainly observed it, but he failed to note its true significance. In large groups of young adult males, many objectified women, and peer pressure coerced conformity among them. Warfare demanded that soldiers set aside traditional, civilized controls of violence. It required only a small leap to relinquishing some control over sexual impulses. Thus, soldiers became heavily fixated on the opposite sex. The heavy flow of choice anatomical expressions represented part of the response; the quest for sexual experiences, well beyond what they might have attempted at home, exemplified another.[11]

Nor did Warren recognize the link between military and sexual conquest. Confederate soldiers sought more than just the defeat of their Yankee enemy; they hoped to dominate them, and for that first year under Lee's command, they accomplished it. While the spirit of domination enhanced the army's collective sense of power, it affected individual egos as well.[12]

How much could they manage to get away with? Men with wives at home committed bigamy by marrying women around Hanover Junction, Virginia, where they were stationed. According to Sgt. William G. Parker of the 11th North Carolina Infantry, a yeoman farmer with a wife and young son, their company commander "told one or more of the Ladies that they were married men and they took it as a joke and told him he could not fool her out of a husband that way." One woman married a soldier from Greenville, North Carolina, and lived with him awhile, until she found a letter of his from his original wife. She then "discountenanced him and he left for his Regiment." Parker chalked up the entire mess by writing his wife, "the war brings about many strange things."[13]

In an unconvincing attempt to reassure his mother that he behaved well, Pvt. Eli Landers wrote, "Mama don't you be uneasy about me for I have got as much sense as I ever had but that's not much." For many soldiers in Lee's army, however, the war and military service brought out their worst qualities. Future division commander Lafayette McLaws, with nineteen years of service in the U.S. Army before joining the Confederacy, knew from experience when he divulged to his wife, "being a Soldier is a very severe test of character to which very many men give way under, exhibiting themselves in Such unenviable characteristics that if they could see themselves as others see them, and have [n]ot lost their instincts of decent humanity not a few would feel very much like committing suicide." Pious young men in peacetime embraced the practices of the disreputable once in uniform. "Few there are who have escaped the contagious effects of being mixed up with the vile and low," an Alabama officer explained to his mother and sisters. "All grades of society and character are here blended indiscriminately together. The bad are not reformed while the good are made bad."[14]

Confederate mythologists endowed their soldiers with unusual character and virtue. After all, nothing could be more ennobling that to risk one's life to preserve liberty. The cause was righteous, the enemy a wicked oppressor, so their soldiers must be honorable, valiant, dutiful, and uncorrupted. Especially early in the war, Confederate people applauded, feted, and showered their noble defenders with acts of kindness. They welcomed them into their homes, fed them, cared for them when ill, and devoted vast amounts of time to nursing them in hospitals. Society placed them on pedestals and allowed them liberties that they would not consider in peacetime. As Warren suggested to his wife, Virginians so embraced their protectors that to wear a uniform "was a pass port to every gentlemens house and to every foolish young girls heart." In reality, as Capt. John T. Thornton confessed to his wife, "I now see that an army is necessarily a school of vice." An absence of traditional controls, prolonged boredom, transgressions of proper moral conduct in peacetime, and the fragile nature of life encouraged misbehavior. What a number of soldiers feared most was that immorality would contaminate Southern society for years to come. "No one can know the guile of this world without having been in the army three years in a Revolution," a Georgia lieutenant instructed his wife. "God grant that present depravity may not survive the army and the Revolution, but I doubt not there is much purity and truth, also."[15]

In an effort to check misconduct in the army, Lee adopted an indirect approach. He sought to remind soldiers that the Confederate nation needed God on its side, invoking God's blessings in congratulatory campaign letters and periodically declaring days of fast. Lee did not disdain the use of alcohol in modest quantities and even thought it therapeutic for the men, but when it disrupted normal discipline or siphoned valuable resources from the army, he cracked down on consumption, production, and sale. In the trenches around Richmond in June 1862, he authorized subordinate officers to issue alcohol if they thought it would benefit the health of the men. Early in the war, Gov. John Letcher of Virginia empowered Lee to revoke liquor licenses of any taverns that refused to cooperate with military authorities, and his office relayed the authority to subordinate commanders. The idea was to punish vendors who plied soldiers with too much liquor. Even in late 1863, as shortages in almost everything except casualties became more severe, Lee complained to Letcher that seven distilleries were in operation in Rappahannock County. His problem was not with alcohol per se, but with the fact that they used scarce grain.[16]

Other officers cracked down as best they could. In summer and fall 1861, Beauregard battled repeatedly with liquor shops that served soldiers excessive quantities of alcohol. At one point, he prohibited the sale of alcohol within five miles of any main camp and within two miles of pickets. Subordinate commanders launched their own periodic campaigns against alcohol when it became a big problem. According to a private in the 1st Texas, it was important that general officers led by example. He and his comrades applauded many high-ranking officers such as Lee, Jackson, and Longstreet who either seldom partook or were teetotalers, and they condemned "Early[,] Magruder, & those Drinkers of Apple Jack, & Whiskey, that wrecked their commands and injured our cause, by their 'Weaknes' in not controlling themselves."[17]

Most high-ranking officers viewed gambling as a less serious offense. Soldiers gambled in camp, and it did not interfere with the performance of their duty. Nonetheless, when gambling became rampant, officers occasionally cracked down on it. Brigadier General James H. Lane, for example, reminded men in mid-November 1863, "Gambling in this Brigade is prohibited and those caught at it will be severely punished."[18]

In the end, though, it took the soldiers themselves to resist temptations. Private John Caperton, then serving in a Virginia militia regiment and later an artillerist in Lee's army, pledged to his mother that he would not drink or gamble. After a couple of months of service, he reported, "I have not touched Liquor I have not touched dice and I have not touched cards except once and then I only touched them whilest I was throwing them out of my shelf." Irishman James Campbell in the 4th Texas announced gleefully that he mended his ways in the army. "I hope that it will gratify you and all my friends to Know that I have stoped all my bad habeds sick [such] as drink and Swairing," he crowed, and "I do not tast licker of no Sort nor don't in tend to till I gat back home." Similarly, Mississippi private John McDonald, with nearly two years of service, declared to his wife that he, too, had improved during his time in the army. "Susan I have not been sensibly converted but I am not as wild as I was before I left home," he informed her, "I don't curse nor gamble nor cheat my fellow soldier nor lust after the base women of this town [Fredericksburg] of which there is a number of them set up here to gather soldiers money and communicate there disease to the soldier which of course renders him unfit for duty." Whether these women believed them, we can only wonder.[19]

AMID THE CORRUPT world of soldiering, many men found solace in God and religion. T. D. Rock of the 1st Texas entered military service carrying a Bible, and he intended to carry it with him as his shield. To his parents, Rock insisted, "relying upon the God of Battles I shall meet this Enemy of my Country fearlessly aye gladly and if I fall I will fall a willing sacrifice upon the altar of my country." Others relied on faith as a means of guarding against immorality and of strengthening themselves in the fight against fundamental military hardships. A company commander was convinced of the opposite dynamic: immorality strengthened religiousness. "Nothing so quickens our spiritual life," he notified his sister, "as the constant sense of approaching dissolution in our mind." Facing death and hardship, many soldiers insisted that God had an ultimate plan. "I know it is a hard thing to give up every thing and cast you[r] self on our savour who is able to save to the utmost everry one that come unto him in sincerty and in truth, but if you hope to be happy after death you must put your trust in him and keep his commandments," a Virginia enlisted man counseled his wife. "My dear and loveing companion trust in god that when we meat again that we may join in prear [prayer] together to our lord and savior."[20]

Many Confederates believed that against the overwhelming resources of the North, they needed God on their side. To a friend who informed Stonewall Jackson that people prayed for the triumph of the army, Jackson replied, "Without God's blessing I look for no success, and for every success my prayer is, that all glory may be given unto *Him* to whom it is properly due." In late 1861, a South Carolinian explained, "In war, we should remember there is a God of Battles, whose displeasure we should dread to incur; whose favor we should live and labor to gain." Lee agreed: "the people must help themselves, or Providence will not help them." Having fought the massive battles of 1862 and the first half of 1863, a number of soldiers had no doubt that a Divine power tilted the scales in their favor. "In God to whom all victories are due I trust," a Virginia private recorded seven weeks after Antietam, "knowing that 'the fight is not to the strong nor the race to the swift' and knowing that He will be on the side of the just." Before the war, a North Carolina surgeon could never have imagined that Providence would aid a side in war. After witnessing several massive battles, however, "I am convinced that no human agency, could have unaided, turned back the tide of invasions so frequently and decisively," he wrote a friend. Twenty-two million Northerners, better supplied and capable of drawing resources from the entire world, should have crushed a population of six million. God must make up the difference.[21]

Others worried that the Confederate people had not done enough to secure

God's blessings. A Virginia captain and company commander thought the people had not prayed enough to earn God's intercession. "We must not rely upon our own right armies," he elaborated to his wife, "but must trust implicitly in the saving mercy of God." Private Eli Landers of Georgia, after fighting in six major battles, arrived at the conviction that "we will have to be more obedient than we are before we can expect to be delivered from this state of trouble. We will have to deny our strength and acknowledge the Almighty."[22]

The contradiction between war and the tenets of their faith challenged some soldiers to justify hatred and acts of violence. "I pray not for the destruction of our enemies & will never inflict personally any injury to any falling into my hands," a South Carolina officer explained to his wife, "but I do pray God to destroy their purposes, to strike fear into their hearts & to turn them from their errors & sins against us & to grant us Peace & independence." In contrast, a Tennessean felt so strongly in the justness of their cause that he believed Confederate soldiers acted with God's blessing as avenging angels to smite their enemy. "I want to avenge as many wrongs committed against those I love as I can," he justified, "for I really believe he who kills the greatest number of abolition thieves and their abbetters is the best Christian."[23]

Many officers encouraged the practice of religion in the army. Stonewall Jackson, probably the most famously pious prominent Confederate, sought to honor the Sabbath whenever possible. When his command marched one Sunday, a private surmised, "The move which we have made must be of great importance as it is said that Old Jack never makes any other on the Sabbath." Jackson attended church regularly with his troops. Throughout the services, he remained motionless, which made him the butt of some teasing. After Jackson stood throughout the entire liturgy, an artillerist commented, "I suppose he was afraid he would go to sleep." Two weeks later, a staff officer described Jackson at worship as "fixed and motionless as a statue." A surgeon once noticed that Jackson sat "as immovable as a block of that material for which he is named."[24]

Like Jackson, Lee professed a deep Christian faith. Throughout the course of the war, Lee not only attended worship regularly, he invoked religious references and reminded others that all success emanated from God. Shortly after the Battle of Fredericksburg, Lee credited God with the Confederate triumph in a note to Jackson and then added, "I pray he may continue it." Three weeks later, he joined Brig. Gen. Isaac Trimble in offering thanks to God and then confessed, "I see his directing hand in all the operations of the war. My constant prayer is that we may deserve his blessings, & that they be continued." In private letters and conversations, too, he expressed a deep conviction in God and regularly sought God's blessings.[25]

In every facet of army life, Lee took seriously his role as a model for the troops. Like Jackson, he believed that they must lead by example, and if the Confederacy were to win the war, it must have God's support. The commanding general could not expect soldiers to embrace habits that he did not practice, and if he wished to encourage certain behavior, he must do so by public deed. On a Sunday in early December 1863, as Lee rode along inspecting some works with A. P. Hill and some staff officers, the commanding general spotted a cluster of soldiers attending divine worship. Even though they were riding at a considerable clip, Lee halted and listened to the men singing hymns. He stayed for the entire sermon, and when the clergyman offered the benediction, Lee removed his hat, received the blessing, and then continued on his way. "It was a striking scene and one well calculated to impress solemnly all who witnessed it," a mildly cynical Walter Taylor noted.[26]

But Taylor's suggestion that Lee attended church simply for show judged him unfairly. Lee embraced religion and genuinely believed that both his soldiers and the Confederacy must gain God's favor. In a lengthy conversation with Pendleton, Lee convinced the clergyman–artillery chief, "He is deeply concerned for the spiritual welfare of the soldiers." In the declaration of a day of fasting, Lee reminded his troops that God had "preserved your lives amidst countless dangers" and had protected them through all their trials and tribulations. He called on them, along with millions of fellow Confederates in and out of uniform, to pray "that he will continue his merciful protection of our cause; that he will scatter our enemies and set at naught their evil designs, and that he will graciously restore to our beloved country the blessings of peace and security." Lee encouraged officers to observe the Sabbath, "not only from a moral and religious duty, but as contributing to personal health and well being of the troops." He responded positively to one soldier's request for a brief leave to celebrate Yom Kippur at the Richmond synagogue, and the commanding general encouraged all officers to release Jewish soldiers in their command for the celebration, if possible.[27]

Other officers, too, felt a responsibility to encourage religious participation in their command. A Virginia cavalry officer advised his brother to join in all the wholesome fun around camp. Sing, dance, introduce games, and "join in with them in all innocent amusement" so that "when you speak on religious subjects the effect is very strong." The 9th Virginia had no chaplain, so on Sundays the colonel read from the Bible for all who wanted to listen. In a North Carolina regiment, the colonel called in the chaplain to lead the men in prayer at dress parade. The chaplain thought it worked so well that he recommended the practice to President Davis.[28]

Young males between seventeen and twenty-five were the least observant segment of Southern society, and many carried this lack of interest with them into uniform. Others had no exposure to organized religion, and they initially perceived services more as a curious spectacle than anything else. Among those who had religious backgrounds and had attended church or synagogue in peacetime, only a modest portion immediately joined prayer meetings and other forms of religious activity. Religion in the South had a private component to it, and many preferred to keep their thoughts and prayers to themselves. As they attempted to project a sense of masculinity to their comrades, young males in Lee's army may have believed that embracing religion openly suggested weakness. Thus, counting heads at religious events in no way reflected spiritual practices or sentiment.[29]

Over the course of the war, however, the demands and brutality of military service encouraged soldiers to seek solace in religion, or at least to feel guilty about their failings. A Virginia hospital steward admitted his sinful behavior and believed he deserved the wrath of the Almighty. "Estranged from God and Godly people, to live without the hope of eternal salvation and the dread of everlasting punishment is a distressing thought," he recorded in a journal. Private Hill Fitzpatrick of Georgia also knew he had not embraced religion as he should. "I have wandered far from the path of duty as a Christian," he confessed to his wife, Amanda, "and am often troubled by it." Others, having reflected on their time in uniform, arrived at the conclusion that they must make amends and change their ways. Private Jasper Gillespie declared to his wife, "C.O. Goodwyne & myself sinse my return from home began to consider our lives sinse we came in the Army, the many hair breadth escapes during two long years here, and the little obligations that we have been to our God as members of his visible Church on earth, and we resolved to begin anew & try to do better." Twice a day they prayed together and they joined in the regimental religious revival.[30]

Not until after Antietam did the army erupt in revivals. During respites from the fighting, religious tremors shook Lee's army into the spring campaign of 1864. In October 1862, an Alabamian reported to his father protracted meetings at Bunker Hill, Virginia, for the past several nights. "There is a good deal of excitement," he wrote. "Large numbers of moaners every night." In February and March 1863, two Mississippi chaplains held extended meetings, gaining converts nightly. The attendance grew so large that the local Methodist church, with a capacity of 300, could not accommodate them, so they shifted it to the nearby Episcopal church, which seated almost 1,000. In mid-March 1863, a soldier attended Sunday church there and estimated 700 soldiers and civilians in attendance, with "over 100 men begging the forgiveness of their sins." After the opening spring campaign in 1863, the army again revived its religious spirit. A Virginian alerted his family, "we have a great revival going on here," with nightly meetings. When campaigning slowed in the late summer and early autumn, meetings resumed. "A revival has commenced in our brigade," a Georgia private jotted in his diary. "I hope [it] will spread from heart to heart till all receives joy and peace." As the spring, 1864 campaign season neared, interest in religion resumed once again.[31]

Although there were some revivals with shouting and emotional outpourings, most were much more dignified events. When soldiers referred to great excitement, they described the joy of seeing a dozen comrades step forward, profess their sins, and pray to God for assistance so that they could do better. One young officer from South Carolina, who boasted to his mother that scarcely a day passed without some religious event in his brigade, could hear hymns resonate through camp as he wrote the letter. "There is no fictitious enthusiasm," he claimed. "I have not heard the word 'revival' since I have been here." He insisted, "No catchwords or devices are resorted to for the purpose of attracting numbers—it is serious solemn awakening of hope—among men who for years have been walking face to face with all the darkness and honor of a sudden and hopeless death." Another junior officer, a Virginian in the Stonewall Brigade, boasted that soldiers in his and an adjoining brigade had created a meeting ground between camps and had convinced an accomplished Presbyterian minister to preach periodically. Soldiers designed and ran the nighttime events. Music from a band alerted soldiers that the meeting was convening. Soldiers stoked campfires and had "lights burning on stands" to guide troops in the dark. As the clergyman picked his way carefully through the crowd of veterans lounging on the ground, "good old fashioned hymns are sung by a hundred stentorian voices" that echoed through the woods. The cleric typically delivered a sermon "adapted particularly to the minds of his hearers all of whom seem to be listening with the deepest attention." There was no sobbing or crying out. Soldiers listened and digested the word of God. Among those in attendance was Jackson himself, "beside a high Private straining to hear the sermon—he is considerably deaf."[32]

The subdued nature of the events may have been the result of the type of clergymen involved. While soldiers sometimes received ministrations from philanthropic or visiting missionaries and preachers, in most instances clergymen from very traditional denominations served as chaplains in Lee's army. Most guest clergymen were Episcopalians and Presbyterians and came from local communities in Virginia. They preferred a more dignified atmosphere at religious events and discouraged revivalist practices.

Early in the war, a number of regiments took chaplains with them to war in Virginia. Within months, however, hardships, boredom, insufficient pay, and low status winnowed down the numbers considerably. After the war, Reverend J. William Jones, who began as chaplain in the 13th Virginia and served as a corps missionary chaplain, counted 205 chaplains in the army, excluding the cavalry. Most of those, however, served for a very brief time. In February 1864, he counted 86 chaplains in Virginia, some of whom were on leave. Soldiers relied increasingly on themselves to run prayer meetings or drew on local clergymen to lead their divine worship.[33]

Without doubt the most influential clergyman in the Army of Northern Virginia was Lee's chief of artillery, William N. Pendleton. A small slaveholder and clergyman in Jackson's hometown of Lexington, Virginia, Pendleton graduated fifth in the West Point class of 1830, a year behind Lee. After the Battle of First Manassas, in which Pendleton served as a colonel of artillery, tales circulated that he exhorted his gunners to aim lower, fire, and then shouted, "Oh, Lord, have mercy on their Souls, for I will have none on their bodies." Pendleton understood the peculiar nature of his dual positions. He reconciled his jobs by insisting, "I do not delight in war and would not hurt the hair of the head of any human being save under conviction of public duty, as by prayer, pleading &

This is the first known wartime photograph of Robert E. Lee, taken in 1862. *Southern Historical Collection, Wilson Library, University of North Carolina*

Confederate president Jefferson Davis appointed Lee army commander after Johnston was wounded. When Lee offered to resign after Gettysburg, Davis replied that to find someone better suited to command the army "is to demand an impossibility." *National Archives*

The commander of the Army of the Potomac, General Joseph E. Johnston, struggled in his relationship with President Jefferson Davis. At Seven Pines in May 1862, he suffered a severe wound that led to Lee's appointment as army commander. *National Archives*

The theatrical John Bankhead Magruder bluffed the Union into advancing slowly up the Peninsula in 1862, enabling Johnston to shift the Confederate army over and block the Yankees. *Battles and Leaders, vol. 5, p. 209*

Private Bennett Rainey Jeffares, Company D, 38th Georgia, suffered a severe leg wound at Gaines's Mill in June 1862. Eighteen months later, Jeffares returned to Lee's army. Unable to walk properly, he drove an ambulance, freeing up another soldier to return to combat. *Personal collection of Michael S. Parks*

Cavalry division commander Major General Fitzhugh Lee, R. E. Lee's nephew, proved his worth by leading Jackson's flank attack at Chancellorsville in 1863 and a year later by beating the Federals to Spotsylvania and holding the crossroads until reinforcements arrived. *Library of Congress*

Cadmus Marcellus Wilcox was a West Point graduate and the author of an important text on the rifled musket. A skillful officer, he directed a brilliant delaying action during the fighting near Fredericksburg during the Chancellorsville Campaign in April and May 1863. *Library of Congress*

Thomas Jonathan "Stonewall" Jackson brilliantly combined speed, surprise, and power in the Shenandoah Valley Campaign. A peculiar personality who was not as attentive to the welfare of his men as Lee would have liked, when he died after Chancellorsville it was a severe loss for the army. *National Archives*

One of the most perceptive diarists of the war, Catherine Edmondston despised Lee until his success during the Seven Days' and Bull Run campaigns, when she began to place her full confidence behind him. *North Carolina Division of Archives and History*

Crotchety Jubal A. Early emerged as an excellent officer and skillfully led the last true Confederate offensive in 1864, until overwhelming Union strength and a breakdown in discipline resulted in several disastrous defeats. *Battles and Leaders, vol. 4, p. 529*

Richard H. Anderson, a solid division commander, struggled as a corps commander and required Lee's careful supervision and steady advice. *Battles and Leaders, vol. 4, p. 717*

Lafayette McLaws, a sound division commander, ran afoul of his corps commander James Longstreet during the Tennessee Campaign of 1863 and was transferred from the army shortly before Lee needed him most, during the Overland Campaign. *Library of Congress*

John B. Gordon, a citizen–soldier in the tru-est sense, entered the army without any mili-tary training and rose from captain to major general. He was instrumental in planning the Confederate attacks at Cedar Creek in October 1864 and Fort Stedman in March 1865. *Battles and Leaders, vol. 4, p. 523*

The most talented of the younger officers, Brigadier General Porter Alexander served in many capacities in the Army of Northern Virginia. *Miller's Photographic History of the Civil War, vol. 5, p. 61*

Robert Rodes, a Virginia Military Institute graduate, emerged as the most talented and innovative division commander in the Army of Northern Virginia. *Miller's Photographic History of the Civil War, vol. 10, p. 145*

Ambrose Powell Hill, according to Lee his very best division commander, never fully mastered the transition to leading a corps. He was killed in action in the final days of the war. *Miller's Photographic History of the Civil War, vol. 10, p. 143*

Stephen Dodson Ramseur, a young West Point graduate, commanded a hard-hitting North Carolina brigade and was a hero at the Battle of Spotsylvania. He was mortally wounded at Cedar Creek in October 1864. *North Carolina Division of Archives and History*

A flamboyant yet popular officer, General P.G.T. Beauregard was acclaimed a hero at First Manassas. He eventually ran afoul of President Jefferson Davis and was sent out west. Later in the war, he commanded exceedingly well at Petersburg in the 1864 campaign against overwhelming Union numbers when Ulysses S. Grant tricked Lee and shifted his army across the James River and advanced on Petersburg. *Miller's Photographic History of the Civil War, vol. 1, p. 143*

William Nelson Pendleton, an Episcopal clergyman, graduated a year behind Lee at West Point. Not a particularly effective chief of artillery, Pendleton served the army well spiritually and was one of the few people with whom Lee could express his true sentiments. *Battles and Leaders, vol. 3, p. 329*

Charles M. Blackford, one of several Blackfords in the Army of Northern Virginia, had attended the University of Virginia and was an attorney before the war. He served as a judge in the First Corps court. *Author's collection*

Richard S. Ewell rose to corps command but, like Hill, never settled into the position comfortably. His diminished physical condition after the loss of a leg contributed to the stress of duty and at times impaired his ability to serve effectively. *Battles and Leaders, vol. 1, p. 251*

Wade Hampton rose from colonel to commander of cavalry in the Army of Northern Virginia. An extremely talented officer, this wealthy South Carolinian disliked his commander, Major General J.E.B. Stuart, and resented what he considered preferential treatment toward Virginians. *Miller's Photographic History of the Civil War, vol. 4, p. 269*

James Ewell Brown Stuart, the acclaimed Confederate cavalryman, possessed an extraordinary tactical eye. He positioned artillery guns on Nicodemus Heights at Antietam, which probably saved Lee's army from defeat. *Library of Congress*

Lieutenant General James Longstreet thrived as corps commander under Lee, but in independent command he struggled. *Library of Congress*

Lee with his son Custis (*left*) and Walter H. Taylor, taken in Richmond not long after Lee's surrender at Appomattox. *Library of Congress*

expostulation I have earnestly tried for peace." More soldiers heard Pendleton discourse on religion than any other cleric, and many credited him with instilling faith in them. A Virginia artillerist recorded in his diary immediately after the opening battle in late spring 1863: "The men were sitting on their guns and listening very attentively to the words of God uttered by Gen. Pendleton." In late summer, a South Carolina lieutenant attended a sermon by Pendleton and found it "searching, eloquent, & just." Pendleton played such a valuable role in the spiritual well-being of the army, traveling throughout the army and offering divine liturgy so frequently, that Lee was loath to remove him as artillery chief, even when more accomplished and capable officers were available.[34]

Although some clergymen failed in their jobs, others performed with noteworthy skill and compassion for their fellow Confederates. The religious and acerbic D. H. Hill informed a friend and minister, "Our Regimental Chaplains as a general thing are as trifling as the Regimental surgeons, which is the strongest denunciation I can use." Others blasted their chaplains for laziness or for long, tedious sermons, and after the war, numerous tales spread among veterans of the cowardly conduct of their religious leaders as they entered battle for the first time. Yet many others earned superb reputations for strong spiritual service and humanitarian concern amidst dangers and hardships. The 18th Georgia had a Methodist chaplain who joined the regiment when it arrived in Virginia and stood by the men in every situation. "He have don[e] much good in tending on our sic and wounded and seeing that tha [they] was proprly tended to," a private informed his brother and sister. "He has all ways bin in the battle field ready to do his part in cearing for the wounded and have spair no pains at the hospital in seeing that tha was all promply tended to." Another Georgian explained how his regimental chaplain earned the respect of the men by taking charge of the ambulance corps and removing wounded from the battlefield to field hospital.[35]

When Dr. Robert Lewis Dabney, a prewar clergyman and professor of theology, joined the 18th Virginia, he justified his service by writing his mother, "I might employ my vocation in helping on the cause of our country's defence with those spiritual weapons which I understand best how to use; and especially that I might be able to care for and comfort the people of my own pastoral charge." Dabney ended up staying with the army longer than he anticipated, serving as a central figure on Jackson's staff until a debilitating fever forced him to resign. Dabney, Pendleton, and numerous others preached the need for a spiritual regeneracy in the Confederacy. Until that happened, God would punish the people. Pendleton spoke eloquently to troops about individual and national sins, and how the people of the Confederacy must rid themselves of both. In a sermon entitled "Procrastination" delivered in late April 1862, he hammered at the men, "A soldier, a man whose very profession it is to face dangers and wounds: whose daily tasks all point to the field of battle, where death holds high revel! Of all men, the soldier can with least reason be thoughtless of his soul." Several weeks later, Dabney argued that the war was "a visitation upon us for our sins and that it would not cease until the purposes of God were accomplished in it," specifically "until our people repent and turn to Him." This message spread throughout the army's religious community. A Georgian proclaimed, "When our people and soldiers turn their hearts to God, He will grant us peace." After listening to Dabney, a Virginian announced to his father, "I think the fate of this country is now in the hands of the praying people, and though I cannot see how or when I believe God will certainly answer the prayers of His faithful people in the land." With everyone embracing God's teachings, the Confederacy would triumph, and its people would suffer until then.[36]

Revivals and prayer meetings notwithstanding, most soldiers avoided public worship. In early 1863, Jackson bragged about 65 in an Alabama regiment seeking salvation since the war began—yet the regimental strength exceeded 400. The Stonewall Brigade built a house for worship, which Jackson termed "well attended," but he admitted the numbers had declined from the previous fall, when they had 100 men "inquiring the way of life." The brigade population numbered slightly below 1,500. A North Carolinian crowed over a revival in his brigade, exclaiming, "The change in the morals of the men is everywhere visible." Yet only about 160 men participated.[37]

The least demanding form of religious initiative was Christian associations formed by regiments and brigades. All one had to do to join was profess belief in Christ, and soldiers did not have to attend meetings unless they wanted to do so. Brigadier General George H. Steuart's brigade of Maryland, North Carolina, and Virginia troops had 200 names on its list. The 2nd Alabama formed one that claimed 60 members, including the regimental commander. Few organizations, though, compared with the 9th Georgia, which had the majority of its men in the organization.[38]

According to the estimates of Chaplain Jones, approximately 15,000 soldiers converted to religion during the war, a number that represents at best about one in twelve men who served in the Army of Northern Virginia or its predecessor. To be sure, converts were a fraction of those who believed in God or prayed with any regularity. Nonetheless, they reflect a generally low level of activity, caused in part by the steadily declining number of chaplains. By March 1863, Jackson complained that more than half the regiments in his corps lacked chaplains. Over time, the problem worsened, so that late in the war, when the army needed them most, few regiments still had one.[39]

For those who continued their peacetime practices or who found religion, it offered a wonderful antidote to the moral challenges of military life. Many troops struggled with the absence of traditional social controls; religion restored them. It eliminated any confusion by reminding men what the proper boundaries for behavior were. Communication with God gave soldiers comfort in times of great emotional need, and various religious practices eased psychological and sometimes physical tension. Most important of all, divine services, meetings, Christian associations, or solitary prayer provided enormous psychological comfort by teaching soldiers that God's will superseded man's, that they could only do their best and then trust in God. They must turn matters beyond their control over to the care of God, thereby lifting the enormous burden of fear and worry from their shoulders. "May God grant that thousands of these our brave comrades may have this weight of doubt and fear taken from their souls," a twenty-three-year-old South Carolinian beseeched, "that they will enter with a still higher and more joyful courage upon the battlefields which still lie stretched before us." They were certain to face great battles. That God would help them, they could only hope.[40]

Chapter 20

CHANCELLORSVILLE

SHORT IN STATURE, Brigadier General Dod Ramseur strained to scan the mass of attentive faces. On a late March day in 1863, an unusually large number of soldiers had come out to hear a sermon. "As I looked upon bold faces and manly forms crowding around the preacher," Ramseur wrote to his fiancée, "I thought the scene might resembled that presented by Moses teaching the children of Israel in the Wilderness." The spring campaign season was approaching rapidly, and concerned soldiers wanted to prepare their souls.[1]

"We certainly have a Stupendous task before us," Ramseur added, one that would test the mettle of every soldier and, if successful, earn every one of them "the full title of Heroes." After two years of fighting and staggering losses, a conclusion to the war appeared nowhere in sight. The troops, so a Georgia private informed his siblings, were "a giting tiard of this thing call war." A Virginian learned that Brig. Gen. William N. Pendleton predicted the war would last another five years. "My only consolation," the Virginian asserted, "is that I believe him to be 'neither a prophet nor the son of one.' "[2]

Emotionally and physically, Confederate soldiers tired of war. Few had conceived that the struggle for independence would last for two long years, and fewer anticipated that the campaigns of 1863 would end it. Yet for all their weariness, most still felt confident in the ultimate outcome. They did, after all, have Robert E. Lee as army commander. The Union army could maintain its position north of the Rappahannock River only while the roads were impassable, a South Carolinian explained to a friend, "for if he dont do something by the time the good weather sets in General Lee will, & when he moves there will be something done." A thirty-three-year-old Texan and father of five shared that faith in the Rebel army's prowess. He assessed his comrades as being in "*miserably* good health and spirits" and admitted that after Antietam they were not "*extremely* anxious to meet the enemy *again*." If the Federals did come, however, "they will find us more determined than ever, not to be whipped."[3]

Come they would. This time, 135,000 Yankees would advance under a new commander, "Fighting" Joe Hooker. Lee would have to confront this massive enemy force with diminished strength. In mid-February, a buildup of Union troops in southeastern Virginia threatened Lee's rail lines to the Carolinas and Georgia. He detached two divisions under Longstreet to block any Federal penetration and to gather supplies for the army.[4]

In January 1863, the Union army had attempted a swing across the Rappahannock River. Heavy downpours for two days stalled the movement in mud, and the Federals called it off. Since then, so a Rebel artillery private noted, "we have been playing the part of the King of France, marched up the hill and then down again." By early March, they were not even marching up the hill. Spring thaw and rains had converted the ground into a quagmire. "Such mud you never saw the like of—" he reported to his cousin, "in some places I am convinced there is no bottom." Five weeks later, roads began to dry. "Virginia's thirsty soil will again be watered by the best blood of our beloved South," a Florida enlisted man forecast, "and will claim fresh victims to the bitter hatred of our despicable foes."[5]

During those few inactive months, the army did not remain completely idle. While a fortunate few returned home on furloughs, all regiments and batteries undertook strenuous efforts to recruit back to their strength the previous spring. Soldiers arrived in steady trickles, some new men, and others recuperated wounded or sick. By April, nearly all units had more bodies in the ranks than six or eight months before. The task facing their officers was to prepare green troops. In mid-April, Jackson laid out a marching schedule for his corps, with the soldiers covering one mile every twenty-five minutes and a ten-minute rest each hour. Jackson, as usual, reminded his men that straggling was a punishable offense. He also prohibited those who left the ranks on a march from taking their weapons with them. In the artillery, Pendleton sought to lighten the load of his batteries and reduce forage consumption and animals by citing Jackson and Lee. "Genl. Jackson takes no trunk himself and allows none in his corps." If a corps commander saw no need for one, no other officer or enlisted man should have one. The clerks in Lee's office did not have horses, and "for all his voluminous papers & all the accommodation of his staff only three or four wagons are employed." If the army commander and staff trimmed their baggage down to several wagons, batteries should do the same.[6]

Every command had to resume training to incorporate the newcomers, to teach basic tactical maneuvers, and to build *esprit de corps*. No doubt, the most impressive instructional regimen during that winter and early spring was the brainchild of Brig. Gen. Robert Emmett Rodes. A VMI graduate and former instructor, Rodes was tough, disciplined, and courageous; he was one of those unusual soldiers who quickly grew into each new assignment. In combat, he exhibited considerable skill, impressing the taskmaster Jackson. A soldier in his command once praised him with the words, "His composure was unsurpassed" and amid heavy fighting, "it was his good tactics, coolness, and judgment that saved us." By spring 1863, when he stepped in as acting division commander, he had already sustained wounds in two different battles. In November 1862,

Rodes rebuked the officers and noncommissioned officers in his brigade for their inattentiveness to the needs of his men. His crackdown caused a rebirth in the brigade. In most divisions, brigade inspectors remained relatively idle. As acting division commander, Rodes put them to work. He ordered them to examine every company once per month, paying careful attention to tactical movements on the drill field, arms and equipment, and officer competency. By his directive, brigade inspectors filed monthly written evaluations to his head-quarters on each company. The object was to spur officers to train their troops more rigorously; otherwise, companies would not pass inspection.[7]

Several months later, Rodes instituted an unusual and thoughtful prac-tice. He placed a four-gun battery near army headquarters "for the purpose of instructing portions of each infantry command in the manual of the Piece." Each brigade commander would have the use of a cannon for a day, with the gun crew there to assist them. He wanted at least one company per regiment to drill on a field gun and to keep up with that training from time to time, so that his men could service a cannon in a crisis.[8]

Despite the absence of two of Longstreet's divisions, the army still suffered supply shortages. By early April, Lee felt the Yankees had stockpiled supplies for an advance and were just waiting for a turn in weather. "I wish I could say the same for ourselves," he wrote his wife. "We are scattered, without forage & provisions, & could not remain long together if united for want of food." A Georgia private agreed with his army commander. "The cearsity [scarcity] of provishons is a cosing a grate deal of uneasiness a mong the soldiers," he com-mented to his brother and sister, although "the Yankees cant whip us only by starving us out."[9]

The private need not have boasted. In late April, Hooker launched his opening gambit with a cavalry raid toward Richmond, which he hoped would distract Lee. Meanwhile, he sent three corps on a wide flanking movement to the west, crossing the Rappahannock and Rapidan rivers before Lee could react. To the east near Fredericksburg, he quietly laid pontoons and crossed the Rappahannock. In three days, the Federals had skillfully shifted the bulk of their army below the Rappahannock-Rapidan line and had created a pincer movement that threatened Lee's rear and supply line.

Lee could have adopted the safe course of action of falling back, most likely behind the North Anna–Pamunkey River line. Yet several factors influenced his decision to attempt something bold. Ever since his retreat across the Potomac River, Lee had sought an opportunity to advance northward into Maryland and Pennsylvania. Although the army had earned a resounding victory in the Battle of Fredericksburg, it had not been able to follow it up. In late February, Lee requested that Jackson have his mapmaker Jed Hotchkiss prepare a map of the Shenandoah Valley extended to Harrisburg and Philadelphia. A month later, the army commander called on authorities in Richmond to repair the Virginia Central Railroad to ship critical supplies for his army, both along the Rappa-hannock and in the event of an advance into Maryland and beyond. Not long afterward, he suggested to Davis and the secretary of war that if Hooker did not assume the offensive by May 1, it would be best for him to seize the initiative. He would recall Longstreet and have him hold Hooker in check while Lee turned the Federal army from its position near the Rappahannock, cleared the lower Shenandoah Valley, and struck northward across the Potomac.[10]

Lee feared yielding the initiative to his enemy. With a competent general at the helm, overwhelming Union forces could force his army back to Richmond, and then it would only be a matter of time before the capital and industrial and railroad hub fell. By resisting farther north, he protected vital rail lines and shielded farmers and citizens from Union occupation and destruction. More important, his army would retain greater flexibility to maneuver and deliver a powerful blow.

Hooker had placed Lee's army in a precarious position, between two large Union forces. Lee's response was his most audacious maneuver of the war. He elected to divide his army into two groups, rather than fall back and give up his dreams of a raid northward. Observing the lack of initiative among the Yankee troops around Fredericksburg, Lee thought that the main thrust would come from the west. He and Jackson would contend with the bulk of the Union army, while Early, commanding his division, William Barksdale's Mississippi Brigade, and some artillery, would cordon the Federals in Fredericksburg. Lee rushed Richard H. Anderson's and McLaws's Divisions westward to block the two main east-west routes from Fredericksburg to a crossroads rooming house called Chancellorsville. To McLaws, Lee said that if the Confederate troops performed up to their standard, they would beat the Yankees back. "McLaws, Let them know that it is a Stern reality now, it must be, Victory or Death, for defeat would be ruinous." With spades and shovels, soldiers threw up earthworks for defense, anticipating a massive attack.[11]

Up to that point, Hooker's campaign plan had succeeded brilliantly. But the next morning, Jackson decided to press the issue. He directed McLaws and Anderson to advance, and he would support them with additional troops. "The first grand advance I made was in view of Genl. Jackson," Mississippi brigade commander Carnot Posey informed his wife, "he sent his compliments to me and directions to 'push on' the only command he ever gives." Once Hooker's forces encountered resistance from Confederates, he recoiled. Despite a two-to-one manpower advantage, greater than two-to-one superiority in artillery, and far more supplies and better equipment, he yielded the initiative to Lee.[12]

Late that night, at the intersection of Chancellorsville and Catharine Furnace roads, Lee and Jackson, seated on Yankee hardtack crates, hatched a scheme for a flank attack. Early seemingly had isolated the Union force around Fredericksburg, which enabled Lee to concentrate on Hooker's main wing. Engineers had reconnoitered that Union front and offered a pessimistic view of prospects there. Stuart had probed the eastern flank of the main body with little success. That left the Yankee right. Brig. Gen. Fitz Lee, a Rebel cavalryman and Lee's nephew, had determined that flank to be unfortified. Lee proposed

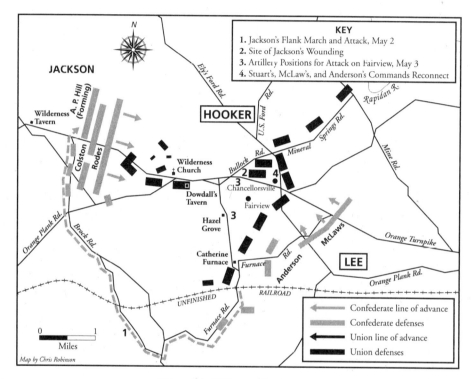

KEY

1. Jackson's Flank March and Attack, May 2
2. Site of Jackson's Wounding
3. Artillery Positions for Attack on Fairview, May 3
4. Stuart's, McLaw's, and Anderson's Commands Reconnect

Battle of Chancellorsville

that Jackson strike it. With locals as guides, Jackson would take 28,000 soldiers on a twelve-mile route around the Federal right. Since the march would take most of the day, Lee, with 13,000 troops and twenty-four cannons, would have to keep the entire Union command at bay.[13]

For ten hours, the lengthy Rebel column hiked along a circuitous route to maneuver around the Federal flank. On several occasions, Yankee troops observed the movement, but no one took serious steps to prepare for the attack. "The day was oppressively hot and many fell on the roadside from exhaustion," an Alabama artillerist described. "Gen. Jackson rode up and down the column telling 'the boys' that every moment was a fortune and they rushed forward throwing away blankets, knapsacks everything but their guns and ammunition." Soldiers nursed their comrades by pouring water on their faces, hoping to revive them and get them back in the march. As they neared the flank, Fitz Lee advanced along a pathway and climbed a hill. Below him were unsuspecting Union troops lounging around camp, protected by some abatis. Fitz Lee rode back to the main flanking column and brought Jackson forward to observe the position for himself.[14]

Fearful of throwing the men into the fight piecemeal and losing the great advantage of surprise, Jackson assembled his forces carefully. Sometime before 6:00 P.M., he unleashed his columns. Down they swooped, hollering the Rebel yell as they swept over the Union position. Some slowed to plunder the Yankee encampment. Quite a number of Jackson's attackers had eaten little over the two previous days and they discovered all they wanted. Passing over the scene afterward, a Virginia artillerist commented, "you could'nt step 10 steps without seeing a big fat Dutchman laying stripped of his outer clothes & a pile of crackers all around him." Fortunately for the Confederates, the majority pressed onward. In the rear, Federals could hear the sound of attack and tossed up works to check the advance. As the front wave of Confederates slowed, succeeding columns passed through them and kept the attack moving. At one point, Brig. Gen. Dorsey Pender seized the colors and on horseback led his men into the Federal entrenchments. "The effect of such examples of daring gallantry at critical moments," division commander A. P. Hill insisted to the army commander, "is incalculable."[15]

As resistance stiffened and the attack slowed, Jackson wanted one more powerful thrust, hoping to cut off the Federals from the fords across the Rappahannock. What Jackson could not observe in the darkness were thousands of well-positioned Yankees blocking his path. Foolishly, he rode forward to observe personally. For some time, troops near the front had skirmished and even come under heavy artillery fire. They were skittish. They had also received orders, according to one of Jackson's staff officers, "to fire upon any cavy [cavalry] coming from the direction of the enemy." Firing at some Federals rippled along the line from the south, and the 18th North Carolina joined in the shooting. They let loose a volley and struck Jackson in three places. With its rider stunned, Jackson's horse bolted, nearly unseating the general on a low tree limb. Two others stopped the horse. Jackson had been hit in his right hand, his left wrist, and above the left elbow. In a peculiar coincidence, less than two weeks earlier Jackson's engineer Capt. James K. Boswell had written to his aunt, "Strange as it may seem, not one of Genl. J's staff has ever been killed, though I doubt not they have been as much exposed as the staff officers of any Major Genl. in the army." Boswell lay dead from the musket fire, and Jackson was badly wounded.[16]

Someone tied handkerchiefs on Jackson's arm, which may have saved him from bleeding to death. Stretcher bearers came up and hauled him away, dropping the general twice as they carried him through the Wilderness in darkness. This may have restarted the bleeding. They gave Jackson some whiskey on the battlefield to dull his senses, and after a rough ambulance ride, Dr. Hunter McGuire amputated his arm about three inches below the shoulder. The next day, probably in the evening, Jackson dictated a note informing the army commander of his injury. In reply, Lee informed Jackson, "I cannot express my regret at the occurrence. Could I have directed events, I should have chosen for the good of the country to have been disabled in your stead."[17]

Later that night, A. P. Hill sustained a shell wound that incapacitated him temporarily for field service. As senior division commander, Rodes agreed with Hill to call on cavalry commander Jeb Stuart to replace Hill.

Despite the wounding, Jackson's flank movement and attack thrilled the Confederate populace. By the end of the day's fighting, the Confederates had certainly inflicted heavy casualties on the Yankees, but nothing astronomical by Civil War standards. Hooker's right wing stood more compact than before, and with concentrated strength, Hooker could achieve greater objectives if he acted boldly. Yet the battle's significance was psychological. Somehow, once again, the Confederacy had foiled a grand Union offensive and attacked on an unsuspecting flank. At First Manassas, Seven Days', Cedar Mountain, and Second Manassas, the Confederacy had snatched victory from a better-armed, better-equipped, and usually larger Union army.[18]

Lee's situation was still perilous. That night, his army lay in three segments. Stuart commanded on the extreme left. Lee oversaw the center. Back near Fredericksburg, Early somehow managed to hold his own. Twice that night, in the most emphatic terms, Lee directed Stuart to take Chancellorsville and unite the two commands. Stuart needed no prodding. Well before Lee's first message, he had begun preparing to launch an attack to drive the Federals back. On the far right of Stuart's lead division, Brig. Gen. James J. Archer's Tennesseans and Alabamians confronted a ridge named Hazel Grove, which separated the two portions of the Confederate army. It was the critical piece of ground on the battlefield, and Hooker gave it to him: The Union commander withdrew his troops from the key terrain in order to tighten his line. Archer's early morning attack, supported by some cannons placed on the northern edge of the clearing by Col. Porter Alexander, caught the tail end of the evacuation, capturing four guns and one hundred prisoners.[19]

With his uncanny ability to recognize valuable terrain features, Stuart immediately understood the value of Hazel Grove. He planted twenty-eight cannons there under the direction of Alexander, and later the two of them rode northward to the Orange Plank Road, where Alexander cobbled together fourteen more guns. This gave the Confederates an extraordinary converging fire on the Union infantry and artillery occupying the cleared high ground appropriately called Fairview.

BY THIS POINT in the war, Federals had proven themselves masters of the long arm. At Seven Days', especially on Malvern Hill, and later at Antietam and Fredericksburg, Yankee superiority in guns and gunnery punished Rebel troops and thwarted Confederate plans. In several battles, Confederate artillerists could boast moments of glory. Colonel Stephen Dill Lee's flanking artillery fire helped repulse an assault on Jackson's position at Second Manassas. Several weeks later, Rebel gunners at Nicodemus Heights and elsewhere punished attacks by Hooker's and John Sedgwick's Corps. When the Yankees tried to break through Jackson's Corps at Fredericksburg, artillerists under Pelham, Pegram, and McIntosh disrupted the attack despite suffering heavy losses. Still, at Fredericksburg, Longstreet shrewdly directed his artillery not to duel with Union gunners, a battle they could not win, but to concentrate instead on Federal infantry.[20]

Chief of Artillery Pendleton lacked genuine ability as an artillerist. Perhaps had he remained in the service of the U.S. Army he would have developed into a skilled gunnery officer, but he had left for a life as a man of the cloth. With the encouragement of some talented junior officers, however, Pendleton did institute two sweeping changes that improved artillery organization and responsiveness to army needs. At Lee's request, in early October 1862 he consolidated batteries, eliminated unsatisfactory officers, and reduced the number of animals the artillery required, thereby cutting the critical burden of supply. Then, in mid-February 1863, after consultation with Alexander and Jackson's Corps artillery chief, Col. Stapleton Crutchfield, Pendleton proposed a farsighted restructuring of artillery. In the past, the Confederacy had frittered away its artillery strength by assigning a battery to each brigade and holding large numbers of batteries as army reserve. Brigade commanders could not use artillery effectively and became territorial about their battery. Pendleton recommended consolidating every four batteries into a battalion, with one battalion assigned to each division. Artillery battalion commanders would report to the chief of the corps artillery, and they reported to the chief of artillery, who in turn worked directly for the army commander. In addition, each corps had two reserve battalions, which it could employ in conjunction with division battalions for heavy, concentrated fire. This structure, Pendleton and others believed, would improve unity and concentration in battle. It was a huge leap forward.[21]

Its first true test was at the Battle of Chancellorsville. In short order, Alexander as acting corps artillery chief and Stuart as acting corps commander collected and positioned large numbers of guns on the plateau at Hazel Grove and along the plank road. As Stuart boasted in his official report, "under the happy effects of the battalion system, it was done quickly." The converging fire devastated the Union gunners and infantrymen who held the Fairview high ground. Union Brig. Gen. John W. Geary, whose division occupied trenches there, insisted his command "was exposed to a terribly raking and enfilading fire from the enemy, who had succeeded in turning the right flank of the army, leaving us exposed to the full fury of his artillery." Division commander Brig. Gen. Alpheus S. Williams, whose Federals also held part of Fairview, explained that Confederates unlimbered batteries at Hazel Grove and "opened a most vigorous fire upon our batteries and our lines of infantry both right and left of this position."[22]

While the artillery pounded the Union forces around Fairview, Confederate infantry launched a series of assaults to dislodge the Yankees. The two arms worked unusually well together this day, shattering the Federal position and after some stiff resistance causing what a North Carolinian called "the second edition of the Bull Run races." Ramseur told his brother his division charged over parts of two Virginia brigades, which he called "timid friends," and drove Yankees from three lines of entrenchments. At one point, Rebel troops could not dislodge the Federals. Lee arrived on the scene and, hat in hand, cheered the men. "Right well you know with such a leader we could not fail," crowed a Georgian. Colonel Bryan Grimes described to his wife how in one sector troops fell back in disorder "until Gen'l Lee took Command in person and with waiving hat in hand charged them driving them helter skelter." With the commanding terrain of Fairview in Stuart's hands, Chancellorsville became untenable for the Union. Alexander posted artillery, which hurled shot after shot into the easy targets. One Confederate shell struck a pillar on which Hooker was leaning, knocking him to the ground senseless for a few minutes. When the Yankee commander regained consciousness and composure, he pulled back into a tighter defensive posture with his back to the river.[23]

After the fighting was over and Confederates controlled the Chancellorsville crossroads, Lee and Stuart rode down the line. Unbroken cheers erupted as Lee passed. "The boys greeted him wherever he went, and it must have been a proud moment for him," a Georgia sergeant speculated to his parents. "He had just routed the enemy and gained a glorious victory; and now to witness with what devotion his men loved him!" He then concluded with the remark, "It was inspiring beyond anything you can imagine." Another soldier agreed. "The sight of the old hero after such a victory was too much," he described to his father. "We had never cheered him before, but now the pride we felt in him must have vent, and of all the cheering ever heard this was our most enthusiastic." Soldiers expressed their belief that, more than anything else, Lee had made the difference between triumph and failure. Charles Marshall, one of Lee's aides, observed the spontaneous outpouring and admitted some years later, "I thought that it must have been from such a scene that men in ancient days rose to the dignity of gods."[24]

The heavy artillery fire caused one of the most disconcerting scenes for veterans and green troops alike. Dry scrub, tangled vine, third-stage timber, and leaves caught fire from exploding shells, and large portions of the battlefield went up in flames. According to a Georgia infantryman, "the wailings of the wounded enemy were horrible—evidencing not only pain from their wounds, but excrutiating tortures of the fire. Many—very many—were burnt to a crisp, as well as many of our dead and wounded." A Virginia veteran admitted it was "One of the most horrible sights I ever witnessed in my life."[25]

Just as Chancellorsville turned dramatically in Confederate favor, Fredericksburg reached a boiling point. Shortly before daylight on April 29, Union troops quickly laid pontoons and crossed the Rappahannock near Deep Run, a couple of miles east of Fredericksburg. Major General Jubal Early with his division, Barksdale's Mississippi Brigade, and some artillery defended the Fredericksburg area, while the rest of the army concentrated on Hooker's principal wing. Union forces had seen Jackson's flanking movement and Hooker's people had mistakenly concluded that Lee planned to fall back from the Rappahannock area. Just before Jackson's people struck the flank, Hooker notified the Union commander of the left wing, Maj. Gen. John Sedgwick, to cross the river at Fredericksburg "as soon as indications permit," seize Fredericksburg, and pursue the enemy. "We know that the enemy is fleeing, trying to save his train," his aide wrote. By 9:00 P.M., after Jackson rolled up his flank, Hooker had changed his tune. He ordered Sedgwick to cross the river immediately and march on Chancellorsville, "until you connect with this army." En route, he would probably strike Lee's rear, "and between us we will use him up." Sedgwick exploited his previous crossing and marched upriver, forcing his way into Fredericksburg by daylight. Additional troops crossed on pontoons at Fredericksburg.[26]

During the initial crossing, Federal troops attacked Rebel pickets so suddenly and laid pontoons so quickly that they had crossed the Rappahannock before anyone notified Early, two miles away. Rebel forces responded by erecting field works. "During that day and the next," a Georgian reported, "I never worked harder in my life." They cut logs, piling them along the railroad, with whatever ties and rails they could find. They tossed up mounds of dirt, loosened by bayonets and scooped by hand. Confusion in the transmission of orders nearly withdrew the bulk of Early's command on May 1, but Early corrected the staff error and returned in time to retain possession of the line.[27]

On the morning of May 3, the Federals launched their attack. Louisianans foiled one attempt to break out to the northwest of town, which would have turned the entire Confederate position. Twice, Barksdale's men with some guns from the Washington Artillery repulsed Union assaults at Marye's Heights, the scene of great slaughter more than four months earlier. Finally, after a truce to remove the wounded revealed the manpower weakness of the Rebel position,

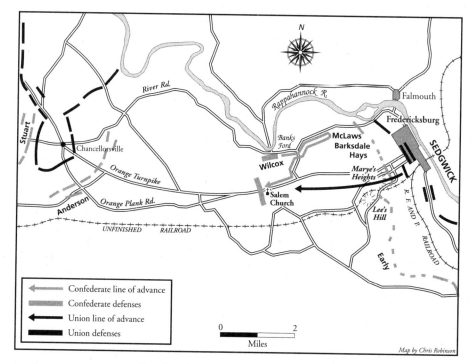

N

River Rd.

Rappahannock R.

Falmouth

Stuart

Banks
Ford

Fredericksburg

Chancellorsville

McLaws
Barksdale
Hays

SEDGWICK

Wilcox

Orange Turnpike

Marye's
Heights

Anderson

Orange Plank Rd.

Salem
Church

R. F. AND P. RAILROAD

UNFINISHED   RAILROAD

Lee's
Hill

Early

Confederate line of advance
Confederate defenses
Union line of advance
Union defenses

0   2
Miles

Map by Chris Robinson

Battle of Second Fredericksburg

a determined frontal assault crashed through the line. A Confederate artillerist claimed the Mississippians "fought like tigers. Some fought with rocks after the enemy reached the Stone Wall. They had a hand to hand fight, clubbing their guns." Ultimately, they succumbed to overwhelming numbers. Federals were "so infuriated" at the Rebels' stubborn resistance that "They fired on us after we surrendered, killing Corpl Lutzman and wounding I. C. Florence severely in the leg."[28]

With his line broken, Early conducted a skillful withdrawal to the south along Telegraph Road. From upriver, he received some valuable help from Brig. Gen. Cadmus M. Wilcox. Wilcox's Alabama brigade guarded Banks's Ford over the Rappahannock between Fredericksburg and Hooker's position. Once he spotted the haversacks on enemy pickets, he realized the Yankees at Banks's Ford did not intend to stay there long. They were abandoning their old position and were marching toward Chancellorsville. Under instructions from Lee, he notified the commander and marched to Fredericksburg, leaving behind fifty men and two artillery guns to watch the crossing. With a couple of cannons and some skirmishers, Wilcox blocked the movement of three Yankee regiments just north of town. The lack of aggressiveness on the part of these Federals led Wilcox to surmise that this was merely a feint. He rode over to Marye's Heights and witnessed a substantial Union buildup in the streets below. Not long after he returned to his command, Barksdale requested reinforcements. Wilcox immediately detached the 10th Alabama and personally accompanied it, when they learned from some Louisiana infantry north of the Mississippians that Barksdale's line had given way.

Much like Rodes, Wilcox had proven himself a resourceful officer. A West Point graduate, he became an expert on rifled muskets and wrote an important book on the subject before the war. At Antietam, his men occupied a sunken road and fought valiantly, but when Yankees penetrated, his men were easy targets. In the next fight, at Fredericksburg in December 1862, he directed his men to dig zig-zag trenches, to prevent the same disaster. In the area near Fredericksburg once more, Wilcox now conducted perhaps the most skillful delaying action of the war. Rather than fall back with Early's command along Telegraph Road, he elected to block Federal movements along Orange Plank Road, a route that would take Yankee troops into Lee's rear and toward Hooker at Chancellorsville. Twice, Wilcox's men checked a Federal advance, both times falling back in excellent order to a new defensive position. Each time, he dragged out the action, to give the Confederates more time to bring reinforcements to the scene. His third position was around Salem Church, some five miles from Fredericksburg. Here, troops from McLaws's Division occupied a concealed position perpendicular to the plank road. Wilcox's own Alabamians occupied the center. In the late afternoon, Sedgwick attacked with three waves. At one point, a portion of the Alabamians fell back, exposing the flank of the adjacent regiments. Troops quickly refused (bent back) their line, and a counterattack from the 9th Alabama hammered out the bulge. Despite a "spirited" attack, the Confederates held their ground, and Sedgwick's assault fizzled.[29]

The initiative then shifted to the Confederates. That night, Early attempted to coordinate an attack with McLaws. He struck in the early morning hours, regaining Marye's Heights and threatening the Union rear. Sensing an opportunity to crush Sedgwick's command, Lee rushed R. H. Anderson's division over to collaborate with the two veteran commanders. By the time Anderson got in position, forming the third side of a box, it was near 6:00 P.M., about the time of Jackson's flank attack several days earlier. This time, however, Early struck aggressively, Anderson half-heartedly, and McLaws barely budged. With limited threats in two of three avenues of attack, the Union concentrated much of its musket and artillery fire on Early's brigades, which suffered heavy losses. Hays's Louisiana Brigade, badly victimized, lost 40 percent of its men in the battle. One Louisiana lieutenant informed his father, "I was struck five times and once a ball flattened on my sword belt buckle (which would have gone through my stomach) which I have and will send to you by the first opportunity, the 2nd ball cut the skin on my throat. A third on my left check the fourth through my coat on my side fifth through the fleshy part of my hand inflicting a severe flesh wound." A round passed through a tightly wrapped blanket and barely penetrated a friend's chest, the blanket saving his life. His brother Charlie also had a close scare. He picked up a small box in a Yankee knapsack and moments later a ball crashed through his blanket, knapsack, and then deflected off the box.[30]

It was the last significant fighting in the Battle of Chancellorsville. Left to his own devices, Sedgwick evacuated his forces across the Rappahannock early the next morning. That night, Hooker decided to retreat as well. On May 5, his dispirited soldiers shuffled back across the pontoons.

The Confederates were astounded at the Union collapse of will at the top. Better to call him "'Fighting'—*fainting*—fleeing" Joe Hooker, claimed Virginia private Thomas Petty. A Georgian insisted instead that they nickname him "*General Running Joe Hooker*." Another Georgian who fought around Fredericksburg could not believe the Union retreat. "I never have saw Yankees skeedadle so in all my life," he wrote to friends, "when they hear the Rebels Come Chargeing and hollowing they Cant stand."[31]

THE VIEW FROM the battlefield was soon trumped by news from the hospital. Stonewall Jackson appeared to be doing better after his arm was amputated, until fever and discomfort struck. Pneumonia had entered his lungs before the wounding. In his weakened condition, after so much loss of blood, he could not resist. Steadily, his health declined. By midafternoon, May 10, Jackson was no more.[32]

It was a crushing blow to the new nation. Jackson had become a larger-than-life figure for the Confederate people, and he rallied spirits like no one else in the army. A forlorn Catherine Edmondston wrote: "He was the nation's idol, not a breath even from a foe has ever been breathed against his fame. His very enemies reverenced him. God has taken him from us that we may lean more upon *Him*, feel that He can raise up to Himself instruments to work His Divine Will."[33]

In an elegant tribute, a captain in the 60th Georgia explained to his sister what Jackson had meant to the army. "If I live a hundred years and remain sane, I shall never forget his look mounted on a noble horse and a most elegant rider. His eagle eye seemed to take in all at a glance. He rode up to a battery and in a few moments it was thundering death among our enemies." He concluded, "General Lee is a far greater General than 'Old Stonewall' but he can never excite the enthusiasm which this old war horse did with his faded coat and cap and his sun burnt cheek,—'*Requiescat in Pace.*'"[34]

Still, these were soldiers, and no matter how regrettable, death was part of their trade. Upon hearing of Jackson's passing, a Texan down in the Suffolk area with Longstreet hoped the news was false, yet was resigned to the fact that "we cannot halp it for thier is many good man gon up a spout since the ware com manced." When Robin Berkeley's sister declared the victory at Chancellorsville "dearly bought," the Virginia artillerist snapped back, "All our victories have been very dearly won, and may [many] brave and good men have fallen in them but because they happen not to be quite so high on the ladder of fame are soon forgot." He then instructed her, "You cannot walk over a single field about here without passing over some poor soldiers grave who though he has fallen fighting for his country has not so much as plank to tell who lies beneath the fresh mound." Similarly, a Georgian vented his annoyance over the fuss about Jackson's death. "It is wrong to make so much noise about one man When thousands of privates have been killed unknown to glory, more meritorious and equally as patriotic as he." When he heard people say they would rather lose 25,000 soldiers than Jackson, it outraged him. "This is all nonsense and toadyism."[35]

The Army of Northern Virginia sustained nearly 13,500 casualties at Chancellorsville, more than 1,700 of them killed or mortally wounded in action. Lee specifically requested that officers not report slight wounds in their statement of casualties, reminding them that casualties were not necessarily indicative of good or hard fighting. They still submitted numbers that tallied well over 9,000 wounded soldiers. A week after the fighting, a soldier in the 10th Virginia, Col. Edward Warren's command, spotted only 6 officers and 80 men present for drill, when the regiment had taken 430 into the battle. A captain commanded his regiment. The soldier could only comment, "O this horrible War."[36]

Officially, the 10th Virginia lost 157 men in the battle, second highest in its brigade. The 3rd North Carolina suffered 232 casualties, 215 of whom were killed or wounded. After the fight, the regimental chaplain of the 3rd North Carolina reported to a friend, "I have heard such sounds, & seen such sights, as make my flesh almost crawl when I think of them. Such suffering, agonizing and terrible in the extreme, I never had the least idea before." All told, the seven highest regimental losses, killed and wounded, fell to North Carolina infantry regiments. Among the three North Carolina brigades, Lane's suffered 910 casualties, Pender's 756, and Ramseur's almost 800. Only Rodes's Alabamians and Warren's brigade of Virginia and North Carolina tabulated casualties at that tragic rate.[37]

The strain on officers and men during the fight was tremendous. Mississippi brigade commander Carnot Posey informed his wife that over the seven days of campaigning, he ate one small meal per day and slept a total of twelve hours. Five days after the fighting, a private in the 3rd North Carolina apologized to his wife for his terse letter. "I shant write much now for I cant right," he scripted badly, "I have Got the trimbles." Nearly a month later, a Virginian in Heth's Brigade recalled his close scares with death, including two bulletholes through his pants and one that tore up his shoe. "It was by far the hottest place I ever was in and I am not very anxious to get in another such place." Several days after the fighting ended, one of Ramseur's staff officers contrasted the fury of the battle with the present calm. "I was in imminent and fearful peril, with all the emotions ablaze, the death shot whistling around, the roar of artillery shaking the ground like the mighty throes of an earth-quake, and the groans of the wounded and dying rending the air and piercing the skies," he explained to his wife. "To-day, —serene, and soft, and quiet,—I could lift up my voice gratefully in the temple of God, far removed from the maddening excitements and the immediate danger which but a few days since ruled the hour. Blessed contrast!"[38]

The loss of Jackson loomed above all other casualties. Among other things, it meant Lee would need a new corps commander. Stuart had stepped in and fought Jackson's troops superbly, but he already directed the cavalry, and it seems unlikely that Lee considered him seriously. As senior division commander, A. P. Hill appeared to be the logical choice. Lee appreciated his aggressiveness in combat and his brilliant march from Harpers Ferry to save the army at Antietam. Lee regarded Hill, all factors considered, "the best soldier of his grade with me." When Jackson fell, Hill had stepped into the job, until he, too, suffered a wound. Within a week after Hooker retreated north, Hill had recovered sufficiently to return to duty. The drawback to Hill was that he had tangled with Jackson and Longstreet.[39]

Ever since Lee assumed command of the army, he had believed that the two corps or wings of the army were too big. Each contained approximately 30,000 men. "These are more than one man can properly handle and keep under his eye in battle in the country that we have to operate in," Lee wrote to President Davis. "They are always beyond the range of his vision, and frequently beyond his reach." Lee had not approached Davis previously on the subject because he had no one to recommend as the third corps commander. With Jackson's death, Lee suggested breaking the army into three corps, to be commanded by Longstreet, Hill, and Richard S. Ewell, an old Regular Army officer who had fought well with Jackson in the Valley and ever since, until sustaining a severe leg wound at Groveton during the Second Manassas operation. Ewell had his leg amputated, but by late May, he felt healthy enough to return to active duty. Lee described him as "an honest, brave soldier, who has always done his duty well." In reality, while Ewell was a bit cautious and a great worrier, Hill was impetuous.

To balance the three corps, Lee consolidated brigades to form two new divisions, which joined Anderson's Division to form the Third Corps under Hill. Longstreet retained his First Corps with divisions under Hood, Pickett, and McLaws, and Ewell took over Jackson's Second Corps, with Early, Johnson, and Rodes as his division commanders.[40]

The Confederates now depended more than ever on Lee. "Our army [is] in the finest spirits & health," Pendleton's nephew and staff officer Dudley asserted to his mother. "Will go any where with Genl Lee & its comdrs [commanders]." Young Willie Pegram agreed. Jackson's death cast a gloom over the army. Soldiers did not fully understand how much they loved him till he died. Nonetheless, "His death will not have the effect of making our troops fight any worse," Pegram insisted to his sister. "Besides being the bravest troops in the world, they have the most unbounded confidence in their *great leader*, Genl. Lee."[41]

In the minds of Confederates in and out of uniform, Lee's army had emerged as the one great nationalizing institution. Ever since Lee assumed command, the Army of Northern Virginia had not failed its citizens. Its great success had given life to the Rebels in their darkest hours; its victories had pulled together Southern people from ten states into a Confederate nation. When some argued that Joe Johnston was the best general, Pauline Heyward of South Carolina challenged them: "Lee has *never* lost a battle; give me that kind of a man for my Hero General." Chancellorsville was yet another in a string of successes for Lee and his Army of Northern Virginia. As William Pitt Ballinger, a distinguished Galveston, Texas, lawyer marveled, "what a glorious army that of Lee is."[42]

Chapter 21

⸺◦⸺

ARMS AND AMMUNITION

Aformer student at the University of Virginia and prewar teacher, William Allan began his wartime service as a quartermaster clerk in the Stonewall Brigade. An individual of extraordinary capacity, Allan's competence soon caught the eye of Stonewall Jackson. In December 1862, Jackson appointed him the ordnance officer on his staff.[1]

Allan did not bring expertise in ammunition to the headquarters staff. He did, however, exhibit an uncanny knack for organization. Somehow, he managed to instill order among ordnance personnel. He kept the corps brimming with ammunition, supervised its efficient distribution to regiments and batteries, and oversaw all the essential paperwork. A quick study and an observant officer, Allan spotted a serious problem during the fighting at Chancellorsville. With Jackson's chief of artillery, Stapleton Crutchfield, wounded, Allan paid more careful attention to how well his ordnance worked in the battle. He noticed that Confederate shells and case shot exploded prematurely, sometimes almost immediately after they exited the cannon's mouth, inflicting casualties on the wrong side. A few weeks after the campaign, Allan filed an official notice of what he had witnessed, one that set the Confederate Ordnance Bureau spinning.[2]

The Ordnance Bureau had been a source of Confederate pride. Largely through the tireless work of Josiah Gorgas and a handful of others, the Confederacy erected a massive ordnance production program from scratch. At the start of the war, state and national governments controlled approximately 150,000 shoulder weapons of various calibers, of which little more than one in six had rifling for superior range and accuracy. Southern states did not mass-produce arms, ammunition, or gunpowder, and they had few trained workers in the field. Only the Federal installation at Harpers Ferry made weapons in any appreciable quantity. The Confederacy initially relied on gunpowder, weapons, and ammunition seized from U.S. government installations.[3]

In time, the Confederate States drew on their own supplies for basic chemical and mineral ingredients and began to turn out considerable quantities of weapons and ammunition. The South had one lead mine operating in Virginia, and copper mines had just opened in eastern Tennessee. It collected niter in caves and cultivated niter beds. The nation mined sulfur and iron and set up a Nitre and Mining Bureau to oversee extraction and smelting. Confederates struggled to develop a reliable source of nitric acid, essential in the manufacturing of percussion caps, which ignited the gunpowder in small arms. Officials scoured university campuses and chemistry laboratories with limited success. Ultimately, they had to import much of the nitric acid.

Richmond housed the only major cannon foundry in the South, Tredegar Iron Works. Upon orders from Lee, Jackson seized and began removing the manufacturing equipment for rifled muskets at Harpers Ferry, a process that Johnston completed. Part of the machinery went to Richmond and another set was shipped to Fayetteville, North Carolina. Eventually, the Confederacy manufactured 55,000 rifled muskets per year. The rest would have to come from importation, modification of outmoded smoothbores, or captured Yankee weapons.[4]

To convert raw materials into usable products, the Confederacy had to build factories, most of them from the ground up. With Tredegar and the small-arms manufacturing equipment seized at Harpers Ferry, Richmond quickly emerged as the great industrial center of the Confederacy, producing half the Confederacy's ordnance. In Augusta, Georgia, the Confederacy erected a massive gunpowder factory that serviced most of the armies in the field. It also established arsenals and ordnance plants across the nation.[5]

Other than what it captured from the Yankees, Lee's army received the vast majority of its weapons and ammunition from Richmond. Through January 1, 1865, the Richmond Arsenal and Tredegar Iron Works had produced, refitted, repaired, or issued 341 Columbiad and large siege guns; 1,306 artillery guns either manufactured or captured; 1,375 gun carriages; 875 caissons for carrying field ammunition; 921,441 rounds of field, siege, and coastal artillery ammunition, 1,456,190 friction primers to spark the explosion; 1,110,966 fuses; 323,231 infantry arms that were mostly captured and turned in to the Ordnance Department; 72,513,854 small-arms cartridges; 146,901,250 percussion caps to ignite small-arms cartridges; and assorted other items.[6]

At the start of the war, the Rebel forces in Virginia relied heavily on antiquated weapons dating back to the War of 1812. Arsenals soon began converting them from flintlock to percussion caps, but varying calibers made it difficult for the army to procure ammunition. Original volunteers, moreover, brought with them into military service weapons from home—shotguns, rifles, muskets, and pistols—again varying in caliber and quality.[7]

The machinery Jackson seized at Harpers Ferry enabled the Confederate States to produce some rifled muskets, but still the majority of small arms would have to come from outside the country. Davis's government began importing Enfield rifles from England and inferior rifled muskets from other countries. Ultimately, however, Lee's troops would also use the Yankee army as a major supplier of quality small arms. Through 1862, the 100,000 small arms that

Rebels picked up from battlefields and captured from Yankee prisoners, in addition to the 174 field pieces, proved critical for the war effort in the East and helped offset weapons shortages elsewhere in the Confederate States.[8]

Despite their incredible haul, Lee's army continually suffered from shortages. Weapons wore out or were damaged. Others fell into Union hands, or men discarded them in haste to avoid capture. A Georgian wrote his mother that in the Battle of Antietam, officers assigned him and a few comrades to guard the wagons. A party of Yankees attacked. "I tell you that we had to cut out faster than I Ever did Before in my life." Federals launched several shots at him and missed. In flight, he lost his gun and "my shoes came untide and I did not have time to stop and tie them so they got them."[9]

The Ordnance Bureau labored heroically; nonetheless, shortages continued. Davis discouraged a raid northward in fall 1861 in part because Johnston's army lacked weapons. At the beginning of the Peninsula Campaign, Wilcox's Brigade alone had 300 unarmed men. The best his commander Magruder could do was to procure 100 smoothbore muskets, mostly flint and steel. On the eve of the Battle of Fredericksburg, Lee called on the secretary of war for 3,000 rifles for unarmed soldiers. In a sad state of affairs, the 4th Virginia Cavalry mustered 462 enlisted men present in January 1863, yet it had carbines and rifles for only 148. The vast majority fought with pistols and sabers. Two months later, twelve men in the 33rd Georgia Infantry had no weapons on a dress parade, and an inspection of the 26th North Carolina uncovered a shortage of forty muskets. That August, Lee reported 1,700 unarmed men in his army and predicted a need for 10,000 more rifles in a month. In fact, virtually every infantry and cavalry regiment in Lee's army lacked a full complement of firearms on any given day.[10]

Regiments and even companies carried into battle a mix of arms, a dangerous situation and a nightmare for ordnance officers and sergeants. Early in Lee's tenure as army commander, he sought to ensure uniformity. When it became apparent that he could not obtain enough weapons for all his troops, he determined in March 1863 that "measures be taken to bring about homogeneous armament in Regts where practicable and certainly so in Companies." Yet even within companies it was an impossibility. An inspection in the 26th North Carolina, for example, uncovered three companies with mixed weapons, some rifled muskets and others smoothbores. The regimental commander probably could have traded weapons to reduce the problem to a single company, but he could not eliminate it without an influx of sufficient arms to standardize the entire regiment.[11]

Throughout the war, officials failed to provide the same uniform quality of weapons to its troops as the federal government issued. "You would be astonished to see at what distance our men are sometimes shot down," a lieutenant in the 3rd Georgia explained. A Federal marksman had killed one of his men at a range of 500–600 yards. In the aftermath of Chancellorsville, his entire regiment was finally able to arm all the men with rifles. "I am glad we are now on an equal footing with them." Other units were not so lucky. The following June, Company A, 14th Virginia Cavalry, had three unarmed men, one with a .69 caliber weapon, thirteen with .54 Mississippi rifles, two .577 Enfield rifles, and ten .52 Sharp's carbines. Throughout the war, many soldiers in infantry regiments carried the smaller cavalry musket into battle, because there were not enough infantry muskets available.[12]

With a variety of small arms, ammunition problems haunted the Confederate army. In the early stages of the war, soldiers fired a considerable amount of .69 or .71 caliber balls, or buck and ball cartridges, heavy rounds that required nearly double the amount of gunpowder to fire as an Enfield .577 rifled musket. Once the Confederate government used up all its U.S.-made gunpowder, it had to rely on its own production. Yet not until 1864 did its gunpowder match the quality of that manufactured in the North.[13]

Despite the closeness in caliber, .577 and .58, the army had to issue different ammunition and loading instructions for Enfields and Springfields. During the Antietam Campaign, Hill Fitzpatrick struggled to load a Yankee round in his Enfield rifle. "To my greatest mortification my gun failed to fire," the private reported to his wife, "but I soon recollected that it was charged with a Yankee cartridge which had to be ram[m]ed hard. I drew my stick gave it a hard ram tried it again and went clear as a whistle." After the battle, Lee's headquarters explained that officers and men could recognize the Enfield ammunition because it had a wooden plug at the cavity. Soldiers were to insert it into the barrel of the musket with the paper. The Springfield ammunition had grooves around it, full of grease. "The .58 caliber will be inserted naked," or without the paper, Lee instructed them.[14]

Nor did Confederate troops have the advantage of Williams cleaners, which Union soldiers carried. With black-gunpowder weapons, ten or twelve rounds would foul the musket, so that soldiers would have to clean the weapon in order to load another round. In the Federal army, soldiers received two Williams cleaners with every twenty rounds. The cleaner scoured the barrel and enabled soldiers to fire up to twenty rounds before they had to clean their muskets, an enormous advantage in combat. Dissatisfied with their effectiveness, the Union stopped issuing Williams cleaners in 1864, but they unquestionably gave Yankee infantrymen an edge for the first three years of the war. By then large numbers of Federals carried repeating rifles, which enabled their soldiers to fire between seven and sixteen rounds in the time a Rebel could load and fire one.[15]

Even worse, the Confederacy had serious problems manufacturing its small-arms ammunition. In December 1862, the Ordnance Bureau issued a circular, warning arsenals that they must limit the size of Enfield ammunition. "Complaints are made that the guns will not load after 6 or 7 Rounds," it stated. Seven months later, in June 1863, Gorgas's top assistant, Maj. J. W. Mallet, received a complaint from a general officer in Lee's army, probably his old friend Robert Rodes, that Enfield ammunition clogged too frequently, most likely from the gunpowder and grease from cartridge boxes. "I have been informed by a letter from a General Officer in the Army of Northern Virginia," Mallet alerted Gorgas, "that the men have repeatedly sought to obtain Miss. Rifle ammunition (cal. 54) for their Enfield rifles and rifled muskets (cal. 577 & .58)—such was the general fear of the jamming of bullets in the bore derived from previous experience." The smaller ammunition would not grip the walls of the barrel and exploit the spiral rifling grooves, which spun the bullet for greater distance and accuracy, but they would not jam, either. The problem became so serious that Lee alerted his subordinate commanders about it.[16]

Around the same time, the Ordnance Department also learned that it had issued molds for lead that varied slightly in size. It was the Ordnance Department's intent that everyone produce a projectile that was .565 in size, suitable for both the .577 Enfield and the .58 Springfield. Officials at the Richmond Laboratory issued a standard gauge for use at all arsenals. After workers removed the bullet from the mold, they passed it through the gauge to make sure it was of the proper size. Yet the Augusta Arsenal made bullets that were too large. At other arsenals, they produced bullets that were too small. "The balls made accurately to moulds and gauges lately issued," Gorgas complained to Mallet in early July, "are I have decided too small for efficient use in arms of precision." This would not have been a particular problem for Lee's army, except that it consumed such enormous amounts of small-arms ammunition that the Confederate Ordnance Department had to ship ammunition from Augusta to Richmond at times. In one month, May 1864, Augusta Arsenal sent 935,000 rounds of Enfield (.577), Mississippi (.54), and Belgian ammunition (.69) to Lee's army. Gorgas attempted to stem these manufacturing problems by requiring all arsenals to ship a batch of ammunition monthly to the Richmond Labs for testing. At least that way, the Confederacy could identify a production problem before it proved disastrous in the field.[17]

With mixed weapons and ammunition problems throughout the army, Lee opposed soldiers' exchanging their muskets for superior ones found on the battlefield. Shortly after Seven Days', he directed officers to halt the practice to ensure uniformity within their commands. Before the spring campaign of 1863, the Confederate government officially forbade it, no doubt with Lee's consent, warning, "Disaster may easily result from a disregard of this necessary order." After Chancellorsville, Lee again complained to Stuart that his cavalry had adopted captured weapons and reminded him the practice was not in the best interest of the army.[18]

Similar ordnance troubles afflicted the field artillery. Early in the war, Confederate artillerists functioned at a severe disadvantage. Federals had superior artillerists, ammunition, and field guns. By the time of Fredericksburg, Confederate artillery crews had acquired considerable expertise, and the ammunition had improved. The great disadvantage that Confederates still faced, Lee suggested, was in the guns themselves. The Confederacy had too many different types of cannons, which required too many different types of ammunition. Worst of all, two of the most common types of guns, the 6-pounder smoothbore and 12-pounder howitzer, were either too small or had a range too limited for regular campaigning. "I am greatly in need of longer range smoothbore guns," the army commander wrote the secretary of war. "The best guns for field service, in my opinion, are the 12-pounder Napoleons, the 10-pounder Parrotts, and the approved 3-inch rifles." Lee suggested that the Confederacy could melt down its 6-pounder smoothbores and 12-pounder howitzers. Several weeks earlier, Gorgas had arrived at the same conclusion and ordered the manufacture of Napoleons, 10-pounder banded Parrotts, and some 20- and 30-pounder Parrotts. Three-inch rifled guns had the best range of the medium-sized field guns—up to a few miles—but they could not deliver canister and fired smaller projectiles, and the relatively limited open spaces over which Civil War armies contended restricted their usefulness. Due to their weight and the size of the projectile they fired, muzzle-loading, smoothbore Napoleons, based on a model used by Napoleon III, proved the most serviceable artillery weapons.[19]

Napoleons used four types of projectiles. The first, called canister, had the shortest maximum range, perhaps 200 yards. Canister consisted of tightly packed lead balls in a thin can. The container ripped apart as it sped out of the barrel, spraying the lead like a giant shotgun blast. The second type was spherical case shot. Spherical case shot was tightly packed, marble-size pieces of lead in a thin iron container with a fuse attached to it. Gunners fired the container, the fuse igniting an explosion that scattered the small balls of lead. Although gunners could fire it two-thirds of a mile, they more often employed it for targets a half mile away or closer. Shells were the third kid of ammunition. Artillerists fired each shell over their enemy, and when the fuse burned down, it exploded, usually into four big chunks. Lee's batteries fired shells at targets up to three-quarters of a mile away. The final projectile was solid shot. A Napoleon could hurl one a mile, but because it did not explode, it caused the least damage. Gunners fired solid shot at long-range targets, into columns of the enemy, and at fieldworks and fixed fortifications. The Ordnance Department recommended that batteries carry eight solid shots, sixteen spherical case shots, four shells, and four canister rounds, although after surveying field commanders, Gorgas believed batteries should carry three times as many shells as case shot. Ultimately, he recommended equal numbers of shell and case shot. Batteries retained the privilege of adjusting the ammunition they carried into battle.[20]

To fire weapons, gun crews placed bags of premeasured gunpowder down the barrel, packed the projectile with a ramrod, and then pulled a lanyard, which exploded a friction primer. That small blast ignited the powder, which in turn hurled the ammunition downrange. Gunners then swabbed the barrel to extinguish any sparks before loading gunpowder bags for the next round. Shot and spherical case required 2.5 pounds of gunpowder per firing, while shells necessitated a two-pound charge. Shells and case shot had fuses that ignited during the firing and then exploded the projectile over the target. Each of these types of ammunition had a hole with a plug made of wood or metal. The fuse fit into the plug snugly to prevent premature explosion of ammunition. One category of fuse, of which there were a few variations, consisted of metal and gunpowder. They were fairly complex devices that required adjustment for distances, and they often had a complicated metal fuse igniter. The other type of fuse was much simpler. It consisted of paper with gunpowder rolled tightly and placed in a thin wooden sheath or cover. Gunners cut them particular lengths, based on the estimated distance of the target. For very long distances, gunners had to employ paper fuses; metal fuses could not burn that long.[21]

Artillery was both a science and an art. Artillerists became expert at estimating distances and cutting fuses, but other factors impaired their precision. According to tests, a variation in the amount of gunpowder alone could affect the distance by 161 feet. Wind, terrain, and other factors also influenced the distance and accuracy of shots.[22]

In the first year of the war, the army suffered from repeated problems with friction primers and artillery ammunition. Magruder grumbled to Gorgas in late September that he had tried out a new shipment of friction primers made at the Richmond Arsenal and none of them exploded. A fresh batch of friction primers arrived, and Magruder complained, to "Supply the place of others, which were *worthless*, [which] turned out to be *worthless* themselves." In northern Virginia, Pendleton encountered a similar problem; Gorgas blamed it on unskillful troops and the difficult design of iron six-pounder cannons. Alexander, whose fascination with and mastery of every working part of the army demonstrated the depth of his intellect, discovered defective fuses for shells "which would have been useless in a fight." He devised a partial solution to the problem and forwarded his remedy to the Ordnance Department. Still, the Bormann mechanical fuses that the Confederacy attempted to construct were simply too complicated to produce. Their manufacture required extremely precise equipment, something the Confederacy lacked. By late December 1862, Gorgas terminated their production.[23]

Confederates also experienced problems with the manufacture of their largest cannons. During the Peninsula Campaign, a Georgian complained that five or six large guns burst during firing. In one mishap, seven or eight men sustained wounds. "Our cannon are greatly defective," he dejectedly admitted. Nearly eight months later, the Confederacy still had not mastered production of huge cannons. Lee announced that two new thirty-pound rifled guns burst after use. One had been fired fifty-five times, the other only thirty-nine.[24]

Gorgas and his people strove tirelessly to improve the weapons, ammunition, and firing products. They upgraded the quality of various equipment and products and worked the kinks out of the manufacturing system. Because the Confederacy suffered from a defective rail system, they developed arsenals around the country from the bottom up, and somehow they managed to hire experienced workers or train others in the production process. Still, problems in production persisted, sometimes with tragic consequences on several levels.

On Friday, March 13, 1863, some eighty to a hundred Ordnance Bureau employees, all of them women and girls, labored in a large room, approximately seventy feet long and twenty feet wide, at the Richmond Laboratory. Some were waxing friction primers to prevent them from getting wet in the field. Others boxed musket percussion caps, filled with explosive fulminate of mercury. A group extracted lead from condemned small-arms cartridges, and a few sewed up cannon cartridge bags with gunpowder. Because it was a cold day, other employees regularly dropped by the large room to warm themselves near the stove, before returning to work in another part of the arsenal.

Mary Ryan, a forty-six-year-old Irish immigrant and mother of three, was employed that day waxing friction primers. She worked with a kind of peg-board, in which she placed primers with the exposed end into the board. Ryan would then cover each primer with wax and remove them individually. In an effort to increase speed, she decided to try to hit the bottom of the perforated board with another board, thinking the friction primers would pop out all at once and save time. After the first whack, Elizabeth Dorson, a twenty-eight-year-old coworker and mother of two, "saw Mary Ryan knocking two boards together twice, one of them filled with friction primers. I said to one of the other girls that she, Mary Ryan, ought to be more careful." Catharine Cavanaugh, a twelve-year-old, swept the floor directly behind Mary. When she saw Mary hit the board, she told her not to hit it so hard. Mary called Catharine foolish, and hit it again, driving a wire into the primer. The first blast drove Mary into the ceiling, and as she fell to the ground, that explosion triggered a chain reaction.[25]

Elizabeth Dorson had barely uttered her warning when the explosion occurred. Witnesses claimed that she escaped from the inferno by climbing out the window and trying to swim the James River. As she began to struggle, a passerby jumped in and pulled her to shore. Elizabeth had no recollection of her flight from the building.[26]

The explosion ripped off the roof and knocked down the walls. With specks of gunpowder floating through the air, the entire room became a ball of flame. Forty-three women were killed, and twenty-five others sustained serious injuries. Mary lingered on for four days before she died. Elizabeth survived with severe burns. When military officials questioned her in a hospital, young Catharine "could scarcely speak by reason of the severe burns about her face." Several months after the war, a reporter met a young woman in Richmond who had been in the explosion; "her hands and face were covered with cruel scars," he noted. For five weeks, doctors could not tell if she would live or die, she told him. "But I did not mind, for it was in a good cause," the young woman asserted.[27]

The blast caused such devastation and so unnerved the workers that the Confederate government shut down the arsenal temporarily. It took almost a month before workers returned in full strength. In the meantime, the War Department had to ship vast quantities of ammunition and fuses from Charleston to offset the loss, taxing the railroads at a critical time, but at least ensuring Lee's army would have sufficient ordnance for the spring and summer campaigns.[28]

The replacement ammunition proved problematic, often exploding prematurely. An investigation focused primarily on the case shot themselves and the plugs. Major Allan suggested that the wooden plugs often shrank or jiggled loose in firing, causing the projectile to explode too early. Once officials in Richmond examined the case shot with wooden plugs, they condemned all the rounds. Subsequent studies concluded that wooden plugs with the McEvoy Fuse Igniter attachment exploded prematurely. "The igniter tests severely the tightness of the plug and fuse," the report elaborated. The flame from the McEvoy Igniter "rushes with much force upon the plug and when either it or the fuze itself is at all loose, it makes its way into the magazine." In a separate examination, Mallet also called into question the filler in the case shot. At the Charleston Arsenal, they used resin as a filling material, which softened and mixed with powder during warm weather, and in cold weather it cracked if handled roughly.[29]

Even though Gorgas had directed Mallet in early May 1863 to inspect the manufacture of friction primers and fuses at various laboratories, no one suspected either as the cause of problems. Mallet suggested two months later that the holes bored into the shell for the plug and fuse may have been too large, and he proposed that artillery officers oversee the final reaming in the field to guarantee a proper fit.[30]

Allan's complaint and the initial investigation certainly demonstrated the varying quality of ammunition throughout the Confederacy. The incident occurred at a time when the Ordnance Department had recognized problems in the manufacture of small-arms ammunition from one arsenal to another, and Gorgas assumed that the Confederacy might have a problem in the production of artillery ammunition and supporting materials as well. In early June 1863, Gorgas ordered each arsenal to send a batch of everything it manufactured to the Richmond Laboratories for regular testing.[31]

No doubt, Gorgas and his subordinates in the Ordnance Department accomplished extraordinary feats. With limited resources and inexperienced laborers to fuel it, they built a munitions industry from scratch. Problems that emerged were typical manufacturing flaws that in time they would have overcome. Unfortunately, the war afforded them little time or margin for error.

These ordnance difficulties also placed in sharper relief the truly impressive performance of the combat arms in Lee's army. While the Union encountered its own manufacturing problems, they paled in comparison to the Confederacy's. Confederates went to war with inferior weapons, if any at all, and they fought with ammunition that failed to measure up to Union standards. To compensate, Lee's army had to rely on superior leadership and combat effectiveness. But as the army drained manpower in battle after battle, and its pool of talented officers and enlisted men diminished, these advantages became harder to sustain. The Union could rely on better equipment and greater resources and manpower to compensate for its battlefield losses. The Confederacy had no such luxury.

Chapter 22

—◦◦—

THE FAILURE AT GETTYSBURG

P ERHAPS IT WAS an omen. Lee's army was still basking in the glow of victory at Chancellorsville when Federal horsemen caught Stuart's cavalry unaware. Three weeks earlier, Stuart had directed that one regiment from each brigade be held in a state of readiness at all times, while the other regiments grazed their horses in the rear. Evidently, the cavalrymen failed to take his directive to heart. In early June, while on a mission to determine whether Lee had begun to shift his army, Federal cavalry caught Stuart's mounted troops by surprise at Brandy Station (or Beverly Ford). The two-pronged attack penetrated Stuart's screen and discovered that Lee had maneuvered his army to the northwest, perhaps as a springboard for a raid into Maryland and Pennsylvania. The Yankees had struck so suddenly that medical officers "were invariably without their instruments and other appliances necessary [for] the proper performance of their duties," so the army medical director confessed. Fighting in many instances was hand to hand, and it was so close and widespread that Stuart's famed horse artillery could not deploy.[1]

Ultimately, Stuart's command regrouped and launched a potent counterattack, driving the Yankees back across the Rappahannock River. Confederate infantrymen rushed to the aid of their stunned comrades. The fact that the infantry had to bail out the cocky horsemen caused further embarrassment. Infantrymen saw it as a great comeuppance. "It is amusing to hear the cavalry fellows, trying to bluff their way out of it," a sergeant major in the 1st Virginia Infantry wrote to his mother. "They say it was the hardest & most successful fight of the war, that more ability was displayed &c &c &c. if there were any military genius displayed at all, it was in stopping the runaway & stampeded cavalry." In their panic, wagons crashed into one another and drivers cut loose their horses. "It's a 'bitter pill' to the 'chivalry.' Genl Stuart will lose his *feather* if he does not mind." The *Richmond Enquirer* rebuked Stuart for being caught off guard, suggesting "If Gen Stuart is to be the eyes & ears of the army, we advise him to see more, and be seen less." In one blow, the Federals had shattered the aura of invincibility that Confederate cavalry had earned. As a member of

Stuart's staff pithily summed up the affair, the Battle of Brandy Station *"made the Federal cavalry."*[2]

The rest of Lee's army, however, remained confident. "We looked forward to victory under him as confidently as to successive sunrises," recalled Porter Alexander. After the stunning victory at Chancellorsville, spirit among the infantry and artillery ran high. They had crushed the massive Union offensive without Longstreet and his two divisions. Once they returned, the army would be unbeatable. They might have lost Jackson, but not Lee. "We can not be whipped with bob lee at the had [head] of this armay," a Texas private wrote to his sweetheart, "for we dont think of anything als but to whip tham and that badly."[3]

Lee had multiple objectives for launching a raid into Maryland and Pennsylvania. At the time, a Union general named Ulysses S. Grant had executed a brilliant campaign and hammered Confederate armies in Mississippi and threatened to besiege Vicksburg, the critical Confederate position on the Mississippi River. When the secretary of war proposed Lee ship a division to Mississippi, the army commander resisted. "The uncertainty of its arrival and the uncertainty of its application cause me to doubt the policy of sending it," Lee responded. His army could accomplish more with the troops than the commanders in Mississippi. If they could instill fear among the people of Pennsylvania, the Lincoln administration might feel compelled to detach large forces from Grant to save critical industrial centers back east and to protect potential voters from an invading enemy. Certainly a raid northward would spare Southern farmers and ease commissary burdens by enabling the Confederate government to feed its largest army on Northern grain and livestock. Lee also sought an opportunity to defeat the Federal army far away from its base, where he could follow up his victory with repeated attacks and extinguish the Army of the Potomac. A series of crushing defeats in Pennsylvania could very well offset the fall of Vicksburg in the public mind.[4]

Soldiers reacted to the march northward with mixed sentiments. The prospect of any major campaign instilled uneasiness. "I dread this summers campaign   every thing seemes to indicate a bloody time," a private wrote his aunt. "I have no doubt but what we will be successful but it will cost a great many lives." Though McLaws understood why they were going to Pennsylvania, he still worried that a giant raid on the North might revive the faltering spirit of the Union. Others had an unsatisfying taste of Northern raids from the previous fall and wanted no part of any more. "Our army is a twistin a round a triying to get whiped a gain I fear," a Georgian private predicted to his mother and sister. Another soldier reported to his wife that he thought they were destined for Maryland. "I don't intend to go if I can help it and I think I can," he reassured his wife. Army officials thought otherwise, and he went.[5]

Yet most troops, particularly the Virginians, eagerly awaited a chance to take the war to the North. For two years, these soldiers had battled on native soil. They had witnessed widespread destruction of property and tens of thousands of lives lost or comrades maimed. The citizens of Virginia had suffered overwhelming hardships and indignities, while their men could do little to halt them. It was time for the Union populace to endure the brutal effects of war. After the Battle of Chancellorsville, a Virginia private scanned what was once a beautiful landscape, now pockmarked from artillery fire, with fences vanished and homes destroyed. "Would that our Enemy's could feel the effects of war as we do, perhaps they would stop fighting," he intimated to a cousin. A Virginia infantryman predicted "it will be useless to try to keep the men from going into orchards, etc. as they did last summer & I don't think they should hesitate to take anything they may wish for the army. We have been too lenient all the time & I go in for causing all the suffering we can in their country." He had become convinced, "It's the only way to bring them to their senses."[6]

On the march northward in mid-June, troops stirred up clouds of dust that coated clothing and hair and caked on faces. Everyone, it seemed, had doused their hair, eyebrows, and eyelashes with white. Only streams of perspiration disrupted the uniform pale facial mask, creating a macabre appearance. "A demon or ghost could not have looked worse," recorded a soldier. Mile after mile they trudged, as scorching June heat and choking dirt particles sucked energy from the men in gray. Two weeks later, rains came, and troops grumbled over "mud and mire" and soaked clothing. Still, on they pushed.[7]

The Potomac River offered an opportunity for Lee's troops to cleanse themselves of Virginia soil. In a frolicsome event, much like their first crossing into Maryland, thousands of buck-naked men holding clothing and accouterments above their heads plunged into the brisk, waist-deep river, "yelling & screaming like school children." One South Carolina officer noticed the difference between the Union and Confederates. "The Yankees carry pontoon trains along with them," he quipped, "but our boys say every man in General Lee's Army carried his own pontoons." When soldiers emerged on the opposite bank, they once again occupied Maryland soil, this time with few illusions.[8]

As soldiers marched northward, even in Virginia, the problem of plundering reared its ugly head once more. McLaws worried that the army could degenerate into a mob if officers did not control the men. "It is absolutely necessary however to our Salvation that our Army should not become demoralized," he asserted to his wife, "which would be the case should our men be permitted to rob and take at pleasure." In mid-June, Ewell had warned his corps that "this plundering must be repressed or our discipline is gone." Three days later, when the provost marshal entered Martinsburg, "there was a mob breaking open stores," committing all sorts of depredations. While local citizens huddled in their homes "frightened nearly to death," wrote an officer, "the streets were crowded with hundreds of drunken men as there are any number of bar rooms & distilleries in town." The practice continued in Maryland. Across the Potomac in Sharpsburg, a soldier noted in his diary, "our boys have nearly all supplied themselves with articles of some use or necessity. The stores have been opened &," he vaguely admitted, "the prices have been to us-Dixie boys' remarkably moderate."[9]

Lee intended to disperse his forces, drawing on the local population for foodstuffs, fresh horses and fodder, and any other equipment that his army might need. He permitted only official confiscation. Lee directed officers to pay Northerners for goods. Those who refused to sell would have the necessary property confiscated and a receipt issued to them. Any citizen who attempted to conceal or remove food or useful equipment would have the property seized and their name submitted to headquarters. Lee wanted no mob activity.[10]

Even though Maryland had remained in the Union, it was a sister slave state, and many Confederates maintained a more tolerant attitude toward its residents, particularly since the army had several regiments and batteries from that state. Pennsylvania, on the other hand, lay above the Mason-Dixon Line. It was the undisputed land of the enemy, and Lee's troops eagerly anticipated an opportunity to cross over into Pennsylvania and invade the North. The problem of plundering would loom large.

Quartermasters and commissaries did their best to implement Lee's directive. They scoured the countryside in search of foodstuffs, livestock, and anything usable. "Our Army is living off the country and the Quarter Masters are taking every thing that the Army can use," a Mississippi private jotted in his diary. A North Carolinian could not get over the lengths to which Pennsylvanians went to hide their livestock. On impressment duty for horses, "they were hidden in most extraordinary places," he wrote a friend. "Some in upper stories of barns & others in cellars of houses Some even in haystacks all of which was very ludicrous." So thorough was their search that an Alabamian thought they took every horse, mule, and cow in the area.[11]

Officers authorized the collection of necessities and the destruction. As the army passed the property of Congressman Thaddeus Stevens, an archenemy of slavery, they burned his iron works and confiscated his property. A week later, Confederate troops entered Mechanicsburg, Pennsylvania, just outside Harrisburg, and ordered fifteen hundred rations for the men. "It was very Humiliating and yet amusing to see persons walk up with their baskets of Ham, bread, butter, and whatever else they chose to bring," a local resident commented. Other soldiers thought that army officers did not go far enough. In Carlisle, a soldier was upset when the army did not burn down Dickinson College. "For my part," he commented in his journal, "I wanted to see the building burned to the ground, for it is one of the most intense abolition literary institutions in the whole North."[12]

Both officers and men exceeded the bounds of authorized foraging and began to plunder. A soldier declared that he and his comrades "enjoyed ourselves finely," admitting that "although positive orders were issued prohibiting soldiers from disturbing private property, they paid no attention to any order of the kind, and took everything they could lay their hands on in the eating line." Troops plundered abandoned buildings and occasionally took items from civilians. "Numbers of our soldiers exchanged hats with citizens to day, without a willingness on part of citizens," a soldier confessed. "Some of them who were bare footed made citizens pull off shoes and boots." Soldiers seized what they wanted. "We press every thing that we think that will be beneficial to our cause and cuntry," boasted a Rebel. Officers frequently joined in. "Stringent orders have been issued against such conduct by our generals," recorded a company-level officer, "though it is rather a hard matter to restrain our troops when they remember the devastated plains of Virginia and the conduct of the Federals in other portions of our country." As an officer stated baldly, "in short we killed, captured, and destroyed everything that came in our way."[13]

The conduct of both officers and men disgusted a Virginia captain. "Our soldiers acted very disgracefully in Pennsylvania towards the citizens altho very stringent orders were issued for the protection of private property," he complained to his mother. "I did not hear of the first man who suffered for taking anything he wanted from the people which proves that officers were as guilty as the men." One officer admitted that some of Ewell's staff plundered abandoned buildings and took items from civilians. If a corps commander could not or would not restrain his own staff, how could the army expect enlisted men to do so?[14]

For most Confederates, this was their first trip to the North, and the natural beauty and wealth of the region surprised them. They had accepted unquestioningly arguments about the superiority of slave labor. What they saw, however, belied those tales. Soldier after soldier wrote home of stunning landscape, with hardwood forests and lush pasture land and tidy fields scattered along the gentle slopes and valley floors. "This is the finest country I have ever saw yet," a Virginian informed his brother. "Every thing looks fine." In Pennsylvania, the soil was rich and the livestock fat. Impressive stone homes and enormous barns dotted the land. A North Carolinian considered Pennsylvania and Maryland the "best contry I ever saw" and thought "ther barns is finer than any house in NC." Evidently, these middle-class farmers in a free-labor society did quite well for themselves.[15]

Lee's soldiers were not nearly as impressed with the local inhabitants. Typical was the comment of a private who wrote to his sister, "We passed through some of the prettiest country that I ever saw in my life they has [some] of the finest land in it in the world and some of the ugliest women that I ever saw." An artillerist possessed similar hostile views. "Sister I will Give you a description of the Girls in pensylvania thay are all nothing but Dutch and Irish and the durty and Sturnest menest looking Creaturs that I ever saw to Call them selves white Girs [Girls]." As he observed them working the fields, he realized "them is the Girls that is writing to their husbands and Sweehearts and brothers to fight on and restore the union." Many were surprised in talking to the women that "they care but little about the Niggers—wish they may be kept in the South." Soldiers usually treated the residents respectfully, except when locals acted a bit too forceful in their support of the Union. According to the British military observer Lt. Col. Arthur Fremantle, one Pennsylvania woman, adorned with a miniature flag affixed to her blouse, cast contemptuous glances at Confederate troops as they marched past. Finally, a Texan had enough. Pointing his finger at the woman, he announced, " 'Take care, madam, for Hood's boys are great at storming breastworks when the Yankee colors is on them.' " She retreated into her home.[16]

On the Union side, after a lackluster pursuit into Pennsylvania by Hooker, the War Department replaced him with Maj. Gen. George G. Meade. With Meade at the helm, the chase suddenly took on a sense of mission and urgency. He had orders to target Lee's army, all the while shielding Baltimore and Washington. At Piping Creek, some twenty miles southeast of Gettysburg, Meade laid out a strong defensive position, in case his army had to retire, and then pushed beyond it. Skillfully, he fanned his forces out in all directions in search of the enemy, always keeping his six corps in support of one another. By the morning of July 1, Meade's corps were anywhere from five to twenty-five miles from Gettysburg, and he had instructed Maj. Gen. John Reynolds to take charge of the three forward corps and be prepared for offensive or defensive operations.[17]

The roles had suddenly shifted. Lee's army had become the invaders, and Federal troops fought in defense of hearth and home. In Virginia, so noted a Yankee soldier, the women had been "our bitterest enemies, where they never look on us except with contempt and never speak but in derision." Guerrillas had wandered the countryside, and Yankees always had to be on their guard. Anyone who wandered away from camp carelessly did so at his peril. Now in Pennsylvania, locals opposed Lee's army. They became a source of information for the Yankees, and militia units converged on Lee's foragers. Federal soldiers perceived a major battle in Pennsylvania as a great opportunity for them. With the Confederates such a long distance from home, a decisive victory and a vigorous pursuit by Union forces could devastate Lee's forces.[18]

The Battle of Gettysburg was something of a surprise. Neither side anticipated a large-scale fight there, and Lee had specifically instructed his subordinates not to bring on a general engagement. It began almost by accident, with some skirmishing on June 30. Full-fledged combat commenced the following day. Confederates in Maj. Gen. Harry Heth's Division of A. P. Hill's Corps trudged into town in search of plunder; Federal cavalry under Brig. Gen. John Buford opposed them. Once the two sides exchanged fire, however, reinforcements poured into the area, deploying without any specific plan in mind, merely to take advantage of visible openings. Heth deployed his two lead brigades on either side of the Chambersburg Pike. Buford's men, supported by some artillery, fought aggressively and held their position until infantry replaced them. The weary horsemen then passed rearward through town.[19]

Federals in the First Corps arrived on the scene and filtered through cavalry lines. The Iron Brigade of Wisconsin, Michigan, and Indiana troops, which had fought so valiantly at Groveton the previous August, crashed through some

274 / GENERAL LEE'S ARMY

woods and overwhelmed James J. Archer's Brigade of Tennesseans and Alabamians in front and flank, capturing a sizable portion of the command, including Archer. On the other side of the Chambersburg Pike, where Joseph R. Davis's Brigade of Mississippians and North Carolinians offered stiff resistance, reinforcements from the Iron Brigade waded through a withering fire and stormed a railroad cut to dislodge Davis's men, seizing the prized ground and a few hundred Confederates along with it. The price, however, was immense—over one-third of the Federal reinforcements appeared on the casualty list.[20]

To the north, Maj. Gen. Robert Rodes's Division of Ewell's Corps suddenly materialized on Oak Hill. One of Lee's premier division commanders, Rodes had received orders the previous day to withdraw from Carlisle and concentrate at Cashtown. With the fight well underway, he deployed three brigades in front and two in support and pressed forward without skirmishers, much as Jackson had done with Rodes's troops two months earlier. Rodes's right wing helped to clear the railroad cut and drive the Federals back to a gentle slope near town. The Rebels east of the road attacked feebly and fell back rapidly, thus opening the door for a Union concentration on the middle brigade.

After the Yankee First Corps, men from the Eleventh Corps arrived on the scene. They secured Cemetery Hill south of town with their artillery and rushed to the sounds of gunfire, forming part of an L-shaped position that shielded Gettysburg on the north and west sides. As Brig. Gen. Alfred Iverson's North Carolinians in Rodes's center advanced, Union troops who had opposed the weak attack east of the Mummasburg Road swung around and concealed themselves along a stone wall directly on Iverson's left flank. The Tar Heels stepped right into the trap. Federals rose up and poured a devastating fire into the Confederates. The next morning, a Rebel artilleryman recorded the tragic sight. Seventy-nine North Carolinians lay dead in a perfectly straight line, apparently killed by a single volley. Other victims were scattered across the field. The scene was "perfectly sickening" and "would have satiated the most blood-thirsty and cruel man on God's earth," he wrote. It was a turkey shoot with human targets. "Great God!" he added, "When will this horrid war stop?"[21]

With Rodes's Division stalled, victory on the first day seemed within Union grasp, until a Confederate division under Jubal Early rolled around the Federal right wing. Down the road from Heidlersburg, northeast of Gettysburg, Early's troops pressed, penetrating the Yankee rear and threatening to cut off the retreat route through the town. Panic gripped thousands of bluecoats from the Eleventh Corps, who broke ranks and raced rearward. That compelled soldiers in the First Corps to flee also, heavily pressed by Heth's and Rodes's columns. A Virginia enlisted man described to his parents how they shot down the fleeing Yankees "like Rabbits in a snow." It was "the first time I ever had a good fair shoot at a man I took up good aim as if I have been shotting at game." Some Federals passed through town to safety, while others were cut off or tried to hide. A soldier claimed the Confederates "draged as many as five hundred from the cellars." All told, over three thousand Yankees fell into Confederate hands that day.[22]

Those Federals who escaped formed a new line, south of town, anchored at Cemetery Hill, where the Eleventh Corps had positioned its artillery as it passed through the town. Lee gave Ewell an order to carry the position "if practicable." Ewell examined the ground and declined to launch an attack.

The first day came to an end with this Confederate success, yet it was only a mild precursor of the fighting to come. That evening and throughout the night, Federal forces streamed into the Gettysburg area, anchoring the right and extending along a ridge to form a fishhook-shaped position. Soldiers piled logs, branches, and stones to form barricades or exploited existing walls as protection against Confederate advances. By sunrise, five of the six Union corps, along with the army commander, had reached the scene.[23]

Although Lee had arrived in the vicinity of Gettysburg in midafternoon of the first day, he could not organize his army well enough to launch a coordinated attack before nightfall. Losses were so severe that regiments and in a few cases brigades almost disintegrated. Davis's hard-fought brigade entered the fight with nine field officers and emerged with two unhurt. Pettigrew's North Carolinians suffered nearly 1,100 casualties in the first day's fighting, more than a third of the total strength. The 26th North Carolina took 800 soldiers into the battle and lost 549 of them. The 11th North Carolina endured 250 casualties, nearly half its strength. Rodes's Division took 2,500 casualties, with Daniel's and Iverson's North Carolina brigades sustaining two-thirds of them. Confederate units had converged from the west, north, and northeast on the Yankee position, and in the rout, commands got mixed up. Structure dissolved as units searched house to house. Soldiers uncovered pockets of resistance, crushed them, and gathered and escorted prisoners to the rear. Even worse, Confederates continued their pillaging. They broke into shops and homes and appropriated so many items that a soldier boasted, "I assure you that city is well plundered. The Louisianians left nothing that human hands could destroy." Other Confederates complained about how their comrades dropped out of ranks to rob Yankees killed and wounded. A Maryland man grumbled, "Very often you could see some of our boys go down on a dead yank and take his money out of his pocket." An officer on Early's staff scanned the battlefield and was disgusted with what he saw. "The Yankee dead were stripped, almost to utter nakedness," he wrote with shame. "It seems strange that the champion of liberty, can be the prostitute of avarice. Yet such is the case." He went on to state that "The hand that shoots from the front rank of battle is frequently the first to find the pockets of the dead and this pilfering of the fallen is by no means confined to the skulkers, & followers in the rear."[24]

By nightfall, Lee had concentrated most of his infantry and artillery near Gettysburg. He had not intended to bring on a general engagement, but success on the first day of fighting and his belief that most of the Federal army had not reached Gettysburg induced the Confederate commander to renew the

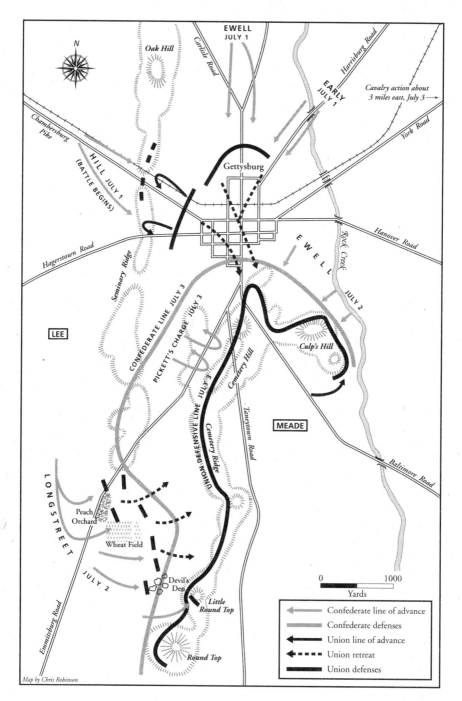

Battle of Gettysburg

battle the following day. Early the next morning, after reconnaissance indicated that the Union had neglected to secure its south wing, Lee ordered two of Longstreet's divisions to swing around and roll up the Federal left flank. To position themselves properly for a surprise attack, Confederate troops had to backtrack, wasting all morning and much of the afternoon. The lengthy trek under a broiling sun and stifling humidity drained the attackers of precious energy. By 4:00 P.M., when the attack finally began, Longstreet's troops were tired.[25]

In defense, Maj. Gen. Daniel Sickles, commander of the Federal Third Corps, had foolishly projected his forces out from the original line to occupy some high ground where locals had planted peach trees. The new bow in the Union position doubled the length of his defense, forcing him to commit all his reserves and to pull troops away from a natural southern anchor, Little Round Top, to maintain a contiguous line. Meade's chief engineer, Gouverner K. Warren, noticed the problem, and a division from the Fifth Corps raced over to secure the position as the assault began.

On the Confederate right flank, Hood's men struggled through difficult terrain just to reach Union lines. At Devil's Den, a rocky outcropping guarded by huge boulders several hundred yards north of Little Round Top, Union guns poured such an effective fire into the attackers that it drew front-line and follow-on units like a magnet. Eventually, Confederates carried Devil's Den, but carefully positioned artillery and infantry to the rear prevented the attackers from exploiting the gain. The severe resistance siphoned valuable troops from the extreme Confederate right by drawing away two Alabama regiments from the initial assault and a brigade of Georgians who composed the second wave.

At Little Round Top, Alabamians and Texans finally deployed for attack after their long and circuitous march. In their haste to position themselves, these men had pressed right through Plum Creek and had taken no time to replenish their canteens. As they waited to charge, Col. William C. Oates of the 15th Alabama ordered twenty-two men to collect canteens and return to Plum Creek for fresh water. Before the water detail returned, orders directed the brigades to advance. Lumbering back to the assembly point with that heavy load of water, the detachment discovered no one there. As they searched for their regiment, the party stumbled into Yankee hands.[26]

Meanwhile, Oates and his Confederate comrades attempted to seize the position by storm. They had carried such difficult places before, but this time they failed. According to the adjutant of the 48th Alabama, five times they charged, and five times they were beaten back. Disorganized from the cut-up terrain, and fatigued by the long, hot day, they were too few and too weary to wrest the position from the Federals.[27]

Oates later admitted his men "suffered greatly for water," and "the loss of those twenty-two men and the lack of water contributed largely to our failure." Yet it was not simply a matter of thirst. Without water, Confederates could not clean their weapons of the black powder residue that caked the inside of their rifle barrels. The sooty crust impaired their ability to ram down charges. They were nearly defenseless. So exhausted and demoralized were these Confederates that 400 of them surrendered to a counterattack by perhaps 200 men with fixed bayonets.[28]

Elsewhere on the field that day, Union and Confederate forces battled with similar results. Several times Confederates pierced the Federal line, only to falter at the critical moment. McLaws's Division led the fight around the Peach Orchard. Reconnaissance early in the morning led him to believe that only two regiments and an artillery battery defended the area. Once his division arrived in the vicinity, however, it became apparent the Union held the ground in strength. An immediate attack would have been foolhardy, and after some give-and-take he convinced Longstreet that the Federals had brought up considerable force. McLaws then received authorization to wait until Hood's Division rolled up the flank, before he attacked directly ahead. Unfortunately, Hood went down with a serious wound early in the fight and his division could not dislodge Federals from little Round Top. Those Rebel troops who plunged into Devil's Den ultimately carried the position and pressed on into a wheat field, where they bogged down in heavy fighting. Coordination between divisions and even brigades and sometimes regiments collapsed, and McLaws had to launch an attack into the Peach Orchard without the benefit of a flank attack. They carried the ground, but with great loss, and stout Union resistance prevented a true breakthrough.[29]

Throughout the day, the story remained the same. Tired from the prolonged delays and sapped by the heat, Confederate columns fought aggressively at first, but simply could not muster the resolve or the effective coordination with adjacent commands to exploit any advantage. Lee's army suffered some 6,500 losses that day, all in vain.[30]

The entire affair frustrated Lee. It was a battle on a field not of his choosing. Success on July 1 had convinced him to continue to fight. The Confederates had squandered too much daylight on the second day and had failed to exploit opportunities. He could withdraw in the face of an undefeated enemy, a risky proposition at best that would most likely end the campaign, or he could attempt one more desperate fight. Audacious to the core, Lee placed his faith in the officers and men of the Army of Northern Virginia. They would fight yet one more day.

Fortunately, Jeb Stuart and his cavalry finally arrived at Gettysburg. Ten days earlier, Longstreet and Stuart had proposed a cavalry movement into Hooker's rear, and on June 23, Lee granted approval. The next day, Stuart left two brigades to assist Lee's army and took three brigades with him on a lengthy ride between the Union army and Washington, D.C., with the objective of confusing the enemy, destroying supplies, and linking up with Ewell's Corps once the horsemen crossed the Potomac River. As he had done at Second Manassas after the humiliating Union raid that nearly captured him, Stuart seized a chance to redeem himself from the embarrassment at Brandy Station less than two weeks earlier. His cavalry had accomplished the feat before against a stationary army, but this time the Federals were marching northward in pursuit of Lee's main force. It took the Rebel horsemen much longer to pass beyond the Army of the Potomac, and then he had difficulty locating his own army. Without those three brigades and their cavalry leader, Lee had struggled to ascertain the location of the Union army during the march into Pennsylvania. On July 2, Stuart's three brigades could have provided valuable reconnaissance of the Union left flank and opened more options for Lee's attack.[31]

Lee's plan for the third day was to place pressure on the two Union flanks and crack through the Federal center. Near success in the middle of the Union line convinced the Confederate commander that Meade had weakened the center to fortify the wings. Ewell's Corps, on the northern end, would strike at Culp's and Cemetery hills. Stuart's cavalry, tired after a very lengthy journey, would swing around to the northeast of the Union position and threaten Meade's rear. An extensive bombardment, followed by a massive assault, would rupture the middle of the Yankee line.

The previous day, Ewell's action at Culp's Hill had failed to coordinate with Longstreet's grand movement. This time, Lee wanted his entire army working together. During the night, however, a firefight broke out that completely disrupted Lee's agenda. Before the Confederates on Culp's Hill could launch their attack, the Yankees struck. At 3:30 A.M., two brigades supported by fourteen artillery guns assailed some Confederate troops and drove them back. Reinforcements rushed to the scene, and the fight raged until midmorning, when fire on both sides slackened.[32]

At 1:00 P.M., Lee finally unveiled his attack. The Confederates fired a signal salvo, followed by a massive barrage of shot and shell. Longstreet entrusted Alexander with as many as 170 field guns to blast away at the Union defenses before the assault, informing him that if the bombardment did not "drive the enemy or greatly demoralize him so as to make our effort pretty certain, I would prefer that you should not advise Gen Pickett to make the charge." Alexander replied that because of the dense smoke and the position of the Union infantry, he could only judge the effectiveness of the bombardment by the return fire. "If as I infer from your note there is any alternative to this attack it should be carefully considered before opening our fire, for it will take all the arty ammunition we have left to test this one thoroughly & if the result is unfavorable we will have none left for another effort & even if this is entirely successful it can only be or at a very bloody cost." Longstreet then answered that the plan was to advance the infantry if the artillery drove the enemy from the position or if it had the effect "such as to warrant us in making the attack." Federals cannons replied vigorously at first, but gradually tapered off to conserve ammunition. A Mississippian recalled that "the smoke was so thick that I could not see our battery horses between our lines and the guns." From Culp's Hill, a Connecticut soldier reported, "All at once it seemed as though all the artillery in the universe had opened fire and was belching forth its missiles of death and destruction." The thunderous sound, recorded a Yankee officer, reminded him of Niagara Falls. "The hole earth Seem to Be in a perfect Motion," a Confederate artillerist described. Soldiers along Cemetery Ridge hunkered down as best they could, to shield themselves from the deadly projectiles.

Solid shot struck among the Federals or in front and bounced through the lines, as Rebel gunners intended. But the ammunition that Confederates depended on for success was the shells. With time fuses, shells exploded into roughly four large chunks of lead, making them some four times as effective against those defenders as solid shot. This time, they failed the Confederacy. Only those shells that struck well up in the trees rained shards of lead on the defenders. According to a Minnesotan, the enemy "tried to explode their shells directly over us, but fortunately, most of them just went far enough to clear us." Wagons, rear-area personnel, and Meade's headquarters, hundreds of yards behind the front line, endured a pounding, while the Confederate gunners failed to soften up the Union defenders. Smoke and clouds of dirt obscured the view. The attackers did not realize that the greatest bombardment in the history of warfare failed to fulfill its design.[33]

As the Union artillery shelled the Rebel line in turn, Brig. Gen. James L. Kemper of Pickett's Division ordered his men to hug the ground. The Federal shells were accurate, bearing down on his troops and cutting them to shreds even though they lay on the opposite side of the crest. Looking up, Kemper saw Longstreet in front of the Confederate line, astride his great horse, completely impervious to the danger. "His bearing was to me the grandest moral spectacle of the war." Years later, people accused Longstreet of sulking over the infantry assault, but when Kemper saw and spoke to him, Longstreet was a tower of strength, concerned not for his own safety but for Kemper's men.[34]

At 1:25 P.M., as his ammunition began to run out, Alexander sent word to Pickett, "if you are to advance at all you must come at once or we will not be able to support you as we ought, but the enemy's fire has not slackened materially & there are still 18 guns firing from the cemetery." When Alexander saw no movement from Pickett's Division, he sent another message, fifteen minutes later. "The 18 guns have been driven off. For Gods sake come on quick or we cannot support you Ammunition nearly out."[35]

Soldiers rose to their feet and aligned. Eleven brigades joined in the attack, led by troops in George Pickett's and J. J. Pettigrew's divisions. Alexander supported them as best he could with the artillery, but to little effect. One of the most famous of the Civil War's tragic tableaux was set to unfold. "I never was scard as bad in my life," confessed a Mississippian in Pettigrew's Division. Over several fences and up and down gentle slopes elegant formations of Confederates marched. Union guns carved gaping holes in these ranks, only to have them close up rapidly. The various angles of approach and the different distances that the attackers had to cover began to disrupt formations. At a range of approximately 250 yards, Union infantry opened fire. Rather than continue the charge, pockets of Confederates halted in open ground and exchanged rifle fire.[36]

On the Confederate left, brigades converged on the target area. The attackers did not extend beyond the Union line, so Federals could concentrate their fire on the outer Rebel flank, withering away first J. M. Brockenbrough's Virginians, then Davis's depleted ranks. As the remainder of Pettigrew's Division struck the principal Federal line, Yankees poured fire from two and sometimes three directions. The Confederate left buckled. "Suddenly the column gave way," described an Ohioan, "the sloping landscape appeared covered, all at once, with the scattered and retreating foe. A withering sheet of missiles swept after them, and they were torn and tossed and prostrated as they ran. It seemed as if not one would escape."[37]

In the center and on the Confederate right, miscommunication caused serious problems. Pickett's brigades angled sharply to the left, while Wilcox's Alabamians and Perry's Brigade of Floridians charged directly ahead, splitting the assault columns. Some Vermonters seized the opening. On orders from their brigade commander, they struck Pickett's men on the flank. Then the 16th Vermont pivoted and poured a wicked fire on Wilcox's and Perry's brigades, shattering their charge.

Led fearlessly by their brigade commanders, the bulk of Pickett's troops rushed onward. With a shout, they raced double-quick toward the works. Blasts of canister and volley after volley of Federal rifle fire struck them down by the hundreds. Some halted in the open field and blazed away. Others dropped to the earth, shielding themselves from the hail of lead. The situation was hopeless.

Yet somehow, a portion of the wave pressed on. At twenty yards from the wall they endured a burst, recoiled, and then surged forward yet farther. The sight of this seemingly irresistible mass panicked the defenders. Suddenly, some Pennsylvanians broke and rushed rearward, leaving a handful of their comrades to repel the onslaught. Several hundred intrepid Confederate souls crashed over a low stone wall and penetrated the Union works. Remnants of the Pennsylvania regiments battled them with rifle butts and bayonets, as if they were warring for sacred ground, but the Northerners were outmanned.

Too few and too far from support, this small band of Rebels could not hold the break. Yankee reinforcements quickly gathered and smashed into the Southerners. The struggle lasted just a few minutes. The Confederates fought valiantly. Many fell right there; others yielded. Some foolishly attempted to run the gauntlet back to Confederate lines and became easy targets.

Lee's attack had failed. Over 6,500 were killed, wounded, or captured, more than half of all the men involved in the assault. Bodies littered the field. Union riflemen and artillery picked off the few remaining as they worked their way rearward. "Many noble spirits who had passed safely through the fiery ordeal of the advance and charge, now fall on the right and on the left," a soldier described. As Pickett rode off the field, tears rolled down his cheeks. "Taylor," he sobbed to a staff officer, "we've lost all our friends."[38]

MERCIFULLY, DARKNESS SETTLED over the battlefield, and Union forces engaged in the horrible task of attending to the dead and wounded. On Culp's Hill, Federal troops built fires to light up the field. They buried gray and blue alike and carried the injured to hospitals. Over the next few days, soldiers gazed at the battlefield in shock and dismay. "Part of the field, across which I had occasion to ride twice, presented a horrible spectacle," recorded Confederate staff officer Campbell Brown. "Corpses so monstrously swollen that the buttons were broken from the loose blouses & shirts, & the baggy pantaloons fitted like a skin—so blackened that the head looked like an immense cannon ball, the features being nearly obliterated." A Virginian in Pickett's Division, who mourned the passing of his closest friends, confessed, "I feel perfectly lost."[39]

Physicians poured into the Gettysburg area to lend a hand. They had no idea what awaited them. The foul odors and ungodly sights prompted many to lie down and vomit. Without adequate facilities, wounded lay on the field for days and even weeks until doctors and nurses could care for them. In many cases, the situation was hopeless.

Suffering from pain and slowly expiring, soldiers made amends to their God. A few had the privilege of jotting down some final words to loved ones. "I was wounded in both knees on the 2nd one by a grape & one by a minie ball one fractured by a grap[e] I lay on the field two days," Sgt. Jay Rico Love wrote his father and brother. "I have been treated very kindly by the enemy as a generall thing but owing to the great number of wonded it is imposible to attend to all I don't expect to live & the Doctor has told me I cant recover." He placed his trust in God "& I believe & trust he will receive me in heaven." Love expected to meet his loved ones in heaven and admonished his brother to join a church. He told them he had prayed twice a day, and "I am not afraid to die." He concluded with the words, "I remain your affectionate Son & Brother, J. R. Love." Despite his severe injuries, Love survived the war in a Yankee prison camp. Others were not so fortunate. In a final letter to his mother, one officer who suffered a severe wound to the jaw admitted, "My sufferings and hardships during two weeks that I was kept out in the field hospital were very great." He went on to tell her, "I assure you that it was the greatest consolation whilst lying in pain on the cold and damp ground, to look up to that God to whom you so constantly directed my thoughts in infancy and boyhood, and I feel that I was his son by adoption." Shortly afterward, he passed away. The officer, Col. W. Tazewell Patton, became the idol of his great-nephew, George S. Patton.[40]

To a grieving father whose son lay in rest at Gettysburg, Lee wrote: "I know of no more fitting resting place for a brave soldier that the battle field in which he has laid down his life in the defense of the rights of his Country."[41]

Confederate losses were staggering. Nearly a third of the general officers in the army were killed, wounded, or captured. Heth reported nearly 1,500 casualties in Davis's Brigade and over 1,700 in Pettigrew's Brigade. Attrition among officers was so great that a major commanded Pettigrew's Brigade. In some cases in the army, lieutenants led regiments. A company in the 26th North Carolina had all three of its officers and 83 of 84 men killed or wounded. According to Capt. Henry T. Owen, 29 of 31 officers in the 18th Virginia were killed or wounded. Only he and another man in his company emerged from the battle unscathed. McLaws's Division, which had managed to be in the thick of much of the fighting thus far in the war, suffered its single highest number of casualties—some 2,500. All told, Lee's army lost more than 4,700 killed and almost 13,000 wounded; another 5,800 were prisoners or missing.[42]

After the terrible third day, Lee expected to continue the battle. He waited, hoping the Yankees would come out of their works for an open-field fight. Meade refused to take the bait, and by nightfall Lee began an evacuation. By holding his position, Lee bought some time for his ambulances, wagons, and walking wounded, which stretched for miles southward toward Virginia. After a few more tense days, including a firefight that cost the Confederacy acting division commander Johnston Pettigrew, the Army of Northern Virginia made its escape.[43]

By the time they returned to Virginia soil, the Confederate troops were exhausted. "We had a nice time going into Pa.," a veteran wrote a friend in early August, "but comeing out was quite to the contrary." Union pursuit prevented foraging parties from bringing in food for the men. In Edward O'Neal's Alabama brigade, the rations spoiled, and "when General Oneal was riding up and down the lines they boys wood hollow abut rashins." From the safety of his home state, a Virginian informed his father, "I am as fat as hard service and short rations always makes me." All in all, it had been the most demanding expedition of the war. "I am completely used up indeed," a cavalryman admitted at the end of the retreat. Another soldier, a Georgia infantryman, announced to his sister, "I thought I knew it all, but this last campaign exceeds in hardships anything I ever experienced. I have been cold, hot, wet, dry, ragged, dirty, hungry & thirsty, marched through clouds of dust, waded mud knee deep & suffered from fatigue & loss of sleep." He was glad to be "home," on Confederate soil.[44]

Morale among the soldiers dropped in the wake of the Gettysburg retreat. "Our numbers are terribly reduced and the morale of the army is very low," an officer on Alexander's staff admitted to his mother in late July. "Every one feels how disastrous to us our defeat at Gettysburg was and every body has found out by this time how badly we were repulsed to use the most moderate term for our reverse there and the retreat has been almost as bad for us as the defeat." For the first time since Seven Days', a substantial number of troops entertained the possibility of losing the war. A little over a year before, when Confederates had their backs to Richmond, their situation had been far more desperate, but few of them had discussed the possibility of surrender. The Gettysburg affair jolted them. "I never saw such a change in all my life," a Virginian wrote his wife. He predicted, "We will have to submit to yankee rules, & I do beleave that half of the army is under the same impression." Private John A. Everett of the

11th Georgia divulged to his mother, "the Armey is Broken harted." They had suffered so much in the past year that many troops "Don't Care which way the war Closes." He then concluded, "it Dont look like that we will Ever whip the Yankees they have got too many men for us."[45]

Once they reached Virginia, large numbers wandered way from the army to take "French leave," or unauthorized absence. As a Virginian explained, "it is nearly impossible to keep up a Regt. [Regiment] when near there homes." Over time, many of them would return, after a quick visit home and some good meals. Others, most of whom did not live near the army's route, abandoned ranks with no intention of returning. "Minn are disurtan ever day," a North Carolinian explained, "men are gitten tiard of the war." So many men took flight from Scales's Brigade that Lee requested the secretary of war to picket ferries and bridges over the James River and over the Staunton and Dan rivers farther west, to collect those men and return them to the army.[46]

Yet a large number of soldiers refused to back down from the cause. The same North Carolina private declined to join those deserters. "I doe think that is a poor way to bring the ware to a cloas by dusurtion," he insisted to his wife. "I will make that my last thing desurt from my poast in a time of need after men have suffered as much as we have and them [then] give it up a shame to our cause." Another North Carolina private conceded there was "a heap of Dissatisfaction among the Soldiers" and they wanted peace. He, too, desired the war to end as badly as anyone else, "though I am not Willing to be a Slave for Old ab Linkon and my Children after me."[47]

In evaluating the campaign and its results, some refused to acknowledge defeat. They equated victory with driving the opposing forces from the field. Since the Confederates had retreated voluntarily, they had not lost. "The truth about Gettysburg is that we were *repulsed* at the *final* position of the enemy, & that the *want* of *success* was a *terrible calamity*; but we were *not defeated*," insisted Robert Stiles. "Our men were very much mortified at the result—but say they can whip the Yanks—have done so and can whip them still," justified another soldier. "At no time during the engagement were our men panic stricken or routed." An Alabamian thought the big losses actually occurred out west at Vicksburg and Port Hudson. "It is true we did not accomplish our object," he conceded to his aunt, "but we were not whipped." Gettysburg was merely a setback on the road to independence—nothing more.[48]

Despite the rough treatment the army received in Pennsylvania, many soldiers retained a glimmer of confidence. A Virginia cavalryman admitted, "I don't think we made much by going into Pennsylvania" and that the aftermath of the campaign was the "darkest Hour we have ever had," but he also believed "the darkest hour is just before day." The next time the army fought the enemy, a South Carolinian vowed, "we will give the Yanks a bad whipping" because "they will have to attack us on our own ground and we will give it to them strong."[49]

Once the troops settled in camp in Virginia, and the threat from Meade's army dissipated, morale began to recover. Lee offered furloughs to check desertions and absences without leave. He immediately requested shoes and clothing for the needy, and he made efforts to secure flour, in conjunction with meat they had gathered and brought back from Pennsylvania and Maryland. Basic comforts and relaxation made all the difference. "I feel like the rest of the boys—" a soldier in the 11th Virginia wrote, "That my Patriotism has revived 1000 percent since we have gotten where there will be no fighting." Those who survived the campaign had much for which to be thankful. By mid-August, McLaws claimed with some exaggeration that the men "Have all our old spirit and self confidence."[50]

Within a couple of months, however, the same old problems recurred. Food and clothing shortages plagued the army, and the quartermasters could not secure adequate hay and fodder for the animals. But by then, the army had passed through its most difficult times. It had lost some deserters, but many who had absented themselves returned. The great problem was simply the huge losses from the campaign and the burden that fell on the shoulders of the survivors. They now had to accomplish the same work with far fewer soldiers.[51]

In the end, the Confederate campaign into Pennsylvania failed for several reasons. With the brief exception of the Maryland Campaign, Lee's army had always fought on Virginia soil, amid familiar surroundings and a supportive populace. In the North, Rebels went on the attack on strange ground, among a population that opposed their presence. As one soldier pointed out, "the enemy had the advantage over them in position, & supplies, and were encouraged to fight, because we were invading their soil. Who would not fight on his own '*Dunghill*'[?]" Walter Taylor, Lee's aide-de-camp, divulged to his brother, "I will not hide one truth—that our men are better satisfied on this side of the Potomac. They are not accustomed to operating in an enemy country where the people are inimical to them & certainly every one of them is today worth twice as much as he was three days ago."[52]

Discipline declined and plundering worsened during the march through enemy country. One Confederate pinpointed it in a letter home. "I felt[,] when I saw how our men were going on[,] that nothing but disaster would follow and in truth I was associated with an armed mob with the broadest license and not with a disciplined army such as General Lee has had under his command." As Lee reminded his commander in chief, "Our people are so little liable to control that it is difficult to get them to follow any course not in accordance with their inclinations."[53]

During the invasion of Pennsylvania and Maryland, general officers had to take on unusual responsibilities, such as the creation and oversight of foraging parties and the supervision of independent marches. Two new corps commanders added to the complexity. A Louisianan thought that the generals, not the soldiers, failed at Gettysburg. Others believed the army fought the battles as pieces, but not as a coherent whole. Generals were never able to get the army to execute from the same battle script; instead, individual commands seemed to fight independently or at least with little regard for the adjacent units, let alone more distant commands. Lee himself explained to Davis that in spite of all the difficulties, "I still think if all things could have worked together it would have been accomplished."[54]

Others criticized Lee and his subordinate generals for their tactical ineptness. One soldier was dismayed to think "Lee fought them in there own Country & on their own choice of Position." John Warwick Daniel, an extremely perceptive staff officer, believed the invasion had little to do with Confederate defeat; Lee's army failed tactically. "They were failures in the plans of the battles, not in the larger manuevres in the country, failures which might have occurred as well before Richmond as before Gettysburg." Brigade commander Dod Ramseur concurred with Daniel. "The Enemy occupied a Gibralter of a position," he noted. A perceptive captain asserted, "It was a second Fredericksburg affair, only the wrong way." Others chided their high-ranking officers for mismanaging the battle. "The insanity of our Generals led them to attack," argued Eugene Blackford. To his mind, Confederate tactics at Gettysburg made no sense. The Yankees "are as mere chaff before the wind when ever they come out in the open country And this but makes the policy of attacking them when they are entrenched more criminal." Another soldier called it a "sin" to kill experienced troops in such numbers because "his place could not be filled."[55]

A Virginia artillerist announced his displeasure with his mounted comrades-in-arms. The cavalry, he insisted, "have proven themselves almost totally worthless since we have been here." Although Stuart had helped save the day on several battlefields and campaigns, he disappointed Lee on the movement into Pennsylvania.[56]

By the same token, Confederate artillery fire had failed the infantry on the third day, overshooting the Union forces on Cemetery Ridge and bombing the wagons several hundred yards to the rear. A week after the Battle of Gettysburg, Lt. James Dinwiddie completed his tests at the Richmond Laboratories. In the aftermath of William Allan's complaints, Gorgas had ordered all ammunition, primers, and fuses from around the Confederacy tested monthly at the Richmond Laboratories. Dinwiddie's assignment was ammunition and fuses from Charleston and Selma arsenals. After employing all sorts of tests, Dinwiddie urged "the great necessity of contriving some method by which fuzes may be driven by machinery so as to secure perfect uniformity in their burning." Fuses manufactured in Charleston, which Gorgas shipped to Lee's army after the explosion and closure at the Richmond Laboratories, were made very well. The problem was they burned slower than they were intended. "A spherical case shot with a 4" fuse would burst at 5"— that is at least 200 yards beyond where it was intended to burst." A 5-inch fuse burned at a rate of 5.25 inches, perhaps 100 to 150 yards beyond the target. From mid-July through January the next year, disturbing results continued to trickle into the chief of the Ordnance Department's headquarters: There was a lack of regularity in the performance of artillery shells and fuses. When artillerists fired shells and case shot, they cut the fuses a particular length. The blast that hurled the projectile forward also ignited the fuse, which burned down and caused the shell or case shot to explode over the enemy position. Fuses produced in Charleston, Atlanta, and Augusta, however, usually burned slower and performed more inconsistently than those made in Richmond. Lee's artillerists simply assumed a level of uniformity in the manufacture of fuses—that all fuses burned at roughly the same rate. As experienced gunners, most had estimated the distances correctly and cut the fuses the proper length for shells and fuses manufactured in Richmond. But because many of the shells and fuses had come from the Charleston arsenal, the fuses burned more slowly, and the explosive projectiles carried far beyond the Union line before they burst. Clouds of smoke and dirt obscured visual confirmation of the gunners' accuracy, but the explosion of Yankee caissons and damage to Federal guns by solid shot convinced them that they had determined the range properly. A lack of quality control in the manufacture of fuses undid the Confederate artillery bombardment on the third day at Gettysburg.[57]

For the first time since Seven Days', criticism spilled over onto Lee. Longstreet matter-of-factly explained to his good friend Sen. Louis Wigfall, "Our failure in Pa [Pennsylvania] was due I think to our being under the impression that the enemy had not been able to get all his forces up. Being under this impression Gen. Lee thought it best to attack at onse and we did attack before our forces got up." Longstreet believed other factors contributed to the defeat, but that was the principal issue. Other soldiers offered more direct criticism of Lee. "Gen. Lee is being out-Generaled," a Georgian suggested to his father, "or is playing a very low down game on the Yanks." An Alabama lieutenant who fought at Culp's Hill declared, "it was the worst piece of generalship I ever knew Lee to exercise."[58]

A number of soldiers pinned the blame on Lee for overconfidence. He genuinely believed his troops could carry any position. "Everybody thinks Genl Lee made a great mistake in attacking the enemy in the strong position he fell back to, But I expect he had too much confidence in our army." When soldiers criticized their commanding general, they did so gently. A South Carolina officer thought the men fought magnificently, but the generals failed them through overconfidence. "The greatest misfortune is that it destroyed the unbounded confidence reposed in Gen. Lee," he explained. "Before, the army believed he could not err. They now see that he can once in awhile." Thomas Petty thought the only thing the campaign proved was that Lee was "*human.*" Even those who were more direct in their objections to the way he handled the battle expressed those opinions gingerly. "Gen. Lee was too confident in his men—" conceded a soldier, "expecting them to overcome difficulties too great." Lee himself corroborated that opinion. He assumed full responsibility for the failure of the campaign, stating in his official report, "More may have been required of them than they were able to perform." That same day, he made clear to Davis where the burden fell. "I am alone to blame," he wrote, "in perhaps expecting too much of its prowess & valour."[59]

A little over a month after the battle, newspapers heaped criticism on the administration, and on various officers and commands. Even Lee, despite his status as the national hero, came under fire from the press. As a means of quelling the protests, Lee offered Davis a way out. He tendered his resignation as army commander. "The general remedy for the want of success of a military commander is his removal," Lee wrote. Failure to accomplish his objectives and health problems were his justification. Although there is no evidence to substantiate it, Lee probably knew that Davis would reject the offer, but he gave Davis an opportunity to resolve a delicate issue, if the president so desired. In a warm and generous letter, Davis replied, "To ask me to substitute you by some one in my judgment more fit to command, or who would possess more of the confidence of the army, or of the reflecting men in the country is to demand an impossibility."[60]

Time after time, Lee's army had pulled out victories, despite overwhelming Union advantages in men and materiel. Fighting on Northern soil, Yankee troops exhibited an unusual degree of commitment and tenacity, which enabled them to hold on during the most desperate moments of the battle, to win the critical fights within the fight. For the first time in the war, Confederates lost those decisive encounters. Although the Confederacy suffered disastrous casualties, the impact of Gettysburg may have been more dramatic for Federal soldiers. Union troops had finally demonstrated that they were "good stuff" from which to build an army. They could beat Lee's Army.

Several weeks after Seven Days', Jackson revealed to Dabney, "In God's own time I hope that He will send an army North and crown it with victory, and make its fruits peace, but let us pray that he send it not, except He goes with it." At Gettysburg, neither God nor Mars nor good fortune shone on the Confederacy. Lost opportunities and near successes plagued the Army of Northern Virginia during its Northern invasion. Lee commanded below his usually high standards, subordinates failed to cooperate and made poor tactical decisions, and the troops lacked their normal focus and execution. Little seemed to go right for the Confederacy. Yet for all that, Lee's army nearly won the battle.[61]

The Army of Northern Virginia perceived Gettysburg more as an aberration. In a series of major engagements throughout the war, Lee's army had lost only one, and in that instance the Federals had failed to drive them from the field. No one doubted they would win again, especially on their own soil, among their own people. Without the distractions of duty as an invading force, without the breakdown of discipline, the Army of Northern Virginia was an extremely formidable force.

Chapter 23

HOME FRONT

A T SIX FEET one inch tall, with brown hair and brown eyes, Frederick Augustus Habersham possessed a commanding presence, particularly in uniform. An avid supporter of secession, he had responded to the first call for volunteers. Selected as lieutenant of the Georgia Hussars, he mobilized with them and occupied Fort Pulaski for a week. After returning home for several months, the unit reassembled to protect one of the coastal islands for thirty more days.

Habersham came from a prominent Savannah family. The thirty-year-old worked as a bookkeeper in his uncle's merchant business, and by 1860 he had amassed considerable wealth, including ten slaves. He married Eliza "Leila" Elliott, also from a substantial slaveholding family, and they had three children, two boys and a girl. Her mother and family, worth over $30,000, lived next door. When Lee came to Savannah during his service in the winter of 1861–62, he spent considerable time with the Habershams. Leila's uncle was John Mackay, an old friend of Lee's from Regular Army days, and Lee visited and took meals with the extended family whenever he could.[1]

After occupation duty, the cavalrymen debated whether to go to the defense of Virginia as an artillery battery. Fred was eager to serve his Confederate nation, and the newly reformed unit once again offered him a lieutenancy, but Leila implored him to remain at home. She simply was not ready to give up her man to national service. Fred regretfully declined the commission. Instead, he joined a militia company that enabled him to remain in town and at work. During the successful Federal invasion at nearby Hilton Head, South Carolina, Fred participated as a volunteer aide, and although the island fell to Union hands, he escaped with a friend to fight another day.

As threats persisted, Fred sent the family inland and joined the Chatham Artillery with the rank of private. During re-election in May 1862, Fred declined a nomination as battery captain. His old commander in the Georgia Hussars, Capt. J. P. W. Read, wrote from Virginia that the battery had a lieutenancy for him, and he preferred to be in the heart of the fight rather than to serve locally with the Chatham Artillery. By this time, the war had taken some dark turns, and Leila knew she could not detain her husband from his duty any longer. Before Fred left, the captain informed Fred that someone else had been chosen lieutenant, but he invited Fred to come anyway as a volunteer aide. Shortly after the Seven Days' closed, Fred entrained for Richmond. He left behind Leila, three children, and a fourth one on the way.

From the front Fred wrote beautiful, touching letters to Leila. He reported rumors, stories, and news about friends and acquaintances. He also offered descriptions of the dreadful battlefields around Richmond. The massive destruction awed Fred. He always inquired of his children and admitted to Leila, "I should be sorry if the war ended now, sorry that I've not had an opportunity of doing something which my children would be proud of." Despite the hectic pace, he did not forget his son's birthday. He also kept the family apprised of "Your old friend Gen'l Lee" whenever he saw or heard stories about him. On the march northward toward Second Manassas, Fred received a letter from Leila, informing him of his cousin's death from illness. Fred went off to the woods to be alone, "in order not to show my weakness." Several days later, he heard that Leila had contracted a serious sickness, and the two awful events caused "a hard blow on my spirits," he admitted.[2]

He witnessed the battles of Second Manassas and then Harpers Ferry. As a volunteer aide to Read, he did whatever the captain needed, and as an experienced soldier, he offered much-appreciated advice. Fred listened to the shouts and cheers of Virginians as the army forced the enemy into retreat, observed the sights and sounds of a major battle at Second Manassas, and then walked the battlefield and examined the destruction. On the eve of Antietam, he marveled, "What a change has taken place since Lee took command."[3]

The next day, the battery entered combat, and only half walked away from the fight unscathed. Among the dead was his friend Lt. Breck Parkman. The experience jolted Fred like nothing he had ever endured. When the soldiers buried Parkman, he was "shocked at the levity around his grave." What stunned him most was their ready acceptance of death. The soldiers liked Parkman, yet his passing appeared to create little sensation among them. "These men seem to have no thought of the future," he conveyed in amazement. "During the engagement they cursed in the most awful manner and one man, after he fell severely wounded, cursed and yelled at the top of his voice to the others to go on and give the Yanks Hell."[4]

Fred's concern for his wife's health convinced him to return to Georgia. He visited the family at the inland house near Cartersville. The sight of Fred overjoyed Leila. He stayed two months, playing with his children, taking afternoon walks with the pregnant Leila, and chatting with Leila's brother, who was on leave from Georgia Military Institute. While on that visit, Fred learned that another had won the vote for the vacant lieutenancy, but Read insisted the fellow was incompetent and would fail an examination. He urged Fred to remain patient, that the commission would ultimately be his. Fred, however, could not wait, and he returned to Savannah alone to see if he could find an appropriate position in a combat unit, preferably one bound for Virginia. While Fred worked in Savannah, Leila gave birth a bit prematurely to their third son, whom she named Frederick Augustus Habersham, Jr. Less than a day later, the infant passed away while Leila's mother cradled him. She carried Little Fred into the bedroom, and Leila "took the little baby in my arms & *wept*, as only Mothers weep over their dead infants." It was New Year's Day, 1863. Fred received a cryptic note from her sister, expressing sorrow for his loss. In a panic, he rushed to Cartersville, where he learned of the birth and death. Fred stayed with his wife until she was up and well.[5]

The demands of work for the Confederacy compelled Fred to return to Savannah, while the family remained at the house near Cartersville. In mid-February, a letter arrived announcing that Read's Battery had chosen him unanimously for a lieutenancy, and he must report as soon as possible. Fred left in the middle of the night to catch a train for Virginia. He vowed to Leila, " 'I will come back.' " Over the next two and a half months, Fred reported on his studies for the lieutenancy examination, their mutual friends, including Lee, and war news.[6]

Inside Fred's letter describing the Battle of Antietam, he scribbled a separate note, telling his wife and his mother, "I prayed upon going into action and returned thanks upon coming out safe. I trust it may prove a lesson to me by which I may be saved." Yet when his battery defended Marye's Heights at Fredericksburg as part of the Chancellorsville Campaign, a shell fragment crushed the back of Fred's skull, killing him instantly.[7]

Leila knew a great battle was taking place in Virginia, and she was understandably on edge. Two days after the attack on Marye's Heights, as Leila wandered through the garden of her neighbor's, Aunt Sally Mackay stuck her head out the window and called for Leila to come home. Her aunt met her at the door and broke the news. She had barely time to react when Fred's mother, brother, and numerous family members burst into the house, "weeping and wailing." Leila hoped it was a mistake, that he had only suffered a wound, but soon the fateful telegram arrived. He had fallen working his gun against fearful odds.[8]

Fred's brother Robert traveled to Virginia to retrieve the body. He learned that Fred had acted heroically, and his men had buried him some three miles to the rear. After some searching with the help of Fred's slave, they found the spot. One soldier from his battery had placed a wooden sign above his grave:

Frederick A. Habersham
2nd Lieut. Read's Battery
Cabell's Battalion
McLaws Division

Savannah, Georgia
Killed Sunday 3rd May 1863

Reginescat In Pace
Buried May 6th 1863

They dug up his body, which his men had wrapped in a blanket and placed in a wooden box. Robert transferred it into a casket for the journey home. Everyone offered condolences, including Lee.[9]

Once Leila learned that they had secured his remains, she and her brother traveled by carriage to Laurel Grove Cemetery, where they selected a grave plot. She chose one next to Fred's cousin Stephen, with whom he was close. Stephen would lie on one side of Fred. The plot on the other side she secured for herself.[10]

When the body arrived, Robert refused to let her look at her husband's face. He brought back her last letter, with a picture of her for him, unopened. It had arrived too late. Among his belongings, she found a chain and locket that Robert had cut. The chain was stained with Fred's blood. Inside the locket was a picture of Leila. His overcoat and uniforms had bloodstains, too.

Sunday afternoon, they held a funeral at Christ Church. Everyone tried to discourage Leila from attending, fearing it would be too difficult for her and she would make a scene. She promised to control herself, and they could not dissuade her. When the religious service concluded, the party traveled to the cemetery. They lowered the casket of her beloved husband into the grave and laid the tiny coffin of their infant son at his feet. Leila then watched as they tossed dirt on his casket. She remained as calm "as if my heart had turned to stone."[11]

After the funeral, she tried to visit her sister and her husband's family, but her grief was too strong. She returned to Savannah to be with her family and her in-laws. The next year, she changed the name of her eldest son, Ralph, to Frederick Augustus Habersham, Jr. She never remarried.[12]

ARMY AND HOME life were reflexive forces in the lives of Confederates. Combat and camp duty shaped and altered perceptions of the war among civilians, while events and opinions at home fed and influenced army life in positive and negative ways. If loved ones were suffering unnecessarily, then Confederate troops felt that they had failed in their purpose for entering military service. Everyone knew that those in uniform and those who remained behind would have to endure sacrifices for the sake of the war effort, and some would even give their lives for the cause, but when the hardships at home became too severe, it posed a severe distraction to soldiers. Rebel troops could not fight effectively if they had one eye on the Yankees and another on loved ones at home. Deteriorating conditions on the home front help explain the desertion and absence without leave rates in Lee's army and had a major impact on the war.

At the same time, letters and information from home offered a valuable escape from the burdens and brutalities of armed conflict. Amid the killing, maiming, hating, and destruction, life back home offered them a sense of peace, serenity, love, growth, and construction—all positive visions to counterbalance the hostility of war and refresh soldiers' memories. When no information arrived from home, soldiers became frustrated. They felt disconnected from the central community in their lives. North Carolinian John Damron pledged not to write his father again until he received a letter from home, but then he decided that approach would sever all communication. "As I have given up all idea of receiving a scratch from your very reserved pen," he teased, "you certainly should be appointed Superintendent over some Asylum of Mutes as I verryly believe your experience in such matters would be highly beneficial to such an instruction."[13]

Some soldiers merely assumed that military service would be a pause in their home life, but inevitably the two became intertwined. Close to two of every three soldiers in Lee's army entered military service unwed. They hoped that when the war ended, they would have fair prospects of resuming a fulfilling life. Unmarried Lt. Ezekial Graham complained that women cared too much about rank. "With most ladies now-a-days, it takes a field officer to be called 'Handsome,'" he commented, "the personal appearance of a General, who is of course, *par excellence*, the embodiment of perfection, being considered indescribable; Captains are usually termed 'Good Looking' or 'Fine Looking' and Lieutenants 'tolerable' while privates are considered being almost disgusting." As he was a second lieutenant, not many women would express interest in him. Quite a number like Graham were eager to find a spouse after the war concluded. A Georgian admitted to a woman that before the war, he had ample opportunities to marry but was not ready. "I am now ready and so soon as I am out of the army I intend to do so or get awfully repulsed," he informed her. Another Georgian declared to his sister that a buddy had gone to Louisiana and returned with a beautiful, rich wife. He and another friend pledged to visit Louisiana once the war ended and "you may look out for a Sister- in-Law 'be she pretty or be she ugly.'"[14]

What particularly disturbed unwed soldiers in Lee's army was that women who had pledged to wait for the volunteers did not always do so. "I thought the girls had agreed not to marry until the volunteers returned," a Louisianan protested to his sister, "but it appears that they have broken or forgotten their pledge." A Virginia officer was not nearly so forgiving of women who failed to support soldiers and their cause. "To those ladies who said they wd. [would] not have lovers *in the war*," he argued, "I wd. Say *lovers out of the war* are not *worth having*, and to the lady who wd. Break an engagement for such a cause, is incapable of appreciating patriotism, and does not deserve the protection of the brave."[15]

In a horrid tale, Frank Barron and a school chum who was betrothed joined the 6th South Carolina. At Frazier's Farm, a case shot severed his friend's leg. Barron bound the wound. When his friend returned home, his fiancée broke off the engagement and married someone else, a speculator who had hired a substitute rather than serve in the army. His parents were dead, his uncle had passed away, his fiancée had dumped him, and all he had was his friendship with Barron. "Oh! Frank I was wrong, very wrong for thinking that anyone could love a cripple like myself for life," he confessed to Barron. The veteran's depression grew deeper, to the point where he did not blame his fiancée at all for breaking off their engagement. Eventually, he entered a lunatic asylum and died shortly afterward. His experiences must have sent a chill throughout the old company.[16]

When their sisters began courting, soldiers felt compelled to weigh in on the merits and demerits of their boyfriends, as if they were home. Sarah Scurry took a fancy to a soldier, and her brother John could not resist presenting a different side of her beau. "If you were to take a look at him in camp—Ragged, dirty and l——y [lousy] you wouldn't think him so good looking." Another soldier's sister fell in love with a Northerner, and he conveyed his sentiments bluntly to their mother: "My opinion is Freed is no better than any other Yankee, he does no fighting for us." Launcelot Blackford approved his sister Mary's choice for a husband. His concern was the wedding announcement. "Be sure to let Church's regiment appear on the card," he insisted. "I would not have it appear you married anybody but a soldier; particularly now. Men that ain't soldiers may be very well in their way, but I prefer not to have any such in the family."[17]

Lewis Blackford, Launcelot's older brother, had no trouble finding a bride. His problem was trying to get his mother to accept his choice. His mother replied "almost with horror" when she learned he had proposed to a young woman. Blackford, however, refused to back down. He reminded her that while he hoped his selection would please her, "one will fall in love for oneself and one that would please you might not please me." Blackford then frankly stated, "I think it would be easier for you to learn to love my choice after marriage than for me to learn to love your choice."[18]

Troops needed to know that those at home supported and appreciated their sacrifices and service. A South Carolina private found comfort in the knowledge that his wife coped with two small children and a farm while he went off to war. "Would to God all women could See the necesities of our country as you Seem to view them," he lauded her, "& in the Same noble Spirit, that actuated you, Say to their husbands & Sons & even their fathers, *dear* as your Society is to me, & *painful* as your absence will certainly prove yet you must march to the battlefield, & thare contend with all of your might, against the vile foe, that is invading our land, for the purpose of robing us of every thing that renders life really desirable." Two years into the struggle for Confederate independence, a Virginia horseman took great pride in the patriotism of Confederate women, presenting their predicament as a choice between freedom and sexual slavery. "I think the women of the South have shown very little despondency in spite of the great stakes they have in the game, even greater than we have," he asserted. "For in no event will we have to live under the despot's rod, while for them there is no escape, in case we fail to sustain our cause with our arms."[19]

True to the cause, civilians supported the war in any way they could. Women and older men volunteered in hospitals to ease the suffering of the sick and wounded. They conveyed valuable information about Union forces and their movements to Confederate troops. In one instance, near Monterey, Virginia, women assisted Jackson's columns during the Valley Campaign by chopping down trees to block the road. The Union troops had to backtrack and change course. In a handful of instances, women disguised themselves as men and served in the army. According to a Union serviceman, a doctor discovered that a wounded Rebel soldier at Gettysburg was a woman. She lost a leg. Mostly, though, women and some men aided the fight by shaming eligible men into taking up arms and joining their neighbors in defense of homes.[20]

Soldiers understandably loathed those at home who failed to support them, Unionists (that is, Union sympathizers) above all. A Floridian vowed to "go home and whip every body there that in the least is opposed to us" as soon as the war was won. An Alabama lieutenant wanted "all those tories in northern Alabama caught and hunge to one large pole." He felt sure the Confederacy would have secured its independence by early 1864 had it not been for the Unionists.[21]

Likewise, those who simply lost interest earned the wrath of soldiers. Early in the war, during the *rage militaire*, white people in the South largely banded together to support their soldiers in the field. Except for pockets of Unionists, the population enthusiastically rallied around the secessionist cause. As body counts and hardships rose astronomically, many still clung to the revolution, but some people lost faith, while others lost interest. Far removed from the fighting, civilians worried more about loved ones than soldiers did about themselves. Morale fluctuated more steeply than it did for soldiers, and word of disaffection or dissatisfaction at home spread quickly to those in uniform. "I am astonished at the state of public feeling in Georgia as represented by the returned furloughed men," a junior officer complained to his wife in late August 1863. "They say Georgia is now almost whipped, and she has hardly ever had an armed heel on her soil." Launcelot Blackford informed his father, "The men are in much better spirits than their people at home, who are, I fear, in some if not many instances foolish and wicked enough to write discouraging and craven letters to their representatives in the army." Soldiers had more control over the fate of their country than did civilians, and they had come to terms with the chance of war. As a Virginian explained in November 1863, "At home all is long face & despondency, dreary imaginations and visions of disasters & misfortunes. In the army all is hopes, cheerfulness & high expectations and I may interestingly say the best cure for the hypochondriac is to visit the army." After two years of fighting, soldiers began to feel as though the Confederate public had forgotten them. It seemed as though only immediate family members exhibited interest in the welfare of troops, even though the Yankees would have overrun the Confederacy without their armed defenders. "But for some few I wouldnot care if the Yankees did come & take every negro & horse they had," a Virginia private confided. "I feel some consolation in believeing there is A day coming when every tub will have to stand upon its own bottom."[22]

Troops needed reinforcement from family and friends. They relished outward support—cheering crowds, lining up along the side of the road as they marched past, offering hearty welcomes, water, food, and blessings for a safe campaign. Soldiers rejoiced when the folks at home sent individual care packages, or when a comrade on furlough returned with boxes of shoes and clothing from organized donation drives in their local community. "The ragged sentinel who may pace his weary rounds this winter on the bleak spurs of the Blue Ridge, or along the frozen valleys of the Shenandoah and Rappahannock, will also be your sentinels, my friends, at home," journalist Peter Alexander reminded his readership. "It will be for you and your household that he encounters the wrath of the tempest and the dangers of the night," and he urged the people to provide for the needs of the soldiers.[23]

Despite the gap that evolved between military reality and perceptions of war at home, a gulf that exists in all wars, reflexive relationships formed between soldiers and civilians. Events and attitudes of war among the troops deeply affected citizens, even if they struggled to understand the true nature of military life. Soldiers, by contrast, came into the service from home and returned occasionally on furloughs, which kept them abreast of events in their community. They could readily comprehend what transpired there, but as the war dragged into 1864, furloughs became less frequent and that gulf widened as well. Just like the troops, loved ones at home concealed some hardship for fear of distracting their men from the critical duty of soldiering. Although troops could better imagine the plight of civilians—and word of the difficulties almost always reached the men in the army—the events and burdens at home still influenced troop morale and the way these men met their obligations as soldiers. Thus, soldiers worried about citizens at home, and they in turn feared for their men in the field.

By supporting their cause enthusiastically, people at home felt like a vibrant force in the war effort. Virginian Sara Ann Fife declared the Union "rotted to the core." She complained that the tariff taxed Southerners excessively and then the North "must attack our social system, incite our slaves to rebellion circulating abolition volumes among that class here, who will read & explain them to the slaves." She believed either restriction of slaveholders' access to the territories or efforts to destroy slavery were grounds for disbanding the Union. Throughout the war, she maintained an intense hatred of the enemy. After Yankee soldiers occupied her home, she vented, "Oh! If I was a boy, to fight them." A month after the war ended, Fife remained wholly unreconstructed. "I truly believe that African slavery is right," she jotted in her diary. "I love it & all the South loves it. It suits us, & I do not see how we can do without it." A Louisiana woman concurred with Fife's sentiments. "I despise every thing that is connected with the Yankees in any way," she wrote a friend in Lee's army. "If I had a *drop* of yankee blood in my veins I would have it taken out." Amid the secession crisis, Catherine Edmondston resented her sister's visit because she was so pro-Union. Her sister argued, "This glorious Union, broken up for the sake of a few negroes! Rather let them go than destroy the Union." Edmondston responded in her diary, "This is to me treason against Liberty. In the first place, it is not a 'few negroes.' It is the country, for I should like to know who could live here were they freed?—& then the principle involved!" She then concluded with the potent words, "I *yield nothing*—no compromise—where my *liberty*, my *honour*, dearer than life is concerned!" Edmondston remained an ardent secessionist to the end.[24]

In the same way, opportunities to give advice and guidance in farm and work activities or family matters thrust soldiers back into the heart of home life and made them feel like vital contributors once again. Despite heavy fighting, Pvt. C. C. High took time to make some shoes for his wife, justifying his labor by asserting, "you may be shure I wouldnot draw a woman Barefooted for you [k]now that I donte like them kind of wiming [women]." In farm households, the usual division of labor meant that women were unused to planting, tilling, and harvesting. Husbands tried to reassure their wives that they could handle these tasks. When Pvt. Marcus Hefner's wife suggested she could plow some plots for cultivation, he encouraged her: "try to satisfy the bely before the back." Sergeant Hill Fitzpatrick urged his wife not to shy away from the task of butchering the hogs. "Pitch in like a man an attend to it, and every thing of that sort," he encouraged her. "You must be the man and the woman both now you know." Margaret McCollum expressed concern over the rent, and her husband Thomas told her to visit the landlord and "ask of him not to be hard about the rent, with you as we don't get paid of regular." In the case of a North Carolina cavalryman, his wife and children moved in with his parents, and his mother turned on him for leaving his family for army duty. His wife complained to him about her mother-in-law's continual, bitter remarks and shabby treatment. From Virginia, all he could suggest was to endure it. "This war compels us to submit to many other hardships besides those of actual battle and army life and this unhappy condition is our plague while others have theirs."[25]

Some women possessed a knack for good management and directed an effective and efficient business in their husbands' absence. Amanda, Hill Fitzpatrick's wife, ran a store and the farm, supervised the slaves, and raised the children with only a modest amount of help and some occasional advice and encouragement from him. But for most households, the loss of a primary breadwinner, declining production and importation, and spiraling costs placed tremendous strain on civilians, even if opposing armies never marched through the community. Limited supplies altered the chemistry in those communities. Individuals hoarded for their own purposes, which worsened the shortages and drove prices up. With confidence in Confederate paper money slipping and a grave shortage of hard currency, sellers padded prices substantially. Colonel J. Q. A. Nadenbousch viewed it as a breakdown in values, and he feared for the present and the future. "This war has opened the gap for crimes which would never have entered the mind of man," he complained to his wife. "It has not only desolated empires & swept millions from the earth but it has demoralized the whole country[,] opened the way to all manner of vices and when peace may be concluded we will find ourselves in the midst of a community which will wink at no evil however so corrupt it may be." In his opinion, they had "abandoned all principles of honesty[,] decency & pride."[26]

Wives left in charge of farms often had difficulty dealing with slaves, and soldier-husbands did not hesitate to offer management advice. Nadenbousch suggested that his wife rely on Sol to keep Louise straight. Later, as his wife relayed more difficulties, he instructed her bluntly, "if Jack attempts to put on any airs ask Mr. Grey to thrash him" and remind the slaves that he would return someday and "attend to these matters." When Pvt. Sambo Short learned that his mother had livestock and poultry stolen, he immediately blamed the slaves. "Have them properly thrashed," he advised his wife, and lay down the law with them. Hill Fitzpatrick learned that his slaves had participated in a "negroe frolic." He reacted by informing wife Amanda, "It made me broil to think of it. I think I shall have to whip some of them yet if I ever get back."[27]

From afar, soldiers continued to weigh in on the rearing of their children. An officer counseled his wife about their six-year-old boy, "give my love to Carter & tell him to Keep his mind on his books if he ever expects to be a man." Another soldier employed old-fashioned bribery by sending his children money for behaving well for their mother, warning them, "if you don't bee smart and mind hur I wont never send you and Charley no more money." After serving for some time, it became apparent to many soldiers that they might not make it home to help raise their children, and they reminded their wives just what kinds of values they wanted their children to exhibit. "O Fanny if it should be my lot never to see you any more I want you to raise Charley in an honest and upright manner," a North Carolina soldier wrote, "teach him to do right and correct him if he needs it." Less than two weeks later, he warned Fanny not to idolize Charlie in case something happened to him. Another North Carolinian, a prewar farmer, admonished his children "to be smart and doo as your mother tells you, for she knows better how to farm it then you doo for I dont know when if ever I will get home again."[28]

Men in Lee's army had seen the hardships that Virginia residents had suffered. They were thankful that most of their own loved ones had avoided that disaster, but troops from other states also feared that the war would spread to their homes. Nearly all of them had witnessed streams of refugees, armed only with a few bundles of precious items, fleeing the advance of the Union army. Lee's own family members were forced to abandon their home, as had many of his soldiers' loved ones. They had gazed upon the destruction in the wake of Yankee retreats, and they had viewed the devastation that their own soldiers wrought on the private property of the people they were supposed to defend.[29]

Whether compassion or a hope that someone would reciprocate if their loved ones were in distress motivated them, some of Lee's soldiers were particularly kind to the civilians they encountered. Among the beneficiaries were the residents of Fredericksburg, for whom Lee's army had developed an unusual fondness. According to a South Carolinian, the people of Fredericksburg had acted especially charitably toward the army. He judged the ladies there very patriotic: "they gave our soldiers a great many hats, shoes[,] boots & a great many other articles of clothing which they very much needed." When citizens evacuated their homes in late November and December 1862, Lee employed wagons and ambulances "day and night" to move citizens away. Troops then took up collections, providing thousands of Confederate dollars as relief for the people of Fredericksburg.[30]

The burdens of war fell heavily on civilians, especially the poor and lower middle class, and many of them had to take severe measures for their own welfare. In Richmond, with soaring prices and severe shortages, a food riot broke out. President Davis confronted the crowd and scattered his pocket change among them. In Salisbury, North Carolina, a large group of soldiers' wives armed with hatchets and other small weapons forced their way into various merchant shops and demanded and received donations of flour, molasses, and salt. An eyewitness of the event called for an end to all speculation and "hoped that yesterday's work will be the means of persons exercising more sympathy for their fellow man. They cannot save their souls by money." Other towns and cities faced similar crises.[31]

In an unusual instance during wartime, the states' rights mentality worked to the benefit of the poor and hungry in the Confederacy. As the war extended into its third year, the power of the national government began to wane, and state and local governments, in conjunction with family networks and voluntary organizations, attempted to relieve the hardships by purchasing foodstuffs for the poor and aiding those in need. In Mississippi, a group of people formed the Confederate Society to check extortion and corruption, publicizing their efforts and hoping to spark the creation of similar groups across the Confederacy. Nadenbousch, a wealthy farmer and slaveholder in peacetime, directed his wife to give their surplus to the poor families of his company. He understood that everyone must sacrifice during wartime and that his troops could not focus on the mission at hand if they were worried about the basic necessities for loved ones at home. "We cant live to & for ourselves these times," he advised his wife, but "we must all work together for good." Even the national Confederate government did its part. In mid-February 1864, Congress required all farms with fifteen or more able-bodied adult field slaves that took advantage of an exemption from conscription for one adult white male to sell to the government 100 pounds of beef or pork per slave at a rate fixed by the state government. These farms also had to sell all their surplus foodstuffs to soldiers' families or the government at that same fixed rate.[32]

Despite national, state, local, and voluntary efforts to feed and clothe everyone, families at home endured great hunger and hardship. A Tennessean received a letter from his wife, imploring him to "soon com home for if you dont we will starve for we ar on the border of starving now, and since the Yanks has stopped round hear I cant get sewing work to do." Unfortunately for him, he was stuck in a Yankee prison camp and had no means of alleviating her burdens. When a Confederate soldier learned from his wife that their only cow had died, his world came crashing down. "I have never heard any newse from home that hurt me like that did but I cant help it," he replied. He could not sleep, worrying about the welfare of his wife and children. "I see no chance but for you to suffer," he relayed sadly. Neither she nor he had enough money to buy a new cow, and it broke his heart to think of them in such dire straits.[33]

More than the physical hardships, it was mental anguish that tormented civilians. Many spouses had never been apart from their husbands since they married. The loneliness grated on them severely. Ann Nelson, who managed a farm, six slaves, and two children, thought she would go "deranged" unless her husband returned. A woman informed her husband, "Bluford i am a getting very tired of liveing by my self it is the loncemess time i ever saw i dont think i can standet mutch longer." Martha Futch tried to keep her mind occupied, but inevitably, her thoughts drifted to her husband in Lee's army. "My injoyement ant [aint] much," she admitted, "fore my study is about you in the day and dreme of you at nite."[34]

Those in the field could move, execute, and act for themselves—to some extent, they could control their own destiny and their physical activity eased the stress of battle. People at home could only await the news. When Mem Cohen's son joined a regiment that was assigned to Stonewall Jackson, the news unraveled her. Her friend Mary Chesnut recorded that "she has persistently wept ever since she heard the news. It is no child's play, she says, when you are with Stonewall. He don't play at soldiering. He don't take care of his men at all. He only goes to kill the Yankees." The women were helpless to affect the process. "Oh! The anxiety of mind I have endured," Fanny Scott expressed to her husband after the initial battle at Yorktown. "I have never before been so unhappy." Kate Scales complained of nightmares about the welfare of her husband, Brig. Gen. Alfred M. Scales. He tried to ease her fears, explaining, "it is but a dream which had its origin in your anxiety for me & to be affected by it is to suffer in anticipation." As the battle for Richmond began, William Parker urged his wife Emaline to be cheerful. "I have tried; and do try," she responded, "but there is a solomn feeling, in my heart I can not help and I think I can see it in every intelligent face." Eleven months later, Parker finally understood his wife's fundamental sadness: "I verily believe the people at home suffer most in anticipation of trouble to there friends."[35]

News would spread by telegraph and newspapers of a great battle or skirmish fought in the Virginia Theater. For days, people waited in trepidation to learn who had gone down in the fight. Finally, a report arrived, as it did with Fred Habersham, followed soon by a letter or telegram from an officer or friend, explaining how a loved one died and what happened to his body. In time, the family of the deceased would receive his trappings and back pay. Those whose loved ones survived felt an exhilarating sense of relief. The fix was temporary. It merely meant that they would have to undergo the same emotional trauma again, when the armies fought once more.[36]

In rare instances, cases of mistaken identity resulted in false reports that a loved one had fallen. Marcus Hefner's wife received word that he was killed in action at Chancellorsville. The stunning news soon turned to her joy and someone else's sorrow when she learned it was the wrong Marcus Hefner. Private George G. Young of the 2nd South Carolina Cavalry received a telegram informing him that his brother was desperately ill and urging him to come immediately. The very words jolted Young. As he read the message a second time, and the horrible news had just begun to sink in, he noticed the message was for a Joseph Young. The messenger had delivered it to the wrong Young.[37]

Unless military officials were confident that a soldier had died in battle or fallen into enemy hands, they listed him as missing. The lack of detailed information may have been more agonizing for the folks at home than anything else. It prolonged the news blackout and extended the anxiety. A Virginia woman heard rumors that Federals had taken her son prisoner. "The idea of your ever falling into the hand of our cruel & treacherous enemy is more distressing to me than you can imagine," she divulged to him. Yet for those who had heard nothing from their loved one for weeks after the battle, news that he had been captured was infinitely better than word that he had fallen in combat. After receiving a letter from her husband that the Yankees had taken him prisoner and he was alive and well, Bettie Burroughs responded joyfully, "I can assure you that it afforded me the most Exquisite pleasure imaginable to Learn what had become of you for I have been kept in the most dreadful suspense aver since [you] was captured." In late May 1864, Union forces captured Lt. J. L. McCrorey in a counterattack. Authorities reported him killed in action and newspapers in South Carolina had listed him as dead. Not until two and a half months later, when a friend of his was captured and arrived at Point Lookout, did McCrorey learn that loved ones thought he was no more. It mattered little. Pneumonia seized McCrorey's lungs and five days later, he passed away.[38]

In a strange way, the battlefield claimed the lives of those who survived. Some sustained wounds from which they recovered and eventually returned to combat or the army, while others lost limbs or endured injuries that prevented them from contributing effectively to the war effort. Disabled veterans returned to the home front and faced an exceedingly difficult transition to wartime civil life. An officer from the 7th Georgia complained to Jefferson Davis that one of his privates, Frank M. Daniel, suffered a wound at First Manassas that required an amputation near the shoulder. "He is a poor man with a large family," his former captain wrote, "and I found him the other day in circumstances of actual indigency." He thought it was awful that a man who had given so much of himself for his country "should be thrown aside and turned out like a broken down plough horse, to subsist on charity." He called for disabled veterans' pensions, which the Confederacy ultimately authorized. Other disabled veterans experienced even worse problems. A mother with a son in Lee's army mentioned to Davis that an officer had sustained a terrible head wound that left him with "the light of day & reason gone." She admitted being terribly worried about her son's suffering the same fate. Another mother complained that her eldest son received a severe wound at Antietam that required the amputation of his arm. "All the bright dreams of my poor boy were crushed," she divulged. "He returned home disabled for life, his mind a prey to bitter regret that he could no longer serve his country."[39]

No doubt, morale at home waxed and waned with wartime successes and failures. But even in the face of a resounding triumph, casualties cut to the core of wartime support. Five weeks after Gettysburg, Pvt. William H. Proffit of the 1st North Carolina could not believe what he heard about the morale at home. "I understand the people of Wilkes are badly whipped and willing for our patriotic old state to return to the pretended Union and claim Abraham Lincoln as their chief magistrate," he wrote his sister. Rumors also suggested that the countryside was full of deserters and that no one tried to compel these men to return to their commands. Proffit told his sister he would like to believe these reports were untrue, but the evidence was against his wishes. In fact, a considerable opposition spirit had taken hold in North Carolina, a state that had barely voted for secession, and it continued to grow over the course of the war. Lee himself had expressed mild concern in April 1863 over desertion in North Carolina regiments. What fueled the fires of disaffection more than anything, though, were the tremendous casualties among North Carolinians in Lee's army. Behind Virginia, North Carolina sent the most troops to Lee's army that spring and summer. At Chancellorsville, nearly three in every ten North Carolinians were killed, wounded, or captured, by far the greatest total and percentage of any state in Lee's army. The seven highest totals of killed and wounded fell to North Carolina regiments. Two months later, at Gettysburg, after the army had added two large North Carolina brigades, 46.4 percent of all North Carolinians were killed, wounded, or captured. The top four regimental casualty figures and six of the seven highest occurred in North Carolina regiments. North Carolina lost 1,782 more soldiers than the next-highest state, a difference that constituted more casualties than eight states suffered in the entire battle. Then, to worsen the discrepancy, at the Battle of Bristoe Station nearly all the casualties in Lee's army came from North Carolina—well above 10 percent of all troops from North Carolina in the army. While it is difficult to determine a figure with precision, a reasonable calculation over a five-and-a-half-month period from late April to mid-October 1863 indicates seven of every ten North Carolinians who served in the Army of Northern Virginia were casualties. The impact of those losses in the most successful and visible Confederate field command, the Army of Northern Virginia, on the North Carolina home front was devastating and coincided precisely with the rising disaffection in the state.[40]

The combined losses at Vicksburg and Gettysburg drove down morale in every Confederate state, more so among civilians than military personnel. There was a temporary resurgence after Chickamauga, but the rout at Chattanooga and fiasco at Bristoe Station prevented any significant resurgence that winter. Only the dawn of spring 1864, and the belief that the new year would be decisive, could raise hopes. Everyone knew that 1864 was a presidential election year in the Union, and Federal forces would make a giant push to close out the struggle before citizens cast their ballots. If the Confederacy could repel this major thrust on various fronts, it might just convince the Northern states that the price of reunion was simply too high. Folks at home and their loved ones in Lee's army braced for a campaign that might very well win the war.[41]

Chapter 24

BLACKS AND THE ARMY

Before the war, Dr. Elias Davis owned real estate and property worth nearly $12,000, including eight slaves. A physician and father of a young son, he joined the 10th Alabama Infantry, serving as an enlisted man and then as an officer. After two and a half years in the Army of Northern Virginia and its predecessor, Davis refused to back down. "My opinion is that we would have long ago had peace: If The Great Powers beyond the Atlantic Ocean had not been prejudiced against the institution of Negroe slavery," he argued to his mother. Not only was the Confederacy fighting the Union, Davis insisted, but it contended against Great Britain, France, and Russia as well. By respecting the Union blockade, those nations had compelled the Confederate States to fight alone against overwhelming resources drawn from around the world. "We have suffered much during this war," he added, "but I am willing to fight forever, rather than submit to freeing negroes among us; and being tarred to defray expenses of a war waged to wrest from our hands rights and property bequeathed to us by our ancestors." Davis then concluded with the assertion, "I conscienciously believe our cause is just and consequently cant believe that we will not be successful."[1]

The struggle over slavery and freedom lay at the heart of the war. Yet during the war, that peculiar institution Davis pledged to protect, and for which he gave his life in 1864, represented a world of contradictions to Rebels. Confederate States had seceded to protect African slavery, but the ensuing war proved to be the ultimate threat to its existence. They sought to preserve enslavement of blacks, and at the same time fought under the banner of liberty. Southerners fed themselves on a diet of slave loyalty, yet bondsmen by the hundreds of thousands fled the institution once the opportunity arose. Owners professed a deep affection among slaves for their masters, even while Southern whites on the home front lived with the fear of servile insurrection.

Even the primary mission of slavery, to secure inexpensive labor, proved to be a double-edged sword. Confederates counted on slave productivity to offset the massive loss of manpower as white men rushed to arms. While slaves did grow crops and labor for Confederate armies and the war effort, they also slowed their work, caused fear and distress within home communities through their misbehavior and occasional truculence—particularly with a shortage of adult white males at home, produced crops in occupied territories for the Union, and shattered white perceptions of slave fealty by aiding or fleeing to the enemy. Worse yet, 150,000 ex-slaves picked up arms to fight against their former masters.[2]

Since early in the war, slaves had perceived the Union army as their vehicle to freedom, and large numbers fled to Federal lines or used their armies as a shield to secure safety. Any slaveholder whose property was approached by the enemy army witnessed the rapid breakdown of slave "loyalty." Fear among whites over the prospect of Yankee invasion tipped off slaves to the opportunity of escape, and owners soon discovered that their loyal and loving slaves had abandoned their farms and plantations, hiding out anywhere they could until the arrival of the Federal forces. In late July 1861, a Confederate loyalist on the James River complained to an officer that one slave escaped by jumping out a window. A guard shot at him but missed. Nearly a year later, as the Confederates battled to save Richmond, a citizen in the area admitted to his brother that many of his slaves had run away. Three of them, "who have been taking holiday for 6 weeks," returned, but eleven were still missing. He thought "most will make good their escape." Silas, a slave of Lt. C. J. Batchelor's family back in Louisiana, was shot in the arm by an overseer when he ran off. A militia unit captured him, and he confessed that he had escaped from the Batchelors.[3]

Lincoln's Emancipation Proclamation did not surprise Confederates so much as it confirmed their suspicions of Union war aims and reinforced their commitment to the war. A North Carolinian contended the Proclamation would have little effect on slavery, because Lincoln's administration had already freed slaves in areas where the Union army gained control. It merely exposed him as an outright abolitionist. "The proclamation of Lincoln has filled every one with indignation," reported a South Carolina officer and slave owner to his father, "and we are all now in favor of raising the 'black flag' and asking and showing 'no quarter.'" Elias Davis considered it "the death struggle of the monster." Others viewed the Proclamation as removing any basis for a negotiated settlement. Either the Union would win and slavery would be destroyed or the Confederacy would triumph and preserve the institution. Brigadier General Alfred Scales informed his wife he could not resign. If he did, and others followed his lead, "slavery must & would be our doom." A Virginian who owned one slave concurred, explaining to his mother and his wife, "unless we can maintain our independence peace will do us no good for after Lincoln procklamation any man that wouldent fight to the last ought to be hung as high as ham."[4]

After the Emancipation Proclamation, Union armies and recruiters accelerated efforts to bring able-bodied black males into military service, either as soldiers or as stevedores, muleteers, or other laborers who worked for the army. Often the slaves brought their families rather than leaving them behind in bondage, stripping entire communities of African slaves. According to Fred Fleet's mother, his father reacted badly to their flight. "His negroes all leaving him in such a way has mortified him sadly," she informed him. Others resigned themselves to the loss. Thomas Devereaux of North Carolina agreed with his father that "it only means less to feed." He lamely added, "if they knew what was good for them, they would run the other way when they did run." When Federals came nearby and swept his wife's slaves away, Col. Thomas Rosser of the 5th Virginia Cavalry offered cold comfort. "The loss of servants it is true is a great inconvenience but pshaw before the war is over *all* you have will go and it makes no difference how soon they start." Wealthier families had the option of shifting their slaves to a more remote location in the Confederate interior or across the Mississippi River, but if they did so, the entire family would have to abandon their home, too. Otherwise, so a Confederate officer noted, no one would be around to grow the food.[5]

As the peculiar institution slowly broke down from Union invasion and flight, slaves asserted themselves more frequently and more forcefully. With most adult white males off in military service, a power vacuum developed on farms and plantations. Unless white females or elderly males asserted themselves firmly, slaves filled at least part of the void. Increasingly, some challenged white authority, which generated fear among white civilians. A woman whom a hospital steward knew told him, "She has servants that are not as servants ought to be, and which she acknowledged to fear." In North Carolina, a wife pleaded for her husband to come home. "When Spencer leaves us we will [be] left alone no person to provide or protect us in no respect whatever," she complained. "Dr. Brooks will be the only man any where near us we don't know what will become of the women and negroes I guess they will kill us all up they are cursing the Ladies and abusing some of them now and after the men all leave, it will be worse." In response, her husband advised, "you wrote Something a bout the negroes getting So Sassy to the women my advice to you a bout that when they begin their Slack jaw take something & Shoot Branes & leave them for the dogs to eat." One soldier stationed in Virginia placed four slaves under guard. "It is said that one of them abused a lady and threatened the life of her husband." Cases of slave arson and murder heightened fears among family members of Lee's soldiers. In peacetime, these crimes occurred periodically, but with heightened wartime emotions and concerns, the fear of them—and possibly the fact of them—increased.[6]

The greatest terror among Southern whites, particularly with such a dearth of young and middle-aged males at home, was collective violence through insurrection. Throughout the war, no massive insurrection succeeded, but enough of them occurred to cause panic and to play on the minds of soldiers in the field. A Louisiana artillerist, ultimately bound for Virginia, jotted in his diary before any fighting began, "an alarm of negro insurrection." In late May 1861, an Arkansas soldier passing through Lynchburg, Virginia, commented to his wife, "These people here seem to feel no apprehension on account of the negroes and every thing seems as quiet and as satisfactory as with us. You see no manifestation of alarm." Not so with Mary Smiley, whose brother served in the army in Virginia. Three days after the Arkansas soldier wrote his letter, she reported a rumor to her brother that "a parcel of Irishmen and negroes from the Penitentiary that were working on the railroad had broken out and killed thirteen families." Some of these stories were undoubtedly false. Writing to his father in June 1861, young Virginia private James Langhorne challenged a tale that circulated widely in and out of the army. "That report (and the excitement & fear it occasioned) of 80 white men followed by a large number of negroes that we reported to have recollected in Pulaski [Virginia] and were marauding through the Country & committing all manner of depredations and outrages was the most supremely ridiculous affair I ever heard of," he dismissed. "I am asshamed that the people of the country could have been so hoaxed."[7]

Yet in other cases, the insurrections were real. In Natchez, Mississippi, a slave uprising in late September 1861 resulted in the execution of close to three dozen slaves. Lieutenant William Ker, stationed in Virginia, heard about it and told his sister, "I sincerely hope that the insurrection had been effectually put down, and that, for your sakes and mine, the *trial* may soon be over and everything *quiet* again." He blamed masters for allowing their servants to "run wild" and hoped they would act more responsibly in the future. Eleven days later, he declared to her, "I am sincerely rejoiced to know that the last of the wretches have been hung."[8]

Perhaps the most frightening was the attempted insurrection near Bethany Institute, a young lady's school in Louisiana. According to a young woman with kin in Lee's army, "they had every thing planned and were going to murder the people at nine o'clock, but the gentlemen found it out a few hours before the appointed time and caught some of them." A ringleader among the insurrectionists, who turned out to be a slave hired from a Natchez owner, escaped. Men hunted him with dogs but after more than a week they still had not apprehended him. "We are afraid to go to bed now—" she admitted, "some times we get so excited we can't sleep." One night all the girls intended to sleep together but the school head refused to let them.[9]

Many families faced a more subtle form of rebellion: work slowdowns. The lash drove many slaves to work unceasingly, from before sunrise to sunset. Without this threat, as owners and overseers went off to war, slaves felt they no longer had to work as hard, or they refused to do so. One North Carolina woman wrote Brig. Gen. Johnston Pettigrew, seeking the release of her son from his military commitment. She grumbled that "my Slaves will not work without some man to make them." A Georgia soldier concluded to his mother that their slaves had become more of a burden than an asset. He traced his wartime financial decline to the "presence and expense of an idle, lazy, sickly, deceitful, discontented family of negroes. I believe they have been a sponge to soak up all the substance and increase and profits of a few who have always rendered reluctant, compulsory service."[10]

Under the circumstances, Capt. Henry Owen debated with his wife the idea of selling their slaves in late 1862. He realized it might be the best thing to do, but only if it were absolutely necessary. "I think it a sin and prefer retaining them." South Carolinian J. B. Ligon had his uncle sell his mother's slaves, yet his mother "fretted at the disposition." He reassured her it was in her best interest. "I can't see what on earth you want them with you for," he wrote forcefully. "They have been a perfect nuisance and distraction to you for the last four years." Some preferred that loved ones sell a particular slave who was notoriously difficult to handle. "I've written you and now repeat, sell Peter," a husband in Lee's army directed his wife. He would earn $2,500 in Richmond, and "I do not wish you annoyed, and I am very certain there should be no such negro on a place *in such times.*" A Louisiana soldier recommended his father sell a slave named John, who would cause him too much trouble during the war and might convince other slaves to run off to the Yankees. Captain J. Q. A. Nadenbousch counseled his wife, "if Ellen cuts up much I will bring her here and sell her," despite her pregnancy.[11]

At the same time that slaveholding soldiers advised loved ones to sell their bondsmen and women, others asked parents or wives to extend their warm remembrances to them. The great contradiction of slavery—the notion that enslavement was good for people of African descent as well as for whites—enabled them to express genuine support for both. "Mother, give my love to all the family, white and black, also to enquiring friends," a Texan on Longstreet's staff wrote home. A Virginian asked his wife to "tell the negros I have not forgotten them and they must [not] forget me." Many Confederates perceived their slaves as part of a larger extended family and held them in great affection, while accepting their status as slaves and never challenging it. After writing warm wishes to his wife and children, South Carolina infantryman J. W. Tindall requested that his wife "tel the Negroes to be faithful and pray for their master to be returned back their again and if I neve[r] See the again I want them all to meet me in heaven." Indeed, many slaves did return such affection. A slave named Tom on the farm of Edward Burriss's father sent him Christmas greetings and "wishes you much luck in slaying the Yankees." Burriss's father insisted, "So far they hate the Yankees, & if they ever get in their possession will hate them more."[12]

With centuries of experience at employing slaves for various tasks, the army tapped slave labor almost immediately for defense purposes. In fact, Union policy toward slaves altered early in the war due to slave labor on fortifications. At the end of April 1861, when three slaves slipped away from Rebel lines, stole a small boat, and rowed into Fort Monroe, Union commander Brig. Gen. Benjamin Butler refused to return them. Because the Confederates had employed them on military projects, by international law the slaves were subject to confiscation as contraband of war. As Confederate forces prepared for the spring campaign in 1862, they began to impress slave labor for the erection of works and other military purposes. Magruder announced that he would arrest all citizens who refused to cooperate as "treasonable and disloyal subjects." He tapped black males between sixteen and sixty and put them to work in all sorts of military projects, including road repair.[13]

Various states took the lead in permitting the impressment of slaves, and in late March 1863, the Confederate Congress authorized it. The national legislation established pay scales for them and directed compensation for slaves who died in the line of duty. Still, that did not suppress the cries of owners when they discovered the poor conditions under which their valuable slaves lived or the exposure slaves had to enemy lines, which induced so many to run away to the Yankees. The practice of impressment, moreover, had taken on a life of its own long before state legislatures and Congress acted, with literally thousands of slaves employed in Virginia alone. The army found other valuable service than simply digging ditches, repairing roads, and tossing up works. After the medical fiasco at First Manassas, the secretary of war authorized the medical corps to employ slaves as nurses and cooks, with payment to go to their owners. Demands to maintain and repair railroads also necessitated the use of slave laborers. As the war dragged on into 1863 and 1864, slave and food shortages prevented railroads from keeping their lines in satisfactory running order, particularly when they competed for labor with the army constructing defensive works around Richmond. With the manpower crunch in late 1862, the Army of Northern Virginia began to employ slaves and free blacks as teamsters and in other support positions, which freed soldiers for combat roles.[14]

In concentrated numbers for the first time, these slaves fell ill with a host of maladies, just as whites had done when they first entered military service. Most of them came from rural areas and had little immunity to diseases. Interaction with soldiers who had come through urban areas or from military camps spread smallpox, measles, and other highly contagious illnesses, and contaminated water and food spread dysentery, diarrhea, and typhoid fever. The toll on black slaves, like that on white soldiers early in the war, was astronomical, and slave owners howled in protest.[15]

Most slave and free-black laborers worked for a relatively brief period. They came out to perform specific tasks, such as burial details or work on fortifications. When they completed the project, they returned to their owners. Those who remained with the army for longer stints usually acted as "body servants" to wealthy soldiers. The Confederate army failed to compile statistics on body servants, but when units first came to Virginia, it was not unusual for one in twenty or one in thirty soldiers to have one. In rare instances the ratio was closer to one in ten or twelve. Over time, the number and percentage of body servants declined. The war extended longer than most soldiers predicted, the servants grew homesick, and it appeared for many an unnecessary expense. With extremely valuable slaves near enemy lines, owners risked losing their servant-slaves through capture or escape, and numbers curtailed dramatically. These body servants managed the gear of their owner, cooked meals, cleaned clothing, and helped maintain the horses. On the march, servants often drove wagons and carried weapons. In camp, they performed all sorts of household chores.[16]

Some blacks took to the work well and others failed at it. In early October 1861, a South Carolinian declared, "Spencer is well, and is invaluable to me. I do not believe there is a better servant in the Army than he is, and I do not have any fears of his being deceived by the Yankees." Spencer left behind a wife and children on the farm. Brigadier General Scales had a servant whom he liked very much "but he has no more idea of English language than a cage size monkey." Brigadier General Dorsey Pender's body servant Joe proved unusually enterprising. He not only cared for the general but washed clothing for others, and one day he arrived at headquarters with a new suit of clothing that he had purchased for himself. On the other hand, some body servants cared little for the work and, inevitably, failed miscrably at it. "I am sorry to have it to say but Jack is as worthless a negroe as I ever have seen," pronounced a Virginian to his mother. "If I give him anything to carry he will loose it. The boys are afraid to give him any thing to wash he lost or destroyed a new shirt   The first lot of cloths he had to wash, and he is not fit for nothing at all."[17]

Families chose body servants who had grown up with their soldiers and had developed a strong attachment over the years. Slave owners hoped that if the owner or son became ill or if some tragedy befell him, the servant would remain at his side and care for him. When Fred Habersham died in battle, his body servant waited for family members to arrive, helped show them the location of the grave, and assisted in bringing the body back to Savannah. Two brothers took one of their slaves off to war with them. When one brother became ill, the body servant nursed him until he could go on a sick furlough. The slave then returned to the army to look after the other brother. There, he learned that his master had been killed in action during Seven Days' and he discovered fellow soldiers burying him without a coffin. After grieving, he carried the body to a farmhouse, where he procured a coffin and took him to Richmond for a Christian burial. These slaves had unusual freedom and mobility. They came and went from camp with just a written pass, and often they traveled by train, on foot, or on horseback between the family and the army without white escort.[18]

Wash Wills accompanied his owner's son, George Whitaker Wills, into the war. A highly literate and respected body servant, Wash wrote letters home to his wife and carried news and other items back and forth from the army to home. After Wash got married during the war, he informed Wills that he had to return home regularly. According to Wills, "he can't afford to stay away from his *wife* that long." Whenever his master's son got sick, Wash was there to care for him. In a battle in October 1864, as Wash was returning to the army, Lieutenant Wills was killed in action by a shell. For a while, Wash felt terribly guilty for not having been there, but everyone in the company assured him that Wills died instantly. In a beautifully scripted letter to Wills's brother Richard, Wash also took some consolation that George had embraced religion and carried a

New Testament with him into battle. "I think for the last few months we have enjoyed religion more," Wash wrote Richard, and he always believed that the prayers of others had shielded him in battle. Clearly, Wash and Wills had a very special bond within the confines of the institution of slavery.[19]

Body servants often became homesick. They left wives, children, and parents in bondage, which discouraged them from acting up or from running to the Yankees. While at the front, Abel Crawford's slave Jim unraveled emotionally when he learned that he was losing his girlfriend. He had expected to marry her when he received word that Fannie courted another slave named Peter. "The news she sends here has almost put him crazy," Abel communicated to his wife. Life without his love offered no prospects for Jim. He divulged to his master Abel, "Peter has taken his intended wife, And why not come and take his life." Six weeks later, Jim learned that it was all a hoax, perhaps to get Jim to express his true feelings for Fannie. Jim, in his own hand, poured out his heart to Fannie. "My action must have long since told you that you were very dear to me and I flattered myself that I was not indifferent to you." He finally confessed, "it is useless for me to tell you that I love you." Surely, she could tell. "Tell me Fannie must I love in vain   I hope not." He asked that she write him immediately and "let me know if there is room for me to hope with the utmost anxiety."[20]

Like white soldiers, body servants occasionally acted up in camp, according to their masters, but they also added to the quality of life and to its atmosphere. Thomas Petty, who had left his clerk's job in Washington, D.C., to support the Rebel cause, recorded that a body servant "received a merited drubbing for insolence." Captain Porter King of the 4th Alabama had to quell a nighttime drunken ruckus involving slaves. According to King, he "whipped the negro Bob (laid him across his keg and then burned his whiskey)." In other instances, servants were a source of amusement to pass the time. Some played musical instruments for soldiers' entertainment. Other times, they pulled pranks on fellow servants. A regimental commander's servant collected a band of fellow servants and attacked the quartermaster's servant and his cohorts with corncobs. A large group of soldiers gathered to watch the spirited yet good-natured battle.[21]

Just as injuries and acts of violence occurred among white soldiers in Lee's army, they happened between Confederates and body servants as well. A soldier in the 47th North Carolina accidentally shot and killed a slave during drill. The previous evening, he had performed guard duty and failed to remove the load in his musket. He merely removed the percussion cap. The next day during drill, the officer called "fire," and he aimed at the slave a short distance from him. Apparently, some residual fulminate of mercury ignited the charge when the hammer struck it, and the projectile passed through the slave's neck. At Wayside Hospital in Lynchburg, a black man struck Pvt. William J. Burton in the head with a cleaver after an altercation. According to a witness, "The negro was greatly at fault." The following morning, Burton died, and soldiers in the regiment attempted to lynch the black man. The brigade and regimental commanders had to intervene and convince the soldiers to let the law take its course.[22]

Although the Confederate government did not authorize the arming of blacks as soldiers until 1865, occasionally body servants were caught in the midst of real battles. White soldiers usually depicted their conduct as reflecting the twin contradictions of fundamental loyalty and innate cowardice. An Alabama officer relayed to his sister how he had not seen his body servant Joe for four or five days since the onset of the battle around Suffolk. The servant drew rations for his owner and sent forward cooked meals, but "he says Minie balls and bomb shells are too thick for him." The idea that Joe exhibited good judgment by remaining out of harm's way, particularly when the outcome of the war could work against Joe's best interest, never dawned on his owner. While accompanying his owner into battle, a body servant suffered a severe head wound. For years they could not remove the ball, and when they finally did so nine years after the war, he went totally blind. An Arkansan reported meeting a body servant who came off the field with the Washington Artillery at First Manassas. He had obviously stood by his master for the entire battle and "Seemed proud of his performances." In a small firefight, a body servant shot a Yankee who tried to escape. At New Market Bridge, according to an Alabama private, a servant fired on a Yankee, bringing him to the ground, and proceeded to shoot three more rounds at the enemy soldier. During Seven Days', a Union shirker elected to surrender to the first person who passed by, rather than continue fighting. It turned out to be a body servant. A Georgia lieutenant mentioned it in his regular newspaper column, exclaiming how "Col Cumming's boy 'Tom' brought in a Yankee prisoner!" These instances, however, were very unusual. Much more typical was the case of Neptune, a slave whose owner went down in combat. He rushed onto the battlefield amid heavy fire and brought his lifeless body to safety. He had a longstanding relationship with the soldier and they cared for each other deeply.[23]

With Union lines so very near, hundreds of body servants, like fellow slaves employed elsewhere, slipped away to freedom. A body servant named Matt had the "little impudent ways (to others, not to me) of a *town* darkey," so a North Carolina officer wrote his wife. "I have had to give him several scoldings, which have done him good." Within four months, Matt had run off to the Yankees. Often Confederate owners could not imagine why a slave would flee. A South Carolinian admitted Abram had been "a good boy and a faithful one," but recently he had to administer scolding and a light flogging. He sent Abram across the York River for supplies. Armed with a pass from his owner, Abram took advantage of the proximity of Union forces advancing up the Peninsula and never returned. The officer thought Abram had made a grave, perhaps irreparable error. "I am sorry he was such a fool—" the South Carolinian wrote to his wife, "I'll bet he will always be sorry for it." Sergeant Robert Park's servant also escaped to the Yankees, and his master could not imagine why. He sent Charles off to cook a meal, and the body servant never returned. Park speculated, "My opinion is that he was enticed away or forcibly detained by some negro worshipper, as he had always been prompt and faithful, and seemed much attached to me."[24]

Confederate troops acted vigilantly to prevent slaves from running away, but the same porous lines that enabled Rebel troops to go absent without leave or to desert were tempting to body servants and other slaves. The army attempted to check the migration by retrieving runaway slaves and turning them over to authorities, and at times they picked up large numbers who followed Union troops from the field or pursued cavalry raiders on their return to Yankee lines. A member of A. P. Hill's staff reported the seizure of large numbers of runaways in wagons and carriages, loaded down with plunder from homes, along with some Federal troops. He notified his cousin, "if I had been present at that time not a prisoner would have been taken in a carriage or buggy or with any article of stolen property about them and so help me Heaven I would have carried out my threat." He concluded by adding, "I moreover believe that if I were ever to treat them (the Yankees) kindly again I would be a soldier unworthy to wear the Southern uniform." Even on the trip into Pennsylvania, some Confederate cavalry gathered African-Americans, most of whom were probably free blacks, and took them back into Virginia. Just how many they enslaved was unclear, but an eyewitness claimed the Rebel horsemen were "hunting up the contrabands & driving them off by droves."[25]

The problem of escapes led to a significant decline in body servants, as well as a shift from the use of slaves to the employment of free blacks. Free blacks already had secured their liberty and therefore had little incentive to flee. Prices varied, but generally a free black could command between twenty and forty dollars per month or more to cook (a sum far higher than the amount the government paid enlisted soldiers) and with additional money for laundering, they could double that wage.[26]

The issue of body servants and slaves performing all sorts of functions for Lee's army cut both ways. Slaves could labor in various capacities, from driving wagons to unloading trains and other conveyances. In hospitals, they could work as nurses and laborers to ease the burdens of patients. They could perform the myriad tasks that were essential to maintaining a field army, thereby freeing soldiers to tote weapons in battle, a top priority for Lee as the war entered its third year. And they took care of fundamental chores for soldiers who had fought for a couple of years and had been worn down by the everyday grind of military duty and combat.

At the same time, each black with the army, either free or slave, stressed Lee's logistical network that much more. The Rebel army failed to feed its soldiers and its animals adequately. Blacks with the army required yet more food. For Lee, it was another tug of war for competing resources—slaves would free more musket carriers who would then have to live on even more reduced rations.[27]

The conduct of slaves and body servants with the army, moreover, cut at the heart of soldier motivation. Southern states had seceded from the Union to protect their right to own slaves. They had gone to war to protect the independent government they had established, as well as to defend their homeland. This flight of slaves undermined their belief in faithful bondsmen.

By the opening of the third year of war, the institution of slavery had so severely degraded that it was no longer viable in much of Virginia. The same was true in other Border States. Even if the Confederacy had won its independence in 1864, and Abraham Lincoln had lost the 1864 presidential election, slavery in Virginia might well have been a lost cause. It is hard to imagine that the Union's Senate would have generated the necessary two-thirds vote to ratify a peace treaty that returned slaves freed during the war. The Confederacy could never have conquered the Union and dictated peace terms. The best it could hope for was a negotiated solution that secured its independence. In short, even in the best circumstances for the Confederacy, the massive border to the north and west with the United States would have served as a highway to freedom for Virginia slaves.

Fred Fleet, an enlisted man who rose to brevet second lieutenant in the 26th Virginia Infantry and whose father had owned thirty-four slaves, recognized the collapse of slavery in late 1864. "They have been stolen from their masters and have run away of their own accord, to such an extent that the deficiency can only be supplied by reopening the slave trade, to which our people as a class are bitterly opposed. How then are slaves to be obtained?" he asked. "Surely no one will go South, and buy them at a very high price and bring them here, where they can slip across the border with very little trouble & be free." Fred then closed with the assessment from the former governor of the state, "Genl. [Henry] Wise says slavery is a dead issue here in Va., and his opinion has considerable weight with me."[28]

Rebels had little choice but to shift their rationale for the war. They began to view their independence more and more as the ultimate end. Bitterness over the war had elevated the cause of independence. They would rather live apart from the Union, even with their institution of slavery in tatters. Certainly the Lincoln administration had made it easier by elevating the destruction of slavery to a war aim. As Fleet advised his father, "we are not fighting for them, but for our independence and our very lives."[29]

Chapter 25

COMBAT

THE 18TH VIRGINIA Infantry had occupied a central position in the third-day assault at Gettysburg. One of five regiments in Richard Brooke Garnett's Virginia Brigade of Pickett's Division, the 18th had crossed the Emmitsburg Road, swung around the Codori Farm, and helped storm the critical Union defenses on Cemetery Ridge. All the while, Union artillery gouged huge gaps in the lines. As the 18th rushed up that last modest slope to reach the enemy position, Federals pounded them with waves of canister and musket balls that blunted and then shattered the assaulting lines. Those who fled traveled over no-man's-land and exposed themselves as easy targets. Dead and wounded blanketed the field, and some who remained uninjured hugged the ground until nightfall, when they slipped back to Rebel lines. The 18th had entered the fight with 312 men and suffered 245 losses, or more than three of every four soldiers. It tallied the fifth-highest percentage casualties of any Confederate regiment at Gettysburg.

By the time the regiment returned to camp, it was a faint imitation of its former size and condition. Henry T. Owen, a slaveholder before the war and a captain of Company C, described to his wife grimly, "Some squads are all gone and wide gaps are left between the tents." Two years before, 700 had fought at First Manassas. Only sixty-seven of the 18th recrossed the Potomac River into Virginia uninjured. As Owen gazed over the area that once contained a bustling company campsite, the scattered pockets of soldiers broke his heart. The losses were frightful. To his mind, however, "the saddest sight I have witnessed was that of one of my men who had camped near me and when we came in awhile ago he went and sat down all alone and resting his jaw between his hands presented the most disconsolate picture of distress I ever beheld." One of Pvt. William A. Burke's brothers had already died from smallpox, and "The only messmate he had for a long time and who was with him was his [other] brother and he is reported killed."[1]

Burke had enlisted in Company C along with his brothers, and over the course of prolonged service, the Burkes had forged powerful bonds with other soldiers. This was particularly true of his mess, a group of roughly six men who ate and lived together. Day in, day out, the mess shouldered the burdens and joys of military life together as an extremely close-knit group. With the loss of all the other members of his mess, Burke was now more than alone. He felt isolated. He knew others in the company and regiment, but none so well. In time, messmates came to count on each other as brothers, whether or not they were kin, in every aspect of military service. Now, Burke grieved over more than the fate of his brother. His was the mourning of a lost soul, cut adrift within the army after two years of service. The war had stripped Burke of his brothers, his friends, and the comrades who sustained him in the most harrowing moments of battle.

The cohesion that Burke and his messmates had formed provided reassurance that their comrades would stand alongside them in their time of need. It helped shift the burden of fear from the individual to the group. In battle, fear and chaos could overwhelm the solitary soldier. If he banded together in a larger group that demanded selflessness for the good of the whole, then each individual in that unit established some measure of control. Not only would he have comrades to shield him, but if someone in the group were lost at least the group and its goals would survive.[2]

Yet with his band of brothers destroyed, Burke remained at his post and continued to fight and serve his country. Something supported him more than just his small, cohesive group. In fact, motivations for combat among citizen soldiers were much more complicated, particularly in a democratic republic, than many believe.

Group and personal motivations explain why Civil War soldiers fought and what sustained them in combat. The group category included themes, values, perceptions, or experiences that acted as a cohesive force and served as building blocks for a spirit of camaraderie. Personal motivations consisted of aspects of their character that encouraged and sustained them individually. Virtually all soldiers had at least one of these personal motivations, and some had several of them. In fact, personal and group motivations operated hand in hand, supporting each other, from volunteering through battle to the end of the war.[3]

The foundation for group motivation was support of slavery and a vision of Confederate liberty. Whether they owned slaves or not, Confederate soldiers understood and embraced the ideas that Africans were inferior beings who were ideally suited for slavery; that slavery was a right inherited from their ancestors; that the Founding Fathers had secured that right in the Constitution; and that if Southern whites allowed Northerners to strip them of those liberties, then they were no better than slaves themselves. Confederate soldiers held their society and government in exalted positions, believing that they served as a model for the rest of the world. If their nation died, so would that vision of liberty. Their government was, many Confederates believed, the last hope of free government on earth, and their society was ideally suited to the geography, the climate, the crops they grew, and freedom for whites.[4]

Confederates had formed a new government based on that slaveholding ideology, and the shots fired on Fort Sumter and the secession of the Upper South had evoked an outpouring of patriotism. The population rallied around its government and the flag. Husbands pressured wives to let them enlist; sons pleaded with parents to allow them to join; women shamed loved ones into going. Some young men ran off to the army without parental consent. Women sewed flags; huge crowds lined up along the rail lines to cheer Confederate enlistees bound for the front. All caught the furor of the moment.

While the *rage militaire* ultimately evaporated, that essence of patriotism did not. As Lee's army achieved extraordinary early success, it emerged as a symbol of the nation and fostered a spirit and a patriotism all its own. Men in Confederate society continued to feel a sense of obligation to serve their country, a kind of implicit contract for citizens who reaped the benefits of the best government on earth to assume responsibility to defend it. When the Confederacy invoked conscription, there were no major riots. While there was some resistance, most people accepted the implications of a draft and obeyed the call to arms.

Attachment to loved ones and their homes bound soldiers together as well. Federals were invading their homeland, threatening to destroy all they had worked for and subjecting their families to terror and, quite possibly, brutality or death. Home reflected dreams of hundreds of thousands of young men, some of whom had left their mark on their community but many who had not. Home represented a quality of life; the product of love, hard work, economic opportunity, and freedom; and the virtues and values to which they aspired and genuinely believed the war put at risk. Even slaves were part of that home and larger family.[5]

Closely related to images and defense of home were perceptions of manhood. All humans seek to protect loved ones and their community from invasion and destruction, but Southern culture promoted concepts of masculinity that demanded they embrace honor. In the face of hardship and even death, society expected a man to perform his duty with dignity and courage. After three years of tough service, an exhausted Confederate soldier confessed that sometimes he "would almost welcome the bullet which would terminate so much trouble," but to do so, to quit like that, would be an "unmanly" act.[6]

Hatred of the enemy, a powerful emotion among both armies, also helped to unite men. In the eyes of Southerners, Union troops became tyrants, hirelings, Hessians, mercenaries whose object was to suppress the rights of Southerners and to destroy all that they had worked for. "I certainly love to live to hate the base usurping vandals," admitted a North Carolinian. "If it is a Sin to hate them; then I am guilty of the unpardonable one."[7]

These five elements—a slaveholding ideology, patriotism, attachment to loved ones and home, perceptions of manhood, and hatred of the enemy—united prewar and wartime experiences to establish a Confederate culture. That new culture formed building blocks for a spirit of camaraderie among Lee's men.

In wartime, society called on people to act in ways that were unthinkable for most people in peacetime: killing people and destroying property. This Confederate culture and the comradeship it engendered elevated the group above the individual and displaced much of the guilt inherent in this violence. The sounds, the smells, the sights, and the emotions of a battle overwhelmed individuals, but the group sustained them through all its harrowing moments. A soldier's comrades buttressed him emotionally and physically. He could count on his comrades to look out for him, to protect him from their enemies, to care for him if he were wounded, and to comfort him in his final moments of life. If he died, at least the group would live.[8]

The Confederacy recruited most military units from specific localities. Enlistees knew one another before the war, sometimes from childhood. In some instances, a bond had already formed, as it had among the Burke brothers; in other cases, prewar acquaintances or even strangers evolved into wartime comrades. The fact that they came from the same area and state, that the home community embraced them collectively, that outsiders often saw them as one, promoted cohesion. This local tie also acted as a coercive element, compelling men to behave according to the group norm lest the embarrassing word drift back to the home front.

Training and discipline, too, promoted camaraderie. Although officers drilled troops in tactical maneuvers to develop mastery for the battlefield, marching promoted esprit de corps, a pride in the unit that strengthened cohesion. The more they practiced together, the stronger they bonded as a unit; the more proficient they became, the greater the pride they formed for their regiment, battery, or company. Discipline, too, promoted the group by forcing men to keep in line with the rest, preventing any variation, and suppressing or stifling the spirit of individualism. Eventually, officers hoped that training in tactics and discipline would bond the men to one another and assist them to perform their duty in combat.

Through the process of sharing all of these motivations, the army forged a group from solitary soldiers. They helped to create bonds that sustained troops collectively throughout their military service. Yet several other factors motivated individual soldiers: a spirit of adventure, a desire to test one's character in battle, and a reckoning with death. In each instance, though, these personal motivations worked in conjunction with Confederate culture.

A search for adventure had lured many individuals into military service. A twenty-mile circle with their home at the center defined the universe of many Civil War soldiers. The pace of their world was comfortable yet slow. Young men ached for excitement. When the war broke out, few could resist. More than just viewing new sights, soldiers sought the ultimate adventure, combat. They wanted to "see the elephant," as the Civil War generation referred to their initial glimpse of battle. Usually, after a few battles, the novelty wore off, but quite a few loved that thrill of a heightened state of awareness in battle. Combat offered perverse pleasure. A South Carolinian on a reconnaissance party caught some Yankee troops in a surprise flank attack. After the firefight, he crowed to his sister, "I never enjoyed my self so much in a Battle as I did on this occasion." Another soldier described the banter after battles among those who had narrowly escaped. "It is fun to tease them when they are not hurt," he explained. Still another expressed his exhilaration when he told a fellow soldier, "the excitement of battle was glorious: that it flowed like good wine through the veins and roused all his manhood."[9]

Many wanted to test their character in battle. Did they have what it took to stand up and perform under stress? Since youth, many of these men had read and heard tales about battle. Some men of great peacetime standing shrank under fire, while some of lesser stature at home underwent wondrous changes.

The final personal factor that helped encourage men to enlist, supported them throughout their service, and fortified them in combat was a reckoning with death. Not only did Lee's soldiers fall in frightful numbers on the battlefield, they died in almost the same proportions from illness. Close to one in every four soldiers in Lee's army lost their lives. The survivors could not avoid facing death. Some relied on their trust in God's will. They prayed for the salvation of their souls and conceded that if God decided it was their time, so be it. Others embraced simple fatalism. When it was their time, they would die, and nothing they could do would prevent it.

Most men on the Rebel side entered military service in the belief that they were doing God's work. A Georgian asserted to his sister, "Had I not implicit confidence in the justice of our cause, and the final success of our arms[, I] would feel very badly; but knowing the Lord will do right, can face the cannons mouth, and feel that the Lord will watch every one of us, and if it is his will I should die here, can die, like a hero expecting a happy reunion with friends and relatives where there is no war." Through camp life, on the march, and in battle, God sustained them. Those who survived the diseases that roared through camp or who made it through combat when comrades all around them fell could imagine no other reason than God's will. "I have frequently asked myself the question when I have seen men fall near me why that ball or that shell did not strike me," a junior officer pondered. He concluded that "God preserves me for some wise purpose" or "it may be in answer to your prayers." After participating in some desperate combat, a Virginia private surmised, "if god had not been present all of us would have been killed." By surrendering their lives to God's will, the soldiers released control and with it an enormous burden from their shoulders. Another Virginian placed his complete faith in God's will. "Don't be uneasy Mother God has spared me so far for some wise purpose. If it be his will all the bullets of the Yankees can't hurt me. If he has decreed otherwise I could not die in a better cause & at best we all have it to do sooner or later a few days or years make little difference."[10]

Some puzzled over God's ways. One soldier, deeply religious himself, was baffled by their behavior. "I see men, wicked, profane, and depraved go in and fight bravely, too," he wrote. "I don't understand it." For those with weaker faith, fatalism could be deeply pessimistic. Some presumed that they would die and stopped worrying. A Virginia corporal admitted to his cousin in late March 1863 that "I never expect to live to see the end of this war" and therefore "I could face death or the Cannon's mouth with as much indifference as I eat my beef and bread." He was right: He did not survive it. Others simply assumed that when it was their time, they would be killed. "He who falls today is only a few hours before him who falls tomorrow," a captain philosophized. A Virginian revealed his assessment to his aunt: "No one knows, when he rises in the morning, whether he will see noon." A fight might erupt at any time and take men's lives. "Such is the uncertainty attending the soldier in time of war." They would be good soldiers and take sensible precautions while fulfilling their duty. There was no reason to be reckless with their lives, but they would die someday, and it might as well be soon.[11]

LEE'S MEN WENT through a typical progression of feelings over the course of the war, from worry and excitement, to shock, to cooler thinking, to, often, cynicism, and for some fear and desertion. In anticipation of their first exposure to combat, soldiers confessed all sorts of worries. They had unusual images of what it would be like, drawn from readings and conversations with veterans of previous wars and very early battles. A Virginia lieutenant naïvely assumed that the Confederacy would fight a giant battle in late May 1861. "When we do have one it will (in my opinion) be a most desperate one—a hand to hand fight," he predicted. On the verge of First Manassas, a staff officer with Stonewall Jackson imbued with deep religious convictions wrestled with the conflict between fulfilling his obligation to the Confederacy and killing a fellow human being. "God knows if a stern duty ever compels me to take a human life," he worried. "I shall not feel like exulting over it." Colonel Dod Ramseur took his 49th North Carolina Infantry north to join in the Seven Days' fight. After only two months of training, he admitted confidentially to his brother, "I do not put much confidence in my men." The West Point graduate then explained, "They look scared & anxious." The regiment fought on the periphery of the battle, and twice it was exposed to enemy fire. Compared with the devastating experience for other Rebel units, it was a gentle introduction to warfare, and his regiment behaved credibly under fire.[12]

In that first fight, distinctive images became embedded in the minds of the soldiers. Launcelot Blackford came under rifled artillery fire, and he admitted to his mother, "It was about the first time I had ever heard them coming toward me, and though I was not I believe unduly discomposed, I thought all the while that I should be very glad when it was over." A Louisiana lieutenant received his baptism by fire at Yorktown, and artillery loomed largest in his immediate memory as well. "I think the most unpleasant remembrances of the Strife are these same *schrapnell shot*," he declared to his mother. "They get to us some seconds before the report of the powder that sent them so that the first thing we know of them [is] a shrill whistle unlike any thing you or I ever heard, before, then, the sharp bell-like crack of the bomb—the whistle of the little balls like bumble-bees—then the report of the Gun." It all came so close together, though, that "it takes a very *fine ear* to distinguish which is first." Georgia infantryman Eli Landers also tasted his first battle on the Peninsula. "It did not frighten me as bad as I expected," he revealed, "but I tell you the bullets would whistle around my head I felt sort of ticklish." Two days later, the Yankees attacked again, and this time "the bullets sung round our heads like mad bees."[13]

As soldiers gained more experience, they kept cooler heads before battle and acted more systematically. If they had time, they inspected their weapons, wiped off any moisture, and examined their cartridges to ensure they were in good condition. Frequently, the corps or division commander reminded them to remain cool, take proper aim, and obey orders. Occasionally, a company commander would threaten them with execution on the spot if they ran. In time, they developed good composure before the fight, and when troops entered combat, they hardened to its sights and sounds. "I have changed much in my feelings," Hill Fitzpatrick wrote his wife, Amanda, after Second Manassas. "The bombs and balls excite me but little and a battlefield strewed with dead and wounded is an every day consequence." They were fast becoming veterans.[14]

A perceptive Mississippi private informed a young woman that "a battle is really indescribable." He explained that it "is a living moving speaking thing and that without the combination of these parts you cannot make a battle." All the battles within a battle, its thousands of events that composed the whole, extended far beyond the sight and comprehension of a solitary being. Nor were battles ever the same. A Georgia private at Fredericksburg informed family members that "the bullets run a round my head like hornettes." South Carolina officer James Nance, who had fought at First Manassas and then on the Peninsula, attempted to describe the fight at Seven Pines to a loved one. "I was never so much reminded of a hail storm in my life," he wrote her. "The grape and canister striking in the trees and all around us, reminding me of the hail and the flash of the shell and the report from its bursting answering respectively for the lightning and thunder." The booms of cannon, the loud pop of musketry, roaring cheers, shouts of anguish, much of it concealed from view by monstrous, lingering clouds of soft gray smoke, overloaded the human senses. There seemed to be no way for an eyewitness to order it. Yet from the chaos emerged some clarity. "Have you ever imagined a battle field and its vicinity—the throng of men hurrying to & fro—the trains of wagons and artillery passing and repairing apparently in inextricable confusion[?]" one of Stuart's staff officers questioned his wife. "All is bewildering to the spectator. And yet how strange that one man's mind should control all and bring desired results from this chaos of war. At intervals there is a perfect calm, and you might imagine all over, when suddenly the whole heavens reverberate with clamor of the contending hosts."[15]

Battlefield confusion spawned all sorts of disastrous and demoralizing events. On numerous occasions, Confederates fired unwittingly on their own men. Early in the war, nervousness among untrained troops wearing a multitude of uniforms prompted soldiers to fire first and identify later, inflicting some heavy losses within their own ranks. In a panicky state, some soldiers in Cobb's Legion unleashed a volley into the 3rd Virginia Cavalrymen. Private Thomas French had his blanket riddled with bullets and his reins cut. His comrade Pvt. Benjamin Blanton was not so fortunate. "Blanton had two musket balls entirely through his right leg.—1 near thigh joint grazing his bags & end of penis & 1 through the calf of his leg." The eyewitness reported, "He will be quite ill—and may die." Blanton survived, but he never returned to active duty. This was an unusually skittish command, and men in Cobb's Legion had also killed their major and a private and wounded one of their captains in separate incidents as they returned from posting pickets. At Chancellorsville, North Carolinians shot Jackson and some of his staff. Two months later, Yankees had captured some men in the 23rd North Carolina when a Confederate column approached and fired into the mass of gray and blue. A North Carolinian lost his best friend in the barrage. Other times, soldiers fired on civilians who unintentionally wandered into dangerous situations or got caught in the middle of a battle. Pickets shot an elderly fellow who approached Rebel lines. "They com'd [commanded] him to halt and as he was an old man did not notice it and they shot him," reported a North Carolina private. During the course of the Battle of Chancellorsville, as some Yankees retreated, Confederates poured shot and shell into a house. When they reached the house, "it was distressing to hear the cries of the inmates," a Floridian detailed, "the lady of the house had been shot in-to, her head severed from her body. A younger woman, seemingly her daughter, was perfectly frantic and in her fright had run off & lost her two little children." When soldiers observed the scene, "blood boiled in every man," and they placed full blame on the Yankees for taking cover in a home with civilian occupants.[16]

Soon, the specter of entering combat again hung heavily over the heads of soldiers. They would fight for the cause and for their comrades—it was their duty, and their honor and manhood rested on the execution of that duty—but they dismissed the foolishness of early days, when they had talked boldly and behaved with absurd bravado. Veterans had seen too much death and destruction not to dread the coming of the next fight. Twenty-year-old Georgian William H. Norwood informed a loved one in January 1863, "Camp life is a happy life if there was no fighting to do but fighting is very unpleasant thing to do." During the raid into Pennsylvania later that year, Sambo Short alerted his wife, "We are in the enemys country & expect to do some hard fighting soon I hope & trust to god not, I don't wish to Kill any of them & don't want to be killed." A North Carolinian missed the Battle of Fredericksburg because he had no shoes, and his colonel left all barefoot men in the rear until the quartermaster procured some for them. "I can tell you I was glad then that my shoes did not come becaus I would rather loose a hundred dollars than to go in a battle," he admitted to his parents. Although these men hated the idea of returning to battle, they obeyed orders and fought, with the exception of the North Carolinian who had permission to remain in the rear.[17]

Many others, however, failed to meet their soldierly obligations. Virtually every regiment and battery, no matter how well they usually fought, fled from the battlefield at least once. Whether they ran in panic or rushed to the rear and reorganized quickly—a somewhat controlled yet hasty retreat—over the course of a long war circumstances sometimes required men to retreat pell-mell because the enemy had crashed through their line or had suddenly penetrated their rear and they were on the verge of capture. Sensible judgment underlay those desperate acts. But there were also individuals and sometimes groups in every regiment who failed to meet their obligations to their comrades and shirked to the rear.

Two factors motivated soldiers to cowardice: Either they had an unusually low threshold for stress and could not stand the pressure of combat, or they failed to bond significantly with their comrades to disperse the fear of battle and to rely on others for their protection. A lieutenant colonel recorded the travails of a soldier in his regiment in their first fight, who was "shooting wildly nearly straight up" in Seven Days'. According to the officer he feigned illness for the rest of the campaign. In fact, the stress of combat proved too much for the soldier. His erratic battlefield behavior was uncontrollable, and his illness may have been very real—a reaction to stress. Another private received clemency in his general court-martial for cowardice because the court deemed him "a man of such ignorance and weakness of intellect," suggesting he was too ignorant to withstand the stress of the fight.[18]

In other instances, soldiers failed to bond effectively with the other men. This proved particularly true if they entered battle without proper drill. Since such soldiers had little confidence in their comrades, they were more likely to run or shirk their duty. In the 4th Virginia, a captain ran from the field at First Manassas, the only officer in the regiment who did not act gallantly. Somehow, he managed to survive the black mark and served satisfactorily in the regiment throughout the battles of 1862, when he transferred to the Quartermaster's Department. A Virginia cavalryman conveyed his disdain for some of the men in his regiment when he wrote home, "Tell Mammy that I have seen a good many fellows that seem to have pains like her when they hear bad news, especially the words 'Charge!' or 'prepare to fight on foot, dismount,' You can then see some fellows trying to sneak off, but the old major is generally up with them." Numerous regiments had a policy that barefoot men did not have to fight. When an officer learned that soldiers had tossed away their shoes to escape battle, he exploded in rage to his wife. "I never dreamed that such cowardly, base, heartless, vile, covetous, despicable wretches breathed the breath of life & the air of heaven, until I saw their vile qualities developed in this war."[19]

In most regiments soldiers slipped off to the rear, where they banded in groups. A Georgian grumbled that "there were many in all companys as well as ours, that fell out of ranks to keep out of the fight and it has been the case all the time." A regimental commander kept track of the sizable number of shirkers in his regiment, amounting to roughly one in every ten. At a fight during the Peninsula Campaign, Capt. Henry Owen complained, "Some of my men acted most shamefully and deserted me early in the action, but the large portion of the company stood manfully up and fought desperately." A South Carolinian was dismayed by those who ran from the fight without proper cause. "Some of them are men who you would think wouldn't be guilty of such a thing," he asserted to his wife. Just like the men who remained in battle, these soldiers collected in groups and fortified one another's decision to straggle by offering words of comfort or justification to remove the guilt. Nearly always, they devised some tale to cover their conduct: They were stunned by a shell, their weapon was damaged, or they helped a wounded man to the rear. Some even claimed to have sustained injuries, although their bodies exhibited no marks.[20]

The most unusual cases of soldiers' dodging combat were those who regularly fought well. Some of them derived pleasure from the adventure and novelty of combat. These men tended not to bond well with fellow soldiers; the spirit of adventure and the quest for action motivated them. Because they did not fight to protect their comrades, when they got tired or no longer felt like engaging with the enemy, they simply quit. A North Carolinian recorded his role at the Battle of Cedar Mountain in a very matter-of-fact way. He fired seven shots at the Yankees, but when the order came to charge, he elected not to go, "in consequence of an almost intolerable or unindurable thirst." He got some water and then sat down and watched the battle without an ounce of guilt or remorse. When the fight ended, he had enough energy to rummage the battlefield for booty, and he also had a strong enough stomach to draw water from a creek that ran red with blood from the fight. Other times, good soldiers with strong combat records had simply dry-tapped the well of self-discipline. The physical demands of the campaign or the stress of huge battle after huge battle proved too much. Some may have dodged death so many times that they could not imagine doing it one more time, and they fell out. If they had just had some rest, many of them probably would have revived their exhausted bodies and minds and performed their duty well again.[21]

Most soldiers who shirked combat duty escaped punishment, if not scorn, from fellow soldiers. When they were caught, punishment varied dramatically. Some officers had no patience for cowards, while others used public humiliation as the best means of behavioral adjustment. In the 8th Alabama, a private deserted his comrades on the field of battle repeatedly, and a court-martial ordered his execution. A firing squad also shot a soldier in the 12th Virginia for cowardice at Bristoe Station. According to a fellow soldier in the regiment, "the poor fellow seemed little concerned." When a lieutenant committed the same offense, running in the face of the enemy, the regimental commander offered him the choice of resigning or facing a court-martial. In a North Carolina regiment, a cowardly sergeant was thrashed with the blunt end of the brigade commander's sword. The sergeant then ran away temporarily. As punishment for his crimes, the general "wants him published in the news papers & that he give him a whipping with his sword." In the 3rd North Carolina, a soldier had his head shaved and they drummed him around camp every day for thirty days with a big sign that read "coward." A Florida officer tired of threatening a soldier to get him into a fight, and he transferred him to the Commissary Department, where he could do the Confederacy some good.[22]

To avoid combat, soldiers went to unusual lengths, frequently with dire physical consequences. One man was caught behind a tree swinging his arms out wildly from behind it, hoping one of them would get hit. When an officer questioned him about it, he confessed to "'feeling for a furlough.'" Much more serious was the conduct of several individuals in commands that replaced Pickett's Division after Gettysburg. "Some few white Livered Gentry who didn't want to go—shot themselves in the hand, one poor fool picked up an axe & deliberately cut his foot half in two, from the effects of which he soon died," reported a soldier to a friend.[23]

Nothing galled those men who had fought in various battles like accusations or rumors at home that they had dodged combat. The hometown communities buzzed with tales, often false or exaggerated, of how local men measured up in combat. When Rawley Martin's cousin heard that he had behaved badly, she severed their communications. He did not blame her. "You very properly determined you would have nothing to do with a coward," but he insisted that the scuttlebutt was untrue. A soldier on furlough spread false stories about Eli Landers, accusing him of misconduct before the enemy. Landers was furious. He discharged his duties well, and it hurt him that a brother soldier would tell lies about him. He told his mother to check with his officers or any of the other men home on furlough and they would tell her he was a good soldier. "He has never been in but one fight," Landers rebutted his accuser, "but if he don't give me satisfaction when he comes back I think he will be in another one!" Soldiers were very sensitive about their reputation and, like Landers, defended them aggressively, as any man of honor would.[24]

After the war, a perceptive army surgeon commented of his comrades-in-arms in a journal article, "While their intrepidity is displaying itself in deeds of the most exalted courage it can, in the twinkling of an eye, collapse into the most abject cowardice." He attempted to remind his readers that these were human beings, with finite capacities to withstand stress, hunger, cold, heat, hardships, and distractions back home. Even the best-developed and steadiest soldiers were mortal and subject to lapses. Yet day after day, tens of thousands of men in Lee's army performed their duty in battle skillfully, and sometimes heroically. Their ability to stand and fight against overwhelming numbers of well-drilled Federals with superior weapons and resources in so many battles demonstrated their extraordinary prowess and motivation.[25]

Some select individuals conducted themselves with extraordinary bravery, earning the lasting acclaim of fellow soldiers. According to a friend, Pvt. Dan Murphy was a terror in battle, a free spirit who fought with reckless abandon. He was "most conspicuous in daring & a don't care sort of bravery—Dan laid a good many of the Yanks low." Dan also led the charge when it came to collecting Yankee plunder. "I believe he made it a rule to rifle the pockets of every yank he came across," his friend reported to his brother. "He got $6.00 in specie out of one fellows pocket & an excellent pair of buckskin gloves from another—besides taking a dutch Yankee prisoner." Another soldier wrote home of Pvt. L. Chuck Parrish of the 21st Virginia Infantry, who had not distinguished himself in civilian life but, to the surprise of his acquaintance from home, "certainly fought heroically—as few men fight—cooly & calmly." Every shot he fired had a telling effect: "*I donot believe he threw away a Single Shot.*" When he observed a comrade shoot wildly, he challenged the fellow, "damn you what are you wasting your ammunition for. Why don't you shoot at something." Parrish was killed in action at Second Manassas.[26]

The army gave preferential treatment to outstanding combat soldiers. In general courts-martial, Lee remitted or reduced sentences for soldiers who had earned good records of combat service. In mid-1863, the War Department had companies vote for men to receive badges of distinction in combat. Lee then had to fight to ensure that the government actually issued the badges because they conveyed such status in his army. When Hill Fitzpatrick reported to his wife, Amanda, that the company had voted one for him, he admitted, "I shall be right proud of it as a relic of the past and will try to preserve it for my little soldier boy." In other instances, officers recommended soldiers for promotions on the basis of service in combat. Private Robert Tyler Jones, the grandson of President John Tyler, of the 53rd Virginia grabbed the regimental standard at Gettysburg and boldly carried it forward until he fell unconscious from wounds to the head and arm. A soldier in the 25th South Carolina announced to his wife that three privates and two sergeants had been promoted to lieutenant for gallantry. "This has a powerful influence on the men & makes them all anxious to excel."[27]

A very different form of courage was required of men who were not calm under pressure. They feared battle terribly, yet remained at their posts and performed their duty as good and responsible soldiers. In effect, they fought two intense battles, one against themselves and another against the enemy. Caught in an artillery crossfire, Pvt. Pegram Ward admitted to his cousin, "*what a hot place it was, too hot for Pegram, & scared almost out of his sences; but I believe he stood at his post, or rather layed to it.*" He had never hugged the ground so closely in his life. He felt each shell burst overhead, and on every explosion "the ground would gaive way a little." Despite the anxiety, he stayed with his comrades. Virginia corporal Leroy Edwards advanced in an attack during the Battle of Chancellorsville alongside a soldier "who has never been remarkable for his courage." He cried out that the enemy had fired on them from the flank. His comrade tried to reassure him with a cavalier retort, "'I suppose they are and you will get more yet when you get up the hill." The captain, too, sought to compose the soldier by replying calmly. The shaken soldier continued to advance, but his fear was apparent to everyone. "I felt sorry for the poor, white faced coward, and then tried to cheer him up, but at the time his whining cowardice was disgusting," Edwards commented. A North Carolinian noted to his wife that a friend of theirs was so frightened in combat that he soiled his pants, but unlike a number of others, he did not run. "I perceived that his pants is little stained," he elaborated, "But I think that he had washed them since the Battle."[28]

At one time or another virtually every soldier who spent time in Lee's army had narrow escapes in combat. These were such close calls that they left the near victim, as an Alabamian quipped, "Mortally scared to death." A North Carolina infantryman reported to his sister that only kindly God could have protected him in battle, "I had 14 holes shot through my blanket 2 through my over coat and one through my jacket. But by the help of that just God who ruleth all things," he conceded, "I escaped unscratched." At Fredericksburg, a solid shot passed within six inches of an Alabama soldier's thigh. "Boo! It makes my hair stand upon ends to think of it," he admitted to his sister. In the same fight, staff officer Sandie Pendleton had a ball pass through his overcoat and undercoat and strike a knife in his pocket. "It saved my life as the ball would have gone through the groin, & fractured the hip joint," he detailed to his mother. "I am very stiff, & horribly bruised." Corporal Edwards, who so sharply criticized the behavior of a fearful comrade, was taking aim at a Yankee when the fence before him splintered. His rifle dropped from his hands, "followed by a *most disagreeable sensation* in a *most delicate* part of the body," he wrote. "I was satisfied that a *part* of one of my members was gone." He looked down and saw gaping holes in his britches and drawers. In a panicked state, he examined himself further and determined that he was uninjured. He could not contain his delight, announcing "imagine my joy when I found that I was not damaged, though much enfeebled."[29]

In the course of battle, substantial numbers of soldiers in Lee's army fell into Yankee hands. Some 16 percent, slightly fewer than one in every six soldiers, was captured before the final surrender. The single largest loss, at Gettysburg, totaled around 12,000. Nearly 7,000 of those were wounded troops whom the Confederacy could not remove from the field. Although Lee's army lost significant additional prisoners at Bristoe Station, Spotsylvania, in May 1864, and elsewhere, the losses only faintly resembled those at Gettysburg, until the final three weeks of the war. Federals imprisoned Lee's men at various locations. Early in the war, quite a number were held at Fort Warren in Boston Harbor. In time, Federals established large prison camps at Capitol Prison in Washington, Point Lookout in Maryland, Fort Delaware in the Delaware River, and Elmira, New York. Some even ended up at Johnson's Island in Ohio.[30]

After the war, Confederates levied charges of starvation and brutality, partly in response to reports of the horrible conditions that Yankees endured at Andersonville, Georgia. During the war, rumors had circulated throughout the Confederacy of deliberately harsh treatment. Contemporary soldiers' testimony, however, indicated that Lee's soldiers expected worse. No doubt, the limited diet and minimal exercise weakened resistance, and dense populations promoted the spread of disease. And in some instances, particular guards or Union officers treated them shabbily. But on the whole, Confederate prisoners grumbled comparatively little over the Spartan lifestyle in Yankee camps. "No doubt you think this is a very horrible place to live," a Virginian imprisoned at Fort Warren wrote in mid-July 1862, "but on the contrary we have very comfortable quarters and excellent food and are allowed the liberty of the Island." In early July 1863, a soldier complained that at Fort Delaware, which the Yankees built on a low, marshy island, "the stench is intolerable," but a year later, an artillerist declared to his uncle that "[I] have not found imprisonment near as hard as I expected." A North Carolinian declared to his wife in October 1863, "The reports that have been circulated in the South in regard to 'Yankee Cruelty' to prisoners &c &c. are all false, as far as my observation extends."[31]

Living conditions tended to be satisfactory during the warmer months and a little less so during the winter, particularly at prison camps farther north. Food was no worse than in Lee's army, and prisoners at Point Lookout and Fort Delaware could supplement it with seafood. Clothing, again, was poor, but as a cavalryman noted in February 1865, "At the end of the Maryland & Pen. Campaigns I was worse off & more ragged than to day." Soldiers could receive care packages from friends who were Northerners, and greenbacks often allowed them to purchase items. One officer even received money from his colonel's old body servant, who had fled to the Yankees. For those who became ill or the wounded who fell into Federal hands, medical care, largely inadequate for Civil War soldiers, was superior in the Union. As one prisoner wrote his father in 1864, "I think the sick get much better medical attention than they ever did in Dixie."[32]

The greatest enemy that Confederates in prison camps battled was boredom. Day after day, they lounged, slept, ate, and talked to the same people, over and over again. Some turned to religion, which offered structured activities and relieved the burden of the unknown. Others started schools or began to publish prison camp newspapers. The *Fort Delaware Prison Times* and the *Lee Club Gazette* offered facetious news, announcements of various clubs and activities, and even advertisements. The *Fort Delaware Prison Times* avowed its intention to "keep our readers posted upon all incidents in our little world." When the *Lee Club Gazette* released its columns, the rag vowed to "afford the prison public a periodical which may serve in some slight degree to enliven by its novelty if in no other way the ennui of the hours spent here."[33]

Still, the inescapable boredom wore down prisoners. "Time rolls hevily away here," a Virginia cavalryman commented to his wife, "I get very low spirited sometimes." He thought, "if I could look forward to any time of getting to Dixie I would be in better spirits." In his case, the infrequency of mail from home compounded his loneliness, convincing him "the community cares not." A South Carolina lieutenant reported the words of a comrade who said, "he would rather be a negroes dog at home than to be here" at Point Lookout. Another soldier, this one at Johnson's Island, simply resigned himself to his predicament. "I believe we are in prison for the war, & altho' I had rather lose a limb & be free, I see now no alternative, not have I for some time," he admitted to his brother.[34]

When Federals broke off prisoner exchanges over unfair treatment of black soldiers by Confederates, it cut the heart out of prisoners. Other than swearing the oath of allegiance to the United States or escaping, which offered slim possibilities, prisoner exchanges were their only means out. Later in the war, the Union revived the cartel, and the warring sides swapped thousands of soldiers, but in most cases, men were so weak that they failed to return to the ranks before the war ended. For those lucky few thousand, though, it was a time of exhilaration. "Thank God I am free!" trumpeted an Alabamian in March 1865. Despite his illness, he felt as deeply committed to the Confederacy as ever before. "For Dixie I have fought, bled and suffered imprisonment, and for Dixie I am ever ready to die," he reaffirmed to his father. "I assure you the happiest moment of my life was when I stepped on Confederate soil at Savannah, welcomed by the ladies who thronged the wharf," pronounced a prisoner of ten months to a loved one.[35]

So MANY BORE the scars of combat for their remaining years. North Carolina officer William G. Morris got shot at Fredericksburg "through my Left Yeare." He declared to his wife it was not a serious wound, although "I was as bloodey as a Hog." In the end, Morris took the wound in stride, suggesting, "I Doon Not Like to Beare old abes Mark but am thankfull to God that it is no worse." At Chancellorsville, a Georgia enlisted man had two balls graze him and a piece of shell struck him on the upper arm near the shoulder, he explained to his parents. On the battlefield, he had a friend cut it out with a knife and he continued to fight. The soldier refused to permit his name to enter the wounded list, "lest you might see my name in the papers before I had an opportunity of writing, which of course would have caused you a great deal of mental anxiety." Artillery private Allison Spikes suffered a serious wound, but was not hit by a lead projectile. At Cold Harbor in 1864, a Union cannon ball struck the breastworks, knocking off a rail, which struck him in the back and head and injured him so severely that the surgeons hospitalized him for six weeks.[36]

But at least they survived. The final truth about war concerns its dead, and the Civil War killed more than 620,000 men. Some 50,000 came from Lee's army. Private John Futch of the 3rd North Carolina was with his brother when Charley fell at Gettysburg. On the second day, Charley was shot in the head and "suffered Mity Bad before he died" the next day. John toted his brother from the field and never left his side until he expired. "I am at a grate lost since I lost

Charley," he revealed to his wife, "tal I am all Most crasey." John Futch did not survive the war, either. Private Casper W. Boyd came from a wealthy slaveholding family and hoped to become a doctor. He took a liking to military service and thought highly of the officers and men in the 15th Alabama, although he was "shocket by the wicket othes that my fellow soldiers role out." His greatest pleasure, though, was reading the Bible. On the Sabbath, he liked to take a stroll with Bible in hand to some meadow, "where I have no one to desterbe me there I try to worship God in my umble way." At the Battle of Cross Keys, he suffered a critical wound in his side. Despite faltering health, he dictated a final letter to his parents. He urged them not to worry or feel unhappy, "that I am with friends who care for me." If he did die, he reassured his mother, they would meet in another world, "where all is *love, peace* & happiness—There no hearts will be *made sad*, and tears of sorrow shed." His faith in God comforted him through his last hours.[37]

Amid the deep sorrow over the loss of family and friends, there were occasional moments of utter joy that helped ease the blow of losses. At Chancellorsville, a soldier was among many in the 44th Georgia who became separated from his command in the flank attack. When the fighting ceased, everyone in his company presumed he was dead. It took him a couple of hours afterward to locate his comrades. "Just hear let me say to you, that I never seen in all my life, So much rejoicing, as we did over the different men and parts of the companies, as we came up to the reg[iment]," a soldier wrote his friends. "Some of the officers and men gave me a good old fashion hug. Which was reciprocated by me with all my heart."[38]

Out of concern for human decency and for genuine health reasons, soldiers had to pitch in and bury the dead soldiers and animals that often covered the ground of the Civil War's great battlefields. This work was not only disagreeable, at times it proved to be dangerous as well. Unexploded shells littered the battlefield; pestilence from decay spread quickly, contaminating soldiers and their water supply. Confederates usually dug graves a few feet deep for their own men; for Yankees, they merely tossed some dirt over them. In time, it was not unusual for hogs and other animals to root up Federal bodies and scavenge them.[39]

If a victim's friends discovered his body, they usually made a coffin and buried it after a brief, private ceremony in the rear. As in the case of Lt. Fred Habersham, the bodies of officers or wealthy soldiers who died early in the war were more likely to have their corpses shipped home. During the fourth year of the war, as the tally of dead rose dramatically, metallic coffins for shipping bodies became more difficult to obtain, and fewer families could bring home their loved ones for burial. In a hurtful act that illustrates the inferior status of enlisted men, Brig. Gen. Joseph B. Kershaw requested that Pvt. Charles Kerrison escort the bodies of four officers back to South Carolina, but Kerrison was not allowed to bring home the body of his own brother, a mere private.[40]

At first, soldiers exhibited considerable anguish over deceased friends and acquaintances and some squeamishness about dead soldiers in general. One of Longstreet's staff officers informed his sister, "You have no idea of how one feels when he sees persons cold in death on the field, or being borne away wounded with whom a few hours before he was talking & laughing." Tears rolled down the cheeks of a South Carolina surgeon who could only stand helplessly as friends from home died right before his eyes. Even when soldiers did not know the deceased, they had a natural reluctance to be near corpses. Although soldiers had seen dead persons before, war sometimes compelled them to eat near or lie on the ground among corpses, an activity that required some adjustment. At a very crowded rail depot at Warrenton Junction early in the war, a group of soldiers sat on a large box, until someone pointed out that there was a corpse inside. According to a Virginia lieutenant, "the boys vacated their seats 'instanter' but I thought as he was that I could not hurt him and I was not afraid of him hurting me," so he lay down and took a nap.[41]

In time, soldiers hardened their hearts in a way that was incomprehensible before the war. The killings, the maimings, the destruction and devastation on an unprecedented scale, compelled troops to close off their sympathy in order to preserve themselves psychologically. After a year and a half at war, a Virginia cavalryman believed war "deprives thousands upon thousands of life & strips the residue of all that life holds out most dear." In the immediate aftermath of Antietam, a Mississippian explained to his wife in vivid terms, " 'I have supped' so 'full of horrors'—have seen death, crime, shame and despair so busy at their work that my head has whitened and my very soul turned into stone." What shocked them most was how men reacted to the death of friends. "I don't know how people at home feel for their deceased friends, but in the Army men have become so accustomed to looking at the dead and dying, that the loss of a dear friend, scarcely ever elicits more than a sigh, or 'poor fellow,' and though not exactly forgotten, is scarcely ever mentioned after." Having fought on numerous battlefields, a Georgia infantryman admitted, "Sis It was not anything more for me to look at dead & Diing [dying] men than It is for you to look at pebbles between the door and gate at home. At the same time it seemed as natural as anything else that might come under my observation." He concluded, "I did not cear [care] no more for it than if I had ben looking on so many dead rats." In fact, this harshness had reached such a point that at Second Manassas a Louisiana soldier bayoneted a wounded Yankee who begged to be put out of his misery. The Rebel then announced to other wounded Federals "is there any more of you that want my services if so I will take great pleasure in waiting on you." No one said a thing about his misconduct.[42]

As the war ground down their character, soldiers took on a different appearance. The fancy uniforms and caps from the earlier days yielded to slouch hats and faded, threadbare uniforms. Their skin had darkened from winter winds and intense Virginia summer heat, and hair and facial growth, forever untidy, disclosed woeful grooming practices in the field. "Boys who enlisted in their teens," Captain Henry T. Owen noted, "appeared changed now by the weather and hardships & trails [trials] of war into men of middle life." After just one year in the army, a twenty-four-year-old staff officer for Jackson recorded his opinion that "it appears more like ten years than one; the truth is that I have thought[,] felt and acted more in the last year than in all the rest of my life."[43]

The physical and emotional strain mounted. Soldiers felt survivor guilt, and as the war pushed on into its fourth year, that baggage became extremely heavy. "It makes me feel very bad just to think of how many of my old associates is gone and they are all experiencing Eternity while I am yet on the Terms of Time and Probation," a Georgian wrote to his mother. It would not be long, though, before he joined them. Others earned promotions because of the deaths of friends and carried that burden with them into the new rank. When Capt. L. G. Picou was killed in action—the fourth officer in the company who died in battle—Madison Batchelor assumed his position. "Oh! How sad it is to be promoted by the death of your best and dearest friend," he moaned. The worst part of the war, according to a South Carolina lieutenant, was the memories that so distressed him. "*Fighting* is but a small part of the *all* of such a battle," he penned home. "You spoke once of the horrors that must haunt a life time with memories. These scenes, O God, have swept over my soul in successive swoons of horror and blood." More and more, observant troops noticed their comrades reading the Bible and caring for themselves spiritually, not so much in organized religious practices, but in personal and private moments. Increasingly, it was the only way to bring order from the chaos and ease their trauma and guilt. "What a reformation fighting brings about in a Regiment," an Alabamian commented in his diary.[44]

Despite the deaths of comrades and friends, a carefree spirit operated if the core of the company or battery survived. But extremely heavy losses shattered cohesion, and instilled among survivors a sense of abandonment. After the rout and losses at Crampton's Gap, blocking a Union attempt to slice off part of Lee's army in the Maryland Campaign, Eli Landers of the 16th Georgia revealed to his mother, "I feel perfectly lost since the fight for my mess was all killed or wounded that was along but me." Landers's company entered the fight at Antietam with only five men. Elton Decker lost several of his comrades at Antietam. "I do not feel like writing much at this time," he conveyed to his wife. "I feel too lonely & even when I am penciling this my eyes are moistened with tears but it is well to give vent to our feelings." Private William H. Cocke shared those sentiments. After discussing the death of his friends at Gettysburg, he admitted, "I feel perfectly lost."[45]

When Pvt. William Burke sat so forlornly, chin on his arms, he experienced not just a sense of loss, but a spirit of isolation and abandonment. Some weeks later, Burke learned that his brother had actually survived a wound at Gettysburg and was held in a Yankee prison camp. Edwin Burke was eventually exchanged, and after a six-month stint in a hospital, he returned to both the regiment and his brother, only to suffer another wound three months later.

By Civil War standards, he was lucky. For many, comrades never returned. Some were fortunate enough to forge bonds with new groups to sustain them through the ordeal of war. Others relied on their belief in the Rebel cause, and that, or the pride they had in their own reputation, was enough. Yet many soldiers in Lee's army felt their isolation keenly amid the horror of war, shouldering the burdens all alone. As the war dragged on, survival instincts and pressing needs at home grew ever larger. The cause receded, and their comrades died. As casualties continued to mount, disaffection became a specter that haunted Lee's once-mighty force.

Chapter 26

LEE AND THE HIGH COMMAND

I N MID-JUNE 1862, less than two weeks after Lee had assumed command of the army, Louisiana captain Robert H. Miller informed his father the Confederacy would win—he was sure of that—but "no one can doubt either that our Greatest Generals are little better than imbeciles." Thirteen months later, in the aftermath of the Battle of Gettysburg, another officer noticed there was a "want of concert of action on the part of our Generals," believing "The Army was fought by Divisions instead of by Corps, which was a great and most unfortunate mistake." Although soldiers could overcome poor command decisions and suspect leadership, Gettysburg unquestionably demonstrated the difficulty of that task.[1]

At the head of the army stood a genuine American Sphinx. Lee's troops perfectly idolized him. "The General is a perfect model of a gentleman," commented a soldier who knew him. In the eyes of a Tennessean, "Lee the second Washington, but by far a man superior in all respects to Washington, is at the helm of Confederacy and she is bound to ride the waves of strife triumphantly." An Alabamian declared in early June 1864, "LEE is almost worshipped here. He is considered second to no living man—and of the dead[,] Napoleon alone is admitted his superior in point of military talent."[2]

In truth, Lee possessed a complex personality with qualities that both complemented and were at war with one another. He could write charming, chatty letters to his daughter-in-law, Charlotte, and warm, playful letters to his children, expressing his deep affection and concern for them. Lee could play the role of the gracious Virginian, with his lighthearted banter. Still, the same man could be hot-tempered, cold, sarcastic, and almost unbearably irritable. He was renowned as a cautious man, yet he ordered some of the boldest maneuvers in American military history. After meeting Lee's brother and noting his interesting and forthcoming conversation, Mary Chesnut of South Carolina compared the naval officer to his more famous sibling, the general. "Can anybody say they know his brother?" she pondered. "He looks so cold and quiet and grand."[3]

Lee firmly believed in slavery and the Southern cause. His family owned slaves; his wife's family owned slaves; he grew up accepting the institution as simply a way of life. As trustee in his wife's father's will, Lee manumitted his in-laws' slaves because the will specified it. "They are entitled to their freedom," Lee justified to his wife Mary, "& I wish to give it to them." Lee embraced the Southern cause and the right to secede to protect civil liberties. "The war was originated [or] occasioned by a doubtful question of Construction of the Constitution which our wise & cautious forefathers differed about even while framing it, & which was transmitted unsettled to the descendants," he wrote. As the war became more and more destructive, Lee threw his heart and soul into the cause of Southern independence and rights, and his hostility against the Federals grew intense. The war became personal to Lee.[4]

Although Lee's critics have accused him of parochialism—a fixation on a Virginia-centric view of the war—he frequently advocated policies that would aid the entire Confederacy in securing its independence and were bold changes from the past. Lee fully understood that an enemy with overwhelming resource and manpower advantages confronted the Confederacy, and that peace would come only with a political settlement. Yet Lee also recognized that Confederate military forces would play the critical role in securing that political decision. If the Confederacy were to gain its independence, its people would have to endure enormous sacrifices and adopt revolutionary policies "by calling out the full resources of the country." Throughout his Confederate service, Lee advocated more manpower through enlistment and conscription. Not only did he push for troop increases in the Army of Northern Virginia, he urged the Davis administration to raise greater forces across the Confederate States. In a last-ditch effort to augment troop strength, Lee's endorsement persuaded enough legislators to authorize black enlistment late in the war. Lee repeatedly sought government assistance in repairing and improving the operation of railroads to assist all field armies with supplies. He also argued that to feed its armies, the government should adopt a policy of proportional impressment, so that the burden was spread evenly among the people. "If it requires all the meat in the country to support the army, it should be had," Lee insisted, "and I believe this could be accomplished by not only showing its necessity, but that all equally contributed, and that it was faithfully applied."[5]

Even within his own army, Lee always sought to broaden public interest so that the entire Confederacy embraced the Army of Northern Virginia. Although he implemented Davis's wishes to create brigades from regiments from a single state, he voiced his opposition. By mixing regiments from various states in each brigade, the Confederacy would broaden public interest in them. As disease and combat took their toll, Lee urged governors and recruiters to fill the ranks of state brigades from the Deep South, both to increase troop strength and to expand public appeal and interest in his army.[6]

His operational approach was not some Napoleonic scheme to vanquish the enemy army. He sought to punish invaders and discourage Northern support for the war. His raids into Maryland and Pennsylvania were not attempts to capture major Union cities. Lee hoped to maintain his army on Northern soil, drawing supplies from locals and altering political opinions and influencing ballots at election time. In a thoughtful proposal for securing independence, Lee urged Davis to encourage the Northern peace elements. Even those peace advocates who sought a restoration of the Union argued that before serious negotiations begin they must establish peace first. "That after all is what we are interested in bringing about," he advised Davis. "When peace is proposed to us it will be time enough to discuss its terms, and it is not the part of prudence to spurn the proposition in advance, merely because those who wish to make it believe, or affect to believe, that it will result in bringing us back into the Union." Once the Union declared peace, Lee believed, it could not reconstitute its armies, and the Confederacy would be free to reject any terms short of independence.[7]

Lee possessed numerous attributes that enabled him to become a superb army commander. He had worked and studied his craft for over three decades. During that time, he developed a thorough knowledge of all aspects of military service and matured as a military thinker from study, observation, and reflection. Walter Taylor, Lee's assistant adjutant general and frequent critic, admitted, "he has what few others possess—a head capable of planning a campaign and the ability to arrange for a battle." Lee was an excellent worker who devoted careful consideration to every important aspect of the campaign. "I have never known a man more thorough and painstaking in all he undertook," Taylor added. Lee mastered the art of predicting enemy intentions and plans. He knew what choices the opposing generals had, and he gained insight from their decisions. Lee formulated an accurate understanding of what the Union army planned, and thus was able to thwart them. Two tours of service at the right hand of Davis in Richmond exposed him to the true strengths and weaknesses of the Confederacy. Better than any other Confederate field commander, Lee grasped the limits of Confederate military and civilian contributions to the war effort.[8]

Lee knew that if he fought on the defensive, the Union army would overwhelm him with its vastly superior might and resources. All the Federals needed was a competent commander who could control the tempo and flow of a campaign. Lee had to take the initiative and fight on the offensive to dictate the course of the war in his theater. In order to accomplish that, however, Lee understood that he had to take great risks. He had to draw the enemy from Virginia, so that his army could live off their resources while husbanding his nation's limited supplies. He had to fight on advantageous terms. And, finally, when he went into battle, he had to commit all his resources—no holding back. The Union possessed greater numbers. To offset that, he needed to get all his men into every fight and, ideally, have superior strength at the point of contact.[9]

Lee's drawbacks as a military commander were few. Until he had sufficient evidence to understand the enemy's objectives, he hesitated to act. Some contemporaries called this quality cautious, but Lee simply did not want to commit his resources too early. Once he understood his enemy's intentions, then he willingly hurled everything he had at his disposal against them. Others criticized Lee for acting within the confines of acceptable wartime conduct. They wanted him to embrace a harsher war against civilians. In effect, they argued that he was not the revolutionary fighter for these revolutionary times. But from Lee's perspective, the Confederacy had built and was attempting to preserve an independent nation and it should, therefore, fight in the conventional manner. Although guerrilla warfare flourished in some areas of the Confederacy, Lee believed it would merely expose Southerners to sacrifices, brutalities, and the destruction or confiscation of their property, including slaves, on an unprecedented scale, without offering a reasonable chance of success.

As a field commander, Lee allocated as many resources to subordinates as he could and planned and explained matters thoroughly. Sometimes, he was there in person at decisive points to ensure subordinates executed critical attacks properly, but on the whole he did not micromanage. If he had a fault it was his unwillingness to inform specialized staff of his plans in advance. "The movement of the Enemy cannot be anticipated by me, for the General commanding never discloses any of his plans to those around him," complained the army's medical director. "The Chief Officers of the different Departments of his Army are ordered to prepare to move just before the Army takes up its line of march, and everything is done hurriedly and mysteriously." The surgeon felt more information "would add greatly to the efficiency of the [Medical] Corps."[10]

As the war dragged on, physical maladies took a toll on Lee's ability to command. Lee's job was physically demanding. Just before the first march into Maryland, Lee broke both wrists when his horse fell. He could not write—he could not ride—he could not even dress himself. In February 1863, Lee suffered what was most likely a heart attack. Over the next two months, he was weak, and he could not muster the strength to work normal hours. In early March, he confessed to his wife, "I am in indifferent health myself & feel almost worn out, so that I fear I may be unable in the approaching campaign to go through the work before me." More than a month later, just two weeks before the start of the Chancellorsville Campaign, a staff member reported that Lee was doing better but still resided in a house a couple of miles from the army headquarters. Doctors thought Lee had caught pneumonia, which they later rediagnosed as neuralgic rheumatism. Since it was almost campaign season, they kept this information from nearly everyone. In the fall, his rheumatism was so severe that he had to use a wagon to haul himself around the field. After several days, he felt better, "Yet I still suffer," he informed wife Mary.[11]

An individual who prepared for campaigns so painstakingly had to devote extensive time to the task. After his heart attack, his stamina declined, and for a few months he had to cut back on his workload dramatically and rest more. Earlier in the war, the trained engineer in Lee induced him to reconnoiter key positions personally. At Malvern Hill, Federal sharpshooters fired upon him, and at Second Manassas a Union bullet creased his cheek, prompting him to make a joke out of it. After his heart attack Lee was too unwell to attempt reconnaissance, and he justified his replacement as army commander after Gettysburg based on this incapacity. Later in the year, he could no longer resist the temptation, and once again came under fire, this time by artillery.[12]

Lee believed that he must lead by example. If he expected his soldiers to endure hardships, then he must cope with them as well. For the most part, he lived in a tent—"my principal habitation ever since wherever I have been"— and slept on a small, uncomfortable field cot. After three years, his headquarters tent had so many holes that biting winds whipped through it and rain leaking in threatened to damage critical paperwork. It was only then that he sheepishly requested a new one. He ate the same food as his troops and bore the same sacrifices. Once he pitched his tent for the night, it remained and he remained in it, no matter what was available in the neighborhood. "Tis one of my commander's idiosyncracies to suffer any amount of discomfort and inconvenience sooner than to change a camp once established," Taylor grumbled. "So the minor lights must submit, quietly, grin and endure." In fact, his staff called Lee "the Tycoon" behind his back, a sarcastic reference to his grand responsibilities and the Spartan lifestyle at headquarters. Just before Christmas in 1863, Lee had business in Richmond. Taylor suggested that he would return to duty "to show how very self-denying he is." Taylor, a bright staff officer, completely missed the point. If Lee's men could not enjoy Christmas at home, then why should he? Lee maintained a small staff, much to the dismay of Taylor and other staffers, because he sought to maximize the number of shooters in the army and to serve as an example for subordinate officers. As Lee explained to his son, he did not want "a retinue around me who seek nominal duty or an excuse to get off real Service elsewhere. I have a great deal of work to do & want men able & willing to do it."[13]

Eventually, the Union adopted army group commanders, which relieved people like Grant and William T. Sherman from the administration of an army and much of its paperwork so that they could think about and solve the major problems and conduct planning. Lee functioned as an army commander, with all the administrative functions, planning, and execution that position entailed. His workload was simply overwhelming. At the end of March 1863, as he recovered from his heart attack, Lee complained to the secretary of war that he had read 268 court-martial proceedings that week, including the testimony. Some weeks, he had more than that to read. "I have with the necessary correspondence within and out of the Army but little time for the most important of my duties," he stated. From December 5, 1862, to February 26, 1863, his headquarters received and recorded 9,800 papers, all routine matters. In early April, to bring this process under control, Lee directed that all papers for the commanding general were to come to headquarters by regular couriers, "unless it be of importance to the Army, or of urgent private character." Over the next period, from April 10 to June 23, the number of documents that arrived at headquarters declined to 7,604. The next two and a half weeks, it fell to 1,722, but the next two and a half weeks after that the quantity soared to 4,135. His staff could handle some of the paper, but far too much of it required the personal attention of Lee.[14]

The combination of an oppressive workload, declining health, the aches and pains of field life for a man in his midfifties, and the stress of army command brought out the worst in Lee's temper and general disposition. The staff felt that Lee slighted them or made unreasonable demands and then erupted when things went wrong. Major Charles S. Venable, a prewar mathematician who served as Lee's assistant adjutant general, considered returning to the field artillery. "I am too high-tempered to stand a high-tempered man and consequently I become stubborn, sullen, useless and disagreeable." Later in the war, when Venable's wife pressed him to secure a leave, he replied, "if you had the pleasure of Gen. Lee's acquaintance you would debate with yourself about asking for anything." Yet Venable, a more mature man than Taylor, also understood "the old man has much to annoy and worry him" and thought well of Lee. Taylor, on the other hand, found him disagreeable. Early on, Taylor complained, "He is so *unappreciative*." After a while, Taylor admitted he was "annoyed by any imaginery unreasonableness or ill temper on the part of my Chief." A year later, Taylor declared Lee "so unreasonable and provoking at times," concluding, "I might serve under him for ten years to come and couldn't *love* him at the end of that period."[15]

For his subordinate commanders, Lee sought individuals with tactical competence who executed boldly. He wanted general officers who fought aggressively and threw the full weight of their command into combat. Lee insisted on proper tactical training of the troops and demanded that the officers pay careful attention to the well-being of their men. In effect, he could instruct subordinates in the science of military command, but he could not teach them the art of fighting. Early in the war, he sought West Point or Regular Army officers for key positions. They possessed the proper tactical training and had a familiarity with army ways. But as the war went on and vacancies occurred, Lee was much more willing to promote on merit, regardless of West Point credentials. What mattered was competence in battle.

As he had done after Seven Days' when he cleared house of senior officers, Lee continued to pull the personnel strings skillfully. After Ewell suffered a severe wound at Second Manassas, Lawton took over division command as senior brigadier. He fell at Antietam, opening the door for Lee to elevate Early to acting and then division command. Early then complained that Lawton's Brigade needed a new commander. During Lawton's absence, it had fallen into a "deplorable state of disorganization." Lee seized on that and elevated Col. John B. Gordon, a citizen-soldier and a star in combat, to the position. In May, after a seven-month recovery period, Lawton notified Lee he was ready to return to active duty. Lee replied that "I waited for you a long time." There were no vacancies for Lawton, but Lee would keep him in mind. "In view of your present condition," Lee concluded, "should there be any other duty you may prefer, it will give me great pleasure to advocate your wishes." Lawton then grumbled that others received promotions while he was recuperating from a battlefield wound. Lee responded by reminding him that he had not joined the service in quest of rank or fame, but for a cause. "The most honorable position in this war in my opinion is that of the private soldier," he stated emphatically. Everyone must do their duty, at whatever rank and position. Lawton assumed the post of quartermaster general in the Confederate army in February 1864.[16]

In the case of Isaac Trimble, Lee wanted to keep him with the army and found ways to do so. Trimble's service extended back to the Valley Campaign, where he impressed Jackson as a good combat officer. In the Second Manassas Campaign, Trimble's men marched thirty-four miles and attacked a larger force at Manassas Junction. They captured eight artillery guns, more than double their number of Yankees, and huge stockpiles of supplies. In a rare moment of praise, Jackson wrote the adjutant general, "I regard that days achievement, as the most brilliant that has come under my observation during the present War" and urged Trimble's promotion to major general. Jackson congratulated him on the "brilliant success" and stated baldly, "You deserve promotion." Trimble was severely wounded at Second Manassas and he was not promoted because he was unfit for duty. When Trimble complained to Lee, the general replied, "Our Cause is too momentous to allow private considerations to obstruct public interest." Four months later, Lee consolidated troops to form a division for Trimble, among them some Maryland troops, whose "organization has been a failure so far." Lee was confident Trimble could whip all of them into shape. At Gettysburg, Trimble suffered a leg wound and fell into Yankee hands. He remained in a prison camp until early 1865.[17]

Perhaps the one exception to Lee's standards for subordinate officers was Chief of Artillery Pendleton. The clergyman and West Point graduate could not compare with Alexander or a handful of other officers in the artillery in ability and execution. Lee understood that and slowly pushed Pendleton into roles of decreasing importance and responsibility. But Pendleton served two vital functions for Lee, and the commanding general relied on him heavily. Pendleton was an Episcopal minister who counseled Lee on religious matters, and he was also a friend and contemporary. They knew each other from West Point days—Pendleton graduated a year behind Lee and both men came from Virginia—and could communicate with each other in ways that Lee could not with much younger officers like Jackson, Longstreet, Ewell, or Early. In late May 1863, Pendleton visited Lee on duty. In time, their conversation drifted to religion and ultimately to Jackson. As the two men talked of their fallen friend, Lee wept. He could speak candidly and reveal his emotions with Pendleton.[18]

With Jackson gone, Lee relied on two new corps commanders, A. P. Hill and Ewell, along with his "Old War Horse," Longstreet. Both newcomers to the rank of lieutenant general had long histories of service in the U.S. Army and in the war in Virginia. They had proven themselves as division commanders, but as the spring campaign of 1864 approached, Lee had doubts about the fitness of both men.

Ambrose Powell Hill enjoyed a meteoric rise after slow advancement in the Regular Army. He graduated fifteenth in the West Point Class of 1847, and by the time of his resignation, he held the rank of only a first lieutenant in the U.S. Army. Despite limited service at First Manassas, Hill discovered himself commanding a brigade by early 1862, with the rank of brigadier general. He fought well at Williamsburg, which earned him another promotion, to major general and division commander. He continued to serve until his wounding at Chancellorsville. Lee regarded Hill as his best division commander. "He fights his troops well," Lee wrote to Davis, "and takes good care of them."[19]

During the course of his service as a division commander, Hill had separate run-ins with Longstreet and Jackson. After Hill squabbled with Longstreet's staff officer and refused to obey orders from him after Seven Days', Lee shifted Hill and his division to Jackson's wing. Within two months, tensions between Jackson and Hill erupted. The two men had a spat en route to Cedar Mountain, but matters really exploded on September 3, 1862. Jackson gave specific marching instructions for the next day; Hill started late and violated Jackson's system of fifty minutes marching, ten minutes rest per hour. Jackson promptly arrested Hill for violating orders. A few days later, Jackson released Hill so that he could command his division on the Maryland raid, yet the charges remained. Hill's spectacular march from Harpers Ferry and directly into battle to save the Confederate right flank earned him kudos and Jackson's withdrawal of the charges with Lee's consent. His pride scorched, Hill wanted his honor restored by a court-martial. That winter, he pushed the matter to near insubordination. Privately, Hill despised Jackson, calling him "that crazy old Presbyterian fool" and comparing him to a "slumbering volcano" who might erupt and wreak havoc at any moment. Lee attempted to explain the rationale for the dismissal of charges, insisting, "A commanding officer has the right to make an arrest, and to release the officer arrested without prosecuting the matter further, when in his judgment, the exigencies of the service require such a course." Hill had to get in the last word and wrote Lee one more time.[20]

Bearded, long-haired, often puffing on a pipe, Hill suffered severely from an ailment, possibly prostatitis, which could have developed from a bout with gonorrhea as a West Point cadet. Periodically, the pain achieved such severity that it confined him to bed. Perhaps that was why he behaved so testily. North Carolinian Samuel Walkup depicted Hill in his diary by jotting, "He is a proud, haughty, old maidish son, and selfish looking misanthrope and loves to be a tyrant and vixenish, snaps and snarls at everything and everybody." Upon Hill's rise to corps command after Jackson's death, a soldier wondered how he would fare. "Genl. Hill who now commands shows none of striking characteristics of a great leader." He added, "if he can plan and execute I will be very agreeably surprised."[21]

In his first experience as a corps commander, at Gettysburg, Hill stumbled into a fight when Lee had specifically ordered his corps commanders not to bring on a general engagement. Although the Confederacy achieved considerable success that first day, Hill's men sustained terrible losses in the vicious fighting. On the third day, his corps spearheaded the attack and incurred gargantuan casualties once again.

After Lee had detached Longstreet and two divisions to assist Bragg's army near Chattanooga, and Union army commander Meade sent two of his corps to aid the beleaguered forces there in the wake of the rout at Chickamauga, Lee decided to turn the Federals out of their position, similar to his actions in the Second Manassas Campaign. At Bristoe Station, the impetuous Hill blundered into an awful situation in an act of "unpardonable mismanagement," as Walter Taylor called it. He launched an attack without proper reconnaissance, and his attacking division marched directly into a trap, with Federals positioned on the front and flank. By the time he extricated them, nearly 1,000 lay killed and wounded and well over 400 were missing. Over 1,300 of the casualties were from two North Carolina brigades. To his credit, Hill openly admitted his mistake, but it did little to repair the damage to his reputation. Sandie Pendleton, a staff officer for Ewell, proclaimed, "Hill is a fool & a woful blunderer." When Lee arrived on the scene, he seethed with anger. The next day, Lee and his staff rode to a knoll overlooking the field, and barked at Hill to bury his dead.

Hill then confessed, "This is all my fault, General."

"Yes, it *is* your fault," snapped Lee. "You committed a great blunder yesterday, your line of battle was too short, too thin, and your reserves were too far behind."[22]

For division commanders, Hill had a mixed bag. His best was Wilcox. When it appeared that Wilcox and Rodes were competing for the same division command, Rodes predicted Wilcox, the West Pointer, would get the slot. "I would prefer being beaten by a baboon but will submit to it quietly, unless they place [him] in command of this Div[ision]." Both men eventually got a division, and both earned them. Wilcox had commanded skillfully on numerous battlefields, including Salem Church. When Dorsey Pender died of wounds at Gettysburg, Wilcox transferred over to command his division.[23]

Henry Heth secured a division before the Gettysburg Campaign. A West Point graduate who had earned renown for his frontier service, he was liked by both Davis and Lee. Still, he competed against Pender, who had served superbly with the army and sustained four wounds yet never left the field. Both Lee and Hill preferred Pender, and they resolved the matter by building a division for Heth and awarding another to Pender. Heth's Division was mauled on the first day at Gettysburg, and when he abdicated his command to Pettigrew after suffering a relatively minor wound, there was some grumbling. On the third day, under Pettigrew, the division stormed Cemetery Ridge and was repulsed. Apparently, Pickett blamed Pettigrew's command at least in part for his defeat. In fairness, Heth's Division had already suffered huge losses in the battle; Pickett's men were fresh. Pettigrew, moreover, had to storm the Union position with his left flank exposed to heavy Union fire. As he advanced, his men were outflanked more and more. The division then endured heavy casualties once again at Bristoe Station. After two fights, Heth had yet to distinguish himself or even demonstrate that he was capable of effective division command.[24]

The third division commander in Hill's Corps was a West Pointer and Regular Army officer, Richard "Dick" Anderson. Although Jenkins described him as a beloved but "indifferent officer" and Brig. Gen. A. R. Wright questioned Anderson's courage, he had fought with the army since the Peninsula and had commanded a division since the conclusion of Seven Days'. At Antietam he sustained a wound, but he returned for Fredericksburg. In the Battle of Chancellorsville, he and his men fought extremely well. No one had more division-command experience than Anderson.[25]

The second of Lee's new corps commanders, Richard Stoddard Ewell, had graduated thirteenth in his West Point class of 1840. He fought well in the Mexican War, but his advancement in the Regular Army was slow, reflecting his solid but undistinguished record. Ewell commanded a brigade at First Manassas and received his promotion to major general early in 1862. Despite some frustrating moments, Ewell played a vital role in Jackson's Valley Campaign. He fought with Jackson at Seven Days' and Cedar Mountain, and then suffered a severe wound that cost him a leg at Groveton. He returned to duty to assume corps command after Chancellorsville.

Ewell was an unusually odd fellow. A short man with bulging blue eyes and a bald, domed head, Ewell was eccentric, though not quite in Jackson's league—he called Jackson "that enthusiastic fanatic." He married his cousin, the widowed Lizinka Brown, and referred to her as "Mrs. Brown" even after their nuptials. His staff officer and stepson recorded an incident in which Ewell was waiting for a woman to bring him a glass of milk when he spotted some scissors. He picked them up and began clipping his hair without a mirror. When the woman returned, he put down the scissors, gulped the milk, and rushed off with hair on one side of his head cut short and the other side untouched. It took several days for the staff to convince Ewell to cut the rest.[26]

One soldier called him a "snorter." The private insisted that "sometimes he is quite pleasant and talks quite freely" and other times he "is in bad humor." A Virginia private described him as "Low in stature—a firm and decided look." Deep down, Ewell was a worrier. He often suffered headaches and an upset stomach. After he had his leg amputated, the physical strain of active campaigning bore heavily on him, exacerbating the mental stress.[27]

Ewell's first encounter with the enemy as the new Second Corps commander indicated a relatively seamless transition from Jackson. In an attempt to clear Yankees from the lower or northern part of the Shenandoah Valley, Ewell's troops crushed a Federal command at Winchester in mid-June, inflicting heavy losses and capturing well over 3,000 Yankees with a brilliant flank attack by

Early's Division. A Union officer claimed that the Confederates had lied about Jackson's death: "there was no officer in either army that could have executed that movement but 'Old Jack.'" A soldier in Early's Division confirmed the assessment. "I say Bully for old Ewell he is another Jackson, Bully Bully," he exclaimed to his parents.[28]

At Gettysburg, Ewell did not execute to his standards at Winchester, but neither did any other high-ranking officer. On the first day, after routing the Union troops with Early's flank attack, he declined to press the attack on Cemetery Hill. His great failure was not seizing Culp's Hill, which would have made Cemetery Hill untenable to the Federals. The second day, he failed to coordinate properly with Longstreet's attack and his corps fought piecemeal. On the third day, the Union forces dictated the fighting by assaulting before dawn, and again Ewell never coordinated well with Longstreet, who attacked in the afternoon. Nor did he command skillfully at Bristoe Station. Although he avoided serious blunders, his corps hardly distinguished itself.[29]

By November 1863, Ewell broke down physically once again. Sandie Pendleton referred to him as "our superannuated chieftain, worn out as he is by the prostration incident." Taylor complained that with Jackson dead and Longstreet on detached service, the army had a leadership void just below the top. "I only wish the General had good Lieutenants," he admitted to his future bride. "We miss Jackson & Longstreet terribly. Poor Ewell—a cripple—is now laid up and not able to be in the field."[30]

When Ewell announced in mid-January 1864 that he was ready to resume command of his corps, Lee made clear his reservations. While he admired Ewell's patriotic devotion, "I was in constant fear during the last campaign that you would sink under your duties or destroy yourself. In either event injury might have resulted." The threat of replacement was implicit.[31]

By the spring campaign season, Ewell appeared ready physically, but a peculiar episode no doubt annoyed Lee. An order passed through the staff, but no one notified Early. Early exploded, and Ewell placed him under arrest. By this point, Lee clearly had had enough of petty charges against competent officers. Ewell could not handle a minor interpersonal dispute without dragging the commanding general into the matter. Lee chided Early for "improper & uncalled for" remarks yet he refused to believe that Early meant any "disrespect" toward Ewell or Lee. By Lee's order, Early was released from arrest and returned to duty.[32]

Without doubt, Ewell benefited from the best division commanders in any of Lee's corps. Rodes, arguably the best division commander in the entire army, had settled into the job well since his elevation before Chancellorsville. Early, a West Point graduate and Virginia lawyer, commanded another division. A soldier assigned to his headquarters described him as "About 5 feet, 10 inches high and very much bent with rheumatism. Dark eyes, gray hair and beard. Dark complexion—not very talkative, of great energy and strong mind. Very rough in speech, great swearer and curser." Like Ewell, Early had fought at

First Manassas and continued to serve his country well. Jackson, a tough critic, recommended Early for promotion to major general, stating, "He manages his men well in camp and also in action, and has recently improved very much in promptness which I regarded as wanting in him until within the last few weeks." Young Pendleton, a very perceptive officer who had served on Jackson's staff, believed Early was "far superior" to Ewell as a commander, "more energetic and a good disciplinarian, and withal more agreeable as an associate." Early exhibited the spark that could make him a very valuable officer. The last of the three, Allegheny Johnson, was a hard-bitten veteran who had fought during the Valley Campaign and took over the division for the Gettysburg Campaign. Johnson developed a reputation that when he threw his troops into battle, they struck with the punch of a sledgehammer, exactly the way Lee wanted his commanders to fight.[33]

Longstreet, last but not least, functioned as Lee's right-hand man. Lee had inherited Longstreet from Johnston, and the Georgian had proven himself a conscientious and competent soldier. Over months of service dating back to First Manassas, Longstreet and Johnston had formed a powerful bond. Johnston trusted his subordinate's campaign skills and Longstreet felt that his opinion carried considerable weight with the army commander. In the retreat on the Peninsula, Johnston assigned Longstreet the task of covering the rear, and at Seven Pines, he placed Longstreet in charge of the critical attack. On the first day there, Longstreet confused the plan and botched the execution. Then, in what could only be described as a conspiracy, he and Johnston foisted blame on Huger.

When Lee assumed command, he had listened to Johnston enough to know that Longstreet stood in very high regard throughout the army. At Seven Days', Longstreet commanded admirably, and from that point he emerged as a reliable wing and later corps commander under Lee. Like so many high-ranking field officers, he had to grow into the position. As a wing or corps commander, he kept his forces in hand, and he fought them well on numerous battlefields, particularly Second Manassas and then at Antietam. He administered skillfully and instituted intelligent policies for the care and training of his men, so that when it came time to launch a campaign, his soldiers were fit and ready. Longstreet was also a progressive officer in the development and uses of his staff.[34]

An Alabamian described him as "a large, robust, full faced man who, as he rides by with his old striped blanket, looks more like an old Virginia planter than the great general that he is." After graduating from West Point in 1842, he had served for nearly twenty years in the Regular Army, distinguishing himself particularly in the fighting in Mexico. A staff officer thought that even though he was "as brave as Julius Caesar," his greatest strength was "the seeming ease with which he can handle and arrange large numbers of troops."[35]

Like most commanders, Longstreet had his favorite subordinates whom he advanced as rapidly as he could. Unfortunately, his pet junior officers did not always measure up to their commander's lofty opinion. In the artillery reorganization, each corps received a corps artillery chief at the rank of brigadier general. Longstreet sought Col. J. B. Walton's promotion. Walton had come east with the Washington Artillery and had served with Longstreet for some time. Lee, however, thought Walton's "knowledge of Arty [artillery,] especially science, must be limited, & I think his knowledge of ground defective, & his selection of positions not good." He had to send A. L. Long out to position Longstreet's artillery regularly. Ultimately, Walton received the assignment.[36]

Another of Longstreet's favorites was George Pickett. A West Pointer in the class of 1846, Pickett graduated last in his class and earned an impressive 660 demerits while there. In his final year, Pickett was five demerits shy of expulsion. He entered the Regular Army and earned a solid reputation in Mexico and on the Texas and Pacific Northwest frontier. Pickett commanded ably in the Peninsula Campaign and the struggle for Richmond, and at Gaines's Mill he sustained a serious shoulder wound. Longstreet secured him a division command. But Pickett was also a wretched administrator who failed to care for his troops properly. Twice the army commander rebuked Pickett for his inept care and supervision of his troops. The same carelessness, inattention to detail, and lack of planning that had hurt him at West Point was reflected in the oversight of his division.[37]

A third favorite of Longstreet's was a South Carolinian, Micah Jenkins. A graduate of South Carolina Military Academy, Jenkins established a school in Yorkville, South Carolina, before secession. By 1860 he had amassed a fortune of nearly $30,000, including a dozen slaves. He formed the 5th South Carolina Infantry during the secession crisis and took it to Virginia early in the war.[38]

When he marched off to war, Jenkins left his wife to cope with his business and three small children. Yet he still guided financial concerns. In July 1861, he informed his wife he planned to cut back on slaves' rations once the hard work was done and he intended to buy bacon rejected by the army for his slaves. "It is plenty good for them and will save me a great deal, if the Express does not charge me too much."[39]

Jenkins was ferociously ambitious, forever wrangling for promotion. Unlike so many climbers, though, Jenkins was an excellent combat commander and a skilled leader. Soldiers grumbled about his flagrant desire for promotion and his aggressiveness in battle, but Jenkins achieved results. A soldier wrote his sister that he thought Jenkins "would lose half his Brigade I believe if he could be made a Major Genl." Launcelot Blackford had a "strong repugnance" for him, pronouncing Jenkins ambitious, "unjust & captious," but "in some respects a good officer." At Seven Pines, Jenkins launched a superb attack that sliced deeply into the Union lines. At Seven Days', Jenkins was all over the battlefield. His horse was hit three times, he was shot in the arm, his sword was bent and broken, and shot and shells ripped up his blanket. As one staff officer wrote, "it was of such stuff that soldiers and heroes were made." At the same time, Jenkins took great pride in his soldiers. He attempted to drill them thoroughly and care for them in camp, announcing to his wife in fall 1862, "I have a very fine Brigade, and if I could get one months quiet to work with it would make it the finest in the service." In October 1863, Longstreet assigned Jenkins as acting division commander and recommended him for permanent promotion, stating, "Of all the Brigadiers in the Army, Gen. Jenkins is my first choice as a most active and zealous officer."[40]

When Longstreet attempted to build political support, he aligned himself with the wrong faction. Service with Johnston bonded the two men, and in time President Davis determined that Johnston simply lacked the ability to command a field force effectively. The longstanding hostility between Johnston and the administration spilled over into Congress's anti-Davis faction. Among Longstreet's close friends, there was Louis T. Wigfall, a former brigadier general and a U.S. and C.S. senator from Texas. A heavy-drinking, erratic politician, Wigfall became angry at Davis when the president did not agree with the senator's policies and launched a full-scale attack on Davis and his administration.[41]

Longstreet had long angled for an independent command. Once Lee had achieved such great success in the East, it became apparent to Longstreet that he must look west to fulfill his ambitions. In October 1862, he wrote his old friend Joe Johnston offering to serve with him. Johnston had just received an assignment for a massive region, stretching from the Appalachian Mountains to the Mississippi River and encompassing two significant field commands. In early February 1863, he wrote his friend Wigfall seeking his own command. "I have not consulted Gen Lee but I am quite satisfied that he will not object to my going anywhere where I can have a separate command," he informed his old commander, "But he will not be likely to consent to my going under any one else nor do I desire it as by remaining here I have troops that give me no trouble."[42]

Later that month, Lee tested Longstreet's readiness for an independent command by detaching him as the head of two divisions and sending him to the Suffolk area, where a Union buildup of troops threatened Petersburg and its railroads. Despite attentive coaching by Lee, Longstreet's service wrought mixed results. The Federal force did not seize Petersburg or destroy the railroads, and Longstreet's command did gather some valuable supplies for the army to the north. Yet Longstreet mishandled his first truly solo fight and suffered a defeat at the hands of Union major general J. J. Peck.

Still, Longstreet yearned for his own army. Braxton Bragg had accomplished little as commander of the Army of Tennessee, and Longstreet set his sights on that job. In mid-August 1863, he again informed Wigfall that he wanted to go west to "save the country. If I remain here I fear we shall go, little at a time till all will be lost." His service was not "essential here"; in the west, he could reverse fortunes. He lobbied hard for the detachment of troops and an offensive in Tennessee. If that could not happen, he suggested that he and Bragg swap positions, and that Lee allocate three brigades from his army to Longstreet's new command. From his perch in Virginia, he advised Lee, "I

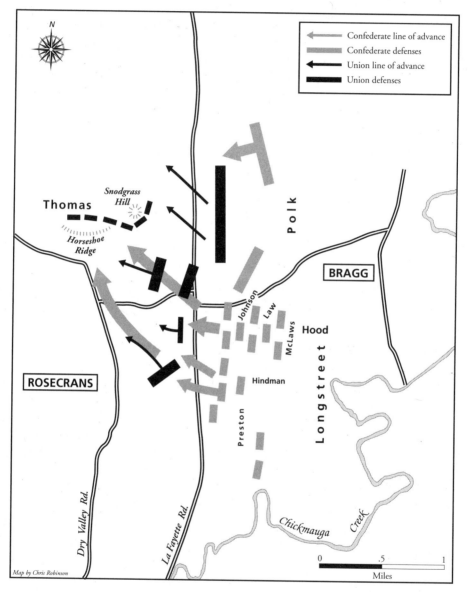

Battle of Chickamauga

doubt Bragg has confidence in his troops or himself either. He is not likely to do a great deal for us." In early September, Lee consented to transport two divisions with Longstreet at their head to reinforce Bragg's army near Chattanooga. A skillful Union maneuver had compelled Bragg to fall back and abandon the important railroad city. If the Confederates did not check the Federal advance, they would push south toward Atlanta, a vital industrial and railroad hub. When Longstreet left, he had great hopes that it was a stepping-stone to the western command.[43]

After a few days' march and roughly an eight-day train ride, three brigades of John Bell Hood's Division and two from McLaws went almost directly to the front. Longstreet arrived at Ringgold on the afternoon of September 19, with heavy skirmishing already taking place. He immediately set out to find Bragg and receive his assignment for the next day. Aided by only a road map and a description of the terrain, Longstreet assumed command of the left wing of the entire army. With McLaws back in Atlanta hurrying troops northward, Hood, as the only division commander present, took charge of his and McLaws's weakened divisions.[44]

In the Battle of Chickamauga, an uncoordinated attack on the right stalled, and Longstreet ordered Hood's advance. Thanks to a staff error that prompted a Federal commander to pull a brigade out of line, Hood's attack unwittingly struck into that gap. With a roar, the detached troops from Lee's army crashed through the Yankee line and wheeled right, rolling up much of the Federal position. Hood went down with a severe thigh wound that would cost him his leg. Brigadier General Evander M. Law, the senior brigade officer present, stepped into Hood's old slot as acting division commander. The loss did not halt the screaming Rebels. Meanwhile, Brig. Gen. Joseph Brevard Kershaw, in command of both McLaws's brigades, did not receive orders to angle to the right, so he pushed directly ahead, further disrupting the Yankee command. Eventually, he ran up against a powerful Federal defense on Snodgrass Hill. Kershaw assailed the works, but they were too strong. Reinforcements arrived; still the Confederates could not gain the position. After dark, the Federals retired to defenses around Chattanooga, having delayed the Rebel onslaught and perhaps saving Chattanooga from evacuation. Some 2,000 men from the Army of Northern Virginia fell that day, but they had caused a breakthrough that led to a rout of most of the Union army. They captured over 3,000 Federals, took forty artillery pieces, and collected 17,645 small arms. Their service had enhanced the luster of the army from Virginia.[45]

At Chickamauga, the Confederates had won a great victory, but they had also squandered an opportunity. Bragg had completely lost control of the battle, and subordinates were furious at his mismanagement. The next day, he temporized once again, finally advanced, and then decided on a different course, wasting any effective chance of inflicting more damage on the enemy or compelling them to retreat from Chattanooga. In a message that circumvented proper channels, Longstreet revealed to the secretary of war his disgust at Bragg's poor generalship. "It seems that he cannot adopt and adhere to any plan or course, whether of his own or of someone else." He added that only Lee could accomplish the task of restoring Tennessee to Confederate control.[46]

As part of the opposition to Bragg, Longstreet conveyed his opinions to Davis's aide, Col. James Chesnut, as he passed near headquarters. Others gathered to sign a round robin, proclaiming their dissatisfaction with Bragg. The situation became so serious that Davis traveled personally to visit the army, speak to the principals, and broker a solution. One witness testified that Longstreet, as a successful corps commander who augmented his reputation by creating the breakthrough at Chickamauga, voiced his dissatisfaction with Bragg, and his opinion apparently carried great weight with the president. Yet in the end, Davis decided to support Bragg and relieved or transferred the key critics, including D. H. Hill.[47]

Bragg assigned Longstreet and his troops to the extreme left of the Confederate line. McLaws arrived to command his division. As senior brigadier and Longstreet's preferred officer, Jenkins took over Hood's Division, with Law returning to his brigade, creating some harsh feelings throughout Hood's Division. Within days, affairs began spiraling out of control. Jenkins removed troops that Law had positioned to cover Brown's Ferry over the Tennessee River, citing outdated instructions from Longstreet as his justification, allowing Federals to cross there and begin accumulating force to strike at Lookout Mountain. In hopes of driving the Federals back across the river, Jenkins led a night attack, but overwhelming Union strength and confusion amid the darkness resulted in failure. Both Jenkins and Longstreet blamed Law, whose brigade suffered only fifteen casualties, and Brig. Gen. Jerome B. Robertson, commander of the Texas Brigade.[48]

A week after the night attack, Longstreet met with Bragg and other corps commanders to discuss a rapid movement on the Union forces at Knoxville, which Bragg approved. Again with McLaws's and Hood's divisions, Longstreet marched toward Knoxville. Severe supply problems and the army's inability to deliver a powerful blow outside Federal fortifications frustrated him. Worse, a strange assortment of events—some due to Longstreet, others because of Bragg and his engineer—delayed the attack and gave Union troops a chance to prepare better. Finally, early in the morning on November 29, the Confederates launched a frontal assault on Fort Sanders, which Yankee engineers and laborers had protected with a ditch six feet deep, in spots reaching eleven feet, and eight to twelve feet wide, with a twelve-foot earth wall, slick with ice. Unaware of the length and depth of the trenches, McLaws's men brought no scaling ladders. With no artillery fire to silence Union guns, the men attacked bravely and became trapped in the ditch. Their only escape was to run back across the ground they had originally traversed, exposing themselves as easy targets for the defenders. All told, Longstreet lost 813 soldiers in the attack.[49]

Several hours after the fiasco, Longstreet received confirmation that a disaster had befallen Bragg's army and that he should retreat to northern Georgia to rendezvous with survivors. That proved impossible, and Longstreet soon learned that Grant's army had sent reinforcements under Sherman to relieve the Yankees in Knoxville. After conferring with senior commanders, Longstreet elected to march toward Bristol, Tennessee, in the direction of Lee's army.[50]

His mission in the west suddenly a disaster, Longstreet took out his frustration on three subordinates—Robertson, Law, and McLaws. In a pathetic display of petulance, he levied charges against each one. Robertson received a reprimand, and Longstreet got him removed as a brigade commander. In Law's case, when Jenkins placed him under arrest, a staff officer commented, "they are at dagger points." The War Department refused to even entertain the initial charges of seeking a leave under false pretenses, nor additional charges for the same offense. Law was restored to brigade command. Longstreet then complained to Lee, asserting that two battlefield failures "were due to want of conduct" by Law. "If my efforts to maintain discipline, spirit, and zeal in the discharge of official duty are to be set aside by the return of General Law and his restoration to duty without trial, it cannot be well for me to remain in command." He demanded that Law undergo a trial or that he himself be relieved of Confederate service. Longstreet then ordered the rearrest of Law. Lee, desperate for a capable corps commander, could not afford to lose Longstreet on the verge of the great spring 1864 offensive. He insisted to Adjutant General Samuel Cooper that this was a grave charge and should be investigated. Cooper passed it on to Davis, who replied in forceful terms that the secretary of war would inform Lee why the War Department dropped the charges. "General Longstreet has seriously offended against good order and military discipline," the president blasted, "in rearresting an officer who had been released by the War Department, without any new offense being alleged."

The McLaws case, on the other hand, actually went to trial. The court exonerated him of all charges except a portion of one and sentenced him to suspension for sixty days. Adjutant General Cooper set aside that decision, stating that the evidence did not sustain the specification. In effect, he ruled the court acted incompetently, and restored McLaws to duty. The War Department evidently had had enough of Longstreet's accusations. McLaws believed the entire fiasco was a vendetta against him for failing to join Longstreet in the clique to oust Bragg.[51]

Unfortunately, at a time when the Army of Northern Virginia needed all its good officers, Longstreet unnecessarily offended and alienated Law and drove McLaws, a slow but skillful division commander, away from the army. He could no longer serve under Longstreet, so he accepted an assignment in Georgia. The second division commander, Hood, a good combat commander but a careless administrator, recovered satisfactorily and advanced to corps command out west. Thus, Longstreet's corps entered the 1864 spring campaign with two new division commanders, Charles W. Field and Kershaw. Field, a West Point graduate, had earned a reputation as "courteous and affable to everyone, but a strict disciplinarian," which annoyed recalcitrant soldiers. He served as a fine brigade commander, but he sustained a severe hip wound, one that his wife, a clairvoyant, dreamed. After a lengthy convalescence—nearly a year and a half—he returned to the field for duty. Twenty years after the war, the bullet worked its way down the leg and a physician removed the ball above the knee. No one knew how well he would stand up to the rigors of the campaign. Longstreet tried to switch him with Maj. Gen. Simon Bolivar Buckner, a personal friend, but Davis would have none of it.[52]

Kershaw earned a reputation as an extremely ambitious officer. At First Manassas, he cursed his troops for not standing and fighting. Then, in a serious breach of military protocol, he submitted his campaign report to the newspapers for publication and publicity before turning it in to his superior officers. Longstreet had groomed him for high command, viewing him as the best brigade commander after Jenkins. Others were not convinced. Earlier in the war, Beauregard called him a "militia idiot." His men had problems with his excessive drinking.[53]

After the Gettysburg Campaign, Lee concluded that the cavalry required some reorganization. Brigades had too many regiments, and despite the depleted numbers of horsemen, more than four regiments were too much for a brigade commander to control in battle and camp. He decided to create seven cavalry brigades, and suggested to Davis that the War Department create two divisions and a corps.

Among the cavalry, Lee still had Stuart at the helm. In September 1863, when the commanding general reorganized the cavalry into a corps, he retained Stuart as its head without a promotion in rank. This was not because he fell out of favor with Lee. Stuart possessed a masterful tactical eye, and despite his flamboyance and love of publicity, he evinced a cool, brave manner in battle that inspired all around him. After serving under fire with him, an infantry officer remarked, "He always speaks kindly & encouragingly to those under his command," an excellent quality under duress. Lee considered him indispensable.[54]

For the first division slot, Lee recommended and Davis approved the choice of Wade Hampton. He was an extremely wealthy and well-connected South Carolinian who had fought with rare skill and gallantry since First Manassas. Over the course of the fighting, Hampton had suffered two wounds, including a shell fragment in the body and two saber cuts, one all the way to the skull, which required physicians to shave half his head. He took it all good-naturedly, declaring it "striking, if not beautiful," although "the flies play the mischief as they wander over the bald side." Lee recommended him for "his services and his gallantry."[55]

Hampton expressed neither fondness nor respect for Stuart. He regularly criticized Stuart for pampering the Virginia regiments and assigning his South Carolinians to the more arduous tasks. Others joined in the chorus, insisting that Virginians monopolized promotions that they did not deserve. In fact,

Hampton's claim was not quite as valid as he supposed. Four of seven cavalry brigades in the army came from Virginia. And the imbalance made sense. When a South Carolinian lost his horse, he had to return all the way home to secure a fresh mount. While he traveled, the Confederacy lost his services. Virginians could get home more quickly. Hampton criticized Stuart for assigning much of the duty during wintertime to non-Virginia horsemen, while he deployed Virginians to their home counties. Yet Virginia cavalrymen could feed their horses at local expense, thereby reducing the supply burden on the army and increasing hay and fodder for the other animals, and in time of crisis reassemble in several days. Stuart simply could not do that for Carolinians, Georgians, and Mississippians.[56]

For the other division command, Lee recommended his nephew, Fitz Lee. A happy-go-lucky student at the U.S. Military Academy when his uncle was superintendent, Fitz Lee evolved into a fine cavalry officer. He rose from staff officer and lieutenant colonel to brigadier general, capping his early service by guiding Jackson on his flanking march at Chancellorsville. Stuart thought Fitz Lee would make a fine division commander and recommended that the War Department elevate him over Hampton, even though Hampton's commission as brigadier general was older and therefore the South Carolinian outranked Fitz Lee. In his letter to Davis, Robert E. Lee hesitated to promote a family member, "but I do not know any other officer in the cavalry who has done better service." Neither Fitz Lee nor Hampton was a strong disciplinarian, but the commanding general excused that fault. "I know how difficult it is to establish rigid discipline in our armies, and therefore make allowances," Lee elaborated.[57]

Civil War officers understood the political nature of their positions. With varying degrees of success, most of them had cultivated ties to prominent politicians by taking them on as volunteer aides. Promotion to brigadier general and above required a presidential appointment and congressional approval, and well-placed or respected patrons within the Confederate Senate could help maneuver the nomination through political minefields or lobby for presidential appointment. John Bell Hood befriended Davis and, with the help of various senators, secured a promotion to lieutenant general and a corps command in the Army of Tennessee after recovering from his severe wound at Chickamauga. Longstreet proposed Hood for promotion in October 1863, which McLaws viewed as an effort to get rid of a climber who was "more of a politician & did not hesitate to denounce Longstreets demerits at Hd Qrs." Competing candidates for promotion regularly accused their opponents of pandering to Congress and the administration during their all-too-frequent trips to Richmond. Less bold officers did not lobby directly; they encouraged or permitted other soldiers or civilians to petition the War Department or administration, seeking the promotion of their champion. One accomplished officer, Brig. Gen. William Mahone, actually had the General Assembly of Virginia petition Davis on his behalf. Politics and generalship went hand in hand in Lee's army, although the towering presence and reputation of Lee largely prevented these matters from bubbling to the surface.[58]

Whether they were politicians turned generals or career officers, they understood that at least part of the process was political, and that it never hurt to have an advocate in the court of politics. When it came to Lee's army, however, Davis hesitated to interfere with personnel decisions. While he would do so if it were in the interests of the service, he much preferred Lee's opinion and consent before promoting or transferring individuals.

Opportunity certainly presented itself for those with talent who aspired to high command. Lee's army crossed into Pennsylvania with fifty-two general officers. Seventeen failed to return. At Chancellorsville, it lost a cluster more, including Jackson. When Lee scanned the casualty list from Chickamauga, he wrote the president, "I am gradually losing my best men."[59]

As he contemplated the spring campaign of 1864, Lee surely understood his predicament. Two of his three corps commanders had thus far failed him, and he observed no evidence of genuine improvement. Four of his division commanders had assumed their posts after Gettysburg, and another had taken over during the battle. Two more commanded divisions for the first time for the Gettysburg Campaign, which left only four major generals who had led divisions during Chancellorsville or earlier. Lee's army bled dry from the top as well as the bottom.

Chapter 27

PREPARING FOR THE
SPRING CAMPAIGN OF 1864

BLUSTERY WINTER WEATHER chilled soldiers to the marrow. They huddled around fires in shanties or the open air, lightly clothed for a frigid February day, warming themselves as best they could. These days were so cold, their veteran army commander commented to his brother that "Ice freezes hard in our tents, even when there is a fire." Yet many of them were old hands at Virginia winters, enduring their second or third cold season at the front. Experience did not soften the elements. The frigid air bit and stung, and like everything else, they would simply have to endure it.[1]

Shortages plagued the army, as they had done for years. "Aunt Frank it is enough to make tears come from the eyes of the most hardened soul to see our brave men marching through the mud & snow almost naked & *barefooted*," a lieutenant in the 3rd Georgia Sharpshooters wrote. Only five or six men in his company had shoes. Two weeks later, in early February, a Virginian estimated that half the men lacked adequate footwear and wondered, "if our government cant do better than that I don't know how we will make out much longer." Lee struggled to get leather or hides to divisions and brigades, where cobblers and handymen among them could make shoes for their command. Twenty-two men in McLaws's old division took a break from traditional soldiering to produce fifteen hundred pairs of shoes and repair hundreds more that winter. Once again, the army took matters into its own hands when the government failed to provide for its men.[2]

When it came to food for the troops and provender for the animals, there was little soldiers could do. In mid-January, a Virginian admitted, "Rations scarce as hens teeth." Ramseur informed his brother later that for the past month soldiers had subsisted on $1\frac{1}{8}$ pounds of flour and between $\frac{1}{8}$ and $\frac{1}{4}$ pound of meat per day and nothing else. By early April, the army curtailed the ration to $\frac{2}{3}$ pound of unsifted flour and $\frac{1}{3}$ pound of bacon, which, so grumbled a soldier, "cose grate dissadisfaction a mong the soldiers. In fack it was barley enuf for one meal per day." Based on recent weather, A. P. Hill joked, "We have no fault to find with the amount of water lately issued to this army, the ration of which has been full to overflowing. I cannot say so much for the other component parts, equally necessary, and much more acceptable when *dry*."[3]

Horses and mules suffered as badly as the troops. In mid-February, Lee warned Quartermaster General Lawton that the army had received only 6½ days' rations since the first of the month, forcing him to tap his meager reserve. Two days later, Pendleton reported 600 to 700 artillery horses in infirmaries in Lynchburg and North Carolina out of a total of 3,000. Stuart's horsemen, too, had serious problems sustaining their mounts, and when Longstreet sought additional animals for a proposed dash into Kentucky, Lee replied with the revealing question: "If horses could be obtained for you, where is the forage & equipment to be procured?"[4]

Two main factors determined the shortage. According to reasonable estimates, Richmond had a population of 130,000, with an infrastructure capable of handling only 50,000. That huge population and its animals had to be fed. The larger problem lay with the railroads. Track failed, mechanics and laborers joined the army or, in the case of slaves, fled to the Yankees, and winter weather washed out portions of lines or temporarily stifled transit. On February 8, the Department of Subsistence reported less than one-third of all food for man and beast shipped in January had reached Lee's army. Along the line from Greensboro to Danville, a freshet had washed out the railroad, causing a ten- to fifteen-day delay for repairs.[5]

Even without bad weather, the rail system impeded Lee's ability to feed and supply his army. Travel was so slow that it took a soldier almost sixty hours by rail to go from Raleigh to Orange Court House. On the verge of the spring campaign, a knowledgeable source notified a general that North Carolina alone had 30,000 tons of long forage for army use with "efficient collection & distribution," but that failed to address the difficulty of getting the animal feed to the army.[6]

All of this boded ill for the Confederacy as the campaign season neared. On March 9, the assistant to the commissary general warned, "If supplies are not accumulated here a demoralized Army pillaging its countrymen may be looked for, with the loss of Richmond." His fears reflected more than a kernel of truth. A Georgia private confirmed that soldiers had begun to take matters into their own hands. Troops began pilfering chickens and meat from locals. "The thing went on for several days, the men all hungry and mad." Eventually, they went to the brigade commander and threatened to charge the commissary and take the food by force if he did not issue more. "He had us a extray days rashins ishued and got us all sorty pasafide," the private conveyed. Still, he warned, "Hungry will cose a man to do all most any thing."[7]

Lee attempted to protect and assist local farmers in their production by halting common practices among his troops. He ordered roads through farmers' fields closed and preserved fencing—if soldiers were going to trample fields, why would any farmer waste the labor to till the soil and sow food crops? Lee also announced that in the future the army would not bury the dead in cultivated fields. He instructed the men that they could dig graves only in church cemeteries or some remote location, such as woods.[8]

For all that, morale remained stable that winter. For three years, soldiers in Virginia had repeatedly battled back Yankee onslaughts and had even taken the war across the Potomac. This year gave them a new opportunity; 1864 would be a campaign season that could make or break the Confederacy. It was a Northern presidential election year, and Confederates anticipated a huge push to close out the war or dramatically shift Yankee fortunes before citizens cast their ballots. "This is to be the big fight," a Georgia private instructed his mother, "the fight that is to restore peace to our land, or to be our everlasting ruin." A Texas private bubbled with eagerness for the upcoming campaign. "We are still flushed with the pleasing anticipation that this summer will cast the die for our great deliverance from Yankee tyranny," he exclaimed. A diarist concurred. "Our soldiers are in the highest kind of spirits and confident of victory. All believe that this campaign will *end the war*."[9]

Some soldiers believed that the new Union commanding general, Ulysses S. Grant, would launch a titanic struggle to win the war in this campaign. "The army seem to expect a harder time," an Alabama lieutenant conveyed. A Georgian agreed. "Officers and men believe that Grant is the enemies' last man." After handicapping the campaign, he concluded with the words, "The opinion seems general in both armies that this year will end the war." Not only did the Federals have the presidential and congressional elections hanging over their heads, but terms of service for three-year Union enlistments expired that summer. It would take months and months to get fresh recruits up to pace, during which time the advantage would shift dramatically to the Confederates. Everyone agreed that Grant would press as hard as possible to seize Richmond in this spring campaign. Less than four weeks before the start of the Union advance, an Alabamian predicted that Lee's army "Will have some bloody work to do before very long."[10]

Other soldiers had their own reasons to begin the fight. Lieutenant Colonel Willie Pegram was eager to get out of camp and get the war over. A private in the Powhatan Artillery hoped they would deliver the "greatest whipen ever they haf got in their lives" so he could plunder them. He also wanted Yankee food. "I will get as fat as a pig or as fat as that pig that bit your mother's finger." Pendleton's nephew informed his parents, "We are all making our lists of 'articles to be procured in Pennsylvania,'" in anticipation of success.[11]

At the prospect of bringing the war to a close, soldiers exhibited a new exuberance. Led by Hart's South Carolina Battery, Cullen Battle's Alabama Brigade, George P. Doles's Georgia Brigade, and the North Carolina brigades of Ramseur, Robert D. Johnston, and Junius Daniel, the army erupted in a flurry of re-enlistments for the war. Although the act was more symbolic than real—the Confederacy would never have let them leave the service by expiration of their terms—it represented a passion to see the war through to victory in this, the decisive year. As a North Carolina enlisted man wrote to his father, "Pa we have all Reinlisted for the 'War' we had to do it and I thought I would come on as a patriot soldier of the South." He concluded, "We are soldiers and we have to stay as long as there is any 'war' there is no way to escape it." Certainly some felt they had endured enough and wanted to leave the service. An enlisted man in the 26th North Carolina doubted fifty men would re-enlist and the colonel "would not let it come to a vote because he knew it would not pass." As he explained, "they are tired of this war and don't want to stay any longer." They were the exceptions, though.[12]

After three years of fighting, Confederates still harbored a deep hatred for Yankees. The hardships, sacrifices, and fatalities intensified those feelings over time. Mississippian Jesse Sparkman shuddered at the thought of more fighting, but he believed God would permit Confederate to avenge losses in this unnecessary and unholy war. "Surely a just God will punish these Northern fanatics for the misery and death they are spreading over our land," he jotted in his diary. "Yes, a day of retribution must come when they shall be made to feel the curse of their own evil doing. I sometimes wish that the earth might engulf them as the wicked were in the Red Sea." Private Samuel Walsh resented the Union for "trying to force us to live as the colered race of our land." In concurrence, a Virginia private from a slaveholding family insisted the war "will either show clearly that Slavery is a divine law, or that it is an 'abomination,' as the 'Abolitionist' say it is." A Georgia enlisted man who had run his father's plantation with thirty-two slaves before the war pledged to fight as long as the Confederacy had an army, "rather than the South should agree to a dishonorable peace." He sincerely hoped the Confederacy would secure its independence "from the tyrannical yoke of abolitionism. I want to have the explicit pleasure of telling the Yankee wherever I may meet him that his people were not able to Subjugate the South."[13]

Despite all the losses, this was still a veteran army, composed primarily of men who had joined the service in 1861 and 1862. The old soldiers dominated the tone and the key positions. A crusty veteran described himself to a loved one with the assessment, "I am a pretty hard looking case, a regular *hard-up* confederate." His wardrobe consisted of anything he could "borrow," including shirt, boots, and hat. "I go to church every Sunday weather permitting, Don't drink any liquors, stronger than water because Confederate shin plasters are too scarce (not because liquor is to[o] scarce)." As April rolled around, staff officer Osmun Latrobe believed, "Our troops are in magnificent condition, full of confidence in their leaders and themselves, and better still full of bitter hate to the enemy."[14]

Those who entered the service in 1863 and 1864 composed a small portion, about one in every six, of those who ultimately served in Lee's army. Although their median age was considerably older than those who had joined earlier in the war, the soldiers of 1863 and 1864 tended toward the edges of the age curve. Almost two of every three men were in their thirties or were minors when the

South seceded from the Union. Compared to 1861 and 1862, the percentage of those who entered the service in their thirties doubled. Close to half the men of '63 and '64 left spouses behind. On the other hand, census takers in 1860 listed nearly three in every ten as students. And more of the new recruits came from parts of the Upper South—the states of Maryland, Virginia, and North Carolina. As wartime logistics strained the transportation network, it proved easier to assign new troops nearest to Virginia to Lee's army.[15]

Reflecting both their age and youth, the soldiers of 1863 and 1864 had a higher median personal and family wealth than did those of 1861 and 1862. The men in their thirties had accumulated more property than younger heads of household, and the younger men still lived with their parents or other family members. When it came to slaveholding, however, the results were mixed. Twenty percent more soldiers who entered the war in 1863 or 1864 personally owned slaves. Yet when those who lived with their parents enter the equation, the statistic reverses. Twenty percent more of the recruits of 1861 and 1862 and their families owned slaves. Compared to their later comrades, 25 percent more men from the 1861 and 1862 groups lived in households with slaves. Despite the significant overrepresentation of soldiers from the planter class in Lee's army, the percentage of new soldiers from families with twenty or more slaves also declined by nearly 15 percent in the last two years of the war.[16]

Beneath their surface enthusiasm lay some serious problems. Many of the troops who joined in 1863 had fought in some of the largest and most destructive battles on this continent; others had entered military service in the aftermath of Gettysburg, and they had experienced little action. Those who joined in early 1864 knew nothing about soldiering. Due to attrition among veterans, those who donned the uniform for the first time in 1863 or 1864 constituted a heavier proportion of manpower. Their actual strength within the army for that spring campaign may have been close to one in every four, and in some commands, the proportion was much higher. Company A, 11th Virginia Infantry, for example, opened the campaign with twenty-five new recruits out of forty-four men. They entered military service and underwent the typical cycle of green soldiers. Many suffered from measles and other highly contagious diseases, so that Lee tried to detain them at Camp Lee in Richmond, to make sure they did not carry those pathogens into camp. Those "childhood" illnesses, along with the usual winter bouts with colds, pneumonia, rheumatism, and other ailments, took a severe toll on the army. In Kershaw's old South Carolina brigade, one-third of the effectives were ill just a month before the campaign opened, and despite the best efforts of the Medical Department, measles broke out in William T. Wofford's Brigade.[17]

Both officers and men grumbled over the lack of quality officers in the army. A signal corpsman claimed that every private knew if Lee had "good and active executive officers," they would defeat the Federals. Because congressional law imposed seniority on the army, Lee's only means of ridding the service of poor officers or blocking the elevation of mediocre ones were examination boards.

The backlog, however, proved disastrous. In February, Lee complained that the War Department reviewed decisions by boards of examiners at such a glacial pace that he had just received a report ten months after the examination. The board had tested the officer before the Chancellorsville Campaign.[18]

Inspections in very early spring uncovered serious shortcomings among company officers. Attrition in battle and promotion to field grade had thinned the ranks of quality officers, and inspectors uncovered severe administrative problems. In B. G. Humphreys's Mississippi Brigade (Barksdale's old brigade), three of four regiments had captains in command, which meant they were not overseeing their companies. No officer had undertaken efforts to work on tactics since Chickamauga. Inspectors uncovered a serious inattention to troops in Goode Bryan's Georgia Brigade. "Many company commanders are not sufficiently familiar with the condition of the men," a lieutenant colonel observed. Kershaw's old brigade suffered the same fate. General Braxton Bragg, removed as commander of the Army of Tennessee and serving as Davis's military advisor, uncovered similar problems throughout McLaws's old division, which Kershaw had commanded since mid-December.[19]

Once again, Rodes surpassed his comrades in efficient oversight of his command. This time, he counseled officers in proper leadership in battle and on the march. He complained that company-grade officers abdicated their responsibilities in battle by not directing the fire of their men. They permitted their men to fire at random and, reverting to their role as enlisted men, grabbed muskets and fought alongside their troops. Officers, Rodes insisted, must remain calm, redirect errant fire, keep troops in line and at their work, and preserve good order. Field-grade officers must supervise the march more carefully, keeping the unit compact and preventing straggling. If the column arrived at a difficult crossing during the march, Rodes demanded that the commanding officer wait there to ensure everyone made it through. By adopting these procedures, Rodes anticipated, the army would develop a greater esprit de corps and enhanced efficiency in battle and on the march.[20]

Three years of fighting had taken their toll, not just on officers and men, but also on the tools to make war. In the Third Corps, for example, an inspector deemed the artillery in bad condition, pronouncing Pegram's battalion "unserviceable." All the guns had suffered from severe wear and tear and demanded immediate repair. With such poor cannons, the men took little pride in maintaining their guns, all of which were badly in need of a proper cleaning. Extensive campaigning, a tough winter, and severely limited food had also debilitated the animals. The army could nurse the horses back to strength with additional food, when it became available, but Pegram's men would simply have to maintain the guns as best they could. No new weapons, carriages, or barrels would replace them.[21]

Long before the weather warmed and the roads began to dry, Lee's army undertook steps to prepare for active campaigning. At their commander's insistence, officers and men pared down their possessions to reduce baggage before the campaign. General officers again hounded their men about the unnecessary waste of ammunition, threatening to hold regimental commanders responsible for unnecessary damage to ammunition unless they punished troops for it. The Ordnance Department issued a circular for soldiers who fired Enfield rifled muskets, reminding them as Lee had done eighteen months earlier that when they loaded the weapon, they could not ram the charge with the paper cartridge. Soldiers must pour the gunpowder, drop the projectile without the paper down the barrel, and then pack it down with the ramrod. The circular reported that "many of them ram the charge home with the paper between the bullet and the powder. As this paper is a very stiff hollow cylinder it will not crumple up, therefore a considerable space in the barrel" developed. Either the projectile lacked adequate velocity when fired—a spent round—or if the powder packed near the bullet, a hang fire (a delayed, inaccurate firing) would occur.[22]

The army took steps to increase troop strength and prepare soldiers for the coming struggle. Lee requested that Davis remit the sentences of a number of enlisted men languishing in prison, consuming supplies and not contributing to the war effort. "I am desirous of having the men returned to the army," the commanding general wrote, "in time to take part in the approaching campaign." Kirkland's North Carolina Brigade underwent company drill in the morning, battalion or brigade drill in the evening, and then dress parade to refresh the veterans, train the recruits, and bond the two groups. A soldier in the 44th North Carolina, in the same brigade, reported that they practiced skirmishing and took target practice at ranges up to 900 yards. Sharpshooters in other regiments also worked on their marksmanship, firing at targets up to 600 yards away. Stuart directed Fitz Lee to practice with his cavalrymen charging in column, "solid and compact, so as *to shock*." He wanted them to dismount and deploy on foot, and to "urge commanders to *command their men* in *action* from Corpl up to Brigadier." Lee instructed his men if the Yankees captured them, not to give the name of their regiment, brigade, division, or corps. Simply tell them your name and company, and while in Union prisons, do not discuss any military matters.[23]

Spiritually, too, soldiers prepared themselves for the bloodiest struggle of the war. Throughout the month of April revivals seized hold of the army—not the kind with shouts and emotional outbursts, but calm, serious affairs. One soldier argued that officers pledged to the Presbyterian church while "the privates Join the mud heads," presumably the Baptists. Since the conversions began, thievery of rations had ceased in his company. A North Carolinian explained to his wife that nightly religious service packed the chapel, and if a soldier wanted a seat, he had to get there early. Another North Carolinian, a private, declared to his aunt and uncle "if our people at home would only be as attentive in serving God is[as] the soldiers I think we will prosper in all our efforts, and undertakings." Yet another soldier trumpeted to his parents, "a great change is taking place in our Brigade. I feel like we will be victorious on the battlefield. I feel like the God of battles will help us out in our great difficulty and deliver us from our enemies." Soldiers went to church to help get all things in order for the campaign season, and many of them came away with newfound inspiration and a conviction that God would aid their side. Lee himself encouraged these religious activities by attending them when he could.[24]

Throughout the first four months of 1864, Lee devoted a large portion of his time and energy to solving his logistical problems. Shortages in food for men and animals dominated his concerns, and he tried every means to reduce them. In early January, he forbade the use of ordnance wagons except under great necessity. Lee wanted the animals out foraging. In early April, he imposed a weight limit of eighteen hundred pounds per wagon unless "the distance is short and the load constantly decreasing." Two weeks later, he slightly modified that directive, but the principle remained the same. So severe were supply problems that Lee had to keep Longstreet's two divisions near Gordonsville, some ten miles to the rear. If he concentrated the army near the Rapidan River, he could not supply it. By midmonth, Lee admitted to Davis, "My anxiety on the subject of provisions for the army is so great that I cannot refrain from expressing it to your Excy. [Excellency]. I cannot see how we can operate with our present supplies." Any disruption of the supply route or failure on the railroad would place his army in a desperate situation and might force him to abandon all of Virginia. He had stockpiled rations for that day and tomorrow and had nothing more. "Every exertion should be made to supply the depots at Richmond and at other points," he urged. He pleaded with Davis to earmark all available space on trains for supplies.[25]

The hot-tempered Lee grew unusually testy. Had logistics been his sole concern, Lee would have compartmentalized it better, but he had to direct and administer the entire army, serve as advisor to Davis whenever the president called for his opinion, and worry about supply, a problem over which he had little control. Under the strain, Lee lashed out at his wife for her miscounting the number of pairs of socks she and her friends had knitted and sent to him for needy soldiers. The mere fact that the army commander, with all his work, would count twenty-six pairs of socks in a box and then take time to rebuke her for the incorrect number indicated both his reaction under stress and the dynamics of his relationship with his wife. Less than a week later, a new shipment of socks arrived, and Lee verified those numbers as well. Although the incident probably revealed more about Lee's frustration with his wife's imprecision than anything else, it also demonstrated Lee's increasing intolerance with inefficiency around him.[26]

Lee correctly forecast that the Union would advance in Virginia on several fronts. Not only would Grant strike southward across the Rapidan and Rappahannock rivers, but the Federals would hurl forces west from the coast toward Richmond and south up the Shenandoah Valley. Lee erred, however, when he underestimated the size, strength, and sustaining power of the Union. The Confederate general believed the Federals would concentrate on a single objective first, probably the Army of Tennessee, now under Joseph E. Johnston.

He knew enough to wait for the Union to tip its hand, but his initial guess was wrong. Lee did not realize that the Union possessed enough power to launch several major campaigns simultaneously.[27]

More than seven months earlier, two divisions under Longstreet had entrained for Georgia, eager to demonstrate their mettle to their western comrades. Although they spearheaded a rout of the Federals at Chickamauga, events soon turned sour. Many concluded that the soldiers in the Confederate Army of Tennessee were not bad material, but a knowledgeable officer asserted that they were a year behind the Army of Northern Virginia in organization, marching, and fighting. Then, the Army of Tennessee suffered a disastrous defeat at Chattanooga, and Longstreet's men were repulsed in their assault on Knoxville, largely due to mismanagement by general officers. A rough winter in Tennessee sapped any remaining enthusiasm for service in the West.[28]

On April 7, 1864, Longstreet received orders to rejoin the Army of Northern Virginia. Troops in Virginia and Tennessee were delighted. Even though they were destined for heavy fighting, they were also going home, and that added spring in their step made the trip all the more easy. As they arrived in the vicinity of Gordonsville, a South Carolina officer admitted "he felt as if the right arm of the army had been restored."[29]

On April 29, Longstreet assembled his command for a giant review by Lee. Across an expansive field assembled 10,000 to 12,000 soldiers, with a large crowd of civilians to see the event. Once Lee appeared on horseback, waves of cheers roared down the line, "a feeling that thrilled all hearts," a soldier reported. Men tossed their hats into the air in honor of their old commander. As the soldiers marched past the reviewing party, men violated propriety to cast a sideways glance at their beloved leader. When the review ended, the crowd rushed to Lee. According to a soldier, some women announced, "they had Shuck handes with the gratest general in the world."[30]

For all the headaches and stress that Lee endured, the long wait was almost over. His army once more reunited, the thought of combat seemed to pick up Lee's spirits.[31]

Chapter 28

———◦⬦◦———

THE OVERLAND CAMPAIGN

O N MAY 2, 1864, the 28th North Carolina marched out of camp to a
nearby field, surrounded by tall trees. Just as they had done repeatedly for some time, the troops began to practice tactical maneuvers with their
green recruits, so that the newcomers could execute critical movements in battle. Without much warning, a dark sky overwhelmed them. The temperature
dropped quickly, and in the distance, they could see a tornado funnel ripping
gaps in the trees. The soldiers immediately broke for quarters, but before they
reached them, "it was upon us," as a company officer wrote. Thick clouds of
dust and dirt nearly suffocated them, while the rattling of tall trees and flying debris convinced them to stand in open ground. Several massive timbers
uprooted by the funnel came crashing down. Good fortune shone on the 28th
that day: none of the regiment was injured, aside from minor scrapes and cuts.

Neighboring 37th North Carolina was not so lucky. It, too, had begun drilling in a nearby field when the storm suddenly engulfed it, tossing a massive
pine tree into its ranks. The dirt clouds so blinded the men that no one saw the
tree falling on them. By a miracle, only one man was killed. Three others suffered serious wounds, and several more sustained slighter injuries.[1]

The tornado paled in comparison with the storm several days later. On May
4, the Union army under Grant crossed the Rapidan River and began pushing
through the Wilderness, the area around the old Chancellorsville battlefield,
in hopes of stealing a march on Lee and maneuvering into more open ground
to the southeast. Lee responded by pushing Ewell's Corps northeastward along
the Orange Turnpike, the most direct route to the Wilderness. Hill's Corps
advanced along the Orange Plank Road, which would carry his men to the
south of Ewell's columns. Longstreet's forces, the farthest away and the last to
move, exhibited their usual ponderous pace, but when they arrived, they were
ready to deliver a powerful punch.[2]

Lee selected wisely when he decided to fight Grant's forces in the Wilderness. The tangled, second-generation growth made travel off the roads
extremely difficult, and Lee and his officers knew the confusing road network
far better than their Yankee adversaries. The terrain, moreover, neutralized

two of the Union's greatest strengths. Even though Federals possessed a two-to-one manpower advantage, they could not deploy those masses effectively there. Nor could the Yankees exploit their artillery superiority. Just as Lee would have wished, the battle would become an infantry fight, and Lee had no doubt that he commanded the finest infantrymen in the world. The Confederate commander intended to hold the enemy in the Wilderness with Ewell and Hill and have Longstreet deliver the crushing blow on the left flank of the Yankee army.[3]

En route to the Wilderness, a Virginian in Ewell's Corps jotted a potentially final note to his mother, stating, "I hope we will be able to give them a good thrashing, for on this fight depends greatly our future safety." Later that day, May 5, a portion of Ewell's Corps reached the Wilderness and tossed up some field works along the Orange Turnpike. Federals, assuming this was a token party, attempted to sweep them aside, and the battle began. Ewell's Corps quickly engaged in heavy fighting, with several brigades suffering extensive casualties. Over the course of two days, fighting varied from difficult to savage. At one point, fires scorched an open field with hundreds of dead and wounded soldiers. Two Confederate brigades, Cullen Battle's Alabamians and John M. Jones's Virginians, piled up heavy casualties and fell back under mistaken orders. Georgians under Brigadier Generals John B. Gordon and George Doles not only plugged the gap but routed the acclaimed Iron Brigade of Wisconsin, Indiana, and Michigan soldiers in the process. Despite considerable losses, Ewell's Corps accomplished its mission. It fixed and held the enemy in place.[4]

Hill's troops, led by Heth's Division, neared the intersection of Orange Plank and Brock roads, several miles to the southeast of Ewell, and after some skirmishing Heth's men began tossing up field works several hundred yards back along a low ridge. The Federals concentrated overwhelming strength on Heth's command, ultimately forcing Hill to throw Wilcox's Division into the fight to prevent a disaster. "I sat in one place and shot my riful 61 times," a private in the 55th North Carolina informed his wife. His company went into the fight with thirty men and came out with eight, and only two fell into Union hands. His regiment lost nearly two-thirds of its men that afternoon. By nightfall, Wilcox's men had staved off disaster, but Hill's Corps had suffered badly against superior Federal strength.[5]

By dawn's first light, Union troops on Hill's front launched their attack. Grant had correctly divined Hill's precarious situation, and he concentrated on shattering that command early in the morning. With the Union juggernaut finally rolling, Hill faced disaster. Worn down by the previous day's fighting, and horribly outnumbered, he could not last against this massive Union steamroller. As Hill's line fell back, the corps commander cobbled together a dozen cannons to check the Union advance. It was not enough. They delayed, but could not disrupt, the Yankee wave. As his line threatened to buckle, Longstreet's Texas Brigade raced up from the rear. Lee rushed among them, cheering them on, calling out that Texans had always driven the foe. The commanding general

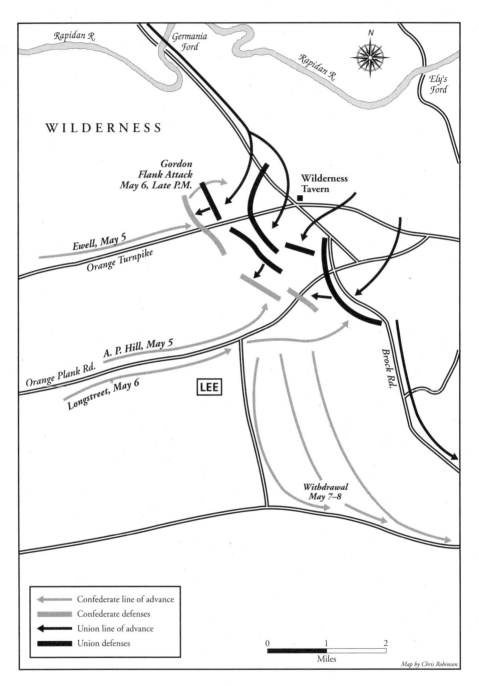

Battle of the Wilderness

then tried to lead them into battle, but the Texans would have none of it. With bullets whizzing by them, "now some one seizes the Genl Lee's bridel & says he must go no father. he stops & to our great relief turns back." According to one of Hill's staff officers, "Genl Lee started to lead one Brigade in a charge, they told him to go back or they *would n't fight*. He did not go back tho' till two of Lee's staff led his horse off." Longstreet's columns struck like a sledge-hammer and pounded back the Federals. His men picked up Yankee rifles and with several loaded weapons at their side they repulsed renewed attacks. As one Georgian depicted the scene, "the 'blue bodies' were piled up."[6]

Despite the difficult terrain, Lee sought an opportunity to strike the Yankees' flank. A staff officer discovered a railroad cut, and several brigades maneuvered through it. Nearly two years earlier, Hill had squabbled with Longstreet's staff officer Moxley Sorrel to the point where he would not accept any communication from him. This time, Sorrel led an assault that rolled up the Union flank and relieved pressure on Hill's exhausted men. Hill never forgot the favor, and in October when a vacancy occurred in one of his Georgia brigades, he arranged for Sorrel to receive the promotion and appointment.[7]

Longstreet, "with his usual contempt for life, could be seen where the bullets flew thickest," a Georgian commented in his diary. As Longstreet advanced forward with Jenkins, Kershaw, and some staff, troops from Mahone's Brigade assumed they were Yankees and fired from fifty to sixty yards away. Their shots were telling. Longstreet, Jenkins, and two staff officers were hit. The staff officers died at the scene. Jenkins, shot through the skull, uttered the words, "'steady men steady,'" and he expired. Meanwhile, a projectile had punched through Longstreet's throat and exited through his right shoulder. Three of Longstreet's staff officers lifted the two-hundred-pound general from his horse and laid him on the ground. At that moment a lull in the fight occurred, and Lee detected something was wrong. "In a few moments," a South Carolinian in Jenkins's Brigade described for his mother, "this Great Chief was among us, calm, noble, a quiet confidence resting upon his face. I saw him then, and will never forget the scene." That night, Longstreet endured sheer agony, admitting he had no idea "men were liable to such pain." They administered opiates to alleviate his suffering, and in fitful dreams he gasped out, "Those are extra regiments, the line is formed let it advance." Longstreet would live, but he would not return to the army for some months, and when he did, he still could not use his arm. Disaster had befallen the Confederacy once again at the hands of its own men, four miles from where some of their own troops had shot Jackson a year earlier. Lee appointed Richard H. "Dick" Anderson as the acting corps commander.[8]

Once Longstreet went down, the attack stalled. Confederate forces were in disarray, and it took several hours to sort out things. In the late afternoon, the Federals mounted a final thrust on the Confederate right. Despite making some headway, they could not inject sufficient manpower to exploit the opening. That night, Rebel troops braced for yet another early morning attack.

Men stockpiled weapons—two to five loaded guns they had picked up on the battlefield that day—ready to pour a devastating fire on those blue lines. But there would be no attack.[9]

On the Confederate left, Gordon had lobbied hard for a flank attack, much like the one Jackson had employed at Chancellorsville a year earlier. His superiors were hesitant, but the persistent Georgian finally received authorization to strike late in the afternoon with two brigades. He plowed back part of the Union line, creating a minor scare, but his attack lacked the strength necessary to inflict serious damage. Jackson had taken 28,000 men on his famous flank march, achieved surprise, and still could not make it decisive. Ewell's entire corps had far fewer men than Jackson had employed, and he could not extricate enough of them from the line to deliver a meaningful blow.[10]

The next day, Grant planned a night march to slide his columns around Lee's right flank and occupy the area near Spotsylvania Court House. That would position his army between Lee and Richmond and compel the Confederate commander to attack him on Grant's choice of ground. Fitz Lee raced his men to the crossroads northwest of the village, moving faster and fighting with greater resolve than the Federals, even though many of the Yankee horsemen carried Spencer repeating carbines. It may have been Fitz Lee's greatest accomplishment of the war.[11]

Infantry followed rapidly to support Stuart's cavalrymen. A sergeant major noted it was very hot and water was scarce en route. "The only signs of life I have seen in this desolate country was a dog," an artillerist claimed. "It did me good to see it." Bands banged out national airs as the army moved throughout the night. Wounded Yankees cried hurrah as they assumed the Confederates were retreating for Richmond, badly underestimating Lee and his army.[12]

Once again, Lee's planning and knowledge of the roads reaped dividends. Anderson arrived to bolster the cavalrymen, assuming a position that Lee had selected over a month earlier. Federal infantry, assuming only cavalry opposed them, attacked recklessly and Anderson's men hammered them back. Additional Rebel and Yankee commands filtered into the area, and both sides began tossing up works. Lacking spades, the Confederates loosened earth with bayonets, shoveled with cups, and scooped by hand. Nonetheless, they erected some formidable works, with abatis, logs protected by dirt mounds, and headlogs, which enabled soldiers to fire their rifles without exposing the tops of their heads. The line extended in a broad-shaped inverted V, with a bulging salient known as the Muleshoe at the portion where the two wings connected.[13]

On May 10, a Union assault on the Muleshoe crashed through Doles's Georgians and seized several hundred prisoners. Federals had forced Doles's men back behind Confederate works, enabling the attackers to conceal themselves in the woods as they moved up close to the fortifications. A combined effort by North Carolinians, Alabamians, Virginians, and the remnants of Doles's Brigade snuffed out the penetration, but the initial success set the stage for a massive assault two days later.[14]

Grant selected May 12 for an attack to seize the Muleshoe and its men. To prevent Lee from dispatching troops from other sectors to reinforce the area, he directed four corps to attack along the line. Lee had received intelligence that led him to believe Grant intended to shift his army toward Fredericksburg, and in order to move rapidly, Lee ordered Ewell to remove his cannons from the Muleshoe. Ewell elected not to do so, because of heavy rain and mud, but his artillery chief, Brig. Gen. A. L. Long, shifted them rearward and placed the horses out to graze. After midnight, Allegheny Johnson detected Union movement into position for an attack, and Long returned some guns, but they arrived just in time for the Yankees to seize them.[15]

Shortly after 4:30 A.M., overwhelming numbers of Federals appeared from the mist and crashed though Confederate barriers and into the Muleshoe. Perhaps 2,000 graycoats fell into Union hands, including Johnson and brigade commander George Steuart. On the tip of the salient, undermanned Louisianans resisted well until their exposed right flank forced them to fight in two directions. The Stonewall Brigade, just to the left of the Louisianans, also fought valiantly but could not match the Federals. Along the line, Confederate brigades toppled. Next in line was Hays's old brigade of Louisianans. They had collected multiple rifles and loaded them in anticipation of just such an attack. With unusual firepower and considerable help from Junius Daniel's North Carolinians, they held their ground long enough for Gordon's Division, the corps reserve, to stem the tide. Gordon pushed a North Carolina brigade into Steuart's old position and as he prepared a counterthrust with two other brigades, Lee arrived to lead them into the fight. For a second time in less than a week, soldiers shouted for Lee to return, and the army commander relented. It was a wise decision. No one could have executed better than Gordon. His brigades slammed into the Federals and restored virtually the entire right portion of the salient to Rebel control. On the left part of the Muleshoe, Rodes sent Battle's Alabama Brigade to buttress Daniel's men. They not only stabilized that front but regained ground. Then, Ramseur's North Carolinians entered the fight. Using the fog and mist to conceal themselves, the brigade swung around Daniel's right and charged the works that the Stonewall Brigade had vacated. Despite heavy losses and vicious fighting, they gained a foothold in the old works and began prying Federals from them. Further reinforcements helped solidify those reconquered trenches, but at a very heavy cost. Ramseur, who suffered a serious arm wound in the fight, earned the title "hero of the day" from Ewell as well as Lee's personal thanks.[16]

Not since the Seven Days' Battle had fighting been so intense for such a prolonged period. Unlike Seven Days', though, every command saw extensive action, and soldiers were continually at risk. Lines were very close together, and sharpshooters posed a constant threat. Union artillery proved uncannily accurate. A Georgia private slept next to one of his friends one night. Suddenly, he awoke as his friend struggled to breathe. Before he could get light on him, his friend died of a chest wound from a musket ball.[17]

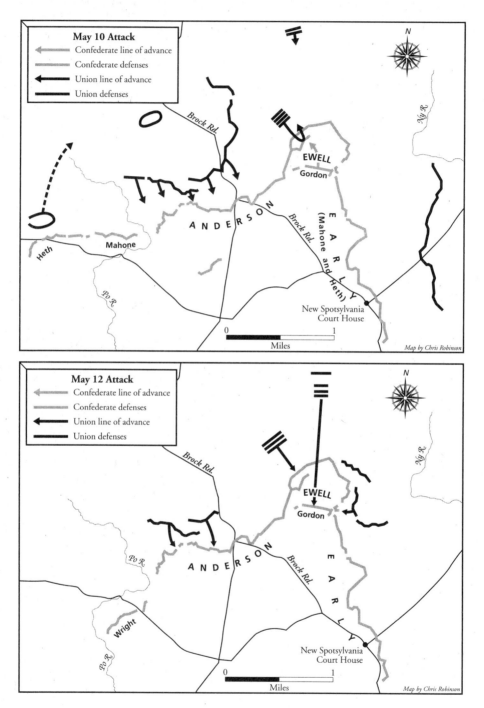

Battle of Spotsylvania

Even for the old veterans, this series of battles was some very tough fighting. "You can imagine what a hard struggle it is when I say Gettysburg cannot be compared to it," a Georgia officer wrote to his wife. One Virginia cavalryman explored a pine forest after the evacuation at Spotsylvania and found almost every shot embedded in trees within the height of a man, exhibiting "remarkably accurate firing." For newcomers, it was a brutal introduction to war. Venable, on Lee's staff, gazed upon the seventeen-year-olds who had only joined the army that winter. "It is sad to see their little faces in many instances girl like, all powder begrimed & then see them forlorn & broken down unable to follow other veterans & looking in the wilderness for their regiments," he wrote. "God bless the brave boys. Their first battle frightened them but they make soldiers in a week." Several days later he scripted, "I saw a poor little young soldier this afternoon crying by his dead comrade." He did not know if it was his brother or father and did not have time to ask. As a Florida private traveled to the front for his first fight, he admitted it was a sobering experience. "I am the most miserable man in the world for I am now standing on the brink of Eternity without the love of god," he confided to his wife. He suddenly became aware that he had not prepared himself for death and feared "I may be launched in to an etearnell hell." As he listened to the pounding of artillery and the boom of small-arms fire, he concluded with the admission, "Oh you cant imagine my feelings at this time." To observe the inexperienced troops in battle, so commented another Floridian, pained him. "The new troops have suffered heavily," he explained to his wife, "because they have been needlessly exposed and are too careless." Without the knowledge of veterans, they made mistakes that cost them their lives.[18]

On May 15, a Rebel captain wrote his wife, "This is the eleventh day of this great fight and still we are at it." That same day, Venable underestimated Lee's casualties at "not more than 15,000," and claimed they had inflicted almost double that number. Bodies piled up beyond Confederate lines, most of them Yankees, and the stench proved nearly unbearable. A staff officer complained to his wife, "The suffering of the wounded indescribable; the mental anxiety & solicitude almost insupportable. It *must* end before many days." He had no idea how wrong he could be.[19]

Soldier after soldier reported just how exhausting this campaign had become. According to an old friend, Brig. Gen. Goode Bryan "is looking badly—the campaign is using him up I think." Alexander never took off his pants or vest for two weeks straight. A North Carolina regimental commander, Bryan Grimes, conceded to his wife, "Am well and safe—but so much exhausted from our exertion and loss of sleep that I can but assure you of my welfare." Like Alexander, he had not changed clothes in two weeks. Louisianan Robert Stafford understood why the campaign wore him out badly: "I am so black up with powder and mud, we march, fight, eat & sleep in the mud and rain."[20]

Despite the bloodshed, Lee's army still felt sure of the outcome. The commanding general sent an inspiring circular, recounting the initial successes in

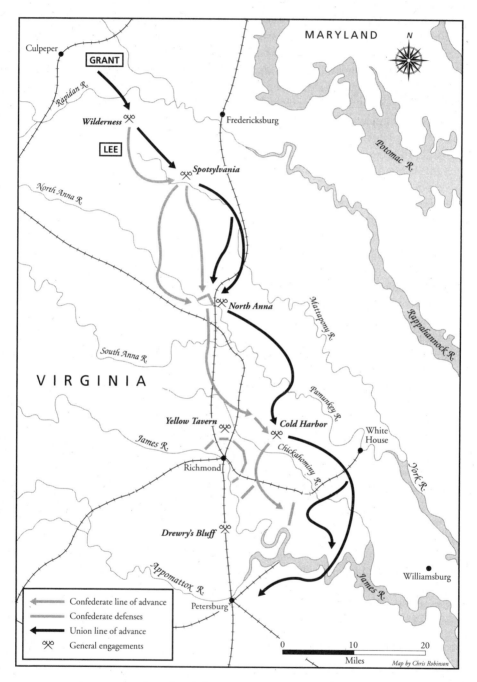

Overland Campaign to Petersburg

other theaters and intimating that if they were to defeat Grant the war could come to a close. A North Carolinian vowed that he might be worn out from the fighting, but, "We can whip the whole yankee nation, and we will do it." By this stage of the war, the Confederacy had already lost so many lives that artillery private William Routt did not want those countrymen to have died in vain. So confident were Confederates they would defeat Grant that Routt overheard one soldier joke that he " 'would give *$1.25 in gold for $1. in Confederate money!'* "[21]

Grant both baffled and frightened soldiers in Lee's army. "Grant is a perfect Bull-dog," a Virginian alerted his mother. "We have met a man this time," a Louisiana lieutenant wrote, "who either does not know when he is whipped, or who cares not if he looses his whole Army, so that he may accomplish his end." A North Carolinian who survived the tornado thought, "Grant is not like other Yankees. Half such a whipping would have sent McClellan, Hooker, Burnside or Meade crossing to the other side of the Rappahannock, but Grant may join us again in battle at any moment." Walter Taylor agreed. "He alone of all would have remained this side of the Rappahannock after the Battle of the Wilderness," he wrote his fiancée. In a perverse way, they admired his persistence, but the ease with which he ran up his butcher's bill surprised them. "Gen Grant has no idea of going back yet & never will until he is the worst whipped man that ever fought Gen. Lee," forecast a Virginian. An Alabama lieutenant declared, "Grant is a strange soldier perfectly reckless of human life and rushes his men against impregnable points without seeming to care for their loss so that the point is carried." Even Taylor, who in some respects admired Grant for his fighting spirit, exclaimed, "Grant is beating his head against a wall."[22]

For two weeks more, it continued. Grant attempted to turn Lee's right flank and in each instance Lee's troops beat the Federals to the critical spot. The sluggish nature of the Union army, overloaded with wagons and impedimenta, and the incapacity of its general officers to transform orders into quick movements prevented them from outpositioning the Confederates. As Lee's chief engineer explained, "Grants movements have been slow as compared with ours and this has in some instances, apparently been our salvation." Lee's soldiers arrived in advance, and despite a lack of equipment, tossed up works that saved Rebel lives and enabled them to punish their enemy. They repulsed Union attack after Union attack, expending close to a million rounds of small-arms ammunition that May alone. In the rare instances that Lee's forces ventured outside works for a fight, they did not fare so well. "All we want is to get on the defensive—" a North Carolina private instructed his uncle, "we think if we have to charge them, that we are ever ruined—we cannot recruit much more." All he wanted was one night and "with our bayonets and tin plates we can put up splendid works." An Alabamian insisted that behind breastworks, "we do not in the least dread" Yankee attacks. In the past, his Confederate comrades had launched into their Rebel yell as they attacked the enemy, but "now they cheer whenever the enemy make a charge and the nearer the Yankees get the more they yell," so testified a Virginian.[23]

Although the Confederates had punished their Yankee attackers, they had suffered severe losses themselves. Accurate statistics have never surfaced, but fragments that exist suggest casualties in the realm of a little more than half those in the Union army. Lane's North Carolina Brigade endured over 1,000 casualties in May; Battle's Alabamians declined from 1,600 men at the opening of the campaign to 800 in late May. The army medical director reported Ewell's Second Corps as suffering almost 4,500 men killed and wounded in May. Ramseur, one of its brigade commanders, informed his wife that the Second Corps had declined from 17,000 to 7,000 in strength. Jenkins's South Carolinians took 529 casualties in the first six weeks of action, probably a bit over one-third of its men. Other commands, such as Heth's Division, once again suffered a mauling, but no specific statistics seem to have survived. Perhaps Taylor stated it best when he wrote his fiancée, "our list of casualties is a sad one to contemplate."[24]

Fortunately, Lee replaced many of those losses with other commands. Major General John C. Breckinridge arrived from the Shenandoah Valley with troops, and after a victory by Beauregard over Union forces near Petersburg, Pickett's Division joined the army as well. Before Petersburg, some Georgians referred to Hagood's South Carolinians as the "Pound Cake Regt.," because it had seen such little service. After the resistance at Petersburg, those same troops cheered when they learned the "Pound Cake" Regiment was joining their brigade.[25]

Among the general officers, that first month of combat proved utterly disastrous. After two weeks of campaigning, Lee's army had six generals killed, nine wounded, and three captured. Worse yet were the consequences of war on Lee's high command. Among the army's top five generals, not one of them emerged unscathed by the war. Longstreet, Lee's most reliable corps commander, suffered a severe wound on May 6 that kept him out of action for months. Anderson took his place, but he lacked the capability, as Lee soon discovered, for the position. Hill's ailment flared up during the stress of the campaign and kept him out for days at a time. Early initially filled his shoes ably. The third corps commander, Ewell, seldom had good health and crashed under the weight of the campaign. Lee discovered him exhausted and incapable of formulating decisions. At the end of the month, Ewell went on sick leave with dysentery. Early replaced him permanently. Then, disaster struck when Stuart suffered a mortal wound at the Battle of Yellow Tavern on May 11. Among combat commanders, Stuart possessed the best eye for terrain in the army, and his loss was truly a tragedy for the Army of Northern Virginia. Temporarily, Lee would direct all three cavalry divisions: Hampton's, Fitz Lee's, and that of Lee's son Rooney, who had received an assignment to head a third division just before the campaign began. "I feel the loss of Stuart more than you do & wish indeed his place could be supplied," Lee informed his nephew in July. "I trust his zeal, activity,

& attention at least is left us." Eventually, he selected Hampton to oversee the cavalry, and the South Carolinian performed expertly. But Stuart had held a position of great responsibility for a long time and would have been a logical choice to head a corps.[26]

Amid those heavy losses, Lee felt compelled to lead Confederate troops into battle at critical moments on three separate occasions. In addition to the Wilderness when Texans demanded he return to the rear, twice during the Battle of Spotsylvania soldiers intervened to prevent the army commander from pressing an attack personally. On May 10, Virginians demanded that he retire before they advanced, and Maj. Gen. John B. Gordon had to grab his bridle and insist that he head to the rear, vowing to lead the charge himself. Two days later, Lee came under artillery fire while urging Rodes's men into the fight. Mississippians once again insisted that he head to safety, and the army commander relented. The importance of victory and the dearth of excellent combat leaders drove Lee to assume duties far below the level of responsibility of an army commander.[27]

Lee himself suffered badly during the campaign. From May 5 to 25, Lee had not gotten two consecutive hours of sleep. He assumed much of the burden of commanding the First Corps, and he grew increasingly uneasy over Ewell's handling of his corps. On May 25, Pendleton reported Lee unwell, although he believed some rest and a better diet would restore him. The illness turned out to be dysentery, and it afflicted Lee for a week. He rode around camp in an ambulance and growled at the incompetence of his driver, even though he had ridden with the same soldier for two years. Troops saw him poring over maps in the back of the ambulance, and he still devoted enormous attention to detail. Finally, he had to remain in his tent. Taylor allowed him to "attend to nothing except what was absolutely necessary for him to know & act upon." By the end of the month, Lee had begun to improve.[28]

After informing his fiancée that Lee "has remained more quiet & directs movements from a distance," Taylor hurled a barb at the army's corps commanders by writing, "This is as it should be, & if he had capable lieutenants 'tis the course he might always pursue." None of the three—Anderson, Ewell, or Hill—proved satisfactory.[29]

Initially, Lee seemed relatively confident with Anderson as a combat commander. His uneasiness stemmed from Anderson's inability to handle the myriad details of directing a corps. Lee provided him with all the pertinent information regarding other corps, but he also felt it was necessary to instruct Anderson on basic tasks, of which he would never remind Hill, Ewell, or Early. Day after day during May and June, Lee sent notes ordering Anderson to rest his men, resupply the troops, post pickets along certain roads to prevent surprise attacks, or familiarize himself with the local transportation network. On occasion, he even directed movement of troops within Anderson's Corps. Clearly, Lee felt uncomfortable with Anderson as an acting corps commander. The problem was that he had no one else he could trust for the job.[30]

To Lee's mind, Ewell's major shortcoming was his indecisiveness, rather than his health. In point of fact, Ewell handled his corps well at the Wilderness, but Lee thought he should have acted more boldly and launched Gordon's flank attack sooner and with more troops. When Lee arrived at the Muleshoe on May 12, he evidently believed that Ewell was "too overwhelmed to be efficient." Six days later, Ewell mismanaged his troops in a fight at Harris Farm, particularly the retreat. When Rodes came to Lee and protested the restoration of Ewell to command after his bout with dysentery, Lee agreed. He had placed Early in charge of the corps when Ewell took leave, and the commanding general refused to replace him. Ewell kept pressing Lee to restore him to corps command, and Lee, reluctant to hurt the feelings of a tried and true soldier, kept skirting the issue, until he finally made it clear no change would take place. Ramseur took over Early's Division, and Ewell then assumed command of the Department of Richmond.[31]

In contrast to Ewell, Hill acted too decisively—some might have said rashly. Hill fought aggressively, as Lee would expect, but he sometimes exhibited poor judgment. At Jericho Mills on May 23, he directed Wilcox's Division to attack what turned out to be a Union corps without consulting Lee. Hill certainly received faulty information on the size of the enemy force, but he threw his men into a fight precipitously, with no reinforcements available, and the fight cost Wilcox's Division some 700 men. Still, at this point in the war, Lee could not afford to take on the added burden of overseeing Hill's Corps as he did with Anderson. Nor did he have a viable replacement.[32]

The burdens of extended combat affected all ranks. Soldiers regularly lived on four hours of sleep during the campaign. After two weeks with Lee's army, a North Carolina private grumbled that he had not slept more than two or three hours per night "and some nights we dont get to shut our eyes." Amid intense May and June heat, with breezes blocked by fortifications and bursting sunshine or heavy rains and deep mud, it proved exceedingly difficult for soldiers to find a comfortable place to rest. Duty required extensive manual labor, erecting fortifications everywhere they went. For meals, men received meat and plenty of flour, but nothing else, day after day. Just for a change in diet, soldiers in the 2nd Florida proposed cooking some "rock soup." The longer they remained in one location, the worse vermin, sanitation, and illness problems became.[33]

Officers tried to rotate troops so that one-third of the men in every regiment and battery would be awake at any given time. The problem was they had no place to hide. Enemy lines were so near that Lee's troops could not move back out of range for a reprieve, and soldiers found it very difficult to sleep or relax in the trenches. They had to be vigilant all the time. The slightest mistake could expose them to a Yankee sharpshooter or enable Federals to force an advantage over them. This kind of continual wariness exhausted troops physically and mentally. A lieutenant in the 5th South Carolina, who had taken over as company commander, labored so intensively that he "'broke down'" and had to go to the division hospital. An Alabama enlisted man conveyed the same message to his father. "Our army is in fine spirits," he revealed, "but many a poor fellow is breaking down from fatigue loss of sleep &c." After three weeks of almost incessant combat under Allegheny Johnson, Capt. Alfred D. Kelly had to return to the rear because he was so "worn down." Kelly closed a brief note to his brother, explaining his condition, with the words: "My shattered nerves will not allow my writing more."[34]

After the first month of the spring campaign, soldiers in Lee's army realized they had not experienced anything quite like this in the war. Over the course of fighting, some of the very best regiments and brigades in Lee's army broke and ran from the battlefield. How others remained in the killing fields was a mystery.

Rather than face the danger and stress of the front any longer, soldiers began shooting themselves to get out of action. The problem became so serious that Pickett issued a circular, warning his men if "any one that shoots or Hurts himself a [on] purpose and the facts can be substantiated they shall be shot to Death *immediately*." Soldiers declined or avoided opportunities for promotion because the new rank would take them away from such sinecures as ordnance sergeant and place them in the front ranks. Worst of all, such heavy loss of life disrupted cohesion among the troops. Men who entered the campaign with a core of dependable comrades emerged from a single fight completely lost and abandoned. As South Carolinian Charles Kerrison explained to his sister after their brother was killed in action, "Since his death life has lost half its interest."[35]

Chapter 29

———◦◦———

THE TRENCHES

"**H**IS TALENT & STRATEGY**," Lee wrote about Grant, "consists in accumulating overwhelming numbers." After hammering Lee's army day
after day, piling up losses on both sides of the line, as Grant's forces slowly crept
toward a point northeast of Richmond, the Union general attempted something
bold. He had hoped to turn the Rebel flank and position his forces between the
Confederate capital and Lee's men, but each time Lee was one step ahead of
him. Frustrated with the bloody dance, Grant pulled his army back so that it
broke contact with Lee, then stole a march across the James River, swinging
around to Petersburg, thirty miles south of Richmond. If Grant's army could
seize Petersburg, it would sever several rail connections to Richmond from the
south and have a chance to take the capital from below. Around Petersburg,
Grant could also inject needed strength into his army by joining forces with
Maj. Gen. Benjamin Butler's Army of the James, which had been stymied by
Beauregard since May.[1]

Beauregard detected the presence of men from the Army of the Potomac
outside Petersburg on June 10 and blocked them with what few troops he could
concentrate. Lee reacted cautiously. If Grant's move was a feint and Lee shifted
his troops across the James River, he would open the door to the fall of Richmond. He had to be certain that Grant had moved his entire army, or at least
a large portion of it, before he could risk transferring his columns from the
present line. While Lee struggled to divine Grant's true intentions, Beauregard executed a brilliant defense. His small forces put up a great front, which
discouraged the Yankees and won praise from Lee's veterans. Beauregard and
his men also benefited from the stout resistance Lee's army had demonstrated
for the past five weeks. The Army of Northern Virginia had stopped so many
Union assaults that when it came time to storm Beauregard's works south of
Petersburg, Federal troops were extremely hesitant. Grant had created a situation that would allow his soldiers to attack with overwhelming advantages, but
his officers and men balked. They looked across the line and observed the kinds
of trenches and defenses that they had assailed repeatedly, and that had cost
them thousands of lives, and their collective efforts were half-hearted at best.

Union troops did not know that Beauregard had perpetrated a skillful deception with relatively weak defenses and insufficient troop strength.[2]

In mid-June, Lee swung his army below Petersburg and merged with the flamboyant Beauregard. The siege of Petersburg had begun. "The enemy has a strong position, & is able to deal us more injury than from any other point he has ever taken," Lee informed Davis a week later. "Still we must try & defeat them. I fear he will not attack us but advance by regular approaches. He is so situated that I cannot attack him." Two years earlier, Lee the engineer had warned Davis and Johnston that once the Yankees besieged Richmond, with their vast advantage in strength, it would simply be a matter of time before the city fell. After two and a half months of trench warfare, Lee reported to a recuperating Longstreet, "We have but little enjoyment here. Our enemy is very cautious & he has become so proficient in entrenching that he seems to march with a system already prepared." By laying siege to Petersburg, Grant shifted the contest from Lee's superb infantry to Union engineering, artillery, and numbers, and the everyday grind of life in the trenches began to take its toll on Lee's superb army. "He threatens dreadful things every day," Lee concluded to his absent corps commander, "but thank God he has not expunged us yet."[3]

Soldiers in Lee's army admired the way their commander had shielded them so well while they had cut down Yankees in droves, but the continual fighting had enervated Rebels badly. Since the campaign opened in early May, Lee's troops had enjoyed little relief from danger. With Federal troops so close, men had to look out for a Union attack at any moment. Observers exposed themselves as targets for Yankee sharpshooters, as did those who moved around the fortifications. Once they settled into position around Petersburg, the risk of all-out assaults diminished, but new hazards and burdens emerged, making life in the trenches dangerous and exhausting.[4]

Both armies hauled in mortars, which lofted huge shells high into the air, dropping on unsuspecting troops. Soldiers could no longer protect themselves from these massive rounds by hunkering down in trenches. A North Carolinian was sleeping one night when a mortar round crashed into his chest and exploded, hurling his body to the other side of the breastworks. These mortars also had considerable range, so that soldiers far to the rear, beyond musket range, were in considerable danger. When Benning's Georgia Brigade occupied a reserve position, it lost twenty-five men in two days from mortar fire. What frustrated these men most was that they could not even fire a shot in return. Confederates, too, tapped mortars for retaliatory fire. They would conceal them in the daytime—superior Union fire might zero in on them—and haul them out after sunset, lofting a slow and steady fire throughout the night.[5]

Sharpshooters on both sides heightened the tension by firing with uncanny accuracy, exploiting the slightest openings and taking down soldiers who barely exposed themselves. A captain and a private in the 17th Georgia passed each other in the trench, the tops of their heads becoming visible to Federal snipers. A single round crashed through both of their skulls, killing them instantly.

Federals gunned down cattle eleven hundred yards away, and when Confederate troops slipped back to secure some fresh meat, they were shot, too. One soldier in the 27th South Carolina suffered a severe wound when a round deflected off a tree and went through one cheek and out the other, removing a couple of teeth in the process. Evidently, the soldier was "a great talker" and was gabbing at the time, which may have saved his life. "He was never very good looking," an acquaintance commented. "This may improve his appearance." Confederate snipers were no less deadly. A black sharpshooter fired at a target through a rifle hole. When he removed the rifle to examine the results, a Confederate marksman drilled a bullet directly through the opening and into his head, killing him.[6]

DURING THE SPRING and summer of 1864, the ceaseless danger, the staggering loss of life, and the enormous psychological strain of continuous combat wrought changes on the spiritual attitudes of soldiers in Lee's army. In the past, fighting had lasted several days, at worst a week, and then the campaign came to a close, so that troops could undertake organized services and prayer meetings at somewhat regular intervals. About one in every four men participated in these religious activities. Amid the extensive fighting of 1864, more and more soldiers sought spiritual guidance and offered divine thanks, but they seldom had an opportunity to practice religion in an organized or structured way. To meet their spiritual and emotional needs, they relied more on private prayer. The randomness of death and destruction on such a huge scale helped soldiers personalize their survival with their divine creator. Only the hand of God could have shielded them, for whatever reason, they insisted, and this sort of personal focus encouraged a very private relationship with God. Major Robert Stiles reported the spontaneous singing of hymns in the trenches at dusk. A Georgia private offered a classic millennialist argument to his sister when he wrote, "This war you know was designed by all wise Providence as a chastisement for our past wickedness & until we bow our stubborn necks we can but expect a farther punishment." He insisted, "If every man & woman prayed for the war's end, peace would come for an independent Confederate state." Along similar lines, a South Carolina private who wrote of soldiers praying in the trenches every night argued, "O my Dear I believe if the people at home would Engage with us in fervent prayer to God for deliverance from this war it would not be long before we would be delivered." Faith and prayer, a Georgian wrote his home county Baptist Association, would ensure victory for the Confederacy. "The same people that supplied manna in the desert, that sent the ravens to Elijah, and staid the widow's scant supply, can succor us, if we trust him," he predicted.[7]

Not only did private religion help them to draw God to their cause, it also sustained soldiers as heavy losses dissolved cohesion within their units. A Virginian lost his two closest friends during the siege. All three had embraced

Christ as their savior and supported one another with pledges to be there for one another, both physically and spiritually. One of them was killed in action, and a second was wounded and fell into Union hands. Despite the loss of his comrades, the last soldier relied on a Higher Power to protect him. "God has given me my life a little bit longer without a wound whilst many of my companions lives have been stricken down[,] killed or wounded," he recorded in his diary. "I am as grateful as I can be for this sacred instance of His mercy."[8]

Captain Will Biggs of the 17th North Carolina lost his closest comrades and nearly unraveled psychologically during the siege, but faith helped keep him together. For two weeks straight, he wrote his sister, "we have been in the trenches exposed to all kinds of weather, without scarcely any sleep at night, cooped up in narrow pits, & fearful every moment to be struck by a bullet from their sharp shooters." His cousin and lieutenant, Arch Staton, was shot and killed, as were his other lieutenant and friend, John D. Perry, and the regimental commander, Lt. Col. John C. Lamb. After a third consecutive week on the front lines, his command rotated out of the trenches for thirty-six hours. "For my own part," he admitted to his sister, "it was absolutely necessary for me, for I don't think I could have stood it a day longer. I was completely broken down in body & almost in spirit." By June 22, his company had lost twenty-eight men, the most in his regiment, but worst of all, nearly all of them were his best men, which placed an even greater responsibility on his shoulders. The death of Staton, though, left him prostrate for a few days and he had not recovered from it two weeks later. "He was the only *friend* & *comrade* I had in the company so now I am alone."[9]

Biggs suggested that he wanted a new assignment, perhaps on a general's staff. Because his father was a prominent North Carolina politician, he might be able to arrange it. But the fact was he refused to leave his company. Only he and the acting regimental commander had not gone to the field hospital during the campaign. "Some body must stay with the men and cheer them up for upon them depends our all and when they once give up our Cause is gone and with it all we hold most sacred and dear," he wrote. Only God could have provided him with the strength. He credited "a Kind Providence" with preserving his health despite the deaths and hardships all around him and enabling him to continue serving the men. In early July, he came down with a bout of dysentery, but he returned promptly. With trusted officers dead, and no one qualified to take the slot, he had assumed all the duties of the company and did not believe it could function without him. Biggs had come to the conclusion that he must manage everything. "The company needs me *all the time* and I dislike to be absent from them even the shortest time. When I am away, Something is *sure* to go wrong." With the burden of an enormous workload, Biggs was on the verge of exhausting himself, when he fell ill with typhoid fever. It took him nearly eight weeks to recover his physical and mental health.[10]

More than simply combat, Lee's army had to battle harsh conditions in the trenches. A late spring to midsummer drought parched the earth and transformed dirt into dust ten inches deep in some areas. Movement by man or beast stirred up huge, choking clouds of dust. "We live in it, lie in it, sleep in it, breathe it, drink it, & eat it, until it has almost become second nature," a South Carolina quartermaster sergeant informed his wife. The trenches offered no shade. Soldiers tried stretching blankets over poles to cast shade, but it did not work well. Earthworks, some of which dipped below ground, protected them from enemy fire but also blocked breezes, creating grueling conditions during hot days. Ingeniously, Yankee sharpshooters targeted water sources, which discouraged soldiers from venturing out in the daytime. Troops would simply have to endure their thirst until nightfall. When rain finally fell, it converted dust into thick mud, at times so deep that "not half the company could get a place to lye last night or even sit without being from four to eight inches in mud," an Alabama private complained. Soldiers looked so shabby that one quipped, "I imagine that there is very little here to encourage any marriageable young lady, could she see Lee's Army, to 'wait until the war is over.'"[11]

Initially, soldiers barely slept at all during the campaign, but eventually sleep deprivation caught up to the men, and their bodies demanded rest. Troops fell asleep despite the conditions. The army also established an effective trench rotation policy. During the night, for example, Kirkland's North Carolina Brigade assigned one in every ten men on post as sentinels, and another tenth in the trenches, along with one in every three officers. The rest of the command could remain in the rear but had to be awake at 4:00 A.M. in case of an attack at first light. It was, as a Virginian noted, "a terribly methodical life."[12]

Other commands were not quite so lucky. Due to combat losses and sickness, troop strength in many units had been reduced dramatically, placing greater burdens on those who remained with their commands. The length of line that regiments had to protect extended as well. The Federals, with greater manpower and resources, gradually stretched their lines farther out, and Lee's army had to compensate or be outflanked. By late August, the 35th Georgia had to protect almost two miles, and according to an inspector, "most of the command is all the time on duty." Strength in other regiments and brigades had fallen so low that men had to perform excessive duty to compensate for their weakened condition. A Virginian grumbled that due to diminished manpower, his regiment had to go on twenty-four hour picket duty every two days. To ease the workload, Lee tried to prevent officers from sending men to the rear unless it was vital. Each soldier pulled out of the front lines placed an additional burden on fellow soldiers.[13]

Nor did commands always occupy good terrain for trenches. The natural contours of the land compelled some units to build trenches along low ground, while their more fortunate comrades tossed up field works on hills. Soldiers on lower ground were more susceptible to sniper fire and had much greater problems with flooding. Hagood's South Carolina Brigade occupied a trench that was so much lower than adjacent fields that "it is impossible by any means at hand to prevent the accumulation of water," reported an inspector.[14]

Prolonged service in the trenches taxed their endurance. An Alabamian grumbled of the restricted space, "It is a miserable life to be in the trenches all the time—so confining." A Virginian complained of the prolonged service: "this is the 69th day we was in the diches [ditches] & no prospect of any relief Soon." The men in his company "are completely worn out."[15]

Just as it exhausted men physically and mentally, trench warfare took its toll on resources and basic necessities for the men. Although Lee's soldiers received a disproportionate share of the Confederacy's clothing, it was not nearly enough. Shoes, submerged in trench water for extended periods of time, broke down much more rapidly than they normally did in the field. Pants, shirts, socks, and drawers wore out under siege conditions, so that the shortages that plagued Lee's army during the first three years worsened. One Louisiana captain, angered over the inadequate shoes and clothing for his men, argued that military personnel in Richmond should give up their uniforms for the soldiers in the field. "Our men are shoeless, pantless, jacketless, sockless and miserable and resembled Falstaff's Army more than any Corps in the Confederacy, while every man in Richmond, or any other city connected with the Army are dressed in the best of all. God grant that our leaders may soon learn that men cannot march and fight when they are half naked and with feet that leave bloody marks wherever they step."[16]

Problems with clean water and sufficient rations plagued the army around Petersburg. A Georgia private pronounced the water the worst the army ever had to drink. He claimed "the use of it bring on various diseases besides contagious diseases raging violent here small-pox, measles, mumphs, itch & hoping cough." Food was even more problematic. For months, rations consisted of bread and salt beef, clearly deficient of proper nutrients, doled out in quantities insufficient to satisfy hungry troops. Portions of food in each ration were so meager that soldiers sometimes ate the entire amount in one sitting and fasted the next day. On occasion, they received an adequate quantity, but it was the same old diet of beef and bread. Only those with greenbacks for currency, taken from Union prisoners of war or sent through the lines by Northern friends, could supplement their diets at all. Signs of scurvy appeared throughout the army, and many soldiers suffered bouts of night blindness due to vitamin deficiency.[17]

Much of the beef for Lee's army came from the Caribbean islands, oddly enough for a Confederacy rich in cattle. Texas had a superabundance of beeves, but the Confederacy had no way of transporting them to Virginia. It made more sense to ship meat to an Atlantic seaport and then by rail to Petersburg or Richmond. Over the course of this long haul, meat sometimes spoiled and had to be discarded, reducing the amount available for hungry troops.[18]

On a mid-September morning, Hampton and some 4,000 Rebel horsemen slipped out of Confederate lines on an unusual raid. Armed with accurate intelligence, they targeted a huge herd of Union cattle near City Point, Virginia. Moving quickly, Hampton caught the Federals unprepared, and after a firefight he and his command brought off 2,468 beeves. "They are certainly the greatest sight in the way of cattle that I ever saw," a South Carolinian crowed, a "number of them will weight over 1,000 lbs and the whole lot are supposed will average 700 [to] 800 lbs round." The men rejoiced at Hampton's achievement. The cattle would normally have lasted two and a half weeks, but Lee's commissaries stretched that to nearly a month. Almost as important, the army secured nearly twenty-five hundred hides for the production of shoes. In effect, Hampton's raid relieved the Confederacy of one-twelfth its annual burden for meat, an extraordinary achievement.[19]

Throughout most of June and July, much of Virginia suffered a severe drought. Week after week, many areas received little rainfall, drying up creeks and streams, and worst of all, destroying crops. Nearly all the vegetable crops were ruined, and corn production declined so badly that the army had to provide corn from its measly stockpile to care for civilians in Petersburg. With the railroads already taxed by shipments of meat, corn, and ammunition to Richmond, the idea of hauling vegetables and having to ship corn from distant states seemed disastrous to commissary and quartermaster officers. Cavalrymen took matters into their own hands and "all become rogues in order to steal something to eat for their horses." Lee complained that the army received 2,000 bushels of corn per day, when it needed 3,200. In mid-June, he informed Davis, "I think it is clear that the railroads are not working energetically & unless some improvement is made, I do not know what will become of us." A month later, animals still did not receive enough. The army issued six to eight pounds of corn per day, but no hay or oats.[20]

With soldiers living all day, every day in trenches—many of them referred to them appropriately as "pits"—and horses maintained nearby, sanitary conditions deteriorated horribly, and flies and other vermin soon infested trenches and camps. The stationary nature of the campaign kept horses and wagons in a fixed location, always near the troops for fear of thievery, and animal manure literally piled up in camp to the rear of trenches. Waste attracted flies and rodents, and the warm weather provided a perfect breeding environment for them. A South Carolinian grumbled that a cloud of flies hovered around camp and in the trenches, a quarter of a mile thick in any direction. A Virginia artillery private complained, "our camp is swarming with flies, generated by filth from the horses. Confound them, they torture me to death." Officers tried to ease the discomfort of soldiers who rotated from the trenches to the rear by shifting campsites, but the flies made the move as well.[21]

Amid wretched sanitary conditions, soldiers had little opportunity to keep clean. Only the most vigilant officers could maintain some reasonable level of cleanliness in trench warfare. And even when officers tried to concern themselves with the personal hygiene of their soldiers, the lack of soap made it impossible. On August 9, Lee notified Davis that throughout the entire campaign, his troops had received only three daily issues of soap. "The great want of cleanliness which is a necessary consequence of these very limited issues is now producing sickness among the men in the trenches, and must effect their self respect & morale," the commanding general argued. The government had an opportunity to purchase 24,000 pounds of soap at $3.75 per 100 pounds, but the commissary general thought the price was too high. He only wanted to pay $2.50 per 100 pounds and passed on the offer, even though the commissary general "holds out no definite prospect of sending an adequate supply."[22]

As a result, illnesses broke out across the army. "I think the excessive heat and the disagreeableness of the trenches are enough to make the hardiest men sick," a Virginia infantryman claimed; "an iron constitution sometimes gives way." Some illnesses were due to unsanitary practice; others were the result of dietary deficiency; and still other diseases had more to do with the extended service in poor locations. Along with bouts of scurvy, such ailments as diarrhea and dysentery, products of vitamin deficiency and poor sanitary practices, plagued Lee's command. "Diarrhoea and Dysentery prevail to a very great extent throughout our Army," the medical director wrote the surgeon general, "officers of the highest rank have not been exempt, and our strength is being much impaired." He blamed diet as the primary cause. Troops occupying portions of the lines near the James River, particularly those from Pickett's Division, suffered from severe malarial problems that extended from August, after the drought ended, into October. To make matters worse, soldiers endured chiggers and other skin parasites, collectively called "camp itch," that caused almost unbearable discomfort. As one cavalryman described it, the "Scratch Affliction" was "a great annoyance and keeps me hard at work with both hands many nights." All told, brigades and divisions reported anywhere from 5 to 20 percent of the men present who were sick, to say nothing of the additional 25 to 60 percent on sick furlough or in hospitals away from the army. If just half of them returned, it would have been an infusion of a couple of divisions.[23]

The loss of so many men cut deeply into the strength and quality of the army. Losses in some commands were utterly devastating. Wilcox's Division opened the campaign in May with 9,331 troops, with 7,088 bearing arms and 630 officers. By September 18, it had fallen to 5,727 men present, with 3,855 servicing weapons and 396 officers. Lane's North Carolina Brigade, part of Wilcox's Division, fell from, 2,050 on May 4 to 833 at the end of August. That same day, Hagood's South Carolina Brigade did not number as many men for duty as the smallest regiment it had brought to Virginia three months earlier. The strength of Cooke's Brigade of North Carolinians had fallen below 1,000 men, and the 27th North Carolina totaled fewer than 200 troops. The 9th Alabama, a veteran regiment that had arrived in Virginia in May 1861, counted only 110 men in late July. When Captain Biggs of the 17th North Carolina nearly succumbed to stress, his problem was more than just the loss of a few friends. He regularly bemoaned the death and serious wounding of his best soldiers, who often exposed themselves more than others in the line of duty.[24]

These losses, moreover, had gutted the regimental officer corps. Brigade inspections uncovered countless inexperienced officers. They simply did not grasp their duties. Many of them had proven themselves as excellent combat soldiers, but their obligations as officers ranged far from the battlefield. In addition to an understanding of tactics, an officer must also command the respect and obedience of his men, impose discipline on the march, and control his troops in battle. All commands had poor officers, but incompetent ones dominated dozens of regiments, sometimes ranking as high as regimental commander. In other instances, officers had proven themselves capable, yet attrition compelled them to assume responsibilities far beyond their qualifications, as in the case of a lieutenant in the 61st Alabama, who commanded the regiment in early October.[25]

Lee recognized the problem. "What our officers most lack is the pains & labour of inculcating discipline," Lee alerted Davis. "It is a painful tedious process, & is not apt to win popular favour." Officers came from a society that failed to promote self-discipline, and because few senior commanders emphasized discipline enough, very few subordinates embraced it. "Many officers have too many selfish views to promote to induce them to undertake the task of instructing & disciplining their Commands," Lee insisted. They would have to remain with the troops all the time and attend to detail, a prospect that appealed to very few of them. As an inspector of a Virginia brigade in the First Corps claimed, "the Inspector does not believe that there is 'discipline,' as he understands it, in any Regiment in the Corps, as far as, he has been able to judge." Other corps were no better.[26]

With all these losses, Lee's army exhibited signs of losing its edge for the first time. Both officers and men noticed that troops no longer possessed the same fighting spirit as they had previously. "I Sometimes of late think that they are not quite so full of ardour & spirit as they were the first two years of the war," Wilcox confessed to his sister. Soldiers openly grumbled about charging breastworks and some refused to do so. Relief forces failed to familiarize themselves with fields of fire, would not repair the guns, failed to maintain a six-man crew per gun, or keep vigilant, according to Pendleton. Morale had dropped considerably. "I wish I cood throw down my Gun to never pick hit [it] up again," announced a South Carolina private. Another soldier told his wife he would abide by any arrangement she could broker to get him out of the war. He was killed in action weeks later. Others offered between $500 and $600 for another man's furlough.[27]

Trench warfare simply enervated the men. "I never was so sick and tired of anything on my life as I am of this war," sighed a Virginia private to his mother. He had been in the army so long "My life previous to the war seems but a dream." A company officer felt the same way. "My dear cousin, are you not very tired of this war?" he posed in October. "The life I lead is so very different to that in which I was reared, it is so antagonistic to my nature, that sometimes when I think of its probable duration for four for five years to come, I am nearly overcome by its depressing weight, and would at times almost welcome the bullet which terminated so much trouble." He admitted that his sentiments were "unmanly" and that he still believed in the Confederate cause, "yet there are times when the heart is sick, sick of this life in the wilderness." A Virginia artillerist complained to his father along similar lines. "Ah! Dearest Father, how dead *dead dead* my youth is!" Utterly exhausted, a Virginia officer excused himself to his sister with the words, "I wish I could write you a better letter but I have been strangled in dust[,] scorched in the sun and demoralized continually by 'bumin' that I am completely stewed[,] dryed and withered up and am now fit for nothing and hav'nt got more half sense."[28]

As soldiers watched their comrades fall, many sought sinecures where they would not regularly come under enemy fire. As one soldier informed his loved ones, he sought "the safest honorable scheme to save my bark." Hospitals filled with shirkers, and doctors had to drive them back to their commands. A Georgian shot himself in the hand to escape further combat duty. Others, nominated for promotions, declined them, because new ranks would require them to return to the trench. Soldiers in the fighting grew increasingly resentful of those in the rear. When former Texas governor and aide to President Davis Francis Lubbock delivered a rousing, patriotic address to the Texas Brigade, one of their ranks belittled him by recording that he "made a *Speech* to our boys to day, 'very vindictive toward the *Yankees*,'—but he takes good care to keep *so far* in the rear, that he wont get hurt." A junior officer from South Carolina formulated a similar argument when he declared to his mother, "If all who are able to do service were at their posts we could 'laugh him to scorn,' but as it is we who are here will have to keep him from making farther progress, and are ready to do our duty."[29]

Physical demands had reached a level of severity that an officer declared that he and his comrades had become so "hardened" that "we can hardly be said to act & feel like men." Conditions in the trenches were so bad that in early July, a North Carolina private confessed to his brother, "if I was fit to dye & had no family to cear [care] for I wood reather dye than live."[30]

Chapter 30

MEDICAL CARE

WHEN THE WAR broke out, William H. Taylor, a twenty-six-year-old physician from Richmond, volunteered for hospital duty in the Confederate nation's capital, but he could not resist the call to field service. He joined the 19th Virginia as its assistant surgeon. Throughout the course of the conflict, he remained with the regiment, despite opportunities for promotion elsewhere. Taylor had gone to war with the men, earned their respect and trust, and refused to leave them in someone else's hands.[1]

Taylor held early morning sick call and issued his diagnoses quickly. For the most part, he treated ill soldiers in one of two ways. In one pocket, he carried a ball of blue mass, a medicine with blue chalk, calomel, and mercury, which of course was toxic. In the other pocket Taylor had a ball of opium. If the patient's bowels functioned, he received opium; if he were constipated, Taylor issued a plug of blue mass. If the patient got worse, the physician referred him to a brigade hospital or to a general hospital, often in Richmond.[2]

Some years after the war, armed with the new knowledge of germs and antiseptics, Taylor winced at the thought of the medical care that physicians had offered to soldiers. Civil War surgeons struggled to care for soldiers with illnesses or injuries, and few of their practices worked. Other than vaccinating for smallpox, administering quinine for malaria, issuing foods rich in vitamin C for scurvy, and amputating limbs for shattered bones and severed arteries, physicians seldom cured patients by design. With his two courses of action, at best Taylor eased pain; at worst, he unwittingly poisoned his patients.[3]

Taylor did promote good health during the war by encouraging cleanliness around camp and in hospitals. He reminded his regimental commander to have troops police the camp well, and he tried to keep his patients clean. Still, sanitation did not assume a level of importance as it did some decades later, and when it came to trench warfare, physicians had little incentive or authority to improve conditions dramatically.[4]

In the combat environment, Taylor functioned much more effectively. As an assistant surgeon, he traveled around the battlefield, stanching the flow of blood and binding wounds as best he could. He also oversaw evacuations to the field hospital. There, surgeons would operate, if necessary, to repair injuries. Once the wounded had stabilized enough for transportation, the army shipped them by wagon and sometimes rail to general hospitals.[5]

By and large, physicians in Lee's army received professional training in medical schools, usually a two-year course. When regiments were formed, soldiers often asked individual civilians to serve as surgeons or assistant surgeons. To ensure quality, the War Department established a medical board to examine physicians. Army doctors immediately complained, arguing that forcing surgeons and assistant surgeons to prove themselves was an insult to their professionalism. They much preferred that those who were incompetent appear before a board of inquiry or a general court-martial. A medical board, they insisted, would act too subjectively. Nonetheless, the directive stood. Opinions on the effectiveness of these boards varied considerably. In late 1862, the surgeon general began systematizing the regulation of physicians. Doctors filed applications listing name, age, length of time in practice, year and school of graduation, position they sought, and testimonials of character. They would then appear before a medical board, and "no unsuccessful candidate will be granted a second examination in less than six months." For promotion from assistant surgeon to surgeon, the surgeon general required all candidates to have five years of medical experience before appearing before the board, except in the case of a vacancy within the regiment. Those seeking promotions would need to apply with the same basic information.[6]

Surgeons and assistant surgeons often came from wealthy families who could afford to send a son to a medical college. Dr. Preston Roane, a nineteen-year-old student when the war broke out, joined the 26th Virginia Infantry Battalion in 1864 after studying medicine. His father, also a physician, owned nineteen slaves and nearly $100,000 of property. The thirty-one-year-old Dr. Holmes Hunter left his family for extensive wartime service. Although he entered the war with a wife and two children, they were in good standing, with sixteen slaves and $21,000 worth of property. By contrast, Dr. Taylor had recently hung his shingle. He lived in a boardinghouse in Richmond and claimed $500 worth of property to his name, but he possessed a good mind, a conscientious work ethic, and the promise of financial success.[7]

Army doctors had access to hospital stewards and, in hospitals, nurses. Hospital stewards were enlisted men who oversaw medical equipment, assisted surgeons in their surgical duties, and functioned as pharmacists. Sometimes they accompanied the command into battle, helping the assistant surgeons in their duties, and other times they remained in the rear and helped set up field hospitals and assisted in the surgeries. In addition, officers and enlisted men whose duties were not quite so critical during battle, such as commissary and quartermaster personnel, often labored in the operating rooms, holding down patients during surgeries and performing other essential tasks.[8]

Of all those involved in healing, nurses earned the greatest praise from the sick and wounded. Women and some men volunteered to work in hospitals, where they bathed soldiers, changed bandages, clothes, and linens, fed and cared for the men, wrote letters home on their behalf, and offered gentle words of comfort. Launcelot Blackford believed that without the nurses the sick and wounded would not recover, insisting they were "to many of the patients really angels of mercy." His brother Lewis concurred. He wrote their mother, "were it not for them, there would be enormous suffering and neglect." A Texas private praised the women of Fredericksburg hospital for their "angelic ministrations." In Richmond hospitals, "they seemed to be nursed with the utmost care, especially so by the ladies," a Virginia officer recorded. Some soldiers were fortunate enough to have a family member who nursed them back to health. "What I should have done without Ma I do not know," wounded Virginian William N. Ward commented to his sister Eddy. "Men don't know much about nursing."[9]

As the numbers of sick and wounded in the Virginia Theater compounded, medical authorities could not rely just on volunteers to care for the men. Military hospitals began to hire slaves and free blacks, men and women, to labor in the hospitals. Blacks had experience ministering to the needs of whites, and they could perform an array of duties from caring for soldiers and cooking food to chopping firewood, doing laundry, and scrubbing floors. Often the government hired them for a year-long contract, to establish continuity and secure steady and reliable care.[10]

When soldiers first suffered wounds or fell seriously ill, regimental doctors transferred them to mobile brigade or field hospitals. According to a hospital steward, "Here distinctions between the wealthy and the poor, the learned and ignorant, the distinguished and the unknown are merged into one lot." During the first year of the war, the army medical director complained that surgeons kept patients too long before sending them to the general hospital. Because the army set them up in the field, conditions were not as good as in permanent hospitals, but soldiers were loath to leave them. They lay alongside comrades, and surgeons in their regiment, brigade, or division cared for them. When fighting ended or troops were off duty, comrades could visit them more easily and keep up their morale.[11]

Quite a number of soldiers and physicians suspected patients at the field hospital of malingering. A South Carolina surgeon noted that a soldier claimed to suffer from colic. "He was actually playing what we call possum." A Virginian accused his comrades who crowded into hospitals of "playing 'old soldier,' a species of deceit which I found out by painful experience is very common among our patriotic soldiers." Yet with the few diagnostic techniques available it was very difficult to distinguish truth from fiction unless the doctor knew the patient very well. In so many instances, soldiers came down with illnesses that seemed treatable, but in a few days, symptoms became more severe, and patients quickly passed away. Surgeons therefore reacted to complaints with prudence.[12]

After First Manassas and the massive outbreak of illness in Johnston's army, various hospitals popped up in Richmond to care for soldiers, called general hospitals. Yet the initial casualties paled by comparison with those the army suffered in the late spring and summer of 1862, the number and severity of which overwhelmed Confederate authorities. Complaints flooded the War Department. Congress authorized states to erect hospitals for troops from their state. Georgia and South Carolina quickly established hospitals in Richmond, followed by Louisiana, North Carolina, and Texas, but these were ultimately dwarfed by the massive hospitals named Chimborazo and Winder in Richmond and a third named Jackson, just outside the capital. These three hospitals offered over 15,000 beds. Dozens of smaller facilities in Richmond closed down, as the surgeon general much preferred larger hospitals. Other communities, such as Charlottesville, Lynchburg, Danville, and Petersburg, also serviced Lee's troops.[13]

Although Southerners did not manufacture medicines before the war, they possessed ample medical equipment and supplies to provision hospitals and field surgeons reasonably well at the outset of the war. In time, demand compelled Confederates to manufacture their own medicines, such as blue mass. The quality proved so poor that the mercury separated from the pill—a bona fide advantage to the patient, but a serious problem in the eyes of doctors. The Confederacy then imported blue mass and other medicines on blockade runners or secured them from captured Federal supplies.[14]

On the whole, soldiers received satisfactory medical care based on the knowledge and skill of the time, but that seldom lived up to the standards demanded by soldiers or their families. An unimpressed Alabamian grumbled, "I have bin in aplace call a hospital, but I would purnounce it a hog pen." Many soldiers referred to it as a "horse pittle," a reference to the animal's urine. The treatment Pvt. Sambo Short's brother received absolutely outraged him. His brother Oscar took sick and was delirious. Physicians at the hospital stripped him of his clothes and doused him with basin after basin of cold water. What galled Short was that fifteen or twenty people were close witnesses to his naked brother and another hundred observed from a distance. "The surgeons don't show a man any respect at all," he fumed. Eight days later, his brother died.[15]

In contrast to these massive hospitals, Sallie Tompkins of Richmond converted the home of the Robertson family into the Robertson Hospital. The structure could hold only one hundred patients at a time, which enabled her and her associates to provide the sick and wounded with personal attention. Tompkins's greatest achievement was simply keeping the men clean at all times, and well fed, the best medical care a patient could receive in most instances. When Mary Chesnut and some friends brought food to the men, she marveled, "The men under Miss Sally's kind care looked so clean and comfortable. Cheerful, one might say." In the immediate aftermath of the Battle of First Manassas, private homes took in wounded and sick, and when the Medical Department took steps to transfer patients to military hospitals, the directive threatened Robertson Hospital. Davis intervened by awarding Tompkins a captain's commission for her service and preventing attempts to close her doors. Later, in her effort to fend off detractors and protect the hospital, she demonstrated that over the past year, only eight soldiers had died under her care. Altogether, according to her records, she admitted 1,333 soldiers during the war, of whom 73 died.[16]

Based on the state of medical knowledge at the time, physicians could cure very few ailments. In addition to keeping careful records of patients so that family members could locate loved ones or receive their private property, army doctors maintained and studied cases and shared information. In late June 1862, the surgeon general reminded them to preserve thorough case books and records of gunshot wounds and surgery. "This is demanded not only in justice to the corps of which they are members, and from which much interesting and useful statistical information will be expected at the close of the war, but also for the benefit of the science of surgery at large, which should not be robbed of the advantages supposed to accrue from so extended a field of observation as that which now presents itself." The war offered a rare glimpse into a huge array of illnesses and injuries, and surgeons and assistant surgeons needed to document information to advance the field. The surgeon general called on physicians to collect indigenous botanical remedies, in part because the blockade made it difficult to bring in medicines from Europe, but also as a means of improving the treatment of the sick.[17]

After Seven Days', the medical director for Lee's army launched his own campaign for records of gunshot injuries and surgical operations. "The subject requires every attention," he insisted, "and it is due not only to the science of surgery at large, but to the professional reputation of each Medical Officer in this District, that he should carefully examine, closely watch, and keep an accurate record of each case of this nature, that comes under his observation and treatment." Later that year, he embarked on a quest to gather information on the "Surgical Pathology of the Nervous System." He wanted surgeons in charge of hospitals to examine records and reports of their medical officers pertaining to all cases of "local or general diseases of the Nerves which have been treated or observed by them, resulting from or subsequent upon wounds or surgical operations." He then ordered them to submit this data along with monthly reports of sick and wounded.[18]

Through official and unofficial channels, army surgeons attempted to improve their science. They shared stories of cases and successful cures. Together, they worked on ways to compensate for the difficulty of procuring recommended medicines for their patients. Physicians harangued fellow officers over unsanitary conditions around camp, and they complained to the War Department over poor food and the outbreak of easily preventable diseases such as scurvy. They established a Medical and Surgical Association and published *Confederate States Medical and Surgical Journal.*[19]

To a large extent, the workload for physicians was frightful. Periodic outbreaks of childhood illnesses—mumps, measles, chicken pox, and others—

overwhelmed doctors early in the war, and waves swept through the army as new recruits joined the ranks. Two months before the spring campaign in 1863, the army suffered a deadly outbreak of spinal meningitis, which physicians mercifully contained. Vaccinations and eruptions of smallpox regularly plagued Lee's army. Medical officers received instructions to vaccinate troops and children who lived near the army to prevent exposure. Still, they could not suppress the disease. In early April 1863, the Second Corps Field Hospital housed 543 patients, 31 of whom died of smallpox. In winter months, barefoot, ill-clad, and undernourished soldiers could not resist pneumococcus, the bacteria that generated into pneumonia. Add to that a host of discomforts from colds to camp itch and the usual problem with venereal diseases, and surgeons and assistant surgeons seldom enjoyed rest periods.[20]

Word of an upcoming march triggered a flurry of activity. Army doctors scurried about, removing the sick who could not march, loading medical supplies, and checking to ensure they had all the proper equipment. Wagons were at a premium in Lee's army, and medical officers always coped with shortages. Not only were they concerned with hauling their supplies and tents on the march, but they also had to calculate how to transport the wounded back to general hospitals, a very difficult proposition. The army lacked sufficient ambulances, and those they did have never seemed to have enough springs, so that the infirm bounced around in the back, heightening their agony as they traveled the difficult roads to safety. Not until after the Battle of Chancellorsville did ambulances carry splints. Combat victims with shattered femurs would bang around during the ride, and "splints would protect them from the most excrutiating suffering." Unless the fighting took place near Richmond, wagons and ambulances would often haul wounded soldiers to field hospitals or railroad junctions, where trains would take them to Richmond hospitals. When Francis W. Dawson suffered a gash four inches long and one inch deep in his leg, he bound it with a handkerchief, finished the battle, and then walked seven miles to receive medical aid. Anticipating large numbers of wounded after battle, hospital workers moved current patients into one area and thoroughly cleaned furniture and floors with disinfectants and lime and aired out bedding.[21]

After battle, the case load for surgeons was astronomical, and their reports demonstrated remarkable feats and an impressive level of care and concern for the wounded, as well as many terrible ordeals. Dr. Warner Lewis Baylor recorded the case of Pvt. James Johnston, 17th Georgia, who received two gunshot wounds to the arm at Second Manassas. An ulcer developed and a bone protruded from it. Dr. Baylor sought to keep the wound clean with a concoction of "Chlorat Potash" twice per day, and he tried elder leaves and charcoal to keep the flies and maggots from infesting the injury, but that failed. Soon, infection grew severe and the "Discharge became heavy." He gave Johnston some opiates for the pain and milk and brandy for a cough. The infection spread, his breathing became more labored, and on September 11, Johnston expired. Much later in the war, Baylor battled the same problem, whether to save the limb and risk the life, or amputate the limb. Thirty-year-old Corp. Thomas N. Knight sustained a wound on March 25, 1865, at Fort Stedman that fractured the tibia in his right leg. For nearly two weeks, he was nursed, but the infection grew worse. "We attempted to save the leg," Baylor recorded, "but on 7 of April we decided that the only chance to save the life of the patient was to amputate the thigh in the lower third, which was done by myself, while the patient was under the influence of chloroform." Knight "suffered so much pain, and from such excessive discharge that this, was considered the only chance of recovery." Baylor had waited too long. Once again, infection had spread through the patient's bloodstream, and Knight showed signs of fever. By April 18, he died, leaving behind his mother and three sisters who depended on him.[22]

Tales also indicate that the wounded suffered terribly. Corp. L. J. Shaw of the 3rd North Carolina, one of his regiment's 215 soldiers killed or wounded in a battle, suffered a severe wound. Doctors saved his leg, but five months later, physicians continued to pick bone fragments out of his leg and predicted there were "more to come out yet." The site of the wound, he elaborated to his captain, "has Enflamed and looks very angry." He hoped to return for the spring campaign, but it took him until early 1865 before he could resume any field duty.[23]

From September 1862 to July 1864, hospitals in Virginia admitted almost 413,000 patients due to illness or injury, which kept doctors in a frantic state for much of Lee's tenure as army commander. This figure did not include those who were sick but remained in camp, were killed in action, or suffered wounds that did not require hospital care.[24]

Throughout the war, nearly one in every four men who served in Lee's army died on the battlefield or from disease. Slightly more soldiers died in combat, a phenomenally high proportion considering that disease claimed two of every three fatalities among all Confederate troops. Within Lee's army, age indicated how men were likely to die—the earlier their year of birth, the more likely they were to die of disease. Younger men, usually more aggressive and less concerned with mortality or injury, lost their lives more frequently in battle. Men born after 1835 were more likely to die in battle while those born before 1835 succumbed more often to disease.[25]

Disease tended to strike down soldiers in the earlier part of their service career. Just over half of all soldiers who died of disease did so in their first twelve months of service, and more than five of every six who fell to illness did so within their first two years in the army. Among the men who entered the service in 1863 and 1864, a higher percentage died of disease, rather than in battle. That had partly to do with the length of service. Soldiers who entered in 1861 or 1862 fought in more large battles and were at greater risk of losing their lives in action. But enlistees and conscripts in 1863 and 1864 also tended toward more extremes in age, with unusually high percentages of older and very young men. Those disproportionate numbers of older soldiers struggled to fend off diseases in the army.[26]

In preparation for the 1864 campaign, the medical director of the Army of Northern Virginia, Dr. Lafayette Guild, instituted a number of changes, some under Lee's recommendation. In December 1862, Lee had complained to the adjutant general that soldiers returned to camp carrying contagious diseases. A year later, after consulting with Guild, Lee proposed the creation of a quarantine camp and hospital as a holding facility to guarantee that returning soldiers did not infect their comrades. Guild justified the plan to the surgeon general by mentioning a recent bout of sixty cases of smallpox, a problem that clearly warranted a quarantine camp. With Lee's support, in mid-January, Guild announced the creation of a "Sanitary Camp," a practical solution to a serious problem and one that probably aided in the reduction of illnesses in Lee's army that winter and early spring.[27]

Guild also took steps to prepare the medical corps to respond more efficiently to army campaign needs. After Gettysburg, the Confederates left behind a considerable number of physicians to tend to wounded Confederates. A year earlier, Lee and McClellan had agreed to treat physicians as noncombatants, but the arrangement broke down over a dispute about a Virginia Unionist, and Lee's army endured a severe shortage of medical officers at Bristoe Station. Although they did restore the agreement, Lee could not chance the loss of a significant number of physicians for a month or two. Guild requested that the War Department close several smaller hospitals, and some of those physicians receive assignments to Lee's army. Two weeks before the campaign opened, because of the "unprecedented health" of the army, the medical corps announced it could pack lighter and reduce its transportation. The army required less medicine for troops and could concentrate on hauling material surgeons would need to treat wounds. At the same time, the surgeon general announced the creation of a Reserve Surgical Corps, composed of "the most skillful and efficient operative Surgeons," in proportion of one per 500 hospital beds, who would go to the army and care for wounded on the battlefields and supervise their removal and transportation to hospitals.[28]

Despite the best efforts of Guild and his subordinates, no one could have anticipated the deluge of casualties and sick during the Overland Campaign. In May 1864, the number of soldiers who entered hospitals in Virginia peaked at over 48,000, a figure that was 33 percent higher than that for any other month (June 1864 ranked second). During the months of May, June, and July 1864, Virginia hospitals admitted more than 102,000 soldiers. So many troops required hospitalization that the army had to ship more than 50,000 of those cases to hospitals outside the department during that three-month period. The army could neither care for nor feed them in Richmond. On Guild's recommendation, hospitals in three states—Danville and Farmville, Virginia; Raleigh and Greensboro, North Carolina; and Kingsville, Tennessee—began to receive direct shipments of wounded from the battlefields of Virginia. Once the battlefield shifted to Petersburg, the hospital there became unsafe, and Guild had to shift many sick and wounded to Richmond.[29]

The problem, as both Lee and Guild knew, was that once soldiers went to general hospitals, particularly those outside Richmond, it was very difficult to get them to return to the army. Early in the war, physicians returned soldiers to the field too soon, and too many relapsed or required transportation for the march. By early 1864, too many soldiers failed to return from hospitals or sick furloughs. Guild requested the surgeon general create commissions composed of physicians to check patients in hospitals in Virginia, North Carolina, South Carolina, and Georgia and send those men able for duty back to the army. As part of Lee's effort to increase troop strength for the upcoming campaign, he complained that too many furloughed soldiers failed to rejoin their comrades, and he suggested a policy prohibiting sick and wounded furloughs in all cases. Yet the army could not terminate leaves for the sick and wounded. At a time when the army had reduced meat rations to a quarter pound of bacon or beef per day, it made no sense to keep badly wounded soldiers in Richmond, when their families could better feed and care for them. In August, Guild complained on behalf of Lee that when physicians treated soldiers in infirmaries and field hospitals, they returned to their units promptly. When they went to general hospitals, he asserted, "it seems to require almost supernatural efforts to force the men back to their regiments in the field."[30]

All told, some 4,200 soldiers died in hospitals during the first three months of the 1864 campaign, and thousands more died on the battlefield—a combined total well above 10 percent of the army that took the field in early May. Many of the wounded never healed properly and could not return to duty. Six months later, Lee learned of a serious problem with those they sent home on wounded furloughs. After an extensive investigation, the Medical Department of the Army of Northern Virginia discovered that a "very large number" of soldiers became permanently disabled from wounds that should have healed properly. Surgeons treated wounds to the extremities properly, but when patients received furloughs to go home, medical care was inadequate and muscular and bone problems resulted in permanent disabilities. "At least three fourths of the slighter wounds of the extremities have permanently disqualified the recipients for active field service on account of the resulting muscular contractions," explained Surgeon W. S. Mitchell of Rodes's Division. Wounds to the hands or wrists increased the chances of improper healing. Mitchell believed his division alone lost 100 combat troops from improper healing. "The appeals of a wounded soldier to be permitted to return to kind friends at home, are hard to resist," Guild argued, "but it is false humanity to yield to such appeals in the present emergency of the country when we know that the soldier will return to his command crippled and deformed for life."[31]

At a time when Lee needed more troops, medical policies, charitable though they were, inhibited wounded soldiers from recovering properly and returning to their combat commands.

Chapter 31

MANPOWER

"I HAVE THE HONOR to represent to you the absolute necessity that exists, in my opinion, to increase our armies, if we desire to oppose effectual resistance to the vast numbers that the enemy is now precipitating upon us," Lee notified the secretary of war in January 1863. Over the previous seven months, the Army of Northern Virginia had paid an excessive price in blood to block enemy advances and had lost opportunities to inflict much greater damage, all because the army lacked the necessary manpower. Casualties and disease had thinned Lee's ranks, while their enemy tapped a much larger population to bolster theirs. That imbalance would cost "the most precious blood of the country," because "every man who remains out of service increases the dangers to which the brave men, who have so well borne the burden of the war, are exposed." Lee believed the Confederate people "must put forth their full strength at once." He requested that the secretary of war call on governors to appeal to their constituents to fill the ranks, using "shame" against "those who will not heed the dictates of honor and of patriotism."[1]

Ever since he assumed command of the army in June 1862, Lee had struggled to increase his troop strength. Secretary of War George W. Randolph had ordered soldiers to serve as clerks in Richmond, and shortly after Seven Days' Lee, unaware of Randolph's directive, insisted that they return to the ranks immediately, in accordance with President Davis's earlier policy that civilians should perform clerical duties. Randolph charged Lee with disobedience, but Lee explained to the secretary that in the past seventeen days his army had lost 168 men—approximately half a regiment—to discharges for medical reasons and details of this kind. "This constant drain," he argued, "reduces the ranks of the Army, forces it to inaction & may result in disaster." Randolph withdrew the charges.[2]

Lee waged a continual war to halt the siphoning of combat soldiers for peripheral duties. He encouraged civilians ineligible for military service to perform clerical duties. When he learned that topographical engineers detailed privates to assist them, Lee blocked the order. "Company and other intermediate commanders are constantly demurring in consequence of the reduction of their commands by details," Lee wrote Longstreet, "and I desire to make only such as are absolutely necessary." The army commander halted the practice of allowing infantry and other soldiers to transfer from his department, and he stripped the quartermaster and commissary departments of what he considered excess personnel. He encouraged subordinate commanders to crack down on soldiers who remained at home on frivolous pretexts and he reminded civilians through his officers that soldiers who deserted, were absent without leave, or overstayed their furloughs prevented others from receiving furloughs, hoping locals would pressure absentees to return to the army. It became so difficult for men to obtain release from their military obligation that a soldier informed his wife, "they wont discharge a man as long as he can put one foot before the other." In fact, they even found military jobs for soldiers who had lost a leg or an arm. As the army passed through communities, Lee instructed his corps commanders to enroll all citizens who were not exempt from the draft. Forever vigilant, Lee informed the secretary of war after Gettysburg, "Every subterfuge is being adopted to withdraw men from military service. It ought to be stopped." Even those within the military felt Lee's ire. When Lee saw an old family acquaintance, staff officer William McWillie, on foot and searching for a new mount to replace his dead horse, Lee bluntly told him to go to the chief of ordnance "and he will give you a good musket and you may do a great deal of good."[3]

The original Conscription Law, which passed Congress in April 1862, generated some frustration among those who had enlisted in 1861. It compelled them to stay in the army two more years. But it also drove large numbers of civilians into the military ranks who might not have enlisted at that time. However much the law violated Confederate sensibilities regarding civil liberties, it saved the Confederacy from defeat that summer.[4]

Large numbers of men whose ages fell within the prescribed limits of eighteen to thirty-five sought exclusion from conscription on various grounds. Many had already claimed exemption from the militia for frivolous reasons—one man argued he should not have to serve because he was a coffin maker. With the conscription law in place, the volume of proposed exemptions soared. Along with legal claims by clergy, politicians, teachers, and slave owners with fifteen or more slaves, others claimed medical disability. Abuse of disability claims became so rampant that the Medical Department announced that a certificate of disability from a doctor was not sufficient cause for rejecting a recruit. Only medical officers specifically designated for that role could exclude individuals from conscription. "Recruit[s] must not be rejected for trivial defects," the medical director instructed authorized physicians, "but all passed who are capable of bearing arms." Nor did the military tolerate lenient medical examiners. When a few doctors dismissed an entire batch of conscripts as physically unfit, officers refused to let those doctors examine any new cases.[5]

Among those exempt from the draft due to specifications in the addendum to the law, a small number of men sought to avoid military service as conscientious objectors. Just before the passage of the Conscription Act, Jackson encountered three religious denominations that opposed all wars. Taking a practical and not a moral position, Jackson conceded, "They can be made to fire, but they can very easily take bad aim." Many of those conscientious objectors professed loyalty to the Confederacy and possessed noncombat skills that the army needed, so Jackson directed his subordinates to organize them into hundred-man companies. They could perform labor for the army that would free others to return to combat units, and drill in tactics without weapons.[6]

Much later in the war, tolerance for conscientious objectors receded. Private Maben Hinshaw in the 6th North Carolina, a professed Quaker, received much worse treatment at the hands of officers in 1865. Although Hinshaw, a prewar painter and father of four, had refused to take up arms, they coerced him. "I had to take a gun and drill or die," Hinshaw explained. He had heard from several witnesses that they had hung his Quaker friend by his thumbs, bucked him, run him double-quick with a gun tied to him, and flogged him. When his fellow Quaker still resisted, they knocked him down with a club twice and then hung him. "They did not frite or sker me to it," Hinshaw explained to his wife, "but I discovered they wod punish me til it wod kill me and Linda for thy sake and the childrens I wod not go to surten deth at that time and I am inhopes I shal not be condemd in the site of heven for it."[7]

After two years of service, Pvt. Joel B. Ragsdale of the 4th Texas wrote Davis in September 1863, requesting that the president relieve him from bearing arms. His officers were skeptical of his sudden morals. After all, "He has been two years aiding, abetting, & countenancing the Slaughter of the enemies of freedom." A lieutenant thought his request was the "product of *a delicately nervous temperament*; or of an emotion less creditable to his manhood." Lieutenant Colonel J. P. Bane declared, "If Private Ragsdale's conscientious scruples are So great as to prevent him from Killing one of his greatest enemies, he will do to stop the bullet that otherwise might Kill a better man."[8]

Ten months later, Ragsdale again wrote Davis, asking the president to let him leave the service for "consciencious scruples." If Davis would not release him, Ragsdale asked that the president remove him from an arms-bearing assignment. He looked upon killing as murder, "a sin in direct violasion of the laws of God." He admitted having fought in numerous battles "yet it has not been without remorse of conscience." Davis replied that Ragsdale exhibited some confusing ideas, and if his officers could not reconcile with him, his regimental commander should find an appropriate assignment for him.[9]

Yet another way to avoid military service was to hire a substitute. Even though many soldiers expressed a wish to find a substitute, and some actually pleaded with loved ones for help locating one, less than 1 percent of the soldiers in Lee's army accomplished it. After the Conscription Act retained his services for another two years, Virginia private Howell Nelson conceded to his wife, "If I had the money I would give two thousand for someone to take my place." In point of fact, Nelson owned six slaves and boasted assets of $13,000, but he did not want to pay the price. A Georgia private implored his father not to be tempted by offers to serve in someone else's stead. He was too old to withstand the hardships of army life. "I will advise you to stay at home," he penned just before Second Manassas. "Do not go in no man's place as a substitute."[10]

Clearly, wealthy soldiers had an advantage in securing substitutes. Private Seth Combs, a thirty-six-year-old Virginian worth some $20,000 and owner of twenty slaves, secured a substitute after two years of service. South Carolinian William Tenant enjoyed financial success with twenty-seven slaves, when he elected to hire a substitute. Private John J. Dunning of the 5th South Carolina Cavalry owned nothing himself, but his father was a master butcher with considerable wealth and eleven slaves, and he chipped in the money to release his son from the army. Not all soldiers who hired substitutes possessed considerable wealth, though. In a very different circumstance, James R. Bentley secured Crawford Talley to act as his substitute. Talley must have agreed for personal reasons, because neither of them nor their families had any appreciable wealth.[11]

With money available for substitution, cases of fraud and unethical behavior developed. Private D. J. Lemmon of the 1st South Carolina Sharpshooters brought in an individual named Joe Bell to serve as his substitute. Several soldiers commented that Bell was very intelligent but resembled a woman; the officers dismissed it as usual campground commentary. When it came time for the physical, Bell resisted and eventually refused to proceed beyond a very rudimentary examination. Lemmon was informed that the surgeon could not approve the substitute without a proper physical exam, and the two confronted Bell. At that point, Bell admitted she was a woman. It turned out that Bell had been imprisoned as a Union spy under the name Mrs. Underwood, and was quickly handed over to authorities at Castle Thunder, the Richmond prison.[12]

In most cases of corruption, however, individuals sought a chance to claim a prize and desert. Patrick McGee took $500 from a soldier to substitute in the 40th Virginia while he served in a different regiment. McGee claimed he was a foreigner based on his Irish nationality and demanded release from his original regiment, the 1st Virginia. Then, he brokered a deal for $1,000 to substitute for a soldier in the 47th Virginia. Once he arrived at the 47th Virginia, he learned that part of the money was being withheld to ensure he did not desert. McGee became furious and refused to serve. The ruckus attracted a crowd, and someone recognized him as a bounty jumper. Officials arrested him, a court-martial found him guilty, and he was executed. L. S. Childers of the 5th Florida committed a similar offense, but timing worked in his favor. He took money as a substitute for a wealthy Floridian named George Raysor. Childers deserted, was caught, and a court-martial sentenced him to die. To induce deserters to return to the ranks, Davis offered a general amnesty, and unintentionally, it covered Childers. Authorities not only released him from death row, they reinstated him in his old regiment, where he resumed his service.[13]

The army and the War Department attempted to regulate the substitution process carefully, so that when good men left the service, they were not replaced by scoundrels. Even before conscription, the army allowed substitution with the permission of the company commander. As Congress discussed the new conscription legislation, the War Department terminated substitution, then reauthorized it. Substitutes were to be individuals in good health who were not previously eligible for military service, such as persons younger or older than the draft age or foreigners. In early September 1862, the War Department prohibited men younger than eighteen from becoming substitutes. In July 1863, to ensure that the army received adequate service from substitutes, those who hired them became liable for their term of service if the substitute left the army for any reason other than as a casualty of war. Meanwhile, Lee directed captains and colonels to "accept no substitute, unless his moral, physical and soldierly qualifications are clearly equal to those of the soldier for whom he is offered." By late December 1863, Congress outlawed the process of substitution and eight days later made those who hired substitutes once again eligible for conscription.[14]

Some soldiers felt that substitutes were poor replacements for the original soldiers. "There are a great many 'subs' in the Regiment now or have been put in," a Virginia private wrote, "but nearly all have deserted and I am glad of it as I don't want to fight side by side with the Rich mans sub." Yet for substitutes like Edward S. Dean in the 3rd Virginia Cavalry, the deal he brokered as a substitute established him financially for the rest of his life. A pro-Confederate from Delaware, Dean received land from the Osborne family in Nottoway County, Virginia, to act as a substitute for Richard S. Osborne. With hard work after the war, Dean became a successful farmer by 1870, worth nearly $10,000. Dean, moreover, fought well for the Confederacy, suffering a gunshot wound to the arm in May 1864 at Yellow Tavern.[15]

In the months leading up to the spring campaign in 1864, Lee pared down wasted manpower and placed excess personnel back in the fighting army. Due to the decline in strength, Lee forbade the election of any new second lieutenants without permission from the secretary of war. This would keep more shooters in the ranks. When officers resigned their commissions for any reason other than a permanent disability, Lee directed that they must enroll immediately and choose a new company in which to serve as a conscript. The commanding general offered a thirty-day furlough for any soldier who brought in an able-bodied recruit, as long as the enlistee possessed good moral character and was neither a deserter nor absent without leave from another command. With Davis's cooperation, Lee secured pardons for many soldiers who had committed certain offenses with justifiable reasons, such as overstaying leaves at home because a parent was ill, and had served part of their prison sentences. At a time when beef was scarce anyway, the army even reduced the number of butchers it required. By shifting the work to the division from the brigade level, the army placed many butchers back in the line.[16]

The results were impressive. One Virginian boasted in late April that his company had 80 men. An officer in the 45th Georgia maintained that the regiment had come to Virginia with roughly 1,000 men in April 1862, and fell back from Antietam with only 200 left. At the start of the spring campaign, the regiment listed 425 men on its rolls as present. The army found homes not just for recruits but for old and injured soldiers as well. Private Bennett Rainey Jeffares of the 38th Georgia suffered a severe leg wound in Seven Days'. After months in Chimborazo and the hospital at Stone Mountain, Georgia, and a medical furlough at home, he elected to return to Lee's army. Unable to walk well enough for the infantry, Jeffares was convinced he could still contribute, and he drove wagons for the remainder of the war, freeing an able-bodied soldier for combat duty.[17]

Directly and indirectly, the Conscription Act drove large numbers of men into Lee's army. Five months after Congress passed its first Conscription Act, it raised the age limit of those subject to conscription from thirty-five to forty-five. Individuals like Philip Brady, who had enlisted in the 1st Louisiana in 1861 at thirty-five and received a discharge for age at reorganization in 1862, found himself conscripted in 1864 and serving in the Richmond Howitzers. In mid-February 1864, Congress not only extended the terms of service for men who had enlisted in 1861 to the end of the war, it expanded the conscription age to include seventeen-year-olds and placed men between forty-five and fifty in reserve organizations. Rather than wait and risk the draft, young men volunteered promptly upon coming of age while older men braced for the call to duty.[18]

Evidence tracking conscripts has proven difficult to compile. With the exception of North Carolina, which kept records of its conscripts in official personnel documents, conscription information for Confederate soldiers was haphazard at best. The Camp of Instruction at Camp Lee outside Richmond, which opened on the last day of October 1862 and became the point of concentration for Virginia conscripts, maintained strong collective records. Through January 31, 1864, 7,153 conscripts received assignments, most of them with the Army of Northern Virginia. From February 1864 to February 1865, another 8,653 passed through Camp Lee for Lee's army. Of the conscripts joining Lee's army over those thirteen months, the infantry drew nearly three-fourths, and the cavalry another one in every five. The artillery received about one in every fourteen. Through February 28, 1865, physicians deemed 6,316 conscripts ineligible for service because of physical disabilities. The state also drafted 1,561 free blacks and assigned them to support duties for the military.[19]

Statistics up to November 1863 indicated that more than half of all those who reported for conscription were ultimately exempted from duty. In addition to those with physical disabilities, only 2 percent claimed an exemption as overseers under the Fifteen Slave Law, which permitted a household with fifteen or more slaves to keep an adult white man at home. Eight percent of the conscripts were railroad workers, millers, and farmers who avoided military service. Shoemakers composed more than 10 percent of the legal exclusions, and government officials made up another 11 percent. Even doctors and those who sought exceptions on religious grounds doubled the number of overseer exemptions. The largest category of exemptions, making up almost 42 percent, were those who hired substitutes, a practice outlawed by Congress the following month. Drunkards were allowed an exemption if they paid $300 and then $500, but only a few men exploited the loophole each month. Although statistics on justification for exemptions survive for only two other time periods, they indicate that comparatively few slaveholders exploited the Fifteen Slave exemption. In November 1863, for example, twenty-seven more sought overseer exemptions, and from August 1 through 17, 1864, a dozen more did.

Earlier in the war, until November 1, 1863, the army detailed 7,311 conscripts to noncombat work. That number declined as more pressing needs for manpower arose. But as military shortages increased throughout 1864, the army retained more skilled workers as soldiers and detailed them to military production. In a two-month period in late 1864, almost 1,300 conscripts received detail assignments from Camp Lee.[20]

Over the last two years of the war, perhaps 12 percent of the soldiers were conscripts. More than half were in their thirties and fewer than one in five were under twenty. Nearly two-thirds were married, and a majority disclosed their occupation as farmer. Conscripts were much poorer and had a smaller attachment to slavery than their fellow volunteers. The median personal and, if they lived with their parents, family wealth was $400, far below the $1,250 of Lee's army as a whole. Less than a quarter of conscripts either owned or lived with parents who owned slaves, and 35 percent lived in households with slaves, again well below the figure of 44 percent for the Army of Northern Virginia as a whole.[21]

Many people in and out of the army stigmatized conscripts. They felt these men lacked patriotism and honor, that there was something unmanly about an individual who refused to fight willingly for his country and hearth and home. Yet many volunteers did so to avoid the stigma of conscription, while others would have left the army if the government had not extended their enlistment term to three years and then the duration of the war. In late August 1862, the *Richmond Examiner* discussed the motivations and quality of conscripted soldiers. "It is not a forced inference to suppose that the conscripts recently brought into the army are unequal in spirit and zeal to the volunteers who enlisted from a sense of patriotic duty," the editors concluded. "When men are forced into service they are not apt to exhibit those higher qualities of the soldier, of which voluntary enlistment affords some indication, and only long training can ensure. The conscripts are men possessing neither native enthusiasm nor trained efficiency in it." Somehow, argued the editor, the army must instill in its conscripts the zeal and ambition that they inherently lacked.[22]

By contrast, the *Mobile Register* presented a very different assessment of conscript motivation. "There are many—who shall say not a majority proportion— among the conscripts, whose hearts are as fully in their country's cause, and who would as fearlessly battle for it as any volunteer, but who have not engaged in the war simply for the reason, that their private obligations and the necessities of their dependents rendered it absolutely impossible for them to do so without sacrifices which they had no moral right to make, and without reducing helpless persons looking to them for support to want and suffering." The *Register* portrayed a different side of conscription, one of integrity and conscience. Reminding its readers that Napoleon's army was composed of conscripts who had certainly fought well, the *Register* predicted, "There are thousands of conscripts who will prove, before the war is over, that they are worthy to be the 'comrades in battle' of our bravest volunteers."[23]

Some did lack the will to fight, and some had greater priorities at home. Roughly one in every fourteen conscripts deserted at Camp Lee, and with those desertions from the field army, the proportions of their desertions far exceeded those of volunteers. A soldier in the 2nd Washington Artillery from Louisiana, assuming poetic license, set his feelings about conscripts to verse.

> *They took me for a soldier and are going to make me fight*
> *Though I never could believe myself that shooting folks was right.*

He much preferred his life as a gambler. When the conscript official seized him, the conscript tried to bribe him with all his money. The official took the money and turned him in anyway. The conscript complained that the other soldiers cursed and kicked him and treated him shabbily. They insisted:

> *The only thing I'll ever learn, is, how to run away—*
> *Then they say they've found me out, that I am a stupid lout,*
> *I have so many orders, I don't Know what I'm about.*

He urged others not to try to bribe the guards:

> *But get some foreign Gentlemen, by paying in advance,*
> *To swear you come from Germany, or Ireland, or France.*
> *To set the matter right, have it writ in black and White*
> *That you're a foreign fellow, and they cannot make you fight.*[24]

Others had obligations to their families that superseded their duty in the war. John Berryman Crawford was a thirty-five-year-old Mississippian and father of four young children, one an infant, when he was conscripted in January 1863. A comfortable nonslaveholding farmer in Jasper County, Crawford boasted around $1,800 in total wealth. Crawford supported the secessionist cause, but with no one to tend the farm other than himself, he felt an overpowering sense of responsibility to his family. Despite his attachment to wife Martha and the farm, he went willingly when called upon to serve and devoted himself to becoming the best soldier he could.[25]

Crawford joined Company F, 16th Mississippi Infantry, a veteran regiment that had fought the battles of 1862. After his first fight—at Chancellorsville—he wrote to Martha that "the shot and shell an menny balls com round me like hail stones but no time for doging." A religious man, Crawford "expected ever miute [minute] our companey would be blown into attums but I think kind providents smiled on us." After eight days in battle, he described it as "aslaughter pen." To Martha, he conceded, "it is enough to make old master weep." A month later, he had come to grips with mortality and the place of God in his life. "I don't know what minute I may lunch in eturnite though I feel I am prepared," he declared to Martha.[26]

Paramount in Crawford's mind was the well-being of his family. Shortly after Chancellorsville, he received a letter from his wife informing him that someone, probably a relative of hers, had beaten their little boy Tommy and threatened to whip her. Initially, he was hurt, but soon grew angry. "It all most break my heart to think about it to think I am so far from home," he wrote. "The tears I have shed since I read your letter would flood a mill O my god my god what will become of my family." A week later, he confessed, "eber time I think of his whiping tomy my blood boils to the top of my mettle I think at that time I could murder him."[27]

Like so many soldiers with wives and children at home, Crawford longed for them and thought about them all the time. He often looked at the lock of hair she had given him and maintained, "it looks very natural but I wood like to see the place it com off of much more." Martha implored him to obtain a furlough and visit them, but he replied it would be impossible. "They wount give furlough til they are dead three days and then they have to examine the grave to see if he thiere or not," he quipped. What worried him most was the fear that she and the children would suffer from a shortage of necessities. He insisted, "that wood make me desert an com home."[28]

After Gettysburg, he was hospitalized with fever. The combination of illness, poor treatment in the hospital, and the fight at Gettysburg discouraged him about the outcome of the war. In early August, he announced to Martha, "our confederacy is gon up the spout and I don't car[e] how soon the sooner the better for ous."[29]

When the rumor mill ground out tales of the army shifting to Tennessee, Crawford delighted in the prospect. "I wish they wood go[,] then I wood be nier home so I could runaway and come home," he told her. "it is too fur from hear to runaway." The 16th Mississippi did not go.[30]

Crawford eagerly awaited the campaign of 1864. "Wee exspect a big fight next spring," he predicted in late January, "and if wee whip them I think they will quit waring the yankee are giting tiard of it as much as wee arre." He informed Martha, "the yankee says on to Richmond are [or] to hell I think it will be the latter with agrate many of them." He confidently believed they would repulse the grand Union advance, and when Lincoln's term expired "something will be don towards peace but not until then."[31]

Crawford was killed in action at Spotsylvania on May 12, 1864.[32]

After the Battle of Fredericksburg, A. P. Hill declared, "The conscripts showed themselves desirous of being thought worthy comrades of our veteran soldiers." His opinion, however, did not reflect the majority sentiment among volunteers. "I am ashamed of these poor fellows who stays at home until the Enrolling officer takes them by the hair of the head & pulls them in the Army," a Georgian decreed. It galled an Alabamian that those who cried for secession and war were "planning sum skeem to give the conscripting officer the slip." When Congress extended the conscription age and designated those between forty-six and fifty for the reserves, a Virginian rejoiced. "I presume Isaac Baker will limp most awfully now since congress has extended the conscript law to fifty. I almost wish it may reach Harrison Coyner, as [he] seemed anxious that every body else should be in the service."[33]

In many cases, prospective conscripts reinforced common opinion by violently resisting conscripting officers. A captain in the 7th Virginia led a squad of eleven men to Rappahannock County to collect some conscripts. As they approached the door of a house owned by a fellow named Carter, he, his sons, and his son-in-law came out with guns blazing. A shotgun blast killed a sergeant, but the soldiers eventually subdued the Carter family and dragged them back to camp for punishment. Even more bizarre were some conscripts in Essex County, Virginia, who tried to strike a deal with authorities. Led by two wealthy slaveholders, they proposed that if the officials would not try to press them into the army, they would ensure that soldiers did not overstay their leaves. One sergeant pronounced such an offer "too mean and contemptible for any white man." He insisted, "If they want to [be] useful to the cause let them take their muskets and come to the army instead of running after soldiers who go to see their friends." The sergeant and his comrades pledged to settle the score when they got home.[34]

Conscripts would get Lee only part of the combat manpower he needed. At the end of April 1864, the superintendent of the Bureau of Conscription informed the secretary of war that "fresh material for the armies can no longer be estimated as an element of future calculation for their increase." Essentially, all men who could serve were serving, except for deserters. Although he overstated his argument, he was correct to suggest that dissolving military details, returning deserters, and expanding the age limits for service were the only real solutions. Many men who would have been exempt from conscription sent substitutes anyway as gestures of patriotism, and when those who hired substitutes became eligible for conscription, they possessed legitimate exemptions. The superintendent argued that the Fifteen Slave Law had not produced the sorts of food surpluses the army needed or Congress expected. "My opinion is that the agriculture of the country cannot safely spare more than a very small additional draft." Over a period of four months, from December 1863 to March 1864, officials assigned only 7,513 conscripts to all Confederate armies, and the superintendent estimated about 50 percent more, some 3,700 conscripts, went directly to the army, bypassing Camps of Instruction. According to his statistics, almost as many soldiers returned from desertion during that period as the Conscription Bureau funneled into the army.

The Confederacy was running out of men. "For conscription from the general population," the superintended stated baldly, "the functions of this Bureau may cease with the termination of the year 1864."[35]

Chapter 32

DESERTION

I N THE AFTERMATH of the Gettysburg Campaign, Lee warned Davis, "The number of desertions from this army is so great and still continues to such an extent, that unless some cessation of them can be caused, I fear success in the field will be seriously endangered." With cavalry carefully positioned to block crossing at fords and bridges, and through a systematic policy of rest, refitting, and food, Lee was able to stanch the flow of bodies away from his army. Yet three weeks before the opening of the spring campaign of 1864, Lee complained about the same problem: "Desertion and absence without leave are nearly the only offences ever tried by our Courts. They appear to be the only vices in the army." During the previous month, Lee reported 5,474 men absent without leave—soldiers who left the army but were likely to return shortly—and 322 deserters.[1]

The impact of desertion, however, was more severe than Lee suggested. Soldiers who took to flight almost always carried their weapons with them, often reducing the number of quality arms in an army already hard-pressed for good rifles and pistols. They rode or hiked to the homes of family and friends, drawing foodstuffs from the local population en route. Frequently, they abandoned the army in groups, which increased the hardships they inflicted on civilians and injured public support for the war effort. Among the greatest wartime plunderers were deserters. As one Virginian wrote his wife, they "are a terror to the inhabitants." Once at home, deserters often gathered in gangs to shield one another from local and military officials who sought their arrest and return. This frequently polarized communities, with the disaffected and friends and family of deserters on one side and those who supported the war or whose loved ones fought in the army on the other. Lee complained that authorities "were not prosecuting civilians for harboring or protecting known deserters, even when the cases were clear," but the army commander failed to weigh the impact and support within the local community for punishing their neighbors and friends as the hardships at home and in the army increased.[2]

Substantial numbers of soldiers fled to Union lines, either from shame or for convenience, where they provided a bounty of information. On September 9, 1863, the Union Army of the Potomac learned of Lee's plans to reinforce Bragg's army, a few days before Lee's men embarked on trains for north Georgia. In mid-December 1863, a Federal colonel in the Provost-Marshal General's Office crowed, "our Knowledge of the army is so complete" from the interrogation of deserters, prisoners of war, spies, and scouts. On two consecutive days in mid-July 1864, the First Corps called off attacks because troops had deserted to Yankee lines with knowledge of the plan. In November, one of Grant's aides admitted, "Deserters are arriving in sufficient numbers to keep us very well posted regarding the movements and positions of the enemy's brigades in our front."[3]

Soldiers who lived in Virginia or North Carolina often took "French leave," as they sometimes called it, slipping away for a brief time and then returning on their own, while their comrades from more distant states had no such opportunity. Proximity of the march to their home, the conclusion of an arduous campaign, better medical care, or prolonged absence from loved ones induced men to go absent without leave. Generally, punishment was mild—pay docked for a month or two and confinement to camp or some form of extra duty. In the eyes of many soldiers, the punishment was worth it. Private John N. Old of the Charlottesville Artillery left on March 27 and arrived home three days later. After a week-long visit, he returned to the army and immediately reported to the battery commander. The captain told Old he was sorry he had run away but was glad he returned on his own. "He was quite Friendly and told me to hold on until he could See about my case," Old wrote his wife. "I Recon tha will take my wages for a month."[4]

No one will ever know just how many soldiers in Lee's army went absent without leave or deserted. Regimental and battery commanders sometimes handled unauthorized absences in the unit, and some service records frequently failed to include that information. While muster rolls often contained desertions, during the final seven months of the war either recordkeeping broke down in Lee's army or muster rolls were destroyed, so that statistics on desertion most certainly undercount the actual numbers. Approximately one in every seven soldiers in Lee's army deserted. Fewer than 10 percent of all deserters returned to the army either voluntarily or by arrest.[5]

Although desertion cut across all social and economic lines, several factors emerged to help distinguish deserters from those who remained with the army. Deserters tended to be poorer and had a weaker connection to slavery. Deserters had personal and, if they lived with their parents, combined personal and family median wealth of $730, compared to nearly $1,350 for nondeserters. Those who stayed with the army were almost twice as likely to own slaves or reside with parents who did, and were nearly twice as likely as deserters to reside in slaveholding households. As deserters tended to be poorer than other soldiers, the hardships of war, particularly the loss of the principal breadwinner, weighed more heavily on deserters and their families. Many also frequently had weaker bonds with their home community.[6]

Yet financial difficulties told just part of the story. Deserters were only 10 percent more likely to be married than nondeserters, but almost 50 percent more likely to have children. In fact, 98 percent of all married deserters had children.[7]

Age, too, affected rates of desertion. Active duty and even camp life took a physical toll on the men, and older soldiers had a much more difficult time coping with the strain of military life. One in every five deserters in the infantry and artillery were born in the 1820s, which meant that by 1864, they were in their late thirties or early forties. In the cavalry, nearly two of every five deserters were born in the 1820s.[8]

The cavalry had the highest percentage of deserters, with almost one in every five, and artillery had the fewest at less than one in every eight. Mounted on horseback, cavalrymen had the easiest means of escaping the army. Most likely, artillerists deserted the least because they worked as a team more than did soldiers in other branches. They forged tighter bonds than the infantry or cavalry because they worked in such close proximity to one another and relied on each other to execute the artillery mission.[9]

Not surprisingly, those who entered the service in 1861 and 1862 deserted less frequently than those who joined Lee's army in 1863 and 1864. Despite prolonged service and increased sacrifices, fewer than 14 percent of the men of 1861 and 1862 fled the army. Most of them had joined voluntarily, and that commitment sustained them through the most trying circumstances of the war. Even though soldiers who entered in 1863 and 1864 served much shorter lengths of time, close to one in every four of them deserted. Many of them refused to volunteer and were conscripted or felt compelled to enlist.[10]

Wealth, slave ownership and exposure, age, fatherhood, and even year of entry into the service were indicators of the type of soldier who would desert. Yet men who joined the Confederate army did so for a variety of reasons, and as the war extended into its fourth year, with the enormous hardships of the campaign that spring and summer, the forces and pressures to desert increased as well. Abner Vance, a forty-six-year-old father of eight, volunteered in the 60th Virginia Infantry. After a month of service, Vance realized he could neither handle the demands of army life nor walk away from his obligations at home and deserted. Others learned they were ill suited for military life. Private Julian Hamilton's family "really pushed him" into enlisting in the 38th North Carolina, where his brothers served. Julian decided he "couldnt stand it any longer, so he left" without telling his brother. Julian headed for Yankee lines, where he took the oath of allegiance and settled in Ohio. In the 19th Georgia, Pvt. Bud Nash could not cope with the paralyzing fear of combat any longer and fled the army. "He run out of fights just as long as he could without being courtmartialed so I reckon he thought he would leave for good," an acquaintance from home informed his mother. As tales spread of the brutal nature of combat in Virginia, soldiers voted with their feet rather than go into that war zone. Shortly after Seven Days', some 150 men bolted from Raleigh when word spread that they were Richmond bound. Once the 1864 campaign began, and the lengthy rosters of men killed in action appeared in Confederate newspapers, troops panicked at the thought of a transfer to Lee's army. Despite warnings that authorities would punish deserters with execution by firing squad, quite a few South Carolina soldiers leaped from moving trains to make their escape.[11]

Soldiers believed that their enlistment or conscription amounted to a contract with the government. They would serve their country, incurring risks and enduring hardships for Confederate independence and the preservation of slavery. In return, troops expected their country—both the government and the people—to feed and clothe them, to provide them with good weapons to fight for those causes, and to ensure their loved ones were looked after in their absence. By the third year of the war, the Confederacy had violated that pact. Soldiers constantly went without. They were often partially clothed and barefoot, and their diet was unappetizing, insufficient, and lacking in proper nutrition. Even as late as 1864, some troops marched off to battle with barely serviceable weapons, some with none at all. Many had agreed to serve for one year. The government then compelled them to perform that duty for two more years, and as that period was about to expire, it chose to keep them in uniform for the duration of the war. And then, to make matters worse, many of their families at home were suffering. Southerners had seceded from the Union to protect their civil liberties, yet the Confederacy trampled the rights of its soldiers.

Meanwhile, more Confederate territory had fallen under Yankee control. Much of Virginia, Mississippi, and Louisiana were under Union rule, and all of Tennessee. Arkansas and Georgia, along with Virginia, were now battleground states. Only Alabama, the Carolinas, Florida, and Texas remained under predominantly Rebel control. If the army and the government could no longer protect its citizens, so soldiers concluded, why should they remain in uniform?

All along, soldiers had felt the tug of dual loyalties: one to their fledgling nation and another to their family. In mid-1862, when Capt. Ujanirtus Allen heard that his wife was struggling without him, he stated emphatically where his ultimate obligation would rest. "I love my country as dear as anyone," he informed his wife, "but am unwilling to sacrifice domestic happiness to good public opinion. Anyone that would do it is unworthy of either." In the eyes of many Confederates, their premier duty rested with family. Those who had children at home felt an even greater burden. "Nancy if i dont git home in the spring to help you to make something to eate i am A feare that you & my deare little children will starve," a Virginian worried in February 1864. "But I hope to god you will never Come to that." A month later, he deserted. Shortages and rising prices raised concern among soldiers for loved ones at home. Meager army pay did not go far amid spiraling inflation, and their families struggled to overcome the hardships. "They are bound to suffer unless he comes home

& does something for them," a sympathetic officer explained to his parents. The act of desertion did not necessarily mean that soldiers had lost faith in the cause. They simply obeyed a higher call, an obligation to their families.[12]

No doubt, much of the suffering in the ranks and on the home front was beyond Lee's capacity to solve, but neither he nor Johnston embraced an effective furlough program that would have curtailed considerable flight from the army. After the Gettysburg Campaign, Lee instituted furloughs of one per 100 soldiers based on merit and need, a solution so paltry that it was almost worthless. Meanwhile, good soldiers who could not receive furloughs were resentful. "I do not want to desert," a North Carolinian asserted, "but I cannot bear quite to be treated like a brute." Eventually, he was captured in battle, took the oath of allegiance to the Union, and settled in Bethlehem, Pennsylvania. Another soldier, this one a private, informed his wife, "if they Dont gave me more to eat than they have bin a giving I will have to make my furlow my self." Six weeks later, he still had not received a furlough, and his spirits were broken: "I am cowd Down completely for it Dont look like I will ever get home without I runaway."[13]

Quite a number of soldiers felt they had paid a steep price for their military service already. Sixteen percent had suffered at least one wound before they deserted. Even though comrades had fallen, many soldiers had never confronted their own mortality until being wounded themselves. Suddenly alarmed by the consequences of battle, they could not stomach the idea of another fight.[14]

There was an accelerating pattern of desertion, following the progress of the war. A steady, modest number of desertions occurred until after the Maryland Campaign. The last quarter of 1862 witnessed a doubling of the desertion rate from its highest total in the four previous quarters. The three major campaigns of late 1862—Seven Days', Second Manassas, and Maryland, culminating in the Battle of Antietam—took an enormous toll on Lee's army.

Although desertion rates declined in early 1863, they increased after Chancellorsville and then reached new heights in the last half of the year. Those who lived anywhere near the army had opportunities to desert, and many seized that chance. Soldiers who resided great distances from the army's position had little hope of escaping to home and stayed with the army.

After Gettysburg and the fall of Vicksburg in July and August 1863, Virginians, North Carolinians, and Tennesseans abandoned the army for home in droves, convinced that the victories they had won mattered little when other Confederates armies suffered disaster after disaster. Unit cohesion dissolved in many regiments and batteries, as cataclysmic losses cut the heart out of these commands. During the spring and summer of 1863, total casualties among Virginians ranked second. Ten Virginia regiments lost more than half their men, and the 8th Virginia Infantry sustained 92 percent casualties. Among Tennesseans, the three highest regimental totals for prisoners of war came from Archer's Brigade. Although small in troop strength, Tennessee lost the highest percentage of casualties of the Confederate States at Gettysburg.[15]

By far, the worst situation existed among North Carolina troops. A Virginian admitted that his fellow statesmen, Louisianans, and Alabamians deserted in considerable numbers, but he insisted, "The North Carolinians seem to be the most discontented of any." At Chancellorsville and then at Gettysburg, North Carolina regiments sustained the greatest number of casualties. At Gettysburg, North Carolina lost nearly 6,600 of its fathers and sons. In fact, the difference between North Carolina's losses and the losses of the next highest, Virginia, surpassed the total losses for Mississippi, which ranked fifth among states in total casualties at Gettysburg. North Carolina had more men killed, more men wounded, and more men captured or missing (most of the missing were likely killed) than any other state in any of those categories. It left some of its finest men and soldiers on that battlefield. Eleven regiments from the Tar Heel State lost over 60 percent of their men, accelerating a desertion trend that had begun after Chancellorsville. Casualties fostered massive discontent in the army and on the North Carolina home front. More than 10,000 men from that state had fallen in the two battles. Rumors spread throughout the remnants of the 23rd North Carolina, which had lost almost 90 percent of its men at Gettysburg, that with no peace in sight their home state might return to the Union. "I have no doubt but desertion will ruin our Army," a captain in the 26th North Carolina, which sustained 82 percent casualties in Pennsylvania, wrote to his brother. He had lost confidence in the troops from home. "They all speak favorably of desertion (with few exceptions) and I fear they will endeavor to get home after they draw their pay." After reporting 100 soldiers from Daniel's North Carolina Brigade deserting the previous night, an Alabamian commented with dismay, "I am sorey to say our noble old army is becoming verey tierd of the war and Deserting like hel."[16]

Private John W. Wright of the 7th North Carolina felt a disloyalty on the part of the Confederate States as well. A nonslaveholder, he had joined a regiment that had fought and suffered very heavy losses from Seven Days' to the trenches around Petersburg. The 7th sustained nearly 16 percent casualties at Seven Days' and lost substantially at Second Manassas, Antietam, and Fredericksburg. A third of the remaining regiment fell at Chancellorsville, and another 55 percent went down at Union hands at Gettysburg. Nearly 150 more were casualties at the Wilderness and Spotsylvania. Wright had missed none of it. "I have been with the Regt in every engagement and on every march that it has been in," he informed his father. In the late summer 1864, he asked for a furlough of eighteen days to straighten out personal affairs that required his attention. The army rejected his request, and he exploded in outrage. "It makes me think hard to be denied the privilege of 18 days furlough after doing what I have done for the Confederacy and nothing myself to fight for and being exposed to all the camp diseases and shot of every description and had to run to keep from being taken prisoner," he fumed to his father. "What heart have I to fight for any people that treats me so unjustly," he wondered. "It is with much reluctance that I take up my gun to go to battle to fight for such people." He vowed not to expose himself or fight very hard until the army awarded him a furlough. "I have paid for one and I think I ought to have it," he insisted. The previous winter, he alerted his father that if conditions got too severe, he might slip off to the enemy, or if they did not hear from him for a while, not to panic. He might have fallen into enemy hands. He now warned his father that if they went into battle again, he might not escape the Yankees, since "I cant run fast." Not long afterward, he was taken prisoner. Whether the Union actually captured him, or he allowed himself to be taken, was unclear.[17]

The desertion calculus was a complex one. Private John Futch was a small slaveholder and father of two who had joined the 3rd North Carolina with his three relatives. One of them was killed in action at Seven Days', and a brother, Charley, perished at Gettysburg. Futch's commitment began to waver: "I never wanted to come home so bad in my life, but it is so that I cant come at this time but if we come down south I will try to come eny how for I want to come home so bad that I am home sick." Twelve days later, he decided he would try to return home without authorization. "I am going to come before long if I have to Runaway to do it," he wrote his wife. "I am at very great loss since the death of Charley I am so lonesome I do not know what to do." By mid-August, he had received word from his wife that she was concerned about finances, and the news drove him over the edge. "Marthy, I Want to come home the worst I ever Did in my Life I am vary uneasy about you." He and his remaining relative, Hanson, slipped out of camp, headed for coastal North Carolina and home. Authorities seized them, and both soldiers were tried and convicted of desertion, although from his letters it appears uncertain whether he intended to stay at home permanently. The court sentenced them to die by firing squad. Hanson caught smallpox at Castle Thunder, the prison in Richmond, and died. John Futch was executed.[18]

From September through December 1863, two divisions in Lee's army transferred to Georgia and then Tennessee. For the first time since leaving their native state, soldiers from the Deep South had a chance to make it home. From September 1863 to April 1864, half of all deserters came from the Lower South, the first time soldiers from South Carolina, Georgia, Alabama, Mississippi, and Louisiana deserted in appreciable numbers.[19]

From January through September 1864, desertion rates remained high. Private George W. Angel of the 21st Virginia decided he had had enough. He had agreed to serve three years, and his term expired. Because the Confederacy refused to respect its end of their contract, he deserted to the Yankees. In mid-September, an inspector affixed blame for frequent desertions to "the condition of their families at home" and "their hard life in the trenches." Reliable soldiers began to show signs of war weariness and deserted, much to the dismay of their officers. When a division inspector declared, "I am mortified to report several more cases of desertion to the enemy," it was not merely that they fled to Yankee lines, but that they were dependable soldiers, not the usual malcontents, scoundrels, conscripts, or substitutes. Private James Oswald confessed amazement when an old acquaintance deserted. "I was very much surprised at his conduct—" he divulged to his friend, "as he was a *good soldier*." According to a soldier in Company K, 28th Virginia, once soldiers who were vested in the community deserted, it opened the floodgates. When those men who had standing in their community left the army, what would keep someone who had little or no property or reputation in the ranks?[20]

With hardships compounding, more and more soldiers fled to the Federals. "They left on account of hard treatment," the interrogator reported to Meade's chief of staff on the motivations of two deserters, "and they say they are poorly provided for in both food and clothing." Many of the deserters in 1863 were Southerners who expressed little sympathy for the rebellion. They had longstanding ties to the Northern states or had lived in pro-Union regions of Virginia, North Carolina, and Tennessee and had been forced into the army against their wishes. One soldier from the 8th Louisiana had been raised in New York and had resided in the South for only five years. Mistreated by his officers, he left for the Union army. Two soldiers from the 12th Georgia deserted, but were arrested in north Georgia and returned to their regiment. Rather than fight again, they fled for the Yankees. By mid-September 1864, Confederates were trickling into Union lines in steady numbers. Meade suggested ten per day as a "liberal estimate."[21]

Within Lee's army, soldiers began encouraging others to stay away from the army or to desert. A Virginian implored his brother on sick leave "to stay as long as he can" and urged him to visit a hospital to extend his sick furlough. Three months later, he urged his brother "to be as Complaining as possibly and tell them that he gets *worse and try* and get a discharge." Others began advising their comrades to desert. Authorities prosecuted Pvt. John M. Harrison for telling the men in his regiment "it would be better if all the men in the 44th Regiment of North Carolina Troops would go home and take their guns with them." Another private wrote his brother, telling him not to return to the army, as he intended to flee. Officers intercepted the letter and prosecuted him for inciting others to desert.[22]

If the army were to curb desertion, it needed the full cooperation of the local population. Various newspapers ran notices with the names of deserters and offered a thirty-dollar reward for their apprehension. This kind of public notification put pressure on families to encourage their sons or husbands to return to the army. Yet as the burdens and dangers of military service increased and problems on the home front intensified, locals were loath to surrender kin and neighbors, both out of sympathy for the hazards of duty and because of the severity of punishments, which included execution. In an attempt to check runaways near the source, Lee's headquarters relayed messages of desertions and possible destinations, and the commanding general positioned cavalry and sometimes infantry at key fords and spans to apprehend runaways before they escaped too far. He also positioned teams consisting of an officer from the provost guard and three enlisted men on each train, with instructions to maintain order and arrest all soldiers without proper authorization.[23]

On August 1, 1863, Davis announced a proclamation of amnesty for all deserters, providing they returned within twenty days. The pardon also covered all those who were under arrest or sentenced for desertion. According to one Virginian, the proclamation brought large numbers of soldiers back to the army, "though I am sorry to say that about an equal number ran away as soon as the Proclamation was received, supposing perhaps that they would be pardoned if they returned in twenty days, but they are very much mistaken about it."[24]

With the threat of a death sentence if convicted, deserters had nothing to lose by resisting capture with violence. Well armed with Confederate rifled muskets and ample ammunition, they often banded together and formed outlaw parties. In an effort to enhance their strength, deserters sometimes tapped escaped conscripts and slave runaways to join forces with them, since both parties sought to resist Confederate authority. Family and close friends often aided and protected them. At times, these bands terrorized entire communities, committing armed robbery and other offenses and intimidating anyone they did not trust. Their successful resistance only served to encourage others to desert and create bands, and according to a Rebel official, they existed in varying strength, especially along the Atlantic seaboard.[25]

To combat this growing power, the army had to send parties to collect deserters. It did not take long for the situation to degenerate into small-scale guerrilla warfare. Captain Henry W. Wingfield of the 58th Virginia was sent to Patrick County, Virginia, to capture runaways. Even before he started the search, friends warned him that deserters shot officers. Waiting for a party of cavalry to assist him, Wingfield caught his first deserter when the man unwittingly walked right past their concealed position. Once they arrested one deserter, news of their operation spread throughout the county and "every body is looking out for us," Wingfield recorded. Several days of hard work by a party of cavalrymen and an officer resulted in the capture of only four men in five days, but at least no one suffered injuries. Lieutenant Henry Ringstaff and a party of five soldiers experienced firsthand the desperation of deserters. They approached the house of a notorious deserter, Pvt. John Medlin of the 28th North Carolina. Ringstaff called for admittance to the house, and Medlin shouted back " 'damn you,' " firing a round into Ringstaff's face. Medlin and his three comrades then shot and wounded two other soldiers, one of them mortally, and made their escape.[26]

To deal with the desperate nature of deserters and their depredations on the local population, Lee detached two regiments, the 1st South Carolina and the 12th Georgia, to track down deserters and conscripts on both sides of the Blue Ridge near Front Royal, Virginia. "The mountains are covered with these rascals & they should be sent to the proper authorities for summary punishment," wrote a South Carolina officer. Scaling the mountains was hard, but the troops enjoyed it. The mission got them out of camp and provided them with access to better food. Their numbers were large enough that deserters would not be able to challenge them effectively. "The tried veterans of Lee's army are a terror to all traitors and will meet with little if any trouble from there," the officer wrote his father. "Our greatest trouble comes from the feminine gender, several of that sex having pleaded against the arrest of sons, brothers, etc., whom we have taken up as conscripts fit for the army."[27]

In certain areas of North Carolina, large numbers of deserters, supported by friends and families, formed bands that resisted all authority. Home Guards failed to break them up initially, and the fighting proved savage. Detachments of regular soldiers searched and found little. As a soldier from Lee's army commented, "they ar too Smart for us." Since Home Guards could not locate the bands, they began confiscating slaves and horses and harassing or torturing wives of notorious deserters, tying them up, slapping them around, and placing them in large groups under close guard as hostages. According to one letter of complaint to the North Carolina governor, "Women have been frightened into abortions almost under the eyes of their terrifiers."[28]

Those soldiers whom authorities apprehended for desertion and absence without leave received punishments in various forms, from fines and extra duty or restrictions to execution by firing squad. Some soldiers received whippings for running from the army. Twenty-five lashes on a bare back, well laid on, was a fairly common means of punishment. Strangely enough, Stonewall Jackson, who had a reputation for harsh punishments, remitted the sentence of Pvt. Thomas G. Shaver in the 27th Virginia. A court directed that Shaver receive thirty lashes, have his head shaved, and then be drummed out of the service. Jackson overturned this decision by stating, "the execution of it would be detrimental to the service," particularly the dismissal of a soldier when the army needed manpower. Private Tillman F. Beggarly slipped off to home after Chancellorsville, and it may have saved his life. After he was caught, a court-martial sentenced him to several months in Castle Thunder in Richmond, and he missed the Gettysburg Campaign because of it. "You her [hear] a heap of talk a bowt that place a being such a bad place," he explained to his wife, "I had as soon bee in thar as any other place in Richmon." Private Marcus Hefner ran home, and a court sentenced him to two months' hard labor and loss of pay. "Ther is one thing that I hate," he informed his wife in March 1864. "I hate that it taint longer   I wish it was for 12 months or in durin the war."[29]

Although a South Carolinian had attempted to desert twice in the past, a court-martial only sentenced him to twelve months of hard labor with a ball and chain upon a third infraction. His company commander testified that he had conducted himself well in the regiment's battles, and that earned him favor with the court. Others were not so fortunate. The precise number of soldiers from Lee's army who received death sentences will never be known, but many lost their lives at the hands of a firing squad. Lee and other government officials endorsed the death penalty to discourage desertion.[30]

As they waited for their death sentence to be carried out, soldiers and loved ones lobbied for assistance from any source they could find. Deserters pleaded with the president for commutation or pardon, pledging to fight with all their power if Davis would let them live. "We have too few men to sacrifice, save in defence of their country & rights," a Louisiana chaplain wrote the commander in chief; "particularly is this true in regard to the decimated ranks of our regiment." Parents drafted letters to Lee, begging for his intervention. Marchal and Jane Trent informed Lee that their son returned home for new shoes and clothing and was waiting on the cobbler to finish the pair when their son was arrested. They traveled to Richmond and received a reprieve from Davis for Trent's death sentence, but he was still confined at Castle Thunder, where rations were meager. They asked Lee to return him to duty with his comrades, where he belonged. Two Virginians implored Davis to spare their lives, claiming they were not prepared to meet their Maker, and that they wanted the opportunity to see the war through to victory before they died. Davis asked the secretary of war to inquire into their cases, but by the time he saw the president's endorsement, it was too late. A firing squad had executed them the previous day.[31]

The night before their execution, some soldiers continued to plead desperately for clemency, while others, resigned to their fate, sought to make amends and communicate to family and friends one last time. Colonel Bryan Grimes received a request from some men on death row to visit them the day before the army would execute them for desertion. "It was heart rending to listen to their piteous appeals for Mercy," he described to his wife, but he informed them he could not seek suspension of their sentence, "for I conscientiously believed that the good of the Service absolutely demands the infliction of the Severest penalties of the law to prevent desertions." Jacob and Elkana Lanier were arrested for leaving camp to go foraging. A court convicted them of desertion and sentenced them to death. Deeply religious soldiers, they accepted their fate with surprising calmness. With execution a mere thirty-six hours away, Elkana reassured his wife and others, "I can take it tolerably patiently, knowing that the Lord died for me." He urged them, "Do not grieve for me nor brother—we are going to meet our good brother who went before." What concerned him was his children's welfare. "I want you to help Elizabeth to raise my children for I cannot." His brother, Jacob, expressed a powerful belief in religion, which comforted him in these last moments. He insisted, "there is not a man in the regiment that will say we got justice, but the officers have determined to have a better disciplined army than heretofore, and so it must need be that they make example of some to check the remainder, and it has fell on our unhappy lot to be an example." He then resigned himself to that fate: "It is hard but we have to bear it." He advised his father how to dispose of his few possessions, and he counseled each family member directly to embrace God so that they could all be united again someday. He signed off with the words, "Farewell to friends and the world." Both men were executed on the morning of September 26, 1863.[32]

Private James Wright had the misfortune of guarding prisoners on death row. His officers detailed him to oversee four men for sixteen consecutive hours. The prisoners had a ball and chain attached to their leg, and guards carried loaded weapons during duty. "O Fanny you don't know how bad I felt to see them in that condition," he expressed to his wife, "and having to guard them the last night that they had to live!" The army fed them a last dinner of dry bread, and he felt so awful that he gave them his roasted potatoes and butter. "It done me good to see them eat it," he told her. Another soldier who guarded death row inmates witnessed the mother of one of the prisoners arrive to say farewell to her son. She had traveled all the way from Mobile. "It was an unpleasant sight to see this old Lady embrace her condemned Son," he divulged to his sister. Officers assigned Pvt. William Chancely to a firing squad, a most detestable duty. He and nineteen others had their muskets loaded out of sight. Ten had blanks and ten had bullets, so that soldiers did not feel too guilty over executing a fellow soldier. The commanding officer marched out to a field, with companies drawn up to witness the act. Guards brought out the prisoner and tied him to a stake. The offender usually had a chance to say some final words. On command, the squad fired, and a party then buried him. In a case of desertion in October 1864, officers simply executed a soldier from the 59th Alabama right in the trenches.[33]

Watching the execution of someone who had fought for the same cause and had incurred comparable, perhaps even greater sacrifices, was deeply disturbing to Lee's men. A Virginia sergeant whose company had the brutal task of forming the firing squad declared to his sister, "Nanny I have witnessed 3 of the awfullest Sights I ever saw." After describing the event in some detail, he announced, "you cant amagine what feelings I had." A North Carolinian attempted to analyze why soldiers, accustomed as they were to death, found executions so offensive. "It is much more shocking to me than in Battle, for in Battle the blood is up and men excited and as no one expects to be hit positively, he feels a hope," he wrote to his wife. "But in these military executions the blood is cool and the doom of the victim certain and it freezes the blood to witness it." In many cases, comrades in arms expressed sympathy for the victim. "Saw a man shot today for desertion," a Virginia private recorded in his diary. "Poor fellow. His crime was only going home to see after his wife and children." Though it was his third or fourth offense, the private sympathized with his plight. "Did he not die for his country?" he wondered.[34]

The day after the army executed some of his soldiers, Colonel Grimes filed a complaint to Lee's headquarters about the sentencing of deserters. He objected to the idea of punishing deserters with hard labor and suggested that capital punishment achieved little, too. "Labor and confinement is no punishment to a coward or to a man so devoid of principle as to desert," he argued. "In my opinion from what I hear among the men," he continued, "it would be much better to inflict all punishments in camp requiring the offender at the same time to participate in all fights in which his regiment is engaged." Many deserters considered jail time preferable to battle, and they were "thinking the chances of Capital punishment as being no greater than that encountered in any one pitched battle." The solution, he argued, was to make men perform their duty by extending their terms of service.[35]

Still, no matter how difficult the conditions, most men pledged they would never desert the flag. The cause was too important and their reputation too valuable to damage either by running away. "I love you and my children as I do my life and would like to see you," a Virginia private explained, "but I shall never desert to see you." Despite dwindling manpower and territory, the Confederacy was not prepared to surrender in 1864.[36]

Chapter 33

————⊃◦⊂————

THE GRIND OF WAR

NEITHER LEE NOR GRANT sought the kind of grinding campaign that developed in the spring of 1864 and culminated that summer in a prolonged siege. Both commanders wanted an open-field fight. Grant hoped to bring his overwhelming forces against the Confederates, and Lee desperately sought for an opportunity to seize the initiative and exploit his greater mobility and superior quality of infantrymen. When Lee read a Northern newspaper article in mid-July claiming that Grant would engage the Army of Northern Virginia in the open field, he replied that he "hoped that Gen. Grant was of the same way of thinking. That there was nothing he desired more than a 'fair field fight' and that if Grant would meet him on equal ground he would give him *two to one*," unusually strong words from Lee. Yet the campaign evolved in accordance with General Meade's expectations. A topographical engineer by training, Meade had hoped for greater Union success at the Wilderness but assumed that both sides would counteract each other's strengths. Eventually, the campaign would lapse into a siege around Richmond, where the advantage would and did shift to the Union.[1]

Initially, Confederates felt a sense of frustration over Union resilience. "We have whipped Grant twice," a Floridian wrote his wife in late May, "but he has such a tremendous army that we cannot *rout* him and consequently victories don't amount to much." From Spotsylvania, Grant had pledged to "fight it out on this line if it takes all summer." The fighting shifted from there to below Petersburg, with no relenting from the Union commander. "It seems to me that Grant having 'fought it out all summer' is going to try and hold on to his present line all fall too, bombing away every day, with no purpose but to keep up appearances and employ our army, in watching him, and holding him in," a Virginian assessed in early September. Despite enormously heavy losses, the Yankees appeared to fight better this campaign than ever before. What shocked Confederates most, and what some simply could not fathom, was the seemingly endless supply of Union soldiers, equipment, ammunition, and materiel. The Federal forces absorbed the beating and kept pressing. Still, the Confederates had Lee, who had pulled out victories from precarious situations many times

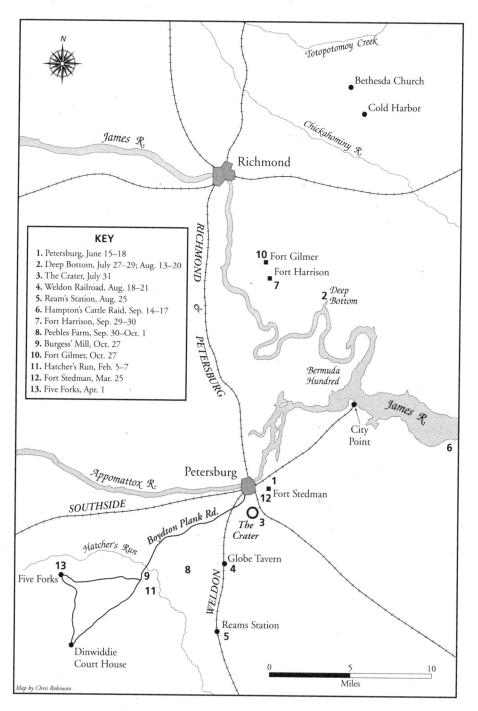

KEY

1. Petersburg, June 15–18
2. Deep Bottom, July 27–29; Aug. 13–20
3. The Crater, July 31
4. Weldon Railroad, Aug. 18–21
5. Ream's Station, Aug. 25
6. Hampton's Cattle Raid, Sep. 14–17
7. Fort Harrison, Sep. 29–30
8. Peebles Farm, Sep. 30–Oct. 1
9. Burgess' Mill, Oct. 27
10. Fort Gilmer, Oct. 27
11. Hatcher's Run, Feb. 5–7
12. Fort Stedman, Mar. 25
13. Five Forks, Apr. 1

Siege of Petersburg, with battles denoted

before, and they believed he would do so again. "The darkest clouds it seems are darkening the horizon—" an Alabamian depicted to his father, "and while to the cold reason there seems no escape from subjugation yet the greatest resolution to continue the struggle to death seems to pervade this army As much as ever."[2]

With Union and Confederate forces locked around Petersburg, Grant extended the tentacles of his army northward toward Richmond and westward to sever the rail connections to Petersburg from the south and west. If the Yankees could destroy or sufficiently damage rail links to Petersburg, Lee would have to abandon not just that city but the Confederate capital as well. Lee's men fought viciously to keep the railroads open. Just as important, Federals had to emerge from their trenches to cut the rail lines, and Lee perceived a golden opportunity to strike. Throughout the summer and into the fall, Union troops attempted to destroy the Weldon and the Southside railroads. Each time, Confederate forces punished them. Infantry delivered powerful blows, but it was Hampton's Cavalry that detected the movement and held up the Yankee columns long enough for infantry to arrive. Yet with each Federal advance, the trench lines extended, stretching Confederate defenses. In August, the Union secured a portion of the Weldon Railroad, restricting the Rebels to the Southside line. Lee compensated by drawing supplies along the Weldon Railroad to a point sixteen miles below the city and hauling them by wagon along Boydton Plank Road. Although the alternative proved cumbersome and costly, and the Boydton Plank Road fell into disrepair from heavy use, it enabled Lee to keep two pipelines into Petersburg open. Several more times in 1864, Grant's troops attempted to shatter that roundabout supply route. Eventually, they damaged it, but they could not shut it down.[3]

To the northeast, above the James River, the Union army pounded its way toward Richmond. Grant had positioned Maj. Gen. Benjamin Butler's Army of the James in that sector, and the lieutenant general was unsure of its ability to achieve a major breakthrough without reinforcements from the Army of the Potomac. Nonetheless, these advances toward Richmond served as an excellent diversion for the movements against the supply lines to the southwest, and they compelled Lee to allocate considerable numbers of troops to shield Richmond and the Richmond & Petersburg Railroad. Heavy fighting took place around Deep Bottom Run in late July, with support from Maj. Gen. Winfield Scott Hancock's Second Corps and Maj. Gen. Philip Sheridan's cavalry. Wilcox's and Kershaw's divisions blocked the way. Three weeks later, Hancock's men joined in an attack again. This time, the Federals made greater progress, but confusion amid the woods and stout resistance by Rebel infantry and cavalry repulsed the movement.

Fighting continued in that sector in late September and October. Federals attacked Forts Harrison and Gilmer to prevent Lee from shifting more troops from north of the James. In the attack on Fort Harrison, there were so few Confederate defenders that they stood ten feet apart. Artillery could not support them effectively because the Union troops had advanced so close under the cover of timber, they received protection from the terrain. They only had to advance another few hundred yards before they swamped Fort Harrison. In the effort to retake the fort, Richard Anderson's people neglected to synchronize the attacking columns with each other and the Rebel artillery. The attempt failed miserably. Twice more the Rebels tried to capture the lost fort, yet both attacks were feeble. The absence of enthusiasm and aggressiveness among the Confederates in the First Corps shocked Porter Alexander, who had recently returned to the army after several months away recuperating from a wound. "Our troops have fought so long behind breastworks," he surmised, "that they have lost all spirit in attacking or would have carried it easily." The army commander himself witnessed the half-hearted attacks. "Gen Lee was more worried at this failure," Alexander wrote to his wife, "than I have ever seen him under similar circumstances." Trench warfare was taking its toll on Lee's army, and the army commander could do little to check it. One week later, Lee assailed the Federal position, hoping to regain control of the Darbytown Road. His troops drove back Union cavalry, but an uncoordinated attack on Yankee defenders in fortified works merely tallied another 1,350 casualties, with little else to show for it.[4]

In the course of these fights, many of Lee's soldiers confronted a new enemy for the first time: black soldiers. Confederates had learned of the debate and plans to recruit African-Americans into the Union army, and many of them thought of the idea as preposterous. They believed blacks would make terrible soldiers, and the notion that former slaves would fight against them raised their ire to new levels. "If they bring them black scoundrels here there will be more buzzard meat in this part of the country than ever was before," a Virginian vowed to his mother in February 1863. "And they say they are going to put them in front, just like the cowardly skunks."[5]

During the Petersburg Campaign, most of Lee's soldiers had their first exposure to U.S. Colored Troops. An Alabamian predicted, "They will prove nothing but 'food for our bullets,'" and to some extent he was correct. Lee's men took special delight in engaging black soldiers. They were able to demonstrate their power over former slaves and sought retribution for those who joined the Union army and fought against them. "Our boys could not stand for negroes to be so near them and pitched into them and drove them off," Hill Fitzpatrick informed his wife. Whenever Confederates discovered black troops on the skirmish or picket lines, they launched a hailstorm of bullets to drive them away. According to a Virginian, "as soon as our men saw them, they were worse than a blood hound when he smells blood." Any time a black soldier exposed himself, a barrage of musketry followed. Quiet sectors suddenly heated up, simply because black soldiers went out on picket duty. "Our men are very indignant very naturally—" a Virginia private commented to his mother, "but for my part I had rather Kill one Yankee than a dozen Negroes."[6]

At the infamous Battle of the Crater on July 30, Confederate soldiers slaughtered blacks and whites in combat and then murdered large numbers of black soldiers without qualms or regrets. It began when some Pennsylvania troops dug a mine shaft under the Confederate works and filled it with four tons of gunpowder. The explosion at 4:44 A.M. destroyed a portion of the line some sixty yards long, leaving in its wake a giant crater. Federal troops stormed into the breach—first white troops, then black—and were so horrified by the destruction that they slowed to gawk instead of exploiting the fissure. Mahone's Division came crashing down on them and with the help of troops on either flank, the Rebels quickly sealed the breach and retook the terrain. Whites and blacks in Union blue made easy targets in the Crater, and Confederates followed up with bayonet assaults. An Alabama veteran pronounced to his wife, "I have never seen such slaughter since the war commenced on so small a space (2 acres)." Confederate soldiers claimed black troops called for no quarter, but many attempted to surrender and were simply cut down. "It gows mighty against our boys to take Negro prisoners," a private insisted. A South Carolinian admitted to his mother that the Rebels literally butchered them. Mahone had to intervene personally to stop the murder. A North Carolinian claimed, "our boys showed them no quarters after we had taken the black rascals till our General Mahone rushed forward and ordered it to be stoped." A company commander informed his sister that Mahone "begged his men to stop the killing of negroes." Artillerist Col. Willie J. Pegram witnessed the affair and felt not a twinge of guilt over the slaughter. "It seems cruel to murder them," he wrote his fiancée, "but I think the men who did it had very good cause for doing so." In fact, Pegram thought it would invigorate the troops. "I have always said that I wished the enemy would bring some negroes against this army. I am convinced, since Saturday's fight, that it has a splendid effect on our men." Lee surely must have heard tales of the killing of black soldiers, yet he authorized no investigation and punished no one. After Confederates stripped the bodies for usable items, those black soldiers who were taken prisoner buried the dead.[7]

Although there were instances in which soldiers executed their captives, Lee's men and their adversaries usually respected the right of individuals to surrender and receive protection. Unusual was the case of Gus Clewell, a North Carolina private who asserted to his sister, "I don't think that I will ever trouble myself in taking a prisoner, while I have a cartridge in my box, and can get my gun to fire off." He thought the best practice was to have Yankees disappear. He justified his stance by writing, "I am not anyways bloodthirsty or anything of the kind but I am tired of the war, and want it brought to a close one way or the other, as soon as possible." From their perspective, Union soldiers felt indignant when they recovered bodies of their comrades, stripped of shoes and clothing, under flags of truce. It gave Yankees the feeling that Rebels did not respect their dead. But Union and Confederate soldiers possessed an extraordinary ability to compartmentalize the war. Despite their opposition on the battlefield, many formed bonds as fellow soldiers. They could exchange gunfire, trying to kill each other, and under flag of truce exchange newspapers or swap tobacco for coffee. Lee's headquarters strictly forbade the practice, but soldiers did not care. Occasionally, pickets negotiated truces among themselves, without the knowledge of their officers, so that soldiers did not have to remain on their guard. In one instance, a Confederate soldier tried to steal some brush from the abatis for fuel, an act that was illegal among Confederates, and a Yankee told him to drop it or he would shoot. When the Rebel asked why, he replied that if Union generals perceived a gap in the enemy works, the Federals would have to attack, "and I don't want to do it."[8]

Day in, day out, trench warfare took its toll on soldiers on both sides. And as Lee certainly understood, the advantage rested with the Federals. The Union army lost 60,000 casualties in seven weeks in the Overland Campaign, and the Northern government was able to replace them. Lee's army sustained a bit more than half that number, but replacements did not come so easily. Federals built a railroad behind their lines to supply their troops during the siege. The Confederacy had a single rail line that ran into Petersburg and could not procure the equipment, clothing, ammunition, or food its troops needed. With the upcoming presidential election several months away, Lee had to break Grant's stranglehold on the Army of Northern Virginia. "Our safety depends upon ourselves alone," Lee insisted to Davis in early July. "If we can defeat or drive the armies of the enemy from the field, we shall have peace. All our efforts & energies should be devoted to that object."[9]

On June 13, Lee detached Early with the objectives of driving a Federal force away from Lynchburg, where the Virginia & Tennessee, Southside, and Orange & Alexandria railroads intersected, and advancing northward to threaten Maryland and pull forces away from Grant's command around Petersburg. Ten months earlier, John Warwick Daniel described Early with some choice words: "Gen Early is constitutionally a fault finder—querolous, dissatisfied & meddling in his disposition, and with no spark of that high strong cordial, generous nature which is the special object of my admiration." Early, however, had paid his dues. He fought at First Manassas and throughout the war. A lifelong bachelor with an acid tongue, he had proven himself a skillful commander, one of those few who actually gained Jackson's support and trust. Early's people not only repulsed the Union attack outside Lynchburg, but compelled the enemy to retreat so hastily that it fled completely out of the theater of operations.[10]

Early drove his men hard in pursuit of his foe. Food was in short supply, and the men simply did without. When Early or Rodes rode by, men chanted, "'bread, bread, bread.'" Scorching heat in late June dried and cracked fields. Roads became shoe-mouth-deep dust. Yet Early continued to push his men. By July 4, they had had seized the heights around Harpers Ferry and compelled a Yankee evacuation that night. "The Yankees made a great preparation for a July dinner so we had the pleasure of eating it for them," crowed a satisfied Rebel. Pies, cakes, candies, pickles, wine, beers, breads, molasses, and other delicacies awaited hungry troops.[11]

From there, they crossed into Maryland, whipped a Union command at Monocacy, and rushed toward Washington, D.C. Once again, the Union had to deal with a threat to the nation's capital, this time in a presidential election year. No one had ever gotten this close. "'Tis the boldest & most successful move of the war," a Virginian wrote in his diary. But the long, tough campaign began to take its toll on Early's men. "Troops much broken down by excessive heat, long marching, dusty roads and exceedingly dry country through which we passed," one of Early's aides described. Ramseur claimed that his men marched forty-two miles with only two hours' rest. Men were too fatigued, their numbers were too few, and Union defenses were too strong for Early to attempt an assault. The hopes of so many Confederates, that "he may capture and burn the place to the ground, for it truly is a perfect Sodom and Gomorrah," proved impossible.[12]

When Early fell back into Maryland, his command had achieved extraordinary successes, but the men had paid a heavy price in exhaustion. "I had no idea that the human frame was capable of sustaining fatigue that Early's Maryland campaign has demonstrated," a Georgian admitted to his parents. They had marched all day and sometimes throughout the night. He wrote that "the days were extremely hot and the dust arose in such clouds as to obscure objects a short distance off almost suffocating the soldiers." The threat to the Union capital that deep into the war unnerved many Washington officials and caused severe distress throughout the North. Gold soared to its highest price in the entire war, and Lincoln formed serious doubts that his side would actually win the war. "I don't expect the old fellow [Lincoln] has cracked a joke since we were there," a North Carolinian quipped a few weeks later.[13]

The aggressive Early refused to rest on his laurels. In his first trip into Maryland, he had extracted payments of $220,000 from two Maryland towns in restitution for destruction to the Valley, especially Lexington. After defeating Federals again near Winchester, his cavalry penetrated all the way to Pennsylvania, demanding a large cash payment from the people of Chambersburg. When the people failed to comply, his men burned down the town.[14]

Yet even before the burning of Chambersburg, Early's command had exhibited shakiness on the battlefield as discipline began to erode. At Stephenson's Depot on July 20, Ramseur's Division of veterans broke and ran after barely returning fire when Union forces appeared on their flank. Ramseur was humiliated. Rodes came to his defense, maintaining seven weeks later that "this result would not occur one time in a hundred with these same troops under the same circumstances" and that "they were under the influence of panic." A month later, a North Carolina veteran alerted his father, "our Army is losing its discipline which is causing life & limbs of many a good man, because they have to expose themselves to get the sorry ones to do any part of their duty." Attrition from the 1864 campaign had cut deeply into their ranks, and replacements failed to instill a feeing of security, eroding confidence in their own and adjacent commands.[15]

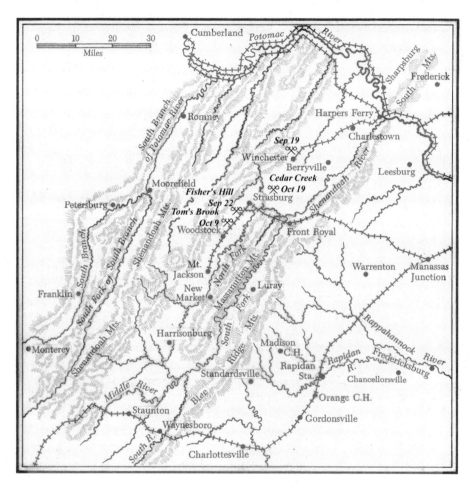

Early's Valley Campaign

In what had once been the lushest of valleys, soldiers and their animals went hungry regularly. Active campaigning had discouraged farmers as far south as Bunker Hill from planting crops. Between New Market and Staunton, the wheat crop was superb, but a drought had devastated the corn crop. A Virginian estimated the corn production at one-third its usual harvest in the area, which spelled disaster for Lee's army. "Our battery horses, are in a terrible condition," an artillerist complained. "They scarcely get corn enough to sustain life." Men received nothing but beef and bread, and not much beef.[16]

Continual combat in trenches had eroded discipline, and without control of the battlefield, they lost the ability to secure clothing and other items from the enemy dead, wounded, and prisoners. Once freed from the confines of trenches, soldiers compensated for the restrictions by taking what they wanted, without regard to authorization. Wade Hampton fumed over reports that cavalrymen robbed citizens in Maryland, even those with family members in Lee's army. "Some of our troops, when last there behaved in the most shameful manner to our friends," he wrote, "stealing their stock & in some cases even taking jewelry from ladies who had brothers in our service." He requested that Lee allow him to travel up there to straighten them out, but the army commander refused to let him go. A North Carolinian thought Early's command the "greatest army in the country. Think of infantry surprising cavalry and plundering their camp!" An Alabama lieutenant, on the other hand, complained of wholesale straggling: "the troops here would not fight, being too much bent on plundering, and not having their own officers with them, they are under no subjection or discipline, and do pretty much as they choose." He argued that plunder was the only incentive soldiers had for campaigning. An inspector in Pegram's Brigade uncovered the same problem. Men plundered and then sold items, and the practice demoralized the best soldiers. "This great desire for plunder, in anticipation of *gain*, induce many men to swerve from their proper line of duty, leaving their comrades to do the duty that would otherwise have assisted to do."[17]

In early August, Grant placed Sheridan in charge of seven infantry and three cavalry divisions—more than 40,000 troops. He directed the feisty Union general to crush Early's command and advance south to the Virginia Central Railroad, destroying everything so that the Confederacy could not draw foodstuffs from it the following year. In response to the huge Federal buildup, Lee detached First Corps commander Anderson with Kershaw's Division and Fitz Lee's Cavalry Division to bolster Early's forces.[18]

Although Anderson outranked Early, Lee had much greater faith in the ability of the crusty Virginia bachelor and wanted him in command. Lee clearly liked Anderson and appreciated his efforts, but at the same time he knew that Anderson held the position of corps command out of necessity, not ability. He required coaching and careful supervision. In late August, Early saw an opportunity to strike Sheridan's command. While he pressed northward with his forces, Anderson's command, poised on the Union flank near Front Royal, could deliver a crushing blow to the retreating enemy. Yet Anderson probed the

Federal position with part of his command, determined it was too strong, and refrained from attack. When Lee learned of Anderson's actions, he patiently forwarded advice on how to fight his troops. "I think in all cases it is the best to employ all our available force without reference to the weakness of the enemy," the commanding general instructed. "If we have the advantage of numbers, it renders success more certain, and the loss less. I hope that you will always endeavor to bring your whole force to bear upon the enemy when practicable, as in that way alone can superiority of numbers be made valuable."[19]

With Early confronting vastly superior numbers, and Anderson uncomfortable in his role, Lee seriously contemplated taking command in the Valley. Evidently, Fitz Lee had written to the commanding general requesting that he come and take charge of the situation. Lee was sorely tempted. "A victory over Sheridan is very important if it Can be obtained," Lee replied confidentially to his nephew, "& I have hoped it might have been accomplished. It is with that view that I have Continued A[nderson]." Had Beauregard been at Petersburg, Lee would have gone to the Valley and taken charge. At the time, though, Beauregard was in Wilmington, and if Lee left, no one could oversee operations at Petersburg.[20]

Sending Anderson with Kershaw's Division to bolster Early's forces left Lee's army facing nearly a two-to-one Federal advantage around Petersburg. As he explained to Early, "I am in great need of his troops, and if they can be spared from the Valley, or cannot operate to advantage there I will order them back to Richmond." Yankee scouts had picked up intelligence that Anderson could not remain in the Valley very long, and once Sheridan saw evidence that Anderson had left, he launched an advance on Early's columns.[21]

On September 19, Union troops struck Early's command around Winchester. Throughout the morning, Confederates fought bravely against more than triple their number, repulsing Yankee attackers. Fitz Lee had two horses shot from beneath him. Rebels inflicted double the number of killed and wounded that their command suffered. Yet it was not enough. By midafternoon, the tide of battle had shifted decisively toward the Federals. Sheridan massed his vast cavalry superiority against the Rebel left flank, and the sheer weight and firepower of the blow crumbled resistance. As Yankee horsemen threatened their rear, the Rebel line buckled. In the opening hours of the fight, Rodes was killed, and according to an Alabamian, his death resulted in the crushing defeat. "The men after they were flanked, gave up thinking that their only hope of extrication was his Generalship, and he being gone, their only trust was legs, of which they made good (or rather bad) use," he explained to his wife. Private Henry Beck of the 57th North Carolina called it "the grandest stampede I ever saw in my life." The women of Winchester rushed into the streets, pleading with Rebel troops to make a stand. According to a Louisiana captain, they just brushed aside these women, "resisting tears, entreaties, and reproaches." A noncommissioned officer admitted he ran twelve miles. "I would run a while and stop and laugh at others and think what fools we were making of our selves when some shell would come tearing among us and every thing would start off again," he described to his parents. "It was equal to the 1st Manassa stampede," he argued. "I never saw any thing like it." Ramseur rallied his division and organized it to make a stand and even launch a counterattack. It merely delayed the pursuit.[22]

Early's command regrouped at Fisher's Hill, the last relatively defensible position far enough north to control gaps in the Blue Ridge. Even Fisher's Hill, however, had serious problems for the small Confederate force. The position was nearly four miles long, and Early lacked the strength to anchor both flanks on the high ground. Three weeks earlier, Ramseur had criticized the Rebel mounted force, complaining, "Our cav is greatly inferior in numbers equipments & efficiency to the Yankee cav y   The consequence is, that our Inf is constantly called on to do work that the Cav y should perform." This time, Early positioned Lunsford Lomax's cavalrymen on the far left to hold as best they could, fighting as infantry.

On September 22, Sheridan, benefiting from a four-to-one advantage, swung some 5,500 troops under Maj. Gen. George Crook onto the high ground west of Lomax's position. Late that afternoon, Yankee cavalrymen armed with repeating rifles struck Lomax's command in the front, while Crook's men swept down on the flank. Lomax's horsemen, fighting on foot, had to allocate one of every four men to hold the horses, a critical reduction in strength. His cavalrymen, moreover, carried only Enfields, excellent weapons, but single shot. They had neither sabers nor pistols. Lomax's cavalry broke, and efforts to repair the damage failed. In no time, the Confederate line unhinged, and the second stampede in three days began.[23]

The Winchester and Fisher's Hill debacles were galling to soldiers in Early's command. Even by Confederate standards, they felt like poor stepchildren—undermanned, undersupplied, and inadequately resourced. One Louisiana captain argued that with 4,000 more men, they never would have lost at Winchester, let alone Fisher's Hill. Instead of fleeing from Fisher's Hill, they would be watering their animals from the opposite bank of the Potomac River with proper strength. He and others found it reprehensible that Rebel troops lacked so badly in almost every area. An Alabama lieutenant noted a week before the Battle of Third Winchester, "Nearly all of my company are barefoot, and most of them are destitute of pants. Such constant marching on rough, rocky roads, and sleeping on the bare ground, will naturally wear out the best shoes and the thickest of pants." He had picked up a worn-out shoe on the march and put it on because it was in better condition than one that he owned. A North Carolinian reported 200 barefoot men in his brigade and a large number without pants. Another officer oversaw a camp with 600 barefoot men at Gordonsville. "God grant that our leaders may soon learn," the Louisisiana officer expressed, "that men cannot march and fight when they are half naked, with feet that leave bloody marks whenever they step."[24]

Other supply problems plagued the army in the Valley as well. A cavalry brigade commander who had lived in nearby Charlottesville was shocked by the scene. To his wife, he revealed, "no forage for horses and no food for men. The people in a starving condition." He concluded, "I have never believed anything like it possible in this country." A noncommissioned officer of infantry, disgusted at the lack of combat prowess of the cavalry, proposed a solution to the food shortage. "They never will fight so I think it useless to have them in the Army eating rations from the Government." Grimes had great hopes when Thomas Rosser arrived with his men that he would whip all the cavalry into shape, "but his also appears to have become demoralized." Grimes then concluded there "must be something contagious in this atmosphere." Yet in fairness to the cavalry, it had suffered badly. Strength had been worn by attrition, horses were emaciated, and the equipment had so deteriorated that disaster was almost inevitable. In one brigade alone, almost one in every six horsemen carried an unserviceable weapon into combat. If they fought on foot, they could adapt, but on mounts, they entered combat at an extreme disadvantage, especially against Federals on excellent animals and armed with repeating weapons.[25]

While Sheridan's men began torching anything of military usefulness, Early began to rebuild his shattered command. Grimes, who commanded a North Carolina brigade, believed that Early had to act circumspectly before he undertook a new campaign. As he explained to his wife, "our great danger lies in the fact that since our recent reverses the troops do not have that unbounded confidence in his judgment which is necessary for a successful military leader—for without that he can hardly expect his men to act well their part, when they think he is deficient in judgment." At the same time, Lee counseled Early, "One victory will put all things right." He returned Kershaw's Division, minus Anderson, to the Valley commander, and urged him to reinvigorate his command and bring absentees back into the ranks. Maneuver to buy time, Lee advised, and strike propitiously and powerfully.[26]

With Federal troops scattered in camp north of Cedar Creek, Early sent Jackson's mapmaking expert Jed Hotchkiss with Gordon to scout the Union left. They returned with a bold plan. At night, Gordon with three divisions would cross the Shenandoah River, follow a little-known pathway around the base of Three Top Mountain, and recross the winding Shenandoah to roll up the Union left flank. Kershaw's Division would also march at night and attack the enemy directly. Wharton's Division with artillery would prepare to attack farther west. Tom Rosser's cavalry would swing far beyond Wharton and open the fight. Early endorsed the concept and the particulars, and on the night of October 18, the Confederates undertook the most impressive night movement of the war.[27]

Early's Confederates struck the unsuspecting Yankees at 5:00 A.M., and by sunrise they had routed the enemy and were in full possession of two corps camps. The army promptly became a plundering mob. With winter approaching, and soldiers so short on basic items to help them cope with the upcoming cold weather, huge numbers of men embarked on the spree. An assistant surgeon witnessed Gordon's aide pilfering from Yankee camps for the headquarters, and the physician even admitted succumbing to the lure himself. The thrill of victory against double their own strength, the long night march, and the availability of food and clothing for soldiers in need dissolved any discipline that remained.[28]

Early hesitated to pursue the Federals, because of the strength of their cavalry, and by the time he organized forces to challenge the Yankees again, they had secured a strong defensive position. The momentum shifted back to the Yankees. Sheridan, who was returning from a trip to Washington, rallied his retreating soldiers and launched a vicious counterattack that completely routed Early and his soldiers. The Yankees had transformed one of the great marches and victories in the entire war into "one of the most shameful and disgraceful stampedes on record," as one Confederate described it. "The simple fact is," a staff officer of Early's wrote to his wife, "that this army has become like a team of horses that are in the habit of running away, which will often run when there is no occasion for it." The soldiers in Early's command had lost confidence in themselves, their comrades, and their officers. One of Early's men, in the rear and not present at the fight, commented to his sister, "On that day our Army won the greatest victory of this war, & the same day was more disgracefully beaten than an Army ever was." Although Early inflicted double the casualties on his enemy, he lost twenty-five field guns and nearly all his ammunition, baggage, and foraging wagons. Among the mortally wounded was Ramseur.[29]

In days past, recalled one of Longstreet's staff members, they used to refer to Banks as Jackson's commissary; "equally as appropriately the Yankees could call Early Sheridan's ordnance officer" for all the artillery and ammunition he had lost. Discipline in Early's command collapsed. Early "is one of the best military men of the present time. Take Genl. Lee out and I don't think he has his equal," a North Carolinian declared. "That movement was the most excellent planned affair that was ever known and I am sure we would have been successful but for the men plundering." Nonetheless, he felt the army had to change commanders, "for Genl Early is no disciplinarian." After stabilizing his command, Early and subordinate officers tried to crack down on discipline, but as an Alabamian commented, " 'The stable door is to be locked, after the horse has been stolen.' " Ultimately, officers were to blame for the Cedar Creek fiasco. They failed to discipline their men, and company commanders permitted their soldiers to fall out and plunder.[30]

A month after Early's disaster, Lee schemed to seize the initiative one more time. He considered sneaking Early down from the Valley to join with Hampton's cavalry for a surprise attack. He wondered if Hampton could find a vulnerable point without having to pass over breastworks. Yet the cavalry commander could find no exposed flank, nor could Early readily extricate his command at that time. Lee's last major effort to seize the initiative from Grant was finished, a failure.[31]

Throughout the late summer and fall, Confederate soldiers had begun to prepare for the winter months ahead. They had erected formidable works that, Grant informed Meade, "come near holding themselves without troops." On either side, one defender every six feet, supported by artillery, could hold the line, Grant believed. Although the works varied due to terrain and the proximity of the enemy, they generally consisted of a main line about breast high and fifteen feet thick at the top, with large logs stacked horizontally and fortified by an occasional vertical log. Ideally, troops built them aboveground, so that water did not collect in the bottom of the trench, although topography sometimes required otherwise. Some one hundred or more yards to the rear they slept in tents or on the open ground. As winter began to creep near, soldiers tossed up cabins for better comfort. They also carved out bunks within the wall of the main line, so that troops could sleep while others remained on watch. At determined intervals along the principal defense, Confederates erected small earth forts, which protected artillery guns. On the enemy side of the main line, soldiers had scooped out a ditch four and a half feet deep and six feet wide. Just beyond the ditch Lee's soldiers embedded a line of palisades, or sharpened sticks, in the ground. Anywhere between 200 and 800 yards beyond the main line they positioned pickets, who rotated regularly. They also had their own slighter works for protection. Between these outposts and the palisade, Confederates placed abatis, sharpened branches tied together to slow passage. In some locations, they built numerous rows of abatis.[32]

Throughout the siege, trench warfare remained dangerous and extremely uncomfortable. Both sides continued to employ snipers and hurled shells at each other, and anyone who exposed himself incurred risks. When Brig. Gen. Archibald Gracie peered over the lines, a shell exploded above him, with one fragment passing through his body and another through his head, killing him on the spot. Those who served in trenches or on picket duty endured heat and thirst in the summer, but nothing compared to the brutality of winter cold. Soldiers manned trenches without shoes or blankets and without fires, and enemy gunfire made it difficult for them to move about and keep comfortable. Fires to warm them were simply out of the question. Rain or snow sometimes lined the bottom and soldiers, many of them barefoot, had no means of protecting their feet. Other times the elements caused bombproofs to leak or cave in on unsuspecting soldiers. Pests, moreover, were a huge problem. "Rats are running riot, over the whole camp," complained a Virginian with a facetious tone. "Don't mind the *rats* so *much*, but cant *afford* to *board* them." He asked his wife to send a cat.[33]

Lee kept active, inspecting lines, examining enemy positions for weaknesses, and he continued to carry an unusually heavy burden. After the army commander came down to look over the works, a Texan jotted in his diary that "whenever the *big men* begin to stir around on the front we think that 'Death is in the wind.'" In absence of the brigade commander, a staff officer toured Lee around their position, with the commanding general drawing on his engineering skills for suggestions and alterations. "He is anxious yet he says he is confident of success," the officer wrote his wife in mid-October. "All we want is men & these are coming in now."[34]

Lee's brother reported in late September that "Brother Robert has not been very well lately." Fortunately for Lee, the workload eased a bit two weeks later when Longstreet, his arm and hand still paralyzed and in a sling, returned to duty. Since the opening of the spring campaign, Lee had borne an excessive burden because of his corps commanders. The one on whom he could absolutely rely was Longstreet, and he had gone down at the Wilderness. His arrival at Petersburg removed a huge weight from Lee's shoulders. Immediately, Longstreet took charge of his corps and ordered adjustments. The Confederates had already positioned abatis between the pickets and the main line. Longstreet ordered them placed in front of the picket line as well, to prevent Confederates from deserting to the enemy. He planked critical supply roads before the winter mud mired their wagons, and he attempted to restore the York River Railroad to help ease the transportation problems from Richmond. A man with little regard for African-Americans, Longstreet determined that the Confederates should employ their worst units opposite black troops, since an attack by the U.S. Colored Troops was unlikely and Rebel soldiers hated to desert to them. He ordered all rifle pits constructed seven feet high with platforms for pickets. They would keep pickets dryer and still give protection. Longstreet also demanded stern penalties for desertion and absence without leave. "Remedies of the most severe kind," he wrote, "are required to keep the army together this winter."[35]

Lee, meanwhile, wrestled with the never-ending battle for manpower. In the summer months, the army commander had pushed for an increase in troop strength to offset combat losses. They released prisoners from Castle Thunder to place them in the ranks. Authorities retained one musician per brigade, and all others marched to the front, where the ordnance officers issued them muskets. The army stripped orderlies and clerks and reduced the number of hospital stewards to the minimum level, just to maximize the number of rifle toters.[36]

Those steps checked the decline, but only temporarily. Combat, illness, and desertion reduced strengths dramatically by early fall. Heth's Division, for example, opened the spring with approximately 6,500 and suffered 5,376 casualties in the 1864 campaign. Law's old brigade tallied fewer than 800 men in early September, of whom 93 were present but sick. Still, even when those ill soldiers returned to duty, the brigade of five regiments had a total strength below what Confederate officials originally intended for a single regiment. A Maryland cavalry battalion entered the spring campaign with approximately 330 officers and men, and by mid-September it tabulated 71 bodies. A North Carolina captain averaged 10 to 12 men in his company that fall. He had three times as many soldiers in Yankee prison camps as he had present with the army. As Lee warned Davis at the beginning of November, "Unless we can obtain a reasonable approximation to his [Grant's] force I fear a great calamity will befall us." In August, conscription contributed only a modest number. After traveling around Richmond, Launcelot Blackford commented to his mother that nearly all the men he saw on the streets were invalids. Conscription had swept away everyone else, except for government employees, and they served in the local defense brigade.[37]

Lee did what he could. He directed the consolidation of small regiments. Although soldiers identified with their units and took great pride in their accomplishments, the duplication of officer and staff positions cost the army too many combatants. Soldiers grumbled about consolidation, and it undoubtedly injured morale, but there was no choice. Lee also looked toward African-Americans to ease the burden on his men. Free blacks and slaves had long served as teamsters and manual laborers, and Lee pushed to increase those numbers. By the end of October, some 2,000 blacks were working to build or repair fortifications alone, while others were restoring or upgrading railroads to reduce derailments.[38]

On October 8, Lee issued a circular to draw all men back into the ranks. "With a view to increase effective strength of this army, which is regarded as of the first importance at this time," Lee ordered officers to supervise rolls of all detailed soldiers. He wanted only men incapable of performing regular duty to act as clerks, hospital attendants, and couriers, and to perform other support duties. Excess artillerists suddenly found muskets in their hands. Authorities pressed men, soldiers and civilians, into companies—called "Snatchups"—and forwarded them to the front. Each month, hospital patients underwent a physical examination to determine who could return to Petersburg. A brigade commissary officer had all his people transferred back to the line, and disabled soldiers replaced them. Private George Lawless of the 27th Virginia had suffered wounds at Antietam and again at Gettysburg. He requested assignment rounding up deserters in his home county, rather than lie around the hospital. Officials determined if he were fit enough to search for deserters, he could carry a musket in the trenches.[39]

In conjunction with a strong push to move conscripts out of Camp Lee and into the army, units suddenly experienced a huge surge in troop strength. In October, the War Department assigned 2,847 conscripts to Lee's army, more than the total number of conscripts who had joined the army since May. Of those October soldiers, 2,627 went to the infantry. Wright's Brigade boasted an increase of 200 men in October, which it credited to the circular. By the end of November, Pickett's Division had augmented its strength by 2,000 through new soldiers and the return of detailed troops. Hill's Third Corps picked up 5,000 more men.[40]

Although Lee had scoured the region for what one soldier called "'Long Tails'" to bump up his combat strength, supply problems continued to spiral downward. His tenuous hold on the Weldon line left him with the Southside

Railroad into Petersburg and the Richmond & Danville, which frequently washed out and derailed from poor repair. This strain on logistics spilled over into the business of ammunition procurement. Taxed as badly as they were, railroads had great difficulty hauling sufficient quantities of lead and other metals to produce ammunition. To offset this shortfall, the Ordnance Department began paying soldiers to glean lead and unexploded shells from battlefields. Soldiers would receive ten cents per pound for lead or a fixed rate for shot from the Nitre and Mining Bureau. They also paid for all useful metals. Unfortunately, incautious handling sometimes resulted in fatal injuries with unexploded shells. Pendleton's headquarters urged soldiers to bring in shells with care and let ordnance personnel unload any explosives. By recycling lead, the army reduced cargo space and weight dramatically, which it could then allocate for food for man and beast.[41]

As they had throughout most of Lee's tenure, food shortages continued to plague his army. "I can eat three times what I get for we only get anuft for one meal in twenty four hours," a North Carolinian grumbled in early December. Shaky rail lines from the south, combined with the Virginia drought and Sheridan's destructive march, limited the amount and kinds of edibles that reached the Army of Northern Virginia. Just as they had appeared in each of the three previous years, scurvy and "scorbutic dysentery" cases surfaced in the army, along with other manifestations of malnutrition and vitamin deficiency.[42]

Pangs of hunger and shivers from cold temperatures drove soldiers once again to take for themselves, hurting discipline and burdening the local population. The troops realized that men in the trenches would have little opportunity to support themselves at Yankee expense this winter, unlike previous winters, and they would have to take from civilians whenever they had the chance. By this stage of the war, it had become part of their culture, as well as a necessity. "Asking a Soldier where he got anything is a very unfair question, & generally not to be answered," a Georgia private instructed his sister. "Always ask is there any more there."[43]

Not long after Longstreet returned to duty, he cracked down on the looting of prisoners, deserters, and civilians. He assumed that the culprits were independent scouts, and he ordered subordinates to limit the numbers of scouts each division permitted. Exactly one month later, he lashed out at the same misbehavior, this time recognizing that the problem was more widespread than he had initially believed. "The extent of the depredations committed by Soldiers from the 1st Corps upon stock, gardens and other property of the citizens around Richmond call for the most rigid measures of correction," he demanded. "If allowed to continue the result will be the demoralization of the Army." He forbade soldiers to leave camp without written authority and ordered roll calls at irregular hours. Yet Longstreet's efforts did little to halt the practice. Three weeks later, Lee announced his shock that "outrages and depredations, amounting in some cases to flagrant robbery, have been perpe-

trated upon citizens living within the lines, and near the camps of the army."
In a recent episode, a band of ruffians intent on plundering killed a child. Lee
sought the complete cooperation of all soldiers, insisting "we cannot escape the
disgrace that attends these evil-doers, except by the most strenuous exertions
on our part to restrain their wickedness and bring upon them the just punishment of their offenses." Lee charged the officer corps with particular culpabil-
ity, since ultimate responsibility for "prevention and detection of unlawful acts"
fell on its shoulders.[44]

Discipline had broken down in the vast majority of regiments and batteries,
largely as a consequence of grinding combat and inadequate supply. Approximately one in every four officers in Lee's army throughout the war was killed
in battle, and five of every nine survivors suffered wounds. By factoring out
those who failed in the 1862 re-election—very few of them had commanded
in combat—close to nine of every ten officers in Lee's army were either killed
or wounded. About 86 percent of all company-grade officers—lieutenants and
captains—were killed, wounded, or captured. Officers felt an obligation to lead
their men, and that subjected them to heavy enemy fire. "I have to expose myself
a great deal with my present Brigade to make it fight," Brig. Gen. James Dearing admitted to his wife in late November. Several months later, he was killed
in action. In many commands, officer slots were revolving doors as officers
went down and new ones stepped into place. One brigade had had six different
commanders in the seven months since the spring campaign had opened. Not
surprisingly, inefficiency, lax discipline, and unsoldierly bearing were virtually
universal themes in inspection reports.[45]

Once again, some inspectors harped on the election of officers as the source
of the problem. "Many of the officers are grossly ignorant and negligent of
their duties, owing to a great degree to the unfortunate system of elections by
which these officers are chosen," groused an inspector of Brig. Gen. William
Terry's Brigade. A lieutenant colonel formulated the argument that many of
those officers who had lost election two years earlier had returned to the army
through conscription as privates. Soldiers had rejected them because they were
stern disciplinarians, and they would make excellent company commanders
once again. His assertion and faith were misplaced. Why should fellow soldiers
trust them now, after they had sat out two years of war and the government
had to compel them to return to service? Many of those officers who lost re-
election had never been in combat and had commanded under the very best
circumstances in the entire war. While their veteran comrades had slugged
it out on a dozen battlefields, they had sat on the sidelines stewing over the
re-election failure. At that stage of the war, what would prompt experienced
soldiers to serve under someone who had dodged military duty those past two
and a half years?[46]

As the siege dragged on, soldiers worried deeply about their loved ones.
They witnessed the burdens of war on the people of Virginia, and they knew

how devastating circumstances could become. Troops observed Union mortar and cannon fire into Petersburg, and the devastation it caused among civilians there. They saw how runaway inflation priced goods beyond the means of the poor in Richmond. A Virginia private reported that a boy from Richmond informed him that "people have ceased eating meat, it being out of their power to purchase meat at $12 and $15 pr pound." The next day, he recorded, "Some of the fellows who have been up near Richmond say that a piece of bacon will get a soldier anything he wants. It is also reported that some of the women about here will *trade* for bacon or meal. What a pity!" The artillerists in the 1st Virginia Regiment agreed to donate one ration over the next seven days to the Richmond poor. Lee's headquarters, as well as his soldiers, worried over relief for the poor. When word spread that the people of Richmond had decided to collect food for a good Christmas dinner for the men in Lee's army, soldiers worried that "the demand for every kind of eatables has put them so high" that "it will deprive many poor devils in this City the pleasure of a Christmas Dinner."[47]

They received reports that many civilians had grown dispirited over the war and its losses. "I am pained to hear so much despondency & gloom in the country," a Virginian revealed. "It comes up to us from all quarters." A Georgia private complained, "I have Herd that all Houston County is ready to go rite back in to the Union." He was sorry to hear it. "If our Peeple at Home cant Stand this war tell me What we Poor Soldiers air to do." Once William T. Sherman's army destroyed Atlanta and he began his march from there to Savannah, morale in states like Georgia plummeted. "For God sake use your influence to send every man that is able to bare arms to the front," a Georgian implored his sister. "You have a part in this war to do and now is the time for you to use every effort to swell the ranks of our depleted Regiments," he insisted.[48]

Soldiers particularly feared for loved ones along the paths of Union invasions or raids. In the Shenandoah Valley where Sheridan's command had passed, not only did the people lose their crops, but the Union troops also destroyed their tools and ran away with their slaves, so that they had no means of cultivating the soil the next year. For three and a half years, people in Virginia had endured the destructive presence of armies battling in their neighborhoods. The war now spilled into relatively untouched regions, both in that state and elsewhere, and soldiers could not bear the idea of remaining in the army while their families hungered or suffered badly. When a private learned that Yankee forces had marched near his home and had seized food, slaves, and livestock and left his family "scarcely anything to live on at all," he described the thought as "Horrible to Contemplate." The destructive nature of war challenged soldiers in ways they did not anticipate. They had entered the army to protect their rights, specifically the right to own slaves, and to defend their homes. It appeared as if they were failing on both scores. Once their families suffered severe hardships, the war challenged soldiers to determine where their loyalty ultimately rested, with their country and comrades or with their families. More and more soldiers opted for the welfare of their families over that of their fledgling country.[49]

DESPITE A BAD turn in the struggle for independence that year, war-weary Confederates still had hope that they would pull out a stalemate, thanks to the upcoming Union presidential campaign. Lincoln sought re-election against George B. McClellan, the commander whom they had fought on the Peninsula, in the Seven Days' Battle, and at Antietam. Although McClellan vowed to continue the war, his party included peace planks in its platform. "This is the long looked for day on which our fortunes are to be so much influenced for good or evil," an Alabamian reported on Election Day. "We have thought for the last three years that the Northern people would become certainly convinced of the impossibility of subjugating us by the time of another presidential election should come around, we will soon know whether we have been deceived." Sentiments in his camp varied, he wrote, with a majority predicting Lincoln's re-election. They were right. Lincoln carried the popular vote and swept the Electoral College.[50]

Lincoln's re-election placed the Confederates on notice that any chance of negotiating a compromise with the Yankees would require far more fighting. "War—unrelenting, cruel, and horrid war, still claims the floor, and will probably hold high carnival during another term of four years," a North Carolinian wrote. The combination of the election and Sherman's march through Georgia triggered a mass exodus of soldiers from the army. Desertion from Lee's army during the final quarter of 1864 soared at least 50 percent higher than in any previous three-month period. Evidence indicates that the overwhelming majority deserted in November and December. On October 22, for example, Maj. Gen. Bushrod Johnson's Division tabulated an aggregate present strength of 4,075. Four weeks later, it reported 4,040 as aggregate present, but by December 19, the division total had declined to 2,674. "Thar is more disafection among the men then you think thare is," Pvt. Jacob West wrote a friend in early December. "Tha most all say that will not go through a nother campaign throuout this brigade thare is a good meny leving now som going home and som to the yankees." Two months earlier, the Federals had received fewer than ten deserters per day. By late November, they averaged ten to fifteen, and only a fraction of all deserters surrendered to the Yankees. Worse yet, while some of these men were conscripts or detailed troops who refused to perform field duty any longer, many had earned excellent reputations as soldiers. A man in the 48th Georgia who bore scars from two battlefields and who was "looked upon as one among the first" in his company deserted near the end of the year. For some time, he had complained over the quantity and quality of rations. Each man had his limits, and he simply had had enough.[51]

In December, a staff officer termed 1864 "The dying year." The title was more precise than he realized, representing issues beyond fatalities in combat and hospital tents. Very early in the war, farsighted officers like Lee had recognized the Confederacy had a narrow margin of error in its effort to win the war. The Confederacy needed a much higher percentage of its manpower and productivity in agriculture and manufacturing to fuel its war effort, and it had obtained it. But was it enough? As the fourth New Year's Day at war passed, signs of the unraveling Confederate war effort were plainly visible. The battles, the hardships, the suffering at home, and the prospect of more years of difficult service shattered the resolve of some of the most devoted Confederates. The margin of error that had so concerned Lee had disappeared, while the enemy seemed ever to expand.[52]

Chapter 34

SPIRAL OF DEFEAT

O N JANUARY 1, 1865, Pvt. Thomas Devereux marveled at the changes that had taken place over the last decade. "Who would have thought ten years ago today, that we would now be engaged in a bloody and ruthless war; almost whipped but still jubilant; Men who had been used to the best that money could buy living on meat & bread, and scarcely enough of that, sleeping out, in all weather with not a blanket part of the time, and always poorly clad." A twenty-year-old volunteer who had completed his first year of service, Devereux clung to the Confederate cause. Their ancestors had held out against enormous hardships and won their independence, and so could the Confederates.[1]

Private Spencer Barnes was in no mood to celebrate the coming of the new year. That month, he would complete three years of service for the Confederacy. Over that time, he had fought in all the major battles and campaigns since Seven Pines, sustaining a wound at Bristoe Station in November 1863. He had seen where the Confederacy had been, and could assess its current state. The future offered little to inspire him. In solemn tones, the thirty-one-year-old miller explained to his sister, "every thing looks quite gloomy at the present & prospects don't seam to get no brighter I hav hoped for peace and I fear that peace is never for me to se again I hav become disheartend like a great many others that is don't care which away the war goes." Having fought for three years, he pronounced with disgust, "a mans life has become so here it is not vallied [valued] no more than we woud a dog there."[2]

Soldiers like Devereux and Barnes held on, but for tens of thousands of troops in Lee's army, service had become so burdensome that they did so barely, and many others simply could endure no more. As conditions steadily deteriorated in the army and on the home front, soldiers deserted en masse, convinced that their cause was lost and loved ones needed them. The Federals extended their lines, interdicting Confederate supply routes and worsening shortages within the army, which sparked more desertions. Union forces marched through the Confederate States, destroying rail lines, disrupting communications, and confiscating food and property from civilians. Torn between their loyalty to their families and obligations to their fledgling nation and their comrades, many more of Lee's soldiers headed home to look after the welfare of their kin, further weakening the army. With so many of their buddies dead, wounded, or imprisoned, and evidence of a collapsing Confederacy all around them, the desertion floodgates opened wide.

Many soldiers still felt enormous pride in the Army of Northern Virginia. Lee's army had earned a superb battlefield record and emerged as a symbol of effective resistance in both Confederate and Union eyes. They took special satisfaction in besting the Yankees time after time with inferior numbers of troops and resources, delaying the onset of this downward spiral. But once it began, it ultimately dragged down the Army of Northern Virginia.

Conditions in the trenches, always poor, worsened during the winter months. As a Louisiana private described it, "this place is enough to Kill the devil." Although soldiers could sometimes sleep in winter quarters, duty along the front lines became more burdensome as the weather turned inclement. Rain, snow, and thaw triggered minor landslides and collapsed bombproofs, out of which soldiers had to dig without proper tools, and trenches filled several inches deep with water. In some areas, the troops had to place tents at the same level as the trench floor, which flooded them as well. For firewood, soldiers often had to hike a mile to the rear and carry the wood manually. Off-duty soldiers would have to make two or three trips just to collect enough firewood for the night. Snipers continued to pick off careless men who unwittingly exposed themselves or who crossed open terrain. Yankees also lobbed huge mortar rounds, eight-and twelve-inch shells, among pockets of troops. "You can imagine what a scatteration they make, sometimes burying themselves four feet in the Earth and the[n] bursting," a soldier described. "It looks like a small volcano." Rats and mice overran the camp. "They rumbled over everything, neither did they spare my blankets," a soldier complained. "It would do you no good to mount a stool here and scream! The mice would only stare at you in amazement and probably hitherto unseen, one would drop upon you from the roof." One even shared his pillow. He feared they would eat his meager rations before he got to them.[3]

As Rebel numbers diminished and Grant's army stretched its lines, soldiers had to perform heavy duty on a more regular basis, and they openly grumbled about it. One officer reported that men rotated from one assignment to the next, day after day, with no break between duties. They expressed open resentment over the practice. It became more difficult for officers to compel troops to perform these duties. Cold, hungry, and inadequately clothed, their soldiers protested any assignment that was risky or took them out in harsh weather. "It is very trying to me to have to require duties of the men," a South Carolina captain admitted. "I feel like I had rather be a private myself than to have to do what I have to do."[4]

That winter, the length of the Rebel line and the lack of manpower to defend it became a huge problem for Lee. By the beginning of February, Lee alerted

Longstreet, "our force is inadequate for our length of line every where, and we must endeavor to make up by energy and promptness for our paucity of numbers." Early and correct information, Lee instructed his corps commander, was the key to their defense. As the Federals stretched their position westward, Lee elongated and attenuated his defenses to a critical degree. By early spring, the Petersburg-Richmond defenses extended forty-five miles. Generally, Rebel defenders stood in the works five to six feet apart. In late February, Maj. Gen. Custis Lee reported in one brigade he had 932 privates to defend 1,405 yards of main line and 2,600 yards of picket line. Another brigade was worse off. With 1,187 privates it manned 2,401 yards of parapet and 2,300 yards of picket.[5]

To supply these troops and the populations of Richmond and Petersburg, the Confederacy relied largely on railroads. Civilians drew supplies via the Virginia Central Railroad, which ran from west of Staunton to Richmond, and the Richmond & Fredericksburg line. They provided just enough food. Lee's army drew its food and forage from the Southside Railroad, which ran from Lynchburg to Petersburg, and the Richmond & Danville Railroad. In May 1864, the Confederates completed the construction of the Piedmont Railroad, which linked Greensboro and the North Carolina Railroad with the Richmond & Danville line. The Piedmont, however, had a four-foot-eight-and-one-half-inch gauge, while the width of the Richmond & Danville track was five feet. Despite its new construction, the Piedmont Railroad functioned poorly. In late December, the line was in "such bad condition" that it took forty-eight hours to travel from Greensboro to Danville, an average of one mile per hour. In January, heavy rains and ensuing floods knocked out the Piedmont line for fifteen days. In desperation, the army commander called on local farmers east of the Blue Ridge and south of the James to contribute food. Combined with the amount the commissary officers had stockpiled, the local gifts were barely sufficient. To improve transportation, Lee once again requested that Davis detail 500 laborers under a competent engineer to get the line back in service, but problems continued. Poor construction, compounded by overweight and excessive numbers of cars, caused frequent derailments, which wrecked valuable rolling stock and delayed shipments. The Southside and the Richmond & Danville railroads shared the same gauge and intersected at Burkeville, but they could not switch cars from one line to the other and convey direct shipments to the army at Petersburg. Instead, they had to employ black laborers to transfer cars from one track to the other manually. Not until February did anyone suggest the use of shifting engines, which would be more efficient and "facilitate the shipments to A.N.V. in a much greater degree." The solution came too late to make a difference.[6]

With Lee's army reliant almost exclusively on these railroads for food and supplies, prolonged shortages plagued the army as never before. In the past, men had gone cold or barefoot in winter and hungry for extended periods of time, but nothing compared to the winter of 1864–65.

In late January 1865, Quartermaster General Alexander Lawton reported that over the last seven months, his office had allocated enough supplies for each soldier to have received approximately two pairs of shoes, two shirts, two sets of drawers, two pairs of socks, two pairs of pants, one blanket, and more than one jacket. Yet inspection after inspection uncovered a lack of shoes and clothing in serious, often critical numbers. "The men are suffering for clothing," relayed an inspector in late November 1864, "many are very ragged and in some instances, strictly speaking, unfit for the field." He considered the delay in delivery of clothing "inexcusable." Late in December, some men in the 9th Alabama attended inspection with no pants at all, and fifteen men in the 10th Alabama were barefoot. The same was true in Kershaw's Division. "Some of the men are without pants and others nearly so," an inspector reported.[7]

In mid-March, Lawton insisted that "a larger supply of clothing has been issued to the armies in the last three months than in any similar period during the war," yet men in Lee's army still suffered severe shortages. According to an inspector, "Experience has shown that the semi-annual allowance of clothing which would be sufficient to clothe men comfortably in less onerous duty will last scarcely three months in the Trenches, from the greater wear of material in rubbing against the sides of the ditches." During January and February, inspectors uniformly determined the condition of clothing as poor. In Robert Ransom's Brigade at the end of January, one in every six soldiers had shoes that were irreparable, and others were barefoot. Pickett's Division needed 757 jackets and 1,359 pairs of pants. Rufus Barringer's Cavalry Brigade had "a large number of the men" barefoot. As late as the end of March, soldiers like Pvt. Peter Cross complained, "I can tell you I am naked fur pants you oit [ought] to see mea then you would see a raged [ragged] man."[8]

The quality of the material tended to be poor. For a long time, brigades and divisions had manufactured their own shoes, which by all accounts were superior to what the government issued. As an officer commented on the inspection report of Lane's Brigade at the end of 1864, "It has been satisfactorily demonstrated after a Year's experience that *better* shoes can be made in camp than are supplied by the Q.M. Dept." Both Rodes's and Early's divisions ran shoe and tailoring shops for the men, something their commanders would never have established if the clothing and shoe shortage had not reached a grave status. To be sure, the problem at any given moment varied by unit and even by state. In Wilcox's Division at the end of November 1864, the two North Carolina brigades had received clothing allotments from their state and were "much better supplied" than the other two brigades, from Georgia and South Carolina. At the end of February 1865, the quartermaster of Georgia had issued clothing to Anderson's Brigade, while the Texas Brigade, Bratton's Carolinians, and Law's Alabamians endured serious clothing shortages.[9]

Feed for horses reached critical lows during the winter months. Lee established a standard of ten pounds of corn and ten pounds of long forage per day. The army seldom achieved half that goal. By late December 1864, artillery horses were already starving in Hill's Corps, and an inspector pronounced the animals in "miserable condition." Horses in Poague's Battalion consumed only five pounds of feed per day, which amounted to slow starvation, and he predicted that unless more forage arrived, Pegram's Battalion "will be without horses for the Spring Campaign." In Early's Valley District, twenty-eight artillery horses died over a ten-day stretch in December on a diet of less than five pounds. By January, Early had to disband much of his artillery to care for his horses. According to a quartermaster officer, "The men have been permitted to take the horses to their homes, and remain there during the winter, on condition that they feed & care for them. Nothing but a desperate condition of affairs could make such an arrangement for the good of the country," he explained. "But the horses would inevitably starve here." Hampton complained to Lee that many of his horses received between two and a half and five pounds of feed per day, and they often had to substitute unthrashed wheat for feed. Even in areas where hay and corn were relatively plentiful, his horses never received a day of full rations. In order to maximize the limited feed available, the army had to send Butler's Division with nearly 4,000 horses to South Carolina to feed and recover from active campaigning and near starvation. Authorities in Richmond restricted the use of horses among officers to those who entered the battlefield or who had to perform duties in places that were widely separated. Despite all these efforts at pinching, the situation did not improve much. During the last week of February, animals in Fitz Lee's Cavalry Division had received eight pounds of feed per day. "This is insufficient to keep the horses in condition—" an inspector wrote, "they must go down."[10]

Humans fared no better than animals, but at least they had the power to protest. Throughout 1864, rations seldom exceeded a pound of corn meal and a quarter pound of beef or bacon, and only occasionally did men receive vegetables. By early 1865, the commissary could not sustain even that meager bounty. Many days, the government could supply troops with either meat or a starch—cornmeal or flour—but not both. Quantities, too, declined, so that the government often issued a pound of bread or three-quarters of a pound of cornmeal per day, between nine hundred and twelve hundred calories. As one captain commented, "Nothing has a greater tendency to create discontent and dissatisfaction than the want of the usual quantities of nourishment." After four or five meatless days at a time, the government often attempted to provide troops with sorghum or sugar to defuse unrest. Other times, two or three days passed without any flour or corn for bread.[11]

No matter what the case, troops were always hungry, and they resented it. Kershaw conceded the link between food and morale when he commented for the record, "To these deficiencies of food I attribute the number of desertions daily occurring and a general feeling of depression existing." In late February, Longstreet's headquarters instructed division commissary officers not to request food until the day they needed it. "It is unsafe to Keep them on hand," an officer admitted, "the troops having taken by armed force the supplies of one of the C.S. [Commissary of Subsistence] of the Div during the month and several times indicated a disposition to do so." If they had no food around, armed mobs of soldiers would not steal it.[12]

Even worse, shortages became so severe that the government diverted corn intended for horses to go to soldiers. "The corn received [sic] in Richmond and intended for animals," a major explained, "is turned over to the Comsry. [Commissary] Dept to be converted into subsistence for the men." Usually, this corn contained dried leaves and stalks from the corn plant, roughage that offered additional nourishment for horses. Soldiers found it unpalatable. "We get Corn Bread now in place of wheat Bread," a soldier informed his family. "It is Baked in town and it looks like a pile of Cow dung Baked in the sun   I could nock down a cow with a pone of it." He concluded, "I have Come to the beleafe that the Confederacy is plaid out."[13]

The problem was not a food shortage so much as it was transporting the food to the army. In mid-December, Commissary General Lucius B. Northrop, who had long since lost Lee's confidence as an effective officer, sought Lee's help in procuring food for the Army of Northern Virginia. With Virginia's limits tapped, the army would have to look elsewhere. East Tennessee could furnish 100,000 bushels of corn and 5,000 barrels of flour, if the Confederacy possessed the wagons and draft animals to haul them, which it did not. Troubles in the Carolinas made it difficult to purchase and ship foodstuffs, especially at the fixed prices of the government with paper currency, and Sherman's march had cut off Georgia as a source of supply. As Northrop explained in mid-January, "The feeding 'from hand to mouth' is our permanent condition—with a ravaged country, broken-down teams, and R.R. transportation not sufficient for bringing forward current supplies, and an indebtedness rapidly increasing—with a credit impaired."[14]

During the next couple of months, Lee struggled to feed his soldiers adequately. He thought the public should do without certain foods that the army could cook readily in the field. Civilians could consume other foods that required more preparation time or spoiled relatively quickly. Seddon wanted Lee to impress food for his army; Northrop discouraged it. The commissary general believed that Lee had earned a reputation throughout the nation as its great leader, around whom all Confederates rallied. If Lee impressed food from civilians, it would ruin his reputation and cause even more damage to the Rebel war effort than hungry soldiers. Northrop preferred that Lee use his standing and make a public appeal to civilians to provide for the army, while his agents impressed food. Several weeks later, the situation reached such a level that Davis ordered the secretary of war to have food impressed immediately for Lee's army. "The distress of our brave defenders renders me uncontrollably anxious," admitted the president.[15]

Reduced rations with severely limited vitamin intake and excessive exposure to cold temperatures spawned widespread illness that winter. Many soldiers in various brigades suffered bouts of scurvy. At the height of winter, "Pneumonia has been more prevalent of late than usual from exposure, and want of proper garments," an officer reported. Personal hygiene nearly disappeared, which also bred illness. Soap was so scarce that a division and a brigade began manufacturing it for their men. In mid-January, a soldier commented that some men had not put on a clean shirt since August. And once troops became seriously ill, field hospitals lacked supplies and adequate accommodations. Even the hospitals in Richmond suffered from a shortage of wood and coal and were extremely cold.[16]

As the Federal noose tightened and its blockade closed the last major port of Wilmington, North Carolina, Confederates had to rely on their own productivity and transportation system, a fatal combination for Lee's army. The Second Corps had not recovered from its loss of wagons in the Valley Campaign, and its mobility and supply became a severe problem for Early's successor, Gordon. Among the cavalry, quite a number of horsemen lacked arms as late as the first of March. Some never received weapons, and others turned them in to the ordnance officer when they went to the hospital, only to find them reissued upon their return. In Rooney Lee's Division, cavalrymen possessed a striking mix of weapons, including breech-loaders from the Yankees, rifled muskets, rifles, and muzzle-loading carbines. In one brigade, two regiments sported seven different types of weapons and two others carried six kinds. Even worse, every regiment in the brigade required at least three different calibers of ammunition. Soldiers seldom possessed bayonets or knapsacks, and the lead shortage created a severe ammunition shortfall. Men did their best by scavenging old battlefields, but by February, Josiah Gorgas reported only eighty to ninety rounds of small-arms ammunition in the hands of units in the field. He tried to play down that low figure by arguing that the average expenditure at Chancellorsville and Gettysburg amounted to twenty-five to thirty rounds per man, which must have been small comfort to Lee and his senior officers. In fact, thousands straggled and thousands more were killed and wounded and never fired close to that number of shots, so that some soldiers and regiments certainly fired sixty or seventy rounds. If the army fought a major battle and did not control the battlefield or seize a large portion of an enemy ordnance train, it could scarcely survive a second major battle.[17]

Lee took every possible step to expand supply, improve conditions, augment manpower, and buoy morale. He appealed to Davis, worked the supply network, and devoted an enormous amount of time to providing for the welfare of his men. On February 9, he assumed the rank of general-in-chief of all Confederate armies, and one of his first acts was to attempt to increase manpower. He convinced Davis to authorize amnesty for all deserters who returned to the army within twenty days or reported to an enrolling officer in areas where transportation back to their respective army was difficult. Lee even appealed to manhood and "the liberty transmitted by their forefather" to secure their fullest cooperation and service.[18]

Yet for all his efforts, Lee could not check the spiraling morale. Conditions in the army were so bad, sacrifices so many, and the resulting confidence in the

Confederacy so low that faith in the cause began to crumble among stalwart troops. In early February, the medical director for the Third Corps commented on an inspection report, "I regret that I cannot bear favourable testimony as regards the cheerfulness of the troops—, dejection and dissatisfaction were too manifest,—short rations, insufficient clothing, etc. may be enumerated among the causes which operate to produce this state of things." Soldiers spoke openly about wanting to see the war close, and they no longer insisted on a favorable outcome. "It has been the death of a many fine man that has went to fight for his sweet heart and country calls," a North Carolinian wrote to his girlfriend. "I hav wished that their had never been a gun in the world and what is ought to be plunged in the bottom of the sea." A month later, two veterans announced in camp "they wod not go in a nother such fite for all the negors in the confederacy and they sed they wous interested in Negros property." Virginia enlisted man John Perkins confided to a friend, "the men are very much demoralized and dissatisfied. Rations are short, and prospects of gaining our Independence beyond a hope, so think most of the men."[19]

Morale at home, too, was sinking, and it affected the spirit of the men severely. In certain areas, Southern whites had coped for some time with the depredations of deserters and their own armies. Sherman's command inflicted excessive damage over a wider swath. His Union soldiers roared through portions of Georgia and the Carolinas, confiscating foodstuffs and animals, disrupting slavery, destroying railroads and mills, and committing petty acts of thievery, harassment, and occasionally physical abuse. In South Carolina, they carried their destructiveness to new heights, wrecking or burning numerous towns and hundreds of homes. Everywhere they went, Sherman's army created mayhem and terrorized large numbers of citizens.[20]

The march of Sherman and his army through Georgia to the coast in November and December and then through the Carolinas from the end of January into late March had a devastating impact on support for the war at home. A resident of Rome, Georgia, a town destroyed during Sherman's march, explained to his absent brother, "there was *almost universally* through our own country a *wanton destruction* of *private property*, and our soldiers were caused to desert on account of the suffering of their families at home than by all other causes combined." Union soldiers took what they wanted and left little, insulted wives and parents, and instigated the collapse of the slave system. They left chaos in their wake.[21]

Strategically, it was brilliant. Sherman's march was comparatively bloodless, and psychologically devastating. As Sherman's army approached, loved ones left little doubt about the level of panic at home. "I can hardly tell you my anxieties and fears for a few days past," Annie Evans of Cheraw, South Carolina, wrote to her husband in Lee's army. "I feel sometimes almost ready to faint by the way—so much excitement, so many thousand rumors, and so much turmoil every way." Within two weeks, Sherman's army arrived there. Once Sherman's forces were situated between the Army of Northern Virginia and loved ones, the lengthy delays in communication heightened anxiety for Confederate soldiers and civilians. Rumors ran rampant, and a lack of firm information spurred desertion.[22]

So many impassioned letters reached Lee's troops that many abandoned the army in droves to go home and protect their families. "There are too many soldiers, who receive the most discouraging Kind of letters from home entreating them, in some cases to return even if they must desert to do so," a soldier admitted to a loved one. The Confederate inspector general, after perusing inspection summaries from Lee's army, noted, "Reports from the Army exhibit the fact, that many desertions occur which are induced by appeals from friends at home." The problem reached such serious proportions that Lee wrote to North Carolina governor Zebulon Baird Vance in late February as Sherman's soldiers prepared to enter that state, conceding "The state of despondency that now prevails among our people is producing a bad effect upon the troops. Desertions are becoming very frequent and there is good reason to believe that they are occasioned to a considerable extent by letters written to the soldiers by their friends at home." Lee urged Vance to attempt to alter public spirit in North Carolina, a hopeless task that the good Confederate governor undertook nonetheless.[23]

For many of those in and out of the army, the inability of the Confederacy to check Sherman's advance shattered their remaining faith in the government. Quartermaster General Lawton received a letter in mid-January from his wife, reporting the decline of spirit in Georgia. He replied, "The infection has spread every where; and the opinions expressed to-day by prominent men would have driven them out of Society a month since." Lawton then admitted that people had begun to arrive at the conclusion that "the Government is powerless to continue the struggle." Lee's headquarters and his troops maintained a steady awareness of the advancing Union army, and the Confederacy's inability to block it damaged faith in the viability of resistance. A Georgia infantryman insisted his regiment had lost "several of our best Soldiers" and predicted, "as long as sherman has no one to oppose him our boys here will keep it up (desertion) till there will be no one left to fight." A Virginia sergeant conveyed the opinions of his comrades when he wrote his mother two days after the fall of Columbia, South Carolina, "The success of Sherman in the South is causing the soldiers to grow more despondent. They think that if it was necessary to feed them upon short rations while we had Georgia & South Carolina to draw supplies from, and could get a large amount of provisions through the blockade vessels, now that both of these sources will probably be lost to us, it will be impossible to keep the army provisioned." Two weeks later, Alexander wrote, "Sherman however has troubled us greatly. We are now living on corn meal made from what ought to go to our horses, & the horses—poor things have to fill up with only four lbs of hay a day, & are pretty nearly starved." Lee monitored the advance carefully and sent Butler's Cavalry Division to rejuvenate his animals and to resist Sherman, but he lacked the strength to detach any more soldiers, for fear that Grant would crush his lines.[24]

Private Joseph Cox described "with the most hearte felt Sorrow" the "Deplorable condition" of his beloved Army of Northern Virginia. "Her once Galant men are fleeing to the mountains as though the Last Day had come," he lamented. "If Gabriel had already blown his Trumpet it Does not seame to me Grater Constination [consternation] Could Reign." Over the course of February and March, Lee's army lost on average about 120 men to desertion every day—comparable to an infantry brigade present for duty every ten days. Although Lee picked up an almost equal number through prisoner exchange in late February, most of those men were unfit for field duty, while many of the deserters at this stage of the war had fought long and hard for the Confederacy. Because of the limited food supply, the great distance home, or to avoid the stigma of desertion, substantial numbers fled to the Yankees, where at least they received respectable quantities of food. In one day in late February, 144 Rebels deserted to the Army of the Potomac, and two days earlier, 127 had fled to their lines. The Army of the James collected smaller numbers, but regularly a couple of dozen per day. "No army can endure such a drain, and ours will approach inevitable ruin if this thing is not remedied," a North Carolinian determined. "The men have an idea that all is lost, and that further carnage is useless."[25]

Not only did this mass exodus strip the army of valuable personnel, but it challenged those who stayed to rethink their commitment. Many were convinced that their comrades who left had simply admitted what should be apparent: The Confederate cause was hopeless. The mere fact that the Confederacy had to post pickets in the rear of the army spoke volumes. "It is useless to conceal the truth any longer," a North Carolinian declared. "Most of our people at home have become so demoralized that they write to their husbands, sons and brothers that desertion *now* is not *dishonorable*." A Virginian claimed that 2,200 men from Longstreet's Corps had deserted since the fall and that at least 100 per night abandoned the army. "In my opinion every man killed or wounded after this it will be cold blooded murder," he argued. "All know that it is useless for the war to be further persisted." When a captain from an Alabama regiment planned and executed a desertion, a fellow soldier exhibited great compassion. "Captain Reaves was not disloyal," the soldier insisted. "He could not stand the coming campaign." The soldier then elaborated, "He is like many another man. He may pass through 49 battles and in all conduct himself with courage and gallantry and in the 50 he may fail—his courage may be gone." Reaves had been a good officer who could no longer endure the strain of combat, and he gained sympathy. Pickets refused to fire on comrades who were deserting to the enemy or deliberately fired away from them. Troops even spoke and joked about it matter-of-factly, calling it "sending over commissioners."[26]

After all the sacrifices, suffering, and fallen comrades, many could not bring themselves to abandon the flag. Those old soldiers still possessed their reputation, one that they had earned on dozens of battlefields and through countless hardships. They had too much pride to throw it away in this final time of crisis. A Virginian informed his wife that if the army evacuated Virginia, desertion "would be ten times greater in such a case I can tell any one what I would do if I were to desert it would be a disgrace on me and my children for ever." A month later, as the situation worsened, he remained steady to the cause. "I still have faith," he wrote his wife in late February, "that god will not suffer the manful struggle that we are making in vane." An Alabamian felt likewise, even though he had no clothing, lived on short rations, and had not received pay in six months. "I can't See what a man can premise himself to desert his own Flag, bring *Disgrace* [upon] himself & family." At the end of March, a Texas sergeant and prewar physician detailed the sense of isolation he experienced as a result of losses. "I have friends here still," he wrote, "but all the nearest & dearest are gone & I am left alone, solitary among thousands." Yet he refused to leave the ranks. As a Virginian insisted to his sister, "We have no other alternative left us now, but to fight on with a determination and a will."[27]

And so they hoped that, somehow, a peace conference might bring an honorable end to the war. In early February, Lincoln met with Confederate Vice President Alexander Stephens and other officals as a preliminary discussion about terms of peace. Lincoln insisted on reunion and an end to slavery, and the meeting ended without progress. Agitation over the peace conference gave soldiers some hope. Its collapse did the opposite. Some of Lee's troops could not imagine another campaign like that of 1864. For others, it reaffirmed their belief that they must fight it out till they achieved victory. A month later, a Union general suggested to Longstreet that Lee and Grant open a dialogue. Lee made overtures to Grant, but the Union commander declined, stating that he had power to negotiate only on matters of a purely military nature. This exchange lacked the publicity of the Hampton Roads meeting of Lincoln and Stephens, and few of the soldiers knew about it.[28]

In desperation, the rebellion turned to African-Americans to offset the loss of manpower. Various official and unofficial debates had taken place over black military service in the Confederacy since the war began. Davis had suppressed a proposal by a talented general officer to develop this untapped source of manpower.

By early 1865, matters had changed. "Nearly every one succumbs to the notion that *slavery* is a doomed institution in any event," wrote Lawton to his wife, "though they differ much as to its slow or rapid death." The war had virtually destroyed slavery in Virginia, Tennessee, Louisiana, and Arkansas, and it had severely injured the institution in much of Mississippi and parts of Alabama, Georgia, Florida, South Carolina, and North Carolina. Even if the Confederacy gained its independence, slavery probably could not have existed in much of Virginia, Tennessee, and Arkansas, where the nation's boundaries abutted the Union. Only a war could have changed Southern attitudes so rapidly among some residents. After admitting that he had become "rather 'squeemish' now about fighting to uphold slavery," a soldier wrote, "This is an age of progress, and Slavery and 'progress' don't go together very well." He anticipated that ultimately, they would have to provide slaveholders with compensation for their bondspeople.[29]

In a strange way, the Confederacy had come around to a position that Lincoln had confronted more than two and a half years earlier. In response to a letter from New York newspaperman Horace Greeley, Lincoln had made it clear that saving the United States was paramount to him. He would free all the slaves, or none, toward that end. If he had to free some and keep others in slavery, he would do that, too. "What I do about slavery and the colored race, I do because I believe it helps to save the Union." So it had become for the Confederacy. What the nascent nation did with slavery, it did to preserve independence, even though it had sought independence to protect slavery. War had taken such a toll on Confederates and had generated so much animosity toward the Union that the ends and means of the war had reversed. As one of Lee's staff officers, Charles Marshall, argued in justification for the concept of black military service, "What benefit they expect their negroes to be to them, if the enemy occupy the country, it is impossible to say."[30]

The key to the legislative debate over the employment of black soldiers rested with Lee. Desperate for increased manpower, the army commander endorsed black military service to a state legislator and then supported the legislation, which had the approval of the Davis administration, in a letter to a congressman. "I think the measure not only expedient but necessary," Lee announced. "The enemy will certainly use them against us if he can get possession of them, and as his present numerical superiority will enable him to penetrate many parts of the country, I cannot see the wisdom of the policy of holding them to await his arrival, when we may, by timely action and judicious management, use them to arrest his progress." He believed the white population could not supply the manpower necessary for a protracted struggle, and under proper circumstances he believed blacks would make "efficient soldiers," as the Union had proven, though most Confederates denied it. With Lee's endorsement, the legislation wiggled through the House and narrowly passed by a solitary vote in the Senate. Davis signed it into law.[31]

For the most part, soldiers in Lee's army endorsed the concept. "I would rather join with the devil himself rather than submit to Yankee rule," a Virginian wrote. Hill Fitzpatrick, himself a small slave owner, acted the pragmatist when he wrote his beloved wife, Amanda, "I had much rather gain our independence without it but if necessary I say put them in and make them fight." Private Devereux endorsed the idea. "Put into the army every free negro in the country and as many slaves as Lee wants," he wrote to his sister. "Any thing to keep back the Yankees." He concluded, "it is our only chance and I would make them my equals rather than submit." It was an astonishing thought in 1865 in the South. Most Confederates were less high-minded, and agreed with a Georgia captain, who stated, "I am more than willing that a negroe should be shot at in my place."[32]

Lee was "anxious" to begin recruiting black soldiers, and he wanted to ensure that only competent and qualified white men received authorization to form units. Many candidates volunteered their services, and the 49th Georgia Infantry offered to integrate its regiment with black soldiers to bring it up to full strength and to have veterans work with the blacks to make them good troops quickly. "When in former years, for pecuniary purposes, we did not consider it disgraceful to labor with negroes in the field or at the same work bench," its officers attested, "we certainly will not look upon it in any other light at this time, when an end so glorious as our independence is to be achieved."[33]

Yet at the same time, a fair number of officers and men expressed doubts about the merits of the plan. Alexander thought it was "inhumane & unchristian & bad policy" to make blacks into soldiers, and he much preferred the government conscript 5,000 as a work force for the army. A North Carolina private had serious problems with the idea of black military service. A friend of his had spent eight months in a Yankee prison camp and "he was garded evry third day by the African beast." One day, his friend asked the black guard, "what ar you afighting us for[?] his reply is too mean for me to repete but in a mild manner," he wrote his brother and sister-in-law. "To Seduce your Sister." The Confederate then asked his brother and sister-in-law if they could live on equal terms with their family slave. For him, the notion of black armed service was outrageous. A Virginia soldier concurred. The act of bringing blacks into uniform undercut the entire purpose of the war. "For one," he recorded in his diary, "I prefer to fight on even to the end of my existence rather than submit to this hated idea of negro equality, and the employment of slaves as soldiers is nothing less." In an inspection report around the same time, a lieutenant warned the brigade officers not to assign a black teamster to ordnance wagons. The ordnance wagons sometimes came under fire, and if a teamster abandoned the field in fright, soldiers could not replenish their ammunition. Although he did not raise the issue of black soldiers directly, his remark alerted people to the question of reliability among black troops.[34]

A year after the war ended, Peter Alexander, a prominent journalist, suggested that had the Confederacy adopted black enlistment a year earlier, the Confederate government might have survived. In early March, Virginia private James Perkins challenged the effectiveness of the progress with a simple comment: "all the Kuffy's in the Confederate States might be armed organized and sent to to [sic] the field, but it would only be to starve to death." Then, he wondered where and how the Confederacy intended to feed 200,000 black soldiers "when the present Army scarcely gets enough to keep soul and Body together."[35]

His number was wildly wrong. By the end of the war, the Confederacy had raised only a few hundred black troops. They had no impact on fighting or campaigning. As Davis informed Lee on April 1, 1865, "I have been laboring, without much progress, to advance the raising of negro troops."[36]

There were no more men. The soldiers were exhausted. Hundreds of quality officers were killed or severely wounded. Supplies were scarce. Morale was all but crushed.[37]

In late February 1865, Lee attempted one more time to alter the culture of his army. He had to squeeze every ounce of performance from those he had on hand, and renewed discipline and commitment might just plug the desertion leak. Lee reminded officers and men that efficiency and safety required that everyone remain at their assigned posts. Congress had just passed legislation that removed from soldiers the power to elect junior second lieutenants. He would see to it that the individual chosen for the commission had distinguished himself for courage, discipline, and attention to duty. In addition, he would create file closers—one in every ten men per company—who would receive careful instruction in their duties. He would issue them Lance appointments and they would wear distinctive badges for their duty. On the march, they would prevent straggling. In battle, they would keep two paces behind the troops, with loaded guns and fixed bayonets. They would preserve order, enforce directives from officers, and "permit no man to leave his place, unless wounded." Lee authorized file closers to fire on delinquents and plunderers, who had seriously impaired the army's ability to fight with full strength. To general officers, Lee issued a circular that sought much greater discipline. The army commander believed that Confederate soldiers possessed great courage, but they relied on it too much, to the detriment of "those measures which would increase their efficiency and contribute to their safety." In a struggle against a much larger enemy force, it was imperative that the Confederacy bring the largest proportion of its men into battle. Soldiers needed to understand that discipline improved efficiency and also increased safety. "Disastrous surprises and those sudden panics which lead to defeat and the greatest loss of life, are of rare occurrence among disciplined troops," he insisted. Experience on many battlefields proved conclusively that commands that attacked most vigorously suffered fewer losses and almost always won. "The appearance of a steady, unbroken line is more formidable to the enemy, and renders his aim less accurate, and his fire less effective." He urged officers to impress upon the minds of their subordinate officers that they could foster discipline only through "constant watchfulness." Officers "must attend to the smallest particulars of detail." The key, Lee argued, was, "Men must be habituated to obey, or they cannot be controlled in battle, and the neglect of the least important order impairs the proper influence of officers." Troops did begin to drill and train, as much as their trench duties permitted. Perhaps under the right conditions, Lee's demands for change might have worked. Yet with an army living on so little, clothed so badly, and in a continual state of combat, it was too late. The Confederacy was in a death spiral, and it dragged Lee's army down with it.[38]

Still, tens of thousands stayed on to the very end. Many of them, like their army commander, placed their faith in God to see them through the crisis. As Sherman advanced through South Carolina, and Maj. Gen. John M. Schofield led an invasion of North Carolina, while Grant's giant command slowly strangled the Army of Northern Virginia, Lee held to that conviction, writing, "trusting in a Merciful God, who does not always give the battle to the strong, I pray we may not be overwhelmed." Veteran soldiers had witnessed how the hand of God had saved them in battle, when others fell. If the Omnipotent had shielded their lowly life, then surely God would intervene to save a worthy cause like the Confederacy. It was their last refuge. "It is in vain to trust any arm of the flesh for deliverance," a Virginian wrote his aunt in mid-March. God had delivered into Gideon's hand the power to crush his vast enemies. Surely he could save the Confederacy.[39]

Others took too much pride in their service to give up at this critical hour. A Georgia private vowed to his mother that he did not want any man or woman to "look at me with Scorn and contempt" because he deserted. In February 1865, Hill Fitzpatrick earned a well-deserved furlough. On his way back to Virginia, he was cut off by Sherman's army. It would have been easy for Fitzpatrick to remain at home. In fact, the other seventeen in his group never made it back. But Fitzpatrick had long harbored resentment for deserters. In May 1863, he had pledged to his wife, "So help me God Cout, my bones will bleech the hills of Virginia before they shall have me up for that." He had to walk 180 of the 550 miles from his home outside Macon, Georgia, to Virginia. The trip took him eighteen days, and he arrived just in time for the final battles around Petersburg. Fitzpatrick suffered a mortal wound on April 2 and fell into Yankee hands. They buried him in Manchester, Virginia.[40]

Soldiers stayed, too, because of their implicit faith in Lee. Time after time, he had led the Army of Northern Virginia to victory. He had earned their trust and confidence, and the burdens of military service in late winter and early spring 1865 could not shake that belief. "But of one thing I am sure," a private wrote his mother, "I will follow where Bob Lee leads. He will do what is best." After a camp discussion in which most Virginians argued they would desert if the Army of Northern Virginia evacuated the state, a sergeant informed his sister he would not be one of them. "I have thought the matter over calmly & seriously & have made up my mind to follow that great & good man Robt. E. Lee wherever he may lead[,] to success or to ruin if it must be."[41]

Chapter 35

---◦◦---

THE FINAL DAYS

Lee knew he could not hold out much longer. In a letter to the aggrieved widow of Brig. Gen. John Pegram, who fell at Hatcher's Run on February 6, Lee hinted at the coming of the end when he consoled her, "As dear as your husband was to you, as necessary apparently to his Country & as important to his friends, I feel assured it was best for him to go at the moment he did." Ten days later, he exhibited concern for his wife, Mary, and the children, who boarded in Richmond. After expressing his fear of the Grant-Sherman-Schofield combination converging on the Army of Northern Virginia, maintaining that they "seem to have everything their own way," he pledged, "I shall however endeavour to do my duty & fight to the last." He then wondered about the fate of his wife and family. "Should it be necessary to abandon our position to prevent being surrounded, what will you do? Will you remain in the city? You must consider the question & make up your mind. You will be able to retain nothing in the house, & I do not see how you can live, or where to go." He then admitted, "It is a fearful condition & we must rely for guidance & protection upon a kind Providence."[1]

Several days before writing to his wife, Lee had already begun preparations for the flight of his army. He suspended all leaves of absence and furloughs south of North Carolina, fearing Sherman's army would cut anyone beyond that off and would keep them from returning. Lee warned the secretary of war that the government should prepare in the event that Confederate armies had to abandon their cities. He gave Walter Taylor orders to ready the headquarters for a march. Within days, the army commander told authorities that he might have to abandon Richmond toward Burkeville and Lynchburg, and that officials should transfer supplies from the capital.[2]

Lee had come to the conclusion that the fall of Richmond would not necessarily end the war. "If the army can be maintained in an efficient condition," he wrote the secretary of war on March 9, "I do not regard the abandonment of our present position as necessarily fatal to our success." His army required food and forage, positioned to the west along his route of retreat, and he would count on victory to secure ordnance from the enemy and buoy spirits to compensate for no pay and inadequate clothing. The Commissary Department believed it could supply enormous amounts of food, plenty to sustain the army into the next harvest, with proper money and transportation. Although both major Confederate armies drew supplies from the State of North Carolina, placing a great burden on its people, Quartermaster General Lawton thought the state could sustain the army's animals for three months. Lawton also suggested that despite its insufficiency, the army had received more clothing in the previous three months than ever before, and his supplies of shoes were larger than those of any other article. That, too, would have to sustain them for some time to come.[3]

With the Sherman juggernaut slashing through the Carolinas, and Schofield in Wilmington prepared to reinforce Sherman, the Confederacy could temporize no longer. Once Sherman's columns reached the Roanoke River, the Army of Northern Virginia would have to abandon the Richmond-Petersburg line due to supply problems. Lee decided to attack and penetrate Grant's works and roll up his line. This would force the Yankee commander to constrict his position, which would free Lee to detach substantial reinforcements to North Carolina. There, Lee's old friend, Joseph E. Johnston, was back in command. With significantly increased strength, Johnston could then attempt to crush Sherman's columns. It was a desperate, almost preposterous undertaking, but it was also their best option. After careful planning, John B. Gordon launched a surprise predawn attack on the Union lines at Fort Stedman, to the northeast of Petersburg. With nearly his entire corps and two additional brigades, plus a cavalry division waiting to exploit a breakthrough, Gordon sent advance parties to open pathways through Confederate abatis and seize the advanced Union pickets. Axmen then cleared Union obstructions, and attackers stormed the works. Gordon planned superbly, and his lead elements executed brilliantly. In the moments before sunrise, they quickly secured Fort Stedman and some surrounding batteries. But the Federals were too numerous, too well equipped, and too responsive for the plan to work. Once the sun rose and Union batteries targeted Confederates by sight, the attack collapsed. The Rebels lost some 2,700 men, the vast majority as prisoners of war. Grant, moreover, assumed that Lee had denuded other portions of his line to accumulate enough force to launch the attack on Fort Stedman. He ordered an attack to the west, which seized Confederate pickets but could not penetrate the main line.[4]

Within days of Lee's failed attack at Fort Stedman, Grant undertook a new movement on the western flank. Sheridan had returned from northern Virginia with his potent cavalry, mounted well and armed with repeating rifles. Grant hoped to exploit this mobility and firepower with a crushing blow to sever the Southside Railroad and turn Lee out of Petersburg. Under Sheridan's command, the horsemen would swing on a wide flank to Dinwiddie Court House while infantry advanced on a tighter loop past old battlegrounds to secure the crossroads. To counter this movement, Lee detached Pickett with five infantry brigades and two cavalry divisions under Fitz Lee. On March 31, after Sheridan occupied Dinwiddie Court House, the two sides clashed, with the Confederates pushing back the Yankees. That night, Union reinforcements from the Fifth Corps marched to Sheridan. Early on April 1, Pickett withdrew to Five Forks, a valued crossroad, and fortified a position near White Oak Road, the east-west thoroughfare. It took much of the day for Sheridan to position his forces, but shortly after 4:00 P.M. he struck around the Confederate left flank and into the rear. At the time, Pickett had assumed no major fighting would take place and was far to the rear, enjoying baked shad with Fitz Lee and Brig. Gen. Thomas Rosser. He had left no one in charge. Hearing distant gunfire, he responded only slowly. Without someone to direct action, his men failed to coordinate effectively and suffered a disastrous rout, losing more than 3,000 casualties—again, most as prisoners. Lee rushed reinforcements out to protect the remnants of Pickett's columns and began planning his army's retreat. A few days later, he ordered Pickett relieved from the Army of Northern Virginia.[5]

The next day at 4:00 A.M., Grant followed up the success at Five Forks with an assault all along the line. From the picket areas Federals had seized a week earlier, Union forces crashed through the Rebel works. A. P. Hill had rushed into the fight, attempting to rally his men, when a bullet struck him down. A mile and a half to the northeast at Fort Gregg, Confederates fought desperately against white and black soldiers, exhausting their ammunition and then using rocks, clubs, and bayonets to keep back the blue tide. They failed. Lee tried to inspire and direct his men in the early afternoon, and in the course of the fight he exposed himself to a "most terrific fire from the enemy light batteries." Shells and solid shot showered him, although he escaped uninjured. Lee's personal intervention accomplished nothing. The Federals had crushed his line and secured control of the Southside Railroad. Late that night, Lee ordered the Confederate defenders to abandon Richmond and Petersburg.[6]

RICHMOND SMOLDERED. AMID the crackle of burning tobacco warehouses and the periodic explosion of ignited ammunition and arms that the Confederacy could not carry, skittish and dispirited soldiers scurried toward safety westward. Lee's men knew the end was near. For some days, they had expended excessively large amounts of ammunition in battle, rather than risk their own lives. "In fact in all our recent fights," reported Lee's ordnance officer, "I noticed an apparent nervousness on the part of our men and of the enemy causing an unusual rapidity of fire either at random or at ranges too great to be effective." No one wanted to be killed or wounded in the closing moments of a losing war. Somehow, against all evidence, a few clung to hope of some miracle that Lee or God would save them and the Confederacy. "I must not despair," a Louisiana private scribbled in his diary. "Lee will bring order out of chaos, and with the help of our Heavenly Father, all will be well."[7]

Although Lee may have wanted to abandon Richmond and Petersburg sooner, he could not do so. His animals were too weak and too few to chance a

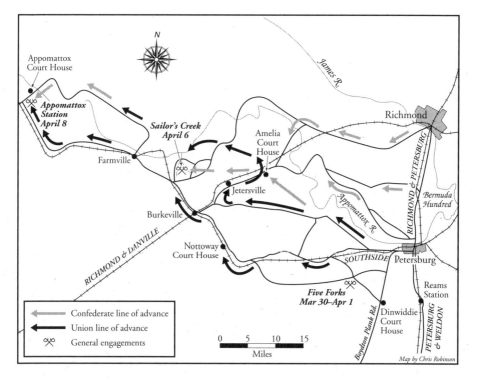

Retreat to Appomattox

retreat. Now, he had no choice, and the reduced numbers and strength of his animals, on top of the poor conditions of the roads, slowed the advance painfully and made each day's march more difficult.[8]

His beloved soldiers, too, fared disastrously on the retreat. Their physical deterioration from poor conditioning prevented thousands from keeping up over the next few days. Unlike previous campaigns during which soldiers purposely straggled, many just could not keep up on this march. For months, Lee's army had lived on a diet that lacked half of the necessary protein to maintain muscle mass and provided less than two-thirds the necessary calories to sustain body mass. The diet, largely a quarter pound of beef, two pints of coarse cornmeal, and occasional small amounts of molasses, was woefully deficient in most vitamins, resulting in weakness and problems in absorbing protein, minerals, and vitamins, with soldiers suffering skin ailments, night blindness, anemia, scurvy, and diarrhea. In a telling assessment, Dr. J. W. Powell, medical director for the Third Corps, commented on the corps inspection report in February, "While there was not found much absolute sickness existing, there were many weak and feeble men, who cannot be relied upon to undergo any great physical exertions." Thousands dropped out of the retreat march, some falling into Yankee hands and others working their way toward home.[9]

At Amelia Court House, close to fifty miles from Richmond and Petersburg, Lee's army arrived on the morning of April 4, looking for food. Several weeks earlier, Lee had prepositioned ammunition and, he thought, food and fodder there. Upon his arrival with the army, he was dismayed to discover nothing to eat. Lee's troops had to spend the day hunting up food and forage with limited success. Meanwhile, Ewell, the commander of the Department of Richmond, had picked up Kershaw's Division and moved with his own troops from Richmond toward Amelia Court House. When he reached the Appomattox River, no pontoon bridge awaited him, and his command had to trudge southward and plank the Richmond & Danville Railroad bridge to cross. His supply wagons, however, took a "safer" route, and much was lost to a Union cavalry raid. Custis Lee's Division would go without food that day.[10]

This delay to forage gave Sheridan a chance to slice off a large chunk of Lee's army at Saylor's Creek on April 6. Union troops occupied Jetersville, which blocked Lee's route to Burkeville. Instead, Lee swung around toward Farmville, where supplies in Burkeville could reach his dwindling army by rail, and he could then head south to link with Johnston's command in North Carolina. Harassment from Union cavalry slowed Anderson's Division, along with Ewell's troops and Gordon's Division, and they lost contact with Longstreet's columns ahead of them. On Ewell's directive, Gordon, the rear guard, took the supply train and his division along a safer route. Before Anderson and Ewell could determine how to proceed, a combination of Union infantry, artillery, and cavalry enveloped both Confederate flanks and utterly crushed them. Anderson, Pickett, and Bushrod Johnson escaped. Ewell stayed behind, trying to rally his whipped men, and fell into Union hands. Federals then caught up to Gordon and struck with superior numbers. Gordon fought them off until early evening, when Federals delivered a crushing blow and "drove him from the field in much confusion."[11]

The Saylor's Creek disaster marked the beginning of the very end for Lee's army. Not only did it lose 8,000 men and large numbers of guns and wagons, but the battle was emblematic of the collapse of the army's fighting prowess. Exhausted physically and emotionally, the men of the Army of Northern Virginia could no longer resist the vicious strikes of the Union army. Sheridan and his command sensed the Confederates' enervated condition and closed for the kill. An artillery lieutenant who lost most of his battalion at Saylor's Creek informed his girlfriend, "For eight days, I have been in the saddle—night & day—sword in hand, & we have had more desperate fighting than I have ever seen before." On the night of April 6, Lee told Pendleton, "it was all over— Ewell's Corps captured, Anderson dispersed, Gordon's the only organized body of troops in the whole left wing." Only Longstreet's Corps remained intact.[12]

Once again, the army continued its march at night, stumbling into Farmville that morning. There, officials issued rations, but before everyone could receive food, Lee had to withdraw the trains, fearing the Union would attack once more. Lee resumed the retreat toward Appomattox Court House. Longstreet continued to issue marching orders, insisting that his men travel according to the tactics manual. "Straggling will be prevented by the exercise of every exertion," Lee's "Old War Horse" insisted. By nightfall on April 8, the lead elements had filtered into Appomattox Court House. Yet straggling persisted. The army was dissolving.[13]

On April 7, Grant made an overture to Lee for the surrender of the Army of Northern Virginia, suggesting that "the last week must convince you of the hopelessness of further resistance." Lee thought it was premature, but asked what terms Grant would offer. The Union army commander replied the next day that all he insisted upon was "that the men and officers surrendered shall be disqualified for taking up arms again against the Government of the United States until properly exchanged." He offered to meet Lee personally or to designate representatives to draft terms at any location Lee suggested. On the evening of the eighth, Lee refused to surrender, stating, "To be frank, I do not think the emergency has arisen to call for the surrender of this army." He still had some sliver of hope of slipping through the Union dragnet. Lee did offer to negotiate on behalf of all Confederate armies, a proposal Grant quickly rebuffed. Lincoln had conveyed to Grant that he was not in favor of any negotiations for surrender beyond those for the army in his front.[14]

Lee still had one final chance. He laid his correspondence before his corps commanders, with Fitz Lee present. Yankee cavalrymen had blocked their passage westward, and the group decided that Fitz Lee's men, supported by Gordon's troops, would spearhead an attack to rock back the Union horsemen enough for the army to slip through the pursuit. If Federal infantry had arrived, they were to notify Lee, who would then agree to terms. The original intention was to strike at 1:00 A.M., but the muffled sound of troops shuffling into place convinced the army commander to delay the movement until first light, so that Fitz Lee and Gordon could see what kind of opposition confronted them. At first, the attack drove back enemy cavalry, but then resistance stiffened. Large bodies of Union infantry arrived to close off the escape route.

Around 10:00 A.M., as Fitz Lee directed the fighting, a Federal volley from one hundred yards zipped past everyone, except for one projectile that struck Charles Minnigerode, Fitz's aide-de-camp and the son of a distinguished Episcopal clergyman in Richmond, in the back. Minnegerode went down with a shriek, and Fitz Lee dropped from his horse to comfort his favorite staff member. The cavalry commander stayed with him, weeping, until the Union troops were nearly on top of them, and they had to leave. Shortly afterward, Fitz Lee received a note from his uncle stating all were to cease fire. He was surrendering the army.[15]

Minnegerode lived, only to commit suicide twenty-three years later. At least he survived the war. John Wesley Richards, a twenty-five-year-old private in the 58th North Carolina, the son of a poor laborer, was not so lucky. According to official sources, he had survived Saylor's Creek, only to suffer a mortal wound at Appomattox. They were two among 500 casualties on both sides that day.[16]

Lee requested Grant meet him to accept the surrender of the Confederate army on the terms the Union commander had offered. It took some time to arrange a temporary truce and to contact Grant. Lee, resplendent in his best uniform, along with his aide Charles Marshall and Grant's aide Orville Babcock, settled on the McLean House, owned by the same family who lived amid the battleground at First Manassas, for the drafting of terms. Grant arrived an hour later in a dirty uniform with only the insignia of a lieutenant general on his shoulders. After some slightly awkward conversation, Lee drew them to the business at hand. Grant drafted terms that paroled the men of the Army of Northern Virginia as long as they agreed not to take up arms against the United States unless properly exchanged. According to the terms, "officers and men will be allowed to return to their home, not to be disturbed by U.S. authority so long as they observe their paroles and the laws in force where they may reside." They would surrender weapons, although officers could keep their sidearms, and those who owned horses could take them home. While staff copied the agreement, Lee commented that his men and their Yankee prisoners needed food. Grant directed Sheridan to provide it.[17]

In General Orders, No. 9, a farewell to his troops, Lee stated they had been "compelled to yield to overwhelming numbers and resources." To President Davis ten days later, Lee blamed the "moral condition" of the army for the defeat. "The operations which occurred while the troops were in the entrenchments in front of Richmond and Petersburg were not marked by the boldness and decision which formerly characterized them. Except in particular instances, they were feeble; and a want of confidence seemed to possess officers and men.

This condition, I think, was produced by the state of feeling in the country and the communications received by the men from their homes, urging their return and the abandonment of the field." Both were correct. The Rebels confronted vast Union superiority, and over the course of four years, it had worn down the Confederacy. Yet, as Lee also knew, Confederate defeat was no foregone conclusion.[18]

The war might have turned out differently. As Alexander later explained Confederate strategy, the objective was "that the desperation of her resistance would finally exact from her adversary such a price in blood & treasure as to exhaust the enthusiasm of its population for the objects of war." He then elaborated, "We could not hope to *conquer* her. Our one chance was to wear her out." The Confederacy had to punish Union attempts to conquer it so severely that those blows would discourage the Yankees from further attempts and lead them to give up. It was not an impossible hope. The Army of Northern Virginia came close to convincing the Union to quit the fight. More than one in every three Union soldiers (approximately 36.4 percent) who died in battle fell at the hands of Lee's troops, and they inflicted well over half (56.4 percent) of all Yankee wounds in combat. In the last year of the war, Grant's forces sustained almost 127,000 casualties against the Army of Northern Virginia.[19]

Throughout the war, the Army of Northern Virginia was the most successful institution in the Confederacy. For nearly four long years, it fought off Union commands with vastly superior numbers and resources. Over time, Lee and his troops came to symbolize the viability of their rebellion. They drew the Confederate people together and fostered a spirit of nationalism. The Confederate Constitution created a government; Lee's army built a nation. Rebel soldiers and civilians believed Lee's army was unconquerable. Even Yankees grasped the central role of Lee's army in the Confederacy. As long as Lee's army existed, the rebellion survived.

"Certainly never was there such an Army in ancient or modern times," an artillerist informed his mother. A Virginian pronounced in February 1863, "the idea of a defeat never occurs to them so great is their confidence in their own prowess, and the skill of their generals." As a surgeon wandered through the camps, he could not help but marvel to his children, "these are the men who won victories around Richmond and in Northern Virginia, and in truth whenever they have met the enemy, I ask myself the question, am I in truth in the midst of these actors in those immortal deeds." Before Appomattox, one soldier knew the defeat of the Army of Northern Virginia would spell the collapse of the Confederacy, but he did not think it possible. Lee "is a hard oald hors to handel." Another soldier, in Tennessee with Longstreet and longing for service with Lee again, called him "my favorite Gen (Robert E. Lee) [and] the best man of the age." On the eve of the spring offensive in 1864, a North Carolinian boasted that Grant "had better look sharp for Genl. Robert E. Lee when he attempted to cross the river. He will find a different set of men to fight here than he ever fought in Tennessee. He will fight men who never heard of the[m] being whipped and more than that men who love to obey and follow their leader." As late as mid-December 1864, when Sherman's army was on the verge of capturing Savannah, A. P. Hill resigned himself to the notion that it all rested on the shoulders of Lee's army. "I suppose now we shall, in addition to Grant, have Sherman on our hands too," he commented to his wife. "Well, the Army of Northern Virginia is equal to it, and however much you task its powers will always respond, and I hope successfully."[20]

In the eyes of the Confederate people, Lee's army emerged as the embodiment of its revolutionary cause. Confederate civilians developed such unbounded faith in Lee and his soldiers that up until the end they could not imagine the destruction of the army. Catherine Edmondston recalled how people once referred to Lee as " '*old-stick-in-the-mud*' " and recited a litany of his failures, perceived or real. "Should any one now dare to remember or to apply that sobriquet to him their heads would to a certainty be broken, if not by one of his men by a civilian. Such is [the] confidence & affectionate trust we all repose in him," she wrote. " 'Marse Robert' can do any & all things." Reports of those bloody battles in Virginia during the spring of 1864 reached Monroe, Louisiana, where Sarah Lois Wadley kept the faith. "Our confidence in Lee has never once faltered," she wrote approvingly, "may he prove victorious again!" Even as late as mid-March 1865, Emma LeConte in South Carolina maintained her faith in the Army of Northern Virginia. When she heard rumors that Richmond had fallen, she recorded in her diary, "where is the ray of hope? Only to Gen. Lee and his poor little half-starved army can the people look—yet an army that has never suffered defeat, a contrast to the Western Army."[21]

Lee's army achieved such extraordinary success that it altered Union policies and perceptions. Through the Battle of Gettysburg, the army had fought so well that opposing generals believed Lee's army outnumbered the Army of the Potomac. Secretary of War Edwin M. Stanton insisted "peace can be had only when Lee's army is beaten, captured, or dispersed." Prominent Republican senator Charles Sumner agreed: "when Lee's army is out of the way, the whole Rebellion will disappear." The Army of Northern Virginia was so successful that Lincoln, Stanton, and others fixated on its destruction.[22]

As the Union commanders applied those overwhelming Federal numbers and resources more efficiently, culminating with the work of Grant and Sherman, they began to tear the Confederate national fabric to shreds. The continual strain on the army and the entire nation unraveled almost every facet of the war effort and Confederate life. No one remained untouched by the calamity. Against this, the Confederacy had to mobilize a greater preponderance of its men and supplies and maximize their usage. It had a much narrower margin for error than the Union, and it had to use its soldiers and supplies much more carefully.

Confederates embraced the notion that Southern society and culture imbued them with superior martial skills, including courage. Early in the war, they had little doubt that each Confederate soldier was worth at least three times as many Yankees. In time, they tempered that ratio, but battle after battle demonstrated their martial prowess against overwhelming Federal numbers and resources. In a test of true character, such as hand-to-hand combat, there was no competition. "Southern steel proves too much for them when born by men moved with more than human strength," a Virginian argued. Confederates were confident that they fought for a just cause and believed that men struggling for independence possessed great moral advantages over their oppressors. And they had great hopes that a just God would look kindly upon a people battling oppression.[23]

Repeatedly, Lee drew on his troops' confidence and courage to defeat much larger enemy forces. On many occasions, Lee touted them as the best combat soldiers in the world, and as late as May 1864, Lee reported to Davis, "The courage of this army was never better, and I fear no injury to it from any retrograde movement that may be dictated by some sound military policy." Confederate soldiers possessed unusual confidence in their military prowess. They fought audaciously, often compensating for tactical errors and insufficient or inadequate supplies, equipment, and numbers.[24]

But Southern culture brought with it a baggage that Lee never seemed to combat effectively. Confederates came from a society that encouraged independence and independent-mindedness. They did not take orders or discipline well and often did what they wanted, not what their officers directed. It took hard work by Lee to convince them that manual labor was not beneath them and that it saved lives. When it came to breaking soldiers of the practices of leaving the line with wounded comrades, just drifting away from combat because they did not feel like fighting, or plundering in the midst of battle, he failed.

Efforts to discipline the soldiers never took hold because the officers, even some of the West Pointers, came from Southern society and had many of the same values as their men. Southerners applauded a kind of profligacy and inattention to detail, an attitude they brought into the Confederate army. Many officers acted as though details were beneath them, and this behavior undercut effective leadership and administration. Great in battle, they tended to be poor and unresponsive in camp, when they should have been busy disciplining and drilling their troops, mastering their own responsibilities, and preparing the men for the next campaign. On the regimental and battery level, soldiers chose officers from that society, men who reflected their values. Replacement officers came from the enlisted ranks, and the fresh influx of recruits and occasional furloughs revived those cultural links to the world at home. By the time Lee took command in June 1862, that army culture had already set firmly. Lee tried to crack it, but without the full and constant support of vigilant officers, he merely chipped away at the edges.

No doubt, supply shortages and declining productivity hurt the Confederate war effort. Agricultural productivity unquestionably slipped over the course of the war as the Confederacy placed 18 percent of its white population in uniform, the majority of them farmers. Women compensated for some of that loss, but they had other obligations to their families and could not bring in the same-size harvest. To offset the loss of personnel to the army, the Confederacy hoped to rely on slave labor. Many slaves instead ran off to Union lines, slowed their work pace, or labored for the railroads or the army.

Still, the Confederacy did not fail from a lack of agricultural output; it simply had to use what it produced more efficiently. Although people at home wrote letters to loved ones and politicians expressing fear of starvation, and in some cases claiming it, there is no evidence of any significant starvation, other than in prisoner-of-war camps. War, like all cataclysms, affected the poor more than any other element of society. The poorest people, most likely, suffered from a very slow starvation much as Lee's soldiers did. Those in rural areas fared better than urban dwellers. At least they could grow their own nourishment. People in cities, like those in Lee's army around Petersburg, relied on a faltering currency and a failing transportation network to supply them. In the last weeks of the war, the Confederacy possessed plenty of rations for Lee's troops and hay and fodder for its animals; it lacked reliable money to pay for it and the transportation system to deliver it. Trains ran so slowly, derailed so frequently, and could pull so few cars that the army could not accumulate enough supplies in Richmond. In February 1865, Davis finally removed the unpopular Commissary General Northrop and replaced him with Isaac M. St. John. Almost immediately, supplies improved a bit, and everyone credited him. In fact, logistics was a very complicated and slow process with a lengthy lead time. St. John merely benefited from actions that others had undertaken weeks, sometimes months, earlier. He certainly might have improved upon the work of Northrop—virtually everyone seemed to like him more and expected matters to improve—but he had been in office only six weeks when Lee abandoned Richmond and Petersburg.[25]

Industry suffered a similar fate. During the course of the war, the Confederacy developed factories to produce war's necessities, and they achieved phenomenal results, but they suffered from ineffective quality control, particularly in ordnance and clothing. As Federal armies marched through the Confederacy, disrupting communities, destroying railroads, and severing commercial ties with the outside world, it became more and more difficult for factories to procure raw materials, let alone produce munitions and clothing. Once they did produce these military necessities, there was no assurance they could deliver them to the armies in the field with their decrepit transportation network.[26]

This inability of the Confederacy to provide its soldiers with basic items—food, clothing, and quality weapons and ammunition—compelled them to take matters into their own hands. Much of that indiscipline about which Lee complained consisted of citizen-soldiers taking for themselves what their nation failed to give them.

THE INSTITUTION OF slavery, upon which the Confederacy hoped to rely, suffered disastrously during the war. In some states, such as Virginia, it was critically injured; elsewhere, with the exception of Texas and perhaps Florida, slavery was badly damaged. The fealty that some Confederates expected, moreover, proved illusory. Slaves ran away, slowed their work, and were more aggressive as they partially filled the power void that formed when huge numbers of white males rushed off to the army. The war proved transformative, and though the Confederacy undertook secession to preserve slavery, after nearly four years of war, the government narrowly decided to employ slaves as soldiers, just as their enemy had done two and a half years earlier.[27]

There was broad support for the war in all economic strata of Confederate society. It was hardly a rich man's war and a poor man's fight. Three of every four households in the slaveholding states did not own slaves in 1860, yet four of every nine soldiers in Lee's army came from slaveholding households. Over 37 percent either owned slaves themselves, or the parents or family members with whom they resided in 1860 owned slaves. There certainly were poor people in Lee's army. Nearly 20 percent had no appreciable wealth, according to the 1860 census, but 20 percent of the soldiers in the army, or their family with whom they lived, were worth more than $10,000, a very substantial sum. Fewer than one in every twenty farmers in Lee's army owned no land. It was, in short, a rich, poor, and middle-class war. Rich and poor tended to be overrepresented, because the skilled workers were kept at their jobs by design. All social classes supported the institution of slavery for racial, familial, friendship, and economic reasons. Once war broke out, all those groups rallied around the flag. Those who were killed or wounded in action were 20 percent more likely to be from a slaveholding family, and they were more than 10 percent richer than noncasualties. Deserters tended to own fewer slaves and came from poorer households than those who stayed with the army, representing the centrality of the slave issue. No doubt, the harsh conditions of war fell harder on the poor, but the wealthy did not dodge their obligations to serve and fight.[28]

The Army of Northern Virginia had some of the toughest fighting and incurred some of the greatest losses in American history. For the entire war, close to 30,000 of these soldiers were killed in action and more than 125,000 were wounded. Nearly one in every four soldiers died, with a slightly higher percentage falling in battle rather than succumbing to disease. Four of every ten soldiers in Lee's army were either killed in battle or wounded at least once, and five of every nine soldiers were killed, wounded, or captured before the final surrender. Six percent of Lee's army suffered multiple wounds and almost another 10 percent endured some combination of wounds and imprisonment. By factoring in those who were discharged for disabilities, almost three of every four soldiers who ever served in the Army of Northern Virginia were killed, died of disease, wounded, captured, or discharged for a disability. That statistic rises to more than 80 percent when those who deserted are factored out of the equation.[29]

The Confederacy could not replace those men lost to combat or illness. Virginia and neighboring states had largely emptied their manpower pools and had very little in the pipeline. A study by the Conscription Bureau on September 30, 1864, determined that in Virginia only 2,719 males would reach the age of seventeen over the next year. Demographics worked against the Army of Northern Virginia, and Lee knew it.[30]

Over time, the powerful link between the military and civilian worlds damaged the spirit of commitment within Lee's army. Civilians lived in fear for the well-being of loved ones in military service, and soldiers grew increasingly concerned about the impact of wartime hardships on family and friends. North Carolina was divided over the benefits of secession, and that split spilled over into the early stages of the war. The staggering battlefield losses of North Carolina soldiers in 1863 and 1864 fueled those tensions. In 1864, the destruction from Sheridan's Valley Campaign and especially from Sherman's march through Georgia triggered substantial desertions as soldiers returned home to care for their families. As Sherman's army pushed into South Carolina, the devastation sparked massive desertions and denied Lee's army valuable food and other supplies, worsening conditions in the field and inducing more soldiers to flee for home or the enemy. The spiral of defeat dragged down the Confederacy and Lee's army with it. And once the army yielded Richmond and Petersburg to the Yankees, huge number of Virginians gave up and headed home.[31]

Ultimately, the Army of Northern Virginia did not collapse because of Southern culture, industry, agriculture, slavery, motivations, manpower shortages, discontent at home, or any other solitary factor. Intense and sustained Union pressure caused serious fissures in all these areas, collectively bringing down the army and the Confederacy. Four long years of war damaged or disrupted virtually every aspect of Confederate life. The demoralization to which Lee referred was a consequence of all these problems, not a cause.

The men in Lee's army faced incredibly difficult service. Barely two weeks after Appomattox, Pvt. Carl Henninghausen, a German-born soldier in the 15th Virginia, wrote his mother about his military experiences. "My idea at the beginning of this was that it would come to two or three battles at most and in three months everything would be over," he admitted. "We soon found out that military service in southern America is no child's play, and we had to sweat for having bound ourselves to it for a year." Henninghausen reported, "Old German soldiers in our company would rather have served five years of German service than one year here." He recalled his first fight, at Bethel Church, where an inferior number of Confederates routed the Yankees from the field. "Would to God they had won then," he wrote in frustration, "but there was no courage in the fellows."[32]

At the McLean house, Grant signed the copied agreement. Lieutenant Colonel Marshall drafted a brief acceptance of those terms and handed it to the army commander. Lee signed the document, surrendering the Army of Northern Virginia, and handed it to Grant. Four years of hardship and sacrifice were over.[33]

As Lee returned to his camp, Rebel soldiers rushed to him. He confirmed what all had suspected—the army had capitulated. When he reached camp, Lee gravitated toward an apple tree, where he remained all afternoon. Alexander, meanwhile, formed his artillerists along the road, where Lee would have to pass to reach his headquarters, hoping to pay a silent tribute. As Lee rode along the peaceful gauntlet, discipline failed them one last time. Men broke ranks and rushed to their commander.[34]

The next day, Lee and Marshall wrote General Orders, No. 9, Lee's farewell to the army, in his ambulance. "After concluding the tears ran down the old hero's cheeks," staff officer Giles B. Cooke recorded, "and he gave way—for the first time that I ever knew him to do so since my connection with him." He was not the only Confederate who wept that day. Lee spent much of his remaining time signing copies of General Orders, No. 9, for soldiers who sought it, and greeting visitors at his headquarters. He preserved his dignity and coolness throughout the day.[35]

Before the fighting in late March, Lee commanded approximately 67,000 men, according to his estimate. Only 7,892 infantrymen and a couple of thousand artillery and cavalry kept up with the army. Over the next few days, as Yankees paroled them, large numbers poured into Appomattox to surrender. By April 12, 26,018 had consented to a parole.[36]

On April 20, Lee reported to Davis that in his opinion, "an army can not be organized and supported in Virginia," and so far as he could tell the people east of the Mississippi River had no heart left for war. "A partisan war may be continued, and hostilities protracted," he advised the president, "causing individual suffering and the devastation of the country; but I see no prospect by that means of achieving a separate independence." Of course, Lee reassured Davis respectfully, the decision was the president's. "To save useless effusion of blood, I would recommend measures be taken for suspension of hostilities and the restoration of peace."[37]

Word of the army's surrender struck Confederate supporters like a bolt of lightning. Many had thought that Lee's army was invincible, and that somehow, the general and his men would extricate themselves from the disastrous loss of Richmond. The army had come to symbolize a dream, which now vanished with the news. "How can I write it?" Catherine Edmondston expressed her feelings. "How find words to tell what has befallen us? *Gen Lee has surrendered!* Surrendered the remnant of his noble Army to an overwhelming horde of mercenary Yankee knaves & foreigners." She simply could not believe it. That *"Lee,* Lee upon whom hung the hopes of the whole country, should be a prisoner seems too dreadful to be realized!" When Sarah Dawson learned the news, she wrote,

"Everyone cried, but I would not," trusting that God would save them "even though all should apparently be lost." From the prison camp in Elmira, New York, Pvt. W. W. Gramling of the 5th Florida Infantry described prisoners' reactions to the news as mixed. "Some seem to rejoice—" he recorded, "while others lament the capture of so noble an army." As rumors circulated throughout Tyler, Texas, about the surrender of the Army of Northern Virginia, Kate Stone admitted, "All this is too dreadful to believe." Five days later, she insisted that everyone was depressed. Unwilling to accept the outcome, Stone revealed, "I cannot bear to hear them talk of defeat." But they were.[38]

Soldiers signed paroles and headed home. Many families waited for weeks, sometimes months, as soldiers in Lee's army walked home. Along the way, they took food from civilians. They had no choice.[39]

Lee and his staff signed their paroles and began the dreary ride home. On April 16, around 3:00 P.M., Lee and his remaining staff rode into Richmond. They were greeted by the smell of charred ruins and the sights of wholesale destruction. According to an eyewitness, "The chieftain looked fatigued, and rode along at a jaded gait." People applauded and doffed hats respectfully, and Lee responded with "affable dignity." Several times, people attempted to rally cheers for him, but failed. Near his home on Franklin Street, crowds cheered him with greater success. As he pulled up to the house, he descended from his horse and immediately uncovered his head in acknowledgment of them. A small crowd rushed him to shake hands. Lee responded courteously but silently. When he had greeted all of them, Lee bowed to the crowd, turned, and ascended the steps. Several cried out for a speech, but he paid no heed. He extended his hand, opened the door, and entered the house. For Robert E. Lee, the war was over.[40]

PRIVATE THOMAS PETTY, the Washington, D.C., clerk who lost friendships over secession, gazed at the stars on a warm July night in 1861. Suddenly, a comet rocketed through the night sky. The next day, he read in the Richmond newspapers that no one had anticipated the passing of a celestial body. He wondered what it meant. "*Perhaps* it portends or foreshadows the speedy acknowledgment of our C.S. independence," he pondered, "& by its sudden apparition typifies the C.S. which has come into the host of nations like the comet blazing gloriously."[41]

Petty was wrong about independence, but correct about the comet as a metaphor. In the grandeur of time, the Army of Northern Virginia, like the Confederate States of America, was a short-lived shooting star. It appeared as a powerful illumination and quickly passed into the darkness. Yet it left an indelible mark on the landscape and psyche of the American nation far beyond its four years. Perhaps 200,000 men stepped into its ranks throughout the course of the war. Undermanned, underfed, poorly clothed, and inadequately equipped, the Army of Northern Virginia kept a significantly larger and better-resourced Union army at bay for almost four years. Its success was so great that in the minds of Northerners and Southerners alike it came to symbolize the viability of the Confederate States.

Even today, many decades after its last veteran expired, Lee's army continues to live in the imagination of the American public, not so much for what it represented, but for what it accomplished on the field of battle under the most difficult conditions and circumstances.

The sacrifices, tragedies, and achievements of General Lee's army provided that essential kernel of truth from which the myth of the Lost Cause blossomed.

APPENDIX I:

THE SAMPLE

THE SAMPLE WAS designed by Dr. Kent Tedin, the former chairman of the Department of Political Science at the University of Houston. The sample consists of 600 soldiers who served in Lee's army. Because there was no single list of names, we chose a stratified cluster sample. Each infantry, cavalry, and artillery unit that ever served in Lee's army received a number. I then determined through army strength throughout the war that 81.8 percent of all troops were in the infantry, 11.3 percent were in the cavalry, and 6.9 percent were in the artillery. We then randomly selected fifty artillery batteries and fifty cavalry regiments and seventy-five infantry regiments. We then randomly selected three names from each chosen battery and cavalry regiment and four from each infantry regiment. The sample consists of 150 artillerists, 150 cavalrymen, and 300 infantrymen. The artillery and cavalry samples are large enough to make them statistically significant. The infantry sample is much larger because of the proportion of infantrymen in Lee's army.

I then gathered all the information I could locate on soldiers from Compiled Service Records, Census Records, Pension Files, obituaries, county histories, family histories, and other sources. Dr. Michael S. Parks, a professor of Decision and Information Sciences in the Bauer School of Business at the University of Houston, set up an Access Document to hold the data and calculated hundreds of charts based on the data. I then calculated dozens more. All results were determined by branch of service, and the percentage was multiplied by the percentage of representation within Lee's army to provide accurate totals for the army.

Although the sample is not designed to represent the precise percentage of units from each state, the sample does include units from each Confederate state, plus Maryland, Kentucky, and West Virginia. The breakdown by home state is:

Ala.: 24	Ga.: 83	Md.: 12	N.C.: 97	Tenn.: 16	Va.: 187
Ark.: 4	Ky.: 5	Miss.: 20	S.C.: 77	Tex.: 4	W.Va.: 42
Fla.: 4	La.: 16				

The data were grouped into fifty-four categories ranging from prewar to wartime to postwar. They are: census records found; last name; first name;

middle name; branch; unit name; state of unit; company; officer or enlisted man; ranks; other units; year of birth; state of birth; state at time of enlistment; how he entered service; date of entry; marital status; number of children; pre-war occupation; class status; personal wealth; family wealth; nonfamily wealth; personal slaves owned; family slaves owned; nonfamily slaves owned; occupation of head of household; name of nonfamily head of household; county of soldier; slave-to-white ratio in county; date soldier left service; how soldier left service; battle in which soldier was killed in action; number of times wounded in action; locations of wounds; battle(s) in which wounds occurred; number of absences without leave (AWOL); date of AWOL(s); length of AWOL(s); number of desertions; date of desertion(s); length of desertion(s); numbers of illnesses; types of illnesses; number of times prisoner of war (POW); length of time POW; number of general courts-martial; postwar occupation; postwar residences; location of death; state of death; date of death; manner of death; and general remarks. For some of the data recorded I did not have a separate category. For example, I recorded real property (land) and personal property (all other wealth) from U.S. Census and state tax records, but in the database, I combined them into wealth. Nonetheless, because I recorded them separately, I could calculate how many farmers did not own land, which enabled me to determine how many were tenant farmers.

	With Clustering and Stratification (poststratification weights) 95% Confidence Intervals			With No Design Effects (poststratification weights) 95% Confidence Intervals	
	Estimate	LCB	UCB	LCB	UCB
Own slaves? (personal & family)	36.7%	31.6%	42.1%	32.1%	41.5%
Own slaves? (including nonfamily)	42.2%	38.0%	47.7%	36.4%	47.2%
Excluding nonfamily wealth					
<$400	37.0%	32.5%	41.8%	32.4%	41.9%
$400–$799	5.9%	3.7%	9.3%	3.9%	8.8%
$800–$1,199	6.3%	4.3%	9.1%	4.3%	9.2%
$1,200–$3,999	16.1%	12.3%	20.8%	12.8%	20.1%
$4,000–$10,000	14.6%	11.5%	18.4%	11.5%	18.4%
>$10,000	20.1%	16.2%	24.6%	16.4%	24.2%
Including nonfamily wealth					
<$400	27.8%	23.5%	32.5%	23.5%	32.4%
$400–$799	6.6%	4.3%	10.0%	4.3%	10.0%
$800–$1,199	6.6%	4.4%	9.6%	4.5%	9.6%
$1,200–$3,999	16.3%	12.4%	21.1%	12.4%	21.1%
$4,000–$10,000	17.1%	13.7%	21.1%	13.7%	21.1%
>$10,000	25.7%	21.6%	30.3%	21.6%	30.3%

n=547
Confidence Intervals are adjusted for design effects of clustering on unit and stratification by branch.
Using Taylor series linearization as implemented in STATA® 8.0/S.E. survey estimation procedures.
LCB=Lower confidence bound
UCB=Upper confidence bound

Intraclass correlations:

Wealth	0.06671
Wealth (including nonfamily)	0.04957
Number of slaves	0.06919
Number of slaves (including nonfamily)	0.06382

Intraclass correlation is the variance between clusters over the total variance. The adjusments of the standard errors and confidence intervals for design effects are small because the intraclass correlation is relatively small. Most of the variance occurs within clusters at the individual level rather than between clusters. In this situation, the assumption of simple randomness and the use of algorithms based on SRS give answers similar to those with adjustment for design effects.

Weights are poststratification weights that reproduce the distribution to the branches at 81.8 percent infantry, 11.3 percent cavalry, 6.9 percent artillery, after deleting missing values.

Branch	Freq.	Percent	Cum.	Weight
A	37.743001	6.9	6.9	0.2948672
C	61.811002	11.3	18.2	0.4446835
I	447.446	81.8	100	1.598021
Total	547	100		

NOTES

Abbreviations Used

A&IGO	Adjutant and Inspector General's Office
AAR	After-Action Report
ADAH	Alabama Department of Archives and History
AGO	Adjutant General's Office
AHQ	*Alabama Historical Quarterly*
AHS	Atlanta Historical Society
ALR	*Alabama Review*
ANV	Army of Northern Virginia
C	Confederate
CAH	Center for American History
CI	Circulars Issued
CL, UMI	Clements Library, University of Michigan
CWMC	Civil War Miscellaneous Collection
CWTIC	Civil War Times Illustrated Collection
DU	Duke University
EU	Emory University
FHQ	*Florida Historical Quarterly*
FSA	Florida State Archives
FSNBP	Fredericksburg and Spotsylvania National Battlefield Park
FSU	Florida State University
GDAH	Georgia Department of Archives and History
GHQ	*Georgia Historical Quarterly*
GHS	Georgia Historical Society
GO	General Orders
HQ	Headquarters
IR	Inspection Report
LC	Library of Congress
LR	Letters Received
LS	Letters Sent

LSU	Louisiana State University
LV	Library of Virginia
M	Microfilm Group
MC	Museum of the Confederacy
MDAH	Mississippi Department of Archives and History
MDHS	Maryland Historical Society
ML	Morgan Library
NA	National Archives and Records Administration
NCDAH	North Carolina Division of Archives and History
NPL	Norfolk Public Library
NYHS	New-York Historical Society
NYPL	New York Public Library
OR	*War of the Rebellion*
R	Microfilm
RG	Record Group
RNBP	Richmond National Battlefield Park
SCHS	South Carolina Historical Society
SHC, UNC	Southern Historical Collection, University of North Carolina
SHSW	State Historical Society of Wisconsin
SO	Special Orders
SW	Secretary of War
TNSL	Tennessee State Library
TS	Telegrams Sent
TU	Tulane University
UAL	University of Alabama
USAMHI	U.S. Army Military History Institute
USC	University of South Carolina
USMA	U.S. Military Academy at West Point
UVA	University of Virginia
VHS	Virginia Historical Society
VMHB	*Virginia Magazine of History and Biography*
VMI	Virginia Military Institute
W&L	Washington and Lee University
W&M	College of William & Mary

Prologue

1. Theodore Lyman to wife, 18 May 1864. Lyman, *Meade's Headquarters, 1863–1865*, 100.
2. Lee to Davis, 19 Apr. 1864. Dowdey and Manarin, eds., *Wartime Papers*, 704.
3. Ellen Renshaw House diary, 23 Apr. 1865. House, *A Very Violent Rebel*, 161–62.
4. I believe the Confederacy lost due to external causes. It would not have imploded if the war had not come along. The war, however, generated severe internal and external problems that impaired Confederates in resisting Union invasion. This external pressure caused virtually every Confederate institution to break down and accentuated some fissures that existed before the war.
5. H. A. Deweerd, "Leaders Who Rode with Lee." *New York Times Book Review*, 8 Oct. 1944, 23.
6. J. Tracy Power has written *Lee's Miserables: Life in the Army of Northern Virginia from the Wilderness to Appomattox* (Chapel Hill: University of North Carolina Press, 1998).

1. Comedy of Errors, Tragedy of Triumph

1. Records of James S. Petty. U.S. Census, 1860. M653, R1381, 983; U.S. Census, 1850. M438, R978, 24.
2. See J. Thomas Petty diary, 1 Jan.–20 Apr. 1861. J. Thomas Petty Papers, MC; Lee A. Wallace, Jr., *17th Virginia Infantry*, 132.
3. Petty diary, 1 Jan. 1861. J. Thomas Petty Papers, MC.
4. Petty diary, 5 Jan. 1861. J. Thomas Petty Papers, MC.
5. Petty diary, 9 and 16 Apr. 1861. Also see Petty diary, 12 and 14 Apr. 1861. J. Thomas Petty Papers. MC.
6. Petty diary, 17, 14, and 24 Apr. 1861. J. Thomas Petty Papers, MC; Records of John B. Petty. U.S. Census, 1860. M653, R1381, 991; U.S. Slave Census, 1860. Warren County, Virginia, 448.
7. Petty diary, 15, 21, 22, and 27 Apr.; 21 and 22 June; 1, 6, and 8 July 1861. J. Thomas Petty Papers, MC.
8. Frank Potts journal, 27 July 1861, 34–35. Frank Potts Papers, LV; Record of Frank Potts. U.S. Census, 1860. M653, R1352, 114.
9. Petty diary, 19 July 1861. J. Thomas Petty Papers, MC. For accounts of the Battle of Blackburn's Ford, see William C. Davis, *The Battle at Bull Run: A History of the First Major Campaign of the Civil War*, 112–31; Thomas Goree to Uncle Pleas, 2 Aug. 1861. Thomas Jewitt Goree, *The Thomas Jewitt Goree Letters, Volume I: The Civil War Correspondence*, 56–58; Wallace, *17th Virginia*, 18–19.
10. Petty diary, 21 July 1861. J. Thomas Petty Papers, MC. Also see Frank Potts journal, 27 July 1861. Frank Potts Papers, LV; Samuel L. West to Pop, 8 Aug. 1861. CWMC, USAMHI.
11. Records of Jesse G. Jordan. U.S. Census, 1860. Madison County, AL, 191; U.S. Slave Census, 1860. Madison County, AL, 471; "An Alabama Mother," *Confederate Veteran*, v. 5, 523.
12. Jesse [Jordan] to Sister, 15 Apr. 1861. Jordan-Bell Papers, VHS.
13. See "An Alabama Mother," *Confederate Veteran*, v. 5, 523; J. Gary Laine and Morris M. Penny, *Law's Alabama Brigade in the War Between the Union and the Confederacy*, 4–5; CSR of Jesse Jordan, 4th Alabama Infantry. M311, R124, NA.
14. Jesse [Jordan] to Sister, 15 Apr. 1861. Jordan-Bell Papers, VHS.
15. Laine and Penny, *Law's Alabama Brigade*, 5–6.
16. Hussen [A. C. Davidson] to Darly, 9 July 1861. James A. Davidson Papers, ADAH; James G. Hudson journal, July [n.d.]. James G. Hudson Papers, ADAH; John [Fort] to Mother, 20 July 1861. Tomlinson Fort Papers, EU; J. H. Langhorne to Father, 18 June 1861. Langhorne Family Papers, VHS; Davis, *Battle at Bull Run*, 134–35; SO, No. 1. HQ, Army of the Shenandoah. 18 July 1861. Jeffrey D. Stocker, ed., *From Huntsville to Appomattox: R. T. Cole's History of the 4th Regiment, Alabama Volunteer Infantry, C.S.A., Army of Northern Virginia*. 18–19.
17. A.C. Davidson to Pit, 23 July 1861. James A. Davidson Papers, ADAH; James G. Hudson journal, July [n.d.]. James G. Hudson Papers, ADAH; Laine and Penny, *Law's Alabama Brigade*, 6–7.
18. Jesse [Jordan] to Sister, 4 Aug. 1861. Jordan-Bell Papers, VHS.
19. Jesse [Jordan] to Sister, 4 Aug. 1861. Jordan-Bell Papers, VHS; Laine and Penny, *Law's Alabama Brigade*, 6–7.
20. A. C. Davidson to Pit, 23 July 1861. James A. Davidson Papers, ADAH; Laine and Penny, *Law's Alabama Brigade*, 6–8.
21. CSR of James Thomas Petty, 17th Virginia Infantry. M324, R593, NA.
22. "An Alabama Mother," *Confederate Veteran*, v. 5, 523.

2. Secession and Mobilizing for War

1. For the coming of the war, see David Potter, *The Impending Crisis, 1848–1861*, and James M. McPherson, *Battle Cry of Freedom: The Civil War Era*; Don E. Fehrenbacher, *The Dred Scot Case: Its Significance in Law and Politics*.
2. For John Brown, see Stephen Oates, *To Purge This Land with Blood: A Biography of John Brown*.
3. *Richmond Enquirer*, 20 Oct. 1859; Journal of the Senate: Report of Gov. Wm. H. Gist, South Carolina, 29 Nov. 1859. *Microfilm of Early State Records*. South Carolina, A. la, R30, 21; Journal of the Senate:

Report of Gov. Robert C. Wickliffe, Louisiana, 1860. *Microfilm of Early State Records*. Louisiana, A. la. R3, 9. Also see Journal of the Assembly: Report of Gov. M. S. Perry, Florida, 1859. *Microfilm of Early State Records*. Florida, A. 1b, R3, 31. By contrast, Governor Robert C. Wickliffe of Louisiana disagreed. Southerners had battled the irrepressible conflict for years, he asserted. Brown's deeds were merely the most blatant. "For more than a quarter of a century," he insisted, "a sectional conflict, based upon hatred of the institution of slavery, has been waged by the North upon the South."

4. Report of Florida Governor M. S. Perry, Nov. 1859. *Microfilm of Early State Records*. Florida, A. 1b, R3, 33–34; Report of Louisiana Gov. Robert C. Wickliffe, Jan. 1860. Journal of the Senate. *Microfilm of Early State Records*. Louisiana, A. 1a, R3, 8–9; Report of Alabama Governor to Senate, 16 Nov. 1859. *Microfilm of Early State Records*. Alabama, A. la, R4, 22; Wilbur Davis reminiscences, 35. Davis Family Papers, UVA. Also see J. Thompson Brown to wife, 27 Nov. 1859. J. Thompson Brown Papers, VHS; B. F. Howard Record Book. B. F. Howard Record Book, MC; Edward Baker Loring reminiscence, 2. Edward Baker Loring Papers, LV; A. B. Francis reminiscences. Kate Mason Rowland Papers, MC.

5. Mississippi Committee on the Militia, 30 Nov. 1859. *Microfilm of Early State Records*. Mississippi, A. 1a, R8, 164–65 and 254; W. L. Sykes to Gov. John J. Pettus, 18 Jan. 1861. *OR* 4, (1): 61; Report of the Governor of Alabama to Senate, 16 Nov. 1859. Alabama Joint Committee on Militia. *Microfilm of Early State Records*. Alabama, A. la, R4, 22, 103, 111, 147, and 185; Proposal to build an Arsenal at Alexandria, Journal of the Senate, 2 Mar. 1860. *Microfilm of Early State Records*. Louisiana, A. la, R3, 96; Lee to Col. T. J. August, 20 Dec. 1859. Lee Family Papers, VHS; Cromwell Giles, *The Virginia Manufactory of Arms*, 61–62; Report of Gov. John Letcher, 7 Jan. 1861. Journal of the Senate, 1861 Extra Session. *Microfilm of Early State Records*. Virginia, A. la, R6, 35; A law to finance the purchase of $100,000 new arms, 16 Jan. 1861. Journal of the Senate. *Microfilm of Early State Records*. Arkansas, A. la. R5, 568.

6. Report of Gov. William McWillie, 8 Nov. 1859. Journal of the Senate. *Microfilm of Early State Records*. Mississippi, A. la, R8, 20; J. Hampden Chamberlayne to ?, 27 Nov. 1859. Bagley Family Papers. VHS.

7. Report of Florida Governor M. S. Perry, Nov. 1859. *Microfilm of Early State Records*. Florida, A. 1b, R3, 33–34.

8. Report of Gov. William McWillie, 8 Nov. 1859. Journal of the Senate. *Microfilm of Early State Records*. Mississippi, A. la, R8, 25; Report of Louisiana Gov. Robert C. Wickliffe, Jan. 1860. Journal of the Senate. *Microfilm of Early State Records*. Louisiana, A. la, R3, 8–9.

9. Resolution of the Senate and House of Representatives, 2 Dec. 1859. *Microfilm of Early State Records*. Florida, A. la, R3, 51, 182, and 204; Journal of the Senate. Joint Resolution of Louisiana Senate and House. *Microfilm of Early State Records*. Louisiana, A. la, R3, 112; Journal of the Senate: A. B. Moore, Governor, to Senate, 17 Jan. 1860. *Microfilm of Early State Records*. Alabama, A. la, R4, 176. Also see William L. Barney, *The Secessionist Impulse: Alabama and Mississippi in 1860*; J. Mills Thornton, III, *Politics and Power in a Slave Society: Alabama, 1800–1860*; Steven A. Channing, *Crisis of Fear: Secession in South Carolina*.

10. *Report of the Joint Committee of the General Assembly of Virginia on the Harpers Ferry Outrages, 26 January 1860*, 22. Gilder-Lehrman Collection, ML; Eric Foner, *Free Soil, Free Labor, Free Men: The Ideology of the Republican Party Before the Civil War*, 312–13.

11. Executive Resolution of A. B. Moore, Governor of Alabama, 28 Nov. 1860. Gilder-Lehrman Collection, ML. Also see Foner, *Free Soil, Free Labor, Free Men*, and William E. Gienapp, *Origins of the Republican Party, 1852–1856*.

12. "Declaration of the Immediate Causes of Secession," Frank Moore, ed., *Rebellion Record*, I, 3–4; Journal of the Georgia Convention, *OR* 4 (1): 84; "A Declaration of the Immediate Causes Which Induce and Justify the Secession of the State of Mississippi from the Federal Union," *Journal of the State Convention and Ordinances and Resolutions Adopted in January 1861*, 86–88; "Declaration of the Causes which Impel the State of Texas to Secede from the Federal Union," E. W. Winkler, ed., *Journal of the Secession Convention of Texas*, 61–66. Also see Charles B. Dew, *Apostles of Disunion: Southern Secession Commissioners and the Causes of the Civil War*.

13. Gary W. Gallagher, *Stephen Dodson Ramseur: Lee's Gallant General*, 17–18; Robert [Stafford] to Sister, 17 Nov. 1860. Gilder-Lehrman Collection, ML.

14. Paul J. Semmes to Gov. Joseph E. Brown, 11, 21, 22, and 25 Dec. 1860; 18 and 22 Jan. 1861. Paul J. Semmes to Col. H. C. Wayne, State Adjutant General, 1 Feb. 1861. Gilder-Lehrman Collection, ML; Report of Governor John Letcher, Virginia, 7 Jan. 1861. 1861 Special Session, Journal of the Senate. *Microfilm of Early State Records*. Virginia, A. la, R6, 35; R. L. Dabney to Rev. Hodge, 23 Jan. 1861. Box 2, Folder 4, Robert Lewis Dabney Papers, Union Theological Seminary; John W. Davis to Brother, 1 Mar. 1861. John W. Davis Papers, UVA; Sykes to Governor Pettus, 18 Jan. 1861. *OR* 4 (1): 61–62; William E. Moore diary, 4 Jan. 1861. CWTIC, USAMHI. According to Charles W. Ramsdell, only Texas did not prepare for war, due largely to Governor Sam Houston. See Ramsdell, "The Texas State Military Board, 1862–1865," *Southwestern Historical Quarterly* 27, No. 4 (April 1924), 255–56.

15. See Emory M. Thomas, *The Confederate Nation: 1861–1865*, 99–102; William C. Davis, *Jefferson Davis: The Man and His Hour*, 327–30; William J. Cooper, Jr., *Jefferson Davis, American*, 341–44.

3. The Volunteers of '61

1. Jesse Jordan to Sister, 15 April 1861. Jordan-Bell Papers, VHS; H. W. Barclay reminiscences, 5. H. W. Barclay. CAH; J. T. Smith to Mother, 27 July 1861. Smith-Johnson Papers, MC; John M. Kent to Capt., 20 May 1861. Edmundson Family Papers, VHS.

2. Chesnut., *Mary Chesnut's Civil War*, 83; Davis to Congress, 25 Feb. 1862. *OR* 4 (1): 951; An Act to further provide for public defense, 8 Aug. 1861. It authorized up to 400,000 more volunteers. *OR* 4.(1): 537.

3. W. R. Bivins to Davis, 18 Nov. 1861. A. H. Stephens Papers, LC; Records of John T. Bivins. U.S. Census Records, 1860. Wilkes County. Ga. 853. Hancock County, Ga., 232; on Ruffin in the war, see Eric H. Walther, *The Fire-Eaters*, 265–67, and David Allmendinger, Jr., *Ruffin: Family and Reform in the Old South*. See Sample, Appendix I.

4. See Sample in Appendix I. Records of James D. Gilliam. U.S. Census, Amherst Co., Va. M653, R 1332, 391; Records of William E. Herring. U.S. Census Records, Lisbon Co., NC. M653, R913, 838. Slave Census, 1860, Lisbon County, N. C. 164.

5. Some 23.5 percent of all enlistees in 1861 had children, according to the Sample in Appendix I. Records of J. W. Dickinson. U.S. Census, 1860. Virginia. M653, R 1338, 448; Records of Elbert Leech. U.S. Census, 1860. Lowndes (W) Co., Mississippi. M653, R 586, 50; Jno M. Tilley to Wife, 26 Aug. 1861. John M. Tilley Papers, GDAH; Records of John M. Tilley. U.S. Census, 1860. Taliaferro Co., Ga., 720–21; Records of John M. Tilley. U.S. Slave Census, 1860. Taliaferro Co., Ga. 16.

6. See Sample in Appendix I; Records of George Webb. U.S. Census, 1860. East Baton Rouge, La. M653, R408, 627. Records of Amelia Webb. Slave Census, 1860. Louisiana, East Baton Rouge, 192; Records of Ganam S. Lyons. U.S. Census, Marion Co., Ala. M653, R16, 724.

7. See sample in Appendix I.

8. See Sample in Appendix I. Records of William T. Kerfoot. U.S. Census Records, 1860. Fauquier Co., Va. M653, R1344, 180.

9. See sample in Appendix I. The exact figures are 10.27 percent, 25.62 percent, and 35.89 percent. There were approximately 393,000 slave owners (I excluded Delaware, Kansas, and Nebraska), and about 7,945,000 white people in those slaveholding states, which means 4.95 percent owned slaves.

10. See sample in Appendix I. Some people who were included in nonfamily households may have been related to the soldier, but I could not determine that from the census data and other sources. James M. Jasper in *The Art of Moral Protest: Culture, Biography, and Creativity in Social Movements* (Chicago: University of Chicago Press, 1997), 12, describes culture as "shared mental worlds and their physical embodiments." Surely images on paper currency are cultural symbols.

11. See sample in Appendix I. While there were distinctions between officers and enlisted men, only 4.4 percent of the random sample held commissions in 1861, making those numbers too small for accurate statistical comparison, but they are in rough proportion with the number of enlisted men.

12. Records of Howlit Irvin. U.S. Census Records, 1860. Baldwin County. Ga., 146; Records of William R. Phillips. U.S. Census Records, 1860. Norfolk County, Va., 190. Irvin served in the Irvin Battery, named for his father.

13. Records of Patrick Brennan. U.S. Census, Chatham Co., Ga. M653, R115, 56; Records of William Forner and Lewis Eichner. U.S. Census Records, Baltimore, Md. M653, R465, 820.

14. Frank Potts journal, 14 July 1861, 25. Frank Potts Papers, LV; Records of Frank Potts. Records of John Dooley. U.S. Census Records, Henrico County, Va. M653, R1352, 114 and 329; Records of Frank Potts and Records of John Dooley. Slave Census, Virginia. Henrico County, 18 and 40.

15. Frederick Law Olmsted, *A Journey in the Seaboard Slave States in the Years 1853–1854*, II, 150.

16. John Dooley journal, 5 July 1863. Dooley, *John Dooley, Confederate Soldier: His War Journal*, 115; An English Combatant, *Battle-Fields of the South from Bull Run to Fredericksburg*, xi; James B. Sheeran journal, 11 Aug. 1862. Joseph T. Durkin, S.J., *Confederate Chaplain: A War Journal of Rev. James B. Sheeran. c.s.s.r., 14th Louisiana, C.S.A.*, 5. See Kelly J. O'Grady, *Clear the Confederate Way!: The Irish in the Army of Northern Virginia*; Terry L. Jones, *Lee's Tigers: The Louisiana Infantry in the Army of Northern Virginia*; Cornelius M. Buckley, S.J., ed. and trans., *A Frenchman, A Chaplain, A Rebel: The War Letters of Pere Louis-Hippolyte Gache, S.J.*

17. Philip David Kohn to Son, 5 Feb. 1861, in Helen Kohn Hennig, *August Kohn: Versatile South Carolinian*, 9–10; L. Leon, *Diary of a Tar Heel Confederate Soldier*, 71.

18. See sample in Appendix I.

19. Frank Dunbar Ruggles to Father. 22 Oct. 1862. J. R. Richardson Papers, MC; Records of D. D. Ruggles. U.S. Census Records. 1860. New Orleans, 4th Ward. 144.

20. Dewees Ogden to Uncle Sam. 22 Apr. 1863. Dewees Ogden Papers. LV. For insights into the closed nature of Northern society during the secession crisis, see "Memy" [Seaton Gales] to [wife], 10 May 1863. Gales Papers, NCDAH.

21. Anderson Merchant to Mother, 9 Jan. 1862. Lewis Leigh Collection. USAMHI: Robert H. Miller to Mother. 31 Jan. 1862. Robert H. Miller, "Letters of Lieutenant Robert H. Miller to His Family, 1861–1862," *VMHB* 70 (No. 1, 1962), 66.

22. Unknown diarist. 1 Aug. 1861. Diary, 1st Maryland Artillery Papers, New York State Library.

23. Jimmie [Langhorne] to Mother, 12 June [1861]. Langhorne Family Papers, VHS.

24. William M. Blackford diary, 17 Apr. 1861. Vol. 5, Box 2, William M. Blackford Papers. UVA. Also see D. C. Love, *Prairie Guards*, 1.

25. Miscellaneous Records, Mrs. M. C. Emerson Papers, LV; E. P. and N. T. Miller. Papers, 17th Mississippi Infantry File, FSNBP.

26. Laine and Penny, *Law's Brigade*, 4–5; R. A. Bryant to Eugenia, 15 June 1861. Bryant Family Papers, LV.

27. Laine and Penny, *Law's Brigade*, 5–6; Order No. 27. 15th Va. Vols. 21 June 1861. Orderly Book, 15th Virginia Infantry, NYHS.

28. Davis to Congress, 18 Aug. 1862. *OR* 4 (2): 55; G. B. Johnston to James H. Lane, 21 Sep. 1861. James H. Lane Papers, Auburn University.

29. Letter to the Editor of the *Enquirer*, 30 Dec. 1863. W. S. Morris Papers, MC; Richard M. McMurry, *Two Great Rebel Armies: An Essay in Confederate Military History*, 98–105; James H. Lane, "Sketch of North Carolina Military Institute." James H. Lane Papers, Auburn University; Lee to Beauregard, 19 June 1861. Letters Sent, Virginia Forces. R1, RG 109; Davis to Congress, 18 Aug. 1862. *OR* 4 (2): 55.

30. 29–30 Apr. 1861. Unidentified Member of Company K. 3rd Alabama Infantry, "A Sketch of 12 Months," *Alabama Historical Quarterly* 25 (No. 1 & 2, 1963), 152; Sam [Melton] to wife, 25 Apr. 1861. Samuel Wicliffe Melton Papers, USC. See Milledge L. Bonham Papers, Box 3, Apr. and early May 1861, USC, for some interesting restrictions that Gov. Francis Pickens placed on South Carolina troops, particularly Pickens to Secretary of War, 23 Apr. 1861, and Bonham to Pickens. 3 May 1861.

31. Letter from the Muscogee Rifles. 22 June 1861. William B. Styple. ed., *Writing & Fighting*, 20: Ivy Duggan to Editor, *Central Georgian*, 29 July 1861. Civil War Miscellany: 48th Georgia File. GDAH; Patrick Crawford Hoy. *A Brief History of Bradford's Battery*, 6.

32. McLaws to Wife, 24 June 1861. McLaws Papers, SHC, UNC. See McLaws, *A Soldier's General: The Civil War Letters of Major General Lafayette McLaws*, 86–87.

33. Robert H. Miller to Mother, 31 Jan. 1862. Miller, "Letters of Lieutenant Robert H. Miller to IIis Family, 1861–1862," *VMHB* 70 (No. 1, 1962), 66; Terry L. Jones, *Lee's Tigers: The Louisiana Infantry in the Army of Northern Virginia*, 17–19.

34. J. H. Langhorne to Mother, 13 May 1861. Langhorne Family Papers, VHS; C. M. Wilcox to Sister Mary, 18 Nov. 1861. Cadmus M. Wilcox Papers, LC; [A. R. H. Ranson] to Henry, 4 June 1861. Lewis Leigh Collection, USAMHI; T. Rowland to Mother, 15 May 1861. Kate Mason Rowland Papers, MC.

35. Chesnut, *Mary Chesnut's Civil War*, 83.

4. Why They Enlisted

1. Speech by Miss Josie V. Thrasher and Captain Gazaway B. Knight. 25 July 1861. Company G, Cobb's Legion File, Roll 2-2560, Civil War Miscellany, GDAH.

2. Address by Dr. B. M. Palmer at City Hall, 27 May 1861. Louisiana Historical Collection: Battalion, Washington Artillery, Box 11. TU; GO, No. 73. HQ, 1st Corps, Army of the Potomac, 28 Nov. 1861. C.S.A. Army, Richmond Howitzers, 1st Company. Order Book. VHS.

3. Letter from the Muscogee Rifles, 22 June 1861. William B. Styple, ed., *Writing & Fighting from the Army of Northern Virginia*, 20; William Ephraim Smith, undated, wartime. William Ephraim Smith Papers, DU.

4. The calculation is for soldiers who enlisted in 1861. The statistic includes individuals who owned slaves themselves or whose parents owned slaves. When I refer to "exposure to slavery," I mean they own slaves, their parents own slaves, or they live with a slaveholder. See Appendix I for detailed information about the sample. Overseers worked for slave owners. The sample included eleven overseers, four of whom lived independently from their employer. Just how many others rented land from slave owners, or how many served a slave-owning clientele, cannot be determined from the census records. Also, some future soldiers may have lived with family, but because they did not have the same last name as the head of household, I could not determine that.

5. Records of James B. W. Foster, William J. Taylor, Amos Stevenson. Martha Whitehead, and E. W. Edwards. U.S. Census Records, 1860. Northampton County, N.C., 158; Records of William J. Taylor, Amos Stevenson, Martha Whitehead, and E.W. Edwards. Slave Census Records, 1860. Northampton County, N.C., 344; Records of John B. Petty. U.S. Census Records. 1860. Warren County, Va., 991; Records of John B. Petty. Slave Census, 1860. Warren County. Va., 448; Eugene D. Genovese, *The World the Slaveholders Made: Two Essays in Interpretation*, 99–102.

6. McPherson, *Battle Cry of Freedom*, 99.

7. McPherson, *Battle Cry of Freedom*, 196.

8. J. D. B. DeBow, *The Interest in Slavery of the Southern Non-Slaveholder*. 1860 Association, Tract No. 5, 4–5 and 8. Gilder-Lehrman Collection, ML.

9. McPherson, *Battle Cry of Freedom*. 243. See Edmund S. Morgan, *American Slavery, American Freedom: The Ordeal of Colonial Virginia*, for a shrewd discussion of the use of racism by slaveholders. For the origins of racism and its influences, see David Brion Davis, *The Problem of Slavery in the Age of Revolution, 1775–1823* and *The Problem of Slavery in the Western Culture*; Winthrop Jordan, *White Over Black: American Attitudes toward the Negro, 1550–1812*.

10. R. L. Dabney to Rev. Hodge, 23 Jan. 1861, Box 2, F4, Robert Lewis Dabney Papers, Union Theological Seminary; John E. Armstrong reminiscence, CWTIC, USAMHI.

11. Richard Henry Watkins to Wife, 20 Dec. 1861. Richard Henry Watkins Papers, VHS, courtesy of James McPherson; R. G. Haile diary, 12 June [1862]. Robert Gaines Haile Papers, WM; James M. McPherson, *For Cause and Comrades: Why Men Fought in the Civil War*, 19–21. See William J. Cooper, Jr., *Liberty and Slavery: Southern Politics to 1860*, and Chandra Manning, *What This Cruel War Was Over: Soldiers, Slavery, and the Civil War*.

12. J. J. Archer to Mother, 17 Mar. 1861. James J. Archer Papers, MDHS: William Blair, *Virginia's Private War: Feeding Body and Soul in the Confederacy, 1861–1865*, 12.

13. W. E. Rogers to Father, n.d. [June or July 1861]. Styple, ed., *Writing & Fighting*, 27; John T. Thornton to [wife], 18 July 1861. John T. Thornton Papers, UVA; Milton Barrett to Brother and Sister, 2 Aug. 1861. Barrett *The Confederacy Is On Her Way Up the Spout: Letters to South Carolina, 1861–1864*, 22.

14. Albert Batchelor to Mother, 13 May 1861. Albert A. Batchelor Papers, LSU.

15. W. R. Redding to Lizzie, Aug. 1861. W. R. Redding Papers, UNC, courtesy of James McPherson. While the primary burden rested with adult males, in times of crisis adult females could also assume a front-line role in family defense.

16. Rawley W. Martin to Darling, Sweet, Precious Love, undated [1861]. Rawley White Martin Papers, Duke U.; J. H. Langhorne to Father, 18 June 1861. Langhorne Family, VHS. Also see Poem of Wm. G. Cabaniss, 38th Virginia Infantry, Nov. 1862. Anderson Folder, CWTIC, USAMHI.

17. ASM[organ] to wife, 19 May 1861. Asa Stokely Morgan Papers, FSNBP; Henry Lewis to

Mother, 9 Aug. 1862. Harry Lewis Papers, UNC, courtesy of James McPherson. Also see McPherson, *For Cause and Comrades*, 22.

18. George Loyal Gordon to Wife. 3 July 1861. George L. Gordon Papers. UNC. George Knox Miller to Celestine McCann, 10 June 1861. George Knox Miller Papers. UNC, both courtesy of James McPherson. Also see Blair, *Virginia's Private War*, 6.

19. The best study on honor is Bertram Wyatt-Brown. *Southern Honor: Ethics and Behavior in the Old South* (New York: Oxford University Press, 1982). Also see Kenneth Greenberg, *Honor and Slavery*: Eric Walther, "Southerners' Honors," *Southern Studies* (new series), 12 (Fall/Winter. 2005), 129–54; Jacqueline Glass Campbell, *When Sherman Marched North from the Sea: Resistance on the Confederate Home Front*. Although Southern society often perceived males as the sex that did or did not possess honor, and women were more the objects of honorable deeds, females could exhibit honor as well. Southern white women did not believe they were the more fragile sex. They simply accepted the notion in public in order to promote stability at home and in the family. In unusual circumstances, when white women had to exhibit qualities that showed honor, they did so, and males applauded them for it.

20. Jno. M. Tilley to Wife, 18 July 1861. John M. Tilley Papers, GDAH; J. M. Tate to Sister, 12 May 1861. Gilder-Lehrman Collection, ML; Eli Landers to Mother, 24 Sep. 1863. Landers, *Weep Not for Me, Dear Mother* (Gretna, La; Pelican Publishing Company, 1996), 118; Felix Buchanan to Father, 27 Apr. 1863. Quoted in Randall C. Jimerson, *The Private Civil War: Popular Thought During the Sectional Conflict*, 19.

21. John S. Apperson journal, 2 Feb. 1861. Apperson, *Repairing the March of Mars: The Civil War Diaries of John Samuel Apperson*, 34; Jimmie [Langhorne] to Mother, 12 June [1861]. Langhorne Family Papers, VHS; Husband [J. Griffin] to Leila, 26 Feb. 1862. CWTIC, USAMHI. Also see Ivy W. Duggan to Editor, *Central Georgian*, 7 Sep. 1861. Civil War Miscellany: 48th Georgia, GDAH.

22. Davis speech in Jackson, Miss, 26 Dec. 1862. Lynda Laswell Crist et al., *Papers of Jefferson Davis*, 8, 573; J. Nance to Laura, 18 Aug. 1863. James D. Nance Papers, USC; Thomas J. Goree to Robert D. Goree, 20 Dec. 1861. Langston James Goree V, ed., *Thomas Jewett Goree Letters*, 135; J. Keith to Mother, 3 Oct. [1863]. Keith Family Papers, VHS. Also see Will [Crutcher] to Evangeline. 19 Mar. 1862. Crutcher-Shannon Papers, CAH; Samuel Walsh to Miss R. L. Proffitt, 11 Apr. 1864. Proffitt Family Papers, SHC, UNC.

23. Statistics derived from the sample in Appendix I. Enlisted men were supposed to get fifty dollars in clothing allowance. See Walther, "Southerners' Honor." 129–54.

24. Statistics specifically are 5.1 percent foreign born, and 16 percent born and enlisted from different states. See sample in Appendix I. Of course, being born and residing in the same state does not mean that a soldier did not move away and come back or travel extensively anyway. But based on their ages, wealth, and what we know of nineteenth-century society, it is exceedingly unlikely that a majority traveled much.

25. On manhood and combat, see McPherson, *For Cause and Comrades*, 25–26. Also see Gerald F. Linderman, *Embattled Courage: The Experience of Combat in the American Civil War*; Earl J. Hess, *The Union Soldier in Battle: Enduring the Ordeal of Combat*.

26. JHC to Sister, 1 Aug. 1861. Bagby Papers, VHS; Richard Henry Watkins to Wife, 23 Sep. 1861. Richard Henry Watkins Papers, VHS, courtesy of James McPherson; Goree, ed., 98. See McPherson, *For Cause and Comrades*, 25–26.

27. J. H. Langhorne to Mother, 8 May 1861, and to Father, 18 June 1861. Langhorne Family Papers, VHS. Langhorne's letters also reveal how he related to each of his parents based on sex.

28. Records of Henry Lethcoe. U.S. Census Records, 1860. Washington County, Va. 550; CSR of Henry Lethcoe, 48th Virginia Infantry. M324. R913, NA. The census record did not state what Lethcoe's offense in Abingdon was, but he was in jail with two of his brothers.

29. Jno. Winfield to Wife, 2 Sep. 1861. John J. Winfield Papers, SHC, UNC; Samuel F. Tenney to Alice Toomer, 18 Jan. 1862. E. B. Duffee, Jr., ed., "War Letters of S. F. Tenney, a Soldier in the Third Georgia Regiment," *Georgia Historical Quarterly*, 57 (Summer 1973), 280; Daniel A Grimsley to Cousin, 18 Aug. [1861]. Grimsley Family Papers, LV; J. V. Fuller to Wife, 18 May 1862. Confederate Miscellany, EU; G. M. C. Lee to Jordan, 26 Aug. 1861. Frank E. Vandiver, ed., "A Collection of Louisiana Confederate Letters," *Louisiana Historical Quarterly* 26, No. 4 (1943), 941; Ivy W. Duggan to Editor, *Central Georgian*, 29 July 1861. Civil War Miscellany: 48th Georgia File, GDAH; John P. Welsh to Brother, 23 May 1861. Welsh Family Papers. LV.

30. J. J. Davis to Father and Mother, 29 May 1861. Jeremiah Jefferson Davis Papers, GDAH; A Daughter of the South, "Women of the South," *Richmond Enquirer*, 7 Mar. 1862, P2C2; Lucy Wood Butler diary, 24 May 1861. Lucy Butler Papers, UVA, also quoted in Blair, *Virginia's Private War*, 38.

31. E. K. Smith to Mother, 21 May 1861. R2, Edmund Kirby-Smith Papers, SHC, UNC; John Futch to Martha, 9 March 1862. Futch Brothers Papers, NCDAH; W. Y. Hopkins to Aunt, 8 June 1861. George W. Hopkins Papers, MDAH; Benj. F. White to Dear Young Friend, 5 Jan. 1862. James J. Phillips Papers, USC; Wife [Mrs. Hawks] to Husband, 24 Feb. 1862. Thomas J. Jackson Papers, DU. Also see EKS to Mother, 2 June 1861. R2, Edmund Kirby-Smith Papers, SHC, UNC: B. J. Pack to Salina, 2 Nov. 1861. Joseph B. and Andrew Pack Papers, USC; Holmes to ?, 25 June 1861. Styple, ed., *Writing & Fighting*, 21.

32. Congratulatory Address of Maj. Gen. Ransom, 18 Dec. 1862. Kate Mason Rowland Papers, MC; R. T. Scott to Fan, 18 Mar. 1862. Keith Family Papers, VHS; Will [Crutcher] to darling, 26 Oct. 1861. Crutcher-Shannon Papers, CAH. Although most Western nations had given up slavery, Southerners thought those countries were in error. It was the Confederacy that was the progressive country, so Southerners thought, because it recognized the inferiority of Africans and used them to uplift its white population. Nor were the benefits one-sided. Daily exposure of these people of African descent to Southern whites steadily improved them, too.

33. John L. Hardman to Uncle, 22 Aug. 1861, in *Southern Confederacy*, 28 Aug. 1861, and letter of

13 Aug. 1861 in *Southern Confederacy*, 16 Aug. 1861; General Orders, No. 1. HQ, Dept. of Alexandria, 2 June 1861. General Orders and Circulars, Army of the Potomac, June 2, 1861–Jan. 30, 1862. RG 109, NA.

34. Oscar E. Stuart to Sister, 19 Feb. 1862. Oscar J. E. Stuart Papers, MDAH; Ivy W. Duggan to Editor, *Central Georgian*, 13 Sep. 1861. Civil War Miscellany: 48th Georgia File, GDAH.

35. Henry T. Owen, "Reminiscences of the War," Box 1. Henry T. Owen Papers, LV.

36. J. S. Newman diary, 30 July 1861. J. S. Newman Papers, LV; Thomas J. Owen to Sallie, 12 Nov. 1861. Thomas J. Owen Papers, GDAH; T. R. Lightfoot to Uncle, 14 July 1861. Cody, "Letters of the Three Lightfoot Brothers, 1861–1864," *Georgia Historical Quarterly* 25, No. 4 (1941), 394; James W. Baldwin to Lee, 15 Aug. 1861. Box 1, Bound Series, Lee Headquarters Papers, VHS; George Washington Hall diary, 1 Apr. 1862. George Washington Hall Papers, LC; H. C. Kendrick to Sister, 19 Nov. 1861. H. C. Kendricks Papers, SHC, UNC, courtesy of James McPherson.

37. James Stanley Newman diary, 30 July 1861. James Stanley Newman Papers, MC; F. B. Moore to Ann, 7 June 1861. Richard Anderson File, CWTIC, USAMHI; Eli Landers to Mother, [?] Aug. 1861. Landers, *Weep Not for Me*, 24; R. A. Smith to Sir, 9 Dec. 1861. Graves Family Papers, EU; James T. Thompson to Mother and sisters, 12 Aug. 1861. Thompson, "A Georgia Boy with 'Stonewall' Jackson, the Letters of James Thomas Thompson," *VMHB* 70, No. 3 (1962), 316.

38. John T. Thornton to wife, 23 Aug. 1861. John T. Thornton Papers, UVA; Husband [J. Griffin] to Leila, 26 Feb. 1862. CWTIC, USAMHI; C. C. Blacknall to Captain, 23 Mar. 1863. Oscar W. Blacknall Papers, NCDAH.

5. Becoming Soldiers

1. Col. D. H. Hill to Col. Winston, 19 June 1861. Letters and Telegrams Sent, Army of the Peninsula. RG 109. NA; Charles Batchelor to Albert, 10 Oct. 1861. Albert A. Batchelor Papers, LSU.

2. Jas. P. Williams to Aunt Mary, 9 May 1861. J. Peter Williams Papers, UVA.

3. John Esten Cooke to Maria, 14 Sep. 1861. John Esten Cooke Papers, LC.

4. Order of John Letcher, 23 April 1861. General Orders, No. 1. HQ, 23 Apr. 1861. *OR* 2: 775–76; Walker to Lee, 10 May 1861. GO, No. 13. HQ, Virginia Forces, 10 May 1861. Entry 64, Box 87, Virginia Forces, RG 109, NA; Douglas Southall Freeman. *R. E. Lee; A Biography*, I, 463–64. On Lee, see Freeman, *R. E. Lee*, 4 vols.; Emory M. Thomas, *Robert E. Lee: A Biography*; Michael Fellman, *The Making of Robert E. Lee*.

5. Joseph T. Glatthaar, "Edmund Kirby Smith," in Gary W. Gallagher and Joseph T. Glatthaar, eds., *Leaders of the Lost Cause: The Confederate Full Generals*, 210–11.

6. GO, No. 11. HQ, Virginia Forces. 5 May 1861. Entry 64, Marked Box 87, Virginia Forces, RG 109, NA; F. W. S[mith] to Boyd, 4 June [1861]. David F. Boyd Papers, LSU; John Rayburn to father, 25 June 1861. Samuel King Rayburn Papers, ADAH; Edmund Kirby Smith to Mother, 21 May 1861. R2, Edmund Kirby-Smith Papers, SHC, UNC.

7. Lee to Jackson, 27 Apr. 1861. *OR* 2: 784–85; Records of Thomas J. Jackson. U.S. Census, 1860. Rockbridge Co., Va., 38; James J. White to [Mary], undated. Rockbridge Historical Society Collection, W&L; James I. Robertson, Jr., *Stonewall Jackson: The Man, The Soldier, The Legend*, 191–92. On Jackson, see Robertson, *Stonewall Jackson*; Frank E. Vandiver, *Mighty Stonewall*.

8. Garnett to Jackson, 28 Apr. 1861. Lee to Jackson, 1, 6, 9, and 10 May 1861. Jackson to Lee, 6, 7, and 9 May 1861. *OR* 2: 786, 793–94, 806–07, 809–10, 814–15, 822, 824–25, and 832–33.

9. Cooper to Johnston, 15 May 1861. *OR* 2: 844–45; J. E. Johnston to Sir, 8 Feb. 1875. David Ezra Papers, VHS; *Chesnut, Mary Chesnut's Civil War*, 799. For the best biography of Johnston, see Craig Symonds, *Joseph E. Johnston: A Civil War Biography*. One need only read the letters of Edmund Kirby Smith, Johnston's chief of staff, to see the Lee bashing. R2, Edmund Kirby-Smith Papers, SHC, UNC.

10. R. H. Gray to Father, 10 July 1862. Robert H. Gray Papers, MC; Theodore [Fogle] to Father, 4 Oct. 1861. Theodore T. Fogle Papers, EU; Thos. L. Preston to Wife, 10 June 1861. Preston-Davis Family, UVA; Chesnut, *Mary Chesnut's Civil War*, 268.

11. Johnston to Garnett, 26 May 1861, with Memorandum in relation to Harper's Ferry; 28 May 1861, with a Consultation on the condition of Harper's Ferry and its defenses reduced to writing, 28 May 1861. Lee to Johnston, 30 May, 3 June 1861. Johnston to Lee, 31 May 1861, 6 June 1861. *OR* 2: 880–81, 889–90, 894–96, 901, 907–8

12. Order of John Letcher, 20 April 1861. *OR* 51, 2: 21; Douglas Southall Freeman, *Lee's Lieutenants*, I (New York: Charles Scribner's Sons, 1942), 91; Records of Philip St. Geo. Cocke. U.S. Census, 1860. Powhatan Co., Va., 816; U.S. Census, 1860. Yazoo Co., Miss. 956.

13. Lee to Cocke, 13 May 1861. Inspection Report (hereafter IR) of Geo. Deas, 23 May 1861. Cocke to Lee, with enclosure, 8 May 1861. AAR of Maj. Gen. C. W. Sandford, 28 May 1861. Beauregard to Davis, 3 June 1861. *OR* 2: 837, 867–68, 818–19, 37–39, and 901–2; D. G. Duncan to L. P. Walker, 27 May 1861. *OR* 51, 2: 113–14.

14. Cocke to Garnett, 8 and 14 May 1861. Cocke to Lee, 24 Apr. and 15 May 1861. Lee to Cocke, 3, 10, and 15 May 1861. Cocke to Ruggles, 11 May 1861. *OR* 2: 818, 776–77, 798–99, 824, 831–32, 845–47, 841.

15. Lee to Cocke, 13 May 1861. *OR* 2: 836–37; Freeman, *Lee's Lieutenant*, 90–91.

16. See L. M. Blackford to Mother, 23 Oct. 1861. Launcelot Minor Blackford Papers, UVA; Crenshaw Hall to Father, 19 July 1861. Bolling Hall Family Papers, ADAH; Thomas. J. Goree to Uncle Pleas, 2 Aug. 1861. Goree, ed., 56; E. B[lackford] to Bro, 25 July 1861. Lewis Leigh Collection, USAMHI.

17. Special Orders, No. 95. HQ, Virginia Forces. 21 May 1861; Special Orders, No. 149. HQ, Virginia Forces. 31 May 1861. *OR* 2: 879–80 and 896; Alexander, *Fighting for the Confederacy: The Personal Recollections of Edward Porter Alexander*, 38; W. L. Barrett to Brother & Sister, 22 Nov. 1861. Heller and

Heller, eds., *The Confederacy*, 43–44; Freeman, *R.E. Lee*, I, 229; Charles P. Roland, "P.G.T. Beauregard," in Gallagher and Glatthaar, *Leaders of the Lost Cause*, 45.

18. Chesnut, *Mary Chesnut's Civil War*, 80; R. B. B[uck] to Ma, 12 June 1861. Richard Bayly Buck Papers, UVA; T. R. Lightfoot to Uncle, 14 July 1861. Burnett, ed., *GHQ* 25, 394. Also see Davis to Bettie, 12 June 1861. Bidgood Family Papers, VHS; Crenshaw Hall to Father, 19 July 1861. Bolling Hall Family Papers, ADAH.

19. Beauregard to Davis, 3 June 1861. *OR* 2: 901–2.

20. EKS[mith] to ?, 29 May 1861. EK Smith to Mother, 21 May 1861. R2, Edmund Kirby-Smith Papers, SHC, UNC; Beauregard to Lee, 23 June 1861. F16, C.S.A. Records, CAH; Beauregard to Davis, 3 June 1861. Johnston to Lee, 6 June 1861. *OR* 2: 901–2 and 907–8; Beauregard to Davis, 16 June 1861. Beauregard Papers, LC.

21. E. T. H. Warren to wife. 26 Apr. 1861. E. T. H. Warren Papers. UVA; Crenshaw Hall to Father, 26 June 1861. Bolling Hall Family Papers, ADAH; James J. White to Mary, 15 June 1861. Rockbridge Historical Society Collection, W&L.

22. Jno. Winfield to Wife, 19 May 1861. John J. Winfield Papers, SHC, UNC; EK Smith to Mother, 24 June 1861. R2, Edmund Kirby-Smith Papers, SHC, UNC; John K. McIver to Col., 18 June 1861. John K. McIver Papers, MC; Order, No. 27. 15th Virginia Vols. 21 June 1861. Orderly Book, 15th Virginia Infantry, NYHS.

23. Ted [Barclay] to Mother, 1 July 1861, and to Sister, 25 June 1861. Alexander Tedford Barclay Papers, W & L U; Reg. Order, No. 9. HQ, 4th Inf. [Va.]. 21 May 1861. Regimental Order, No. 29. HQ, 4th Inf. [Va.]. 29 May 1861. A. P. Hill Papers, VHS; J. H. Langhorne to Mother, 2 May and 21 July 1861, and to Father, 16 July 1861. Langhorne Family Papers, VHS; Regt. Order, No. 19. HQ, 1st Inf. [Va.]. 17 May [1861]. Company B, 2nd Virginia Infantry Order Book, VHS; G.O., No. 9. HQ, Yorktown. 31 May 1861. General Orders, Army of the Peninsula, May 1861–Apr. 1862. RG 109, NA.

24. Beauregard to Davis. 11 July 1861. Davis Collection, EU; Davis to Beauregard, 18 July 1861. *OR* 2: 981; William C. Davis, *The First Battle of Manassas*, 6.

25. R. A. Bryant to Eugenia, 28 Apr. 1861. Bryant Family Papers, LV; [William McKnight] to Mother, 28 May [1861]. McKnight Papers, originals at Alexandria, Va., Library. Vol. 139, FSNBP; J. Thomas Petty diary, 23 June 1861. J. Thomas Petty Papers, MC; Sam to wife, 28 June 1861. Samuel Wicliffe Melton Papers, USC; George [Robertson] to Ma, 25 Sep. 1861. George Lee Robertson Papers, CAH.

26. Ike [Bell] to Cass, 31 May 1861. Jordan-Bell Papers, VHS; J. S. Newman diary, 18 Apr. 1861. J. S. Newman Papers, LV.

27. T. R. Lightfoot to Uncle, 14 July 1861. Burnett, ed., *GHQ* 25: 395.

6. "To Slaughter One Another Like Brutes"

1. Unknown journal, 10 June 1861. Unidentified, "A Sketch of 12 Months," *AHQ* 25 (No. 1 & 2). 156.

2. E. T. H. Warren to Jennie, 6 June 1861. Edward T. H. Warren Papers, UVA. Also see J. H. Langhorne to Father, 18 June 1861. Langhorne Family Papers, VHS.

3. Samuel L. West to Pop, 8 Aug. 1861. CWMC, USAMHI.

4. Milton [Smith] to Mother, 7 July 1861. Smith Papers, 18th Mississippi Infantry, FSNBP; James Langhorne to Mother, 26 June 1861. Langhorne Family Papers, VHS; *Richmond Dispatch*, 21 Sep. 1861.

5. James M. McPherson, "Ethnic Versus Civic Nationalism in the American Civil War," in McPherson, *Is Blood Thicker Than Water? Crisis of Nationalism in the Modern World*, 45 and 50–51; *Charleston Mercury*, 7 July 1862, P1C2.

6. Sam to wife, 14 July 1861. Samuel Wicliff Melton Papers, USC.

7. Milton [Smith] to Father, 24 July 1861. Smith Papers, 18th Mississippi Infantry, FSNBP; [William Hollingsworth] to Brother, 24 July 1861. William Hollingsworth Papers, Gilder-Lehrman Collection, MC; Lee to Johnston, 24 July 1861. Lee Letters, UVA.

8. Robertson, "First Bull Run," in Heller and Stofft, eds., *America's First Battles*, 104; AAR of Johnston, 14 Oct. 1861. AAR of Beauregard, 26 Aug. [14 Oct.] 1861. Thomas Jordan, Strength of the Union Army July 21, 1861, as reported by Confederate authority. E. P. Alexander, Return of captures and prisoners taken, 12 Oct. 1861. *OR* 2: 475, 503, 569, 571.

9. John [Fort] to Mother, 26 July 1861. Tomlinson Fort Papers, EU; J. H. Newman diary, 21 July 1861. J. H. Newman Papers, LV.

10. R. B. B[uck] to Ma, 24 July 1861. Richard Bayly Buck Papers, UVA; Jackson to Anna, 22 July 1861. Charles W. Dabney Papers, SHC, UNC; JOC[ollins] to wife, 20[1] July 1861. John Overton Collins Papers, VHS.

11. Frank Potts journal, 6 Aug. 1861. Frank Potts Papers, LV. For months, sometimes more than a year afterward, soldiers continued to talk about First Manassas.

12. J. W. Reid to [Family], 24 July [1861]. J. W. Reid, *History of the Fourth Regiment of S.C. Volunteers*, 25.

13. J. M. Tate to Mother, 27 July 1861. Jeremiah M. Tate Papers, Gilder-Lehrman Collection. ML.; Hamilton Couper to Maggie, 25 July 1861. Hamilton Couper Papers, 8th Georgia Infantry File. FSNBP; [Thomas Goree] to Mother, 23 July 1861. Goree, ed., 54; John Newton Lyle, "Sketches Found in a Confederate Veteran's Desk." WLU in Robertson, *Stonewall Jackson*, 263.

14. B. G. Brown to Papa, n.d. [July 1861]. Brown Family Papers. UVA; E. T. H. W[arren] to [wife], 30 July 1861. Edward T. H. Warren Papers, UVA; J. W. Reid to [family], 30 July 1861. Reid, *History of the Fourth S.C.*, 29.

15. Ugie Allen to Susie, 31 July 1861, Randall Allen and Keith S. Bohannon, ed., *Campaigning with "Old Stonewall": Confederate Captain Ujanirtus Allen's Letters to his Wife*, 16.

16. William [Terry] to Ma, 1 Sep. 1861. William Terry and Family, LSU; J. Wm. Murray to Ellen, 18 July 1861. Murray Family Papers, LV.

17. H. A. Carrington to Wife, 22 July 1861. Carrington Family Papers, VHS; Hunter H. McGuire to Father, 24 July 1861. Hunter H. McGuire Papers, UVA; James G. Hudson journal, July 1861. James G. Hudson Papers. ADAH.

18. Geo. Field diary, 23 July 1861. George Field Papers, 11th Alabama Infantry File, FSNBP.

19. Private to ?, 26 July 1861. Styple, ed., *Writing & Fighting*, 34.

20. J. W. Murray to Ellen, 23 July 1861. Murray Family Papers, LV.

21. J. H. Newman diary, 22 July 1861. J. H. Newman Papers, LV; Henry to Parents, 23 July 1861. Henry Shanklin Papers, LV.

22. B. F. White to Jimmie, n.d. [late July or Aug. 1861]. James J. Phillips Papers, NCDAH.

23. John [Fort] to Mother, 26 July 1861. Tomlinson Fort, EU.

24. Hunter McGuire to Father, 24 July 1861. Hunter H. McGuire Papers, UVA; R. A. Hardaway to [home], n.d.[July 1861]. R. A. Hardaway Papers, MC; James G. Hudson journal, July 1861. James G. Hudson Papers, ADAH; J. W. Murray to Ellen, 23 July 1862, describing what he saw at First Manassas. Murray Family Papers, LV; Dr. James L. Cabell to Sir, 21 Sep. 1861. C.S.A. Archives. Hospital Records. Charlottesville, DU; St. George Tucker Brooke reminiscences, 20. St. George Tucker Brooke Papers, LV.

25. B. F. White to Jimmie, n.d. [late July or Aug. 1861]. James J. Phillips Papers. NCDAH.

26. Jesse Jordan to sister, 4 Aug. 1861. Jordan-Bell Family Papers, VHS.

27. *Richmond Dispatch*, 26 July 1861. Willie P. Mangum Papers, LC; AAR of Col. J. B. Kershaw, 26 July 1861. *OR* 2; 522: Henry Burst to Mrs. Smith, 22 July 1861. EKS to Mother, 31 July and 16 Aug. 1861. R2, Edmund Kirby-Smith Papers, SHC, UNC; Anita Withers diary, 21 Sep. 1861. Anita Withers Papers, SHC, UNC. Thanks to Robert K Krick and Robert. E. L. Krick for this reference.

28. J. A. Maddox to Miss E. J. Smith, 4 Aug. 1861. Letters of Confederate Soldiers, FSU; Elias Davis to Sweet Georgia, 30 July 1861. Elias Davis Papers, SHC, UNC; Ted to Mother, 6 Aug. 1861. Alexander Tedford Barclay Papers, W&L; R. V. Kidd to Ginnie, [July 1861]. Alice V. Pierrepont, *Reuben Vaughan Kidd, Soldier of the Confederacy*, 295.

29. AAR of Joseph E. Johnston, 14 Oct. 1861. Return of captures and abstract of prisoners taken by Capt. E. P. Alexander, 12 Oct. 1861. *OR* 2: 477 and 571. Alexander lists the number of muskets at 4,000; Johnston lists them at a later date at 5,000. P. H. Powers to Wife, 23 July 1861. Lewis Leigh Collection, USAMHI; Phil Haxall to Parke, 26 July 1861. George William Bagby Papers, VHS; Report of Artillery Equipment Captured on the 21st July, & received by Col. Pendleton on the 23rd. William N. Pendleton Papers, DU; E. T. H. Warren to wife, 26 July 1861. Edward T. H. Warren Papers, VHS.

30. Bob Houston to Friends, 24 July 1861. Confederate Soldiers Collection. Coleman Family File, MC; Johnston to Davis, 30 Aug. 1861. Joseph E. Johnston Papers, DU.

31. Theodore to Father, 29 Aug. 1861. Theodore T. Fogle Papers, EU; [John Esten Cooke to Maria], 14 Sep. 1861. John Esten Cooke Papers, LC; John [Steger] to Mollie, 10 Dec. 1861. Carter Family Papers, VHS; Ivy Duggan to Editor, *Central Georgian*, 13 Sep. 1861. Civil War Miscellany: 48th Georgia File, GDAH; G. Campbell Brown to Aunt, 20 Aug. 1861. Polk-Brown-Ewell Papers, SHC, UNC; Johnnie [Buchanan] to Mother, 18 June 1861. John Buchanan Papers, USC.

32. In World War II in the Pacific Theater, collecting human trophies was not unusual. See John W. Dower, *War Without Mercy: Race & Power in the Pacific War*; E. B. Sledge, *With the Old Breed at Peleliu and Okinawa*; J. Glenn Gray, *The Warriors: Reflections on Men in Battle*.

33. D. W. Halliday to Anne, 23 Sep. 1861. Confederate Miscellany, EU.

34. Johnston to Sir, 5 Aug. 1861. Joseph E. Johnston Papers, Gilder-Lehrman Collection, ML; Eugene Blackford to Father, 22 July 1861. Lewis Leigh Collection, USAMHI; Johnston to Davis, 3 Aug. 1861. Joseph E. Johnston Papers, DU. For corroboration on Yankees' firing too high due to sights, sec Claud W. Fuller, *The Rifled Musket*; David F. Butler, *United States Firearms: The First Century, 1776–1875*; "Someone firing at men 100 yds. away was liable to have perfectly-aimed rounds passing 3+ feet above his point of aim." Memo from LTC Dana Mangham, U.S.A. to author, 17 Aug. 2004. Copy in possession of author.

35. B. G. Brown to Papa, n.d.[July 1861]. Brown Family Papers, UVA; W. H[ampton] to [Mrs. Singleton], 5 Sep. 1861. Hampton Family Papers, USC.

36. C. W. Dabney to Brother, 24 Aug. 1861. Charles W. Dabney Papers, SHC, UNC; Ben Hubert to Miss Letitia M. Bailey, 31 July 1861. Ben Hubert Papers, DU.

37. Johnston to Sir, 5 Aug. 1861. Joseph R. Johnston Papers, Gilder-Lehrman Collection, MC.

38. AAR of Micah Jenkins, 22 July 1861. AAR of D. R. Jones, 23 July 1861. *OR* 2: 542 and 538; Sam to wife, 25 July 1861. Samuel Wicliffe Melton Papers, USC.

39. AAR of Johnston, 14 Oct. 1861. *OR* 2: 477; Johnston to Davis, 10 Aug. 1861. *OR* 5: 777.

40. Davis, *Jefferson Davis*, 351; Bratton to Wife, 23 July 1861. Bratton, *General John Bratton: Sumter to Appomattox in Letters to His Wife*, 30; G. T. Beauregard to Dabney, 6 Aug. 1861. Box 2, F4, Robert Lewis Dabney Papers, Union Theological Seminary; General Orders, No. 45. HQ, Dept. Northern Virginia. 18 Dec. 1861. Jubal Early Papers, VHS.

41. Johnston to Davis, 30 Aug. 1861. Joseph E. Johnston Papers, DU.

42. Davis to Maj. Campbell Brown, 14 June 1866. George Washington Campbell Papers, LC.

7. "A Great Canvass City"

1. [Ned] to Dear Parents, 21 Nov. 1861. Bayol Family Papers, VHS; William E. Bird to Sallie, 19 Aug. 1861. Rozier, *Granite Farm Letters*, 15. A different version of this chapter appeared in William C. Davis and James I. Robertson, Jr., eds., *Virginia at War, 1861*.

2. John [Fort] to Kate, 15 July 1861. Tomlinson Fort Papers, EU. At peak, the army had about 90,000 men. http://www.census.gov/population/documentation/twps0027/tab09.txt.

3. Conversation with John Hennessy, National Park Service, 20 Apr. 1999. Notes in author's possession; Emory Thomas, *Confederate State of Richmond: A Biography of the Capital*, 128; *OR* 4 (1): 822; Samuel L. West to Pop, 8 Aug. 1861. CWMC, USAMHI. http://www.census.gov/population/documentation/twps0027/tab09.txt. Richmond was 6.12 square miles. Civil War armies often organized in a linear fashion, with less attention to depth.

4. Six percent were from urban areas. See sample, Appendix I. Records of Barry Lynch. U.S. Census Records, Louisiana. M653, R421, 326. Records of Addison Tinsley. U.S. Census Records, Georgia. M653, R115, 233. Records of Daniel C. Wright. U.S. Census Records, Maryland. M653, R463, 142; Obituary in *Baltimore Sun*, 20 Feb. 1922; 16.

5. CSR of George S. High, 13th Mississippi Infantry; Records of George S. High. U.S. Census, Mississippi, M653, R589, 8.

6. J. Vance to Cousin Kate, 22 Aug. 1861. Walker Collection, USAMHI; Benj. F. White to Dear Young Friend, 2 Dec. 1861. James J. Phillips Papers, NCDAH.

7. A. L. P. Vairin diary, 14 June 1861. A. L. P. Vairin Papers, MDAH; R. Channing Price to Mother, 18 Aug. 1861. R. Channing Price Papers, SHC, UNC; J.B.H. to Confederacy, 31 Aug. 1861. *Southern Confederacy*, 6 Sep. 1861; Magruder to Mayor et.al of Williamsburg, 11 Oct. 1861. Letters and Telegrams Sent, Army of the Peninsula, May–November 1861. RG 109, NA; John Sewell Anglin to Parents, 27 Nov. 1861. John S. Anglin Papers, LC; D. W. Baine to Colonel, 28 Dec. 1861. Pettigrew Family Papers, NCDAH; R. Taylor Scott to Fan, 13 Jan. 1862. Keith Family Papers, VHS; Johnston to Davis, 23 Aug. 1861. C. C. Jones, Jr., Papers, DU; Robert G. Kean diary, 5 Oct. 1861. Robert G. H. Kean Papers, UVA.

8. Johnston to Davis, 16 June 1861. Jefferson Davis Collection, EU; Beauregard to Davis, 23 Aug. 1861. Beauregard Papers, LC; F. W. Thompson to Sister, 13 Aug. 1861. Fleming W. Thompson Papers, CAH; Lee to Dr. De Leon, 20 June 1861. R1, Letters Sent. Virginia Forces, RG 109. NA; J. P. Hamilton to Henry, 27 Nov. 1861. J. R. Dorros to Mother, 26 July 1861. Lewis Leigh Collection, USAMHI. For basic information on measles, see http://kidshealth.org/parent/infections/bacterial_viral/measles.html.

9. Ivy W. Duggan to Editor, *Central Georgian*, 12 Oct. 1861. Civil War Miscellany: 48th Georgia File, GDAH. Bedford Brown to Lee, 15 Oct. 1861. Series B. Box 3, Lee Headquarters Papers, VHS; Capt. F. F. Montgomery to Davis, 12 Feb. 1862. Letters Received, Secretary of War. M437, R28, F859–62. RG 109, NA. For information on typhoid fever, see http://www.cdc.gov/ncidod/dbmd/diseaseinfo/typhoidfever_g.htm.

10. Thos. H. Williams to Sir, 22 Jan. 1862. Letters Sent, Medical Director's Office, ANV; A. P. Mason to Maj. J. R. G. Cole, 25 Jan. 1862. Letters and Telegrams Sent, ANV. RG 109, NA. For information on scurvy, see http://www.people.virginia.edu/~rjh9u/vitac.html.

11. General Order, No. 5. Army of the Potomac. 18 Aug. 1861. M921, R1, F3, GSOCI, ANV; Thos. H. Williams to Sir, 22 Nov. and 18 Dec. 1861. LS, Medical Director's Office, ANV. RG 109, NA.

12. Dr. J. L. Cabell to Surg. Moore, 30 Sep. 1861. CSA Archives. Hospital Records. Charlottesville. DU; Thomas G. Rhett to General, 2 Sep. 1861. SO, No. 55. Medical Director's Office, Manassas Junction. 14 Oct. 1861. Order Book, Thomas H. Williams Papers, Schenectady County Historical Society.

13. B. F. White to Jimmie, n.d.[Aug. 1861]. James J. Phillips Papers, NCDAH; John S. Apperson journal, 24 Oct. 1861. Roper, ed., 144–45; J. Vance to Cousin Kate, 22 Aug. 1861. Walker Collection, USAMHI; Cornelius [Kollock] to Henrietta, 20 June 1861. Cornelius Kollock Papers, SCHS; Elbert to ?, 24 Sep. 1861. *Southern Confederacy*, 3 Oct. 1861; A Soldier to the Confederacy, 30 Oct. 1861. *Southern Confederacy*, 8 Nov. 1861; McLaws to Children, 21 July 1861. McLaws Papers, SHC, UNC; GO, No. 7. Medical Director's Office, Manassas Junction. 1 Oct. 1861. Order Book, Thomas H. Williams, Schenectady County Historical Society.

14. William V. Williams et al., to Davis, 3 Sep. 1861. LR, CSW. M437, R14, F1179. RG 109, NA.

15. Joe D. Shields, Jr., to Pa Ma & family, 16 Sep. [1861]. Joseph D. Shields Papers, LSU; William A. Clarke to Friend, 7 Sep. 1861. Mrs. Clarke to ?, 22 Dec. 1861 and 24 Aug. 1861. Cody, "Letters of Barnett Hardeman Cody and Others, 1861–1864," *GHQ*, No. 3 (Sep. 1939), 289; G. W. Hopkins to Mother, 19 Oct. [1861]. George W. Hopkins Papers. MDAH; Richard [Habersham] to little Brother, 25 Aug. 1861. Richard Habersham Papers, LC; John Sewell Anglin to Parents, 27 Nov. 1861. John S. Anglin Papers, LC; Milton Barrett to Brother and Sister, 14 Oct. 1861. Heller, eds., 27–28. Also see [A. J. McBride] to Cousin, 16 July 1861. Andrew Jay McBride Papers, DU; Unknown diarist, 23 Sep. 1861. Unidentified, "A Sketch of 12 Months," *AHQ* 25, 165; Edge to Sal, 21 Nov. 1861. Rozier, *Granite Farm Letters*, 45.

16. John H. Griscom, *The Sanitary Condition of the Laboring Class of New York, With Suggestions for its Improvement*.

17. W. H. Mitchell to Doctor, 12 Aug. 1861. *Southern Confederacy*, 12 Sep. 1861; Private to ?, 26 July 1861. Styple, ed., *Writing & Fighting*, 34.

18. J. T. Thompson to ?, 23 July 1861. Austin, ed., *VMHB* 70, No. 3, 315; J. I. Cooper to Sir, 23 Aug. 1861. Fishburne Family Papers, UVA.

19. J. Hays to Mother, 4 Aug. 1861. James Hays Papers, VHS; James G. Hudson journal, July 1861. James G. Hudson Papers, ADAH; S. A. Smith to Sir, 1 Sep. 1861. Record Book of the Hospital of the 7th Louisiana Infantry, RG 109, NA; Johnston to Davis, 30 Aug. 1861. Joseph E. Johnston Papers, DU; George Field diary, 23 July 1861. George Field Papers, 11th Alabama Infantry Volume, FSNBP; John S. Apperson journal, 25 July 1861. Apperson, 118.

20. S. A. Smith to Sir, 1 Sep. 1861. Record Book of the Hospital of the 7th Louisiana Infantry, RG 109, NA; Richard W. Waldrop diary, 3 Dec. 1863. Richard Waldrop Papers, SHC, UNC, quoted in Bell I. Wiley, *Life of Johnny Reb: The Common Soldier of the Confederacy*, 248.

21. Thos. H. Williams to Sir, 19 Nov. 1861. Report of Medical Director of 2nd Corps, included in Thos. H. Williams to Sir, 22 Jan. 1862. Letters Sent, Medical Director's Office, ANV; General Orders, No. 2. HQ, 1st Corps, Army of the Potomac, 17 Jan. 1862. General Orders and Circulars, Army of the Potomac. RG 109, NA; Geo. W. Lay to General, 25 Jan. 1862. J. B. Walton Papers, F5, Louisiana Historical Association, TU.

22. GO, No. 8. HQ, 2nd Brigade, 1st Division, 1st Corps, Army of the Potomac. 26 Oct. 1861. GO Issued by Subcommands, Army of the Potomac. RG 109, NA.

23. Otis D. Smith to Sir, 8 Feb. 1862. Otis David Smith Papers, ADAH; Reminiscences of James M. Holloway, n.p. Holloway Family Papers, VHS; Johnnie to Mother, 22 Feb. 1862. John Buchanan Papers, USC; E. A. Davis to Sir. 12 Feb. 1862. Ezekiel Andrew Davis, "Confederate Life at Home and in Camp: Seven Letters." *GHQ* 40, No. 3 (Sep. 1956), 304.

24. Benj. F. White to Dear Young Friend, 5 Jan. 1862. James J. Phillips Papers, NCDAH; Chas. S. Venable to darling boy, 8 Aug. 1861. Memoir of Mary Cantey, 29. UVA; Theodore to Father & Mother, 30 June 1861. Theodore T. Fogle Papers. EU; T. R. Lightfoot to cousin Hennie, 24 Oct. 1861. Cody, *GHQ* 26, No. 1, 68.

25. Milton Barrett diary, 1 Nov. 1861. Barnett, 31; James P. Williams to Aunt Mary, 24 June 1861. J. Peter Williams Papers, UVA; Jas. W. Bacon to Friend, 26 Jan. 1862. Hugh Conway Browning Papers, DU; W. B. Young to Aunt, 29 July 1861. William Dunlap Simpson Papers, DU; Robert [Stafford] to Sister, 12 July 1861. Robert Stafford Papers, Gilder-Lehrman Collection, ML; Daniel J. Hileman to Miss R. A. McCutcheon, 13 Sep. 1861. Daniel Hileman Folder, Rockbridge Historical Society Manuscripts, W&L; Soldier Jim to Cousin, 17 Sep. 1861. *Southern Confederacy*, 29 Sep. 1861.

26. William V. Williams et al. to Davis, 3 Sep. 1861. Letters Received by the Secretary of War, M437, R14, F1180. RG 109, NA; Beauregard to Davis, 23 Aug. 1861. Beauregard Papers, LC; Thos. H. Williams to Sir, 19 Nov. 1861 and 22 Jan. 1862. Letters Sent, Medical Director's Office, ANV. RG 109, NA; Johnston to Davis, 23 Aug. 1861. C. C. Jones, Jr., Papers, DU; Henry [Graves] to Mother, 11 Aug. 1861. Graves Family Papers, EU; H. R. Berkeley diary, 25 May 1861. H. R. Berkeley Papers, MC; L. B. Northrop to Sir, 22 June 1861. C.S.A. Army. Infantry. Tomlinson's Battalion, VHS; Edge to [Sallie], 10 Jan. 1862. Rozier, *Granite Farm Letters*, 51; J. H. Bayol to Parents, 2 Oct. 1861. Bayol Family Papers, VHS; James Hays to Ma, 30 Sep. 1861. James Hays Papers, VHS.

27. James P. Williams to Aunt Mary, 14 Oct. 1861. James Peter Williams Papers, UVA; L. M. Blackford to Mother, 11 Jan. 1862. Launcelot Minor Blackford Papers, UVA.

28. J. M. Tate to sister, 3 June 1861. Jeremiah Tate Papers, Gilder-Lehrman Collection, ML; Lloyd Powell to Father, 30 June 1861. Powell Family Papers, W&M; A. S. Morgan to wife, 4 Oct. 1861. Asa S. Morgan Papers, 1st Arkansas Infantry Volume, FSNBP; S. P. Hillhouse to wife, children, and friends, 29 June and 12 July 1861. CWMC, USAMHI; J. R. McCutcheon to Kate, n.d. [1861]. Rockbridge Historical Society Papers, W&L, copy at FSNBP.

29. Hussen to Darly, [July 1861]. James A. Davidson Papers, ADAH; W.P.S. to Brother, 21 Aug. 1861. *Southern Confederacy*, 29 Aug. 1861; GO. No. 61. Virginia Forces, 5 May 1861. Virginia Forces, Entry 64, Marked Box 87, RG 109, NA; William P. Heflin, *Blind Man*, 17.

30. L. McLaws to children, 21 July 1861. Lafayette McLaws Papers, SHC, UNC.

31. E. K. Smith to Wife, 15 Nov. 1861. R2, Edmund Kirby-Smith Papers, SHC, UNC; McLaws to Wife, 18 Aug. 1861. Lafayette McLaws Papers, SHC, UNC; W. G. Kisling to Ginnie, 5 Jan. 1862. W. G. Kisling Papers, MC; Shields to Major, 17 June 1861. Isaac Howell Carrington Papers, DU; GO, No. 61. Army of the Potomac, 20 Nov. 1861. General and Special Orders Issued, ANV. M921, R1, F33–35. RG 109, NA; Charges and Specifications preferred against Lt. Col. C. M. Bradford, 3rd La. Batt. Vols., by Maj. Gen. Huger. Benjamin Huger Papers, MC; Milton Barrett to Brother and Sister, 28 Mar. 1862. Barnett, 55; J. Scurry to Sarah, 3 Jan. 1862. John G. Scurry Papers, Gilder-Lehrman Collection, ML; R. H. Jones to wife, 7 Dec. 1861. R. H. Jones Papers, GDAH.

32. Daniel J. Hileman to Miss R. A. McCutcheon, 13 Sep. 1861. Daniel Hileman Folder, Rockbridge Historical Society Manuscripts, W&L; J. J. Hileman to Brother, 22 Sep. 1861. Lewis Leigh Collection, USAMHI; R. Fairfax to Mamma, 11 Oct. 1861. Fairfax Brothers Papers, MC; M. H. Fitzpatrick to Amanda, 17 Apr. 1863. Jeffrey C. Lowe and Sam Hodges, eds., *Letters to Amanda: The Civil War Letters of Marion Hill Fitzpatrick, Army of Northern Virginia*, 62; J.W.F.L. to Confederacy, 25 Aug. 1861. *Southern Confederacy*, 7 Sep. 1861; Orders No. 2, Col. Wm. N. Levy, 7 Sep. 1861. Col. William N. Levy Orders, LV; J.B.H. to Confederacy, 31 Aug. 1861. *Southern Confederacy*, 6 Sep. 1861.

8. Keeping the Army Together

1. CSR of Daniel Hileman. 27th Virginia Infantry. M324, R730, NA; [Daniel Hileman] to Kate, 22 Sep. 1861. Daniel Hileman Folder, Rockbridge County Historical Manuscripts, W&L.

2. CSR of James A. Maddox, 20th Georgia Infantry. M266, R329, NA; J. A. Maddox to Miss E. J. Smith, 4 Aug. 1861. Letters of Confederate Soldiers, FSU.

3. G. W. Smith Memorandum, circa 1 Oct. 1861. *OR* 5: 884–86.

4. [Crenshaw Hall] to Laura, 14 Nov. 1861. Bolling Hall Family, ADAH; A. P. Hill to Lute, 26 Sep. 1861. A. P. Hill Papers, VHS; L. G. Young to Uncle Robert, [?] Nov. 1861. Robert Newman Gourdin Papers, EU.

5. Jno. to Charley, 28 July 1861. Box 2, Papers of the Army of Northern Virginia, Louisiana Historical Association, TU; [Daniel Hileman] to Kate, 22 Sep. 1861. Daniel Hileman Folder, Rockbridge County Historical Manuscripts, W&L; James K. Edmondson to wife, 7 Aug. 1861. James K. Edmondson Family, W&L; Edge to Sallie, 22 Sep. 1861. Rozier, *Granite Farm Letters*, 29; Circular. 19 Oct. 1861. GO&C, Army of the Potomac. RG 109, NA; John S. Robertson to Jim, 6 Sep. 1861. Richard Anderson

Folder, CWTIC, USAMHI; Early to LTC Cummings, 22 Jan. 1862. Early Papers, Gilder-Lehrman Collection, ML.

6. Barnett H. Cody to Father, 20 Aug. 1861. Thos. R. Lightfoot to Cousin Hennie, 10 Oct. 1861. Cody, *GHQ* 23, No. 3: 286; 25, No. 4: 399; R. Fairfax to Mamma, 11 Oct. 1861. Fairfax Brothers Papers, MC.

7. James K. Edmondson to wife, 7 Aug. 1861. James K. Edmondson Family Papers, W&L; H. R. Berkeley diary, 26 May 1861. H. R. Berkeley Papers, MC; Jimmie [Langhorne] to Father, 5 June 1861. Langhorne Family Papers, VHS; C. C. Blacknall diary, 13 Aug. 1861. Oscar W. Blacknall Papers, NCDAH.

8. R. B.B[uck] to Pa, 18 Nov. 1861. Richard Bayly Buck Papers, UVA; A. J. McBride to Cousin Fannie, 8 June 1861. Andrew Jay McBride Papers, DU; Will [Crutcher] to wife, 2 Nov. 1861. E. R. Crockett Papers, CAH; Officers of the 20th Miss. Inf. to Davis, 27 Nov. 1861. Letters Received, Secretary of War. M437, R17, F355–57. RG 109, NA.

9. Bolling Hall to father, 26 Dec. 1861. Bolling Hall Family, ADAH; Mary S. Livingston to Davis, 25 Jan. 1862. Letters Received, Secretary of War. M437, R26, F990–91. RG 109, NA; Robert [Stafford] to Sister, 5 Dec. 1861. Robert Stafford Papers, Gilder-Lehrman Collection, ML; Will T. Martin to Nep, 12 Feb. 1862. Box 19, F216, Joseph F. Waring Papers, GHS.

10. E. K. Smith to wife, 14 Dec. 1861. R2. Edmund Kirby-Smith Papers, SHC, UNC [his name was Edmund Kirby Smith, but the collection is entitled Edmund Kirby-Smith Papers]; E. A. Davis to Sir, 12 Feb. 1862. E. A. Davis, *GHQ* 40, No. 3: 304.

11. Jno. J. Reev to Parke, 11 Jan. 1862. George William Bagby Papers, VHS; L. M. Blackford to Mother, 16 Jan. 1862. Launcelot Minor Blackford Papers, UVA; Glatthaar, *Partners in Command*. 15–16; Robertson, *Stonewall Jackson*, 301–13.

12. R. G. Strickland to Brother, 22 Dec. 1861. CSA. Russell G. Strickland File. NYPL; Jas. H. Brown to Sister, 12 May 1861, James H. Brown Folder, Gilder-Lehrman Collection, ML; Ivy W. Duggan to Editor, *Central Georgian*, 7 Sep. 1861. Civil War Miscellany: 48th Georgia File, GDAH; Theodore to Sister, 26 Oct. 1861. Theodore T. Fogle Papers, EU.

13. R. Fairfax to Mama, 31 Jan. 1862. Fairfax Brothers Papers, MC; John S. Foster to Lizzie, 29 June 1861. James Foster and Family, LSU.

14. R. H. Miller to Mother, 3 Feb. 1862. Robert H. Miller, *VMHB* 70 (1): 67; Ben Hubert to Miss Bailey, 18 Aug. 1861. Ben Hubert Papers. DU.

15. Jno. M. Tilley to Wife, 11 Sep. 1861. John M. Tilley Papers, GDAH; Thos. S. Preston to Wife, 13 Mar. 1862. Preston-Davis Papers, UVA; Ivy W. Duggan to Editor, *Central Georgian*, 13 Aug. 1861. Civil War Miscellany: 48th Georgia File, GDAH. For just a sample of the orders against destruction, see General Orders, No. 57. HQ, Bethel Church, 9 Aug. 1861. GO, Army of the Peninsula, May 1861–Apr. 1862. RG 109, NA; Circular, Department of Fredericksburg. 17 and 26 Aug. 1861. HQ, Dept. of Fredericksburg. Order Book, John B. Brown Papers, NCDAH.

16. James Stanley Newman diary, 10 Aug. 1861. James Stanley Newman Papers, MC; Edward to Sister, n.d. [1861]. Bayol Family, VHS; J. H. Everett to wife, 9 July 1861. John A. Everett Papers, EU; B. J. Pack to dear, 5 July 1861. Joseph B. and Andrew Pack Papers, USC; F. P. Johnson to Father & Mother, 22 Sep. 1861. CWTIC, USAMHI.

17. [Daniel Hileman] to Rate, 22 Sep. 1861. Daniel Hileman Folder, Rockbridge County Historical Manuscripts, W&L; J. H. Newman diary, 11 Aug. 1861. J. H. Newman Papers, LV; R. A. Bryant to Eugenia, 30 Oct. 1861. R. A. Bryant Papers, LV.

18. Joe D. Shields, Jr., to Pa, 1 July 1861. Joseph D. Shields Papers, LSU; Wm. T. Williams to Jennette, 6 June 1861. CWTIC, USAMHI; Eli Landers to Napoleon, n.d. [1861]. Landers, *Weep Not for Me*. 128: Charles [Batchelor] to Albert, 25 Aug. 1861. Albert A. Batchelor Papers, LSU; J. M. Tate to Mother, 27 July 1861. Jeremiah Tate Papers, Gilder- Lehrman Collection, ML; J. R. Gilham to Mother, 7 Nov. 1861. Ella Francis Daniels Papers, ADAH; J.B.H. to Confederacy, 9 Aug. 1861. *Southern Confederacy*, 18 Aug. 1861.

19. Rhaddie to Parents and Brother, 7 Jan. 1862. W. R. M. Slaughter Papers, VHS; Theodore T. Fogle to Mother, 8 Feb. 1862. Theodore T. Fogle Papers, EU; Lt. J. T. Stephens to Davis, 10 Feb. 1862. Letters Received, Secretary of War. M437, R27, F99–106. RG 109, NA; Moore, *Conscription and Conflict*, 6–8.

20. Ned to Father, 2 Feb. 1862. Bayol Family Papers, VHS; Jos. B. McCutcheon to Cousin, 20 Feb. 1862. FSNBP, original in Rockbridge Historical Society Papers, WL; Robert [Stafford] to Sister, 19 Jan. 1862. Robert Stafford Papers, Gilder-Lehrman Collection, ML.

21. R. A. Bryant to Eugenia, 5 Jan. 1862. Bryant Family Papers, LV; Records of Richd. A. Bryant. U.S. Census Records, Cumberland County, Va. M653, R1341, P958.

22. G. L. Robertson to Pa, 2 July 1861. George Lee Robertson Papers, CAH; Records of G. L. Robertson. U.S. Census Records, Travis County, Tex. M653, R1306, P269; S. B. Waring to Cora, 8 Feb. 1862. Powell-Waring Papers, MDHS; Records of Bartlett Waring. U.S. Census, Mobile County. M653, RI7, P395.

23. To the Army of the Peninsula. HQ, Army of the Peninsula. 4 Mar. 1862. Orders Received by the 15th Regiment Virginia Volunteers, Dec. 1861–Apr. 1862. RG 109, NA; H. S. Figures to Pa, 9 Feb. 1862. Donald Tiedeken Papers, VHS. Laine and Penny, *Law's Alabama Brigade*, 9.

24. A. S. Cameron to Madam, 1 Mar. 1862. Letters of Confederate Soldiers, FSU; G. T. Brown to Miss, 6 Dec. 1861. Jane Fisher Papers, DU.

25. Randolph to Davis, 12 Aug. 1862. *OR* 4(2): 42–49; An Act to provide for the public defense, 16 Apr. 1862. GO, No. 30. Adj. and Insp. General's Office. 28 Apr. 1862. *OR* 4(1): 1094–97.

26. Edward S. Cox to Miss Porter, 3 Mar. 1862. William H. Jones Papers, DU; Spencer C. Barnes to Father, 3 Mar. 1862. Spencer Barnes Papers, MC; Records of Spencer Barnes. U.S. Census, Edgecombe County, N. C. M653, R896, P207.

27. [E. T. H. Warren] to Jennie, 15 Feb. 1862. E. T. H. Warren Papers, UVA; John S. Foster to Sinah, 19 Nov. 1861. Box 18, F194, Joseph F. Waring Papers, GHS: Records of John S. Foster. U.S. Census, Spalding County. Ga. M653. R136, P283.

28. W H[ampton] to [Mrs. Singleton], 5 Sep. 1861. Hampton Family Papers, USC; Jimmie [Griffin] to Leila, 25 Apr. 1861. CWTIC, USAMHI.

29. JST diary, 27 Apr. 1862. G. Ward Hubbs. ed., *Voices from Company D: Diaries by the Greensboro Guards, Fifth Alabama Infantry Regiment, Army of Northern Virginia*, 81; W. Preston Johnston to Rosa, 3 May 1862. Mason Barret Collection, TU; List of Officers Relieved from duty by the reorganization of the 18th Regt. N.C.T., 25 Apr. 1862. Robert H. Cowan to Major, 5 June 1862. Lawrence O'Brien Branch Papers, NCDAH. There was no standard or single elections day. In fact, units received virtually no guidance from the War Department or state governments.

30. Krick, *Lee's Colonels*, 19; Franklin Gaillard to Maria, 31 Dec. 1861. Franklin Gaillard Papers, SHC, UNC.

31. Records of Wiley P. Robertson. U.S. Census Records, 1860. Caswell County, N.C., 716; Records of S. F. Robertson. U.S. Slave Census, 1860. Caswell County, N.C., 355; Records of Thomas Beall [spelled Bell in census but Beall in slave census]. Records of Jesse Hargrave. U.S. Census Records, 1860. Davison Co., N.C., 775 and 986; Records of Thomas Beall and Jesse Hargrave. U.S. Slave Census, 1860. Davidson County, N.C., 26 and 37–38. Statistics are based on a random sample of seventeen regiments and batteries, approximately one in ten, that served in Virginia on 30, Apr. 1862 and became part of the Army of Northern Virginia. The units were Chew's Battery, 1st Virginia Bn., Wooding's (Danville) Battery, 21st North Carolina, 1st Louisiana Bn., 3rd Virginia, 12th Alabama, Jeff Davis Legion, Fredericksburg Artillery, 16th North Carolina, Loudon Artillery, 21st Virginia, 46th Virginia, 8th Louisiana, 2nd South Carolina (2nd Palmetto), 42nd Virginia, and Armistead's Battery; Franklin Gaillard to Maria, 31 Dec. 1861. Franklin Gaillard Papers, SHC, UNC.

32. Wm[Murray] to Ellen, 22 Feb. 1862. Murray Family Papers, LV; James M. Daniel to John, 28 May 1862. Daniel Family Papers, USC. Also see R. V. Kidd, diary, 27 May 1862. Pierrepont, *Reuben Vaughan Kidd*, 312; William C. Oates, *The War Between the Union and the Confederacy and Its Lost Opportunities*, 83; CSR of 16th and 21st North Carolina Infantry. M270, R241–48 and 278–84. CSR of William Keith. M270, R244 and 556. RG 109, NA.

33. CSR of John C. Gilmer, 21st North Carolina Infantry. M270, R280. RG 109, NA.

34. CSR of 42nd Virginia Infantry. M324, R871–76. RG 109, NA.

35. For proof, one need only scan published rosters of regiments and batteries to see the large number of original officers who failed to retain their positions in the spring elections of 1862 and who ended up as officers of new units. See Dewees Ogden to Cousin Mary, 3 Mar. 1863, for an officer who served, did not run for re-election, and joined an artillery battery as a private instead. Dewees Ogden Papers, LV.

36. William R. Smith diary, 15 Apr. 1862. CWTIC, USAMHI; C. J. W[inston] to Aunt, 16 Feb. 1862. Winston-Clark Family Papers, VHS.

37. J. T. Thompson to Mother and sisters, 26 Mar. 1862. Thompson, "A Georgia Boy," *VMHB* 70, No. 3: 322.

9. Clashes within the High Command

1. EKS to Mother, 16 Aug. and 31 July 1861. Henry Burst[?] to Mrs. Smith, 22 July 1861. Reel 2. Edmund Kirby-Smith Papers, SHC, UNC; *Richmond Dispatch*, 6 Aug. 1861, 3; Joseph T. Glatthaar, "Edmund Kirby Smith," in Gary W. Gallagher and Joseph T. Glatthaar, eds., *Leaders of the Lost Cause: New Perspectives on the Confederate High Command*, 213–14.

2. EKS to Mother, 3 Nov. 1861. Reel 2, Edmund Kirby-Smith Papers, SHC, UNC.

3. See Edward M. Coffman, *The Old Army: A Portrait of the American Army in Peacetime, 1784–1898*; William B. Skelton, *An American Profession of Arms: The Army Officer Corps, 1784–1861*; Donald B. Connelly, *John M. Schofield and the Politics of Generalship*, 1–11.

4. See Robert E. L. Krick, *Staff Officers in Gray: A Biographical Register of the Staff Officers in the Army of Northern Virginia*, 1–56, for an outstanding survey of the history of staff positions.

5. R. B. Lee to Davis, 23 July 1861. G. T. Beauregard to Colonels, 29 July 1861. Alfred Roman, *The Military Operations of General Beauregard*, I, 121–22. Beauregard certainly knew that the two congressmen would raise a ruckus on the issue in Congress.

6. Davis to Cobb, 1 Aug. 1861. Resolution of Hon. James Chesnut, 1 Aug. 1861. *Journal of the Congress of the Confederate States of America. 1861–1865*, I, 309 and 305.

7. See William Davis, *Jefferson Davis*, 97 and 306.

8. Davis to Beauregard, 10 [4] Aug. 1861. Roman, *Military Operations*, I, 122–23.

9. Beauregard to Davis, 10 Aug. 1861. *OR* 51 (2): 1071–72.

10. AAR of Beauregard, 26 Aug. [14 Oct.] 1861. *OR* 2: 484–85. Beauregard had also failed to alter the date of the original draft, so it seemed to Davis that it had been completed months earlier and never forwarded to him.

11. *Journal of Confederate Congress*, I, 478 and 486; Undated Indsmt to AAR of Beauregard, [Oct. or Nov. 1861]. Chesnut to Beauregard, 16 July 1861. Davis to Beauregard, 30 Oct. 1861. Davis to Chesnut, 30 Oct. 1861. Chesnut to Davis 9 Nov. 1861. Davis to Cooper and Lee, 4 Nov. 1861. Cooper to Davis, 9 Nov. 1861. Lee to Davis, 24 Nov. 1861. *OR* 2: 504–15.

12. Beauregard to *Richmond Whig*, 3 Nov. 1861. Roman. *Military Operations*, I. 163–64; Beauregard to Davis, 7 Nov. 1861. Crist and Dix, eds., *Papers of Jefferson Davis*, 7. 399–401: T. Harry Williams. *P.G.T. Beauregard: Napoleon in Gray*, 108.

13. Chesnut to Davis, 9 Nov. 1861. Davis to Chesnut, 11 Nov. 1861. *OR* 2: 509–11, and 513–14.

14. Beauregard to Benjamin, 9 Oct. 1861. *OR* 51(2): 339; Benjamin to Beauregard, 17 Oct. 1861. Davis to Beauregard, 17, 20, and 25 Oct. 1861. *OR* 5: 903–6 and 920. Roman, *Military Operations*, I, 158–63.

15. Davis to Beauregard, 10 Nov. 1861. *OR* 5: 945.

16. Benjamin to Johnston and Beauregard, 26 Jan. 1862. *OR* 5: 1048; Thomas Bragg diary, 31 Jan. 1862. Thomas Bragg Papers, SHC, UNC.

17. H. S. Foote, *War of the Rebellion' or Scylla and Charybdis*, 357; Eli N. Evans, *Judah P. Benjamin: The Jewish Confederate*, 154–55; Cooper, *Jefferson Davis*, 382–83.

18. Crist and Dix, eds., *Papers of Jefferson Davis*, 7, 335, Fn. 3; Johnston to Cooper, 29 July 1861, *OR* 2: 1007; William C. Davis, *Jefferson Davis*, 357.

19. Edmund Kirby Smith to Mother, 17 Aug. 1864. Reel 4, Edmund Kirby-Smith Papers. SHC, UNC; Alexander, *Fighting for the Confederacy*, 89.

20. Krick, "Snarl and Sneer and Quarrel," in Gallagher and Glatthaar, eds., *Leaders of the Lost Cause*, 170–73.

21. An Act for the establishment and organization of the Army of the Confederate States of America, 6 Mar. 1861. An Act amendatory of an act for the organization of the staff departments of the Army and an act for the establishment and organization of the Army of the Confederate States of America, 14 Mar. 1861. *OR* 4 (1): 131 and 164; Steven H. Newton, *Joseph E. Johnston and the Defense of Richmond*, 5–7.

22. Johnston to Davis, 12 Sep. 1861. *OR* 4(2): 605–8.

23. Davis to Johnston, 14 Sep. 1861. *OR* 4(2): 611.

24. Davis to Johnston, 22 June 1861. *OR* 2: 945; Johnston to Wigfall, 12 Nov. 1863. Wigfall Family Papers, LC.

25. Johnston to Jackson, 28 Jan. 1862. *OR* 5: 1050.

26. Johnston to Jackson, 28 Jan. 1862. *OR* 5: 1050; Cooper to Johnston, 18 June 1861. *OR* 2: 934; Davis to Smith, 19 Nov. 1863. *OR* 22 (2): 1072; Glatthaar. *Partners in Command*, 101 and 110–11; Symonds, *Joseph E. Johnston*, 140.

27. Johnston to Secretary of War, 26 Sep. 1861. Recollections of Council of War of 1 Oct. 1861, dated 31 Jan. 1862. *OR* 5: 881–82 and 884–86.

28. Benjamin to Johnston, 26 Jan. 1862. Taliaferro et al. to Loring, 25 Jan. 1862. Indsmts by Loring, 26 Jan. 1862, and Jackson, 4 Feb. 1862. Beauregard to Hill, 23 Jan. 1862. Fulkerson to Staples, 23 Jan. 1862. Taliaferro to Staples, 23 Jan. 1862. Reynolds to Benjamin, 23 Jan. 1862. Davis to Benjamin, 29[?] Jan. 1862. Johnston to Benjamin, 29 Jan. 1862. Benjamin to Jackson, 30 Jan. 1862. Jackson to Benjamin, 31 Jan. 1862. Indsmt by Johnston, 7 Feb. 1862. Loring to Benjamin, 31 Jan. 1862. Loring to Jackson, 28 Jan. 1862, with Inclosure by S. M. Barton. Benjamin to Johnston, 3 Feb. 1862. Johnston to Jackson, 3 Feb. 1862. Johnston to Davis, 5 Feb. 1862. Johnston to Benjamin, 7 Feb. 1862. Johnston to Cooper, 7 Feb. 1862, with Inclosure of Charges against Loring. Loring to Benjamin, 12 Feb. 1862. Davis to Johnston, 14 Feb. 1862. *OR* 5: 1040–43, 1046–50, 1053–56, 1059–60, 1065–66, and 1070–72.

29. Special Orders, No. 252. A & IGO, 3 Dec. 1861. Johnston to Benjamin, 13 Dec. 1861. *OR* 5: 979 and 993–94; Order of Battle, 21 July 1861. *OR* 2: 469–70; Order of Battle, [31?] Aug. 1861. Cooper to Johnston, 2 Sep. 1861. Benjamin to Johnston, 7 Oct. 1861. Davis to Smith, 10 Oct. 1861. Davis to Beauregard, 17 Oct. 1861. GO, No. 15. A & IGO, 22 Oct. 1861. GO, No. 18. AIGO, 16 Nov. 1861. Johnston to Cooper, 6 Dec. 1861. Benjamin to Johnston, 9 and 27 Dec. 1861. Johnston to Benjamin, 1 and 14 Jan. 1862. Benjamin to Johnston, 7 Jan. 1862. *OR* 5: 825–27, 892, 894, 903–4, 913–14, 960–61, 979, 985, 987–88. 1011–12, 1015–16, 1023, 1028. Davis to Johnston, 11 May 1862. *OR* 11, (3): 507–8.

30. Johnston to Benjamin, 18 Jan. 1862. Benjamin to Johnston, 25 Jan. 1862. Johnston to Davis, 1 Mar. 1862. Davis to Johnston, 4 Mar. 1862. *OR* 5: 1037, 1045–46, 1086–87, and 1089.

31. Johnston to Davis, 5 Feb. 1862. *OR* 5: 1062.

32. Thomas Bragg diary, 20 and 19 Feb. 1862. Thomas Bragg Papers, SHC, UNC; Johnston to Davis, 16, 22, 23, 25, and 28 Feb. 1862 and 3 Mar. 1862. Davis to Johnston, 28 Feb. 1862. *OR* 5: 1074, 1079, 1081, 1083–85, and 1088; Joseph E. Johnston, *Narrative of Military Operations* (New York: D. Appleton and Company, 1874), 96–99; Stephen W. Sears, *To the Gates of Richmond: The Peninsula Campaign*, 12–14.

33. Thomas Bragg diary, 20 Feb. 1862. Thomas Bragg Papers, SHC, UNC; Davis to Johnston, 28 Feb. and 10 Mar. 1862. Johnston to Davis, 3 Mar. 1862. A. C. Myers to Davis, 7 Mar. 1862. *OR* 5: 1083–85, 1088–89, 1093, 1096.

34. Johnston to Davis, 13 Mar. 1862. *OR* 51 (2): 1073–74; R. G. Cole to Johnston, 7 Feb. 1871. Johnston, *Narrative*, 98–99; AAR of Johnston, 12 Mar. 1862. *OR* 5: 526–27; Jeffrey N. Lash, *Destroyer of the Iron Horse: General Joseph E. Johnston and the Confederate Rail Transport, 1861–1865*, 29–33.

35. Wm. T. Breeze to Mollie, 12 Mar. 1862. Carter Family Papers, VHS; Tho. S. Preston to Wife, 13 Mar. 1862. Preston-Davis Papers, UVA; E. S. Cox to Miss Porter, 23 Mar. 1862. William H. Jones Papers, Duke U; Johnnie to Mother, n.d. [March 1862]. John Buchanan Papers, USC; J. Hays to Ma, 8 Mar. 1862. James Hays Papers, VHS; Robert [Stafford] to Ma, 21 Mar. 1862. Robert Stafford Papers, Gilder-Lehrman Collection, ML.

36. Husband to Wife, 30 Mar. 1862. Thaddeus Oliver Papers, MC; Records of Thaddeus Oliver. U.S. Census Records, Marion County, Ga. M653, R130, F289; Tho. S. Preston to wife, 13 and 15 Mar. 1862. Preston-Davis Papers, UVA.

37. Davis to Johnston, 15 and 15 Mar. 1862. *OR* 5: 527–28.

38. GO, No. 14. AIGO, 13 Mar. 1862. *OR* 5: 1099; Thomas Bragg diary, 19 Feb. 1862. Thomas Bragg Papers, SHC, UNC; Stanton to McClellan, 13 Mar. 1862. Roy P. Basler, ed., *The Collected Works of Abraham Lincoln*, V, 157–58.

10. Playing Troops Like Fireflies

1. Winston to Bryan, 24 Mar. 1862. Magruder to Randolph, 24 Mar. 1862. *OR* 11 (3): 394 and 392–93.

2. There are numerous books on the famous naval battle. The best and most readable is probably William C. Davis, *Duel Between the First Ironclads.*

3. E. K. Smith to Wife, 8 Dec. 1861. R2, Edmund Kirby-Smith Papers, SHC, UNC; Tho. S. Preston to Wife, 28 Mar. 1862. Preston-Davis Papers, UVA; Lee to Johnston, 25 Mar. 1862. GLC, ML.

4. Robert H. Miller to Mother, 28 Sep. 1861. Confederate Miscellany, EU; Woodward, ed., *Mary Chesnut's Civil War*, 352; D. H. Hill to Wife, 8 Jan. 1862. Daniel Harvey Hill Papers, USAMHI. The only published biography of Magruder is Paul D. Casdorph, *Prince John Magruder: His Life and Campaigns.*

5. Thos. Preston to Wife, 21 Apr. 1862. Preston-Davis Papers, UVA; Magruder to Randolph, 24 Mar. 1862. *OR* 11 (3): 392–93.

6. For an excellent discussion of the Confederate defenses, see McLaws to Wife, 31 Mar. 1862. Oeffinger, ed., *A Soldier's General*, 135–36; Magruder to Randolph, 25 March 1862. Lee to Huger, 25 Mar. 1862. Lee to Magruder, 26 Mar. 1862. Magruder to Lee, 5 Apr. 1862. *OR* 11 (3): 395, 396–97, 398–99, and 422.

7. Chesnut, *Mary Chesnut's Civil War*, 401; Alexander, *Fighting for the Confederacy*, 74; R. H. Miller to Mr. Campbell, 27 Apr. 1862. Robert H. Miller *VMHB*, 70 (1): 82.

8. Lee to Johnston, 4 Apr. 1862. *OR* 11 (3): 420; Lee to Johnston, 7 Apr. 1862. Telegram Book, Box 1, Lee's Headquarters Papers, VHS.

9. Edwin to Laura, 2 May 1862. Soldier Letters Collection, MC; John G. Scurry to Sarah, 11 May 1862. John G. Scurry Papers, Gilder-Lehrman Collection, ML; H. T. Owen to Harriet, 24 Apr. 1862. Henry T. Owen Papers, LV; Johnston to Lee, 27 Mar. 1862. Lee to Northup, 27 Mar. 1862. Lee to Johnston, 4 Apr. 1862. *OR* 11 (3): 405–6; John S. Tucker diary, 6 Apr. 1862. Hubbs, ed., *Voices from Company D*, 76; AAR of Magruder, 3 May 1862. *OR* 11 (1): 408–9; R. H. Miller to Mr. Campbell, 27 Apr. 1862. Miller, *VMHB*, 70 (1): 81; Husband to Wife, 22 Apr. 1862. Daniel Harvey Hill Papers, NCDAH; C. W. Dabney to Brother, 19 Apr. 1862. Robert Lewis Dabney Papers, Union Theological Seminary; George to Ma, 28 Apr. 1862. George Lee Robertson Papers, CAH; Hammie to Mother, 12 Apr. 1862. Mauriel Phillips Joslyn, ed., *Charlotte's Boys: Civil War Letters of the Branch Family of Savannah*, 111.

10. In fairness to Johnston, at this stage of the war he did not stand alone, and only experience would provide contradictory evidence. The attack on Forts Henry and Donelson demonstrated the susceptibility of gunboats, even ironclads, on the river to land-based artillery. The most obvious example of the strength of defenders was the Petersburg Campaign of 1864–65. There is some evidence that Lee thought Johnston should have stood firm and held on to the Peninsula. See Mosby to Fitzhugh Lee, 17 Dec. 1895. Mosby, *The Letters of John S. Mosby*. 77–78.

11. Johnston to Lee, 22 Apr. 1862. Special Orders, No. 6. Headquarters, 12 Apr. 1862. *OR* 11 (3): 438 and 455–56; Johnston, *Narrative*, 111–13.

12. Summary discussions are in Johnston, *Narrative*, 111–16; Davis, *Rise and Fall*, II, 86–88.

13. See EKS to Mother, 21 May 1861. EKS to ?, 29 May 1861. R2, Edmund Kirby-Smith Papers, SHC, UNC.

14. Benjamin to Johnston, 9 Feb. 1862. Special Orders, No. 26. A&IGO, 5 Nov. 1861. *OR* 5: 1066–67 and 938; Jackson to Doctor, 11 Feb. 1862. Thomas J. Jackson Papers, VMI; A. S. W[ade] to Lou, 10 Feb. 1862. Lewis Leigh Collection, USAMHI; R. W. Waldrop to Father, 14 Feb. 1862. Richard W. Waldrop Papers, SHC, UNC. Also see James I. Robertson, Jr., *The Stonewall Brigade.*

15. D. H. Hill to Wife, 7 Mar. 1862. Gilder-Lehrman Collection, ML; J. R. McCutchan to Sister, 13 Mar. 1862. RHSM, W&L, copy at FSNBP; Robertson, *Stonewall Jackson*, 343–44, 346–47, and 349–50; Garnett to Cooper, 20 June 1862. Richard Brooke Garnett Papers, MC.

16. *OR* 11 (3): 57–62; C. G. Coleman to Anna, 25 Mar. 1862. Confederate Soldiers: Coleman Family File, MC.

17. Jas. C. Gamble to Mort, 20 Dec. 1861. Lewis Leigh Collection, USAMHI; Chesnut, *Mary Chesnut's Civil War*, 444; Jimmie [Griffin] to Wife, 11 July 1861. CWTIC, USAMHI; Ewell to Miss Lizzie, 13 May 1862. Ewell Papers, LC; quotation also in Vandiver, *Mighty Stonewall*, 228–29. For a first-rate biography of Ewell, see Donald C. Pfanz, *Richard S. Ewell: A Soldier's Life.*

18. See Glatthaar, *Partners in Command*, 20–21.

19. Lee to Johnston, 28 Mar. 1862. *OR* 11 (3): 409.

20. Lee to Jackson, 25 Apr. 1862. Jackson to Ewell, 10 Apr. 1862. Lee to Jackson, 21 Apr. 1862. Lee to Ewell, 21 Apr. 1862. *OR* 12 (3): 845, 858–60, and 865–66. Jackson had expressed interest in seizing the offensive in early April. See Jackson to Longstreet, 5 Apr. 1862. *OR* 12 (3): 844.

21. Jackson to Lee, 29 Apr. 1862. Ewell to Lee, 30 Apr. 1862. Lee to Jackson, 1 May 1862. Jackson to Ewell, 3 and 4 May 1862. *OR* 12 (3); 872 and 876–79; AAR of Brig. Gen. Robert H. Milroy, 14 May 1862. AAR of Jackson, 7 Mar. 1863. *OR* 12 (1): 465–67 and 470–73.

22. Lee to Jackson, 16 May 1862. Taylor to Jackson, 14 May 1862. Jackson to Johnston, 17 May 1862. *OR* 12 (3): 892–95 and 889.

23. Johnston to Ewell, 17 May 1862. Jackson to Ewell, 18 May 1862. Jackson to Lee, 20 May 1862. *OR* 12 (3): 896–98; Freeman, *Lee's Lieutenants*, 371. The reply message from Lee to Jackson is missing, but it must have been sent promptly, because Jackson began moving his various components the next day.

24. Joseph Franklin Kauffman diary, 7 May 1862. Joseph Franklin Kauffman Papers, SHC, UNC; Ugie to Wife, 24 Apr. 1862. Allen and Bohannon, eds., *Campaigning with "Old Stonewall,"* 88; Wm. B. Burress to wife, 8 June 1862. William B. Burress Papers, MC; L. M. Blackford to Mother, 25 May 1862. Launcelot Minor Blackford Papers, UVA. See Circular, HQ, Army V.D., 13 May 1862. Record Book of Gen. W. B. Taliaferro. RG 109, NA, for Jackson's instructions on marching.

25. E. T. H. Warren to Wife, 25 [May] 1862. E. T. H. Warren Papers, UVA; Charles W. Trueheart to Mother, 4 July 1862. Edward B. Williams, ed., *Rebel Brothers: The Civil War Letters of the Truehearts*, 59–60; L. M. Blackford to Father, 7 June 1862. Launcelot Minor Blackford Papers, UVA; AAR of Jackson, 10 Apr. 1863. *OR* 12 (1): 701–9. For a description of the battles, see Robertson, 400–402; Vandiver, 250–55.

26. AAR of Jackson, 10 Apr. 1863. *OR* 12 (1): 706–8; Glatthaar, *Partners in Command*, 25–27.

27. Lincoln to McDowell, 28 May 1862. *OR* 12 (3): 267; Ugie to Wife, 6 June 1862. Allen and Bohannon, eds., 100; Charles S. Winder diary, 30 May 1862. Charles S. Winder Papers, MDHS; Jedediah Hotchkiss diary, 1 June [1862]. Jedediah Hotchkiss, *Make Me a Map of the Valley: The Civil War Journal of Stonewall Jackson's Cartographer*, 51.

28. AAR of Jackson, 10 Apr. 1863. Statement of A. S. Pendleton, [n.d.] 1862. *OR* 12 (1): 705–7 and 709–10. See Vandiver, 268–72, for a detailed explanation of Jackson's plan and position.

29. AAR of Jackson, 14 Apr. 1863. *OR* 12 (1): 711–16. For a brilliant depiction of the fighting, see Robert K. Krick, *Conquering the Valley: Stonewall Jackson at Port Republic*; Robertson, *Stonewall Jackson*, 428–45; Vandiver, *Mighty Stonewall* 275–83; Robert G. Tanner, *Stonewall in the Valley: Thomas J. "Stonewall" Jackson's Shenandoah Valley Campaign, Spring 1862*.

30. Lee to Jackson, 8 and 11 June 1862. *OR* 12 (3): 908 and 910.

31. Richd to Father, 26 May 1862. Richard W. Waldrop Papers, SHC, UNC; Ugie to Susie, 12 June 1862. Allen and Bohannon, eds., 106; Barnett H. Cody to Sister Hennie, 13 June 1862. Cody, *GHQ* 23(4): 365; A. A. Clewell to Parents, 13 June 1862. Augustus Clewell Papers, NCDAH.

32. The three previous retreats were from Harpers Ferry, from Fairfax Court House to the Centerville line, and from Centerville-Manassas to the Rappahannock.

33. William R. Smith diary, 5 May 1862. CWTIC, USAMHI; C. J. Winston to Uncle, 10 May 1862. Winston-Clark Family, VHS; Edward S. Cox to ?, 11 May 1862. William H. Jones to Wife, 12 May 1862. William H. Jones Papers, DU; Henry to Wife, 6 May 1862. Henry T. Owen Papers, LV; AAR of Longstreet, 16 May 1862. AAR of A. P. Hill, 10 May 1862. AAR of R. H. Anderson, 10 May 1862. AAR of Pickett, ? May 1862. *OR* 11 (1): 564–69, 575–79, 580–81 and 584–87.

34. AAR of D. H. Hill, undated [Jan. 1863]. AAR of Jubal Early, 9 June 1862. AAR of Col. D. K. McRae, 10 May 1862. *OR* 11 (1): 601–11; P. J. S[inclair] to Alexander, 12 May 1862. P. J. Sinclair Papers, NCDAH.

35. Henry to Wife, 6 May 1862. Henry T. Owen Papers, LV; Edward S. Cox to ?, 11 May 1862. William H. Jones Papers, DU. Confederates reported 1,560 casualties, while the Union claimed 2,239. *OR* 11 (1): 450 and 568. While it is difficult to estimate the number of soldiers who were actually involved in the fight, approximately 15,000 Confederates and somewhere between 20,000 and 25,000 Yankees were.

36. P. H. Powers to Wife, 15 May 1862. Lewis Leigh Collection, USAMHI; John S. Tucker diary, 4 May 1862. Hubbs, ed., *Voices*, 83.

37. Johnston to Wigfall, 12 Nov. 1863. Louis T. Wigfall Papers, LC.

38. See Steven H. Newton. *The Battle of Seven Pines, May 31–June 1, 1862*, for the battle.

39. Johnston to Huger, 30 and 31 May 1862. *OR* 11 (1): 938; Johnston to Smith, 30 May 1862. Pinckney to D. H. Hill, 31 May 1862. Hill to Rodes, 31 May 1862. Mason to Whiting, 31 May 1862. *OR* 11 (3): 563–64. See Johnston to Wigfall, 12 Nov. 1863. Louis T. Wigfall Papers, LC, for evidence that Smith had lost his standing with Johnston.

40. Johnston to Smith, 30 May 1862. Hill to Rains, 31 May 1862. Hill to General, 31 May 1862. *OR* 11 (3): 563–64; AAR of Longstreet, 10 June 1862, with indorsement of Huger. AAR of D. H. Hill. n.d. 1862. AAR of Robert E. Rodes, 7 June 1862. *OR* 11 (1): 939–43 and 970–71. Johnston asked Smith to alter his AAR to omit Longstreet's mistakes, which meant that Johnston participated with Longstreet in a scheme to cover up Longstreet's error and to make Huger the scapegoat. See Johnston to Smith, 28 June 1862. Original AAR of Smith. Gustavus W. Smith, *The Battle of Seven Pines*, 19–21, 64, and 177–78.

41. AAR of D. H. Hill, n.d. 1862. AAR of Micah Jenkins, n.d. 1862. *OR* 11: 944 and 947–50; James K. Swisher, *Prince of Edisto: Brigadier General Micah Jenkins, CSA*, 47–51.

42. Freeman, *R. E. Lee*, II, 67–71; Johnston, *Narrative*, 136–39.

43. Alexander, *Fighting for the Confederacy*, 88; Johnston, *Narrative*, 138–39.

44. Davis to Winnie, 2 June 1862. Jefferson Davis Papers, MC; H. L. P. King diary, 22 June 1862. H. L. P. King Papers, SHC, UNC; Symonds, *Johnston*, 163–74; Glatthaar, *Partners in Command*, 116–17.

45. Johnston to Davis, 19 Aug. 1861 and 16 Feb. 1862. *OR* 5: 797 and 1074; Sam to Wife, 22 Nov. 1861. Samuel Wicliff Melton Papers, USC; On Smith's wife captivating the cadets, see Peter W. Houck, ed., *Duty, Honor, Country: The Diary and Biography of General William P. Craighill at West Point, 1849–1853*, 420, 481–82, 487, and 518. Thanks to Robert E. L. Krick for directing me to the information on Mrs. Smith.

46. Smith claimed that he intended to fight but the administration and certain commanders, specifically Longstreet, hindered his efforts. Lee stated otherwise. See Private Memorandum of Benjamin S. Ewell, 20 Oct. [1862?]. Benjamin S. and Richard S. Ewell Papers, DU; Jaspar Whiting to Lee, 2 June 1862. William N. Pendleton Papers, SHC, UNC; AAR of D. H. Hill, n.d. 1862. *OR* 11 (1): 945–46.

47. The only account of this is Davis, *Rise and Fall*, II, 130.

11. Lee in Command

1. RE Lee to [Charlotte Lee], 2 June 1862. Robert E. Lee Papers, VHS.

2. EKS to Mother, 20 Oct. 1855. Edmund Kirby-Smith Papers, SHC, UNC.

3. Justus Scheibert, *Seven Months*, 39; R. E. Lee to Geo. W. S. Fly, 23 Nov. 1866. Robert E. Lee Papers, CAH.

4. D. H. Hill to Wife, 6 June [1861]. Daniel Harvey Hill Papers, USAMHI; James Keith to Mother, 7 June [1861]. Keith Family Papers, VHS; William P. Parker diary, 16 Aug. 1861. William P. Parker Papers, WL; Frank [Barron] to Annie, 20 May 1864. Barron Papers, FSNBP.

5. EKS to Mother, 10 and 16 May 1861. R2, Edmund Kirby-Smith Papers, SHC, UNC; Sam to wife, 29 May 1861. Samuel Wicliffe Melton Papers, USC; F. W. Pickens to Bonham, 7 July 1861. Milledge Luke Bonham Papers, USC; Walter Taylor to [Bettie], 4 Mar. 1864. Walter H. Taylor Papers, NPL.

6. Jay Luvaas, "Lee and the Operational Art: The Right Place, the Right Time." *Parameters* (Autumn 1992), 2–18, for a marvelous introduction to Lee and the operational art.

7. Wm. E. Jones to Loring, 4 Aug. 1852. Typescript copy in possession of author by way of Robert K. Krick.

8. Edward A. Pollard, *The First Year of the War*, 168; Ben Allston to Father, 9 Dec. 1861. R. F. W. Allston Papers, SCHS; A. C. Haskell to Mother, 22 Jan. 1862, Alexander C. Haskell Papers. SHC, UNC; *Richmond Enquirer*, 20 Sep. 1861, P1, C3; Armand [Beauregard] to [General Beauregard], 14 Oct. 1863. *OR* 30 (4): 746.

9. Lee to wife, 7 Oct. 1861. Robert E. Lee, Jr., *Recollections and Letters of General Robert E. Lee*, 51; R. E. Lee to [Charlotte], 25 Dec. 1862. Lee Family Papers, VHS; Freeman, *R. E. Lee*, I, 598.

10. GO, No. 14. WD, A & IGO. 13 Mar. 1862. OR by 15th Virginia Infantry, Dec. 1861–Apr. 1862. RG 109, NA; [Andrew Wardlaw] to wife, 12 Mar. 1862. CWMC. USAMHI; *Charleston Mercury*, 11 Mar. 1862, P1, C3–4 and 17 Mar. 1862, P1, C3; Davis to Lee, 2 Mar. 1862. *OR* 6: 400; Freeman, *R. E. Lee*, I, 605–31.

11. Tho S Preston to Wife, 28 Mar. 1862. Preston-Davis Papers, UVA; Catherine Edmondston diary, 6 May 1862. Edmondston *"Journal of a Secesh Lady,"* 169; McClellan to Lincoln, 20 Apr. 1862. George B. McClellan, *The Civil War Papers of George B. McClellan: Selected Correspondence. 1860–1865*, Stephen Sears, ed., 244–45.

12. John H. Reagan, *Memoirs: With Special Reference to Secession and the Civil War*, 139; Josiah Gorgas, "Extracts from my notes written chiefly soon after the close of the war," 1, 6, 19–21, 24–25, 31, 33–35. Gorgas Family Papers, UAL; Alexander, *Fighting for the Confederacy*, 512. Some scholars have suggested that Lee was fixated on protecting Richmond and Virginia, at the expense of other areas of the Confederacy. I believe the Confederacy could not have sustained the struggle for long without the manufacturing in Richmond.

13. Lee to Son, 23 Feb. 1862. Markham Papers, MC. For Lee on slavery and slave ownership, see Thomas, *Robert E. Lee*, 12, 173, 177 79, 183–84, 273–74; Fellman, *The Making of Robert E. Lee*, 54–75.

14. GO, No. 15, A & IGO, 22 Oct. 1861. *OR* 5: 913–14; 3O, No. 22, HO 1 June 1862. *OR* 11 (3): 569. Lee called it the Army of Northern Virginia in SO, No. 4. HQ, Richmond, Va., 5 Apr. 1862. DO, Virginia Forces, 29 Apr. 1861–30 May 1862. RG 109, NA.

15. Lee to Myers, 10 June 1862. GO, No. 68. IIQ, Dept. of Northern Virginia, 14 June 1862. Circular. HQ, 10 June 1862. *OR* 11 (3): 585–86, 599, and 588; Henry J. Mugler diary, 30 [?] May 1862. Henry J. Mugler Papers, Virginia, V. 13, FSNBP; GO, No. 63. HQ, Dept. of No. Va. 5 Jun. 1862. M921, R1, F172 and 174, GSOCI, ANV, RG 109, NA.

16. GO, No. 64. GO, No. 67. HQ, ANV, 5 and 12 June 1862. M921, R1, F172 and 174, General and SO&CI, ANV, RG 109, NA. The order states that 800,000 were issued.

17. GO, No. 68. HQ, Dept. of No. Va., 14 June 1862. *OR* 11 (3): 599. Earlier in the campaign, Magruder complained of a "wasteful expenditure of ammunition, "as did Lee. GO, No. 177. HQ, Army of Peninsula, 9 Apr. 1862. Orders Received, 15 Va. GO, No. 28, HQ of the Forces, 20 June 1861. Virginia Forces. RG 109, NA.

18. GO, No. 66, HQ, Dept. of No. Va., 8 June 1862. GO, No. 67. HQ, Dept. of No. Va., 12 June 1862. M921, Rl, F173–74, GSOCI, ANV, RG 109, NA.

19. Circular. HQ, 10 June 1862. Lee to Stuart, 11 June 1861. Lee to Randolph, 11 June 1862. *OR* 11 (3): 588, 590–91; Alexander, *Fighting for the Confederacy*, 68–69.

20. Stevens to Campbell, 9 June 1862, in Richard W. Stephenson, "General Lee's Forgotten Mapmaker: Major Albert H. Campbell and the Department of Northern Virginia's Topographical Department." *North & South* 8, No. 2 (Mar. 2005): 66 and 69; Davis Inclosure, 18 Feb. 1865. *OR* 47 (2): 1306.

21. H. L. P. King diary, 15 June 1862. Thomas Butler King, Papers, SHC, UNC; Ch. Friend to Wife. 15 June [1862]. Blanton Family Papers, VHS; AAR of Stuart, 17 June 1862. *OR* 11 (1): 1036–40.

22. Circular. HQ, 10 June 1862. Lee to Stevens, 5 June 1862. Lee to Gorgas, 5 June 1862. Lee to Mallory, 21 June 1862. Minor to Lee, 24 June 1862. *OR* 11 (3): 588, 574, 610, and 615. By 24 June, the navy had completed an iron-plated, rifled 32-pounder, with 200 shells.

23. Lee to Davis. 5 June 1862. R. E. Lee Papers, USMA; GO, No. 62. HQ, Dept. of Northern Va. 4 June 1862. M921, R1, F167, GSOCI, ANV. RG 109, NA; Circular. HQ, 10 June 1862. AIGO, 13 June 1862. *OR* 11 (3): 588 and 597; H. L. P. King diary, 14 June 1862. Thomas Butler King Papers, SHC, UNC; W. S. Grady, 12 July 1862. Henry Woodfin Grady Papers, EU; Jno. T. Smith to Cic. Heath, 20 June 1862. Smith- Johnson Papers, MC; Longstreet to Hill, 13 and 16 June 1862. D. H. Hill Papers, LV.

24. GO, No. 68. HQ, Dept. of Northern Virginia, 14 June 1862. M921, R1, F177, GSOCI, ANV. RG 109. NA.

25. GO, No. 63. HQ, Dept. of Northern Virginia, 5 June 1862. *OR* 11 (3): 576–77; D. H. Hill to Wife, 10 June 1862. D. H. Hill Papers, USAMHI; J. B. Magruder to Hill, 13 June 1862. Letters Sent, Right Wing of Army of Northern Virginia. RG 109, NA; John [Scurry] to Sarah, 19 June 1862. John G. Scurry Papers, Gilder-Lehrman Collection, ML.

26. GO. No. 68. HQ, 1st Div., 1st Corps, 2 June 1862. GO & C, Gen. W. H. C. Whiting's Command, Feb.–July 1862. RG 109, NA; GO, No. 10. HQ, Longstreet's Div., 2 June 1862. James Longstreet Papers, MC; SO No., HQ, Longstreet's Division, 3 June 1862. Bryan Grimes Papers, NCDAH; Circular, Inspector General's Office, Dept. of N V, 9 June 1862. William N. Pendleton Papers, SHC, UNC;

GO, No. 63. HQ, Dept. of Northern Virginia, 5 June 1862. M921, R1, F170, GSOCI, ANV. RG 109, NA; *Augusta Constitutionalist*, 2 July 1862, P2. C2.

27. Lee to Davis, 7 June 1862. Douglas Southall Freeman, ed., *Lee's Dispatches*, 11; Confidential Circular, HQ, Army of Northern Virginia, 7 June 1862. M921, Rl, F1372, GSOCI, ANV. RG 109, NA.

28. Davis to Lee, 2 June 1862. *OR* 11 (3): 569; Davis to Varina, 19 June 1862. War Department Collection of Confederate Records: Confederate Papers Relating to Citizens or Business Firms ("Citizens File"): Davis, Jefferson, Box 20681, RG 109, NA.

29. Wm. Preston Johnston to Wife, 1–2 June 1862. Mason Barret Collection, TU.; W. N. Pendleton to Darling love, 3 June 1862, William N. Pendleton Papers, SHC, UNC; H. L. P. King diary, 8 June 1862. Thomas Butler King Papers, SHC, UNC; D. H. Hill to Wife, 16 June 1862. D. H. Hill Papers, USAMHI.

30. Samuel to Cousin, 22 June [1862]. John Oakey Papers, DU.

31. R. Haile Journal, 6 June 1862, *Tell the Children I'll Be Home When the Peaches Get Ripe: The Journal and Letters of Robert Gaines Haile, Jr.*, 39–40.

32. Catherine Edmondston diary, 8 June 1862. Edmondston, *"Journal of a Secesh Lady,"* 189; Chesnut, *Mary Chesnut's Civil War*, 387. The absence of comments in soldiers' letters and diaries on Johnston's wounding and Lee's elevation and work is striking.

33. *Richmond Examiner*, 17 June 1862, John M. Daniel, *The Richmond Examiner During the War*, 56; *Richmond Enquirer*, P4, C1; Davis to Varina, 11 June 1862. Jefferson Davis Papers, MC.

12. The Battle for Richmond: The Seven Days' Campaign

1. Lawton to wife, 23 June 1862. A. R. Lawton Papers, SHC, UNC; U.T. to Editor, 22 June 1862, in *Savannah Republican*, 2 July 1862, P1, C2. For the best studies of the campaign, see Sears, *To the Gates of Richmond*, and Brian K. Burton, *Extraordinary Circumstances: The Seven Days Battles*; Records of Alexander R. Lawton. U.S. Census, 1860. Savannah, Chatham Co., Ga. 260. Records of Alexander R. Lawton. Slave Census, 1860. Savannah, Chatham Co., Ga., 491.

2. Lee to Jackson, 8 and 11 June 1862. *OR* 11 (3): 583 and 589; Conversation between Lee and William Allan, 17 Dec. 1868. Gallagher, ed., *Lee the Soldier*, 15–16.

3. See Vandiver, 293–303; Freeman, *Lee's Lieutenants*, I, 496–502; Robertson, *Stonewall Jackson*, 460–66; Glatthaar, *Partners in Command*, 33–34; Conversation between Lee and William Allan, 17 Dec. 1868. Gallagher, ed., *Lee the Soldier*, 15–16.

4. GO, No. 75. HQ, ANV, 24 June 1862. *OR* 11 (2): 498–99. For a nice, brief overview of the campaign, see William J. Miller, *Richmond, 1862*. In what is largely a good book, Burton in *Extraordinary Circumstances* criticizes the order because it differs with Lee's letters to Jackson on June 11 and 16. The General Order was the official battle plan, and an officer would know that it superseded comments in those letters.

5. See James I. Robertson, Jr., *General A.P. Hill: The Story of a Confederate Warrior*, for the best biography of Hill. It is unclear whether Lee ordered or later endorsed Hill's attack.

6. AAR of LTC L. A. Grant, 9 July 1862. *OR* 11 (2): 478–79.

7. Chilton to Magruder, 1 July 1862. AAR of Lewis Armistead, 14 July 1862. *OR* 11 (2): 677 and 819; Robert K. Krick, "Armistead and Garnett: The Parallel Lives of Two Virginia Soldiers," in Gary W. Gallagher, ed., *The Third Day of Gettysburg and Beyond*, 99–101.

8. Lee to Davis, 2, 3, and 4 July 1862. Dowdey and Manarin, eds., *Wartime Papers*, 206–8; Lee to Davis, 6 July 1862. *OR* 11 (3): 635; Campbell Brown diary, 22 Apr. 1867. George Washington Campbell Papers, LC.

9. Charles to Etta, 19 June 1862. Kerrison Family Papers, USC; [Jasper A. Gillespie] to wife, 5 July 1862. Jasper A. Gillespie Papers, GDAH; R. E. Wilkinson to sister, 7 July 1862. Mary E. Wilkinson Papers, LV; Records of Charles Kerrison. U.S. Census Record, 1860. Charleston, S.C., 8; Records of Jasper Gillespie. U.S. Census Records. 1860. Monroe Co., Ga., 709.

10. R. H. Gray to Father, 10 July 1862. R. H. Gray Papers, NCDAH; Records of Robert H. Gray. U.S. Census Records, 1860. Randolph Co., N.C., 349; Records of Robt. Gray. U.S. Slave Census, 1860. Western Div., Randolph Co., N.C. 6. He had twenty-two slaves. C. S. Powell, "Seven Days Fighting Around Richmond in 1862," 2. C. S. Powell Papers, MC; C. P. P [oppenheim] to Mary, 24 July [1862]. C. P. Poppenheim Papers, SCHS.

11. WWC to Mac, 24 July 1862. Alexander M. McPheeters Papers, DU; D. R. E. Winn to Fannie, 4 July 1862. David Read Evans Winn Papers, EU; A. H. Colquitt to Col, 11 July 1862. Alfred Hoyt Colquitt Papers, FSNBP; Records of A. H. Colquitt. U.S. Slave Census, 1860. Newton Dist., Baker Co., Ga., 20–1. For a great explanation of Southern courage and Northern cowardice, see *Richmond Examiner*, 2 July 1861. Daniel, *The Richmond Examiner During the War*, 16–17.

12. B. Wylie Scott to Ella, 5 June and 20 July 1862. Ella Merryman Papers, VHS; Return of Casualties. *OR* 11 (2): 972.

13. Samuel H. Walkup diary, 25 June 1862. Samuel H. Walkup Papers, SHC, UNC; AAR of Robert Ransom, 19 July 1862. *OR* 11 (2): 792–93.

14. D. R. E. Winn to Fannie, 14 July 1862. David Read Evans Winn Papers, EU; Records of D. R. E. Winn. U.S. Census, 1860. Sumter Co., Ga., 461; Records of D. R. E. Winn. Slave Census, 1860. Sumter Co., Ga., 54. He owned three slaves and was worth $22,000 in 1860.

15. F. Saunders to Mother, 5 July 1862. Irvine-Saunders Papers, UVA; J. W. D[avidson] to ?, 3 Aug. 1862. James Wood Davidson Papers, USC. Also see Ivy W. Duggan to Editor, *Central Georgian*, 8 July 1862. Civil War Miscellany: 48th Georgia, GDAH; [W. C. Allen] to [Father], 11 July 1862. Allen Family Papers, UAL; GO, No 78. HQ, Dept. of NV, 12 July 1862. Order Book, Wright's Brigade. CWTIC, USAMHI.

16. James R. Boulware diary, 27 June 1862. James R. Boulware Papers, LV; Brother to Sister, 8 July 1862. Kerrison Family Papers, USC.
17. Ch. Friend to Wife, 29 June 1862. Blanton Family Papers, VHS; G. K. Harlow to Father & Family, 3 July 1862. Harlow Family Papers, VHS; [Wm. Fisher Plane] to [wife], 8 July 1862. Lewis, ed., *GHQ*, 48, 223; L. L. Hawk to Miss, 11 July 1862. Jane Fisher Papers, DU.
18. Wade Hampton to Mrs. Cheves, 14 July 1862. Beverly Randolph Wellford Papers, VHS; [Wm. Fisher Plane] to [wife], 8 July 1862. Lewis, ed., *GHQ*, 48, 223. Plane owned six slaves and owned $28,000 of property. Records of W. F. Plane. U.S. Census Records, 1860. Baker Co., Ga., 105. Slave Records of W. F. Plane. Slave Census, 1860. Baker Co., Ga., 16.
19. H. R. Foster to Brother and sister, 26 July 1862. Wills Family, W&M; N. J. Brooks to Mother & all, 4 July 1862. Brooks Family Papers, GDAH. Also published in *Confederate Reminiscences and Letters*, XX, 232–34. Thanks to Keith Bohannon for providing me with a fuller copy of the letter.
20. J. Foster Marshall to Brigadier General Gregg, 13 July 1862. J. Foster Marshall Papers, USC; "Rebel Yell," *News Leader*, 17 Aug. 1936. MC; Report of Casualties, 25 June–1 July, 1862. *OR* 11 (2): 973–84; Henry to Harriett, 30 June 1862. Henry T. Owen Papers, LV.
21. James Keith Boswell diary, 12 Feb. 1863. *Diary of James Keith Boswell*, MC; [Addison Burnside] to Mother, 8 July 1862. Addison M. Burnside Papers, GDAH; Charles Scott Venable diary, 26 June 1862. Charles Scott Venable Papers, USC.
22. Lee Conversation with William Allan, 17 Dec. 1868. Gallagher, ed., *Lee the Soldier*, 15–16; Lee to Magruder, 28–29 June 1862. Dowdey and Manarin, eds., *Wartime Papers of R.E. Lee*, 204–5. AAR of Lee, 6 Mar. 1863. *OR* 11 (2): 490–97; Edward P. Alexander, *Fighting for the Confederacy*, 104.
23. E. T. H. Warren to wife, 2 July 1862. E. T. H. Warren Papers, UVA; AAR of Lee, 6 Mar. 1863. AAR of W. N. Pendleton, 21 July 1862. AAR of D. H. Hill, n.d., 1862. Enclosure of Lee in Lee to Randolph, 14 Aug. 1862, with Magruder's reply, 5 Sep. 1862. Magruder to Lee, 1 July 1862. AAR of Capt. William G. Crenshaw, 14 July 1862. *OR* 11 (2): 497, 629, 679–81, 686, and 902; An English Officer [Wolseley], "A Month's Visit to the Confederate Headquarters." *Blackwood's Magazine*, XCIII (Jan. 1863), 12; Campbell Brown reminiscences, 188. Ewell Papers, TNSL; Alexander, *Fighting for the Confederacy*, 110–11; Burton, *Extraordinary Circumstances*, 318–20.
24. Lee to wife, 9 June [July] 1862. Dowdey and Manarin, eds., *Wartime Papers*, 229–30; AAR of Lee, 6 Mar. 1863. Lee to Randolph, 14 Aug. 1862. Lee to Magruder, 29 June 1862. *OR* 11 (2): 495, 497, 679, and 687
25. Pendleton to Lee, 2 Oct. 1862. SO, No. 209. HQ, ANV, 4 Oct. 1862. *OR* 19 (2): 647–54. See Harsh, *Confederate Tide Rising*, 195–96.
26. AAR of Lee, 6 Mar. 1863. Report of Capt. Smith Stansbury, 15 July 1862. Inclosure of Lt. Frank E. Jones, 15 July 1862. *OR* 11 (2): 497–98 and 510–11.
27. W. G. Kisling to Cousin, 20 July 1862. W. G. Kisling Papers, MC; L. McLaws to wife, 28 June 1862. Lafayette McLaws Papers, SHC, UNC.
28. John T. Thornton to [wife], 4 July 1862. John T. Thornton Papers, UVA; Thos. J. Goree to Mother, 21 July 1862. Goree, ed., 164; R. H. Gray to Father, 10 July 1862. R. H. Gray Papers, LV.
29. Sue Branch to Aunt, 1 July 1862. Vol. II, 31, Mrs. Lawrence O'Brien Branch Papers, NCDAH; Samuel Horace Hawes diary, 1 July 1862. Katherine H. Hawes Papers, VHS.
30. Charleston *Mercury*, 1 July 1862, P1, C2, and 8 July 1862, P1, C2; *Augusta Constitutionalist*, 28 June 1862, P2, C1; *Atlanta Southern Confederacy*, 10 July 1862, P2, C2–3, and 11 July 1862, P2, C1–2. For this section, I read the four Richmond newspapers and half a dozen papers from throughout the Confederacy.
31. Justice to Editors of the *Enquirer*, n.d. *Richmond Enquirer*, 1 July 1862, P2, C2.
32. *Richmond Whig*, 14 July 1862. P1, C1–2.
33. *Richmond Enquirer*, 1 July 1862, P2, C1; Soldier Jim to Editor, 20 July 1862 in *Atlanta Southern Confederacy*, 26 July 1862. Styple, ed., *Writing & Fighting*, 121.
34. Ch. Friend to Wife, 1 July 1862. Blanton Family Papers, VHS.

13. Taking War to the Enemy

1. Jas. P. Williams to Aunt Mary, 6 July 1862. James Peter Williams Papers, LV.
2. Thomas to nephew, 26 Jan. 1861. Thomas Jackson Arnold, *Early Life and Letters of General Thomas J. Jackson*, 293–94 (original at VMI, which includes the idea of taking no prisoners); Jackson to Boteler, [Feb. 1862] and 3 Mar. 1862. Thomas J. Jackson Papers, New-York Historical Society; William McWillie Journal, n.d. William McWillie Papers, MDAH; L. Guild to Surg. Gen. Moore, 22 May 1863. LS, Med. Director's Office, ANV. RG 109, NA. See Charles Royster, *The Destructive War: William Tecumseh Sherman, Stonewall Jackson, and the Americans*, 40–41. James I. Robertson, Jr., depicts Jackson as seeing himself as an Old Testament avenger in his *Stonewall Jackson*.
3. Quoted in Wiley, *Life of Johnny Reb*, 308; William McWillie Journal, n.d. William McWillie Papers, MDAH.
4. Prescott to Sister, 29 Nov. 1861. Prescott-Jones Family, GDAH.
5. Thos. Green Penn to Ma, 27 June 1862. Green W. Penn Papers, DU.
6. Glatthaar, *Forged in Battle: The Civil War Alliance of Black Soldiers and Their White Officers*, 1–9. Later, only those who proved their loyalty to the Union could secure their runaway slaves, and they could receive no help from Yankee soldiers, which made the process of retrieval extremely difficult.
7. Edmund Ruffin diary, 18 June [1862]. Ruffin, *The Diary of Edmund Ruffin*, II, 346; Benjamin Fleet journal, 9 Jun. 1862. Betsy Fleet and John D. P. Fuller, eds., *Green Mount: A Virginia Plantation Family During the Civil War*, 133; Hanover to Editor of the *Enquirer*, 11 Oct. 1862. *Richmond Enquirer*, 21 Oct. 1862, P2, C3; Joseph T. Glatthaar, "Black Glory: The African-American Role in Union Vic-

tory," in Gabor S. Boritt, ed., *Why the Confederacy Lost*, 142–43; William Blair, *Virginia's Private War*, 78.

8. Husband [D. H. Hill] to Wife, 30 Nov. 1861. Daniel Harvey Hill Papers, USAMHI; C. M. Wilcox to Sister Mary, 18 Nov. 1861. Cadmus M. Wilcox, LC; Longstreet to Soldiers, 17 June 1862. *OR* 11 (3): 605–6.

9. A [Lawton] to [wife], 16 July 1862. A. R. Lawton Papers, SHC, UNC; R. Fairfax to Mama, 22 Aug. [1861]. R. & E. Fairfax Papers, MC; Wm. H. Hill diary, 3 Aug. 1861. William D. Hill Papers. MDAH; D. H. Hill to Wife, 20 June 1861. Daniel Harvey Hill Papers, USAMHI; D. H. Hill to Beauregard, 18 Dec. 1861. Daniel Harvey Hill Papers, LV; M.H. to Amanda, 9 June 1862. Lowe and Hodges, eds., *Letters to Amanda*, 13; *Augusta Constitutionalist*, 2 July 1862, P3, C1; ? to Lafayette, 30 July 1862. Marquis Lafayette Young Papers, LV; Robt. H. Miller to Mother, 14 Aug. 1862. Connor, ed., *VMHB* 70, 1, 90; Anne Kinchloe memo, 6 Nov. 1862. 49th Virginia Infantry, Co. C Papers, GDAH.

10. J. Q. A. Nadenbousch to Wife, 28 Apr. 1862. J. Q. A. Nadenbousch Papers, MC; John T. Thornton to [wife], 3 Feb. 1862. John T. Thornton Papers, UVA. While some might argue that protecting one's home and property is central to honor, I regard it as a duty above and beyond honor. Males need not embrace the concept of honor to feel an obligation to protect hearth and home.

11. Powhatan B. Whittle to Sister, 14 Feb. 1862. Whittle Papers, FSNBP; Otis D. Smith to Mrs. Allen, 20 May 1862. Otis David Smith Papers, ADAH; W. B. Bailey to Brother, 12 July 1862. Coco Collection, HCWRT, USAMHI.

12. Brother to Sister, 8 July 1862. Kerrison Family Papers, USC; Husband [D. H. Hill] to wife, 3 July 1862. Daniel Harvey Hill Papers, NCDAH; [W. C. Allen to Father], 4 Jul. 1862. Allen Family Papers, UA. Also see R. B. B[uck] to Ma, 16 Feb. 1862. Richard Bayly Buck Papers, UVA; Thos. J. Goree to Uncle, 15 Feb. 1862. Goree, ed, 131; Henry Bryan to Col. Charles Smith, 7 Nov. 1861. L & T Sent, Army of the Peninsula, May–Nov. 1861. RG 109, NA. For a new soldier who brought all the stereotypes, see Thos. C. Elder to Wife, 27 Apr. 1862. Elder Family Papers, VHS.

13. Robt. H. Miller to Mary Anna, 25 Nov. 1861. Confederate Miscellany, EU; GO, No. 9. HQ, 2nd Div., 12 Apr. 1862. Orders Rec'd by 15th Virginia, Dec. 1861–Apr. 1862. RG 109; NA; Wm. J. Pegram to Brother, 11 Feb. 1862. Pegram-Johnson-McIntosh Family Papers, VHS; Stephens Smith to Julia, 14 Jul. 1862. Stephens Calhoun Smith Papers, DU; J. S. A[nglin] to Parents, 6 Jun. 1862. John S. Anglin Papers, LC; "The Master Race," *Richmond Whig*, 25 June 1862, P2, C2. See James McPherson, *Is Blood Thicker Than Water?* 27–69, on the widespread nature and falsity of the claim of Southerners as a separate race.

14. Excerpt of Leroy Pope Walker Speech, 12 Apr. 1861. Excerpts from *Richmond Enquirer*, 18 Apr. 1861. *New Orleans Picayune*, 18 Apr. 1861. *Vicksburg Whig*, 20 Apr. 1861. *Richmond Examiner*, 23 Apr. 1861. *Goldsboro Tribune*, 24 Apr. 1861. *Raleigh Standard*, 24 Apr. 1861. *Eufala Express*, 25 Apr. 1861. *Wilmington Daily Journal*, 27 Apr. 1861. *Milledgeville Southern Recorder*, 30 Apr. 1861. Message from Jefferson Davis to Congress, 29 Apr. 1861. Frank Moore, ed., *The Rebellion Record: A Diary of American Events with Documents, Narratives, Illustrative Incidents, Poetry, etc.*, I, 175 and 188–90; William C. Harris, *Leroy Pope Walker: Confederate Secretary of War*, 26; Davis to the Army of Eastern Virginia, 5 Jul. 1862. *OR* 11 (3): 690; *Richmond Dispatch*, 5 July 1862, P2, C1; *Mobile Advertiser*, 19 Aug. 1862, P2, C1; *Augusta Daily Constitutionalist*, 8 July 1862, P2, C1. Also see *Augusta Daily Constitutionalist*, 9 July 1862, P2, C1. In *Athens Southern Banner*, 16 July 1862, P3, C1. The *Southern Banner* quotes Davis's letter slightly differently, 16 July 1862, P4, C2.

15. John [Magruder] to Henry, 8 June 1862. Magruder Family Papers, LV; Jimmie [Johnston to Miss Green], 2 Sep. 1862. Mercer Green Johnston Papers, LC; Ned to Parents, 9 Sep. 1862. Bayol Family Papers, VHS. By this stage of the war, others believed similarly. See J. G[orgas] to Dearest, [8 Aug. 1862]. G to Dearest, [Sep. 1862]. Box 675, F 10, Gorgas Papers, UAL.

16. J. F. Marshall to Davis, 8 July 1862. Davis to Marshall, 11 July 1862. J. Foster Marshall Papers, USC; Davis to John Fosyth, 18 July 1862. Crist, ed., *Papers of Jefferson Davis*, 8, 293–95.

17. R. E. Lee to [wife], 28 July 1862. Lee Family Papers, VHS; S. McLean to Cousin, 25 July 1862. Civil War Miscellaneous Collection, USAMHI. Also see R. F Eppes to wife & children, 13 July 1862. Confederate Papers, SHC, UNC; H. R. Foster to Brother and sister, 26 July 1862. Willis Family Papers, WMU; James Campbell to Martha, 17 July 1862. John Campbell Papers, Rice U.

18. Lee to Col. G. W. Lay, 11 and 12 July 1862. L&TS, ANV. General Orders, 1862–63, D. H. Hill's Command. Orders & Circulars of Subcommands, ANV. RG 109, NA; Special Orders, No. 155, 156, 159. AIGO, 5, 7 and 10 July 1862. *OR* 51 (2): 587–89; Lee to Hill, 4 July 1862. Randolph to Holmes, Preston, and Dorman, Mallett and Dunwody, 4 July 1862. Davis to Lee, 5 July and 5 July 1862. Guild to Surgeon-General, 5 July 1862. Lee to Davis, 6 July 1862. Special Orders, No.——,——, and No. 146. HQ, Dept. of No. Va. 7, 8, and 9 July 1862. Lee to Randolph, with Randolph's endorsement. 11 July 1862. Randolph to Finnegan, 11 July 1862. GO, No. 77. HQ, Dept. of No. Va. 11 July 1862. Long to Semmes, 15 July 1862. *OR* 11 (3): 630–39 and 643; Lee to Davis, 5 July and 25 July 1862 (three letters). Crist, ed., *Papers of Jefferson Davis*, 8, 278–79 and 301.

19. "Longstreet and A.P. Hill" in Houston *Daily Post*, 31 Jan. 1888. Sorrel to Goree, 5 Mar. and 2 Apr. 1888. Goree, 305–10; Hill to Lee, 12 July 1862, with indsmt. of Longstreet, 14 July 1862. *OR* 11 (3): 639–40.

20. Special Orders. No. 150. HQ, Dept. of No. Va. 13 July 1862. Lee to Jackson, 23, 25, 26 and July 1862. Special Orders, No. 164. HQ, Dept. of No. Va. 27 July 1862. *OR* 12 (3): 915–19; AAR of Lee, 18 Apr. 1863. AAR of Jackson, 2 Apr. 1863. *OR* 12 (2): 176–77 and 181–82.

21. F. Saunders to Mother, 12 Aug. 1862. Irvine-Saunders Papers, UVA; Charles M. Blackford to wife, 11 Aug. 1862. Blackford, *Letters from Lee's Army*, 101; William Ellis Jones diary, 9 Aug. 1862. William E. Jones Papers, FSNBP (originals at Schoff Collection, Clements Library, University of Michigan); Chapman Maupin to Father, 10 Aug. 1862. Maupin Family Papers, UVA; Noah Collins journal, 9 Aug. 1862. Isaac S. London Papers, 28–29, FSNBP. See Robert K. Krick, *Stonewall Jackson at Cedar Mountain*, for the battle and casualty numbers in Appendix III.

22. Lee to Davis, 24 Aug. 1862. *OR* 12 (3): 942; Jackson to Trimble, 27 Aug. 1862, with addendum by Trimble. Fitzhugh Lee Opie Papers, UVA; AAR of R. E. Lee, 8 June 1863. AAR of Jackson, 27 Apr. 1863. *OR* 12 (2): 553–54 and 645.

23. Richard to Father, 26 June 1862. Richard W. Waldrop Papers, SHC, UNC. See John Hennessy, *Return to Bull Run: The Campaign and Battle of Second Manassas*, 168–90; AAR of Jackson, 26 Apr. 1863. *OR* 12 (2): 644–45.

24. Longstreet to Fitz John Porter, 23 Sep. 1866 and 31 Oct. 1877. Box 2, Clippings File, Cadmus Wilcox Papers, LC; AAR of Lee, 8 June 1863. AAR of Longstreet, 10 Oct. 1862. AAR of Jackson, 26 Apr. 1863. *OR* 12 (2): 555, 564–65, and 645–46.

25. D. M. McIntire to Colonel Hoke, 29 Sep. 1862. William J. Hoke Papers, SHC, UNC; T. J. McGeorge reminiscences. T. J. McGeorge Papers, MC; AAR of Jackson, 26 Apr. 1863. *OR* 12 (2): 646–47.

26. AAR of Col. Stephen D. Lee, 2 Oct. 1862. AAR of Longstreet, 10 Oct. 1862. *OR* 12 (2): 577–78, 565–66.

27. Chris [Winsmith] to Father, 3 Sep. 1862. Christopher Winsmith Papers, MC; Potomac to *Athens Southern Confederacy*, 23 Sep. 1862. Styple, ed. *Writing and Fighting*, 142–43; AAR of Longstreet, 10 Oct. 1862. *OR* 12 (2): 565–66.

28. Lee to Davis, 30 Aug. 1862. Dowdey and Manarin, eds., *Wartime Papers*, 268.

29. Robt [Tondee] to Sister Hattie, 3 Sep. 1862. Robert P. Tondee Papers, DU; Ivy W. Duggan to Editor, *Central Georgian*, 1 Oct. 1862. Civil War Miscellany: 48th Georgia File, GDAH; *OR* 12 (2): 249–62, 560–62, 568, and 810–14.

30. Thomas J. Clark to wife, 7 Sep. 1862. Thomas A. Clark Papers, FSA; John S. Foster to Katie, 23 Sep. 1862. John S. Foster to Father, [Sep. 1862]. F 194, Box 18. Joseph F. Waring Papers, GHS; R. Fairfax to mama, 7 Sep. 1862. Fairfax Brothers Papers, MC; Eli Landers to Mother, 25 Sep. 1862. Eli P. Landers, *Weep Not for Me*, 83–84.

31. Isaac Hirsch diary, 4 Sep. 1862. Isaac Hirsch Papers, LV.

32. Walter to Sister, 30 Aug. 1862. Walter H. Taylor Papers, NPL; Your loving Husband [Dorsey Pender] to Wife, 7 Sep. 1862. William Dorsey Pender, *The Civil War Letters of William Dorsey Pender*, 173; R. H. Jones to Wife, 5 Sep. 1862. R. H. Jones Papers, GDAH.

33. Maj. B. P. Noland to Chilton, 23 Aug. 1862. CSA. Commissary Department, NYPL; Chilton to Randolph, 2 Sep. 1862. Lee to Davis, 4 Sep. 1862. *OR* 19 (2): 588 and 591–92; AAR of Lee, 19 Aug. 1863. *OR* 19 (1): 144.

34. Lee to Randolph, 3 Sep. 1862, with Randolph's Indorst., 9 Sep. 1862. *OR* 19 (2): 589–90.

35. AAR of Lee, 19 Aug. 1863. *OR* 19 (1): 144; Lee to Davis, 3 and 4 Sep. 1862. *OR* 12 (2): 390–92.

36. W. R. Stilwell to Molly, 10 Sep. 1862. Stilwell Papers, FSNBP; T. Rowland to Mother, 7 Sep. 1862. Kate Mason Rowland Papers, MC; Samuel Walkup diary, 7 Sep. 1862. Samuel H. Walkup Papers, SHC, UNC; Jed Hotchkiss diary, 5 Sep. 1862. Hotchkiss, *Make Me a Map*, 78–79; Osmun Latrobe diary, 6 [Sep. 1862]. Osmun Latrobe Papers, MDHS; Isaac Hirsch diary, 7 Sep. 1862. Isaac Hirsch Papers, LV; I. M. Auld to Mother, 9 Sep. 1862. CWMC, USAMHI.

37. V. A. S. P[arks] to *Savannah Republican*, 7 Sep. 1862. Styple, ed., *Writing and Fighting*, 147; Will to Sister, 9 Sep. 1862. Will Papers, MC; Dorsey Pender to Wife, 7 Sep. 1862. Pender, *One of Lee's Best Men*, 173; Charles Cormier to ?, 15 Sep. 1862. Louisiana Historical Collection: Papers of Army of Northern Virginia, Box 2. TU.

38. Wife [Elizabeth Phoebe Key Howard] to [Husband], [n.d.] Sep. [1862]. Elizabeth Phoebe Key Howard Papers, MDHS; Records of Charles Howard. U.S. Census, 1860. Ward 11, Baltimore, Md., 473; Records of Charles Howard. Slave Census, 1860. Ward 11, Baltimore, Md., 66.

39. W. J. Pegram to Mother, 7 Sep. 1862. Pegram-Johnson-McIntosh Family Papers. VHS; Jed Hotchkiss diary, 6 Sep. 1862. Hotchkiss, *Make Me a Map*. 79; John S. Foster to Kate, 23 Sep. 1862. Box 18, F194. Joseph F. Waring Papers, GHS; J. S. Johnston to [Miss Green], 22 Sep. 1862. Mercer Green Johnston Papers, LC; Walter Taylor to [Sister], 7 Aug. [Sep.] 1862. Walter H. Taylor Papers, NPL; J. D. Nance to Laura, 24 Sep. 1862. Nance Papers (orig. at USC), FSNBP. Dorsey Pender claimed half the people supported the Confederacy. He seems to be exaggerating. Pender to Wife, 7 Sep. 1862. Pender, *One of Lee's Best Men*, 172. See Robert K. Krick, "The Army of Northern Virginia in September 1862: Its Circumstances, Its Opportunities, and Why It Should Not Have Been at Sharpsburg," in Gary W. Gallagher, ed., *Antietam: Essays on the 1862 Maryland Campaign*, 38; Lee to Davis, 7 Sep. 1862. *OR* 19 (2): 596.

40. Pockets still existed along the southern bank of the Potomac River around Washington and along the coastline, such as those at Norfolk and Fort Monroe.

41. Lee to Davis, 13 and 7 Sep. 1862. Pleasanton to Marcy, 6 Sep. 1862. *OR* 19 (2): 606, 597–98, and 194–95; Christopher to Kate, 23 Sep. 1862. Christopher Winsmith Papers, MC.

42. Lee to Myers, 21 Sep. 1862. *OR* 19 (2): 614; Ivy W. Duggan to Editor, *Central Georgian*, 1 Oct. 1862. Civil War Miscellany: 48th Georgia File, GDAH; P.W.A. to *Savannah Republican*, 26 Sep. [1862]. R2, Edmund Kirby-Smith Papers, SHC, UNC; [William Fisher Plane] to [wife], 5 Sep. 1862. Plane, *GHQ* 48, No. 2, 224–25; James E. Phillips memoirs, 9.

43. Charles Cormier to ?, 15 Sep. 1862. Louisiana Historical Collection: Papers of Army of Northern Virginia, Box 2. TU; Krick, in Gallagher, ed. *Antietam*, 41 and 43–44. Krick sees more opposition to the concept of crossing into the Union than I do.

44. Lee to Davis, 9 and 12 Sep. 1862. *OR* 12 (2): 602 and 605; McLaws to Wife, 29 Aug. and 4 Sep. 1862. Lafayette McLaws, *A Soldier's General*, 153–55.

45. Alexander, *Fighting for the Confederacy*, 141–42; George Templeton Strong diary, 24 Sep. 1862. Strong, *The Diary of George Templeton Strong*, 3, 261. For weather, see Krick, in Gallagher, ed. *Antietam*, 41–42. Corn in Maryland in September was ripe. Soldiers did not eat unripe or green corn; they prepared it improperly, which caused bowel problems. Bob Krick to author, 20 Jan. 2007. Copy in possession of author.

46. Lee to Davis, 16 Sep. 1862. *OR* 19 (1): 141–42; Timothy J. Reese, *High-Water Mark: The 1862 Maryland Campaign in Strategic Perspective*, 16–21.

47. AAR of Lee, 19 Aug. 1863. AAR of Jackson, 23 Apr. 1863. *OR* 19 (1): 147–48 and 954–55; Channing Price to Mother, 18 Sep. 1862. R. Channing Price Papers, SHC, UNC; Jackson to McLaws, 14 Sep. 1862. Chilton to McLaws, 14 Sep. 1862. A. L. Long to McLaws, 15 Sep. 1862. McLaws Papers, SHC, UNC; L. M. McLaws to Miss Lizzie, 20 Sep. 1862. Ewell Papers, LC.

48. Osmun Latrobe diary, 15 Sep. 1862. Osmun Latrobe Papers, VHS. Harsh, a careful historian of Lee's decisions, suspects Lee was contemplating an attack from this position. The evidence could be interpreted either way. Harsh, *Taken at the Flood*, 330–35.

49. For the best battle account, see Stephen Sears, *Landscape Turned Red: The Battle of Antietam*. Also see Jay Luvaas and Harold W. Nelson, *The U.S. Army War College Guide to the Battle of Antietam: The Maryland Campaign of 1862*. For the political and international context, see James M. McPherson, *Antietam: Crossroads of Freedom*.

50. Thomas McCarty journal, 17 Sep. 1862. Thomas L. McCarty Papers, CAH; T. Rowland to Mother, 21 Sep. 1862. Kate Mason Rowland Papers, MC; Gilmer Crutchfield diary, 17 Sep. 1862. Gilmer W. Crutchfield Papers, UVA; [T. Fogle] to Father & Mother, 28 Sep. 1862. Theodore T. Fogle Papers, EU; Jos. Q. Burton, "A Sketch of the 47th Regt. Ala. Vols.," 3. Auburn University; T. F. Botsford, *Memories*, 7; T. Ruffin, Jr., to wife, 19 Sep. 1862. Thomas Ruffin, Jr., Papers, NCDAH; G. P. Ring to Wife, 20 Sep. 1862. Box 2, Louisiana Historical Collection: Papers of the Army of Northern Virginia, TU; Harsh, *Taken at the Flood*, 432–33; H. L. P. King diary, 17 Sep. 1862. H. L. P. King Papers, FSNBP.

51. Alexander, *Fighting*, 239; James R. Boulware diary, 17 Sep. 1862. James R. Boulware Papers, LV; J. D. Nance to Laura, 24 Sep. 1862. Nance Papers (Originals at USC), FSNBP; W. N. Pendleton to Colonel, 17 Sep. 1862. J. Thompson Brown Papers, VHS; Incomplete Tabulation of Artillery, ANV. *OR* 19 (1): 836–37; J. B. Richardson diary, 17 Sep. 1862. J. B. Richardson Papers, MC; Osmun Latrobe diary, 17 Sep. 1862, with newspaper clippings. Osmun Latrobe Papers, VHS.

52. J. E. B. Stuart to wife, 19 Aug. 1862. Stuart Papers, VHS; R. Channing Price to Mother, 18 Sep. 1862. R. Channing Price Papers, SHC, UNC; AAR of Jackson, 23 Apr. 1863. AAR of Stuart, 13 Feb. 1864. *OR* 19 (1): 956–57, 818–19; William Woods Hassler, *Colonel John Pelham: Lee's Boy Artillerist*; Robert H. Moore II, *The First and 2nd Stuart Horse Artillery*, 33–35.

53. [Lee] to Sir, 15 Feb. 1870, incomplete. Series A, Box 4, Lee Headquarters Papers, VHS; Army Correspondent to *Savannah Republican*, 19 Sep. 1862; W. L. Claybrooks to Mother & Father, 17 Oct. 1862. Lewis Leigh Collection, USAMHI. CSR of William L. Claybrooks, 2nd Miss. Inf., fails to mention a wound. RG 109, NA.

54. T[homas Rowland to Home], 30 Sep. 1862. Kate M. Rowland Papers, MC; Walter Taylor to [Sister], 21 Sep. 1862. Walter H. Taylor Papers, Norfolk PL; Alexander, *Fighting*, 145; W. H. H. Winston to Aunt, 22 Oct. 1862. Winston-Clark Family Papers, VHS.

55. Taylor to ?, 28 Sep. 1862. Walter H. Taylor Papers, NPL.

56. Ivy W. Duggan to Editor, *Central Georgian*, 1 Oct. 1862. Civil War Miscellany: 48th Georgia File, GDAH. Here, I agree with Gallagher in *The Confederate War*, 10–11 and 127–28, and Royster, *The Destructive War*, that Confederates in and out of the army sought an aggressive war.

14. A Failure of Discipline

1. James H. Hoyt to Sir, 17 Dec. 1862. Robert A. Lancaster Papers, VHS; CSR of James H. Hoyt. M311, R108, RG 109, NA.

2. Burnside to Cullum, 7 Nov. 1862. *OR* 19 (2): 552–53; J. M. C[oker] to Wife, 18 Dec. 1862. Coker Papers, FSNBP (originals in Hodgson Heidler Collection, UGA); Milton Barrett to Brother and Sister, 28 Jan. 1863. Barrett, 82–83; Summary of Casualties in First Corps. Report of Casualties of Second Corps. Report of Casualties in Union Army. *OR* 21: 572, 635, and 142; J. B. Magruder to Papa, 20 Dec. 1862. Magruder Family, LV. For a superb and insightful study of Fredericksburg, see George C. Rable, *Fredericksburg! Fredericksburg!* The best battle study is Francis Augustin O'Reilly, *The Fredericksburg Campaign: Winter War of the Rappahannock*.

3. W. L. Davis to S. W. Smythe, 16 Dec. 1862. William L. Davis Papers, MDAH; C. C. Blacknall to Jinny, 18 Dec. 1862. Oscar W. Blacknall Papers, NCDAH; Jno. W. Daniels to Grandmama, 22 Dec. 1862. John Warwick Daniel Papers, UVA; H. R. Berkeley diary, 18 Dec. 1862. H. R. Berkeley Papers, MC; [Thos. Elder] to wife, 21 Dec. 1862. Thomas Elder Papers, VHS; James R. Boulware diary, 28 Dec. 1862. Dr. James Richmond Boulware Papers, LV; John S. Foster to Sister Lissie, 12 Jan. 1863. Box 18, F194, Joseph F. Waring Papers, GHS.

4. See Escott, *After Secession*, 102; David H. Donald, "Southerner As a Fighting Man," in Charles Sellers, *Southerner As American*.

5. For organizational culture, see Joanne Martin, *Organizational Culture: Mapping the Terrain*; Mats Alvesson, *Understanding Organizational Culture*. Also see Wyatt-Brown, *Southern Honor*. Even within a modern army, after boot camp tears down individual will and resurrects it into a collective mindset that leadership designs, military trainers cannot suppress all aspects of individualism, particularly if it draws personnel from a society that prizes civil liberties and independence. This is called differentiation.

6. This assessment of why soldiers voted officers out is based on the examination of officers' records for seventeen randomly selected units. The single most pronounced factor in officers' losing elections was a prolonged absence from the unit. I derived the issue of those who neglected to care for the men from soldiers' letters.

7. Peter Kivisto, "The Revival of Assimilation in Historical Perspective," in Peter Kivisto, ed., *Incorporating Diversity: Rethinking Assimilation in a Multicultural Age*, 22–23. This consensus on honor is called integration theory; conflict, as represented in profligacy, self-indulgence, and a lack of discipline is called differentiation theory. See Martin, *Organizational Culture*, Chapter 4. While not all Southern whites could fulfill these objectives, most embraced the concepts and aspired to do so. In addition to Wyatt-Brown, *Southern Honor*, see Eric Walther, "Southerners' Honor," *Southern Studies*, 129–54. Thanks to Mel Deaile for aiding me with the readings.

8. R. Fairfax to Jenny, 7 June 1862. Fairfax Brothers Papers, MC.

9. Edsy to [wife], 18 Mar. 1862. E. P. Alexander Papers, SHC, UNC; H. T. Holladay to Jeannie, 23 May 1862. Holladay Family Papers, VHS; A [Lawton] to [wife], 16 July 1862. A. R, Lawton Papers, SHC, UNC; L. M. Blackford to Mother, 3 Apr. 1862. Launcelot Minor Blackford Papers, UVA.

10. J. A. Cotton to Uncle, 16 Sep. 1861. Martin, ed., "The Cotton Letters," *VMHB* 37, No. 1, 21; Jno. W. Daniel to Father, 13 Jan. 1862. John Warwick Daniel Papers, UVA; C. C. Blacknall to Jinny, 18 May 1862. Oscar W. Blacknall Papers. NCDAH.

11. G. Gache to Philip, P.C., 20 Aug. 1862. Buckley, ed., *Frenchman*, 132; R. Fairfax to Jenny, 7 June 1862. Fairfax Brothers Papers, MC; James P. Williams to Nannie, 17 June 1862. J. Peter Williams Papers, UVA; Charles to Uncle, 4 July 1862. Kerrison Family Papers, USC; Personne, 16 July 1862. *Charleston Courier*, 22 July 1862. Newspapers, Vol. 1, RNBP; James R. Boulware diary, 28 June 1862. James R. Boulware Papers, LV; GO, No.___. HQ, [D. H. Hill's] Division, 12 July 1862. GO, 1862–63. D. H. Hill's Division. O&C of Subcommands, ANV. RG 109, NA.

12. Ugie to Susie, 13 Aug. 1862. Allen and Bohannon, eds., 143–44; S to ?, 5 Jan. 1865. J. E. B. Stuart Papers, LC.

13. [Chris Winsmith] to Kate, 5 Sep. 1862. Christopher Winsmith Papers, MC; Henri J. Mugler journal, 28 June 1862. Virginia, Vol. 13, RNBP; G. Berkeley Greene to Oscar, 1 Sep. [1862]. Oscar J. E. Stuart Papers, MDAH; Alexander, *Fighting*, 164.

14. Isaac Hirsch diary, 27 Aug. 1862. Isaac Hirsch Papers, LV; Jerry [Harris] to ?, 27 Dec. 1862. Harris Papers, FSNBP; M. H. Fitzpatrick to Amanda, 27 Sep. 1863. "Letters to Amanda," CWMC, USAMHI; Robert [Stafford] to Ma, 13 Sep. 1862. Gilder-Lehrman Collection, ML; Richard J. Davis to Wife, 11 and 15 Aug. 1862. Preston Davis Papers, UVA.

15. E. T. H. Warren to Jennie, 18 Apr. 1863. E. T. H. Warren Papers, UVA; [Pender] to wife, 19 Sep. 1862. Pender, 175

16. W. W. Gordon to Nellie, 29 Sep. 1862. Don 18, F196, Joseph F. Waring Papers, GHS; J. J. Halsey to Sir, 14 and 17 Mar. 1863. Morton-Halsey Papers, UVA; James Nixon to Wife, 26 July 1867 James Nixon Papers, FSU; Charles E. Waddell diary, 3 Aug. 1863. Charles E. Waddell Papers, MC; Richard T. Davis to wife, 10 Jan. 1864. Preston-Davis Papers, UVA; [Walter Taylor to Bettie], 25 Oct. 1863. Walter H. Taylor Papers, NPL.

17. Napoleon Maxim 107. Conrad H. Lanza, *Napoleon and Modern War: His Military Maxims*, 136; Wilcox to Sister, 7 June 1862. Wilcox to John, 26 Sep. 1862. Cadmus M. Wilcox Papers, LC; AAR of D. H. Hill, n.d., 1862. *OR* 19 (1): 1026; [Pender to wife, 19 Sep. 1862]. Pender, 175.

18. [Pender to wife, 19 Sep. 1862]. Pender, 175; Christopher [Winsmith] to Kate, 23 Sep. 1862. J. S. Johnston to Mary, 11 Nov. 1862. Mercer Green Johnston Papers, LC.

19. Lee to Davis, 7 Sep. 1862. *OR* 19 (2): 597.

20. Lee to Davis, 21 Sep. 1862. *OR* 19 (1): 143; Lee to Davis, 22 Sep. 1862. J. R. Jones to Major Paxton, 27 Sep. 1862. *OR* 19 (2): 617–18 and 629–30.

21. SO, No. 20. HQ, 7 July 1862. F7, J. B. Walton Papers, Louisiana Historical Association, TU; GO, 94. HQ, Dept. of Northern Va. 11 Aug. 1862. Box 11, Battalion, Washington Artillery, Louisiana Historical Association, TU; GO, No. 38. HQ, 3rd Brigade. 24 Aug. 1862. Garland's Brigade. O&C of Subcommands, ANV. RG 109, NA; Circular. Right Wing, ANV. 6 Sep. 1862. Box 11, Battalion, Washington Artillery: Louisiana Historical Association, TU.

22. Lee to Longstreet and Jackson, 22 Sep. 1862. *OR* 19 (2): 618–19.

23. Davis to Lee, 28 Sep. 1862. Lee to Davis, 2 Oct. 1862. Crist, Dix, and Williams, eds., *Papers of Jefferson Davis*, 8, 408–9 and 421.

24. Lee to Randolph, 27 Oct. 1862. Lee to Randolph, 27 Oct. 1862. SO, No. 234. HQ, ANV, 6 Nov. 1862. Lee to Davis, 6 Nov. 1862. *OR* 19 (2): 683–84 and 697–99; Lee to Cooper, 7 Dec. 1862. L&TS, ANV. RG 109, NA. Tabulation based on a comparison of the division and brigade commanders.

25. Lee to Longstreet, 2 and 5 Dec. 1862. L&TS, ANV. RG 109, NA; GO. HQ, Iverson's Brigade. 2 Dec. 1862. GO, Iverson's Brigade. Orders & Circulars of Subcommands. ANV. RG 109, NA; Circular. HQ. 1st Army Corps. 13 Nov. 1862. Battalion, Washington Artillery, Box 11, Louisiana Historical Association, TU; J. M. Tate to sister, 29 Sep. 1862. Jeremiah Tate Papers, Gilder-Lehrman Collection, ML.

26. Davis to Senate and House of Representatives, 11 Sep., 8 Oct., and 10 Oct. 1862. An Act to relieve the Army of disqualified, disabled and incompetent officers, 13 Oct. 1862. *OR* 4 (2): 80–81, 110–11, 114, and 205–6; Davis to Lee, 28 Sep. 1862. *OR* 19 (2): 633–34; Crist, Dix, and Williams, eds., *Papers of Jefferson Davis*, 8, 409–10.

27. *OR* 2: 571; *OR* 5: 350; *OR* 11 (1): 935; *OR* 11 (2): 510–11; *OR* 12 (1): 708 and 716; *OR* 12 (2): 179; *OR* 19 (1): 558 and 955; *OR* 21: 568 and 635; Ivy Duggan to Editor, *Central Georgian*, 1 Oct. 1862. Civil War Miscellany: 48th Georgia File, GDAH; R. E. Lee per G. W. C. Lee to Annie & Agnes, 30 Sep. 1862. R. E. Lee to Mary, [Oct. 1862]. Lee Family Papers, VHS; John S. Rucker diary, 31 May 1862. Ralph G. Poriss Papers. USAMHI; GO, No. 78. HQ, Dept. of No. Va., 12 July 1862. *OR* 11 (3): 640–41.

28. AAR of Capt. Greenlee Davidson, Letcher's Artillery, undated, section dated 19 Sep. 1862. Greenlee Davidson Folder, RHSM, WL; James P. Williams to Aunt Mary, 18 Nov. 1862. James Peter Williams Papers, UVA; W. B. Bailey to Bro, 20 Nov. 1862. Coco Collection, HCWRT, USAMHI; Edward S. Duffey diary, 17 Dec. 1862. Edward S. Duffey Papers, VHS; [John W. Daniel] to Sister, 5 Dec. 1863. John Warwick Daniels Papers, UVA.

29. Charles T. Furlow journal, 3 Sep. 1862. Charles T. Furlow Papers (originals at Yale University), Vol. 376, FSNBP; F. Saunders to Mother, 24 Sep. 1862. Irvine-Saunders Papers, UVA. See Kivisto, 18.

30. [Pender to his wife, 19 Sep. 1862]. Pender, 175; H. T. Owen to Harriett, 27 July 1862. Henry T. Owen Papers, LV; Hennessy, *Return to Bull Run*, 122–23; Robertson, *Stonewall Jackson*, 557.

31. Here, I challenge the "leader-focused" culture.

15. Lee's Officer Corps and Army Culture

1. Lee to Randolph, 23 Sep. 1862. Lee to Davis, 2 Oct. 1862. *OR* 19 (2): 622 and 643–44.

2. Lee to Letcher, 23 Sep. 1861. Series B, Box 2, Lee Headquarters Papers, VHS; Lee to Davis, 7 Sep. 1862. *OR* 19 (2): 597.

3. Lee to Magrath, 24 Dec. 1861. *OR* 6: 350; Joseph T. Glatthaar, "A Dynamic for Success and Failure: Discipline, Cause, and Comrades in the Relationship Between Officers and Enlisted Men in Lee's Army," a paper delivered at a Symposium in Honor of James M. McPherson. Princeton University, April 2005, 1–2.

4. General Orders, No. 70. HQ, First Corps, Army of the Potomac, 3 Nov. 1861. GO & Circulars, Army of the Potomac. RG 109, NA; Letter to the Editor of the *Enquirer*, 30 Dec. 1863. W. S. Morris Papers, MC; Davis to Congress, 18 Aug. 1862, *OR* 4, 2: 55. The Texas regiments originally had the Confederate government appoint their officers, much to the dismay of the soldiers. See Charles E. Brooks, "Popular Sovereignty in the Confederate Army: The Case of Col. John Marshall and the Fourth Texas Regiment," in Aaron Sheehan-Dean, ed., *The View from the Ground: The Experiences of Civil War Soldiers*.

5. Lee to Beauregard, 19 June 1861. Letters Sent, Virginia Forces. R1, RG 109; An Act to Amend an act entitled an act to further provide for the public defense, 16 Apr. 1862. An Act to further provide for the public defense, 16 Apr. 1862. *OR* 4, 1: 1081–82 and 1095–96; Davis to Congress, 18 Aug. 1862. *OR* 4, 2: 55. With citizen-soldiers, there had to be some elective system. This was the least intrusive for the army.

6. 50.6 percent owned or their parents with whom they resided owned slaves, compared to 35.7 percent of all enlisted men. Some 67.9 percent of all officers came from households that owned slaves. That compares to about 41.5 percent of all enlisted men. 14.6 percent of officers held professional occupations. Some 36.3 percent of all officers were married; just under a third of all enlisted men were married.

7. Some 19 percent of all officers had less than $800 personal total wealth, and if they lived with family, combined personal and family wealth. 54.8 percent of all enlisted men had more than $800 personal total wealth. by the same means of measurement.

8. Joe D. Shields, Jr., to Pa, 28 June 1861. Joseph D. Shields Papers, LSU; John S. Foster to Dr. James Foster, 2 Aug. 1861. Box 18, F194, Joseph F. Waring Papers, GHS.

9. Frank [Barron] to Jennie, 23 July 1863. Barron Papers, FSNBP; Dick [Phelps] to Aunt, 12 Mar. 1862. Dick to Sister, 6 Nov. 1862. Charles R. Phelps Papers, UVA; Carter [Braxton] to Sisters, 11 Oct. 1862. Carter Braxton Papers, originals in Ann Brown Memorial Collection, Brown U.

10. Wm. H. Ker to Sister, 10 May 1863. William H. Ker Papers, LSU; E. D. Ryan to Senators & Representatives, 21 Apr. 1862, LR. CA&IG. M474, R23, F933–36. RG 109, NA;

11. Jno. J. Reeve to Park, 9 Dec. 1861. George William Bagby Papers, VHS; Cornelius McLaurin to Sister, 8 May [1861]. Lewis Leigh Collection, USAMHI; J. W. M[urray] to wife, 15 Sep. 1861. Murray Family Papers, LV.

12. Wolf Lichtenstein memoir, n.p. CWTIC, USAMHI; W[Cocke] to parents. 20 May 1862. Cocke Family Papers, VHS; Sarah H. Walker to Davis, 2 Dec. 1862. LR, CA&IG. M 474, R9, F1431–433. RG 109, NA; Henry D. Puckett to wife and children, 30 Jan. 1863. Henry D. Puckett Papers, FSNBP.

13. Charlie to Ma, 31 May 1861. Ward Family Papers, LC; Davis to Lee, 12 June 1862. Rowland, V, 274–75; T. Jim [Linebarger] to [Ann], 6 Oct. 1864. Anne Linebarger Snuggs Papers, SHC, UNC; Oates, *War Between the Union*, 69–70.

14. Grey Back to Editor of *Grape Shot*, 24 Apr. 1864. *Grape Shot* by Willis Bolls, MC; Elliott [Welch] to Mother, 14 Feb. 1864. Elliott Stephen Welch Papers, DU.

15. O. C. Hamilton to Father, 30 May 1863. Colier Green and Oliver Clark Hamilton Papers, NCDAH; J. S. Anglin to Parents, 4 July 1862. John S. Anglin Papers, LC. Records of William Anglin. U.S. Slave Census, 1860. Iredell County, N.C., 547.

16. Jno. M. Tilley to Wife, 31 Dec. 1861. John M. Tilley Papers, GDAH; Council to wife, 2 Oct. 1863. Council A. Bryan Papers, FSA; R. E. Mobley to Bettie, 1 Jan. 1865. Lewis Leigh Collection, USAMHI; J. E. B. Stuart to Darling One, 11 Sep. 1863. Stuart Papers, VHS; E. T. H. Warren to wife, 7 Nov. 1861. E. T. H. Warren Papers, UVA; R. E. Lee to Fitzhugh, [May 1863?]. R. E. Lee Papers, UVA.

17. Wm. E. Bird to [Sallie], 19 Aug. 1861. Rozier, *Granite Farm*, 15; A. D. Kelly to Brother, 4 Dec. 1862. Williamson Kelly Papers, DU.

18. John C. Towles journal, n.d., 1862, 45–46. John C. Towles Papers, LV; John S. Apperson journal, 25 Jan. 1862. Apperson, 190; Thos. J. Goree to Sister Frank, 8 Dec. 1861. Goree, ed., 107; J. F. Coghill to Mit, 10 Sep. 1863. Jonathan F. Coghill Papers. Auburn U.

19. James Campbell to Martha, 28 May 1863. John Campbell Papers, Rice University; O. C. Hamilton to Father, 30 May 1863. Colier Green and Oliver Clark Hamilton Papers, NCDAH.

20. Robt. H. Miller to Father, 23 July 1862. Miller, *VMHB* 70(1): 87; John Bellinger Patrick journal, 18 Sep. 1863. John Bellinger Patrick Papers, USC. Large numbers of others had similar, yet less colorful assessments of Jenkins's ambition.

21. R. Fairfax to Jenny, 3 Apr. 1862. Fairfax Brothers Papers, MC; GO, No. 63. HQ, ANV. 14 May 1863. *OR* 25 (2): 798–99.

22. GO, No. 69, 120, 123, 126, 4, 6, and 7. HQ, ANV. 23 July [June] 1862. 21 and 28 Oct. 1862. 12 Nov. 1862. 13, 20, and 21 Jan. 1863. G&SO&C Issued, ANV. M921, RI, F180, 262, 268, 275–76, 290–91, 368–69, 379, 393, and 398. Letter of resignation of Lieut. J. H. Copeland, 20 Sep. 1862 with endsmt. By Col., 22 Sep. 1862. CSR of J. H. Copeland, Holcombe Legion. RG 109, NA.

23. *CSA* v. *Col. V. D. Groner, 61st Virginia,* 9 and 18, Records of the Military Court, Longstreet's Corps, MC; Memo by Col. Bryan Grimes re: Lt. Jones, G, 4th NC, 21 Feb. 1864. Bryan Grimes Papers, NCDAH.

24. Magruder to Sir, 22 June 1861. L&TS, ANV, May–Nov. 1861. RG 109, NA; Jno. E. Hall to Father, 27 Nov. 1861. Bolling Hall Papers, ADAH; GO, No 26 and 28. HQ, ANV. 23 and 27 Feb. 1863. G&SO&CI, ANV. M921, R1, F538 and 587. RG 109, NA.

25. R. T. Scott to Fan, 4 Feb. 1862. Keith Family Papers, VHS; Court-Martial of Lt. Harvey E. Jones, 3rd Alabama. A. P. Hill to Davis, 14 Oct. 1864. LR, CA&IG. M474, R27, F425–55 and R114, F590–91. Morning Report of Capt. Jno. S. Swan, 59 VA, 19 Jan. 1862. CSR of Lt. Col. Francis P. Anderson. M331, R6. Copy at FSNBP. RG 109, NA; Jim O. T[hurman] to John, 20 Oct. 1863. John G. Scurry Papers, Gilder-Lehrman Collection, ML; IR collection of Lane's Brigade by Capt. E. T. Nicholson, 31 Aug. 1864. IR, R10, F377. RG 109, NA; Campbell Brown remin., 170. Ewell Papers, TNSL.

26. H. R. Berkeley diary, 18 Aug. and 1 Oct. 1862. H. R. Berkeley Papers, MC. Evidently, Nelson had changed his ways, because the private recorded their justification: "We thought him rather too strict and exacting."

27. Report of Board of Examiners of Maj. J. H. J. Williams, 9th Alabama. Testimony of Capt. T. W. E. Winn, Wilcox's Staff, and Capt. G. C. Smith, 9th Alabama. Williams to Davis, 29 June 1863. William Preston Johnston to Seddon, 29 June 1863. Lee and Davis endsmts. LR, CA&IG. M474, R88, F64–77 and 93–99.

28. Orders, No. ?, HQ, Yorktown, 3 July 1861. Cary Letter Book, MC; James P. Williams to Ma, 13 May 1863. James Peter Williams Papers, UVA.

29. William A. Heirs to?, 18 Nov. 1862. William A. Heirs Papers, Gilder-Lehrman Collection, ML. Thanks to Bob Krick for showing me this.

30. Will [Crutcher] to Evangeline, 17 Oct. 1861. Crutcher-Shannon Family Papers, CAH; John O'Farrell diary, 20 May 1862. John O'Farrell Papers, MC; Bert to Nim, 26 Apr. 1864. Fairfax Brothers Papers, MC; J. Q. A. Nadenbousch to Wite, 28 Apr. 1062. J. Q. A. Nadenbousch Papers, MC; Jno. T. Smith to Lucie & May, 4 June 1862. Smith-Johnson Papers, MC.

31. Jas. F. Cameron to Father and Mother, 21 Dec. 1861. James F. Cameron Papers, ADAH.

32. Husband to Wife, 2 July 1862. CWTIC, USAMHI; John Rayburn to Father, 10 Nov. 1861. Samuel King Rayburn Papers, ADAH.

33. Theodore to Mother, 23 June 1861. Theodore T. Fogle Papers, EU.

34. B. F. White to Friend, 28 Feb. 1862. James J. Phillips Papers, NCDAH.

35. [Wm. Fisher Plane] to [wife], 25 May 1862. Plane, *GHQ* 48 (2): 221; S. F. Harper to Genl., 28 Aug. 1862. Pettigrew Family Papers, NCDAH.

36. GO, No. 4. HQ, Iverson's Brigade, 6 Jan. 1863. Order Book, 23rd North Carolina Infantry. RG 109, NA.

37. GO, No. 22. HQ, Second Army Corps. 25 Mar. 1863. Second Army Corps, Orders and Circulars of Subcommands, ANV. RG 109, NA; GO, No. 10. HQ, 23rd NCI. 4 Feb. 1863. Order Book, 23rd North Carolina Infantry. RG 109, NA; GO, No. 10. HQ, Iverson's Brigade. 26 May 1863. Iverson's Brigade. Special Orders No.___. HQ, 3rd Brigade, 3rd Division. 12 Aug. 1862. Garland's Brigade. Orders and Circulars of Subcommands, ANV. RG 109, NA; J. J. W[ilson] to Brother, 22 Oct. 1862. J. J. Wilson Papers, MDAH; Chilton to General, 22 Sep. 1862. Wright's Brigade Order Book, CWTIC, USAMHI.

38. John C. Towles journal, 26 June 1862. John C. Towles Papers, LV; W. H. S. Burgwyn to Harry, 23 Sep. 1862. W. H. S. Burgwyn Papers, NCDAH; Thos. C. Elder to Wife, 8 July 1862. Elder Family Papers, VHS; Lee to Davis, 14 Dec. 1862. AAR of LTC R. L. Walker, 21 Dec. 1862. *OR* 21: 547 and 649–50; Petition of the officers of 44 NC, I. I. Crump et al. 21 Nov. 1863, M474, LR, CA&IG, R72, F542–46. RG 109, NA.

39. Based on the sample, 23.3 percent of officers were KIA, and 55.6 percent were WIA at least once (no repeats, so a person who was wounded in one battle and killed in a later fight was counted as one, in KIA column). For enlisted men, 10.6 percent were KIA and 34.3 percent were WIA at least once. In statistics compiled in *OR* 11 (1); 12 (1 and 2); and 19 (1), some 480 union officers were KIA and 1,857 officers were WIA.

40. G. R. Pickett's Comments to IR of Pickett's Division by Acting Adjutant and Inspector General Walter Harrison, 30 Jan. 1865. Inspection Reports. Reel 14, Frame 449. Lt. Col. H. E. Peyton to Gen. Cooper, 29 Nov. 1864. Inspection Reports. Reel 11, Frames 452–53. RG 109, NA. These statistics, which are unavailable in precise form, are based on a percentage of officers KIA to total casualties (1.68 percent) and officers WIA (7.04 percent) to total casualties that I tabulated for the battles from Seven Pines through Antietam. I then took the total casualties of Fredericksburg, Chancellorsville, Gettysburg, and Chickamauga, which would give 755 officers KIA and 3,183 WIA. When you factor in the Overland Campaign, a rough estimate gives those numbers.

41. Circular. HQ, Armies of the C.S., 22 Feb. 1865. Lee's Order Book, Ser. A, Lee's Headquarters Papers, VHS.

42. Lee to Davis, 13 Aug. 1864. Freeman, ed., *Lee's Dispatches,* 369.

16. The Soldiers of '62

1. Records of James Campbell and J. J. Campbell. U.S. Census, 1860, Guadalupe County, Tx., 34; Record of John Campbell. U.S. Slave Census, Guadalupe Co., Tx., 10.

2. James Campbell to Martha, 29 May 1862. John Campbell Papers, Rice U.

3. James Campbell to Martha, 29 May and 16 July 1862. John Campbell Papers, Rice U.; AAR of W. H. C. Whiting, n.d. July 1862. AAR of Hood, 10 July 1862. *OR* 11 (2): 562–64 and 568–69; CSR of James Campbell, 4th Texas Infantry. RG 109, NA.

4. James Campbell to Martha, 12 Aug. and 18 Nov. 1862 and 20 May 1863. John Campbell Papers, Rice U.

5. Records of Nancy Fitzpatrick. U.S. Census for 1860, Crawford County, Ga., 64; Records of Nancy Fitzpatrick. U.S. Slave Census for 1860, Crawford County, Ga., 32.

6. Fitzpatrick to Amanda, 1 July. 2 Sep., 4 Dec., and 15 Dec. 1862, 3 and 15 June 1863, 21 March 1864, and 27 March 1865. Lowe and Hodges, eds., 17–18, 24–25, 32–33, 36–37, 72–73, 128, and 204; GO, No. 131. A&IGO, 3 Oct. 1863. *OR* 25 (1): 1052–53.

7. Introduction and M. H. Fitzpatrick to Amanda, 17 Apr. 1863. Lowe and Hodges, eds., ix–xvi and 62.

8. Fitzpatrick to Amanda, 20 July 1863 and 7 Jan. 1864[5]. William Fields to Mrs. Fitzpatrick, 8 June 1865. Lowe and Hodges, eds., 79, 196, and 209–10.

9. See Sample in Appendix I. Thos. C. Elder to Wife, 27 Apr. 1862. Elder Family Papers, VHS; Records of Thomas C. Elder. U.S. Census, 1860, City of Petersburg, 171; Records of T. C. Elder. U.S. Slave Census, 1860. City of Petersburg, 11; Records of Thos. C. Elder. U.S. Slave Census, 1860. Lunenburg Co., 42. Of course, not all 1861 regiments served in Virginia early in the war or stayed with the army the entire war.

10. See Sample in Appendix I. The actual percentages from the Deep South—Texas, Louisiana, Mississippi, Alabama, Georgia, Florida, and South Carolina—were 39.9 percent in 1861 and 42.6 percent in 1862.

11. Thomas J. Clark to wif, 29 July 1862. Thomas Clark Papers, FSA; Records of Thomas J. Clark. U.S. Census, 1860. Hamilton Co., Fla., 621; Jody Norman to author, 16 June 2006.

12. See Appendix I. In 1861, 44.8 percent were farmers or farmhands; in 1862, it was 59 percent. In 1861, 27.8 percent of volunteers were married; in 1862, that number rose to 53.6 percent. Fatherhood rose from 23.9 percent to 42.5 percent. In 1861, 34.4 percent were born before 1836; in 1862, 43.8 percent were born before 1836.

13. See Sample in Appendix I. Records of Arthur Wachob. U.S. Census. 1860, Washington Co., 1015; Records of Thomas R. Dew and William W. Hart. U.S. Census Records, 1861. Albemarle Co., Va., 599. U.S. Slave Census, 1860. Albemarle Co., Va., 96–97 and 100; CSR of Thomas R. Dew, 47th Virginia Infantry. RG 109, NA; Records of Cicero Farrar. U.S. Census, 1860. Itawamba Co., Miss., 18; CSR of Cicero Farrar, 42nd Mississippi Infantry. RG 109, NA. Dew enlisted in March and was promoted to captain in June 1862.

14. See Sample in Appendix I. Record of Eli Mayfield. U.S. Census, 1860. Walton Co., Ga., 173.

15. In saying 60 percent more wealth, I am comparing median wealth. See sample in Appendix I.

16. Records of Hunter H. Holmes, U.S. Census, 1860. Gates Co., N.C., 214; Records of Otis Mills. U.S. Census, 1860. Polk Co., N.C., 198; Records of Thomas J. Corbin. U.S. Census, 1860. Pittsylvania Co., Va., 247.

17. Benjamin to Shorter et al., 2 Feb. 1862. A Proclamation to the People of the State of Georgia from Gov. Joseph E. Brown, 11 Feb. 1862. Gov. Henry T. Clark to Benjamin, 11 Feb. 1862. *OR* 4, 1: 902–3 and 918–22. Thanks to friend Keith Bohannon for explaining Georgia's policy.

18. Some 47 percent were born in 1841 or after. Record of Seaborn Swann. U.S. Census, 1860. Clarke Co., Ga., 1037; Records of Lemuel Swann. U.S. Slave Census, 1860. Clarke Co., Ga., 14.

19. Records of John P. Givens. U.S. Census, 1860. Gaston Co., 163; Records of William J. Hope. U.S. Census, 1860. Fluvanna Co., Va., 656; Records of William J. Hope and Sarah B. Davis. U.S. Slave Census, 1860. Fluvanna Co., 78.

20. Sam to Mary, 9 Dec. 1861. Samuel Wicliffe Melton Papers, USC; Thos. C. Elder to Wife, 12 June 1863. Thomas Elder Papers, VHS. See Appendix I for birth. Cavalry had 25.7 percent born before 1831 and 34.7 percent born after 1840, the largest percentage for any of the branches.

21. Longstreet to Soldiers, 17 June 1862. *OR* 11 (3); 605–6.

22. See Sample in Appendix I. CSR of James Septimus Ackis, Brooks (S.C.) Artillery. CSR of John P. Givens, 48th North Carolina Infantry. RG 109, NA. Even though Ackis was wounded twice, I counted him only once. Givens suffered a wound, a capture, and then died of disease. He counted once as well. I did not count surrender at Appomattox in the prisoner of war category.

23. Statistics for 1861 were 57.7 percent of artillerists, 57.1 percent of cavalrymen, and 71.4 percent of infantrymen. In the class of 1862, they were 57.4 percent for artillerists, 54.4 percent for cavalrymen, and 79.3 percent for infantry. In the army as a whole, for 1861 volunteers it was 71.4 percent; for those who entered in 1862, it was 75.0 percent.

24. C. A. Hege to father, 17 Aug. and 15 Nov. 1862. Lewis Leigh Col., USAMHI; Tom[Aiton] to Pa, 11 Aug. 1862. *Recollections and Reminiscences, 1861–1865, through World War 1*, 6, 491.

25. Theodore T. Fogle to Father & Mother, 13 Oct. 1862. Theodore T. Fogle Papers, EU.

17. Supplying the Army

1. Records of Charles M. Blackford. U.S. Census, 1860. Campbell, Co., Va., 296; Records of Charles M. Blackford. U.S. Slave Census, 1860. Campbell Co., Va., 17, 33, and 72. Albemarle Co., Va., 112; Records of William M. Blackford. U.S. Slave Census, 1860. Campbell Co., Va., 33.

2. J. T. Thompson to Mother and Sisters, 26 Mar. 1862. Thompson, "A Georgia Boy," *VMHB* 70, 3, 322; Records of James T. Thompson. U.S. Census, 1860. DeKalb Co., Ga., 30; Records of Thos. Thompson. U.S. Slave Census, 1860. DeKalb Co., GA., 274.

3. John A. Everett to Ma, 8 Sep. 1861. John A. Everett Papers, EU; [McLaws] to Wife, 19 Feb. 1862. McLaws Papers, SHC, UNC. Although Beauregard and Johnston had grumbled about supply issues at Manassas after the battle, most initial difficulties stemmed from struggles to establish a system that would collect and distribute food and supplies to their "mobile city"—a problem of poor planning, confusion, and sloppy paperwork.

4. Colonel Ro. Johnston to Major Corley, 23 Aug. 1861. L&TS, Dept. of the Peninsula, Aug. 1861–May 1862. RG 109, NA; E. T. H. Warren to wife, 27 Aug. 1861. E. T. H. Warren Papers, UVA; James McClinton to friend, 30 Sep. 1861. Harris Family Papers, USC; George to Sister, 10 Oct. 1861. George Lee Robertson Papers, CAH.

5. Magruder to Sir, 25 Oct. 1861. Magruder to Gorgas, 28 Sep. 1861. L&TS, Army of the Peninsula, May–Nov. 1861. R. F. Sturdivant to Capt. H. Bryan, 17 Mar. 1862. Bryan to Lt. Col. Goode, 17 Mar. 1862. L&TS, Army of the Peninsula. RG 109, NA; John T. Thornton to [wife], 3 Oct. 1861. John T. Thornton Papers, UVA; GO, No. 2. HQ, First Corps, Army of the Potomac. 17 Jan. 1862. GO& C, Army of the Potomac. RG 109, NA; C. J. W[inston] to Aunt, 16 Feb. 1862. Winston-Clark Family Papers, VHS; G. W. Smith to Hill, 9 Mar. 1862. D. H. Hill Papers, LV; W. N. Pendleton to Maj. Corley, 31 Mar. 1862. W. N. Pendleton Letterbook, MC.

6. W. Carvel Hall to Captain, 1 Apr. 1862. Keiley Family Papers, VHS.

7. [W. T. Casey] to Mama, 5 June 1862. William T. Casey Papers, VHS; Benj. H. Freeman to Farther, 18 Oct. 1862. Freeman, Benjamin, *Confederate Letters of Benjamin H. Freeman*, 14.

8. J. T. Thompson to [Family], 5 Oct. 1862. Thompson, "A Georgia Boy," *VMHB*, 70, 3, 331: Fannie Page Hume diary, 20 Nov. 1862. Fannie Page Hume papers, LC; Sarah Ann Fife diary, 24 Nov. 1862. Strickler Family Papers, UVA; C. M. Wilcox to John, 26 Sep. 1862. Cadmus M. Wilcox Papers, LC; R. F. Lee to [Mary], 13 Nov. 1862. Lee Family Papers, VHS; Harvie [Hightower] to Sister, 11 Nov. 1862. Hightower, *GHQ* 40, 2, 179; Whitfield Kisling to Cousin, 1 Nov. 1862. Whitfield Kisling Papers, MC; Charles [Kerrison] to Sister, 28 Nov. 1862. Kerrison Family Papers, USC; [Warren] to Jennie, 27 Oct. 1862. E. T. H. Warren Papers, UVA; W to Parents, 7 Oct. 1862. Cocke Family Papers, VHS; Tommie [Reeder] to Sister, 28 Nov. 1862. Reeder Papers, FSNBP (originals at USC); James Campbell to Uncle, 20 Oct. 1862. John Campbell Papers, Rice U.; Thos. S. Garnett to Emma, 27 Oct. 1862. Garnett Family Papers, LV. Thompson's father, Thomas, was worth $8,050. See Records of Thos. Thompson. U.S. Census, 1860. DeKalb Co., Ga., 30.

9. [Wm. H. Cocke] to [Parents], 25 Dec. 1862. Cocke Family Papers, VHS; B. H. Freeman to Farther and Mother and Sisters, 24 Nov. 1862. Freeman, Benjamin, *Confederate Letters of Benjamin H. Freeman*, 19; Circular. Medical Director & Inspector's Office. 22 Nov. 1862. Orders & Circulars Rec'd & Issued, Medical Director's Office. RG 109, NA; J. Scurry to Sarah, 13 Feb. 1863. John G. Scurry Papers, Gilder-Lehrman Collection, ML; Louis Leon diary, 7 Feb. 1863. Leon, *Diary*, 16. By the first winter, locals had become pretty much tapped out. See Christopher to Kate, 1 Nov. 1861. Christopher Winsmith Papers, MC.

10. L. B. Northup to Randolph, 3 Nov. 1862. CSA. Commissary Department. NYPL; Lee to Seddon, 12 Jan. 1863. L&TS, ANV. RG 109, NA; Theodore to Father, 18 Oct. 1861. Theodore T. Fogle Papers, EU.

11. McPherson, *Ordeal by Fire*, 206; Maj. Francis Rawle to Lieut., 10 Dec. 1862. Frank Rawle Papers, MC; SO, No.___. HQ, Colquitt's Brigade. 20 Dec. 1862. Colquitt's Brigade, Orders and Circulars of Subcommands, ANV. RG 109, NA; G. M. Logan to Colonel, 1 Mar. 1863. G. M. Logan Papers, USC.

12. E. Fontaine to Davis, 19 Mar. 1863. M437, R91, F727. LR, SW. Johnston to War Department, 3 Dec. 1861. LR, SW. WD-8229-1861. RG 109, NA; Report of Forage Received at Milford Station by railroad for the Arty. of the Second Corps, 29 Jan.–13 Apr. 1863. W. H. Kirker Papers, LV.

13. W. H. Kirker to Col., 2 Feb. 1863. George G. Thompson to Kirker, 17 Mar. 1863. W. H. Kirker Papers, LV; Lee to Lawton, 10 Mar. 1864. L&TS, ANV. RG 109, NA; Willie to Father, 28 Mar. 1863. Willie Dame Papers, FSNBP; Thos. C. Elder to wife, 6 Apr. 1863. Thomas Elder Papers, VHS; Augustus L. Coble to Turley Coble, 25 Feb. 1863. HCWRT, USAMHI; George H. Sharpe to General, 21 Mar. 1863. Information from Examination of Scouts, Deserters, etc., Army of the Potomac. RG 108, NA; W. R. Montgomery to Aunt Frank, n.d. Apr. 1863. W. R. Montgomery Papers. V242, FSNBP; R. E. Lee to [Mary], 6 Mar. 1863. Lee Family Papers, VHS.

14. GO, No. 119. HQ, ANV. 16 Oct. 1862. GSOCI, ANV. M921, R1, F259. RG 109, NA; Lee to Custis, 5 Jan. 1863. R. E. Lee Papers, DU; Lee to Seddon, 7 Dec. 1862. Box 1, Telegraph Book, Ser. a, Lee's Headquarters Papers, VHS; Lee to Davis, 24 Feb. 1863. Freeman, ed., *Lee's Dispatches*, 72; Lee to Colonel Lawrence Baker, 1 Mar. 1863. Lee to Longstreet, 10 Mar. 1863. Lee to Myers, 21 Mar. 1863. Lee to Seddon, 25 Mar. 1863. Lee to Jackson, 27 Mar. 1863. Lee to Anderson, 28 Mar. 1863. L&TS, ANV. RG 109, NA; GO, No. 24. HQ, ANV. 21 Mar. 1863. Wright's Brigade Order Book, CWTIC, USAMHI; SO, No. ___. HQ, Arty. Corps. 29 Jan. and 4 Feb. 1863. Pendleton Order Book, MC; Lee to Longstreet, 18 Feb. and 27 Mar. 1863. Longstreet to Lee, 18 and 24 Mar. 1863. *OR* 18: 883–84, 924–25, 933, and 943.

15. Circular. HQ, Right Wing, ANV. 26 Oct. 1862. Louisiana Historical Collection: Battalion, Washington Artillery, Box 11, TU; SO, No. 242 and 243. HQ, ANV. 14 and 15 Nov. 1862. GSOCI, ANV. M921, R2, F133–36. RG 109, NA; GO, No. 47. HQ, Right Wing, ANV. 7 Nov. 1862. Wright's

Brigade Order Book, CWTIC, USAMHI; Charles [Kerrison] to Sister, 13 Nov. 1862. Kerrison Family Papers, USC; A. S. Pendleton to Mother, 11 Dec. 1862. William N. Pendleton Papers, SHC, UNC.

16. Chilton to Myers, 12 Jan. 1863. Lee to Seddon, 7 and 27 Oct. 1863. Lee to Lawton, 28 Sep. and 6 Nov. 1863. Lee to Ewell, 19 Jan. 1863. L&TS, ANV. RG 109, NA; Special Orders No.___. HQ, Colquitt's Brigade. 7 Dec. 1862. Colquitt's Brigade, Orders the Circulars of Subcommands, ANV. RG 109, NA.

17. A. C. Haskett to Pa, 27 Oct. 1863. Alexander C. Haskell Papers, SHC, UNC; M. Hill Fitzpatrick to Amanda, 16 Apr. 1864. "Letters to Amanda," CWMC, USAMHI; Tom to Sir, 18 Apr. 1863. Tom Aiton Papers, USC; James A. Gillespie to Sallic, 9 May 1863. Gillespie Papers, FSNBP (orig. at GDAH); N. J. Brooks to father & all, 10 May 1863. Brooks Family Papers, GDAH; S. R. Flynt to Brother, 15 Aug. 1863. Flynt Papers, FSNBP; Ivy C. Duggan to Editor, *Central Georgian*, 25 Apr. 1864. Civil War Miscellany: 48th Georgia, GDAH; E[dgar Ashton] to Sister, 6 Dec. 1863. Cocke Family Papers, VHS.

18. W. J. H[atchett] to Parents, 15 July 1863. Hatchett Family Folder, CWTIC, USAMHI; Halsey [Wigfall] to Louly, 18 July 1863. Louis T. Wigfall Papers, LC; [E. T. H. Warren] to darling, 17 July 1863. E. T. H. Warren Papers, UVA; M. Hill Fitzpatrick to Amanda, 2 Nov. 1863. "Letters to Amanda," CWMC, USAMHI; D. J. Hileman to Miss Rate A, McCutcheon, 15 Dec. 1863. Daniel Hileman Folder, Rockbridge Historical Society Collection, W&L; W. J. Seymour journal, 3 Dec. 1863. Schoff Collection CL, UMI; J. M. Tate to sister, 26 Aug. 1863. Jeremiah Tate Papers, Gilder-Lehrman Collection, ML; Inspection Reports. R7, F22 and 52. Inspection Records, RG 109, NA: GO, No. 49. HQ, Corse's Brigade. 31 July 1863. Corse's Brigade Order Book, MC.

19. Lee to Seddon, 7 Aug. 1863. L&TS, ANV. RG 109, NA; Lee to Davis, 26 Aug. 1863. Louisiana Historical Association: Jefferson Davis Papers, TU; W. C. Allen to Farther, 8 Aug. 1863. Allen Family Papers, UAL; Rawleigh to Sister, 20 Aug. 1863. Rawleigh Dunaway Papers, LV; Walton to Pendleton, 22 Aug. 1863. Endsmt. by J. L. Corley. Walker to Captain, 29 Aug. 1863. Walton to Capt. Jno. Wood, 29 Sep. 1863. Cooper to Davis, 1 Oct. 1863, with Davis's endsmt. Walton to Sorrel, 6 Oct. 1863. Walton to Lt., 3 Oct. 1863. Louisiana Historical Association: J. B. Walton Letter Book, TU; Report of Transportation belonging to the Arty. Second Corps, Army of Northern Virginia, undated. W. H. Kirker Papers, LV.

20. Jno. W. Daniel to Father, 23 Sep. 1863. John Warwick Daniel Papers, UVA; [John] to Catherine, 3 Oct. 1863. John Old Papers, FSNBP; Records of John Old. U.S. Census, 1860. Albemarlc Co., Va., 92.

21. James M. Compton to Parence, 18 May 1862. Hunter-Milhous Papers, ADAH; Francis G. Ruffin to Lt. Col. R. G. Cole, 9 Jan. 1864. Francis G. Ruffin Memorandum, 8 Feb. 1864. Northup to Cole summary, Feb. 1864. Francis Gildard Ruffin Letterbook, Department of Subsistence, Francis G. Ruffin Papers, VHS; P. P. Duncan to General, 10 Sep. 1863. Wright's Brigade Order Book, CWT1C, USAMHI; A. Evans to Wife, 24 Mar. 1864. Arthur Evans Papers, MC; T. P. Devereaux to father, 18 Dec. 1863. Thomas Pollock Devereaux Papers, NCDAH; W. H. Taylor to Maj. D. B Bridgford, 31 Dec. 1863. Taylor to Anderson, 31 Dec. 1863. L&TS, ANV. RG 109, NA.

22. A. Evans to Wife, 24 Mar. 1864. Arthur Evans Papers, MC; T. P. Devereaux to father, 18 Dec. 1863. Thomas Pollock Devereaux Papers, NCDAH; M. H. Fitzpatrick to Amanda, 4 and 15 Dec. 1862. Lowe and Hodges, eds., 33 and 40; Edwin Kerrison to Sister, 6 Sep. 1863. Kerrison Family Papers, USC.

23. W. N. Pendleton to Darling Love, 13 Nov. 1863. William N. Pendleton papers, SHC, UNC; Lee to Davis, 26 Aug. 1863. Louisiana Historical Association: Jefferson Davis Papers, TU; Lee to Davis, 25 Nov. 1863. Telegrams Received by Confederate SW. M6I8, R16, F447; Extract from Reports of Butlers Brigade from December 20th, 1863 to Jany 30th 1864. Hampton's Reply to Lee Circular, Hampton Family Papers, USC; Maj. C. E. Snodgrass to J. L. Corley, 10 Dec. 1863. LT& Other Papers Received by Lee. RG 109, NA.

24. Wm. Porcher Miles to Beauregard, 12 Dec. 1863. Civil War Miscellany, CAH; Davis to Northrop, 4 Jan. 1864. B. P. Noland to Northrop, 14 Nov. 1863. CSA. Commissary Department, NYPL; Lee to Northrop, 13 Jan. 1864. Confidential Letters Sent, ANV. RG 109, NA; Lee to Letcher, 31 Oct. 1863. Lee to Northrop, 23 Nov. 1863. L&TS. ANV. RG 109, NA; Lee to Kemper, 29 Jan. 1864. Dowdey and Manarin, eds., *Wartime Papers*, 663.

25. S.B. French to Colonel, 9 Jan. 1864, endsmt. by Northrop, 11 Jan. 1864. R. W. N. Noland, undated note. CSA. Commissary Department, NYPL; Lee to Lawton, 17 Jan. 1864. Box 1, Telegraph Book. Lee's Headquarters Papers, VHS; Lee to Hill, 10 Dec. 1863. L&TS, ANV. RG 109, NA; Robert C. Black III, *The Railroads of the Confederacy*, 198.

26. Lee to Seddon, 12 Apr. 1864. Dowdey and Manarin, eds., *Wartime Papers*, 696–97.

27. GO, No. 7. HQ, ANV. 22 Jan. 1864. GSOC1. ANV. M921, R1, F 1116. RG 109, NA.

18. Camp and Recreation

1. [J. C. Featherston], 8 [?] Mar. 1864. Irvine-Saunders Family Papers, UVA: Junius [Taylor] to Sue, 27 Mar. 1864. Pine Hill Plantation Papers, FSU. See B. L. Mobley to Mother, 31 Dec. 1861, Benjamin L. Mobley Papers, EU, for a discussion of the impact of a band in inspiring soldiers to fight.

2. Charles [Kerrison] to Sister, 30 Jan. 1862. Kerrison Family Papers, USC.

3. Schiebert, *Seven Months*, 36.

4. Theo Frank to Wife, 24 Mar. 1864. Frank Family Papers, SHC, UNC; James R. Boulware diary, 29 Jan. 1863. James R. Boulware Papers, LV; Thomas [Caffet] to Mary, 30 Jan. 1863. Hugh William Caffey Papers, ADAH; Willie [Dame] to Mother, 31 Jan. 1863. Dame Papers, FSNBP; James [Mobley] to Beny, 1 Feb. 1863. Benjamin Mobley Papers, EU; Samuel A. Firebaugh diary, 23–24 [24–25] Feb. 1863. CWMC, USAMHI; J. L. Taylor to Sue?, 26 Feb. 1863. Pine Hill Plantation Papers, FSU; Saml. Walkup diary, 24 Mar. 1864. Samuel H. Walkup Papers, SHC, UNC; J. P. Verdery to Sister, 28

Mar. 1864. Verdery Family Papers, DU; F [Shaffner] to Carrie, 27 Mar. 1864. J. E. Shaffner Papers, NCDAH.

5. Frank B. Jones diary, 14 Apr. 1862. Frank P. Jones Papers, MC; James R. Montgomery diary, 11 Feb. and 22 Apr. 1864. James R. Montgomery Papers, MC; Wm C Morgan to Devoted sister, 26 Aug. 1861. Flora Morgan McCabe Papers, LC; W. A. Reid to Miss, 16 Apr. 1864. Civil War Miscellany: 17th Virginia Infantry, Company A, GDAH; J. A. Gillespie to Wife, 23 May 1862. Jaspar A. Gillespie Papers, GDAH; Harvie [Hightower] to Sister, 11 Nov. 1862. Hightower., *GHQ* 40, 2, 179.

6. D. M. McIntosh to little Brother, 16 Apr. 1863. Pegram-Johnson-McIntosh Papers, VIIS; J. H. B[ayol] to Sister, n.d. Dec. 1861. Bayol Family Papers, VHS; Wm. R. Smith diary, 19 June 1862. CWTIC, USAMHI; Frank Lobrano diary, 22 May 1863. Louisiana Historical Association: Civil War Papers, TU; Jesse Sparkman diary, 14 Apr. 1864. Jesse R. Sparkman Papers, FSNBP; Robert T. Douglass diary, 30 May and 2 June 1863. Robert T. Douglas Papers, FSNBP; John T. Thornton to [wife], 1 Oct. 1861. John T. Thornton Papers, UVA; Theophilus Frank to wife, 29 Apr. 1864. Frank Family Papers, SHC, UNC; B. W. Justice to wife, 10 Apr. 1864. Benjamin W. Justice Papers, EU.

7. James R. Montgomery diary, 15 Mar. 1864. James R. Montgomery Papers, MC; Ben to Wife, 7 Sep. 1863. Benjamin W. Justice Papers, EU; Leroy Edwards to Lanny, 29 Mar. 1863. Leroy S. Edwards Papers, VHS.

8. Unidentified diarist, 5, 11, 13, and 14 Sep. 1861. Unknown, *ALHQ*, 25, 1 and 2, 161–64; Wiley, *Life of Johnny Reb*, 52; Programs, Some Rosters of Washington Artillery, Box 11, F16. Concert of the Maryland Line Glee Club, Box 2. Louisiana Historical Association: Washington Artillery, TU; James R. Boulware diary, 10 and 13 Feb. 1863. James R. Boulware Papers, LV; J. Scurry to Sarah, 13 Feb. 1863. John G. Scurry Papers, Gilder-Lehrman Collection, ML; Love, *Prairie Guards*, 15.

9. P. G. Harrison to friend, 13 Oct. [?]. Cabell Family Papers, UVA; Thos. F. Green to Hatty, 6 Mar. 1863. Thomas Fitzgerald Green Papers, GDAH; John O'Farrell diary, 1 Mar. 1863. John O'Farrell Papers, MC; Campbell Brown, "Reminscences," 170. Ewell Papers, TSL; Jas. Christian memoirs, 1. James Christian Hill Papers, VHS; James G. Hudson, *ALHQ* 23, 1 and 2, 175–76.

10. Turner Vaughan diary, 12 Mar. 1863. "Diary," *ALHQ* 18, 4, 574–75; Watkins Kearns diary, 1 Sep. 1863. Watkins Kearns Papers, VHS; W. L. Davis to S. W. Smythe, 16 Dec. 1862. William L. Davis Papers, MDAH.

11. GO, No. 47. HQ, Right Wing, ANV. 7 Nov. 1862. 55B, Box 11, Louisiana Historical Association: Battalion, Washington Artillery, TU.

12. Report of Steuart's Brigade, 20 Mar 1864 Assistant Inspector General File, John B. Brown Papers, NCDAH. My calculations are based on the number of brigades.

13. Ed [Apps] to Friend, 5 Feb. 1862. J. B. Richardson Papers, MC; E. A. Davis to Sir, 12 Feb. 1862. E. A. Davis, *GHQ* 40, 3, 304; W. G. Kisling to Cousin Ginnie, 5 Jan. 1862. W. G. Kisling Papers, MC; J. W. M[urray] to wife, 13 Dec. 1861. Murray Family Papers, LV; Edge to [Sallie], 10 Jan. 1862. Rozier, *Granite Farm Letters*, 52; Charles to Dr. Lee, 18 Mar. 1863. Dr. Lee Papers, DU; Unsigned to Col. J. Thompson Brown, 4 Jan. 1864. Lee Battery File, MC; GO, No. 26. HQ, ANV. 3 Apr. 1864. Order Book. CSA Archives. Army of Northern Virginia, DU.

14. [Henry Owen] to wife, 7 Nov. 1862. Henry T. Owen Papers, LV.

15. R. H. Jones to Wife, 14 Nov. 1861. R. H. Jones Papers, GDAH; Taz [Graham] to Melia, 21 June 1861. Underwood Family Papers, LV.

16. Beverly Ross to Wife, 8 Feb. 1865. Beverly Ross Papers, MC; A. S. Morgan to Wife, 28 Sep. 1861. A. S. Morgan Papers, FSNBP; William H. Nelms to Sister, 27 May 1862. William H. Nelms Papers, MC; [Daniel Hileman] to Rate, 22 Sep. 1861. Daniel Hileman Folder, Rockbridge Historical Society Manuscripts, WL; Arthur Evans to wife, 7 Jun. 1864. Arthur Evans Papers, MC.

17. Thos. T. Green to Elise, 23 Aug. 1864. Greene Family Papers, VHS; Records of Thomas T. Green. U.S. Census, 1860. Franklin Co., Ala., 653; A. M. Scales to darling wife, 25 Mar. 1863. Alfred M. Scales Papers, NCDAH; Josiah B. Patterson to Wife, 4 Dec. 1861. Josiah Blair Patterson Papers, GDAH.

18. J. G. C[ovington] to Wife, 15 July 1863. Joseph G. Covington Papers, MC; W. G. Parker to Ema, 14 May 1863. William G. Parker Papers, NCDAH; Records of William G. Parker. U.S. Census, 1860. Bertie Co., N.C., 74; Records of William G. Parker. U.S. Slave Census, 1860. Bertie Co., N.C., 137.

19. John W. Watson to wife, 5 Oct. 1862. Watson Papers, FSNBP; Walter H. Taylor to Longstreet et al., 8 Jan. 1863. L&TS, ANV, RG 109, NA; GO, No. 107, 110, 4, 6, and 21. HQ, ANV. 9 and 26 Dec. 1863 and 8, 19, and 23 Mar. 1864. GSOCI, ANV. M921, R1, F1036, 1046, and 1191 and GO Order Book, 37th North Carolina Infantry. DU; Thomas to Wife, 5 Aug. 1863. Gordon and Rosser Families, UVA.

20. C. G. Hamilton to Sister, 10 Feb. 1862. Colier Green & Oliver Clark Hamilton Papers, NCDAH; James C. Fisher to Miss, 13 Nov. 1861. Jane Fisher Papers, DU; Report of James C. Fisher. U.S. Census, 1860. Catawba Co., N.C., 180; Will to [Evangeline], 23 Oct. 1861. Crutcher-Shannon Family Papers, CAH; A. B. B[arron] to wife, 14 May 1863. Alfred Benton Barron Papers, FSNBP; Rowland to Rhoda, 24 Jan. 1864. Confederate Papers, SHC, UNC.

21. M. H. Fitzpatrick to Amanda, 15 Dec. 1862. Lowe and Hodges, eds., 39; J. H. Everett to wife, 26 Oct. 1861. John A Everett Papers, EU; J. P. Wilson to Son, 1 Jan. 1865. J. P. Wilson Papers, MC.

22. John A. Everett to Ma, 11 Aug. 1861. John A. Everett Papers, EU; Geo. H. T. Greer diary, 9 Nov. 1862. George H. T. Greer Papers, LV; Robert [Stafford] to Sister, 29 Mar. 1862. Robert Stafford Papers, Gilder-Lehrman Collection, ML; John [Wise] to Cousin, 11 Oct. 1863. Evelyn B. Moore Papers, UVA; Jno. W. Daniel to Sister, 1 Dec. 1861. John Warwick Daniel Papers, UVA.

23. John N. Old to Catherine, 21 June 1863. John Old Papers, FSNBP; Robert Gaines Haile diary, 2 June 1862. King & Queen and Essex County Historical Sketches, UVA; W. R. Stilwell to Mollie, 10 July 1863. Stilwell Papers. FSNBP.

24. I. P[itman] to wife, 5 May 1864. Confederate Papers, SHC, UNC; [Joab Goodson] to Niece, 1 Jan. 1865. Goodson, *Alabama Review* 10, 3, 231; M. E. Wilson to Wife, 13 May 1862. M. E. Wilson Papers, USC.

25. Geo. H. T. Greer diary, 10 Nov. 1862. George H. T. Greer Papers, LV.

26. A. M. Scales to Wife, 5 Apr. 1863. A. M. Scales Papers, NCDAH; R. A. Bryant to Eugenia, 26 Oct. 1861. Richard A. Bryant Family, LV.

27. Husband [Ramseur] to Wife, 9 Dec. 1863. Stephen Dodson Ramseur Papers, SHC, UNC.

19. Religion and Morality

1. Jno. W. Green to ?. 9 Oct. 1862. Munford-Ellis Papers, DU; JQAN to Wife, 19 Dec. 1862. John Q. A. Nadenbousch Papers, MC; James W. Wright to Father and Mother, 24 Apr. 1864. John Wright Family Papers, NCDAH; Records of J. Q. A. Nadenbousch. U.S. Census, 1860. Berkeley Co., Va., 72; Records of J. Q. A. Nadenbousch. Slave Census, 1860. Berkeley Co., Va., 368.

2. James R. Boulware diary, 24 July 1862. James R. Boulware Papers, LV; Quoted in Wiley, *Life of Johnny Reb*, 50; J. M. Weller to Mother, 4 Mar. 1862. Joseph M. Weller Papers, LV; Wiley, *Life of Johnny Reb*, 48–50. One need only examine the Specifications for Courts-Martial to see the prevalence of swearing.

3. J. M. Weller to Mother, 4 Mar. 1862. Joseph M. Weller Papers, LV; Frank Potts journal, 6 Aug. 1861. Frank Potts Papers, LV; A. L. P. Vairin diary, 27–29 Nov. 1862. A. L. P. Vairin Papers, MDAH; J..Q. A. Nadenbousch to wife, 16 and 29 Sep. 1861. J. Q. A. Nadenbousch Papers, MC; Pendleton to Mayor & Council of the City of Petersburg, 31 Oct. 1864. W. N. Pendleton Letter Book, MC; Special Orders, No. 22. HQ of Division, 2 Aug. 1861. R7, F940. SO, Virginia Forces. RG 109, NA; GO, No. 10. HQ, Daniel's Brigade. 19 Oct. 1862. 45th North Carolina Infantry: General and Special Orders Log Book, North Caroliniana Collection, UNC.

4. ASM to Wife, 1 Aug. 1861. Asa S. Morgan Papers, FSNBP; R. Fairfax to Jenny, 12 Nov. 1861. Fairfax Brothers Papers, MC; J. H. L[anghorne] to Mother, 12 Nov. 1861. Langhorne Family Papers, VHS; Wiley, *Plain People*, 26; H. N. Rector to Genl., 6 Feb. 1863. 4th Virginia Cavalry Papers, MC; John G. Scurry to Father, 17 Jan. 1864. John G. Scurry Papers, Gilder-Lehrman Collection, ML; James M. Plumer to Father, 27 Aug. 1861. Lewis Leigh Collection, USAMHI; Jones, *Lee's Tigers*, 15–19 and 36–39; John S. Apperson journal, 26 Nov. 1861. Apperson, *Repairing*, 162.

5. A. S. Pendleton to Rose, 24 Jan. 1862. Sandie Pendleton Papers, Gilder-Lehrman Collection, ML; Eli Landers to Mother, n.d. Aug. 1863. Landers, *Weep Not For Me*, 111; William H. Taylor, "Some Experiences of a Confederate Assistant Surgeon," 95; Marion [Koiner] to Mother, 21 Feb. 1864. David Ezra Papers, VHS; Wm. V. Williams et al., to Davis, 3 Sep. 1861. LR, CSW. M434, R14, F1180; Henri J. Mugler journal, 22 May 1864. Henri J. Mugler Papers, Virginia, V. 13, RNBP.

6. Wiley, *Life of Johnny Reb*, 56; R. A. Bryant to ?, 24 June 1861. R. A. Bryant to Eugenia, 20 Oct. 1861. Bryant Family Papers, LV; "Pants versus Petticoats," *Richmond Enquirer*, 31 Oct. 1864, P2C6; Watkins Kearns diary, 13 July 1862. Watkins Kearns Papers, VHS; D. J. Blanton to wife and children, 16 Nov. 1862. CWMC, USAMHI.

7. T. F. Beggarly to Wife, 23 Dec. 1862 and 11 Apr. 1864. Margaret E. Beggarly to husband, 17 Jan. 1863. Tillman F. Beggarly Papers, DU; J. C. Penn to Ma, 11 Aug. 1861. Green W. Penn Papers, DU.

8. E. T. H. Warren to Jennie, 15 Nov. and n.d. [late Nov.–Dec. 1861]. E. T. H. Warren Papers, UVA; Records of E. T. H. Warren. Records of Mary E. Smith. Records of Mary S. Shands. Records of C. A. Woodward. Records of Mary C. S. Ragan. U.S. Census, 1860. Rockingham Co., Va., 364, 339, 363, 345, and 346. It is apparent that Warren's wife confirmed the story.

9. E. T. H. Warren to Jennie, 15 Nov. 1861. E. T. H. Warren Papers, UVA.

10. E. T. H. Warren to Jennie, 15 Nov. 1861. E. T. H. Warren Papers, UVA; J. Glenn Gray, *The Warriors*, xii and 12–13.

11. Gray, *The Warriors*, 62–63.

12. Gray, *The Warriors*, 68–69.

13. W. G. Parker to Emma, 24 May 1863. William G. Parker Papers, NCDAH; Records of William G. Parker, U.S. Census, 1860. Gates Co., N.C., 122..

14. Eli Landers to Mother, 15 Nov. 1861. Landers, *Weep Not For Me*, 147; L. M[cLaws] to wife, 26 Aug. 1861. Lafayette McLaws Papers, SHC, UNC; John T. Smith to Mother and Sisters, 1 Feb. 1863. Smith-Johnson Papers, MC; John McDonald to Wife, 11 Apr. 1863. V. 80, FSNBP. For a similar experience in World War II, see the classic E. B. Sledge, *With the Old Breed at Peleliu and Okinawa*, 123–24.

15. E. T. H. Warren to Jennie, 15 Nov. 1861. E. T. H. Warren Papers, UVA; John T. Thornton to [Wife], 1 Oct. 1861. John T. Thornton Papers, UVA; Edge to Darling, 18 July 1864. Rozier, *Granite Farm Letters*, 178. Warren did not believe such practices would become general, but he thought the bad influence will be "almost universal."

16. Garnett to Capt. Whittle, 15 May 1861. Geo. Deas to Col. Mott, 20 June 1861. R1, F134, LS, Virginia Forces. RG 109, NA; Lee to Letcher, 31 Oct. 1863. L&TS, ANV. RG 109, NA; GO, No. 63. HQ, Dept. of NV. 5 Jun. 1862. William N. Pendleton Papers, SHC, UNC.

17. GO, No. 18. HQ, Dept. of Alexandria, 18 June 1861. GO, No. 59. HQ, 1st Corps, Army of the Potomac, 29 Sep. 1861. GO&C, Army of the Potomac. RG 109, NA; Special Orders, No.——. HQ, Dept. of Fredericksburg. 20 Aug. 1861. Orders, 1861–65, John B. Brown Papers, NCDAH; Gen. Orders, No. 10. HQ, Daniel's Brig. n.d. [1863]. Log Book of G & SO, 45th North Carolina Infantry, 1862–63. NCDAH; Thomas McCarty journal, n.d. Thomas L. McCarty Papers, CAH.

18. Special Orders, No. 3. HQ, Lane's Brigade. 18 Nov. 1863. GO Book, 37th North Carolina Infantry. DU; Special Order, No.——. HQ, 4th Virginia Cavalry. 23 Apr. 1863. 4th Virginia Cavalry Papers, MC.

19. John Caperton to Ma, 30 May 1861. Caperton Family Papers, VHS; James Campbell to My Dear, 14 May 1862. John Campbell Papers, Rice U.; John McDonald to Wife, 11 Apr. 1863. John McDonald Papers, V. 80, FSNBP.

20. T. D. Rock to Father & Mother, 20 Aug. 1861. T. D. Rock Papers, MC; J. R. Manson to Sister, 13 Nov. 1863. CWM, USAMHI; John W. Watson to Wife, 16 Nov. 1863. Watson Papers, FSNBP; Taylor [Scott] to Fan, 15 Apr. 1862. Keith Family Papers, VHS.

21. T. J. Jackson to Doctor, 31 July 1862. Thomas J. Jackson Papers, VMI; Jimmie to Laura, 25 Nov. 1861. James D. Nance Papers, USC; Lee to Son, 22 Nov. 1862. R. E. Lee Papers, DU; Geo. H. T. Greer diary, 9 Nov. 1862. George H. T. Greer Papers, LV; J. E. Shaffner to Friend, 16 May 1863. J. E. Shaffner Papers, NCDAH; W. G. Parker to Ema, ? May 1863. William G. Parker Papers, NCDAH.

22. Thos. McDowell to Wife, 16 May 1862. McDowell Family Papers, UVA; Eli Landers to Mother, 21 Aug. 1863. Landers, *Weep Not for Me*, 159.

23. George to Liz, 5 Aug. 1864. George H. Moffett Papers, SCHS; Jno. F. Goodner to Lizzie, 9 Mar. 1863. Goodner, *The Goodner Family*, 264.

24. Geo. H. T. Greer diary, 9 Nov. 1862. George H. T. Greer Papers, LV; Thos. M. Wade to Son, 13 May 1862. Lewis Leigh Collection, USAMHI; [Launcelot] to Mother, 29 May 1862. Launcelot Minor Blackford Papers, UVA; S.M.B. to Fran, 15 Apr. 1863. Bemiss Family Papers, VHS; W. G. Kisling to Cousin, 1 Nov. 1862. W. G. Kisling Papers, MC.

25. Lee to Jackson, 13 Dec. 1862. Lee Papers, MC; Lee to Trimble, 2 Jan. 1863. Isaac R. Trimble Papers, MDHS; W. N. Pendleton to Dear Rose, 17 Nov. 1862. W. N. Pendleton Papers, SHC, UNC; [J. P. Verdery] to Sister, 24 Feb. 1864. Verdery Family Papers, DU.

26. [Walter Taylor to Bettie], 5 Dec. 1863. Walter H. Taylor Papers, NPL.

27. [Walter Taylor to Bettie], 5 Dec. 1863. Walter H. Taylor Papers, NPL; W. N. Pendleton to Wife, 1 June 1863 and 17 Nov. 1862. William N. Pendleton Papers, SHC, UNC; GO, No. 15. HQ, ANV. 7 Feb. 1864. GO, No. 46. HQ, ANV. 23 Mar. 1863. G&SO&CI, ANV. M921, R1, F1158 and 685. RG 109, NA; Lee to Rev. M. I. Michelbach., 29 Aug. 1861. Rosen. *Jewish Confederates*, 234–35; Louis Leon diary, 29 Sep. 1863. Leon, *Diary of a Tar Heel*, 48–49.

28. Wm. W. Blackford to Lanty, 30 May 1861. Blackford Family Papers, UVA; James [Collier] to Mother, 28 July 1863. James Marshall Collier Papers, ADAH; John H. Tillighast to Davis, 14 Nov. 1862. LR, CSW. M437, R75, F697–99. RG 109, NA.

29. R. Channing Price to Sister, 1 Aug. 1861. Richard Channing Price Papers, VHS; Wm. to Susie, 15 June 1861. William D Elder Papers, MDAH; Jno M. Tilley to wife, 5 Aug. 1861. John M. Tilley Papers, GDAH.

30. John S. Apperson journal, 11 Aug. 1861. Apperson, *Repulsing the "March of Mars,"* 127; M. Hill Fitzpatrick to Amanda, 2 Sep. 1862. "Letters to Amanda," CWMC, USAMHI; J. A. Gillespie to Wife, 24 Apr. 1864. Jaspar A. Gillespie Papers, GDAH.

31. Barnett H. Cody to Father, 9 Oct. 1862. Cody, *GHQ* 23, 4, 366; Marcus Hefner to Wife, 17 Oct. 1862. Marcus Hefner Papers, NCDAH; Wm. H. Hill diary, 19 and 25 Feb. and 8 and 15 Mar. 1863. William D. Hill Papers, MDAH; H. J. David to Mother, 12 Mar. 1863. Horatio J. David Papers, FSNBP; G. K. Harlow to Father & Family, 27 May 1863. Harlow Family Papers, VHS; George Washington Hall diary, 15 Aug. 1863. George Washington Hall Papers, LC. Robert K. Krick, at the time chief historian at Fredericksburg and Spotsylvania National Battlefield Park, told me that the capacities of the two churches in Fredericksburg were 300 and 1,000. Bob has seen no evidence of J. William Jones's claims and agrees with me that his account is grossly exaggerated. For a brilliant and provocative analysis of revivalism in the Confederate army, see Drew Gilpin Faust, "Christian Soldiers: The Meaning of Revivalism in the Confederate Army," *Journal of Southern History* 53, No. 1 (Feb. 1987), 63–90.

32. A. C. Haskell to Ma, 14 Sep. 1863. Alexander Cheves Haskell Papers, SHC, UNC; Whitfield Kisling to Cousin, 1 Nov. 1862. W. G. Kisling. Papers, MC.

33. J. William Jones, *Christ in the Camp: Religion in the Confederate Army*, 358, 529–34; Robert Lewis Dabney, "Chaplains in the Army of Northern Virginia: A List Compiled in 1864 and 1865." *VMHB* 71, 327–40.

34. Thomas J. Goree to Uncle Pleas, 2 Aug. 1861. Goree, 62; Sam to Wife, 23 Dec. 1861. Samuel Wicliff Melton Papers, USC; E. K. Smith to Wife, 9 Nov. 1861. R2, Edmund Kirby-Smith Papers, SHC, UNC; W. N. Pendleton to Nan, 27 Nov. 1862. William N. Pendleton Papers, SHC, UNC; Lucien [S. J. Owen] to Mother, 3 Oct. 1863. CWTIC, USAMHI; B. W. Justice to wife, 21 Aug. 1863. Benjamin W. Justice Papers, EU; Aaron T. Hess diary, 10 May 1863. Confederate Miscellaneous Papers, SHC, UNC.

35. D. H. Hill to Dabney, 26 Mar. 1862. Robert Lewis Dabney Papers, Union Theological Seminary; Edwin C. Edwards diary, 27 July 1863. Edwards Family Papers, LV; Walter Addison, "Anecdotes." 17th Virginia Infantry File, Kate Rowland Papers, MC; Fred C. Foard, reminiscences, 7. Fred C. Foard Papers, NCDAH; Thoms. J. Goree to Uncle Pleas, 2 Aug. 1861. Goree, ed., 63; Husband [Shaffner] to [wife], 19 Mar. 1865. J. E. Shaffner Papers, NCDAH; Milton Barrett to Brother and sister, 14 Apr. 1863. Barrett, 96; Lorraine to Father, 7 May 1863. 3rd Regiment Georgia Volunteer Infantry, Company C, GDAH; Geo. Patterson to Bishop, 9 May 1863. Josiah Collins Papers, NCDAH.

36. R. L. Dabney to Mother, 14 June 1861. Dabney Family Papers, VHS; B. W. Justice to wife, 21 Aug. 1863. Benjamin W. Justice Papers, EU; "Procrastination" by R. L. Dabney, 26 Apr. 1862 to 2nd Virginia Brigade at Swift Run Gap, 14. Box 6, F3, Robert Lewis Dabney Papers, Union Theological Seminary; R. Fairfax to Pa, 16 May 1862. Fairfax Brothers Papers, MC; Lorraine Hillyer to Shaler, 28 May 1863. Francis Lorraine Hillyer Papers, FSNBP; J. F. Coghill to Mit, 4 Sep. 1863. Jonathan F. Coghill Papers, Auburn U.

37. T. J. Jackson to Col., 23 Feb. 1863. Margaret Preston Junkin Papers, SHC, UNC; Jackson to Dabney, 5 Dec. 1862. Robert Lewis Dabney Papers, Union Theological Seminary; Robertson, *Stonewall Brigade*, 175; B. W. Justice to Wife, 4 Oct. 1863. Benjamin W. Justice Papers, EU; [C. A. Conn] to Mr.

Brantley, 4 Jan. 1863. William Thomas Conn, *GHQ* 465, No. 2, 186–87; Fleming W. Thompson to Sister. 14 Aug. 1863. Fleming W. Thompson Papers, CAH.

38. Whit to Cousin, 26 Aug. 1863. W. G. Kisling Papers, MC; Robert to Sister, 28 Aug. and 5 Sep. 1863. Robert to Aunt, 27 Aug. 1863. Robert Stafford Papers, Gilder-Lehrman Collection, ML; Jno. G. Webb to Mother, 7 Mar. 1863. Lewis Leigh Collection, USAMHI; Samuel A. Firebaugh diary, 9 Apr. 1863 and 3 Mar. 1864. CWMC, USAMHI; [Warren] to Wife, 24 May 1863. T. J. Warren Papers, USC; Chaplain's diary, 26 Oct. 1864. Henry Carter Lee Papers, MC.

39. Jones, *Christ in the Camp*, 390; T. J. Jackson to General Cooper, 10 Mar. 1863. Thomas J. Jackson Papers, MC; IR of Heth's Division by Capt. Robt. M. Gruinell, 12–13 Aug. 1864. IR, R10, F225, RG 109. NA; Creed T. Davis diary, 7 Nov. 1864. Creed T. Davis Papers, VHS. Jones claims his number of 15,000 was conservative. My use of the figure 180,000 for men who ever served in the Army of Northern Virginia is unquestionably on the low side. Gardiner Shattuck in *A Shield and a Hiding Place* and Steven Woodworth in *While God is Marching On* suggest a higher percentage of religious attendance.

40. See Faust, "Christian Soldiers," 81. This is the same basic principle of Alcoholics Anonymous, which teaches practitioners to turn matters beyond their control over to a higher power, thereby easing the burden on them.

20. Chancellorsville

1. Dod to [Nellie], 26 Mar. 1863. Stephen Dodson Ramseur Papers, SHC, UNC.

2. [Ramseur] to Nellie, 8 Feb. 1863. Stephen Dodson Ramseur Papers, SHC, UNC; Milton Barrett to Brother and sister, 14 Apr. 1863. Barrett, 93; John [Wise] to Cousin, 11 Jan. 1863. Evelyn B. Moore Papers. UVA: B. H. McGuire to Lucy, 21 Feb. 1863. Byrd Family Papers, VHS.

3. L. Maudlin to friend, 4 Feb. 1863. Heller, ed., 85; W. F. Ford to George, 14 Mar. 1863. George Lee Robertson Papers, CAH; Records of William F. Ford. U.S. Census, 1860. Marion Co., Tex., 22.

4. Lee to Longstreet, 18 Feb. and 27 Mar. 1863. Longstreet to Lee, 18 and 24 Mar. 1863. *OR* 18: 883–84, 924–25, 933, and 943.

5. Dewees Ogden to Cousin Mary, 3 Mar. 1863. Dewees Ogden Papers, LV; F. P. Fleming to Aunt Tilly, 11 Apr. 1863. Fleming, *FHQ* 27, 1 (July 1949), 50.

6. John P. Welsh to Mother & Wife, 19 Jan. 1863. Welsh Family Papers, LV; Leroy S. Edwards to Father, 15 Feb. 1863. Leroy S. Edwards Papers, VHS; [Warren] to Jennie, 5 Jan. 1863. E. T. H. Warren Papers, UVA; GO, No. 30. HQ, 2nd AC. 18 Apr. 1863. Jubal Early Papers, VHS; GO, No. 26. HQ, 2nd AC. 13 Apr. 1863. Second Army Corps, O&C of Subcommands, ANV. RG 109, NA; Order No.——. HQ, Arty Corps. 15 Apr. 1863. Louisiana Historical Association: J. B. Walton Letterbook, TU.

7. H.K. to [Editor], n.d. [May 1863]. *Richmond Sentinel*, 27 May 1863; GO, No. 7. HQ, Hill's Div. 9 Mar. 1863. GO, D. H. Hill's Division, 1862–63, O&C of Subcommands, ANV. RG 109, NA.; Robert K. Krick, "Was Robert E. Rodes the Army's Best Division Commander?" in Krick, *Smoothbore*, 117–43; Robertson, *Stonewall Jackson*, 698. In GO, No. 675. HQ, ANV. 21 May 1863, Lee abolished brigade inspectors. *OR* 25 (2); 815.

8. Circular. HQ, Rodes's Division. 8 Sep. 1863. 45th North Carolina Infantry: General and Special Order Log Book, 1862–63, North Caroliniana Collection, UNC.

9. Lee to wife, 3 Apr. 1863. Lee to Seddon, 27 Mar. 1863. Dowdey and Manarin, eds., *Wartime Papers*, 427 and 418; Milton Barrett to Brother and sister, 14 Apr. 1863. Barrett, 96.

10. Hotchkiss diary, 23 Feb. 1863. Hotchkiss, *Make Me a Map*, 116; Lee to Seddon, 25 Mar. 1863. L&TS, ANV. RG 109, NA; Lee to Davis, 16 Apr. 1863. *OR* 25 (2): 713–14 and 724–25.

11. AAR of Lee, 21 Sep. 1863. *OR* 25 (1): 797: Lee to R. H. Anderson, 29 Apr. 1863. Markham Papers. MC; L. M. McLaws to Sweetheart, 29 Apr. 1863. McLaws Papers, SHC, UNC; Leroy S. Edwards to Lanny. 10 May 1863. Leroy S. Edwards Papers, VHS; Charles to Sister, 7 May 1863. Kerrison Family Papers, USC; Alexander, *Fighting*, 200.

12. Carnot to Wife, 7 May 1863. Carnot Posey Papers. MC; AAR of Lee, 21 Sep. 1863. AAR of Maj. Gen. R. H. Anderson, 6 June 1863. AAR of Posey, 12 May 1863. AAR of Brig. Gen. William Mahone, 27 May 1863. *OR* 25 (1): 797, 850–51, 870–71, and 862. For the best volume on Chancellorsville, see Stephen W. Sears, *Chancellorsville*. Still useful is John Bigelow, Jr., *The Campaign of Chancellorsville*. For a terrific, brief summary and analysis, see Gary W. Gallagher, *The Battle of Chancellorsville*.

13. Lee to Dr. A. T. Bledsoe, 28 Oct. 1867. Fitzhugh Lee, *Chancellorsville*, 28: T. M. R. Talcott to Long. 19 July 1886. Talcott Family Papers, VHS; AAR of Lee, 21 Sep. 1863. *OR* 25 (1): 798; William Allan, Memorandum of Conversations with Lee, in Gallagher, *Lee the Soldier*, 9.

14. Wm. J. Reese to ?, 15 May 1863. William J. Reese Papers, FSNBP (originals at UAL); F. Lee, *Chancellorsville*, 29–32.

15. F. Lee. *Chancellorsville*, 29–33; A. P. Hill to Lee, 24 May 1863. M474, R135, F305–6. LR, CA&IG. RG 109, NA.

16. R. E. Willbourn to Sir, 12 Dec. 1863. Dabney-Jackson Papers, LV; [Lane] to Augustus C. Hamlin, n.d. James Lane Papers, Auburn U.; [O. C. Hamilton] to Father, 17 May 1863. Colier Green and Oliver Clark Hamilton Papers, NCDAH; Statement of Maj. Sandie Pendleton, 18 July 1863. John Esten Cooke Papers, UVA; H. H. McGuire. "Some Notes in regard to the Last Days of Jackson." Thomas J. Jackson Papers, NYHS; Krick, "The Smoothbore Volley That Doomed the Confederacy," in *Smoothbore Volley*, 1–41, especially 16–18; Robertson, *Stonewall Jackson*, 725–36; J to [Aunt], 21 Apr. 1863. *Diary of James Keith Boswell*, MC.

17. Lee to Jackson, 4 May [1863]. Lee Family Papers, VHS; Robertson, *Stonewall Jackson*, 736–39; Krick, "Smoothbore Volley," in *Smoothbore Volley*, 33–37.

18. AAR of Lee, 21 Sep. 1863. *OR* 25 (1): 799. On the actual battlefield of First Manassas, Confederates had more troops engaged.

19. AAR of Stuart, 6 May 1863. AAR of Brig. Gen. James J. Archer, 2 June 1863. *OR* 25 (1): 887–88 and 925.

20. Sorrel to Walton, 11 Dec. 1862. F9, Louisiana Historical Association: J. B. Walton Papers, TU.

21. Lee to Randolph, 4 Oct, 1862. Pendleton to Lee, 2 Oct. 1862. SO, No. 209. HQ, ANV. 4 Oct. 1862. *OR* 19 (2): 646–54; Pendleton to Lee, 11 Feb. 1863. GO. No. 26. HQ, ANV. 15 Feb. 1863. *OR* 25 (2): 614–19 and 625–26: Alexander, *Fighting*, 104–5.

22. AAR of Stuart, 6 May 1863. AAR of Brig. Gen. John W. Geary, 10 May 1863. AAR of Brig. Gen. Alpheus S. Williams, 15 May 1863. AAR of Brig. Gen. E. Porter Alexander, 7 Mar. 1864. *OR* 25 (1): 887–88, 730–31, 680–81, and 823–24.

23. John C. Ussery to Father, 8 May 1863. Ussery Papers, FSNBP; S.D.R. to Brother, 10 Apr. [1863]. Stephen Dodson Ramseur Papers, SHC, UNC; G to Father, 10 May 1863. Styple, ed., *Writing & Fighting*, 197; Husband to Wife, 6 May 1863. Bryan Grimes Papers, SHC, UNC; AAR of Alexander, 7 Mar. 1864. *OR* 25 (1): 823–24.

24. Micajah D. Martin to Father and Mother, 8 May 1863. Martin, "Chancellorsville." *VMHB* 37, 3, 226; G to Father, 10 May 1863. Styple, ed., *Writing and Fighting*, 197: Charles Marshall, *Lee's Aide-de-Camp*, 173.

25. G.E.K. to Mr. Editor, 9 May 1863. George E. Kelley[?] Papers, FSNBP; Jno. Tiffany to Parents, 8 May 1863. John Tiffany Papers, FSNBP; Robert to Pa, 10 May 1863. Robert Stafford Papers, Gilder-Lehrman Collection, ML; Thomas M. Smiley to Aunt, 12 May 1863. Smiley Family Papers, UVA; A. L. DeArmond to Wife, 7 May 1863. CWMC, USAMHI; James A. Gillespie to Sallie, 9 May 1863. Gillespie Papers, FSNBP (originals at GDAH).

26. J. H. Van Alen to Butterfield, 2 May 1863 (4:10 P.M.). Van Alen to Sedgwick, 2 May 1863. *OR* 25 (2): 363 and 365; AAR of Maj. Gen. John Sedgwick, 15 May 1863. *OR* 25 (1): 557.

27. Jno. W. Daniel to Father, 1 May 1863. John Warwick Daniel Papers, UVA; Urbanus Dart to Horace, 7 May 1863. Dart Family Papers. FSNBP (originals at GDAH); AAR of Maj. Gen. Jubal A. Early, 7 May 1863. AAR of Brig. Gen. William Barksdale, 15 May 1863. *OR* 25 (1): 1000–1001 and 839–40.

28. AAR of Brig. Gen. William Barksdale, 15 May 1863. *OR* 25 (1): 839–40; Edward Owen diary, 2 [3] and 12 May 1863. Edward Owen Papers, MC; R[obert] to Betty. 9 May 1863. Anna Habersham Wright Smith. ed., *A Savannah Family. 1830–1901*, 165.

29. AAR of Brig. Gen. Cadmus M. Wilcox, 10 May 1863. AAR of McLaws, 10 May 1863. *OR* 25(1): 855–57 and 826–27; Hilary A. Herbert, "History of the 8th Alabama," written at Orange Court House, Virginia. winter/spring 1864, 27–31. Hilary A. Herbert Papers. SHC, UNC.

30. AAR of Early. 7 May 1863. *OR* 25 (1): 1001–2; W. J. Seymour journal, 4 May 1863. Schoff Collection, University of Michigan; Mad [Batchelor] to Father, 22 June 1863. Albert A. Batchelor Papers, LSU. Hoke's Brigade suffered 445 casualties, most of them here. Sears, *Chancellorsville*, 498.

31. J. Thomas Petty diary, 5 May 1863. J. Thomas Petty Papers, MC; AJB[ell] to Editor, 28 May 1863. *Southern Banner*, 6 June 1863. Copy in FSNBP; G. M. Bundy to Brother & Sister, 15 May 1863. Confederate Miscellany. EU.

32. Krick, "Smoothbore Volley That Doomed the Confederacy," *Smoothbore Volley*, 39–40; Robertson, *Stonewall Jackson*, 737–54; Lee to Seddon. 10 May 1863. *OR* 25 (2): 791.

33. Catherine Edmondston diary, 11 May 1863. Edmondston, "*Journal of a Secesh Lady*," 392.

34. John B. Colding to Sister, 29 May 1863. 60th Regiment Georgia Volunteer Infantry, Company G, GDAH.

35. James Campbell to Martha, 11 May 1863. John Campbell Papers, Rice University; Robin to Sister, 17 May [1863]. Berkeley Family Papers, VHS; L. C. Cooper to Mother, 18 May 1863. Cooper Papers, FSNBP (originals at Kenesaw Mountain National Battlefield Park).

36. GO. No. 63. HQ, ANV. 14 May 1863. Record Book of Gen. W. B. Taliaferro. RG 109, NA; Samuel A. Firebaugh diary, 13 [12] May 1863. CWMC, USAMHI; John [Wise] to Cousin, 7 May 1863. Evelyn B. Moore Papers, UVA; John Esten Cooke, Obituary of Channing Price. J. E. B. Stuart to Cousin, 11 May 1863. Bryan Grimes Papers, SHC, UNC. For casualties statistics, see Sears, *Chancellorsville*, 492–501.

37. [George Patterson] to Friend, 19 May 1863. Josiah Collins Papers, NCDAH. See Sears, *Chancellorsville*, 492–501. The regiments were 1st, 2nd, 3rd, 4th, 7th, 13th, and 37th North Carolina Infantry. The 37th North Carolina had 230 men killed or wounded, the highest total.

38. Carnot to Wife, 7 May 1863. Carnot Posey Papers, MC; Daniel Brown to wife, 10 May 1863. Isaac Brown Papers, NCDAH; [William Hatchett] to Aunt & Uncle, 2 June 1863. Hatchett Family Folder, CWTIC, USAMHI; Memy [Seaton Gales] to [wife], 10 May 1862. Seaton Gales Papers, FSNBP (originals at NCDAH).

39. Lee to Davis, 20 May 1863. *OR* 25 (2): 810.

40. Lee to Davis, 20 May 1863. SO, No. 129. A&IGO. 30 May 1863. *OR* 25 (2): 810 and 840.

41. D.D.P. to Mama. 7 May 1863. Dudley D. Pendleton Papers, DU; W. J. Pegram to Sister, 11 May 1863. Pegram-Johnson-McIntosh Papers, VHS.

42. Pauline Heyward diary, 2 June 1863. Heyward, *A Confederate Lady Comes of Age: The Journal of Pauline De Caradeuc Heyward, 1863–1888*, 15; William Pitt Ballinger diary, 18 May 1863. William Pitt Ballinger Papers, CAH; Caroline W. Eubank to Cousin Charles, 5 May 1863. Box 5, Munford-Ellis Papers, DU; *Augusta Daily Constitutionalist*, 5 May 1863, P2, C1.

21. Arms and Ammunition

1. Robert E. L. Krick, *Staff Officers in Gray: A Biographical Register of the Staff Officers of the Army of Northern Virginia*, 60.

2. Although the report of Allan is missing from its proper location at the National Archives, its contents may be determined by reading responses of persons who read the report. See Maj. J. W. Mallet to Col. J. Gorgas, 14 July 1863. LS, Superintendent of Laboratories. Macon, Ga.; Col. T. S. Rhett to Major J. W. Mallet, 28 July 1863. LR, Superintendent of Laboratories, Macon, Ga. RG 109, NA.

3. Josiah Gorgas, "Extracts from my notes written chiefly soon after the close of the war," 1–3, 5, and 28. See Frank E. Vandiver, *Ploughshares into Swords: Josiah Gorgas and Confederate Ordnance*, for a wonderful book on the subject. Also see Josiah Gorgas, *The Journals of Josiah Gorgas, 1857–1878.*

4. Gorgas, "Extracts." 9 and 11–14. Josiah Gorgas Papers, MC; Lee to Lt. Col. B. J. Ewell, 15 June 1861. RI, LS, Virginia Forces. RG 109, NA Gorgas to Seddon, 31 Dec. 1864. Josiah Gorgas Papers, MC; Report of Brig. Genl. Josiah Gorgas to Sec. of War, 9 Feb. 1865. Josiah Gorgas File, Southern Historical Society Papers, MC.

5. J. W. Mallet, "Work of the Ordnance Bureau of the War Department of the Confederate States, 1861–1865," *The Alumni Bulletin of the University of Virginia* (Apr. and Aug. 1910), 164–67; Gorgas, "Extracts," 9–10. Josiah Gorgas Papers, MC.

6. Excerpt from *Richmond Enquirer*, 1 Apr. 1865, in Gorgas, "Extracts," 20–21. Josiah Gorgas Papers, MC.

7. Maj. H. B. Tomlin to Col. R. S. Garnett, 25 May 1861. CSA. Army. Infantry. Tomlin's Battalion. VHS; GO, No. 128. HQ, Army of the Peninsula. Orders Received, 15th Virginia. RG 109, NA; Garnett to Jackson, 28 Apr. 1861. RI, LS, Virginia Forces, RG 109, NA; AGO. 23 Aug. 1861. LS, Army of the Peninsula. RG 109, NA.

8. Gorgas, "Extracts," 4–5 and 10. Josiah Gorgas Papers, MC. See Chapter 14, Ff. 27.

9. J. A. Everett to May, 1 Oct. 1862. John A. Everett Papers, EU.

10. Memo of meeting of 26 Sep. 1861 between Smith, Johnston, and Beauregard with Davis, 31 Jan. 1862. Alfred Roman Papers, LC; Magruder to Lee, 14 Apr. 1862. A. G. Dickinson to Wilcox, 15 Apr. 1862. L&TS, Dept. of the Peninsula, Aug. 1861–May 1862. RG 109, NA; Seddon to Lee, 4 Dec. 1862. Box 1, Lee Papers. RG 109, NA: Arms of the 4th Virginia Cavalry, 25 Jan. 1863. 4th Virginia Cavalry Papers, MC; Louis G. Young to Pettigrew, 2 Mar. 1863. Pettigrew Family Papers, NCDAH; Lee to Seddon, 7 Aug. 1863. L&TS, ANV. RG 109, NA; IR of Bryan's Brigade by Lt. Col. Archer Anderson, 7 Apr. 1864. IR of Wofford's Brigade by Lt. Col. Archer Anderson, 11 Apr. 1864. R2, F108–11 and 124–25, IR, RG 109, NA.

11. Chilton to Early, 16 Mar. 1863. L&TS, ANV. RG 109, NA; Louis G. Young to Pettigrew, 2 Mar. 1863. Pettigrew Family Papers, NCDAH.

12. Lorraine Hillyer to Shaler, 28 May 1863. Francis Lorraine Hillyer Papers, FSNBP (originals at GDAH); Thos. L. Feamster diary, 27 June 1864. Feamster Family Papers, LC; IR of Anderson's Brigade by Lt. John F. Green, 28 Aug. 1864. IR of Perry's Brigade by Capt. H. H. Perry, Sep. 1864. IR of Gary's Cavalry Brigade by Lt. J. C. Mills, 27 Feb. 1865. R4, F711. R10, F34. R16, F339, IR. RG 109, NA; Alexander, *Fighting*, 60–61.

13. J. H. H. Hodges to Col. J. L. White, 11 May 1863. L&TR, Superintendent of Laboratories, Macon, Ga., May–Oct. 1863. RG 109, NA; W. N. Smith to Lt. Col. LeRoy Brown, 17 June 1864. CSR of W. N. Smith. Confederate General and Staff Officers,. M331, R232. RG 109, NA; James Chesnut to Mary, 22 June 1861. Chesnut, *Mary Chesnut's Civil War*, 90; Halsey to Mama, 13 Aug. 1863. Louis T. Wigfall Papers, LC.

14. M. H. Fitzpatrick to Amanda, 27 Sep. 1862 and 5 Mar. 1863. Lowe and Hodges, eds., *Letters to Amanda*, 28 and 55; GO. No. 108. HQ, ANV. 21 Sep. 1862. Wright's Brigade Order Book, CWTIC, USAMHI.

15. Glatthaar, "Battlefield Tactics," in McPherson and Cooper, eds., *Writing*, 79–80 and 276.

16. Circular. Ordnance Bureau. 12 Dec. 1862. O&CR, Macon Arsenal. RG 109, NA: Mallet to Gorgas, 9 June 1863. LS, Superintendent of Laboratories, Macon, Ga., Apr. 1863–Apr. 1864. RG 109, NA; Circular. HQ, ANV. 15 June 1863. Rodes's Division Circulars, O&C of Subcommands, ANV. RG 109, NA.

17. J. W. Mallet to Gorgas, 13 June 1863. LS, Superintendent of Laboratories, Macon, Ga., Apr. 1863–Apr. 1864. Smith to Mallet, 25 July 1863. LR, Superintendent of Laboratories, Macon, Ga., Apr. 1863–Apr. 1864. RG 109, NA; Issues of Ammunition for May by Augusta Arsenal, 1864. J. W. Mallet Papers, MC; Vandiver, *Ploughshares*, 189–91; Mallet, "Work of Ordnance Bureau," 168; Gorgas to Mallet, 4 June 1863. L&TR, Superintendent of Laboratories, Macon, Ga., May–Oct. 1863. RG 109, NA.

18. GO, No. 78. HQ, Dept. of N. Va. 12 July 1862. Record Book of Gen. W. B. Taliaferro. RG 109, NA; GO, No. 19. A&IGO. 17 Feb. 1863. GO Book, 37th North Carolina Infantry, DU; Lee to Stuart, 23 May 1863. L&TS. ANV. RG 109, NA.

19. Lee to Seddon, 5 Dec. 1863. Endorsement by Seddon. 9 Dec. 1862. Reply by Gorgas, 10 Dec. 1862; Circular. Bureau of Ordnance. 13 Nov. 1862. *OR* 21: 1046–47.

20. See Joseph T. Glatthaar. "Battlefield Tactics," in James M. McPherson and William J. Cooper, Jr., eds., *Writing the Civil War: The Quest to Understand*, 65–66; Circular. Ordnance Bureau. 4 June 1863. J. W. Mallet Papers, MC; Gorgas to Mallet, 31 Mar. 1863. L&TR, Superintendent of Laboratories, Macon, Ga., June 1862–May 1863. RG 109, NA.

21. Second Report of the Board of Artillery Officers Assembled at Augusta, Georgia. J. W. Mallet Papers, MC; Table of Range, Richmond Arsenal, 17 Oct. 1863. MC3, M-599, MC.

22. Second Report of the Board of Artillery Officers Assembled at Augusta, Georgia. J. W. Mallet Papers, MC.

23. Magruder to Gorgas, 28 Sep. 1861. Magruder to Sir, 25 Oct. 1861. L&TS, Army of the Peninsula. May–Nov. 1861. RG 109, NA; Gorgas to Pendleton, 25 Oct. 1861. Box 675, F23, Gorgas Papers, UAL; [Alexander] to [wife], 11 Dec. 1861. Alexander to Beauregard, 14 Jan. 1862. E. P. Alexander Papers, SHC, UNC; Alexander, *Fighting*, 36 and 62; Circular. Ordnance Bureau. 24 Dec. 1862. O&CR, Macon Arsenal. RG 109, NA.

24. [William Fisher Plane] to [wife], 25 Apr. 1862. Plane, *GHQ* 48, 2: 220; Lee to Seddon, 18 Dec. 1862. L&TS, ANV. RG 109, NA.

25. Special Orders, No. 2. A&IGO. 14 Mar. 1863. Report of Board to Examine the Explosion, 18 Mar. 1863. J. W. Mallet File, Record and Pension Office. RG 94, NA; Josiah Gorgas diary, 13 Mar. 1863, Gorgas, *The Civil War Diary of Josiah Gorgas*, 25–26; Records of Mary Ryan. U.S. Census, 1860. City of Richmond, Va., 225; Records of Elizabeth Dorson. U.S. Census, 1860. City of Richmond, Va., 28.

26. Report of Board to Examine the Explosion, 18 Mar. 1863. J. W. Mallet File, Record and Pension Office. RG 94, NA.

27. Report of Board to Examine the Explosion, 18 Mar. 1863, J. W. Mallet File, Record and Pension Office. RG 94, NA; Gorgas diary, 21 Mar. 1863. Gorgas, *Diary*, 26; Capt. James Ker et al., Report of the Board to Examine the Explosion at Richmond Laboratory, 25 Mar. 1863. Box 4, Richmond Arsenal File, RG 109, NA; John T. Trowbridge, *The Desolate South, 1865–1868; A Picture of the Battlefields and of the Devastated Confederacy*, 91–92.

28. Mar.–Apr. 1863. Ordnance Department, Time Book, Women Employees, Richmond Arsenal. RG 109, NA.

29. Mallet to Gorgas, 14 July 1863. Mallet to Gorgas, 9 June 1863. Mallet to J. T. Trezevant, 9 June 1863. LS, Superintendent of Laboratories, Macon, Ga., Apr. 1863–Apr. 1864. RG 109, NA; Gorgas to Captain, 7 June 1863. T. S. Rhett to Mallet, 28 July 1863. L&TR, Superintendent of Laboratories, Macon, Ga., May–Oct. 1863, RG 109, NA.

30. Gorgas to Mallet, 2 May 1863. J. W. Mallet Papers, MC; Mallet to Gorgas, 14 July 1863. LS, Superintendent of Laboratories, Macon, Ga., Apr. 1863–Apr. 1864. RG 109, NA.

31. Gorgas to Mallet, 7 June 1863. L&TR, Superintendent of Laboratories, Macon, Ga., May–Oct. 1863. RG 109, NA.

22. The Failure at Gettysburg

1. GO, No. 17. HQ, Cavalry Division. 20 May 1863. Order Book, Hampton's Cavalry Brigade, Lewis Leigh Collection, USAMHI: L. Guild to Surg. Gen. Moore. 14 June 1863. LS, Medical Director's Office, ANV. RG 109, NA. A very different version of this chapter appears in Gabor S. Boritt, ed., *The Gettysburg Nobody Knows*.

2. C. R. Phelps to Aunt, 11 June 1863. Charles R. Phelps Papers, UVA; W. O. H[arvie] to Ma, 14 June 1863. Harvie Family Papers, VHS; Quotation in Mac to Bill, 22 June 1863, Box 18, F197. Joseph F. Waring Papers, GHS; H. B. McClellan, *I Rode With Jeb Stuart*; Thomas [Rosser] to [Sister], 11 June 1863. Gordon and Rosser Families. UVA.

3. Alexander, *Fighting*, 222; James Campbell to Martha, 28 May 1863. John Campbell Papers, Rice University.

4. Lee to Seddon, 10 May 1863. Lee to Davis, 11 May 1863. Dowdey and Manarin, eds., *Wartime Papers*, 482–84; Lee to Davis, 7 June 1863. Lee to Cooper, 31 July 1863. *OR* 27 (2): 293–94 and 305.

5. W. H. H. Winston to Aunt, 21 May 1863. Winston-Clark Family Papers, VHS; McLaws to Emily, 19 June 1863. McLaws Papers, SHC, UNC; E. J. Martin to Mother & sister, 25 June 1863. C.S.A. Army Papers, NYPL; Charles A. Wills to Wife, 12 June 1863. Wills Family Papers, W&M.

6. Pegram Ward to Cousin, 19 May 1863. Ward Family Papers, LC; B[uck] to [Parents], 18 May 1863. Cocke Family Papers, VHS; B. L. Farinholt to Lelia, 1 July 1863. Benjamin Lyons Farinholt Papers, VHS; A member of Cutshaw's Battery to Father, 7 July 1863, in *Richmond Enquirer*, 17 July 1863; Wm. H. Routt to Bettie, 23 June 1863. William H. Routt Papers, MC; F. J. Dunlap to Sister, 22 June 1863. CWMC, USAMHI.

7. W. James Kincheloe diary, 12 June 1863. 49th Virginia Infantry, Company C Papers, GDAH; Sambo to Babie, 26 June 1863. Confederate Soldiers: William B. Short File, MC.

8. W. J. Seymour journal, 23 June 1863. Schoff Collection, Clements Library, U. of Michigan; Franklin Gaillard to Sonny, 28 June 1863. Franklin Gaillard Papers, SHC, UNC.

9. L. McLaws to Emily, 15 June 1863. Lafayette McLaws Papers, SHC, UNC; GO, No. 45. HQ, Second Army Corps. 15 June 1863. 45th North Carolina Infantry. Log Book of G&SO, 1862–1863, NCDAH; C. C. Blacknall to Bro George, 18 June [1863]. Oscar W. Blacknall Papers, NCDAH; Watkins Kearns diary, 21 June 1863. Watkins Kearns Papers, VHS.

10. See GO, No. 72. HQ, ANV. 21 June 1863. *OR* 27 (3), 912–13.

11. Wm. H. Hill diary, 29 June 1863. William H. Hill Papers, MDAH; George P. Collins to Miss Mary, 18 Aug. 1863. Pettigrew Family Papers, NCDAH; K to Sue. 17 July 1863. Alice V. D. Pierrepont, *Reuben Vaughan Kidd*, 329.

12. Isaac Seymour diary, 24 June 1863. Coco Collection, HCWRT, USAMHI; C. B. Niesley to Parents, 1 July 1863. HCWRT, USAMHI; Charles T. Furlow journal, late June 1863. V 376, Charles T. Furlow Papers, FSNBP (originals at Yale U.).

13. K to Sue, 17 July 1863. Pierrepont, *Reuben Vaughan Kidd*, 329; Elias Davis to Georgia, 27 June 1863. Elias Davis Papers, SHC, UNC; Taylor to Fan, 16 July 1863. Keith Family Papers, VHS; L. M. Blackford to Father, 28 June 1863. Launcelot Minor Blackford Papers, UVA; Turner Vaughan diary, 28 June 1863. "Diary of Turner Vaughan," *AHQ* 18, No. 4, 588; J. M. Tate to Ma, 28 June 1863. Jeremiah Tate Papers, Gilder-Lehrman Collection, ML; Wiley, *Plain People*, 23–24; Thomas L. Ware diary, 27 June 1863, Brake Collection, USAMHI (originals in SHC, UNC); Charles T. Furlow journal, 1, 3, and 4 July 1863. V 376, Charles T. Furlow Papers, FSNBP (originals at Yale U.); Billie M. to Friend, 27 Aug. 1863. John McIntoch Kell Papers, DU; James H. Wilkes to [Mary], 16 July 1863. Ward Family Papers, LC.

14. J. R. Manson to Mother, 30 July 1863. Lewis Leigh Collection, USAMHI; Campbell Brown journal, late June 1863. Copy in Brake Collection. USAMHI.

15. Bro. Dil to Brother, 25 June 1863. Leonard-Koiner Papers, FSNBP; Marcus Heffner to wife, 19 July 1863. Marcus Heffner Papers, NCDAH.

16. Bud to Sister, 18 July 1863. Michael Musick Collection, USAMHI; John J. Chandler to Sister, 17 July 1863, John J. and Silas Chandler Papers, LV; Wm. Pigman diary, 27 June 1863. William Pigman Papers, GDAH; Halsey to Louly, 18 July 1863. Louis T. Wigfall Papers, LC; Arthur J. L. Fremantle diary, 27 June 1863. Fremantle, *The Fremantle Diary*, 191.

17. Charles E. Belknap diary, 29 June 1863. Copy in Brake Collection, USAMHI. Also see Charles C. Perkins diary, 30 June 1863. CWTIC, USAMHI. See also Circular, HQ, Army of the Potomac. 30 June 1863; Meade to [Reynolds], 30 June 1863. *OR* I 27 (3): 417 and 420.

18. Elon Francis Brown diary, 26 June 1863. Also see entry for 21 June 1863. Elon Francis Brown Papers, SHSW; Horatio Dana Chapman diary, 30 June 1863. Copy in Brake Collection, USAMHI.

19. Flavius J. Bellamy diary, 1 July 1863. Copy in Brake Collection, USAMHI.

20. AAR of Brig. Gen. Joseph R. Davis, 26 Aug. 1863. *OR* 27 (2): 648–50; Edwin B. Coddington, *The Gettysburg Campaign: A Study in Command*, 271; Alan T. Nolan, *The Iron Brigade: A Military History*, 239; Rufus R. Dawes, *Service with the Sixth Wisconsin Volunteers*, 169.

21. Henry Berkeley diary, 2 July 1863. Henry Berkeley, *Four Years in the Confederate Artillery: The Diary of Private Henry Robinson Berkeley*, 50.

22. W.J.H. to Parents, 7 July 1863. Hatchett Family Folder, CWTIC, USAMHI; Jas. H. Wilkes to [Mary], 16 July 1863. Ward Family Papers, LC.

23. AAR of Lee, Jan. 1864. *OR* 27 (2): 317–18.

24. AAR of Davis, 26 Aug. 1863. AAR of Rodes, n.d, 1863. *OR* 27 (2): 649–50, 552–55, and 562; Louis G. Young to Maj. Barker, 10 Feb. 1864. Francis D. Winston Papers, NCDAH; Jas. H. Wilkes to [Mary], 16 July 1863. Ward Family Papers, LC; Thomas J. Webb to Brother, 18 July 1863. Brake Collection, USAMHI; John W. Daniel on Gettysburg, 20 Nov. 1863. John Warwick Daniel Papers, VHS.

25. AAR of Lee, Jan. 1864. *OR* 27 (2): 318–19.

26. William C. Oates, *The War Between the Union and the Confederacy and Its Lost Opportunities*, Robert K. Krick, ed., 212; Maj. Homer R. Stoughton to Capt. John M. Cooney, 27 July 1863. *OR* 27 (1): 519; AAR of Col. William C. Oates, 8 Aug. 1863. *OR* 27 (2): 392–93; J. H. H[endrick] to Mother, 8 July 1863. Robert James Lowry diary, 2 July 1863. Brake Collection, USAMHI; W. B. Sturtevant to Jimmy, 27 July 1863. W. B. Sturtevant Papers, MC.

27. H. S. Figures to Father & Mother, 8 July 1863. H. S. Figures Papers, Gilder-Lehrman Collection, ML.

28. Oates, *The War*, 212; AAR of Oates, 8 Aug. 1863. *OR* 27 (2): 393.

29. McLaws to Wife, 7 July 1863. McLaws Papers, SHC, UNC; S. R. Johnston to Fitz Lee, 11 Feb. 1878. Samuel R. Johnston Papers, VHS; Alexander, *Fighting*, 236–40; Osmun Latrobe diary, 2 July 1863. Osmun Latrobe Papers, MDHS.

30. AAR of Wilcox, 17 July 1863. AAR of Brig. Gen. A. R. Wright, 28 Sep. 1863. *OR* 27 (2): 618–19 and 622–23.

31. Longstreet to Lee, 22 June 1863. J. E. B. Stuart Papers, VHS; Lee to Stuart, 23 June 1863. *OR* 27 (3): 923; AAR of Stuart, 20 Aug. 1863. *OR* 27 (2): 692–97; N. R. Fitzhugh to Sister, 16 July 1863. Montgomery D. Corse Papers, SHC, UNC; Alexander, ed., *Fighting*, 228 and 231–32.

32. AAR of Brig. Gen. John W. Geary, 29 July 1863. *OR* 27 (1): 827–29; AAR of Ewell, n.d. 1863. AAR of Maj. Gen. Edward Johnson, 30 Sep. 1863. *OR* 27 (2): 447–48 and 504–5.

33. W. P. Heflin, *Blind Man "On the Warpath,"* 24; Horatio Dana Chapman diary, 3 July 1863. John W. Plummer to brother, n.d., in Minneapolis *State Atlas*, 26 Aug. 1863. Brake Collection, USAMHI; John N. Old to Catherine, 16 July 1863. Old Papers, FSNBP; Longstreet to Alexander, 3 July 1863, 11:45 A.M. and 12:15 P.M. Alexander to Longstreet, 3 July 1863, around noon. Edward Porter Alexander Papers, LC. Also see Charles Wainwright, *A Diary of Battle: The Personal Journals of Colonel Charles S. Wainwright, 1861–1865*, 249.

34. Kemper to Alexander, 20 Sep. 1869. Frederick Dearborn Collection, Harvard University.

35. Alexander to Pickett, 3 July 1863, 1:25 and 1:40 P.M. Edward Porter Alexander Papers, LC.

36. J. B. Crawford to wife, 8 July 1863, J. B. Crawford Papers, MDAH. See Earl J. Hess, *Pickett's Charge—Last Charge at Gettysburg*. For a fascinating depiction over time, see Carol Reardon, *Pickett's Charge in History and Memory*.

37. Franklin Sawyer, *A Military History of the 8th Regiment Ohio Vol. Infy*, 132; Smith [Brown] to Parents, 4 July 1863. Morris Brown Papers, Hamilton College; AAR of Maj. J. Jones, 9 Aug. 1863. AAR of Davis, 22 Aug. 1863. *OR* 27 (2): 643–44 and 650–51. Officially, three soldiers in the regiment received Medals of Honor for capturing flags. *OR* I 27 (2): 282.

38. Hess, *Pickett's Charge*, 335; A to ?, in *Richmond Enquirer*, 24 July 1863; Taylor [Scott] to Fan, 5 Aug. 1863. Keith Family Papers, VHS.

39. Horatio Dana Chapman diary, 3 July 1863. Campbell Brown journal, 4 July 1863. Copy in Brake Collection, USAMHI; [William H. Cocke] to ?, 11 July 1863. Cocke Family Papers, VHS; John Henry [Burrill] to Parent, 13 July 1863. Joseph [Twitchell] to Sis, 5 July 1863. Brake Collection, USAMHI.

40. J. R. Love to Father & Brother, 10 July 1863. Elizabeth Ann Love Wilson Papers, FSA; Excerpts of W. Tazewell Patton to Mother, n.d. George E. Cary Papers, MC. Also see James I. Robertson, Jr., *Soldiers Blue and Gray*, 226.

41. Lee to Sir, 26 Nov. 1863. Robert E. Lee Papers, SHC, UNC.

42. Report of casualties in Heth's division at Gettysburg, 1 and 3 July. Harry Heth Papers, MC; J. J. Young to Governor, 4 July 1863. W. H. S. Burgwyn Papers, NCDAH; A. M. Scales to Wife, 10 Aug. 1863. Alfred M. Scales Papers. NCDAH; Henry to Wife, 21 Dec. 1863. Henry T. Owen Papers, LV; Report of Casualties. *OR* 27 (2): 346; McLaws to Wife, 7 July 1863. McLaws Papers, SHC, UNC; John W. Busey and David G. Martin, *Regimental Strength and Losses at Gettysburg*, 258.

43. Latrobe to Walton, 4 July 1863. Louisiana Historical Association: J. B. Walton Papers, TU; W. J. Seymour journal, 5 July 1863. Schoff Collection, U. of Michigan; AAR of Lee, Jan. 1864. *OR* 27 (2): 322–24; John C. Donahue diary, 4 July 1863. John C. Donahue Papers, LV; Alexander to Walton, 18 July 1863. Louisiana Historical Association: J. B. Walton Papers, Register of Papers Forwarded, TU; Robert P. Myers diary, 6 July 1863. Robert P. Myers Papers, MC; Alexander, *Fighting*, 267 and 271; G. P. Collins to Sir, n.d. [1863]. Pettigrew Family Papers, NCDAH. See Kent Masterson Brown, *Retreat from Gettysburg: Lee. Logistics, and the Pennsylvania Campaign*, for coverage of the retreat.

44. ? to Absent Friend, 4 Aug. 1863. Bowles-Jordan Papers, UVA; [Tate] to Mary, 19 July 1863. Jeremiah Tate Papers, Gilder-Lehrnman Collection, ML; Heath to Father, 13 July 1863. Heath Jones Christian Papers, LV; M. Elton Decker to Ella, 11 July 1863. Decker Family Papers, LV; T. T. Fogle to Sister, 16 July 1863. Theodore T. Fogle Papers, EU; Lee to Davis, 10 July 1863. Dowdey and Manarin, eds., *Wartime Papers*, 545.

45. Jos. C. Haskell to Ma, 26 July 1863. Rachel Susan Cheves, DU; J. G. C[ovington] to Wife, 15 July 1863. Joseph G. Covington Papers, MC; J. A. Everett to ma, 4 Aug. 1863. John A. Everett Papers, EU; Unsigned to Absent Friend, 4 Aug. 1863. Bowles-Jordan Papers, UVA. Gary W. Gallagher, "The Impact of Gettysburg" in Gallagher, *Lee and His Army in Confederate History*, argues that the impact of the Gettysburg defeat on the army and civilian world has been overestimated. I agree with that, but I believe more soldiers were upset by the defeat than Gary asserts, particularly in those units that had suffered disastrous losses at Chancellorsville as well as Gettysburg. We disagree by degrees.

46. Harvey [Hightower] to Sister, 3 Aug. 1863. Hishtower, *GHQ* 40, 2, 185; Cousin Whit to Cousin, 26 July 1863. W. G. Kisling Papers, MC; A. L. DeArmond to wife, 17 Aug. 1863. CWMC, USAMHI; Lee to Seddon, 30 July 1863. *OR* 27 (3): 1052.

47. A. L. DeArmond to wife, 17 Aug. 1863. CWMC, USAMHI; E. R. Sloan to Wife, 18 Aug. 1863. Edwin R. Sloan Papers, DU; Records of Edwin R. Sloan. U.S. Census, 1860. Mecklenburg Co., N.C., 119; Records of Edwin R. Sloan. U.S. Slave Census, 1860. Mecklenburg Co., N.C., 18. He owned one slave and rented four others. J to Laura, 18 Aug. 1863. James D. Nance Papers, USC; H. H. Howard to Mother, 30 Jul. [1863]. Lewis Leigh Collection, USAMHI.

48. Robert [Stiles] to Mother, 29 July [1863]. Robert A. Stiles Papers. VHS; Caspar C. to Cousin, 12 July 1863. Caspar C. Hinkel Papers, MC; W. B. Young to Aunt, 6 Aug. 1863. William Dunlap Simpson Papers, DU.

49. S. W. N. Feamster to Mother, 27 July 1863. Feamster Family Papers, LC; J. Walker Vinson to William, 30 Aug. 1863. John Walker Vinson Papers, MC; Watkins Kearns diary, 16 July 1863. Watkins Kearns Papers, VHS.

50. ? to John, n.d. Aug. 1863. John G. Scurry Papers, Gilder- Lehrman Collection, ML; McLaws to Wife, 14 Aug. 1863. McLaws Papers, SHC, UNC; Eugene Blackford to Mary, 4 Aug. 1863. Lewis Leigh Collection, USAMHI; [Rosser] to Wife, 31 Aug. 1863. Gordon and Rosser Families Papers, UVA; Husband to [Wife], 14 Aug. 1863. Seaton Gales Papers, NCDAH.

51. John Futch to Wife, 31 July 1863. John Futch to Wife and to Mother, 2 Aug. 1863. Futch Brothers Papers, NCDAH; S. R. Flynt to Brother, 15 Aug. 1863. Flynt Papers, FSNBP; A. C. Haskell to Pa, 27 Oct. 1863. Alexander C. Haskell Papers, SHC, UNC; Council to Wife, 24 July 1863. Council A. Bryan Papers, FSA.

52. W. B. Sturtevant to Jimmie, 27 July 1863. W. B. Sturtevant Papers, MC; Walter to [Dick], 17 July 1863. Walter Herson Taylor, *Lee's Adjutant*, 62. Thanks to friend Gary Gallagher for mentioning the Taylor letter.

53. Dick [Manson] to Mother, 30 July [1863]. CWMC, USAMHI; Lee to Davis, 29 July 1863. Dowdey and Manarin, eds., *Wartime Papers*, 563.

54. Isaac G. Seymour diary, 2 July 1863. Coco Collection, HCWRT, USAMHI; E. McG. Burress to Kate, 27 July 1863. John C. Burress and Family, LSU; Lee to Davis, 31 July 1863. Freeman, ed., *Lee's Dispatches*, 110.

55. James E. Green diary, 3 July 1863. Brake Collection, USAMHI; Jno. W. Daniel to Father, 5 Sep. 1863. John Warwick Daniel Papers, UVA; Dod [Ramseur] to Darling, 8 July 1863. Stephen Dodson Ramseur Papers, SHC, UNC; AAR of Capt. J. J. Young, 4 July 1863. *OR* 27 (2): 645; Eugene [Blackford] to Mother, 8 July 1863. Lewis Leigh Collection, USAMHI; James E. Phillips memoirs, 26. James Eldred Phillips Papers, VHS; Leroy S. Edwards to father, 28 July 1863. Leroy S. Edwards Papers, VHS; Edge to precious darling, 19 July 1863. Rozier, *Granite Farm Letters*, 125.

56. Charles Figgat to ?, 12 July 1863. Brake Collection, USAMHI.

57. Report on Sample of Ammunition &c. received from Charleston and Selma by Lt. Jas. Dinwiddie, 10 July 1863. R18, F11, IR. RG 109, NA; Gorgas to Mallet, 4 June 1863. Personal Papers. J. W. Mallet. Records and Pension Office, Document File # 568, 231. RG 94, NA; Mallet to Gorgas, 14 July and 3 Aug. 1863. LS, Superintendent of Laboratories, Macon, Georgia, Apr. 1863–Apr. 1864. W. N. Smith to Mallet, 25 July 1863. LR, Superintendent of Laboratories, Macon, Georgia. RG 109, NA; SO, No. 175, HQ. Department of South Carolina. Ga. & Fla. 6 Sep. 1863. E. P. Alexander to Gorgas, 7 Nov. 1863. Experiments on rate of burning of fuzes, Dec. 1863 and Jan. 1864. MC3, M600, J. W. Mallet Papers, MC; Louis G. Young to Maj. Barker, 10 Feb. 1864. Francis D. Winston Papers. NCDAH.

58. J. Longstreet to General, 2 Aug. 1863. Louis T. Wigfall Papers, LC; W. J. J. Webb to Father, 7 July 1863. Lewis Leigh Collection, USAMHI; David Ballenger to Mother, 18 July 1863. V294, FSNBP (original at Clemens Library).

59. [G. T. Rust] to Wife, 18 July 1863. George T. Rust Papers, VHS; Frank Gaillard to Maria, 17 July 1863. Franklin Gaillard Papers, SHC, UNC; J. Thomas Petty diary, 11 Aug. 1863. J. Thomas Petty Papers, MC; Caspar C. to Cousin, 12 July 1863. Caspar C. Hinkel Papers, MC; Lee to Davis, 31 July 1863. Freeman, ed., *Lee's Dispatches*, 110; AAR of Lee, 31 July 1863. *OR* 27 (2): 309; S. W. N. Feamster to Mother, 27 July 1863. Feamster Family Papers, LC.

60. Lee to Davis, 8 Aug. 1863. Dowdey and Manarin, eds., *Wartime Papers*, 589–90; Crist et al., *Papers of Jefferson Davis*, 9, 337–38.
61. Jackson to Dabney, 24 July 1862. Robert Lewis Dabney Papers, Union Theological Seminary.

23. Home Front

1. Records of Frederick A. Habersham. U.S. Census, 1860. Chatham Co., Ga., 293; Records of Frederick A. Habersham. U.S. Slave Census, 1860. Chatham Co., 84; Records of Mrs. Margaret Elliott. U.S. Census, 1860. Chatham Co., Ga., 293; Records of Mrs. Margaret Elliott. U.S. Slave Census, 1860. Chatham Co., 84; Discharge Papers of Pvt. Frederick Habersham, May 1862. Anna Smith, ed., *A Savannah Family*, 77.
2. Fred to Leila, n.d. [late July–early Aug. 1862]. Fred to Leila, 13, 20, and 25 Aug. 1862. Smith, ed., *A Savannah Family*, 93–94 and 101.
3. Fred to Leila, 5, 16, and 18 Sep. 1862. Smith, ed., *A Savannah Family*, 111–13, and 115–16.
4. Fred to Leila, 18 and 22 Sep. 1862. Smith, ed., *A Savannah Family*, 115–17.
5. Leila memoirs, n.d. [circa 1863]. Smith, ed., *A Savannah Family*, 132–33.
6. Leila memoirs. Fred to Leila, 14, 16, and 25 Mar. 2, 8, 15, and 23 Apr. 1863. Smith, ed., *A Savannah Family*, 137–59.
7. Fred to Wife and Mother, [18 Sep. 1862]. Leila's memoirs. R to Carrie, 1863. Smith, ed., *A Savannah Family*, 116, 160, and 165–66.
8. Leila's memoirs. Smith, ed., *A Savannah Family*, 116 and 160.
9. R to Carrie, 12 May 1863. Smith, ed., *A Savannah Family*, 169.
10. Leila's memoirs. Smith, ed., *A Savannah Family*, 172.
11. Leila's memoirs. Smith, ed., *A Savannah Family*, 173–74.
12. Smith, ed., *A Savannah Family*, 285.
13. Jno. D. Damron to Father, 17 Dec. 1862. Damron Papers, FSNBP (originals in Ann Penn Wray Collection, University of Tennessee); S. W. Walkup to Minnie, 13 June 1862. Samuel H. Walkup Papers, SHC, UNC. See Reid Mitchell, *The Vacant Chair: The Northern Soldier Leaves Home*, for a perceptive discussion of this link.
14. E. D. G[raham] to Friend, 26 Nov. 1864. Ezekial Dunigan Graham Papers, FSNBP; Jas. H. Wilkes to [Mary], 16 July 1863. Ward Family Papers, LC; James P. Verdery to Sister, 7 Nov. 1864. Verdery Papers, DU; R. H. Miller to Mrs. Campbell, 23 Dec. 1861. Robert H. Miller, *VMHB* 70, 1, 65.
15. George [Lee] to Sister, 16 Jan. 1861[2]. Vandiver, ed., *Louisiana Historical Quarterly* 26, 4, 947; F. W. C[ox] to Mollie, 15 Aug. [1861]. Fleet W. Cox Papers. UVA.
16. [Frank Barron] to Jennie, 20 May 1863. Barron Papers, FSNBP; Mother to Son, 13 Oct. 1862. David F. Boyd Papers, LSU; Fannie Bossiere to Davis, 10 Mar. 1863. M437, R82, F191–95. LR, CSW. RG 109, NA.
17. John to Sarah, 28 May 1863. John G. Scurry Papers, Gilder-Lehrman Collection, ML; Robert to Mother, 8 May 1863. Robert Stafford Papers, Gilder-Lehrman Papers, ML; L. M. Blackford to Mary, 14 Feb. 1865. Blackford Family Papers, UVA.
18. Lewis Blackford to Mother, 25 Feb. 1862. Blackford Family Papers, UVA.
19. [B. J. Pack] to Salina, 2 Jan. 1862. Joseph B. and Anthony Pack Papers, USC; Records of B. J. Pack. U.S. Census, 1860. Clarendon Co., S.C., 92; James W. Magruder to Eva, 8 Aug. 1863. Magruder Family Papers, LV; W. W. Gordon to Nellie, 29 July 1862. Box 18, F196. Joseph F. Waring Papers, GHS.
20. Eliza Moses diary, 24 July [1861]. Moses, *Last Order of the Lost Cause*, 111–12; G to [newspaper], 9 May 1863. T. M. Gorman Papers, FSNBP; [Frank] to wife, 31 May 1863. F. M. Parker Papers, FSNBP (original, in NCDAH); [William Preston Johnston] to wife, 15 May 1862. Mason Barret Collection, TU; Hannah M. Berry to Thomas, n.d. Smiley Family Papers, UVA; Affectionate Husband to Wife, 17 Jan. 1862. D. H. Hill Papers, NCDAH; Thomas Reid to father and mother, 20 Aug. 1863. Brake Col., USAMHI.
21. J. A. Maddox to esteemed friend, 5 Mar 1863. Letters of Confederate Soldiers, FSU; John Rogers to Sister, 17 Apr. 1864. Confederate Miscellany, EU; Uncle Joab Goodson to Niece, 20 Jan. 1864. Hoole, ed., Goodson, *AR*, 10, 3, 217; R. Channing Price to Mother, 5 Mar. 1862. R Channing Price Papers, SHC, UNC.
22. Edge to Sallie, 28 Aug. 1863. Rozier, *Granite Farm Letters*, 145; L. M. Blackford to Father, 13 Aug. 1863. Launcelot Minor Blackford Papers, UVA; W. G. Kinchloe to Annie, [Nov. 1863]. John Warwick Daniel Papers, UVA; Wm. H. Routt to Bettie, 10 May 1863. William H. Routt Papers, MC.
23. PWA to *Savannah Republican*, 26 Sep. [1862]. R2, Edmund Kirby-Smith Papers, SHC, UNC; Wm. R. Smith diary, 23 Mar. 1862. CWTIC, USAMHI; *Macon Daily Telegraph*, 2 Jan. 1863, P1; L. G. Batchelor to Father, 17 Feb. 1864. Albert A. Batchelor Papers, LSU; Jno. E. Hall to Father, 1 May 1864. Bolling Hall Family Papers, ADAH.
24. Sara Ann Fife, diary, 13 Nov. 1861, 4 Mar. and 16 May 1865. Strickler Family Papers, UVA (also cited in Blair, *Virginia's Private War*, 35); Nannie C to Friend, [n.d.] Apr. 1864. Albert A. Batchelor Papers, LSU; Catherine Edmondston diary, 16 Feb. 1861. Edmondston, *"Journal of a Secesh Lady."* 36–37; Cornelia Peake McDonald, *A Woman's Civil War: A Diary with Reminiscences of the War from March 1862*, 253; E. Martin to Nephew, 28 Apr. 1861. Smiley Family Papers, UVA; Joab Goodson to Neice, 5 Feb. 1863. Goodson, *Alabama Review* 10, 2, 139.
25. C. C. High to wife, 5 Aug. 1864. C. C. High Papers, NCDAH; Marcus Hefner to Wife, 27 Mar. 1863. Marcus Heffner Papers, NCDAH; M. Hill Fitzpatrick to Amanda, 16 Dec. 1863 and 16 June 1862. Lowe and Hodges, eds., *Letters*, 104 and 14; Thos. McCollum to Margaret, 25 Nov. 1862. Thomas McCollum Papers, GDAH; Records of Thomas McCollum. U.S. Census, 1860. Chatham Co., Ga., 269–70; Husband to Wife, 18 Aug. 1863. Ann Marie Stewart Turner Papers, Rice U.
26. M. H. Fitzpatrick to Amanda, 27 Apr. 1863. Lowe and Hodges, eds., *Letters*. 64–65; J. Q. A.

Nadenbousch to Wife, 4 June 1863. J. Q. A. Nadenbousch Papers, MC; E. T. H. Warren to wife, 19 and 21 Feb. 1862. E. T. H. Warren Papers, UVA.

27. J. Q. A. Nadenbousch to Wife, 29 Sep. 1861 and 7 Aug. 1862. J. Q. A. Nadenbousch Papers, MC; Sambo to Babie, 4? Apr. 1863. Confederate Soldiers: William B. Short Papers, MC; Lowe and Hodges, ed., *Letters*, 22.

28. Y. M. Moody to Dear and Confiding Wife, 26 July 1864. Young Marshall Moody Papers, Rice U.; Records of Y. M. Moody. U.S. Census, 1860. Merenga Co., Ala., 40; G. W. Pearsall to Wife, 23 Dec. 1863. George W. Pearsall Papers, NCDAH; James W. Wright to Fanny, 5 and 17 May 1863. John Wright Family Papers, NCDAH; Theophilus Frank to wife, 16 June 1864. Frank Family, SHC, UNC; J. B. Patterson to Sons, 31 Oct. 1863. Josiah B. Patterson Papers, GDAH; C. S. Venable to son, 20 Nov. 1864. McDowell- Miller-Warner Family Papers, UVA; Records of Charles Venable. U.S. Census, 1860. Richland Co., S.C., 102; Records of C. S. Venable. U.S. Slave Census, 1860. Richland Co., S.C., 105; C. S. Venable to Son, 9 Feb. 1862. Memoir of Mary Cantey, UVA; Franklin Gaillard to Sonny, 27 Oct. 1861. Franklin Gaillard Papers, SHC, UNC.

29. A. S. Morgan to Wife, 10 Sep. 1861. A. S. Morgan Papers, FSNBP; James H. Nelson to Uncle, 18 Apr. 1862. Howell S. Nelson Papers, MC; L. E. Jones to husband, 13 Apr. 1862. Jones to wife, 19 Apr. 1862. R. H. Jones Papers, GDAH; J. N. Old to Catherine, 19 Sep. 1863. Old Papers, FSNBP; Mother to Son, n.d. [May? 1862]. David S. Boyd Papers, LSU; John S. Apperson journal, 20 July 1864. Apperson, *Repairing*, 580; Joab Goodson to Niece, 30 Nov. 1862. Goodson, *ALR* 10, 2, 131; G. J. Wright to Dorothy, 2 May 1862. Gilbert J. Wright Papers, VHS; Joab Goodson to Niece, 30 Nov. 1862: Goodson, *ALR*, 10, 2, 131.

30. Jesse to Mollie, 21 Nov. 1862. Jesse McGee Papers, FSNBP (originals at USC); Joab Goodson to Niece, 30 Nov. 1862. Goodson, *ALR* 10, 2, 131; C.E.D. to ?, 22 Nov. 1862. Denoon Family Papers, LV; John [Wise] to Cousin, 22 Nov. 1862. Evelyn B. Moore Papers, UVA; W.L.D. to S. W. Smythe, 16 Dec. 1862. William L. Davis Papers, MDAH; William to Wife, 23 Dec. 1862. William H. Jones Papers, DU; F.M.C. to wife, 16 Dec. 1862. Coker Papers, FSNBP (originals in Hodgson Heidler Collection, UGA); Charles to Uncle Edwin, 18 Dec. 1862. Kerrison Family Papers, USC; W. W. Hopkins to Mayor of Fredericksburg, 2 Mar. 1863. W. M. Hopkins Papers, FSNBP; W. H. S. Burgwyn diary, 18 Dec. 1862. W. H. S. Burgwyn Papers, NCDAH; [C. A. Conn] to Mr. Brantley, 4 Jan. 1863. Conn, *GHQ* 46, 2, 187; *Macon Daily Telegraph*, 2 Feb. 1863, P4.

31. Jas. S. Corley to Major, 11 Jan. 1863. Irvine-Saunders Papers, UVA; John S. Apperson journal, 3 Apr. 1863. Apperson, *Repairing*, 402; Milton Barren to Brother and sister, 11 Apr. 1862. Barrett, *Confederacy*, 93–96; Robert H. Miller to Pa. 30 Sep. 1861. Confederate Miscellany, EU; Col. Henry Thomas Garnett to Emma, [Summer 1862]. Garnett Family Papers, LV; L. McLaws to Lizzie, 18 Feb. 1863. Ewell Papers, LC; Sharpe to Bowers, 13 Jan. 1864. Information from examination of scouts, deserters, etc., Army of the Potomac. RG 108, NA; Thomas, *Confederate State of Richmond*, 119–22; S to Editor, 19 Mar. 1863. *Raleigh Standard*, 20 Mar. 1863; Daniel Brown to Wife, 5 Apr. 1863. Isaac Brown Papers, NCDAH; *North Carolina Standard*, 20 Mar. 1863; Mary J. Wills to my affectionate husband, 1 June 1863. Wills Family Papers, W&M; Paul Escott, *Many Excellent People: Power and Privilege in North Carolina, 1850–1900*, 64–67.

32. William [Dame] to Mother, 1 Sep. 1863. Dame Papers, FSNBP; Wiley, *Plain People*, 41–42; J. Q. A. Nadenbousch to Wife, 28 Apr. 1862. J. Q. A. Nadenbousch Papers, MC; An Act to organize forces to serve during the war, 17 Feb. 1864. GO, No. 20. A&IGO. 1 Mar. 1864. *OR* 4 (3): 179–80; Blair, *Virginia's Private War*, 104; Thomas, *Confederate State of Richmond*, 121–22; Coulter, *Confederate States of America*, 422–28.

33. B.G.D. to Husband, 14 June 1863. AGO Record Office: Personal Letters to Prisoners at Point Lookout. RG 109, NA; Records of Solomon Durham. U.S. Census, 1860. Franklin Co., Tenn., 26; H. G. Richardson to Chilton, 4? Jan. 1864. L, T & Other Papers Received by Lee. RG 109, NA; Roster entry for Andrew Randlett, aka Andrew Randolph. Kevin C. Ruffner, *44th Virginia Infantry*, 103; Adelia A. Etheridge to Davis, 22 Dec. 1863. M437, R126, F223–25. LR, CSW. RG 109, NA; Records of Thomas S. Etheridge. U.S. Census, 1860. Princess Anne Co., Va., 595; Records of Thomas S. Etheridge. U.S. Slave Census, 1860. Princess Anne Co., Va., 103; Rowland to Rhoda, 30 May 1863. Confederate Papers, SHC, UNC; John Futch to Wife, 20 Apr. 1863. Futch Brothers Papers, NCDAH; Lee to Geo. P. Hise, 26 Oct. 1862. Copy in 1937 W.P.A. Project, Campbell Co., Va. Copy provided author by Robert K. Krick.

34. Ann J. Nelson to Beloved One, 12 Apr. 1862. Howell S. Nelson Papers, MC; Records of Howell Nelson. U.S. Census, 1860. Mecklenburg Co., Va., 204; Records of Howell Nelson. U.S. Slave Census, 1860. Mecklenburg Co., Va., 24; B. A. Blisset to husband, 23 July 1862. Blissit Family Papers, GDAH; Martha Futch to husband, 5 Mar. 1862. Futch Brothers Papers, NCDAH; Margaret E. Beggarly to husband, 28 Sep. 1862. Tillman F. Beggarly Papers, DU; Mary J. Wills to my affectionate husband, 1 June 1863. Wills Family Papers, W&M; M. H. Fitzpatrick to Amanda, 7 Nov. 1862. Lowe and Hodges, eds., *Letters to Amanda*, 29; Horatio Dana Chapman diary, 4 July 1863. Brake Collection, USAMHI; Thos. McCollum to Wife, 10 Jan. 1863. Thomas McCollum Papers, GDAH; W. E. Wilson to rindia, 25 Jan. ? W. E. Wilson Papers, USC; M. C. Hutchinson to Davis, 18 Feb. 1863. Charles W. Taylor to Davis, [Apr.? 1863]. M437, R113, F774–75 and R95, F23–27. LR, CSW. RG 109, NA; Records of J. A. Hutchinson. U.S. Census, 1860. Claiborne Co., Miss., 557; Records of J. A. Hutchinson. U.S. Slave Census, 1860. Claiborne Co., Miss., 93; Records of J. A. Shields. U.S. Census Records, 1860. Claiborne Co., Miss., 559; Records of William H. Taylor. U.S. Census, 1860. Charles City Co., Va., 143; Records of William H. Taylor. U.S. Slave Census, 1860. Charles City Co., Va., 15; J. A. Kibler to Sister, 30 Mar. 1863. James A. Kibler Papers, LV.

35. Mary Chesnut diary, 16 June 1862. Chesnut, *Mary Chesnut's Civil War*, 387; Fanny [Scott] to Taylor, 19 Apr. 1862. Keith Family Papers, VHS; A. M. Scales to Wife, 10 Aug. 1864. Alfred M. Scales Papers, NCDAH; Carrie [Fries] to Friend, 19 Jan. 1863. J. E. Shaffner Papers, NCDAH; Emaline Parker to William, 16 June 1862. W. G. Parker to Ema, 14 May 1863. William G. Parker Papers, NCDAH.

36. G. W. Pearsall to Wife, 2 June 1864. J. W. Powell to Mrs. Sarah Pearsall, 5 May [June] 1864. George W. Pearsall Papers, NCDAH: Records of George W. Pearsall. U.S. Census, 1860. Wayne Co., N.C., 124; Geo. T. Wier to Mrs. Hopkins, 17 June 1862. George W. Hopkins Papers, MDAH; Robert C. Towles to Father, [May 1864]. Comrade to editor, n.d. Excerpted from a Richmond paper. Sallie Y. Conner to Madam, 13 June 1864. Jno. Wm. to Aunt, 20 June 1864. Towles Family Papers, Manuscript Volume Diaries, W&M; Records of E. R. Hopkins. U.S. Census, 1860. Noxubee Co., Miss., 2; Records of E. R. Hopkins. U.S. Slave Census, 1860. Noxubee Co., Miss., 337. She owned twenty-one slaves.

37. Marcus Hefner to Wife, 23 May 1863. Marcus Hefner Papers, NCDAH; G. G. Young to Brother, 10 Feb. 1863. Young Family Papers, USC.

38. Alice Saunders to [Fleming], 4 Dec. 1863. Irvine-Saunders Family Papers, UVA; Bettie Burroughs to my dear Husband, 30 Sep. 1864. AGO Record Office: Personal Letters to Prisoners at Point Lookout. RG 109, NA; J. L. McCrorey diary, [30 May] and 15 Aug. 1864. J. L. McCrorey Papers, USC.

39. W. Proctor Hughey to Davis, 18 Apr. 1862. LR, CSW. M437, R103, F38–40. RG 109, NA; Mother to Son, 13 Oct. 1862. David F. Boyd Papers, LSU; Fannie Bossiere to Davis, 10 Mar. 1863. M437, R82, F191–95. LR, CSW. RG 109, NA; [Frank Barron] to Jennie, 20 May 1863. Barron Papers, FSNBP.

40. W. H. Proffit to Sister Louisa, 10 Aug. 1863. Proffit Family Papers, SHC, UNC; Nannie to Brother, 22 July 1863. J. Peter Williams Papers, UVA; Lee to Seddon, 18 Apr. 1863. *OR* 18: 998; Busey and Martin, *Regimental Losses*, 499, 501, and 603; Return of Casualties of Third Corps, in the Engagement at Bristoe Station, Va., October 14. *OR* 29 (1): 428 and 433. At Chancellorsville, North Carolina suffered 3,801 casualties out of 13,460 men. At Gettysburg, the state lost 6,582 of 14,182. At Bristoe Station, the state lost 1,300, which was over 10 percent. The percentage losses cannot be added because new troops joined the army.

41. Gabriel M. Farmer to Mother, 22 Jan. 1864. Gabriel Farmer Papers, GDAH.

24. Blacks and the Army

1. Elias Davis to Mother, 17 Dec. 1863. Elias Davis Papers, SHC, UNC; Records of Elias Davis. U.S. Census, 1860. Jefferson Co., Ala., 821; Records of Elias Davis. U.S. Slave Census, 1860. Jefferson Co., Ala., 468; CSR of Elias Davis, 10th Alabama. M311, R193. RG 109, NA.

2. Dudley T. Cornish, *The Sable Arm: Negro Troops in the Union Army*; James M. McPherson, *The Negro's Civil War: How American Negroes Felt and Acted During the War for the Union*; Joseph T. Glatthaar, *Forged in Battle: The Civil War Alliance of Black Soldiers and Their White Officers*; Noah Andre Trudeau, *Like Men of War: Black Troops in the Civil War*.

3. Ro. Johnson to Major, 27 July 1861. Order Book, Robert Johnson Papers, MC; [William B. Sydnor] to Bro, 2 July 1862. William B. Sydnor Papers, VHS; H. R. McLean to Mr. Batchelor, 13 Dec. 1863. L. G. Batchelor to Father, 18 Feb. 1864. Albert A. Batchelor Papers, LSU.

4. Tom [Branson] to Emily, 14 Oct. 1862. Branson Family Papers, NCDAH; Christopher to Father, 4 Oct. 1862. Christopher Winsmith Papers, MC; Elias Davis to Georgia, 5 Oct 1862. Elias Davis Papers, SHC, UNC; A. M. Scales to Kate, 11 Jan. 1863. Alfred M. Scales Papers, NCDAH; John P. Welsh to Mother & wife, 30 Jan. 1863. Welsh Family Papers, LV; Records of John P. Welsh. U.S. Census, 1860. Rockbridge Co., Va., 232; Records of J. P. Welsh. U.S. Slave Census, 1860. Rockbridge Co., Va., 52.

5. Charles I. Batchelor to Cousin James, 6 Aug. 1863. Ma and Pa to Fred, 12 June 1864. Fleet and Fleet, *Green Mount*, 331; T. P. Devereux to father, 27 Feb. 1864. Thomas Pollock Devereux Papers, NCDAH; Thomas to Wife, 15 July 1863. Gordon and Rosser Families Papers, UVA; W. R. Barksdale to Fenell, 30 Nov. 1862. William R. Barksdale Papers, MDAH; E. Shelby Jeffries, Jr., to Ma, 9 Aug. 1863. William Terry and Family Papers, LSU; Edmund Fontaine to Davis, 19 Feb. 1863. M437, R91, F726–32. LR, CSW. RG 109, NA.

6. John Apperson journal, 1 Feb. 1863. Apperson, *Repairing*, 355; R. F. Evans to husband, 1 Jan. 1864. Arthur Evans to Wife, 10 Jan. 1864. Arthur Evans Papers, MC; Records of Arthur Evans. U.S. Census, 1860. Edgecombe Co., N.C., 415; Records of Evans & Payne. U.S. Slave Census, 1860. Edgecombe Co., N.C., 145; Ro. Johnston to Major, 31 July 1861. Order Book, Robert Johnson Papers, MC; I. M. Auld to Mamie, 14 July 1862. CWMC, USAMHI; John Letcher to Senate and House, 5 May 1862. Bradley T. Johnson Papers, DU; George J. Johnston, n.d. [Dec. 1863 or early 1864]. George J. Johnston Papers, AHS; M. Hill Fitzpatrick to Amanda, 1 Aug. 1862. "Letters to Amanda," CWMC, USAMHI.

7. Wm. E. Moore diary, 12 Jan. 1861. CWTIC, USAMHI; ASM[organ] to Wife, 20 May 1861. Asa Stokely Morgan Papers, FSNBP; Mary A. Smiley to Brother, 23 May 1861. Smiley Family Papers, UVA; Jimmie [Langhorne] to Father, 5 June [1861]. Langhorne Family Papers, VHS.

8. Wm. H. Ker to Sister, 27 Oct. and 7 Nov. 1861. Excerpts in Winthrop D. Jordan, *Tumult and Silence at Second Creek: An Inquiry into a Civil War Slave Conspiracy*, 321–22 (originals in William Ker and Family Papers, LSU).

9. Nannie C. to Friend, n.d. Apr. 1864. Albert A. Batchelor Papers, LSU; Samuel H. Walkup diary, 18 Nov. 1862. Samuel H. Walkup Papers, SHC, UNC.

10. Marcy Wade to Gen. Pettigrew, 6 Apr. 1863. Pettigrew Family Papers, NCDAH; Samuel H. Wiley to Mother, 26 Nov. 1864. Rozier, *Granite Farms Letters*, 215.

11. Henry to Harriet, 21 Dec. 1862. Henry T. Owen Papers, LV; J. B. Ligon to Mother, 25 Aug. 1864. James Blackmon Ligon Papers, USC; Edge to Darling, 8 Aug. 1863. Rozier, *Granite Farm Letters*, 133; L. G. Batchelor to Father, 17 Feb. 1864. Albert A. Batchelor Papers, LSU; J. Q. A. Nadenbousch to Wife, 29 Sep. 1861. J. Q. A. Nadenbousch Papers, MC.

12. Thomas J. Goree to Mother, 8 Dec. 1861. Goree, ed., 104–5; J. W. Murray to wife, 25 Aug. [1861]. Murray Family Papers, LV; J. W. Tindall to Wife, 16 June 1864. J. W. Tindall Papers, USC; John W. Burriss to Edward, 26 Dec. 1862. John C. Burriss and Family, LSU.

13. Glatthaar, *Forged in Battle*, 4; Henry Bryan to Stafford G. Cook, Esq., and to William Smith, 24 Feb. 1862. L&TS, Army and Department of the Peninsula. RG 109, NA; Letcher to Davis, 14 Mar. 1863, Inclosure, "An Act to amend and re-enact 'An Act further to provide for the public defense, 3 Oct. 1862,'" 13 Mar. 1863. *OR* 4, 2:426–30.

14. Randolph to Vance, 10 Nov. 1862. Vance to General Assembly, 17 Nov. 1862. Davis to Brown and other Governors, 26 Nov. 1862. "An Act to organize and supply negro labor for coast defense, &c." State of South Carolina, 4 Nov. 1862. "An act to press into service negroes," State of Louisiana, 1 Jan. 1863. "An act to authorize the impressment of slaves," State of Mississippi, 3 Jan. 1863. Seddon to Vance, 4 Feb. 1863. Vance to Seddon, 12 Feb. 1863. "An act and re-enact 'An act further to provide for public defense,'" State of Virginia, 13 Mar. 1863. An Act to regulate impressments, 26 Mar. 1863. GO, No. 37. A&IGO. 6 Apr. 1863. *OR* 4, 2: 175–76, 181, 211, 266–70, 278–79, 296–97, 385–86, 393–94, 426–430, 469–71, 469–72; Chas. H. Smith to Surg. Thos. H. Williams, 3 Aug. 1861. Order Book, Thomas H. Williams, Schenectady County Historical Society; *Richmond Whig*, 7 July 1862, P1C2; John R. Chambliss and Thomas H. Urquhart to Davis, 27 Jan. 1863. Fontaine to Davis, 19 Mar. 1863. Seddon to Davis, 19 Aug. 1863. Crist et al., *Papers of Jefferson Davis*, 9: 41–42, 105, and 349; Davis to Letcher, 26 Nov. 1863. Crist et al., *Papers of Jefferson Davis*, 10:88. Kent Masterson Brown, *Retreat from Gettysburg*, 49–50, argues that 6,000 to 10,000 teamsters with Lee's army during the Gettysburg campaign were black. His figure is too high. The army could not have fed that many. In March 1864, the War Department hoped to increase the number of blacks performing all sorts of jobs for the Confederate army to 20,000. While it is very difficult to estimate, the actual number would have been well below the lower limit.

15. [Sally McDowell] to husband, 21 Sep. 1861. McDowell Family Papers, UVA; Capt. R. P. Archer to Magruder, 2 Mar. 1862. L&TS, Army of the Peninsula. RG 109, NA.

16. See Confederate Pension Applications Act of 1902 for Body Servants. LV; Winchester & Potomac Rail Road, 9 Jun 1861. M346. Confederate Citizens and Business Firms, Winchester & Potomac RR. RG 109, NA; [James] to Sister, 14 Oct. 1864. Verdery Family Papers, DU.

17. Christopher to Kate, 3 Oct. 1861. Christopher Winsmith Papers, MC; A. M. Scales to Kate, 5 Apr. 1863. Alfred M. Scales Papers, NCDAH; John T. Smith to Lucie & Ma, 8 Mar. 1862. Smith-Johnson Papers, MC; Husband [Pender] to Wife, 22 Sep. 1862. Pender, *One of Lee's Best Men*, 177–78; William J. to Mama, 5 Dec. 1863. CWTIC: Hatchett Family Folder, USAMHI; K to Sue, 17 July 1863. Pierrepont, *Reuben Vaughan Kidd*, 330; R. A. Bryant to Eugenia, 5 Jan. 1862. Bryant Family Papers, LV.

18. Thomas J. Goree to Mother, 18 Oct. 1861. Goree, ed., 92; Letter quoted in William Hanlon, "Levi Miller: Black Confederate Veteran," *Winchester Star*, 26 Feb. 1997, 2. FSNBP; "Loyal Black Servant," *Richmond Dispatch*, 7 July 1862, P1, C1; Theodore to Sister, 7 Jan. 1863. Theodore T. Fogle Papers, EU.

19. Wash to Master Richard, 31 Oct. 1864. Cary Whitaker to Br Billy, 5 Aug. 1861. G. W. Wills to Pa, 4 June 1862. G. W. Wills to Mother, 14 Sep. 1862. G. W. Wills to Sister, 16 Jan. and 16 Sep. 1863. William Henry Wills Papers, SHC, UNC; Records of William Henry Wills. U.S. Census, 1860. Halifax Co., N.C., 80; Records of William Henry Wills. U.S. Slave Census, 1860. Halifax Co., N.C., 25.

20. Abel to Dora, 26 Aug. 1864. Jim Crawford to Fannie, 8 Oct. 1864. Abel H. Crawford Papers, DU.

21. J. Thomas Petty diary, 24 Aug. 1863 and 30 May 1862. J. Thomas Petty diary, MC; Porter King diary, 24 Nov. 1861. CWMC, USAMHI; Memy to [wife], 15 Apr. 1864. Seaton Gales Papers, NCDAH.

22. Cousin Ben to Wife, 7 Sep. 1863. Benjamin W. Justice Papers, EU; J. Thomas Petty Papers, 1–2 Oct. 1863. J. Thomas Petty Papers, MC.

23. R. V. Kidd to Sister, 28 Apr. 1863. Pierrpont, *Reuben Vaughan Kidd*, 321; A.S.M. to Wife, 27 July 1861. Asa S. Morgan Papers, FSNBP; P. H. Powers to Wife, 4 July 1861. P. H. Powers Papers, FSNBP; David L. Anderson to Sister, 26 June 1862. Confederate Miscellany, EU; Excerpt from Thomasville, *Georgia Herald*, reprinted in *Augusta Chronicle*, 25 July 1874. J. H. Seegars and Charles Kelly Barrow, *Black Southerners in Confederate Armies: A Collection of Historical Accounts*, 140; V. A. S. P[arks] to Editor, 2 July 1862. Styple, ed., 115; Peter Carmichael, "We Were 'Men': The Ambiguous Place of Confederate Slaves in Southern Armies," presented at the 2005 Southern Historical Association, 11–12.

24. Memy to [Wife], 15 Apr. and 14 Aug. 1864. Seaton Gales Papers, NCDAH; Jimmie [Griffin] to Leila, 21 May 1862. CWTIC, USAMHI; Robert E. Park diary, 10 July 1864. *Southern Historical Society Papers*, Vol. I, 379; Melville [Walker] to Lucy, 23 Sep. 1863. Melville Walker Papers, LV.

25. Richard to Mother, 27 May 1862. Richard W. Waldrop Papers, SHC, UNC; Murray to Cousin, 3 July 1864. Murray F. Taylor Papers, VHS; Rachel Carmony diary, 15 June 1863. James C. Mohr, ed., *The Carmony Diaries: A Northern Family in the Civil War*, 329–30; Frank to Wife, 7 July 1864. Frank Riley Papers, UVA.

26. R. A. Bryant to Eugenia, 5 Jan. 1862. Bryant Family Papers, LV; Richard J. Davis to wife, 25 Aug. 1862. Preston-Davis Family Papers, UVA; John S. Apperson journal, 10 Oct. 1862 and 6 Jan. 1863. Roper, ed., *Repairing*, 255, 339; Christopher to Father, 17 Oct. 1862. Christopher Winsmith Papers, MC; A. W. Winston to Aunt, 19 Oct. [1861] and 7 Feb. 1864. Winston-Clark Family Papers, VHS.

27. Circular. HQ, ANV. 21 Mar. 1863. M921, R1, F1391. RG 109, NA.

28. Fred to Pa, 9 Dec. 1864. Fleet and Fleet, *Green Mount*, 349; Records of Benjamin Fleet. U.S. Census, 1860. King & Queen Co., Va., 32; Records of Benjamin Fleet. U.S. Slave Census, 1860. King & Queen Co., Va., 225–26.

29. Fred to Pa, 9 Dec. 1864. Fleet and Fleet, *Green Mount*, 349.

25. Combat

1. Henry to Harriet, 24 July 1863. Henry T. Owen Papers, LV; Records of H. T. Owen. U.S. Census, 1860. Nottaway Co., Va. 944; Records of H. T. Owen. U.S. Slave Census, 1860. Nottaway Co., Va., 342.

2. See Samuel Stouffer et al., *The American Soldier: Adjustment During Army Life* and *The American Soldier: Combat and Its Aftermath*, for information on ideology and unit cohesion. That study is predated by a few hundred years by Charles Ardant du Picq. *Battle Studies*; see also Charles Moskos, *The American Enlisted Man*; Anthony Kellett, *Combat Motivations*; Richard Holmes, *Acts of War: The Behavior of Men in Battle* (New York: Free Press, 1985); James I. Robertson, Jr., *Soldiers Blue and Gray*; Reid Mitchell, *Civil War Soldiers*; Randall C. Jimerson, *The Private Civil War: Popular Thought During the Sectional Conflict*; Joseph T. Glatthaar, *The March to the Sea and Beyond: Sherman's Troops in the Savannah and Carolinas Campaigns*; Gerald E. Linderman, *Embattled Courage: The Experience of Combat in the American Civil War*; Earl J. Hess, *The Union Soldier in Battle*; John Keegan, *The Face of Battle: A Study of Agincourt, Waterloo, and The Somme*; James M. McPherson, *What They Fought For, 1861–1865*; James M. McPherson, *For Cause and Comrades: Why Men Fought in the Civil War*; John A. Lynn, *The Bayonets of the Republic: Motivation and Military Tactics in the Army of Revolutionary France, 1791–1794*. Stouffer et al. ignore cause or ideology, yet their study is clearly biased against recognizing it. They argue that soldiers fight for comrades, that they never discussed what it was all about. As ex-captain Charles P. Roland explained at the Southern Historical Association Annual Meeting of 1991, soldiers did not talk about it because everyone knew what it was all about. There was no dispute. One obvious example from Stouffer is the question of whether soldiers ever experience doubt about whether the war is worth fighting. The question presumes the World War II soldiers knew what the war was about. Only then could they weigh the reasons for the war with the sacrifices. Ideology may be defined as a body of ideas on which a political, economic, or social system is based.

3. I first proposed this in a paper, "Combat Motivations in the Civil War," a Symposium at the Library of Congress, 2002. I have avoided calling the category "individual" because by definition the word contrasts with group.

4. Jno. Winfield to Wife, 2 Sep. 1861. John J. Winfield Papers, SHC, UNC; McPherson, *What They Fought For*, 30 and 48; Jimerson, 18.

5. Jimerson, 24; Mitchell, *Civil War Soldiers*, 77; Glatthaar, *The March to the Sea and Beyond*, 164. Also see Reid Mitchell, *The Vacant Chair: The Northern Soldier Leaves Home*.

6. P. T. Vaughan to Ginnie, 11 Oct. 1864. Pierrepont, *Reuben Vaughan Kidd*, 358; Jimmie Langhorne to Mother, 12 June 1861. CWTIC, USAMHI.

7. H. C. Kendricks to [Father], [Apr.–May 1863]. H. C. Kendricks Papers, SHC, UNC; Ben to Lettie, 25 Apr. 1862. Ben Hubert Papers, DU; Gary W. Gallagher, *The Confederate War*, 105; Wiley, *Life of Johnny Reb*, 309.

8. The literature on this subject is vast. Along with Stouffer, see Roy R. Grinker and John P. Spiegel, *Men Under Stress* (Philadelphia: Blakiston, 1945); Edward A. Shils and Morris Janowitz, "Cohesion and Disintegration in the Wehrmacht in World War II," *Public Opinion Quarterly* 12, No. 2 (Summer 1948), 280–315; Glatthaar, *Forged in* Battle, 21; J. A. Gillespie to wife, 5 July 1862. GDAH; Holmes, *Acts of War*, 26, 272–73, 293, and 300.

9. Edwin to Sister, 21 Dec. 1862. Kerrison Family Papers, USC; Jas. A. Daniel to wife, 28 July 1864. Daniel Family Papers, FSNBP; J.H.R to Mother, 12 Nov. 1862. James Henry Rice Papers, USC; James Campbell to Martha, 18 Nov. 1862. John Campbell Papers, Rice U.

10. [W. T. Conn] to Sister, 25 July 1861. Conn, *GHQ* 46, 2, 171; J. R. Manson to Mother, 30 July [1863]. Lewis Leigh Collection, USAMHI; John Collins to wife, 16 Nov. 1862. John Overton Collins Papers, VHS; James Keith to Mother, 24 May 1864. Keith Family Papers, VHS; J. R. Manson to Mother, 30 July [1863]. Lewis Leigh Collection, USAMHI; Creed T. Davis diary, 5 June 1864. Creed T. Davis Papers, VHS; Joab Goodson to Niece, 14 Sep. 1862. Goodson, *ALR* 10, 2, 129; A. M. Scales to Kate, 9 Apr. 1864. Alfred M. Scales Papers, NCDAH; James T. Thompson to Mother and sisters, 12 Aug. 1861. Thompson, "A Georgia Boy," *VMHB* 70, 3, 316; Eli Landers to Mother, n.d. May 1863. Landers, *Weep Not for Me*, 103; R. F. Eppes to Wife & children, 13 July 1862. Confederate Papers, SHC, UNC; [W. J. Webb] to Mother, 23 May 1863. Lewis Leigh Collection, USAMHI; Wiley, *Life of Johnny Reb*, 35.

11. G. S. Magruder to Cousin, 29 Mar. [1863]. Magruder Family Papers, LV; Thos. S. Garnett to Emma, 13 Oct. 1862. Garnett Family Papers, LV; Ruffner [Morrison] to Aunt Susan, [9 Sep. 1861?]. CWTIC, USAMHI.

12. James K. Edmondson to wife, 19 May 1861. Edmondson Family Papers, W&L; E. G. Lee to [Sue], 15 July 1861. Lewis Leigh Collection, USAMHI; Dod to Brother, 5 June 1862. Stephen D. Ramseur Papers, SHC, UNC.

13. L. M. Blackford to Mother, 11 Jan. 1862. Launcelot M. Blackford Papers, UVA; Robert H. Miller to Mother, 9 Apr. 1862. Miller, *VMHB* 70, 1, 80; Eli Landers to Mother, 23 and 25 Apr. 1862. Landers, *Weep Not for Me*, 73.

14. W. S. Long, reminiscence, 1214. Breckinridge Long Papers, LC; J. S. Johnston to [Miss Green], 20 July 1862. Mercer Green Johnston Papers, LC; GO, No. 49. HQ, 1st AC. 16 Nov. 1862. Box 11, Louisiana Historical Collection: Battalion, Washington Artillery, TU; Undated, Unsigned,. Flora Morgan McCabe Papers, LC; M. Hill Fitzpatrick to Amanda, 2 Sep. 1862. "Letters to Amanda," CWMC, USAMHI.

15. Jimmie to [Miss Green], 2 Sep. 1862. Mercer Green Johnston Papers, LC; E. J. Martin to Mother & brothers, 19 Dec. 1862. CSA. Army Papers, NYPL; James D. Nance to Laura, 21 June 1862. Nance Papers, FSNBP (orig. at USC); P. H. Powers to [wife], 4 May [1864]. Lewis Leigh Collection, USAMHI.

16. Robert T. Hubard to Father, 14 Nov. 1861. Hubard Family Papers, UVA; R. Channing Price to Mother, 17 Nov. 1861. R. Channing Price Papers, SHC, UNC; [J. F. Coghill] to Pappy Ma and Mit, 9 July 1863. Jonathan F. Coghill Papers, Auburn U.; Colquitt to Cary, 17 June 1861. Cary Letter Book, MC; John S. Anglin to Pop & Mother, 31 Oct. 1861. John S. Anglin Papers, LC; Joel C. Blake to Laura, 8 May 1863. CWTIC, USAMHI.

17. W. H. Norwood to Emily, 24 Jan. 1863. Letters of Confederate Soldiers, FSU; Sambo [William B. Short] to Babie, 26 June 1863. Confederate Soldiers: William B. Short File, MC; C. A. Hege to Parents, 18 Dec. 1862. Lewis Leigh Collection, USAMHI.

18. Samuel Walkup diary, 18 Nov. 1862. Samuel H. Walkup Papers, SHC, UNC; Lee endsmt., 28 Mar. 1863, to Trial of Pvt. James E. Witcher, F, 4th Georgia, for cowardice at Sharpsburg. L&TS, ANV. RG 109, NA.

19. Jas. H. Langhorne to Lizzie, 2 Feb. 1862. Langhorne Family Papers, VHS; CSR of Albert Gallatin Pendleton. M324, R410. RG 109, NA; B. K. Whittle to All, 4 Nov. 1863. Whittle Family Papers, UVA; B. W. Justice to wife, 1 Dec. 1863. Benjamin W. Justice Papers, EU.

20. J. A. Gillespie to Wife, 14 Aug. 1862. Jasper A. Gillespie Papers, GDAH; Samuel H. Walkup diary, 12 Dec. 1862 (the diary is filled with entries about soldiers' dodging battle). Samuel H. Walkup Papers, SHC. UNC; Henry to Wife, 6 May 1862. Henry T. Owen Papers, LV; A. M. McIllwain to Sallie, 23 Sep. 1862. Andrew McIllwain Papers, USC; B. W. Justice to wife, 1 Dec. 1863. Benjamin W. Justice Papers, EU.

21. Noah Collins journal, 9 Aug. 1862. Isaac S. London Papers, FSNBP; GO, No. 88. HQ, ANV. 17 Sep. 1863. M921, R1, F934–35. G&SO&CI, ANV. RG 109, NA.

22. Leroy S. Edwards to father, 10 Nov. 1863. Leroy S. Edwards Papers, VHS; GO, No. 19. HQ, ANV. 14 Feb. 1863. GO, No. 13, HQ, ANV. 2 Feb. 1863. GO, No. 26. HQ, ANV. 23 Feb. 1863. GO, No. 88. HQ, ANV. 17 Sep. 1863. M921, R1, F490–91, 445–46, 497, 934, and 547–48. G&SO&CI, ANV. RG 109, NA; T. C. Brady to wife, 29 Sep. 1862. Brady Family Papers, CAH; D. M. McIntire to Col. Hoke, 29 Sep. 1862. William J. Hoke Papers, SHC, UNC; J. Futch to Father, 26 Feb. 1863. Futch Brothers, NCDAH; Council to wife, 2 Apr. 1863. Council A. Bryan Papers, FSA.

23. John H. Munford to Sallie, 24 Oct. 1862. Munford-Ellis Papers DU; ? to John, n.d. Aug. 1863. John G. Scurry Papers, Gilder-Lehrman Collection, ML.

24. R. W. Martin to Nellie, 4 Aug. 1862. Rawley White Martin Papers, DU; Eli Landers to Mother, n.d. [late 1862]. Landers, *Weep Not for Me*, 84.

25. William Henry Taylor, "Some Experiences of a Confederate Assistant Surgeon," *Transactions of the College of Physicians of Philadelphia*, 28, 110–11. Also see Taylor, *De Quibus: Discourses and Essays*.

26. Carr [Gamble] to Brother, 30 Dec. 1861. Lewis Leigh Collection, USAMHI; A. D. Kelly to Bro, 3 Oct. 1862. William Kelly Papers, DU; CSR of L. C. Parrish. M324, R641. RG 109, NA.

27. Petition of Officers to the 10th Mississippi, 1 Aug. [1863]. M471, R09, F002 03. LR, CA&IGO. RG 109, NA; Bunch, *Roster of the Courts-Martial*, 385; Trial of Pvt. Leonidas R. Bowyer, B, 19 Virginia. GO, No. 69. HQ, Dept. of NV. 23 July 1862. GO, No. 88. Dept. of NV. 28 July 1862. M921, R1, F181 and 203. G&SO&CI, ANV. RG 109, NA; Lee to Seddon, 17 Aug. 1863. L&TS, ANV. RG 109, NA; A. J. Cloud to Davis, 21 May [1863]. M474, R77, F16–23. LR, CA&IGO. RG 109, NA; M. H. Fitzpatrick to Amanda, 3 June 1863. Lowe and Hodges, eds., 72; Wm. R. Aylett Recommendation of Pvt. Robert Tyler Jones, 22 Sep. 1863. Box 2, Lee Papers. RG 109, NA; [J. Adger Smythe] to Darling, 23 June 1864. Smythe-Stoney-Adger Papers, SCHS.

28. J. Pegram Ward to Cousin, 18 Dec. 1862. Ward Family Papers, LC; Leroy S. Edwards to Lanny, 10 May 1863. Leroy S. Edwards Papers, VHS; John Futch to wife, 28 May 1863. Futch Brothers Papers, NCDAH.

29. John Elmore Hall to Laura, 16 Sep. 1864. Bolling Hall Papers, ADAH; George [Cherry] to Sister, 20 Dec. 1862. Lunsford R. Cherry Papers, DU; Rhaddie to Sister, 4 Jan. 1863. W. R. M. Slaughter Papers, VHS; A. S. Pendleton to Mother, 14 Dec. 1862. William N. Pendleton Papers, SHC, UNC; Leroy S. Edwards to Lanny, 10 May 1863. Leroy S. Edwards Papers, VHS; Robert to Mother, 8 May 1863. Robert Stafford Papers, Gilder-Lehrman Collection, ML.

30. Point Lookout technically was Camp Hoffman, but everyone called it Point Lookout.

31. William [McKnight] to Mother, 15 July 1862. McKnight Papers (originals at Alexandria Public Library), FSNBP; W. Pigman diary, 8 July 1863. William Pigman Papers, GHS; A. L. Holladay to Uncle James, 13 June 1864. Holladay Family Papers, VHS; C. C. Blacknall to Jinnie, 10 Oct. [1863]. Oscar W. Blacknall Papers, NCDAH; Francis A. Boyle diary, 1 July 1864. Barron Papers, FSNBP; John to Mother, 10 Mar. 1864. John Taylor Papers, USC.

32. H. F. Keidel to Louis, 12 Feb. 1865. Keidel Family Papers, LC; T. S. Belvin to Father, 1 Mar. 1864. Pansy Aiken Slappey Folder, CWTIC, USAMHI; John C. Allen journal, 4 Nov. and 11 Dec. 1864. John C. Allen Papers, VHS; Joseph E. Purvis diary, 11 July 1863. CWTIC, USAMHI; J. L. McCrorey diary, 1 and 16 July 1864. J. L. McCrorey Papers, USC; B. H. Coffman to Wife, 23 Aug. 1864. CWMC, USAMHI; C. C. Blacknall to Bro George, 24 May [1863]. Oscar W. Blacknall Papers, NCDAH; Frank A. Boyle diary, 15 Jul. and 3 Aug. 1864. Barron Papers, FSNBP; John G. Scurry to Father, 27 July 1863. John G. Scurry Papers, Gilder-Lehrman Collection, ML; W. W. Grambling diary, 19 Aug. 1864. W. W. Grambling Papers, FSA; J. O. Collins to wife, 7 Feb. and 12 Oct. 1864. John Overton Collins Papers, VHS; Thomas J. Wilkins diary, 18 Aug.–5 Sep. 1864. Thomas J. Wilkins Papers, MDAH; CSR of Thomas J. Wilkins, 11th Mississippi Infantry. M269, R200. RG 109, NA. On 22 Aug. 1864 the Union suspended Confederates' ability to supplement their allowances with purchases, in retaliation for alleged treatment of Union prisoners of war.

33. *Fort Delaware Prison Times*, Apr. 1865. *Fort Delaware Prison Times*, MS and *Fort Delaware Prison Times*, SHC, UNC; *Lee Club Gazette*, Mar. 1865. *Lee Club Gazette*, MC; John to Mother, 10 Mar. and 27 Aug. 1864. John Taylor Papers, USC; J. O. Collins to wife, 24 June and 20 July 1864. John Overton Collins Papers, VHS; Joseph E. Purvis diary, 5 Aug. 1863. CWTIC, USAMHI; Thomas Herndon diary, 1 Jan. and 6 and 20 Mar. 1864. Herndon Papers, FSNBP; Francis A. Boyle diary, 15 July 1864. Barron Papers, FSNBP.

34. J. O. Collins to wife, 28 Feb., 5 Apr., and 29 July 1864. John Overton Collins Papers, VHS; J. L. McCrorey diary, 24 July 1864. J. L. McCrorey Papers, USC; John to Alex, 30 July [1864]. John Taylor Papers, USC.

35. H. Vaughan to Father, 1 March 1865. Paul Turner Vaughan Papers, SHC, UNC; Edwin Henshaw to Madam, 16 Dec. 1864. Ft. Delaware Prisoners, MC; Lewis H. Andrew diary, 15 Apr. 1865. Lewis H. Andrews Papers, AHS.

36. W. G. Morris to Companion, 18 Dec. 1862. William Groves Morris Papers, SHC, UNC; Micajah D. Martin to Father and Mother, 8 May 1863. Martin, "Chancellorsville," *VMHB* 37, 3, 227; Application of Allison Spikes, Manley Artillery. Soldier's Applications for Pension, 24 May 1901 and 25 June 1902. NCDAH.

37. John Futch to wife, 2 Aug. 1863. Futch Brothers Papers, NCDAH; C. W. Boyd to Brother, 14 May 1862, and to mother & Father (written by Miss C. V. Brand), 21 June 1862. *AHQ* 23, 3, and 4, 296–97; Records of A. Boyd. U.S. Census, 1860. Montgomery Co., Ala., 87; Records of A. Boyd. U.S. Slave Census, 1860. Montgomery Co., Ala., 263. His father owned thirteen slaves. Also see Unsigned, n.d. [June 1863]. Ward Family Papers, LC.

38. Unsigned, probably W. B. Haygood to friends, 18 May 1863. Edward Harden Papers, FSNBP (originals at DU).

39. Edward to Vir, 30 June 1862. Clarke Family Papers, VHS; Rhaddie to Sister, 4 Jan. 1863. W. R. M. Slaughter Papers, VHS; Brother to Sister, 8 July 1862. Kerrison Family Papers, USC; SO, No. 2. HQ, Arty Corps. 23 June 1862. William N. Pendleton Order Book, MC; G. K. Harlow to Mother and Family, 21 June 1863. Harlow Family Papers, VHS; Osmun Latrobe diary, 16 Dec. 1862. Osmun Latrobe Papers, VHS; Harvey to Sister, 20 Dec. 1862. Hightower, *GHQ* 40, 2, 180.

40. Charles to Sister, 19 May 1864. Kerrison Family Papers, USC; John [Wise] to Cousin, 7 May 1863. Evelyn B. Moore Papers, UVA.

41. Thos. J. Goree to Sister, 17 June 1862. Goree, ed., 154; James R. Boulware diary, 30 June 1862. James R. Boulware Papers, LV; W. G. Kisling to Cousin, 26 Mar. 1862. W. G. Kisling Papers, MC.

42. M. Elton Decker to Ella, 22 Sep. 1862. Decker Family Papers, LV; J. M. Greene to [Annie], 21 Sep. 1862. Green W. Penn Papers, DU; J. S. Johnston to [Miss Green], 29 Sep. 1862. Mercer Green Johnston Papers, LC; [Calhoun Cooper] to Mother, 10 Jan. 1863. Cooper Papers, FSNBP (originals at Kenesaw NBP); James [Binion] to Sis, 11 Jan. 1863. Michael Musick Collection USAMHI; William McWillie journal, n.d., William McWillie Papers, MDAH; J. F. Shaffner to ?, 5 Apr. 1863. J. E. Shaffner Papers, NCDAH; [John T. Smith] to ?, 9 Feb. 1863. Kate Mason Rowland Papers, MC; Edge to [Sallie], 9 July 1863. Rozier, *Granite Farms Letters*, 119; W. H. to Fisher, 2 Jan. 1863. Hampton Family Papers, USC; Louis Leon diary, 19 Dec. 1862. Leon, *Diary of a Tar Heel*, 14.

43. Eli Landers to Mother, 8 May 1863. Landers, *Weep Not for Me*, 103; Henry T. Owen, "Pickett's Division at Gettysburg," 1. Henry T. Owen Papers, LV; James Keith Boswell diary, 25 Feb. 1863. *Diary of James Keith Boswell*, MC.

44. Eli Landers to Mother, 8 Aug. 1863. Landers, *Weep Not for Me*, 112; Mad to Father, 22 June 1863. Albert A. Batchelor Papers, LSU; J. W. Davidson to ?, 16 July 1862. James Wood Davidson Papers, USC; John S. Tucker diary, 20 July 1862. Ralph G. Poriss Collection, USAMHI; Richard T. Davis to Wife, 28 June 1863. Preston-Davis Papers, UVA.

45. Eli Landers to Mother, 25 Sep. 1862. Landers, *Weep Not for Me*, 88; M. Elton Decker to Ella, ? Sep. 1862. Decker Family Papers, LV; Wm. H. Cocke to ?, 11 July 1863. Cocke Family Papers, VHS.

26. Lee and the High Command

1. Robert H. Miller to Father, 13 June 1862. Miller, *VMHB* 70, 1, 84; Isaac G. Seymour diary, 2 July 1863. Coco Collection, HCWRT, USAMHI.

2. H. E. Young to Uncle, 27 Jan. 1863. Robert Newman Gourdin Papers, EU; J. P. Hamilton to Sister, 31 Oct. 1862. Lewis Leigh Collection, USAMHI; J. Elmore Hall to Laura, 5 June 1864. Bolling Hall Family, ADAH; Eli Landers to Mother, 10 Aug. 1863. Miller, *Weep Not for Me*, 112.

3. Anyone who peruses Dowdey and Manarin, ed., *Wartime Papers*, will see a host of examples of letters to his children, his daughter-in-law Charlotte, and their friends. Lee to Son, 23 Feb. 1862. Markham Papers, MC; Lee to Rooney, 24 Apr. 1864. Lee Papers, Gilder-Lehrman Collection, ML; W. R. Fitzhugh to Sister, 30 Apr. 1864. Montgomery D. Corse Papers, SHC, UNC; R. E. Lee to Captain, 16 Nov. 1864. Walter Herron Taylor Papers, Stratford Hall; Longstreet to Latrobe, 28 May 1886. Osmun Latrobe Papers, VHS; Lucy Minnegerode & Lou Haxall to Lee, [Dec. 1863]. Lee to Pvt. Cary Robinson, 8 Dec. 1863. Robinson Family Papers, VHS; A. C. Haskell to Ma, 11 Nov. 1863. Alexander C. Haskell Papers, SHC, UNC; Wm. Porcher Miles to Beauregard, 13 Dec. 1863. Civil War Miscellany, CAH; Mary Chesnut diary, 24 July 1861. Chesnut, *Mary Chesnut's Civil War*, 116. Thomas L. Connelly entitled his book *The Marble Man: Robert E. Lee and His Image in American Society.* Freeman considered him a simple man in his four-volume *R. E. Lee*, IV, 493–505; Fellman sees much greater complexity in his *The Making of Robert E. Lee.*

4. Lee to [Mary], 8 Jan. 1863. Lee Family Papers, VHS; R. E. Lee meditations, undated and incomplete. Ser a, Box 4. Lee Headquarters Papers, VHS; L. Guild to Surg. Gen. Moore, 22 May 1863. LS, Medical Director's Office, ANV. RG 109, NA; S. M. B[emiss] to Children, 10 Apr. 1863. Bemiss Family Papers, VHS.

5. Lee to Kemper, 29 Jan. 1864. Lee to McGrath, 24 Dec. 1861. Lee to Benjamin, 6 Feb. 1862. Lee to Seddon, 10 Jan. and 12 Nov. 1863 and 22 Jan., 16 Feb., and 23 Aug. 1864. Lee to Davis, 13 Jan. and 2 Sep. 1864. Dowdey and Manarin, eds., *Wartime Papers*, 663, 93–94, 110, 388–90, 622–23, 650–51, 659–60, 663, 672–73, 843–44, 847–50; Gallagher, *Lee and His Army in Confederate History*, 170–71. Although postwar Virginians embraced Lee as their own, Lee functioned on behalf of the Confederacy. For arguments of Lee parochialism and Virginia-centrism, See J. F. C. Fuller, *Lee and Grant: A Study in Personalities*; T. Harry Williams, "The Military Leadership of North and South," in David H. Donald, ed., *Why the North Won the Civil War*; Russell F. Weigley. *The American Way of War: A History of the United*

States Military Strategy and Policy; Thomas L. Connelly, *The Marble Man: Robert E. Lee and His Image in American Society*; Connelly, "Robert E. Lee and the Western Confederacy: A Criticism of Lee's Strategic Ability," *Civil War History* 15 (June 1869), 116–32; Alan T. Nolan, *Lee Considered: General Robert E. Lee and Civil War History*. The best response is Gallagher, *Lee and His Army in Confederate History*, 151–90.

6. Lee to Davis, 7 June 1862. Crist et al., *Papers of Jefferson Davis*, 8, 229–30; Davis to Lee, 25 July 1862. *OR* 51 (2): 597;

7. Lee to Davis, 10 June 1863. Dowdey and Manarin, eds., *Wartime Papers*, 507–9. T. Harry Williams in his essay "The Military Leadership of the North and South" in Donald, ed., *Why the North Won the Civil War*, argues that Lee was a Jominian. Fuller in *Grant and Lee* insists that Grant was a modern general and Lee an antiquated one. Weigley in *American Way of War* sees Lee as a Napoleonic general, a military leader behind his time.

8. Walter Taylor to [Bettie], 4 Mar. 1864. W. H. Taylor to B. Saunders, 27 Apr. 1864. Walter H. Taylor Papers, NPL; Charles Marshall, reminiscences of Lee in *Richmond Dispatch*, 26 Jan. 1896, 11. Fitzhugh Lee Papers, UVA.

9. Walter Taylor to Sally, 17 Sep. 1861. Walter H. Taylor Papers, Gilder-Lehrman Collection, USAMHI; Alexander, *Fighting*, 265.

10. Walter Taylor to [Bettie], 4 Mar. 1864. Walter Taylor to [Bettie], 20 Feb. 1862. Walter H. Taylor Papers, NPL; L. Guild to Surg. Gen. Moore, 22 Nov. 1862. LS, Medical Director's Office, ANV. RG 109, NA.

11. Lee to [Mary], 6 Mar. and 19 Oct. 1863. Lee Family Papers, VHS; H. E. Y[oung] to Uncle, 18 Apr. 1863. Robert Newman Gourdin Papers, EU; C. S. Venable to wife, 13 Apr. 1863. McDowell-Miller-Warner Papers, UVA; D. D. P[endleton] to Mama, 16 Oct. 1863. Dudley D. Pendleton Papers, DU.

12. Chas. S. Venable diary, 4 July 1862. Charles Scott Venable Papers, USC; Charles S. Venable journal, 29 Aug. 1862. Personal Reminiscences of the Confederate War," 55–56. Charles S. Venable Papers, UVA (thanks to R. K. Krick for his help on this); C.E.D. to Brother, 4 Dec. 1862. Denoon Family Papers, LV; Lee to Davis, 8 Aug. 1863. Dowdey and Manarin, eds., *Wartime Papers*, 589–90; W. J. Seymour journal, 26 Nov. 1863. Schoff Collection CL, UMI.

13. Lee to Lawton, 21 July 1864. A. R Lawton Papers, SHC, UNC; Lee to Lawton, 27 July 1864. Lewis Leigh Collection, USAMHI; Robert E. Lee, List of Staff Officers, Army of Northern Virginia, 1866. R. E. Lee to Son, 29 Dec. 1861. R. E. Lee Papers, DU; Robert P. Myers diary, 21 Sep. 1861. Robert P. Myers Papers, MC; Mary Chesnut diary, 30 Nov. 1863, Chesnut, *Mary Chesnut's Civil War*, 495; Walter Taylor to [Bettie], 25 Oct. 1863. 20 Dec. 1863, and 21 Feb. 1864. Walter H. Taylor Papers, NPL; Chas. S. Venable to Taylor, 10 Jan. 1866. Walter Herron Taylor Papers, Stratford Hall.

14. Walter Taylor to [Bettie], 27 Dec. 1863. Walter H. Taylor Papers, NPL; Lee to Seddon, 28 Mar. 1863. L&TS, ANV; Miscellaneous Record of Papers Received & Referred, 5 Dec. 1863–26 Feb. 1863; 10 Apr.–23 June 1863; 28 July–14 Aug. 1863. 15 Aug.–3 Sep. 1863. Miscellaneous Record of Papers Received & Referred, 1862–63, ANV, RG 109, NA; Circular. HQ, Dept. of Northern Virginia. 6 Apr. 1863. M921, R1, F1396. G&SO&C1. ANV. RG 109, NA.

15. C. S. Venable to wife, 21 June 1863 and 18 Dec. 1864. McDowell-Miller-Warner Papers, UVA, Walter Taylor to Bettie, n.d. [Oct. 1862?], 21 Aug. 1863, 15 Nov. 1863, 1 June 1864, and 15 Aug. 1864. Walter H. Taylor Papers, NPL; Alexander, *Fighting*, 481–82.

16. Early to Jackson, 17 Feb. 1863. J. A. Early Papers, NYHS; Lee to Lawton, 11 May 1863. A. R. Lawton Papers, SHC, UNC; Lee to Lawton, 26 May 1863. L&TS, ANV. RG 109, NA.

17. Jackson to Trimble, 27 Aug. 1862. Jackson to Cooper, 22 Sep. 1862. Lee to Trimble, 2 Jan. 1863. Lee to Trimble, 20 May 1863. Isaac R. Trimble Papers, MHS.

18. W. N. Pendleton to Darling Love, 1 June 1863. William N. Pendleton Papers, SHC, UNC.

19. Lee to Davis, 2 Oct. 1862. *OR* 19 (2): 643.

20. Hill to Chilton, 30 Sep. 1862, with Endsmt. by Jackson, 30 Sep. 1862. Jackson to Chilton, 3 Oct. 1862. Hill to Chilton, 8 Jan. 1863. Lee to Hill, 12 Jan. 1863. Hill to Chilton, 29 Jan. [1863]. *OR* 19 (2): 729–33; Krick, *Stonewall Jackson at Cedar Mountain*, 24–36. There is evidence that Jackson and Hill reconciled to some extent at Second Fredericksburg during the Chancellorsville Campaign. Jed Hotchkiss interview with Maj. Conway R. Howard, 16 Apr. 1864. Typescript copy in possession of author, given to him by Robert K. Krick. Original at UVA.

21. Robertson, *General A. P. Hill*, 3–4 and 11–12: Samuel Walkup diary, 29 May 1864. Samuel H. Walkup Papers, SHC, UNC; Charlie MF to wife, 15 May 1863. Donald Tiedeken Papers, VHS.

22. Walter to [Bettie], 17 Oct. 1863. Walter Taylor Papers, NPL; AAR of Hill, 26 Oct. 1863. Return of Casualties of Third Corps, in the Engagement at Bristoe Station, Va., October 14. AAR of Heth, 24 Oct. 1863. List of Casualties of Heth's Division. October 14, 1863. *OR* 29 (1): 426–28 and 430–33; A. S. Pendleton to ?, [16 Oct. 1863]. William N. Pendleton Papers, SHC, UNC; W. J. Seymour journal, 15 Oct. 1863. Schoff Collection, CL, UMI.

23. Robt. Rodes to General, 22 Mar. 1863. Polk-Brown-Ewell Papers, SHC, UNC.

24. Edward M. Coffman, *The Old Army: A Portrait of the American Army in Peacetime, 1784–1898*, 60; Lee to Davis, 20 May 1863. Lee to Davis, 25 May 1863. A. P. Hill to Lee, 24 May 1863. Davis to Lee, 26 May 1863. Lee to Davis, 28 May 1863. M474, R135, F302–9. LR, A&IG. RG 109, NA.

25. Micah Jenkins to Wife, 22 June 1862. Micah Jenkins Papers, USC; A. R. Wright to Daughter, 7 Feb. 1864. Ambrose R. Wright Papers, MC.

26. Husband to Wife, 15 Apr. 1864. Bryan Grimes Papers, SHC, UNC; Campbell Brown reminiscence, 15. Ewell Papers, TNSL; Ewell to Miss Lizzie, 13 May 1862. Ewell Papers, LC.

27. John [Steger] to Mollie, 10 Dec. 1861. Carter Family Papers, VHS; Edwin Edwards diary, 1 Oct. [1863]. Edwards Family Papers, VHS; [Stuart] to Darling, 24 Jan. 1862. Stuart Papers, VHS; Ewell to

Miss Lizzie, 13 May 1862. Ewell Papers, LC; A. S. Pendleton to ?, [16 Oct. 1863], William N. Pendleton Papers, SHC, UNC. Ewell's correspondence in the early part of the Valley Campaign reveals this.

28. W. J. Seymour journal, 14 and 15 June 1863. Schoff Collection, Clements Library, UM; J. K. Walker to Farther & Mother, 17 June 1863. Confederate Miscellany, EU.

29. A. S. Pendleton to ?. [16 Oct. 1863], William N. Pendleton Papers, SHC, UNC.

30. A. S. Pendleton to Mary, 25 Nov. 1863. William N. Pendleton Papers, SHC, UNC; Walter to [Bettie], 15 Nov. 1863. Walter H. Taylor, NPL.

31. Lee to Ewell, 18 Jan. 1864. *OR* 33: 1095–96.

32. Indorsement by R. E. Lee, 27 Apr. 1864. Markham Papers, MC; John Warwick Daniel diary, 26 and 28 Apr. 1864. John Warwick Daniel Papers, VHS.

33. George N. T. Greer diary, after 15 Nov. 1862 entry. CWTIC, USAMHI; Jackson to Cooper, MC-1, A-B, Southern Historical Society Papers, MC; Jas. C. Gamble to Mort, 20 Dec. 1861. Lewis Leigh Collection USAMHI; W. J. Seymour journal, 5 May 1864. Schoff Collection, CL, UM; Mary Chesnut diary, Sep. 1863. Chesnut, *Mary Chesnut's Civil War*, 444.

34. Richard L. DiNardo, "Southern by the Grace of God but Prussian by Common Sense: James Longstreet and the Exercise of Command in the U.S. Civil War," *Journal of Military History* 66 (Oct. 2002), 1011–32.

35. Joab Goodson to Niece, 5 Feb. 1863. Goodson, *ALR* 10, 2, 140; Thos. J. Goree to Mother, 14 Dec. 1861. Goree, 110; W. B. Pettit to Wife, 16 Dec. 1862. William B. Pettit Papers, SHC, UNC.

36. Lee to Davis, 7 Mar. 1863. Freeman, *Lee's Dispatches*, 79–80.

37. Lesley J. Gordon, *General George E. Pickett in Life & Legend*, 14–15; Deborah McKeon-Pogue, USMA manuscripts Librarian, to author, 24 Aug. 2006. Copy in possession of author; Lee to Pickett, 18 Nov. 1862. L&TS, ANV. RG 109, NA; Lee to Longstreet, 19 Jan. 1865. John W. Fairfax Papers, VHS.

38. Records of Micah Jenkins. U.S. Census, 1860. York Co., S.C., 12; Records of Micah Jenkins. U.S. Slave Census, 1860. York Co., S.C., 5.

39. M. Jenkins to Wife, 7 July 1861. Micah Jenkins Papers, USC.

40. D. F. Jamison to Daughter, 11 July 1862. Micah Jenkins to wife, 24 Aug. 1862. Micah Jenkins Papers, USC; James [McFall] to Sister, 31 May 1863. McFall Papers, EU; L. M. Blackford to Mother, 12 Feb. 1864. Launcelot Minor Blackford Papers, UVA; William McWillie journal, n.d., William McWillie Papers, MDAH; Longstreet to McLaws, 18 Oct. 1863. McLaws Papers, SHC, UNC; Husband to Wife, 26 March 1864. Samuel Wicliffe Melton Papers, USC; Thos. J. Goree to Sister, 17 June 1862. Thos. J. Goree to Mother, 21 July 1862. Thomas J. Goree, *Longstreet's Aide: The Civil War Letters of Major Thomas J. Goree*, 87 and 94–95.

41. For a discussion of various political blocs, see Thomas Lawrence Connelly and Archer Jones, *The Politics of Command: Factions and Ideas in Confederate Strategy*, xiii–xiv and 49–86.

42. Longstreet to Johnston, 6 Oct. 1862. James Longstreet Papers, DU; J. Longstreet to General, 4 Feb. 1863. Louis T. Wigfall Papers, LC.

43. Longstreet to Wigfall, 18 Aug. and 12 Sep. 1863. Louis T. Wigfall Papers, LC; Longstreet to Lee, 5 Sep. 1863. Lee to Davis, 6 Sep. 1863. Davis to Lee, 8 Sep. [1863]. Lee to Davis, 9 Sep. 1863. *OR* 29 (2): 699–702 and 706.

44. Maj. Frederick A. Eiserman, "Longstreet's Corps at Chickamauga: Lessons in Inter-Theater Deployment," 35–65.

45. AAR of Longstreet, n.d. Oct. 1863. AAR of Kershaw, 15 Oct. 1863. *OR* 30 (2): 287–91 and 503–5.

46. Circular. HQ, Army of Tennessee. 21 Sep. 1863. Circular. HQ, Army of Tennessee. 22 Sep. 1863. Longstreet to Seddon, 26 Sep. 1863. Polk to Lee, 27 Sep. 1863. *OR* 30 (4): 679, 689, 705–6, and 708.

47. Longstreet to Hill, 4 and 4 Oct. 1863. Mackall to Johnston, 13 Oct. 1863. Armand to Beauregard, 14 Oct. 1863. *OR* 30 (4): 728 and 743.

48. AAR of Longstreet, 25 Mar. 1864. Insmt. 25 Dec. 1863. AAR of Law, 3 Nov. 1863. AAR of Col. J. Bratton, 1 Nov. 1863. AAR of Brig. Gen. J. B. Robertson, 5 Nov. 1863. *OR* 31 (1): 216–20, 224–28, and 231–35; Wert, *General James Longstreet*, 334–39; Swisher, *Prince of Edisto*, 108–15.

49. AAR of Longstreet, 1 Jan. 1864. Return of Casualties in Longstreet's Corps, November 14–December 4. *OR* 31 (1): 455–66 and 475.

50. AAR of Longstreet, 1 Jan. 1864. *OR* 31 (1): 461–62.

51. Charge and Specification Against Brig. Gen. J. B. Robertson. Husband to wife, 13 Dec. 1864[3]. Samuel Wicliff Melton Papers, USC; *Atlanta Southern Confederacy*, 29 Apr. 1864, P1, C1; Longstreet to Cooper, 22 Mar. 1864, with Indorsement by Cooper, to Charge and Specification Prepared Against Brig. Gen. E. M. Law. Longstreet to Cooper, 8 Apr. 1864, with Indorsement by Cooper to Additional Charge and Specification Preferred Against Law. Cooper to Buckner, 18 Apr. 1864. Longstreet to Cooper, 26 Apr. 1864. Cooper to Longstreet, 27 Apr. 1864. Lee to Cooper, 30 Apr. 1864. Indorsement of Cooper, 5 May 1864. Indorsement of Davis, 18 May 1864. Longstreet to Lee, 27 Apr. 1864. GO, No. 46. A&IGO. 4 May 1864. *OR* 31 (1): 470–75 and 505–6. Robert K. Krick, "Longstreet Versus McLaws—and Everyone Else—About Knoxville." in Krick, *Smoothbore Volley*, 85–116; L. McLaws to Lizzie, 29 Feb. 1864. Ewell Papers, LC.

52. Lee to Davis, 20 May 1863 and 12 July 1864. Dowdey and Manarin, eds., *Wartime Papers*, 488–89 and 823–24; Alexander, *Fighting*, 135; Jimmie [Griffin] to Wife, 11 July 1861. CWTIC, USAMHI; D.D.P. to Mama, 10 Oct. 1861. Dudley D. Pendleton Papers, DU; SO, No. 36. A&IGO. 12 Feb. 1864. Longstreet to Cooper, 25 Feb. 1864. *OR* 32 (2): 726 and 801–2; Longstreet to Cooper, 4 Mar. 1864. Cooper to Longstreet, 4 Mar. and 4 Mar. 1864. *OR* 32 (3): 583.

53. Longstreet to McLaws, 18 Oct. 1863. McLaws Papers, SHC, UNC; Longstreet to Lee, 23 Apr. 1864. Longstreet Order Book, CAH; Mary Chesnut diary, 4, 8, and 18 Aug. 1861 and 13 Jan. 1862. Chesnut, *Mary Chesnut's Civil War*, 130, 135, 151, and 278; E. McGehee to Ned, 15 June 1864. John C.

Burruss and Family Papers, LSU; Charles [Kerrison] to Uncle, 19 Sep. 1864. Kerrison Family Papers, USC.

54. SO, No. 226. HQ, ANV. 9 Sep. 1863. *OR* 29 (2): 707–8; Chas. E. Waddell diary, 2 Aug. 1863. Charles E. Waddell Papers, MC; Lee to Fitz, 10 July 1864. Fitzhugh Lee Papers, UVA; P. H. Powers to Wife, 17 May 1864. Lewis Leigh Collection USAMHI.

55. WH to Fisher, 16 July 1863. Hampton Family Papers, USC; Lee to Davis, 1 Aug. 1863. *OR* 27 (3): 1068–69.

56. WH to [Mrs. Singletary], 5 Sep. 1861. WH to Fisher, 2 and 27 Jan. 1863 and 5 Jan. 1864. Hampton Family Papers, USC; Hampton to Wigfall, 12 May 1863. Louis T. Wigfall Papers, LC; Hampton to Fisher, 22 Nov. 1862 and 19 May 1863. Box 18, F22, Joseph F. Waring Papers, GHS; JEB Stuart to Wife, 27 Jan. 1864. J. E. B. Stuart Papers, UVA.

57. Stuart to Lee, 27 May 1863. Box 2, Lee Papers. RG 109, NA; Lee to Davis, 1 Aug. 1863. *OR* 27 (3): 1068–69.

58. Longstreet to McLaws, 18 Oct. 1863, with notation by McLaws, undated. McLaws Papers, SHC, UNC; W. S. Featherston to Seddon, 3 Dec. 1862. CSR of Cadmus M. Wilcox; R. H. Anderson to Cooper, 30 Mar. 1862. Wm. A. Carraway et al. to Davis, 13 Jan. 1863. Chas. H. Lynch et al. to Davis, 8 Mar. 1864. CSR of William Mahone. RG 109, NA; [Bryan Grimes] to Wife, 24 Apr. and 15 Aug. 1864. Bryan Grimes Papers, SHC, UNC; McLaws to Munford, 20 Apr. 1895. Munford-Ellis Papers, DU; Lee to Pickens, 29 May 1862. Lee Papers, Gilder-Lehrman Collection, ML; Bryan Grimes to Wife, 27 Nov. 1862. Bryan Grimes Papers, NCDAH; J. J. Archer to Bob, 5 Nov. 1862. James J. Archer Papers, MHS; Brother [Ramseur] to Brother, 10 Oct. 1864. Stephen Dodson Ramseur Papers, SHC, UNC.

59. Lee to Davis, 23 Sep. 1863. *OR* 29 (2): 742–43.

27. Preparing for the Spring Campaign of 1864

1. R. E. Lee to Carter Lee, 20 Feb. 1864. Lee Papers, W&M.

2. W. R. Montgomery to Aunt Frank, 19 Jan. 1864. William R. Montgomery Papers, FSNBP; Geo. K. Harlow to Father Mother & Family, 1 Feb. 1864. Harlow Family Papers, VHS; Robert E. Park diary, 7 Jan. 1864. *Southern Historical Society Papers*, 26, 29; Lee to Lawton, 1 and 13 Jan. and 2 Feb. 1864. L&TS, ANV. RC 109, NA; ITC Archer Anderson to Colonel, 12 Apr. 1864. IR of Kershaw's Brigade by Lt. Col. Archer Anderson, 5 Apr. [1864]. R2, F64–65 and 75–76. IR. RG 109, NA.

3. C. E. DeNoon to ?, 16 Jan. 1863[4]. DeNoon Family Papers, LV; Dod to Brother, 28 Jan. 1864. Stephen D. Ramseur Papers, SHC, UNC; [Milton Barrett] to Brother and sister, 1 Apr. 1864. Heller, ed., 115–16; A. P. Hill to Sir, 30 Mar. 1864. A. P. Hill Papers, MC; T. P. Devereaux to father, 3 Jan. 1864, and to mother, 13 Jan. 1864. Thomas Pollock Devereaux Papers, NCDAH.

4. Lee to Lawton, 15 Feb. 1864. L&TS, ANV. RG 109, NA; Pendleton to General, 17 Feb. 1864. W. N. Pendleton Letter Book, MC; Stuart to Fitz Lee, 24 Mar. 1864. Fitzhugh Lee Papers, UVA; Lee to Longstreet, 8 Mar. 1864. R. E. Lee Papers, LV; Davis to Longstreet, 25 Mar. 1864. Crist et al., *Papers of Jefferson Davis*, 10, 290–92.

5. Pendleton to Darling Love, 23 Apr. 1864. William N. Pendleton Papers, SHC, UNC; Francis Gildard Letterbook, Department of Subsistence, Report, 8 Feb. 1864. Northup to Lt. Col. Cole, summary, Feb. 1864. Report of 19 Jan. 1864. Francis G. Ruffin Papers, VHS; George H. Sharpe to Col. Bowers, 13 Jan. 1864. Information from examination of scouts, deserters, etc., Army of the Potomac, RG 108, NA.

6. George Washington Hall diary, 27–29 Mar. 1864. George Washington Hall Papers, LC; James Stanton? To Brig. Gen. Gordon, 28 Apr. 1864. James B. Gordon Papers, NCDAH.

7. Francis G. Ruffin to Maj. A. M. Allen, 9 Mar. 1864. Francis Gildard Ruffin Letterbook, Francis G. Ruffin Papers, VHS; [Milton Barrett] to Brother and sister, 1 Apr. 1864. Barrett, 115–16.

8. GO, No. 10. HQ, ANV. 28 Jan. 1864. Order Book, 23rd North Carolina Infantry. RG 109, NA; GO, No. 23. HQ, Rodes's Division. 18 Apr. 1864. Rodes's Division, O&C of Subcommands, ANV. RG 109, NA.

9. Jerry M. Tate to Ma, 27 Apr. 1864. Jeremiah Tate Papers, Gilder-Lehrman Collection, ML; Seaborn Dominey to Caroline, 4 Mar. 1864. http://history- sites.com/cgi-bin/boards/txcwmb/index. cgi?read=1488; Joab Goodson to Niece, 3 May 1864. Goodson, *ALR* 10, 3, 221; unknown diarist, n.d. [spring 1864], 126. Lewis Leigh Collection, USAMHI; Taylor to [Bettie], 1 May 1864. Walter H. Taylor Papers, NPL.

10. Thos. Greene to Elise, 9 Apr. 1864. Greene Family Papers, VHS; Ivy W. Duggan to Editor, *Central Georgian*, 25 Apr. 1864. Civil War Miscellany; 48th Georgia, GDAH; Robert to Pa, 11 Apr. 1864. Robert Stafford Papers, Gilder-Lehrman Collection, ML; [Dod] to Nellie, 8 Feb. 1863. Stephen D. Ramseur Papers, SHC, UNC; C. G. Coleman to Anna, 24 Apr. 1864. Confederate Soldiers: Coleman Family, MC; Samuel Walkup diary, 29 Mar. 1864. Samuel H. Walkup Papers, SHC, UNC; A. M. Scales to Kate, 9 Apr. 1864. Alfred M. Scales Papers, NCDAH.

11. W. J. Pegram to Sister, 11 Feb. 1864. Pegram-Johnson-McIntosh Papers, VHS; Wm. H. Robertson to Friend & dear miss, 19 Apr. 1864. William H. Robertson Papers, VHS; D.D.P. to Mama & Papa, 21 Mar. 1864. Dudley D. Pendleton Papers, DU; Charles to Sister, 23 Apr. 1864. Kerrison Family Papers, USC.

12. GO, No. 14. HQ, ANV. 3 Feb. 1864. G&SO&CI, ANV. RG 109, NA; Dod to Brother, 28 Jan. 1864. Stephen D. Ramseur Papers, SHC, UNC; Benjamin H. Freeman to Farther and family, 19 Feb. 1864. Benjamin Freeman, *Confederate Letters of Benjamin H. Freeman*, 35; B. K. Whittle to Father, 15 Feb. 1864. Whittle Family Papers, UVA; Resolution of 10th VA Inf., 24 Feb. 1864. Box 2, Louisiana Historical Collection: Papers of ANV, TU. James W. Wright to Brother, 12 Feb. 1864. John Wright Family Papers, NCDAH.

13. Jesse Sparkman diary, 14 Apr. 1864. Jesse Sparkman Papers, FSNBP; Samuel Walsh to Miss R. L. Proffit, 11 Apr. 1864. Proffit Family Papers, SHC, UNC; John to Mother, 13 Feb. 1864. John Scurry Papers, Gilder-Lehrman Collection, ML; Records of James Scurry. U.S. Census, 1860. Campbell Co., Va., 323; Records of James Scurry. U.S. Slave Census, 1860. Campbell Co., Va., 43; F. M. Howard to Brother, 19 Apr. 1864. Lewis Leigh Collection, USAMHI; Records of Asa J. Howard. U.S. Census, 1860. Oglethorpe Co., Ga., 675; Records of Asa J. Howard. U.S. Slave Census, 1860. Oglethorpe Co., Ga., 63; Thos. Greene to Elise, 10 Apr. 1864. Greene Family Papers, VHS. See Aaron Sheehan-Dean, *Creating Confederates: Family and Nation in Civil War Virginia.*

14. F. A. B[rode] to [Josephine], n.d. [late 1863-early 1864]. J. B. Richardson Papers, MC; Osmun Latrobe to [Mattie], 9 Apr. 1864. Ward Family Papers, LC.

15. See sample in Appendix I: 17.7 percent of the sample entered the service in 1863 or 1864; 53.4 percent were single, and 46.6 percent were married, compared to 36 percent married and 64 percent single in 1861-62. For 1863-64, mean birth year was 1834 and median birth year was 1834.9. For 1861-62, median birth year was 1837.8 and median was 1835.9. In 1863-64, 63.7 percent were born before 1831 or after 1843. In 1861-62, 55.5 percent were from the Upper South, and in 1863-64 the number climbed to 61 percent. Students made up 28 percent of all occupations for 1863-64 soldiers.

16. See Sample in Appendix I. Median personal and family (if they lived with them) wealth in 1861-62 was $1,303, and in 1863-64 it was $1,577. Personal slaveholding in 1861-62 was 12.33 percent, and for 1863-64 troops it was 16.4 percent. Personal and family slaveholding was 36.8 percent in 1861-62 and 30.4 percent in 1863-64. For households with slaves, 1861-62 was 44.28 percent and 1863-64 was 34.6 percent. Among slaveholders, soldiers who were planters or resided with parents who were planters were 9.38 percent in 1861-62 and 8.27 percent in 1863-64. This challenges arguments about narrow-mindedness of planters in Escott, *After Secession*, 90-91, and others. They certainly risked their own lives and those of their sons out of proportion to their numbers.

17. John to Sarah, 27 Mar. 1864. John G. Scurry Papers, Gilder-Lehrman Collection, ML; IR of Wofford's Brigade by Lt. Col. Archer Anderson, 11 Apr. [1864]. IR of Kershaw's Brigade by Lt. Col. Archer Anderson, 5 Apr. [1864]. IR, R2, F124-25 and 78-79. RG 109, NA.

18. Daniel [Bestor] to Sister, 17 Jan. 1864. Linda Bestor Robertson Papers, ADAH; Lee to Seddon, 30 Oct. 1863 and 8 Feb. 1864. L&TS, ANV. RG 109, NA.

19. IR of Humphreys's Brigade by Anderson, 6 Apr. [1864]. IR of Bryan's Brigade by Anderson, 7 Apr. [1864]. IR of Kershaw's Brigade by Anderson, 5 Apr. [1864]. IR of McLaws's Division by Bragg, 14 Apr. 1864. IR, R2, 90-91, 108-11, 74-75, and 71-72. RG 109, NA.

20. GO, No. 23. HQ, Rodes's Division. 18 Apr. 1864. GO, HQ, to Armies of the Confederate States. Entry 64. RG 109, NA.

21. C. S. Venable to A. L. Long, 30 Jan. 1864. L&TS, ANV. RG 109, NA.

22. Circular. HQ, Johnston's Brigade. 13 Apr. 1864. Circular. HQ, Johnston's Birgade. 1 Jan. 1864. Second Army Corps, O&C of Subcommands, ANV. RG 109, NA; IR of Heth's Division by Sidney H. Davies, AA&IG, 28 Feb. 1865, referring to contents of circular in early 1864. IR, R16, F59. RG 109, NA.

23. Lee to Davis, 7 Apr. 1864. Freeman, ed., *Lee's Dispatches*, 149; J. W. Wright to Father, Mother and Fanny, 1 May 1864. John Wright Family Papers, NCDAH; Benj. H. Freeman to Farther, Mother, Sisters, 26 Apr. 1864. Benjamin Freeman, *Confederate Letters of Benj. H. Freeman*, 37; Stuart to Fitz Lee, 24 Mar. 1864. Fitzhugh Lee Papers, UVA; J. M. Tate to sister Mary, 17 Apr. 1864 and 1 Jan. 1864. Jeremiah Tate Papers, Gilder-Lehrman Collection, ML; M. Hill Fitzpatrick to Amanda, 15 and 29 Apr. 1864. Lowe & Hodges, eds., *Letters to Amanda*, 141 and 144; [J. P. Verdery] to Sister, 18 Apr. 1864. Verdery Family Papers, DU.

24. A. J. Proffit to Father & Mother, 30 Apr. 1864. Proffit Family Papers, SHC, UNC; Benj. H. Freeman to Father, Mother, Sisters, 26 Apr. 1864. Benjamin Freeman, *Confederate Letters of Benj. H. Freeman*, 38; B. W. Justice to Wife, 10 Apr. 1864. Benjamin W. Justice Papers, EU; B. A. Withers to Uncle & Aunt, 19 Apr. 1864. Ralph G. Poriss Collection, USAMHI; James W. Wright to Father and Mother, 24 Apr. 1864. John Wright Family Papers, NCDAH; Samuel Walkup diary, 17 Apr. 1864. Samuel H. Walkup Papers, SHC, UNC; Thos. J. Luttrell diary, 23 Apr. 1864. Thomas J. Luttrell Papers, FSNBP; Taylor to [Bettie], 25 Mar. 1864. Walter Herron Taylor, 144.

25. GO, No. 2. HQ, ANV. 2 Jan. 1864. GO Book, 37th North Carolina Infantry, DU; GO, No. 27. HQ, ANV. 5 Apr. 1864. GO, No. 32. HQ, ANV. 19 Apr. 1864. G&SO&CI, ANV. RG 109, NA; Lee to Davis, 12 Apr. 1864. Rowland, ed., 224.

26. Lee to Mary, 27 Mar. and 2 Apr. 1864. Lee Family Papers, VHS; Taylor to [Bettie], 3 Apr. 1864. Tower, ed., 148. In January 1865 Lee was still counting socks, and when he did not get the right number, he asked a major to count them, too. Finally, after rebuking his wife, he suggested she sew up the bag and declared, "I have not time to Count its Contents." Lee to Mary, 8 Jan. 1865. Beverly Randolph Wellford Papers, VHS. Normally, an incident like this would indicate some controlling, perfectionist nature. Although Lee did emerge from West Point without any demerits, his service in the war indicates that Lee understood the chaotic and imprecise nature of warfare, and while he strove to eliminate it, as any good commander would, it did not obsess him as it did other Civil War commanders. Since his relationship with his wife was loving, and he did not demonstrate any other signs of perfectionism, I assume this was one of those hot-button items in a marriage. Thanks to friend Dr. Peggy Thoits, a medical sociologist who specializes in mental health issues, for clarifying this for me.

27. Lee to [Custis Lee], 29 Mar. 1864. Hunter H. McGuire Papers, UVA; Lee to Davis, 25 Mar. 1864. Crist et al., *Papers of Jefferson Davis*, 10, 295-97.

28. Eli Landers to Mother, 24 Sep. 1863. Eli Landers, *Weep Not for Me*, 117; FH [Frank Huger] to Mother, 30 Sep. 1863. Gary Gallagher Personal Papers (copy in author's possession); J. E. Johnston to General, 18 Apr. 1863. R3, Edmund Kirby-Smith Papers, SHC, UNC; W. B. Young to Aunt, 29 May 1863. William Dunlap Simpson Papers, DU.

29. Longstreet, *From Manassas to Appomattox*, 547; Franklin Gaillard to Maria, 24 Apr. 1864. Franklin Gaillard Papers, SHC, UNC.

30. R to [Editor], 1 May 1864. *Daily South Carolinian*, 10 May 1864, P3, C3–4; [A. H. Young] to Sister, 30 Apr. 1864. Young, "Civil War Letters of Abram Hayne Young." *SCHM* 78, 1 (Jan. 1977), 70; William R. Stilwell to Molly, 29 Apr. 1864. William Stilwell, *The Stilwell Letters: A Georgian in Longstreet's Corps, Army of Northern Virginia*, 254; Sallie to Brother, 5 May 1864. John Alexander Barry Papers, SHC, UNC.

31. Taylor to [Bettie], 3 Apr. 1864. Walter Herron Taylor, 148.

28. The Overland Campaign

1. Jim [Linebarger] to [family], 3 May 1864. Anne Linebarger Snuggs Papers, SHC, UNC.

2. For the best book on the Battle of the Wilderness, see Gordon C. Rhea, *The Battle of the Wilderness, May 5–6, 1864*. For a good, short overview, see Gordon C. Rhea, *The Battles of Wilderness & Spotsylvania*.

3. W. J. Seymour journal, 6 May 1864. Schoff Collection, CL, UM; Taylor to Anderson, 27 May 1864. E. P. Alexander Papers, SHC, UNC.

4. Will A. Yeager to Mother, 5 May 1864. Roy Bird Cook Papers, MC; Campbell Brown Memorandum, 1 July 1864. Ewell Papers, TNSL; W. J. Seymour journal, 5 May 1864. Schoff Collection, CL, UM.

5. G. W. Pearsall to Wife, 7 May 1864. George W. Pearsall Papers, NCDAH; Robertson, *General A. P. Hill*, 253–62; Rhea, *Battle of the Wilderness*, 188–208.

6. AAR of Longstreet, 23 Mar. 1865. AAR of Kershaw, n.d. *OR* 36 (1): 1054–55 and 1061–62; E. R. Crockett diary, 6 May 1864. E. R. Crockett Papers, CAH; Finley [Harper] to Father, 6 May 1864. Samuel Finley Harper Papers, NCDAH; Bob to Rad, 26 May 1864. Joachin R. Saussy, Jr., Papers, DU; B. W. Justice to wife, 9 May 1864. Benjamin W. Justice Papers, EU; G. W. C. Lee to Taylor, 13 Nov. 1872. Walter Herron Taylor Papers, Stratford; Thos. L. McCarty diary, 7 May 1864. Thomas L. McCarty Papers, CAH; H. B. McClellan to Editor of the *Times*, 15 Jan. 1878. G. W. C. Lee memo to Fitz Lee, 11 Feb. 1898. R2, Fitz Lee Papers, UVA.

7. AAR of Longstreet, 23 Mar. 1865. AAR of Mahone, n.d. *OR* 36 (1): 1054–55 and 1090–91; C. F. Denoon to Father, 15 May 1864. Denoon Family Papers, LV.

8. Joseph Pryor Fuller diary, 6 May 1864. W.P.A. Papers: Joseph Pryor Fuller, LC; William McWillie journal, [May 1864], William McWillie Papers, MDAH; Francis W. Dawson to Mother, 1 June 1864. Francis Warrington Dawson Papers, DU; Christopher to Mother, 15 May 1864. Christopher Winsmith Papers, MC; Rhea, *Battle of the Wilderness*, 370–74.

9. Thos. L. McCarty diary, 7 May 1864. Thomas L. McCarty Papers, CAH.

10. AAR of Gordon, 5 July 1864. *OR* 36 (1): 1077–78.

11. Alexander, *Fighting*, 366; James Keith to Mother, 8 May 1864. Keith Family Papers, VHS. For the best book on Spotsylvania, see Gordon C. Rhea, *The Battle for Spotsylvania Court House and the Road to Yellow Tavern, May 7–12, 1864*.

12. Creed T. Davis diary, 8 May 1864. Creed T. Davis Papers, VHS; Joseph McMurran diary, 8 May 1864. Joseph M. McMurran Papers, LV.

13. Taylor to Anderson, 27 May 1864. E. P. Alexander Papers, SHC, UNC; W. J. Seymour journal, 8 May 1864. Schoff Collection, CL, UM; Diary of 1st Army Corps, 7–11 May 1864. *OR* 36 (1): 1056–57; Lee to Genl., 10 May 1864. George Washington Campbell Papers, LC.

14. AAR of Ewell, 20 Mar. 1865. *OR* 36 (1): 1071–72; G. C. Brown to Mother, 11 May 1864. Polk-Brown-Ewell Papers, SHC, UNC.

15. AAR of Ewell, 20 Mar. 1865. *OR* 36 (1): 1072; Campbell Brown "Memoirs," 194–95. Ewell Papers, TNSL; Joseph McMurrin diary, 12 May 1864. Joseph McMurrin Papers, LV.

16. AAR of Ewell, 20 Mar. 1865. AAR of Gordon, 5 July 1864. AAR of Ramseur, 3 Aug. 1864. *OR* 36 (1): 1072–73 and 1078–83; W. J. Seymour journal, 11 May 1864. Schoff Collection, CL, UM; G. P. Ring to Wife, 15 May 1864. Box 2, Louisiana Historical Collection: Papers of ANV, TU; James to Annie, 9 June 1864. John Warwick Daniel Papers, UVA; Husband to Wife, 30 May 1864. Stephen D. Ramseur Papers, SHC, UNC.

17. W. R. Stilwell to Mollie, 16 May 1864. Stilwell Papers, FSNBP; [Alexander] to wife, 19 May 1864. E. P. Alexander Papers, SHC, UNC.

18. M. G. Bass to wife, 9 May 1864. Bass Papers, FSNBP; Franklin D. Walter diary, 20 May 1864. Walter Papers, FSNBP; C. S. Venable to wife, 11 and 15 May 1864. Charles S. Venable Papers, SHC, UNC; R. H. Tate to Mrs. Lizzie Tate, 7 May 1864. Robert H. Tate Papers, FSA; Council to Wife, 10 June 1864. Council A. Bryan Papers, FSA.

19. George [Ring] to Darling, 15 May 1864. Box 2, Louisiana Historical Collection: Papers of ANV, TU; B. W. Justice to Wife, 11 May 1864. Benjamin W. Justice Papers, EU; C. S. Venable to wife, 15 May 1864. Charles S. Venable Papers, SHC, UNC; T. M. Gorman journal, 13 May 1864. T. M. Gorman Papers, FSNBP; Willie to Mother, 18 May [1864]. Willie Dame Papers, FSNBP.

20. Robert Tooler Myers diary, 16 May 1864. Robert Tooler Myers Papers, MC; [Alexander] to Wife, 19 May 1864. E. P. Alexander Papers, SHC, UNC; Husband to Wife, 9, 17, and 18 May 1864. Bryan Grimes Papers, SHC, UNC; Robert to Sister, 20 May 1864. Robert Stafford Papers, Gilder-Lehrman Collection, ML.

21. T. P. Devereux to [Folks], 13 [May 1864]. Thomas Pollock Devereux Papers, NCDAH; J. D. Joyner to Bro, 17 May 1864. Joyner Family. SHC, UNC; Wm. H. Routt to Bettie, 21 May 1864. William H. Routt Papers, MC; Finley to Sister, 21 May 1864. Samuel Finley Harper Papers, NCDAH.

22. Willie to Mother, 18 May [1864]. Willie Dame Papers, FSNBP; G. P. Ring to Wife, 15 May

1864. Louisiana Historical Collection: Papers of ANV, TU; Jim to [family], 15 May 1864. Anne Line-barger Snuggs Papers, SHC, UNC; Taylor to [Bettie], 23 and 15 May 1864. Walter H. Taylor Papers, NPL; R. W. Dunaway to Sister, 12 May 1864. Rawleigh Dunaway Papers, LV; TG to Elise, 22 May 1864. Greene Family Papers, VHS.

23. M. L. Smith to Mrs. Lawton, 6 June 1864. A. R. Lawton Papers, SHC, UNC; Issues of Ammunition During May 1864 to Gen'l Lee's Army, Va, by U.S. Finney, Capt. & Inspector. J. W. Mallett Papers, MC; Ansalum Withers to Uncle Banks, 31 May 1864. Ralph G. Poriss Collection, USAMHI; Alexander, *Fighting*, 370; Jack Brown to Mr. Saulsburg, 26 May 1864. Jack Brown Papers, FSNBP; T. Greene to Elise, 31 May 1864. Greene Family Papers, VHS; Dudley to Mama, 5 June 1864. Dudley D. Pendleton Papers, DU. For very good coverage on this, see Gordon C. Rhea, *To the North Anna River: Grant and Lee, May 13–25, 1864* and *Cold Harbor: Grant and Lee, May 26–June 3, 1864*.

24. L. Guild to Brown, 5 Jan. 1865. Polk-Brown-Ewell Papers, SHC, UNC; Husband to Wife, 4 June 1864. Stephen D. Ramseur Papers, SHC, UNC; James H. Lane to Wilcox, 20 June 1867. Cadmus M. Wilcox Papers, LC; Henry R. Shorter to Doctor, 26 May 1864. Henry R. Shorter Papers, MC; List of Casualties in Brig. Gen. E. A. Perry's Brigade on the 6th of May 1864 in the Battle of the Wilderness, Va. Council A Bryan Papers, FSA, Taylor to [Bettie], 23 May 1864. Walter H. Taylor Papers, NPL; Partial Returns of Casualties for the First Corps. *OR* 36 (1): 1060.

25. Devoted husband to Wife, 29 May 1864. Smythe-Stoney-Adger Papers, SCHS.

26. Stuart to Cooper, 23 Mar. 1864. Davis and Bragg endsmts., 23 and 14 Apr. 1864. War Department Collection of Confederate General and Staff Officers' Papers, J–M, 439–43. RG 109, NA; R. E. Lee to Fitz, 10 July 1864. Fitzhugh Lee Papers, UVA; Robertson, *General A. P. Hill*, 260 and 268; SO, No. 123. HQ, ANV. 8 May 1864. *OR* 36 (2): 974; Thomas, *Bold Dragoon*, 292–95.

27. W. W. Smith, "Lee to the Rear," *Southern Historical Society Papers* 8, 562–66; C. S. Venable to N. H. Harris, 24 Nov. 1861. *SHSP* 8, 106–8; Azarian Bostwick to Sister, 5 June 1864. Gregory C. White Personal Collection. Thanks to Keith Bohannon for providing the letter and permission.

28. William McWillie journal, 28 May [1864]. William McWillie Papers, MDAH; W. N. Pendleton to Wife, 25 May 1864. William N. Pendleton Papers, SHC, UNC; May 1864 Folder. E. P. Alexander Papers, SHC, UNC; Henry Beck diary, 27 May. 1864. Henry Beck Papers, AHS; B. L. Wynn diary, 28 May 1864. B. L. Wynn Papers, MDAH; Creed to Davis diary, 27 May 1864. Creed T. Davis Papers, VHS; Taylor to [Bettie], 30 May 1864. Walter H. Taylor Papers, NPL.

29. Taylor to [Bettie], 1 June 1864. Walter H. Taylor Papers, NPL.

30. Lee to Anderson, 21, 24, 27, 29, and 30 May 1864. Venable to Anderson, 21 and 27 May 1864. Marshall to Anderson, 22 and 26 May 1864. Taylor to Anderson, 23, 29, and 29 May 1864. Circular. HQ [ANV]. 31 May 1864. E. P. Alexander Papers, SHC, UNC. Alexander's Papers describe similar efforts on Lee's part to run Anderson's Corps in June.

31. G. C. Brown to Mother & Sister, 20 May 1864. Marshall to Ewell, 5 May 1864. Taylor to Ewell, 7 May 1864. Cowles to Gordon, 6 May 1864, with endsmt. by Gordon to Ewell and Early. Lee to Ewell, 29 and 31 May and 1 June 1864. Ewell to Lee, 1 June 1864. Ewell to Lizinka, 22 May 1864. G. C. Brown to Ewell, 13 June 1864. Early to Ewell, 5 June 1864. SO, No——. [HQ, ANV], 4 June 1864. Polk-Brown-Ewell Papers, SHC, UNC; Robert to Sister, 20 May 1864. Robert Starford Papers, Gilder-Lehrman Collection, ML; Lee Conversation to William Allan, 3 Mar. [1868]. Gallagher, ed., *Lee the Soldier*, 11–2; Gallagher, ed., *Spotsylvania*, 14–7; G. C. Brown to Mother & Sister, 20 May 1864. Polk- Brown-Ewell Papers, SHC, UNC; D. S. Freeman to Dr. Hamlin, 19 Nov. 1936. D. S. Freeman Papers, UVA.

32. See Rhea, *To the North Anna*, 304–19.

33. John W. Hampton to Uncle and Family, 9 June 1864. Caleb Hampton Papers, DU; [William Chancely] to Cousin, 8 June 1864. CWMC, USAMHI; Sam P. Collier to Parents, 29 May 1864. Samuel P. Collier Papers, NCDAH; [James Oswald] to John, 8 June 1864. John G. Scurry Papers, Gilder-Lehrman Collection, ML; Council to Wife, 10 June 1864. Council A. Bryan Papers, FSA.

34. Circular. HQ, 1st AC. 17 May 1864. Longstreet Order Book, CAH; Christopher to Mother, 8 June 1864. Christopher Winsmith Papers, MC; E. A. Thompson to Mr. & Mrs. R. J. Thompson, 4 June 1864. Thompson Family Papers, FSNBP; Robert to Pa, 26 May 1864. Robert Stafford Papers, Gilder-Lehrman Collection. ML; A. D. Kelly to Brother, 25 May 1864. Williamson Kelly Papers, DU; G. W. Pearsall to Wife, 23 May 1864. George W. Pearsall Papers, NCDAH.

35. [James Oswald] to John, 8 June 1864. James O. Thurman, Jr., to John, 25 May 1864. Jeremiah Tate Papers, Gilder-Lehrman Collection, ML; Charles to Sister, 19 May 1864. Kerrison Family Papers, USC; Thos. McCarty diary, 6 June 1864. Thomas L. McCarty Papers, CAH; Henri J. Mugler journal, 31 May 1864. Henri J. Mugler Papers, West Virginia University; J. W. Tindall to Wife, 31 May 1864. J. W. Tindall Papers, USC; R. Rouzie to Sister, n.d. [1864]. Rouzie Family Papers, W&M.

29. The Trenches

1. Lee to Son, 24 July 1864. R. E. Lee Papers, DU.

2. Beauregard to Bragg, 10 June 1864. Davis endsmt. ZM 747–48. Louisiana Historical Association: Jefferson Davis Papers, TU; Alexander, *Fighting*, 424–25.

3. Lee to Davis, 21 June 1864. Freeman, ed., *Lee's Dispatches*, 254–55; Lee to Longstreet, 29 Aug. 1864. James Longstreet Papers, GDAH.

4. Seaborn S. Dominey to Wife. 25 July 1864. http://history-sites.com/cgi-bin/boards/txcwmb/index.cgi?read=1501; C.E.D. to Father & Mother. 28 May 1864. Denoon Family Papers, LV.

5. Sam R. Lockhart to Mother, 5 July 1864. Confederate Papers, SHC, UNC; Charles to Dr. Lee, 21 June 1864. Dr. Lee Papers, DU; GO, No.——. HQ, Arty, ANV, 30 Sep. 1864. W. N. Pendleton Papers, LV.

6. Edge to Darling, 17 July 1864. Rozier, *Granite Farm Letters*, 176; Husband to Liz, 3 Aug. 1864.

George H. Moffett Papers, SCHS; Thomas Morris Chester article, 30 Aug. 1864. Chester, 113; Christopher to Father, 19 June 1864. Christopher Winsmith Papers, MC.

7. Robt. To Sister, 20 May 1864. Robert A. Stiles Papers, VHS; Jas. P. V. to Sister, 27 Sep. 1864. Verdery Family Papers, DU; J. W. Tindall to Wife, 16 June 1864. J. W. Tindall Papers, USC; Ivy W. Duggan to Washington [County, Ga.] Baptist Association, 1 Sep. 1864. Civil War Miscellany: 48th Georgia Infantry, GDAH; E. R. Crockett diary, 25 Sep. 1864. E. R. Crockett Papers, CAH.

8. J. R. Manson diary. 28 Oct. 1864. CWMC, USAMHI; Whig to esteemed Cousin, 2 Aug. 1864. Proffit Family Papers, SHC, UNC; Seaborn S. Dominey to Wife, 25 July 1864. http://history-sites.com/cgi-bin/boards/txcwmb/index.cgi?read=1501.

9. Will to Sister, 5 June 1864. Will Biggs to Father, 21 and 22 June 1864. Asa Biggs Papers, DU.

10. Will Biggs to Father. 22 June, 14 and 19 July, and 29 Sep. 1864. Will Biggs to Pat, 27 June and 8 July 1864. Will Biggs to Ma, 5 July and 2 Aug. 1864. Asa Biggs Papers, DU.

11. Husband to Wife, 10 July 1864. Smythe-Stoney-Adger Papers, SCHS; Wm. Biggs to Pat, 27 June 1864. Asa Biggs Papers, DU; Council to Wife, 10 June 1864. Council A. Bryan Papers, FSA; B. Mason to Wife, 16 Aug. 1864. Mason Family Papers, Auburn U.; E. D. Graham to Friend, 18 June 1864. Ezekial Duncan Graham Papers, FSNBP.

12. E. R. Crockett diary. 25 June 1864. E. R. Crockett Papers, CAH; Circular. HQ, Kirkland's Brigade. 6 Sep. [1864]. C.S.A. Archives. ANV. Order Book. DU; Charley to Mother, 23 Sep. 1864. Charles Baughman Papers, MC.

13. IR of Thomas's Brigade by Lt. Edward L. Lewis, 29 Aug. 1864. IR, R10, F400. RG 109, NA; A. N. Proffit to esteemed sister and cousin. 1 Sep. 1864. Proffit Family Papers, SHC, UNC; C. J. Winston to Aunt and Uncle, 12 Oct. 1864. Winston-Clark Family Papers, VHS; Circular. HQ, ANV. 5 June 1864. M921, R1, F1459. G&SO&CI, ANV. RG 109, NA.

14. IR of Hagood's Brigade by Capt. G. H. Moffett, 8 Aug. 1864. IR, R16, F532. RG 109, NA; Will Biggs to Sister, 5 June 1864. Asa Biggs Papers, DU; Uncle Joab to Nannie, 27 June 1864. Goodson, *Alabama Review* 10, 3, 224–25.

15. J. Elmore Hall to Laura, 14 July 1864. Bolling Hall Papers, ADAH; C. T. Dewese to father, n.d. Aug. 1864. Dewese Family Papers, LV; Leonidas C. Haden to Mama, 15 Oct. 1864. Leonidas C. Haden Papers, MC; G. Moffett to [Liz], 18 and 28 July 1864. George H. Moffett Papers, SCHS; W. S. Long reminscences, 124–25. Breckinridge Long Papers, LC.

16. Issues of Clothing to armies in the field. *OR* 4 (3): 1041; J. Elmore Hall to father, 6 Oct. 1864. Bolling Hall Family, ADAH; IR of Bratton's Brigade by Capt. J, Banks Lyle, 20 Sep. 1864. IR, R9, F615. RG 109, NA; G. P. Ring to Darling, 21 Sep. 1864. George P. Ring Papers, FSNBP (originals at TU).

17. George Washington Hall diary, 18 July 1864. George Washington Hall Papers, LC; [A. E. Shore] to Brother, 17 July 1864. Augustine E. Shore Papers, EU; A. N. Proffit to esteemed sister and cousin, 1 Sep. 1864. Proffit Family Papers, SHC, UNC; IR of Benning's Brigade by Capt. H. H. Perry, 9 Aug. 1864. IR, R10, F22. RG 109, NA; George Washington Hall diary, 21 Aug. 1864. George Washington Hall diary, LC; IR of Two Divs. Of Infy. & Artillery under Beauregard ay Petersburg, Va., 10 Sep. 1864. IR of Colquitt's Brigade by Capt. E. Burnet, 11 Aug. 1864. IR, R16, F459 and 495. RG 109, NA; R. Scarbrough to cousin, 28 Aug. 1864. Confederate Miscellany, EU; Henry to Parents, 24 June 1864. Henry I & Robert Greer Papers, LC; A. P. Hill to Ruffin, 23 Aug. 1864. Francis G. Ruffin Papers, VHS; Christopher to Kate, 3 Sep. 1864. Christopher Winsmith Papers, MC.

18. A. P. Hill to Ruffin, 23 Aug. 1864. Northup to A. P. Hill, 23 Aug. 1864. Francis G. Ruffin Papers, VHS.

19. AAR of Wade Hampton, 27 Sep. 1864. Hampton's Reply to Lee's Circular Letter. Hampton Family Papers, USC; M. Stokes to Wife, 18 Sep. 1864. William Stokes Papers, USC; Jas. P. V to Sister, 23 Sep. 1864. Verdery Family Papers, DU; Thos. C. Elder to wife, 18 Sep. 1864. Thomas Elder Papers, VHS; Benj. H. Freeman to Farther, Mother. Sis. 24 Sep. 1864. Benjamin Freeman, *Confederate Letters of Benj. H. Freeman*, 53; Fred [Fleet] to Ma, 11 Oct. 1864. Fleet and Fleet, *Green Mount*, 344; Charley to Ma, 18 Sep. 1864. Charles Baughman Papers, MC.

20. Joseph Pryor Fuller diary, 19 July 1864. Joseph Pryor Fuller Papers, LC; R. A. Young to Sir. 27 July 1864. R. A. Young Papers, MC; Creed T. Davis diary, 12 July 1864. Creed T. Davis Papers, VHS; Richard Davis to wife, 22 July 1864. Richard J. Davis Papers, UVA; Henri J. Mugler journal, 22 May 1864. Henri J. Mugler Papers, VA, Vol. 13, RNBP; Lee to Davis, 16 June 1864. Freeman, ed., *Lee's Dispatches*, 246–47.

21. B. J. Justice to Wife, 20 May 1864. Justice Papers, FSNBP (original at EU); Wm. Stokes to Wife, 4 and 9 Aug. 1864. William Stokes Papers, USC; Creed T. Davis diary, 19 June 1864. Creed T. Davis Papers, VHS; Husband to Liz, 3 and 5 Aug. 1864. George H. Moffett Papers, SCHS.

22. Lee to Davis, 9 Aug. 1864. Freeman, ed., *Lee's Dispatches*, 288–89; Lee to Secretary of War, 19 Jan. 1865, with endsmts. by Seddon, 26 Jan. 1865, Dudley, 28 Jan. 1865, Guerin, 5 Feb. 1865, and Northrop, 13 Feb. 1865. *OR* 46 (2): 1099–1100.

23. Edward [Bagby] to Pa, 6 July 1864. Clarke Family Papers, VHS; Creed T. Davis diary, 5–6 July 1864. Creed T. Davis Papers, VHS; L. Guild to Surg. Gen. Moore, 30 May and 8 Aug. 1864. LS, Med. Dir. Office, ANV. RG 109. NA; Henry to Father, 28 June 1864. Henry I. and Robert Green Papers, LC; I. Pitman to Wife, 6 Sep. 1864. Confederate Papers, SHC, UNC; Frank Huger to Celly, 3 Aug. 1864. Frank Huger Papers, Gary Gallagher Personal Collection; H. Meade to Mother, 14 Oct. 1864. Meade Family Papers, VHS; IR of Texas Brigade by Capt. Jno. W. Kerr, 28 Nov. 1864. IR, R14, F320, IR of Pickett's Division by Maj. Walter Harrison, 28–29 Aug. 1864. IR, R10, F276 and 283–84. IR of Field's Division by Maj. L. Morton, 30 Aug. 1864. IR, R10, F329–32. IR of Finnegan's and Perry's Brigades by Capt. James G. Spann, 16 Aug. 1864. IR, R10, F128–29 and 133–34. RG 109, NA; W. H. H. Ewing to Uncle, 18 Aug. 1864. Henry T. Owen Papers, LV.

24. IR of Wilcox's Division by Maj. Jos. A. Englehard, 31 Dec. 1864. IR, R14, F88 and 91–92. IR of Lane's Brigade by Capt. E. T. Nicholson, 31 Aug. 1864. IR, R10, F374 and 376. RG 109, NA; Samuel

P. Lockhart to Ellen, 9 July 1864. Hugh Conway Browning Papers, DU; Husband to Liz, 30 Aug. 1864. George H. Moffett Papers, SCHS; [J. C. Featherston] to wife, 24 July 1864. Irvine-Saunders Family Papers, UVA; Wm. Biggs to Father, 21 June 1864. Asa Biggs Papers, DU.

25. IR of Benning's Brigade by Capt. H. H. Perry, 9 Aug. 1864. IR, R10, F22–23. IR of Finnegan's and Perry's Brigades by Capt. James G. Spann. 16 Aug. 1864. IR, R10, F128–29 and 133–34. IR of Hays's and Stafford's Brigade by Capt. R. J. Barton, 19 Aug. 1864. IR, R10, F179. IR of Evans's Brigade by J. Mitchell, 20 Aug. 1864. IR, R10, F167. IR of Pickett's Division by Maj. Walter Harrison. 28–29 Aug. 1864. IR, R10, F281. IR of Harris's Mississippi Brigade by Capt. James Hayes, 30 Aug. 1864. IR, R10, F121. IR of Benning's Brigade by Capt. H. H. Perry, 8 Sep. 1864. IR, R10, F8–10. IR of McGowan's Brigade by Capt. L. C. Haskell, 27 Sep. 1864. IR, R10, F520. IR of Wright's Brigade by Lt. D. H. Pope, 28 Sep. 1864. IR, R10, F593. Extract from IR of ANV: Artillery Corps, 31 Oct. 1864. IR, R8, F260–61. RG 109, NA; Thos. T. Greene to Elise, 7 Oct. 1864. Green Family Papers, VHS.

26. Lee to Davis, 13 Aug. 1864. Freeman, ed., *Lee's Dispatches*, 369; IR of Hunton's Brigade by Capt. E. C. Fitzhugh, 9 Aug. 1864. IR, R 10, F350. RG 109, NA.

27. C. M. Wilcox to Sister, 15 Aug. 1864. Cadmus M. Wilcox Papers, LC; Henry to Mother, 3 Oct. 1864. Henry I. and Robert Green Papers, LC; [G. Moffett] to [Liz], 14 Sep. 1864. George H. Moffett Papers, SCHS; Jas. A. Daniel to Wife, 26 June 1864. Daniel Family Papers, FSNBP; A. H. Dalton to father, 16 May 1864. Dalton Family Papers, USC; J. W. Tindall to Wife, 13 June 1864. J. W. Tindall Papers, USC; Pendleton to Colonel Mosely, 20 Sep. 1864. W. N. Pendleton Letter Book, MC; L. R. Dalton to par, 25 July 1864. Lewis Leigh Collection, USAMHI.

28. Louis [Wise] to Mother, 27 July 1864. Evelyn B. Moore Papers, UVA; P. T. Vaughan to Ginnie, 11 Oct. 1864. Pierrepont, *Reuben Vaughan Kidd*, 358; Robert Stiles to Mother, 12 Sep. [1864]. Robert Stiles Papers, VHS; Sam Brooke to Sister, 3 July 1864. John M. Binckley Papers, LC.

29. Linsey T. Wells to ?, 16 Sep. 1864. Linsey T. Wells Papers, VA, Vol. 8, RNBP; Creed T. Davis diary, 14 May 1864. Creed T. Davis Papers, VHS; [D. N. Sills] to Mother, 28 Aug. 1864. Vernon Howell Papers, NCDAH; John A. Everett to Ma, 7 July 1864. John A. Everett Papers, EU; Thomas McCarty diary, 10 Sep. 1864. Thomas L. McCarty Papers, CAH; Christopher to Mother, 11 Sep. 1864. Christopher Winsmith Papers, MC; H. Meade to Mother, 23 Oct. 1864. Meade Family Papers, VHS; Henri J. Mugler journal, 14 June 1864. Henri J. Mugler Papers, Va. Vol. 13. RNBP.

30. W. S. Grady to Wife, 12 July 1864. Henry Woodfin Grady Papers, EU; J. W. Calton to Brother, 6 July 1864. John Washington Calton Papers, NCDAH.

30. Medical Care

1. Records of William H. Taylor. U.S. Census. 1860. Henrico Co., Va., 78; William Henry Taylor. M.D., "Some Experiences of a Confederate Assistant Surgeon," *Transactions of the College of Physicians of Philadelphia* 28, 91 and 105. See H. H. Cunningham, *Doctors in Gray: The Confederate Medical Service.*

2. Taylor, "Some Experiences," 94–95 and 104–5.

3. Taylor, "Some Experiences," 104.

4. Taylor, "Some Experiences," 104.

5. Taylor, "Some Experiences," 114–16.

6. Wm. E. Coffin to Davis, 21 Oct. 1861. M437, R14, F1314–17. LR, CSW. RG 109, NA; Saml. Preston Moore. Instructions to Applicants for Appointment in the Medical Dept. of the Army, 20 Nov. 1862. Saml. Preston Moore, Instructions to Asst. Surgeons applying for promotion in the Medical Department, 28 Nov. 1862. L, T, and Other Papers Received by Lee. RG 109, NA; Cunningham, *Doctors in Gray*, 32–35.

7. Records of Preston Roan. U.S. Census, 1860. Casswell Co., N.C., 713. Records of N. M. Roan. U.S. Slave Census, 1860. Casswell Co., N.C., 354; Records of H. H. Hunter. U.S. Census, 1860. Gates Co., N.C., 214. Records of H. H. Hunter. U.S. Slave Census, 1860. Gates Co., N.C., 238; Records of William H. Taylor. U.S. Census, 1860. Henrico Co., Va., 78.

8. Edge to [Sallie], 7 July 1863. Rozier, *Granite Farm Letters*, 116. For an excellent journal of a hospital steward, see Apperson, *Repairing the "March of Mars."*

9. L. M. Blackford to ?, n.d. Launcelot M. Blackford Papers, UVA; B. Lewis Blackford to Mother, 4 June 1862. Blackford Family Papers, UVA; A. Lee to Sister, 31 Mar. 1862. George Lee Robertson Papers, CAH; Robert Gaines Haile diary, 7 June 1862. King & Queen and Essex County Historical Sketches, UVA; W. N. Ward to Eddy, 3 Aug. [1863]. Ward Family Papers, LC; J. Thomas Petty diary, 7 June 1862. J. Thomas Petty Papers, MC.

10. AN ACT to authorize the employment of cooks and nurses, 21 Aug. 1861. *OR* 4 (1): 579–80; Circular. Office of Insp. of Hospitals. 2 July 1862. Brock Collection: Samuel P. Moore Papers, Huntington Library; GO, No. 13. HQ, AP. 14 Dec. 1861. GO&C, AP. RG 109, NA; GO, No. 95. A&IGO. 25 Nov. 1862. *OR* (2): 209–10; Cunningham. *Doctors in Gray*, 72.

11. John S. Apperson journal, 8 May and 1 Apr. 1863. Apperson, *Repairing*, 437 and 401; Thos. H. Williams to Sir, 13 Dec. 1861 and 22 Jan. 1862. LS, Med. Dir., ANV. RG 109, NA.

12. James R. Boulware diary, 27 Feb. 1863. James R. Boulware Papers, LV; R. Fairfax to Mama, 31 Jan. 1863. Fairfax Brothers Papers, MC; Case Book of Dr. Warner Lewis Baylor, 24 July–2 Aug. 1863. Baylor Family Papers, VHS; W. to Ellen, 25 May 1862. Murray Family Papers, LV.

13. An Act to provide for the sick and wounded of the Army in hospitals, 27 Sep. 1862. *OR* 4 (2): 199–200; Emory M. Thomas, *Confederate State of Richmond*, 54–59; Cunningham, *Doctors in Gray*, 45–54; Carol C. Green, *Chimborazo: The Confederacy's largest Hospital.*

14. Taylor, "Some Experiences," 93 and 107.

15. J. M. Tate to sister, 15 Nov. 1862. Jeremiah Tate Papers, Gilder-Lehrman Collection, ML; W. H. Darby to frind, 24 Sep. 1816[61]. A. H. Dalton to Father, 31 Sep. 1861. Dalton Family Papers, USC;

W. B. Short to Babie, 6 Mar. 1863. Confederate Soldiers: William B. Short, MC; Edwin Kerrison to Sister, 28 July 1863. Kerrison Family Papers, USC; Creed T. Davis diary, 5–6 July 1864. Creed T. Davis Papers, VHS; William H. Robertson to Friend & dear miss, 19 Apr. 1864. Donald Tiedeken Papers, VHS.

16. Mary Chesnut diary, 26 Aug. 1861. Chesnut, *Mary Chesnut's Civil War*, 164; Statement by Sallie Tompkins (probably), early 1863. C. W. Downing to Sallie Tompkins, 10 Nov. 1864. R. Townshend Dodson to Miss Sallie, 10 Aug. 1862. Sallie Tompkins Papers, MC; Elizabeth Coleman, "The Captain Was a Lady," *Virginia Cavalcade*, 6, 1, 35–41.

17. S. Moore to Sir, 17 June 1862. Brock Collection: Samuel Preston Moore Papers, Huntington Library; Circular. Surgeon General's Office. 25 June 1862. Circular. Surgeon General's Office. 22 July 1862. O&CR&OI, Med. Dir. Office, AP. RG 109, NA.

18. GO, No. 9. Med. Dir. &IO. 30 July 1862. GO, No. 20. Med. Dir. & IO. 21 Nov. 1862. O&CR & CI, Med. Dir. Office, AP. RG 109, NA.

19. R. H. Chilton to Surg. L. Guild, 14 Jan. 1864. L&TS, ANV. RG 109, NA; J. S. D. Cullen, Med. Dir. Of First Corps to Sir, 25 May 1863. L&OI&R, Chief Surgeon's Office, Gen. McLaws Division, 1862–64. RG 109, NA; *Richmond Examiner*, 2 Oct. 1861, P3; GO, No. 41. HQ, Huger's Division. 11 July 1862. Wright's Brigade Order book, CWTIC, USAMHI; A. S. Mason to Sir. 28 Nov. 1862. Brock Collection: Samuel Preston Moore Papers, Huntington Library; Medical and Surgical Assn. in Confederacy. File MC, S 788. MC; Addition to Medical Regulations. War Dept. 26 Mar. 1863. Jubal Early Papers, VHS. For a complaint of unsystematic procedures, see John S. Apperson journal, 23 Jan. 1863. Apperson, *Repairing*, 348.

20. Lee to Davis. 14 Aug. 1862. Freeman, ed., *Lee's Dispatches*, 48; Wm. J. Griggs to Pa., n.d. Griggs Family Papers, VHS; Henry to Wife, 20 Apr. 1862. Henry T. Owen Papers, LV; L. Guild to Gen. Moore, 15 Aug., 14 and 9 Jan., and 24 Mar. 1863. LS. Med. Dir. Office, ANV. RG 109, NA; John S. Apperson journal, 1 Apr. 1863. Apperson, *Repairing*, 401; GO, No. 8. Med. Dir. & I Office. 28 July 1862. Circular. Surgeon General's Office. 29 Nov. 1862. O&CR&OI, Med. Dir. Office, AP. RG 109, NA; James R. Boulware diary, 24 Dec. 1862 and 1 Jan. 1863. Dr. James R. Boulware Papers, LV; Joseph G. Covington to Wife, 14 Feb. 1863. Joseph G. Covington Papers, MC; Circular. Med. Dir. Office. 23 Mar. 1863. L&OI&R, Chief Surgeon's Office. Gen. McLaws Division, 1862–64. RG 109, NA; Thos. C. Elder to wife, 13 Apr. 1863. Thomas Elder Papers, VHS; Wm. B. Short to Babie, 18 Aug. 1863. Confederate Soldiers: William B. Short File, MC; Circular. Med. Dir. Office, ANV. 23 Mar. 1863. Wright's Brigade Order book, CWTIC, USAMHI; Robert P. Myers diary, 26 Dec. 1862. Robert P. Myers Papers, MC; Surg. Jno. H. Claiborne, "On the Use of Phytolaccor Desandra in Camp Itch," *Confederate States Medical and Surgical Journal* (Mar. 1864), 39.

21. Circular. Office of Inspector of Hospitals. Richmond, 12 Aug. 1862. Brock Collection: Samuel Preston Moore, Huntington Library; L. Guild to Surg. Gen. Moore, 30 Sep. 1864. L. Guild to Major A. H. Cole, 11 Apr. 1863. LS, Med. Dir. Office, ANV. RG 109, NA; SO, No. 12. Med. Dir. Office. 19 Aug. 1861. SO, No. 198. A&IGO. 31 Oct. 1861. Order Book, Thomas W. Williams Papers. Schenectady County Historical Society; Thos. H. Williams to Sir, 21 Oct., 17 Nov., and 16 Dec. 1861. Thos. H. Williams to Col., 8 Nov. 1861. LS, Med. Dir., ANV. RG 109, NA; GO, No. 110. HQ, ANV. 24 Sep. 1862. Wright's Brigade Order Book, CWTIC, USAMHI; J. T. Gilmer to Sir, 16 May 1863. Circular. Division HQ. 7 Jan. 1863. L&OI&R, Chief Surgeon's Office, Gen. McLaws Division, 1862–64. RG 109, F. W. Dawson to Mother. 1 July 1862. Francis Warrington Dawson Papers, DU; NA; Cunningham, *Doctors in Gray*, 118–20.

22. Case Book of Pvt. James Johnston. 17th Georgia, admitted 29 Aug. 1862. Case Book of Corp. T. N. Knight, 45th North Carolina, admitted 25 March 1865. Dr. Warner Lewis Baylor Papers, VHS; Records of Thomas Knight. U.S. Census, 1860. Rockingham Co., N.C., 88.

23. L. J. Shaw to Capt. Brown, 18 Oct. 1863. Individual Soldier Files: John B. Brown, NCDAH; J. G. Williford to Friend, 11 Sep. 1862. HCWRT, USAMHI.

24. Statistical Reports of Hospitals in Virginia. Cunningham, *Doctors in Gray*, Appendix II, 277–78.

25. Statistics compiled from Sample in Appendix I.

26. Statistics from Sample in Appendix I. Special thanks to Michael Rothman for charting the deaths by age.

27. Lee to Cooper, 26 Dec. 1862. Lee to Cooper, 26 Dec. 1863. L&TS, ANV. RG 109, NA; L. Guild to Sir, 9 and 15 Jan. 1863. LS, Med., Dir. Office, ANV. RG 109, NA.

28. L. Guild to Surg. Gen. Moore, 3 Sep. and 23 Oct. 1863 and 9 Apr. 1864. L. Guild to Lt. Col. Taylor, 13 Feb. 1864. LS, Med. Dir. Office, ANV. RG 109, NA; Samuel Preston Moore to Medical Directors in the Field & of Hospitals, 15 Mar. 1864. Box 4, Chase Family Papers, LC.

29. L. Guild to Surg. Gen. Moore, 19 and 30 June 1864. LS, Med. Dir. Office, ANV. RG 109, NA; J. Haring to my dear friend, 22 May 1864. Robertson Papers, GHS.

30. Circular. HQ, AP Med. Dir. Office. 20 Dec. 1861 O&CR&OI, Med. Dir. Office, AP. RG 109, NA; L. Guild to Surg. Gen. Moore, 23 Feb. 1864. L. Guild to Taylor, 13 Feb. 1864. L. Guild to Surg. Gen. Moore, 8 Aug. 1864. LS, Med. Dir. Office, ANV. RG 109, NA.

31. L. Guild to Co. Taylor, 27 Jan. 1865. LS, Med. Dir. Office, ANV. RG 109, NA.

31. Manpower

1. Lee to Seddon, 10 Jan. 1863. *OR* 21: 1085–86.

2. Lee to Hon. G. W. Randolph, 25 July 1862. L&TS. ANV. RG 109, NA.

3. Lee to Northrup, 11 Sep. 1863. Lee to Col. J. F. Gilmer, 8 Dec. 1862. Lee to Longstreet, 6 Mar. 1863. Lee to Seddon, 22 Oct. and 28 July 1863. Mason to Maj. Gen. Smith et al., 5 Feb. 1862. L&TS,

ANV. RG 109, NA; J. D. Imboden to Lee, 7 Feb. 1863. D. H. Hamilton to Major, 29 Dec. 1862. L, T&Other Papers Received by Lee. RG 109, NA; Endsmt by R. E. Lee to recommendation of Col. Wm. Peyton Johnston seeking a transfer, n.d. R. E. Lee Papers, Gilder-Lehrman Collection, ML; Thos. S. Mills to General, 12 Jan. 1863. Wright's Brigade Order Book, CWTIC, USAMHI; W. B. S[hort] to Babie, 10 Apr. 1863. Confederate Soldiers Papers: William B. Short, MC; GO, No. 21. HQ, ANV. 16 Feb. 1863. M921, R1, F504. G&SO&CI, ANV. RG 109, NA; William McWillie journal, n.d. [July 1862]. William McWillie Papers, MDAH.

4. N. F. Register to Father, 15 May 1862. Walker Collection: Pratt Folder, USAMHI; J. M. Weller to Laura, 18 Apr. 1862. Joseph M. Weller Papers, LV; J. M. Tate to sister, 23 Apr. 1862. Jeremiah Tate Papers, Gilder-Lehrman Collection, ML.

5. [Hill] to Wife, 22 Jan. 1862. Daniel Harvey Hill Papers, NCDAH; Circular. Med. Dur. & I Office. 7 July 1862. O&CR&OI, Med. Dir. Office, AP. RG 109, NA; W. B. Short to Babie, 6 Mar. 1863. Confederate Soldiers Papers: William B. Short, MC.

6. Jackson to Colonel, 21 and 31 Mar. 1862 Thomas J. Jackson Papers, DU.

7. Maben Hinshaw to Wife, 29 and 22 Jan. 1865. Meban Hinshaw Papers, DU; Records of Mebane Hinshaw. U.S. Census, 1860. Randolph Co., 142.

8. Ragsdale to Davis, 11 Sep. 1863. Endsmt. by 1st Lt. T. J. Selman, n.d. [Sep.–Oct. 1863]. Lt. Col. J. P. Bane, 17 Oct. 1863. M474. R80, F560–61. LR, CA&IGO. RG 109, NA.

9. J. B. Ragsdale to Davis, 4 July 1864. M474, R80, F551–57. LR, CA&IGO. RG 109, NA; Endsmt., Davis to Secretary of War, 28 July 1864. Crist et al., *Papers of Jefferson Davis*, 10, 497.

10. H. S. Nelson to wife, 9 Apr. 1862. Howell S. Nelson Papers, MC; Records of Howell S. Nelson. U.S. Census, 1860. Mecklenburg Co., Va., 60; Records of Howell S. Nelson. U.S. Slave Census, 1860. Mecklenburg Co., Va., 24; H. B. Blisset to father, 22 Aug. 1862. Blisset Family Papers, GDAH; Robert to Pa, 10 May 1863. Robert Stafford Papers, Gilder-Lehrman Collection, ML.

11. Records of Seth Combs. U.S. Census. 1860. Stafford Co., Va., 934: Records of Seth Combs. U.S. Slave Census. 1860. Stafford Co., Va., 351, 355, and 362–63; Records of John Dunning. U.S. Census. 1860. Charleston, S.C., 373, Ward 5; Records of James Dunning. U.S. Slave Census. 1860. Charleston. 462–63.

12. Alexander Colclough diary, 23–26 July 1862. Alexander Colclough Papers, USC.

13. GO, No. 136. HQ, ANV. 27 Dec. 1862. M921. RI, F326 and 330–31. G&SO&CI, ANV. RG 109, NA; CSR of George Raysor, B, 5th Florida. CSR of L. S. Childers, B, 5th Florida. M251, R50 and R66. RG 109, NA.; Records of George Raysor. U.S. Census, 1860. Jefferson Co., Fla., 902; Records of George Raysor. U.S. Slave Census, 1860. Jefferson Co., Fla., 214.

14. Judah P. Benjamin, Regulations concerning substitutes in the Army, 20 Oct. 1861. SO, No. 51. AIGO. 5 Mar. 1862. GO, No. 29. AIGO. 26 Apr. 1862, An ACT to provide for the public defense, 16 Apr. 1862. GO, No. 37. AIGO. 19 May 1862. *OR* 4 (1): 694–95, 971, 1093, 1099, and 1124; GO, No. 64. AIGO. 8 Sep. 1862. GO, No. 98. AIGO. 20 July 1863. Jefferson Davis to House of Representatives, 7 Dec. 1863. *OR* 4 (2): 78, 648, and 1040–41; GO, No. 60. HQ, ANV. 8 May 1863. M921, R1, F822. C&SO&CI, ANV. RG 109, NA; An Act to prevent the enlistment of substitutes in the military service of the Confederate States, 28 Dec. 1863. An Act to put an end to the exemption from military service of those who have heretofore furnished substitutes., 5 Jan. 1864. *OR* 4, 3: 11–12. See Moore, *Conscription and Conflict*, 27–45.

15. JS to Sarah, 16 May 1863. John G. Scurry Papers, Gilder-Lehrman Collection, ML; CSR of Edward S. Dean. M324, R28. Records of Edward S. Deane. U.S. Census, 1870. Nottaway Co., Va., R1669, 128.

16. GO, No. 86. HQ, ANV. 20 Aug. 1863. Corse's Brigade Order Book, MC; Taylor to Col., 3 Jan. 1864. Taylor to Sir, 30 Dec. 1863. L&TS, ANV. RG 109, NA; GO, No. 1. HQ, ANV. 1 Jan. 1864. General Order Book. 37th North Carolina Infantry. DU; Lee to Davis, 13 Apr. 1864. Freeman, ed., *Lee's Dispatches*, 155–56; IR of Bryan's Brigade by Lt. Col. Archer Anderson, 7 Apr. [1864]. IR of McLaws Division by Lt. Col. Archer Anderson, 12 Apr. 1864. R 2, F 110 and 65–66. IR. RG 109, NA; An Act to organize forces to serve the war, 17 Feb. 1864. *OR* 4 (3): 178.

17. Lee to Cooper. 15 Feb. 1864. B1, Telegraph Book. Ser. A. Lee's Headquarters Papers, VHS; Watkins Kearns diary, 14 Feb. 1864. Watkins Kearns Papers, VHS; Rawleigh to Sister, 29 Apr. [1864]. Rawleigh Dunaway Papers, LV; Lt. Joel Arthur Walker, "Forty-Fifth Georgia Infantry Regiment." 5 and 11. Civil War Miscellany: 45th Georgia Infantry, GDAH; CSR of Pvt. Bennett Rainey Jeffares, 38th Georgia Infantry. M266, R437.

18. CSR of Philip Brady, 1st Louisiana Infantry. M320, R73; CSR of Philip Brady, 2nd Richmond Howitzers. M324, R315; An ACT to amend an act entitled "An Act to provide further for the public defense," 27 Sep. 1862. *OR* 4 (2): 160; An Act to organize forces to serve during the war, 17 Feb. 1864. *OR* 4 (3): 178–81.

19. I. C. Shields to Page, 1 Oct. 1863. Monthly Progress Reports, from Before September 1862 through February 1865. Progress Reports for Conscription. Ch. I, Vol. 250. RG 109, NA; Report on the Number of Exemptions for Physical Disabilities to November 1, 1864 in Virginia. Ch. I, Vol. 239, Bureau of Conscription. Letters, Reports & Endorsements Sent, Nov. 1864–Mar. 1865. RG 109, NA. In CSR, North Carolina indicates its conscripts; other states do it seldom.

20. Some 51.2 percent were deemed physically ineligible to serve. Ch. I, Vol. 250. Report of the Number of Exemptions and of Each particular Class in the State of Virginia to November 1863. Progress Made in the Execution of the Conscription Law in Virginia, Month of November 1863. Revised Report Through 1 Nov. 1863 on conscription, 19 Nov. 1863. Ch. I, Vol. 235½. List of Exemptions in Virginia to 17 August 1864, Virginia Exemptions & Details to 17 Aug. 1864. Ch. I, Vols. 223–29. Special Orders, Camp of Instruction, Richmond, Virginia. RG 109, NA.

21. See Appendix I. According to the random sample, just below 3 percent were conscripts as indi-

cated in their military service records. Some 52.9 percent of soldiers and their parents were worth $400 or less. By contrast, 18.2 percent were worth over $10,000, and one of these was a merchant whose worth included his inventory. Some 59 percent were farmers; 65 percent were married, I would guess that between 6 percent and 8 percent of all soldiers who served in Lee's army were conscripts, but that is an informed guess. Seddon to Pillow, 12 Oct. 1863, LS, CSW, RG 109, NA; GO, No. 112. HQ, ANV. 31 Dec. 1863. M921, R1, F1055. G&SO&CI, ANV. RG 109, NA; T. C. Brady to Wife & Ben, 7 Jan. 1865. Brady Family Papers, CAH.

22. *Richmond Daily Examiner*, 22 Aug. 1862.

23. *Mobile Register*, n.d., reprinted in *Richmond Whig*, 23 Aug. 1862.

24. Monthly Progress Reports, from Before September 1862 through February 1865. Progress Reports for Conscription. Ch. I, Vol. 250. RG 109, NA; "The Conscript," by A. G. Knight, 2nd Co. W Arty. Box 11, F55B. Louisiana Historical Collection: Washington Artillery Papers, TU.

25. Records of J. B. Crawford. U.S. Census. 1860. Jasper Co., Miss., 399.

26. J. B. Crawford to Wife, 7 May and 12 June 1863. John Berryman Crawford Papers, MDAH; CSR of J. B. Crawford. 16th Mississippi Infantry. M269, R240. RG 109, NA. For another good conscript soldier, see CSR of Henry Thomas Hodges, 61st North Carolina Infantry. M270, R546. RG 109, NA.

27. J. B. Crawford to Wife, 16 and 23 May 1863. John Berryman Crawford Papers, MDAH.

28. J. B. Crawford to Wife, 12 June, 18 Oct., and 24 Nov. 1863 and 9 Feb. 1864. John Berryman Crawford Papers, MDAH.

29. J. B. Crawford to Wife, 8 July and 9 Aug. 1863. John Berryman Crawford Papers, MDAH.

30. J. B. Crawford to Wife, 17 Sep. and 7 and 14 Oct. 1863 and 18 Mar. and 15 Jan. 1864. John Berryman Crawford Papers, MDAH.

31. J. B. Crawford to Wife, 24 Jan., 18 Mar., and 9 Feb. 1864. John Berryman Crawford Papers, MDAH.

32. CSR of J. B. Crawford, 16th Mississippi Infantry. M269, R240. RG109, NA.

33. AAR of A. P. Hill, 24 Dec. 1862. *OR* 21: 647; J. A. Gillespie to Wife, 28 Apr. 1864. Jaspar A. Gillespie Papers, GDAH; [Tate] to sister Mary, 12 Sep. 1863. Jeremiah Tate Papers, Gilder-Lehrman Collection, ML; Marion [Koiner] to Mother, 21 Feb. 1864. David Ezra Papers, VHS: Husband to Wife, 10 Nov. 1864. Bryan Grimes Papers, SHC, UNC; Charles to Sister, 16 May 1863. Kerrison Family Papers, USC; L. S. Childers to Davis, 9 June 1863. M474, R61, F312–16. LR, AIGO. RG 109, NA; F to ?, 4 Feb 1864, I, E. Shaffner Papers, NCDAH.

34. B. G. Brown to Father & Mother, 22 Jan. 1867. Brown Family Papers, UVA; Lee to Longstreet, 22 Jan. 1863. L&TS, ANV. RG 109, NA; La Gayden Batchelor to brother M, 30 Aug. 1803. Albert A. Batchelor Papers, LSU; Richard Rouzie, Jr., to Sister, 5 Oct. 1863. Rouzie Family Papers, WM; Records of Hugh Billups. Records of Peter Campbell. U.S. Census, 1860. Essex Co., Va., 36 and 84. Records of Hugh Billups. Records of Peter Campbell. U.S. Slave Census, 1860. Essex Co., Va., 36 and 70.

35. Col. John S. Preston to Secretary of War Seddon, 30 Apr. 1864, with enclosures. *OR* 4 (3): 354–64. Gallagher, *Confederate War*, 34–35.

32. Desertion

1. Lee to Davis, 17 Aug. 1863. Dowdey and Manarin, eds., *Wartime Papers*, 591; Lee to Davis, 13 Apr. 1864. Freeman, ed., *Lee's Dispatches*, 157–58. The classic study on desertion is Ella Lonn, *Desertion During the Civil War*, More recently. Mark A. Weitz, in *More Damning than Slaughter: Desertion in the Confederate Army*, argues essentially the same thing. Weitz tries more forcefully to support the argument in McWhiney and Jamieson. *Attack and Die*, and others that the Confederacy lost because of manpower. Where McWhiney and Jamieson place the blame on Confederate generals who bled the nation to death, Weitz affixes it to desertion. In Lee's army, desertion was a problem, but it became critical after Lincoln's re-election, and it was reflective of all sorts of other problems. Lee's army could barely feed and clothe the soldiers that it had long before Lincoln's re-election, let alone attend to concerns on the home front.

2. Richard T. Davis to wife, 3 June 1863. Preston-Davis Papers, UVA; Lee to Cooper, 4 Jan. 1864. C. S. Venable Papers, CAH.

3. Moxley Sorrel diary, 17 and 18 July 1864. Moxley Sorrel Papers, MC; Col. George H. Sharpe to Gen. Humphreys, 9 Sep. 1863, and General Martindale, 12 Dec. 1863. Bab[cock] to McEntee, 14 Nov. 1864. Information from examination of scouts, deserters, etc., Army of the Potomac. RG 108, NA.

4. Coulter, *Confederate States of America, 1861–1865*, 463; GO, No, 58, 51, and 62, HQ, AP, 1st Corps. 8 and 29 Sep. 1861. GO&C, AP. RG 109, NA; Thomas L. Feamster diary, 15 Jan. 1864. Feamster Family Papers, LC; Wm to Wife, [5 Jan. 1863?]. Murray Family Papers, LV; John Nelson Old diary, 27 Mar. 1863. J. N. Old to Catherine, 10 Apr. 1863. John N. Old Papers, FSNBP; John E. Armstrong remin., CWTIC, USAMHI; Wills Lee remin., 6–7. Wills Lee Papers, FSNBP. AWOL offenses often were not listed on muster rolls or CSRs, so it is difficult to get some numbers. Lee's statements of over 5,000 AWOL in a month speaks volumes of the numbers.

5. Some 15.48 percent of the army deserted. Of all deserters, only 8.7 percent returned, which means that 91.3 percent did not return. The U.S. government reported statistics that Ella Lonn included in Table II of her classic study, *Desertion During the Civil War*, 232. Those statistics are absurd.

6. Sample in Appendix I. Among deserters, 21.2 percent either owned slaves, or their parents with whom they resided owned slaves, compared to 39.2 percent of nondeserters. About 26.2 percent of deserters lived in slaveholding households, compared to 46.7 percent of nondeserters.

7. Sample in Appendix I. According to the sample, 98 percent of all married deserters had children, compared to 69 percent of married nondeserters. In the sample, 28.88 percent of nondeserters had children, compared to 41.84 percent of deserters. Some 40.3 percent of deserters in the sample were married, compared to 36.27 percent of nondeserters.

8. See sample in Appendix I. Some 37 percent of cavalrymen who deserted were born in the 1820s or earlier, compared 19.6 percent of infantry and 20 percent of artillery.

9. Artillerists deserted at a rate of 12 percent, cavalry at 18.7 percent, and infantry at 15.3 percent.

10. See sample in Appendix I. By years of enlistment, 14.2 percent of soldiers from 1861, 13.6 percent in 1862, and 22.6 percent in 1863 and 1864 deserted.

11. CSR of Abner Vance, 60th Virginia Infantry; Records of Abner Vance. U.S. Census, 1860. Monroe Co., Va., 1009; C. G. Hamilton to Father, 23 June 1863. Colier Green and Oliver Clark Hamilton Papers, NCDAH; *North Carolina Troops*, 9, 10, 79; Eli Landers to Mother, n.d. Landers, *Weep Not for Me*, 104; Marcus Hefner to Wife, 10 July 1863. Marcus Hefner Papers, NCDAH; Daniel Wilson to Friends, 1 Aug. 1862. Constantine A. Hege File, Lewis Leigh Collection, USAMHI; J. W. Tindall to Wife, 25 May 1864. J. W. Tindall Papers, USC; J. Babcock to General, 5 Sep. 1863. Information from examination of scouts, deserters, etc., Army of the Potomac. RG 108, NA.

12. Allen and Bohannon, eds., *Campaigning with "Old Stonewall,"* 101; James F. Knick to Wife and Children, 21 Feb. 1864. James F. Knick Papers, LV; T. B. Barron to Parents, 8 Aug. 1863. T. B. Barron Papers, MC.

13. C. A. Hege to Parents, 7 Sep. 1863. Lewis Leigh Collection, USAMHI; W. D. Smith to wife, 27 July 1863, and Father, 2 Sep. 1863. William D. Smith Papers, DU.

14. See sample in Appendix I.

15. Busey and Martin, *Regimental Strengths and Losses at Gettysburg*, 599–602 and 506.

16. Thomas C. Elder to wife, 21 Aug. 1863. Thomas Elder Papers, VHS; Busey and Martin, *Regimental Strengths and Losses at Gettysburg*, 599–602 and 506; J. F. Coghill to Pappy Ma and Mit, 10 Aug. 1863. Jonathan F. Coghill Papers, Auburn U.: [H. C. Albright] to Brother, 21 Aug. 1863. Henry Clay Albright Papers, NCDAH; J. W. Wright to Father Mother and Fanny, 17 and 22 June 1863. John Wright Family Papers, NCDAH; Marcus Hefner to Wife, 19 May and 10 July 1863. Marcus Hefner Papers, NCDAH; John Rogers to Brother, 20 Aug. 1863. Confederate Miscellany, EU.

17. J. W. Wright to [Father], n.d. [Sep. 1864], John Wright Family, NCDAH: 7th North Carolina Infantry. http://www.itd.nps.gov/cwss/regiments.cfm.

18. John Futch to Wife, 19 and 31 July and 6 and 16 Aug. 1863. Futch Brothers Papers, NCDAH; *North Carolina Troops*, 3, 593; Records to John Futch. U.S. Census, 1860. Hanover Co., N.C., 842; Records of John Futch. U.S. Slave Census, 1860. Hanover Co., N.C., 282.

19. David Ballenger to Nancy, 30 July 1863, V. 294, David Ballenger Papers, FSNBP (originals, at CL, UM); CSR of Cicero Farrar, 42nd Mississippi Infantry. M269, R394. RG 109, NA; Records of Cicero Farrar. U.S. Census, 1860. Itawamba Co., Miss., 18.

20. James F. Knick to Wife and children, 21 Feb. 1864. James F. Knick Papers, LV; Col. Geo. H. Sharpe to Maj Gen Humpreys, 23 Apr. 1864. Information from the examination of scouts, deserters, etc. RG 108, NA; IR of Two Divs of Infy. & Artillery under Beauregard at Petersburg, 10 Sep. 1864, by Lt. Col. A. Truman. IR, R16, F460. IR of Pickett's Division by Maj. Walter Harrison, 28–29 Aug. 1864. R10, F276 and 283–84. RG 109, NA; James Oswald to John, 15 July 1864. John G. Scurry Papers, Gilder-Lehrman Collection, USAMHI; Anthony to Sue, 23 Aug. [1864]. Anthony Graybill Papers, V. 335, FSNBP.

21. Sharpe to Humphreys, 24 Aug. and 8 Oct. 1863 and 19 Apr. 1864. Sharpe to General Martindale, 12 Dec. 1863. Statement of S. B. Flandreau, 8th Louisiana, 22 May 1863. Information from examination of scouts, deserters, etc., Army of the Potomac. RG 108, NA; Meade to Wife, 15 Sep. 1864. Meade, *Life and Letters of Gen. Geo. Gordon Meade*, II, 228; M. B. Steele diary, 22 Oct. 1863. Henry Carter Lee Papers, MC.

22. Geo. K. Harlow to father Mother & Family, 4 Oct. 1862 and 21 Jan. 1863. Harlow Family Papers, VHS; William J. Brightwell to Dear and Devoted Wife, 9 Dec. 1862. Donald Tiedeken Papers, VHS; GO, No. 66. HQ, ANV. 25 May 1863. GO, No. 87. HQ, ANV. 10 Sep. 1863. GO, No. 88. 17 Sep. 1863. GO, No. 9. HQ, ANV. 27 Jan. 1864, M921, R1, F862, 919, 935–36, and 1136–137. RG 109, NA; F to ?, 4 Feb. 1864. J. E. Shaffner Papers, NCDAH.

23. *New York Herald*, 19 Feb. 1862, P4; *Atlanta Southern Confederacy*, 4 Jan. 1863; GO, No. 43. AIGO. 13 June 1862. Wright's Brigade Order Book, CWTIC, USAMHI; Circular. HQ, Valley District. 23 Oct. 1862. General Order Book, 37th North Carolina Infantry, DU; G. K. Griggs to Biller, 11 Nov. 1862. Anderson Folder, CWTIC, USAMHI; *Wilmington Journal*, 1 Oct. 1862; Lee to Cooper, 12 Jan. 1863. Taylor to Elzey, 20 May 1863. L&TS, ANV. RG 109, NA; Lee to Stuart, 20 May 1863. Lee to Jones, 26 May 1863. Lee to Jones, Stuart, Davisdon & Lane, 4 June 1863. Box 1, Telegraph Book, Ser. a, Lee's Headquarters Papers, VHS; GO, No. 127. HQ, ANV. 14 Nov. 1862. *OR* 19 (2): 722; List of Absentees from 38th North Carolina. *State Journal*, 1 Oct. 1862. William Dorsey Pender Papers, NCDAH.

24. Proclamation [1 Aug. 1863]. *OR* 4 (2): 687–88; H. Meade to Mother, 15 Aug. 1863. Meade Family Papers, VHS. Johnston's Brigade issued a Circular encouraging deserters to return. Circular. HQ, Johnston's Brigade. 28 Jan. 1864. Second Army Corps, O&C of Subcommands, ANV. RG 109, NA.

25. Lt. Col. J. W. Lay to Cooper, 24 June 1863. IR, R2, F358–60. RG 109, NA; A. C. Haskell to Ma, 19 Sep. 1863. Alexander C. Haskell Papers, SHC, UNC; Capt. T. Scott to Col. Latrobe, 1 Mar. 1865. Box 4, Series a, Lee's Headquarters Papers, VHS; Ema to William, 8 June 1863. William G. Parker Papers, NCDAH; F to Carrie, 25 Sep. 1863. F to ?, 1 Nov. 1863. J. E. Shaffner Papers, NCDAH; Joseph Harper to [Davis], 25 Sep. 1863. M437, R96, F799–800. LS, CSW. RG 109, NA; Lt. W. Fish to Col. Grimes, 3 Oct. 1863. Vol. II, 1863–70. Bryan Grimes Papers, NCDAH; W. Walsh to Miss R. L. Proffit, 29 Sep. 1863. Proffit Family Papers, SHC, UNC; S. M. Kermit? to Capt., 23 May 1864. William Ephraim Smith Papers, DU; A. M. Scales to Wife, 10 Aug. 1864. Alfred M. Scales Papers, NCDAH.

26. Henry Wingfield diary, 30 Aug–18 Sep. 1863. Vol. 167, Henry Wingfield Papers, FSNBP; H. Ringstaff to Sir, 10 June 1863. Box 5, Chase Family Papers, LC; Special Order, No. 532. HQ, AP. 19 Nov. 1862. SOI, AP, Dec. 1861–Sep. 1863. RG 109, NA; Renshaw, *Louisiana Historical Quarterly*, 10, 2, 241–48.

27. Chars. J. C. Hutson to Father, 7 Nov. 1863. Charles J. C. Hutson Papers, Gilder-Lehrman Collection, NYHS. Thanks to Peter Carmichael for passing along this document.
28. J. W. Calton to Brother, 30 Dec. 1863. John Washington Calton Papers, NCDAH; Thos. Settle to Gov. Vance, 4 Oct. 1864. Thomas J. Settle, Jr., Papers, NCDAH (originals in Hampton L. Carson Collection, Free Library of Philadelphia); J. L. Wright to Father, 2 Sep. 1864. John Wright Family Papers, NCDAH; Calvin J. Cowles to W. W. Holden, 25 July 1864. Letterbook "L," Feb.–Nov. 1864. Calvin J. Cowles Papers, NCDAH; Tom [Branson] to Emily, 14 Oct. 1862. Branson Family Papers, NCDAH; Margaret E. Baggarly to husband, 23 Nov. 1863. Tillman F. Baggarly Papers, DU.
29. Louis Leon diary, 26 Feb. and 23 Mar. 1863. Leon, *Diary of Tar Heel*, 18 and 20; John O'Farrell diary, 20 Feb. 1863. John O'Farrell Papers, MC; Jno. J. Reev to Miss Parke, 8 June 1862. George William Bagby Papers, VHS; C. A. Hege to Parents, 30 Sep. 1863. Lewis Leigh Collection, USAMHI; GO, No. 102. HQ, Army Valley District. 8 Oct. 1862. Miscellaneous T. J. Jackson Papers, MC; Saml. H. Walkup diary, 23 June 1863. Samuel Hoey Walkup Papers, SHC, UNC; Tillman F. Beggarly to Wife, 28 July 1863. Tillman F. Beggarly Papers, DU; Marcus Hefner to [wife], 29 [Aug.?] 1863. Marcus Hefner Papers, NCDAH; A. M. Miller to Sister, 5 Dec. 1863. Confederate Papers, SHC, UNC.
30. Christopher to Father, 6 Sep. 1864. Christopher Winsmith Papers, MC.
31. Robert Hatchie, Jr., to Davis, 18 May 1863. M437, R86, F585–88. LR, CSW. RG 109, NA; Marchal and Jane Trent to Lee, 2 Mar. 1864. Box 2, Lee Papers, NA.
32. Husband to Darling, 23 Apr. 1864. Bryan Grimes Papers, SHC, UNC; Jacob E. Lanier to father and Mother, 2 Sep. 1863. J. C. Lanier to Father, Mother, Brother and Sister and Friends, 20 Sep. 1863. Elkana Lanier to Wife, 20 Sep. 1863. E. Mc. Lanier to Wife, 24 Sep. 1863. J. E. Lanier to Friends, 24 Sep. 1863. Lanier Family Letters, Typescripts in possession of the author.
33. James W. Wright to Fanny, 24 Mar. 1864. John Wright Family, NCDAH; W. C. McClellan to Sister, 20 Feb. [1863]. Buchanan-McClellan Papers, SHC, UNC; William F. Chancely to Cousin, 27 Sep. 1863. CWMC, USAMHI; F to ?, 30 Apr. 1864. J. E. Shaffner Papers, NCDAH; Samuel Walkup diary, 24 Mar. 1864. Samuel H, Walkup Papers, SHC, UNC; Records of Thomas W. Deal. U.S. Census, 1860. Burke Co., N.C., 396; J. Elmore Hall to father, 6 Oct. 1864. Bolling Hall Family Papers, ADAH. Tom Lowry, the leading expert on courts-martial, believed 338 soldiers in Lee's army were sentenced to death. Lee rarely remitted sentences, according to Lowry. Tom Lowry to author, 22 Jan. 2007. Copy in author's possession.
34 John W. Watson to Sister, 7 Apr. 1864. Watson Papers, FSNBP; S. H. Walkup to Wife, 28 Jan. 1864. Samuel H. Walkup Papers, SHC, UNC; H. R. Berkeley diary, 0 Jan. 1064. H. R. Berkeley Papers, MC; James E. Phillips memoirs, 40.
35. Bryan Grimes to Taylor, 25 Apr. 1864. Bryan Grimes Papers, DU.
36. Silas Chandler to wife, 5 Aug. 1863. John J. and Silas Chandler Papers, LV.

33. The Grind of War

1. W. J. Pegram to Jennie, 14 July 1864. Pegram-Johnson-McIntosh Papers, VHS; Meade to Wife, 7 July 1864. Meade, *Life and Letters*, II, 211.
2. Council to wife, 23 May 1864. Council A. Bryan Papers, FSA; Grant to Halleck, 11 May 1864. *OR* 36 (2): 627; E. Fairfax to Ma, 3 Sep. 1864. Fairfax Brothers Papers, MC; Henry to Mother, 3 Oct. 1864. Henry I. and Robert Greer Papers, LC; Rob to Mother, 2 Oct. 1864. Robert Stiles Papers, VHS; Crenshaw Hall to Father, 26 Sep. 1864. Bolling Hall Family Papers, ADAH.
3. Lee to Anderson, 22 June 1864. Taylor to Anderson, 22 June 1864. Edward Porter Alexander Papers, SHC, UNC; John C. Donahue diary, 29–30 June 1864. John C. Donahue Papers, LV; Lee to Davis, 5 July 1864. Freeman, ed., *Lee's Dispatches*, 274–75; Frank to wife, 7 July 1864. Frank Riley Papers, UVA; L. A. Dalton to par, 29 July 1864. Lewis Leigh Collection, USAMHI; [Wade] to Fisher, 10 Sep. and 5 Oct. 1864. Hampton Family Papers, USC; Lee to Fitz Lee, 17 Sep. 1864. Fitzhugh Lee Papers, UVA; Lee to Hampton, 8 Oct. 1864. R. E. Lee Papers, Gilder-Lehrman Collection, ML; Lee to Hampton, *The Destruction of the Weldon Railroad; Deep Bottom, Globe Tavern, and Reams Station, August 14–25, 1864.*
4. Linden Kent to Ma, 2 Oct. 1864. Linden Kent Papers, MC; Alexander to [Wife], 3 Oct. 1864. Edward Porter Alexander Papers, SHC, UNC. See Richard J. Sommers, *Richmond Redeemed: The Siege at Petersburg.*
5. Willie to Mother, 10 Feb. 1863. William Dame Papers, FSNBP; John Keely to John, 25 Sep. 1863. John G. Scurry Papers, Gilder-Lehrman Collection, ML.
6. Robert E. Pack diary, 6 June 1864. *Southern Historical Society Papers*, vol. 1, 371; M. Hill Fitzpatrick to Amanda, 24 Sep. 1864. "Letters to Amanda," CWMC, USAMHI; [J. C. Featherston] to wife, 24 July 1864. Irvine-Saunders Papers, UVA; R. W. Royall to Mother, 24 Aug. 1864. Royall Family Papers, MC; J. E. Hall to Father, 27 Aug. 1864. Bolling Hall Papers, ADAH; John to Mother, 6 Dec. 1864. John G. Scurry Papers, Gilder-Lehrman Collection, ML; William A. Davis to Sister. 8 Dec. 1864. Lewis Leigh Collection, USAMHI; Rice D. M. Lucas to ?, 5 Dec. 1864. "Grape and Canister," newsletter of Civil War Round Table of Wilmington, Feb. 1984. HCWRT, USAMHI; Chesnut, *Mary Chesnut's Civil War*, 159.
7. J. C. Featherston to Wife, 1 and 2 Aug. 1864. Irvine-Saunders Papers, UVA; Sydnor to Omis, 1 Aug. 1864. Sydnor Barksdale Papers, MC; Frank Huger to Mother, 2 Aug. 1864. Frank Huger Papers, copy in possession of Gary Gallagher, who shared them with the author; J. W. Wright to Fanny, 2 Aug. 1864. John Wright Family Papers, NCDAH; Henry Biggs to Sister, 3 Aug. 1864. Asa Biggs Papers, DU; D. N. Binion to Sister, 10 Aug. 1864. Confederate Miscellany, EU; C. T. Dewese to farther, n.d. Aug. 1864. Dewese Family Papers, LV; [J. P. Verdery] to Sister, 31 July 1864. J. P. Verdery Papers, DU; W. J. Pegram to Jennie, 1 Aug. 1864. Pegram-Johnson-McIntosh Papers, VHS; Robt. W. Hicks diary, 31 July 1864. Robert W. Hicks Papers, MC. Freeman does not deal with Lee and the atrocity. Emory Thomas,

in *Robert E. Lee*, 342, feels Lee must have known and did nothing about it. Michael Fellman in *The Making of Robert E. Lee*, 205, states, "If General Lee knew of this significant incident, he did not respond to it." J. C. Featherston in his letter dated 2 Aug. 1864 stated, "It is said that Genl Lee who was looking on when he saw we were successful pulled off his hat and waved it & said 'well done' I heard Genl Pendleton of the artillery say it was 'one of the most brilliant successes of the campaign, for the enemy expected great results from it & had been caught in their own trap.'" See Michael A. Cavanaugh and William Marvel, *The Battle of the Crater: "The Horrid Pit," June 25–August 6, 1864*.

8. G to Sister, 6 Nov. 1864. Augustus Clewell Papers, NCDAH; Thomas Morris Chester story, 18 Aug. 1864. Thomas Chester, *Thomas Morris Chester*, 106; Lewis to Mother, 8 March 1865. Launcelot M. Blackford Papers, UVA; [John C. Ashton] to friends, 25 Oct. 1864. Cocke Family Papers, VHS; SO, No. 167. HQ, ANV. 18 July 1864. Box 4, Ser. a, Lee Headquarters Papers, VHS; E. S.[?] Tapp to George, 14 June 1864. Tapp Papers, MC; A. W. Wallace to Hen, 17 July 1864. Armistead-Blanton-Wallace Papers, VHS; John W. Hampton to Uncle and Family, 9 June 1864. Caleb Hampton Papers, DU. See Gray, *The Warriors*, 142–48.

9. Lee to Davis, 6 July 1864. Freeman, ed., *Lee's Dispatches*, 368.

10. Jno. W. Daniel to Father, 9 Aug. 1863. John Warwick Daniel Papers, UVA; Jackson to Cooper, MC-1, A–B, Southern Historical Society Papers, MC; Husband to Darling, 12 June 1864. Bryan Grimes Papers, SHC, UNC; [Thomas Goree] to Sister, 21 Oct. 1864. Goree, ed., 233; Charles M. Squire memoirs, 6. CWTIC, USAMHI.

11. Husband to Wife, 22 June 1864. Bryan Grimes Papers, SHC, UNC; John S. Apperson journal, 25 June 1864. Apperson, *Repairing the "March of Mars,"* 506; S.D.R. to Bride, 30 June 1864. Stephen Dodson Ramseur Papers, SHC, UNC; Robert [Stafford] to Sister Anna, 15 July 1864. Robert Stafford Papers, Gilder-Lehrman Collection, ML.

12. Joseph McMurren diary, 14 July 1864. Joseph McMurren Papers, LV; William N. Old diary, 11 July 1864. William W. Old Papers, LC; Giles Buckner Cooke diary, 14 July 1864. Giles Buckner Cooke Papers, VHS; Brother to Brother, 1 Aug. 1864. S.D.R. to Bride, 30 June and 23 July 1864. Stephen D. Ramseur Papers, SHC, UNC.

13. Tom to Parents, 23 July [1864]. Bomar Family Papers, EU; C. C. Blacknall to Captain, 31 July 1864. Oscar W. Blacknall Papers, NCDAH.

14. Early to Edward Bok, n.d. Early Family Papers, VHS; Narration of Francis West Chamberlayne. Chamberlayne Family Papers, VHS.

15. Husband to Wife, 23 July and 18 Aug. 1864. Stephen D. Ramseur Papers, SHC, UNC; Rodes to Ewell, 12 Sep. 1864. *OR* 36 (1): 353–54; G. W. Wills to Pa, 24 Aug. 1864. William Henry Wills Papers, SHC, UNC; William Stokes to Wife, 27 Sep. 1864. William Stokes Papers, USC.

16. Isaac Prillaman to Brother, 30 July 1864. Prillaman Papers, FSNBP; Creed T. Davis diary, 8 Sep. 1864. Creed T. Davis Papers, VHS; Husband to Wife, 20 Aug. 1864. Bryan Grimes Papers, SHC, UNC; C. C. Blacknall to Captain, 31 July 1864, and Jenny, 7 Aug. [1864]. Oscar WW. Blacknall Papers, NCDAH; [T. Rowland] to Mother, 1 Aug. 1864. Kate Mason Rowland Papers, MC.

17. [Wade Hampton] to Fisher, 10 Sep. 1864. Hampton Family Papers, USC; Joseph [Trundle] to Sister, 25 July 1864. Lewis Leigh Collection, USAMHI; Thos. T. Greene to Elise, 12 and 14 July 1864. Greene Family Papers, VHS; T. P. Devereux to father, 1 Sep. 1864. Thomas Pollock Devereux Papers, NCDAH; IR of Pegram's Brigade by Lt. W. B. McNumas, 30 Sep. 1864. IR, R10, F717. RG 109, NA.

18. See Glatthaar, "U.S. Grant and the Union High Command During the 1864 Valley Campaign," in Gary W. Gallagher, ed., *The Shenandoah Valley Campaign of 1864*, 48–50.

19. Lee to Anderson, 29 Aug. 1864. R. E. Lee Papers, Gilder-Lehrman Collection, ML; G. H. Moffett journal, n.d., 48–49. George H. Moffett Papers, SCHS.

20. Lee to Fitz Lee, 17 Sep. 1864. Fitzhugh Lee Papers, UVA. For a good account of these actions, see Jeffry D. Wert, *From Winchester to Cedar Creek: The Shenandoah Valley Campaign of 1864*.

21. Lee to Early, 26 Aug. 1864. *OR* 43 (1): 1006.

22. S. S. Lee to Carter. 30 Sep. 1864, Fitzhugh Lee Papers, UVA; Thos. T. Green to [Elise], 20 Sep. 1864. Greene Family Papers, VHS; Brother to Brother, 10 Oct. 1864. Stephen D. Ramseur Papers, SHC, UNC; Henry Beck diary, 19 Sep. 1864. Henry Beck Papers, AHS; G. P. Ring to Wife, 21 Sep. 1864. Box 2. Louisiana Historical Collection: Papers of ANV, TU; Sam to Parents, 21 Sep. 1864. Samuel P. Collier Papers, NCDAH. See Roger U. Delauter and Brandon H. Beck. *The Third Battle of Winchester*.

23. Early to Lee, 9 Oct. 1864. Lee to Seddon, 20 and 23 Sep. 1864. *OR* 43 (1): 554–56 and 552; Husband to Wife, 7 Sep. 1864. Stephen D. Ramseur Papers, SHC, UNC; Richard T. Davis to Wife, 20 Sep. 1864. Preston-Davis Papers, UVA; Husband to Wife, 22 Sep. 1864. Bryan Grimes Papers, SHC, UNC. Robert E. L. Krick, "A Stampeede of Stampeeds: The Confederate Disaster at Fisher's Hill," Gallagher, ed., *The Shenandoah Valley Campaign of 1864*, 166–99.

24. G. P. Ring to Wife, 21 Sep. 1864. Box 2, Louisiana Historical Collection: Papers of ANV, TU; Robert E. Park diary, 11 Sep. 1864. *Southern Historical Society Papers*, vol. 1, 435; Tom to Kate, n.d. [Sep. 1864]. Thomas Pollock Devereux Papers, NCDAH; Robert Tooler Myers diary, 26 Sep. 1864. Robert Tooler Myers Papers, MC.

25. Husband to Wife, 10 Oct. 1864. Gordon and Rosser Families Papers, UVA; Sam P. Collier to Parents, 11 Oct. 1864. Samuel P. Collier Papers, NCDAH; Husband to Wife, 10 Oct. 1864. Bryan Grimes Papers, SHC, UNC; Field Returns of Lomax's (Old) Cavalry Brigade, 24 Oct. 1864. IR, R8, F461. RG 109, NA.

26. B. K. Whittle diary, 6 Oct. 1864. Whittle Family Papers, UVA; Husband to Wife, 3 Oct. 1864. Bryan Grimes Papers, SHC, UNC; Lee to Early, 27 Sep. 1864. *OR* 43 (1): 558–59.

27. Early to Lee, 21 Oct. 1864. Hotchkiss journal, 17–19 Oct. 1864. *OR* 43 (1): 561 and 1030–31.

28. Robert Tooler Myers, 19 Oct. 1864. Robert Tooler Myers Papers, MC; P. A. McMichael diary, 19 Oct. 1864. McMichael Papers, SCHS; Hotchkiss journal, 17–19 Oct. 1864. *OR* 43 (1): 1031.

29. Charles to Fluvanna Friend, 2 Nov. 1864. Bowles-Jordan Papers, UVA; Saml. J. C. Moore to

wife, 25 Oct. 1864. Samuel J. C. Moore Papers, SHC, UNC; Samuel M. Sublett to Sister, 3 Nov. 1864. William H. Jones Papers, DU; Early to Taylor, 20 Oct. 1864. Early to Lee, (twice) 21 Oct. 1864. Hotchkiss journal, 17–19 Oct. 1864. *OR* 43 (1): 560–64 and 1031.

30. [Thomas Goree] to Sister, 21 Oct. 1864. Goree, ed., 233; Thos. Greene to Elise, 28 Oct. 1864. Greene Family Papers, VHS; Sam P. Collier to Parents, 22 and 26 Oct. 1864. Samuel O. Collier Papers, NCDAH; John S. Apperson journal, 19 Oct. 1864. Apperson, *Repairing the "March of Mars"*, 601 and 599; Husband to Wife, 23 and 19 Oct. 1864. Bryan Grimes Papers, SHC, UNC.

31. Lee to Hampton, 19 Nov. 1864 (Confidential). Hampton Family Papers, USC. Early was busy at the time dealing with Union cavalry. See *OR* 43 (2): 918–25.

32. Grant to Meade, 30 July 1864. *OR* 40 (3): 638–39; L. M. Blackford to Mother, 16 Oct. 1864. Launcelot M. Blackford Papers, UVA; Taylor, "Some Experiences," 96; IR of Hoke's Division by Maj. James M. Adams, 29 Oct. 1864. 1R, R11, F359. IR of Johnson's Division by Capt. W. H. Whitner, 30 Oct. 1864. IR, R11, F474. RG 109, NA; Lowe and Hodges, eds., *Letters to Amanda*, 181–82.

33. John C. Evans to Annie, 3 Dec. 1864. John C. Evans Papers, AHS; Fred Fleet to Lou, 26 Nov. and 21 Dec. 1864. Fleet and Fleet, *Green Mount*, 347–48 and 350; [Q. S. Adams] to Mother, 23 Nov. 1864. Addams Family Folder, CWTIC, USAMHI; John G. Scurry to Sarah, 25 Nov. 1864. John G. Scurry Papers, Gilder-Lehrman Collection, ML; Y. M. Moody to Wife, 26 Dec. 1864. Young Marshall Moody Papers, Rice U.

34. E. R. Crockett diary, 16 July 1864. E. R. Crockett Papers, CAH; Husband to Liz, 19 Oct. 1864. George H. Moffett Papers, SCHS; John E. Hall to Father, 10 Nov. 1864. Bolling Hall Family, ADAH.

35. S. S. Lee to Carter, 30 Sep. 1864. Fitzhugh Lee Papers, UVA; Francis W. Dawson to Mother. 13 Oct. 1864. Francis Warrington Dawson Papers, GU; Taylor to Sister, 21 Oct. 1864. Goree, 232; John T. Stott diary, 29 Mar. 1865. CWTIC, USAMHI; Latrobe to Field & Hoke, 12 Nov. 1864. Longstreet to Taylor, 28 Nov. 1864. Longstreet to Lee, 7 Dec. 1864. Latrobe to Ewell, 17 Dec. 1864. Latrobe to Col. J. L. Davis, 25 Dec. 1864. Longstreet Order Book, CAH; IR of Pickett's Division by Maj. Walter Harrison, 30 Nov. 1864. IR, R13, F60. RG 109, NA.

36. Henri J. Mugler journal, 1, 3, and 5 June 1864. Henri J. Mugler Papers, VA, Vol. 13. RNBP; Taylor to [Bettie], 1 June 1864. Walter H. Taylor Papers, NPL.

37. Report of Casualties of Heth's Division during campaign of 1864. Henry Heth Papers, MC; Rhea, *Wilderness*, 194; IR of Law's Brigade, Field's Division, Longstreet's Corps, 8 Sep. 1864. IR, R3, F361–63. RG 109, NA; Morning Report of Capt. John B. Brown's Company ("B") 3rd Regt. N.C. Troops for November 1864. Morning Reports, 1861–64. John B. Brown Papers, NCDAH; R. Stuart to ?, 13 Sep. 1864. Osman Latrobe Papers, LC; Lee to Davis, 2 Nov. 1864. Freeman, ed., *Lee's Dispatches*, 305; L. M. Blackford to Mother, 14 June 1864. Launcelot Minor Blackford Papers, UVA; Moore, *Conscription and Conflict*, 319–20.

38. Geo. to Lucy, 27 Oct. 1864. Bowles-Jordan Papers, UVA; Confidential Circular. HQ, ANV. 29 Dec. 1864. Bryan Grimes Papers, NCDAH; Longstreet to Lee, 30 Dec. 1864. Longstreet Order Book, CAH; Alexander to Wife, 30 Oct. 1864. Edward Porter Alexander Papers, SHC, UNC; Seddon to Davis, 15 Dec. 1864. LSW, CSW to President, 1861–1865. M523, R1, F174. RG 109, NA; George W. Brent to Beauregard, 18 Dec. 1864. C. W. C. Reeve Papers, MC.

39. Circular. HQ, ANV. 9 Oct. 1864. G&SO&CI, ANV. M921, R1, F1473. RG 109, NA; Charlie [Baughman] to Mother, 14 Oct. 1864. Charles Baughman Papers, MC; Joseph Hilton to Coz, 14 Oct. 1864. Confederate Miscellany, EU; IR of Richmond hospitals by Lt. Col. John Saunders, n.d. Dec. 1864. IR, R17, F162–80. RG 109, NA; Thos. C. Elder to Wife, 16 Oct. 1864. Thomas Elder Papers, VHS; Lee to Davis, 9 Sep. 1864. Freeman, ed., *Lee's Dispatches*, 294; Geo. W. Lawless to Davis, 15 Nov. 1864. M437, R133, F619–21. LR, CSW. RG 109, NA; B. B. Alsworth to Davis, n.d. M474, R153, F199–200. LR, CA&IGO. RG 109, NA.

40. Progress Reports of Conscripts, May–Oct. 1864. Ch. I, Vol. 250. RG 109, NA; IR of Wright's Brigade by Lt. D. H. Pope, 28 Oct. 1864. IR, R11, F753. IR of Pickett's Division by Maj. Walter Harrison, 30 Nov. 1864. IR, R13, F60. Lt. Col. H. E. Peyton to Cooper, 29 Nov. 1864. IR, R11, F452. IR of Barringer's Cav. Brigade by Maj. Lee. [1 Nov.] 1864. IR, R11, F890. IR of Wilcox's Division by Maj. L. H. Hunt, 30 Nov. 1864. IR, R12, F685. RG 109, NA.

41. John to Father, 7 Nov. 1864. John G. Scurry Papers, Gilder-Lehrman Collection, ML; Lee to Davis, 21 July and 22 Aug 1864. Freeman, ed., *Lee's Dispatches*, 285–86 and 292–93; Lee to Chas. G. Talcott, 7 July 1864. Lee to Davis, 23 July 1864. Box 1, Ser. a, Lee Headquarters Papers, VHS; Alexander, *Fighting*, 124 and 473; Circular. HQ, ANV. 13 Oct. 1864. M921, R1, F1479. G&SO&CI, ANV. RG 109, NA; GO, No.——. HQ, Arty ANV. 21 Sep. 1864. W. N. Pendleton Order Book, MC.

42. Jacob West to friend, 6 Dec. 1864. N.C., Vol. 5, RNBP; S. D[ominey] to Sister, 20 Dec. 1864. Letters from Company M, 1st Texas. http://history-sites.com/cgi-bin/boards/txcwmb/index. cgi?read=1480; IR of Anderson's Brigade by Lt. Thos. G. Jackson, 28 Nov. 1864. IR of Lane's Brigade by Lt. E. B. Meade, 28 Dec. 1864. IR, R14, F335 and F415. RG 109, NA; Pendleton to Corley, 20 July 1864. W. N. Pendleton Order Book, MC.

43. Jas. P. V. to Sister, 4 Sep. 1864. Verdery Family Papers, DU; Jim to wife, 27 Sep. 1864. Daniel Family Papers, FSNBP; Henri J. Mugler journal, 23 May 1864. Virginia, Vol. 13. RNBP; Randolph H. McKim diary, 15 Dec. 1864. Henry Carter Lee Papers, MC; Eugene H. Levy diary, 13 May 1864. Marcus, ed., *Memoirs of American Jews*, III, 301.

44. Circular. HQ, First Corps, 20 Oct. 1864. GO, No. 71. HQ, ANV. 12 Dec. 1864. *OR* 42 (3): 1155 and 1270; GO, No. 21. HQ, 1st Army Corps. 20 Nov. 1864. First Corps, O&C of Subcommands, ANV. RG 109, NA.

45. IR of Archer's and Walker's Brigades by Capt. William Brown, 28 Nov. 1864. IR, R13 F37. IR of Pickett's Division by Maj. Walter Harrison, 28–29 Aug. 1864. IR, R10, F276 and 283–84. Extract from IR of ANV; Artillery Corps, 31 Oct. 1864. IR, R8, F260–61. RG 109, NA; IR of Texas Brigade by Capt. Jno. W. Kerr, 28 Nov. 1864. IR, R14, F321. IR of Corse's Brigade by Capt. J. C. H. Bryant, 30

Nov. 1864. IR, R13, F74. IR of Cavalry Corps, ANV, by Maj. Geo. Breamer, Dec. 1864. IR, R13, F637. IR of Pickett's Division by Maj. Walter Harrison, 30 Nov. 1864. IR, R13, F57. IR of Cooke's Brigade by Capt. H. A. Butler, 26 Dec. 1864. IR, R14, F175. IR of Elliott's Brigade by Capt. James Lowndes, 29 Dec. 1864. IR, R14, F237. IR of Rodes's Division by Maj. H. A. Whiting, 30 Dec. 1864. IR, R13, F432. RG 109, NA; Creed T. Davis diary, 8 Dec. 1864. Creed T. Davis Papers, VHS. The exact percentages in the sample were 23.2 percent KIA and 55.6 percent WIA, which totaled 78.8 percent. For lieutenants and captains, the precise figure in the sample was 86.005 percent. According to Robert Krick in *Lee's Colonels*, about 56 percent of the field officers were killed or wounded, and by factoring in those who lost elections, it was closer to 60 percent.

46. IR of Terry's Brigade by Capt. R. J. Barton, 29 Dec. 1864. IR, R13, F384. Lt. Col. H. E. Peyton to Cooper, 29 Nov. 1864. IR, R11, F452–53. RG 109, NA.

47. Thos. C. Elder to Wife, 11 July and 11 Sep. 1864. Thomas Elder Papers, VHS; Henri J. Mugler journal, 4, 5, 11, and 15 June 1864. Virginia, Vol. 13, RNBP; Creed T. Davis diary, 9 June 1864. Creed T. Davis Papers, VHS; C. S. Venable to Wife, 6 Jan. 1865. Memoir of Mary Cantey, UVA; Taylor to Co. J. W. Milton, 10 Aug. 1864. Lee Headquarters Papers, VHS; M. Lynch to Sir, 24 Dec. 1864. William Ephraim Smith Papers, DU; Lizzie to dearest friend, 30 June 1864. Albert A. Batchelor Papers, LSU; N.E.W. to Brother, 4 June 1864. J. Peter Williams Papers, UVA. Soldiers also worried about the poor suffering. See [Wade] to Fisher, 5 Oct. 1864. Hampton Family Papers, USC; Mother to [John], 12 July and 1 Sep. 1864. John to Mother, 8 Aug. 1864. John Taylor Papers, USC.

48. Thomas W. Gilmer to Dabney, 9 Jan. 1864[5]. B2, F2, Robert Lewis Dabney Papers, Union Theological Seminary; John A. Everett to Ma. 23 Sep. [1864]. John A. Everett Papers, EU; E. M. Walden to Sister, 3 Dec. 1864. E. M. Walden Papers, W&M; Th. Bragg to Lt. Gen. Holmes, 9 June 1864. IR, R2, F374–80. RG 109, NA; George to Liz, 28 Nov. 1864. George H. Moffett Papers, SCHS.

49. James H. Burgess. Esq., on Winchester, Virginia [1865]. *Report of the Secretary of the Baltimore Agricultural Aid Society*, 15; W. S. Camden to Wife, 28 June 1864. William H. Jones Papers, DU; J. P. Wilson to wife, 2 Nov. and 20 Dec. 1864. John P. Wilson Papers, MC.

50. Q. S. Adams to Sir, 8 Nov. 1864. Adams Family Folder, CWTIC, USAMHI; R. H. Anderson to Mrs. Mills, 6 Sep. 1864. Richard H. Anderson Papers, USC.

51. F to ?, 3 Dec. 1864. J. E. Shaffner Papers, NCDAH; Cadmus Wilcox to Sister Mary, 21 Nov. 1864. Cadmus M. Wilcox Papers, LC; Jas. P. Verdery to Friend, 9 Nov. 1864. Verdery Family Papers, DU; John to Father, 11 Nov. 1864. John G. Scurry Papers, Gilder-Lehrman Collection, USAMHI; Luther L. Swank to Kate, 19 Nov. 1864. Luther L. Swank Papers, LV; Rawleigh to Sister, 5 Nov. [1864]. Rawleigh Dunaway Papers, LV; Benj. F. Duncan to Cousin, 4 Dec. 1861. Grimsley Family Papers, LV; Johnson's Division Strength, 22 Oct., 16 Nov., and 19 Dec. 1864 and 3 and 18 Jan. 1865. MCI, AB, SHSP, MC; Jacob West to frend, 6 Dec. 1864. N.C., Vol. 5, RNBP; Meade to Wife, 15 Sep. 1864. Meade, *Life and Letters of Gen. Geo. Gordon Meade*, II, 228; J.C.B. to Col, 30 Nov. 1864. Information from examination of scouts, deserters, etc., Army of the Potomac. RG 108, NA; James P. Verdery to Sister, 31 Dec. 1864. Verdery Family Papers, DU. From Oct. to Dec. 1864, fifteen soldiers in the sample deserted. The previous high occurred in Oct.–Dec. 1863, when the army moved two divisions west and ten deserted. July–Sep. 1864 had eight. There is no way to uncouple Lincoln's election from Sherman's march, because the march began days after news of the election results reached the Confederates.

52. George to Liz, 1 Dec. 1864. George H. Moffett Papers, SCHS; John P. Lockhart to Pattie, 4 Dec. 1864. Willie P. Mangum Papers, LC.

34. Spiral of Defeat

1. T. P. Devereux to [Parents], 1 Jan. 1865. T.P.D. to Nan, 9 Jan. [1865]. Thomas Pollock Devereux Papers, NCDAH.

2. S. C. Barnes to sister, 1 Jan. 1865. Spencer Barnes Papers, MC; Records of Spencer Barnes, U.S. Census, 1860. Edgecombe Co., N.C., 415; *Southern Historical Society Papers*, vol. 15, 259 and 267.

3. [Theodore Hoyt Woodard] to Sister, 8 Jan. 1864[5]. Ed [Apps] to Josephine, 19 Jan. 1865. J. B. Richardson Papers, MC; IR of Evans's Brigade by Capt. Corty, 30 Jan. 1865. IR, R14, F761. IR of Wise's Brigade by Lt. Richard A. Wise, 29 Jan. 1865. IR, R15, F239. RG 109, NA; Crenshaw Hall to Laura, 20 Feb. 1865. Bolling Hall Family Papers, ADAH; T. to Precious Wife, 22 Mar. 1865. Greene Family Papers, VHS; John Kennedy Coleman diary, 15 Feb. 1865. CWTIC, USAMHI; Husband to [Wife]], 19 Mar. 1865. J. E. Shaffner Papers, NCDAH.

4. John B. Brown to Capt., 27 Jan. 1865. Correspondence Letterbook, 1864–65. John B. Brown Papers, NCDAH; John C. Evans to Annie, 18 Jan. 1865. John C. Evans Papers, AHS.

5. Lee to Longstreet, 3 Feb. 1865. R. E. Lee Papers, VHS; Conversation with Will Greene, Director Pamplin Park Civil War Soldier Museum; G. W. C. Lee to Latrobe, 25 Feb. 1865. Box 4, Lee Headquarters Papers, VHS.

6. Capt. J. McEntee to Col. Bowers, 11 and 15 Dec. 1864. George H. Sharpe to Col. Bowers, 27 Dec. 1864 and 21 Jan. 1865. JCB[abcock] to Col. Sharpe, 17 Jan. 1865. Information from examination of scouts, deserters, etc., Army of the Potomac. RG 108, NA; Lee to Vance, 28 Dec. 1864. *OR* 42 (3): 1334–35; Husband to [Wife], 16 Jan. 1864. A. R. Lawton Papers, SHC, UNC; Lee to Farmers East of the Blue Ridge and South of the James River, 12 Jan. 1865. Dowdey and Manarin, eds., *Wartime Papers*, 883; Lee to Davis, 20 Jan. 1865. Freeman, ed., *Lee's Dispatches*, 325–26; J.S. to Ma, 22 Jan. 1865. J. H. Stewart Papers, DU; Lt. Col. A. S. Cunningham to Chilton, 2 Feb. 1865. IR, R4, F2. RG 109, NA. For the Piedmont Railroad, see Black, *Railroads*, 149–53.

7. Clothing Issued to Lee's Army, 1 July 1864–21 Jan. 1865. *OR* 4 (3): 1041; IR of Butler's Cavalry Brigade by Capt. James I. Gregg, 29 Nov. 1864. IR, R12, F23. IR of Sander's Old Brigade by Lt. B. F.

Sides, 29 Dec. 1864. IR, R14, F283. Lt. Col. H. E. Peyton, endsmt. 10 Jan. 1865, to IR of Kershaw's Division by Maj. E. L. Colston, 28 Dec. 1864. IR, R13, F269. RG 109, NA.

8. Lawton to Breckinridge, 10 Mar. 1865, with Lawton to Alexander, 9 Oct. 1866. Peter Wellington Alexander Papers, Columbia U.; IR of Elliott's Brigade by W. L. Gondelook[?], 26 Jan. 1865. IR, R15. F277. IR of Ransom's Brigade by S. H. Gee, 29 Jan. 1865. IR, R15, F244, 250, and 253. IR of Barringer's Brigade by Capt. Chiswell Dabney, 30 Jan. 1865. IR, R15, F366. Endsmt by Maj. R. J. Scott to IR of Pickett's Division by Maj. Waltter Harrison. 30 Jan. 1865. IR, R14, F437. IR of Wise's Brigade by Lt. Richard A. Wise, 29 Jan. 1865. IR, R15, F236. IR of Field's Division by Capt. Roswell Ellis, 27 Feb. 1864[5]. IR, R15, F452. IR of Lewis's Brigade by Capt. W. W. Beard, 29 Jan. 1865. IR, R14, F682. IR of Rodes's Division by Maj. H. A. Whiting, 30 Jan. 1865. R14, F793. RG 109, NA; Lt. Col. H. E. Peyton to Cooper, 29 Nov. 1864. IR, R11, F453. IR of Ham's Mississippi Brigade by Capt. Jas. Hays, 25 Nov. 1864. IR, R12, F359. RG 109, NA; GO, No. 4. HQ, Johnston's Brigade. 17 Jan. 1865. Johnston's Brigade, O&C of Subcommands, ANV. RG 109, NA; Lee to Longstreet, 19 Jan. 1865. John W. Fairfax Papers, VHS; Peter Cross to wife & children, 26 Mar. 1865. John Wright Family Papers, NCDAH; Fred [Brodé] to Sister, 29 Jan. 1865. J. B. Richardson Papers, MC.

9. Endsmt. by R. J. Wingate to IR of Lane's Brigade by Lt. E. B. Meade, 28 Dec. 1864. IR, R14, F236 and 250. IR of Lewis's Brigade by Capt. W. W. Beard, 29 Jan. 1865. IR, R14, F682. IR of Rodes's Div. by Maj. H. A. Whiting, 30 Jan. 1865. IR, R14, F793. IR of Wilcox's Division by Maj. H. L. Hunt, 30 Nov. 1864. IR, R12, F685. IR of Field's Div. by Capt. Roswell Ellis, 27 Feb. 1864[5]. IR, R15, F452. RG 109, NA.

10. IR of Artillery of 3rd Corps by AA&IG Walker, 31 Dec. 1864. IR, R15, F426–27. IR of Army of the Valley District by Maj. Edwin L. Moore, n.d. Dec. 1864. IR, R13, F603. Consolidated Report of Cavalry Horses at Recruiting Camps in Virginia in the year ending 31 Dec. 1864 by Maj. G. Paxton, 10 Feb. 1865. IR, R9, F923–24. Maj. Campbell to Cooper, 25 Jan. 1865. IR, R3, F2. IR of Fitzhugh Lee's Cav. Div. by Maj. Geo. Treanor, 1 Mar. 1865. IR, R16, F245. IR of Butler's Cav. Div. by Maj. John Preston, 31 Dec. 1864. IR, R13, F690. IR of 1st Corps by Capt. R. M. Sims, 31 Han. 1865. IR, R15, F331. IR of Grimes's Brigade by A. W. Green[?], n.d. Feb. 1865. IR, R15, F622. Comments of Capt. J. T. Averell to IR of Stuart's Brigade by Brig. Gen. Geo. H. Stuart, 28 Jan. 1865, R14, F461. IR of Gracie's Brigade by Capt. H. H. Lengstak, 23 Dec. 1864. IR, R14, F217. RG 109, NA; Thomas W. Gilmer to Dabney, 9 Jan. 1864[5]. B2, F4. Robert Lewis Dabney Papers, Union Theological Seminary. Hampton's reply to Lee's Circular, SO, No. 80. HQ, ANV. 29 Dec. 1864. Hampton Family Papers, USC; Lee to Davis, 15 Jan. 1865. Dowdey and Manarin, eds., *Wartime Papers*, 881; T. Rowland to Mother, 7 Mar. 1865. Kate Mason Rowland Papers, MC; Wm. Stokes to Wife, 6 Dec. 1864. William Stokes Papers, USC; Richard T. Davis to Wife, 30 Dec. 1864. Preston-Davis Papers, UVA; B. K. Whittle to Father, 9 Jan. 1865. Whittle Family Papers, UVA.

11. IR of Bryan's Brigade by Capt. Jas. Walker, 30 Dec. 1864. IR, R13, F307 and 310. Lt. Col. H. E. Peyton endsmt., 10 Jan. 1865, of IR of Kershaw's Division by Maj. E. L. Costen, 28 Dec. 1864. IR, R13. F269. Endsmt. of J. B. Kershaw to IR of Kershaw's Division by Maj. E. L. Costen, 28 Feb. 1865. IR, R15, F524. IR of Ham's Mississippi Brigade by Capt. Jas. Hays, 25 Nov. 1864. IR, R12, F359. Endsmt. by Capt. B. W. Justice, 1 Feb. 1865 to IR of MacRae's Brigade by Capt. Louis Young, 27 Jan. 1865. IR, R15, F162. Endsmt. by Capt. R. N. Lawrence, 1 Mar. 1865, of IR of Kershaw's Division by Maj. E. L. Costen, 28 Feb. 1865. IR, R15, F524. Lt. Col. H. E. Peyton edsmt. of IR of Elliott's Brigade by Capt. James Lowndes, 29 Dec. 1864. IR, R14, F229. Comment of Lt. H. W. Bell to IR of Du Bose's Brigade by Capt. J. S. Hackett, 26 Feb. 1865. IR, R15, F591. IR of Lane's Brigade by Lt. E. B. Meade, 28 Dec. 1864. IR, R14, F416. RG 109, NA. By comparison, the U.S. Army considers 4,000 calories per day as necessary for an adult male in a combat environment to maintain his weight and health.

12. Jefferson Hedrick to Sister, 31 Dec. 1864. Frank Family Papers, SHC, UNC; Endsmt. of J. B. Kershaw to IR of Kershaw's Division by Maj. E. L. Costen, 28 Feb. 1865, and Comments of Capt R. N. Lawrence, 1 Mar. 1865. IR, R15, F524. RG 109, NA; Lt. Col. Cole to Northrop, 30 Nov. 1864. Francis G. Ruffin Papers, VHS; Lee to Davis, 14 Dec. 1864. Freeman, ed., *Lee's Dispatches*, 307–8; [Theodore Hoyt Woodard] to Sister, 8 Jan. 1864[5]. J. B. Richardson Papers, MC.

13. IR of Fitzhugh Lee's Cav. Div. by Maj. Geo. Treanor, 1 Mar. 1865. IR, R16, F245. RG 109, NA; T. C. Brady to Wife & Son, 13 Jan. 1865. Brady Family Papers, CAH.

14. Northrop to Cole, 10 Dec. 1864. Northrop to Lee, 13 Dec. 1864. Northrop to Cooper, 11 Jan. 1865. Francis G. Ruffin Papers, VHS; Lee to Seddon, 11 Jan. 1863. Dowdey and Manarin, eds., *Wartime Papers*, 881; Northrop to Seddon, 6 Jan. 1865, endsmt. by Seddon. Trenholm to Seddon, 10 Jan. 1865. C.S.A. Commissary Department, NYPL.

15. Northrop to Seddon, 11 Jan. 1865. Francis G. Ruffin Papers, VHS; Davis to Breckinridge, 8 Feb. 1865. Lee Headquarters Papers, VHS.

16. IR of Finnegan's Brigade by B. F. Simmons, 25 Feb. 1865. IR, R16, F165. IR of Wise's Brigade by Lt. Richard A. Wise, 29 Jan. 1865. IR, R15, F238. IR of Battle's Brigade by Lt. Daniel Partridge, 26 Feb. 1865. IR, R15, F637. IR of Hoke's Division by Maj. Jas. M. Adams, n.d. Nov. 1864. IR, R12, F205. IR of Johnston's Brigade by Lt. E. Hayne Davis, 28 Jan. 1865. IR, R14, F709. IR of Gary's Brigade by Lt. J. C. Miller, 27 Feb. 1865. IR, R16, F340. IR of Gordon's Division by Capt. R. I. Barton, 30 Jan. 1865. IR, R14, F719. IR of Law's Brigade by Lt. L. A. Morgan, 27 Dec. 1864. IR, R13, F259 and 267. IR of Third Corps by Maj. R. J. Wingate, n.d. Jan. 1865. IR, R15, F299. IR of Winder & Jackson Hospital by Lt. Col. Jno. Saunders, 29 Dec. 1864 and 9 Jan. 1865. IR, R17, F188–89 and 194. RG 109, NA; B. K. Whittle to Father, 9 Jan. 1865. Whittle Family Papers, UVA; T. C. Brady to Wife & Son, 13 Jan. 1865. Brady Family Papers, CAH.

17. Extract of IR for 2nd Corps, Feb. 1865. IR, R15, F608. IR of Fitzhugh Lee's Cav. Div. by Maj. Geo. Treanor, 1 Mar. 1865. IR, R16, F245. IR of W. H. E. Lee's Brigade by Maj. J. M. Lee, 31 Jan. 1865. IR, R15, F353 and 363. IR of Field's Division by Capt. Roswell Ellis, 27 Feb. 1864[5]. Comments by Capt. James Pleasants, Ordnance Officer. IR, R15, F455. Extract from IR of Wright's Brigade, 31 Oct.

1864. IR, R11, F461. RG 109, NA; GO, No. 1. HQ, Heth's Division. 1 Feb. 1865. Morning Report and Order Book, 1st Tennessee Infantry. RG 109, NA; Gorgas to Mallet, 10 Mar. 1865. Personal Papers, J. W. Mallet. Records and Pensions Office, Document File #568,231. RG 94, NA; Report of Brig. Gen. Josiah Gorgas to Sec. of War, 9 Feb. 1865. Josiah Gorgas File, SHSP. MC.

18. GO, No. 1. HQ Confederate Armies. 9 Feb. 1865. Davis to Lee, 10 Feb. 1865. GO, No. 2. HQ, Armies of the Confed. States. 11 Feb. 1865. *OR* 46 (2): 1226–30; Lee to Davis, 9 Feb. 1865. *OR* 51 (2): 1082–83.

19. J. W. Powell, Medical Director of A. P. Hill's Corps [Feb. 1865], addendum to IR of 3rd Corps by Maj. R. J. Wingate, Jan. 1865. IR, R15, F286. RG 109, NA; M.H. to Companion & children. 22 Feb. 1865. Mebane Hinshaw Papers, DU; Abel to Wife, 5 and 9 Mar. 1865. Abel H. Crawford Papers, DU; Willie Ellis to friend, 19 Feb. 1865. John Wright Family Papers, NCDAH; Ben Mason to Wife, 21 Jan. 1865. Mason Family Papers, Auburn U.; J. A. P[erkins] to Friend, 4 Mar. 1865. Bowles-Jordan Family Papers, UVA; [Thomas] to Sir, 19 Jan. 1865. Greene Family Papers, VHS; G. Prillaman to Father, 15 Mar. 1865. Prillaman Papers, FSNBP.

20. See Glatthaar. *The March to the Sea and Beyond*; Campbell, *When Sherman Marched North from the Sea*.

21. [Melvin Dwinell] to Brother Albert, 30 Sep. 1865. Dwinell, "Vermonter in Gray," *Vermont History* 30, 3, 229–30; John Kennedy Coleman diary, 14 Mar. 1865. CWTIC, USAMHI; Peter Cross to wife & children. 26 Mar. 1865. John Wright Family Papers, NCDAH; Huldah A. Briant to Chris, 25 Jan. 1865. M. C. Briant to Annie, 12 Feb. 1865. Huldah Anne (Fain) Briant Papers, DU; Marion [Koiner] to Sister, 18 Jan. 1865. David Ezra Papers, VHS; J. Stewart to Ma, 20 Mar. 1865. James H. Stewart Papers, DU.

22. Annie [Evans] to Husband, 22 Feb. 1865. John C. Evans Papers, AHS.

23. H. Meade to Lottie, 11 Mar. 1865. James H. Lane Papers, Auburn U.; R. H. Chilton endsmt., 21 Mar. 1865, to IR of Johnston's Brigade by Lt. A. F. Lawhout[?], 27 Feb. 1865. Extract from Johnston's Brigade, Feb. 1865. IR, R15, F731 and 721–22. RG 109, NA; Lee to Vance, 24 Feb. 1865. Vance to Lee, 2 Mar. 1865. *OR* 47 (2): 1270–71 and 1312; Samuel Walkup diary, 21 Feb. 1865. Samuel H. Walkup Papers, SHC, UNC. Sec Jason Philips, "The Grape Vine Telegraph: Rumors and Confederate Persistence," *Journal of Southern History* 72, 4, 753–88.

24. Joe to Lizzie, 25 Feb. 1865. Joel Thomas Pierce Papers, GDAH; T.P.D. to Father, 20 Feb. [1865]. Thomas Pollock Devereux Papers, NCDAH; Thomas Green to Ma, 19 Feb. 1865. Green W. Penn Papers, DU; Alexander to [wife], 2 Mar. 1865. F. P. Alexander Papers, SHC, UNC; Wm. A. Penn to Ma, 19 Feb. 1865. Green W. Penn Papers, DU; Lee to William P. Miles, 19 Jan. 1865. Dowdey and Manarin, eds., *Wartime Papers*, 885–86.

25. Joseph Cox, Jr., to Brothers, 26 Feb. 1865. Prillaman Papers, FSNBP; Sharpe to Colonel, 25 Feb. 1865. Sharpe to Bowers, 25 Feb. 1865. Information from examination of scouts, deserters, etc., Army of the Potomac. RG 108, NA; Cooper to Lee, 21 Feb. 1865. Lee to Breckinridge, 28 Feb. 1865. Taylor to Lee, 8 Mar. 1865. *OR* 46 (2): 1245, 1265, and 1292–93; Lee to Secretary of War, 27 Mar. 1865. Davis to Lee, 1 Apr. 1865. *OR* 46 (3): 1353 and 1370; IR of Wilcox's Brigade by Maj. L. H. Hunt, Feb. 1865. IR, R16, F142. IR of Bushrod Johnson's Division by Capt. Wm. H. Whittier[?], Feb. 1865. IR, R16, F365. RG 109, NA; Monthly Report, Corse's Brigade. Corse's Brigade Order Book, MC; Husband to [Wife], 19 Mar. 1865. J. E. Shaffner Papers, NCDAH; [R. P. Scarbrough] to Cousin Araminta, 31 Jan. 1865. Confederate Miscellany, EU. On 24 Feb., the Army of the Potomac received 134 deserters. Webb to Bowers, 25 Feb. 1864. *OR* 46 (2): 693. Statistics for desertion are very difficult to tabulate. Even those that Lee offered to the secretary of war undercounted or failed to include cavalry. Those from the Army of the James are based on *OR* 46 (2) and (3).

26. Thos. Green to Ma, 2 Mar. 1865. Green W. Penn Papers, DU; Jim to Billy, [Mar.? 1865], Griggs Family Papers, VHS; Crenshaw Hall to Boiling, 22 Feb. 1865. Box 10, Bolling Hall Papers, ADAH; B. W. Justice to Wife, 15 Mar. 1865. Benjamin W. Justice Papers, EU; Beverly Ross to Wife, 8 Feb. 1865. Beverly Ross Papers, MC.

27. Silas Chandler to wife, 25 Jan. 1865. John J. and Silas Chandler Papers, LV; R. E. Mobley to Bettie, 1 Jan. 1865. Lewis Leigh Collection, USAMHI; [Edward] to Aggie, 26 Mar. 1865. E. R. Crockett Papers, CAH; Marion to Sister, 23 Feb. 1865. Leonard-Koiner Papers, FSNBP; A. N. Proffit to Sister, 15 Feb. 1865. Proffit Family Papers, SHC, UNC.

28. Lincoln to House of Representatives, 10 Feb. 1865, with various communications. Longstreet to Lee, 1 Mar. and 1 Mar. 1865. Lee to Grant, 2 Mar. and 2 Mar. 1865. Grant to Lee, 4 Mar. 1865. Davis to Lee, 28 Feb. 1865. *OR* 46 (2): 505–13, 824–25, 1264, and 1276; Beverly Ross to Wife, 8 Feb. 1865. Beverly Ross Papers, MC; Abel to Dora, 17 Feb. 1865. Abel H. Crawford Papers, DU; B. K. Whittle to Father, 10 Feb. 1865. Whittle Family Papers, UVA; W. Taylor to Bettie, 5 and 19 Mar. 1865. Walter H. Taylor Papers, NPL; S. S. Sarvis, "Reminiscences of a Confederate Officer," 28. Sarvis Papers, USC.

29. Husband to [wife], 16 Jan. 1865. A. R. Lawton Papers, SHC, UNC; John G. Scurry to Matthew, 29 Jan. 1864. John G. Scurry Papers, Gilder-Lehrman Papers, ML.

30. Lincoln to Horace Greeley, 22 Aug. 1862. Roy P. Basler, ed., *Collected Works of Abraham Lincoln*, vol. 5 (New Brunswick, N.J.: Rutgers University Press, 1953), 388; Charles Marshall to Ewell, 27 Mar. 1865. George W. Campbell Papers, LC.

31. Lee to Hon. E. Barksdale, 18 Feb. 1865. St. Paul's Church Vestry Book, VHS.

32. Rawleigh to Sister, 20 Feb. 1865. Rawleigh Dunaway Papers, LV; M. Hill Fitzpatrick to Amanda, 3 Nov. 1864. Lowe and Hodges, eds., *Letters to Amanda*, 182; T.P.D. to Kate, 8 Feb. 1865. Thomas Pollock Devereux Papers, NCDAH; M. C. Briant to Huldah, 29 Mar. 1865. Huldah Anne (Fain) Briant, DU; Joe to Sister, 15 Feb. 1865. Vol. 21, FSNBP; Gordon to Taylor, 18 Feb. 1865. *OR* 51 (2): 1063.

33. Taylor to Longstreet, 29 Mar. 1865. Ser. a. Box 4, Lee Headquarters Papers, VHS; Lee to Secretary of War, 27 Mar. 1865. Longstreet to Taylor, 30 Mar. 1865. *OR* 46 (3): 1356 and 1367; Col. J. T. Jordan et al., to Taylor, 15 Mar. 1865, *OR* 46 (2): 1315–17; Vance to Secretary of War, 18 Mar. 1865. W.

H. S. Burgwyn Papers, NCDAH; William Smith to Davis, 1 Apr. 1865. CSR of Andrew J. Rodgers, 32nd Bn. Virginia Cavalry. RG 109, NA; Lane W. Brandon to Davis, 29 Mar. 1865. M437, R146, F717–18. LR, CSW. RG 109, NA.

34. Alexander to [wife], 7 Nov. 1864. E. P. Alexander Papers, SHC, UNC; J. W. Calton to Brother & Sister, 27 Mar. 1865. John W. Calton Papers, NCDAH; John W. Stott diary, 30 Oct. 1864. CWTIC; USAMHI; Comments of Lt. J. M. Young to IR of Du Bose's Brigade by Capt. J. S. Hackett, 26 Feb. 1865. IR, R15, F590. RG 109, NA. To this, an unidentified soldier jotted, "Wait awhile old fellow, we will have negroe soldiers."

35. Peter Wellington Alexander, "The State of the Confederate Cause," 17 May 1865, 1. Peter Wellington Alexander Papers, Columbia U.; JAP[erkins] to Friend, 4 Mar. 1865. Bowles Jordan Papers, UVA.

36. Davis to Lee, 1 Apr. 1865. *OR* 46 (3); 1370.

37. IR of 2nd Army Corps by Capt. R. J. Barton, 31 Jan. 1865. IR, M2166, R14, F869. Lt. Col. H. E. Peyton, endsmt. [Jan. 1865] to IR of Pickett's Div. by Maj. Walter Harrison, 20–23 Dec. 1864. IR, R13, F132. IR of Rodes's Div. by Maj. H. A. Whiting. 30 Jan. 1865. IR, R14, F791. Endsmt. by Lt. Col. H. E. Peyton, 10 Jan. 1865 to IR of Gordon's Div. by Capt. J. M. Pace, 30 Dec. 1864. IR, R13, F364 and 372. IR of Early's Div. by Maj. John H. New, 30 Jan. 1865. IR, R14, F665. IR of Terry's Brig. by Capt. R. J. Barton, 28 Jan. 1865. IR, R14, F780 and 782. Comments by Col. Thomas Munford to IR of Munford's Brig. by Henry Lee, 27 Feb. 1865. IR, R16, F312. G. R. Pickett's Comments to IR of Pickett's Div. by Maj. Walter Harrison, 30 Jan. 1865. IR, R14, F449. IR of Third Corps by Maj. R. J. Wingate, Jan. 1865. IR, R15, F297. IR of Thomas's Brig. by Lt. E. L. Lewis, 26 Jan. 1865. IR, R15, F134. Endsmt. by Maj. Gen. Heth, 1 Feb. 1865 to IR of Heth's Div. by Sidney H. Davies, 29 Jan. 1865. IR, R15, F150. IR of Wilcox's Div. by Maj. L. H. Hunt, Feb. 1865. IR, R16, F140. IR of Dearing's Brig. by Jas. C. Rutherford, 30 Jan. 1865. IR, R15, F388 and 390. IR of Pickett's Div. by Maj. Walter Harrison, 30 Jan. 1865. IR, R14, F446. Brig. Gen. W. MacRae to Colonel, 25 Jan. 1865. IR, R9, F932–38. IR of Elliott's Brig. by W. L. Gondelook[?], 26 Jan. 1865. IR, R15, F280. IR of Battle's Brig. by Lt. Daniel Partridge, 26 Feb. 1865. IR, R15, F638. RG 109, NA.

38. GO, No. 4. HQ, Armies of the Confederacy, 22 Feb. 1865. Circular. HQ, Armies of the Confederacy, 22 Feb. 1865. Lee Papers, Army Headquarters, 1865. Entry 64. Marked Box 87. RG 109, NA; Venable to darling, 23 Mar. [1865]. Memoir of Mary Cantey, 56–57. UVA; IR of McGowan's Brigade by Capt. Reddick, 27 Jan. 1865. IR, R15, F123. IR of McGowan's Brigade by Capt. Reddick, 28 Feb. 1865 IR, R16, F113. RG 109, NA; R. J. Wingate to General, 8 Mar. 1865. Lewis Leigh Collection, USAMHI.

39. Lee to Mary, 21 Feb. 1865. Dowdey and Manarin, eds., *Wartime Papers*, 907; James P. Williams to Aunt Mary, 16 Mar. 1865. James P. Williams Papers, LV; Samuel Walkup diary, 6 Mar. 1865. Samuel H. Walkup Papers, SHC, UNC; Billie to Sister Maggie, 9 Feb. 1865. Confederate Papers, SHC, UNC; GO, No. 65. 7 Nov. 1865. G&SO&CI, ANV. M921, R1, F1273. RG 109, NA; W. N. Pendleton to Darling Love, 25 May 1864. William N. Pendleton Papers, SHC, UNC.

40. John A. Everett to Ma, 16 Mar. 1865. John A. Everett Papers, EU; M. H. Fitzpatrick to Amanda, 16 May 1863. M. Hill Fitzpatrick to Amanda, 4 Mar. 1864. William Fields to Mrs. Fitzpatrick, 8 June 1865. Lowe and Hodges, eds., *Letters to Amanda*, 71, 202, and 209–10.

41. John to Mother, 16 Jan. 1865. John G. Scurry Papers, Gilder-Lehrman Collection, ML; Rawleigh to Sister, 20 Feb. 1865. Rawleigh Dunaway Papers, LV; Alexander, *Fighting*, 502.

35. The Final Days

1. Lee to Mrs. Pegram, 11 Feb. 1865. Wyman-Cary-Keyser Papers, MDHS; Lee to Mary, 21 Feb. 1865. Dowdey and Manarin, eds., *Wartime Papers*, 907.

2. Circular. HQ, ANV. 18 Feb. 1865. Lee to Breckinridge, 22 Feb. 1865. *OR* 46 (2): 1240 and 1247; Lee to Breckinridge, 19 Feb. 1865. *OR* 47 (1): 1044; Walter Taylor to [Bettie], 20 Feb. 1865. Walter H. Taylor Papers, NPL.

3. Lee to Breckinridge, 9 Mar. 1865. S. B. French to General I. M. St. John, 10 Mar. 1865. *OR* 46 (2): 1295 and 1297; Lawton to Breckinridge, 10 Mar. 1865. Peter Wellington Alexander Papers, Columbia U.

4. Lee to Breckinridge, 22 Feb. 1865. Lee to Longstreet, 22 Feb. 1865. *OR* 46 (2): 1247 and 1250; Lee to Davis, 26 Mar. 1865. Dowdey and Manarin, eds., *Wartime Papers*, 916–17; John B. Gordon, *Reminiscences of the Civil War*, 386–413; Chris M. Calkins, *The Final Bivouac: The Surrender Parade at Appomattox and the Disbanding of the Armies, April 10–May 20, 1865*, 205–6; John Horn, *The Petersburg Campaign, June 1864–April 1865*, 212–16; AAR of Bvt. Maj. Gen. J. F. Hartranft, 14 Apr. 1865. *OR* 46 (1): 345–49; William H. Hogkins, *The Battle of Fort Stedman*.

5. AAR of Maj. Gen. Gouverneur Warren, 21 Feb. 1865[6]. AAR of Sheridan, 16 May 1865. Lee to Breckinridge, 1, 2, and 2 Apr. 1865. *OR* 46 (1): 796–800, 1101–5, and 1263–65; Thomas Rosser, extract for *Philadelphia Weekly Times*, 5 Apr. 1884. John Bolling Folder, CWTIC, USAMHI; Thomas T. Munford to Captain, 2 Aug. 1870. W. H. Taylor to General, 19 Feb. 1903. Fitzhugh Lee Papers, UVA; Fitz Lee to Taylor, 9 Jan. 1903. Taylor to Lee, 15 Jan. 1904. Walter H. Taylor Papers, NPL; John C. Evans to Annie, 30 Apr. 1865. John Craig Evans Papers, AHS; Gordon, *General George E. Pickett in Life & Legend*, 149–55; William Marvel, *Lee's Last Retreat; The Flight to Appomattox*, 214–17. There is no contemporary written evidence of Pickett's dismissal, but there are pieces of inferential evidence, which Marvel develops well. Also see Edward L. Ayers, Gary W. Gallagher, and David W. Blight, *Appomattox Court House*.

6. AAR of Grant, 22 July 1864. Lee to Breckinridge, 2 and 2 Apr. 1865. AAR of Lee, 12 Apr. 1865. *OR* 46 (1): 54–55 and 1264–65; A. Howard to Lane, 3 June 1867. Geo. H. Snow to Lane, 13 May 1867. James H. Lane Papers, Auburn U.; Giles Buckner Cooke diary, 2 Apr. 1865. Giles Buckner Cooke Papers, VHS.

7. Briscoe G. Baldwin to General [Gorgas], 31 Mar. [1865]. Briscoe Baldwin Papers, VHD; AAR of Lt. Col. Briscoe Baldwin, 14 Apr. 1865. Box 3, Lee Headquarters Papers, VHS; Eugene F. Levy diary, 3 Apr. 1865. Marcus, ed., *Memoirs of American Jews*. III, 312; Taylor, "Sonic Experiences of a Confederate Assistant Surgeon," 112–13; Edward C. Anderson to wife, 19 Nov. 1864. Joseph F. Waring Papers, GHS.

8. Peter Wellington Alexander, "The State of the Confederate Cause," 17 May 1865. Columbia U.; Lee to Breckinridge, 22 Feb. 1865. *OR* 46 (2): 1247; AAR of Lee, 12 Apr. 1865. *OR* 46 (1): 1265–66.

9. AAR of Lee, 12 Apr. 1865. *OR* 46 (1): 1265–66; J. W. Powell, Medical Director of A. P. Hill's Corps, [Feb. 1865], addendum to IR of Third Corps by Maj. R. J. Wingate, Jan. 1865. IR, R15, F286. RG 109, NA. Thanks to Dr. Boyd Switzer, Professor of Nutrition at UNC Medical School, who assisted me here. Lee's men consumed about 35 to 40 grams of protein per day and needed 55 to 70 grams. Based on requirements for an adult male, average size five feet, eight inches tall, 150 pounds, the average soldier in the Army of Northern Virginia received 62.5 percent of calories, 6 percent of vitamin A, 15 percent of vitamin E, 3 percent of vitamin K, 9.9 percent of calcium, 8.8 percent of iodine, 41 percent of potassium, 32.5 percent of folate, along with all sorts of B-vitamin shortages. Conversation with Dr. Boyd Switzer, 12 Dec. 2006 and printout.

10. Capt. B. H. Smith, Jr., to Lt. Col. Latrobe, 13 Mar. 1865. Ser. a, Box 3, Lee Headquarters Papers, VHS; Pfanz, *Richard S. Ewell*, 428–35; Marvel, *Lee's Last Retreat*, Appendix B, 207–13, challenges Lee's statement in his AAR. It seems extremely unlikely that Lee would order ammunition stockpiled for the army at Amelia Court House and not food and forage.

11. Gordon to Lee; 6 Apr. 1865. Ser. a, Box 1, Lee Headquarters Papers, VHS; AAR of Lee, 12 Apr. 1865. *OR* 46 (1): 1265–66; Pfanz, *Ewell*, 436–39.

12. W. G. M[cCabe] to Miss Mary, 7 Apr. 1865. Early Family Papers, VHS; Maj. Campbell Brown diary, 26 Jan. 1866. George Washington Campbell Papers, LC; Taylor, "Some Experiences of a Confederate Assistant Surgeon," 111–13.

13. AAR of Lee, 12 Apr. 1865. *OR* 46 (1): 1266; GO, No.——. HQ, 1st Army Corps. 8 Apr. 1865. Osmun Latrobe Papers, MDHS; Alexander, *Fighting*, 527.

14. Grant to Lee, 7 Apr. 1865. Lee to Grant, 7 Apr. 1865. Grant to Lee, 8 Apr. 1865. Lee to Grant, 8 Apr. 1865. Grant to Lee, 9 Apr. 1865. *OR* 46 (1): 56–57.

15. AAR of Fitz Lee, 12 Apr. 1865. Fitzhugh Lee Papers, UVA; Llewellyn Saunderson journal, 9 Apr. 1865. Llewellyn Saunderson Papers, VHS; AAR of Lee, 12 Apr. 1865. *OR* 46 (1): 1266–67.

16. Krick, *Staff Officers in Gray*, 222; CSR of John Wesley Richards, 56th North Carolina Infantry, M270, R524, RG 109, NA; Records of John Richards. U.S. Census, 1850. Caldwell Co., N.C., 22; Summary of the Fight at Appomattox. http://www.nps.gov/apco/final-battles.htm. Richards does not seem to appear in the census of 1860.

17. AAR of Grant, 22 July 1865. Grant to Lee, 9 Apr. 1865. Lee to Grant, 9 Apr. 1865. *OR* 46 (1): 57–58; Marshall, *Lee's Aide-de-Camp*, 268–74.

18. GO, No. 9. HQ, ANV. 10 Apr. 1865. *OR* 46 (1): 1267; Lee to Davis, 20 Apr. 1865. Letterbook No. 3, Robert E. Lee Papers, LC.

19. Alexander, *Fighting*, 415. Although it is impossible to be precise, my rough tabulation calculates some 36,000 Union soldiers killed in action or died of wounds fighting Lee's soldiers, and they wounded at least 150,000 Federals. By tabulating losses within Fox, *Regimental Losses*, 543–49, I calculated approximates 32,200 KIA; 162,000 WIA (including mortally), and 79,300 POW/MIA for the Union. My guess is that some 40,000 Union soldiers were KIA or mortally WIA, and close to 155,000 were wounded. Some MIA, of course, were killed. Some 36.4 percent of all Union KIA and 56.4 percent of all WIA were inflicted by Lee's army, which constituted less than 25 percent of all Confederate soldiers (estimated at 200,000 of 900,000, or 22.2 percent). The tabulation of losses from the Wilderness to the fighting at Appomattox comes from Gary Gallagher. The Union calculated mortally wounded as wounded; Confederates calculated them as killed in action.

20. Gallagher, *Confederate War*, 11; L. C. Cooper to Mother, 18 May 1863. Cooper Papers, FSNBP (originals at Kenesaw Mountain National Battlefield Park); Leroy S. Edwards to father, 15 Feb. 1863. Leroy S. Edwards Papers, VHS; S.M.B. to Children, 10 Apr. 1863. Bemiss Family Papers, VHS; W. A. Templeton to Sister, 8 Aug. 1863. Templeton Family Papers, USC; W. R. Montgomery to Aunt Frank, 16 Oct. 1863. William R. Montgomery Papers, FSNBP; Sam P. Collier to Sister, 4 Mar. 1864. Samuel P. Collier Papers, NCDAH; APH[ill] to Lute, 17 Dec. 1864. A. P. Hill Papers, VHS.

21. Chesnut, *Mary Chesnut's Civil War*, 442–43; Catherine Edmondston diary, 11 June 1864. Edmondston, *"Journal of a Secesh Lady,"* 577; Sarah Lois Wadley diary, 18 June 1864. Sarah Lois Wadley Papers, SHC, UNC; Emma LeConte diary, 11 Mar. 1865. LeConte, *When the World Ended*, 77.

22. GO, No. 68. HQ, Army of the Potomac. 4 July 1863. *OR* 27 (3): 519; Gary W. Gallagher, "'Upon Their Heads Hang Momentous Interests': Generals," in Gabor S. Boritt, ed., *Why the Confederacy Lost*. 100; Beverly Wilson Palmer, ed., *The Selected Letters of Charles Sumner*, 2, 268; T. Harry Williams, *Lincoln and His Generals*. Lincoln and Stanton demanded that Grant launch a direct attack on Lee's army, when the adoption of alternative strategies could have proven more effective and mitigated the extraordinary combat losses of the Overland Campaign and Petersburg siege.

23. J.H.L. to Mother, 26 June 1861. Langhorne Family Papers, VHS; John C. Towles journal of 1862, 27. John C. Towles Papers, LV; L. Guild to Lee, 5 May 1865. LS, Med. Dir. Office, ANV. RG 109, NA; William McKnight to Mother, 19 May 1862. Virginia, Vol. 139. FSNBP.

24. Lee to Davis, 23 May 1864. Freeman, ed., *Lee's Dispatches*, 195.

25. Circular. HQ, ANV. 28 Feb. 1865. Ser. a, Box 4. Lee Headquarters Papers, VHS; J. P. Wilson to wife, 20 Dec. 1864. John P. Wilson Papers, MC; IR of Post of Weldon by Lt. Col. E. Murray, 30 Jan. 1865. IR, R9, F867–69. Comments by Maj. Chas. Waite, QM, in IR of W. H. F. Lee's Division by J. M. Lee, 28 Feb. 1865. IR, R16, F261. RG 109, NA; *OR* 4 (3): 1183. Scholars have particularly misjudged the supply situation, largely because they have not understood the huge lead time in placing food in the hands of soldiers.

26. See Jas. H. Benton to Gorgas, 11 Feb. 1865, on the inability to import machinery to manufacture quality arms. Box 676, F25. Gorgas Papers, UAL.

27. Robert F. Durden, *The Gray and the Black: The Confederate Debate on Emancipation*; Bruce Levine, *Confederate Emancipation; Southern Plans to Free and Arm Slaves during the Civil War*.

28. See sample in Appendix I: 44.3 percent came from slave households; 37.11 percent either owned slaves themselves or resided with family members who did; 19.0 percent were worth $0, which usually meant they owned no appreciable wealth; 20.0 percent were worth over $10,000. Only 4.8 percent of all farmers owned no real estate. Exactly 67 percent were single. The median birth year was 1838, and the mean was 1835.7. Only 8.7 percent of the soldiers were skilled workers. Some 52.3 percent of deserters (or their families if they resided with them) possessed less than $800 of total wealth; nondeserters owned close to $1,300. About 38.2 percent of nondeserters owned slaves. Deserters had personal and, if they lived with their parents, combined personal and family median wealth of $730, compared to a figure of nearly $1,350 for nondeserters. Among deserters, 21.2 percent either owned, or their parents with whom they resided owned, slaves. That compared to 39.2 percent of nondeserters. Some 26.2 percent of deserters lived in slaveholding households, compared to 46.7 percent of nondeserters. The median wealth of soldiers killed or wounded in action was $1,380, compared to $1,200 for noncasualties. More than 43 percent of all soldiers killed or wounded owned slaves, or their parents did, even though these soldiers made up 36 percent of the army. See Escott, *After Secession*, 94, 99–104, and 113 on class resentment and the "Rich Man's War" thesis. He blends speculators into the equation, though all soldiers regardless of wealth loathed speculators. A small number of soldiers believed the thesis, but many scholars, including Escott, Bell Wiley, and Paul Williams, have oversold the argument, at least based on the evidence in Lee's army.

29. About 7.8 percent suffered some combination of wounds and imprisonment and 6.00 percent suffered multiple wounds—wounds on two or more battlefields. These statistics do not include repeats. If a soldier was killed in action, he was not counted as wounded, even if he suffered a wound on a different battlefield, for example. If a soldier was wounded and died of disease later, he was counted only once. My statistics for killed and wounded for the entire war are rough figures drawn from available and imprecise evidence, but are a good approximation.

30. Report of the number of youths in Virginia arriving at the age of seventeen in the next twelve months, 30 Sep. 1864. Ch. I, Vol. 239. Bureau of Conscription Letters, Reports & Endorsements Sent, Nov. 1864–March 1865. RG 109, NA.

31. Lee to Vance, 14 Feb. 1865 *OR* 47 (2): 1270–71; [William Chancely] to Cousin, 8 June 1864. CWMC, USAMHI; Wm. J. Mosely diary, 8 July 1864. William Jefferson Mosely Papers, GDAH; W. S. Camden to Wife, 28 June 1864. William H. Jones Papers, DU; J.P.V. to Listen, 27 May 1864 Verdery Family Papers, DU; M. C. Briant to Father, 21 Sep. 1864. Huldah Anne (Fain) Briant Papers, DU, Samuel H. Wiley to Mother, 26 Nov. 1864. Rozier, *Granite Farm Letters*, 215; Richard T. Davis to Wife, 18 Nov. 1864. Preston-Davis Papers, UVA; Longstreet to Taylor. 25 Mar. 1865. James Longstreet, *From Manassas to Appomattox: Memoirs of the Civil War in America*, 651–52; Marvel, *Lee's Last Retreat*, 205–6. Marvel's tabulation of losses in the last few weeks of the war is excellent.

32. Carl Henninghausen to Mother, 24 Apr. 1865. Charles A. Henninghausen Papers, VHS.

33. Lee to Grant, 9 Apr. 1865. *OR* 46 (1): 57–58.

34. E. P. Alexander to Longstreet, 26 Oct. 1892. James Longstreet Papers, NCDAH; Goree to Alexander, 6 Dec. [1877]. Goree, 301–3.

35. Giles B. Cooke diary, 9 Apr. 1865. Giles Buckner Cooke Papers, VHS: AG [Amelia Gorgas] to Dick, 21 Apr. 1865. Box 680, F79, Gorgas Papers, UAL; Giles B. Cooke to Albert H. Robberts. 21 Sep. 1930. Giles B. Cooke Papers, MC; Marshall, *Lee's Aide-de-Camp*, 278.

36. Lee to Davis, 20 Apr. 1865. Lee Letterbook No. 3. Robert E. Lee Papers, LC.

37. Lee to Davis, 20 Apr. 1865. Lee Letterbook No. 3, Robert E. Lee Papers, LC; Alexander, *Fighting*, 532–33.

38. Catherine Edmondston diary, 16 Apr. 1865. Edmondston, *"Journal of a Secesh Lady,"* 694–95; Eliza Andrews diary, 18 Apr. 1865. Eliza Frances Andrews, *War-Time Journal of a Georgia Girl*, 151–52; Sarah Morgan Dawson diary, 19 Apr. 1865. Sarah Morgan Dawson, *A Confederate Girl's Diary*, 435; W. W. Gramling diary, 13 Apr. 1865. W. W. Gramling Papers, FSA; Kate Stone diary, 23 and 28 Apr. 1865. Kate Stone, *Brokenburn: The Journal of Kate Stone, 1861–1868*, 330–31 and 333–34.

39. Eliza J. Darden to darling Jimmie, 26 Apr. 1865. AGO Record Office: Personal Letters to Prisoners at Point Lookout. RG 109, NA.

40. Chester, Thomas Morris Chester, 308–9.

41. J. Thomas Petty diary, 3 July 1861. J. Thomas Petty Papers, MC.

BIBLIOGRAPHY

MANUSCRIPTS

Alabama Department of Archives and History, Montgomery

Hugh William Caffey
James F. Cameron
James Marshall Collier
Ella Francis Daniel
James A. Davidson
George Field
Josiah Gorgas
Bolling Hall Family
James G. Hudson
Hunter-Milhous Family
Robert M. Jones
James H. McMath

Thomas Winfrey Oliver IV
Samuel King Rayburn
W. E. Riser
Rives Family
Linda Bestor Robertson
Marion Rushton
John J. Seibels
Martha Simpson
Otis David Smith
Turner Vaughan
Henry F. Wilson
William Yancey

Atlanta Historical Society, Atlanta, Georgia

Ivan Allen
Lewis H. Andrew
Henry Beck
Davidson-Terry
John Craig Evans
Foreacre-Willett
N. W. Harbin

Myra S. Harper
Johnson Family
George J. Johnston
Jones Family
Josiah Blair Patterson
Zachariah A. Rice

Auburn University, Auburn, Alabama

Starrand Brown Family
Joseph Q. Burton
Jonathan F. Coghill
B. R. Jeffares
Robert Jemison

Johnston Family
James H. Lane
Mason Family
Ross Family

Center for American History, University of Texas at Austin

William Pitt Ballinger
H. W. Barclay
Brady Family
Civil War Miscellany
Edward Richardson Crockett
Crutcher-Shannon Family
C.S.A. Records, Soldiers'
    Correspondence
Wilmot Walter Curry
Annie B. Giles
O. T. Hanks

Robert E. Lee
James Longstreet
Thomas L. McCarty
M. F. McNair
Nicholas Pomeroy
A. S. Roberts
George Lee Robertson
James T. Rogers
George F. Shuford
Fleming W. Thompson
Charles S. Vernable

Clemens Library, University of Michigan, Ann Arbor

Schoff Collection:
  W. J. Seymour

College of William & Mary, Williamsburg, Virginia

Mark Alexander
Calfee Family
Civil War Collection
Robert Gaines Haile
Hatfield
Henry C. Hoar
Joseph E. Johnston

Powell Family
Rouzie
Robert C. Towles
John Tyler Scrapbook
F. N. Walker
Wills Family
Asa John Wyatt

Columbia University, New York, New York

Peter W. Alexander

Duke University, Durham, North Carolina

William M. Anderson
William B. G. Andrews
Tillman F. Baggerley
Asa Biggs
John Malachi Bowden
Huldah Anne (Fain) Briant
Hugh Conaway Browning
Isaac Howell Carrington
Lunsford R. Cherry
Rachel Susan Cheves
Job Cobb
Thomas R. R. Cobb
John Esten Cooke
Abel H. Crawford
C.S.A. Archives. Army Units
Francis Warrington Dawson, I
James H. De Votie
Dr. Lee
Benjamin Stoddard and Richard
  Stoddard Ewell
Jane Fisher
Frederick Fraser
General Order Book, 37th North Carolina
  Infantry
Bryan Grimes
Caleb Hampton
James H. Hewett
Meban Hinshaw
Ben Hubert
Thomas J. Jackson
Micah Jenkins
Bradley T. Johnson
Joseph E. Johnston
William H. Jones
John McIntosh Kell

Williamson Kelly
Moses Warren Kenyon
Evander M. Law
Fitzhugh Lee
Robert E. Lee
James Longstreet
William Mahone
Rawley White Martin
Andrew J. McBride
Lafayette McLaws
Alexander M. McPheeters
Thomas Gibbes Morgan, Jr. and Sr.
Munford-Ellis Family
John Oakey
Lizzie Nelms (Smith) Parker
Dudley Diggs Pendleton
William N. Pendleton
Green W. Penn
George Edward Pickett
Joachim R. Saussy, Jr.
Annie R. Shoemaker
William Dunlap Simpson
Stephen Calhoun Smith
William D. Smith
William Ephriam Smith
George H. Steuart I and II
James H. Stewart
Robert A. Stiles
James Ewell Brown Stuart
Robert P. Tondee
Verdery Family
Samuel Hoey Walkup
Joseph Julius Wescoat
Ambrose Ransom Wright

Emory University, Atlanta, Georgia

Bomar Family
Camp Family
Confederate Miscellany
John A. Everett
Featherston Family
Theodore Fogle
Tomlinson Fort
Georgia Miscellany
Robert Newman Gourdin
Henry Woodfin Grady

Graves Family
Benjamin W. Justice
James H. Lee
McFall Family
Benjamin L. Mobley
James A. Patton
Augustine E. Shore
William Henry Stiles
David Read Evans Winn

Florida State Archives, Tallahassee

Council A. Bryan
Byrd Family
Thomas Clark
William Wightman Gramling

Randolph Family
Robert Henry Tate
West Family
Elizabeth Ann Love Wilson

Florida State University, Tallahassee

W. W. Gramling
Letters of Confederate Soldiers

James Nixon
Pine Hill Plantation

Fredericksburg and Spotsylvania National Battlefield Park, Fredericksburg, Virginia

J. C. Allen
William Allen
Francis P. Anderson
Thomas J. Armstrong
W. Ashley
Isaac M. Auld
Alexander Baird
David Ballenger
T. G. Barham
William Barksdale
Alfred Benton Barron
James Frank Barron
Nathan T. Bartley
M. G. Bass
James E. Beard
George Rust Bedinger
Andrew J. Bell
Thomas Belue
George S. Bernard
William J. Black
Francis A. Boyle
S. W. Branch
Sanford W. Branch
Carter Braxton
Martin W. Brett
William Domas Brewer

Jack Brown
R. A. Bryant
Edward M. Burress
James Calloway
William Clegg
Samuel C. Clyde
F. M. Coker
Noah Collins
Alfred Holt Colquitt
Charles J. McDonald Conway, Jr.
L. Calhoun Cooper
Hamilton Couper
Leroy Wesley Cox
Dame
John D. Damrow
James Alexander Daniel
John W. Daniel
John Warwick Daniel
W. L. Daniel
Ancil Darnell
Dart Family
Horatio J. David
Simeon B. David
Thomas P. Devereux
Robert T. Douglas
C. R. Dudley

Fredericksburg and Spotsylvania National Battlefield Park, Fredericksburg, Virginia (*cont'd*)

T. J. Efford
James H. Elliott
Richard S. Ewell
George Field
Henry L. Figures
Gus Floyd
S. R. Flynt
J. R. Forbus
Charles T. Furlow
Seaton Gales
A. W. Garber
Robert K. Garnett
Jasper A. Gillespie
John F. Goodner
T. M. Gorman
Ezekial Dunigan Graham
Anthony Thomas Graybill
John D. Greever
A. G. Grier
George W. Hall
C. G. Hamilton
George W. Hammer
Harden-Edward
Jere Malcom Harris
Nathaniel H. Harrris
Owen T. Hedges
Eli Hemphill
Albert Wymer Henley
Thomas Herndon
Andrew Hero
Harry Hightower
A. P. Hill
Francis Lorraine Hillyer
William H. Hodnett
James Alexander Holmes
Hood Family
W. M. Hopkins
W. B. Howard
Wiley C. Howard
Benjamin Jacob Huddle
P. L. Huddleston
F. L. Hudgins
Thomas J. Jackson
Joe
Aaron F. Jones
John Haw Jones
William Ellis Jones
Joseph D. Joyne
William B. Judkins
B. W. Justice
John Keely
George F. Kelley
Joseph B. Kershaw
Henry Lord Page King
B. R. Kinney

James S. Kirkland
James J. Kirkpatrick
William H. Kirkpatrick
Jacob Lanier
R. E. Lee
Stephen D. Lee
Wills Lee
Leonard-Koiner
Lunsford Lomax
Thomas J. Luttrell
William Mahone
Charles A. Mallow
Thomas Alfred Martin
William L. Masten
William Carey Maupin
M. H. May
Thompson McAllister
Charles W. McArthur
John McDonald
Jesse McGee
McKnight Brothers
Lafayette McLaws
E. P. Miller
N. T. Miller
William R. Montgomery
Asa Stokely Morgan
William Graves Morris
Morrison Family
Henri J. Mugler
Amos Washington Murray
James Drayton Nance
William Lewis Nuckolls
V. J. Nunnelie
R. C. Oakes
John N. Old
F. M. Parker
Tully F. Parker
Josiah B. Patterson
J. J. Pettigrew
Granville P. Porter
P. H. Powers
R. Channing Price
Prillaman
Shepard Green Pryor
R
Henry D. Puckett
John Andrew Ramsay
W. F. Randolph
"Rappahannock"
Daniel S. Redding
Thomas Reeder
Tom Reeder
Anderson W. Reese
William J. Reese
Richard M. V. B. Reeves

George P. Ring
Edward Rowe
S
Alfred Lewis Scott
William S. Shockley
M. Shuler
Edward E. Sill
George W. Smith
James P. Smith
Martin L. Smith
Milton W. Smith
William W. Smith
"A Soldier"
Jesse R. Sparkman
A. N. Steele
George H. Steuart
W. P. Stillwell
William Terry
Thompson Family
J. J. Tibbetts

John Tiffany
John C. Ussery
James D. Van Valkenburg
Henry C. Walker
Thomas T. Wallace
Franklin Gardner Walter
Louis Warlick
John William Watson
Powhatan Bolling Whittle
A. S. C. Williams
George F. Williams
H. H. Williams
R. J. Wilson
Henry Wingfield
David Read Evans Winn
John B. Wise
John L. Wood
Joseph White Woods
Leander G. Woollard
John H. Worsham

Georgia Department of Archives and History, Atlanta

Blissit Family
Brooks Family
Addison Burnside
W. J. H. Carter
Civil War Miscellany Collection:
  3rd Georgia Infantry
  9th Georgia Infantry
  10th Georgia Infantry
  11th Georgia Infantry
  12th Georgia Infantry
  13th Georgia Infantry
  14th Georgia Infantry
  16th Georgia Infantry
  17th Georgia Infantry
  18th Georgia Infantry
  20th Georgia Infantry
  21st Georgia Infantry
  22nd Georgia Infantry
  23rd Georgia Infantry
  24th Georgia Infantry
  26th Georgia Infantry
  27th Georgia Infantry
  28th Georgia Infantry
  31st Georgia Infantry
  35th Georgia Infantry
  38th Georgia Infantry
  44th Georgia Infantry
  45th Georgia Infantry
  48th Georgia Infantry
  49th Georgia Infantry
  50th Georgia Infantry
  51st Georgia Infantry
  60th Georgia Infantry
  61st Georgia Infantry
  2nd Battalion Georgia Infantry

Cobb's Legion
Phillips's Legion
16th Mississippi Infantry
17th Virginia Infantry
49th Virginia Infantry
Jeremiah Jefferson Davis
Erwin Eldridge
Gabriel Farmer Family
R. W. Freeman
Jasper A. Gillespie
Thomas Fitzgerald Green
George Thomas Cottengin Grey
Jones Family
Abraham Jones
R. H. Jones
John H. J. Knowles
John Larkin
James Longstreet
Nancy O. and Thomas Mann Family
Samuel McCarroll
Thomas McCollum
Megarity Family
D. D. Morris
W. B. Morris and R. H. McGinty
John S. Mosby
William Jefferson Mosely
Jaspar A. Norris
Robert W. North
Thomas J. Owen
Josiah Blair Patterson
Andrew J. Perkins
Joel Thomas Pierce
Prescott-Jones Family
John M. Tilley
Samuel Prestly Waits

Georgia Historical Society, Savannah

Langdon Cheves
Pigman

Robertson
Joseph F. Waring

Huntington Library, San Marino, California

Brock Collection

Library of Congress, Washington, D.C.

Edward Porter Alexander
John S. Anglin
James D. and David R. Barbee
John M. Binckley
George Washington Campbell
Chase Family
John Esten Cooke
DeButts Ely
Feamster Family
Henry I. and Robert Green
Habersham Family
George Washington Hall
R. E. Hardie
Burton Harrison
Jed Hotchkiss
Fannie Page Hume
John Auchincloss Ingliss
Joseph C. Ives
Thomas J. Jackson
Joseph E. Johnston
Mercer Green Johnston
Keidel Family
Edmund Kirby-Smith

Osmun Latrobe
Breckinridge Long
Willie P. Mangum
Flora Morgan McCabe
Charles Harvey McManaway
John S. Mosby
Naval Historical Foundation
    Miscellany
Alfred Roman
W. H. Rowan
W. C. Shackelford
M. Shuler
James Power Smith
Charles W. Squires
Walter Ralph Steiner
J. E. B. Stuart
Walter H. Taylor
Robert A. Toombs
Ward Family
Louis T. Wigfall
Cadmus M. Wilcox
Works Progress Administration
Thomas L. Wragg

Library of Virginia, Richmond, Virginia

James C. Birdsong
James Bolton
Dr. James Richmond Boulware
Robert R. Bragg
St. George Tucker Brooke
Bryant Family
John J. and Silas Chandler
Richard F. Chapman
Heath Jones Christian
Company B, 2nd Virginia Infantry
    Order Book
Confederate States of America
A. N. B. Cosby
Dabney-Jackson
John Davis
Decker Family
Denoon Family

Dewese Family
John C. Donahue
Raleigh Dunaway
Edwards Family
Mrs. M. C. Emmerson
Family Budget
Garnett Family
R. H. Gray
George H. T. Greer
Grimsley Family
Edwin H. Harmar
John Hart
Daniel Harvey Hill
Isaac Hirsch
William H. Itrby
Jackson Family
W. O. Johnson

J. William Jones
James A. Kibler
William H. Kirker
James F. Knick
Robert E. Lee
William M. Levy
Edwin Baker Loving
Magruder Family
F. M. McMullen
Joseph McMurran
Enoch A. McNair
Judge Eustace C. Moncure
Thomas T. Munford
Murray Family
J. S. Newman
Dewees Ogden
Henry T. Owen
Wesley W. Palmore
William W. Parsons
W. N. Pendleton
J. P. Perin

Frank Potts
John Wesley Puryear
Thomas S. Ruffin
Henry S. Shanklin
Special Orders, Thirteenth
     Brigade, Virginia Militia
John D. Summers
Luther L. Swank
Sally Tompkins
John C. Towles
Underwood Family
Melville Walker
Ware Family
Joseph M. Weller
Welsh Family
Mary E. Wilkinson
James Peter Williams
Wise Family
James Wood
Marquis Lafayette Young

Louisiana State University, Baton Rouge

Albert A. Batchelor
P. G. T. Beauregard
David F. Boyd
John C. Burruss and Family
James Foster and Family
John Ker and Family
William H. Ker
George Kleinpeter and Family

Gustavus Schmidt
Joseph D. Shields
Benjamin Smith
John F. Stephens
Joel A. Stokes
Jefferson W. Stubbs and Family
Miles Taylor and Family
William Terry and Family

Maryland Historical Society, Baltimore

James J. Archer
Mary Caroline Bell
J. G. Brodwell
Civil War Miscellaneous
Gaddess
John Gibbon
Harry Gilmor
Howard Family

Elizabeth Phoebe Key Howard
Latrobe Family
Powell-Waring
Winfield Scott Thompson
Isaac Trimble
Noah Dixon Walker
Charles S. Winder
Wyman-Cary-Keyser

Miscellaneous Collection

Seaborn Dominey
     http://history-sites.com/mb/cw/txcwmb

Mississippi Department of Archives and History, Jackson

Eugene Baldwin
Ethelbert Barksdale
William R. Barksdale
John Berryman Crawford
William L. Davis
William D. Elder
William H. Griffin
William H. Hill
George W. Hopkins
S. A. Jonas
Archibald K. Jones
Jesse Rubel Kirkland

D. C. Love
McWillie Family
John C. Rietti
Joseph Sessions
James Hardeman Stuart
Oscar J. E. Stuart and Family
Joseph F. Terry
A. L. P. Vairin
Thomas J. Wilkins
J. J. Wilson
B. L. Wynn

Morgan Library, New York, New York

Gilder-Lehrman Collection (now at New-York Historical Society)

Richard H. Anderson
Turner Ashby
Auburn, Alabama Guard
Augusta, Ga., *Southern Cultivator*
P. G. T. Beauregard
Bud
Camden, S.C., *Confederate*
James M. Campbell
T. P. Cleveland
Alfred H. Colquitt
Columbia, S.C., *Confederate Baptist*
Columbus, Ga., *Daily Sun*
Confederate Collection—Florida
G. B. Cook
Samuel Cooper
Nat. R. Davidson
V. S. Denson
Jubal Early
Nathan G. Evans
Richard S. Ewell
Henry L. Figures
John W. Flinn
Josiah Gorgas
Wade Hampton
Daniel Harvey Hill
William T. Hollingsworth
Eppa Hunton
Thomas J. Jackson
Albert G. Jenkins
Joseph E. Johnston
Jones Family
Joseph B. Kershaw
Fitzhugh Lee
Mary Lee
Robert E. Lee
James Longstreet
Lynchburg *Virginian*

Charles Marshall
Lafayette McLaws
Andrew B. Moore
Josiah Mosely
Alexander S. Pendleton
People's Press
Petersburg, Va., *Daily Express*
George W. Phillips
Roger A. Pryor
Raleigh, N.C., *Semi-Weekly Standard*
Raleigh, N.C., *Spirit of the Age*
J. Henry Reid
Report of Joint Committee . . . of Virginia
   and Harpers Ferry Outrages
Robert E. Rodes
John G. Scurry
James A. Seddon
Paul J. and Elizabeth J. Semmes
Gustavus W. Smith
William H. Smith
Robert Stafford
Staunton, Va., *Spectator*
Stereocards of Inside Fort Mahone
Whitfield Stevens
James E. B. Stuart
Substitute for Confederate Service
Jeremiah Tate
Walter H. Taylor
Isaac R. Trimble
Gerrit Van Valkenburgh
John A. Washington
Julius White
William Whiting
George M. Williams
William L. Wilson
George Wortham

Museum of the Confederacy, Richmond, Virginia

Robert C. Allen
R. P. Allen
Mary Carter Deas Archer
Edward H. Armstrong
Thomas I. Armstrong
Army of the Peninsula Order Book,
    15 Oct.–22 Dec. 1861
Edward R. Baird
Sydnor Barksdale
Spencer Barnes
T. B. Barron
Randolph Barton
Charles Baughman
H. R. Berkeley
Henry F. Bobo
Leander S. Bobo
J. A. Braddock
J. M. Brice
Thomas W. Brice
J. A. Brickhouse
J. Thompson Brown
Philip C. Brown
Edward Clifford Bruch
C. D. Burks
William B. Burress
C. W. Butler
George E. Cary
John B. Cary Letter Book
W. H. Caskie
William Wilson Chamberlaine
Charles
Robert H. Chilton
Thomas W. Colley
Company E, 1st Virginia Cavalry
Company 1, 60th Virginia Infantry
Confederate States Medical and Surgical
    Journal
Confederate Soldiers
James A. Connor
Copies of Letters, Army of Northern
    Virginia
Roy Bird Cook
Giles B. Cooke
John B. Corell
Corse's Brigade Order Book,
    1863–65
Joseph G. Covington
N. J. Cundiff
Alfred E. Doby
John P. Dunnavant
C. A. Dunnington
F. H. Duquercron
Jubal A. Early
Arthur Evans
Maurice Evans

R. K. Evans
Fairfax Brothers
G. W. Finley
N. R. Fitzhugh
Fort Delaware Prisoners
Fort Delaware Prison Times
4th Virginia Cavalry
Edwin Galt
R. B. Garnett
T. S. Garnett
J. C. Granbery
Martin W. Gary
D. E. Gordon
John W. Gordon
Grape Shot by William Willis Bolls
Robert H. Gray
Edward A. Green
George H. T. Greer
William T. Gregory
George K. Griggs
Milo Grow
James M. Gunn
Leonidas C. Haden
Robert G. Haile
R. A. Hardaway
Hiram W. Harding
C. C. Harrison
Harry Heth
Robert W. Hicks
A. P. Hill
D. H. Hill
Caspar C. Hinkel
James R. Holley
Robert G. Holloway
B. F. Howard
Andrew J. Howell
Benjamin Huger
David Hunter
Robert W. Hunter
Thomas J. Jackson
Elijah Saunders Johnson
Peyton Johnson, Jr.
Richard Johnson
Robert Johnson Order Book
Frank B. Jones
Lewis A. Jones
K
Linden Kent
Bob Kilpatrick
Junius Kimble
Christian S. Kinser
Whitfield G. Kisling
Ben T. Lacy
George Lalane
Lee Battery

Museum of the Confederacy, Richmond, Virginia (*cont'd*)

Lee Club Gazette
Henry Carter Lee
Mary Custis Lee
R. E. Lee
R. E. Lee Telegrams
William Peter Francis Lee
C. Lewis
Richmond A. Lewis
William F. Lewis
Daniel D. Logan
David Logan
James Longstreet
M. S. Lynn
J. W. Mallett
Markham Collection
Charles Marshall
J. Y. Mason
Joseph W. Mauck
William McComb
McGehee
T. J. McGeorge
James D. McIntire
John K. McIver
David H. Mitchell
James Robert Montgomery
Joseph C. Morris
Lawson Morrissett
John S. Mosby
Joseph Mullen
Thomas T. Munford
Robert Tooler Myers
John Q. A. Nadenbousch
W. N. Nelms
Howell S. Nelson
James Stanley Newman
W. J. Oats
John O'Farrell
Thaddeus Oliver
Edward Owen
William N. Pendleton
William N. Pendleton Order Book
W. W. Perry
John Daniel Petty
J. Thomas Petty
Thomas Pinckney
Green Berry Pockress
John L. Porter
Carnot Posey
C. S. Powell
A. T. Preston
R. Channing Price
Tucker Randolph
Frank Rawle
W. J. Ready

Records of the Military Court, Longstreet's
    Corps, 20 Dec. 1862–26 Jan. 1864
C. W. C. Reeve
J. B. Richardson
Samuel A. Riddick
G. E. Robertson
Rosser F. Rock
T. D. Rock
James B. Roden
Beverly Ross
Z. T. Ross
William H. Routt
Kate Mason Rowland
Royall Family
W. H. Sanders
James M. Shackelford
Henry R. Shorter
Caleb M. Smith
Smith-Johnson
Moxley Sorrel
Southern Historical Society Papers
Henry R. Spann et al.
George H. Steuart
J. E. B. Stuart
Sidney S. Stringer
W. B. Sturtevant
Luther L. Swank
T.
William B. Taliaferro
J. S. Tanner
Tapp
M. F. Taylor
Walter H. Taylor
Sally Tompkins
Melville Vaidan
Jefferson Davis Van Benthuysen
John Henry Vest
John Walker Vinson
Charles E. Waddell
J. F. Waddell
J. B. Walton
P. C. Waring
Richard Weaver
James R. Werth
William W. Westwood
Will
David E. Williams
D. C. Williams
John P. Wilson
John Christopher Winsmith
A. R. Wright
H. E. Young Book
R. A. Young

National Archives, Washington, D.C.

Record Group 108

Information from Examination of Scouts, Deserters, etc.

Record Group 109

Abstracts of Communications Received and Endorsements, Conscript Inspector's Office, 1864
Accounts for Telegrams Sent by Gen. Robert E. Lee, Apr. 1862–June 1864
Adjutant General's Record Office, Personal Letters to Prisoners at Pt. Lookout
Battle Reports, Army of Northern Virginia, 1863
Bureau of Conscription. Letters, Reports and Endorsements Sent, Nov. 1864–Mar. 1865
Camp Lee. Progress Reports for Conscription
Circulars and Correspondence Received by the Enrolling Officer at Richmond, 1863–64
Compiled Service Records
Confidential Letters Sent, Army of Northern Virginia, June 1863–Oct. 1864
Conscription Bureau Circulars
Department Records, Army of Northern Virginia, Virginia State Forces
Diary and Account Book of Col. John Lea, 5th North Carolina Infantry
General and Special Orders and Circulars Issued, Army of Northern Virginia
General and Special Orders, Gen. W. H. C. Whiting's Command, Sep. 1861–Feb. 1862
General Information Index, Flattened and Laminated Files (Entry 454)
General Orders and Circulars, Confederate War Department
General Orders and Circulars, Gen. W. H. C. Whiting's Command, Feb.–Jul. 1862
General Orders Issued by Subcommands, Army of the Potomac
General Orders, Army of the Peninsula, May 1861–Apr. 1862
Inspection Reports and Related Records
Letters and Orders Issued and Received, Chief Surgeon's Office, General McLaws's Division, 1862–64
Letters and Telegrams Received, Superintendent of Laboratories, Macon, Georgia, June 1862–Apr. 1865
Letters and Telegrams Sent, Army and Department of the Peninsula, May 1861–May 1862
Letters and Telegrams Sent, Army of Northern Virginia, Jan. 1862–Mar. 1864
Letters and Telegrams Sent, Confederate Quartermaster General
Letters Received by Medical Director, 9 Apr. 1864–30 Mar. 1865
Letters Received by Surg. Thomas H. Williams, 7 June 1861–6 Dec. 1862
Letters Received, Confederate Secretary of War
Letters Received, Ordnance Depot, Richmond, Virginia, June 1864–Jan. 1865
Letters Received, Ordnance Depot, Richmond, Virginia, Mar.–July 1864
Letters Sent and Received, Gen. W. H. C. Whiting's Command, Mar.–July 1862
Letters Sent by Col. Robert Johnston, Commanding the Cavalry, Army of the Peninsula, July 1861–Apr. 1862
Letters Sent by Dr. Lafayette Guild, 28 June 1862–1 Apr. 1865
Letters Sent by Gen. Richard H. Anderson, Feb. 1861–Aug. 1863
Letters Sent by Gen. W. H. C. Whiting, Mar.–Apr. 1862
Letters Sent by Robert E. Lee, Mar.–Aug. 1862
Letters Sent by Surg. Thomas H. Williams, Inspector of Hospitals in Virginia, 17 May 1862–22 Jan. 1863
Letters Sent by the Medical Director's Office, Army of Northern Virginia, 1862–65
Letters Sent, Army of the Peninsula, 1862

National Archives, Washington, D.C.,
  Record Group 109 (*cont'd*)

Letters Sent, Macon Arsenal, 20 Nov. 1862–2 Jan. 1864
Letters Sent, Medical Director's Office, Sep. 1861–May 1862
Letters Sent, Ordnance Depot, Richmond, Virginia, Apr.–Sep. 1864
Letters Sent, Right Wing of the Army of Northern Virginia, June–Oct. 1862
Letters Sent, Superintendent of Laboratories, Macon, Georgia, Apr. 1863–Apr. 1864
Letters, Telegrams and Other Papers Received by Gen. Lee, 1862–65
List of Enrollments at Camp Lee, 1 Jan.–1 Jul. 1864
Medical Department Hospital Records, 21st Mississippi Infantry
Memoranda, Orders, and Letters Sent by the Assistant Inspector General, Army of the
    Peninsula, Feb.–Apr. 1862
Miscellaneous Letters Received, 7th Tennessee Infantry
Miscellaneous Orders, 7th Tennessee Infantry
Morning Report and Order Book, 1st Tennessee Infantry
Official Diary of the First Corps, Army of Northern Virginia,
    May–Oct. 1864
Order Book, 23rd North Carolina Infantry
Orders and Circulars Issued, Army of the Potomac, 2 June 1861–2 Mar. 1862
Orders and Circulars of Subcommands, Army of Northern Virginia
Orders and Circulars Received and Issued, Surg. Thomas H. Williams, 1861–62
Orders and Circulars Received and Orders Issued, Medical Director's Office, Army of the
    Potomac, 1861–62
Orders and Circulars, Department and Army of Northern Virginia, 1861–65
Orders Received by the 15th Regiment Virginia Volunteers,
    Dec. 1861–Apr. 1862
Orders Received, 15th Virginia Infantry
Orders Rodes's and Battle's Brigade, Army of Northern Virginia, 1861–65
Orders, Telegrams, and Circulars Issued by Medical Director, 19 Mar. 1863–15 Mar. 1865
Record Book of Gen. Thomas T. Munford, Apr. 1862–Sep. 1865
Record Book of Gen. W. B. Taliaferro, 1862–63
Record Book of the Hospital of the 7th Louisiana Infantry
Record of Enlisted Men Detailed, Ordnance Department, Jan.–Nov. 1864
Record of Papers Received and Referred, Army of Northern Virginia, 1862–63
Record of Quartermaster Stores Issued and Condemned in Units of the Army of
    Northern Virginia, 1862–63
Records of the Virginia Forces
Register of Assignments of Medical Officers, Medical Director's Office, Army of
    Northern Virginia
Register of Letters and Telegrams Received, Army of Northern Virginia, 1862–65
Register of Letters and Telegrams Received, Army of Northern Virginia
Register of Letters Received by Medical Director, Aug. 1863–Apr. 1865
Register of Letters Received, Department of Northern Virginia, 1862–64
Roster of Officers of Local Defense Troops and of Artillery Battalions, Army of
    Northern Virginia
Special Orders and Circulars Received, Medical Director, 1864–65
Special Orders Camp of Instruction, Richmond, Virginia
Special Orders Issued by Gen. W. B. Taliaferro, Apr. 1862–Mar. 1863
Special Orders, Army of Northern Virginia, Dec. 1861–Sep. 1863
Special Orders, Department of the Peninsula, Feb.–Apr. 1862
Special Orders, Gen. W. H. C. Whiting's Command, Feb.–July 1862
Statistical Reports of Hospitals in Virginia, 1862–64
Telegram Account Book, Army of Northern Virginia
Virginia Exemptions and Details to 17 Aug. 1864
War Department Collection of Confederate General and Staff Officers' Papers

Record Group 249

Letters Received, Office of Commissary General of Prisoners

Record Group 393

Army of the Potomac: Miscellaneous Letters, Reports and Lists Received
(Deserter Statements)

New York Public Library, New York, New York

Confederate States of America Collection:
Army Papers
Commissary Department
Miscellaneous Headquarters Papers of A. P. Hill

New-York Historical Society, New York, New York

Henry B. Dawson
Jubal A. Early
Thomas J. Jackson

Orderly Book, 15th Virginia Infantry,
1861–62
Regiments—24th Georgia Volunteers
War, 1861–1865

Norfolk Public Library, Norfolk, Virginia

Walter Herron Taylor

North Carolina Division of Archives and History, Raleigh

Henry Clay Albright
Isaac Erwin Avery
Oscar W. Blacknall
Lawrence O'Brien Branch
Mrs. Lawrence O'Brien Branch
Branson Family
Henry Brantingham and W. H. S.
Burgwyn
Isaac Brown
John B. Brown
W. H. S. Burgwyn
John Washington Calton
James P. Campbell
Henry A. Chambers
Augustus Clewell
Samuel P. Collier
Josiah Collins
Calvin J. Cowles
Thomas Pollock Devereux
Fred C. Foard
Futch Brothers
Gales Family
James B. Gordon

R. H. Gray
Bryan Grimes
James Gordon Hackett
Colier Green and Oliver Clark Hamilton
Samuel Finley Harper
Marcus Hefner
C. C. High
Daniel Harvey Hill
Robert F. Hoke
Vernon Howell
Paul E. Hubbell
H. G. Hutchinson
R. H. Hutspeth
Thomas S. Kenan
James A. King
James Longstreet
Albert Moses Luria
F. M. Y. McNeely
B. F. Medley
Raphael J. Moses
Peter M. Mull
John Owen
William G. Parker

North Carolina Division of Archives and History, Raleigh, North Carolina (*cont'd*)

George W. Pearsall

William Dorsey Pender

Pettigrew Papers

Stephen Dodson Ramseur

Robert Ransom

Marquis Lafayette Redd

Thomas Rowland

Thomas J. Ruffin, Jr.

Alfred M. Scales

Thomas Settle, Jr.

J. E. Shaffner

P. J. Sinclair

Herman W. "Pop" Taylor

Thomas C. Wester

Stephen Whitaker

H. H. A. Williams

Francis D. Winston

John Wright Family

John A. Young

John G. Young

Rice University, Houston, Texas

W. E. Barry

Edwin Howard Brigham

John Campbell

Val C. Giles

William Harrison Hamman

John W. Hutchinson

Young Marshall Moody

Ann Marie Stewart Turner

Richmond National Battlefield Park, Richmond, Virginia

Benjamin Blackwell

J. E. Cooke

Josiah Frank Cutcheon

Langston Lorenzo Epstein

Samuel Fulkerson

Georgia

William Gibson

E. A. Klipstein

Charles Silas Morton

Henri J. Mugler

Newspaper Volume

North Carolina

John Omenhausser

Sylvester J. Roberts

Linsey T. Wells

Jacob West

James Calvin Zimmerman

Schenectady County Historical Society, Schenectady, New York

Thomas H. Williams Order Book, 1861

South Carolina Historical Society, Charleston

R. F. W. Allston

Foster Family

Dr. Cornelius Kollock

P. A. McMichael

Moffett

Christopher P. Poppenheim

Mrs. St. Julien Ravenel

Smythe-Stoney-Adger Family

John H. A. Wagener

Charles F. Whilden

South Caroliniana Library, University of South Carolina, Columbia, South Carolina

Thomas Aiton

Richard Herron Anderson

James Morris Bivings

Milledge Luke Bonham

Box Family

Brabham Family

John Andrew Buchanan

M. C. Butler

Alexander Colclough

Confederate States Army

Dalton Family

Daniel Family

James Wood Davidson
Rebecca Easterling
Fall Family
Farr Family
A. Gilliland
John Nicholas Griffis
Harry Hammond
Hampton Family
Harris Family
Miles H. Hunter
Micah Jenkins
Jennings Family
Kerrison Family
Joseph B. Kershaw
John N. Knight
James Blackmon Ligon
G. M. Logan
William H. Lowrance
Matthew Simonton Lynn
R. B. Lyons
J. Foster Marshall
J. L. McCrorey
Andrew McIllwain
Means Family
Samuel Wicliffe Melton
E. A. Miller
Daniel S. Moffett

Thomas John Moore
James Drayton Nance
John Osmut
Joseph B. and Andrew Pack
James Ramsey
Thomas Reeder
James Henry Rice
Samuel Sarvis
Sheppard Family
John M. Smith
South Carolina Volunteers, 15th South
  Carolina Record Book
South Carolina Volunteers, 1st Regiment
William Stokes
William M. Taggert
John Forsythe Talbert
John Taylor
Templeton Family
Thomson Family
J. W. Tindall
James Tinkler
Charles Scott Venable
W. E. Wilson
Andrew Wallace
Thomas J. Warren
Young Family

Southern Historical Collection, University of North Carolina at Chapel Hill, Chapel Hill, North Carolina

Edward Porter Alexander
William Allan
Henry P. Alves
Waightstill Avery
Thomas Bragg
Buchanan-McClellan Family
Confederate Papers
Raleigh E. Colston
Montgomery D. Corse
Moses Ashley Curtis
Charles W. Dabney
Elias Davis
Fort Delaware Prison Times
Frank Family
Franklin Gaillard
Bryan Grimes
Alexander C. Haskell
Hilary A. Herbert
Daniel Harvey Hill
William J. Hoke
Thomas J. Jackson
Margaret Preston Junkin
Joseph Franklin Kauffman
H. C. Kendricks
Richard M. Kennedy
T. Butler King

Edmund Kirby-Smith
Alexander Lawton
Robert E. Lee
Armistead L. Long
James Longstreet
Lafayette McLaws
Neill McLeod
Samuel J. C. Moore
William Groves Morris
William N. Pendleton
William B. Pettit
Polk-Brown- Ewell Family
R. Channing Price
Proffit Family
Stephen Dodson Ramseur
Anne Linebarger Snuggs
Paul Turner Vaughan
Charles S. Venable
Sarah Lois Wadley
Richard W. Waldrop
Samuel Hoey Walkup
William Henry Wills
John J. Winfield
Anita Withers
Asa John Wyatt

State Historical Society of Wisconsin, Madison

Harriet Hamilton Bayly
Letters by Confederate Soldiers
Wisconsin Miscellaneous Manuscripts of the Civil War
Return of Captain James M. B. Stewart's Company F, Archer's Battalion Reserves

Stratford Hall, Stratford, Virginia

Lee Family
Walter Herron Taylor

Tulane University, New Orleans, Louisiana

Louisiana Historical Association:
    Battalion, Washington Artillery
    Civil War Papers
    C.S. Medical Department
    Papers of Army of Northern Virginia
    J. B. Walton

United States Army Military History Institute, Carlisle Barracks, Pennsylvania

Battle of Gettysburg Collection
Berry Family
Braxton Bragg Collection:
    R. E. Lee
Charles Bednar Collection:
    D. H. Hill
Civil War Miscellaneous Collection:
    Nehemiha Atwood
    I. M. Auld
    Ann Barineau
    Atwell J. Barrow
    James Beeler
    Dorsey Binion
    W. L. Blakely
    D. J. Blanton
    Donald Bruce
    William Floyd Chancellor
    Robert Chapman
    B. H. Coffman
    Auvergne D'Antignac
    Aaron Leonidas DeArmond
    William Dickey
    Ferdinand Dunlap
    Henry Figures
    Samuel Angus Firebaugh
    Jacob A. Fisher
    Marion Hill Fitzpatrick
    James M. Goggin
    William H. Gregory

Edwin Harris
Samuel Hillhouse
Porter King
Philip P. Lewis
Christopher Goodhand Lynch
Charles Malloy
Joseph Richard Manson
T. S. McAllister
David G. McIntosh
Solomon McLean
William Lafayette Morgan
John Young Reilly
Elbert Riddick
Samuel B. Rucker, Sr.
Logan H. N. Salyer
James Sheeran
Charles D. Sides
William B. Smithson
James C. Stone
William R. Stone
Van Deck
Charles Walsh
Howard Malcolm Walthall
Andrew Bowie Wardlaw
Samuel L. West
John Goldsborough White
Harry G. Williams
Herschel B. Wilson
C. R. Woolwine

Civil War Times Illustrated Collection:
  Adams Family
  Richard Anderson
  John E. Armstrong
  Novall Baker
  William A. Barger
  James W. Barnes
  Joel C. Blake
  John Blue
  John Bolling
  John Malachi Bowden
  R. C. Bristow
  William A. Clendening
  John Kennedy Coleman
  Samuel Cooper
  Claude Denson
  Orrin L. Ellis
  Georgia Infantry:
    Blanchard's Brigade Order Book
    Wright's Brigade Order Book
  Gettysburg File
  Charles Gratton
  George H. T. Greer
  James Griffin
  Hatchett Family
  William T. Huff
  Clarence L. Hutchins
  H. A. Jackson
  F. P. Johnson
  Benjamin A. Jones
  W. C. Lawrie
  R. E. Lee
  Wolf Lichtenstein
  William Mahone
  Robert G. McAuley
  John F. Milhollin
  William E. Moore
  Henry Ruffner Morrison
  Frank M. Myers
  John F. Neff
  Charles A. Nuttall
  Lucian S. J. Owen
  Pitzer Family
  Joseph E. Purvis
  Pansey Aiken Slappy
  William Randolph Smith
  Charles W. Squire
  Roger Stavis
  John W. Stott
  M. F. Taylor
  Elijah Tyler Tollison
  William H. Ware
  William T. Williams
T. O. Crockett Collection
D. B. Easley Collection
Earl M. Hess Collection:
  Joseph A. Englehard
  James Vance

Gregory Coco Collection:
  James M. Anderson
  William Britton Bailey, Jr.
  John W. Bosworth
  J.G.C.
  Charles W. Currie
  Thomas Galphin
  John Hardeman
  Henry C. Kirkman
  Romain O. Landry
  W. Burton Owen
  Robert Yates Ramsey
  Edwin Selvage
  Isaac G. Seymour
  Valentine W. Southall
  John B. Whitley
Harrisburg Civil War Round Table Collection:
  Augustus L. Coble
  Harvey A. Davis
  John Fontaine
  Rice D. M. Lucas
  C. B. Niegley
  Elbert Madison Williamson
  Joseph G. Williford
Daniel Harvey Hill Collection
John Gregg Collection
Thomas J. Jackson Collection
Lewis Leigh Collection:
  Abram
  A.D.A.
  J. B. Allston
  James Thorp Amil?
  Anthony
  C. M. Anderson
  E.B.
  Neill A. Baker
  Robert T. Bates
  Berry Family
  Eugene Blackford
  Bobby
  George G. Brooks
  James H. Campbell
  Charlie
  G. E. Christ
  W. L. Claybrooks
  R. T. Crenshaw
  William D. Colvin
  W. T. Conn
  A. H. Dalton
  L. R. Dalton
  Wells M. Dalton
  William B. Darst
  Auvengue D'Autignac
  William A. Davis
  J. R. Dorros
  Edward?
  Thomas E. Elliott

United States Army Military History Institute, Carlisle Barracks, Pennsylvania
Lewis Leigh Collection: (*cont'd*)

Jasper Ellis
Henry S. Figures
G. W. Finley
J. S. Flanders
James C. Gamble
William L. Gentry
F. Pinkney Gillespie
Thomas M. Golden
Thomas H. Grayson
Greene
J. G. Hadin
J. H. Hamilton
Norman Harrold
Constantine A. Hege
E. P. Hendner
Henry C. Hicks
Daniel Hileman
J. J. Hileman
Philip Hileman
Ambrose Hite
Warner Hockaday
Alexander Hogan
James W. Hommick?
David L. Hopkins
R. E. Horn
Francis Marion Howard
Harrison H. Howard
R. Ioe, Jr.
R. E. Isbell
William E. Isbell
Bob Ishiah
A. P. Johnson
H. F. Jones
Reynold M. Kirby
D. M. H. Landston
E. G. Lee
R. E. Lee
R. M. Logan
James M. Magruder
James R. Manson
S. McGowan
Cornelius McLaurin
George McNiell
Anderson Merchant
William T. Morgan
Radford Eugene Motley
Joseph M. Muse
Order Book, Hampton's Cavalry
    Brigade
A. S. Pendleton
E. V. Perry
James M. Plumer
Philip H. Powers
G. Julian Pratt

T. T. Raines
Thomas R. Randolph
A. R. H. Ransom
Redmer
Ira Reece
W. N. Rose
J. R. Rowland
John L. Runzir
William D. Ryan
Paul J. Semmes
Absey Simonton
T. J. Smith
Overton Steger
Peter B. Stickley
Jacob Stoutmire
F. L. Stuard
L. F. Stuard
Stuart's Horse Artillery
Philip A. Taliaferro
Walter Taylor
A. C. Thompson
Joseph H. Trundle
Unknown Author
A. S. Wade
Benjamin F. Wade
Horace M. Wade
Thomas M. Wade
J. G. Walker
W. T. Walker
F. B. Ward
E. T. H. Warren
T. H. Warren
John G. Webb
W. Johnson J. Webb
W. Virgil Wells
C. N. Williams
C. W. Williams
Charles Wesley Wilson
R. J. Wingate
J. H. Woods
Robert S. Young
Henry B. McClellan Collection
James and Charlotte Pratt Collection:
    N. F. Register
Michael Musick Collection:
    Dorsey N. Binion
    James T. Binion
    Bud?
    Wade G. Chick
    I. C. Craig
    Alfred Thornton Forbes
    R. D. Funkhauser
    Janney Family
    J. S. McGhea

Thomas Moore
J.N.N.
George W. Wood
Willie Workman
Milton Wylie Humphreys Collection
MOLLUS Collection:
  H. B. McClellan
John S. Mosby Collection
Murray J. Smith Collection:
  Joseph E. Johnston
  Charles Page
R. E. and G. W. C. Lee Collection:
  R. E. Lee
Ralph G. Poriss Collection:
  W. T. Hollingsworth
  Josiah (John) Mosely
  Molly Smart File
  Nick W. West
  Withers Family
Robert L. Brake Collection:
  E. P. Alexander
  William Beavens
  Granville W. Belcher
  Berry Benson
  John Malachi Bowden
  Campbell Brown
  W. H. S. Burgwyn
  William Calder
  Franklin Chunn
  Jacob Click
  Correspondent for *Augusta Daily
    Constitutionalist*
  William Delony
  Henry Kyd Douglas
  Jubal Early
  Rufus K. Felder
  Charles Figgat
  William Fitzgerald
  John Futch
  Weston R. Gales
  John Garibaldi
  G. B. Gerald
  James E. Green
  Joseph P. Haskell
  James Henry Hendrick
  William H. Hill
  Ambrose Hite
  Jed Hotchkiss
  M. A. Hubert
  John Imboden
  Cadwalader J. Iredell
  W. B. Judkins
  James J. Kirkpatrick
  Zach Landrum

Fitz Lee
John H. Lewis
William E. Lofton
James Longstreet
Robert James Lowry
J. R. Manson
Harmon Martin
Lafayette McLaws
Alex McNeill
Charles Moore
Raphael Moses
W. B. Murphy
William C. Ousby
William H. Payne
George Pickett
Shephard G. Pryor
A.W.R.
W. J. Seymour
A. C. Sims
J. Mark Smither
Charles Thompson Stuart
Fleming W. Thompson
Robert L. Thompson
W. G. Thompson
"Tout-Le-Monde"
Thomas L. Ware
Thomas J. Webb
Halsey Wigfall
William H. Winn
T. D. Witherspoon
David Zable
Rod Gregg Collection:
  Joseph M. Amos
  Ignatius
Steljes Collection:
  J. E. B. Stuart
  Robert H. Wilson
Thomas Clemens Collection:
  S. Z. Annon
  Charles W. Hodges
  D. R. Howard
  T. H. Tolson
West-Stanley-Wright Family Collection:
  William W. West
Wiley Sword Collection:
  Joseph A. Englehard
William Walker Collection:
  John B. Dodd
  Jubal Early
  Richard Edwards
  A. S. Pendleton
  Newton F Register in Pratt Folder
  James Vance

United States Military Academy, West Point, New York

Robert E. Lee

University of Alabama, Tuscaloosa

Allen Family
Gorgas Family
Thomas H. Hobbs

University of Virginia, Charlottesville

Blackford Family
Launcelot Minor Blackford
Bowles-Jordan
Brown Family
Richard Bayly Buck
Burwell Family
Cabell Family
Chandler Family
Cooke
Fleet W. Cox
Gilmer W. Crutchfield
John Warwick Daniel
John W. Davis
Davis Family
Joseph W. Embrey
Fitzhugh Family
Freeman
Gildersleeve
Gordon and Rosser Families
Hodges
Josiah Hodges
Hubard Family
Irvine-Saunders Family
Jones
Robert Garlick Hill Kean
James L. Kemper

King and Queen and Essex County
    Historical Sketches
 Leftwich Family
Letters Regarding Confederate
    Organizations, etc.
Maupin Family
McDowell Family
McDowell-Miller-Warner
McGuire
Minor-Carr-Terrell Family
Evolyn B. Moore
Morton-Halsey
Charles R. Phelps
Preston-Davis Family
Riley
Edmund Ruffin
Smiley Family
Randolph Smith
Steptoe Family
Stuart
John T. Thornton
Waddell
Ware
E. T. H. Warren
Whittle Family
J. Peter Williams
James H. Wilson

Virginia Historical Society, Richmond

John C. Allen
William Wharton Archer
Armistead-Blanton-Wallace
Aylett Family
George William Bagby
Bailey Family
Briscoe G. Baldwin
William Selwyn Ball
Bayal Family
Robert Payne Baylor
Warner Lewis Baylor
Beale Family

Bemiss Family
Berkeley Family
Bidgood Family
Benjamin L. Blackford
Blanton Family
Bolling Family
James W. Bonner
Robert A. Boyd
John Thompson Brown
St. George Tucker Coalter Bryan
Burke Family
John E. Burwell

Byrd Family
C.S.A. Army. Infantry, Anderson's Brigade
    Order Book, 1862
C.S.A. Army. Richmond Howitzers, 1st
    Company Order Book, 1861
C.S.A. Army. Richmond Howitzers, 2nd
    Company Records, 1863–64
C.S.A. Army. Virginia Engineers, 1st Regi-
    ment, Company F Letter Book, 1864
C.S.A. Army. Virginia Infantry, Tomlin's
    Battalion Letter Book, 1861
Cabell Family
Caperton Family
John T. Cappell
Carrington Family
Carter Family
William T. Casey
Chamberlayne Family
Chisholm Family
Chisolm Family
Claiborne Family
Clarke Family
Hugh Lawson Clay
Cocke Family
John Overton Collins
Confederate States of America
Conrad Family
Holmes Conrad
Giles Buckner Cooke
Cooper
Leroy Wesley Cox
Richard H. Cunningham
Dabney Family
John Warwick Daniel
Creed T. Davis
Dearing Family
James Dearing
Harman Dinwiddie
Charles A. Douglas
Edward Samuel Duffey
Jubal Early
Edmundson Family
Edrington Family
Julian T. Edwards
Leroy S. Edwards
Thomas Elder
Maurice Evans
Ezell Family
David Ezra
Fairfax Family
Benjamin Lyons Farinhold
Garnett Family
Mary Ober Gatewood
Charles Jones Green
Greene Family
Griggs Family
Grinnan Family
Gwathmey Family

Hankins Family
Harlow Family
Harrison Family
Randolph Harrison
Harvie Family
Harwood Family
Richardson Wallace Haw
Katherine H. Hawes
John S. Hayes
James Hays
Charles A. Henninghausen
A. P. Hill
Daniel Harvey Hill
James Christian Hill
Hobson Family
Holladay Family
Holloway Family
Hundley Family
Irving Family
Thomas J. Jackson
Unkle Jim
Elijah S. Johnson
Samuel R. Johnston
Alexander Caldwell Jones
Benjamin Anderson Jones
Jordan-Bell Family
Watkins Kearns
Keiley Family
Keith Family
William T. Kinzer
Joseph Harrison Lambeth
Robert A. Lancaster
John Landstreet
Langhorne Family
Osmun Latrobe
Lee Family
Edwin Gray Lee
George Bolling Lee
Robert Carter Lee
Lomax Family
Lucas Family
Majette Family
William B. Mansfield
Marrow Family
George A. Martin
Mason Family
Charles Taylor Mason
W. Gordon McCabe
H. B. McClellan
John Van Lew McCreery
Hunter H. McGuire
Lafayette McLaws
Meade Family
Ella Merryman
Josiah Stanton Moore
Neblett Family
Henry Thweatt Owen
Pegram-Johnson-McIntosh

Peyton Family
James Eldred Phillips
Charles Pickett
Philip Henry Powers
Preston Family
Richard C. Price
R. E. Lee Headquarters Papers
Rives Family
Robertson Family
Robinson Family
Francis G. Ruffin
George T. Rust
Llewellyn Saunderson
Alfred Lewis Scott
J. R. Sheldon
W. R. M. Slaughter
Francis W. Smith
St. Paul's Church Vestry Book
Joseph D. Stapp

Robert A. Stiles
J. E. B. Stuart
William B. Sydnor
Talcott Family
Erasmus Taylor
Murray Forbes Taylor
Thomas Family
Lucy Thornton
Donald Tiedeken
Tompkins Family
Upshaw Family
Beverly Randolph Wellford
Charles Urquhart Williams
Winston-Clark Family
Woolfolk Family
Wright Family
Gilbert J. Wright
Mortimer M. Young

Virginia Military Institute, Lexington

Thomas J. Jackson

Virginia Theological Seminary, Richmond

Robert Lewis Dabney

Washington and Lee University, Lexington, Virginia

M. H. Achord
Alexander Tedford Barclay
John W. Brockenbrough
John P. Dull
Edmondson Family
August Forsberg
William Alexander Gordon
John Henry Boswell Jones
William P. Parker
Rockbridge Historical Society Papers:
    Blair Family
    Albert Davidson
    Charles Andrew Davidson
    Greenlee Davidson

J. D. Davidson
William Weaver Davidson
Edward Dix
James B. Dorman
L. A. Harper
Daniel Hileman
Philip C. Hileman
David Gardiner Houston, Jr.
James B. McCutchan
J. Sherwood Raymond
James Jones White
Rufus T. Wilhelm
E. M. Walden
Withrow Family

GOVERNMENT PUBLICATIONS

Henderson, Lillian, ed. *Roster of Confederate Soldiers from Georgia, 1861–1865.* 6 vols. Hopeville, Ga.: Longina and Porter, 1959.

Journal of the Congress of the Confederate States of America, 1861–1865. 5 vols. Washington, D.C.: Government Printing Office, 1904.

Journal of the State Convention and Ordinances and Resolutions Adopted in January 1861. Jackson: E. Barksdale, 1861.

Microfilm of Early State Records.

National Park Service, Civil War Soldiers and Sailors System, http://www.itd.nps.gov/cwss/.

North Carolina Troops: A Roster. 15 vols. Raleigh: North Carolina Division of Archives and History, 1966–2003.

Official Records of the Union and Confederate Navies. Washington, D.C.: Government Printing Office, 1900.

U.S. Census Records. http://www.ancestry.com.

War of the Rebellion: Official Records of the Union and Confederate Armies. Washington, D.C.: Government Printing Office, 1880–1901.

Winkler, E. W., ed. *Journal of the Secession Convention of Texas.* Austin: Austin Printing Company, 1912.

PUBLISHED PRIMARY SOURCES

Alexander, Edward Porter. *Fighting for the Confederacy.* Gary W. Gallagher, ed. Chapel Hill: University of North Carolina Press, 1989.

Allbritton, Orval E. "The Third Arkansas Regiment from Formation to Fredricksburg." *Arkansas Historical Quarterly,* 16 (1957), 150–67.

Allen, Randall, and Bohannon, Keith S., eds. *Campaigning with "Old Stonewall": Confederate Captain Ujanirtus Allen's Letters to His Wife.* Baton Rouge: Louisiana State University Press, 1998.

Andrews, Eliza Frances. *War-Time Journal of a Georgia Girl.* New York: D. Appleton & Co., 1908.

Apperson, John Samuel. *Repairing the "March of Mars."* John Herbert Roper, ed. Macon: Mercer University Press, 2001.

Archer, James Jay. "The James J. Archer Letters: A Marylander in the Civil War." C. A. Porter Hopkins, ed. *Maryland Historical Magazine,* 56 (1961), 72–93 and 352–83.

Barrett, Milton. *The Confederacy Is On Her Way Up the Spout: Letters to South Carolina, 1861–1864.* J. Roderick Heller and Carolynn Ayres Heller, eds. Athens, Ga.: University of Georgia Press, 1992.

Barrow, Henry W. "Civil War Letters of Henry W. Barrow to John W. Fries." Marian H. Blair, ed. *North Carolina Historical Review,* 34 (1957), 68–85.

Basler, Roy P., ed. *The Collected Works of Abraham Lincoln.* 9 vols. New Brunswick, N.J.: Rutgers University Press, 1953.

Batts, William. "A Foot Soldier's Account: Letters of William Batts, 1861–1862." Jane Bonner Peacock, ed. *Georgia Historical Quarterly,* 50 (1966), 87–100.

Bean, William Gleason. *The Liberty Hall Volunteers.* Charlottesville: University Press of Virginia, 1964.

Behan, Charles I. "A Louisiana Soldier Comments on Unionist Sentiment in East Tennessee." L. Moody Simms, ed. *Louisiana History,* 21 (1980), 92–93.

Berkeley, Henry Robinson. *Four Years in the Confederate Artillery: The Diary of Private Henry Robinson Berkeley.* William H. Runge, ed. Chapel Hill: University of North Carolina Press, 1961.

Black, John Logan. *Crumbling Defenses.* Macon, Ga.: [J.W. Burke Co.], 1960.

Blackford, Susan Leigh. *Letters from Lee's Army.* New York: Charles Scribner's Sons, 1947.

Blackford, William Willis. *War Years with Jeb Stuart*. New York: Charles Scribner's Sons, 1945.

Bond, Priscilla. *A Maryland Bride in the Deep South*. Kimberly Harrison, ed. Baton Rouge: Louisiana State University Press, 2006.

Borcke, Heros von. "Memoirs of the Confederate War for Independence." *Blackwood's Edinburgh Magazine*, 97 (1865), 269–88, 389–437, and 557–80.

Boyd, Casper W. "Casper W. Boyd, Company I, 15th Alabama Infantry, C.S.A.: A Casualty at Cross Keys. His Last Letters Written Home." *Alabama Historical Quarterly*, 23 (1961), 291–99.

Bratton, John. *General John Bratton: Sumter to Appomattox in Letters to His Wife*. J. Luke Austin, ed. Sewanee, Tenn.: Proctor's Hall Press, 2003.

Bridges, Richard C. "Letters from Private Richard C. Bridges, C.S.A. 1861–1864." William L. Huettel, ed. *Journal of Mississippi History*, 33 (1971), 357–72.

Brunson, Joseph W. *Historical Sketch of the Pee Dee Light Artillery*. Winston-Salem, N.C.: Stewart Printing House, 1927.

Buck, Lucy Rebecca. *Shadows on My Heart: The Civil War Dairy of Lucy Rebecca Buck*. Elizabeth R. Baer, ed. Athens: University of Georgia Press, 1997.

Buckley, Cornelius M., ed. *A Frenchman, A Chaplain, A Rebel: The War Letters of Père Louis-Hippolyte Gache, S.J.* Chicago: Loyola University Press, 1981.

Cage, William L. "The Civil War Letters of William L. Cage." T. Harry Williams, ed. *Louisiana History*, 39 (1956), 113–30.

Casler, John Overton. *Four Years in the Stonewall Brigade*. Guthrie, Okla.: State Capital Printing Co., 1903.

Cavett, Emmet Duvergne. "A Ring Tournament in 1864. A Letter from a Mississippian in the Army of Northern Virginia." Joseph C. Robert, ed. *Journal of Mississippi History*, 3 (1941), 289–96.

Chamberlayne, John Hampden. *Ham Chamberlayne, Virginian*. Richmond: Press of the Dietz Print Co., 1932.

Chesnut. Mary. *Mary Chesnut's Civil War*. C. Vann Woodward, ed. New Haven, Conn.: Yale University Press, 1981.

Chester, Thomas Morris. *Thomas Morris Chester, Black Correspondent: His Dispatches from the Virginia Front*. Richard J. M. Blackett, ed. Baton Rouge: Louisiana State University Press, 1989.

Clark, George. *A Glance Backward: Or, Some Events in the Past History of My Life*. Houston, Tex.: Press of Rein & Sons Co., 1914.

Clark, Walter. *Histories of the Several Regiments and Battalions from North Carolina*. 5 vols. Goldsboro: Published by the State, 1901.

Clement, Abram Wilson. "Diary of Abram Wilson Clement." Slann L. C. Simmons, ed. *South Carolina Historical Magazine*, 59 (1958), 78–83.

Cody, Barnett Hardeman. "Letters of Barnett Hardeman Cody and Others, 1861–1864." *Georgia Historical Quarterly*, 23 (1939), 265–99; 362–80.

Cole, R. T. *From Huntsville to Appomattox: R. T. Cole's History of the 4th Regiment, Alabama Volunteer Infantry, C.S.A., Army of Northern Virginia*. Jeffrey D. Stocker, ed. Knoxville: University of Tennessee Press, 1996.

"A Collection of Louisiana Confederate Letters." Frank E. Vandiver, ed. *Louisiana Historical Quarterly*, 26 (1943), 937–74.

Confederate Reminscences and Letters. 14 vols. Atlanta: Georgia Division of UDC, 1995.

Confederate States Medical and Surgical Journal. Richmond: Ayres & Wade, 1864–65.

Confederate Veteran. 40 vols. Nashville, 1893–1932.

Conn, Charles Augustus. "Conn-Brantley Letters, 1864." T. Conn Bryan, ed. *Georgia Historical Quarterly*, 55 (1971), 437–41.

Conn, William Thomas, and Conn, Charles Augustus. "Letters of Two Confederate Officers." *Georgia Historical Quarterly*, 46 (1962), 169–95.

Conner, James. *Letters of General James Connner, C.S.A.* Columbia, S.C.: State Company, Printers, 1933.

Cooke, John Esten. *Wearing the Gray.* Bloomington: Indiana University Press, 1959.

Crist, Lynda Lasswell, Dix, Mary Seaton, et al., eds. *The Papers of Jefferson Davis,* vols. 7–11. Baton Rouge: Louisiana State University Press, 1992.

Croom, Wendell D. "The War-History of Company 'C,' Sixth Georgia Regiment." Published by the survivors of the Company, 1879.

Dabney, Robert Lewis. "Chaplains in the Army of Northern Virginia: A List Compiled in 1864 and 1865." W. Harrison Daniel, ed. *Virginia Magazine of History and Biography,* 71, 327–40.

Daniel, John M. *The Richmond Examiner During the War.* New York: Arno Press, 1970, reprinted from 1868 edition.

Davidson, Greenlee. *Captain Davidson Greenlee, C.S.A.: Diary and Letters, 1851–1863.* Charles W. Turner, ed. Verona, Va.: McClure Press, 1975.

Davis, Ezekiel Andrew. "Confederate Life at Home and in Camp. Seven Letters." George W. Clower, Jr., ed. *Georgia Historical Quarterly,* 40 (1956), 298–309.

Davis, Jefferson. *Rise and Fall of the Confederate Government.* 2 vols. New York: D. Appleton & Company, 1881.

Dawes, Rufus R. *Service with the Sixth Wisconsin Volunteers.* Madison: State Historical Society of Wisconsin, 1962.

Dawson, Francis Warrington. *Reminiscences of Confederate Service, 1861–1865.* Bell I. Wiley, ed. Baton Rouge: Louisiana State University Press, 1980.

Dawson, Sarah Morgan. *A Confederate Girl's Diary.* Boston: Houghton Mifflin Company, 1913.

DocSouth. http://www.docsouth.com/.

Dooley, John. *John Dooley, Confederate Soldier.* Joseph T. Durkin, ed. Washington, D.C.: Georgetown University Press, 1945.

———. *John Dooley, Confederate Soldier: His War Journal.* Joseph T. Durkin, ed. Notre Dame: University of Notre Dame Press, 1963.

Douglas, Henry Kyd. *I Rode with Stonewall.* Chapel Hill: University of North Carolina Press, 1940.

Dowdey, Clifford, and Manarin, Louis H., eds. *Wartime Papers of Robert E. Lee.* Boston: Little, Brown, and Company, 1961.

Dwinell, Melvin. "Vermonter in Gray, the Story of Melvin Dwinell." *Vermont History,* 30 (1962), 220–37.

Dwinell, Melvin. "Letters of Melvin Dwinell, Yankee Rebel." Virginia Griffin Bailey, ed. *Georgia Historical Quarterly,* 47 (1963), 193–203.

Early, Jubal Anderson. *War Memories: Autobiographical Sketch and Narrative of the War Between the States.* Frank E. Vandiver, ed. Bloomington, Ind.: Indiana University Press, 1960.

Edmondston, Catherine Ann Devereux. *"Journal of a Secesh Lady."* Beth Gilbert Crabtree and James W. Patton, eds. Raleigh: North Carolina Division of Archives and History, 1979.

Eggleston, George Cary. *A Rebel's Recollection.* David Donald, ed. Bloomington, Ind.: Indiana University Press, 1959.

Ellison, Joseph M. "Joseph M. Ellison: War Letters (1862)." Calvin J. Billman, ed. *Georgia Historical Quarterly,* 48 (1964), 229–38.

An English Combatant. *Battle-Fields of the South from Bull Run to Fredericksburg.* New York: John Bradburn, 1864, reprinted by Time-Life Books, 1984.

An English Officer [Wolseley]. "A Month's Visit to the Confederate Headquarters." *Blackwood's Magazine,* 43 (Jan. 1863).

Fleet, Benjamin, and Fleet, Fred. *Green Mount: A Virginia Plantation Family During the Civil War.* Betsy Fleet and John D. P. Fuller, eds. Lexington: University of Kentucky Press, 1962.

Fleming, Francis Phillip. "Fleming in the War for Southern Independence." Edward C. Williamson, ed. *Florida Historical Quarterly*, 28 (1949/50), 38–52, 143–55, 205–10.
———. "Soldiering with the Second Florida Infantry Regiment." John P. Ingle, Jr., ed. *Florida Historical Quarterly*, 59 (1981), 335–39.
Fontaine, Lamar. "The Prison Life of Major Lamar Fontaine." Clarksdale, Miss.: Daily Register Print, 1910.
Foote, H. S. *War of the Rebellion or Scylla and Charybdis*. New York: Harper & Brothers, Publishers, 1866.
Ford, Arthur Peronneau. *Life in the Confederate Army*. New York: Neale Publishing Co., 1905.
"The 4th Alabama Regiment at the Battle of Manassas." *Alabama Historical Quarterly*, 23 (1961), 208–10.
Freeman, Benjamin H. *Confederate Letters of Benjamin H. Freeman*. Susan T. Wright, ed. Hicksville, N.Y.: Exposition Press, 1974.
Freeman, Douglas Southall, ed. *Lee's Dispatches*. New York: G. P. Putman's Sons. 1957.
Fremantle, Arthur J. L. *The Fremantle* Diary. Walter Lord, ed. Boston: Little, Brown and Company, 1954.
Frobel, Anne S. *The Civil War Diary of Anne S. Frobel*. McLean, Va.: EPS Publication, 1992.
Goodner, John F. *The Goodner Family*. Hubert Wesley Lacey, ed. Dayton, Ohio: 1960.
Goodson, Joab. "The Letters of Captain Joab Goodson, 1862–1864." W. Stanley Hoole, ed. *Alabama Review*, 10 (1957), 127–53 and 215–31.
Gordon, John Brown. *Reminiscences of the Civil War*. New York: Charles Scribner's Sons, 1903.
Goree, Thomas Jewett. *Longstreet's Aide: The Civil War Letters of Major Thomas J. Goree*. Thomas W. Cutrer, ed. Charlottesville: University Press of Virginia, 1995.
———. *The Thomas Jewett Goree Letters*, I. Langston James Goree, ed. Bryan, Tex.: Texas Family History Foundation, 1981.
Gorgas, Josiah. *Civil War Diary of General Josiah Gorgas*. Frank E. Vandiver, ed. University, Ala.: Alabama University Press, 1947.
———. *The Journals of Josiah Gorgas, 1857–1878*. Sarah Wiggins, ed. Tuscaloosa, Ala.: University of Alabama Press, 1995.
Grimes, Bryan. *Extracts of Letters of Major- General Bryan Grimes to His Wife*. Gary Gallagher, ed. Wilmington, N.C.: Broadfoot Publishing Company, 1986.
Griscom, John H. *The Sanitary Condition of the Laboring Class of New York, With Suggestions for Its Improvement*. New York: Harper & Brothers, 1845, reprinted by Arno Press, 1970.
Haile, Robert Gaines, Jr. *Tell the Children I'll Be Home When the Peaches Get Ripe: The Journal and Letters of Robert Gaines Haile, Jr.*. Robert M. Tombes, ed. Richmond: Tizwin, 1999.
Harrison, Walter. *Pickett's Men: A Fragment of War History*. Gaitherburg, Md.: Butternut Press, 1984.
Haynes, Draughton Stith. *The Field Diary of a Confederate Soldier*. Darien, Ga.: Ashantilly Press, 1963.
Heflin, W. P. *Blind Man "On the Warpath."* Published in 1903.
Hennig, Helen Kohn. *August Kohn: Versatile South Carolinian*. Columbia, S.C.: The Vogue Press, 1949.
Heth, Henry. *The Memoirs of Henry Heth*. Westport, Conn.: Greenwood Press, 1974.
Heyward, Pauline DeCaradeuc. *A Confederate Lady Comes of Age*. Mary D. Robertson, ed. Columbia: University of South Carolina Press, 1992.
Hightower, Harvey Judson. "Letters from H. J. Hightower: A Confederate Soldier, 1862–1864." Dewey W. Grantham, Jr., ed. *Georgia Historical Quarterly*, 40 (1956), 174–89.

Hinson, William Godber. "The Diary of William G. Hinson During the War of Secession." Joseph Ioor Waring, ed. *South Carolina Historical Magazine*, 75 (1974), 14–23 and 111–20.

"A Historical Sketch of the Quitman Guards, Company E, Sixteenth Mississippi Regiment." New Orleans, La.: Isaac T. Hinton, 1866.

Holt, Davis. *A Mississippi Rebel in the Army of Northern Virginia*. Thomas D. Cockrell and Michael B. Ballard, eds. Baton Rouge: Louisiana State University Press, 1995.

Hood, John Bell. *Advance and Retreat: Personal Experiences in the United States & Confederate States Armies*. Bloomington, Ind.: Indiana University Press, 1959.

Hosford, John W. "A Florida Soldier in the Army of Northern Virginia: The Hosford Letters." Knox Mellon, Jr., ed. *Florida Historical Quarterly*, 46 (1968), 243–71.

Hotchkiss, Jedediah. *Make Me a Map of the Valley: The Civil War Journal of Stonewall Jackson's Topographer*. Archie P. McDonald, ed. Dallas: Southern Methodist University Press, 1973.

Houck, Peter W., ed., *Duty, Honor, Country: The Diary and Biography of General William P. Craighill at West Point, 1849–1853*. Lynchburg, Va.: Warwick House, 1993.

Houghton, Mitchell Bennett. *From the Beginning Until Now*. Montgomery, Ala.: M. B. Houghton, 1914.

House, Ellen Renshaw. *A Very Violent Rebel: The Civil War Diary of Ellen Renshaw House*. Daniel E. Sutherland, ed. Knoxville, Tenn.: University of Tennessee Press, 1996.

Howard, McHenry. *Recollections of a Maryland Confederate Soldier and Staff Officer Under Johnston, Jackson and Lee*. Dayton, Ohio: Morningside Bookshop, 1975.

Hoy, Patrick Crawford. *A Brief History of Bradford's Battery*. Petersburg, Va.: P. C. Hoy, 1903.

Hubbert, Mike M. "The Travels of the 13th Mississippi Regiment: Excerpts from the Diary of Mike M. Hubbert of Attala County (1861–1862)." John E. Fisher, ed. *Journal of Mississippi History*, 45 (1983), 288–313.

Hubbs, G. Ward, ed. *Voices from Company D: Diaries by the Greensboro Guards, Fifth Alabama Infantry Regiment, Army of Northern Virginia*. Athens: University of Georgia Press, 2003.

Huckaby, Leander. "A Mississippian in Lee's Army: The Letters of Leander Huckaby." Donald E. Reynolds, ed. *Journal of Mississippi History*, 36 (1974), 53–67, 165–78, and 273–88.

Hudson, James G. "A Story of Company D, 4th Alabama Infantry Regiment, C.S.A." Alma H. Pate, ed. *Alabama Historical Quarterly*, 23 (1961), 139–79.

Humphreys, Benjamin G. "Delayed Report of an Important Eye-Witness at Gettysburg—Benjamin G. Humphreys." Frank E. Everett, Jr., ed. *Journal of Mississippi History*, 46 (1984), 305–21.

Hurst, M. *History of the Fourteenth Regiment Alabama Vols., With a List of Names of Every Man that Ever Belonged to the Regiment*. Richmond, Va.: M.B. Hurst, 1863.

Johnston, Joseph E. *Narrative of Military Operations Directed in the War Between the States*. Bloomington: University of Indiana Press, 1959.

Jones, Charles T. "Five Confederates, the Sons of Bolling Hall in the Civil War." *Alabama Historical Quarterly*, 25 (1963), 133–231.

Jones, J. William. *Christ in the Camp: Religion in the Confederate Army*. Harrisonburg, Va.: Sprinkle Publications, 1986; orig. B. F. Johnson & Co., 1887.

Jones, John Beauchamp. *A Rebel War Clerk's Diary*. New York: Sagamore Press, 1958.

Jordan, Allen C., and Jordan, Thomas. "The Thomas G. Jordan Family During the War Between the States." *Georgia Historical Quarterly*, 59, 135–40.

Jordan, William C. *Some Events and Incidents During the Civil War*. Montgomery, Ala.: Paragon Press, 1909.

Jordan, Winthrop D. *Tumult and Silence at Second Creek: An Inquiry into a Civil War Slave Conspiracy*. Baton Rouge: Louisiana State University Press, 1993.

Joslyn, Mauriel Phillips, ed. *Charlotte's Boys: Civil War Letters of the Branch Family of Savannah*. Berryville, Va.: Rockbridge Publishing Company, 1996.

Kean, Robert Garlick Hill. *Inside the Confederate Government: The Diary of Robert Garlick Hill Kean*. New York: Oxford University Press, 1957.

Lamar Rifles, a History of Company G, Eleventh Mississippi Regiment, C.S.A. Roanoke, Va.: Stone Print and Mfg. Co., 1903.

Landers, Eli Pinson. *Weep Not for Me, Dear Mother*. Elizabeth Whitley Roberson, ed. Gretna, La.: Pelican, 1996.

Lang, David. "Civil War Letters of Colonel David Lang." Bertram H. Groene, ed. *Florida Historical Quarterly*, 54 (1976), 340–66.

LeConte, Emma. *When the World Ended*. Earl Schenck Miers, ed. New York: Oxford University Press, 1957.

Lee, Fitzhugh. *Chancellorsville*. Richmond: Virginia Division of the Army of Northern Virginia, 1879.

———. *General Lee*. Greenwich, Conn.: Fawcett Publications, 1961.

Lee, Robert E., Jr. *Recollections and Letters of General Robert E. Lee*. New York: Doubleday, Page & Co., 1904.

Leon, Louis. *Diary of a Tar Heel Confederate Soldier*. Charlotte, N.C.: Stone Publishing Co., [1913].

Lightfoot, Thomas Reese. "Letters of the Three Lightfoot Brothers." *Georgia Historical Quarterly*, 25 (1941), 65–90.

Lightsey, Ada Christine. *The Veteran's Story*. Meridian, Miss.: Meridian News, 1899.

Longstreet, James. *From Manassas to Appomattox*. Bloomington, Ind.: Indiana University Press, 1960.

Love, D. C. *The Prairie Guards*. Columbus, Ga.: 1890.

Lowe, Jeffrey C., and Hodges, Sam, eds. *Letters to Amanda: The Civil War Letters of Marion Hill Fitzpatrick, Army of Northern Virginia*. Macon, Ga.: Mercer University Press, 1998.

Lyman, Theodore. *Meade's Headquarters, 1863–1865: Letters of Colonel Theodore Lyman from Wilderness to Appomattox*. George R. Agassiz, ed. Boston: Massachusetts Historical Society, 1922.

Mahone, William. "On the Road to Appomattox." William C. Davis, ed. *Civil War Times Illustrated*, 9 (1971), 4–11 and 42–47.

Mallet, J. W. "Work of the Ordnance Bureau of the War Department of the Confederate States, 1861–1865." *The Alumni Bulletin of the University of Virginia* (Apr. and Aug. 1910), 164–67.

Malone, Bartlett Yancey. *Whipt 'Em Everytime: The Diary of Bartlett Yancey Malone*. Jackson, Tenn.: McCowat-Mercer Press, 1960.

Marcus, Jacob Rader, ed. *Memoirs of American Jews, 1775–1865*. 3 vols. Philadelphia: Jewish Publication Society of America, 1955–56.

Marshall, Charles. *Lee's Aide-de-Camp*. Lincoln: University of Nebraska Press, 2000.

Martin, Abbot C. "Chancellorsville, a Soldier's Letter." *Virginia Magazine of History and Biography*, 37 (1929), 221–28.

———. "The Cotton Letters." *Virginia Magazine of History and Biography*, 37 (1929), 12–22.

Maxwell, David Elwell. "Some Letters to His Parents By a Floridian In the Confederate Army." Gilbert Wright, ed. *Florida Historical Quarterly*, 36 (1958), 353–72.

McCarthy, Carlton. *Detailed Minutiae of Soldier Life in the Army of Northern Virginia, 1861–1865*. Richmond: Carlton McCarthy and Co., 1884.

McClellan, George B. *The Civil War Papers of George B. McClellan: Selected Correspondence, 1860–1865*. Stephen Sears, ed. New York: Ticknor & Fields, 1989.

McClellan, Henry Brainerd. *I Rode with Jeb Stuart*. Bloomington: Indiana University Press, 1958.

McDonald, Cornelia Peake. *A Woman's Civil War: A Diary with Reminiscences of the War from March 1862*. New York: Grammercy Books, 1992.

McKim, Randolph H. *A Soldier's Recollections*. New York: Longmans, Green, 1910.

McLaws, Lafayette. *A Soldier's General: The Civil War Letters of Major General Lafayette McLaws*. John C. Oeffinger, ed. Chapel Hill: University of North Carolina Press, 2002.

McNeill, James M. "The Prison Notebook of Captain James M. McNeill, C.S.A." Louise McNeill Pease, ed. *West Virginia History*, 31 (1970), 180–84.

Meade, George Gordon. *Life and Letters of George Gordon Meade* 2 vols. George G. Meade, ed. New York: Charles Scribner's Sons, 1913.

Miller, Robert H. "Letters of Lieutenant Robert H. Miller to His Family, 1861–1862." Forrest P. Connor, ed. *Virginia Magazine of History and Biography*, 70 (1961), 62–91.

Mills, Luther Rice. "Letters of Luther Rice Mills, a Confederate Soldier." *North Carolina Historical Review*, 4 (1927), 285–310.

Mitchell, James Madison. "A Confederate Soldier's Letters." *Georgia Historical Quarterly*, 30 (1952), 286–88.

Mohr, James C., ed. *The Carmony Diaries: A Northern Family in the Civil War*. Pittsburg: University of Pittsburg Press, 1982.

Moore, Frank, ed. *The Rebellion Record: A Diary of American Events with Documents, Narratives, Illustrative Incidents, Poetry, etc.* 11 vols. New York: G. P. Putnam, 1864–68.

Moore, Robert A. *A Life for the Confederacy*. James W. Silver, ed. Jackson, Tenn.: McCowat-Mercer Press, 1959.

Morgan, Stephen A. "The Civil War Journal of Stephen A. Morgan." *West Virginia History*, 22 (1960–61), 207–16.

Morrisett, Aldernon Sydney. "A Confederate Soldier's Eye-Witness Account of the Merrimack Battle." Leonora Dismukes Parish and Camillus J. Dismukes, eds. *Georgia Historical Quarterly*, 54 (1970), 430–32.

Mosby, John Singleton. *The Letters of John S. Mosby*. Adele H. Mitchell, ed. NP: Stuart-Mosby Historical Society, 1986.

———. *Memoirs*. Bloomington: Indiana University Press, 1959.

Moses Raphael Jacob. *Last Order of the Lost Cause*. Mel Young, ed. Lanham, Md.: University Press of America, 1995.

Nisbet, James Cooper. *4 Years on the Firing Line*. Bell I. Wiley, ed. Jackson, Tenn.: McCowat-Mercer, 1963.

Northrop, Lucius Bellinger. "Some Letters of Lucius Bellinger Northrop, 1860–1865." Willard E. Wright, ed. *Virginia Magazine of History and Biography*, 68 (1960), 456–77.

Oates, William C. *The War Between the Union and the Confederacy and Its Lost Opportunities*. New York: Neale Publishing Co., 1905.

Oden, John Piney. "The End of Oden's War: A Confederate Captain's Diary." Michael Barton, ed. *Alabama Historical Quarterly*, 43 (1981), 73–98.

Olmsted, Frederick Law. *A Journey in the Seaboard Slave States in the Years 1853–1854*, II. New York: G. P. Putnam's Sons, 1904.

Park, Robert Emory. *Sketch of the Twelfth Alabama Infantry of Battle's Brigade, Rodes's Division, Early's Corps, of the Army of Northern Virginia*. Richmond, Va.: William Ellis Jones, 1906.

Parker, James C., Wood, Lawrence E., and Strain, Willard E., eds. *The Strain Family: A Genealogy of the Descendants of Andrew Strain, Sr. of North Carolina*. Toccoa, Ga.: Commercial Printing Company, 1985.

Patterson, Joseph Blair. "Irrepressible Optimism of a Georgia Confederate in 1864, a Letter." *Georgia Historical Quarterly*, 37 (1953), 348–50.

Paxton, Elisha Franklin. *The Civil War Letters of General Frank "Bill" Paxton, CSA, a Lieutenant of Lee & Jackson*. John Gallatin Paxton, ed. Hillsboro, Tex.: Hill Junior College Press, 1978.

Pender, William Dorsey. *The Civil War Letters of William Dorsey Pender to Fanny Pender*. William W. Hassler, ed. Chapel Hill: University of North Carolina Press, 1965.

Pendleton, William Frederic. *Confederate Diary*. Bryn Athyn, Pa., 1957.

Pierrepont, Alice V. *Reuben Vaughan Kidd: Soldier of the Confederacy*. Petersburg, Va., 1947.

Plane, William Fisher. "Letters of William Fisher Plane, C.S.A., to His Wife." *Georgia Historical Quarterly*, 48 (1964), 215–28.

Poague, William Thomas. *Gunner with Stonewall*. Jackson, Tenn.: McCowat-Mercer Press, 1957.

Post, John Eager Howard. [Letter to His Mother, 17 June 1862]. *Maryland Historical Magazine*, 40 (1945), 290–94.

Putnam, Sallie Brock. *Richmond During the War*. Lincoln: University of Nebraska Press, 1996.

Reagan, John H. *Memoirs: With Special Reference to Secession and the Civil War*. Austin, Tex.: The Pemberton Press, 1968.

Recollections and Reminiscences, 1861–1865. 12 vols. South Carolina Division, United Daughters of the Confederacy, 1990.

Renshaw, James A. "Major John B. Prados." *Louisiana Historical Quarterly*, 10 (1927), 241–48.

Report of the Secretary of the Baltimore Agricultural Aid Society.

"Roll Company A (Pensacola Rifle Rangers)." *Florida Historical Quarterly*, 37 (1958/59), 369–70.

Roman, Alfred. *Military Operations of General Beauregard, in the War Between the States, 1861 to 1865*. 2 vols. New York: Harper & Brothers, 1884.

Rosen, Robert N. *The Jewish Confederates*. Columbia: University of South Carolina Press, 2000.

Ross, John De Hart. "Harpers Ferry to the Fall of Richmond: Letters of Colonel John De Hart Ross, C.S.A., 1861–1865." *West Virginia History*, 45 (1984), 159–74.

Rowland, Dunbar, ed. *Jefferson Davis, Constitutionalist: His Letters, Papers and Speeches*. Jackson, Miss.: Mississippi Department of Archives and History, 1922.

Rozier, John. *Granite Farm Letters: The Correspondence of Edgeworth and Sallie Byrd*. Athens: University of Georgia Press, 1988.

Ruffin, Edmund. *The Diary of Edmund Ruffin*. 2 vols. William Kauffman Scarborough, ed. Baton Rouge: Louisiana State University Press, 1971 and 1976.

Sawyer, Franklin. *A Military History of the 8th Regiment Ohio Vol. Infy*. Cleveland: Fairbanks & Co., 1881.

Scheibert, Justus. *Seven Months in the Rebel States*. Tuscaloosa, Ala.: Confederate Publishing Co., 1958.

Segars, J. H., and Barrow, Charles Kelly. *Black Southerners in Confederate Armies: A Collection of Historical Accounts*. Madison, Ga.: Southern Lion Press, 2001.

Sheeran, James B. *Confederate Chaplain: A War Journal*. Joseph T. Durkin, ed. Milwaukee: Bruce Publishing Company, 1960.

"A Sketch of 12 Months Service in the Mobile Rifle Company by and Unidentified Member." *Alabama Historical Quaterly*, 25 (1963), 149–89.

Smith, Anna Habersham Wright, ed. *A Savannah Family, 1830–1901*. Milledgeville, Ga.: Boyd Publishing, 1999.

Smith, Gustavus W. *The Battle of Seven Pines*. New York: C. G. Crawford, Printers, 1891.

Sorrel, Gilbert Moxley. *Recollections of a Confederate Staff Officer*. Jackson, Tenn.: McCowat-Mercer Press, 1958.

Southern Bivouac.

Southern Historical Society Papers. Richmond, Va.: Published by the Society.

Stamp, J. B. "Ten Months in Northern Prisons." *Alabama Historical Quarterly*, 18 (1956), 486–98.

Stiles, Robert. *Four Years Under Marse Robert*. Dayton, Ohio: Morningside Press, 1977.

Stilwell, William R. *The Stilwell Letters: A Georgian in Longstreet's Corps, Army of Northern Virginia*. Ronald H. Moseley, ed. Macon, Ga.: Mercer University Press, 2002.

Stone, Kate. *Brokenburn: The Journal of Kate Stone, 1861–1868*. John Q. Anderson, ed. Baton Rouge: Louisiana State University Press, 1995.

Strayhorn, Thomas Jackson. "Letters of Thomas Jackson Strayhorn." *North Carolina Historical Review*, 13 (1936), 311–34.

Strong, George Templeton. *The Diary of George Templeton Strong*. Vol. 3. Allan Nevins and Milton Halsey Thomas, eds. New York: The Macmillan Company, 1952.

Styple, William B., ed. *Writing & Fighting from the Army of Northern Virginia*. Kearny, N. J.: Bell Grove Publishing Company, 2003.

Suddath, James Butler. "From Sumter to the Wilderness: Letters of Sergeant James Butler Suddath, Company E, 7th Regiments S.C.V." Frank B. William, Jr., ed. *South Carolina Historical Magazine*, 63 (1962), 1–11 and 93–104.

Taylor, Richard. *Destruction and Reconstruction*. New York: Longmans, Green, 1955.

Taylor, Walter Herron. *Four Years with General Lee*. Bloomington: Indiana University Press, 1962.

———. *Lee's Adjutant: The Wartime Letters of Colonel Walter Herron Taylor, 1862–1865*. R. Lockwood Tower, ed. Columbia: University of South Carolina Press, 1995.

Taylor, William Henry. *De Quibus: Discourses and Essays*. Richmond: The Bell Book and Stationery Company, Publishers, 1908.

———. "Some Experiences of a Confederate Assistant Surgeon." *Transactions of the College of Physicians of Philadelphia*, series 3, 28 (1906), 91–121.

Tenney, Samuel Fisher. "War Letters of S. F. Tenney, a Soldier in the Third Georgia Regiment." E. B. Duffee, Jr., ed. *Georgia Historical Quarterly*, 57 (1973), 277–95.

Thompson. James Thomas. "A Georgia Boy with 'Stonewall' Jackson." Aurelia Austin, ed. *Virginia Magazine of History and Biography*, 70 (1962), 314–31.

Torrence, Leonidas. "The Road to Gettysburg: The Diary and Letters of Leonidas Torrence of the Gaston Guards." Haskell Monroe, ed. *North Carolina Historical Review*, 36 (1959), 476–517.

Townsend, Harry C. *Townsend's Diary, Last Months of the War, January–May 1865*. Richmond: Wm. Ellis Jones, Printer, 1907.

Trimble, Isaac. "The Civil War Diary of Isaac Trimble." William Starr Myers, ed. *Maryland Historical Magazine*, 17 (1922), 1–20.

Trowbridge, John T. *The Desolate South, 1865–1868; A Picture of the Battlefields and of the Devastated Confederacy*. Gordon Carroll, ed. Freeport, N.Y.: Books for Libraries Press, 1956.

Trundle, Joseph H. "Gettysburg Described in Two Letters from a Maryland Confederate." *Maryland Historical Magazine*, 54 (1959), 210–12.

Tucker, John S. "The Diary of John S. Tucker: Confederate Soldier from Alabama." Gary Wilson, ed. *Alabama Historical Quarterly*, 43 (1981), 5–33.

Vaughan, Alfred J. *Personal Record of the Thirteenth Regiment Tennessee Infantry*. [Memphis: Press of S.C. Toof & Co., 1897].

Vaughn, Turner. "Diary of Turner Vaughn, Co. C, 4th Alabama Regiment, C.S.A." *Alabama Historical Quarterly*, 18 (1956), 573–604.

Vinson, Uriah T. "The Vinson Confederate Letters." Hugh Buckner Johnston, ed. *North Carolina Historical Review*, 25 (1948), 100–110.

Wainwright, Charles S. *A Diary of Battle: The Personal Journals of Colonel Charles S. Wainwright, 1861–1865*. Allan Nevins, ed. New York: Harcourt, Brace & World, 1962.

Welch, Spencer Glasgow. *A Confederate Surgeon's Letters to His Wife*. New York: Neale Publishing Co., 1911.

Welsh, John P. and James Welsh. "A House Divided: The Civil War Letters of Virginia Family." W. G. Bean, ed. *Virginia Magazine of History and Biography*, 59 (1951), 397–422.

Wescoat, Joseph Julius. "Diary of Captain Joseph Julius Wescoat, 1863–1865." Anne King Gregorie, ed. *South Carolina Historical Magazine*, 59 (1958), 11–23 and 84–95.

Williams, Edward B., ed. *Rebel Brothers: The Civil War Letters of the Truehearts*. College Station: Texas A&M University Press, 1995.

Wilson, Legrand James. *The Confederate Soldier*. Memphis: Memphis State University Press, 1973.

Wise, John Sergeant. *The End of an Era*. New York: T. Yoseloff, 1965.
Withers, John. "One Year of the War: The Civil War Dairy of John Withers." H. E. Sterkx and L. Y. Trapp, eds. *Alabama Historical Quarterly*, 29 (1967), 133–84.
Woolwine, Rufus J. "The Civil War Diary of Rufus J. Woolwine. Louis H. Manarin, ed. *Virginia Magazine of History and Biography*, 71 (1963), 416–48.
Worsham, John H. *One of Jackson's Foot Cavalry*. Jackson, Tenn.: McCowat-Mercer Press, 1964. (Originally published New York: Neale Publishing Co., 1912.)
Young, Abram Hayne. "Civil War Letters of Abram Hayne Young." Mary Wyche Burgess, ed. *South Carolina Historical Magazine*, 78 (1977), 56–70.

NEWSPAPERS

Athens Southern Banner
Atlanta Southern Confederacy
Augusta Constitutionalist
Baltimore Sun
Charleston Courier
Charleston Mercury
Daily South Carolinian
Eufala Express
Goldsboro Tribune
Macon Daily Telegraph
Minneapolis State Atlas
Mobile Advertiser

New Orleans Picayune
New York Times
North Carolina Standard
Raleigh Standard
Richmond Dispatch
Richmond Enquirer
Richmond Examiner
Richmond Sentinel
Richmond Whig
Savannah Republican
Vicksburg Whig
Wilmington Daily Journal

CITED SECONDARY SOURCES

Allmendinger, David Jr. *Ruffin: Family and Reform in the Old South*. New York: Oxford University Press, 1990.
Alvesson, Mats. *Understanding Organizational Culture*. London: Sage Publications, 2002.
Arnold, Thomas Jackson. *Early Life and Letters of General Thomas J. Jackson*. New York: Fleming H. Revell Company, 1916.
Ayers, Edward K., Gallagher, Gary W., and Blight, David W. *Appomattox Court House*. Harpers Ferry, Va.: National Park Service, 2002.
Ayers, Edward L. *In the Presence of Mine Enemies: War in the Heart of America, 1859–1863*. New York: W. W. Norton & Company, 2003.
Barney, William L. *The Secessionist Impulse: Alabama and Mississippi in 1860*. Princeton: Princeton University Press, 1974.
Bigelow, John Jr. *The Campaign of Chancellorsville*. New Haven: Yale University Press, 1910.
Black, Robert C., III. *The Railroads of the Confederacy*. Chapel Hill: University of North Carolina Press, 1998.
Blair, William. *Virginia's Private War: Feeding Body and Soul in the Confederacy, 1861–1865*. New York: Oxford University Press, 1998.
Boritt, Gabor S., ed. *The Gettysburg Nobody Knows*. New York: Oxford University Press, 1997.
———, ed. *Why the Confederacy Lost*. New York: Oxford University Press, 1992.
Brown, Kent Masterson. *Retreat from Gettysburg: Lee, Logistics, and the Pennsylvania Campaign*. Chapel Hill: University of North Carolina Press, 2005.
Bunch, Jack A. *Roster of the Courts-Martial in the Confederate States Armies*. Shippensburg, Pa.: White Mane Books, 2001.
Burton, Brian K. *Extraordinary Circumstances: The Seven Days Battles*. Bloomington: Indiana University Press, 2001.

Busey, John W., and Martin, David G. *Regimental Strength and Losses at Gettysburg*. Hightstown, N.J.: Longstreet House, 2005.

Butler, David F. *United States Firearms: The First Century, 1776–1875*. New York: Winchester Press, 1971.

Calkins, Chris M. *The Final Bivouac: The Surrender Parade at Appomattox and the Disbanding of the Armies, April 10–May 20, 1865*. Lynchburg, Va.: H. E. Howard, 1988.

Campbell, Jacqueline Glass. *When Sherman Marched North from the Sea: Resistance on the Confederate Home Front*. Chapel Hill: University of North Carolina Press, 2003.

Carmichael, Peter S. *The Last Generation: Young Virginians in Peace, War, and Reunion*. Chapel Hill: University of North Carolina Press, 2005.

———. *Lee's Young Artillerist: William J. Pegram*. Charlottesville: University Press of Virginia, 1995.

Casdorph, Paul D. *Prince John Magruder: His Life and Campaigns*. New York: John Wiley & Sons, 1996.

Cavanaugh, Michael A., and Marvel, William. *The Battle of the Crater: "The Horrid Pit," June 25–August 6, 1864*. Lynchburg, Va.: H.E. Howard, 1989.

Channing, Steven A. *Crisis of Fear: Secession in South Carolina*. New York: Simon & Schuster, 1970.

Coddington, Edwin B. *The Gettysburg Campaign: A Study in Command*. New York: Charles Scribner's Sons, 1968.

Coffman, Edward M. *The Old Army: A Portrait of the American Army in Peacetime, 1784–1898*. New York: Oxford University Press, 1986.

Coleman, Elizabeth. "The Captain Was a Lady." *Virginia Cavalcade*, 6, 1, 35–41.

Connelly, Donald B. *John M. Schofield and the Politics of Generalship*. Chapel Hill: University of North Carolina Press, 2006.

Connelly, Thomas L. *The Marble Man: Robert E. Lee and His Image in American Society*. Baton Rouge: Louisiana State University Press, 1977.

———. "Robert E. Lee and the Western Confederacy: A Criticism of Lee's Strategic Ability," *Civil War History*, 15 (June 1969), 116–32.

Connelly, Thomas Lawrence, and Jones, Archer. *The Politics of Command: Factions and Ideas in Confederate Strategy*. Baton Rouge: Louisiana State University Press, 1973.

Cooper, William J., Jr. *Jefferson Davis, American*. New York: Alfred A. Knopf, 2000.

———. *Liberty and Slavery: Southern Politics to 1860*. New York: Alfred A. Knopf, 1983.

Cornish, Dudley T. *The Sable Arm: Negro Troops in the Union Army*. New York: Longmans, 1956.

Coulter, E. Merton. *Confederate States of America, 1861–1865*. Baton Rouge: Louisiana State University Press, 1950.

Cunningham, H. H. *Doctors in Gray: The Confederate Medical Service*. Baton Rouge: Louisiana State University Press, 1958.

Davis, David Brion. *The Problem of Slavery in the Age of Revolution, 1775–1823*. Ithaca, N.Y.: Cornell University Press, 1975.

———. *The Problem of Slavery in the Western Culture*. Ithaca, N.Y.: Cornell University Press, 1966.

Davis, William C. *The Battle at Bull Run: A History of the First Major Campaign of the Civil War*. Baton Rouge: Louisiana State University Press, 1977.

———. *Duel Between the First Ironclads*. New York: Doubleday and Company, 1975.

———. *The First Battle of Manassas*. Conshohocken, Pa.: Eastern National Press, 1995.

———. *Jefferson Davis: The Man and His Hour*. New York: HarperCollins, 1991.

Davis, William C., and Robertson, James I., Jr., eds. *Virginia at War, 1861*. Lexington, Ky.: University Press of Kentucky, 2005.

Delauter, Roger U., and Beck, Brandon H. *The Third Battle of Winchester*. Lynchburg, Va.: H. E. Howard, 1997.

Dew, Charles B. *Apostles of Disunion: Southern Secession Commissioners and the Causes of the Civil War*. Charlottesville: University Press of Virginia. 2001.

Donald, David H., ed. *Why the North Won the Civil War*. Baton Rouge: Louisiana State University Press, 1960.

Dower, John W. *War Without Mercy: Race and Power in the Pacific War*. New York: Pantheon Books, 1986.

du Picq, Charles Ardant. *Battle Studies*. Reprint, Harrisburg, Pa.: The Military Service Publishing Company, 1947.

Durden, Robert F. *The Gray and the Black: The Confederate Debate on Emancipation*. Baton Rouge: Louisiana State University Press, 1972.

Eiserman, Maj. Frederick A. "Longstreet's Corps at Chickamauga: Lessons in Inter-Theater Deployment." MMAS thesis, U.S. Army Command and General Staff College, 1985.

Escott, Paul. *Many Excellent People: Power and Privilege in North Carolina, 1850–1900*. Chapel Hill: University of North Carolina Press, 1985.

Escott, Paul D. *After Secession: Jefferson Davis and the Failure of Confederate Nationalism*. Baton Rouge: Louisiana State University Press, 1978.

Evans, Eli N. *Judah P. Benjamin: The Jewish Confederate*. New York: Free Press, 1988.

Faust, Drew Gilpin. "Christian Soldiers: The Meaning of Revivalism in the Confederate Army," *Journal of Southern History*, 53, No. 1 (Feb. 1987), 63–90.

———. *Mothers of Invention: Women of the Slaveholding South in the American Civil War*. Chapel Hill: University of North Carolina Press, 1996.

Fehrenbacher, Don E. *The Dred Scott Case: Its Significance in Law and Politics*. New York: Oxford University Press, 1978.

Fellman, Michael. *The Making of Robert E. Lee*. New York: Random House, 2000.

Foner, Eric. *Free Soil, Free Labor, Free Men: The Ideology of the Republican Party Before the Civil War*. New York: Oxford University Press, 1970.

Fox, William F. *Regimental Losses in the American Civil War, 1861–1865*. Dayton, Ohio: Morningside Books, 1985.

Freeman, Douglas Southall. *Lee's Lieutenants*. 3 vols. New York: Charles Scribner's Sons, 1942–44.

———. *R. E. Lee: A Biography*. 4 vols. New York: Charles Scribner's Sons, 1934–35.

Fuller, Claud W. *The Rifled Musket*. Harrisburg, Pa.: Stackpole Press, 1958.

Fuller, J. F. C. *Lee and Grant: A Study in Personalities*. Bloomington: Indiana University Press, 1957, orig. pub. in 1932.

Gallagher, Gary W., ed. *Antietam: Essays on the 1862 Maryland Campaign*. Kent, Ohio: Kent State University Press, 1989.

———. *The Battle of Chancellorsville*. Conshoshocton, Pa.: Eastern National Press, 1995.

———. *The Confederate War: How Popular Will, Nationalism, and Military Strategy Could Not Stave Off Defeat*. Cambridge: Harvard University Press, 1997.

———. *Lee and His Army in Confederate History*. Chapel Hill: University of North Carolina Press, 2001.

———. *Lee the Soldier*. Lincoln: University of Nebraska Press, 1996.

———. *The Shenandoah Valley Campaign of 1864*. Chapel Hill: University of North Carolina Press, 2006.

———. *The Spotsylvania Campaign*. Chapel Hill: University of North Carolina Press, 1998.

———. *Stephen Dodson Ramseur: Lee's Gallant General*. Chapel Hill: University of North Carolina Press, 1985.

———. *The Third Day of Gettysburg and Beyond*. Chapel Hill: University of North Carolina Press, 1994.

Gallagher, Gary W., and Glatthaar, Joseph T., eds. *Leaders of the Lost Cause: The Confederate Full Generals*. Harrisburg, Pa.: Stackpole Press, 2004.

Genovese, Eugene D. *The World the Slaveholders Made: Two Essays in Interpretation*. New York: Vintage Books, 1969.

Gienapp, William E. *Origins of the Republican Party, 1852–1856*. New York: Oxford University Press, 1987.

Glatthaar, Joseph T. *Forged in Battle: The Civil War Alliance of Black Soldiers and Their White Officers*. New York: Free Press, 1990.

———. *The March to the Sea and Beyond: Sherman's Troops in the Savannah and Carolinas Campaigns*. New York: New York University Press, 1985.

———. *Partners in Command: The Relationships Between Leaders in the Civil War*. New York: Free Press, 1994.

Gordon, Lesley J. *General George E. Pickett in Life & Legend*. Chapel Hill: University of North Carolina Press, 1998.

Gray, J. Glenn. *The Warriors: Reflections on Men in Battle*. New York: Harcourt, Brace, 1959.

Green, Carol C. *Chimborazo: The Confederacy's Largest Hospital*. Knoxville: University of Tennessee Press, 2004.

Greenberg, Kenneth. *Honor and Slavery*. Princeton: Princeton University Press, 1996.

Grinker, Roy R., and Spiegel, John P. *Men Under Stress*. Philadelphia: Blakiston, 1945.

Harris, William C. *Leroy Pope Walker: Confederate Secretary of War*. Tuscaloosa, Ala.: Confederate Publishing Company, Inc., 1926.

Harsh, Joseph L. *Confederate Tide Rising: Robert E. Lee and the Making of Southern Strategy, 1861–1862*. Kent, Ohio: Kent State University Press, 1998.

———. *Taken At the Flood: Robert E. Lee and Confederate Strategy in the Maryland Campaign of 1862*. Kent, Ohio: Kent State University Press, 1999.

Hassler, William Woods. *Colonel John Pelham: Lee's Boy Artillerist*. Richmond, Va.: Garrett and Massie, Inc., 1960.

Heller, Charles E., and Stofft, William A., eds., *America's First Battles, 1776–1965*. Lawrence: University Press of Kansas, 1986.

Hennessy, John. *Return to Bull Run: The Campaign and Battle of Second Manassas*. New York: Simon & Schuster, 1993.

Hess, Earl J. *Pickett's Charge—Last Charge at Gettysburg*. Chapel Hill: University of North Carolina Press, 2001.

———. *The Union Soldier in Battle: Enduring the Ordeal of Combat*. Lawrence, Kans.: University Press of Kansas, 1997.

Hogkins, William H. *The Battle of Fort Stedman*. Boston: privately printed, 1889.

Holmes. Richard. *Acts of War: The Behavior of Men in Battle*. New York: Free Press, 1985.

Horn, John. *The Destruction of the Weldon Railroad: Deep Bottom, Globe Tavern, and Reams Station, August 14–25, 1864*. Lynchburg, Va.: H. E. Howard, 1991.

Horn, John. *The Petersburg Campaign, June 1864–April 1865*. Conshohocken, Pa.: Combined Books, 1993.

Jasper, James M. *The Art of Moral Protest: Culture, Biography, and Creativity in Social Movements*. Chicago: University of Chicago Press, 1997.

Jimerson, Randall C. *The Private Civil War: Popular Thought During the Sectional Conflict*. Baton Rouge: Louisiana State University Press, 1988.

Jones, Terry L. *Lee's Tigers: The Louisiana Infantry in the Army of Northern Virginia*. Baton Rouge: Louisiana State University Press, 1987.

Jordan, Winthrop. *White Over Black: American Attitudes Toward the Negro, 1550–1812*. Chapel Hill: University of North Carolina Press, 1968.

Keegan, John. *The Face of Battle: A Study of Agincourt, Waterloo, and The Somme*. New York: Viking Press, 1976.

Kellett, Anthony. *Combat Motivations: The Behavior of Soldiers in Battle*. Boston: Kluwer-Nijhoff Publications, 1982.

Kivisto, Peter, ed. *Incorporating Diversity: Rethinking Assimilation in a Multicultural Age.* Boulder, Colo.: Paradigm Publishers, 2005.

Krick, Robert E. L. *Staff Officers in Gray: A Biographical Register of the Staff Officers in the Army of Northern Virginia.* Chapel Hill: University of North Carolina Press, 2003.

Krick, Robert K. *Conquering the Valley: Stonewall Jackson at Port Republic.* New York: Morrow, Inc., 1996.

———. *Lee's Colonels: A Biographical Register of Field Officers of the Army of Northern Virginia.* Dayton, Ohio: Morningside Press, 1992.

———. *The Smoothbore Volley That Doomed the Confederacy.* Baton Rouge: Louisiana State University Press, 2002.

———. *Stonewall Jackson at Cedar Mountain.* Chapel Hill: University of North Carolina Press, 1990.

Laine, J. Gary, and Penny, Morris M. *Law's Alabama Brigade in the War Between the Union and the Confederacy.* Shippensburg, Pa.: White Mane Publishing Co., Inc., 1996.

Lanza, Conrad H. *Napoleon and Modern War: His Military Maxims.* Harrisburg, Pa.: Military Service Publishing Company, 1943.

Lash, Jeffrey N. *Destroyer of the Iron Horse: General Joseph E. Johnston and the Confederate Rail Transport, 1861–1865.* Kent, Ohio: Kent State University Press, 1991.

Levine, Bruce. *Confederate Emancipation: Southern Plans to Free and Arm Slaves during the Civil War.* New York: Oxford University Press, 2006.

Linderman, Gerald F. *Embattled Courage: The Experience of Combat in the American Civil War.* New York: Free Press, 1985.

Lonn, Ella. *Desertion During the Civil War.* Lincoln: Bison Publishing, 1998 reprint.

Luvaas, Jay. "Lee and the Operational Art: The Right Place, the Right Time." *Parameters* (Autumn 1992), 2–18.

Luvaas, Jay, and Nelson, Harold W. *The U.S. Army War College Guide to the Battle of Antietam: The Maryland Campaign of 1862.* New York: Harper & Row, Publishers, 1987.

Lynn, John A. *The Bayonets of the Republic: Motivation and Military Tactics in the Army of Revolutionary France, 1791–1794.* Urbana: University of Illinois Press, 1984.

Manning, Chandra. *What This Cruel War Was Over: Soldiers, Slavery, and the Civil War.* New York: Alfred Knopf, 2007.

Martin, Joanne. *Organizational Culture: Mapping the Terrain.* Thousand Oaks, Calif.: Sage Publications, 2002.

Marvel, William. *Lee's Last Retreat: The Flight to Appomattox.* Chapel Hill: University of North Carolina Press, 2002.

McMurry, Richard M. *Two Great Rebel Armies: An Essay in Confederate Military History.* Chapel Hill: University of North Carolina Press, 1989.

———. *Virginia Military Institute Alumni in the Civil War.* Lynchburg, Va.: H. E. Howard, 1999.

McPherson, James M. *Antietam: Crossroads of Freedom.* New York: Oxford University Press, 2002.

———. *Battle Cry of Freedom: The Civil War Era.* New York: Oxford University Press, 1988.

———. *For Cause and Comrades: Why Men Fought in the Civil War.* New York: Oxford University Press. 1997.

———. *Is Blood Thicker Than Water? Crisis of Nationalism in the Modern World.* New York: Vintage Books, 1998.

———. *The Negro's Civil War: How American Negroes Felt and Acted During the War for the Union.* New York: Vintage Books, 1965.

———. *Ordeal by Fire: The Civil War and Reconstruction.* New York: McGraw-Hill, 2001.

———. *What They Fought For, 1861–1865.* Baton Rouge: Louisiana State University Press, 1994.

McPherson, James M., and Cooper, William J., Jr., eds. *Writing the Civil War: The Quest to Understand*. Columbia: University of South Carolina Press, 1998.

McWhiney, Grady, and Jamieson, Perry D. *Attack and Die: Civil War Military Tactics and the Southern Heritage*. University: University of Alabama Press, 1982.

Miller, William J. *Richmond, 1862*. Conshohoken, Pa.: Eastern National Park and Monument Association, 1996.

Mitchell, Reid. *Civil War Soldiers*. New York: Viking, 1988.

———. *The Vacant Chair: The Northern Soldier Leaves Home*. New York: Oxford University Press, 1993.

Moore. Albert Burton. *Conscription and Conflict in the Confederacy*. New York: Hillary House Publishers. 1963.

Moore, Robert H., II. *The 1st and 2nd Stuart Horse Artillery*. Lynchburg, Va.: H. E. Howard, 1985.

Morgan, Edmund S. *American Slavery, American Freedom: The Ordeal of Colonial Virginia*. New York: W. W. Norton & Company, 1975.

Moskos, Charles. *The American Enlisted Man*. New York: Russell Sage Foundation, 1970.

Newton, Steven H. *The Battle of Seven Pines, May 31–June 1, 1862*. Lynchburg, Va.: H. E. Howard, 1993.

———. *Joseph E. Johnston and the Defense of Richmond*. Lawrence, Kans.: University Press of Kansas, 1998.

Nolan, Alan T. *The Iron Brigade: A Military History*. Bloomington: Indiana University Press, 1994.

———. *Lee Considered: General Robert E. Lee and Civil War History*. Chapel Hill: University of North Carolina Press, 1991.

Oates, Stephen. *To Purge This Land with Blood: A Biography of John Brown*. New York: Harper & Row, 1970.

O'Grady, Kelly J. *Clear the Confederate Way!: The Irish in the Army of Northern Virginia*. Mason City, Iowa: Savas Publishing Company, 2000.

O'Reilly, Francis Augustin. *The Fredericksburg Campaign: Winter War of the Rappahannock*. Baton Rouge: Louisiana State University Press, 2003.

Palmer, Beverly Wilson, ed. *The Selected Letters of Charles Sumner*. Vol. 2. Boston: Northeastern University Press, 1990.

Pfanz, Donald C. *Richard S. Ewell: A Soldier's Life*. Chapel Hill: University of North Carolina Press, 1998.

Philips, Jason. "The Grape Vine Telegraph: Rumors and Confederate Persistence." *Journal of Southern History*, 72, 4, 753–88.

Pollard, Edward A. *The First Year of the War*. New York: Charles B. Richardson, 1863, reprinted from 1862 edition.

Potter, David. *The Impending Crisis, 1848–1861*. New York: Harper & Row, 1976.

Power, J. Tracy. *Lee's Miserables: Life in the Army of Northern Virginia from the Wilderness to Appomattox*. Chapel Hill: University of North Carolina Press, 1998.

Rable, George C. *Fredericksburg! Fredericksburg!* Chapel Hill: University of North Carolina Press, 2002.

Ramsdell, Charles W. "The Texas State Military Board, 1862–1865." *Southwestern Historical Quarterly*, 27 (1924), 255–56.

Reardon, Carol. *Pickett's Charge in History and Memory*. Chapel Hill: University of North Carolina Press, 1997.

Reese, Timothy J. *High-Water Mark: The 1862 Maryland Campaign in Strategic Perspective*. Baltimore: Butternut and Blue, 2004.

Reid, Brian Holden. *Robert E. Lee: Icon for a Nation*. London: Weidenfeld & Nicolson, 2005.

Rhea, Gordon C. *The Battle for Spotsylvania Court House and the Road to Yellow Tavern, May 7–12, 1864*. Baton Rouge: Louisiana State University Press, 1997.

———. *The Battle of the Wilderness, May 5–6. 1864*. Baton Rouge: Louisiana State University Press, 1994.

————. *The Battles of Wilderness & Spotsylvania*. Conshohocken, Pa.: Eastern National Press, 1995.

————. *Cold Harbor: Grant and Lee, May 26–June 3, 1864*. Baton Rouge: Louisiana State University Press, 2002.

————. *To the North Anna River: Grant and Lee, May 13–25, 1864*. Baton Rouge: Louisiana State University Press, 2000.

Robertson. James I., Jr. *General A. P. Hill: The Story of a Confederate Warrior*. New York: Random House. 1987.

————. *Soldiers Blue and Gray*. Columbia: University of South Carolina Press, 1988.

————. *The Stonewall Brigade*. Baton Rouge: Louisiana State University Press, 1991.

————. *Stonewall Jackson: The Man, The Soldier. The Legend*. New York: Macmillan Publishing U.S.A., 1997.

Royster, Charles. *The Destructive War: William Tecumseh Sherman, Stonewall Jackson, and the Americans*. New York: Alfred A. Knopf, Inc., 1991.

Ruffner, Kevin C. *44th Virginia Infantry*. Lynchburg, Va.: H. E. Howard, 1987.

Sears, Stephen W. *Chancellorsville*. Boston: Houghton Mifflin Company. 1996.

————. *Landscape Turned Red: The Battle of Antietam*. New York: Ticknor & Fields, 1983.

————. *To the Gates of Richmond: The Peninsula Campaign*. New York: Ticknor & Fields, 1992.

Sellers, Charles Grier. *Southerner As American*. Chapel Hill: University of North Carolina Press, 1960.

Shattuck, Gardiner H., Jr. *A Shield and a Hiding Place: The Religious Life of the Civil War Armies*. Macon: Mercer University Press, 1987.

Sheehan-Dean, Aaron. *Creating Confederates: Family and Nation in Civil War Virginia*. Chapel Hill: University of North Carolina Press, 2008.

————. *The View from the Ground: The Experiences of Civil War Soldiers*. Lexington: University Press of Kentucky, 2007.

Shils, Edward A., and Janowitz. Morris. "Cohesion and Disintegration in the Wehrmacht in World War II." *Public Opinion Quarterly*, 12, No. 2 (Summer, 1948), 280–315.

Skelton, William B. *An American Profession of Arms: The Army Officer Corps, 1784–1861*. Lawrence, Kans.: University Press of Kansas, 1992.

Sledge, E. B. *With the Old Breed at Peleliu and Okinawa*. New York: Oxford University Press, 1990.

Sommers, Richard J. *Richmond Redeemed: The Siege at Petersburg*. Garden City, N.Y.: Doubleday & Co., 1981.

Stephenson, Richard W. "General Lee's Forgotten Mapmaker: Major Albert H. Campbell and the Department of Northern Virginia's Topographical Department." *North & South*, 8, No. 2 (Mar. 2005). 64–74.

Stouffer, Samuel, et al., *The American Soldier: Adjustment During Army Life*. Princeton: Princeton University Press, 1949–50.

————. *The American Soldier: Combat and Its Aftermath*. Princeton: Princeton University Press, 1949–50.

Swisher, James K. *Prince of Edisto: Brigadier General Micah Jenkins, CSA*. Berryville, Va.: Rockbridge Publishing Company, 1996.

Symonds, Craig. *Joseph E. Johnston: A Civil War Biography*. New York: W. W. Norton, 1992.

Tanner, Robert G. *Stonewall in the Valley: Thomas J. "Stonewall" Jackson's Shenandoah Valley Campaign, Spring 1862*. New York: Doubleday & Company, Inc., 1976.

Thomas, Emory M. *Bold Dragoon: The Life of J. E. B. Stuart*. New York: Harper & Row, 1986.

————. *The Confederate Nation: 1861–1865*. New York: Harper & Row, 1979.

————. *Confederate State of Richmond: A Biography of the Capital*. Austin: University of Texas Press, 1971.

————. *Robert E. Lee: A Biography.* New York: W.W. Norton & Company, 1995.

Thornton, J. Mills, III. *Politics and Power in a Slave Society: Alabama, 1800–1860.* Baton Rouge: Louisiana State University Press, 1978.

Trudeau, Noah Andre. *The Last Citadel: Petersburg, Virginia, June 1864–April 1865.* Baton Rouge: Louisiana State University Press, 1991.

————. *Like Men of War: Black Troops in the Civil War.* Boston: Little, Brown, 1998.

Vandiver, Frank E. *Mighty Stonewall.* New York: McGraw-Hill Book Company, 1957.

————. *Ploughshares into Swords: Josiah Gorgas and Confederate Ordnance.* Austin: University of Texas Press, 1952.

Wallace, Lee A., Jr. *17th Virginia Infantry.* Lynchburg, Va.: H. E. Howard, Inc., 1990.

Walther, Eric. *The Fire-Eaters.* Baton Rouge: Louisiana State University Press, 1992.

————. "Southerners' Honors." *Southern Studies* (new series), 12 (2005), 129–54.

Weigley, Russell F. *The American Way of War: A History of the United States Military Strategy and Policy.* New York: Macmillan, 1973.

Weitz, Mark A. *More Damning than Slaughter: Desertion in the Confederate Army.* Lincoln: University of Nebraska Press, 2005.

Wert, Jeffry D. *From Winchester to Cedar Creek: The Shenandoah Valley Campaign of 1864.* Carlisle, Pa.: South Mountain Press, 1987.

————. *General James Longstreet: The Confederacy's Most Controversial Soldier—A Biography.* New York: Simon & Schuster, 1993.

Wiley, Bell I. *Life of Johnny Reb: The Common Soldier of the Confederacy.* Baton Rouge: Louisiana State University Press, 1978.

————. *Plain People of the Confederacy.* Columbia: University of South Carolina Press, 2001.

Williams, T. Harry. *Lincoln and His Generals.* New York: Knopf, 1952.

————. *P. G. T. Beauregard: Napoleon in Gray.* Baton Rouge: Louisiana State University Press, 1954.

Woodworth. Steven E. *While God Is Marching On: Religious World of Civil War Soldiers.* Lawrence: University Press of Kansas, 2001.

Wyatt-Brown, Bertram. *Southern Honor: Ethics and Behavior in the Old South.* New York: Oxford University Press, 1982.

ACKNOWLEDGMENTS

I T IS HARD to believe how many years I have been working on Lee's army. When I began this book project, Danielle was in elementary school. She is now in her fourth decade. Over the years, two repositories have actually changed their names. It truly has been a long journey.

Even though I have not worked continuously on the project, it has never strayed far from my thoughts. Over those many years, I have tabulated countless debts, and space does not permit me to recognize all of them. The Virginia Historical Society gave me a Mellon Fellowship for research back in 1989. The late Waverly Winfrey, Howson Cole, Frances Pollard, Nelson Lankford, and Charles Bryan were most supportive. More recently, Lee Shepard has been very helpful in continuing research.

The staffs at the Library of Virginia and the Museum of the Confederacy have been wonderful. Very special thanks go to two archivists and friends, Guy Swanson and John Coski. Very different in their approach and demeanor, both could not have been more helpful to me.

Robert Kenneth Krick, now retired from the National Park Service, has trained a generation of extraordinary Civil War historians for the Park Service and collected a vast manuscript holding at Fredericksburg and Spotsylvania National Battlefield Park. Bob, a great friend, could not have been more accommodating in granting me access to his holdings. Bob also read the entire manuscript in draft and provided very lengthy and helpful comments.

Two others in the Park Service deserve special mention as well. Donald Pfanz, the author of an outstanding book on Richard S. Ewell, gave me access to material when he was in Charleston and later helped me during research at Fredericksburg. When we had the chance, Don has always proved to be great company. Bob Krick (Robert E. L. Krick) at the Richmond National Battlefield Park has followed in his father's footsteps by collecting wonderful materials of his own. Bob is a great supporter of serious researchers and has aided me on countless occasions.

At the National Archives, I benefited greatly from the assistance of my friend Michael P. Musick. To my good fortune, Mike, now retired, saw me through most of my research there and was exceedingly helpful.

Richard Sommers, perhaps the dean of military history archivists, provided friendship, support, ideas, and guidance through the vast holdings of the U.S. Army Military History Institute. A year there as the Harold K. Johnson Professor, arranged by Col. Tom Sweeney and Lt. Col. Marty Andresen, helped me to exploit those holdings, as well as the fabulous book collection.

At the Jefferson Davis Papers Project at Rice University, longtime friends Lynda Crist, Mary Dix, and Captain (now Colonel) Mat Moten gave me access to their records, insights into the documents, and great conversation.

Other archivists around the country, too numerous to mention, have merited my grateful acknowledgment for their terrific service.

Jim McPherson generously swapped research notes. Because Jim decided not to undertake a project, I was the sole beneficiary of the trade. He and Pat have been terrific friends, and I count this as one of many kindly acts the two have done for me over the past two decades.

Over the years, extensive conversations with Drs. Jay Luvaas and the late Archer Jones were both stimulating and delightful.

My buddies at the New River (R.R.R.) prodded me annually for my glacial progress. Their not-so-subtle chiding and great conversation made this a better book.

Niels and Barbara Holch and Charlie, Ben, and Jack Goodman, all wonderful friends, tolerated me on various research trips to Washington, D.C., and let me bunk in the infamous "Joseph T. Glatthaar Memorial Suite." The same is true for other great friends, Steve, Marlin, Sam, and Luci Perkins.

At the University of Houston, the college awarded me a semester leave and a limited-grant-in-aid to work on the project. Sam Hyde of the library staff helped procure books and Keiko Horton and her interlibrary loan people fulfilled requests with vigilance and skill.

At the University of Houston, Tom Hughes, at the time my graduate student but whose subsequent work at Maxwell AFB has earned him a great name in the U.S. Air Force, made extensive photocopies from microfilm or newspaper articles and published letters. Eric Walther, my dear friend of two decades, read a chapter and offered helpful comments. Kent Tedin of Political Science designed my sample. Most of all, Michael S. Parks helped set up my database, crunched numbers, encouraged me over the years, and offered terrific friendship. Purely from friendship and interest in the Civil War, Parks contributed an enormous amount of time toward the project.

At the University of North Carolina at Chapel Hill, my colleagues in History gave me a chance based on research on this topic. They impress me every day with their scholarship, professionalism, and cordiality.

My All-Star student, Laura Marie Leonard, proved to be a gem at independent work. She painstakingly went through every note card with me to verify the accuracy of the quotations and the correct citations. Her extraordinary attention to detail made me proud. Laura also read the entire manuscript with a discerning eye and even convinced me to change a few chapter titles.

Two great friends, Jim Jones and John Moretta, listened patiently as I spoke, perhaps *ad nauseam*, about the book. These are marvelous people, and anyone who can claim just one of them as a friend is a lucky person.

Thanks to Chris Robinson for preparing excellent maps.

At the Free Press, I signed so many years ago that I lost my terrific editor, Joyce Seltzer, to Harvard University Press. Bruce Nichols filled the void superbly. He has been as conscientious, as supportive, and as patient as any editor could be. He and his assistant, Elizabeth Perrella, deserve my lengthy applause.

So, too, does Gary Gallagher. Gary and I have been extremely close friends for many years. In addition to that personal friendship, we have shared ideas, research notes, documents, sources, and speculations. Gary read the entire manuscript and gave me excellent comments, suggestions, and even an occasional challenge. Every time we get together or gab on the phone is a delight.

I have dedicated the book to Jackie, who deserves it.

INDEX

588 / *Index*

ABOUT THE AUTHOR

Joseph T. Glatthaar received a B.A. from Ohio Wesleyan University, an M.A. in History from Rice University, and a Ph.D. from the University of Wisconsin-Madison in History. He has taught at the U.S. Army Command and General Staff College, the U.S. Army War College, the U.S. Military Academy at West Point, and the University of Houston, and is currently the Stephenson Distinguished Professor of History and chair of the Curriculum in Peace, War, and Defense at the University of North Carolina at Chapel Hill.